Key Cases and Comments On

CRIMINAL PROCEDURE

1994 ANNUAL EDITION

Marvin Zalman

Professor of Criminal Justice
Wayne State University

Larry Siegel

Professor of Criminal Justice
University of Massachusetts at Lowell

West Publishing Company

Minneapolis/St. Paul   New York   Los Angeles   San Francisco

WEST'S COMMITMENT TO THE ENVIRONMENT

In 1906, West Publishing Company began recycling materials left over from the production of books. This began a tradition of efficient and responsible use of resources. Today, up to 95% of our legal books and 70% of our college texts and school texts are printed on recycled, acid-free stock. West also recycles nearly 22 million pounds of scrap paper annually—the equivalent of 181,717 trees. Since the 1960s, West has devised ways to capture and recycle waste inks, solvents, oils, and vapors created in the printing process. We also recycle plastics of all kinds, wood, glass, corrugated cardboard, and batteries, and have eliminated the use of Styrofoam book packaging. We at West are proud of the longevity and the scope of our commitment to the environment.

Production, Prepress, Printing and Binding by West Publishing Company.

 TEXT IS PRINTED ON 10% POST CONSUMER RECYCLED PAPER  PRINTED WITH SOY INK™

KEY CASES AND COMMENTS ON CRIMINAL PROCEDURE

1994 Annual Edition

Table of Contents

CHAPTER 3

EXIGENCY AND OTHER SEARCH WARRANT EXCEPTIONS 225

Table of Cases

[Case and Comments in CAPITAL, pages in **bold**]

PREFACE

Criminal procedure is an important area of constitutional law. It has undergone immense shifts in the years since the 1960s, when the Supreme Court established a large body of doctrine under the Fourth, Fifth, Sixth and Eighth Amendments. The continuous changes of doctrine in these areas make it necessary to present students with teaching materials that reflect the most important and the most recent developments in the law. To meet this need, we offer a casebook in a simple format that will be updated annually to reflect these changes.

Several different methods, equally valid, are used to teach law courses to students not enrolled in professional law schools. Some instructors prefer to use textbooks or hornbooks, or texts with very brief excerpts of the cases. Others use traditional casebooks which contain a variety of materials that embed the cases in a wider body of law and scholarship. In 1991 we developed such a "full model" casebook specially designed for programs in criminal justice, criminology, law enforcement and the like. *Criminal Procedure: Constitution and Society* (West, 1991) surrounded the key cases of criminal procedure with historical background, explanations of doctrinal development in the law, discussions of social science relevant to criminal procedure, and biographies of the justices.

An important innovation in that casebook was the "case and comment," a running comment that appeared in the margin of the major cases. In *Key Cases and Comments on Criminal Procedure* we build on this feature, in modified form, to present a useful and unique tool to non-law students confronted with legal materials. Comments are inserted into the case with bracketed bold letters. They are not overly intrusive so that, at the option of the instructor or student, they can be ignored. On the other hand, the comments are designed to assist the undergraduate student with arcane points of law or terminology that a student is not expected to know in advance. The comments also point out specific areas of conflict between justices. In addition, the comments furnish pointers on the styles of legal reasoning. The comments DO NOT recite the holding of the case, so it does not undermine the pedagogical goal of the instructor who uses the casebook approach to teaching law.

In *Key Cases* we offer a text to instructors who desire the "raw material" of the law, with little of the filler provided by standard casebooks. More cases are included than can normally be taught in a semester in order to give instructors the opportunity to shape their course in accord with their best judgment of how to present the materials. The case selection for *Key Cases* provides the instructor with the "classic" cases in constitutional criminal procedure. Some additional cases provide variation on a theme that allow the instructor to explore areas in depth, as desired.

The selection of materials in this volume is weighted toward those areas that have the most to do with police procedure. Books designed for a law school audience balance this area with pretrial, trial and post-trial materials that are of lesser interest to criminal justice students, who have a greater concern with the way in which constitutional norms and rules impinge on the police function.

Once selected, the cases are carefully edited. The facts are normally condensed so as to minimize confusion in reading a case and to help the student focus on the important constitutional discussion. Where the Court's statements of the facts are indispensable to understanding the case, we leave it uncut. Generous portions of dissents are included to give the student an opportunity to explore the constitutional and values conflicts. Finally, we have attempted to keep cases to manageable length without eliminating the critical portions of the opinions of the justices. Footnotes are cut from the cases without indication, but all other omissions are marked by ellipses marks of three asterisks. The lower court history of the cases are truncated or, at times, cut.

In order to make this volume as useful as possible, we are eager to receive comments from instructors using the text or who are contemplating its adoption. We would like to know if there are cases not included that you believe are critical. Are other cases not used? Are the cases edited to meet your needs? Are there some areas of law which you think should be added? Although it may not be possible to satisfy the needs of every instructor in every respect, your comments will be taken into account. We can be reached at: Marvin Zalman, Criminal Justice Program, Wayne State University, Detroit, MI 48202; e-mail: MZALMAN@CMS.CC.WAYNE.EDU; Larry J. Siegel, Criminal Justice Department, University of Massachusetts at Lowell, Lowell, MA 01854.

ACKNOWLEDGEMENTS

The preparation of this casebook was greatly enhanced by the contributions of our colleagues who helped by reviewing the material and providing cogent comments on our work. They include: Charles Chastain, Finn Hornum, Candace Howell, William Shulman, and Larry Woods. We also wish to thank our student, Ms. Elizabeth Ferguson, for her intelligent and diligent editorial assistance. And of course, we wish to thank the editorial staff at West Publishing Company for the outstanding job they did in the development of this text. Mary Schiller, our outstanding senior executive editor, provided the encouragement and advice that made this endeavor efficient and pleasant.

KEY CASES

ON

CONSTITUTIONAL

CRIMINAL PROCEDURE

Chapter One

DUE PROCESS, INCORPORATION
AND THE EXCLUSIONARY RULE

Criminal procedure is a branch of public law that facilitates the prosecution of criminal cases and regulates certain aspects of police work. As a branch of constitutional law, criminal procedure is bound up with the Bill of Rights. The Fourth Amendment to the United States Constitution prohibits unreasonable searches and seizures. The Fifth Amendment establishes the federal grand jury, prohibits double jeopardy, includes the privilege against self-incrimination, and contains the federal due process clause. The Sixth Amendment contains seven rights guaranteed in "all criminal prosecutions:" a speedy and public trial, a jury from the venue of the crime, notice of the crime charged, confrontation of witnesses, subpoena supporting witnesses, and the assistance of counsel. The Eighth Amendment prohibits excessive fines, excessive bail, and cruel and unusual punishments. In addition to the Bill of Rights, ratified in 1791, the due process clause of the Fourteenth Amendment, ratified in 1868, guarantees that no state shall deprive any person of life, liberty, or property without due process of law.

As a branch of constitutional law, then, criminal procedure is concerned not simply with facilitating prosecutions, but with safeguarding the rights of criminal suspects. Constitutional criminal procedure, as we now know it, did not exist in 1791 or in 1868. Rather, modern criminal procedure has evolved through the development of legal doctrines by the United States Supreme Court. The major historical process was the development of what is known as the "incorporation doctrine." What this meant was that rights under the Bill of Rights that were formerly available only in federal cases became protections to suspects and defendants in state and local cases. As a result, the impact of the Bill of Rights expanded enormously. After about three-quarters of a century of intellectual struggle, most of the "criminal" provisions of the Bill of Rights were "incorporated" into the due process clause of the Fourteenth Amendment between 1961 and 1969. So sharp was the doctrinal change that the 1960s are known as the period of the "Due Process Revolution" in criminal procedure. After that "revolution" has come a period of consolidation and some retrenchment, but no wholesale abandonment. Thus, the law of criminal procedure is still evolving today.

* * *

After the ratification of the Bill of Rights in 1791 the Supreme Court had little opportunity to apply the Fourth and Fifth Amendments. Indeed, in *Barron v. Baltimore*, 32 U.S. (7 Pet.) 243 (1833) the Court made it clear that the Bill of Rights applied to the federal government but not to the states. The Fourteenth Amendment, ratified in 1868 in the aftermath of the Civil War, changed this. It created federal guarantees, including "due process," "equal protection of the laws," and the "privileges and immunities of citizenship," for all citizens, who were explicitly made citizens of the United States *and* of the state of residence. These protections were particularly designed to guarantee rights to newly freed slaves, but the rights applied to all. Soon after, the argument was raised that the Fourteenth Amendment was designed to apply *all* the protections of the Bill of Rights to all persons against state and local courts and law enforcement agencies. The idea was advanced that these were the "privileges and immunities" of citizenship. This later became known as the "total incorporation" doctrine.

This argument was initially rejected by the Supreme Court. *Hurtado v. California*, 110 U.S. 516 (1884) held that the Fifth Amendment grand jury was not required for state prosecutions and *Twining v. New Jersey*, 211 U.S. 78 (1907) ruled that the constitutional self-incrimination rule does not apply to the states. But in the course of deciding these cases the Court's opinions contained language that allowed future litigants to claim that where "fundamental" rights were trampled by the states, the federal courts could act to protect persons who were, under the Fourteenth Amendment, citizens of both the states and the United States.

The cases in this chapter involve several separate but intertwined doctrinal developments. The first involved the development of the *federal* search and seizure exclusionary rule. *Boyd v. United States*, *Weeks v. United States*, and *Silverthorne Lumber v. United States*, decided between 1886 and 1914 established this important remedy for Fourth Amendment violations by federal officers. As a result, federal courts offered greater protections of defendants' rights than state courts. If a state had no *state* exclusionary rule, defendants argued that the introduction of illegally seized evidence against them violated their *federal* constitutional rights.

But before this idea was accepted by federal courts, a second doctrine had to develop—that the Fourteenth Amendment due process clause itself applies directly to gross violations of "fundamental fairness." This position, established in *Moore v. Dempsey,* was resisted because it gave federal courts jurisdiction over state courts and officers in an era when states' rights were more salient. The application of the Fourteenth Amendment gave federal courts entry, so to speak, into state criminal procedure where that procedure fell far below the mark of civilized standards. The application of the Fourteenth Amendment directly to state action was the conceptual backbone of the coerced confession cases [see Chapter 5, this volume] and widened the intrusion of federal law into state criminal justice.

The so-called "due process approach," exemplified in the search and seizure area by *Rochin v. California*, still allowed a disparity between the greater rights generally afforded to federal defendants and fewer rights allowed in many state courts. As the Supreme Court began to expand the federal right to counsel, the privilege against self-incrimination, and the Fourth Amendment exclusionary rule, cases came before the Court urging the incorporation of these federal rights and standards into the Fourteenth Amendment due process clause. The argument for incorporation was again rejected in *Palko v. Connecticut* (double jeopardy), *Adamson v. California* (self-incrimination) and *Wolf v. Colorado* (Fourth Amendment exclusionary rule). But in these cases, advances favoring incorporation were made. *Palko* recognized that First Amendment rights had been incorporated in the 1920s; in *Adamson* four justices voted for incorporation; and in *Wolf* the Court appeared to incorporate the substantive "right" of the Fourth Amendment but not the exclusionary rule "remedy" of *Weeks* and *Silverthorne*. Most importantly, several justices indicated a willingness to use the concept of fundamental justice as the basis to incorporate particular elements of the Bill of Rights rather than loading the entire Bill of Rights on the states. Thus, the vehicle for incorporation was to be "partial" rather than "total" incorporation.

Mapp v. Ohio (Fourth Amendment exclusionary rule) "broke the dam" so to speak, and set in motion the incorporation of most of the important rights in the Fourth, Fifth, Sixth and Eighth Amendments during the 1960s. The theory for rejecting incorporation in *Palko* was replaced by the theory expressed in *Duncan v. Louisiana*, that to be incorporated, rights need not be fundamental in an abstract sense but must be fundamental to the American system of justice in its historic context.

The partial incorporation doctrine cannot be abstract but has to be worked out through each specific constitutional right. This Chapter indicates how incorporation developed as to the Fourth Amendment exclusionary rule. *Rochin v. California* was a failed attempt to deal with illegal searches and seizures through the due process approach. *Wolf* and *Mapp* trace the development of its incorporation. These cases of the 1960s reflected the work of an activist and liberal Supreme Court.

United States v. Leon is indicative of a newer trend. As the Supreme Court has become more conservative it has moved to limit the expansion of defendant's rights. It has done this not by overruling the incorporation of the Bill of Rights but by limiting it in detail. *Leon* thus created a "good faith" exception to the exclusionary rule, allowing the introduction of evidence seized in violation of Fourth Amendment requirements where a police officer relied on a judicial warrant in good faith. This indicated a tightening of the Court's interpretation of defendants' rights.

Finally, *Michigan v. Long* (dealing with an interpretation of the plain view and *Terry v. Ohio* [this volume] "stop and frisk" doctrine) made an important contribution to our understanding of the federal dimension of constitutional rights. It established more precise guidelines for the application of the "adequate and independent state ground" rule, under which states must adhere to the minimum requirements of the incorporated Bill of Rights as set forth by the United States Supreme Court, but may, entirely under their own state constitutions, allow greater rights to suspects and defendants. *Long* reminds us that the United States is a federal republic and that the states, as well as the United States, are sources of law and rights.

BOYD v. UNITED STATES

116 U.S. 616, 29 L.Ed. 746, 6 S.Ct. 524 (1886)

MR. JUSTICE BRADLEY delivered the opinion of the court.

[Boyd, an importer, had his goods seized for nonpayment of import duties. Boyd was also charged with making false invoices to facilitate this fraud and was found guilty and subject to a fine. The federal district attorney, to prove the case of fraudulent nonpayment of the taxes against Boyd, obtained a court order requiring Boyd to turn over invoices of previous importations. A federal statute allowed the prosecuting attorney to require the defendant or claimant to produce in court his private books, invoices and papers, or else the allegations of the attorney "shall be taken as confessed." Boyd complied with the order but complained that his constitutional rights were violated.]

The clauses of the Constitution, to which it is contended that these laws are repugnant, are the Fourth and Fifth Amendments. * * * **[a]**

But, in regard to the Fourth Amendment, it is contended that, * * * [the law] is free from constitutional objection, because it does not authorize the search and seizure of books and papers, but only requires the defendant or claimant to produce them. That is so; but it declares that if he does not produce them, the allegations which it is affirmed they will prove shall be taken as confessed. This is tantamount to compelling their production; for the prosecuting attorney will always be sure to state the evidence expected to be derived from them as strongly as the case will admit of. It is true that

certain aggravating incidents of actual search and seizure, such as forcible entry into a man's house and searching amongst his papers, are wanting; * * * but it accomplishes the substantial object of those acts in forcing from a party evidence against himself. **[b]** It is our opinion, therefore, that a compulsory production of a man's private papers to establish a criminal charge against him, or to forfeit his property, is within the scope of the Fourth Amendment to the Constitution, in all cases in which a search and seizure would be; because it is a material ingredient, and effects the sole object and purpose of search and seizure. **[c]**

The principal question, however, remains to be considered. Is a search and seizure, or [its equivalent,] to be used in evidence against [a man] in a proceeding to forfeit his property for alleged fraud against the revenue laws—is such a proceeding for such a purpose an "*unreasonable* search and seizure" within the meaning of the Fourth Amendment of the Constitution? or, is it a legitimate proceeding? **[d]** It is contended by the counsel for the government, that it is a legitimate proceeding, sanctioned by long usage, and the authority of judicial decision. No doubt long usage, acquiesced in by the courts, goes a long way to prove that there is some plausible ground or reason for it in the law. * * * But we do not find any long usage, or any contemporary construction of the Constitution, which would justify any of the acts of Congress now under consideration. **[e]** * * * The search for and seizure of stolen or forfeited goods, or goods liable to duties and concealed to avoid the payment thereof, are totally different things from a search for and seizure of a man's private books and papers for the purpose of obtaining information therein contained, or of using them as evidence against him. * * * In the one case, the government is entitled to the possession of the property; in the other it is not. **[f]** The seizure of stolen goods is authorized by the common law. * * * So, also, the laws which provide for the search and seizure of articles and things which it is unlawful for a person to have in his possession for the purpose of issue or disposition, such as counterfeit coin, lottery tickets, implements of gambling, &c., are not within this category. * * * **[g]**

* * * In the case of stolen goods, the owner from whom they were stolen is entitled to their possession; and in the case of excisable or dutiable articles, the government has an interest in them for the payment of the duties thereon, and until such duties are paid has a right to keep them under observation, or to pursue and drag them from concealment; and in the case of goods seized on attachment or execution, the creditor is entitled to their seizure in satisfaction of his debt; * * * **[f]** Whereas, by the proceeding now under consideration, the court attempts to extort from the party his private books and papers to make him liable for a penalty or to forfeit his property.

In order to ascertain the nature of the proceedings intended by the Fourth Amendment to the Constitution under the terms "unreasonable searches and seizures," it is only necessary to recall the * * * history of the controversies on the subject, both in this country and in England. * * * **[h]**

* * *

The principles laid down in this opinion affect the very essence of constitutional liberty and security. They reach farther than the concrete form of the case then before the court, with its adventitious circumstances; they apply to all invasions on the part of the government and its employes of the sanctity of a man's home and the privacies of life. It is not the breaking of his doors, and the rummaging of his drawers, that constitutes the essence of the offence; but it is the invasion of his indefeasible right of personal security, personal liberty and private property, where that right has never been forfeited by his conviction of some public offence,—it is the invasion of this sacred right which underlies and constitutes the essence of Lord Camden's judgment [in *Entick v. Carrington*]. Breaking into a house and opening boxes and drawers are circumstances of aggravation; but any forcible and compulsory extortion of a man's own testimony or of his private papers to be used as evidence to convict him of crime or to forfeit his goods, is within the condemnation of that judgment. In this regard the Fourth and Fifth Amendments run almost into each other. **[i]**

* * *

Reverting then to the peculiar phraseology of this act, and to the information in the present case, which is founded on it, we have to deal with an act which expressly excludes criminal proceedings from its operation (though embracing civil suits for penalties and forfeitures), and with an information not technically a criminal proceeding, and neither, therefore, within the literal terms of the Fifth Amendment to the Constitution any more than it is within the literal terms of the Fourth. Does this relieve the proceedings or the law from being obnoxious to the prohibitions of either? We think not; we think they are within the spirit of both. **[j]**

* * * Though the proceeding in question is divested of many of the aggravating incidents of actual search and seizure, yet, as before said, it contains their substance and essence, and effects their substantial purpose. It may be that it is the obnoxious thing in its mildest and least repulsive form; but illegitimate and unconstitutional practices get their first footing in that way, namely, by silent approaches and slight deviations from legal modes of procedure. This can only be obviated by adhering to the rule that constitutional provisions for the security of person and property should be liberally construed. A close and literal construction deprives them of half their efficacy, and leads to gradual depreciation of the right, as if it consisted more in sound than in substance. It is the duty of courts to be watchful for the constitutional rights of the citizen, and against any stealthy encroachments thereon. **[k]**

* * *

We think that the notice to produce the invoice in this case, the order by virtue of which it was issued, and the law which authorized the order,

were unconstitutional and void, and that the inspection by the district attorney of said invoice, when produced in obedience to said notice, and its admission in evidence by the court, were erroneous and unconstitutional proceedings. We are of opinion, therefore, that

The judgment of the Circuit Court should be reversed, and the cause remanded, with directions to award a new trial. **[l]**

MR. JUSTICE MILLER, with whom was the CHIEF JUSTICE, concurring:

[JUSTICE MILLER argued that because there was no search and seizure authorized by the statute, it did not violate the Fourth Amendment.]

I concur in the judgment of the court, reversing that of the Circuit Court, and in so much of the opinion of this court as holds the [statute] void as applicable to the present case.

I am of opinion that this is a criminal case within the meaning of that clause of the Fifth Amendment to the Constitution of the United States which declares that no person "shall be compelled in any criminal case to be a witness against himself." **[m]**

And I am quite satisfied that the effect of the act of Congress is to compel the party on whom the order of the court is served to be a witness against himself. * * *

*   *   *   *   *   *   *   *   *   *   *

COMMENTS

[a] The Court referred specifically to the "self-incrimination" clause of the Fifth Amendment.

[b] Unlike the concurrence, the majority does not adhere to a literal reading of the Fourth Amendment.

[c] This may no longer be good law. A summons to appear is not the equivalent of an arrest, *United States v. Dionisio*, 410 U.S. 1 (1973).

[d] The Fourth Amendment contains two clauses, a "warrant clause" and a "reasonableness clause." To find a violation of the Amendment, a search and seizure must be "unreasonable."

[e] If a law or practice is unconstitutional, the fact that the government and the courts mistakenly enforced it for long periods of time does not make it constitutional.

[f] In these examples the Court sets great store on the *property* right of the defendant to the goods. For a long time, the Court based its Fourth Amendment cases on property right notions. But this conceptual basis was overturned by *Katz v. United States* [this volume] which found that Fourth Amendment rights are essentially personal rights.

[g] A person has no property right to possess contraband or illegal goods, and so, under the Court's reasoning has no Fourth Amendment protection. This approach is no longer entirely in force, *i.e.*, police must have a warrant or probable cause to seize contraband which is not in plain view, *Stanley v. Georgia*, 394 U.S. 557 (1969).

[h] The Court reviewed the history of *Paxton*'s case, a famous 1761 Boston case, where James Otis argued unsuccessfully that the English writs of assistance used to authorize searches of merchants' warehouses by "Redcoats" enforcing the Stamp Act violated fundamental principles of the British constitution. It also reviewed, at length, the 1765 English case of *Entick v. Carrington*, in which the English courts held the searches of houses for seditious materials were illegal. These events were very much on the minds of the framers of the Bill of Rights when the Fourth Amendment was proposed.

[i] The close coupling of the Fourth and Fifth Amendment is not now taken as an operative legal norm. Nevertheless, this concept was the hinge on which a majority was cobbled together in *Mapp v. Ohio* [this volume].

[j] The Fourth Amendment applies against all governmental intrusions, whether by police or civil agents; see *Camara v. Municipal Court* [this volume].

[k] James Madison, in proposing the Bill of Rights to the House of Representatives, said that judges "will consider themselves in a peculiar manner the guardians of those rights. * * *" Randy E. Barnett, ed., *The Rights Retained by the People*, p. 61 (Fairfax, Va.: George Mason University Press, 1989).

[l] The Fifth Amendment effect of *Boyd* has been weakened subsequently by the

Supreme Court. It is now clear that the protections of the Fifth Amendment against the compulsory production of documents applies only to natural persons and not to corporations [*Hale v. Henkel*, 201 U.S. 43 (1906)], unincorporated organizations [*United States v. White*, 322 U.S. 694 (1944)], or partnerships [*Bellis v. United States*, 417 U.S. 85 (1974)]. Physical, as opposed to testimonial, evidence is not protected from seizure [*Holt v. United States*, 218 U.S. 245 (1910)]. In *Fisher v. United States*, 425 U.S. 391 (1976), the Court ruled that the privacy protections of the Fourth Amendment do not apply to the subpoena of documents; as the Fifth Amendment protects against compulsion, a custodian of a person's records who has not fear of incrimination may be compelled to give up a person's records.

[m] It was not entirely clear whether the federal statute established a civil or a criminal fine for maintaining false invoices; the Supreme Court is not bound by the declaration of a legislature, but can look to the actual effect of a statute to determine whether it is civil or criminal in nature. *Allen v. Illinois*, 478 U.S. 364 (1986).

WEEKS v. UNITED STATES

232 U.S. 383, 58 L.Ed. 652, 34 S.Ct. 341 (1914)

MR. JUSTICE DAY delivered the opinion of the court.

[Weeks was convicted in federal court for mailing lottery tickets interstate, a federal crime. Local police officers, and later a United States marshall, without a warrant or Weeks' consent, obtained a key, entered his house, searched it and seized both incriminating and nonincriminating evidence. Before trial Weeks filed a petition for the return of his private property, claiming violations of both the Missouri and the United States Constitutions. The nonincriminating items were returned before trial but the incriminating lottery tickets seized from his house were entered into evidence.]

* * * [T]he framers of the Amendments to the Federal Constitution [intended] to provide for that instrument a Bill of Rights, securing to the American people, among other things, those safeguards which had grown up in England to protect the people from unreasonable searches and seizures, such as were permitted under the general warrants issued under authority of the Government by which there had been invasions of the home and privacy of the citizens and the seizure of their private papers in support of charges, real or imaginary, made against them. Such practices had also received sanction under warrants and seizures under the so-called writs of assistance, issued in the American colonies. * * * Resistance to these practices had established the principle which was enacted into the fundamen-

tal law in the Fourth Amendment, that a man's house was his castle and not to be invaded by any general authority to search and seize his goods and papers. * * *

The effect of the Fourth Amendment is to put the courts of the United States and Federal officials, in the exercise of their power and authority, under limitations and restraints as to the exercise of such power and authority, and to forever secure the people, their persons, houses, papers and effects against all unreasonable searches and seizures under the guise of law. This protection reaches all alike, whether accused of crime or not, and the duty of giving to it force and effect is obligatory upon all entrusted under our Federal system with the enforcement of the laws. The tendency of those who execute the criminal laws of the country to obtain conviction by means of unlawful seizures and enforced confessions, [a] the latter often obtained after subjecting accused persons to unwarranted practices destructive of rights secured by the Federal Constitution, should find no sanction in the judgments of the courts which are charged at all times with the support of the Constitution and to which people of all conditions have a right to appeal for the maintenance of such fundamental rights. [b]

What then is the present case? Before answering that inquiry specifically, it may be well by a process of exclusion to state what it is not. It is not an assertion of the right on the part of the Government, always recognized under English and American law, to search the person of the accused when legally arrested to discover and seize the fruits or evidences of crime. This right has been uniformly maintained in many cases. * * * Nor is it the case of testimony offered at a trial where the court is asked to stop and consider the illegal means by which proofs, otherwise competent, were obtained—of which we shall have occasion to treat later in this opinion. Nor is it the case of burglar's tools or other proofs of guilt found upon his arrest within the control of the accused. [c]

* * * If letters and private documents can * * * be seized and held and used in evidence against a citizen accused of an offense [as in this case], the protection of the Fourth Amendment declaring his right to be secure against such searches and seizures is of no value, and, so far as those thus placed are concerned, might as well be stricken from the Constitution. The efforts of the courts and their officials to bring the guilty to punishment, praiseworthy as they are, are not to be aided by the sacrifice of those great principles established by years of endeavor and suffering which have resulted in their embodiment in the fundamental law of the land. [d] The United States Marshal could only have invaded the house of the accused when armed with a warrant issued as required by the Constitution, upon sworn information and describing with reasonable particularity the thing for which the search was to be made. Instead, he acted without sanction of law, doubtless prompted by the desire to bring further proof to the aid of the Government, and under color of his office [e] undertook to make a seizure

of private papers in direct violation of the constitutional prohibition against such action. Under such circumstances, without sworn information and particular description, not even an order of court would have justified such procedure, much less was it within the authority of the United States Marshal to thus invade the house and privacy of the accused. In *Adams v. New York*, 192 U.S. 585, this court said that the Fourth Amendment was intended to secure the citizen in person and property against unlawful invasion of the sanctity of his home by officers of the law acting under legislative or judicial sanction. This protection is equally extended to the action of the Government and officers of the law acting under it. (*Boyd* case, [this volume]) [f] To sanction such proceedings would be to affirm by judicial decision a manifest neglect if not an open defiance of the prohibitions of the Constitution, [b] intended for the protection of the people against such unauthorized action.

[The federal trial court operated on the principle] that the letters having come into the control of the court, it would not inquire into the manner in which they were obtained, but if competent would keep them and permit their use in evidence. Such proposition, the Government asserts, is conclusively established by certain decisions of this court, the first of which is *Adams v. New York*. [In *Adams*, officers seized incriminating papers acting under a search warrant authorizing the seizure of "policy" or betting slips. The Court in that case] put its decision upon the ground that the papers found in the execution of the search warrant, which warrant had a legal purpose in the attempt to find gambling paraphernalia, were competent evidence against the accused, and their offer in testimony did not violate his constitutional privilege against unlawful search or seizure, for it was held that such incriminatory documents thus discovered were not the subject of an unreasonable search and seizure, and in effect that the same were incidentally seized in the lawful execution of a warrant and not in the wrongful invasion of the home of the citizen and the unwarranted seizure of his papers and property. * * * [g]

[In many state cases, the principle is] "* * * that the court, when engaged in the trial of a criminal action, will not take notice of the manner in which a witness [h] has possessed himself of papers or other chattels, subjects of evidence, which are material and properly offered in evidence. * * * Such an investigation is not involved necessarily in the litigation in chief, and to pursue it would be to halt in the orderly progress of a cause, and consider incidentally a question which has happened to cross the path of such litigation, and which is wholly independent thereof."

It is therefore evident that the *Adams* Case affords no authority for the action of the court in this case,

when applied to in due season for the return of papers seized in violation of the Constitutional Amendment. The decision in that case rests upon incidental seizure made in the execution of a legal warrant and in the application of the doctrine that a collateral issue will not be raised to ascertain the source from which testimony, competent in a criminal case, comes.

* * *

We therefore reach the conclusion that the letters in question were taken from the house of the accused by an official of the United States acting under color of his office in direct violation of the constitutional rights of the defendant; that having made a seasonable application for their return, which was heard and passed upon by the court, there was involved in the order refusing the application a denial of the constitutional rights of the accused, and that the court should have restored these letters to the accused. In holding them and permitting their use upon the trial, we think prejudicial error was committed. * * *

It results that the judgment of the court below must be reversed, and the case remanded for further proceedings in accordance with this opinion.

* * * * * * * * * * *

COMMENTS

[a] The problem of the "third degree" or confessions obtained by beatings or torture were seen as a significant social problem throughout the first half of the twentieth century. Attitudes toward the police were ambivalent not only among the lower classes but among the middle and upper classes as well. See, *e.g.*, *Brown v. Mississippi* [this volume].

[b] The concept of "judicial propriety" is central to the development of the exclusionary rule. It was seen in *Weeks* and *Mapp* [this volume] to have constitutional

weight.   Nevertheless, in cases such as *United States v. Leon* [this volume], this rationale vanished. Why did this occur? This is an example of both the dynamic quality of legal reasoning and the political aspects of constitutional law, as the law shifts with the changing makeup of the Supreme Court.

[c] Later cases specified more clearly the scope of exceptions to the warrant requirement of the Fourth Amendment [see Chapter 3, this volume]. Nevertheless, those exceptions were part of the common law heritage of this branch of law and in a sense "built into" the Constitution by assumption. A strictly literal reading of the Constitution on this point would make law enforcement impossible.

[d] Without using the term, the Court is here balancing the needs of law enforcement with the civil liberties of all citizens.

[e] Keep this language in mind when reading Comment [h], below.

[f] The reference to the "Government" here is to the United States government and not to the governments of the states or localities. This case applies only to federal authorities.

[g] The Court here rules that the real principle of the decision in *Adams* was "plain view" and not the broader concept that the courts will never inquire into the way in which evidence was obtained.

[h] Note the difference between the reference to "a witness" here and an officer "acting under color of his office" at Comment [e] above. The Court, in effect, preserves the general rule, but finds an exception when the persons who have gathered evidence by illegal search and seizures are state officers. This is part of the more fundamental principle that in most cases private parties cannot violate the constitutional rights of another; constitutional violations presuppose state action. See *Burdeau v. McDowell*, 256 U.S. 465 (1921); *Walter v. United States*, 447 U.S. 649 (1980); and *United States v. Jacobsen*, 466 U.S. 109 (1984). The general rule, that the court will not stay a prosecution because the means of apprehension are illegal, is still the case in the law of arrest, *Frisbie v. Collins*, [this volume]; *United States v. Alvarez-Machain*, [this volume].

SILVERTHORNE LUMBER COMP. v. UNITED STATES

251 U.S. 385, 64 L.Ed. 319, 40 S.Ct. 182 (1920)

MR. JUSTICE HOLMES delivered the opinion of the court.

[Federal officers illegally searched the petitioners' offices and incriminating evidence was seized. The Silverthornes made a motion for the return of the papers. The papers were photographed and returned. Based on the photographic evidence, new indictments were returned against the Silverthornes.] The Government now, while in form repudiating and condemning the illegal seizure, seeks to maintain its right to avail itself of the knowledge obtained by that means which otherwise it would not have had.

The proposition could not be presented more nakedly. It is that although of course its seizure was an outrage which the Government now regrets, it may study the papers before it returns them, copy them, and then may use the knowledge that it has gained to call upon the owners in a more regular form to produce them; that the protection of the Constitution covers the physical possession but not any advantages that the Government can gain over the object of its pursuit by doing the forbidden act. *Weeks v. United States*, [this volume]* * * to be sure, had established that laying the papers directly before the grand jury was unwarranted, but it is taken to mean only that two steps are required instead of one. In our opinion such is not the law. It reduces the Fourth Amendment to a form of words. The essence of a provision forbidding the acquisition of evidence in a certain way is that not merely evidence so acquired shall not be used before the Court but that it shall not be used at all. Of course this does not mean that the facts thus obtained become sacred and inaccessible. If knowledge of them is gained from an independent source they may be proved like any others, but the knowledge gained by the Government's own wrong cannot be used by it in the way proposed. * * *

Judgment reversed.

THE CHIEF JUSTICE and MR. JUSTICE PITNEY dissent.

*   *   *   *   *   *   *   *   *   *   *

COMMENT

The government's ploy seems unduly "legalistic." Given the recency of the *Weeks* exclusionary rule, the government was testing the Supreme Court to see whether it was holding steadfastly to its rule. There is nothing to prevent parties from testing established rules. Indeed, this regularly occurs and injects an element of dynamism into the law. For example, compare *Wolf v. Colorado* with *Mapp v. Ohio* [this volume] with *United States v. Leon* [this volume], *Spinelli v. United States* [this volume] with *Illinois v. Gates* [this volume], and *Betts v. Brady* [this volume] with *Gideon v. Wainwright*.

MOORE v. DEMPSEY

261 U.S. 86, 67 L.Ed. 543, 43 S.Ct. 265 (1923)

MR. JUSTICE HOLMES delivered the opinion of the Court.

This is an appeal from an order of the District Court for the Eastern District of Arkansas dismissing a writ of *habeas corpus* upon demurrer, the presiding judge certifying that there was probable cause for allowing the appeal. * * * The appellants are five negroes who were convicted of murder in the first degree and sentenced to death by the Court of the State of Arkansas. The ground of the petition for the writ is that the proceedings in the State Court, although a trial in form, were only a form, [a] and that the appellants were hurried to conviction under the pressure of a mob without any regard for their rights and without according to them due process of law.

The case stated by the petition is as follows, and it will be understood that while we put it in narrative form, we are not affirming the facts to be as stated but only what we must take them to be, as they are admitted by the demurrer: On the night of September 30, 1919, a number of colored people assembled in their church were attacked and fired upon by a body of white men, and in the disturbance that followed a white man was killed. The report of the killing caused great excitement and was followed by the hunting down and shooting of many negroes and also by the killing on October 1 of one Clinton Lee, a white man, for whose murder the petitioners were indicted. They seem to have been arrested with many others on the

same day. The petitioners say that Lee must have been killed by other whites, but that we leave on one side as what we have to deal with is not the petitioners' innocence or guilt but solely the question whether their constitutional rights have been preserved. [b] They say that their meeting was to employ counsel for protection against extortions practiced upon them by the landowners and that the landowners tried to prevent their effort, but that again we pass by as not directly bearing upon the trial. [c] It should be mentioned however that O. S. Bratton, a son of the counsel who is said to have been contemplated and who took part in the argument here, arriving for consultation on October 1, is said to have barely escaped being mobbed; that he was arrested and confined during the month on a charge of murder and on October 31 was indicted for barratry, [d] but later in the day was told that he would be discharged but that he must leave secretly by a closed automobile to take the train at West Helena, four miles away, to avoid being mobbed. It is alleged that the judge of the Court in which the petitioners were tried facilitated the departure and went with Bratton to see him safely off.

A Committee of Seven was appointed by the Governor in regard to what the committee called the "insurrection" in the county. The newspapers daily published inflammatory articles. On the 7th a statement by one of the committee was made public to the effect that the present trouble was "a deliberately planned insurrection of the negroes against the whites, directed by an organization known as the 'Progressive Farmers' and House-hold Union of America' established for the purpose of banding negroes to-gether for the killing of white people." According to the statement the organi-zation was started by a swindler to get money from the blacks.

Shortly after the arrest of the petitioners a mob marched to the jail for the purpose of lynching them but were prevented by the presence of United States troops and the promise of some of the Committee of Seven and other leading officials that if the mob would refrain, as the petition puts it, they would execute those found guilty in the form of law. The Com-mittee's own statement was that the reason that the people refrained from mob violence was "that this Committee gave our citizens their solemn promise that the law would be carried out." According to affidavits of two white men and the colored witnesses on whose testimony the petitioners were convicted, produced by the petitioners since the last decision of the Supreme Court hereafter mentioned, the Com-mittee made good their promise by calling colored witnesses and having them whipped and tortured until they would say what was wanted, among them being the two relied on to prove the petitioners' guilt. However this may be, a grand jury of white men was organized on October 27 with one of the Committee of Seven and, it is alleged, with many of a posse orga-nized to fight the blacks, upon it, and on the morning of the 29th the indict-ment was returned. On November 3 the petitioners were brought into Court, informed that a certain lawyer was appointed their counsel and were

placed on trial before a white jury—blacks being systematically excluded from both grand and petit juries. The Court and neighborhood were thronged with an adverse crowd that threatened the most dangerous consequences to anyone interfering with the desired result. The counsel did not venture to demand delay or a change of venue, to challenge a juryman or to ask for separate trials. He had had no preliminary consultation with the accused, called no witnesses for the defence although they could have been produced, and did not put the defen-dants on the stand. The trial lasted about three-quarters of an hour and in less than five minutes the jury brought in a verdict of guilty of murder in the first degree. According to the allega-tions and affidavits there never was a chance for the petitioners to be acquit-ted; no juryman could have voted for an acquittal and continued to live in Phillips County and if any prisoner by any chance had been acquitted by a jury he could not have escaped the mob. [e]

[Post-trial events also indicated the existence of a mob spirit abroad in Arkansas. The state Governor was petitioned by members of the Commit-tee of Seven, the American Legion and the Rotary Club to 'let justice take its course' and not to commute the death sentences. In their petitions that said that the defendants were not lynched on the "solemn promise" that "justice would be done and the majesty of the law upheld."]

In *Frank v. Mangum*, 237 U.S. 309 (1915), [f] it was recognized of course that if in fact a trial is dominated by a mob so that there is an actual interfer-ence with the course of justice, there is a departure from due process of law;

and that "if the State, supplying no corrective process, carries into execution a judgment of death or imprisonment based upon a verdict thus produced by mob domination, the State deprives the accused of his life or liberty without due process of law." [g] We assume in accordance with that case that the corrective process supplied by the State may be so adequate that interference by *habeas corpus* ought not to be allowed. [h] It certainly is true that mere mistakes of law in the course of a trial are not to be corrected in that way. But if the case is that the whole proceeding is a mask—that counsel, jury and judge were swept to the fatal end by an irresistible wave of public passion, and that the State Courts failed to correct the wrong, neither perfection in the machinery for correction nor the possibility that the trial court and counsel saw no other way of avoiding an immediate outbreak of the mob can prevent this Court from securing to the petitioners their constitutional rights. [i]

[The state courts found no violations of defendants' right on appeal. A *habeas corpus* petition to the federal district court followed.] We shall not say more concerning the corrective process afforded to the petitioners than that it does not seem to us sufficient to allow a Judge of the United States to escape the duty of examining the facts for himself when if true as alleged they make the trial absolutely void. We have confined the statement to facts admitted by the demurrer. We will not say that they cannot be met, but it appears to us unavoidable that the District Judge should find whether the facts alleged are true and whether they can be explained so far

as to leave the state proceedings undisturbed.

Order reversed. The case to stand for hearing before the District Court.

MR. JUSTICE McREYNOLDS, dissenting.

* * *

The matter is one of gravity. If every man convicted of crime in a state court may thereafter resort to the federal court and by swearing, as advised, that certain allegations of fact tending to impeach his trial are "true to the best of his knowledge and belief," thereby obtain as of right further review, another way has been added to a list already unfortunately long to prevent prompt punishment. The delays incident to enforcement of our criminal laws have become a national scandal and give serious alarm to those who observe. Wrongly to decide the present cause probably will produce very unfortunate consequences. [j]

[JUSTICE McREYNOLDS stated that he agreed with the principle of *Frank v. Mangum*, and quoted from that opinion]:

* * *

"* * * Under the terms of [the federal *habeas corpus* statute] in order to entitle the present appellant to the relief sought, it must appear that he is held in custody in violation of the Constitution of the United States. . . . Mere errors in point of law, however serious, committed by a criminal court in the exercise of its jurisdiction over a case properly subject to its cognizance, cannot be reviewed by *habeas corpus*. That writ cannot be employed as a substitute for the writ of error. * * *

"As to the 'due process of law' that is required by the Fourteenth Amendment, it is perfectly well settled that a criminal prosecution in the courts of a State, based upon a law not in itself repugnant to the Federal Constitution, and conducted according to the settled course of judicial proceedings as established by the law of the State, so long as it includes notice, and a hearing, or an opportunity to be heard, before a court of competent jurisdiction, according to established modes of procedure, is 'due process' in the constitutional sense. * * *

* * *

"We of course agree that if a trial is in fact dominated by a mob, so that the jury is intimidated and the trial judge yields, and so that there is an actual interference with the course of justice, there is, in that court, a departure from due process of law in the proper sense of that term. And if the State, supplying no corrective process, carries into execution a judgment of death or imprisonment based upon a verdict thus produced by mob domination, the State deprives the accused of his life or liberty without due process of law. * * *"

"But the State may supply such corrective process as to it seems proper. * * *"

Let us consider with some detail what was presented to the court below.

There was the complete record of the cause in the state courts—trial and Supreme—showing no irregularity. After indictment the defendants were arraigned for trial and eminent counsel appointed to defend them. He cross-examined the witnesses, made exceptions and evidently was careful to preserve a full and complete transcript of the proceedings. The trial was unusually short but there is nothing in the record to indicate that it was illegally hastened. * * * **[k]**

* * *

[JUSTICE McREYNOLDS went on to detail both the "insurrection" at Elaine, Arkansas in September 1919 and the procedural steps afforded to the defendants after the trial.]

The Supreme Court of the State twice reversed the conviction of other negroes charged with committing murder during the disorders of September, 1919. The first opinion came down on the very day upon which the judgment against petitioners was affirmed, and held the verdict so defective that no judgment could be entered upon it. The second directed a reversal because the trial court had refused to hear evidence on the motion to set aside the regular panel of the petit jury. * * * Years have passed since they were convicted of an atrocious crime. Certainly they have not been rushed towards the death chair; on the contrary there has been long delay and some impatience over the result is not unnatural. The recent execution of assassins in England within thirty days of the crime, affords a striking contrast.

With all those things before him, I am unable to say that the District Judge, acquainted with local conditions, erred when he held the petition for the writ of *habeas corpus* insufficient. His duty was to consider the whole case and decide whether there appeared to be substantial reason for further proceedings.

Under the disclosed circumstances I cannot agree that the solemn adjudications by courts of a great State, which this Court has refused to review, can be successfully impeached by the mere *ex parte* affidavits made upon information and belief of ignorant convicts joined by two white men— confessedly atrocious criminals. [l] The fact that petitioners are poor and ignorant and black naturally arouses sympathy; but that does not release us from enforcing principles which are essential to the orderly operation of our federal system.

I am authorized to say that MR. JUSTICE SUTHERLAND concurs in this dissent.

*   *   *   *   *   *   *   *   *   *

COMMENTS

[a] A frequent criticism of the law is its excessive formality. A fundamental premise of criminal procedure is that the formal procedures of due process are essential to preserving the rights of defendants to fair trials against popular and political pressure. Here, the Court recognizes the reverse; that the mere form of law can be a cover for unfairness and injustice. In other words, the formalities of due process have to be carried out in the spirit of a "fair fight."

[b] Laypersons often think that the role of a Supreme Court is to "correct injustice" or to finally determine the facts of a case. State supreme courts and the federal Supreme Court exist to review questions of law and thereby settle the rights of the parties, but not to retry the facts. The Supreme Court has almost total discretion over its docket and therefore takes cases in order to modify law and constitutional policy. The Supreme Court hears no witnesses and decides a case entirely on the written arguments in the lawyers' "briefs" and on oral arguments.

[c] JUSTICE HOLMES makes it clear that the decision of the Court is not an exercise of partisan politics, *i.e.*, the Court is not deciding as it does out of sympathy of the cause of the defendants; nevertheless, in some cases it is necessary to understand the social or political background of a case in order to understand its legal importance. The brief account of an attempt by African Americans in 1919 to organize for economic and social justice in the deep South, coming in a tumultuous year that experienced a Wall Street bombing and the deportation of over 500 "Reds" to Russia, enables the reader to understand the likelihood and intensity of mob violence.

[d] Barratry is the "offense of frequently exciting and stirring up quarrels and suits, either at law or otherwise." *Black's Law Dictionary*, Fifth Edition, p. 137. Attorneys could be charged with barratry for stirring up unnecessary litigation. Bratton was apparently charged with barratry as a pressure tactic to frighten him into dropping his

Bratton was apparently charged with barratry as a pressure tactic to frighten him into dropping his defense on behalf of the defendants.

[e] Even omitting the more lurid facts of the case concerning the torture of witnesses and the organization of the mob, JUSTICE HOLMES' dry recounting of what the defense attorney did *not* do raises a question about the fairness of the proceedings in a murder case.

[f] In *Frank v. Mangum* the majority found no due process violation and thus no grounds for a federal *habeas corpus* action. JUSTICE HOLMES, joined by JUSTICE HUGHES, dissented, arguing that a mob atmosphere in the courtroom, with evidence of a palpable fear of violence, renders the trial a mere form. "Mob law does not become due process of law by securing the assent of a terrorized jury."

[g] The core holding of the case is that *state* citizens in *state* proceedings are protected by the due process clause of the Fourteenth Amendment and that in state proceedings the *national* standards of due process must be upheld.

[h] In *Frank v. Mangum* the Court relied on the finding of the Georgia courts that the disturbances in the courtroom were not serious. In this case the Court is more willing to whether the state, by its appellate process (including direct appeal and *habeas corpus* hearings), can correct any trial errors.

[i] A "good motive" of avoiding a lynching is not a good excuse for conducting a trial that violates due process. A federal court has clear jurisdiction to hear such a case to guarantee *federal* rights, even if the state has adequate appellate courts.

[j] The practical consideration of delays of justice is a staple argument against extending access to federal rights. In the 1960s the Supreme Court expanded access to justice by state petitioners; in the following years, the Court has contracted the ability of state petitioners to have their cases heard in federal court.

[k] From reading the same record, the dissenting justices draw a different conclusion than that drawn by the majority.

[l] The dissent places greater weight on the authority of the state courts and is less willing to interfere with the state courts; thus giving greater weight to "federalism." The majority, on the other hand, were more willing to exercise federal judicial power.

PALKO v. CONNECTICUT

302 U.S. 319, 58 S.Ct. 149, 82 L.Ed. 288 (1937)

MR. JUSTICE CARDOZO delivered the opinion of the Court.

[Palko, indicted for first degree murder, was found guilty by a jury of murder in the second degree and given a life sentence. The state appealed under a law that allowed it to appeal "in the same manner and to the same effect as if made by the accused." The appellate court found legal errors at trial that prejudiced the prosecution. A second trial was granted; Palko was found guilty of murder in the first degree and sentenced to death.] **[a]**

[The] statute * * * is challenged by appellant as an infringement of the Fourteenth Amendment of the Constitution of the United States. Whether the challenge should be upheld is now to be determined. * * *

[Palko] made the objection that the effect of the new trial was to place him twice in jeopardy for the same offense, and in so doing to violate the Fourteenth Amendment of the Constitution of the United States. * * *

The argument for appellant is that whatever is forbidden by the Fifth Amendment is forbidden by the Fourteenth also. The Fifth Amendment, which is not directed to the states, but solely to the federal government, creates immunity from double jeopardy. No person shall be "subject for the same offense to be twice put in jeopardy of life or limb." The Fourteenth Amendment ordains, "nor shall any State deprive any person of life, liberty, or property, without due process of law." To retry a defendant, though under one indictment and only one, subjects him, it is said, to double jeopardy in violation of the Fifth Amendment, if the prosecution is one on behalf of the United States. From this the consequence is said to follow that there is a denial of life or liberty without due process of law, if the prosecution is one on behalf of the People of a State. * * *

[The Supreme Court had held, in split opinions, that in a federal case a new trial obtained on the government's motion, rather than the defendant's, violated the double jeopardy clause of the Fifth Amendment]. Even more plainly, right-minded men could reasonably believe that in espousing that conclusion they were not favoring a practice repugnant to the conscience of mankind. Is double jeopardy in such circumstances, if double jeopardy it must be called, a denial of due process forbidden to the states? The tyranny of labels, * * * must not lead us to leap to a conclusion that a word which in one set of facts may stand for oppression or enormity is of like effect in every other. **[b]**

We have said that in appellant's view the Fourteenth Amendment is to be taken as embodying the prohibitions of the Fifth. His thesis is even broader. Whatever would be a violation of the original bill of rights (Amendments I to VIII) if done by the federal government is now equally unlawful by force of the Fourteenth Amendment if done by a state. There is no such general rule. **[c]**

The Fifth Amendment provides, **[d]** among other things, that no person shall be held to answer for a capital or otherwise infamous crime unless on presentment or indictment of a grand jury. This court has held that, in prosecutions by a state, presentment or indictment by a grand jury may give way to informations at the instance of a public officer. *Hurtado v. California*, 110 U.S. 516. * * * The Fifth Amendment provides also that no person shall be compelled in any criminal case to be a witness against himself. This court has said that, in prosecutions by a state, the exemption will fail if the state elects to end it. *Twining v. New Jersey*, 211 U.S. 78, * * * The Sixth Amendment calls for a jury trial in criminal cases and the Seventh for a jury trial in civil cases at common law where the value in controversy shall exceed twenty dollars. This court has ruled that consistently with those amendments trial by jury may be modified by a state or abolished altogether. * * *

On the other hand, the due process clause of the Fourteenth Amendment may make it unlawful for a state to abridge by its statutes the freedom of speech which the First Amendment safeguards against encroachment by the Congress; * * * or the like freedom of the press; or the free exercise of religion; * * * or the right of peaceable assembly, without which speech would be unduly trammeled * * * ; or the right of one accused of crime to the benefit of counsel. * * * In these and other situations immunities that are valid as against the federal government by force of the specific pledges of particular amendments have been found to be implicit in the concept of ordered liberty, and thus, through the Fourteenth Amendment, become valid as against the states.

The line of division may seem to be wavering and broken if there is a hasty catalogue of the cases on the one side and the other. Reflection and analysis will induce a different view. There emerges the perception of a rationalizing principle which gives to discrete instances a proper order and coherence. [e] The right to trial by jury and the immunity from prosecution except as the result of an indictment may have value and importance. Even so, they are not of the very essence of a scheme of ordered liberty. To abolish them is not to violate a "principle of justice so rooted in the traditions and conscience of our people as to be ranked as fundamental." * * * Few would be so narrow or provincial as to maintain that a fair and enlightened system of justice would be impossible without them. What is true of jury trials and indictments is true also, as the cases show, of the immunity from compulsory self-incrimination. * * * This too might be lost, and justice still be done. Indeed, today as in the past there are students of our penal system who look upon the immunity as a mischief rather than a benefit, and who would limit its scope, or destroy it altogether. No doubt there would remain the need to give protection against torture, physical or mental. *Brown v. Mississippi*, [this volume]. Justice, however, would not perish if the accused were subject to a duty to respond to orderly inquiry. The exclusion of these immunities and privileges from the privileges and immunities protected against the action of the states has not been arbitrary or casual. It has been dictated by a study and appreciation of the meaning, the essential implications, of liberty itself.

[f]

We reach a different plane of social and moral values when we pass to the privileges and immunities that have been taken over from the earlier articles of the federal bill of rights and brought within the Fourteenth Amendment by a process of absorption. These in their origin were effective against the federal government alone. If the Fourteenth Amendment has absorbed them, the process of absorption has had its source in the belief that neither liberty nor justice would exist if they were sacrificed. * * * This is true, for illustration, of freedom of thought, and speech. Of that freedom one may say that it is the matrix, the indispensable condition, of nearly every other form of freedom. With rare aberrations a pervasive recognition of that truth can be traced in our history, political and legal. So it has come about that the domain of liberty, withdrawn by the Fourteenth Amendment from encroachment by the states, has been enlarged by latter-day judgments to include liberty of the mind as well as liberty of action. The extension became, indeed, a logical imperative when once it was recognized, as long ago it was, that liberty is something more than exemption from physical restraint, and that even in the field of substantive rights and duties the legislative judgment, if oppressive and arbitrary, may be overridden by the courts. * * * Fundamental too in the concept of due process, and so in that of liberty, is the thought that condemnation shall be rendered only after trial. * * * The hearing, moreover, must be a real one, not a sham or a pretense. *Moore v. Dempsey* [this volume]. For that reason, ignorant defendants in a capital case were held

to have been condemned unlawfully when in truth, though not in form, they were refused the aid of counsel. *Powell v. Alabama*, [this volume]. The decision did not turn upon the fact that the benefit of counsel would have been guaranteed to the defendants by the provisions of the Sixth Amendment if they had been prosecuted in a federal court. The decision turned upon the fact that in the particular situation laid before us in the evidence the benefit of counsel was essential to the substance of a hearing.

Our survey of the cases serves, we think, to justify the statement that the dividing line between them, if not unfaltering throughout its course, has been true for the most part to a unifying principle. On which side of the line the case made out by the appellant has appropriate location must be the next inquiry and the final one. Is that kind of double jeopardy to which the statute has subjected him a hardship so acute and shocking that our polity will not endure it? Does it violate those "fundamental principles of liberty and justice which lie at the base of all our civil and political institutions"? * * * The answer surely must be "no." What the answer would have to be if the state were permitted after a trial free from error to try the accused over again or to bring another case against him, we have no occasion to consider. We deal with the statute before us and no other. The state is not attempting to wear the accused out by a multitude of cases with accumulated trials. It asks no more than this, that the case against him shall go on until there shall be a trial free from the corrosion of substantial legal error. * * * This is not cruelty at all, nor even vexation in any immoderate degree. If the trial had been infected with error adverse to the accused, there might have been review at his instance, and as often as necessary to purge the vicious taint. **[g]** A reciprocal privilege, subject at all times to the discretion of the presiding judge, * * * has now been granted to the state.

There is here no seismic innovation. The edifice of justice stands, its symmetry, to many, greater than before.

* * *

The judgment is
Affirmed.

MR. JUSTICE BUTLER dissents.

* * * * * * * * * *

COMMENTS

[a] The increase in penalty from life imprisonment to the death penalty did not affect any Justice except for Pierce Butler. Could you decide this case without considering this consequence?

[b] Specific legal decisions are made in the context of general rules; generalities themselves are not legal rules. JUSTICE CARDOZO here tries to separate the generality of the federal rule from the specific application of this case, which involves a competing general principle of when a provision of the Bill of Rights is so fundamental as to violate the due process clause of the Fourteenth Amendment.

[c] This is the concept of "total incorporation" of the Bill of Rights into the Due Process Clause of the Fourteenth Amendment. Although the Court has never accepted this doctrine, by the time of the *Palko* case it had to accept the reality of "selective incorporation."

[d] This paragraph lists elements of the Bill of Rights that are "out," *i.e.*, not "absorbed" or "incorporated" into the due process clause of the Fourteenth Amendment by the process of selective incorporation. The following paragraph lists elements of the Bill of Rights that are "in."

[e] One of the chief tasks of a Supreme Court is to provide principles so that specific case decisions fit into a body of law; if cases do not fit together logically, lower courts and administrators will have difficulty in deciding cases. Thinking through the principles that explain a group of cases can lead to the conclusion that some of the cases were incorrectly decided. In this case, JUSTICE CARDOZO's opinion for the Court provides a justification for all the decisions.

[f] In this paragraph JUSTICE CARDOZO, relying in part on critics of the Anglo-American justice system, plausibly argues that the elimination of the specific rights listed does not transform a nation of political liberty into an autocracy. Many free and democratic nations do not enjoy these rights. What he did not ask was how the loss of all these rights at the state level would transform the nature of the American justice system. The Supreme Court took up this question three decades later in *Duncan v. Louisiana* [this volume].

[g] The Court holds open the possibility that if a state prosecuted a defendant numerous times after a conviction or an acquittal simply to get a conviction or a more severe sentence, that such action might violate the defendant's due process rights under the Fourteenth Amendment.

ADAMSON v. CALIFORNIA

332 U.S. 46, 67 S.Ct. 1672, 91 L.Ed. 1903 (1947)

Mr. Justice REED delivered the opinion of the Court.

The appellant, Adamson, a citizen of the United States, [a] was convicted * * * by a jury in * * * California of murder. * * * The provisions of California law which were challenged in the state proceedings as invalid under the Fourteenth Amendment to the Federal Constitution * * * permit the failure of a defendant to explain or deny evidence against him to be commented upon by court and by counsel and to be considered by court and jury. The defendant did not testify. * * *

The appellant was charged * * * with former convictions [b] for burglary, larceny and robbery and [his acknowledgement] barred allusion to these [prior] convictions on the trial. * * * [H]owever, if the defendant * * * takes the witness stand to deny or explain away other evidence that has been introduced, [the prior crimes can be] "revealed to the jury on cross-examination to impeach his testimony." * * * This forces an accused who is a repeated offender to choose between the risk of having his prior offenses disclosed to the jury or of having it draw harmful inferences from uncontradicted evidence that can only be denied or explained by the defendant.

In the first place, appellant urges that the provision of the Fifth Amendment that no person "shall be compelled in any criminal case to be a witness against himself" is a fundamental national privilege or immunity protected against state abridgment by the Fourteenth Amendment or a privilege or immunity secured, through the Fourteenth Amendment, against deprivation by state action because it is a personal right, enumerated in the federal Bill of Rights. [c]

Secondly, appellant relies upon the due process of law clause of the Fourteenth Amendment to invalidate the provisions of the California law * * * (a) because comment on failure to testify is permitted, (b) because appellant was forced to forego testimony in person because of danger of disclosure of his past convictions through cross-examination, and (c) because the presumption of innocence was infringed by the shifting of the burden of proof to appellant in permitting comment on his failure to testify. [d]

We shall assume, but without any intention thereby of ruling upon the issue, that permission by law to the court, counsel and jury to comment upon and consider the failure of defendant "to explain or to deny by his testimony any evidence or facts in the case against him" would infringe defendant's privilege against self-incrimination under the Fifth Amendment if this were a trial in a court of the United States under a similar law. [e] Such an assumption does not determine appellant's rights under the Fourteenth Amendment. It is settled law that the clause of the Fifth Amendment, protecting a person against being compelled to be a witness against himself, is not made effective by the Fourteenth Amendment as a protection against state action on the ground that freedom from testimonial compulsion is a right of national citizenship, or because it is a personal privilege or immunity secured by the Federal Constitution as one of the rights of man that are listed in the Bill of Rights.

[JUSTICE REED then traced the history of such cases as *Barron v. Baltimore*, 7 Pet. 243 (1833), *Twining v. New Jersey*, 211 U.S. 78 (1908), and *Palko v. Connecticut* (this volume).]

* * * For a state to require testimony from an accused is not necessarily a breach of a state's obligation to give a fair trial. * * * [f] The due process clause forbids compulsion to testify by fear of hurt, torture or exhaustion. It forbids any other type of coercion that falls within the scope of due process. * * *

Generally, comment on the failure of an accused to testify is forbidden in American jurisdictions. * * * [g] However, * * * we see no reason why comment should not be made upon his silence. It seems quite natural that when a defendant has opportunity to deny or explain facts and determines not to do so, the prosecution should bring out the strength of the evidence by commenting upon defendant's failure to explain or deny it. * * *

It is true that if comment were forbidden, an accused in this situation could remain silent and avoid evidence of former crimes and comment upon his failure to testify. We are of the view, however, that a state may control such a situation in accordance with its own ideas of the most efficient administration of criminal justice. The purpose of due process is not to protect an accused against a proper conviction but against an unfair conviction. * * * [I]t does not seem unfair to require him to choose between

leaving the adverse evidence unexplained and subjecting himself to impeachment through disclosure of former crimes. * * * [h]

* * *

Affirmed. [i]

Mr. Justice FRANKFURTER (concurring). * * *

For historical reasons a limited immunity from the common duty to testify was written into the Federal Bill of Rights. * * * [j] But to suggest that such a limitation can be drawn out of "due process" in its protection of ultimate decency in a civilized society is to suggest that the Due Process Clause fastened fetters of unreason upon the States. * * *

Between the incorporation of the Fourteenth Amendment into the Constitution and the beginning of the present membership of the Court - a period of 70 years - the scope of that Amendment was passed upon by forty-three judges. Of all these judges, only one, who may respectfully be called an eccentric exception, ever indicated the belief that the Fourteenth Amendment was a shorthand summary of the first eight Amendments theretofore limiting only the Federal Government, and that due process incorporated those eight Amendments as restrictions upon the powers of the States. * * * [k]

Mr. Justice BLACK, dissenting.

* * *

This decision reasserts a constitutional theory spelled out in *Twining v. New Jersey*, * * * that this Court is endowed by the Constitution with boundless power under "natural law" periodically to expand and contract constitutional standards to conform to the Court's conception of what at a particular time constitutes "civilized decency" and "fundamental liberty and justice." * * * [T]he Court concludes that although comment upon testimony in a federal court would violate the Fifth Amendment, identical comment in a state court does not violate today's fashion in civilized decency and fundamentals and is therefore not prohibited by the Federal Constitution as amended.

* * *

* * * I think that [*Twining*] and the "natural law" theory of the Constitution upon which it relies degrade the constitutional safeguards of the Bill of Rights and simultaneously appropriate for this Court a broad power which we are not authorized by the Constitution to exercise. * * * [l]

* * * The amendments embodying the Bill of Rights were intended to curb all branches of the Federal Government in the fields touched by the amendments - Legislative, Executive, and Judicial. The Fifth, Sixth, and Eighth Amendments were pointedly aimed at confining exercise of power by courts and judges within precise boundaries, particularly in the procedure used for the trial of criminal cases. * * * For the fears of arbitrary court action sprang largely from the past use of courts in the imposition of criminal punishments to suppress speech, press, and religion. [m] Hence the constitutional limitations of courts' powers were, in the view of the Founders, essential supplements to the First Amendment. * * *

* * *

My study of the historical events that culminated in the Fourteenth Amendment, and the expressions of those who sponsored and favored, as well as those who opposed its submission and passage, persuades me that one of the chief objects that the provision of the Amendment's first section, separately, and as a whole, were intended to accomplish was to make the Bill of Rights, applicable to the states. With full knowledge of the import of the *Barron* decision, the framers and backers of the Fourteenth Amendment proclaimed its purpose to be to overturn the constitutional rule that case had announced. * * * [n]

* * * "It is never to be forgotten that, in the construction of the language of the Constitution * * *, as indeed in all other instances where construction becomes necessary, we are to place ourselves as nearly as possible in the condition of the men who framed that instrument." [o] [JUSTICE BLACK then stated that the historical research into the adoption of the Fourteenth Amendment by *Twining* was deficient.]

* * *

For this reason, I am attaching to this dissent an appendix which contains a resume * * * of the Amendment's history [which] conclusively demonstrates that the language of the first section of the Fourteenth Amendment, taken as a whole, was thought * * * sufficiently explicit to guarantee that thereafter no state could deprive its citizens of the privileges and protections of the Bill of Rights. * * * [p] And I further contend that the "natural law" formula which the Court uses to reach its conclusion in this case should be abandoned as an incongruous excrescence on our Constitution. I believe that formula to be itself a violation of our Constitution, in that it subtly conveys to courts, at the expense of legislatures, ultimate power over public policies in fields where no specific provision of the Constitution limits legislative power. * * * **[q]**

[A ten-page analysis followed, tracing the expansion of the due process clause by the Court from the 1880s to the 1930s to strike down social legislation, while simultaneously interpreting the due process clause of the Fourteenth Amendment to narrow protections of criminal procedure.]

I cannot consider the Bill of Rights to be an outworn 18th Century "strait jacket" as the *Twining* opinion did. Its provisions may be thought outdated abstractions by some. And it is true that they were designed to meet ancient evils. But they are the same kind of human evils that have emerged from century to century wherever excessive power is sought by the few at the expense of the many. **[r]** In my judgment the people of no nation can lose their liberty so long as a Bill of Rights like ours survives and its basic purposes are conscientiously interpreted, enforced and respected so as to afford continuous protection against old, as well as new, devices and practices which might thwart those purposes. * * * If the choice must be between the selective process of the *Palko* decision applying some of the Bill of Rights to the States, or the *Twining* rule applying none of them, I would choose the *Palko* selective process. * * * **[s]**

* * * I would therefore hold in this case that the full protection of the Fifth Amendment's proscription against compelled testimony must be afforded by California. This I would do because of reliance upon the original purpose of the Fourteenth Amendment.

It is an illusory apprehension that literal application of * * * the Bill of Rights to the States would unwisely increase the sum total of the powers of this Court to invalidate state legislation. * * *

Since *Marbury v. Madison* * * * was decided, the practice has been firmly established, for better or worse, that courts can strike down legislative enactments which violate the Constitution. This process, of course, involves interpretation, and since words can have many meanings, interpretation obviously may result in contraction or extension of the original purpose of a constitutional provision. * * * But to pass upon * * * constitutionality * * * by looking to the particular standards enumerated in the Bill of Rights * * * is one thing; to invalidate statutes because of application of "natural law" deemed to be above and undefined by the Constitution is another. * * * [In the latter instance] "they roam at will in the limitless area of their own beliefs as to reasonableness and actually select policies, a responsibility which the Constitution entrusts to the legislative representatives of the people." **[t]**

MR. JUSTICE DOUGLAS joins in this opinion.

APPENDIX

[The appendix runs to thirty-one pages and covers, among other things, the debate in the Thirty-first Congress over the passage of the Fourteenth Amendment, contemporary opinion, congressional debates in 1871 over a civil rights bill, and some judicial views between 1868 and the *Twining* opinion in 1908.]

[After reviewing the *Barron* doctrine, in the 1866 debate, Mr. Bingham

(R., Ohio) said,] [u]

"The question is, simply, whether you will give by this amendment to the people of the United States the power, by legislative enactment, to punish officials of States for violation of the oaths enjoined upon them by their Constitution?* * * Is the bill of rights to stand in our Constitution hereafter, as in the past five years within eleven States, a mere dead letter? It is absolutely essential to the safety of the people that it should be enforced. * * *

* * * "Gentlemen who oppose this amendment oppose the grant of power to enforce the bill of rights. * * *"

A reading of the debates indicates that no member except Mr. Hale had contradicted Mr. Bingham's argument that without this Amendment the states had power to deprive persons of the rights guaranteed by the first eight amendments.

[Before the Fourteenth Amendment passed, Mr. Bingham opposed a civil rights bill in Congress.] His objection was twofold: First, insofar as it extended the protections of the Bill of Rights as against state invasion, he believed the measure to be unconstitutional because of the Supreme Court's holding in *Barron v. Baltimore, supra.* [v] While favoring the extension of the Bill of Rights guarantees as against state invasion, he thought this could be done only by passage of his amendment. [w] His second objection to the Bill was that, in his view, it would go beyond his objective of making the states observe the Bill of Rights and would actually strip the states of power

to govern, centralizing all power in the Federal Government. To this he was opposed.

[In the Senate debate, Senator Howard argued that the privileges of United States citizenship mentioned in Article IV of the 1789 Constitution included Amendments I through VIII of the Bill of Rights, thus implying that the Fourteenth Amendment would incorporate those rights and they would apply against the states.]

[In 1871, after the Fourteenth Amendment was ratified, in a floor debate over another civil rights bill, Congressman Bingham stated what his intention had been regarding the Fourteenth Amendment:]

* * * "I had read - and that is what induced me to attempt to impose by constitutional amendments new limitations upon the power of the States - the great decision of Marshall in *Barron vs. ... Baltimore.* * * *

* * * I noted and apprehended as I never did before, certain words in that opinion * * * [r]eferring to the first eight * * * amendments* * * : 'Had the framers of these amendments intended them to be limitations on the power of the State governments they would have imitated the framers of the original Constitution, and have expressed that intention.'* * *

"Acting upon this suggestion I did imitate the framers of the original Constitution. * * *

"These eight articles I have shown never were limitations upon the power of the States, until made so by the fourteenth amendment." * * * [x]

MR. JUSTICE MURPHY, with whom MR. JUSTICE RUTLEDGE concurs, dissenting. * * *

I agree that the specific guarantees of the Bill of Rights should be carried over intact into the first section of the Fourteenth Amendment. But I am not prepared to say that the latter is entirely and necessarily limited by the Bill of Rights. Occasions may arise where a proceeding falls so far short of conforming to fundamental standards of procedure as to warrant constitutional condemnation in terms of a lack of due process despite the absence of a specific provision in the Bill of Rights. * * * [y]

*   *   *   *   *   *   *   *   *   *   *

COMMENTS

[a] Why should Justice Reed mention that Adamson is a United States citizen? This calls attention to the provision in section one of the Fourteenth Amendment that "all persons born or naturalized in the United States, and subject to the jurisdiction thereof, are citizens of the United States and the State wherein they reside." The historic importance of this proviso is that it overturned the notorious ruling of *Scott v. Sandford*, 60 U.S. (19 How.) 393 (1857) and made it clear beyond any doubt that Americans of African descent were fully citizens. But the Fourteenth Amendment applies to all persons and the immediate concern in this case is whether a *state* rule of law can be reviewed by a *federal* court. Adamson's U.S. citizenship implies that he is entitled to the protection of the Fourteenth Amendment by the United States government and its courts and thus brings a state conviction under the jurisdiction of a federal court. However, notice that two of the specific guarantees of the Fourteenth Amendment—due process and equal protection—are extended to all "persons," not just to citizens. Thus, the actual protection of the Fourteenth Amendment under its due process clause extends to all persons protected by the Constitution. The actual scope of who is protected depends on the extent to which federal statutes and Court rulings extend the writ of habeas corpus to state petitioners to challenge the constitutionality of their state convictions in federal court.

[b] A defendant's prior criminal record is prejudicial and has no bearing on proof of the crime. The common law frowned on the introduction of such information to juries. However, it may be introduced to the jury to impeach the defendant's credibility as a witness, if the conviction was a felony and had occurred within a reasonable time period in the past.

[c] This expresses a position known as "total incorporation." The other approach is "selective incorporation," by which each provision of the Bill of Rights which is deemed "fundamental" is "incorporated" into the Fourteenth Amendment.

[d] The presumption of innocence is not a right listed in the Constitution; yet it is a constitutional norm that the defendant can draw on to help his case.

[e] *Griffin v. California*, 380 U.S. 609 (1965), held that the Fifth Amendment privilege against self-incrimination prohibited a prosecutor from commenting upon a defendant's failure to testify at trial, thus overruling *Palko*.

[f] Under this "pre-incorporation" view, what is unconstitutional for the federal government under the Fifth Amendment is not unconstitutional for the state government under the Fourteenth Amendment.

[g] Most states did not follow the California procedure at that time. What the majority of states do is persuasive but not binding. A result of our federal system is that important legal rules often differ from one state to another. Should a uniform rule be imposed throughout the United States? Does it seem proper to you that different rules, which might make it easier or more difficult to obtain a conviction, can apply differently in different states? Should this kind of rule be a matter of state sovereignty?

[h] The Court's 1947 decision vindicated states' rights over national uniformity. The fairness and "naturalness" of events are general norms that are translated into constitutional norms by the Justices. They do not perceive the California rule as so unfair as to amount to a constitutional violation.

[i] The Supreme Court affirms or reverses the decision of the court immediately below it, not the conviction.

[j] There are many reasons for concurring. Here, JUSTICE FRANKFURTER adds a reason not given by JUSTICE REED. Notice how he downplays the significance of the privilege against self-incrimination.

[k] This showing that many Justices did not accept Black's interpretation is essentially a static argument, based on tradition. If the Court were to adhere to an iron rule of precedent, it would never innovate; yet, innovation is a matter that a constitutional court must undertake with caution. There is no clear right or wrong on this point. The reference to the "eccentric exception" is to the first JUSTICE HARLAN.

[l] JUSTICE BLACK's view may be called "legal fundamentalism," looking to a very strict interpretation of the Constitution. To his way of thinking, a "natural law" approach to adjudication gives the judiciary too much discretion; he views this basis for adjudication as illegitimate. He is willing to overturn the precedent of *Palko* (whose opinion he joined) and earlier cases because he now believes it is fundamentally wrong.

[m] Here he raises the danger of judicial tyranny; he had two examples in mind: English judges who supported Stuart autocracy in seventeenth-century England and conservative Supreme Court justices who, in the period from 1890 to 1937, used Fourteenth Amendment "substantive due process" doctrines to undermine social reform legislation on the ground that such laws violated the due process property rights of employers and workers.

[n] Justices must have an understanding of the history of the nation and its Constitution. In this case JUSTICE BLACK's scholarship produced a historically important reinterpretation of the intent of the framers of the Fourteenth Amendment. In view of JUSTICE FRANKFURTER's point, it took great self-confidence for JUSTICE BLACK to carefully review the record and say that forty-three previous Justices were wrong.

[o] This is the well-established "intent of the framers" canon of interpretation.

[p] A brief portion of this appendix is given below. The justices may append materials to their opinions that will assist the reader in understanding the case.

[q] Constitutional issues always refer to questions of governmental power; here JUSTICE BLACK raises issues of the relative power of branches of government, with special concern about judicial power.

[r] He writes these words two years after the end of World War II, a great object lesson in how many nations lost their liberties.

[s] This is an important tactical point; JUSTICE BLACK is willing to take "half a loaf" of "selective incorporation" if the "full loaf" of "total incorporation" was not possible. In fact the "incorporation doctrine" that took hold in the 1960s was the selective approach, whereby each incorporated constitutional rule had to be ruled on as fundamental. As a result, a few parts of the Bill of Rights have not been incorporated.

[t] JUSTICE BLACK argues that his position is not against states' rights and not only that the Reed-Frankfurter position gives judges tyrannical powers, but also that of JUSTICEs MURPHY and RUTLEDGE. By interpreting the Bill of Rights, judicial review does not become a huge power to make policy, which is the role of the legislature. JUSTICE BLACK was a U.S. Senator before he was appointed to the bench.

[u] Congressman Bingham was the leading proponent of the Fourteenth Amendment; therefore, his words are given great weight. But is *his* opinion the opinion of the entire Congress?

[v] Like JUSTICE BLACK's, Congressman Bingham's legal logic was quite strict; he would follow the law, even going against his policy desires.

[w] Thus, Bingham intended the Fourteenth Amendment to overrule *Barron*, accepting that Justices make constitutional law in their decisions.

[x] Not all contemporary scholars agree with the key framer of the Fourteenth amendment: "But Black's history falls far short of the 'conclusive demonstration' he thought it to be in his famous *Adamson* dissent." [Raoul Berger, *Government by Judiciary*, p. 137. (Cambridge: Harvard University Press, 1977)]

[y] This is a truly "liberal" and pro-defendant position. It agrees with JUSTICE BLACK's incorporationist view but goes further and gives more protection under a "plenary" interpretation of due process. JUSTICE MURPHY would also find that state procedure considered by the Justices to be unfair violates the Fourteenth Amendment. JUSTICE BLACK would not agree with this position because it gives too much power to judges uncontrolled by law.

WOLF v. COLORADO

338 U.S. 25, 69 S.Ct. 1359, 93 L.Ed. 1782 (1949)

MR. JUSTICE FRANKFURTER delivered the opinion of the Court.

The precise question for consideration is this: Does a conviction by a State court for a State offense deny the "due process of law" required by the Fourteenth Amendment, solely because evidence that was admitted at the trial was obtained under circumstances which would have rendered it inadmissible in a [federal] prosecution * * * [as] an infraction of the Fourth Amendment as applied in *Weeks v. United States*, [this volume] ? * * *

[JUSTICE FRANKFURTER pointed out that the Court rejected the total incorporation idea and that under *Palko v. Connecticut*, this volume], only rights implicit in the concept of ordered liberty are incorporated into the due process clause of the Fourteenth Amendment. Although due process is a flexible and growing concept, determining which rights are fundamental is not a question that can be decided by a formula.]

The security of one's privacy against arbitrary intrusion by the police—which is at the core of the Fourth Amendment—is basic to a free society. It is therefore implicit in "the concept of ordered liberty" and as such enforceable against the States through the Due Process Clause. The knock at the door, whether by day or by night, as a prelude to a search, without authority of law but solely on the authority of the police, did not need the commentary of recent history to be condemned as inconsistent with the conception of human rights enshrined in the history and the basic constitutional documents of English speaking peoples. [a]

Accordingly, we have no hesitation in saying that were a state affirmatively to sanction such police incursion into privacy it would run counter to the guaranty of the Fourteenth Amendment. But the ways of enforcing such a basic right raise questions of a different order. How such arbitrary conduct should be checked, what remedies against it should be afforded, the means by which the right should be made effective, are all questions that are not to be so dogmatically answered as to preclude the varying solutions which spring from an allowable range of judgment on issues not susceptible of quantitative solution. [b]

In *Weeks* * * * this Court held that in a federal prosecution the Fourth Amendment barred the use of evidence secured through an illegal search and seizure. * * * It was not derived from the explicit requirements of the Fourth Amendment; it was not based on legislation expressing Congressional policy in the enforcement of the Constitution. The decision was a matter of judicial implication. Since then it has been frequently applied and we stoutly adhere to it. But the immediate question is whether the basic right . . . demands the exclusion of logically relevant evidence [which would be excluded in a federal case]. When we find that in fact most of the English-speaking world does not regard as vital to such protection the exclusion of evidence thus obtained, we must hesitate to treat this remedy as an essential ingredient of the right. * * *

As of today 31 States reject the Weeks doctrine, 16 States are in agreement with it. * * *

Of 10 jurisdictions within the United Kingdom and the British Commonwealth of Nations which have passed on the question, none has held evidence obtained by illegal search and seizure inadmissible. **[c]**

* * * [T]he exclusion of evidence is a remedy which directly serves only to protect those upon whose person or premises something incriminating has been found. We cannot therefore regard it as a departure from basic standards to remand such persons, together with those who emerge scatheless from a search to the remedies of private action and such protection as the internal discipline of the police, under the eyes of an alert public opinion, may afford. Granting that in practice the exclusion of evidence may be an effective way of deterring unreasonable searches, it is not for this Court to condemn as falling below the minimal standards assured by the Due Process Clause a State's reliance upon other methods which, if consistently enforced, would be equally effective. * * * **[d]**

We hold, therefore, that in a prosecution in a State court for a State crime the Fourteenth Amendment does not forbid the admission of evidence obtained by an unreasonable search and seizure. * * *

MR. JUSTICE BLACK, concurring.

[While the Fourth Amendment is incorporated into the Fourteenth], I agree * * * that the federal exclusionary rule is not a command of the Fourth Amendment but is a judicially created rule of evidence which Congress might negate. * * * **[e]**

MR. JUSTICE MURPHY, with whom MR. JUSTICE RUTLEDGE joins, dissenting.

* * * [A] devotee of democracy would ill suit his name were he to suggest that his home's protection against unlicensed governmental invasion was not "of the very essence of a scheme of ordered liberty." * * * It is difficult for me to understand how the Court can go this far and yet be unwilling to make the step which can give some meaning to the pronouncements it utters.

Imagination and zeal may invent a dozen methods to give content to the commands of the Fourth Amendment. But this Court is limited to the remedies currently available. It cannot legislate the ideal system. * * * [W]e are limited to three devices: judicial exclusion of the illegally obtained evidence; criminal prosecution of violators; and civil actions against violators in the action of trespass. **[f]**

Alternatives are deceptive. Their very statement conveys the impression that one possibility is as effective as the next. In this case their statement is blinding. For there is but one alternative to the rule of exclusion. That is no sanction at all. [Both the *Weeks* and the *Silverthorne* (this volume) cases said as much. He pointed out that prosecutors rarely, if ever, prosecute police for overzealously enforcing the law and that in trespass actions against proven criminals, the amount of damages are likely to be minuscule].

The conclusion is inescapable that but one remedy exists to deter violations of the search and seizure clause. * * * Only by exclusion can we impress upon the zealous prosecutor that violation of the Constitution will do him no good. And only when that point is driven home can the prosecutor be expected to emphasize the importance of observing constitutional demands in his instructions to the police.

[He then noted that in states with the exclusionary rule, police training procedures pay more attention to training about the law than in states without the exclusionary rule].

* * * Today's decision will do inestimable harm to the cause of fair police methods in our cities and states. Even more important, perhaps, it must have tragic effect upon public respect for our judiciary. For the Court now allows what is indeed shabby business: lawlessness by officers of the law. * * *

[JUSTICES RUTLEDGE and DOUGLAS dissented separately.]

* * * * * * * * * * *

COMMENTS

[a] The clear implication of using the *Palko* formula is that the Fourth Amendment right against unreasonable search and seizure *is* incorporated into the Fourteenth Amendment due process clause. This decision, rendered only four years after the Allied victory over Fascist powers and at the onset of the "cold war" with the Soviet bloc, gives resonance to the reference to the "knock at the door."

[b] JUSTICE FRANKFURTER neatly resolves a legal and moral dilemma by severing the basic *right* of the Fourth Amendment from a particular *remedy*. Whether or not this is good constitutional policy, it is a fascinating indication of how legal issues are often decided by how rules and precedents are conceptualized. Thus, the majority has its cake and eats it, too.

[c] The fact that no other common law nations and few states resorted to the exclusionary rule was strong evidence of a common law policy against exclusion. Yet, it begs the questions of whether the common law policy is entirely relevant under the U.S. Constitution. The form of the Constitution and its particular interpretation indicate that it need not be rigidly tied to earlier conceptions. There are no formulas that indicate when and how far a break with the past is appropriate; this is a matter for "constitutional statesmanship."

[d] The majority decision can be seen as an odd balancing act of saying that a right in the Fourth Amendment is fundamental but it cannot be enforced through a constitutionally established remedy. One reason for this was a sensitivity to states' rights on the part of the majority: a desire to disturb as little as possible

rules established by state governments to manage their own affairs. This is a valid perspective on federalism and has been a potent source of federal-state conflict since the founding of the Republic.

[e] Although JUSTICES BLACK and FRANKFURTER were strong rivals on the incorporation issue, as evidenced by their mighty struggle in the 1947 *Adamson* case, we note an interesting accommodation here. JUSTICE BLACK is persuaded by JUSTICE FRANKFURTER's severing of the right from the remedy. As a "constitutional fundamentalist," he adhered more strongly to historic practices than other justices.

[f] The dissenting justices show themselves to be "liberal activists" by their willingness to engraft the remedy onto the right. This continues the "incorporation-plus" position taken by JUSTICE MURPHY in *Adamson*. This approach is not without logical merit, for it is recognized in law and human experience that a rule without a remedy is not much of a rule.

ROCHIN v. CALIFORNIA

342 U.S. 165, 72 S.Ct. 205, 96 L.Ed. 183 (1952)

MR. JUSTICE FRANKFURTER delivered the opinion of the Court.

Having "some information that [the petitioner] was selling narcotics," three deputy sheriffs of the County of Los Angeles, on [one] morning made for the two-story dwelling house in which Rochin lived with his mother, common-law wife, brothers and sisters. Finding the outside door open, they entered and then forced open the door to Rochin's room on the second floor. Inside they found petitioner sitting partly dressed on the side of the bed, upon which his wife was lying. On a "night stand" beside the bed the deputies spied two capsules. When asked "Whose stuff is this?" Rochin seized the capsules and put them in his mouth. A struggle ensued, in the course of which the three officers "jumped upon him" and attempted to extract the capsules. The force they applied proved unavailing against Rochin's resistance. He was handcuffed and taken to a hospital. At the direction of one of the officers a doctor forced an emetic solution through a tube into Rochin's stomach against his will. This "stomach pumping" produced vomiting. In the vomited matter were found two capsules which proved to contain morphine.

[The capsules were admitted into evidence; Rochin was convicted of drug possession and sentenced to sixty days imprisonment.] * * *

* * * [I]n reviewing a State criminal conviction under a claim of right guaranteed by the Due Process Clause of the Fourteenth Amendment, from which is derived the most far-reaching and most frequent federal basis of challenging State criminal justice, "we must be deeply mindful of the responsibilities of the States for the enforcement of criminal laws, and exercise with due humility our merely negative function in subjecting convictions from state courts to the very narrow scrutiny which the Due Process Clause of the Fourteenth Amendment authorizes." *Malinski v. New York*, 324 U.S. 401, 412, 418. * * *

However, this Court too has its responsibility. Regard for the requirements of the Due Process Clause "inescapably imposes upon this Court an exercise of judgment upon the whole course of the proceedings [resulting in a conviction] in order to ascertain whether they offend those canons of decency and fairness which express the notions of justice of English-speaking peoples even toward those charged with the most heinous offenses." * * * These standards of justice are not authoritatively formulated anywhere as though they were specifics. Due process of law is a summarized constitutional guarantee of respect for those personal immunities which, as Mr. JUSTICE CARDOZO twice wrote for the Court, are "so rooted in the traditions and conscience of our people as to be ranked as fundamental." * * * or are "implicit in the concept of ordered liberty." * * * [a]

* * *

The vague contours of the Due

Process Clause do not leave judges at large. We may not draw on our merely personal and private notions and disregard the limits that bind judges in their judicial function. Even though the concept of due process of law is not final and fixed, these limits are derived from considerations that are fused in the whole nature of our judicial process. * * * These are considerations deeply rooted in reason and in the compelling traditions of the legal profession. The Due Process Clause places upon this Court the duty of exercising a judgment, within the narrow confines of judicial power in reviewing State convictions, upon interests of society pushing in opposite directions.

Due process of law thus conceived is not to be derided as resort to a revival of "natural law." To believe that this judicial exercise of judgment could be avoided by freezing "due process of law" at some fixed stage of time or thought is to suggest that the most important aspect of constitutional adjudication is a function for inanimate machines and not for judges, for whom the independence safeguarded by Article III of the Constitution was designed and who are presumably guided by established standards of judicial behavior. * * * To practice the requisite detachment and to achieve sufficient objectivity no doubt demands of judges the habit of self-discipline and self-criticism, incertitude that one's own views are incontestable and alert tolerance toward views not shared. But these are precisely the presuppositions of our judicial process. They are precisely the qualities society has a right to expect from those entrusted with ultimate judicial power.
* * *

Applying these general considerations to the circumstances of the present case, we are compelled to conclude that the proceedings by which this conviction was obtained do more than offend some fastidious squeamishness or private sentimentalism about combatting crime too energetically. This is conduct that shocks the conscience. Illegally breaking into the privacy of the petitioner, the struggle to open his mouth and remove what was there, the forcible extraction of his stomach's contents—this course of proceeding by agents of government to obtain evidence is bound to offend even hardened sensibilities. They are methods too close to the rack and the screw to permit of constitutional differentiation. [b]

* * * Due process of law, as a historic and generative principle, precludes defining, and thereby confining, these standards of conduct more precisely than to say that convictions cannot be brought about by methods that offend "a sense of justice." * * * It would be a stultification of the responsibility which the course of constitutional history has cast upon this Court to hold that in order to convict a man the police cannot extract by force what is in his mind but can extract what is in his stomach.
* * *

We are not unmindful that hypothetical situations can be conjured up, shading imperceptibly from the circumstances of this case and by gradations producing practical differences despite seemingly logical extensions. But the Constitution is "intended to preserve practical and substantial rights, not to maintain theories." * * * [c]

On the facts of this case the conviction of the petitioner has been obtained by methods that offend the Due Process Clause.

The judgment below must be Reversed.

MR. JUSTICE MINTON took no part in the consideration or decision of this case.

MR. JUSTICE BLACK, concurring.

Adamson v. California, [this volume] sets out reasons for my belief that state as well as federal courts and law enforcement officers must obey the Fifth Amendment's command that "No person * * * shall be compelled in any criminal case to be a witness against himself." **[d]**   I think a person is compelled to be a witness against himself not only when he is compelled to testify, but also when as here, incriminating evidence is forcibly taken from him by a contrivance of modern science. * * * California convicted this petitioner by using against him evidence obtained in this manner, and I agree with MR. JUSTICE DOUGLAS that the case should be reversed on this ground.

In the view of a majority of the Court, however, the Fifth Amendment imposes no restraint of any kind on the states. They nevertheless hold that California's use of this evidence violated the Due Process Clause of the Fourteenth Amendment. * * * But I believe that faithful adherence to the specific guarantees in the Bill of Rights insures a more permanent protection of individual liberty than that which can be afforded by the nebulous standards stated by the majority.

What the majority hold is that the Due Process Clause empowers this Court to nullify any state law if its application "shocks the conscience," offends "a sense of justice" or runs counter to the "decencies of civilized conduct." The majority emphasize that these statements do not refer to their own consciences or to their senses of justice and decency. * * * **[e]**

If the Due Process Clause does vest this Court with such unlimited power to invalidate laws, I am still in doubt as to why we should consider only the notions of English-speaking peoples to determine what are immutable and fundamental principles of justice. Moreover, one may well ask what avenues of investigation are open to discover "canons" of conduct so universally favored that this Court should write them into the Constitution? All we are told is that the discovery must be made by an "evaluation based on a disinterested inquiry pursued in the spirit of science, on a balanced order of facts." **[f]**

Some constitutional provisions are stated in absolute and unqualified language. * * * Other constitutional provisions do require courts to choose between competing policies, such as the Fourth Amendment which, by its terms, necessitates a judicial decision as to what is an "unreasonable" search or seizure. There is, however, no express constitutional language granting judicial power to invalidate *every* state law of *every* kind deemed "unreasonable" or contrary to the Court's notion of civilized decencies. * * * I long ago concluded that the accordion-like qualities of this philosophy must inevitably imperil all the individual liberty safeguards specifically enumerated in the Bill of Rights. * * *

[JUSTICE DOUGLAS concurred, agreeing with the reasoning of JUS-TICE BLACK] [g]

* * * * * * * * * *

COMMENTS

[a] What kind of a guide to the courts is this formulation of due process? They can be seen as vague, giving no guidance, and leaving the determination of what constitutes due process in the hands of the judges. JUSTICE FRANKFURTER tries to explain that the due process standard, imprecise at the edges, contains a core that can be known by reading many cases and knowing much of the legal history of England and America.

[b] How easy would this be for a judge or police officer to apply in specific cases? The Supreme Court later held that forcibly taking a blood sample in a medically controlled situation did not shock the conscience, *Breithaupt v. Abram*, 352 U.S. 432 (1957), *Schmerber v. California*, 384 U.S. 757 (1966).

[c] Here JUSTICE FRANKFURTER concedes that the "shocks the conscience" standard is not a "bright line" rule, but accepts this as a normal aspect of the judicial function.

[d] JUSTICE BLACK was keeping alive the concept of incorporation.

[e] Does the justices long-range concern with the impact of their rulings mean that they are "legislating"? JUSTICE BLACK's statement opens the mind to the possibility that if, in the future, a group of justices are not "shocked" by this activity, the ruling of *Rochin* could more easily be reversed than if it were based on a more objective rule.

[f] JUSTICE BLACK punctures the majority's posture that its ruling is an objective measure of society's standards rather than of the justices' own values and feelings.

[g] After *Rochin*, the Court held in *Irvine v. California*, 347 U.S. 128 (1954) that the bedroom electronic eavesdropping of a husband and wife did not "shock the conscience." To many, this indicated that the *Rochin* test was vague and idiosyn-cratic.

MAPP v. OHIO

367 U.S. 643, 81 S.Ct. 1684, 6 L.Ed.2d 1081 (1961)

MR. JUSTICE CLARK delivered the opinion of the Court.

[Cleveland police officers went to Mrs. Mapp's home on a tip that a suspected gambler involved in a bombing was residing there. She refused to let them enter without a warrant. The police broke in after a three-hour wait. There was a scuffle for a piece of paper that the police waved, but no warrant was ever produced. Mrs. Mapp and her daughter were handcuffed and confined to a bedroom while the police ransacked the house (looking into all rooms and into her personal papers and photograph albums). The police found obscene books in a trunk in the basement belonging to a roomer who was no longer living in the house. At trial, the alleged warrant was never produced. Mrs. Mapp was convicted for possession of obscene books seized during a search of her home. [a] The Ohio courts acknowledged that the books and pictures were "unlawfully seized during an unlawful search of [her] home, * * *" but still allowed the evidence to be used, relying on *Wolf v. Colorado* [this volume].]

I.

Seventy-five years ago, in *Boyd v. United States* [this volume], considering the Fourth and Fifth Amendments as running "almost into each other," * * * this Court held that the doctrines of those Amendments

"apply to all invasions on the part

of the government and its employees of the sanctity of a man's home and the privacies of life. * * * *" [b]

The Court noted that

"constitutional provisions for the security of person and property should be liberally construed. * * * * It is the duty of courts to be watchful for the constitutional rights of the citizen, and against any stealthy encroachments thereon."* * *

* * * Concluding, the Court specifically referred to the use of the evidence there seized as "unconstitutional."

[JUSTICE CLARK then quoted from *Weeks v. United States* which established a federal exclusionary rule for illegally seized evidence.]
* * *

There are in the cases of this Court some passing references to the *Weeks* rule as being one of evidence. But the plain and unequivocal language of *Weeks*—and its later paraphrase in *Wolf*—to the effect that the *Weeks* rule is of constitutional origin, remains entirely undisturbed. * * * [c]

II.

[In *Wolf v. Colorado* (1949), the Court first considered the applicability of the Fourth Amendment against the states, and] after declaring that the "security of one's privacy against arbitrary intrusion by the police" is "implicit in 'the concept of ordered liberty' and as such enforceable against the States through the Due Process Clause," * * * and announcing that it "stoutly adhere[d]" to the *Weeks* decision, [nevertheless] the Court decided that the *Weeks* exclusionary rule would not then be imposed upon the States as "an essential ingredient of the right." * * *

[Since 1949, a majority of the states have adopted the exclusionary rule and federal courts no longer allowed into evidence items that were illegally seized by state officers.]

It, therefore, plainly appears that the factual considerations supporting the failure of the *Wolf* Court to include the *Weeks* exclusionary rule when it recognized the enforceability of the right to privacy against the States in 1949, while not basically relevant to the constitutional consideration, could not, in any analysis, now be deemed controlling.

III.

Today we once again examine *Wolf*'s constitutional documentation of the right to privacy free from unreasonable state intrusion, and, after its dozen years on our books, are led by it to close the only courtroom door remaining open to evidence secured by official lawlessness in flagrant abuse of that basic right, reserved to all persons as a specific guarantee against that very same unlawful conduct. We hold that all evidence obtained by searches and seizures in violation of the Constitution is, by that same authority, inadmissible in a state
court.

IV.

Since the Fourth Amendment's right of privacy has been declared enforceable against the States through the Due Process Clause of the Fourteenth, it is enforceable against them by the same sanction of exclusion as is used against the Federal Government. * * * [d] In short, the admission of the new constitutional right by *Wolf* could not consistently tolerate denial of its most important constitutional privilege, namely, the exclusion of the evidence which an accused had been forced to give by reason of the unlawful seizure. To hold otherwise is to grant the right but in reality to withhold its privilege and enjoyment. * * *

V.

Moreover, our holding that the exclusionary rule is an essential part of both the Fourth and Fourteenth Amendments is not only the logical dictate of prior cases, but it also makes very good sense. There is no war between the Constitution and common sense. Presently, a federal prosecutor may make no use of evidence illegally seized, but a State's attorney across the street may, although he supposedly is operating under the enforceable prohibitions of the same Amendment. [e] Thus the State, by admitting evidence unlawfully seized, serves to encourage disobedience to the Federal Constitution which it is bound to uphold. [f] * * * "[The] very essence of a healthy federalism depends upon the avoidance of needless conflict between state and federal courts." * * *

Federal-state cooperation in the solution of crime under constitutional standards will be promoted, if only by recognition of their now mutual obligation to respect the same fundamental criteria in their approaches. "However much in a particular case insistence upon such rules may appear as a technicality that inures to the benefit of a guilty person, the history of the criminal law proves that tolerance of shortcut methods in law enforcement impairs its enduring effectiveness." * * * Denying shortcuts to only one of two cooperating law enforcement agencies tends naturally to breed legitimate suspicion of "working arrangements" whose results are equally tainted. * * *

There are those who say, as did JUSTICE (then Judge) CARDOZO, that under our constitutional exclusionary doctrine "[the] criminal is to go free because the constable has blundered." * * * In some cases this will undoubtedly be the result. But, * * * "there is another consideration - the imperative of judicial integrity." The criminal goes free, if he must, but it is the law that sets him free. Nothing can destroy a government more quickly than its failure to observe its own laws, or worse, its disregard of the charter of its own existence. * * * [g]

The ignoble shortcut to conviction left open to the State tends to destroy the entire system of constitutional restraints on which the liberties of the people rest. * * * [W]e can no longer permit that right to remain an empty promise. * * *

Reversed and remanded.

MR. JUSTICE BLACK, concurring.

[JUSTICE BLACK noted that in

Wolf, he stated that "the federal exclusionary rule is not a command of the Fourth Amendment but is a judicially created rule of evidence which Congress might negate."]

* * *

I am still not persuaded that the Fourth Amendment, standing alone, would be enough to bar the introduction into evidence against an accused of papers and effects seized from him in violation of its commands. For the Fourth Amendment does not itself contain any provision expressly precluding the use of such evidence, and I am extremely doubtful that such a provision could properly be inferred from nothing more than the basic command against unreasonable searches and seizures. Reflection on the problem, however, in the light of cases coming before the Court since *Wolf*, has led me to conclude that when the Fourth Amendment's ban against unreasonable searches and seizures is considered together with the Fifth Amendment's ban against compelled self-incrimination, a constitutional basis emerges which not only justifies but actually requires the exclusionary rule. [h]

[JUSTICE DOUGLAS concurred, emphasizing the inability of any method other than exclusion to deter police illegalities.]

[JUSTICE STEWART expressed no opinion on the search and seizure issue but would have reversed the conviction on First Amendment grounds.]

MR. JUSTICE HARLAN, whom MR. JUSTICE FRANKFURTER and MR. JUSTICE WHITTAKER join,

dissenting.

In overruling the *Wolf* case the Court, in my opinion, has forgotten the sense of judicial restraint which, with due regard for *stare decisis*, is one element that should enter into deciding whether a past decision of this Court should be overruled. Apart from that I also believe that the *Wolf* rule represents sounder Constitutional doctrine than the new rule which now replaces it.   * * *

Essential to the majority's argument against *Wolf* is the proposition that the [exclusionary] rule of *Weeks* * * * derives not from the "supervisory power" of this Court over the federal judicial system, but from Constitutional requirement. This is so because no one, I suppose, would suggest that this Court possesses any general supervisory power over the state courts. Although I entertain considerable doubt as to the soundness of this foundational proposition * * * I shall assume, for present purposes, that the *Weeks* rule "is of constitutional origin."

At the heart of the majority's opinion in this case is the following syllogism: (1) the rule excluding in federal criminal trials evidence which is the product of an illegal search and seizure is "part and parcel" of the Fourth Amendment; (2) *Wolf* held that the "privacy" assured against federal action by the Fourth Amendment is also protected against state action by the Fourteenth Amendment; and (3) it is therefore "logically and constitutionally necessary" that the *Weeks* exclusionary rule should also be enforced against the States.

This reasoning ultimately rests on the unsound premise that because *Wolf* carried into the States, as part of "the concept of ordered liberty" embodied in the Fourteenth Amendment, the principle of "privacy" underlying the Fourth Amendment, * * * it must follow that whatever configurations of the Fourth Amendment have been developed in the particularizing federal precedents are likewise to be deemed a part of "ordered liberty," and as such are enforceable against the States. For me, this does not follow at all.

It cannot be too much emphasized that what was recognized in *Wolf* was not that the Fourth Amendment *as such* is enforceable against the States as a facet of due process, * * * but the principle of privacy "which is at the core of the Fourth Amendment." * * * It would not be proper to expect or impose any precise equivalence, either as regards the scope of the right or the means of its implementation, between the requirements of the Fourth and Fourteenth Amendments. For the Fourth, unlike what was said in *Wolf* of the Fourteenth, does not state a general principle only; it is a particular command, having its setting in a pre-existing legal context on which both interpreting decisions and enabling statutes must at least build. [i]   * * * Since there is not the slightest suggestion that Ohio's policy is "affirmatively to sanction * * * police incursion into privacy" * * * what the Court is now doing is to impose upon the States not only federal substantive standards of "search and seizure" but also the basic federal remedy for violation of those standards. For I think it entirely clear that the *Weeks* exclusionary rule is but a remedy which, by penalizing past official misconduct, is aimed at deterring such conduct in the future. [j]

I would not impose upon the States this federal exclusionary remedy. The reasons given by the majority for now suddenly turning its back on *Wolf* seem to me notably unconvincing.

[JUSTICE HARLAN then put forth several reasons for not extending the exclusionary rule to the states: (1) the fact that many states have voluntarily adopted the exclusionary rule is not determinative of a constitutional question before the Court; (2) "the preservation of a proper balance between state and federal responsibility in the administration of criminal justice" dictates that the federal courts are not constitutionally permitted to develop solutions for the perceived problems of state law enforcement aside from what is strictly required by the Constitution; (3) procedural symmetry between the federal system and the states is not required by the Constitution; and (4) the purported analogy between the exclusion of involuntary confessions under the Fourteenth Amendment and search and seizure cases is spurious.

* * * * * * * * * * *

COMMENTS

[a] This case was appealed to the Supreme Court primarily on First Amendment (free speech) grounds. The Fourth Amendment issue was added perfunctorily. The dissent accused the majority of "reaching out" to settle an issue that was not fully briefed.

[b] Why does JUSTICE CLARK mention the *Boyd* decision's view on the close parallel of Fourth and Fifth Amendment "privacy"?

[c] This critical point remains in contention. The legitimacy of this decision depends on whether the exclusionary rule is seen as inherent in the constitutional prohibition on unreasonable searches and seizures or whether it is viewed as a creation of activist judges, impatient to enforce their view of constitutional behavior on state law enforcement officers. Compare this view to the majority opinion in *United States v. Leon* [this volume].

[d] The "same sanction" phrase is critically important to the entire incorporation doctrine. It means that the U.S. Constitution must be interpreted identically for state as well as for the federal government. Since the Constitution is the "supreme law of the land," the practical effect of incorporation is that the Supreme Court makes specific rules for state courts and law enforcement.

[e] This practice was known as the "silver-platter" doctrine, eliminated the year before in *Elkins v. United States*, 364 U.S. 206 (1960). Under it, federal courts accepted evidence, unlawfully seized by state law enforcement officers, who then turned it over to federal officers not directly involved in the seizure.

[f] This could be done not only by state officers turning over illegally seized evidence to federal agents, but by encouraging federal law enforcement officers to violate the Fourth Amendment and then turn over such illegally seized evidence to state authorities.

[g] It is possible to read the "imperative of judicial integrity" as an independent, nonempirical argument in favor of the exclusionary rule. Yet, in the last decade, the argument is hardly mentioned while the focus of debate has centered on the "effectiveness" and the "costs" of the rule, both empirical issues.

[h] JUSTICE BLACK's vote in favor of the exclusionary rule is the crucial fifth majority vote. IIis explanation makes it clear why JUSTICE CLARK's argument included *Boyd*'s theory that the Fourth and Fifth Amendments deal with different phases of the same issue. It is worth noting that this aspect of the case was treated as obsolete almost from the beginning; the search and seizure exclusionary rule is treated as a Fourth Amendment issue.

[i] JUSTICE HARLAN's point seems more true to the precise wording of the early incorporation cases. However, is the distinction so fine as to be nonexistent? Or, as a practical matter, does the distinction mean that state law enforcement officers are to be given greater leeway to be sloppy or brazen in violating constitutional rights?

[j] In recent years the Court has adopted this view, rather than *Mapp*'s majority view that the exclusionary rule is constitutionally based.

UNITED STATES v. LEON

468 U.S. 897, 104 S.Ct. 3405, 82 L.Ed.2d 677 (1984)

JUSTICE WHITE delivered the opinion of the Court.

This case presents the question whether the Fourth Amendment exclusionary rule should be modified so as not to bar the use in the prosecution's case in chief of evidence obtained by officers acting in reasonable reliance on a search warrant issued by a detached and neutral magistrate but ultimately found to be unsupported by probable cause. To resolve this question, we must consider once again the tension between the sometimes competing goals of, on the one hand, deterring official misconduct and removing inducements to unreasonable invasions of privacy and, on the other, establishing procedures under which criminal defendants are "acquitted or convicted on the basis of all the evidence which exposes the truth."* * * [a]

I

[A facially valid search warrant was obtained from a California judge after a confidential informant told local police that two people known to him were selling large quantities of drugs from their residence and that he personally witnessed some sales. A stakeout of the house revealed that cars parked outside belonged to "Leon," and others who had prior convictions for drug sales. The search warrant affidavit was prepared by an experienced drug enforcement officer and reviewed by several assistant prosecutors. In the federal prosecution, the district court, admitting that the case was a close one, overturned the warrant on the ground that the reliability of the informant was not established and probable cause of drug sales was not independently established despite extensive police corroboration work that did point to suspicious activity. The court stated that the officers acted upon the warrant in the good faith belief that it was based upon probable cause. The federal court of appeals upheld the district court. This case is decided on the understanding that the search warrant was not valid under the Fourth Amendment.]

We have concluded that, in the Fourth Amendment context, the exclusionary rule can be modified somewhat without jeopardizing its ability to perform its intended functions. Accordingly, we reverse the judgment of the Court of Appeals.

II

Language in opinions of this Court * * * has sometimes implied that the exclusionary rule is a necessary corollary of the Fourth Amendment, * * * [or] the conjunction of the Fourth and Fifth Amendments. * * * [Citing *Mapp v. Ohio* [this volume].] These implications need not detain us long. The Fifth Amendment theory has not withstood critical analysis or the test of time, * * * and the Fourth Amendment "has never been interpreted to proscribe the introduction of illegally seized evidence in all proceedings or against all persons." * * * [b]

A

The Fourth Amendment contains no provision expressly precluding the use of evidence obtained in violation of its commands, and * * * the use of [unlawfully seized evidence] "work[s] no new Fourth Amendment wrong." * * * The wrong condemned by the Amendment is "fully accomplished" by the unlawful search or seizure itself, * * * and the exclusionary rule is neither intended nor able to "cure the invasion of the defendant's rights which he has already suffered." The rule thus operates as "a judicially created remedy designed to safeguard Fourth Amendment rights generally through its deterrent effect, rather than a personal constitutional right of the party aggrieved." * * *

Whether the exclusionary sanction is appropriately imposed * * * is "* * * separate from the question whether the Fourth Amendment rights of the party * * * were violated by police conduct." * * * **[c]** Only the former question is currently before us, and it must be resolved by weighing the costs and benefits of preventing the use in the prosecution's case-in-chief of inherently trustworthy tangible evidence obtained in reliance on a search warrant issued by a detached and neutral magistrate that ultimately is found to be defective.

The substantial social costs exacted by the exclusionary rule for the vindication of Fourth Amendment rights have long been a source of concern. * * * "[U]nbending application of the exclusionary sanction to enforce ideals of governmental rectitude would impede unacceptably the truth-finding functions of judge and jury."* * *

Particularly when law enforcement officers have acted in objective good faith or their transgressions have been minor, the magnitude of the benefit conferred on such guilty defendants offends basic concepts of the criminal justice system. * * * Indiscriminate application of the exclusionary rule, therefore, may well "generat[e] disrespect for the law and administration of justice." * * * **[d]** Accordingly, "[a]s with any remedial device, the application of the rule has been restricted to those areas where its remedial objectives are thought most efficaciously served." * * *

B

[JUSTICE WHITE noted that although the Court applies the exclusionary rule in appropriate cases "where a Fourth Amendment violation has been substantial and deliberate," the Court has recently applied the balancing test to refrain from extending the rule, even in instances where it might be appropriate. Thus, federal habeas corpus challenges were limited in *Stone v. Powell*, 428 U.S. 465 (1976); grand jury questions based on evidence from an unlawful search were allowed in *United States v. Calandra*, 414 U.S. 338 (1974); in *United States v. Janis*, 428 U.S. 433 (1976), illegally seized evidence was allowed in federal civil proceedings because in each case the deterrent effect on the police was deemed to be limited; several cases limit standing to challenge the Fourth Amendment even where exclusion would deter police illegality; and finally, illegally obtained evidence may be admitted to impeach a witness.] **[e]**

III

A

* * *

* * * To the extent that proponents of exclusion rely on its behavioral effects on judges and magistrates, * * * their reliance is misplaced. First, the exclusionary rule is designed to deter police misconduct rather than to punish the errors of judges and magistrates. Second, there exists no evidence suggesting that judges and magistrates are inclined to ignore or subvert the Fourth Amendment or that lawlessness among these actors requires application of the extreme sanction of exclusion. **[f]**

Third, and most important, we discern no basis, and are offered none, for believing that exclusion of evidence seized pursuant to a warrant will have a significant deterrent effect on the issuing judge or magistrate. * * * [A]s neutral judicial officers, they have no stake in the outcome of particular criminal prosecutions. * * * Imposition of the exclusionary sanction is not necessary meaningfully to inform judicial officers of their errors. * * * **[g]**

B

If exclusion of evidence obtained pursuant to a subsequently invalidated warrant is to have any deterrent effect, therefore, it must alter the behavior of individual law enforcement officers or the policies of their departments. One could argue that applying the exclusionary rule in cases where the police failed to demonstrate probable cause in the warrant application deters future inadequate presentations or "magistrate shopping" and thus promotes the ends of the Fourth Amendment. Suppress-

ing evidence obtained pursuant to a technically defective warrant supported by probable cause also might encourage officers to scrutinize more closely the form of the warrant and to point out suspected judicial errors. We find such arguments speculative and conclude that suppression of evidence obtained pursuant to a warrant should be ordered only on a case-by-case basis and only in those unusual cases in which exclusion will further the purposes of the exclusionary rule. **[h]**

We have frequently questioned whether the exclusionary rule can have any deterrent effect when the offending officers acted in the objectively reasonable belief that their conduct did not violate the Fourth Amendment. "No empirical researcher, proponent or opponent of the rule, has yet been able to establish with any assurance whether the rule has a deterrent effect * * *" * * * But even assuming that the rule effectively deters some police misconduct and provides incentives for the law enforcement profession as a whole to conduct itself in accord with the Fourth Amendment, it cannot be expected, and should not be applied, to deter objectively reasonable law enforcement activity.

* * *

This is particularly true, we believe, when an officer acting with objective good faith has obtained a search warrant from a judge or magistrate and acted within its scope. In most such cases, there is no police illegality and thus nothing to deter. * * * **[i]**

* * *

C

* * *

Suppression * * * remains an appropriate remedy if the magistrate or judge in issuing a warrant was misled

by information in an affidavit that the affiant knew was false or would have known was false except for his reckless disregard of the truth. * * * The exception we recognize today will also not apply in cases where the issuing magistrate wholly abandoned his judicial role. * * * Nor would an officer manifest objective good faith in relying on a warrant based on an affidavit "so lacking in indicia of probable cause as to render official belief in its existence entirely unreasonable." * * * Finally, depending on the circumstances of the particular case, a warrant may be so facially deficient—*i.e.*, in failing to particularize the place to be searched or the things to be seized—that the executing officers cannot reasonably presume it to be valid. * * * **[j]**
* * *

JUSTICE BLACKMUN, concurring.

[The Court's holding] writes another chapter in the volume of Fourth Amendment law opened by *Weeks v. United States* (1914). * * *
* * * [T]he Court has narrowed the scope of the exclusionary rule because of an empirical judgment that the rule has little appreciable effect in cases where officers act in objectively reasonable reliance on search warrants. * * *

What must be stressed, however, is that any empirical judgment about the effect of the exclusionary rule in a particular class of cases necessarily is a provisional one. By their very nature, the assumptions on which we proceed today cannot be cast in stone. To the contrary, they now will be tested in the real world of state and federal law enforcement, and this Court will attend to the results. If it should emerge from experience that, contrary to our expectations, the good-faith exception to the exclusionary rule results in a material change in police compliance with the Fourth Amendment, we shall have to reconsider what we have undertaken here. The logic of a decision that rests on untested predictions about police conduct demands no less. **[k]**

If a single principle may be drawn from this Court's exclusionary rule decisions, from *Weeks* through *Mapp* * * * to the decisions handed down today, it is that the scope of the exclusionary rule is subject to change in light of changing judicial understanding about the effects of the rule outside the confines of the courtroom. It is incumbent on the Nation's law enforcement officers, who must continue to observe the Fourth Amendment in the wake of today's decisions, to recognize the double-edged nature of that principle.

JUSTICE BRENNAN, with whom JUSTICE MARSHALL joins, dissenting.

Ten years ago in *United States v. Calandra*, 414 U.S. 338 (1974), I expressed the fear that the Court's decision "may signal that a majority of my colleagues have positioned themselves to reopen the door [to evidence secured by official lawlessness] still further and abandon altogether the exclusionary rule in search-and-seizure cases" (dissenting opinion). Since then, in case after case, I have witnessed the Court's gradual but determined strangulation of the rule. It now appears that the Court's victory over

the Fourth Amendment is complete. *
* * [l]

* * *

The majority ignores the fundamental constitutional importance of what is at stake here. * * * [W]hat the Framers understood [in 1791] remains true today—that the task of combating crime and convicting the guilty will in every era seem of such critical and pressing concern that we may be lured by the temptations of expediency into forsaking our commitment to protecting individual liberty and privacy. It was for that very reason that the Framers of the Bill of Rights insisted that law enforcement efforts be permanently and unambiguously restricted in order to preserve personal freedoms. * * * [T]he sometimes unpopular task of ensuring that the government's enforcement efforts remain within the strict boundaries fixed by the Fourth Amendment was entrusted to the courts. * * * [m] If those independent tribunals lose their resolve, however, as the Court has done today, and give way to the seductive call of expediency, the vital guarantees of the Fourth Amendment are reduced to nothing more than a "form of words." * * *

I

* * * [A]s troubling and important as today's new doctrine may be for the administration of criminal justice in this country, the mode of analysis used to generate that doctrine also requires critical examination, for it may prove in the long run to pose the greater threat to our civil liberties.

A

[JUSTICE BRENNAN restated the majority argument here: the exclusionary rule is a mere judicial remedy designed to deter police illegality; the constitutional wrong is complete when the police invade a person's constitutionally protected privacy; and thus there is no constitutional violation if unconstitutionally seized evidence is admitted into evidence.]

Such a reading appears plausible, because, * * * the Fourth Amendment makes no express provision for the exclusion of evidence secured in violation of its commands. * * * [M]any of the Constitution's most vital imperatives are stated in general terms and the task of giving meaning to these precepts is therefore left to subsequent judicial decisionmaking in the context of concrete cases. The nature of our Constitution, as CHIEF JUSTICE MARSHALL long ago explained, "requires that only its great outlines should be marked, its important objects designated, and the minor ingredients which compose those objects be deduced from the nature of the objects themselves." * * * [n]

A more direct answer may be supplied by recognizing that the Amendment, like other provisions of the Bill of Rights, restrains the power of the government as a whole; it does not specify only a particular agency and exempt all others. The judiciary is responsible, no less than the executive, for ensuring that constitutional rights are respected. [o]

* * * Once that connection between the evidence-gathering role of the police and the evidence-admitting function of the courts is acknowledged, the plausibility of the Court's interpretation becomes more suspect. * * * The Amendment therefore must be

read to condemn not only the initial unconstitutional invasion of privacy—which is done, after all, for the purpose of securing evidence—but also the subsequent use of any evidence so obtained.

The Court evades this principle by drawing an artificial line between the constitutional rights and responsibilities that are engaged by actions of the police and those that are engaged when a defendant appears before the courts. According to the Court, the substantive protections of the Fourth Amendment are wholly exhausted at the moment when police unlawfully invade an individual's privacy and thus no substantive force remains to those protections at the time of trial when the government seeks to use evidence obtained by the police. [p]

I submit that such a crabbed reading of the Fourth Amendment * * * rests ultimately on an impoverished understanding of judicial responsibility in our constitutional scheme. For my part, "[t]he right of the people to be secure in their persons, houses, papers, and effects, against unreasonable searches and seizures" comprises a personal right to exclude all evidence secured by means of unreasonable searches and seizures. The right to be free from the initial invasion of privacy and the right of exclusion are coordinate components of the central embracing right to be free from unreasonable searches and seizures.
* * *

B

* * *

* * * [H]owever, the Court since *Calandra* has gradually pressed the deterrence rationale for the rule back

to center stage. * * * [JUSTICE BRENNAN then reviewed the cost-benefit analysis utilized by the majority.] * * *

* * * To the extent empirical data are available regarding the general costs and benefits of the exclusionary rule, it has shown, on the one hand, as the Court acknowledges today, that the costs are not as substantial as critics have asserted in the past, * * * and, on the other hand, that while the exclusionary rule may well have certain deterrent effects, it is extremely difficult to determine with any degree of precision whether the incidence of unlawful conduct by police is now lower than it was prior to *Mapp*. * * * The Court has sought to turn this uncertainty to its advantage by casting the burden of proof upon proponents of the rule. * * *

* * * [B]y basing the rule solely on the deterrence rationale, the Court has robbed the rule of legitimacy. A doctrine that is explained as if it were an empirical proposition but for which there is only limited empirical support is both inherently unstable and an easy mark for critics. The extent of this Court's fidelity to Fourth Amendment requirements, however, should not turn on such statistical uncertainties. * * * Rather than seeking to give effect to the liberties secured by the Fourth Amendment through guesswork about deterrence, the Court should restore to its proper place the principle framed 70 years ago in *Weeks* that an individual whose privacy has been invaded in violation of the Fourth Amendment has a right grounded in that Amendment to prevent the government from subsequently making use of any evidence so obtained. [q]
* * *

JUSTICE STEVENS, * * * dissenting in [*United States v. Leon*].

* * *

Today's decisions do grave damage to [the Fourth Amendment's] deterrent [r] function. Under the majority's new rule, even when the police know their warrant application is probably insufficient, they retain an incentive to submit it to a magistrate, on the chance that he may take the bait. No longer must they hesitate and seek additional evidence in doubtful cases. * * *

* * *

* * * [T]he Court's creation of a double standard of reasonableness inevitably must erode the deterrence rationale that still supports the exclusionary rule. But we should not ignore the way it tarnishes the role of the judiciary in enforcing the Constitution. * * *

* * * Today, for the first time, this Court holds that although the Constitution has been violated, no court should do anything about it at any time and in any proceeding. * * * Courts simply cannot escape their responsibility for redressing constitutional violations. * * * If [unconstitutionally seized] evidence is admitted, then the courts become not merely the final and necessary link in an unconstitutional chain of events, but its actual motivating force. * * * [s]

* * *

* * * * * * * * * * *

COMMENTS

[a] JUSTICE WHITE states the issue *and* establishes a "judicial methodology,"—the "balancing test"—to resolve the issue. The choice assists in producing the desired outcome. The dissent utilizes a different analytic framework to reach its contrary result.

[b] JUSTICE WHITE deflects a major argument of the dissent by "nullifying" the precedential value of *Mapp* as a constitutional rule by relying on later cases. JUSTICE WHITE, a long standing critic of *Mapp*, is now able to use precedents he helped create to weaken its effect. This is typical judicial strategy in the Supreme Court.

[c] In some areas of law the remedy is part of the right. Thus, a complete definition of crime includes the penalty (the public's "remedy"; not the personal remedy of the injured party). For constitutional violations, however, the Court indicates that the public's remedy of exclusion is not an essential part of the right. (In addition to the exclusion of evidence, an aggrieved party can sue the police to recover damages for violations of Fourth Amendment rights, *Soldal v. Illinois* [this volume].) Compare JUSTICE WHITE's reasoning to JUSTICE MURPHY's dissent in *Wolf v. Colorado* [this volume].

[d] The exclusionary rule is "put on the defensive," stressing its costs, limits, and status as a "mere" remedy rather than as a constitutional right. The extent of

social costs involved in the exclusionary rule is an empirical question still open to much debate. Phraseology is important. The "imperative of judicial integrity" of liberal justices becomes the "ideal of governmental rectitude" to conservative justices. The phrases convey different meanings.

[e] Constitutional cases do not stand in isolation; JUSTICE WHITE's recitation of these cases shows that support for a strong exclusionary policy has been eroded.

[f] This can be challenged by arguing that the purpose of the Bill of Rights is to protect the rights of individuals against violations by government officers; who the particular officer is is a secondary matter. Should the Supreme Court invest blanket trust in magistrates?

[g] By way of analogy, judges have immunity from lawsuit for errors made on the bench but are subject to reversal on appeal as a way of correcting their errors and deterring them from not following precedent. Why should magistrates not be concerned when their warrants are overturned as improper? Does this reasoning expand the immunity of a magistrate to insulate erroneous decisions about Constitutional rights from review on appeal?

[h] One could charge the majority with making highly selective factual assumptions. JUSTICE WHITE here brushes aside the "educative" function of the law, that is, the idea that over the long run the law is effective through educating police officers. It is somewhat ironic that the educative function of law and symbolic rules has typically been an important part of conservative belief.

[i] What does police illegality mean here: that no crime has been committed by the police officer? or that no violation of a defendant's constitutional rights has occurred? If the latter, the magistrate could be implicated in the "illegality."

[j] JUSTICE WHITE stresses that the good faith reliance-on-the-warrant exception is not to be interpreted as a blank check to the police. Four cases are set out where the exclusionary rule should apply even if an officer relies on a warrant. Thus, the "good faith exception" is less than a clear-cut rule and more of a guideline. This kind of pronouncement by the Court is likely to produce a good amount of confusion as lower courts hand down divergent rulings on similar factual circumstances.

[k] JUSTICE BLACKMUN's concurrence is unusually frank about the flexibility of this area of law. The majority and the dissent strive to establish both rules and ways of thinking about the Fourth Amendment that will not change. JUSTICE BLACKMUN's less partisan stance recognizes that the pendulum has swung twice on the exclusionary rule; he leaves open the possibility that it might swing back to a more rigid, individual-rights basis once again.

   The concurrence is also a warning to police that widespread Fourth Amendment violations will be the impetus for the Court to once again expand the scope of the exclusionary rule.

[l] This strong language may be discounted in part as a tactic, but it *is* a way of reaching beyond the majority to stir a wider audience and future generations, in the hope that a different Court might overturn this decision.

[m] Does the Court's historic function of preserving the Constitutional liberties of American citizens mean that in every case the only correct rule is that which is most favorable to the criminal defendant? If not, how is a yardstick of constitutional adjudication to be developed?

[n] It could be argued that this point is more applicable to a more open textured right such as "due process" than more narrowly focused rights, such as the Fourth Amendment.

[o] Is this doctrinally plausible? Of course the Fourth Amendment applies with equal force to every governmental officer, magistrate and police alike. But does the *exclusionary rule* so apply? Because of the way in which the majority has characterized the rule, JUSTICE BRENNAN's point here, standing alone, can be discounted by proponents of the view that the rule is "merely" a remedy. Thus, JUSTICE BRENNAN presses his argument forward.

[p] JUSTICE BRENNAN stakes out a different methodology and conclusion from that of the majority. In deciding the correct position do you first look at the nature of the logic used or to the result? In his historic review of the exclusionary rule (parts of which are omitted here) he indicates that even in the era between *Weeks* (1914) and *Mapp* (1961), the pendulum had swung against and then for a constitutional view of the exclusionary rule.

[q] It is now clear that the majority and dissenting justices are arguing this case on different grounds. Although JUSTICE BRENNAN argues that exclusion is the best deterrent of police illegality, the heart of his position is based on constitutional doctrine to which deterrence is irrelevant. If the majority argued the case on the basis established by JUSTICE HARLAN's dissent in *Mapp* would they have established a firmer foundation for the ruling?

[r] Here, JUSTICE STEVENS attacks the majority at one of its central points: deterrence. Does he raise a reasonable doubt in your mind that the holding of this case, rather than strengthening, *undermines* the deterrent effect of the exclusionary rule? Or does his reasoning seem to be more inaccurate than the majority's? Or are both unpersuasive?

[s] Since the constitutional violation occurred in good faith, the majority implies that a civil lawsuit for a rights violation is not possible. Thus, JUSTICE STEVENS raises the specter of a violation of rights without a remedy.

DUNCAN v. LOUISIANA

391 U.S. 145, 88 S.Ct. 1444, 20 L.Ed.2d 491 (1968)

MR. JUSTICE WHITE delivered the opinion of the Court.

Appellant, Gary Duncan, was convicted of simple battery. * * * [The case arose out of a scuffle between black and white teenagers]. Under Louisiana law simple battery is a misdemeanor punishable by a maximum of two years' imprisonment and a $300 fine. Appellant sought trial by jury, but because the Louisiana Constitution grants jury trials only in cases in which capital punishment or imprisonment at hard labor may be imposed, the trial judge denied the request. Appellant was convicted and sentenced to serve 60 days in the parish prison and pay a fine of $150. [The Louisiana Supreme Court found no constitutional error.] [A]ppellant sought review in this Court, alleging that the Sixth and Fourteenth Amendments to the United States Constitution secure the right to jury trial in state criminal prosecutions where a sentence as long as two years may be imposed. * * *

I.

The Fourteenth Amendment denies the States the power to "deprive any person of life, liberty, or property, without due process of law." In resolving conflicting claims concerning the meaning of this spacious language, the Court has looked increasingly to the Bill of Rights for guidance; many of the rights guaranteed by the first eight Amendments to the Constitution have been held to be protected against state action by the Due Process Clause of the Fourteenth Amendment. That clause now protects the right to compensation for property taken by the State; the rights of speech, press, and religion covered by the First Amendment; the Fourth Amendment rights to be free from unreasonable searches and seizures and to have excluded from criminal trials any evidence illegally seized; the right guaranteed by the Fifth Amendment to be free of compelled self-incrimination; and the Sixth Amendment rights to counsel, to a speedy and public trial, to confrontation of opposing witnesses, and to compulsory process for obtaining witnesses. [a]

The test for determining whether a right extended by the Fifth and Sixth Amendments with respect to federal criminal proceedings is also protected against state action by the Fourteenth Amendment has been phrased in a variety of ways in the opinions of this Court. The question has been asked whether a right is among those "'fundamental principles of liberty and justice which lie at the base of all our civil and political institutions;'" * * * whether it is "basic in our system of jurisprudence;" * * * and whether it is "a fundamental right, essential to a fair trial." * * * The claim before us is that the right to trial by jury guaranteed by the Sixth Amendment meets these tests. The position of Louisiana, on the other hand, is that the Constitution imposes upon the States no duty to give a jury trial in any criminal case, regardless of the seriousness of the crime or the size of the punishment which may be imposed. Because we believe that trial by jury in criminal cases is fundamental to the American scheme of justice, we hold that the Fourteenth Amendment guarantees a right of jury trial in all criminal cases which—were they to be tried in a federal court—would come within the Sixth Amendment's guarantee.[14] [b] Since we consider the appeal before us to be such a case, we hold that the Constitution was violated when appellant's demand for jury trial was refused.

* * *

FOOTNOTE 14:

In one sense recent cases applying provisions of the first eight Amendments to the States represent a new approach to the "incorporation" debate. Earlier the Court can be seen as having asked, when inquiring into whether some particular procedural safeguard was required of a State, if a civilized system could be imagined that would not accord the particular protection. For example, *Palko v. Connecticut* [this volume], stated: "The right to trial by jury and the immunity from prosecution except as the result of an indictment may have value and importance. Even so, they are not of the very essence of a scheme of ordered liberty. * * * Few would be so narrow or provincial as to maintain that a fair and enlightened system of justice would be impossible without them." The recent cases, on the other hand, have proceeded upon the valid assumption that state criminal processes are not imaginary and theoretical schemes but actual systems bearing virtually every characteristic of the common-law system that has been developing contemporaneously in England and in this country. The question thus is whether given this kind of system a particular procedure is fundamental—whether, that is, a procedure is necessary to an Anglo-American regime of ordered liberty. It is this sort of inquiry that can justify the conclusions that state courts must exclude evidence seized in violation of the Fourth Amendment, *Mapp v. Ohio* [this volume]; that state prosecutors may not comment on a defendant's failure to testify, *Griffin v. California*, 380 U.S. 609 (1965); and that criminal punishment may not be imposed for the status of narcotics addiction, *Robinson v. California*, 370 U.S. 660 (1962). Of immediate relevance for this case are the Court's holdings that the States must comply with certain provisions of the Sixth Amendment, specifically that the States may not refuse a speedy trial, confrontation of witnesses, and the assistance, at state expense if necessary, of counsel. * * * Of each of these determinations that a constitutional provision originally written to bind the Federal Government should bind the States as well it might be said that the limitation in question is not necessarily fundamental to fairness in every criminal system that might be imagined but is fundamental in the context of the criminal processes maintained by the American States.

When the inquiry is approached in this way the question whether the States can impose criminal punishment without granting a jury trial appears quite different from the way it appeared in the older cases opining that States might abolish jury trial. * * * A criminal process which was fair and equitable but used no jurics is easy to imagine. It would make use of alternative guarantees and protections which would serve the purposes that the jury serves in the English and American systems. Yet no American State has undertaken to construct such a system. Instead, every American State, including Louisiana, uses the jury extensively, and imposes very serious punishments only after a trial at which the defendant has a right to a jury's verdict. In every State, including Louisiana, the structure and style of the criminal process—the supporting framework and the subsidiary procedures—are of the sort that naturally complement jury trial, and have developed in connection with and in reliance upon jury trial.

* * *

[JUSTICE WHITE's opinion reviewed the history of trial by jury in England and America at length. In brief, the right to trial by jury, part of the colonial and Revolutionary heritage, was seen to be at the core of the American constitutional experience, enshrined into the constitution of every state and the federal constitution. It then disposed of the case by adhering to the selective incorporation approach and by determining whether the Louisiana battery misdemeanor was a petty crime or a serious crime.]

It is sufficient for our purposes to hold that a crime punishable by two years in prison is, based on past and contemporary standards in this country, a serious crime and not a petty offense. Consequently, appellant was entitled to a jury trial and it was error to deny it. [c]

The judgment below is reversed and the case is remanded for proceedings not inconsistent with this opinion.

[JUSTICE FORTAS, wrote a concurring opinion; Justice Black wrote a concurring opinion, in which JUSTICE DOUGLAS joined. JUSTICE HARLAN dissented, joined by JUSTICE STEWART.]

* * * * * * * * * *

COMMENTS

[a] With these brief notes (the citations to cases are omitted) the Court reviewed the enormous change that had occurred in less than a decade: the selective incorporation of virtually all the provisions of the Bill of Rights from 1961 to the end of the decade, known as the "Due Process Revolution." This occurred after almost a century of intellectual struggle and development in this area of law in the Supreme Court's jurisprudence.

[b] Significant information is often found in footnotes to Supreme Court opinions. In footnote 14, JUSTICE WHITE lays down a revised theory for incorporation that answers many of JUSTICE CARDOZO's points in *Palko v. Connecticut* [this volume].

[c] The case of *Burch v. Louisiana* [this volume, Chapter 10] traces the development of various aspects of the meaning of the right to a jury in state legal systems under the incorporated Sixth Amendment.

MICHIGAN v. LONG

463 U.S. 1032, 103 S.Ct. 3469, 77 L.Ed.2d 1201 (1983)

JUSTICE O'CONNOR delivered the opinion of the Court.

I

[Sheriff's deputies on patrol after midnight followed Long's speeding automobile as he drove it erratically and into a shallow ditch. Long met the deputies at the rear of the car, leaving the door of the vehicle open. After a delay in producing his license, Long walked to the car, followed by the deputies. They observed a large hunting knife on the floorboard of the car and then subjected Long to a *Terry* protective pat-down, finding no weapons. One deputy shined a flashlight into the car, looking for weapons. He saw something protruding from under the armrest, found marihuana and arrested Long for possession.]

[The marihuana was introduced into evidence. On appeal, the Michigan Supreme Court ruled that "the sole justification of the *Terry* search, protection of the police officers and others nearby, cannot justify the search in this case." The substantive constitutional issue before the United States Supreme Court was whether the search of the auto's passenger compartment was authorized by *Terry v. Ohio* [this volume].] **[a]**

II

Before reaching the merits, we must consider Long's argument that we are without jurisdiction to decide this case because the decision below rests on an adequate and independent state ground. The court below referred twice to the State Constitution in its opinion, but otherwise relied exclusively on federal law. * * * **[b]** Long argues that the Michigan courts have provided greater protection from searches and seizures under the State Constitution than is afforded under the Fourth Amendment, and the references to the State Constitution therefore establish an adequate and independent ground for the decision below.

It is, of course, "incumbent upon this Court * * * to ascertain for itself * * * whether the asserted non-federal ground independently and adequately supports the judgment." * * * **[c]** Although we have announced a number of principles in order to help us determine whether various forms of references to state law constitute adequate and independent state grounds, [see the Court's footnote 4 below] we openly admit that we have thus far not developed a satisfying and consistent approach for resolving this vexing issue. In some instances, we have taken the strict view that if the ground of decision was at all unclear, we would dismiss the case. In other instances we have vacated * * * or continued a case, * * * in order to obtain clarification about the nature of a state court decision. * * * In more recent cases, we have ourselves examined state law to determine whether state courts have used federal law to guide their application of state law or to provide the actual basis for the decision that was reached. * * * In *Oregon v. Kennedy*, 456 U.S. 667, 670-67 (1982), we rejected an invitation to remand to the state court for clarification even when the decision rested in part on a case from the state court, because we determined that the state case itself rested upon federal grounds. We added that "[e]ven if the case admitted of more doubt as to whether federal and state grounds for decision were intermixed, the fact that the state court relied to the extent it did on federal grounds requires us to reach the merits." * * * **[d]**

FOOTNOTE 4:

For example, we have long recognized that 'where the judgment of a state court rests upon two grounds, one of which is federal and the other non-federal in character, our jurisdiction fails if the non-federal ground is independent of the federal ground and adequate to support the judgment.' * * * We may review a state case decided on a federal ground even if it is clear that there was an available state ground for decision on which the state court could properly have relied. * * * Also, if, in our view, the state court "'felt compelled by what it understood to be federal constitutional considerations to construe * * * its own law in the manner it did,'" then we will not treat a normally adequate state ground as independent, and there will be no question about our jurisdiction. * * * Finally, 'where the non-federal ground is so interwoven with the [federal ground] as not to be an independent matter, or is not of sufficient breadth to sustain the judgment without any decision of the other, our jurisdiction is plain." **[e]**

This ad hoc method of dealing with cases that involve possible adequate and independent state grounds is antithetical to the doctrinal consistency that is required when sensitive issues of federal-state relations are involved. Moreover, none of the various methods of disposition that we have employed thus far recommends itself as the preferred method that we should apply to the exclusion of others, and we therefore determine that it is appropriate to reexamine our treatment of this jurisdictional issue in order to achieve the consistency that is necessary. **[f]**

[JUSTICE O'CONNOR next stated several problems with the Court's diverse practices: (1) it requires the Supreme Court to interpret unfamiliar state law, which may not have been discussed by the state courts in the case on appeal; (2) continuances cause delays and lower judicial efficiency; and (3) where a state court interprets the United States Constitution, a dismissal undercuts the United States Supreme Court's obligation to insure uniform interpretation of the Constitution.]

Respect for the independence of state courts, as well as avoidance of rendering advisory opinions, **[g]** have been the cornerstones of this Court's refusal to decide cases where there is an adequate and independent state ground. It is precisely because of this respect for state courts, and this desire to avoid advisory opinions, that we do not wish to continue to decide issues of state law that go beyond the opinion that we review, or to require state courts to reconsider cases to clarify the grounds of their decisions. Accordingly, when, as in this case, a state court decision fairly appears to rest primarily on federal law, or to be interwoven with the federal law, and when the adequacy and independence of any possible state law ground is not clear from the face of the opinion, we will accept as the most reasonable explanation that the state court decided the case the way it did because it believed that federal law required it to do so. If a state court chooses merely to rely on federal precedents as it would on the precedents of all other jurisdictions, then it need only make clear by a plain statement in its judgment or opinion that the federal cases are being used only for the purpose of guidance, and do not themselves compel the result that the court has reached. In this way, both justice and judicial administration will be greatly improved. If the state court decision indicates clearly and expressly that it is alternatively based on bona fide separate, adequate, and independent grounds, we, of course, will not undertake to review the decision.

This approach obviates in most instances the need to examine state law in order to decide the nature of the state court decision, and will at the same time avoid the danger of our rendering advisory opinions. It also avoids the unsatisfactory and intrusive practice of requiring state courts to clarify their decisions to the satisfaction of this Court. [h] We believe that such an approach will provide state judges with a clearer opportunity to develop state jurisprudence unimpeded by federal interference, and yet will preserve the integrity of federal law. "It is fundamental that state courts be left free and unfettered by us in interpreting their state constitutions. But it is equally important that ambiguous or obscure adjudications by state courts do not stand as barriers to a determination by this Court of the

validity under the federal constitution of state action." * * *

The principle that we will not review judgments of state courts that rest on adequate and independent state grounds is based, in part, on "the limitations of our own jurisdiction." * * * The jurisdictional concern is that we not "render an advisory opinion, and if the same judgment would be rendered by the state court after we corrected its views of federal laws, our review could amount to nothing more than an advisory opinion." * * * Our requirement of a "plain statement" that a decision rests upon adequate and independent state grounds does not in any way authorize the rendering of advisory opinions. Rather, in determining, as we must, whether we have jurisdiction to review a case that is alleged to rest on adequate and independent state grounds, * * * we merely assume that there are no such grounds when it is not clear from the opinion itself that the state court relied upon an adequate and independent state ground and when it fairly appears that the state court rested its decision primarily on federal law. [i]

* * *

[The Michigan Supreme Court's opinion and did not rest] upon an independent state ground. Apart from its two citations to the State Constitution, the court below relied *exclusively* on its understanding of *Terry* and other federal cases. Not a single state case was cited to support the state court's holding that the search of the passenger compartment was unconstitutional. * * * The references to the State Constitution in no way indicate that the decision below rested on grounds in any way *independent* from the state court's [j] interpretation of federal law. Even if we accept that the Michigan Constitution has been interpreted to provide independent protection for certain rights also secured under the Fourth Amendment, it fairly appears in this case that the Michigan Supreme Court rested its decision primarily on federal law.

Rather than dismissing the case, or requiring that the state court reconsider its decision on our behalf solely because of a mere possibility that an adequate and independent ground supports the judgment, we find that we have jurisdiction in the absence of a plain statement that the decision below rested on an adequate and independent state ground. [k] It appears to us that the state court "felt compelled by what it understood to be federal constitutional considerations to construe * * * its own law in the manner it did." * * *

JUSTICE STEVENS, dissenting.

* * * The case raises profoundly significant questions concerning the relationship between two sovereigns—the State of Michigan and the United States of America. [l]

The Supreme Court of the State of Michigan expressly held "that the deputies' search of the vehicle was proscribed by the Fourth Amendment to the United States Constitution and *Art. 1, sec. 11 of the Michigan Constitution*." * * * The state law ground is clearly adequate to support the judgment, but the question whether it is independent of the Michigan Supreme Court's understanding of federal law is more difficult. Four possible ways of resolving that question present themselves: (1) asking the Michigan Supreme Court directly, (2) attempting to

infer from all possible sources of state law what the Michigan Supreme Court meant, (3) presuming that adequate state grounds are independent unless it clearly appears otherwise, or (4) presuming that adequate state grounds are *not* independent unless it clearly appears otherwise. This Court has, on different occasions, employed each of the first three approaches; never until today has it even hinted at the fourth. In order to "achieve the consistency that is necessary," the Court today undertakes a reexamination of all the possibilities. * * * It rejects the first approach as inefficient and unduly burdensome for state courts, and rejects the second approach as an inappropriate expenditure of our resources. * * * Although I find both of those decisions defensible in themselves, I cannot accept the Court's decision to choose the fourth approach over the third—to presume that adequate state grounds are intended to be dependent on federal law unless the record plainly shows otherwise. I must therefore dissent. [m]

If we reject the intermediate approaches, we are left with a choice between two presumptions: one in favor of our taking jurisdiction, and one against it. Historically, the latter presumption has always prevailed. * * *

Even if I agreed with the Court that we are free to consider as a fresh proposition whether we may take presumptive jurisdiction over the decisions of sovereign States, I could not agree that an expansive attitude makes good sense. It appears to be common ground that any rule we adopt should show "respect for state courts, and [a] desire to avoid advisory opinions." * * * And I am confident that all Members of this Court agree that there is a vital interest in the sound management of scarce federal judicial resources. All of those policies counsel against the exercise of federal jurisdiction. They are fortified by my belief that a policy of judicial restraint—one that allows other decisional bodies to have the last word in legal interpretation until it is truly necessary for this Court to intervene—enables this Court to make its most effective contribution to our federal system of government. [n]

[JUSTICE STEVENS then argued that because the Michigan Supreme Court ruled in the defendant's favor in this case, there has been no deprivation of a federally protected right. Therefore, the United States Supreme Court should decline jurisdiction.] These * * * are cases in which a state court has upheld a citizen's assertion of a right, finding the citizen to be protected under both federal and state law. The attorney for the complaining

party is an officer of the State itself, who asks us to rule that the state court interpreted federal rights too broadly and "overprotected" the citizen.

Such cases should not be of inherent concern to this Court. * * *

In this case the State of Michigan has arrested one of its citizens and the Michigan Supreme Court has decided to turn him loose. The respondent is a United States citizen as well as a Michigan citizen, but since there is no claim that he has been mistreated by the State of Michigan, the final outcome of the state processes offended no federal interest whatever. Michigan simply provided greater protection to one of its citizens than some other State might provide or, indeed, than this Court might require throughout the country.

* * * Finally, I am thoroughly baffled by the Court's suggestion that it must stretch its jurisdiction and reverse the judgment of the Michigan Supreme Court in order to show "[r]espect for the independence of state courts." * * *

* * * * * * * * * * *

COMMENTS

[a] The Supreme Court ultimately decides the case in favor of the state, holding that the deputies conducted a proper *Terry* search for weapons. At this point, we are concerned with the jurisdictional issue and the relationship between the federal and state authority in determining the rights of parties.

[b] Since Long won his point before the Michigan Supreme Court, this appeal was brought by the state. The appellant must show federal jurisdiction. In this case, the matter was not entirely clear because there was language in the Michigan court's opinion that could have been read to indicate that the decision was based primarily on state, rather than federal, law.

[c] The extent to which the Michigan Supreme Court relied on Michigan's own constitution is a factual question. Compare JUSTICE O'CONNOR's statement at

this point to JUSTICE STEVEN's presentation of this critical factual point, below. Although the adequate and independent state ground doctrine precludes the federal courts from deciding a case, it is up to the same federal courts to decide whether the doctrine applies in the first place. The state court cannot block federal jurisdiction to initially consider the issue.

[d] The three approaches listed here indicate different levels of federal power over state court decisions. Thus, a decision on how the United States Supreme Court should handle such decisions goes to the heart of the federalism issue. Notice that JUSTICE STEVENS, below, in dissent, identifies four approaches. Keep in mind that the existence of federalism means that the extent of constitutional rules may not be the same in every state, *i.e.*, some states may guarantee to their citizens *more* rights than are guaranteed by the basic (*i.e.*, minimum) rights guaranteed by the United States Constitution.

[e] Basic rules in an opinion may be stated in a footnote because it is presumed that lawyers are aware of them, and the textbook-like statement of the general rules are not essential to the development of the reasoning in the case. Judicial styles differ in this regard; sometimes basic rules are written into the opinion of a text. These basic rules are both respectful of the sovereignty of the states and mindful of the legitimate authority of the United States Supreme Court. The key to this delicate balancing act is whether the state supreme court's decision rests on *adequate* and *independent* state grounds.

[f] The Court is in a sense engaged in "judicial housekeeping." Decisions in individual cases made over a period of decades often result in certain inconsistencies. When they are detected and prove to be troublesome to lower courts, it is the responsibility of a supreme court to clarify its rulings, perhaps by overruling one or more approaches taken earlier.

[g] Article III of the United States Constitution limits federal judicial power to "* * * Cases, in Law and Equity, arising under the Constitution [and] * * * to Controversies to which the United States shall be a Party. * * *" In 1793, the justices of the Supreme Court declined to give President Washington a legal opinion requested in a letter. They said, in effect, that the structure of the American government under the Constitution, with its emphasis on checks and balances, precluded the justices from rendering an advisory opinion, that is, a legal opinion where there is no "case or controversy."

[h] Despite the Court's cautionary language, it seems clear that in ambiguous cases, it will review a state supreme court decision instead of "respecting" state sovereignty.

[i] In a footnote JUSTICE O'CONNOR noted that the state courts handle the vast bulk of all criminal litigation in this country. In 1982, for example, more than 12 million criminal actions (excluding juvenile and traffic charges) were filed in the 50 state court systems and the District of Columbia compared to 32,700 in federal courts.

This is a dramatic reminder of the reach of the Supreme Court's authority when it decides state cases.

[j] It is one thing for a state supreme court to interpret its own constitution; it is another for the supreme courts of the states to issue various rulings as to the meaning of the *federal* constitution. If the Michigan Supreme Court simply added one sentence to its opinion, to the effect that its opinion rested on the state ground and that the discussion of federal law was simply to illuminate the issues, would that stop the United States Supreme Court from reviewing the state court opinion?

[k] Should the determination of an adequate and independent state ground depend on whether the state court cited more state than federal citations? Should the adequacy of a state ground depend on the Supreme Court's assessment of the quality of the state court's opinion? There seems to be a level of subjectivity and vagueness in JUSTICE O'CONNOR's opinion in regard to how these issues will be determined. Perhaps such judgment is unavoidable in situations where the state court does not make the basis of its decision absolutely clear.

[l] Federal-state conflict or tension is one of the basic issues of constitutional power, along with conflict between branches of government and the relationship of the individual vis-à-vis the government.

[m] Thus, the majority and the dissenting justices differ essentially in the extent to which they seek to interfere with state court decisions. JUSTICE STEVENS paints the majority as radically upsetting earlier cases that had enhanced states' rights.

[n] JUSTICE STEVENS indirectly accuses the majority of being unnecessarily activist.

Chapter Two

FOURTH AMENDMENT, SEARCH AND SEIZURE

In this Chapter, we examine the constitutional law of search and seizure. The Fourth Amendment to the Bill of Rights states:

> The right of the people to be secure in their persons, houses, papers and effects, against unreasonable searches and seizures, shall not be violated, and no Warrants shall issue, but upon probable cause, supported by Oath or affirmation, and particularly describing the place to be searched, and the person or things to be seized.

Chapter One included several classic Fourth Amendment cases concerning the creation and incorporation of the exclusionary rule (*i.e.*, *Boyd*, *Weeks*, *Silverthorne*, *Wolf*, *Mapp* and *Leon*). To a large extent Fourth Amendment jurisprudence has been intertwined with the development of these two major themes. However, that is far from the entire story.

In Section A we examine the core of what may be called the theory of the Fourth Amendment, the "expectation of privacy" doctrine, also known as the *Katz* doctrine. Before *Katz. v. United States* (1967) it was thought that a violation of Fourth Amendment rights depended upon a physical trespass into a "protected area" (*Olmstead v. United States*, 277 U.S. 438 (1928)). This resulted in rulings that electronic eavesdropping did not violate the Fourth Amendment when conducted without a physical intrusion (*Goldman v. United States*, 316 U.S. 129 (1942)), but did violate the Amendment if the listening device was physically nailed into a protected area (*Silverman v. United States*, 365 U.S. 505 (1961)). The illogic of this position was intolerable and the importance of the issue too great for the law to be left standing in this state. Either the understanding of the Fourth Amendment would have to be expanded to encompass the government listening in on citizens, with the possible effect of outlawing a practice that is difficult to contain under the "particularity clause," or the government could listen in at will as listening devices became more and more sophisticated.

The Court resolved this intellectual impasse by ruling that the Fourth

Amendment did indeed cover electronic eavesdropping and that such activity violated a person's constitutional rights unless the government acted under a judicial warrant based upon the evidentiary standard of probable cause. In *Katz* the Court stated that the Fourth Amendment "protects people, not places" and that what a person "seeks to preserve as private, even in an area accessible to the public, may be constitutionally protected."

That the expectation of privacy doctrine does not cover all Fourth Amendment interests was demonstrated recently in *Soldal v. Cook County* (1993) where the Court ruled, in a case with unusual facts, that a deprivation of property by the government, even when there is no interference with privacy interests, may violate the Fourth Amendment.

The Supreme Court has applied the expectation of privacy doctrine in a variety of settings and circumstances. A prison inmate's subjective or personal interest in the privacy of his cell does not outweigh the objective or public understanding of Fourth Amendment rights. Thus, there is no constitutionally recognized privacy interest in a prison cell (*Hudson v. Palmer* (1984)). Likewise, there is no Fourth Amendment privacy right to abandoned trash (*California v. Greenwood* (1988)), in "open fields" (*Oliver v. United States* (1984)), or in areas that can be viewed by aerial overflights (*Florida v. Riley* (1989)).

The *Katz* doctrine is not the only methodology utilized by the Supreme Court to determine whether the Fourth Amendment has been violated. In *Michigan Dep't. of State Police v. Sitz* (1988) the Court first held that a temporary sobriety checklane did amount to a seizure of persons briefly stopped for a sobriety check. However, it applied a balancing test to determine that this temporary seizure did not violate a stopped person's Fourth Amendment rights because the practice served an important governmental function and was carried out in a reasonable manner. *Sitz* relied on an important mode of Fourth Amendment analysis. The Amendment is divided into two clauses: the "reasonableness clause" and the "warrant clause." Under one theory, a search that is not authorized by a judicial warrant is unconstitutional unless it fits into one of a few limited exceptions (see Chapter Three). But another theory holds that the Fourth Amendment is satisfied by searches and seizures that are "not unreasonable" since the Fourth Amendment prohibits "unreasonable" searches and seizures. Under this theory, the seizure of drivers in *Sitz* was constitutional because deemed reasonable by the Court.

The "reasonableness" theory has also been used in cases where search and seizures occur outside of typical police actions against criminal suspects. Where there are "special needs," the court has allowed searches and seizures without warrant and even without probable cause. In such cases, a lower standard of evidence sufficiency, reasonable suspicion, is sufficient. This standard has been applied in searches of high school students' personal bags by school officials where the search was designed to enforce school rules (*New Jersey v. T.L.O.* (1985)) and in obtaining blood and urine samples from railway employees involved in accidents (*Skinner v. Railway Labor Executives Assn.* (1989)).

A doctrine closely related to the expectation of privacy concept is that of standing. In constitutional law a case in federal court must be a "case or controversy" under Article III (the Judicial Article) of the Constitution. That is, there must be a real conflict between the parties and each party must have a real stake in the outcome of the case. In Fourth Amendment cases, it is possible for a person to have seized evidence used against him at trial without being able to challenge the constitutionality of its seizure, if the defendant has not suffered injury to his personal Fourth Amendment interest (*Rakas v. Illinois* (1978)).

Probable cause is the standard of evidence required for a warrant to issue under the Fourth Amendment. It is also required for most warrantless searches (see Chapter Three) and for arrests made without a warrant (see Chapter Four). It may be generally defined as known facts which allow a reasonably prudent person to draw conclusions about unknown facts. Where police produce a sworn statement to a magistrate containing verified facts regarding contraband, such as the fact that a police agent recently purchased illegal drugs in a specific premises, the magistrate may reasonably conclude that illegal drugs are presently in the premises. The Court has developed cautionary rules where the police must rely on the hearsay of an informer to establish probable cause. In 1969, the Court held in *Spinelli v. United States* that a two-prong test was required, showing sufficient facts to allow the magistrate to determine the informant's basis of knowledge and also showing that the informant is credible or that his information is reliable. This test was overturned in *Illinois v. Gates* (1983) which substituted a "totality of the circumstances" test, in which a failure to establish one prong of the *Spinelli* rule would not necessarily invalidate the warrant. The *Gates* opinion thus expanded the government's ability to have searches based on informants' information upheld.

Plain view is another basic Fourth Amendment doctrine. The doctrine is quite old but was set out in *Coolidge v. New Hampshire*, 403 U.S. 443 (1971) in a plurality opinion. Evidence that is in "plain view" is presumptively not protected by a reasonable expectation of privacy and so may be seized by an officer, without a warrant, if it is contraband or evidence of crime. An officer may not "create" plain view, so it is essential that the officer has a lawful right to be in the place from which the plain view occurs (*Arizona v. Hicks* (1987)). Another plain view element is that it must be immediately apparent to the officer that the item is contraband or evidence of a crime. Prior to *Horton v. California* (1990) it was also thought that the officer's plain view must be inadvertent in that the officer must not have a prior suspicion that the evidence was to be found. In *Horton* the Court decided that the inadvertence rule gave no added protection to individuals and eliminated it. The plain "view" concept applies to any of the senses, such as touch (*Minnesota v. Dickerson* (1993)).

The Supreme Court has on many occasions expressed a preference for search warrants (Johnson v. United States, 333 U.S. 10 (1948); *United States v. Ventresca*, 380 U.S. 102 (1965). The warrant must be issued by a detached and neutral magistrate, not one who is an executive branch officer in charge of investigating a crime (*Coolidge v. New Hampshire*, 403 U.S. 443 (1971)), or a judge who becomes too involved in an investigation (*Lo-Ji Sales, Inc. v. New York*, 442 U.S. 319 (1979), or a magistrate who receives fees for each warrant issued (*Connally v. Georgia*, 429 U.S. 245 (1977)). Warrants are issued after *ex parte* hearings where an officer submits a search affidavit or sworn statement and swears that the basis of information is true. A warrant may be based on hearsay (*Spinelli v. United States* (1969); *Illinois v. Gates* (1983)). Typically the basis of a warrant is not subject to challenge, but the Court held in *Franks v. Delaware*, 438 U.S. 154 (1978) that a challenge is required where a defendant can make a strong showing that it is likely that the police either lied or made statements in reckless disregard for the truth to the magistrate.

A warrant must describe the place to be searched and the items to be seized with particularity. However, there is no civil liability if the warrant is mistaken and the wrong place is entered as long as the error was reasonable (*Maryland v. Garrison*, 480 U.S. 79 (1987)). In executing a search warrant, the general common law rule is that officers must announce their presence, but the "knock and announce" rule may constitutionally be dispensed with when officers have reason to believe that evidence will be destroyed (*Ker v. California*, 374 U.S. 23 (1963)).

Searches for auditory evidence via electronic eavesdropping presents one of the most difficult issues in criminal procedure. It was long feared by the government that telephone wiretapping and "bugging" with listening devices, an important tool against organized and white-collar crime, would not meet the particularity standard of the Fourth Amendment. In *Berger v. New York*, 388 U.S. 41 (1967) the Court cast a shadow over the constitutionality of electronic eavesdropping by striking down an overly broad New York wiretap law as a violation of the particularity requirement of the Fourth Amendment. The Supreme Court forced the issue in *Katz* by ruling that electronic eavesdropping is a Fourth Amendment seizure. On the other hand, *Katz* cited with approval the case of *Osborn v. United States*, 385 U.S. 323 (1966) where agents applied for a judicial warrant for the purpose of wearing an electronic listening device. Also, the search in *Katz* was both particular and supported by probable cause.

Building on the hints provided in these cases, Congress passed an elaborate electronic eavesdropping act that has passed constitutional muster. While in some cases the Court has found that law enforcement has not complied with the exacting requirements of Title III of the Omnibus Crime Control Act of 1968 (*United States v. Giordano*, 416 U.S. 505 (1974) (executive assistant to Attorney General could not authorize warrant)) for the most part the Court has interpreted the law so as to uphold warrants. Thus, *Scott v. United States* (1978) held that federal agents complied with a "minimization requirement" although a large percentage of calls were not of a criminal nature; in *United States v. Ojeda Rios* (1990) a case was not dismissed although post-eavesdropping "sealing" requirements were not followed with precision. Agents do not need an additional search warrant to enter a premises to place a listening device (*Dalia v. United States*, 441 U.S. 238 (1979)).

Federal law does not cover every kind of electronic eavesdropping; so called "body-mikes" do not require prior judicial authorization because the voice of the person who is overheard is not captured surreptitiously, but rather is spoken voluntarily to the listener (*United States v. White* (1971)). Although Title III did not specifically cover "national security" bugging and tapping of citizens within the territory of the United States, the executive branch was still not free to engage in such behavior without prior judicial authorization (*United States v. U.S. District Court* (1972)). A "pen register" which identifies incoming and outgoing telephone calls but does not intercept their content is not a search under the Fourth Amendment (*Smith v. Maryland* (1979)) and was not initially covered by statute. A warrant is now required for the law enforcement use of such devices.

That not every search and seizure issue is encompassed by the Fourth Amendment is made clear by the enormous growth of drug asset forfeiture by state and federal law enforcement. This is the use of civil property forfeiture to deprive those who deal in contraband drugs of the profits derived by their dealing and of any assets used in the illegal enterprise, including houses where drugs were kept and vehicles used to facilitate their transportation. Concerned over growing abuses, the Supreme Court ruled that the amount seized by the forfeiture must bear some relationship to the value of the illegal enterprise, under the Eighth Amendment prohibition on excessive fines (*Austin v. United States* (1993)).

Furthermore, due process requires that a party be given a hearing over the question of innocent ownership before her house is seized by the government (*United States v. Good* (1993)). This is an interesting example of constitutional principles other than the Fourth Amendment playing a role in regulating police seizure activities that involve intrusion on and takings of property.

KATZ v. UNITED STATES

389 U.S. 347, 88 S.Ct. 507, 19 L.Ed.2d 576 (1967)

MR. JUSTICE STEWART delivered the opinion of the Court.

[Katz was convicted of the federal crime of interstate transmission of wagering information by telephone. Evidence was obtained by means of an electronic listening device placed outside a telephone booth that Katz entered at the same time each day and activated by agents only when Katz was in the phone booth. No search warrant was obtained to place the device.] [a]

* * * In affirming his conviction, the Court of Appeals rejected the contention that the recordings had been obtained in violation of the Fourth Amendment, because "[t]here was no physical entrance into the area occupied by [the petitioner]." We granted certiorari in order to consider the constitutional questions thus presented.

The petitioner has phrased those questions as follows:

"A. Whether a public telephone booth is a constitutionally protected area so that evidence obtained by attaching an electronic listening recording device to the top of such a booth is obtained in violation of the right to privacy of the user of the booth.

"B. Whether physical penetration of a constitutionally protected area is necessary before a search and seizure can be said to be violative of the Fourth Amendment to the United States Constitution."

[b]

We decline to adopt this formulation of the issues. In the first place, the correct solution of Fourth Amendment problems is not necessarily promoted by incantation of the phrase "constitutionally protected area." Secondly, the Fourth Amendment cannot be translated into a general constitutional "right to privacy." That Amendment protects individual privacy against certain kinds of governmental intrusion, but its protections go further, and often have nothing to do with privacy at all. Other provisions of the Constitution protect personal privacy from other forms of governmental invasion. But the protection of a person's *general* right to privacy— his right to be let alone by other people— is, like the protection of his property and of his very life, left largely to the law of the individual States.

Because of the misleading way the issues have been formulated, the parties have attached great significance to the characterization of the telephone booth from which the petitioner placed his calls. The petitioner has strenuously argued that the booth was a "constitutionally protected area." The Government has maintained with equal vigor that it was not. But this effort to decide whether or not a given "area," viewed in the abstract, is "constitutionally protected" deflects attention from the problem presented by this case. For the Fourth Amendment protects people, not places. What a person knowingly exposes to the public, even in his own home or office, is not a subject of Fourth Amendment protection. * * * But what he seeks to preserve as private, even in an area accessible to the public, may be constitutionally protected. * * * **[c]**

The Government stresses the fact that the telephone booth from which the petitioner made his calls was constructed partly of glass, so that he was as visible after he entered it as he would have been if he had remained outside. But what he sought to exclude when he entered the booth was not the intruding eye—it was the uninvited ear. He did not shed his right to do so simply because he made his calls from a place where he might be seen. No less than an individual in a business office, in a friend's apartment, or in a taxicab, a person in a telephone booth may rely upon the protection of the Fourth Amendment. One who occupies it, shuts the door behind him, and pays the toll that permits him to place a call is surely entitled to assume that the words he utters into the mouthpiece will not be broadcast to the world. To read the Constitution more narrowly is to ignore the vital role that the public telephone has come to play in private communication. **[d]**

The Government contends * * * that the activity of its agents * * * should not be tested by Fourth Amendment requirements, for the surveillance technique they employed involved no physical penetration of the telephone booth. * * * It is true that the absence of such penetration was at one time thought to foreclose further Fourth Amendment inquiry, * * * for that Amendment was thought to limit only searches and seizures of tangible property. But "[t]he premise that

property interests control the right of the Government to search and seize has been discredited."* * * [O]nce it is recognized that the Fourth Amendment protects people—and not simply "areas"—against unreasonable searches and seizures it becomes clear that the reach of that Amendment cannot turn upon the presence or absence of a physical intrusion into any given enclosure.

We conclude that the underpinnings of *Olmstead* and *Goldman* have been so eroded by our subsequent decisions that the "trespass" doctrine there enunciated can no longer be regarded as controlling. **[e]** The Government's activities in electronically listening to and recording the petitioner's words violated the privacy upon which he justifiably relied while using the telephone booth and thus constituted a "search and seizure" within the meaning of the Fourth Amendment.

[The Court went on to hold that there was no exception to the Fourth Amendment warrant requirement in this case and that therefore the evidence of conversations "seized" in the phone booth was inadmissible.]

MR. JUSTICE HARLAN, concurring.

* * *

* * * The question * * * is what protection [the Fourth Amendment] affords to those people. Generally, as here, the answer to that question requires reference to a "place." My understanding of the rule that has emerged from prior decisions is that there is a twofold requirement, first that a person have exhibited an actual (subjective) expectation of privacy and,

second, that the expectation be one that society is prepared to recognize as "reasonable." * * * **[f]**

* * *

MR. JUSTICE BLACK, dissenting.

* * *

Tapping telephone wires, of course, was an unknown possibility at the time the Fourth Amendment was adopted. But eavesdropping (and wiretapping is nothing more than eavesdropping by telephone) was * * * "an ancient practice which at common law was condemned as a nuisance. . . . " * * * There can be no doubt that the Framers were aware of this practice, and if they had desired to outlaw or restrict the use of evidence obtained by eavesdropping, I believe that they would have used appropriate language to do so in the Fourth Amendment. * * * **[g]**

The Fourth Amendment protects privacy only to the extent that it prohibits unreasonable searches and seizures of "persons, houses, papers, and effects." No general right is created by the Amendment so as to give this Court the unlimited power to hold unconstitutional everything which affects privacy. Certainly the Framers, well acquainted as they were with the excesses of governmental power, did not intend to grant this Court such omnipotent lawmaking authority as that. The history of governments proves that it is dangerous to freedom to repose such powers in courts.

* * *

* * * * * * * * * * *

COMMENTS

[a] The police knew where and when Katz would transmit betting information. The delay in getting a search warrant would not have unreasonably extended the investigation.

[b] The way an issue is phrased is critical in appellate strategy. The choice of an issue can determine the outcome of a case. Here, the attorneys framed their issues to fit existing legal categories. But JUSTICE STEWART looked at this issue in a revolutionary way.

[c] These sentences are often repeated as the core concept of *Katz*. Do these pithy phrases solve all search and seizure issues before the Courts? To be successful, a legal doctrine must assist lawyers and judges in resolving future cases logically and efficiently.

[d] The Court "updates" the Constitution to fit new inventions not conceived of in 1791. Is this updating true to the goals and intent of the 1791 Amendment?

[e] In *Olmstead v. United States*, 277 U.S. 438 (1928) a federal agents' wiretap violated a state law, but did not violate the Fourth Amendment because there was no *trespass*. *Goldman v. United States*, 316 U.S. 129 (1942), held that placing an electronic listening device *against* a wall, was not a trespass while in *Silverman v. United States*, 365 U.S. 505 (1961), *tacking* a mike into a wall was. Such incoherence led the Court to overrule *Olmstead*. Overruling a prior case is rare but typically preceded by ample "warning," *i.e.*, a train of cases that show problems with the application of a doctrine. As a result, cases begin to narrow the scope of a doctrine and thus to "erode" it.

[f] How does JUSTICE HARLAN's point modify JUSTICE STEWART's statements that the decision must turn on what *a person* seeks to keep private? Although a concurrence, JUSTICE HARLAN penned the operative rule of *Katz*.

[g] Is JUSTICE BLACK more true to the Constitution by applying it as it would have been in 1791? If James Madison were sitting on the Court instead of Hugo Black, would he vote with the majority? Does the majority undermine constitutional adjudication by appealing to the underlying values in the Fourth Amendment? Or does the majority enhance the Constitution by its expanded view of the Fourth Amendment? Why is JUSTICE BLACK concerned with granting "omnipotent lawmaking authority" to the Supreme Court?

SOLDAL v. COOK COUNTY

___ U.S. ___, 113 S.Ct. 538, 121 L.Ed.2d 450 (1992)

JUSTICE WHITE delivered the opinion of the Court.

I

[A property company acted to evict Soldal and his family from their rented trailer home, prior to obtaining a court order, a violation of Illinois law. The mobile home park owner notified the Sheriff's Department of the eviction and requested the presence of deputies "to forestall any possible resistance." Sheriff's deputies stood by while trailer park employees disconnected Soldal's trailer from water and sewer connections. A deputy told Soldal that he was present to insure that Soldal did not interfere with the eviction. The officers told Soldal they would not take his criminal trespass complaint because "it was between the landlord and the tenant." The trailer was towed to nearby property. In a later hearing an Illinois judge ruled the eviction unauthorized and ordered the trailer to be returned. It was, however, badly damaged.]

[A federal civil action filed by Soldal under 42 U.S.C. § 1983, **[a]** alleging a violation of Fourth and Fourteenth Amendment rights was dismissed because the court found no conspiracy to deprive Soldal of his rights or the existence of state action necessary under § 1983. The Court of Appeals * * * found state action, **[b]** but held that the removal of the trailer was not a seizure under the Fourth Amendment or a due process deprivation.] On rehearing, the Court of Appeals,] sitting *en banc*, reaffirmed the panel decision. Acknowledging that what had occurred was a "seizure" in the literal sense of the word, the court reasoned that, because it was not made in the course of public law enforcement and because it did not invade the Soldals' privacy, it was not a seizure as contemplated by the Fourth Amendment. * * * Interpreting prior cases of this Court, the Seventh Circuit concluded that, absent interference with privacy or liberty, a "pure deprivation of property" is not cognizable under the Fourth Amendment. * * * Rather, petitioners' property interests were protected only by the due process clauses of the Fifth and Fourteenth Amendments.

We granted certiorari to consider whether the seizure and removal of the Soldals' trailer home implicated their Fourth Amendment rights, * * * and now reverse.

II

* * *

A "seizure" of property, * * * occurs when "there is some meaningful interference with an individual's possessory interests in that property." * * * In addition, we have emphasized that "at the very core" of the Fourth Amendment "stands the right of a man to retreat into his own home." * * *

As a result of the state action in this case, the Soldals' domicile was not only seized, it literally was carried away, giving new meaning to the term "mobile home." We fail to see how being unceremoniously dispossessed of one's home in the manner alleged to have occurred here can be viewed as anything but a seizure invoking the protection of the Fourth Amendment. Whether the Amendment was in fact violated is, of course, a different question that requires determining if the seizure was reasonable. That inquiry entails the weighing of various factors and is not before us. **[d]**

The Court of Appeals * * * concluded that it was a seizure only in a "technical" sense, not within the meaning of the Fourth Amendment. This conclusion followed from a narrow reading of the Amendment, which the court construed to safeguard only privacy and liberty interests while leaving unprotected possessory interests where neither privacy nor liberty was at stake. Otherwise, the court said,

"a constitutional provision enacted two centuries ago [would] make every repossession and eviction with police assistance actionable under—of all things—the Fourth Amendment [, which] would both trivialize the amendment and gratuitously shift a large body of routine commercial litigation from the state courts to the federal courts. That trivializing, this shift, can be prevented by recognizing the difference between possessory and privacy interests." * * * **[e]**

Because the officers had not entered Soldal's house, rummaged through his possessions, or, in the Court of Appeals' view, interfered with his liberty in the course of the eviction, the Fourth Amendment offered no protection against the "grave deprivation" of property that had occurred. *

* *

We do not agree with this interpretation of the Fourth Amendment. The Amendment protects the people from unreasonable searches and seizures of "their persons, houses, papers, and effects." This language surely cuts against the novel holding below, **[f]** and our cases unmistakably hold that the Amendment protects property as well as privacy. * * * [T]he first clause of the Fourth Amendment

"protects two types of expectations, one involving 'searches,' the other 'seizures.' A 'search' occurs when an expectation of privacy that society is prepared to consider reasonable is infringed. A 'seizure' of property occurs where there is some meaningful interference with an individual's possessory interests in that property." * * *

* * * In [*United States v.*] *Place*, [this volume] although we found that subjecting luggage to a "dog sniff" did not constitute a search for Fourth Amendment purposes because it did not compromise any privacy interest, taking custody of Place's suitcase was deemed an unlawful seizure for it unreasonably infringed "the suspect's possessory interest in his luggage." * * * Although lacking a privacy component, the property rights in both instances nonetheless were not disregarded, but rather were afforded Fourth Amendment protection.

Respondents rely principally on precedents such as *Katz v. United States*, * * * to demonstrate that the Fourth Amendment is only marginally concerned with property rights. But the message of those cases is that property rights are not the sole measure of Fourth Amendment violations. * * * There was no suggestion that this shift in emphasis [from property rights to privacy interests] had snuffed out the previously recognized protection for property under the Fourth Amendment. *Katz*, in declaring violative of the Fourth Amendment the unwarranted overhearing of a telephone booth conversation, effectively ended any lingering notions that the protection of privacy depended on trespass into a protected area. In the course of its decision, the *Katz* Court stated that the Fourth Amendment can neither be translated into a provision dealing with constitutionally protected areas nor into a general constitutional right to privacy. The Amendment, the Court said, protects individual privacy against certain kinds of governmental intrusion, "but its protections go further, and often have nothing to do with privacy at all." * * *

* * *

We thus are unconvinced that any of the Court's prior cases supports the view that the Fourth Amendment protects against unreasonable seizures of property only where privacy or liberty is also implicated. What is more, our "plain view" decisions make untenable such a construction of the Amendment. Suppose for example that police officers lawfully enter a house, by either complying with the warrant requirement or satisfying one of its recognized exceptions—*e.g.*, through a valid consent or a showing of exigent circumstances. If they come across some item in plain view and seize it, no invasion of personal privacy has occurred. * * * If the boundaries of the Fourth Amendment were defined exclusively by rights of privacy,

"plain view" seizures would not implicate that constitutional provision at all. Yet, far from being automatically upheld, "plain view" seizures have been scrupulously subjected to Fourth Amendment inquiry. **[g]** Thus, in the absence of consent or a warrant permitting the seizure of the items in question, such seizures can be justified only if they meet the probable cause standard, * * * and if they are unaccompanied by unlawful trespass. That is because, the absence of a privacy interest notwithstanding, "[a] seizure of the article . . . would obviously invade the owner's possessory interest." * * * The plain view doctrine "merely reflects an application of the Fourth Amendment's central requirement of reasonableness to the law governing seizures of property." * * *

The Court of Appeals understandably found it necessary to reconcile its holding with our recognition in the plain view cases that the Fourth Amendment protects property as such. In so doing, the court did not distinguish this case on the ground that the seizure of the Soldals' home took place in a noncriminal context. Indeed, it acknowledged what is evident from our precedents—that the Amendment's protection applies in the civil context as well. * * * **[h]**

* * *

* * * [T]he plain view cases clearly state that, notwithstanding the absence of any interference with privacy, seizures of effects that are not authorized by a warrant are reasonable only because there is probable cause to associate the property with criminal activity. The seizure of the weapons in *Horton* [this volume], for example, occurred in the midst of a search, yet

we emphasized that it did not "involve any invasion of privacy." * * * In short, our statement that such seizures must satisfy the Fourth Amendment and will be deemed reasonable only if the item's incriminating character is "immediately apparent," * * * is at odds with the Court of Appeals' approach.

The Court of Appeals' effort is both interesting and creative, but at bottom it simply reasserts the earlier thesis that the Fourth Amendment protects privacy but not property. We remain unconvinced and see no justification for departing from our prior cases. In our view, the reason why an officer might enter a house or effectuate a seizure is wholly irrelevant to the threshold question of whether the Amendment applies. What matters is the intrusion on the people's security from governmental interference. Therefore, the right against unreasonable seizures would be no less transgressed if the seizure of the house was undertaken to collect evidence, verify compliance with a housing regulation, effect an eviction by the police, or on a whim, for no reason at all. As we have observed on more than one occasion, it would be "anomalous to say that the individual and his private property are fully protected by the Fourth Amendment only when the individual is suspected of criminal behavior." * * * [i]

* * *

* * * * * * * * * * *

COMMENTS

[a] The Soldals brought a federal civil suit against the Sheriff under the Federal Civil Rights Act, which reads in part "Every person who, under color of any statute, ordinance, regulation, custom or usage, of any State * * * subjects, or causes to be subjected, any citizen of the United States * * * to the deprivation of any rights, privileges, or immunities secured by the Constitution and laws, shall be liable to the party injured in an action at law, suit in equity, or other proper proceeding for redress."

[b] The appellate court decided the case *as if* the Sheriffs' deputies participated in physically removing the trailer. Thus, there was "state action."

[c] The full Court of Appeals seems to rule that the deprivation of property, even if "seized," by "state action" against lawful procedure is a civil law matter, unless the kinds of constitutional rights and interests identified in *Katz* are injured.

[d] Note that the Supreme Court is deciding one important issue of general interest; it will not decide the entire case which is of most concern to the petitioner, Soldal. This "division of labor" between trial and appellate courts allows appellate courts to concentrate on issues of law and to focus on novel questions.

[e] The federal circuit court feared that ruling for Soldal would turn every eviction

case into a federal constitutional issue, adding complexity and cost to these cases. Appellate courts have an obligation to consider the practical impact of their rulings, but only to the point where no clear rule of principle is violated by taking a "practical" approach.

[f] "Below" refers to "inferior" courts, *i.e.*, courts "lower" on the judicial hierarchy.

[g] See, for example, *Arizona v. Hicks* and *Horton v. California* in Section D, below.

[h] Some Bill of Rights provisions, like Sixth Amendment rules guiding "criminal prosecutions," apply specifically to criminal cases. Where the Constitution's text does not limit its application, as with the Fourth Amendment, it should be read "liberally" to limit government power to interfere with personal rights. A case like *Camara v. Municipal Court* [this volume] shows the Fourth Amendment restricting the government in civil as well as criminal matters.

[i] This is a reminder that the Bill of Rights criminal justice provisions protect not only "criminals" but "the rest of us."

OLIVER v. UNITED STATES

466 U.S. 170, 104 S.Ct. 1735, 80 L.Ed.2d 214 (1984)

JUSTICE POWELL delivered the opinion of the Court.

The "open fields" doctrine, first enunciated by this Court in *Hester v. United States*, 265 U.S. 57 (1924), permits police officers to enter and search a field without a warrant. We granted certiorari in these cases to clarify confusion that has arisen as to the continued vitality of the doctrine.

I

[The facts in consolidated cases from Kentucky and Maine were similar: police officers without warrants or consent went into the wooded lands owned by defendants and discovered marijuana patches. The privately owned fields were posted with "No Trespassing" signs. The Kentucky site was highly secluded, over a mile from defendant's house, and a gate leading to the fields was locked. To reach the Maine site, officers had to walk a path between the defendant's house and a neighbor's house. The federal Court in the Kentucky case upheld the search while the Maine Supreme Court ruled the evidence obtained from open fields inadmissible.]

II

The rule announced in *Hester v. United States* was founded upon the explicit language of the Fourth Amendment. * * * As JUSTICE HOLMES explained for the Court in his characteristically laconic style: "[T]he special protection accorded by the Fourth Amendment to the people in their 'persons, houses, papers, and effects,' is not extended to the open fields. The distinction between the latter and the house is as old as the common law." * * *

Nor are the open fields "effects" within the meaning of the Fourth Amendment. In this respect, it is suggestive that James Madison's proposed draft of what became the Fourth Amendment preserves "[t]he rights of the people to be secured in their persons, their houses, their papers, and their other property, from all unreasonable searches and seizures. . . ." * * * Although Congress' revisions of Madison's proposal broadened the scope of the Amendment in some respects, * * * the term "effects" is less inclusive than "property" and cannot be said to encompass open fields. [a] We conclude, * * * that the government's intrusion upon the open fields is not one of those "unreasonable searches" proscribed by the text of the Fourth Amendment.

III [b]

This interpretation of the Fourth Amendment's language is consistent with the understanding of the right to privacy expressed in our Fourth Amendment jurisprudence. Since *Katz v. United States* [this volume] the touchstone of Amendment analysis has been the question whether a person has a "constitutionally protected reasonable expectation of privacy." * * * The Amendment does not protect the merely subjective expectation of privacy, but only those "expectation[s] that society is prepared to recognize as 'reasonable.'" * * *

A

No single factor determines whether an individual legitimately may claim under the Fourth Amendment that a place should be free of government intrusion not authorized by warrant. * * * In assessing the degree to which a search infringes upon individual privacy, the Court has given weight to such factors as the intention of the Framers of the Fourth Amendment, * * * the uses to which the individual has put a location, * * * and our societal understanding that certain areas deserve the most scrupulous protection from government invasion. * * * These factors are equally relevant to determining whether the government's intrusion upon open fields without a warrant or probable cause violates reasonable expectations of privacy and is therefore a search proscribed by the Amendment.

In this light, the rule of *Hester v. United States*, that we reaffirm today, may be understood as providing that an individual may not legitimately demand privacy for activities conducted out of doors in fields, except in the area immediately surrounding the home. * * * This rule is true to the conception of the right to privacy embodied in the Fourth Amendment. The Amendment reflects the recognition of the Founders that certain enclaves should be free from arbitrary government interference. For example, the Court since the enactment of the Fourth Amendment has stressed "the overriding respect for the sanctity of the home that has been embedded in our traditions since the origins of the Republic." * * *

In contrast, open fields do not provide the setting for those intimate activities that the Amendment is intended to shelter from government interference or surveillance. There is no societal interest in protecting the privacy of those activities, such as the cultivation of crops, that occur in open fields. Moreover, as a practical matter these lands usually are accessible to the public and the police in ways that a home, an office, or commercial structure would not be. It is not generally true that fences or "No Trespassing" signs effectively bar the public from viewing open fields in rural areas. [c] And [petitioner] * * * concede[s] that the public and police lawfully may survey lands from the air. For these reasons, the asserted expectation of privacy in open fields is not an expectation that "society recognizes as reasonable."

The historical underpinnings of the open fields doctrine also demonstrate that the doctrine is consistent with respect for "reasonable expectations of privacy." As JUSTICE HOLMES, writing for the Court, observed in *Hester*, * * * the common law distinguished "open fields" from the "curtilage," the land immediately surrounding and associated with the home. * * * The distinction implies that only the curtilage, not the neighboring open fields, warrants the Fourth Amendment protections that attach to the home. [d] At common law, the curtilage is the area to which extends the intimate activity associated with the "sanctity of a man's home and the privacies of life," * * * and therefore has been considered part of the home itself for Fourth Amendment purposes. Thus, courts have extended Fourth Amendment protection to the curtilage; and they have defined the curtilage, as did the common law, by reference to the factors that determine whether an individual reasonably may expect that an area immediately adjacent to the home will remain private. * * * Conversely, the common law implies, as we reaffirm today, that no expectation of privacy legitimately attaches to open fields.

We conclude, from the text of the Fourth Amendment and from the historical and contemporary understanding of its purposes, that an individual has no legitimate expectation that open fields will remain free from warrantless intrusion by government officers.

B

* * * [Petitioner argued that a case-by-case analysis should be employed to determine whether an expectation of privacy is reasonable.] The language of the Fourth Amendment itself answers [this] contention.

Nor would a case-by-case approach provide a workable accommodation between the needs of law enforcement and the interests protected by the Fourth Amendment. [e] Under this approach, police officers would have to guess before every search whether landowners had erected fences sufficiently high, posted a sufficient number of warning signs, or located contraband in an area sufficiently secluded to establish a right of privacy. The lawfulness of a search would turn on "'[a] highly sophisticated set of rules, qualified by all sorts of ifs, ands, and

buts and requiring the drawing of subtle nuances and hairline distinctions . . . .'" * * * This Court repeatedly has acknowledged the difficulties created for courts, police, and citizens by an ad hoc, case-by-case definition of Fourth Amendment standards to be applied in differing factual circumstances. * * * The ad hoc approach not only makes it difficult for the policeman to discern the scope of his authority, * * * it also creates a danger that constitutional rights will be arbitrarily and inequitably enforced. * * *

IV

* * * [W]e reject the suggestion that steps taken to protect privacy establish that expectations of privacy in an open field are legitimate. It is true, of course, that petitioner * * * in order to conceal [his] criminal activities, planted the marihuana upon secluded land and erected fences and "No Trespassing" signs around the property. And it may be that because of such precautions, few members of the public stumbled upon the marihuana crops seized by the police. Neither of these suppositions demonstrates, however, that the expectation of privacy was *legitimate* in the sense required by the Fourth Amendment. The test of legitimacy is not whether the individual chooses to conceal assertedly "private" activity. Rather, the correct inquiry is whether the government's intrusion infringes upon the personal and societal values protected by the Fourth Amendment. As we have explained, we find no basis for concluding that a police inspection of open fields accomplished such an infringement.

Nor is the government's intrusion upon an open field a "search" in the constitutional sense because that intrusion is a trespass at common law. The existence of a property right is but one element in determining whether expectations of privacy are legitimate. "The premise that property interests control the right of the Government to search and seize has been discredited.'" *Katz.* * * * "[E]ven a property interest in premises may not be sufficient to establish a legitimate expectation of privacy with respect to particular items located on the premises or activity conducted thereon." * * * **[f]**

The common law may guide consideration of what areas are protected by the Fourth Amendment by defining areas whose invasion by others is wrongful. The law of trespass, however, forbids intrusions upon land that the Fourth Amendment would not proscribe. For trespass law extends to instances where the exercise of the right to exclude vindicates no legitimate privacy interest. Thus, in the case of open fields, the general rights of property protected by the common law of trespass have little or no relevance to the applicability of the Fourth Amendment.

* * *

[JUSTICE WHITE concurred.]

JUSTICE MARSHALL, with whom JUSTICE BRENNAN and JUSTICE STEVENS join, dissenting.

* * *

I

* * *

* * * [T]he Court's reading of the plain language of the Fourth Amendment is incapable of explaining even its own holding in this case. The Court rules that the curtilage, a zone of real property surrounding a dwelling, is entitled to constitutional protection. * * * We are not told, however, whether the curtilage is a "house" or an "effect"—or why, if the curtilage can be incorporated into the list of things and spaces shielded by the Amendment, a field cannot. **[g]**

The Court's inability to reconcile its parsimonious reading of the phrase "persons, houses, papers, and effects" with our prior decisions or even its own holding is a symptom of a more fundamental infirmity in the Court's reasoning. The Fourth Amendment, like the other central provisions of the Bill of Rights that loom large in our modern jurisprudence, was designed, not to prescribe with "precision" permissible and impermissible activities, but to identify a fundamental human liberty that should be shielded forever from government intrusion. We do not construe constitutional provisions of this sort the way we do statutes, whose drafters can be expected to indicate with some comprehensiveness and exactitude the conduct they wish to forbid or control and to change those prescriptions when they become obsolete. Rather, we strive, when interpreting these seminal constitutional provisions, to effectuate their purposes—to lend them meanings that ensure that the liberties the Framers sought to protect are not undermined by the changing activities of government officials. **[h]**

* * *

II

The second ground for the Court's decision is its contention that any interest a landowner might have in the privacy of his woods and fields is not one that "society is prepared to recognize as 'reasonable.'" * * *

As the Court acknowledges, we have traditionally looked to a variety of factors in determining whether an expectation of privacy asserted in a physical space is "reasonable." * * * Though those factors do not lend themselves to precise taxonomy, they may be roughly grouped into three categories. First, we consider whether the expectation at issue is rooted in entitlements defined by positive law. Second, we consider the nature of the uses to which spaces of the sort in question can be put. Third, we consider whether the person claiming a privacy interest manifested that interest to the public in a way that most people would understand and respect. When the expectations of privacy asserted by petitioner * * * are examined through these lenses, it becomes clear that those expectations are entitled to constitutional protection.

A

[Posting laws indicate a societal expectation of privacy.]

B

The uses to which a place is put are highly relevant to the assessment of a privacy interest asserted therein. * * * If, in light of our shared sensibilities, those activities are of a kind in which people should be able to engage without fear of intrusion by private persons or government officials, we extend the protection of the Fourth Amendment to the space in question, even in the absence of any entitlement derived from positive law. * * *

Privately owned woods and fields that are not exposed to public view regularly are employed in a variety of ways that society acknowledges deserve privacy. Many landowners like to take solitary walks on their property, confident that they will not be confronted in their rambles by strangers or policemen. Others conduct agricultural businesses on their property. Some landowners use their secluded spaces to meet lovers, others to gather together with fellow worshippers, still others to engage in sustained creative endeavor. Private land is sometimes used as a refuge for wildlife, where flora and fauna are protected from human intervention of any kind. Our respect for the freedom of landowners to use their posted "open fields" in ways such as these partially explains the seriousness with which the positive law regards deliberate invasions of such spaces, * * * and substantially reinforces the landowners' contention that their expectations of privacy are "reasonable." [i]
* * *

[In Part II C, JUSTICE MARSHALL argued that posting is a sufficient normal precaution to maintain the privacy of "open fields" to create a constitutionally protected expectation of privacy.]

III

* * *

The Fourth Amendment, properly construed, embodies and gives effect to our collective sense of the degree to which men and women, in civilized society, are entitled "to be let alone" by their governments. * * * The Court's opinion bespeaks and will help to promote an impoverished vision of that fundamental right. **[j]**

* * * * * * * * * *

COMMENTS

[a] The intent of the framers of the Constitution is an important, if not the controlling, element of Constitutional interpretation. The conclusion that "effects" refers to personal property and not real estate is based on an assessment that that is what the word meant in 1791 (discussed by JUSTICE POWELL in a footnote) and bolstered by an examination of the activity of the drafters, where the point is strengthened by noting that certain more inclusive language was considered and rejected.

[b] In a constitutional case, the justices will not be content to rest their opinion only on the definition of a term. Because of the gravity of the interests involved, the Court properly feels compelled to explicate the reasons for its holding. This is especially important here because Oliver's position was based on the notion that the *Hester* doctrine was implicitly overruled by the *Katz* expectation of privacy doctrine.

[c] Note that the "open fields" rule takes its dimensions from what people actually and usually do, not from what is strictly legal behavior (*i.e.*, not trespassing), and not on what behavior would ideally enhance the greatest privacy rights of landowners.

[d] The curtilage concept expands the Fourth Amendment definition of a house to a certain "reasonable" amount of land around a house. This gives the constitutional protections of the Fourth Amendment some "breathing room" and prevents the open fields exception from allowing police to tightly surround a house or creep up to windows to peer in (eavesdrop). Are these rules based on common sense?

[e] JUSTICE POWELL noted in a footnote that a place subjected to the exception need not be "open" or a "field," such as a thickly wooded lot. Although the dividing line between a curtilage and an "open field" is somewhat imprecise and must be determined from the particular layout of the property, the defendants here requested an even more open-ended rule: one that eliminates the concepts of open fields and curtilage and rests on a case-by-case analysis of a property owner's expectation of privacy. If the Court accepted this approach, do you think it would end up with results similar to the open fields-curtilage distinction?

[f] This flows naturally from the modern Fourth Amendment interpretation established in *Katz* that technical property rights do not establish the precise contours of Fourth Amendment rights, although in some cases, they offer some evidence of what expectations of privacy are considered objectively reasonable by society and by the courts.

[g] The curtilage "exception" does, indeed, seem to be based more on historical usage than on a strict reading of the constitution. But note that JUSTICE MARSHALL raises this point not to reduce the scope of the curtilage protection, but to increase the protection offered to "open fields."

[h] This reasoning, standing alone, seems compelling. However, so does the reasoning of the majority. Both positions are reasonable and both draw on acceptable canons of interpretation and on sound premises of American constitutional history. Yet, the resolution of the case requires a choice about an important point of constitutional theory; it is in the process of making such a choice that the backgrounds and philosophies of the justices come into play.

[i] Do you accept JUSTICE MARSHALL's contentions that these activities are common or frequent. Even if they are uncommon and infrequent, do they deserve to be accorded a reasonable expectation of privacy by society and the courts (assuming that a subjective expectation of privacy is maintained by posting and the like)?

[j] This is true, but so is the point that the scope of what is a reasonable police search on private land is determined by the collective sense of what is reasonable. Thus, your opinion on this matter is (collectively) an input into the Court's decision.

HUDSON v. PALMER

468 U.S. 517, 104 S.Ct. 3194, 82 L.Ed.2d 393 (1984)

CHIEF JUSTICE BURGER delivered the opinion of the Court.

We granted certiorari * * * to decide whether a prison inmate has a reasonable expectation of privacy in his prison cell entitling him to the protection of the Fourth Amendment against unreasonable searches and seizures. * * *

I

[A prison guard conducted a shakedown search of Palmer's prison cell and seized a ripped pillow case, used to charge Palmer with a violation of destroying state property. In the course of the search Palmer alleged that personal items were taken and destroyed, and the Court decided the case as if these allegations were true. In a 42 U.S.C. §1983 action, Palmer claimed that the search was done only to harass him and that the charge of destroying property was false. The District Court held that destroying an inmate's property is not a due process violation as long as adequate tort remedies existed, citing *Parratt v. Taylor*, 451 U.S. 527 (1981). The Court of Appeals affirmed this but also] held that an individual prisoner has a "limited privacy right" in his cell entitling him to protection against searches conducted solely to harass or to humiliate. * * * The shakedown of a single prisoner's property, said the court, is permissible only if "done pursuant to an established program of conducting random searches of single cells or groups of cells reasonably designed to deter or discover the possession of contraband" or upon reasonable belief that the particular prisoner possessed contraband. * * *

* * *

II

A

* * *

We have repeatedly held that prisons are not beyond the reach of the Constitution. No "iron curtain" separates one from the other. *Wolff v. McDonnell*, 418 U.S. 539, 555 (1974). Indeed, we have insisted that prisoners be accorded those rights not fundamentally inconsistent with imprisonment itself or incompatible with the objectives of incarceration. [a] For example, we have held that invidious racial discrimination is as intolerable within a prison as outside, except as may be essential to "prison security and discipline." * * * Like others, prisoners have the constitutional right to petition the Government for redress of their grievances, which includes a reasonable right of access to the courts. * * *

Prisoners must be provided "reasonable opportunities" to exercise their religious freedom guaranteed under the First Amendment. * * * Similarly, they retain those First Amendment rights of speech "not inconsistent with [their] status as ... [prisoners] or with the legitimate penological objectives of the corrections system." * * * They enjoy the protection of due process. * * * And the Eighth Amendment ensures that they will not be subject to "cruel and unusual punishments." * * * The continuing guarantee of these substantial rights to prison inmates is testimony to a belief that the way a society treats those who have transgressed against it is evidence of the essential character of that society. **[b]**

However, while persons imprisoned for crime enjoy many protections of the Constitution, it is also clear that imprisonment carries with it the circumscription or loss of many significant rights. * * * These constraints on inmates, and in some cases the complete withdrawal of certain rights, are "justified by the considerations underlying our penal system." * * * The curtailment of certain rights is necessary, as a practical matter, to accommodate a myriad of "institutional needs and objectives" of prison facilities, * * * chief among which is internal security. * * *

* * * We must determine here, as in other Fourth Amendment contexts, if a "justifiable" expectation of privacy is at stake. *Katz v. United States* [this volume]. The applicability of the Fourth Amendment turns on whether "the person invoking its protection can claim a 'justifiable,' a 'reasonable,' or a 'legitimate expectation of privacy' that has been invaded by government action." * * * We must decide, in JUSTICE HARLAN's words, whether a prisoner's expectation of privacy in his prison cell is the kind of expectation that "society is prepared to recognize as 'reasonable.'" * * *

Notwithstanding our caution in approaching claims that the Fourth Amendment is inapplicable in a given context, we hold that society is not prepared to recognize as legitimate any subjective expectation of privacy that a prisoner might have in his prison cell and that, accordingly, the Fourth Amendment proscription against unreasonable searches does not apply within the confines of the prison cell. The recognition of privacy rights for prisoners in their individual cells simply cannot be reconciled with the concept of incarceration and the needs and objectives of penal institutions. **[c]**

Prisons, by definition, are places of involuntary confinement of persons who have a demonstrated proclivity for anti-social criminal, and often violent, conduct. Inmates have necessarily shown a lapse in ability to control and conform their behavior to the legitimate standards of society by the normal impulses of self-restraint; they have shown an inability to regulate their conduct in a way that reflects either a respect for law or an appreciation of the rights of others. Even a partial survey of the statistics on violent crime in our Nation's prisons illustrates the magnitude of the problem. During 1981 and the first half of 1982, there were over 120 prisoners murdered by fellow inmates in state and federal prisons. A number of prison personnel were murdered by prisoners during this period. Over 29 riots or similar disturbances were reported in these facilities for the same time frame. * * *

Within this volatile "community," prison administrators are to take all necessary steps to ensure the safety of not only the prison staffs and administrative personnel, but also visitors. They are under an obligation to take reasonable measures to guarantee the safety of the inmates themselves. They must be ever alert to attempts to introduce drugs and other contraband into the premises which, we can judicially notice, is one of the most perplexing problems of prisons today;

they must prevent, so far as possible, the flow of illicit weapons into the prison; they must be vigilant to detect escape plots, in which drugs or weapons may be involved, before the schemes materialize. In addition to these monumental tasks, it is incumbent upon these officials at the same time to maintain as sanitary an environment for the inmates as feasible, given the difficulties of the circumstances.

The administration of a prison, we have said, is "at best an extraordinarily difficult undertaking." * * * But it would be literally impossible to accomplish the prison objectives identified above if inmates retained a right of privacy in their cells. Virtually the only place inmates can conceal weapons, drugs, and other contraband is in their cells. Unfettered access to these cells by prison officials, thus, is imperative if drugs and contraband are to be ferreted out and sanitary surroundings are to be maintained.

Determining whether an expectation of privacy is "legitimate" or "reasonable" necessarily entails a balancing of interests. The two interests here are the interest of society in the security of its penal institutions and the interest of the prisoner in privacy within his cell. The latter interest, of course, is already limited by the exigencies of the circumstances: A prison "shares none of the attributes of privacy of a home, an automobile, an office, or a hotel room." * * * We strike the balance in favor of institutional security, which we have noted is "central to all other corrections goals," * * * A right of privacy in traditional Fourth Amendment terms is fundamentally incompatible with the close

and continual surveillance of inmates and their cells required to ensure institutional security and internal order. We are satisfied that society would insist that the prisoner's expectation of privacy always yield to what must be considered the paramount interest in institutional security. We believe that it is accepted by our society that "[l]oss of freedom of choice and privacy are inherent incidents of confinement." * * * [d]

    * * *

* * * We share the concerns so well expressed by the Supreme Court [of Virginia] and its view that wholly random searches are essential to the effective security of penal institutions. We, therefore, cannot accept even the concededly limited holding of the Court of Appeals.

    * * *

Our holding that respondent does not have a reasonable expectation of privacy enabling him to invoke the protections of the Fourth Amendment does not mean that he is without a remedy for calculated harassment unrelated to prison needs. Nor does it mean that prison attendants can ride roughshod over inmates' property rights with impunity. The Eighth Amendment always stands as a protection against "cruel and unusual punishments." By the same token, there are adequate state tort and common-law remedies available to respondent to redress the alleged destruction of his personal property. * * * [e]

    * * *

[In Part IIB the Court held that the destruction of Palmer's property did not rise to a constitutional due process wrong in this case, given the availability of a postdeprivation remedy.]

III

We hold that the Fourth Amendment has no applicability to a prison cell. * * *

[JUSTICE O'CONNOR concurred.]

JUSTICE STEVENS, with whom JUSTICE BRENNAN, JUSTICE MARSHALL, and JUSTICE BLACKMUN join, concurring in part and dissenting in part.

* * *

I

Even if it is assumed that Palmer had no reasonable expectation of privacy in most of the property at issue in this case because it could be inspected at any time, that does not mean he was without Fourth Amendment protection. For the Fourth Amendment protects Palmer's possessory interests in this property entirely apart from whatever privacy interest he may have in it.

"[The Fourth Amendment] protects two kinds of expectations, one involving 'searches,' the other 'seizures.' A 'search' occurs when an expectation of privacy that society is prepared to consider reasonable is infringed. A 'seizure' of property occurs when there is some meaningful interference with an individual's possessory interests in that property." * * * [f]

There can be no doubt that the complaint adequately alleges a "seizure" within the meaning of the Fourth Amendment. Palmer was completely deprived of his possessory interests in his property; by taking and destroying it, Hudson was asserting "dominion and control" over it; hence his conduct "did constitute a seizure." * * *

The Court suggests that "the interest of society in the security of its penal institutions" precludes prisoners from having any legitimate possessory interests. * * * That contention is fundamentally wrong for at least two reasons.

First, Palmer's possession of the material was entirely legitimate as a matter of state law. There is no contention that the material seized was contraband or that Palmer's possession of it was in any way inconsistent with applicable prison regulations. Hence, he had a legal right to possess it. * * *

Second, the most significant of Palmer's possessory interests are protected as a matter of substantive constitutional law, entirely apart from the legitimacy of those interests under state law or the Due Process Clause. The Eighth Amendment forbids "cruel and unusual punishments." Its proscriptions are measured by society's "evolving standards of decency." * * * The Court's implication that prisoners have no possessory interests that by virtue of the Fourth Amendment are free from state interference cannot, in my view, be squared with the Eighth Amendment. To hold that a prisoner's possession of a letter from his wife, or a picture of his baby, has no protection against arbitrary or malicious perusal, seizure, or destruction would not, in my judgment, comport with any civilized standard of decency.

* * *

II

Once it is concluded that Palmer has adequately alleged a "seizure," the question becomes whether the seizure was "unreasonable." Questions of Fourth Amendment reasonableness can be resolved only by balancing the intrusion on constitutionally protected interests against the law enforcement interests justifying the challenged conduct.

* * * There can be no penological justification for the seizure alleged here. There is no contention that Palmer's property posed any threat to institutional security. Hudson had already examined the material before he took and destroyed it. The allegation is that Hudson did this for no reason save spite; there is no contention that under prison regulations the material was contraband, and in any event as I have indicated above the Constitution prohibits a State from treating letters and legal materials as contraband.

The Court agrees that intentional harassment of prisoners by guards is intolerable. * * * That being the case, there is no room for any conclusion but that the alleged seizure was unreasonable. The need for "close and continual surveillance of inmates and their cells," * * * in no way justifies taking and destroying noncontraband property; if material is examined and found not to be contraband, there can be no justification for its seizure.

When, as here, the material at issue is not contraband it simply makes no sense to say that its seizure and destruction serve "legitimate institutional interests." * * * Such seizures are unreasonable. [g]

The Court's holding is based on its belief that society would not recognize as reasonable the possessory interests of prisoners. Its perception of what society is prepared to recognize as reasonable is not based on any empirical data; rather it merely reflects the perception of the four Justices who have joined the opinion that THE CHIEF JUSTICE has authored. On the question of what seizures society is prepared to consider reasonable, surely the consensus on that issue in the lower courts is of some significance. Virtually every federal judge to address the question over the past decade has concluded that the Fourth Amendment does apply to a prison cell. There is similar unanimity among the commentators. The Court itself acknowledges that "intentional harassment of even the most hardened criminals cannot be tolerated by a civilized society." * * * That being the case, I fail to see how a seizure that serves no purpose except harassment does not invade an interest that society considers reasonable, and that is protected by the Fourth Amendment.

[Justice Stevens' opinion goes on to question the basis for the Court's opinion in the security needs rationale.]

* * * * * * * * * * *

COMMENTS

[a] The Constitution recognizes the deprivation of rights follows from penal incarceration. The 13th Amendment allows involuntary servitude as lawful punishment for crime and the 14th Amendment, §2, recognizes denial of the right

vote for participation in crime.

[b] The extension of such rights to prisoners is a development of the 1970s and 1980s. The Supreme Court's basic position has been that inmates are citizens entitled to rights that are not inconsistent with prison security or reasonable attempts to provide rehabilitation. The prisoner is no longer considered, in the words of an older state case, the "slave of the state."

[c] The dissent takes the majority to task for declaring the social expectation toward prisoners. What is your view?

[d] The balancing test gives the Court a methodology whereby it can "dole out" the Fourth Amendment right, so to speak, to different persons or in different situations. Thus, a Constitutional right is not always a matter of "exists-not exists," but may exist in degrees.

[e] This is a useful statement since it indicates a humane and reasoned approach, despite the withholding of Fourth Amendment Rights from prisoners.

[f] This is an inventive construct. The dissent cannot reasonably argue that a prisoner has the same right as a free citizen to demand that a guard have a warrant before entering a cell! So, it splits the Fourth Amendment into rights against unreasonable (1) searches and (2) seizures. Do you find this plausible or merely clever?

[g] If the dissent does not object to random searches (the lower court felt that searchers should be according to plan or reasonable suspicion) is there any reason not to recognize a limited Fourth Amendment right in prisoners?

NEW JERSEY v. T.L.O.

469 U.S. 325, 105 S.Ct. 733, 83 L.Ed.2d. 720 (1985)

JUSTICE WHITE delivered the opinion of the Court.

* * * [W]e here address only the questions of the proper standard for assessing the legality of searches conducted by public school officials and the application of that standard to the facts of this case.

I

[A 14-year-old public high school student, discovered by a teacher to be smoking in a lavatory in violation of school rules, was ordered by a vice principal to open her purse. He found a pack of cigarettes and a pack of rolling papers. A further search of the purse disclosed a small amount of marijuana, a pipe, plastic bags, many one-dollar bills, an index card with a list of students who owed T.L.O. money, and two letters that implicated her in selling marijuana. The evidence was admitted into juvenile delinquency proceedings. The New Jersey Supreme Court suppressed the evidence on the ground that the Fourth Amendment applied and that the search of the purse was unnecessary to enforce the no-smoking rule and was therefore unreasonable. The United States Supreme Court heard argument on] the broader question of what limits, if any, the Fourth Amendment places on the activities of school authorities. * * * Having heard argument on the legality of the search of T.L.O.'s purse, we are satisfied that the search did not violate the Fourth Amendment.

II

In determining whether the search at issue in this case violated the Fourth Amendment, we are faced initially with the question whether that Amendment's prohibition on unreasonable searches and seizures applies to searches conducted by public school officials. We hold that it does.

It is now beyond dispute that "the Federal Constitution, by virtue of the Fourteenth Amendment, prohibits unreasonable searches and seizures by state officers." * * * Equally indisputable is the proposition that the Fourteenth Amendment protects the rights of students against encroachment by public school officials. * * * [T]he State of New Jersey has argued that the history of the Fourth Amendment indicates that the Amendment was intended to regulate only searches and seizures carried out by law enforcement officers; accordingly, although public school officials are concededly state agents for purposes of the Fourteenth Amendment, the Fourth Amendment creates no rights enforceable against them.

It may well be true that the evil toward which the Fourth Amendment was primarily directed was the resurrection of the pre-Revolutionary practice of using general warrants or "writs of assistance" to authorize searches for contraband by officers of the Crown. * * * But this Court has never limited the Amendment's prohibition on unreasonable searches and seizures to operations conducted by the police. Rather, the Court has long spoken of the Fourth Amendment's strictures as restraints imposed upon "governmental action"—that is, "upon the activities of sovereign authority." * * * Accordingly, we have held the Fourth Amendment applicable to the activities of civil as well as criminal authorities: building inspectors, * * * and even firemen entering privately owned premises to battle a fire, * * * are all subject to the restraints imposed by the Fourth Amendment. As we observed in *Camara v. Municipal Court* [this volume], "[t]he basic purpose of this Amendment, as recognized in countless decisions of this Court, is to safeguard the privacy and security of individuals against arbitrary invasions by governmental officials." * * * Because the individual's interest in privacy and personal security "suffers whether the government's motivation is to investigate violations of criminal laws or breaches of other statutory or regulatory standards," * * * it would be "anomalous to say that the individual and his private property are fully protected by the Fourth Amendment only when the individual is suspected of criminal behavior." * * * [a]

[However], a few courts have concluded that school officials are exempt from the dictates of the Fourth Amendment by virtue of the special nature of their authority over schoolchildren. * * * Teachers and school administrators, it is said, act in loco parentis in their dealings with students: their authority is that of the parent, not the State, and is therefore not subject to the limits of the Fourth Amendment. [b]

Such reasoning is in tension with contemporary reality and the teachings of this Court. We have held school officials subject to the commands of the First Amendment, * * * and the Due Process Clause of the Fourteenth Amendment. * * * If school authorities are state actors for purposes of the constitutional guarantees of freedom of expression and due process, it is difficult to understand why they should be deemed to be exercising parental rather than public authority when conducting searches of their students. More generally, the Court has recognized that "the concept of parental delegation" as a source of school authority is not entirely "consonant with compulsory education laws." * * * Today's public school officials do not merely exercise authority voluntarily conferred on them by individual parents; rather, they act in furtherance of publicly mandated educational and disciplinary policies. * * * In carrying out searches and other disciplinary functions pursuant to such policies, school officials act as representatives of the State, not merely as surrogates for the parents, and they cannot claim the parents' immunity from the strictures of the Fourth Amendment.

III

To hold that the Fourth Amendment applies to searches conducted by school authorities is only to begin the inquiry into the standards governing such searches. Although the underlying command of the Fourth Amendment is always that searches and seizures be reasonable, what is reasonable depends on the context within which a search takes place. The determination of the standard of reasonableness governing any specific class of searches requires "balancing the need to search against the invasion which the search entails." * * * On one side of the balance are arrayed the individual's legitimate expectations of privacy and personal security; on the other, the government's need for effective methods to deal with breaches of public order. We have recognized that even a limited search of the person is a substantial invasion of privacy. * * * We have also recognized that searches of closed items of personal luggage are intrusions on protected privacy interests, for "the Fourth Amendment provides protection to the owner of every container that conceals its contents from plain view." * * * A search of a child's person or of a closed purse or other bag carried on her person, no less than a similar search carried out on an adult, is undoubtedly a severe violation of subjective expectations of privacy. [c]

Of course, the Fourth Amendment does not protect subjective expectations of privacy that are unreasonable or otherwise "illegitimate." * * * To receive the protection of the Fourth Amendment, an expectation of privacy must be one that society is "prepared to recognize as legitimate." * * * [d] The State of New Jersey has argued that because of the pervasive supervision to which children in the schools are necessarily subject, a child has virtually no legitimate expectation of privacy in articles of personal property "unnecessarily" carried into a school. This argument has two factual premises: (1) the fundamental incompatibility of expectations of privacy with the maintenance of a sound educational environment; and (2) the minimal interest of the child in bringing any items of personal property into the school. Both premises are severely

flawed.

Although this Court may take notice of the difficulty of maintaining discipline in the public schools today, the situation is not so dire that students in the schools may claim no legitimate expectations of privacy. * * * We are not yet ready to hold that the schools and the prisons [where prisoners have no reasonable expectation of privacy] need be equated for purposes of the Fourth Amendment.

Nor does the State's suggestion that children have no legitimate need to bring personal property into the schools seem well anchored in reality. Students at a minimum must bring to school not only the supplies needed for their studies, but also keys, money, and the necessaries of personal hygiene and grooming. In addition, students may carry on their persons or in purses or wallets such nondisruptive yet highly personal items as photographs, letters, and diaries. Finally, students may have perfectly legitimate reasons to carry with them articles of property needed in connection with extracurricular or recreational activities. In short, school children may find it necessary to carry with them a variety of legitimate, noncontraband items, and there is no reason to conclude that they have necessarily waived all rights to privacy in such items merely by bringing them onto school grounds. [e]

Against the child's interest in privacy must be set the substantial interest of teachers and administrators in maintaining discipline in the classroom and on school grounds. Maintaining order in the classroom has never been easy, but in recent years, school disorder has often taken particularly ugly forms: drug use and violent crime in the schools have become major social problems. * * * [T]he preservation of order and a proper educational environment requires close supervision of schoolchildren, as well as the enforcement of rules against conduct that would be perfectly permissible if undertaken by an adult. * * * Accordingly, we have recognized that maintaining security and order in the schools requires a certain degree of flexibility in school disciplinary procedures, and we have respected the value of preserving the informality of the student-teacher relationship. * * *

How, then, should we strike the balance between the schoolchild's legitimate expectations of privacy and the school's equally legitimate need to maintain an environment in which learning can take place? It is evident that the school setting requires some easing of the restrictions to which searches by public authorities are ordinarily subject. The warrant requirement, in particular, is unsuited to the school environment: requiring a teacher to obtain a warrant before searching a child suspected of an infraction of school rules (or of the criminal law) would unduly interfere with the maintenance of the swift and informal disciplinary procedures needed in the schools. Just as we have in other cases dispensed with the warrant requirement when "the burden of obtaining a warrant is likely to frustrate the governmental purpose behind the search," [f] * * * we hold today that school officials need not obtain a warrant before searching a student who is under their authority.

The school setting also requires some modification of the level of suspicion of illicit activity needed to justify a search. * * * "[P]robable cause" is not an irreducible require-

ment of a valid search. The fundamental command of the Fourth Amendment is that searches and seizures be reasonable, and although "both the concept of probable cause and the requirement of a warrant bear on the reasonableness of a search, . . . in certain limited circumstances neither is required." * * * Where a careful balancing of governmental and private interests suggests that the public interest is best served by a Fourth Amendment standard of reasonableness that stops short of probable cause, we have not hesitated to adopt such a standard.

[Probable cause to believe there is a law violation is not required for a search of students, a rule adopted by most courts that have decided this issue.] Rather, the legality of a search of a student should depend simply on the reasonableness, under all the circumstances, of the search. Determining the reasonableness of any search involves a twofold inquiry: first, * * * "whether the . . . action was justified at its inception;" * * * second, * * * whether the search as actually conducted "was reasonably related in scope to the circumstances which justified the interference in the first place." * * * Under ordinary circumstances, a search of a student by a teacher or other school official will be "justified at its inception" when there are reasonable grounds for suspecting that the search will turn up evidence that the student has violated or is violating either the law or the rules of the school. Such a search will be permissible in its scope when the measures adopted are reasonably related to the objectives of the search and not excessively intrusive in light of the age and sex of the student and the nature of the infraction. **[g]**

This standard will, we trust, neither unduly burden the efforts of school authorities to maintain order in their schools nor authorize unrestrained intrusions upon the privacy of schoolchildren. By focusing attention on the question of reasonableness, the standard will spare teachers and school administrators the necessity of schooling themselves in the niceties of probable cause and permit them to regulate their conduct according to the dictates of reason and common sense. At the same time, the reasonableness standard should ensure that the interests of students will be invaded no more than is necessary to achieve the legitimate end of preserving order in the schools.

IV

[Applying the standards developed above to the facts of this case, the Court found that the vice principal's search of T.L.O's purse was reasonable. Although possession of cigarettes was not a violation of school rules *per se*, smoking was. T.L.O. denied to the vice principal that she was a smoker at all, and so the presence of cigarettes in her purse would weaken her assertion of innocence. The teacher's report that T.L.O. had been smoking gave the vice principal reasonable suspicion to believe that there were cigarettes in T.L.O.'s purse—more than a mere hunch but less than probable cause. The discovery of the rolling papers made the further search for marijuana reasonable because the presence of rolling papers reasonably indicates the presence of marijuana.]

Because the search resulting in the discovery of the evidence of marihuana dealing by T.L.O. was reasonable, the New Jersey Supreme Court's decision to exclude that evidence from T.L.O.'s juvenile delinquency proceedings on Fourth Amendment grounds was erroneous. Accordingly, the judgment of the Supreme Court of New Jersey is Reversed.

[JUSTICE POWELL concurred, joined by JUSTICE O'CONNOR.]

JUSTICE BLACKMUN, concurring in the judgment.

I join the judgment of the Court and agree with much that is said in its opinion. I write separately, however, because I believe the Court omits a crucial step in its analysis of whether a school search must be based upon probable cause. The Court correctly states that we have recognized limited exceptions to the probable-cause requirement "[w]here a careful balancing of governmental and private interests suggests that the public interest is best served" by a lesser standard. I believe that we have used such a balancing test, rather than strictly applying the Fourth Amendment's Warrant and Probable Cause Clause, only when we were confronted with "a special law enforcement need for greater flexibility." * * * Only in those exceptional circumstances in which special needs, beyond the normal need for law enforcement, make the warrant and probable cause requirement impracticable, is a court entitled to substitute its balancing of interests for that of the Framers. **[h]**

     * * *

JUSTICE BRENNAN, with whom

JUSTICE MARSHALL joins, concurring in part and dissenting in part.

I fully agree with Part II of the Court's opinion. Teachers, like all other government officials, must conform their conduct to the Fourth Amendment's protections of personal privacy and personal security. * * * It would be incongruous and futile to charge teachers with the task of imbuing their students with an understanding of our system of constitutional democracy, while at the same time immunizing those same teachers from the need to respect constitutional protections. * * *

I do not, however, otherwise join the Court's opinion. Today's decision sanctions school officials to conduct full-scale searches on a "reasonableness" standard whose only definite content is that it is *not* the same test as the "probable cause" standard found in the text of the Fourth Amendment. In adopting this unclear, unprecedented, and unnecessary departure from generally applicable Fourth Amendment standards, the Court carves out a broad exception to standards that this Court has developed over years of considering Fourth Amendment problems. Its decision is supported neither by precedent nor even by a fair application of the "balancing test" it proclaims in this very opinion. [i]

I

Three basic principles underly [sic] this Court's Fourth Amendment jurisprudence. First, warrantless searches are per se unreasonable, subject only to a few specifically delineated and well-recognized exceptions. * * *

Second, full-scale searches—whether conducted in accordance with the warrant requirement or pursuant to one of its exceptions—are "reasonable" in Fourth Amendment terms only on a showing of probable cause to believe that a crime has been committed and that evidence of the crime will be found in the place to be searched. * * * Third, categories of intrusions that are substantially less intrusive than full-scale searches or seizures may be justifiable in accordance with a balancing test even absent a warrant or probable cause, provided that the balancing test used gives sufficient weight to the privacy interests that will be infringed. * * *
* * *

[In Part I A, JUSTICE BRENNAN next agreed that the search warrant is not required when school officials and teachers search students to enforce school rules.] * * *

B

I emphatically disagree with the Court's decision to cast aside the constitutional probable-cause standard when assessing the constitutional validity of a schoolhouse search. The Court's decision jettisons the probable-cause standard—the only standard that finds support in the text of the Fourth Amendment—on the basis of its Rohrschach-like "balancing test." Use of such a "balancing test" to determine the standard for evaluating the validity of a full-scale search represents a sizable innovation in Fourth Amendment analysis. This innovation finds support neither in precedent nor policy and portends a dangerous weakening of the purpose of the Fourth Amendment to protect the privacy and security of our citizens. Moreover, even if this Court's historic understanding of the Fourth Amendment were mistaken and a balancing test of some kind were appropriate, any such test that gave adequate weight to the privacy and security interests protected by the Fourth Amendment would not reach the preordained result the Court's conclusory analysis reaches today. Therefore, because I believe that the balancing test used by the Court today is flawed both in its inception and in its execution, I respectfully dissent.

1

An unbroken line of cases in this Court have held that probable cause is a prerequisite for a full-scale search. * * *

Our holdings that probable cause is a prerequisite to a full-scale search are based on the relationship between the two Clauses of the Fourth Amendment. The first Clause ("The right of the people to be secure in their persons, houses, papers, and effects, against unreasonable searches and seizures, shall not be violated . . .") states the purpose of the Amendment and its coverage. The second Clause (". . . and no Warrants shall issue but upon probable cause . . .") gives content to the word "unreasonable" in the first Clause. "For all but . . . narrowly defined intrusions, the requisite 'balancing' has been performed in centuries of precedent and is embodied in the principle that seizures are 'reasonable' only if supported by probable cause." * * *
* * *

Considerations of the deepest significance for the freedom of our citizens counsel strict adherence to the principle that no search may be conducted where the official is not in possession of probable cause—that is, where the official does not know of "facts and circumstances [that] warrant a prudent man in believing that the offense has been committed." * * * The Fourth Amendment was designed not merely to protect against official intrusions whose social utility was less as measured by some "balancing test" than its intrusion on individual privacy; it was designed in addition to grant the individual a zone of privacy whose protections could be breached only where the "reasonable" requirements of the probable-cause standard were met. Moved by whatever momentary evil has aroused their fears, officials—perhaps even supported by a majority of citizens—may be tempted to conduct searches that sacrifice the liberty of each citizen to assuage the perceived evil. But the Fourth Amendment rests on the principle that a true balance between the individual and society depends on the recognition of "the right to be let alone—the most comprehensive of rights and the right most valued by civilized men." *Olmstead v. United States*, 277 U.S. 438 (1928) (Brandeis, J., dissenting). That right protects the privacy and security of the individual unless the authorities can cross a specific threshold of need, designated by the term "probable cause." I cannot agree with the Court's assertions today that a "balancing test" can replace the constitutional threshold with one that is more convenient for those enforcing the laws but less protective of the citizens' liberty; the Fourth Amendment's protections should not be defaced by "a balancing process that overwhelms the individual's protection against unwarranted official intrusion by a governmental interest said to justify the search and seizure." * * *

[The remainder of Parts I and II of JUSTICE BRENNAN's dissent attacks the majority's use of the balancing test and concludes that because the vice principal did not have probable cause to rummage through T.L.O.'s purse after the pack of cigarettes were found, the introduction of the other evidence into the juvenile delinquency hearing violated the Fourth Amendment and should be excluded.] * * *

III

In the past several Terms, this Court has produced a succession of Fourth Amendment opinions in which "balancing tests" have been applied to resolve various questions concerning the proper scope of official searches. **[j]** The Court has begun to apply a "balancing test" to determine whether a particular category of searches intrudes upon expectations of privacy that merit Fourth Amendment protection.   See *Hudson v. Palmer* [this volume] ("Determining whether an expectation of privacy is 'legitimate' or 'reasonable' necessarily entails a balancing of interests"). It applies a "balancing test" to determine whether a warrant is necessary to conduct a search. * * *   In today's opinion, it employs a "balancing test" to determine what standard should govern the constitutionality of a given category of searches. Should a search turn out to be unreasonable after application of all of these "balancing tests," the Court then applies an additional "balancing test" to decide whether the evidence

resulting from the search must be excluded. * * *

All of these "balancing tests" amount to brief nods by the Court in the direction of a neutral utilitarian calculus while the Court in fact engages in an unanalyzed exercise of judicial will. Perhaps this doctrinally destructive nihilism is merely a convenient umbrella under which a majority that cannot agree on a genuine rationale can conceal its differences. * * * And it may be that the real force underlying today's decision is the belief that the Court purports to reject—the belief that the unique role served by the schools justifies an exception to the Fourth Amendment on their behalf. If so, the methodology of today's decision may turn out to have as little influence in future cases as will its result, and the Court's departure from traditional Fourth Amendment doctrine will be confined to the schools.

On my view, the presence of the word "unreasonable" in the text of the Fourth Amendment does not grant a shifting majority of this Court the authority to answer *all* Fourth Amendment questions by consulting its momentary vision of the social good. Full-scale searches unaccompanied by probable cause violate the Fourth Amendment. I do not pretend that our traditional Fourth Amendment doctrine automatically answers all of the difficult legal questions that occasionally arise. I do contend, however, that this Court has an obligation to provide some coherent framework to resolve such questions on the basis of more than a conclusory recitation of the results of a "balancing test." The Fourth Amendment itself supplies that framework and, because the Court today fails to heed its message, I must respectfully dissent. [JUSTICE STEVENS dissented, joined by JUSTICES MARSHALL and BRENNAN, arguing that the statement of the rules by the majority will open the door to intrusive searches by school officials for the most trivial school rules.]

*   *   *   *   *   *   *   *   *   *

COMMENT

[a] Although the Fourth Amendment applies to all governmental actors, it does not apply with the same force to all actors in all situations. Police have greater powers in standard law enforcement situations than do governmental officers in "special needs" situations.

[b] *In loco parentis* reasoning is typically used to exempt public authorities from liability when they take action against minors. In a less authoritarian age, such as the one through which we are now passing, even conservative justices on a conservative Court are reluctant to use in loco parentis reasoning to absolve teachers of liability when they interfere in the liberty or privacy of a student.

[c] Note that the text of the Fourth Amendment applies to "persons, papers, houses, and effects" and thus makes no distinctions between a person or her purse.

[d] New Jersey attempts to apply the *Katz* standard to obliterate the Fourth Amendment rights of students.

[e] In assessing New Jersey's argument, the Court in a general way assesses the mundane reality of what an "average" high school student brings to school. What is left unsaid is an assumption that it is socially unreasonable for school personnel to routinely search through such items, without particularized suspicion, in order to find contraband among the belongings of a few students. Would this assumption apply in a private school? in a military academy-type of school? In schools in a "high crime area"? In any American school where drug use is believed to be rampant?

[f] Reading the Court's language literally produces peculiar results. One could "logically" argue that a warrant *always* frustrates the need for efficient law enforcement or the official enforcement of rules or maintenance of order. Clearly, the Court will not go this far, but if this is so, what standards are supplied by the "balancing test"? Is it merely a form of word that hides the subjective predisposition of the judges? The same criticism can apply to the dispensing of the probable cause standard. This is what JUSTICE BRENNAN argues in dissent.

[g] Does it seem likely that this redefinition of reasonableness creates any yardstick to guide the school administrator, or a guide to the judge to determine when a

schoolchild search is unreasonable?

[h] In the last few years, scholars and commentators on criminal procedure have begun to use the "special needs" label to identify a group of cases that have been exempted from the warrant and probable cause requirements. The label appears to have been taken from JUSTICE BLACKMUN's use of the phrase. This is another example of how the judge-made law system expands: a legal doctrine grows out of the use of a phrase. It appears that JUSTICE BLACKMUN is motivated by a need to answer JUSTICE BRENNAN's trenchant point that the *words* of the Fourth Amendment refer to the warrant and the probable cause and the need of judges to explain their particular decisions in terms of principle and generally applied doctrine.

[i] JUSTICE BRENNAN correctly states the basic Fourth Amendment principles that the Court has applied to searches made by law enforcement officers in the administration of the criminal law. What is occurring in *T.L.O.* and other "special needs" cases is that the Court waters down the stringent Fourth Amendment standards by creating hybrid or special rules for special circumstances. This is an example of judicial activism by a politically conservative Court. JUSTICE BRENNAN, a political liberal, argues here for judicial nonactivism.

[j] In Part III of his dissent, JUSTICE BRENNAN criticizes a group of decisions taken by the Court in the 1980s that use the balancing test to lower the warrant and probable cause standards. By characterizing this process as the application of a "neutral utilitarian calculus" he implies that the majority's rulings in these cases is unprincipled. Since the legitimacy of the Court's ruling ultimately must rest on acceptable principles, JUSTICE BRENNAN sows the seeds of doubt about the legitimacy not only regarding the decision in *T.L.O.* but also in a group of balancing cases. He exploits internal differences among the majority and concurring justices to support this point, although doctrinal differences among justices is hardly novel in constitutional adjudication.

The difficulty of JUSTICE BRENNAN's own position is partially admitted in the last paragraph of his dissent. He is no "constitutional fundamentalist" in the spirit of Hugo Black. As a judicial activist in his own right, he realizes that a simple judicial "yardstick" does not exist (although he uses the term in Part I.B.1. of his dissent, omitted here). Yet, he ardently exhorts the Court, or a future Court, to remain closer to the words of the Fourth Amendment in these cases.

CALIFORNIA v. GREENWOOD

486 U.S. 35, 108 S.Ct. 1625, 100 L.Ed.2d 30 (1988)

JUSTICE WHITE delivered the opinion of the Court.

The issue here is whether the Fourth Amendment prohibits the warrantless search and seizure of garbage left for collection outside the curtilage of a home. We conclude, in accordance with the vast majority of lower courts that have addressed the issue, that it does not.

I

[Based on an informer's tip and corroboration, police suspected drug dealing from Greenwood's residence. An investigator obtained, from Greenwood's trash collector, plastic bags of trash that Greenwood left on the street for collection. Incriminating evidence in the trash was used as a basis for a search warrant, which led to the seizure of cocaine and hashish. The California courts] held that warrantless trash searches violate the Fourth Amendment. * * *

* * *

II

The warrantless search and seizure of the garbage bags left at the curb outside the Greenwood house would violate the Fourth Amendment only if respondents manifested a subjective expectation of privacy in their garbage that society accepts as objectively reasonable. * * * *Katz v. United States,* [this volume] (Harlan, J., concurring). **[a]** Respondents do not disagree with this standard.

They assert, however, that they had, and exhibited, an expectation of privacy with respect to the trash that was searched by the police: The trash, which was placed on the street for collection at a fixed time, was contained in opaque plastic bags, which the garbage collector was expected to pick up, mingle with the trash of others, and deposit at the garbage dump. The trash was only temporarily on the street, and there was little likelihood that it would be inspected by anyone.

It may well be that respondents did not expect that the contents of their garbage bags would become known to the police or other members of the public. An expectation of privacy does not give rise to Fourth Amendment protection, however, unless society is prepared to accept that expectation as objectively reasonable. **[b]**

Here, we conclude that respondents exposed their garbage to the public sufficiently to defeat their claim to Fourth Amendment protection. It is common knowledge that plastic garbage bags left on or at the side of a public street are readily accessible to animals, children, scavengers, snoops, and other members of the public. * * * Moreover, respondents placed their refuse at the curb for the express purpose of conveying it to a third party, the trash collector, who might himself have sorted through respondents' trash or permitted others, such as the police, to do so. Accordingly, having deposited their garbage "in an area particularly suited for public inspection and, in a manner of speaking, public consumption, for the express purpose of having strangers take it," * * * respondents could have had no reasonable expectation of privacy in the inculpatory items that they discarded. **[c]**

Furthermore, as we have held, the police cannot reasonably be expected to avert their eyes from evidence of criminal activity that could have been observed by any member of the public. Hence, "[w]hat a person knowingly exposes to the public, even in his own home or office, is not a subject of Fourth Amendment protection." *Katz.* * * * We held in *Smith v. Maryland*, 442 U.S. 735 (1979), for example, that the police did not violate the Fourth Amendment by causing a pen register to be installed at the telephone company's offices to record the telephone numbers dialed by a criminal suspect. An individual has no legitimate expectation of privacy in the numbers dialed on his telephone, we reasoned, because he voluntarily conveys those numbers to the telephone company when he uses the telephone. **[d]** Again, we observed that "a person has no legitimate expectation of privacy in information he voluntarily turns over to third parties." * * *

* * *

Our conclusion that society would not accept as reasonable respondents' claim to an expectation of privacy in trash left for collection in an area accessible to the public is reinforced by the unanimous rejection of similar claims by the Federal Courts of Appeals. * * * In addition, of those state appellate courts that have considered the issue, the vast majority have held that the police may conduct warrantless searches and seizures of garbage discarded in public areas. * *

*

* * *

[The Court also rejected an argument that a State right should be incorporated into the federal rights and rejected a due process argument. The judgment of the California appellate court was reversed.]

JUSTICE BRENNAN, with whom JUSTICE MARSHALL joins, dissenting.

Every week for two months, and at least once more a month later, the Laguna Beach police clawed through the trash that respondent Greenwood left in opaque, sealed bags on the curb outside his home. * * * Complete strangers minutely scrutinized their bounty, undoubtedly dredging up intimate details of Greenwood's private life and habits. The intrusions proceeded without a warrant, and no court before or since has concluded that the police acted on probable cause to believe Greenwood was engaged in any criminal activity. **[e]**

Scrutiny of another's trash is contrary to commonly accepted notions of civilized behavior. I suspect, therefore, that members of our society will be shocked to learn that the Court, the ultimate guarantor of liberty, deems unreasonable our expectation that the aspects of our private lives that are concealed safely in a trash bag will not become public. **[f]**

I

"A container which can support a reasonable expectation of privacy may not be searched, even on probable cause, without a warrant." * * * Thus, as the Court observes, if Greenwood had a reasonable expectation that the contents of the bags that he placed on the curb would remain private, the warrantless search of those bags violated the Fourth Amendment. * * *

The Framers of the Fourth Amendment understood that "unreasonable searches" of "paper[s] and effects"—no less than "unreasonable searches" of "person[s] and houses"—infringe privacy. As early as 1878, this Court acknowledged that the contents of "[l]etters and sealed packages . . . in the mail are as fully guarded from examination and inspection . . . as if they were retained by the parties forwarding them in their own domiciles." * * * In short, so long as a package is "closed against inspection," the Fourth Amendment protects its contents, "wherever they may be," and the police must obtain a warrant to search it just "as is required when papers are subjected to search in one's own household." * * * **[g]**

With the emergence of the reasonable-expectation-of-privacy analysis, see *Katz v. United States*, * * * we have reaffirmed this fundamental principle. [The dissent cites several cases where the Court either held or made statements supporting the right of privacy in closed containers; but in none of the cases were the containers abandoned].

II

Respondents deserve no less protection just because Greenwood used the bags to discard rather than to transport his personal effects. Their contents are not inherently any less private, and Greenwood's decision to discard them, at least in the manner in

which he did, does not diminish his expectation of privacy. **[h]**

[The dissent produced evidence that the analysis of trash can uncover intimate details about one's life.]

The Court properly rejects the State's attempt to distinguish trash searches from other searches on the theory that trash is abandoned and therefore not entitled to an expectation of privacy. As the author of the Court's opinion observed last Term, a defendant's "property interest [in trash] does not settle the matter for Fourth Amendment purposes, for the reach of the Fourth Amendment is not determined by state property law." * * * **[i]** In evaluating the reasonableness of Greenwood's expectation that his sealed trash bags would not be invaded, the Court has held that we must look to "understandings that are recognized and permitted by society." Most of us, I believe, would be incensed to discover a meddler—whether a neighbor, a reporter, or a detective—scrutinizing our sealed trash containers to discover some detail of our personal lives. * * * **[j]**
* * *

That is not to deny that isolated intrusions into opaque, sealed trash containers occur. When, acting on their own, "animals, children, scavengers, snoops, [or] other members of the public," * * * *actually* rummage through a bag of trash and expose its contents to plain view, "police cannot reasonably be expected to avert their eyes from evidence of criminal activity that could have been observed by any member of the public." * * *
* * *

The mere *possibility* that unwelcome meddlers *might* open and rummage through the containers does not negate the expectation of privacy in their contents any more than the possibility of a burglary negates an expectation of privacy in the home; * * * or the possibility that an operator will listen in on a telephone conversation negates an expectation of privacy in the words spoken on the telephone. "What a person * * * seeks to preserve as private, *even in an area accessible to the public*, may be constitutionally protected." *Katz.* * * * We have therefore repeatedly rejected attempts to justify a State's invasion of privacy on the ground that the privacy is not absolute. * * *

* * *

III

In holding that the warrantless search of Greenwood's trash was consistent with the Fourth Amendment, the Court paints a grim picture of our society. It depicts a society in which local authorities may command their citizens to dispose of their personal effects in the manner least protective of the "sanctity of [the] home and the privacies of life," *Boyd v. United States*, [this volume] and then monitor them arbitrarily and without judicial oversight—a society that is not prepared to recognize as reasonable an individual's expectation of privacy in the most private of personal effects sealed in an opaque container and disposed of in a manner designed to commingle it imminently and inextricably with the trash of others. * * * The American society with which I am familiar "chooses to dwell in reasonable security and freedom from surveillance," * * * and is more dedicated to individual liberty and more sensitive to intrusions on the sanctity of the home than the Court is willing to acknowledge. [k]

I dissent.

* * * * * * * * * * *

COMMENTS

[a] Note the reference to JUSTICE HARLAN's *Katz* concurrence as the operative rule.

[b] What is *your* expectation of trash privacy, keeping in mind, that your expectation will "govern" police searches of both your trash and that of criminal suspects.

[c] Under pre-*Katz* reasoning, there was no Fourth Amendment protection because by setting property on the curb, the owner *abandoned* it and no longer had any *property* interest.

[d] Congress has now provided that government snooping of the telephone numbers called and received (rather than the content of calls) is not proper without a search warrant.

[e] This artful retelling of the facts, as accurate the majority's, adds an emotional

element essential for the dissent's alternate theory of the case.

[f] The Supreme Court used a "shocks the conscience" test in *Rochin v. California* [this volume], but most commentators believe that it proved unworkable. How good a legal standard is one that reads "members of our society will be shocked to learn * * * "?

[g] The mail analogy is weak against the majority's abandonment-expectation theory, but is useful in supporting the dissent's "ethical-shock" theory. Nevertheless, in the dissent's examples, the containers are not abandoned.

[h] This argument radically separates property from privacy by asserting a privacy interest in abandoned property. The majority still links privacy to property. Is this artificial?

[i] This was, nevertheless, a dissenting opinion by JUSTICE WHITE. Thus, the dissent's argument on this point carries logical weight, but is not a statement of legal precedent.

[j] If this is the dissent's constitutional standard, is a non-warranted trash search proper where a public opinion poll shows that 51 percent of the public believes that it is?

[k] If the dissent's rule is somewhat artificial according to common reasoning, is that not the case with many constitutional protections? The dissent does not preclude the application of the plain view doctrine to trash or to the probable cause searches of trash under a warrant.

MICHIGAN DEPARTMENT OF STATE POLICE v. SITZ

496 U.S. 444 110 S.Ct. 2481, 110 L.Ed.2d 412 (1990)

CHIEF JUSTICE REHNQUIST delivered the opinion of the Court.

This case poses the question whether a State's use of highway sobriety checkpoints violates the Fourth and Fourteenth Amendments to the United States Constitution. We hold that it does not and therefore reverse the contrary holding of the Court of Appeals of Michigan.

Petitioners, the Michigan Department of State Police and its Director, established a sobriety checkpoint pilot program [including guidelines] in early 1986. * * *

Under the guidelines, checkpoints would be set up at selected sites along state roads. All vehicles passing through a checkpoint would be stopped and their drivers briefly examined for signs of intoxication. In cases where a checkpoint officer detected signs of intoxication, the motorist would be directed to a location out of the traffic flow where an officer would check the motorist's driver's license and car registration and, if warranted, conduct further sobriety tests. Should the field tests and the officer's observations suggest that the driver was intoxicated, an arrest would be made. All other drivers would be permitted to resume their journey immediately.

[A single checkpoint went into operation for an hour-and-fifteen-minute duration before a citizens' lawsuit against the checkpoint program led the State Police to delay further implementation pending the outcome of the litigation. At trial evidence about the effectiveness of checkpoints was elicited.]

* * * During the * * * checkpoint's operation, 126 vehicles passed through the checkpoint. The average delay for each vehicle was approximately 25 seconds. Two drivers were detained for field sobriety testing, and one of the two was arrested for driving under the influence of alcohol. A third driver who drove through without stopping was pulled over by an officer in an observation vehicle and arrested for driving under the influence.

* * *

[The Michigan courts] performed a balancing test derived from our opinion in *Brown v. Texas*, 443 U.S. 47 (1979). As described by the Court of Appeals, the test involved "balancing the state's interest in preventing accidents caused by drunk drivers, the effectiveness of sobriety checkpoints in achieving that goal, and the level of intrusion on an individual's privacy caused by the checkpoints." * * * [a]

[The Court of Appeals found] that the State has "a grave and legitimate" interest in curbing drunken driving; that sobriety checkpoint programs are generally "ineffective" and, therefore, do not significantly further that interest; and that the checkpoints' "subjective intrusion" on individual liberties is substantial. * * *

* * *

[In deciding this case, *United States v. Martinez-Fuerte*, 428 U.S. 543 (1976)] which utilized a balancing analysis in approving highway checkpoints for detecting illegal aliens, and *Brown v. Texas* [above] are the relevant authorities here. [b]

Petitioners concede, correctly in our view, that a Fourth Amendment "seizure" occurs when a vehicle is stopped at a checkpoint. * * * The question thus becomes whether such seizures are "reasonable" under the Fourth Amendment.

It is important to recognize what our inquiry is *not* about. No allegations are before us of unreasonable treatment of any person after an actual detention at a particular checkpoint. * * * As pursued in the lower courts, the instant action challenges only the use of sobriety checkpoints generally. We address only the initial stop of each motorist passing through a checkpoint and the associated preliminary questioning and observation by checkpoint officers. Detention of particular motorists for more extensive field sobriety testing may require satisfaction of an individualized suspicion standard. * * *

No one can seriously dispute the magnitude of the drunken driving problem or the States' interest in eradicating it. * * * "Drunk drivers cause an annual death toll of over 25,000 and in the same time span cause nearly one million personal injuries and more than five billion dollars in property damage." * * *

Conversely, the weight bearing on the other scale—the measure of the intrusion on motorists stopped briefly at sobriety checkpoints—is slight. [c] We reached a similar conclusion as to the intrusion on motorists subjected to a brief stop at a highway checkpoint for detecting illegal aliens. See *Martinez-Fuerte* [above]. We see virtually no difference between the levels of intrusion on law-abiding motorists from the brief stops necessary

to the effectuation of these two types of checkpoints, which to the average motorist would seem identical save for the nature of the questions the checkpoint officers might ask. [c] The trial court and the Court of Appeals, thus, accurately gauged the "objective" intrusion, measured by the duration of the seizure and the intensity of the investigation, as minimal. * * *

With respect to what it perceived to be the "subjective" intrusion on motorists, however, the Court of Appeals found such intrusion substantial. * * * The court first [held] that the guidelines governing checkpoint operation minimize the discretion of the officers on the scene. But the court also [held] that the checkpoints have the potential to generate fear and surprise in motorists. This was so because the record failed to demonstrate that approaching motorists would be aware of their option to make U-turns or turnoffs to avoid the checkpoints. On that basis, the court deemed the subjective intrusion from the checkpoints unreasonable. * * *

We believe the Michigan courts misread our cases concerning the degree of "subjective intrusion" and the potential for generating fear and surprise. The "fear and surprise" to be considered are not the natural fear of one who has been drinking over the prospect of being stopped at a sobriety checkpoint but, rather, the fear and surprise engendered in law abiding motorists by the nature of the stop. This was made clear in *Martinez-Fuerte*. Comparing checkpoint stops to roving patrol stops [to search cars within 100 miles of the border for illegal aliens] considered in prior cases, we said,

"we view checkpoint stops in a

different light because the subjective intrusion—the generating of concern or even fright on the part of lawful travelers—is appreciably less in the case of a checkpoint stop." * * *

* * * Here, checkpoints are selected pursuant to the guidelines, and uniformed police officers stop every approaching vehicle. [d] The intrusion resulting from the brief stop at the sobriety checkpoint is for constitutional purposes indistinguishable from the checkpoint stops we upheld in *Martinez-Fuerte*.

The Court of Appeals went on to * * * conclude[] that the checkpoint program failed the "effectiveness" part of the test, and that this failure materially discounted petitioners' strong interest in implementing the program. We think the Court of Appeals was wrong on this point as well.

The actual language from *Brown v. Texas*, upon which the Michigan courts based their evaluation of "effectiveness," describes the balancing factor as "the degree to which the seizure advances the public interest." * * * This passage from *Brown* was not meant to transfer from politically accountable officials to the courts the decision as to which among reasonable alternative law enforcement techniques should be employed to deal with a serious public danger.   Experts in police science might disagree over which of several methods of apprehending drunken drivers is preferrable as an ideal.   But for purposes of Fourth Amendment analysis, the choice among such reasonable alternatives remains with the governmental officials who have a unique understanding of,

and a responsibility for, limited public resources, including a finite number of police officers. [e]   *Brown*'s rather general reference to "the degree to which the seizure advances the public interest" was derived, as the opinion makes clear, from the line of cases culminating in *Martinez-Fuerte*, [above]. Neither *Martinez-Fuerte* nor *Delaware v. Prouse* [this volume], however, the two cases cited by the Court of Appeals as providing the basis for its "effectiveness" review, * * * supports the searching examination of "effectiveness" undertaken by the Michigan court.

In *Delaware v. Prouse* [above], we disapproved random stops made by Delaware Highway Patrol officers in an effort to apprehend unlicensed drivers and unsafe vehicles.   We observed that *no* empirical evidence indicated that such stops would be an effective means of promoting roadway safety and said that "it seems common sense that the percentage of all drivers on the road who are driving without a license is very small and that the number of licensed drivers who will be stopped in order to find one unlicensed operator will be large indeed." * * *   We observed that the random stops involved the "kind of standardless and unconstrained discretion [which] is the evil the Court has discerned when in previous cases it has insisted that the discretion of the official in the field be circumscribed, at least to some extent." * * *   We went on to state that our holding did not "cast doubt on the permissibility of roadside truck weigh-stations and inspection checkpoints, at which some vehicles may be subject to further detention for safety and regulatory inspection than are others." * * *

Unlike *Prouse*, this case involves

neither a complete absence of empirical data nor a challenge to random highway stops. * * * [A]pproximately 1.5 percent of the drivers passing through the checkpoint were arrested for alcohol impairment. * * * [E]xperience in other States demonstrated that, on the whole, sobriety checkpoints resulted in drunken driving arrests of around 1 percent of all motorists stopped. * * * By way of comparison, the record from * * * *Martinez-Fuerte*, showed that in the associated checkpoint, illegal aliens were found in only 0.12 percent of the vehicles passing through the checkpoint. * * * * * * We concluded that this "record . . . provides a rather complete picture of the effectiveness of the San Clemente checkpoint", * * * and we sustained its constitutionality. We see no justification for a different conclusion here. **[e]**

In sum, the balance of the State's interest in preventing drunken driving, the extent to which this system can reasonably be said to advance that interest, and the degree of intrusion upon individual motorists who are briefly stopped, weighs in favor of the state program. We therefore hold that it is consistent with the Fourth Amendment. * * *

Reversed.

[JUSTICE BLACKMUN concurred in the judgment.]

[JUSTICE BRENNAN dissented, joined by JUSTICE MARSHALL.]

JUSTICE STEVENS, with whom JUSTICE BRENNAN and JUSTICE MARSHALL join as to Parts I and II, dissenting.

[JUSTICE STEVENS cited evidence to show that sobriety checkpoints had minimal effect, at best, on the problem of drunk driving, and that other more effective means were available.]

In light of these considerations, it seems evident that the Court today misapplies the balancing test announced in *Brown v. Texas* [above]. The Court overvalues the law enforcement interest in using sobriety checkpoints, undervalues the citizen's interest in freedom from random, unannounced investigatory seizures, and mistakenly assumes that there is "virtually no difference" between a routine stop at a permanent, fixed checkpoint and a surprise stop at a sobriety checkpoint. * * *

I

There is a critical difference between a seizure that is preceded by fair notice and one that is effected by surprise. * * * That is one reason why a border search, or indeed any search at a permanent and fixed checkpoint, is much less intrusive than a random stop. A motorist with advance notice of the location of a permanent checkpoint has an opportunity to avoid the search entirely, or at least to prepare for, and limit, the intrusion on her privacy.

No such opportunity is available in the case of a random stop or a temporary checkpoint, which both depend for their effectiveness on the element of surprise. **[f]** A driver who discovers an unexpected checkpoint on a familiar local road will be startled and distressed. She may infer, correctly, that the checkpoint is not simply "business as usual," and may likewise infer, again correctly, that the police have made a discretionary decision to focus their law enforcement efforts upon her and others who pass the chosen point.

* * * The distinction casts immediate doubt upon the majority's argument, for *Martinez-Fuerte* is the only case in which we have upheld suspicionless seizures of motorists.   * * * [T]he [sobriety] checkpoint is most frequently employed during the hours of darkness on weekends (because that is when drivers with alcohol in their blood are most apt to be found on the road) [and] the police have extremely broad discretion in determining the exact timing and placement of the roadblock.

There is also a significant difference between the kind of discretion that the officer exercises after the stop is made. A check for a driver's license, or for identification papers at an immigration checkpoint, is far more easily standardized than is a search for evidence of intoxication. A Michigan officer who questions a motorist at a sobriety checkpoint has virtually unlimited discretion to detain the driver on the basis of the slightest suspicion. A ruddy complexion, an unbuttoned shirt, bloodshot eyes or a speech impediment may suffice to prolong the detention. Any driver who had just consumed a glass of beer, or even a sip of wine, would almost certainly have the burden of demonstrating to the officer that her driving ability was not impaired.
* * *

For all these reasons, I do not believe that this case is analogous to *Martinez-Fuerte*. In my opinion, the sobriety checkpoints are instead similar to—and in some respects more intrusive than—the random investigative stops

that the Court held unconstitutional in * * * *Prouse*. In [that] case the Court explained:

> * * * "Both [immigration roving-patrol stops and stops for license checks on ordinary city streets] generally entail law enforcement officers signaling a moving automobile to pull over to the side of the roadway, by means of a possibly unsettling show of authority. Both interfere with freedom of movement, are inconvenient, and consume time. Both may create substantial anxiety." * * *

We accordingly held that the State must produce evidence comparing the challenged seizure to other means of law enforcement, so as to show that the seizure

> "is a sufficiently productive mechanism to justify the intrusion upon Fourth Amendment interests which such stops entail." * * *

II

The Court, unable to draw any persuasive analogy to *Martinez-Fuerte*, rests its decision today on application of a more general balancing test taken from *Brown v. Texas*, [above]. In that case the appellant, a pedestrian, had been stopped for questioning in an area of El Paso, Texas, that had "a high incidence of drug traffic" because he "looked suspicious." * * * He was then arrested and convicted for refusing to identify himself to police officers. We set aside his conviction because the officers stopped him when they lacked any reasonable suspicion that he was engaged in criminal activity. **[g]** In our opinion, we stated:

> "Consideration of the constitutionality of such seizures involves a weighing of the gravity of the public concerns served by the seizure, the degree to which the seizure advances the public interest, and the severity of the interference with individual liberty." * * *

The gravity of the public concern with highway safety that is implicated by this case is, of course, undisputed. * * * Moreover, I do not understand the Court to have placed any lesser value on the importance of the drug problem implicated in *Texas v. Brown*, [sic] or on the need to control the illegal border crossings. * * * A different result in this case must be justified by the other two factors in the *Brown* formulation. **[h]**

As I have already explained, I believe the Court is quite wrong in blithely asserting that a sobriety checkpoint is no more intrusive than a permanent checkpoint. In my opinion, unannounced investigatory seizures are,

particularly when they take place at night, the hallmark of regimes far different from ours; the surprise intrusion upon individual liberty is not minimal. On that issue, my difference with the Court may amount to nothing less than a difference in our respective evaluations of the importance of individual liberty, a serious albeit inevitable source of constitutional disagreement. **[i]** On the degree to which the sobriety checkpoint seizures advance the public interest, however, the Court's position is wholly indefensible.

* * *

III

The most disturbing aspect of the Court's decision today is that it appears to give no weight to the citizen's interest in freedom from suspicionless unannounced investigatory seizures. Although the author of the opinion does not reiterate his description of that interest as "diaphanous," see *Delaware v. Prouse*, * * * (REHNQUIST, J., dissenting), the Court's opinion implicitly adopts that characterization. * * * **[j]**

* * *

* * * * * * * * * * *

COMMENTS

[a] The majority opinion never indicates the factual basis of *Brown*, which is given by the dissent.

[b] The Court rejected an attempt by the State Police to place checkpoints into the ambit of the "special needs" doctrine.

[c] The dissent disagreed forcefully with these assertions.

[d] Guidelines and uniform procedures are important to prevent the excessive exercise of governmental power.

[e] This may be a low level of effectiveness for a legislature or a commission, but the majority seems to be saying that a court should accept the lowest level of effectiveness and not second guess the executive or legislative branches.

[f] Would you distinguish between a random police stop of your car while driving on the highway and coming to a non-fixed checkpoint in terms of your personal anxiety?

[g] *Brown* had nothing to do with automobile stops. Given the clearly unconstitutional acts of the police in that case (the U.S. Supreme Court decision was unanimous), its language about the balancing test could be seen as dictum.

[h] The dissent implies here that the majority is ruling mainly on the basis of the seriousness of the problem and its approach to not interfering with the executive and legislative branches except in well established areas of constitutional rights.

[i] This is a frank admission of the ideological differences between different members of the Court.

[j] Justices will often use the quote of a fellow-justice in another case either to indicate that judge's predilections or, as here, to show that the judge is biased in the current case.

SKINNER v. RAILWAY LABOR EXECUTIVES' ASS'N

489 U.S. 602, 109 S.Ct. 1402, 103 L.Ed.2d 639 (1989)

JUSTICE KENNEDY delivered the opinion of the Court.

The Federal Railroad Safety Act of 1970 authorizes the Secretary of Transportation to [set standards for railway safety]. Finding that alcohol and drug abuse by railroad employees poses a serious threat to safety, the Federal Railroad Administration (FRA) has promulgated regulations that mandate blood and urine tests of employees who are involved in certain train accidents. The FRA also has adopted regulations that do not require, but do authorize, railroads to administer breath and urine tests to employees who violate certain safety rules. The question presented by this case is whether these regulations violate the Fourth Amendment.

* * *

[Part I reviewed the problem of drinking, drugs, and railway safety and the development of safety regulations. Respondent and its member labor unions obtained an injunction against the blood and urine tests in District Court. A divided Circuit Court held that there was state action that implicated the Fourth Amendment. It held that the automatic post-accident testing procedure was unreasonable as it did not require particularized suspicion.]

II

* * *

A

[The Court found that private railway companies conducted the blood and urine testing under mandatory federal law that allowed no exceptions. This constituted state action and so the Fourth Amendment applied.]

B

Our precedents teach that where, as here, the Government seeks to obtain physical evidence from a person, the Fourth Amendment may be relevant at several levels. * * * The initial detention necessary to procure the evidence may be a seizure of the person, * * * if the detention amounts to a meaningful interference with his freedom of movement. * * * Obtaining and examining the evidence may also be a search, * * * if doing so infringes an expectation of privacy that society is prepared to recognize as reasonable, * * *

We have long recognized that a "compelled intrusio[n] into the body for blood to be analyzed for alcohol content" must be deemed a Fourth Amendment search. See *Schmerber v. California*, 384 U.S. 757, 767-768 (1966). * * * In light of our society's concern for the security of one's person, * * * it is obvious that this physical intrusion, penetrating beneath the skin, infringes an expectation of privacy that society is prepared to recognize as reasonable. The ensuing chemical analysis of the sample to obtain physiological data is a further invasion of the tested employee's privacy interests. * * * **[a]** Much the same is true of the breath-testing procedures required under * * * the regulations. Subjecting a person to a breathalyzer test, which generally requires the production of alveolar or "deep lung" breath for chemical analysis, * * * implicates similar concerns about bodily integrity and, like the blood-alcohol test we considered in *Schmerber*, should also be deemed a search.

Unlike the blood-testing procedure at issue in *Schmerber*, collecting and testing urine samples do not entail a surgical intrusion into the body. It is not disputed, however, that chemical analysis of urine, like that of blood, can reveal a host of private medical facts about an employee, including whether he or she is epileptic, pregnant, or diabetic. Nor can it be disputed that the process of collecting the sample to be tested, which may in some cases involve visual or aural monitoring of the act of urination, itself implicates privacy interests. As the Court of Appeals for the Fifth Circuit has stated:

> "There are few activities in our society more personal or private than the passing of urine. Most people describe it by euphemisms if they talk about it at all. It is a function traditionally performed without public observation; indeed, its performance in public is generally prohibited by law as well as social custom." * * *

Because it is clear that the collection and testing of urine intrudes upon expectations of privacy that society has long recognized as reasonable, * * * these intrusions must be deemed searches under the Fourth Amendment. [b]
* * *

III

A

To hold that the Fourth Amendment is applicable to the drug and alcohol testing prescribed by the FRA regulations is only to begin the inquiry into the standards governing such intrusions. * * * For the Fourth Amendment does not proscribe all searches and seizures, but only those that are unreasonable. * * * What is reasonable, of course, "depends on all of the circumstances surrounding the search or seizure and the nature of the search or seizure itself." * * * Thus, the permissibility of a particular practice "is judged by balancing its intrusion on the individual's Fourth Amendment interests against its promotion of legitimate governmental interests." * * *

In most criminal cases, we strike this balance in favor of the procedures described by the Warrant Clause of the Fourth Amendment. * * * Except in certain well-defined circumstances, a search or seizure in such a case is not reasonable unless it is accomplished pursuant to a judicial warrant issued upon probable cause. * * * We have recognized exceptions to this rule, however, "when 'special needs, beyond the normal need for law enforcement, make the warrant and probable-cause requirement impracticable.'" * * * When faced with such special needs, we have not hesitated to balance the governmental and privacy interests to assess the practicality of the warrant and probable cause requirements in the particular context. * * * The Government's interest in regulating the conduct of railroad employees to ensure safety, like its supervision of probationers or regulated industries, or its operation of a government office, school, or prison, **[c]** "likewise presents 'special needs' beyond normal law enforcement that may justify departures from the usual warrant and probable-cause requirements." * * * The * * * employees covered by the FRA regulations include persons engaged in handling orders concerning train movements, operating crews, and those engaged in the maintenance and repair of signal systems. * * * It is undisputed that these and other covered employees are engaged in safety-sensitive tasks. * * *

The FRA has prescribed toxicological tests, not to assist in the prosecution of employees, but rather "to prevent accidents and casualties in railroad operations that result from impairment of employees by alcohol or drugs." * * * This governmental interest in ensuring the safety of the traveling public and of the employees themselves plainly justifies prohibiting covered employees from using alcohol or drugs on duty, or while subject to being called for duty. This interest also "require[s] and justif[ies] the exercise of supervision to assure that the restrictions are in fact observed." * * * The question that remains, then, is whether the Government's need to monitor compliance with these restrictions justifies the privacy intrusions at issue absent a warrant or individualized suspicion.

B

An essential purpose of a warrant requirement is to protect privacy interests by assuring citizens subject to a search or seizure that such intrusions are not the random or arbitrary acts of government agents. A warrant assures the citizen that the intrusion is authorized by law, and that it is narrowly limited in its objectives and scope. * * * A warrant also provides the detached scrutiny of a neutral magistrate, and thus ensures an objective determination whether an intrusion is justified in any given case. * * * In the present context, however, a warrant would do little to further these aims. Both the circumstances justifying toxicological testing and the permissible limits of such intrusions are defined narrowly and specifically in the regulations that authorize them, and doubtless are well known to covered employees. * * * Indeed, in light of the standardized nature of the tests and the minimal discretion vested in those charged with administering the program, there are virtually no facts for a neutral magistrate to evaluate. * * *

We have recognized, moreover, that the Government's interest in dispensing with the warrant requirement is at its strongest when, as here, "the burden of obtaining a warrant is likely to frustrate the governmental purpose behind the search." * * * As the FRA recognized, alcohol and other drugs are eliminated from the bloodstream at a constant rate, * * * and blood and breath samples taken to measure whether these substances were in the bloodstream when a triggering event occurred must be obtained as soon as possible. * * *

The Government's need to rely on private railroads to set the testing process in motion also indicates that insistence on a warrant requirement would impede the achievement of the Government's objective. Railroad supervisors, like school officials, * * * and hospital administrators, * * * are not in the business of investigating violations of the criminal laws or enforcing administrative codes, and otherwise have little occasion to become familiar with the intricacies of this Court's Fourth Amendment jurisprudence. "Imposing unwieldly warrant procedures * * * upon supervisors, who would otherwise have no reason to be familiar with such procedures, is simply unreasonable." * * *

In sum, imposing a warrant requirement in the present context would add little to the assurances of certainty and regularity already afforded by the regulations, while significantly hindering, and in many cases frustrating, the objectives of the Government's testing program. We do not believe that a warrant is essential to render the intrusions here at issue reasonable under the Fourth Amendment.

C

Our cases indicate that even a search that may be performed without a warrant must be based, as a general matter, on probable cause to believe that the person to be searched has violated the law. * * * When the balance of interests precludes insistence on a showing of probable cause, we have usually required "some quantum of individualized suspicion" before concluding that a search is reasonable. * * * We made it clear, however, that a showing of individualized suspicion is not a constitutional floor, below which a search must be presumed unreasonable. * * * In limited circumstances, where the privacy interests implicated by the search are minimal, and where an important governmental interest furthered by the intrusion would be placed in jeopardy by a requirement of

individualized suspicion, a search may be reasonable despite the absence of such suspicion. We believe this is true of the intrusions in question here.
* * *
* * * [T]he intrusion occasioned by a blood test is not significant, since such "tests are a commonplace in these days of periodic physical examinations and experience with them teaches that the quantity of blood extracted is minimal, and that for most people the procedure involves virtually no risk, trauma, or pain." * * * *Schmerber* thus confirmed "society's judgment that blood tests do not constitute an unduly extensive imposition on an individual's privacy and bodily integrity." * * *

The breath tests authorized by * * * the regulations are even less intrusive than the blood tests. * * * [They] do not require piercing the skin and may be conducted safely outside a hospital environment and with a minimum of inconvenience or embarrassment. Further, breath tests reveal the level of alcohol in the employee's bloodstream and nothing more. Like the blood-testing procedures * * * which can be used only to ascertain the presence of alcohol or controlled substances in the bloodstream, breath tests reveal no other facts in which the employee has a substantial privacy interest. * * * In all the circumstances, we cannot conclude that the administration of a breath test implicates significant privacy concerns.

A more difficult question is presented by urine tests. Like breath tests, urine tests are not invasive of the body and, under the regulations, may not be used as an occasion for inquiring into private facts unrelated to alcohol or drug use. We recognize, however, that the procedures for collecting the necessary samples, which require employees to perform an excretory function traditionally shielded by great privacy, raise concerns not implicated by blood or breath tests. While we would not characterize these additional privacy concerns as minimal in most contexts, we note that the regulations endeavor to reduce the intrusiveness of the collection process. The regulations do not require that samples be furnished under the direct observation of a monitor, despite the desirability of such a procedure to ensure the integrity of the sample. * * * The sample is also collected in a medical environment, by personnel unrelated to the railroad employer, and is thus not unlike similar procedures encountered often in the context of a regular physical examination.

More importantly, the expectations of privacy of covered employees are diminished by reason of their participation in an industry that is regulated pervasively to ensure safety, a goal dependent, in substantial part, on the health and fitness of covered employees. * * * Indeed, the FRA found * * * that "most railroads require periodic physical examinations for train and engine employees and certain other employees." * * *

* * * Though some of the privacy interests implicated by the toxicological testing at issue reasonably might be viewed as significant in other contexts, logic and history show that a diminished expectation of privacy attaches to information relating to the physical condition of covered employees and to this reasonable means of procuring such information. We conclude, therefore, that the testing procedures * * * pose only limited threats to the justifiable expectations of privacy of covered employees. [d]

By contrast, the Government interest in testing without a showing of individualized suspicion is compelling. Employees subject to the tests discharge duties fraught with such risks of injury to others that even a momentary lapse of attention can have disastrous consequences. Much like persons who have routine access to dangerous nuclear power facilities, * * * employees who are subject to testing under the FRA regulations can cause great human loss before any signs of impairment become noticeable to supervisors or others. An impaired employee, the FRA found, will seldom display any outward "signs detectable by the lay person or, in many cases, even the physician." * * * [e] Indeed, while respondents posit that impaired employees might be detected without alcohol or drug testing, the premise of respondents' lawsuit is that even the occurrence of a major calamity will not give rise to a suspicion of impairment with respect to any particular employee.

While no procedure can identify all impaired employees with ease and perfect accuracy, the FRA regulations supply an effective means of deterring employees engaged in safety-sensitive tasks from using controlled substances or alcohol in the first place. * * *

The testing procedures * * * also help railroads obtain invaluable information about the causes of major accidents, * * * and to take appropriate measures to safeguard the general public. * * *

A requirement of particularized suspicion of drug or alcohol use would seriously impede an employer's ability to obtain this information, despite its obvious importance. Experience confirms the FRA's judgment that the scene of a serious rail accident is chaotic. Investigators who arrive at the scene shortly after a major accident has occurred may find it difficult to determine which members of a train crew contributed to its occurrence. Obtaining evidence that might give rise to the suspicion that a particular employee is impaired, a difficult endeavor in the best of circumstances, is most impracticable in the aftermath of a serious accident. * * * It would be unrealistic, and inimical to the Government's goal of ensuring safety in rail transportation, to require a showing of individualized suspicion in these circumstances.

* * *

We conclude that the compelling Government interests served by the FRA's regulations would be significantly hindered if railroads were required to point to specific facts giving rise to a reasonable suspicion of impairment before testing a given employee. In view of our conclusion that, on the present record, the toxicological testing contemplated by the regulations is not an undue infringement on the justifiable expectations of privacy of covered employees, the Government's compelling interests outweigh privacy concerns.

* * *

[JUSTICE STEVENS concurred.]

JUSTICE MARSHALL, with whom JUSTICE BRENNAN joins, dissenting.

* * *

* * * The majority's acceptance of dragnet blood and urine testing ensures that the first, and worst, casualty of the war on drugs will be the precious liberties of our citizens. I therefore dissent.

[In Part I, JUSTICE MARSHALL launched a broad gauged attack on the special needs doctrine] as unprincipled and dangerous.

II

The proper way to evaluate the FRA's testing regime is to use the same analytic framework which we have traditionally used to appraise Fourth Amendment claims involving full-scale searches, at least until the recent "special needs" cases. Under that framework, we inquire, serially, whether a search has taken place; * * * whether the search was based on a valid warrant or undertaken pursuant to a recognized exception to the warrant requirement; * * * whether the search was based on probable cause or validly based on lesser suspicion because it was minimally intrusive; * * * and, finally, whether the search was conducted in a reasonable manner. * * * [f]

* * * The majority's * * * conclusion that the warrant requirement may be dispensed with, however, conveniently overlooks the fact that there are three distinct searches at issue. Although the importance of collecting blood and urine samples before drug or alcohol metabolites disappear justifies waiving the warrant requirement for those two searches under the narrow "exigent circumstances" exception, * * * no such exigency prevents railroad officials from securing a warrant before chemically testing the samples they obtain. Blood and urine do not spoil if properly collected and preserved, and there is no reason to

doubt the ability of railroad officials to grasp the relatively simple procedure of obtaining a warrant authorizing, where appropriate, chemical analysis of the extracted fluids. It is therefore wholly unjustified to dispense with the warrant requirement for this final search. * * *

It is the probable-cause requirement, however, that the FRA's testing regime most egregiously violates, a fact which explains the majority's ready acceptance and expansion of the countertextual "special needs" exception. By any measure, the FRA's highly intrusive collection and testing procedures qualify as full-scale personal searches. Under our precedents, a showing of probable cause is therefore clearly required. But even if these searches were viewed as entailing only minimal intrusions on the order, say, of a police stop-and-frisk, the FRA's program would still fail to pass constitutional muster, for we have, without exception, demanded that even minimally intrusive searches of the person

be founded on individualized suspicion. * * * The federal parties concede it does not satisfy this standard. * * * Only if one construes the FRA's collection and testing procedures as akin to the routinized and fleeting regulatory interactions which we have permitted in the absence of individualized suspicion, * * * might these procedures survive constitutional scrutiny. * * *

[The dissent proceeds to flesh out its conclusion to this point by arguing that the intrusions of blood-, urine- and breath-testing are the kinds of major intrusions protected by warrant and probable cause procedures.]

[In Part III the dissent offers several policy reasons for opposing the FRA testing program: the potential misuse of the samples collected for prosecutions; the fact that less intrusive measures can be used to obtain safety information; and its unfounded assumptions about the deterrent effect of the testing program.] [g]

* * *

* * * * * * * * * * *

COMMENTS

[a] This bifurcation of searches could lead the Court to adopt a rule, desired by the dissent, that would allow an exigency search without a warrant for the taking of blood or urine, but a warrant upon probable cause for its testing. The Court does not go in that direction. Thus, splitting the search into a taking and an analyzing has no practical effect in this case.

[b] Compare the methodology here to that of the Court in *California v. Greenwood* [this volume]. In *Greenwood* the Court refused to assume that most Americans would deem a trash search as an invasion of privacy, but does so here. Should the constitutional protection of privacy depend on the Court's assessment of the common sense of the issue?

[c] See *New Jersey v. T.L.O.* [this volume]; *Hudson v. Palmer* [this volume]. As the "special needs" doctrine expands under cases decisions, it appears more and more

the case that procedural protections shrink. It is clear under these cases that while the basic Fourth Amendment right may be the same in theory, in application the protections offered by the search and seizure amendment differ with differing circumstances.

[d] Is this rationale weaker than the rationales for collection? After all, it is the testing that will yield incriminating evidence, if any, against the employee. Compare this with JUSTICE MARSHALL's dissenting opinion.

[e] If all this is true, post accident testing seems hardly worth the effort compared to testing safety-implicated railway employees routinely or randomly *before* starting their shift. Do you think this is reasonable?

[f] JUSTICE MARSHALL challenges the need for two kinds of Fourth Amendment analysis, traditional criminal law enforcement analysis and "special needs" doctrine analysis. He proceeds to show that this case can be analyzed under traditional analysis. He raises the suspicion that a new mode of analysis was created to bring about a certain result that favors the government in "special needs" cases.

[g] In a case decided the same day, *National Treasury Employees Union v. von Raab*, 489 U.S. 656 (1989), the Court upheld warrantless drug testing of all U.S. Customs Officers who (1) are directly involved in drug interdiction or drug law enforcement, (2) are required to carry firearms, or (3) handle classified materials that would be useful to drug smugglers and could be lost through bribery or blackmail of drug-dependent employees.

FLORIDA v. RILEY

488 U.S. 445 109 S.Ct. 693, 102 L.Ed.2d 835 (1989)

JUSTICE WHITE announced the judgment of the Court and delivered an opinion, in which THE CHIEF JUSTICE, JUSTICE SCALIA, and JUSTICE KENNEDY join.

* * * [T]he Florida Supreme Court addressed the following question: "Whether surveillance of the interior of a partially covered greenhouse in a residential backyard from the vantage point of a helicopter located 400 feet above the greenhouse constitutes a 'search' for which a warrant is required under the Fourth Amendment." * * * The court answered the question in the affirmative. * * *

Respondent Riley lived in a mobile home located on five acres of rural property. A greenhouse was located 10 to 20 feet behind the mobile home. Two sides of the greenhouse were enclosed. The other two sides were not enclosed but the contents of the greenhouse were obscured from view from surrounding property by trees, shrubs, and the mobile home. The greenhouse was covered by corrugated roofing panels, some translucent and some opaque. At the time relevant to this case, two of the panels, amounting to approximately 10% of the roof area, were missing. A wire fence surrounded the mobile home and the greenhouse, and the property was posted with a "DO NOT ENTER" sign.

[Following an anonymous tip Sheriff's deputies could not observe growing marijuana from the road so a helicopter was employed. At the height of 400 feet an investigator observed marijuana with his naked eye and a warrant was obtained based on this evidence, leading to Riley's conviction.]

We agree with the State's submission that our decision in *California v. Ciraolo*, 476 U.S. 207 (1986), controls this case. There, acting on a tip, the police inspected the backyard of a particular house while flying in a fixed-wing aircraft at 1,000 feet. With the naked eye the officers saw what they concluded was marijuana growing in the yard. A search warrant was obtained on the strength of this airborne inspection, and marijuana plants were found. * * * We [held] that the inspection was not a search subject to the Fourth Amendment. We recognized that the yard was within the curtilage of the house, that a fence shielded the yard from observation from the street, and that the occupant had a subjective expectation of privacy. We held, however, that such an expectation was not reasonable and not one "that society is prepared to honor." * * * Our reasoning was that the home and its curtilage are not necessarily protected from inspection that involves no physical invasion. "'What a person knowingly exposes to the public, even in his own home or office, is not a subject of Fourth Amendment protection.'" [Quoting from *Katz v. United States* [this volume]] * * * As a general proposition, the police may see what may be seen "from a public vantage point where [they have] a right to be." * * * Thus the police, like the public, would have been free to inspect the backyard garden from the street if their view had been unobstructed. They were likewise free to inspect the yard from the vantage point of an aircraft flying in the navigable airspace as this plane was. "In an age where private and commercial flight in the public airways is routine, it is unreasonable for respondent to expect that his marijuana plants were constitutionally protected from being observed with the naked eye from an altitude of 1,000 feet. The Fourth Amendment simply does not require the police traveling in the public airways at this altitude to obtain a warrant in order to observe what is visible to the naked eye." * * *

We arrive at the same conclusion in the present case. In this case, as in *Ciraolo*, the property surveyed was within the curtilage of respondent's home. Riley no doubt intended and expected that his greenhouse would not be open to public inspection, and the precautions he took protected against ground-level observation. Because the sides and roof of his greenhouse were left partially open, however, what was growing in the greenhouse was subject to viewing from the air. Under the holding in *Ciraolo*, Riley could not reasonably have expected the contents of his greenhouse to be immune from examination by an officer seated in a fixed-wing aircraft flying in navigable airspace at an altitude of 1,000 feet or, as the Florida Supreme Court seemed to recognize, at an altitude of 500 feet, the lower limit of the navigable airspace for such an aircraft. * * * Here, the inspection was made from a helicopter, but as is the case with fixed-wing planes, "private and commercial flight [by helicopter] in the public airways is routine" in this

country, * * * and there is no indication that such flights are unheard of in Pasco County, Florida. [a] Riley could not reasonably have expected that his greenhouse was protected from public or official observation from a helicopter had it been flying within the navigable airspace for fixed-wing aircraft. [b]

Nor on the facts before us, does it make a difference for Fourth Amendment purposes that the helicopter was flying at 400 feet when the officer saw what was growing in the greenhouse through the partially open roof and sides of the structure. We would have a different case if flying at that altitude had been contrary to law or regulation. But helicopters are not bound by the lower limits of the navigable airspace allowed to other aircraft. Any member of the public could legally have been flying over Riley's property in a helicopter at the altitude of 400 feet and could have observed Riley's greenhouse. The police officer did no more. This is not to say that an inspection of the curtilage of a house from an aircraft will always pass muster under the Fourth Amendment simply because the plane is within the navigable airspace specified by law. But it is of obvious importance that the helicopter in this case was *not* violating the law, and there is nothing in the record or before us to suggest that helicopters flying at 400 feet are sufficiently rare in this country to lend substance to respondent's claim that he reasonably anticipated that his greenhouse would not be subject to observation from that altitude. [c] Neither is there any intimation here that the helicopter interfered with respondent's normal use of the greenhouse or of other parts of the curtilage. As far as this record reveals, no intimate details **[d]** connected with the use of the home or curtilage were observed, and there was no undue noise, and no wind, dust, or threat of injury. In these circumstances, there was no violation of the Fourth Amendment.

* * *

JUSTICE O'CONNOR, concurring in the judgment.

I concur in the judgment reversing the Supreme Court of Florida because I agree that police observation of the greenhouse in Riley's curtilage from a helicopter passing at an altitude of 400 feet did not violate an expectation of privacy "that society is prepared to recognize as 'reasonable.'" * * * I write separately, however, to clarify the standard I believe follows from *California v. Ciraolo* [above]. In my view, the plurality's approach rests the scope of Fourth Amendment protection too heavily on compliance with FAA regulations whose purpose is to promote air safety, not to protect "[t]he right of the people to be secure in their persons, houses, papers, and effects, against unreasonable searches and seizures." * * *

* * *

Ciraolo's expectation of privacy was unreasonable not because the airplane was operating where it had a "right to be," but because public air travel at 1,000 feet is a sufficiently routine part of modern life that it is unreasonable for persons on the ground to expect that their curtilage will not be observed from the air at that altitude. Although "helicopters are not bound by the lower limits of the navigable airspace allowed to other aircraft," * * * there

is no reason to assume that compliance with FAA regulations alone determines "'whether the government's intrusion infringes upon the personal and societal values protected by the Fourth Amendment.'" * * * Because the FAA has decided that helicopters can lawfully operate at virtually any altitude so long as they pose no safety hazard, it does not follow that the expectations of privacy "society is prepared to recognize as 'reasonable'" simply mirror the FAA's safety concerns.

Observations of curtilage from helicopters at very low altitudes are not perfectly analogous to ground-level observations from public roads or sidewalks. While in both cases the police may have a legal right to occupy the physical space from which their observations are made, the two situations are not necessarily comparable in terms of whether expectations of privacy from such vantage points should be considered reasonable. Public roads, even those less traveled by, are clearly demarked public thoroughfares. Individuals who seek privacy can take precautions, tailored to the location of the road, to avoid disclosing private activities to those who pass by. They can build a tall fence, for example, and thus ensure private enjoyment of the curtilage without risking public observation from the road or sidewalk. If they do not take such precautions, they cannot reasonably expect privacy from public observation. In contrast, even individuals who have taken effective precautions to ensure against ground-level observations cannot block off all conceivable aerial views of their outdoor patios and yards without entirely giving up their enjoyment of those areas. To require individuals to completely cover and enclose their curtilage is to demand more than the "precautions customarily taken by those seeking privacy." * * * The fact that a helicopter could conceivably observe the curtilage at virtually any altitude or angle, without violating FAA regulations, does not in itself mean that an individual has no reasonable expectation of privacy from such observation.

[JUSTICE O'CONNOR reasoned that Riley had the burden of proving that the overflight interfered with his expectation of privacy and that because overflights at 400 feet were sufficiently common, that expectation was not made out.]

JUSTICE BRENNAN, with whom JUSTICE MARSHALL and JUSTICE STEVENS join, dissenting.

* * *

I

The opinion for a plurality of the Court reads almost as if *Katz v. United States* [above] had never been decided. * * *

* * * Under the plurality's exceedingly grudging Fourth Amendment theory, the expectation of privacy is defeated if a single member of the public could conceivably position herself to see into the area in question without doing anything illegal. It is defeated whatever the difficulty a person would have in so positioning herself, and however infrequently anyone would in fact do so. In taking this view the plurality ignores the very essence of *Katz*. The reason why there is no reasonable expectation of privacy in an area that is exposed to the public is that little diminution in "the

amount of privacy and freedom remaining to citizens" will result from police surveillance of something that any passerby readily sees. To pretend, as the plurality opinion does, that the same is true when the police use a helicopter to peer over high fences is, at best, disingenuous. Notwithstanding the plurality's statistics about the number of helicopters registered in this country, can it seriously be questioned that Riley enjoyed virtually complete privacy in his backyard greenhouse, and that that privacy was invaded solely by police helicopter surveillance? Is the theoretical possibility that any member of the public (with sufficient means) could also have hired a helicopter and looked over Riley's fence of any relevance at all in determining whether Riley suffered a serious loss of privacy and personal security through the police action?

* * *

It is a curious notion that the reach of the Fourth Amendment can be so largely defined by administrative regulations issued for purposes of flight safety. [e] It is more curious still that the plurality relies to such an extent on the legality of the officer's act, when we have consistently refused to equate police violation of the law with infringement of the Fourth Amendment. But the plurality's willingness to end its inquiry when it finds that the officer was in a position he had a right to be in is misguided for an even more fundamental reason. Finding determinative the fact that the officer was where he had a right to be is, at bottom, an attempt to analogize surveillance from a helicopter to surveillance by a police officer standing on a public road and viewing evidence of crime through an open window or a gap in a fence. In such a situation, the occupant of the home may be said to lack any reasonable expectation of privacy in what can be seen from that road—even if, in fact, people rarely pass that way.

The police officer positioned 400 feet above Riley's backyard was not, however, standing on a public road. The vantage point he enjoyed was not one any citizen could readily share. His ability to see over Riley's fence depended on his use of a very expensive and sophisticated piece of machinery to which few ordinary citizens have access. * * *

II

Equally disconcerting is the lack of any meaningful limit to the plurality's holding. It is worth reiterating that the FAA regulations the plurality relies on as establishing that the officer was where he had a right to be set no minimum flight altitude for helicopters. It is difficult, therefore, to see what, if any, helicopter surveillance would run afoul of the plurality's rule that there exists no reasonable expectation of privacy as long as the helicopter is where it has a right to be.   * * * **[f]**

III

Perhaps the most remarkable passage in the plurality opinion is its suggestion that the case might be a different one had any "intimate details connected with the use of the home or curtilage [been] observed." * * * What,

one wonders, is meant by "intimate details"? If the police had observed Riley embracing his wife in the backyard greenhouse, would we then say that his reasonable expectation of privacy had been infringed? Where in the Fourth Amendment or in our cases is there any warrant for imposing a requirement that the activity observed must be "intimate" in order to be protected by the Constitution?

It is difficult to avoid the conclusion that the plurality has allowed its analysis of Riley's expectation of privacy to be colored by its distaste for the activity in which he was engaged. It is indeed easy to forget, especially in view of current concern over drug trafficking, that the scope of the Fourth Amendment's protection does not turn on whether the activity disclosed by a search is illegal or innocuous. But we dismiss this as a "drug case" only at the peril of our own liberties. * * * If the Constitution does not protect Riley's marijuana garden against such surveillance, it is hard to see how it will prohibit the government from aerial spying on the activities of a law-abiding citizen on her fully enclosed outdoor patio. * * *

* * *

[JUSTICE BLACKMUN dissented, suggesting that in this case the burden of proving the reasonableness of the expectation of privacy was on the prosecutor and that the case should be remanded to determine if the burden was met.]

* * * * * * * * * * *

COMMENTS

[a] In a footnote JUSTICE WHITE noted that as of 1980, 1,500 police helicopters were in operation. When are they used in police work? Is there a difference between a police helicopter called out to pursue robbers or auto thieves and to survey suspected marijuana growers? Are police helicopters more in use in ghetto areas? Should this matter in deciding a case like this one?

[b] What is "reasonable" in such cases is the Court's assessment of what most people commonly believe. Do you think that Riley had a reasonable expectation of privacy?

[c] Do you have a sense of being observed by commercial overflights?

[d] See JUSTICE BRENNAN's remarks on this point in his dissent.

[e] In *Skinner v. Railway Labor Executives' Assn.* [this volume] the purpose of the drug testing was safety and not law enforcement, so that prosecution would not necessarily follow testing (although it could). Here, a flight safety regulation becomes the basis for *pure* law enforcement activity.

[f] Under what circumstances does overflight surveillance becomes unreasonable? Is JUSTICE BRENNAN exaggerating in suggesting that there are no limits to police overflights based on the holding in this case?

AUSTIN v. UNITED STATES

___ U.S. ___, 113 S.Ct. 2801, 125 L.Ed.2d 488 (1993)

JUSTICE BLACKMUN delivered the opinion of the Court.

In this case, we are asked to decide whether the Excessive Fines Clause of the Eighth Amendment applies to forfeitures of property under 21 U.S.C. §§881(a)(4) and (a)(7) [hereinafter, "the statute" or "the sections"]. We hold that it does and therefore remand the case for consideration of the question whether the forfeiture at issue here was excessive.

I

* * * [P]etitioner Richard Lyle Austin * * * pleaded guilty to one count of possessing cocaine with intent to distribute and was sentenced by the state court to seven years' imprisonment. * * * [T]he United States filed an *in rem* action in the United States District Court for the District of South Dakota seeking forfeiture of Austin's mobile home and auto body shop. * * * **[a]** [Austin sold two grams of cocaine to one Engebretson. Police found "small amounts of marijuana and cocaine, a .22 caliber revolver, drug paraphernalia, and approximately $4,700 in cash" in Austin's mobile home.]

II

Austin contends that the Eighth Amendment's Excessive Fines Clause applies to *in rem* civil forfeiture proceedings. * * * **[b]** We have had occasion to consider this Clause only once before. In *Browning-Ferris Industries v. Kelco Disposal, Inc.*, 492 U.S. 257 (1989), we held that the Excessive Fines Clause does not limit the award of punitive damages to a private party in a civil suit when the government neither has prosecuted the action nor has any right to receive a share of the damages. * * * The Court concluded that both the Eighth Amendment and §10 of the English Bill of Rights of 1689, from which it derives, were intended to prevent *the government* from abusing its power to punish, * * * and therefore "that the Excessive Fines Clause was intended to limit only those fines directly imposed by, and payable to, the government." * * *

We found it unnecessary to decide in *Browning-Ferris* whether the Excessive Fines Clause applies only to criminal cases. * * * [The United States] suggests that the Eighth Amendment cannot apply to a civil proceeding unless that proceeding is so punitive that it must be considered criminal. * * * We disagree.

Some provisions of the Bill of Rights are expressly limited to criminal cases. The Fifth Amendment's Self-Incrimination Clause, for example, provides: "No person * * * shall be compelled in any criminal case to be a witness against himself." The protections provided by the Sixth Amendment are explicitly confined to "criminal prosecutions." * * * The text of the Eighth Amendment includes no similar limitation. * * *

Nor does the history of the Eighth Amendment require such a limitation.

JUSTICE O'CONNOR noted in *Browning-Ferris*: "Consideration of the Eighth Amendment immediately followed consideration of the Fifth Amendment. After deciding to confine the benefits of the Self-Incrimination Clause of the Fifth Amendment to criminal proceedings, the Framers turned their attention to the Eighth Amendment. There were no proposals to limit that Amendment to criminal proceedings . * * *" * * * Section 10 of the English Bill of Rights of 1689 is not expressly limited to criminal cases either. * * * The absence of any similar restriction in the other two clauses suggests that they were not limited to criminal cases. * * *

The purpose of the Eighth Amendment, putting the Bail Clause to one side, was to limit the government's power to punish. * * * The Cruel and Unusual Punishments Clause is self-evidently concerned with punishment. The Excessive Fines Clause limits the Government's power to extract payments, whether in cash or in kind, "as *punishment* for some offense." * * * "The notion of punishment, as we commonly understand it, cuts across the division between the civil and the criminal law." * * * "It is commonly understood that civil proceedings may advance punitive and remedial goals, and, conversely, that both punitive and remedial goals may be served by criminal penalties." * * * Thus, the question is not, as the United States would have it, whether forfeiture under [the statute] is civil or criminal, but rather whether it is punishment. [c]

In considering this question, we are mindful of the fact that sanctions frequently serve more than one purpose. We need not exclude the possibility that a forfeiture serves remedial purposes to conclude that it is subject to the limitations of the Excessive Fines Clause. We, however, must determine that it can only be explained as serving in part to punish. * * * "[A] civil sanction that cannot fairly be said solely to serve a remedial purpose, but rather can only be explained as also serving either retributive or deterrent purposes, is punishment, as we have come to understand the term." * * * We turn, then, to consider whether, at the time the Eighth Amendment was ratified, forfeiture was understood at least in part as punishment and whether forfeiture under [the statute] should be so understood today.

III

A

Three kinds of forfeiture were established in England at the time the Eighth Amendment was ratified in the United States: deodand, [d] forfeiture upon conviction for a felony or treason, and statutory forfeiture. * * * Each was understood, at least in part, as imposing punishment.

* * *

B

Of England's three kinds of forfeiture, only the third took hold in the United States. * * *

The First Congress passed laws subjecting ships and cargos involved in customs offenses to forfeiture. It does not follow from that fact, however, that the First Congress thought such forfeitures to be beyond the purview of the Eighth Amendment. Indeed, examination of those laws suggests that the First Congress viewed forfeiture as punishment. For example, [an Act of 1789 punished a person who unloaded goods without permit with fine, disability to hold an office for seven years, publication of his name after conviction, and forfeiture of goods.] It is also of some interest that "forfeit" is the word Congress used for fine. * * *

C

Our cases also have recognized that statutory *in rem* forfeiture imposes punishment. * * *

The same understanding of forfeiture as punishment runs through our cases rejecting the "innocence" of the owner as a common-law defense to forfeiture. * * * In these cases, forfeiture has been justified on two theories—that the property itself is "guilty" of the offense, and that the owner may be held accountable for the wrongs of others to whom he entrusts his property. Both theories rest, at bottom, on the notion that the owner has been negligent in allowing his property to be misused and that he is properly punished for that negligence.

The fiction "that the thing is primarily considered the offender," * * * has a venerable history in our case law. * * *

In none of these cases did the Court apply the guilty-property fiction to justify forfeiture when the owner had done all that reasonably could be expected to prevent the unlawful use of his property. * * * The more recent cases have expressly reserved the question whether the fiction could be employed to forfeit the property of a truly innocent owner. * * * If forfeiture had been understood not to punish the owner, there would have been no reason to reserve the case of a truly innocent owner. Indeed, it is

only on the assumption that forfeiture serves in part to punish that the Court's past reservation of that question makes sense.

* * *

In sum, even though this Court has rejected the "innocence" of the owner as a common-law defense to forfeiture, it consistently has recognized that forfeiture serves, at least in part, to punish the owner. * * * More recently, we have noted that forfeiture serves "punitive and deterrent purposes," * * * and "imposes an economic penalty." * * * We conclude, therefore, that forfeiture generally and statutory *in rem* forfeiture in particular historically have been understood, at least in part, as punishment. [e]

IV

We turn next to consider whether forfeitures under [the sections] are properly considered punishment today. We find nothing in these provisions or their legislative history to contradict the historical understanding of forfeiture as punishment. Unlike traditional forfeiture statutes, [the sections] expressly provide an "innocent owner" defense. * * * These exemptions serve to focus the provisions on the culpability of the owner in a way that makes them look more like punishment, not less. * * * The inclusion of innocent-owner defenses in [the statute] reveals a similar congressional intent to punish only those involved in drug trafficking.

Furthermore, Congress has chosen to tie forfeiture directly to the commission of drug offenses. Thus, under [the statute] a conveyance is forfeitable if it is used or intended for use to facilitate the transportation of controlled substances, their raw materials, or the equipment used to manufacture or distribute them. Under [the statute], real property is forfeitable if it is used or intended for use to facilitate the commission of a drug-related crime punishable by more than one year's imprisonment.   * * *

The legislative history of §881 confirms the punitive nature of these provisions. When it added subsection (a)(7) to §881 in 1984, Congress recognized "that the traditional criminal sanctions of fine and imprisonment are inadequate to deter or punish the enormously profitable trade in dangerous drugs." * * * It characterized the forfeiture of real property as "a powerful deterrent." * * *

The Government argues that [the sections] are not punitive but, rather, should be considered remedial in two respects. First, they remove the "instruments" of the drug trade "thereby protecting the community from the threat of continued drug dealing." * * * Second, the forfeited assets serve to compensate the Government for the expense of law enforcement activity and for its expenditure on societal problems such as urban blight, drug addiction, and other health concerns resulting from the drug trade. * * *

In our view, neither argument withstands scrutiny. * * *

* * *

Fundamentally, even assuming that [the sections] serve some remedial purpose, the Government's argument must fail.   "[A] civil sanction that cannot fairly be said *solely* to serve a remedial purpose, but rather can only be explained as also serving either retributive or deterrent purposes, is punishment, as we have come to understand the term." * * *   In light of the historical understanding of forfeiture as punishment, the clear focus of [the statute] on the culpability of the owner, and the evidence that Congress understood those provisions as serving to deter and to punish, we cannot conclude that forfeiture under [the statute] serves solely a remedial purpose. We therefore conclude that forfeiture under these provisions constitutes "payment to a sovereign as punishment for some offense," * * * and, as such, is subject to the limitations of the Eighth Amendment's Excessive Fines Clause. **[f]**
* * *

[JUSTICE SCALIA, concurred in part and in the judgment.]

[JUSTICE KENNEDY, joined by THE CHIEF JUSTICE and JUSTICE THOMAS, concurred in part and concurred in the judgment.] **[g]**

* * * * * * * * * * *

COMMENTS

[a] An *in rem* action is a civil suit; *in rem* is a "technical term used to designate proceedings or actions *against the thing*, in contradistinction to personal actions, which are said to be *in personam*." [*Black's Law Dictionary*, 5th Edition, p. 713]

[b] The Eighth Amendment reads, "Excessive bail shall not be required, nor excessive fines imposed, nor cruel and unusual punishments inflicted."

[c] The way in which the issue is classified would determine the outcome. The Court rejected the narrower framework (criminal versus civil) for the broader (punitive versus purely remedial damages, or punishment vs. repayment.)

[d] A deodand was a thing that caused injury; at first deodands were forfeit to the king under superstitious and religious theories; later writers rationalized deodand as a penalty for negligence.

[e] By embedding the statute in the Anglo-American legal history of forfeiture, the Court provides a firmer foundation for its ruling regarding the interpretation of the modern forfeiture statute.

[f] The ruling is of great practical importance; it makes it difficult for police to arrest a small or medium level drug dealer and reap large monetary benefits through the forfeiture of houses or cars.

[g] In the 1992 Term the Supreme Court handled other forfeiture cases. In addition to *Austin*, the Court held in *Alexander v. United States*, ___ U.S. ___, 113 S.Ct. 2766 (1993) that the forfeiture of an adult entertainment business for a violation of the Racketeer Influenced and Corrupt Organizations Act (RICO) did not violate the First Amendment, but that the forfeiture was a fine and so came under the Eighth Amendment. In *United States v. 92 Buena Vista Avenue*, ___ U.S. ___, 113 S.Ct. 1126 (1993) the Court held that under federal statutes, it is a defense to the forfeiture of a home that the purchaser did not know that the funds were obtained by illegal drug sales. And *Republic National Bank of Miami v. United States*, ___ U.S. ___ , 113 S.Ct. 554 (1992) held that the transfer of contested drug asset forfeiture funds that had been seized into the United States Treasury did not terminate the jurisdiction of a claimant's appeal.

UNITED STATES v. GOOD REAL PROPERTY

___ U.S. ___, 114 S.Ct. 492, 126 L.Ed.2d 490 (1993)

JUSTICE KENNEDY delivered the opinion of the Court.

The principal question presented is whether, in the absence of exigent circumstances, the Due Process Clause of the Fifth Amendment prohibits the Government in a civil forfeiture case from seizing real property without first affording the owner notice and an opportunity to be heard. We hold that it does.

* * *

I

[Hawaii police officers lawfully seized about 89 pounds of marijuana and other contraband from the home of claimant James Daniel Good. Good pleaded guilty to a state drug crime and was sentenced to one year in jail, five years' probation, and a $1,000 fine. He also forfeited to the State $3,187 in cash found on the premises.]

[Four and one-half years after the drugs were found, the United States filed an *in rem* action in federal court seeking to forfeit Good's house and its four-acre parcel, under 21 U.S.C. §881(a)(7), on the ground that the property had been used to commit or facilitate the commission of a federal drug offense. [a] In an ex parte proceeding, a United States Magistrate Judge found that the Government established probable cause to believe Good's property was subject to forfeiture under the statute and issued a warrant of arrest in rem authorizing its seizure. The warrant was based on an affidavit recounting Good's conviction

and the evidence discovered during the search of his home. The Government seized the property without prior notice to Good or an adversary hearing. At the time of the seizure, Good was renting his home to tenants for $900 per month. The Government permitted the tenants to remain on the premises subject to an occupancy agreement, but directed the payment of future rents to the United States Marshal.

[Good's due process claim was dismissed by the federal District Court on the Government's motion for summary judgment; the property was ordered forfeit. The Court of Appeals unanimously held that the seizure violated the Due Process Clause of the Fifth Amendment.]

II

The Due Process Clause of the Fifth Amendment guarantees that "no person shall . . . be deprived of life, liberty, or property, without due process of law." Our precedents establish the general rule that individuals must receive notice and an opportunity to be heard before the Government deprives them of property. * * *

The Government does not, and could not, dispute that the seizure of Good's home and four-acre parcel deprived him of property interests protected by the Due Process Clause. By the Government's own submission, the seizure gave it the right to charge rent, to condition occupancy, and even to evict the occupants. Instead, the Government argues that it afforded

Good all the process the Constitution requires. The Government makes two separate points in this regard. First, it contends that compliance with the Fourth Amendment suffices when the Government seizes property for purposes of forfeiture. In the alternative, it argues that the seizure of real property under the drug forfeiture laws justifies an exception to the usual due process requirement of preseizure notice and hearing. We turn to these issues. [b]

A

The Government argues that because civil forfeiture serves a "law enforcement purpos[e]," * * * the Government need comply only with the Fourth Amendment when seizing forfeitable property. We disagree. The Fourth Amendment does place restrictions on seizures conducted for purposes of civil forfeiture, * * * but it does not follow that the Fourth Amendment is the sole constitutional provision in question when the Government seizes property subject to forfeiture.

We have rejected the view that the applicability of one constitutional amendment pre-empts the guarantees of another. * * * Here, as in *Soldal [v. Cook County]* [this volume] the seizure of property implicates two "'explicit textual source[s] of constitutional protection,'" the Fourth Amendment and the Fifth. * * * The proper question is not which Amendment controls but whether either Amendment is violated.

[Fourth Amendment cases such as *Gerstein v. Pugh*, [this volume] and *Graham v. Connor*, 490 U.S. 386 (1989), are not pertinent because they]

concerned not the seizure of property but the arrest or detention of criminal suspects, subjects we have considered to be governed by the provisions of the Fourth Amendment without reference to other constitutional guarantees. In addition, also unlike the seizure presented by this case, the arrest or detention of a suspect occurs as part of the regular criminal process, where other safeguards ordinarily ensure compliance with due process. * * *
* * *

It is true, of course, that the Fourth Amendment applies to searches and seizures in the civil context and may serve to resolve the legality of these governmental actions without reference to other constitutional provisions. See *Camara v. Municipal Court* [this volume]; * * * *Skinner v. Railway Labor Executives' Assn.* [this volume]. * * * But the purpose and effect of the Government's action in the present case go beyond the traditional meaning of search or seizure. Here the Government seized property not to preserve evidence of wrongdoing, but to assert ownership and control over the property itself. Our cases establish that government action of this consequence must comply with the Due Process Clauses of the Fifth and Fourteenth Amendments.
* * *

B

Whether *ex parte* seizures of forfeitable property satisfy the Due Process Clause is a question we last confronted in *Calero-Toledo v. Pearson Yacht Leasing Co.*, 416 U.S. 663 (1974), which held that the Government could seize a yacht subject to civil forfeiture without affording prior notice or hearing. Central to our analysis in *Calero-Toledo* was the fact that a yacht was the "sort [of property] that could be removed to another jurisdiction, destroyed, or concealed, if advance warning of confiscation were given." * * * The ease with which an owner could frustrate the Government's interests in the forfeitable property created a "'special need for very prompt action'" that justified the postponement of notice and hearing until after the seizure. * * *

We had no occasion in *Calero-Toledo* to decide whether the same considerations apply to the forfeiture of real property, which, by its very nature, can be neither moved nor concealed. * * *

The right to prior notice and a hearing is central to the Constitution's command of due process. "The purpose of this requirement is not only to ensure abstract fair play to the individual. Its purpose, more particularly, is to protect his use and possession of property from arbitrary encroachment—to minimize substantively unfair or mistaken deprivations of property. * * *" *Fuentes v. Shevin*, 407 U.S., at 80–81.

We tolerate some exceptions to the general rule requiring predeprivation notice and hearing, but only in "'extraordinary situations where some valid governmental interest is at stake that justifies postponing the hearing until after the event.'" * * * Whether the seizure of real property for purposes of civil forfeiture justifies such an exception requires an examination of the competing interests at stake, along with the promptness and adequacy of later proceedings. The three-part inquiry set forth in *Mathews v. Eldridge*, 424 U.S.

319 (1976), provides guidance in this regard. The *Mathews* analysis requires us to consider the private interest affected by the official action; the risk of an erroneous deprivation of that interest through the procedures used, as well as the probable value of additional safeguards; and the Government's interest, including the administrative burden that additional procedural requirements would impose. * * *

Good's right to maintain control over his home, and to be free from governmental interference, is a private interest of historic and continuing importance. * * * The seizure deprived Good of valuable rights of ownership, including the right of sale, the right of occupancy, the right to unrestricted use and enjoyment, and the right to receive rents. All that the seizure left him, by the Government's own submission, was the right to bring a claim for the return of title at some unscheduled future hearing.

* * *

The seizure of a home produces a far greater deprivation than the loss of furniture, or even attachment. It gives the Government not only the right to prohibit sale, but also the right to evict occupants, to modify the property, to condition occupancy, to receive rents, and to supersede the owner in all rights pertaining to the use, possession, and enjoyment of the property.

[The fact that Good was renting his house does] not render the loss insignificant or unworthy of due process protection. The rent represents a significant portion of the exploitable economic value of Good's home. It cannot be classified as *de minimis* for purposes of procedural due process. In sum, the private interests at stake in the seizure of real property weigh heavily in the *Mathews* balance.

The practice of *ex parte* seizure, moreover, creates an unacceptable risk of error. Although Congress designed the drug forfeiture statute to be a powerful instrument in enforcement of the drug laws, it did not intend to deprive innocent owners of their property. The affirmative defense of innocent ownership is allowed by statute. * * *

The *ex parte* preseizure proceeding affords little or no protection to the innocent owner. In issuing a warrant of seizure, the magistrate judge need determine only that there is probable cause to believe that the real property was "used, or intended to be used, in any manner or part, to commit, or to facilitate the commission of" a felony narcotics offense. * * * The Government is not required to offer any evidence on the question of innocent ownership or other potential defenses a claimant might have. * * * Nor would that inquiry, in the *ex parte* stage, suffice to protect the innocent owner's interests. "[F]airness can rarely be obtained by secret, one-sided determination of facts decisive of rights. * * * No better instrument has been devised for arriving at truth than to give a person in jeopardy of serious loss notice of the case against him and opportunity to meet it." * * *

The purpose of an adversary hearing is to ensure the requisite neutrality that must inform all governmental decisionmaking. That protection is of particular importance here, where the Government has a direct pecuniary interest in the outcome of the proceeding. * * * Moreover, the availability of a postseizure hearing may be no recompense for losses caused by erroneous seizure. Given the congested civil dockets in federal courts, a claimant may not receive an adversary hearing until many months after the seizure. And even if the ultimate judicial decision is that the claimant was an innocent owner, or that the Government lacked probable cause, this determination, coming months after the seizure, "would not cure the temporary deprivation that an earlier hearing might have prevented." * * *

This brings us to the third consideration under *Mathews*, "the Government's interest, including the function involved and the fiscal and administrative burdens that the additional or substitute procedural requirement would entail." * * * The governmental interest we consider here is not some general interest in forfeiting property but the specific interest in seizing real property before the forfeiture hearing. The question in the civil forfeiture context is whether *ex parte* seizure is justified by a pressing need for prompt action. * * * We find no pressing need here.

This is apparent by comparison to *Calero-Toledo*, where the Government's interest in immediate seizure of a yacht subject to civil forfeiture justified. dispensing with the usual requirement of prior notice and hearing. Two essential considerations informed our ruling in that case: first, immediate seizure was necessary to establish the court's jurisdiction over the property, * * * and second, the yacht might have disappeared had the Government given advance warning of the forfeiture action. * * * Neither of these factors is present when the target of forfeiture is real property.

Because real property cannot

abscond, the court's jurisdiction can be preserved without prior seizure. It is true that seizure of the res has long been considered a prerequisite to the initiation of *in rem* forfeiture proceedings. * * * This rule had its origins in the Court's early admiralty cases, which involved the forfeiture of vessels and other movable personal property. * * * But when the res is real property, rather than personal goods, the appropriate judicial forum may be determined without actual seizure.

* * * In the case of real property, the res may be brought within the reach of the court simply by posting notice on the property and leaving a copy of the process with the occupant. In fact, the rules which govern forfeiture proceedings under §881 already permit process to be executed on real property without physical seizure. * * *

Nor is the *ex parte* seizure of real property necessary to accomplish the statutory purpose of §881(a)(7). The Government's legitimate interests at the inception of forfeiture proceedings are to ensure that the property not be sold, destroyed, or used for further illegal activity prior to the forfeiture judgment. These legitimate interests can be secured without seizing the subject property [by filing a notice of *lis pendens* under state law [c], by concluding occupancy agreements with occupants, and by executing arrest and search warrants in the criminal action.]
* * *

In the usual case, the Government thus has various means, short of seizure, to protect its legitimate interests in forfeitable real property. There is no reason to take the additional step of asserting control over the property without first affording notice and an adversary hearing.

Requiring the Government to postpone seizure until after an adversary hearing creates no significant administrative burden. A claimant is already entitled to an adversary hearing before a final judgment of forfeiture. No extra hearing would be required in the typical case, since the Government can wait until after the forfeiture judgment to seize the property. From an administrative standpoint it makes little difference whether that hearing is held before or after the seizure. And any harm that results from delay is minimal in comparison to the injury occasioned by erroneous seizure.

C

[In this section, the Court notes that nineteenth century cases authorizing immediate seizure either involved exigent circumstances like seizing contaminated food, or involved tax seizures. The latter rationale has become obsolete with the establishment of the income tax under the Sixteenth Amendment since the federal government's "existence" is no longer placed in jeopardy by the failure to collect immediately on excise taxes and direct confiscations. Under current tax law, the IRS cannot seize a deficient taxpayer's property without affording notice and a hearing, barring exigent circumstances.]

Just as the urgencies that justified summary seizure of property in the 19th century had dissipated, * * * neither is there a plausible claim of urgency today to justify the summary seizure of real property under §881(a)(7). Although the Government relies to some extent on forfeitures as a means of defraying law enforcement expenses, it does not, and we think could not, justify the prehearing seizure of forfeitable real property as necessary for the protection of its revenues.

D

The constitutional limitations we enforce in this case apply to real property in general, not simply to residences. That said, the case before us well illustrates an essential principle: Individual freedom finds tangible expression in property rights. At stake in this and many other forfeiture cases are the security and privacy of the home and those who take shelter within it.

Finally, the suggestion that this one petitioner must lose because his conviction was known at the time of seizure, and because he raises an as applied challenge to the statute, founders on a bedrock proposition: fair procedures are not confined to the innocent. The question before us is the legality of the seizure, not the strength of the Government's case.

In sum, based upon the importance of the private interests at risk and the absence of countervailing Government needs, we hold that the seizure of real property under §881(a)(7) is not one of those extraordinary instances that justify the postponement of notice and hearing. Unless exigent circumstances are present, the Due Process Clause requires the Government to afford notice and a meaningful opportunity to be heard before seizing real property subject to civil forfeiture. **[d]**

* * *

[In Part III Justice KENNEDY ruled that the government filed its action within the statute of limitations and that failure to meet internal timing rules did not require dismissal of the forfeiture action.]

IV

The case is remanded for further proceedings consistent with this opinion.

It is so ordered.

[CHIEF JUSTICE REHNQUIST concurred with the Court's internal timing holding but, joined by JUSTICE SCALIA and JUSTICE O'CONNOR, dissented from the Court's due process holding. He argued that the Fourth Amendment authorized seizure before hearing, that *Mathews* and *Fuentes* do not apply to criminal forfeiture, and would rely on the nineteenth century seizure cases.]

[JUSTICE O'CONNOR concurred and dissented separately, stating that Good received adequate due process and that any perceived deficiencies could be corrected by Congress.]

[JUSTICE THOMAS concurred and dissented; he joined the majority's statement that "individual freedom finds tangible expression in property rights" and also expressed concern over the breadth of the civil forfeiture laws, but found no due process violation.]

* * * * * * * * * * *

COMMENTS

[a] Apart from the legal issues presented, cases like this raise the serious policy question of whether the goal of the government is to use forfeiture to eliminate drug "king pins" under the law or to use forfeiture as a method to raise revenue.

[b] The due process clause of the Fourteenth Amendment will apply to state drug forfeiture proceedings as the Fifth Amendment due process clause applies to federal proceedings.   Therefore, this case will have a major impact on how drug asset forfeitures are conducted throughout the country.

[c] A notice of lis pendens is a notice filed on public records for the purpose of warning all persons that the title to certain property is in litigation. (*Black's Law Dictionary*, Fifth Edition, p. 840).

[d] In a footnote the Court refused to speculate as the kind of hearing that is required by due process.   The elements of due process can vary depending upon the stakes in a case.   A criminal trial, involving the potential loss of life or liberty, is the "full" due process model, of a jury, appointed counsel for indigents and a high degree of formality.   As the stakes for a defendant or claimant decrease, a fair hearing may dispense with jury, counsel, and various formalities.   In prison discipline hearings even the opportunity to be confronted with witnesses and to cross-examine are limited.   The fundamental or essential elements of due process is that before a person is subject to loss, he or she must be given notice that the government is proceeding against his or her interests and must be given a fair hearing in which to challenge the "taking."

RAKAS v. ILLINOIS

439 U.S. 128, 99 S.Ct. 421, 58 L.Ed.2d 387 (1978)

MR. JUSTICE REHNQUIST delivered the opinion of the Court.

* * *

I

[Patrol officers stopped a car fitting the description of a robbery getaway car. Two females, including the car's owner were in the front seats, and Rakas and another man (the petitioners) were passengers. Police found a sawed-off rifle under the front passenger seat and a box of rifle shells in the locked glove compartment, and arrested the petitioners. Petitioners moved to have the rifle and shells excluded from evidence on Fourth Amendment grounds. The petitioners did not] assert that they owned the rifle or the shells seized. The prosecutor challenged petitioners' standing to object to the lawfulness of the search of the car because neither the car, the shells nor the rifle belonged to them. [The Illinois courts found that the petitioners could not challenge the constitutionality of the search and seizure because they did not have standing.]

II

Petitioners first urge us to relax or broaden the rule of standing enunciated in *Jones v. United States*, 362 U.S. 257 (1960), so that any criminal defendant at whom a search was "directed" would have standing to contest the legality of that search and object to the admission at trial of evidence obtained as a result of the search. Alternatively, petitioners argue that they have standing to object to the search under *Jones* because they were "legitimately on [the] premises" at the time of the search.

The concept of standing discussed in *Jones* focuses on whether the person seeking to challenge the legality of a search as a basis for suppressing evidence was himself the "victim" of the search or seizure. Adoption of the so-called "target" theory advanced by petitioners would in effect permit a defendant to assert that a violation of the Fourth Amendment rights of a third party entitled him to have evidence suppressed at his trial. If we reject petitioners' request for a broadened rule of standing such as this, and reaffirm the holding of *Jones* and other cases that Fourth Amendment rights are personal rights that may not be asserted vicariously, we will have occasion to re-examine the "standing" terminology emphasized in *Jones*. For we are not at all sure that the determination of a motion to suppress is materially aided by labeling the inquiry identified in *Jones* as one of standing, rather than simply recognizing it as one involving the substantive question of whether or not the proponent of the motion to suppress has had his own Fourth Amendment rights infringed by the search and seizure which he seeks to challenge. [a] We shall therefore consider in turn petitioners' target theory, the necessity for continued adherence to the notion of standing discussed in *Jones* as a concept that is theoretically distinct from the merits of a defendant's Fourth Amendment claim, and, finally, the proper disposition of petitioners' ultimate claim in this case. [b]

A

We decline to extend the rule of standing in Fourth Amendment cases in the manner suggested by petitioners. As we stated in *Alderman v. United States*, 394 U.S. 165 (1969), "Fourth Amendment rights are personal rights which, like some other constitutional rights, may not be vicariously asserted." * * * A person who is aggrieved by an illegal search and seizure only through the introduction of damaging evidence secured by a search of a third person's premises or property has not had any of his Fourth Amendment rights infringed. * * * And since the exclusionary rule is an attempt to effectuate the guarantees of the Fourth Amendment, * * * it is proper to permit only defendants whose Fourth Amendment rights have been violated to benefit from the rule's protections. * * * There is no reason to think that a party whose rights have been infringed will not, if evidence is used against him, have ample motivation to move to suppress it. * * * Even if such a person is not a defendant in the action, he may be able to recover damages for the violation of his Fourth Amendment rights, * * * or seek redress under state law for invasion of privacy or trespass. [c]

In support of their target theory, petitioners rely on the following quotation from *Jones*:

"In order to qualify as a 'person aggrieved by an unlawful search and seizure' one must have been a victim of a search or seizure, *one against whom the search was directed*, as distinguished from one who claims prejudice only through the use of evidence gathered as a consequence of a search or seizure directed at someone else." * * * (emphasis added). * * *

The above-quoted statement from *Jones* suggests that the italicized language was meant merely as a parenthetical equivalent of the previous phrase "a victim of a search or seizure." To the extent that the language might be read more broadly, it is dictum which was impliedly repudiated in *Alderman v. United States*, and which we now expressly reject. [d] In *Jones*, the Court set forth two alternative holdings: It established a rule of "automatic" standing to contest an allegedly illegal search where the same possession needed to establish standing is an essential element of the offense charged; and second, it stated that "anyone legitimately on premises where a search occurs may challenge its legality by way of a motion to suppress." * * * Had the Court intended to adopt the target theory now put forth by petitioners, neither of the above two holdings would have been necessary since Jones was the "target" of the police search in that case. * * * * * *

Conferring standing to raise vicarious Fourth Amendment claims would necessarily mean a more widespread invocation of the exclusionary rule during criminal trials. The Court's opinion in *Alderman* counseled against such an extension of the exclusionary rule:

> "The deterrent values of preventing the incrimination of those whose rights the police have violated have been considered sufficient to justify the suppression of probative evidence even though the case against the defendant is weakened or destroyed. We adhere to that judgment. But we are not convinced that the additional benefits of extending the exclusionary rule to other defendants would justify further encroachment upon the public interest in prosecuting those accused of crime and having them acquitted or convicted on the basis of all the evidence which exposes the truth." * * *

Each time the exclusionary rule is applied it exacts a substantial social cost for the vindication of Fourth Amendment rights. Relevant and reliable evidence is kept from the trier of fact and the search for truth at trial is deflected. * * * Since our cases generally have held that one whose Fourth Amendment rights are violated may successfully suppress evidence obtained in the course of an illegal search and seizure, misgivings as to the benefit of enlarging the class of persons who may invoke that rule are properly considered when deciding whether to expand standing to assert Fourth Amendment violations. **[e]**

B

* * * [H]aving rejected petitioners' target theory and reaffirmed the principle that the "rights assured by the Fourth Amendment are personal rights, [which] . . . may be enforced by exclusion of evidence only at the instance of one whose own protection was infringed by the search and seizure," * * * the question necessarily arises whether it serves any useful analytical purpose to consider this principle a matter of standing, distinct from the merits of a defendant's Fourth Amendment claim. **[f]** We can think of no decided cases of this Court that would have come out differently had we concluded, as we do now, that the type of standing requirement discussed in *Jones* and reaffirmed today is more properly subsumed under substantive Fourth Amendment doctrine. Rigorous application of the principle that the rights secured by this Amendment are personal, in place of a notion of "standing," will produce no additional situations in which evidence must be excluded. The inquiry under either approach is the same. But we think the better analysis forth-rightly focuses on the extent of a particular defendant's rights under the Fourth Amendment, rather than on any theoretically separate, but invariably intertwined concept of standing. * * * * * *

Analyzed in these terms, the question is whether the challenged search and seizure violated the Fourth Amendment rights of a criminal defendant who seeks to exclude the evidence obtained during it. That inquiry in turn requires a determination of whether the disputed search and seizure has infringed an interest of the defendant which the Fourth Amendment was designed to protect. We are under no illusion that by dispensing with the rubric of standing used in

Jones we have rendered any simpler the determination of whether the proponent of a motion to suppress is entitled to contest the legality of a search and seizure.   But by frankly recognizing that this aspect of the analysis belongs more properly under the heading of substantive Fourth Amendment doctrine than under the heading of standing, we think the decision of this issue will rest on sounder logical footing.

C

Here petitioners, who were passengers occupying a car which they neither owned nor leased, seek to analogize their position to that of the defendant in *Jones v. United States*.   In *Jones*, petitioner was present at the time of the search of an apartment which was owned by a friend.   The friend had given Jones permission to use the apartment and a key to it, with which Jones had admitted himself on the day of the search.   He had a suit and shirt at the apartment and had slept there "maybe a night," but his home was elsewhere.   At the time of the search, Jones was the only occupant of the apartment because the lessee was away for a period of several days. * * * Under these circumstances, this Court stated that while one wrongfully on the premises could not move to suppress evidence obtained as a result of searching them, "anyone legitimately on premises where a search occurs may challenge its legality." * * * Petitioners argue that their occupancy of the automobile in question was comparable to that of Jones in the apartment and that they therefore have standing to contest the legality of the search—or as we have rephrased the inquiry, that

they, like Jones, had their Fourth Amendment rights violated by the search. [g]

We do not question the conclusion in *Jones* that the defendant in that case suffered a violation of his personal Fourth Amendment rights if the search in question was unlawful.   Nonetheless, we believe that the phrase "legitimately on premises" coined in *Jones* creates too broad a gauge for measurement of Fourth Amendment rights.   For example, applied literally, this statement would permit a casual visitor who has never seen, or been permitted to visit, the basement of another's house to object to a search of the basement if the visitor happened to be in the kitchen of the house at the time of the search.   Likewise, a casual visitor who walks into a house one minute before a search of the house commences and leaves one minute after the search ends would be able to contest the legality of the search.   The first visitor would have absolutely no interest or legitimate expectation of privacy in the basement, the second would have none in the house, and it advances no purpose served by the Fourth Amendment to permit either of them to object to the lawfulness of the search.

We think that *Jones* on its facts merely stands for the unremarkable proposition that a person can have a legally sufficient interest in a place other than his own home so that the Fourth Amendment protects him from unreasonable governmental intrusion into that place. * * *   In defining the scope of that interest, we adhere to the view expressed in *Jones* and echoed in later cases that arcane distinctions developed in property and tort law between guests, licensees, invitees, and the like, ought not to control. * * *

But the *Jones* statement that a person need only be "legitimately on premises" in order to challenge the validity of the search of a dwelling place cannot be taken in its full sweep beyond the facts of that case.

Katz v. United States [this volume], provides guidance in defining the scope of the interest protected by the Fourth Amendment. **[h]** In the course of repudiating the doctrine * * * that if police officers had not been guilty of a common-law trespass they were not prohibited by the Fourth Amendment from eavesdropping, the Court in *Katz* held that capacity to claim the protection of the Fourth Amendment depends not upon a property right in the invaded place but upon whether the person who claims the protection of the Amendment has a legitimate expectation of privacy in the invaded place. * * * Viewed in this manner, the holding in *Jones* can best be explained by the fact that Jones had a legitimate expectation of privacy in the premises he was using and therefore could claim the protection of the Fourth Amendment with respect to a governmental invasion of those premises, even though his "interest" in those premises might not have been a recognized property interest at common law. * * *

* * *

* * * [The factor of being "legitimately on premises" is one factor among several that a court may take into account to determine if the defendant had a reasonable expectation of privacy, but it is not a doctrine that controls the outcome of a case.]

D

Judged by the foregoing analysis,

petitioners' claims must fail. They asserted neither a property nor a possessory interest in the automobile, nor an interest in the property seized.
* * *

* * *

[JUSTICE POWELL, joined by the Chief Justice, concurred.]

MR. JUSTICE WHITE, with whom MR. JUSTICE BRENNAN, MR. JUSTICE MARSHALL, and MR. JUSTICE STEVENS join, dissenting.

The Court today holds that the Fourth Amendment protects property, not people, and specifically that a legitimate occupant of an automobile may not invoke the exclusionary rule and challenge a search of that vehicle unless he happens to own or have a possessory interest in it. * * * Insofar as passengers are concerned, the Court's opinion today declares an "open season" on automobiles. However unlawful stopping and searching a car may be, absent a possessory or ownership interest, no "mere" passenger may object, regardless of his relationship to the owner. Because the majority's conclusion has no support in the Court's controlling decisions, in the logic of the Fourth Amendment, or in common sense, I must respectfully dissent. If the Court is troubled by the practical impact of the exclusionary rule, it should face the issue of that rule's continued validity squarely instead of distorting other doctrines in an attempt to reach what are perceived as the correct results in specific cases.
* * * **[i]**

* * *

III

* * *

In sum, one consistent theme in our decisions under the Fourth Amendment has been, until now, that "the Amendment does not shield only those who have title to the searched premises." * * * Though there comes a point when use of an area is shared with so many that one simply cannot reasonably expect seclusion, * * * short of that limit a person legitimately on private premises knows the others allowed there and, though his privacy is not absolute, is entitled to expect that he is sharing it only with those persons and that governmental officials will intrude only with consent or by complying with the Fourth Amendment. * * *

* * * [T]he Court asserts that it is not limiting the Fourth Amendment bar against unreasonable searches to the protection of property rights, but in reality it is doing exactly that. Petitioners were in a private place with the permission of the owner, but the Court states that that is not sufficient to establish entitlement to a legitimate expectation of privacy. But if that is not sufficient, what would be? We are not told, and it is hard to imagine anything short of a property interest that would satisfy the majority. Insofar as the Court's rationale is concerned, no passenger in an automobile, without an ownership or possessory interest and regardless of his relationship to the owner, may claim Fourth Amendment protection against illegal stops and searches of the automobile in which he is rightfully present. The Court approves the result in *Jones*, but it fails to give any explanation why the facts in *Jones* differ, in a fashion material to the Fourth Amendment, from the facts here. More importantly, how is the Court able to avoid answering the question why presence in a private place with the owner's permission is insufficient? * * * [j]

* * *

As a control on governmental power, the Fourth Amendment assures that some expectations of privacy are justified and will be protected from official intrusion. That should be true in this instance, for if protected zones of privacy can only be purchased or obtained by possession of property, then much of our daily lives will be unshielded from unreasonable governmental prying, and the reach of the Fourth Amendment will have been narrowed to protect chiefly those with possessory interests in real or personal property. I had thought that *Katz* firmly established that the Fourth Amendment was intended as more than simply a trespass law applicable to the government. *Katz* had no possessory interest in the public telephone booth, at least no more than petitioners had in their friend's car; *Katz* was simply legitimately present. And the decision in *Katz* was based not on property rights, but on the theory that it was essential to securing "conditions favorable to the pursuit of happiness" that the expectation of privacy in question be recognized.

* * *

IV

* * * The Court's holding is contrary not only to our past decisions and the logic of the Fourth Amendment but also to the everyday expectations of privacy that we all share. * * * If the nonowner were the spouse or child of the owner, would the Court recognize a sufficient interest? If so,

would distant relatives somehow have more of an expectation of privacy than close friends? What if the nonowner were driving with the owner's permission? Would nonowning drivers have more of an expectation of privacy than mere passengers? What about a passenger in a taxicab? *Katz* expressly recognized protection for such passengers. Why should Fourth Amendment rights be present when one pays a cabdriver for a ride but be absent when one is given a ride by a friend? **[k]**

The distinctions the Court would draw are based on relationships between private parties, but the Fourth Amendment is concerned with the relationship of one of those parties to the government. Divorced as it is from the purpose of the Fourth Amendment, the Court's essentially property-based rationale can satisfactorily answer none of the questions posed above. That is reason enough to reject it. The *Jones* rule is relatively easily applied by police and courts; the rule announced today will not provide law enforcement officials with a bright line between the protected and the unprotected. Only rarely will police know whether one private party has or has not been granted a sufficient possessory or other interest by another private party. * * *

More importantly, the ruling today undercuts the force of the exclusionary rule in the one area in which its use is most certainly justified—the deterrence of bad-faith violations of the Fourth Amendment. * * * This decision invites police to engage in patently unreasonable searches every time an automobile contains more than one occupant. Should something be found, only the owner of the vehicle, or of the item, will have standing to seek suppression, and the evidence will presumably be usable against the other occupants. **[l]** The danger of such bad faith is especially high in cases such as this one where the officers are only after the passengers and can usually infer accurately that the driver is the owner. * * *

* * * * * * * * * * *

COMMENTS

[a] Although standing is often viewed as a procedural question, JUSTICE REHNQUIST suggests here that it is really a substantive matter.

[b] In a footnote, JUSTICE REHNQUIST reiterated the fundamental rule of standing, that a party seeking relief "must allege such a personal stake or interest in the outcome of the controversy as to assure the concrete adverseness which Art. III requires." The standing rule in constitutional law is based on the fact that Article III of the Constitution limits the jurisdiction of federal courts to "cases and controversies," thus requiring that a party to a suit must have a *real personal and legal interest* in the case. In some states, persons with very remote connections to a case can bring a suit, as in so-called "taxpayer suits."

[c] JUSTICE REHNQUIST reiterates the familiar rule that a person whose

Fourth Amendment rights have been violated but who is not a criminal suspect may sue the government in civil (tort) law. This is a clever point, for it does not leave the reader with the unpleasant thought that the majority's result will leave a person whose rights have been violated without a legal remedy. This point blunts some of the force of JUSTICE WHITE's powerful dissent.

[d] This is an example of the Court declaring authoritatively how a statement in a prior case is to be interpreted. It shows that the case law system of precedent is a dynamic process of reinterpretation of the meaning of what was written in earlier cases. JUSTICE REHNQUIST and the majority of the Court are concerned here with cutting off an attempt to expand the meaning of the statement in *Jones*, which gave rise to the target theory.

[e] JUSTICE REHNQUIST is also forthcoming about the underlying policy preference of the majority: a wariness, if not outright hostility, to the exclusionary rule because of the costs that the rule extracts in deterring unlawful searches by police officers.

[f] If the outcome of cases do not differ, why does the Court bother clarifying whether the analysis is framed in terms of "standing" or of "substantive Fourth Amendment rights"? The Supreme Court has a felt obligation to maintain the doctrinal clarity and purity of the legal concepts it works with. When a doctrine appears to a court to be incorrectly stated, it is proper to realign it when the court has an opportunity to do so, even if it results in no change in a case. A major example of doctrinal realignment was seen in *Katz v. United States* [this volume] (1967).

[g] Petitioners seek to use *Jones* as a precedent; the application of precedent is rarely an automatic measuring process; instead, the Court must use its judgment to determine whether the case is similar or dissimilar to *Jones*. When courts engage in the process of precedent analysis, they do not merely state the name of the prior case but restate its facts. Here, the Court goes on to point out the dangers that would result in the petitioners' attempt to expand the *Jones* rule or to read it literally. It appears here that the Court not only applies *Jones* but narrows its scope. In the future, therefore, the application of the *Jones* rule has to be read in light of the reassessment in *Rakas*. Thus, the earlier precedent becomes merged into the present case and the general rule of standing (or the application of one's substantive rights under the Fourth Amendment) is now found here.

[h] At times, critical information or reasoning is found in the footnotes to the opinion, such as the following excerpts from Footnote 12: * * * "Legitimation of expectations of privacy by law must have a source outside of the Fourth Amendment, either by reference to concepts of real or personal property law or to understandings that are recognized and permitted by society. One of the main rights attaching to property is the right to exclude others, * * * and one who owns or lawfully possesses or controls property will in all likelihood have a legitimate expectation of privacy by

virtue of this right to exclude. Expectations of privacy protected by the Fourth Amendment, of course, need not be based on a common-law interest in real or personal property, or on the invasion of such an interest. * * * But by focusing on legitimate expectations of privacy in Fourth Amendment jurisprudence, the Court has not altogether abandoned use of property concepts in determining the presence or absence of the privacy interests protected by that Amendment."

It is questionable whether this footnote clarifies the law. On the one hand, JUSTICE REHNQUIST uses expectation-of-privacy analysis to resolve the issue in the case; on the other hand he clouds the *Katz* doctrine by suggesting that it has some relation to property rights.

[i] This opening paragraph goes to the weakest points of the majority opinion: the undermining of the *Katz* doctrine and the side attack on the exclusionary rule. Oddly enough, it is the majority opinion that seems to lack common sense in that the interests of the passenger in the privacy of the car does not seem remote at all.

[j] In the dissenters' view, the majority seems to allow no room for the expectation of privacy doctrine except when the defendant has a property interest. Such a brittle reading of the scope of Fourth Amendment protections seems to have the effect of severely limiting the protections offered by the Amendment. The dissent comes very close to accusing the majority of "instrumental" or "result oriented" reasoning, that is, of generating a rule not in order to produce a doctrinally sound conclusion but to find any result that will cut down the scope of the exclusionary rule. What do you think?

[k] The hypotheticals are examples of legal thinking; the impact of a rule is applied to potential future situations, and the question is posed whether or not the results make any sense. Should a second cousin who visits every five years have a greater reasonable expectation of privacy in your car than your best friend? Undoubtedly, arguments like these are raised at the justices' conferences and between the Justices and their clerks. Some legal arguments based on these kinds of common sense musings, while others are based on broader policy concerns.

[l] This hypothetical has less force since the opinion in *Delaware v. Prouse* [this volume] (1979), which held that police must have at least reasonable suspicion before stopping the occupants of an automobile.

SPINELLI v. UNITED STATES

393 U.S. 410, 89 S.Ct. 584, 21 L.Ed.2d 637 (1969)

MR. JUSTICE HARLAN delivered the opinion of the Court.

[William Spinelli was convicted of the federal crime of interstate travel in aid of racketeering; specifically, that he went to St. Louis, Missouri, from a nearby Illinois suburb to conduct an illegal gambling operation. The Court granted certiorari in order to clarify the rules spelled out in an earlier case, *Aguilar v. Texas*, 378 U.S. 108 (1964).]

In *Aguilar* a search warrant had issued upon an affidavit of police officers who swore only that they had "received reliable information from a credible person and do believe" that narcotics were being illegally stored on the described premises. While recognizing that the constitutional requirement of probable cause can be satisfied by hearsay information, [a] this Court held the affidavit inadequate for two reasons. First, the application failed to set forth many of the "underlying circumstances" necessary to enable the magistrate independently to judge of the validity of the informant's conclusion that the narcotics were where he said they were. Second, the affiant-officers did not attempt to support their claim that their informant was "'credible' or his information 'reliable.'" [b] The Government is, however, quite right in saying that the FBI affidavit in the present case is more ample than that in *Aguilar*. [I]t contain[s] a report from an anonymous informant [and] a report of an independent FBI investigation which is said to corroborate the informant's tip. We are then required

to delineate the manner in which *Aguilar*'s two-pronged test should be applied in these circumstances.

[The affidavit, when reduced to its essential information, contained four facts: (1) that for four of the five days he was followed, Spinelli crossed into Missouri from Illinois at about noon and went to the same apartment house about 4:00 P.M. and was seen to enter a particular apartment; (2) that there were two telephones in the apartment listed under another's name; (3) that Spinelli had a reputation as a bookmaker and gambler among law enforcement agents, including the affiant; and (4) that a "confidential reliable informant" told the FBI agent that Spinelli was operating a gambling operation with the telephones in the apartment.] [c]

There can be no question that the last item mentioned, detailing the informant's tip, has a fundamental place in this warrant application. Without it, probable cause could not be established. The first two items reflect only innocent-seeming activity and data. Spinelli's travels to and from the apartment building and his entry into a particular apartment on one occasion could hardly be taken as bespeaking gambling activity; and there is surely nothing unusual about an apartment containing two separate telephones. Many a householder indulges himself in this petty luxury. Finally, the allegation that Spinelli was "known" to the affiant and to other federal and local law enforcement officers as a gambler is but a bald and unilluminating assertion of suspicion that is entitled to no weight in appraising the magistrate's decision. *Nathanson v. United States*, 290 U.S. 41 (1933). **[d]**

So much indeed the Government does not deny. Rather, * * * the Government claims that the informant's tip gives a suspicious color to the FBI's reports detailing Spinelli's innocent-seeming conduct and that, conversely, the FBI's surveillance corroborates the informant's tip, thereby entitling it to more weight. * * * We believe, however, that the "totality of the circumstances" approach * * * paints with too broad a brush. Where, as here, the informer's tip is a necessary element in a finding of probable cause, its proper weight must be determined by a more precise analysis. **[e]**

The informer's report must first be measured against *Aguilar*'s standards so that its probative value can be assessed. If the tip is found inadequate under *Aguilar*, the other allegations which corroborate the information contained in the hearsay report should then be considered. At this stage as well, however, the standards enunciated in *Aguilar* must inform the magistrate's decision. He must ask: Can it fairly be said that the tip, even when certain parts of it have been corroborated by independent sources, is as trustworthy as a tip which would pass *Aguilar*'s tests without independent corroboration? * * * **[f]**

Applying these principles to the present case, we first consider the weight to be given the informer's tip when it is considered apart from the rest of the affidavit. It is clear that a [magistrate] could not credit it without abdicating his constitutional function. Though the affiant swore that his confidant was "reliable," he offered the magistrate no reason in support of this conclusion. **[g]** Perhaps even more important is the fact that *Aguilar*'s other test has not been satisfied. The tip does not contain a sufficient statement of the underlying circumstances from which the informer concluded that Spinelli was running a bookmaking operation. We are not told how the FBI's source received his information - it is not alleged that the informant personally observed Spinelli at work or that he ever placed a bet with him. Moreover, if the informant came by the information indirectly, he did not explain why his sources were reliable. **[h]** In the absence of a statement detailing the manner in which the information was gathered, it is especially important that the tip describe the accused's criminal activity in sufficient detail so that the magistrate may know that he is relying on something more substantial than a casual rumor circulating in the underworld or an accusation based merely on an individual's general reputation.

The detail provided by the informant in *Draper v. United States*, 358 U.S. 307 (1959), provides a suitable benchmark. While Hereford, the FBI's informer in the case, did not state the way which he had obtained his information, he reported that Draper had gone to Chicago the day before by train and that he would return to Denver by train with three ounces of heroin on one of two specified mornings. Moreover, Hereford went on to describe, with minute particularity, the clothes that Draper would be wearing upon his arrival at the Denver station. **[i]** A magistrate, when confronted with such detail, could reasonably infer that the informant had gained his information in a reliable way. Such an inference cannot be made in the present case.   Here, the only facts supplied were that Spinelli was using two specified telephones and that these phones were being used in gambling operations.   This meager report could easily have been obtained from an off-hand remark heard at a neighborhood bar.

[The allegations resulting from the FBI investigation at most] indicated that Spinelli could have used the telephones specified by the informant for some purpose.   This cannot by itself be said to support both the inference that the informer was gener-ally trustworthy and that he had made his charge against Spinelli on the basis of information obtained in a reliable way.   Once again, *Draper* provides a relevant comparison.   Independent police work in that case corroborated much more than one small detail that had been provided by the informant. There, the police, upon greeting the inbound Denver train on the second morning specified by informer Here-ford, saw a man whose dress corre-sponded precisely to Draper's detailed description.   It was then apparent that the informant had not been fabricating his report out of whole cloth; since the report was of the sort which in com-mon experience may be recognized as having been obtained in a reliable way, it was perfectly clear that probable cause had been established.

We conclude, then, that in the present case the informer's tip—even when corroborated to the extent indicated—was not sufficient to provide the basis for a finding of probable cause. * * * [I]t needed some further support. * * * All that remains to be considered is the flat statement that Spinelli was "known" to the FBI and others as a gambler.   But just as a simple assertion of police suspicion is not itself a sufficient basis of probable cause, we do not believe it may be used to give additional weight to allegations that would otherwise be insufficient. **[j]**

The affidavit, then, falls short of the standard set forth in *Aguilar*, *Draper*, and our other decisions that give content to the notion of probable cause. * * * [W]e do not retreat from the established propositions that only the probability, and not a prima facie showing, of criminal activity is the standard of probable cause; * * * that affidavits of probable cause are tested by much less rigorous standards than those governing the admissibility of evidence at trial; * * * that * * * magistrates are not to be confined * * * by restrictions on the use of their common sense; * * * and that their determination of probable cause should be paid great deference by reviewing courts. * * * **[k]** But we cannot sustain this warrant without diluting important safeguards that assure that the judgment of a disinterested judicial officer will interpose itself between the police and the citizenry.

MR. JUSTICE WHITE, concur-ring.

* * * The tension between *Draper* and the *Nathanson-Aguilar* line of cases is evident from the course followed by the majority opinion. * * *   The *Draper* approach would reasonably justify the issuance of a warrant in this case, particularly since the police had some awareness of Spinelli's past activities.   The majority, however, while seemingly embracing *Draper*, confines that case to its own facts. **[l]** Pending

full scale reconsideration of that case, on the one hand, or of the *Nathanson-Aguilar* cases on the other, I join the opinion of the Court. * * *

[JUSTICES BLACK, FORTAS and STEWART dissented; JUSTICE MARSHALL took no part in the case.]

*   *   *   *   *   *   *   *   *   *

COMMENTS

[a] The important hearsay use rule is mentioned in passing.

[b] The Court next states a two-part rule, stated negatively in terms of what the police failed to do in *Aguilar*. But it establishes a positive and prospective rule to guide police. Restate the two-prong test in your own words. Does the second prong have two elements?

[c] Which of these facts, standing alone, raise a reasonable suspicion that Spinelli was a "bookie?" Do they become more suspicious when taken together? If you were a magistrate, would you allow the police to enter the apartment to search for evidence of crime?

[d] Reputation is, in ordinary life, a kind of hearsay that guides the behavior of most people. Why does the Court virtually banish the use of a person's reputation, upholding the *Nathanson* rule, when other kinds of hearsay may be used to establish probable cause?

[e] Probable cause is a standard of the *weight* of evidence, so JUSTICE HARLAN assumes that an informer's testimony is always less weighty than an officer's or a victim's and thus needs a special framework for analysis, that is, the two-prong test, designed to inquire into the truthfulness of the informant as well as the weight of the evidence. In other cases the "totality of the circumstances" approach is sufficient. Do you agree with this distinction? What are the benefits of a totality of the circumstances approach?

[f] If the tip does not support probable cause, it may be corroborated by other evidence obtained by police investigation; this is evidence that supports the main conclusion that there is probable cause to believe there is evidence of crime in a place.

[g] For a magistrate to accept an affiant's bald assertion and act as a "rubber stamp" is placed on the level of a constitutional error.

[h] The hint here is that informers have reasons to lie or at least to rely on hearsay; there is implied criticism of the FBI agents for failing to be more critical of their informants or more forthcoming with information about them. There is

also the suggestion that an informer may present the police with hearsay and that probable cause could be based on "hearsay upon hearsay." Is this wise?

[i] Why were *Draper's details* so important? None of Hereford's details, except that Draper would be carrying heroin, were inherently suspicious. What did the details indicate about Hereford's relationship with Draper? How do *Draper's* details differ from *Spinelli*'s?

[j] Do you think that reputation evidence is excluded because it is unreliable, because it would allow police to harass people known to be criminals, or a combination of the two? If reputation evidence is ordinarily useful to prudent persons in ordinary life, isn't the exclusion of reputation evidence a policy rule? Or are the consequences of official action too weighty to rely on an individual's reputation?

[k] JUSTICE HARLAN concludes by reiterating several rules that make it clear that the majority does not want to unduly hamper law enforcement in obtaining warrants.

[l] The concurrence points out a flaw in the *Spinelli* opinion: the corroborating details in *Draper* and *Spinelli* are logically similar. The *Spinelli* opinion, then, seems to be a policy statement favoring close scrutiny of informer's tips, rather than a "natural" reading of the information. JUSTICE WHITE's questioning of *Spinelli* was significant fourteen years later.

ILLINOIS v. GATES

462 U.S. 213, 103 S.Ct. 2317, 76 L.Ed.2d 527 (1983)

JUSTICE REHNQUIST delivered the opinion of the Court.

Respondents Lance and Susan Gates were indicted for violation of state drug laws after police officers, executing a search warrant, discovered marihuana and other contraband in their automobile and home. * * * The Illinois Supreme Court * * * held that the affidavit submitted in support of the State's application for a warrant to search the Gateses' property was inadequate under this Court's decisions in *Aguilar v. Texas*, 378 U.S. 108 (1964) and *Spinelli v. United States* [this volume] (1969).

We granted certiorari to consider the application of the Fourth Amendment to a magistrate's issuance of a search warrant on the basis of a partially corroborated anonymous informant's tip. * * *

* * *

II

* * * On May 3, 1978, the Bloomingdale Police Department received by mail an anonymous handwritten letter which read as follows:

"This letter is to inform you that you have a couple in your town who strictly make their living on selling drugs. They are Sue and Lance Gates, they live on Greenway, off Bloomingdale Rd. in the condominiums. Most of their buys are done in Florida. Sue his wife drives their car to Florida, where she leaves it to be loaded up with drugs, then Lance flys down and drives it back. Sue flys back after she drops the car off in Florida. May 3 she is driving down there again and Lance will be flying down in a few days to drive it back. At the time Lance drives the car back he has the trunk loaded with over $100,000.00 in drugs. Presently they have over $100,000.00 worth of drugs in their basement.

"They brag about the fact they never have to work, and make their entire living on pushers.

"I guarantee if you watch them carefully you will make a big catch. They are friends with some big drugs dealers, who visit their house often.

"Lance & Susan Gates
"Greenway
"in Condominiums" [a]

The letter was referred by the Chief of Police * * * to Detective Mader, who decided to pursue the tip. Mader learned * * * that an Illinois driver's license had been issued to one Lance Gates, residing at a stated address in Bloomingdale. He contacted a confidential informant, whose examination of certain financial records revealed a more recent address for the Gateses, and he also learned from a police officer assigned to O'Hare Airport that "L. Gates" had made a reservation on Eastern Airlines Flight 245 to West Palm Beach, Fla., scheduled to depart from Chicago on May 5 at 4:15 p.m.

Mader then made arrangements with an agent of the Drug Enforcement Administration for surveillance of the May 5 Eastern Airlines flight. The agent later reported to Mader that Gates had boarded the flight, and that federal agents in Florida had observed him arrive in West Palm Beach and take a taxi to the nearby Holiday Inn. They also reported that Gates went to a room registered to one Susan Gates and that, at 7 o'clock a.m. the next morning, Gates and an unidentified woman left the motel in a Mercury bearing Illinois license plates and drove northbound on an interstate highway frequently used by travelers to the Chicago area. In addition, the DEA agent informed Mader that the license plate number on the Mercury was registered to a Hornet station wagon owned by Gates. The agent also advised Mader that the driving time between West Palm Beach and Bloomingdale was approximately 22 to 24 hours.

Mader signed an affidavit setting forth the foregoing facts, and submitted it to a judge of the Circuit Court of Du Page County, together with a copy of the anonymous letter. The judge of that court thereupon issued a search warrant for the Gateses' residence and for their automobile. The judge, in deciding to issue the warrant, could have determined that the *modus operandi* of the Gateses had been substantially corroborated. As the anonymous letter predicted, Lance Gates had flown from Chicago to West Palm Beach late in the afternoon of May 5th, had checked into a hotel room registered in the name of his wife, and, at 7 o'clock a.m. the follow-

ing morning, had headed north, accompanied by an unidentified woman, out of West Palm Beach on an interstate highway used by travelers from South Florida to Chicago in an automobile bearing a license plate issued to him. [b]

At 5:15 a.m. on March 7, only 36 hours after he had flown out of Chicago, Lance Gates, and his wife, returned to their home in Bloomingdale, driving the car in which they had left West Palm Beach some 22 hours earlier. [c] The Bloomingdale police were awaiting them, searched the trunk of the Mercury, and uncovered approximately 350 pounds of marihuana. A search of the Gateses' home revealed marihuana, weapons, and other contraband. * * *

The Illinois Supreme Court concluded—and we are inclined to agree —that, standing alone, the anonymous letter * * * would not provide the basis for a magistrate's determination that there was probable cause to believe contraband would be found in the Gateses' car and home. [d] The letter provides virtually nothing from which one might conclude that its author is either honest or his information reliable; likewise, the letter gives absolutely no indication of the basis for the writer's predictions regarding the Gateses' criminal activities. Something more was required. * * *
* * *

[The evidence was suppressed by the Illinois courts, all holding that probable cause was not made out under the *Aguilar-Spinelli* test.]

* * * The Illinois Supreme Court, like some others, apparently understood *Spinelli* as requiring that the anonymous letter satisfy each of two independent requirements before it

could be relied on. * * * According to this view, the letter, as supplemented by Mader's affidavit, first had to adequately reveal the "basis of knowledge" of the letterwriter—the particular means by which he came by the information given in his report. Second, it had to provide facts sufficiently establishing either the "veracity" of the affiant's informant, or, alternatively, the "reliability" of the informant's report in this particular case. The Illinois court, alluding to an elaborate set of legal rules that have developed among various lower courts to enforce the "two-pronged test," found that the test had not been satisfied. First, the "veracity" prong was not satisfied because, "[t]here was simply no basis [for] conclud[ing] that the anonymous person [who wrote the letter to the Bloomingdale Police Department] was credible." * * * The court indicated that corroboration by police of details contained in the letter might never satisfy the "veracity" prong, and in any event, could not do so if, as in the present case, only "innocent" details are corroborated. * * * In addition, the letter gave no indication of the basis of its writer's knowledge of the Gateses' activities: [it] * * * failed to provide sufficient detail to permit such an inference. Thus, it concluded that no showing of probable cause had been made. **[e]**

We agree with the Illinois Supreme Court that an informant's "veracity," "reliability," and "basis of knowledge" are all highly relevant in determining the value of his report. We do not agree, however, that these elements should be understood as entirely separate and independent requirements to be rigidly exacted in every case,

which the opinion of the Supreme Court of Illinois would imply. Rather, as detailed below, they should be understood simply as closely intertwined issues that may usefully illuminate the commonsense, practical question whether there is "probable cause" to believe that contraband or evidence is located in a particular place.

III

This totality-of-the-circumstances approach is far more consistent with our prior treatment of probable cause than is any rigid demand that specific "tests" be satisfied by every informant's tip. Perhaps the central teaching of our decisions bearing on the probable-cause standard is that it is a "practical, nontechnical conception." * * * "In dealing with probable cause, * * * as the very name implies, we deal with probabilities. These are not technical; they are the factual and practical considerations of everyday life on which reasonable and prudent men, not legal technicians, act." * * * **[f]**

* * * [P]robable cause is a fluid concept—turning on the assessment of probabilities in particular factual contexts—not readily, or even usefully, reduced to a neat set of legal rules. * * * "Informants' tips, like all other clues and evidence coming to a policeman on the scene, may vary greatly in their value and reliability." Rigid legal rules are ill-suited to an area of such diversity. "One simple rule will not cover every situation." * * *

Moreover, the "two-pronged test" directs analysis into two largely independent channels—the informant's "veracity" or "reliability" and his "basis of knowledge." There are persuasive arguments against according these two elements such independent   status. Instead, they are better understood as relevant considerations in the totality-of-the-circumstances analysis that traditionally has guided probable-cause determinations: a deficiency in one may be compensated for, in determining the overall reliability of a tip, by a strong showing as to the other, or by some other indicia of reliability. * * * **[g]**

[Justice Rehnquist suggests that an unusually reliable informant should be believed when on occasion he fails to state the basis of knowledge regarding a prediction of crime.] * * *
* * *

We also have recognized that affidavits "are normally drafted by non-lawyers in the midst and haste of a criminal   investigation.   Technical requirements of elaborate specificity once exacted under common law pleadings have no proper place in this area." * * *   Likewise, search and arrest warrants long have been issued by persons who are neither lawyers nor judges, and who certainly do not remain abreast of each judicial refine-ment of the nature of "probable cause." * * * **[h]** The rigorous inquiry into the *Spinelli* prongs and the complex superstructure of evidentiary and analytical rules that some have seen implicit in our *Spinelli* decision, cannot be reconciled with the fact that many warrants are—quite properly,—issued on the basis of nontechnical, common-sense judgments of laymen applying a standard less demanding than those used in more formal legal proceedings. Likewise, given the informal, often hurried context in which it must be applied, the "built-in subtleties," * * * of the "two-pronged test" are particu-

larly unlikely to assist magistrates in determining probable cause.

Similarly, we have repeatedly said that after-the-fact scrutiny by courts of the sufficiency of an affidavit should not take the form of *de novo* review. A magistrate's "determination of probable cause should be paid great deference by reviewing courts." * * *

If the affidavits submitted by police officers are subjected to the type of scrutiny some courts have deemed appropriate, police might well resort to warrantless searches, with the hope of relying on consent or some other exception to the Warrant Clause that might develop at the time of the search. * * * **[i]**

Finally, the direction taken by decisions following *Spinelli* poorly serves "[t]he most basic function of any government": "to provide for the security of the individual and of his property." * * *   If, as the Illinois Supreme Court apparently thought, that test must be rigorously applied in every case, anonymous tips would be of greatly diminished value in police work. * * *

For all these reasons, we conclude that it is wiser to abandon the "two-pronged test" established by our decisions in *Aguilar* and *Spinelli*. In its place we reaffirm the totality-of-the-circumstances analysis that traditionally has informed probable-cause determi-nations. * * *
* * *

JUSTICE BRENNAN's dissent suggests in several places that the approach we take today somehow downgrades the role of the neutral magistrate. * * * Quite the contrary, we believe, is the case. The essential protection of the warrant requirement of the Fourth Amendment, * * * is in "requiring that [the usual inferences which reasonable men draw from evidence] be drawn by a neutral and detached magistrate instead of being judged by the officer. * * *" Nothing in our opinion in any way lessens the authority of the magistrate to draw such reasonable inferences as he will from the material supplied to him by applicants for a warrant; indeed, he is freer than under the regime of *Aguilar* and *Spinelli* to draw such inferences, or to refuse to draw them if he is so minded.

The real gist of JUSTICE BRENNAN's criticism seems to be * * * that magistrates should be restricted in their authority to make probable-cause determinations by the standards laid down in *Aguilar* and *Spinelli*. * * * That such a labyrinthine body of judicial refinement bears any relationship to familiar definitions of probable cause is hard to imagine. * * *

JUSTICE BRENNAN's dissent also suggests that "[w]ords such as 'practical,' 'nontechnical,' and 'common sense,' as used in the Court's opinion, are but code words for an overly permissive attitude towards police practices in derogation of the rights secured by the Fourth Amendment." * * * [N]o one doubts that "under our Constitution only measures consistent with the Fourth Amendment may be employed by government to cure [the horrors of drug trafficking];" * * * but this agreement does not advance the inquiry as to which measures are, and which measures are not, consistent with the Fourth Amendment. "Fidelity" to the commands of the Constitution suggests balanced judgment rather than exhortation. The highest "fidelity" is

not achieved by the judge who instinctively goes furthest in upholding even the most bizarre claim of individual constitutional rights, any more than it is achieved by a judge who instinctively goes furthest in accepting the most restrictive claims of governmental authorities. The task of this Court, as of other courts, is to "hold the balance true," and we think we have done that in this case. **[j]**

IV

Our decisions applying the totality-of-the-circumstances analysis outlined above have consistently recognized the value of corroboration of details of an informant's tip by independent police work. * * *

     * * *

The showing of probable cause in the present case was * * * compelling. * * * **[k]** Even standing alone, the facts obtained through the independent investigation of Mader and the DEA at least suggested that the Gateses were involved in drug trafficking. In addition to being a popular vacation site, Florida is well known as a source of narcotics and other illegal drugs. * * * Lance Gates' flight to Palm Beach, his brief, overnight stay in a motel, and apparent immediate return north to Chicago in the family car, conveniently awaiting him in West Palm Beach, is as suggestive of a prearranged drug run, as it is of an ordinary vacation trip.

In addition, the judge could rely on the anonymous letter, which had been corroborated in major part by Mader's efforts* * *

Finally, the anonymous letter contained a range of details relating not just to easily obtained facts and conditions existing at the time of the tip, but to future actions of third parties ordinarily not easily predicted. The letterwriter's accurate information as to the travel plans of each of the Gateses was of a character likely obtained only from the Gateses themselves, or from someone familiar with their not entirely ordinary travel plans. If the informant had access to accurate information of this type a magistrate could properly conclude that it was not unlikely that he also had access to reliable information of the Gateses' alleged illegal activities. Of course, the Gateses' travel plans might have been learned from a talkative neighbor or travel agent; under the "two-pronged test" developed from *Spinelli*, the character of the details in the anonymous letter might well not permit a sufficiently clear inference regarding the letterwriter's "basis of knowledge." But, as discussed previously, * * * probable cause does not demand the certainty we associate with formal trials. It is enough that there was a fair probability that the writer of the anonymous letter had obtained his entire story either from the Gateses or someone they trusted. And corroboration of major portions of the letter's predictions provides just this probability. It is apparent, therefore, that the judge issuing the warrant had a "substantial basis for * * * conclud[ing]" that probable cause to search the Gateses' home and car existed. The judgment of the Supreme Court of Illinois therefore must be

Reversed.

[JUSTICE WHITE, concurred in the judgment, on grounds that the corroboration in this case supplied information to support both the basis

of knowledge and the veracity prongs of the *Aguilar-Spinelli* rule, which he would not abandon.]

JUSTICE BRENNAN, with whom JUSTICE MARSHALL joins, dissenting.

* * *

I

The Court's current Fourth Amendment jurisprudence, as reflected by today's unfortunate decision, patently disregards Justice Jackson's admonition in *Brinegar v. United States* (1949):

> "[Fourth Amendment rights] are not mere second-class rights but belong in the catalog of indispensable freedoms. Among deprivations of rights, none is so effective in cowing a population, crushing the spirit of the individual and putting terror in every heart. Uncontrolled search and seizure is one of the first and most effective weapons in the arsenal of every arbitrary government. * * *
>
> "But the right to be secure against searches and seizures is one of the most difficult to protect. Since the officers are themselves the chief invaders, there is no enforcement outside of court." * * * (dissenting opinion).

In recognition of the judiciary's role as the only effective guardian of Fourth Amendment rights, this Court has developed over the last half century a set of coherent rules governing a magistrate's consideration of a warrant application and the showings that are necessary to support a finding of probable cause. * * *

In order to emphasize the magistrate's role as an independent arbiter of probable cause and to insure that searches or seizures are not effected on less than probable cause, the Court has insisted that police officers provide magistrates with the underlying facts and circumstances that support the officers' conclusions. * * *

* * *

* * * Properly understood, therefore, *Spinelli* stands for the proposition that corroboration of certain details in a tip may be sufficient to satisfy the veracity, but not the basis of knowledge, prong of *Aguilar*. As noted, *Spinelli* also suggests that in some limited circumstances considerable detail in an informant's tip may be adequate to satisfy the basis of knowledge prong of *Aguilar*.

* * *

Until today the Court has never squarely addressed the application of the *Aguilar* and *Spinelli* standards to tips from anonymous informants. Both *Aguilar* and *Spinelli* dealt with tips from informants known at least to the police. * * * And surely there is even more reason to subject anonymous informants' tips to the tests established by *Aguilar* and *Spinelli*. By definition nothing is known about an anonymous informant's identity, honesty, or reliability. * * *

To suggest that anonymous informants' tips are subject to the tests established by *Aguilar* and *Spinelli* is not to suggest that they can never provide a basis for a finding of probable cause. It is conceivable that police corroboration of the details of the tip might establish the reliability of the informant under *Aguilar*'s veracity prong, as refined in *Spinelli*, and that

the details in the tip might be sufficient to qualify under the "self-verifying detail" test established by *Spinelli* as a means of satisfying *Aguilar*'s basis of knowledge prong. The *Aguilar* and *Spinelli* tests must be applied to anonymous informants' tips, however, if we are to continue to insure that findings of probable cause, and attendant intrusions, are based on information provided by an honest or credible person who has acquired the information in a reliable way.

* * *

II

* * *

At the heart of the Court's decision to abandon *Aguilar* and *Spinelli* appears to be its belief that "the direction taken by decisions following *Spinelli* poorly serves '[t]he most basic function of any government': 'to provide for the security of the individual and of his property.'" * * * This conclusion rests on the judgment that *Aguilar* and *Spinelli* "seriously imped[e] the task of law enforcement," * * * and render anonymous tips valueless in police work. * * * Surely, the Court overstates its case. * * * But of particular concern to all Americans must be that the Court gives virtually no consideration to the value of insuring that findings of probable cause are based on information that a magistrate can reasonably say has been obtained in a reliable way by an honest or credible person. I share JUSTICE WHITE's fear that the Court's rejection of *Aguilar* and *Spinelli* and its adoption of a new totality-of-the-circumstances test, * * * "may foretell an evisceration of the probable-cause standard . * * *" * * *

[JUSTICE STEVENS dissented on the grounds that probable cause did not exist. At the time the magistrate issued the warrant, he did *not* know that Lance and Sue Gates had driven twenty-two hours nonstop from West Palm Beach to Bloomingdale, a suspicious activity in light of the anonymous letter. All he knew was that they had left the Palm Beach area heading north. This fact differed from the anonymous letter's prediction that stated that Sue would fly back to Illinois while Lance drove. To JUSTICE STEVENS, the discrepancy was critical because it indicated: (1) that the Gateses' willingness to leave their house unattended should have been interpreted as indicating that it did not contain drugs; (2) that their activity was not as unusual as if they had left separately; and (3) that the search of their house was improper in light of the absence of probable cause.]

* * * * * * * * * *

COMMENTS

[a] What motivates such an anonymous letter? Motives like envy or revenge might enhance the reliability of such a letter; on the other hand, a false incriminating letter could be written as a prank or to harass someone. The police and the magistrate did not rely exclusively on the letter to initiate the search.

[b] At this point, how certain could the magistrate be that there was probable cause to believe that the Gateses' were involved in drug dealing?

[c] Can you think of any legitimate explanations for this travel plan that may cast doubt on its suspicion? Does the existence of any legitimate explanation negate probable cause?

[d] The Court is wary of information from anonymous tips—yet it does not close the door on the use of such information.

[e] Did the close match between the Gateses' travels and the letter establish the veracity or truthfulness of the anonymous letter writer? If so, was it veracity regarding the Gateses' peculiar travel patterns or veracity as to their drug dealing?

[f] If probable cause is a practical, "nontechnical" search for information, then why is reputation evidence not used? The analysis is clouded by the use of the word "technical." It is better to think of the *Aguilar-Spinelli* and the *Gates* approaches as reflecting different *policy* perspectives. Thus, neither the majority nor the dissenters wish to allow police and magistrates to use reputation evidence, no matter how much nontechnical commonsense it makes to rely on what "everybody knows." What do you think the policy is that lies behind this agreement?

[g] Totality of the circumstances was proposed to the Court by the government in

Spinelli but rejected by the Court at that time. There are many examples of the Supreme Court tracing doctrinal pendulum swings in its cases as events or public opinion dictate a particular outcome or constitutional methodology or both. What do you think caused the shift from the *Aguilar-Spinelli* rule?

[h] Of course, it is true that modern, professional police work requires a good understanding of the subtleties of substantive criminal law, other legal areas, many administrative rules and codes, as well as a good deal of administrative and technical-mechanical information. Is Justice Rehnquist setting his sights too low regarding the mental capacity of lay magistrates and police officers?

[i] Several policy reasons are offered in support of the totality-of-the-circumstances rule: deference to local magistrates; a desire not to push officers to disregard warrants entirely; and more effective police work. Is the second argument "realism," or is it giving in to police intransigence over adhering to the Constitution?

[j] The majority opinion undoubtedly favors law enforcement; there seemed to be no outcry against the two-prong rule; thus, it is not totally implausible to view the real goal of the opinion as expanding the ability of the police to obtain warrants that were blocked by the two-prong test; but Justice Rehnquist turns aside this insinuation by asserting that his position is constitutionally neutral.

[k] Saying that probable cause is compelling is not in full accord with Justice Rehnquist's earlier statement allowing a possibly innocent explanation for the Gateses' behavior. This does not mean that there was not probable cause, but that in many instances magistrates are faced with close calls, where the deciding factor is the nature of the probable cause test, the test's policy orientation, and perhaps the orientation of the magistrate.

ARIZONA v. HICKS

480 U.S. 321, 107 S.Ct. 1149, 94 L.Ed.2d 347 (1987)

Justice SCALIA delivered the opinion of the Court.

In *Coolidge v. New Hampshire*, 403 U.S. 325 (1971), we said that in certain circumstances a warrantless seizure by police of an item that comes within plain view during their lawful search of a private area may be reasonable under the Fourth Amendment. * * * [The issue] in the present case [is] whether this "plain view" doctrine may be invoked when the police have less than probable cause to believe that the item in question is evidence of a crime or is contraband.

I

[Police entered an apartment to search for a person who shot a bullet through the floor, injuring a man in the apartment below]. They found and seized three weapons, including a sawed-off rifle. * * * [a]

One of the policemen, Officer Nelson, noticed two sets of expensive stereo components, which seemed out of place in the squalid and otherwise ill-appointed four room apartment. Suspecting that they were stolen, he read and recorded their serial numbers—moving some of the components, including a Bang and Olufsen turntable, in order to do so—which he then reported by phone to his headquarters. On being advised that the turntable had been taken in an armed robbery, he seized it immediately. * * * Respondent was subsequently indicted for the robbery.

[On a suppression motion, the state trial court and court of appeals held that the view of the serial numbers was an additional search, unrelated to the exigency of search for the shooter, impliedly rejecting the idea that the actions were justified by the plain view doctrine.]

II

[T]he mere recording of the serial numbers did not constitute a seizure. * * * In and of itself * * * it did not "meaningfully interfere" with respondent's possessory interest in either the serial number or the equipment, and therefore did not amount to a seizure. * * *

Officer Nelson's moving of the equipment, however, did constitute a "search" separate and apart from the search for the shooter, victims, and weapons that was the lawful objective of his entry into the apartment. Merely inspecting those parts of the turntable that came into view during the latter search would not have constituted an independent search, because it would have produced no additional invasion of respondent's privacy interest. * * * But taking action, unrelated to the objectives of the authorized intrusion, which exposed to view concealed portions of the apartment or its contents, did produce a new invasion of respondent's privacy unjustified by the exigent circumstance that validated the entry. * * * It matters not that the search uncovered nothing of any great personal value to the respondent— serial numbers rather than (what might conceivably have been hidden behind or under the equipment) letters or photographs. A search is a search, even if it happens to disclose nothing but the bottom of a turntable. **[b]**

III

The remaining question is whether the search was "reasonable" under the Fourth Amendment.

* * * [W]e reject, at the outset, the * * * position * * * that because the officers' action directed to the stereo equipment was unrelated to the justification for their entry into respondent's apartment, it was *ipso facto* unreasonable. That lack of relationship *always* exists with regard to action validated under the "plain view" doctrine; where action is taken for the purpose of justifying entry, invocation of the doctrine is superfluous. * * * **[c]**

We turn, then, to application of the doctrine to the facts of this case. "It is well established that under certain circumstances the police may *seize* evidence in plain view without a warrant," *Coolidge v. New Hampshire* * * * (plurality opinion) (emphasis added). Those circumstances include situations "[w]here the initial intrusion that brings the police within plain view of such [evidence] is supported * * * by one of the recognized exceptions to the warrant requirement. * * * It would be absurd to say that an object could lawfully be seized and taken from the premises, but could not be moved for closer examination." It is clear, therefore, that the search here was valid if the "plain view" doctrine would have sustained a seizure of the equipment.

There is no doubt it would have done so if Officer Nelson had probable cause to believe that the equipment was stolen. The State conceded, however, that he had only a "reasonable suspicion," by which it means something less than probable cause. * * *

We now hold that probable cause is required. To say otherwise would be to cut the "plain view" doctrine loose from its theoretical and practical moorings. The theory of that doctrine consists of extending to nonpublic places such as the home, where searches and seizures without a warrant are presumptively unreasonable, the police's longstanding authority to make warrantless seizures in public places of such objects as weapons and contraband. * * * And the practical justification for that extension is the desirability of sparing police, whose viewing of the object in the course of a lawful search is as legitimate as it would have been in a public place, the inconvenience and the risk—to themselves or to preservation of the evidence—of going to obtain a warrant. Dispensing with the need for a warrant is worlds apart from permitting a lesser standard of *cause* for the seizure than a warrant would require, *i.e.*, the standard of probable cause. No reason is apparent why an object should routinely be seizable on lesser grounds, during an unrelated search and seizure, than would have been needed to obtain a warrant for that same object if it had been known to be on the premises. **[d]**

[There are some searches allowable] on less than probable cause * * * where * * * the seizure is minimally intrusive and operational necessities render it the only practicable means of detecting certain types of crime. * * *

No special operational necessities are relied on here, however—but rather the mere fact that the items in question came lawfully within the officer's plain view. That alone cannot supplant the requirement of probable cause.

The same considerations preclude us from holding that, even though probable cause would have been necessary for a *seizure*, the *search* of objects in plain view that occurred here could be sustained on lesser grounds. A dwelling-place search, no less than a dwelling-place seizure, requires probable cause, and there is no reason in theory or practicality why application of the "plain view" doctrine would supplant that requirement. * * *

[T]o treat searches more liberally would especially erode the plurality's warning in *Coolidge* that "the 'plain view' doctrine may not be used to extend a general exploratory search from one object to another until something incriminating at last emerges." * * * In short, whether legal authority to move the equipment could be found only as an inevitable concomitant of the authority to seize it, or also as a consequence of some independent power to search certain objects in plain view, probable cause to believe the equipment was stolen was required. [e]

* * *

JUSTICE O'CONNOR, with whom THE CHIEF JUSTICE and JUSTICE POWELL join, dissenting.

The Court today gives the right answer to the wrong question. The Court asks whether the police must have probable cause before either seizing an object in plain view or conducting a full-blown search of that object, and concludes that they must. I agree. In my view, however, this case presents a different question: whether police must have probable cause before conducting a cursory inspection of an item in plain view. [f] Because I conclude that such an inspection is reasonable if the police are aware of facts or circumstances that justify a reasonable suspicion that the item is evidence of a crime, I would reverse the judgment of the Arizona Court of Appeals, and therefore dissent.

[A *Coolidge* requirement is that for evidence to be within the "plain view" exception,] it must be "immediately apparent" to the police that the items they observe may be evidence of a crime, contraband, or otherwise subject to seizure. * * *

The purpose of the "immediately apparent" requirement is to prevent "general exploratory rummaging in a person's belongings." * * * If an officer could indiscriminately search every item in plain view, a search justified by a limited purpose—such as exigent circumstances—could be used to eviscerate the protections of the Fourth Amendment. * * *

* * *

* * * When a police officer makes a cursory inspection of a suspicious item in plain view in order to determine whether it is indeed evidence of a crime, there is no "exploratory rummaging." Only those items that the police officer "reasonably suspects" as evidence of a crime may be inspected, and perhaps more importantly, the scope of such an inspection is quite limited. In short, if police officers have a reasonable, articulable suspicion that an object they come

across during the course of a lawful search is evidence of crime, in my view they may make a cursory examination of the object to verify their suspicion. If the officers wish to go beyond such a cursory examination of the object, however, they must have probable cause. [g]

This distinction between a full-blown search and seizure of an item and a mere inspection of the item * * * [is] based on their relative intrusiveness. * * *

* * *

* * * * * * * * * * *

COMMENTS

[a] An exigency—not one of the three standard warrant exceptions of hot pursuit, automobile search or search incident to arrest—made the entry lawful. Thus, a general exigency category exists, based on the reasonableness concept.

[b] JUSTICE SCALIA recognized a thin line between observing and recording a serial number and moving an object to see the serial number. Although search and seizure law has become "interest"-based, this case shows that physical actions remain critical to Fourth Amendment analysis. If the distinction seems trivial, ask if it is annoying for a guest to pick up items on your desk or dresser and inspect them?

[c] Here the defendant argued that the police could only seize items in plain view that related to the shooting; such an argument would destroy the practical value of the plain view doctrine and would not adhere to its logic. Note that both the defense and the prosecution make extreme arguments to the Court in this case.

[d] To the dissent, lifting the stereo is not a search but a "cursory inspection." But the majority fears that to allow police to rummage in a home beyond their lawful purpose to *create* plain view opens a theoretic rift in the plain view doctrine that can have substantial practical consequences.

[e] JUSTICE SCALIA is a "conservative" justice. His decision here is conservative in the sense of "non-activist"—adhering to an established link between a house search and the probable cause standard. "Conservative" is also used to mean pro-law enforcement (and "liberal" to mean pro-defendant) rulings. These dual uses of the terms *conservative* and *liberal* cause some confusion.

[f] The dissent turns on a fine factual distinction, not on a fundamental disagreement with established doctrines; much case law turns on such distinctions.

[g] The dissenters are aware that their approach could undermine constitutional protections if taken too far; they are not hostile to constitutional protection of individual liberty, but believe their rule does not endanger liberty.

HORTON v. CALIFORNIA

496 U.S. 128, 110 S.Ct. 2301, 110 L.Ed.2d 112 (1990)

JUSTICE STEVENS delivered the opinion of the Court.

In this case we revisit an issue that was considered, but not conclusively resolved, in *Coolidge v. New Hampshire*, 403 U.S. 443 (1971): Whether the warrantless seizure of evidence of crime in plain view is prohibited by the Fourth Amendment if the discovery of the evidence was not inadvertent. We conclude that even though inadvertence is a characteristic of most legitimate "plain view" seizures, it is not a necessary condition.

I

[A victim robbed after leaving the San Jose Coin Club annual show identified Horton by his distinctive voice and another witness said that Horton was at the show. The robbers used a machine gun and a "stun" gun in the holdup. Sergeant LaRault, an experienced police investigator determined that probable cause existed and obtained a search warrant from a magistrate that] only authorized a search for the proceeds, including three specifically described rings, [but not for the guns].

Pursuant to the warrant, LaRault searched petitioner's residence, but he did not find the stolen property. During the course of the search, however, he discovered the weapons in plain view and seized them. * * * LaRault testified that while he was searching for the rings, he also was interested in finding other evidence connecting petitioner to the robbery.

Thus, the seized evidence was not discovered "inadvertently."

[The California courts did not suppress the seized evidence, holding that the inadvertence aspect of the plain view doctrine in *Coolidge* was upheld by only four justices and therefore was not binding on the states.]

Because the California courts' interpretation of the "plain-view" doctrine conflicts with the view of other courts, and because the unresolved issue is important, we granted certiorari. * * * [a]

II

* * *

The right to security in person and property protected by the Fourth Amendment may be invaded in quite different ways by searches and seizures. A search compromises the individual interest in privacy; a seizure deprives the individual of dominion over his or her person or property. * * * The "plain view" doctrine is often considered an exception to the general rule that warrantless searches are presumptively unreasonable, but this characterization overlooks the important difference between searches and seizures. If an article is already in plain view, neither its observation nor its seizure would involve any invasion of privacy. * * * A seizure of the article, however, would obviously invade the owner's possessory interest. * * * If "plain view" justifies an exception from an otherwise applicable warrant requirement, therefore, it must be an exception that is addressed to the concerns that are implicated by seizures rather than by searches. **[b]**

The criteria that generally guide "plain-view" seizures were set forth in *Coolidge v. New Hampshire* [above]. The Court held that the Police, in seizing two automobiles parked in plain view on the defendant's driveway in the course of arresting the defendant, violated the Fourth Amendment. Accordingly, particles of gun powder that had been subsequently found in vacuum sweepings from one of the cars could not be introduced in evidence against the defendant. **[c]** The State endeavored to justify the seizure of the automobiles, and their subsequent search at the police station, on four different grounds, including the "plain view" doctrine. The scope of that doctrine as it had developed in earlier cases was fairly summarized in these three paragraphs from JUSTICE STEWART's opinion:

"It is well established that under certain circumstances the police may seize evidence in plain view without a warrant. But it is important to keep in mind that, in the vast majority of cases, *any* evidence seized by the police will be in plain view, at least at the moment of seizure. The problem with the 'plain view' doctrine has been to identify the circumstances in which plain view has legal significance rather than being simply the normal concomitant of any search, legal or illegal.

"An example of the applicability of the 'plain view' doctrine is the situation in which the police have a warrant to search a given area for specified objects, and in the course of the search come across some other article of incriminating character. * * * Where the initial intrusion that brings the police within plain view of such an article is supported, not by a warrant, but by one of the recognized exceptions to the warrant requirement, the seizure is also legitimate. Thus the police may inadvertently come across evidence while in 'hot pursuit' of a fleeing suspect. * * * And an object that comes into view during a search incident to arrest that is appropriately limited in scope under existing law may be seized without a warrant. *Chimel v. California*, [this volume]. Finally, the 'plain view' doctrine has been applied where a police officer is not searching for evidence against the accused, but nonetheless inadvertently comes across an incriminating object. * * *

"What the 'plain view' cases have in common is that the police officer in each of them had a prior justification for an intrusion in the course of which he came inadvertently across a piece of evidence incriminating the accused. The doctrine serves to supplement the prior justification—whether it be a warrant for another object, hot pursuit, search incident to lawful arrest, or some other legitimate reason for being present unconnected with a search directed against the accused—and permits the warrantless seizure. Of course, the extension of the original justification is legitimate only where it is immediately apparent to the police that they have evidence before them; the 'plain view' doctrine may not be used to extend a general exploratory search from one object to another until something incriminating at last emerges." * * *

JUSTICE STEWART then described the two limitations on the doctrine that he found implicit in its rationale: First, "that plain view *alone* is never enough to justify the warrantless seizure of evidence;" * * * and second, that "the discovery of evidence in plain view must be inadvertent." * * *

JUSTICE STEWART's analysis of the "plain view" doctrine did not command a majority and a plurality of the Court has since made clear that the discussion is "not a binding precedent." * * * JUSTICE HARLAN, who concurred in the Court's judgment and in its response to the dissenting opinions, * * * did not join the plurality's discussion of the "plain view" doctrine. * * * The decision nonetheless is a binding precedent. Before discussing the second limitation, which is implicated in this case, it is therefore necessary to explain why the first adequately supports the Court's judgment.

It is, of course, an essential predicate to any valid warrantless seizure of incriminating evidence that the officer did not violate the Fourth Amendment in arriving at the place from which the evidence could be plainly viewed. There are, moreover, two additional conditions that must be satisfied to justify the warrantless seizure. First, not only must the item be in plain view; its incriminating character must also be "immediately apparent." * * * see also *Arizona v. Hicks* [this volume]. Thus, in *Coolidge*, the cars were

obviously in plain view, but their probative value remained uncertain until after the interiors were swept and examined microscopically. Second, not only must the officer be lawfully located in a place from which the object can be plainly seen, but he or she must also have a lawful right of access to the object itself. * * * In all events, we are satisfied that the absence of inadvertence was not essential to the court's rejection of the State's "plain view" argument in Coolidge.

III

JUSTICE STEWART concluded that the inadvertence requirement was necessary to avoid a violation of the express constitutional requirement that a valid warrant must particularly describe the things to be seized. He explained:

"The rationale of the exception to the warrant requirement, as just stated, is that a plain-view seizure will not turn an initially valid (and therefore limited) search into a 'general' one, while the inconvenience of procuring a warrant to cover an inadvertent discovery is great. But where the discovery is anticipated, where the police know in advance the location of the evidence and intend to seize it, the situation is altogether different. The requirement of a warrant to seize imposes no inconvenience whatever, or at least none which is constitutionally cognizable in a legal system that regards warrantless searches as 'per se unreasonable' in the absence of 'exigent circumstances.'

"If the initial intrusion is

bottomed upon a warrant that fails to mention a particular object, though the police know its location and intend to seize it, then there is a violation of the express constitutional requirement of 'Warrants * * * particularly describing . . [the] things to be seized.'" * * *

We find two flaws in this reasoning. First, evenhanded law enforcement is best achieved by the application of objective standards of conduct, rather than standards that depend upon the subjective state of mind of the officer. The fact that an officer is interested in an item of evidence and fully expects to find it in the course of a search should not invalidate its seizure if the search is confined in area and duration by the terms of a warrant or a valid exception to the warrant requirement. If the officer has knowledge approaching certainty that the item will be found, we see no reason why he or she would deliberately omit a particular description of the item to be seized from the application for a search warrant. Specification of the additional item could only permit the officer to expand the scope of the search. On the other hand, if he or she has a valid warrant to search for one item and merely a suspicion concerning the second, whether or not it amounts to probable cause, we fail to see why that suspicion should immunize the second item from seizure if it is found during a lawful search for the first. The hypothetical case put by JUSTICE WHITE in his dissenting opinion in Coolidge is instructive:

"Let us suppose officers secure a warrant to search a house for a rifle. While staying well within the range of a rifle search, they discover two photographs of the murder victim, both in plain sight in the bedroom. Assume also that the discovery of the one photograph was inadvertent but finding the other was anticipated. The Court would permit the seizure of only one of the photographs. But in terms of the 'minor' peril to Fourth Amendment values there is surely no difference between these two photographs: the interference with possession is the same in each case and the officers' appraisal of the photograph they expected to see is no less reliable than their judgment about the other. And in both situations the actual inconvenience and danger to evidence remain identical if the officers must depart and secure a warrant." * * *

Second, the suggestion that the inadvertence requirement is necessary to prevent the police from conducting general searches, or from converting specific warrants into general warrants, is not persuasive because that interest is already served by the requirements that no warrant issue unless it "particularly describ[es] the place to be searched and the persons or things to be seized," * * * and that a warrantless search be circumscribed by the exigencies which justify its initiation. See, e.g., *Maryland v. Buie*, [this volume]. * * * Scrupulous adherence to these requirements serves the interests in limiting the area and duration of the search that the inadvertence requirement inadequately protects. Once those commands have been satisfied and the officer has a lawful right of access, however, no additional Fourth

Amendment interest is furthered by requiring that the discovery of evidence be inadvertent. If the scope of the search exceeds that permitted by the terms of a validly issued warrant or the character of the relevant exception from the warrant requirement, the subsequent seizure is unconstitutional without more. Thus, in the case of a search incident to a lawful arrest, "[i]f the police stray outside the scope of an authorized *Chimel* search they are already in violation of the Fourth Amendment, and evidence so seized will be excluded; adding a second reason for excluding evidence hardly seems worth the candle." * * * Similarly, the object of a warrantless search of an automobile also defines its scope. * * *   In this case, the scope of the search was not enlarged in the slightest by the omission of any reference to the weapons in the warrant. Indeed, if the three rings and other items named in the warrant had been found at the outset—or if petitioner had them in his possession and had responded to the warrant by producing them immediately—no search for weapons could have taken place. **[d]** * * *

As we have already suggested, by hypothesis the seizure of an object in plain view does not involve an intrusion on privacy. If the interest in privacy has been invaded, the violation must have occurred before the object came into plain view and there is no need for an inadvertence limitation on seizures to condemn it. The prohibition against general searches and general warrants serves primarily as a protection against unjustified intrusions on privacy. But reliance on privacy concerns that support that prohibition is misplaced when the inquiry concerns

the scope of an exception that merely authorizes an officer with a lawful right of access to an item to seize it without a warrant.

In this case the items seized from petitioner's home were discovered during a lawful search authorized by a valid warrant. When they were discovered, it was immediately apparent to the officer that they constituted incriminating evidence. He had probable cause, not only to obtain a warrant to search for the stolen property, but also to believe that the weapons and handguns had been used in the crime he was investigating. The search was authorized by the warrant; the seizure was authorized by the "plain-view" doctrine.

The judgment is affirmed.

It is so ordered.

JUSTICE BRENNAN, with whom JUSTICE MARSHALL joins, dissenting.

I remain convinced that JUSTICE STEWART correctly articulated the plain view doctrine in *Coolidge v. New Hampshire*, [above].   The Fourth Amendment permits law enforcement officers to seize items for which they do not have a warrant when those items are found in plain view and (1) the officers are lawfully in a position to observe the items, (2) the discovery of the items is "inadvertent," and (3) it is immediately apparent to the officers that the items are evidence of a crime, contraband, or otherwise subject to seizure. In eschewing the inadvertent discovery requirement, the majority ignores the Fourth Amendment's express command that warrants particularly describe not only the *places* to be searched, but also the *things* to be seized. I respectfully dissent from this rewriting of the Fourth Amendment. **[e]**

I

* * * The [Fourth] Amendment protects two distinct interests. The prohibition against unreasonable searches and the requirement that a warrant "particularly describ[e] the place to be searched" protect an interest in privacy. The prohibition against unreasonable seizures and the requirement that a warrant "particularly describ[e] * * * the * * * things to be seized" protect a possessory interest in property. * * * **[f]**

The Amendment protects these equally important interests in precisely the same manner: by requiring a neutral and detached magistrate to evaluate, before the search or seizure, the government's showing of probable cause and its particular description of the place to be searched and the items to be seized. Accordingly, just as a warrantless search is *per se* unreasonable absent exigent circumstances, so too a seizure of personal property is "*per se* unreasonable within the meaning of the Fourth Amendment unless it is accomplished pursuant to a judicial warrant issued upon probable cause and particularly describing the items to be seized." * * *

The plain view doctrine is an exception to the general rule that a seizure of personal property must be authorized by a warrant. * * * Barring an exigency, there is no reason why the police officers could not have obtained a warrant to seize this evidence before entering the premises. The rationale behind the inadvertent discovery requirement is simply that we

will not excuse officers from the general requirement of a warrant to seize if the officers know the location of evidence, have probable cause to seize it, intend to seize it, and yet do not bother to obtain a warrant particularly describing that evidence. To do so would violate "the express constitutional requirement of 'Warrants * * * particularly describing * * * [the] things to be seized,'" and would "fly in the face of the basic rule that no amount of probable cause can justify a warrantless seizure." * * * **[g]**

Although joined by only three other Members of the Court, JUSTICE STEWART's discussion of the inadvertent discovery requirement has become widely accepted. * * * Forty-six States and the District of Columbia and twelve United States Court of Appeals now require plain view seizures to be inadvertent. There has been no outcry from law enforcement officials that the inadvertent discovery requirement unduly burdens their efforts. Given that the requirement is inescapably rooted in the plain language of the Fourth Amendment, I cannot fathom the Court's enthusiasm for discarding this element of the plain view doctrine.

The Court posits two "flaws" in JUSTICE STEWART's reasoning that it believes demonstrate the inappropriateness of the inadvertent discovery requirement. But these flaws are illusory. First, the majority explains that it can see no reason why an officer who "has knowledge approaching certainty" that an item will be found in a particular location "would deliberately omit a particular description of the item to be seized from the application for a search warrant." * * * But to the individual whose possessory interest has been invaded, it matters not *why* the police officer decided to omit a particular item from his application for a search warrant. When an officer with probable cause to seize an item fails to mention that item in his application for a search warrant—for whatever reason—and then seizes the item anyway, his conduct is *per se* unreasonable. Suppression of the evidence so seized will encourage officers to be more precise and complete in future warrant applications.

Furthermore, there are a number of instances in which a law enforcement officer might deliberately choose to omit certain items from a warrant application even though he has probable cause to seize them, knows they are on the premises, and intends to seize them when they are discovered in plain view. For example, the warrant application process can often be time consuming, especially when the police attempt to seize a large number of items. An officer interested in conducting a search as soon as possible might decide to save time by listing only one or two hard-to-find items, such as the stolen rings in this case, confident that he will find in plain view all of the other evidence he is looking for before he discovers the listed items. Because rings could be located almost anywhere inside or outside a house, it is unlikely that a warrant to search for and seize the rings would restrict the scope of the search. **[h]** An officer might rationally find the risk of immediately discovering the items listed in the warrant—thereby forcing him to conclude the search immediately—outweighed by the time saved in the application process.

* * *

* * * * * * * * * *

COMMENTS

[a] Is it essential for the states to have a uniform rule on the inadvertence element? See *Michigan v. Long* [this volume] and compare the comments of the dissent on point in this case.

[b] All the justices agree that a search and a seizure implicate somewhat different constitutional interests. But, the Court goes on to justify the search here by an implicit reliance on the privacy doctrine, while the dissent focuses on the property interest. Has the majority's ruling here been undermined by the later holding of *Soldal v. Cook County* [this volume] which emphasized the property rights aspects of seizures?

[c] Note that in *Coolidge* there was a seizure of the cars, but the incriminating evidence were the fibre and tissue residues found in the vacuum sweepings, which were the product of a quasi-separate search and seizure within the already seized cars. While the cars were in plain view, the incriminating evidence in them was not. That is, the sweepings were not immediately apparent as incriminating evidence.

[d] This exacting reading of the plain view assumes that police will stop searching as soon as the items listed in the warrant are found. However, items listed in warrants are usually listed in reasonably general or open language (*e.g.*, "a quantity of drugs") and so it is not clear precisely when the police *must* terminate their search.

[e] This statement by implication raises the classic point of why *stare decisis* is limited in constitutional adjudication. While some justices may find that the "rule of *Coolidge*" does not include inadvertence, others can argue that the fundamental law is not *Coolidge* but the Constitution itself, which *requires* particularity as to items seized.

[f] See Comment [b] above.

[g] Does it seem to you that the majority opinion puts the convenience of police officers above the explicit requirements of the Fourth Amendment?

[h] This is not a weighty point, since a warrant for guns and rings will still allow the officers to search into small spaces such as drawers and containers.

MINNESOTA v. DICKERSON

___ U.S. ___, 113 S.Ct. 2130, 124 L.Ed.2d 334 (1993)

JUSTICE WHITE delivered the opinion of the Court.

In this case, we consider whether the Fourth Amendment permits the seizure of contraband detected through a police officer's sense of touch during a protective pat-down search.

I

[Police officers at 8:15 p.m. saw Dickerson leave a building known, on the basis of previously executed warrants, as a notorious "crack house." When Dickerson saw the police he] abruptly halted and began walking in the opposite direction. His suspicion aroused, [the] officer watched as respondent turned and entered an alley on the other side of the apartment building. Based upon respondent's seemingly evasive actions and the fact that he had just left a building known for cocaine traffic, the officers decided to stop respondent and investigate further. **[a]**

The officers pulled their squad car into the alley and ordered respondent to stop and submit to a patdown search. The search revealed no weapons, but the officer conducting the search did take an interest in a small lump in respondent's nylon jacket. The officer later testified:

"[A]s I pat-searched the front of his body, I felt a lump, a small lump, in the front pocket. I examined it with my fingers and it slid and it felt to be a lump of crack cocaine in cellophane." * * *

The officer then reached into respondent's pocket and retrieved a small plastic bag containing one fifth of one gram of crack cocaine. Respondent was arrested and charged * * * with possession of a controlled substance.

[The trial court allowed the introduction of the evidence, finding the initial stop and frisk reasonable.] Finally, analogizing to the "plain-view" doctrine, under which officers may make a warrantless seizure of contraband found in plain view during a lawful search for other items, the trial court ruled that the officers' seizure of the cocaine did not violate the Fourth Amendment:

"To this Court there is no distinction as to which sensory perception the officer uses to conclude that the material is contraband. An experienced officer may rely upon his sense of smell in DWI stops or in recognizing the smell of burning marijuana in an automobile. The sound of a shotgun being racked would clearly support certain reactions by an officer. The sense of touch, grounded in experience and training, is as reliable as perceptions drawn from other senses. 'Plain feel,' therefore, is no different than plain view and will equally support the seizure here." * * *

* * *

[The Minnesota Court of Appeals and Supreme Court suppressed the evidence. They agreed that the initial stop and frisk was proper under *Terry v. Ohio* [this volume]].

[The Minnesota Supreme Court refused to extend the plain view concept to the sense of touch] on the grounds that "the sense of touch is inherently less immediate and less reliable than the sense of sight" and that "the sense of touch is far more intrusive into the personal privacy that is at the core of the [F]ourth [A]mendment." * * * The court thus appeared to adopt a categorical rule barring the seizure of any contraband detected by an officer through the sense of touch during a patdown search for weapons. The court further noted that "[e]ven if we recognized a 'plain feel' exception, the search in this case would not qualify" because "[t]he pat search of the defendant went far beyond what is permissible under *Terry*." * * * As the State Supreme Court read the record, the officer conducting the search ascertained that the lump in respondent's jacket was contraband only after probing and investigating what he certainly knew was not a weapon. * * *

II

A

* * * Time and again, this Court has observed that searches and seizures "'conducted outside the judicial process, without prior approval by judge or magistrate, are *per se* unreasonable under the Fourth Amendment—subject only to a few specifically established and well delineated exceptions.'" * * * One such exception was recognized in *Terry v. Ohio*, [this volume] which held that "where a police officer observes unusual conduct which leads him

reasonably to conclude in light of his experience that criminal activity may be afoot" the officer may briefly stop the suspicious person and make "reasonable inquiries" aimed at confirming or dispelling his suspicions. * * *

Terry further held that "[w]hen an officer is justified in believing that the individual whose suspicious behavior he is investigating at close range is armed and presently dangerous to the officer or to others," the officer may conduct a patdown search "to determine whether the person is in fact carrying a weapon." * * * "The purpose of this limited search is not to discover evidence of crime, but to allow the officer to pursue his investigation without fear of violence. . . ." * * * Rather, a protective search—permitted without a warrant and on the basis of reasonable suspicion less than probable cause—must be strictly "limited to that which is necessary for the discovery of weapons which might be used to harm the officer or others nearby." * * * If the protective search goes beyond what is necessary to determine if the suspect is armed, it is no longer valid under *Terry* and its fruits will be suppressed. *Sibron v. New York*, [this volume].

These principles were settled 25 years ago when, on the same day, the Court announced its decisions in *Terry* and *Sibron*. The question presented today is whether police officers may seize nonthreatening contraband detected during a protective patdown search of the sort permitted by *Terry*. We think the answer is clearly that they may, so long as the officer's search stays within the bounds marked by *Terry*.

B

We have already held that police officers, at least under certain circumstances, may seize contraband detected during the lawful execution of a *Terry* search. * * *

The Court in [*Michigan v.*] *Long* justified this latter holding by reference to our cases under the "plain-view" doctrine. * * * Under that doctrine, if police are lawfully in a position from which they view an object, if its incriminating character is immediately apparent, and if the officers have a lawful right of access to the object, they may seize it without a warrant. See *Horton v. California*, [this volume]. * * * If, however, the police lack probable cause to believe that an object in plain view is contraband without conducting some further search of the object—*i.e.*, if "its incriminating character [is not] 'immediately apparent,'" * * *—the plain-view doctrine cannot justify its seizure. *Arizona v. Hicks*, [this volume].

We think that this doctrine has an obvious application by analogy to cases in which an officer discovers contraband through the sense of touch during an otherwise lawful search. The rationale of the plain view doctrine is that if contraband is left in open view and is observed by a police officer from a lawful vantage point, there has been no invasion of a legitimate expectation of privacy and thus no "search" within the meaning of the Fourth Amendment—or at least no search independent of the initial intrusion that gave the officers their vantage point. * * * The warrantless seizure of contraband that presents itself in this manner is deemed justified by the realization that resort to a neutral magistrate under such circumstances would often be impracticable and would do little to promote the

objectives of the Fourth Amendment. * * * The same can be said of tactile discoveries of contraband. If a police officer lawfully pats down a suspect's outer clothing and feels an object whose contour or mass makes its identity immediately apparent, there has been no invasion of the suspect's privacy beyond that already authorized by the officer's search for weapons; if the object is contraband, its warrantless seizure would be justified by the same practical considerations that inhere in the plain view context.

The Minnesota Supreme Court rejected an analogy to the plain-view doctrine on two grounds: first, its belief that "the sense of touch is inherently less immediate and less reliable than the sense of sight," and second, that "the sense of touch is far more intrusive into the personal privacy that is at the core of the [F]ourth [A]mendment." * * * We have a somewhat different view. First, *Terry* itself demonstrates that the sense of touch is capable of revealing the nature of an object with sufficient reliability to support a seizure. The very premise of *Terry*, after all, is that officers will be able to detect the presence of weapons through the sense of touch and *Terry* upheld precisely such a seizure. Even if it were true that the sense of touch is generally less reliable than the sense of sight, that only suggests that officers will less often be able to justify seizures of unseen contraband. Regardless of whether the officer detects the contraband by sight or by touch, however, the Fourth Amendment's requirement that the officer have probable cause to believe that the item is contraband before seizing it ensures against excessively speculative seizures. The court's second concern—that touch is more intrusive into privacy than is sight—is inapposite in light of the fact that the intrusion the court fears has already been authorized by the lawful search for weapons. The seizure of an item whose identity is already known occasions no further invasion of privacy. See *Soldal v. Cook County*, [this volume]. * * * Accordingly, the suspect's privacy interests are not advanced by a categorical rule barring the seizure of contraband plainly detected through the sense of touch.

III

It remains to apply these principles to the facts of this case. * * * The Minnesota Supreme Court, after "a close examination of the record," held that the officer's own testimony "belies any notion that he 'immediately'" recognized the lump as crack cocaine. * * * Rather, the court concluded, the officer determined that the lump was contraband only after "squeezing, sliding and otherwise manipulating the contents of the defendant's pocket"—a pocket which the officer already knew contained no weapon. * * *

Under the State Supreme Court's interpretation of the record before it, it is clear that the court was correct in holding that the police officer in this case overstepped the bounds of the "strictly circumscribed" search for weapons allowed under *Terry*. * * * Where, as here, "an officer who is executing a valid search for one item seizes a different item," this Court rightly "has been sensitive to the danger . . . that officers will enlarge a specific authorization, furnished by a warrant or an exigency, into the

equivalent of a general warrant to rummage and seize at will." * * * Here, the officer's continued exploration of respondent's pocket after having concluded that it contained no weapon was unrelated to "the sole justification of the search [under *Terry*:] . . . the protection of the police officer and others nearby." * * * It therefore amounted to the sort of evidentiary search that *Terry* expressly refused to authorize, * * * and that we have condemned in subsequent cases. See * * * *Sibron*, [this volume].

Once again, the analogy to the plain-view doctrine is apt. [The Court reviewed *Arizona v. Hicks* [this volume]]. The facts of this case are very similar. Although the officer was lawfully in a position to feel the lump in respondent's pocket, because *Terry* entitled him to place his hands upon respondent's jacket, the court below determined that the incriminating character of the object was not immediately apparent to him. Rather, the officer determined that the item was contraband only after conducting a further search, one not authorized by *Terry* or by any other exception to the warrant requirement. Because this further search of respondent's pocket was constitutionally invalid, the seizure of the cocaine that followed is likewise unconstitutional. * * * **[b]**

IV

For these reasons, the judgment of the Minnesota Supreme Court is
Affirmed.

[Justice SCALIA concurred in a separate opinion; Chief Justice Rehnquist, joined by JUSTICES BLACK-MUN and THOMAS, concurred in

Parts I and II of the majority opinion but would remand the case to the

Minnesota Courts for further proceedings.]

* * * * * * * * * *

COMMENTS

[a] Is this enough reasonable suspicion to justify a *Terry* search?   If so, could police stop anyone who takes "seemingly evasive actions" in a "high crime area"?

[b] Would the search have been justified if there was a larger quantity of contraband in Dickerson's pocket, in a hard lump or container that could be mistaken for a gun or knife?

BERGER v. NEW YORK

388 U.S. 41, 87 S.Ct. 1873, 18 L.Ed.2d 1040 (1967)

MR. JUSTICE CLARK delivered the opinion of the Court.

* * *

I.

[Berger was convicted of conspiracy to bribe the Chairman of the New York State Liquor Authority [SLA]. On the tip of a bar owner that state liquor agents harassed him for failing to pay bribes, investigators uncovered evidence of widespread bribery in the agency. On the basis of this evidence an eavesdrop order was obtained from a state judge and a recording device was placed in the office of an attorney with SLA business for 60 days. On the basis of information from that bugging, the office of SLA official Harry Steinman was bugged under a 60 day warrant and evidence of the conspiracy by SLA chairman Berger was obtained.] Relevant portions of the recordings were received in evidence at the trial and were played to the jury, all over the objection of the petitioner. * * *

II.

Eavesdropping is an ancient practice which at common law was condemned as a nuisance. * * * At one time the eavesdropper listened by naked ear under the eaves of houses or their windows, or beyond their walls seeking out private discourse. The awkwardness and undignified manner of this method as well as its susceptibility to abuse was immediately recognized. [Telegraph eavesdropping by private parties was widespread in the nineteenth century and telephone wiretapping was widespread by police and by private individuals and businesses.]

* * * Illinois outlawed [electronic eavesdropping] in 1895 and in 1905 California extended its telegraph interception prohibition to the telephone. Some 50 years ago a New York legislative committee found that police, in cooperation with the telephone company, had been tapping telephone lines in New York despite an Act passed in 1895 prohibiting it. During prohibition days wiretaps were the principal source of information relied upon by the police as the basis for prosecutions. In 1934 the Congress outlawed the interception without authorization, and the divulging or publishing of the contents of wiretaps by passing § 605 of the Communications Act of 1934. New York, in 1938, declared by constitutional amendment that "[t]he right of the people to be secure against unreasonable interception of telephone and telegraph communications shall not be violated," but permitted by *ex parte* order of the Supreme Court of the State the interception of communications on a showing of "reasonable ground to believe that evidence of crime" might be obtained. * * *

Sophisticated electronic devices have now been developed (commonly known as "bugs") which are capable of eavesdropping on anyone in almost any given situation. They are to be distinguished from "wiretaps" which are confined to the interception of telegraphic and telephonic communications. Miniature in size * * *—no larger than a postage stamp—these gadgets pick up whispers within a room and broadcast them half a block away to a receiver. It is said that certain types of electronic rays beamed at walls or glass windows are capable of catching voice vibrations as they are bounced off the surfaces. Since 1940 eavesdropping has become a big business. * * * [a]

As science developed these detection techniques, lawmakers, sensing the resulting invasion of individual privacy, have provided some statutory protection for the public. [As of 1967, 36 states prohibited wiretapping and seven outlawed all electronic eavesdropping. Most of these states, as New York did, allowed some form of authorized eavesdropping by law enforcement.]

III.

The law, though jealous of individual privacy, has not kept pace with these advances in scientific knowledge. [JUSTICE CLARK recited a brief history of Fourth Amendment law.]

IV.

The Court was faced with its first wiretap case in 1928, *Olmstead v. United States*, 277 U.S. 438 [1928]. There the interception of Olmstead's telephone line was accomplished without entry upon his premises and was, therefore, found not to be proscribed by the Fourth Amendment. The basis of the decision was that the Constitution did not forbid the obtaining of evidence by wiretapping unless it involved actual unlawful entry into the house. Statements in the opinion that a conversation passing over a telephone wire cannot be said to come within the Fourth Amendment's enumeration of "persons, houses, papers, and effects" have been negated by our subsequent cases as hereinafter noted. [b] They found "conversation" was within the Fourth Amendment's protections, and that the use of electronic devices to capture it was a "search" within the meaning of the Amendment, and we so hold. In any event, Congress soon thereafter, and some say in answer to *Olmstead*, specifically prohibited the interception without authorization and the divulging or publishing of the contents of telephonic communications. * * *

[The Court recited the constitutional history of electronic eavesdropping. *Goldman v. United States*, 316 U.S. 129 (1942) held that a listening device placed against an office wall to overhear private conversations did not violate the Fourth Amendment because there was no physical trespass. *On Lee v. United States*, 343 U.S. 747 (1952), held that there is no Fourth Amendment violation when a person voluntarily makes incriminating statements to an agent wearing a "body mike." *Silverman v. United States*, 365 U.S. 505 (1961), held that there was a Fourth Amendment violation, where a microphone attached to a foot long spike was driven through a wall to contact a heating duct that ran through a house, because of the physical trespass.]

In *Wong Sun v. United States*, 371 U.S. 471 (1963), the Court for the first time specifically held that verbal evidence may be the fruit of official illegality under the Fourth Amendment along with the more common tangible fruits of unwarranted intrusion. [*Lopez v. United States*, 373 U.S. 427 (1963), confirmed the holding of *On Lee*.]

V.

It is now well settled that "the Fourth Amendment's right of privacy has been declared enforceable against the States through the Due Process Clause of the Fourteenth" Amendment. *Mapp v. Ohio*, [this volume] * * *

We, therefore, turn to New York's statute to determine the basis of the search and seizure authorized by it upon the order of a state [judge]. Section 813-a authorizes the issuance of an "ex parte order for eavesdropping" upon "oath or affirmation of a district attorney, or of the attorney-general or of an officer above the rank of sergeant of any police department of the state or of any political subdivision thereof. * * *" The oath must state "that there is reasonable ground to believe that evidence of crime may be thus obtained, and particularly describing the person or persons whose communications, conversations or discussions are to be overheard or recorded and the purpose thereof, and * * * identifying the particular telephone number or telegraph line involved." The judge "may examine on oath the applicant and any other witness he may produce and shall satisfy himself of the existence of reasonable grounds for the granting of such application." The order must specify the duration of the eavesdrop—not exceeding two months unless extended—and "[a]ny such order together with the papers upon which the application was based, shall be delivered to and retained by the applicant as authority for the eavesdropping authorized therein."

While New York's statute satisfies the Fourth Amendment's requirement that a neutral and detached authority be interposed between the police and the public, * * * the broad sweep of the statute is immediately observable. It permits the issuance of the order, or warrant for eavesdropping, upon the oath of the attorney general, the district attorney or any police officer above the rank of sergeant stating that "there is reasonable ground to believe that evidence of crime may be thus obtained. * * *" Such a requirement raises a serious probable-cause question under the Fourth Amendment. * * * Probable cause under the Fourth Amendment exists where the facts and circumstances within the affiant's knowledge, and of which he has reasonably trustworthy information, are sufficient unto themselves to warrant a man of reasonable caution to believe that an offense has been or is being committed. * * *

It is said, however, by the petitioner, and the State agrees, that the "reasonable ground" requirement of § 813-a "is undisputedly equivalent to the probable cause requirement of the Fourth Amendment." * * * While we have found no case on the point by New York's highest court, we need not pursue the question further because we have concluded that the statute is deficient on its face in other respects. Since petitioner clearly has standing to challenge the statute, being indisputably affected by it, we need not consider either the sufficiency of the affidavits upon which the eavesdrop orders were based, or the standing of petitioner to attack the search and seizure made thereunder. [c]

The Fourth Amendment commands that a warrant issue not only upon probable cause supported by oath or affirmation, but also "particularly describing the place to be searched, and the persons or things to be seized." New York's statute lacks this particularization. It merely says that a warrant may issue on reasonable ground to believe that evidence of crime may be obtained by the eavesdrop. It lays down no requirement for particularity in the warrant as to what specific crime has been or is being committed, nor "the place to be searched," or "the persons or things to be seized" as specifically required by the Fourth Amendment. The need for particularity and evidence of reliability in the showing required when judicial authorization of a search is sought is especially great in the case of eavesdropping. By its very nature eavesdropping involves an intrusion on privacy that is broad in scope. As was said in *Osborn v. United States*, 385 U.S. 323 (1966), the "indiscriminate use of such devices in law enforcement raises grave constitutional questions under the Fourth and Fifth Amendments," and imposes "a heavier responsibility on this Court in its supervision of the fairness of procedures. . . ." * * * There, two judges acting jointly authorized the installation of a device on the person of a prospective witness to record conversations between him and an attorney for a defendant then on trial in the United States District Court. [d] The judicial authorization was based on an affidavit of the witness setting out in detail previous conversations between the witness and the attorney concerning the bribery of jurors in the case. The recording device was, as the Court said, authorized "under the most precise and discriminate circumstances, circum-

stances which fully met the 'requirement of particularity'" of the Fourth Amendment. The Court was asked to exclude the evidence of the recording of the conversations seized pursuant to the order on constitutional grounds, * * * or in the exercise of supervisory power. * * * The Court refused to do so finding that the recording, although an invasion of the privacy protected by the Fourth Amendment, was admissible because of the authorization of the judges, based upon "a detailed factual affidavit alleging the commission of a specific criminal offense directly and immediately affecting the administration of justice * * * for the narrow and particularized purpose of ascertaining the truth of the affidavit's allegations." * * * The invasion was lawful because there was sufficient proof to obtain a search warrant to make the search for the limited purpose outlined in the order of the judges. Through these "precise and discriminate" procedures the order authorizing the use of the electronic device afforded similar protections to those that are present in the use of conventional warrants authorizing the seizure of tangible evidence. Among other safeguards, the order described the type of conversation sought with particularity, thus indicating the specific objective of the Government in entering the constitutionally protected area and the limitations placed upon the officer executing the warrant. Under it the officer could not search unauthorized areas; likewise, once the property sought, and for which the order was issued, was found the officer could not use the order as a passkey to further search. In addition, the order authorized one limited intrusion rather than a series or a continuous surveillance. And, we note that a new order was issued when the officer sought to resume the search and probable cause was shown for the succeeding one. Moreover, the order was executed by the officer with dispatch, not over a prolonged and extended period. In this manner no greater invasion of privacy was permitted than was necessary under the circumstances. Finally the officer was required to and did make a return on the order showing how it was executed and what was seized. Through these strict precautions the danger of an unlawful search and seizure was minimized. [e]

By contrast, New York's statute lays down no such "precise and discriminate" requirements. Indeed, it authorizes the "indiscriminate use" of electronic devices as specifically condemned in *Osborn*. "The proceeding by search warrant is a drastic one," * * * and must be carefully circumscribed so as to prevent unauthorized invasions of "the sanctity of a man's home and the privacies of life." * * * New York's broadside authorization rather than being "carefully circumscribed" so as to prevent unauthorized invasions of privacy actually permits general searches by electronic devices, the truly offensive character of which was first condemned in *Entick v. Carrington*, 19 How. St. Tr. 1029 [1765], and which were then known as "general warrants." The use of the latter was a motivating factor behind the Declaration of Independence. In view of the many cases commenting on the practice it is sufficient here to point out that under these "general warrants" customs officials were given blanket authority to conduct general searches for goods imported to the Colonies in violation of the tax laws of the Crown. The Fourth Amendment's requirement that a warrant "particularly describ[e] the place to be searched, and the persons or things to be seized," repudiated these general warrants and "makes general searches * * * impossible and prevents the seizure of one thing under a warrant describing another. As to what is to be taken, nothing is left to the discretion of the officer executing the warrant." * * *

We believe the statute here is equally offensive. First, as we have mentioned, eavesdropping is authorized without requiring belief that any particular offense has been or is being committed; nor that the "property" sought, the conversations, be particularly described. The purpose of the probable-cause requirement of the Fourth Amendment, to keep the state out of constitutionally protected areas until it has reason to believe that a specific crime has been or is being committed, is thereby wholly aborted. Likewise the statute's failure to describe with particularity the conversations sought gives the officer a roving commission to "seize" any and all conversations. It is true that the statute requires the naming of "the person or persons whose communications, conversations or discussions are to be overheard or recorded. * * *" But this does no more than identify the person whose constitutionally protected area is to be invaded rather than "particularly describing" the communications, conversations, or discussions to be seized. As with general warrants this leaves too much to the discretion of the officer executing the order. [f] Secondly, authorization of eavesdropping for a two-month period is the equivalent of a series of intrusions, searches, and seizures pursuant to a single showing of probable cause. Prompt execution is also avoided. During such a long and continuous (24 hours a day) period the conversations of any and all persons coming into the area covered by the device will be seized indiscriminately and without regard to their connection with the crime under investigation. Moreover, the statute permits, and there were authorized here, extensions of the original two-month period—presumably for two months each—on a mere showing that such extension is "in the public interest." Apparently the original grounds on which the eavesdrop order was initially issued also form the basis of the renewal. This we believe insufficient without a showing of present probable cause for the continuance of the eavesdrop. Third, the statute places no termination date on the eavesdrop once the conversation sought is seized. This is left entirely in the discretion of the officer.   Finally, the statute's procedure, necessarily because its success depends on secrecy, has no requirement for notice as do conventional warrants, nor does it overcome this defect by requiring some showing of special facts. On the contrary, it permits unconsented entry without any showing of exigent circumstances. Such a showing of exigency, in order to avoid notice, would appear more important in eavesdropping, with its inherent dangers, than that required when conventional procedures of search and seizure are utilized. Nor does the statute provide for a return on the warrant thereby leaving full discretion in the officer as to the use

of seized conversations of innocent as well as guilty parties. In short, the statute's blanket grant of permission to eavesdrop is without adequate judicial supervision or protective procedures.

VI.

It is said with fervor that electronic eavesdropping is a most important technique of law enforcement and that outlawing it will severely cripple crime detection. The monumental report of the President's Commission on Law Enforcement and Administration of Justice entitled "The Challenge of Crime in a Free Society" informs us that the majority of law enforcement officials say that this is especially true in the detection of organized crime. [g] As the Commission reports, there can be no question about the serious proportions of professional criminal activity in this country. However, we have found no empirical statistics on the use of electronic devices (bugging) in the fight against organized crime. Indeed, there are even figures available in the wiretap category which indicate to the contrary. * * *
            * * *

In any event we cannot forgive the requirements of the Fourth Amendment in the name of law enforcement. * * * [I]t is not asking too much that officers be required to comply with the basic command of the Fourth Amendment before the innermost secrets of one's home or office are invaded. Few threats to liberty exist which are greater than that posed by the use of eavesdropping devices. * * *

It is said that neither a warrant nor a statute authorizing eavesdropping can be drawn so as to meet the Fourth Amendment's requirements. If that be true then the "fruits" of eavesdropping devices are barred under the Amendment. On the other hand this Court has in the past, under specific conditions and circumstances, sustained the use of eavesdropping devices. See * * * *Osborn v. United States*, [above]. In the latter case the eavesdropping device was permitted where the "commission of a specific offense" was charged, its use was "under the most precise and discriminate circumstances" and the effective administration of justice in a federal court was at stake. The States are under no greater restrictions. The Fourth Amendment does not make the "precincts of the home or the office * * * sanctuaries where the law can never reach," DOUGLAS, J., dissenting in *Warden, Maryland Penitentiary v. Hayden*, 387 U.S. 294, 321 [1967], but it does prescribe a constitutional standard that must be met before official invasion is permissible. Our concern with the statute here is whether its language permits a trespassory invasion of the home or office, by general warrant,

contrary to the command of the Fourth Amendment. As it is written, we believe that it does. [h]

Reversed.

[JUSTICE DOUGLAS concurred, arguing that electronic eavesdropping was inherently broad, a "dragnet," that could not be made constitutional with warrant procedures.]

[JUSTICE STEWART concurred. He found that the New York law was constitutional and that electronic eavesdropping as permitted by statute is not an illegal search and seizure. However, in this case, probable cause was not established by the investigators' affidavits.]

[JUSTICES BLACK, HARLAN and WHITE each authored a lengthy dissent, arguing that eavesdropping does not come within the ambit of the Fourth Amendment, that the exclusionary rule does not apply, and that the ruling would severely hamper law enforcement.]

* * * * * * * * * * *

COMMENTS

[a] Should telephone wiretapping and electronic eavesdropping or "bugging" be seen as identical to secretly listening to conversations through windows and doors or as inherently different?

[b] *Olmstead* was finally overruled in *Katz v. United States*, [this volume]. But that overruling was the culmination of a series of cases that weakened it, including this decision. When *Katz* is read together with this case, the constitutional basis for electronic eavesdropping is established.

[c] If this case were decided today, would Berger have standing to challenge the eavesdropping? See *Rakas v. Illinois*, [this volume].

[d] The defendant was Jimmy Hoffa, the notorious leader of the Teamster's Union, who had been targeted by the Justice Department for prosecution. This was a major case that the government did not want to lose and so it went beyond the letter of the law to insure that its activity was constitutional.

[e] This lengthy recitation of *Osborn* may seem pedantic. On the contrary, the Court, while striking down what it viewed as an overly broad eavesdropping law and process in this case, took pains to send broad hints to Congress that its ruling did not absolutely prohibit tapping and bugging. Thus, the painstaking recitation of the *Olmstead* ruling was designed to indicate that under carefully controlled authority, eavesdropping was permissible.

[f] At this point the Court gives a point-by-point recitation of the flaws in the law. Again, this is helpful to Congress in that drafters of an electronic eavesdropping law could examine each point as a flaw to avoid in drafting an electronic eavesdropping law that would pass constitutional muster.

[g] JUSTICE WHITE, dissenting, added an Appendix quoting in full the section from the President's Commission on the usefulness of electronic eavesdropping. The justices are not insensitive to major reports and intellectual trends.

[h] The final paragraph was a massive loophole that was picked up by Congress, which passed a constitutional electronic eavesdropping law, that authorized a narrower range of bugging and tapping than did the New York Law.

UNITED STATES v. UNITED STATES DISTRICT COURT

407 U.S. 297, 92 S.Ct. 2125, 32 L.Ed.2d 752 (1972)

MR. JUSTICE POWELL delivered the opinion of the Court.

The issue before us is an important one for the people of our country and their Government. It involves the delicate question of the President's power, acting through the Attorney General, to authorize electronic surveillance in internal security matters without prior judicial approval. Successive Presidents for more than one-quarter of a century have authorized such surveillance in varying degrees, without guidance from the Congress or a definitive decision of this Court. This case brings the issue here for the first time. Its resolution is a matter of national concern, requiring sensitivity both to the Government's right to protect itself from unlawful subversion and attack and to the citizen's right to be secure in his privacy against unreasonable Government intrusion.

[In the heated political atmosphere of the late-1960s and early 1970s, the government engaged in electronic eavesdropping, without judicial warrant, against persons thought to be planning to bomb a Central Intelligence Agency office, on the authorization of the United States Attorney General. The defendants were charged with conspiracy to destroy Government property. The District Court for the Eastern District of Michigan held the eavesdropping illegal and ordered the government to disclose the contents of its tapes of overheard conversations to the defendant. The Court of Appeals upheld the District Court.]

I

Title III of the Omnibus Crime Control and Safe Streets Act, 18 U.S.C. §§2510-2520, authorizes the use of electronic surveillance for classes of crimes carefully specified in 18 U.S.C. §2516. Such surveillance is subject to prior court order. Section 2518 sets forth the detailed and particularized application necessary to obtain such an order as well as carefully circumscribed conditions for its use. The Act represents a comprehensive attempt by Congress to promote more effective control of crime while protecting the privacy of individual thought and expression. * * *

Together with the elaborate surveillance requirements in Title III, there is the following proviso, 18 U.S.C. §2511(3):

"Nothing contained in this chapter or in section 605 of the Communications Act of 1934 * * * shall limit the constitutional power of the President to take such measures as he deems necessary to protect the Nation against actual or potential attack or other hostile acts of a foreign power, to obtain foreign intelligence information deemed essential to the security of the United States, or to protect national security information against foreign intelligence activities. *Nor shall anything contained in this chapter be deemed to limit the constitutional power of the President to take such measures as he deems* *necessary to protect the United States against the overthrow of the Government by force or other unlawful means, or against any other clear and present danger to the structure or existence of the Government.* The contents of any wire or oral communication intercepted by authority of the President in the exercise of the foregoing powers may be received in evidence in any trial hearing, or other proceeding only where such interception was reasonable, and shall not be otherwise used or disclosed except as is necessary to implement that power." (Emphasis supplied.)

The Government relies on §2511(3). It argues that "in excepting national security surveillances from the Act's warrant requirement Congress recognized the President's authority to conduct such surveillances without prior judicial approval." * * *   The section thus is viewed as a recognition or affirmance of a constitutional authority in the President to conduct warrantless domestic security surveillance such as that involved in this case.

We think the language of §2511(3), as well as the legislative history of the statute, refutes this interpretation. [a] The relevant language is that:

"Nothing contained in this chapter * * * shall limit the constitutional power of the President to take such measures as he deems necessary to protect * * *"

against the dangers specified. At most, this is an implicit recognition that the President does have certain powers in the specified areas. Few would doubt this, as the section refers—among other

things—to protection "against actual or potential attack or other hostile acts of a foreign power." But so far as the use of the President's electronic surveillance power is concerned, the language is essentially neutral.

Section 2511(3) certainly confers no power, as the language is wholly inappropriate for such a purpose. It merely provides that the Act shall not be interpreted to limit or disturb such power as the President may have under the Constitution. In short, Congress simply left presidential powers where it found them. This view is reinforced by the general context of Title III. Section 2511(1) broadly prohibits the use of electronic surveillance "[e]xcept as otherwise specifically provided in this chapter." Subsection (2) thereof contains four specific exceptions. In each of the specified exceptions, the statutory language is as follows:

"It shall not be unlawful * * * to intercept" the particular type of communication described.

The language of subsection (3), here involved, is to be contrasted with the language of the exceptions set forth in the preceding subsection. Rather than stating that warrantless presidential uses of electronic surveillance "shall not be unlawful" and thus employing the standard language of exception, subsection (3) merely disclaims any intention to "limit the constitutional power of the President."

The express grant of authority to conduct surveillances is found in §2516, which authorizes the Attorney General to make application to a federal judge when surveillance may provide evidence of certain offenses. These offenses are described with meticulous care and specificity.

Where the Act authorizes surveillance, the procedure to be followed is specified in §2518. Subsection (1) thereof requires application to a judge of competent jurisdiction for a prior order of approval, and states in detail the information required in such application. Subsection (3) prescribes the necessary elements of probable cause which the judge must find before issuing an order authorizing an interception. Subsection (4) sets forth the required contents of such an order. Subsection (5) sets strict time limits on an order. Provision is made in subsection (7) for "an emergency situation" found to exist by the Attorney General (or by the principal prosecuting attorney of a State) "with respect to conspiratorial activities threatening the national security interest." In such a situation, emergency surveillance may be conducted "if an application for an order approving the interception is made . . . within forty-eight hours." If such an order is not obtained, or the application therefor is denied, the interception is deemed to be a violation of the Act.

In view of these and other interrelated provisions delineating permissible interceptions of particular criminal activity upon carefully specified conditions, it would have been incongruous for Congress to have legislated with respect to the important and complex area of national security in a single brief and nebulous paragraph. This would not comport with the sensitivity of the problem involved or with the extraordinary care Congress exercised in drafting other sections of the Act. We therefore think the conclusion

inescapable that Congress only intended to make clear that the Act simply did not legislate with respect to national security surveillances. **[b]**

The legislative history of §2511(3) supports this interpretation. [An excerpt from Senate hearings notes that Senators were not concerned with adding powers to the President, only not taking powers from him].

* * * [V]iewing §2511(3) as a congressional disclaimer and expression of neutrality, we hold that the statute is not the measure of the executive authority asserted in this case. Rather, we must look to the constitutional powers of the President.

II

* * *

Our present inquiry, though important, is therefore a narrow one. It addresses a question left open by *Katz [v. United States*, (this volume)]* * *

"Whether safeguards other than prior authorization by a magistrate would satisfy the Fourth Amendment in a situation involving the national security. * * *"

The determination of this question requires the essential Fourth Amendment inquiry into the "reasonableness" of the search and seizure in question, and the way in which that "reasonableness" derives content and meaning through reference to the warrant clause. * * *

We begin the inquiry by noting that the President of the United States has the fundamental duty, under Art.II, §1, of the Constitution, to "preserve, protect and defend the Constitution of the United States." Implicit in that duty is the power to protect our Government against those who would subvert or overthrow it by unlawful means. In the discharge of this duty, the President—through the Attorney General—may find it necessary to employ electronic surveillance to obtain intelligence information on the plans of those who plot unlawful acts against the Government. The use of such surveillance in internal security cases has been sanctioned more or less continuously by various Presidents and Attorneys General since July 1946. * * *

* * * The covertness and complexity of potential unlawful conduct against the Government and the necessary dependency of many conspirators upon the telephone make electronic surveillance an effective investigatory instrument in certain circumstances. * * *

It has been said that "[t]he most basic function of any government is to provide for the security of the individual and of his property." * * * And unless Government safeguards its own capacity to function and to preserve the security of its people, society itself could become so disordered that all rights and liberties would be endangered. * * *

But a recognition of these elementary truths does not make the employment by Government of electronic surveillance a welcome development—even when employed with restraint and under judicial supervision. There is, understandably, a deep-seated uneasiness and apprehension that this capability will be used to intrude upon cherished privacy of law-abiding citizens. We look to the Bill of Rights to safeguard this privacy. * * *

National security cases, moreover, often reflect a convergence of First and Fourth Amendment values not present in cases of "ordinary" crime. Though the investigative duty of the executive may be stronger in such cases, so also is there greater jeopardy to constitutionally protected speech. * * * History abundantly documents the tendency of Government—however benevolent and benign its motives—to view with suspicion those who most fervently dispute its policies. Fourth Amendment protections become the more necessary when the targets of official surveillance may be those suspected of unorthodoxy in their political beliefs. The danger to political dissent is acute where the Government attempts to act under so vague a concept as the power to protect "domestic security." Given the difficulty of defining the domestic security interest, the danger of abuse in acting to protect that interest becomes apparent. **[c]** Senator Hart addressed this dilemma in the floor debate on §2511(3):

> "As I read it—and this is my fear—we are saying that the President, on his motion, could declare—name your favorite poison—draft dodgers, Black Muslims, the Ku Klux Klan, or civil rights activists to be a clear and present danger to the structure or existence of the Government."

The price of lawful public dissent must not be a dread of subjection to an unchecked surveillance power. Nor must the fear of unauthorized official eavesdropping deter vigorous citizen dissent and discussion of Government action in private conversation. For private dissent, no less than open public discourse, is essential to our free society.

III

As the Fourth Amendment is not absolute in its terms, our task is to examine and balance the basic values at stake in this case: the duty of Government to protect the domestic security, and the potential danger posed by unreasonable surveillance to individual privacy and free expression. If the legitimate need of Government to safeguard domestic security requires the use of electronic surveillance, the question is whether the needs of citizens for privacy and free expression may not be better protected by requiring a warrant before such surveillance is undertaken. We must also ask whether a warrant requirement would unduly frustrate the efforts of Government to protect itself from acts of subversion and overthrow directed against it.

* * *

[The Court reviewed the historic importance of the judicial warrant, grounded in English procedure, and strengthened by judicial interpretations of the Fourth Amendment, in balancing government needs with citizen interests in privacy.]

These Fourth Amendment freedoms cannot properly be guaranteed if domestic security surveillances may be conducted solely within the discretion of the Executive Branch. The Fourth Amendment does not contemplate the executive officers of Government as neutral and disinterested magistrates. Their duty and responsibility are to enforce the laws, to investigate, and to prosecute. * * * The historical judgment, which the Fourth Amendment

accepts, is that unreviewed executive discretion may yield too readily to pressures to obtain incriminating evidence and overlook potential invasions of privacy and protected speech.

* * *

The Government argues that the special circumstances applicable to domestic security surveillances necessitate a further exception to the warrant requirement. It is urged that the requirement of prior judicial review would obstruct the President in the discharge of his constitutional duty to protect domestic security. We are told further that these surveillances are directed primarily to the collecting and maintaining of intelligence with respect to subversive forces, and are not an attempt to gather evidence for specific criminal prosecutions. It is said that this type of surveillance should not be subject to traditional warrant requirements which were established to govern investigation of criminal activity, not ongoing intelligence gathering. * * *

The Government further insists that courts "as a practical matter would have neither the knowledge nor the techniques necessary to determine whether there was probable cause to believe that surveillance was necessary to protect national security." These security problems, the Government contends, involve "a large number of complex and subtle factors" beyond the competence of courts to evaluate. [d]

As a final reason for exemption from a warrant requirement, the Government believes that disclosure to a magistrate of all or even a significant portion of the information involved in domestic security surveillances "would create serious potential dangers to the national security and to the lives of informants and agents. . . . Secrecy is the essential ingredient in intelligence gathering; requiring prior judicial authorization would create a greater 'danger of leaks, . . . because in addition to the judge, you have the clerk, the stenographer and some other officer like a law assistant or bailiff who may be apprised of the nature' of the surveillance." * * *

These contentions in behalf of a complete exemption from the warrant requirement, when urged on behalf of the President and the national security in its domestic implications, merit the most careful consideration. We certainly do not reject them lightly, especially at a time of worldwide ferment and when civil disorders in this country are more prevalent than in the less turbulent periods of our history. There is, no doubt, pragmatic force to the Government's position.

But we do not think a case has been made for the requested departure from Fourth Amendment standards. The circumstances described do not justify complete exemption of domestic security surveillance from prior judicial scrutiny. Official surveillance, whether its purpose be criminal investigation or ongoing intelligence gathering, risks infringement of constitutionally protected privacy of speech. Security surveillances are especially sensitive because of the inherent vagueness of the domestic security concept, the necessarily broad and continuing nature of intelligence gathering, and the temptation to utilize such surveillances to oversee political dissent. We recognize, as we have before, the constitutional basis of the President's domestic security role, but we think it must be exercised in a manner compatible with the Fourth Amendment. In this case we hold that this requires an appropriate prior warrant procedure.

We cannot accept the Government's argument that internal security matters are too subtle and complex for judicial evaluation. Courts regularly deal with the most difficult issues of our society. There is no reason to believe that federal judges will be insensitive to or uncomprehending of the issues involved in domestic security cases. Certainly courts can recognize that domestic security surveillance involves different considerations from the surveillance of "ordinary crime." If the threat is too subtle or complex for our senior law enforcement officers to convey its significance to a court, one may question whether there is probable cause for surveillance. [e]

Nor do we believe prior judicial approval will fracture the secrecy essential to official intelligence gathering. The investigation of criminal activity has long involved imparting sensitive information to judicial officers who have respected the confidentialities involved. * * *

Thus, we conclude that the Government's concerns do not justify departure in this case from the customary Fourth Amendment requirement of judicial approval prior to initiation of a search or surveillance. Although some added burden will be imposed upon the Attorney General, this inconvenience is justified in a free society to protect constitutional values. Nor do we think the Government's domestic surveillance powers will be impaired to any significant degree. A prior warrant establishes presumptive validity of the surveillance and will minimize the burden of justification in post-surveillance judicial review. By no means of least importance will be the reassurance of the public generally that indiscriminate wiretapping and bugging of law-abiding citizens cannot occur.

IV

We emphasize, before concluding this opinion, the scope of our decision. As stated at the outset, this case involves only the domestic aspects of national security. We have not addressed, and express no opinion as to, the issues which may be involved with respect to activities of foreign powers or their agents. **[f]** Nor does our decision rest on the language of §2511(3) or any other section of Title III of the Omnibus Crime Control and Safe Streets Act of 1968. That Act does not attempt to define or delineate the powers of the President to meet domestic threats to the national security.

Moreover, we do not hold that the same type of standards and procedures prescribed by Title III are necessarily applicable to this case. We recognize that domestic security surveillance may involve different policy and practical considerations from the surveillance of "ordinary crime." The gathering of security intelligence is often long range and involves the interrelation of various sources and types of information. The exact targets of such surveillance may be more difficult to identify than in surveillance operations against many types of crime specified in Title III. Often, too, the emphasis of domestic intelligence gathering is on the prevention of unlawful activity or the enhancement of the Government's preparedness for some possible future crisis or emergency. Thus, the focus of domestic surveillance may be less precise than that directed against more conventional types of crime.

Given these potential distinctions between Title III criminal surveillances and those involving the domestic security, Congress may wish to consider protective standards for the latter which differ from those already prescribed for specified crimes in Title III. * * * **[g]**

* * *

The judgment of the Court of Appeals is hereby
Affirmed.

THE CHIEF JUSTICE concurs in the result.

MR. JUSTICE REHNQUIST took no part in the consideration or decision of this case. [JUSTICE REHNQUIST was a high ranking assistant attorney general when the facts of this case arose.]

[JUSTICE DOUGLAS concurred with an opinion detailing the abuses of government sponsored, politically oriented, electronic surveillance.]

MR. JUSTICE WHITE, concurring in the judgment.

* * *

I would affirm the Court of Appeals but on the statutory ground urged by defendant-respondents * * * without reaching or intimating any views with respect to the constitutional issue decided by both the District Court and the Court of Appeals.

* * *

* * * * * * * * * * *

COMMENTS

[a] To support this conclusion, the Court engages in statutory interpretation, to determine the authoritative meaning of the statute. This is a mainstay of the work of most appellate courts. Statutory interpretation involves several "literary" techniques, including ascertaining the common meaning of words, ascertaining the plain meaning of the text, ascertaining the "intent of the legislature," determining the problems that animated the legislation, discovering the policy behind the law, etc. Like all legal reasoning, statutory interpretation involves logic, but is more an art than a science.

[b] This textual analysis rests on reading the single provision of Title III in the context of the entire electronic eavesdropping law.

[c] This appreciation of the danger of governmental overreaching in a sense turns elements of history (such as the Alien and Sedition Acts of 1798, the Palmer raids of 1919, the excesses of the "McCarthy era" in the late 1940s, and the legal harassment of Vietnam War opponents in the late 1960s) into elements of constitutional policy.

[d] Do you think it is good strategy for counsel to tell justices of the Supreme Court that issues of policy are too complex for them to understand?

[e] This is a not so subtle slap at the Government's argument.

[f] Congress has provided for a special warrant court and procedure for electronic eavesdropping orders against foreign powers or their agents in the Federal Intelligence Surveillance Act of 1978, 50 U.S.C. §1801 et seq.

[g] Congress has not done so. If the government wishes to investigate persons, not foreign powers or their agents, for "national security" purposes, it must go through the ordinary processes of investigation.

SCOTT v. UNITED STATES

436 U.S. 128, 98 S.Ct. 1717, 56 L.Ed.2d 168 (1978)

MR. JUSTICE REHNQUIST delivered the opinion of the Court.

In 1968, Congress enacted Title III of the Omnibus Crime Control and Safe Streets Act of 1968, which deals with wiretapping and other forms of electronic surveillance. * * * In this Act Congress, after this Court's decisions in *Berger v. New York*, [this volume], and *Katz v. United States* [this volume], set out to provide law enforcement officials with some of the tools thought necessary to combat crime without unnecessarily infringing upon the right of individual privacy. * * * [a]   This case requires us to construe the statutory requirement that wiretapping or electronic surveillance "be conducted in such a way as to minimize the interception of communications not otherwise subject to interception under this chapter. * * *" 18 U.S.C. §2518(5) (1976 ed.).
* * *

I

* * *   [Government agents obtained a telephone wiretap order in a premises where there was probable cause to believe nine named persons were engaged in a conspiracy to import and distribute drugs.] The order also required the agents to conduct the wiretap in "such away as to minimize the interception of communications that are [not] otherwise subject to interception" under the Act and to report to the court every five days "the progress of the interception and the nature of the communication intercepted." * * *

[b] Interception began that same day and continued [for a month], with the agents making the periodic reports to the judge as required. Upon cessation of the interceptions, search and arrest warrants were executed which led to the arrest of 22 persons and the indictment of 14.
* * * The [district court's suppression of the wiretap evidence] relied in large part on the fact that virtually all the conversations were intercepted while only 40% of them were shown to be narcotics related. This, the court reasoned, "strongly indicate[d] the indiscriminate use of wire surveillance that was proscribed by *Katz* and *Berger.*" * * * [c]
[This ruling was overturned by the court of appeals on the ground that it was too sweeping; on remand the district court excluded the evidence after hearing evidence on minimization; on further appeal, the Court of Appeals itself] examined the intercepted conversations and held that suppression was not appropriate in this case because the [District] court could not conclude that "some conversation was intercepted which clearly would not have been intercepted had reasonable attempts at minimization been made." * * *

II

Petitioners' principal contention is that the failure to make good-faith efforts to comply with the minimization requirement is itself a violation of §2518(5). They urge that it is only after an assessment is made of the agents' good-faith efforts, and presumably a determination that the agents did make such efforts, that one turns to the question of whether those efforts were reasonable under the circumstances. * * * The so-called "call analysis," which was introduced by the Government to suggest the reasonableness of intercepting most of the calls, cannot lead to a contrary conclusion because, having been prepared after the fact by a Government attorney and using terminology and categories which were not indicative of the agents' thinking at the time of the interceptions, it does not reflect the perceptions and mental state of the agents who actually conducted the wiretap. [d]

The Government responds that petitioners' argument fails to properly distinguish between what is necessary to establish a statutory or constitutional violation and what is necessary to support a suppression remedy once a violation has been established. In view of the deterrent purposes of the exclusionary rule, consideration of official motives may play some part in determining whether application of the exclusionary rule is appropriate *after* a statutory or constitutional violation has been established. But the existence *vel non* of such a violation turns on an objective assessment of the officer's actions in light of the facts and circumstances confronting him at the time. Subjective intent alone, the Government contends, does not make otherwise lawful conduct illegal or unconstitutional.

We think the Government's position, * * * embodies the proper approach for evaluating compliance with the minimization requirement. * *

* [A]lmost without exception in evaluating alleged violations of the Fourth Amendment the Court has first undertaken an objective assessment of an officer's actions in light of the facts and circumstances then known to him. The language of the Amendment itself proscribes only "unreasonable" searches and seizures. In *Terry v. Ohio* [this volume], the Court emphasized the objective aspect of the term "reasonable." * * * [e]

* * *

Petitioners do not appear, however, to rest their argument entirely on Fourth Amendment principles. Rather, they argue in effect that regardless of the search-and-seizure analysis conducted under the Fourth Amendment, the statute regulating wiretaps requires the agents to make good-faith efforts at minimization, and the failure to make such efforts is itself a violation of the statute which requires suppression.

This argument fails for more than one reason. In the first place, in the very section in which it directs minimization Congress, by its use of the word "conducted," made it clear that the focus was to be on the agents' actions not their motives. Any lingering doubt is dispelled by the legislative history which, as we have recognized before in another context, declares that sec. 2515 was not intended "generally to press the scope of the suppression role beyond present search and seizure law." * * * [f]

III

We turn now to the * * * analysis of the reasonableness of the agents' conduct in intercepting all of the calls in this particular wiretap. Because of the necessarily ad hoc nature of any determination of reasonableness, there can be no inflexible rule of law which will decide every case. The statute does not forbid the interception of all nonrelevant conversations, but rather instructs the agents to conduct the surveillance in such a manner as to "minimize" the interception of such conversations. * * *

[B]lind reliance on the percentage of nonpertinent calls intercepted is not a sure guide to the correct answer. Such percentages may provide assistance, but there are surely cases, such as the one at bar, where the percentage of nonpertinent calls is relatively high and yet their interception was still reasonable. The reasons for this may be many. Many of the nonpertinent calls may have been very short. Others may have been one-time only calls. Still other calls may have been ambiguous in nature or apparently involved guarded or coded language. In all these circumstances agents can hardly be expected to know that the calls are not pertinent prior to their termination.

In determining whether the agents properly minimized, it is also important to consider the circumstances of the wiretap. For example, when the investigation is focusing on what is thought to be a widespread conspiracy more extensive surveillance may be justified in an attempt to determine the precise scope of the enterprise. And it is possible that many more of the conversations will be permissibly interceptable because they will involve one or more of the co-conspirators. The type of use to which the telephone is normally put may also have some bearing on the extent of minimization required. For example, if the agents are permitted to tap a public telephone because one individual is thought to be placing bets over the phone, substantial doubts as to minimization may arise if the agents listen to every call which goes out over that phone regardless of who places the call. On the other hand, if the phone is located in the residence of a person who is thought to be the head of a major drug ring, a contrary conclusion may be indicated. [g]

Other factors may also play a significant part in a particular case. For example, it may be important to determine at exactly what point during the authorized period the interception was made. During the early stages of surveillance the agents may be forced to intercept all calls to establish categories of nonpertinent calls which will not be intercepted thereafter. Interception of those same types of calls might be unreasonable later on, however, once the nonpertinent categories have been established and it is clear that this particular conversation is of that type. * * *

* * * [I]n this case in the light of these observations, we find nothing to persuade us that the Court of Appeals was wrong in its rejection of [the defendant's] claim. Forty percent of the calls were clearly narcotics [10] related and the propriety of their interception is, of course, not in dispute. Many of the remaining calls were very short, such as wrong-number calls, calls to persons who were not available to come to the phone, and calls to the telephone company to hear the recorded weather message which lasts less than 90 seconds. In a case such as this, involving a wide-ranging conspiracy with a large number of participants, even a seasoned listener

would have been hard pressed to determine with any precision the relevancy of many of the calls before they were completed. A large number were ambiguous in nature, making characterization virtually impossible until the completion of these calls. And some of the nonpertinent conversations were one-time conversations. Since these calls did not give the agents an opportunity to develop a category of innocent calls which should not have been intercepted, their interception cannot be viewed as a violation of the minimization requirement. **[h]**

[JUSTICE REHNQUIST then factually analyzed seven longer telephone calls that did not fall into the categories listed above and noted that each one of them contained references that could reasonably be linked to the drug business]. Although none of these conversations turned out to be material to the investigation at hand, we cannot say that the Court of Appeals was incorrect in concluding that the agents did not act unreasonably at the time they made these interceptions. Its judgment is accordingly

Affirmed.

MR. JUSTICE BRENNAN, with whom MR. JUSTICE MARSHALL joins, dissenting.

* * * [Title III,] for the first time authorizing law enforcement personnel to monitor private telephone conversations, provided strict guidelines and limitations on the use of wiretaps as a barrier to Government infringement of individual privacy. One of the protections thought essential by Congress as a bulwark against unconstitutional governmental intrusion on private conversations is the "minimization requirement" of sec. 2518(5). **[i]** The Court today eviscerates this congressionally mandated protection of individual privacy, * * * [by] dilut[ing] congressionally established safeguards designed to prevent Government electronic surveillance from becoming the abhorred general warrant which historically had destroyed the cherished expectation of privacy in the home. ***

[The agents admitted they made no effort to minimize interceptions. The majority finds that this did not violate Title III]. * * * The basis for [the Supreme Court's] conclusion is a *post hoc* reconstruction offered by the Government of what would have been reasonable assumptions on the part of the agents had they attempted to comply with the statute. Since, on the basis of this reconstruction of reality, it would have been reasonable for the agents to assume that each of the calls dialed and received was likely to be in connection with the criminal enterprise, there was no violation, notwithstanding the fact that the agents intercepted every call with no effort to minimize interception of the noninterceptable calls. That reasoning is thrice flawed.

First, and perhaps most significant, it totally disregards the explicit congressional command that the wiretap be *conducted* so as to minimize interception of communications not subject to interception. Second, it blinks reality by accepting, as a substitute for the good-faith exercise of judgment as to which calls should not be intercepted by the agent most familiar with the investigation, the *post hoc* conjectures of the Government as to how the agent would have acted had he exercised his judgment. **[j]** Because it is difficult to know with any degree of certainty whether a given communication is subject to interception prior to its interception, there necessarily must be a margin of error permitted. But we do not enforce the basic premise of the Act that intrusions of privacy must be kept to the minimum by excusing the failure of the agent to make the good-faith effort to minimize which Congress mandated. In the nature of things it is impossible to know how many fewer interceptions would have occurred had a good-faith judgment been exercised, and it is therefore totally unacceptable to permit the failure to exercise the congressionally imposed duty to be excused by the difficulty in predicting what might have occurred had the duty been exercised. Finally, the Court's holding permits Government agents deliberately to flout the duty imposed upon them by Congress. In a linguistic *tour de force* the Court converts the mandatory language that the interception "shall be conducted" to a precatory suggestion.

[The legislative history indicates a Congressional desire that the minimization provision be strictly construed to deter government overreaching].

      * * *

      * * * [T]he Court manifests a disconcerting willingness to unravel individual threads of statutory protection without regard to their interdependence and to whether the cumulative effect is to rend the fabric of Title III's "congressionally designed bulwark against conduct of authorized electronic surveillance in a manner that violates the constitutional guidelines announced in *Berger v. New York* * * * and *Katz v. United States*. * * *" **[k]** * * * This process of myopic, incremental denigration of Title III's safeguards raises the specter that, as judicially "enforced," Title III may be vulnerable to constitutional attack for violation of Fourth Amendment standards, thus defeating the careful effort Congress made to avert that result.

     *   *   *   *   *   *   *   *   *   *

COMMENTS

[a] JUSTICE REHNQUIST emphasizes the usefulness of wiretapping as a law enforcement tool. Compare this to the beginning of JUSTICE BRENNAN's dissent.

[b] The district court closely controlled the investigation by receiving reports every five days (whether oral or written is not mentioned). There is no indication that the judge asked the agents what steps they were taking to minimize intrusions.

[c] What, if anything, is wrong with a rule that conclusively presumes that agents fail to minimize interceptions when only 40 percent of the calls intercepted are related to the drug selling? Should the outcome be different if only 5 percent of the calls were related to drug dealing? Would the defense argument differ if 75 percent of the calls were criminally related? Does the importance of the percentage depend on the nature of the crime under investigation?

[d] Under this defense argument, if the government agents genuinely and reasonably believe at the outset that minimization is impossible, or if that becomes clear to them as the eavesdropping is conducted, must they still go through the motions of minimization? Or must they file a detailed report based on contemporaneous notes? The second part of the petitioner's argument is similar to the rule that the existence of probable cause is determined by the state of knowledge the officer had before the search rather than after.

[e] The reasonableness approach to the Fourth Amendment is applied. But it applies only where a warrant is not required, as in "stop and frisk" under *Terry v. Ohio*. Since electronic eavesdropping is valid only under a very strict warrant requirement, isn't the majority's application of reasonableness off the mark? The dissent seems not to notice this flaw in the majority's logic.

[f] The Supreme Court can set the tone for the way in which statutes are applied. The Court makes it clear that Title III is not to be interpreted in a rigid way that automatically excludes evidence when a provision is not strictly adhered to.

[g] The use of the *Katz* example is an extreme example of nonminimization. The counter-examples raise the specter that taps of home telephones will hereafter tend to be indiscriminate.

[h] This close factual analysis, favorable to the prosecution, may very well be swayed by the fact that such a large proportion of the calls were related to the drug business. A situation where one family member is selling drugs and others are innocent but their calls were monitored might cast a different light on a subsequent case.

[i] Compare the opening of JUSTICE BRENNAN's dissent with JUSTICE REHNQUIST's. Here, the dangers to individual liberty are stressed. Title III is concerned with balancing legitimate law enforcement needs and the need to protect privacy. The justices' different emphases clearly signal their concerns and whether they would interpret Title III loosely or strictly.

[j] What is wrong with after-the-fact evaluation of reasonableness? Could it result in indiscriminate tapping and bugging with the government later deciding whether or not to use the evidence? This scenario seems to be precluded by many of the provisions of Title III. Thus, why isn't it reasonable for the government to analyze the calls to make a case to show that it did not violate the statute? Don't defendants finely examine the actions of government agents and prosecutors in a post-hoc effort to find error?

[k] JUSTICE BRENNAN links Title III to the Court's prior establishment of Fourth Amendment standards, in order to make a case that the majority's loose interpretation of the statute directly violates the Constitution and not just Title III.

SMITH v. MARYLAND

442 U.S. 735, 99 S.Ct. 2577, 61 L.Ed.2d 220 (1979)

MR. JUSTICE BLACKMUN delivered the opinion of the Court.

This case presents the question whether the installation and use of a pen register [a] constitutes a "search" within the meaning of the Fourth Amendment, made applicable to the States through the Fourteenth Amendment. * * *

I

[A woman was robbed; she gave police a description of the robber and his vehicle. Thereafter she began to receive] threatening and obscene phone calls from a man identifying himself as the robber. On one occasion, the caller asked that she step out on her front porch; she did so, and saw the [automobile] she had earlier described to police moving slowly past her home. * * * By tracing the license plate number, police learned that the car was registered in the name of petitioner, Michael Lee Smith. * * *

The next day, the telephone company, at police request, installed a pen register at its central offices to record the numbers dialed from the telephone at petitioner's home. * * * The police did not get a warrant or court order before having the pen register installed. The register revealed [a date on which Smith placed a call to the robbery victim. That and other evidence was the basis of a search warrant of Smith's home which produced incriminating evidence used to convict him of robbery.]

* * * The pen register tape (evidencing the fact that a phone call had been made from petitioner's phone to [the victim's] phone) and the phone book seized in the search of petitioner's residence were admitted into evidence against him. * * *

[The Maryland Court of Appeals upheld the conviction, holding that there was] no constitutionally protected reasonable expectation of privacy in the numbers dialed into a telephone system and hence no search within the fourth amendment is implicated by the use of a pen register installed at the central offices of the telephone company." * * * Three judges dissented, * * *

II

A

[In this part, the Court reviewed the ruling of *Katz v. United States*, [this volume]. The Court noted in a footnote that because the telephone company placed the pen register at police request, it acted as an agent of law enforcement, establishing state action.]

B

[A pen register does not involve a physical trespass into a home, records only telephone numbers called and does not indicate the content of the call or whether it was completed.] Given a pen register's limited capabilities, therefore, petitioner's argument that its installation and use constituted a "search" necessarily rests upon a claim that he had a "legitimate expectation of privacy" regarding the numbers he dialed on his phone.

This claim must be rejected. First, we doubt that people in general entertain any actual expectation of privacy in the numbers they dial. All telephone users realize that they must "convey" phone numbers to the telephone company, since it is through telephone company switching equipment that their calls are completed. All subscribers realize, moreover, that the phone company has facilities for making permanent records of the numbers they dial, for they see a list of their long-distance (toll) calls on their monthly bills. In fact, pen registers and similar devices are routinely used by telephone companies "for the purposes of checking billing operations, detecting fraud and preventing violations of law." * * * Pen registers are regularly employed "to determine whether a home phone is being used to conduct a business, to check for a defective dial, or to check for overbilling." * * * Although most people may be oblivious to a pen register's esoteric functions, they presumably have some awareness of one common use: to aid in the identification of persons making annoying or obscene calls. * * * Telephone users, in sum, typically know that they must convey numerical information to the phone company; that the phone company has facilities for recording this information; and that the phone company does in fact record this information for a variety of legitimate business purposes. Although subjective expectations cannot be scientifically gauged, it is too much to believe that telephone subscribers, under these circumstances, harbor any general expectation that the numbers they dial will remain secret.

Petitioner argues, however, that, whatever the expectations of telephone users in general, he demonstrated an expectation of privacy by his own conduct here, since he "us[ed] the telephone *in his house* to the exclusion of all others." * * * But the site of the call is immaterial for purposes of analysis in this case. Although petitioner's conduct may have been calculated to keep the *contents* of his conversation private, his conduct was not and could not have been calculated to preserve the privacy of the number he dialed. Regardless of his location, petitioner had to convey that number to the telephone company in precisely the same way if he wished to complete his call. The fact that he dialed the number on his home phone rather than on some other phone could make no conceivable difference, nor could any subscriber rationally think that it would.

Second, even if petitioner did harbor some subjective expectation that the phone numbers he dialed would remain private, this expectation is not "one that society is prepared to recognize as 'reasonable.'" * * * This Court consistently has held that a person has no legitimate expectation of privacy in information he voluntarily turns over to third parties. * * * [This] Court held that a bank depositor has no "legitimate 'expectation of privacy'" in financial information "voluntarily conveyed to ... banks and exposed to their employees in the ordinary course of business [, even if the information is given with the assumption that it will be kept confidential]." * * *

This analysis dictates that petitioner can claim no legitimate expectation of privacy here. When he used his phone, petitioner voluntarily conveyed numerical information to the telephone company and "exposed" that information to its equipment in the ordinary course of business. In so doing, petitioner assumed the risk that the company would reveal to police the numbers he dialed. The switching equipment that processed those numbers is merely the modern counterpart of the operator who, in an earlier day, personally completed calls for the subscriber. Petitioner concedes that if he had placed his calls through an operator, he could claim no legitimate expectation of privacy. * * * We are not inclined to hold that a different constitutional result is required because the telephone company has decided to automate.

* * *

We therefore conclude that petitioner in all probability entertained no actual expectation of privacy in the phone numbers he dialed, and that, even if he did, his expectation was not "legitimate." The installation and use of a pen register, consequently, was not a "search," and no warrant was required. The judgment of the Maryland Court of Appeals is affirmed.

It is so ordered. **[b]**

MR. JUSTICE POWELL took no part in the consideration or decision of this case.

MR. JUSTICE STEWART, with whom MR. JUSTICE BRENNAN joins, dissenting.

* * *

I think that the numbers dialed from a private telephone—like the conversations that occur during a call—are within the   constitutional protection recognized in *Katz*. * * * The information captured by such surveillance emanates from private conduct within a person's home or office—locations that without question are entitled to Fourth and Fourteenth Amendment protection. * * *

The numbers dialed from a private telephone—although certainly more prosaic than the conversation itself—are not without "content." Most private telephone subscribers may have their own numbers listed in a publicly distributed directory, but I doubt there are any who would be happy to have broadcast to the world a list of the local or long distance numbers they have called. This is not because such a list might in some sense be incriminating, but because it easily could reveal the identities of the persons and the places called, and thus reveal the most intimate details of a person's life.

I respectfully dissent.

MR. JUSTICE MARSHALL, with whom MR. JUSTICE BRENNAN joins, dissenting.

* * *

* * * Privacy is not a discrete commodity, possessed absolutely or not at all. Those who disclose certain facts to a bank or phone company for a limited business purpose need not assume that this information will be released to other persons for other purposes. * * *

* * * [T]he Court determines that individuals who convey information to third parties have "assumed the risk" of disclosure to the government. * * * This analysis is misconceived in two critical respects.

Implicit in the concept of assumption of risk is some notion of choice. *

* * [H]ere, unless a person is prepared to forgo use of what for many has become a personal or professional necessity, he cannot help but accept the risk of surveillance. * * * It is idle to speak of "assuming" risks in contexts where, as a practical matter, individuals have no realistic alternative.

More fundamentally, to make risk analysis dispositive in assessing the reasonableness of privacy expectations would allow the government to define the scope of Fourth Amendment protections. For example, law enforcement officials, simply by announcing their intent to monitor the content of random samples of first-class mail or private phone conversations, could put the public on notice of the risks they would thereafter assume in such communications. * * *

In my view, whether privacy expectations are legitimate within the meaning of *Katz* depends not on the risks an individual can be presumed to accept when imparting information to third parties, but on the risks he should be forced to assume in a free and open society. * * *

* * *

* * * * * * * * * *

COMMENTS

[a] In a footnote a pen register was defined as "a mechanical device that records the numbers dialed on a telephone by monitoring the electrical impulses caused when the dial on the telephone is released. It does not overhear oral communications and does not indicate whether calls are actually completed." A pen register is "usually installed at a central telephone facility [and] records on a paper tape all numbers dialed from [the] line" to which it is attached.

[b] In 1986 Congress, despite this ruling, enacted a law stating that "no person may install or use a pen register or a trap and trace device without first obtaining a court order.* * *"   8 U.S.C. §3121(a). However, the only sanction for failure to obtain an order is a criminal penalty of one year imprisonment, 18 U.S.C. §3121(C).   Unlike the general electronic eavesdropping statute, no statutory exclusionary rule is provided.

UNITED STATES v. OJEDA RIOS

495 U.S. 257, 110 S.Ct. 1845, 109 L.Ed.2d 224 (1990)

JUSTICE WHITE delivered the opinion of the Court.

This case arises under Title III of the Omnibus Crime Control and Safe Streets Act of 1968, as amended, 18 U.S.C. §2510 *et. seq.*, (Title III), which regulates the interception of wire, oral, and electronic communications. Except under extraordinary circumstances, * * * electronic surveillance may be conducted only pursuant to a court order. * * * Section 2518(8)(a) requires that "[t]he contents of any wire, oral, or electronic communication intercepted by any means authorized by this chapter shall, if possible, be recorded on tape or wire or other comparable device" and that recording "shall be done in such way as will protect the recording from editing or other alterations." The section further provides that "[i]mmediately upon the expiration of the period of the order, or extensions thereof, such recordings shall be made available to the judge issuing such order and sealed under his directions." * * * Section 2518(8)(a) has an explicit exclusionary remedy for noncompliance with the sealing requirement, providing that "[t]he presence of the seal provided for by this subsection, or a satisfactory explanation for the absence thereof, shall be a prerequisite for the use or disclosure of the contents of any wire, oral, or electronic communication or evidence derived therefrom. * * *" [a]

In this case, a series of court orders authorized electronic surveillance. The tapes later offered in evidence bore seals but the seals on the tapes at issue had not been immediately attached as required by the statute. The issue we address is whether §2518(8)(a) requires suppression of those tapes.

[Respondents are members of a Puerto Rican organization suspected of large scale robberies. Several home electronic interception orders were executed, concerning separate crimes, between April 27 1984 and July 9, 1984, and between July 27, 1984 and September 24, 1984. An order for surveillance of Ojeda Rios' car expired on October 10, 1984.] All tapes created during the surveillance of Ojeda Rios were sealed by the United States District Court for the District of Puerto Rico on October 13, 1984.

[Other members of the conspiracy were also subjected to electronic surveillance, which expired in 1985. Due to the complexity of the case involving many parties to several acts of robbery, prosecutors treated some wiretap requests as extensions of others, and thus did not seal them, when they should have been treated as new orders.]

After respondents were indicted for various offenses relating to the Wells Fargo depot robbery, they moved to suppress all evidence the Government had obtained as a result of electronic surveillance. Following a suppression hearing, the District Court [suppressed some of the tapes on the grounds that they were not extensions of prior orders. The District Court calculated that there had been an 82-day delay in sealing the tapes in one case and 118 days in another.] * * * Without determining the authenticity of these two sets of tapes, the District Court suppressed them on the basis of the delay alone.

The United States Court of Appeals for the Second Circuit affirmed the suppression of the tapes, * * * rejecting the Government's explanation for the sealing delays. Because the scope and role of the sealing provision of Title III has generated disagreement in the lower courts, we granted certiorari, * * * and now vacate and remand.

The Government first argues that because §2518(8)(a) states that as a prerequisite to admissibility, electronic surveillance tapes must either bear a seal or the Government must provide a "satisfactory explanation" for the "absence" of a seal, the "satisfactory explanation" requirement does not apply where the tapes to be offered in evidence actually bear a seal, regardless of when or why the seal was applied. This argument is unpersuasive. The narrow reading suggested by the Government is not a plausible interpretation of congressional intent when the terms and purpose of §2518(8)(a) are considered as a whole. The section begins with the command that tapes shall be sealed "immediately" upon expiration of the underlying surveillance order and then, prior to the clause relied upon by the Government, provides that "the seal *provided for by this subsection*" (emphasis added) is a prerequisite to the admissibility of electronic surveillance tapes. The clear import of these provisions is that the seal required by §2518(8)(a) is not just any seal but a seal that has been obtained *immediately* upon expiration

of the underlying surveillance order. The "absence" the Government must satisfactorily explain encompasses not only the total absence of a seal but also the absence of a timely applied seal. Contrary to what is so plainly required by §2518(8)(a), the Government would have us nullify the immediacy aspect of the sealing requirement.

The primary thrust of §2518(8)(a), * * * and a congressional purpose embodied in Title III in general, * * * is to ensure the reliability and integrity of evidence obtained by means of electronic surveillance. The presence or absence of a seal does not in itself establish the integrity of electronic surveillance tapes. Rather, the seal is a means of ensuring that subsequent to its placement on a tape, the Government has no opportunity to tamper with, alter, or edit the conversations that have been recorded. It is clear to us that Congress viewed the sealing requirement as important precisely because it limits the Government's opportunity to alter the recordings.

The Government's view of the statute would create the anomalous result that the prosecution could delay requesting a seal for months, perhaps even until a few days before trial, without risking a substantial penalty. Since it is likely that a district court would automatically seal the tapes, there would be no "absence" of a seal, in the sense suggested by the Government, and §2518(8)(a) would not come into play, even though the tapes would have been exposed to alteration or editing for an extended period of time. Such a view of the statute ignores the purposes of the sealing provision and is too strained a reading of the statutory language to withstand scrutiny. Like every Court of Appeals that has considered the question, we conclude that §2518(8)(a) applies to a delay in sealing, as well as to a complete failure to seal, tapes.

The Government's second contention is that even if §2518(8)(a)'s "satisfactory explanation" requirement applies to delays in sealing tapes, it is satisfied if the Government first explains *why* the delay occurred and then demonstrates that the tapes are authentic. This submission, however, also is not a sensible construction of the language of §2518(8)(a) and would essentially nullify the function of the sealing requirement as a safeguard against tampering. The statute requires a *satisfactory* explanation, not just an explanation. It is difficult to imagine a situation in which the Government could not explain *why* it delayed in seeking to have tapes sealed. Even deliberate delay would be enough, so long as the Government could establish the integrity of the tapes; yet deliberate delay could hardly be called a satisfactory explanation. To hold that proof of nontampering is a substitute for a satisfactory explanation is foreclosed by the plain words of the sealing provision.

It is true that offering to prove that tapes are authentic would be consistent with Congress' concern about tampering, but even if we were confident that tampering could always be easily detected, we would not be at liberty to agree with the Government, for it is obvious that Congress had another view when it imposed the sealing safeguard.

* * *

We conclude that the "satisfactory \anation" language in §2518(8)(a) be understood to require that the \ment explain not only why a

delay occurred but also why it is excusable. This approach surely is more consistent with the language and purpose of §2518(8)(a).

Finally, we must consider whether the Government established good cause for the sealing delays that occurred in this case. The Government contends in this Court that its delays were the result of a good-faith, objectively reasonable misunderstanding of the statutory term "extension." According to the Government, the attorney supervising the investigation and electronic surveillance of respondents believed that he was not required to seek sealing of the tapes until there was a meaningful hiatus in the investigation as a whole. In arguing that this understanding of the law was objectively reasonable, the Government relies primarily on two Second Circuit cases interpreting the statutory term "extension."

In one case, the Second Circuit held that an electronic surveillance order that was entered at least 16 days after a prior order had expired was to be regarded as an "extension" within the meaning of §2518 because it "was clearly part of the same investigation of the same individuals conducting the same criminal enterprise" as was being investigated under the prior order. * * * In a subsequent case, again involving a gap between the expiration of an order and an "extension," the court indicated that under the circumstances presented later orders could be deemed extensions of prior ones and stated that where an "intercept is of the same premises and involves substantially the same persons, an extension under these circumstances requires sealing only at the conclusion of the whole surveillance." * * *

These cases do not establish that the Government's asserted understanding of the law in this case was correct; indeed, the Second Circuit's decision in this case indicates the contrary, but the cases do support the conclusion that the "extension" theory now pressed upon us was objectively reasonable at the time of the delays.   Thus, we conclude that the excuse now advanced by the Government is objectively reasonable.   In establishing a reasonable excuse for a sealing delay, the Government is not required to prove that a particular understanding of the law is correct but rather only that its interpretation was objectively reasonable at the time.   To the extent the Second Circuit in this case required an absolutely correct interpretation of the law, we think it held the Government to too strict a standard.

Nevertheless, we must remand this case for further proceedings.   A "satisfactory explanation" within the meaning of §2518(8)(a) cannot merely be a reasonable excuse for the delay presented at the appellate level. Rather, our review of the sufficiency of the Government's explanation for a delay should be based on the evidence presented and submissions made in the District Court.   Therein lies the problem in this case.   Whether the supervising attorney actually advanced the Government's "extension" theory in the District Court is not clear. * * * Thus, even though the misunderstanding now pressed by the Government was objectively reasonable, that explanation is not "satisfactory" within the meaning of the statute unless it was relied on at the suppression hearing to explain the sealing delays. Because the Second Circuit did not address this

threshold question, the case must be remanded for a determination whether the Government's explanation to the District Court substantially corresponds to the explanation it now advances.

The judgment of the United States Court of Appeals for the Second Circuit is vacated, and the case is remanded for further proceedings consistent with this opinion.

It is so ordered.

[JUSTICE O'CONNOR, joined by JUSTICE BLACKMUN, concurred.]

JUSTICE STEVENS, with whom JUSTICE BRENNAN and JUSTICE MARSHALL join, dissenting.

The failure to comply with the sealing requirements of Title III was the unfortunate consequence of a Government lawyer's good-faith, but incorrect, understanding of the law. Whether such a mistake should constitute a "satisfactory explanation" for the failure, is, as both the District Court and the Court of Appeals recognized, a close question. Both of those courts resolved their doubts in favor of requiring strict compliance with a statute that was carefully drawn to protect extremely sensitive privacy interests.   I think their resolution of the issue was correct.

The ordinary citizen is often charged with presumptive knowledge of laws even when they are complex and confusing.   A similar presumption should apply to a federal prosecutor responsible for insuring that a prolonged and extensive program of electronic surveillance is conducted in compliance with the law.   Moreover, when issues turn on the details of such an investigation—in this case involving

1,011 tapes made pursuant to 8 separate orders and 17 extensions—I believe we should give special deference to the consistent evaluations of the record by the District Court and the Court of Appeals. Chief Judge Oakes succinctly stated the concern that is decisive for me:

> "We think that unfortunately the failure to seal the Levittown tapes here resulted from a disregard of the sensitive nature of the activities undertaken. The danger here is, of course, that today's dereliction becomes tomorrow's conscious avoidance of the requirements of law. The privacy and other interests affected by the electronic surveillance statutes are sufficiently important, we believe, to hold the Government to a reasonably high standard of at least acquaintance with the requirements of law." * * * [b]

Accordingly, while I agree with the Court's rejection of the Government's construction of Section 2518(8)(a), I would affirm the judgment of the Court of Appeals.

* * * * * * * * * * *

COMMENTS

[a] The Court pointed out that in addition to the §2518(8)(a) exclusionary rule, Title III also contained another "general suppression remedy," under §2518(10), that applies to unlawfully intercepted electronic communications or seizures under facially invalid warrants. The existence of two exclusionary rules in Title III seems to express a Congressional policy of great caution regarding the potential abuses of this practice. The §2518(10) exclusionary rule does not apply in this case.

[b] The lower courts and the dissenters say that in an extremely complex investigation, the government must devote the resources to insure that the statute is complied with, in this regard, to the letter. The reason for such strictness is that errors on the part of the government violate the very important right of privacy in individuals. How would you vote in this case?

UNITED STATES v. WHITE

401 U.S. 745, 91 S.Ct. 1122, 28 L.Ed.2d 453 (1971)

MR. JUSTICE WHITE announced the judgment of the Court and an opinion in which THE CHIEF JUSTICE, MR. JUSTICE STEWART, and MR. JUSTICE BLACKMUN join.

[James White was convicted of drug offenses. He made incriminating statements to a government informer who wore a radio transmitter concealed on his person. Government agents monitored the frequency of the transmitter and overheard the conversations. The informer could not be found to testify, so the government agents testified at trial as to the overheard conversations.]

The Court of Appeals read *Katz v. United States*, [this volume] as overruling *On Lee v. United States*, 343 U.S. 747 (1952), and interpreting the Fourth Amendment to forbid the introduction of the agents' testimony in the circumstances of this case. Accordingly, the court reversed but without adverting to the fact that the transactions at issue here had occurred before *Katz* was decided in this Court. In our view, the Court of Appeals misinterpreted both the *Katz* case and the Fourth Amendment and in any event erred in applying the *Katz* case to events that occurred before that decision was rendered by this Court.

I

Until *Katz v. United States*, neither wiretapping nor electronic eavesdropping violated a defendant's Fourth Amendment rights [unless there was a physical trespass.] [a]

* * * [The *Katz* ruling was briefly restated.]

The Court of Appeals understood *Katz* to render inadmissible against White the agents' testimony concerning conversations that Jackson broadcast to them. We cannot agree. *Katz* involved no revelation to the Government by a party to conversations with the defendant nor did the Court indicate in any way that a defendant has a justifiable and constitutionally protected expectation that a person with whom he is conversing will not then or later reveal the conversation to the police. [b]

Hoffa v. United States, 385 U.S. 293 (1966), which was left undisturbed by *Katz*, held that however strongly a defendant may trust an apparent colleague, his expectations in this respect are not protected by the Fourth Amendment when it turns out that the colleague is a government agent regularly communicating with the authorities. In these circumstances, "no interest legitimately protected by the Fourth Amendment is involved," for that amendment affords no protection to "a wrongdoer's misplaced belief that a person to whom he voluntarily confides his wrongdoing will not reveal it." * * * No warrant to "search and seize" is required in such circumstances, nor is it when the Government sends to defendant's home a secret agent who conceals his identity and makes a purchase of narcotics from the accused, *Lewis v. United States*, 385 U.S. 206 (1966), or when the same agent, unbeknown to the defendant, carries electronic equipment to record the defendant's words and the evidence so gathered is later offered in evidence. *Lopez v. United States*, 373 U.S. 427 (1963).

Conceding that *Hoffa, Lewis,* and *Lopez* remained unaffected by *Katz,* the Court of Appeals nevertheless read both *Katz* and the Fourth Amendment to require a different result if the agent not only records his conversations with the defendant but instantaneously transmits them electronically to other agents equipped with radio receivers. Where this occurs, the Court of Appeals held, the Fourth Amendment is violated and the testimony of the listening agents must be excluded from evidence.

To reach this result it was necessary for the Court of Appeals to hold that *On Lee v. United States* was no longer good law. In that case, which involved facts very similar to the case before us, the Court first rejected claims of a Fourth Amendment violation because the informer had not trespassed when he entered the defendant's premises and conversed with him. To this extent the Court's rationale cannot survive *Katz.* * * * But the Court announced a second and independent ground for its decision; for it went on to say that overruling *Olmstead [v. United States*, 277 U.S. 438 (1928)] and *Goldman [v. United States*, 316 U.S. 129, 135-136 (1942)] would be of no aid to On Lee since he "was talking confidentially and indiscreetly with one he trusted, and he was overheard. * * * It would be a dubious service to the genuine liberties protected by the Fourth Amendment to make them bedfellows with spurious liberties improvised by farfetched analogies which would liken eavesdropping on a conversation, with the connivance of one of the parties, to an unreasonable search or seizure. We find no violation of the Fourth Amendment here." * * * We see no indication in *Katz* that the Court meant to disturb that understanding of the Fourth Amendment or to disturb the result reached in the *On Lee* case, nor are we now inclined to overturn this view of the Fourth Amendment.

Concededly a police agent who conceals his police connections may write down for official use his conversations with a defendant and testify concerning them, without a warrant authorizing his encounters with the defendant and without otherwise violating the latter's Fourth Amendment rights. *Hoffa.* * * * For constitutional purposes, no different result is required if the agent instead of immediately reporting and transcribing his conversations with defendant, either (1) simultaneously records them with electronic equipment which he is carrying on his person, *Lopez v. United States,* * * * (2) or carries radio equipment which simultaneously transmits the conversations either to recording equipment located elsewhere or to other agents monitoring the transmitting frequency. *On Lee v. United States.* * * * If the conduct and revelations of an agent operating without electronic equipment do not invade the defendant's constitutionally justifiable expectations of privacy, neither does a simultaneous recording of the same conversations made by the agent or by others from transmissions received from the agent to whom the defendant is talking and whose trustworthiness the defendant necessarily risks. [c]

Our problem is not what the privacy expectations of particular defendants in particular situations may be or the extent to which they may in fact have relied on the discretion of their companions. * * * Our problem, in terms of the principles announced in *Katz*, is what expectations of privacy are constitutionally "justifiable"— what expectations the Fourth Amendment will protect in the absence of a warrant. [d] So far, the law permits the frustration of actual expectations of privacy by permitting authorities to use the testimony of those associates who for one reason or another have determined to turn to the police, as well as by authorizing the use of informants in the manner exemplified by *Hoffa* and *Lewis*. If the law gives no protection to the wrongdoer whose trusted accomplice is or becomes a police agent, neither should it protect him when that same agent has recorded or transmitted the conversations which are later offered in evidence to prove the State's case. * * *

Inescapably, one contemplating illegal activities must realize and risk that his companions may be reporting to the police. * * * Given the possibility or probability that one of his colleagues is cooperating with the police, it is only speculation to assert that the defendant's utterances would be substantially different or his sense of security any less if he also thought it possible that the suspected colleague is wired for sound. At least there is no persuasive evidence that the difference in this respect between the electronically equipped and the unequipped agent is substantial enough to require discrete constitutional recognition, particularly under the Fourth Amendment which is ruled by fluid concepts of "reasonableness." [e]

Nor should we be too ready to erect constitutional barriers to relevant and probative evidence which is also accurate and reliable. An electronic recording will many times produce a more reliable rendition of what a defendant has said than will the unaided memory of a police agent. * * *

It is thus untenable to consider the activities and reports of the police agent himself, though acting without a warrant, to be a "reasonable" investigative effort and lawful under the Fourth Amendment but to view the same agent with a recorder or transmitter as conducting an "unreasonable" and unconstitutional search and seizure. Our opinion is currently shared by Congress and the Executive Branch, Title III, Omnibus Crime Control and Safe Streets Act of 1968, * * * and the American Bar Association. Project on Standards for Criminal Justice, Electronic Surveillance §4.1 (Approved Draft 1971). It is also the result reached by prior cases in this Court. *On Lee*, *supra*; *Lopez v. United States*, *supra*.

* * *

[The Court ruled in Part II that *Katz* was not retroactive, and so did not apply to this case, whose facts occurred before the *Katz* decision was announced.]

The judgment of the Court of Appeals is reversed.

It is so ordered.

[JUSTICE BLACK concurred on the basis of his dissent in *Katz*.]

[JUSTICE BRENNAN concurring in the result, based on the retroactivity rule, but joined the reasoning of dissenting JUSTICES DOUGLAS and HARLAN, and would go further to overrule *Lopez v. United States.* "In other words, it is my view that current Fourth Amendment jurisprudence interposes a warrant requirement not only in cases of third-party electronic monitoring (the situation in *On Lee* and in this case) but also in cases of electronic recording by a government agent of a face-to-face conversation with a criminal suspect, which was the situation in *Lopez.*"]

MR. JUSTICE DOUGLAS, dissenting.

The issue in this case is clouded and concealed by the very discussion of it in legalistic terms. What the ancients knew as "eavesdropping," we now call "electronic surveillance"; but to equate the two is to treat man's first gunpowder on the same level as the nuclear bomb. Electronic surveillance is the greatest leveler of human privacy ever known. How most forms of it can be held "reasonable" within the meaning of the Fourth Amendment is a mystery. * * *
 * * *

[JUSTICE DOUGLAS reviewed both the extent of electronic eavesdropping in contemporary society and the legal developments in this area, including JUSTICE BRENNAN's dissent in *Lopez v. United States*, where he said "* * * Electronic aids add a wholly new dimension to eavesdropping. They make it more penetrating, more indiscriminate, more truly obnoxious to a free society. Electronic surveillance, in fact, makes the police omniscient; and police omniscience is one of the most effective tools of tyranny." * * *]

MR. JUSTICE HARLAN, dissent-

ing.

 * * *

I think that a perception of the scope and role of the Fourth Amendment, as elucidated by this Court since *On Lee* was decided, and full comprehension of the precise issue at stake lead to the conclusion that *On Lee* can no longer be regarded as sound law. Nor do I think the date we decided *Katz* * * * can be deemed controlling both for the reasons discussed in my dissent in *Desist v. United States*, 394 U.S. 244, 256 (1969). * * * and because, in my view, it requires no discussion of the holding in *Katz*, as distinguished from its underlying rationale as to the reach of the Fourth Amendment, to comprehend the constitutional infirmity of *On Lee*.

I

Before turning to matters of precedent and policy, several preliminary observations should be made. We deal here with the constitutional validity of instantaneous third-party electronic eavesdropping, conducted by federal law enforcement officers, without any prior judicial approval of the technique utilized, but with the consent and cooperation of a participant in the conversation, and where the substance of the matter electronically overheard is related in a federal criminal trial by those who eavesdropped as direct, not merely corroborative, evidence of the guilt of the nonconsenting party. * * * Professor Westin has documented in careful detail the numerous devices that make technologically feasible the Orwellian Big Brother. Of immediate relevance is his observation that "'participant recording,' in which one participant in a conversation or meeting, either a police officer or a co-operating party, wears a concealed device that records the conversation or broadcasts it to others nearby * * * is used tens of thousands of times each year throughout the country, particularly in cases involving extortion, conspiracy, narcotics, gambling, prostitution, corruption by police officials * * * and similar crimes."

* * *

II

* * *

[In Part II A JUSTICE HARLAN carefully dissected the developments in the law of electronic eavesdropping. He concluded that *Katz* was the end point of a series of cases that had eroded the property-trespass basis of the *Olmstead* doctrine; as a result, the holding on *On Lee*, whose facts were virtually identical to those in this case, was undermined and the case was open to reconsideration. "*On Lee* rested on common-law notions and looked to a waning era of Fourth Amendment jurisprudence."]

* * *

By 1963, when we decided *Lopez v. United States*, * * * four members of the Court were prepared to pronounce *On Lee* and *Olmstead* * * * dead. The pyre, they reasoned, had been stoked by decisions like *Wong Sun v. United States*, 371 U.S. 471 (1963), which, on the one hand, expressly brought verbal communication within the sweep of the Fourth Amendment, and, on the other, reinforced our * * * decisions which "refused to crowd the Fourth Amendment into the mold of local property law." * * *

Although the Court's decision in *Lopez* is cited by the Government as a reaffirmation of *On Lee*, it can hardly be thought to have nurtured the questionable rationale of that decision or its much-criticized ancestor, *Olmstead*. To the discerning lawyer *Lopez* could only give pause, not comfort. While the majority opinion, of which I was the author, declined to follow the course favored by the dissenting and concurring Justices by sounding the death knell for *Olmstead* and *On Lee*, our holding, despite an allusion to the absence of "an unlawful * * * invasion of a constitutionally protected area," * * * was bottomed on two premises: the corroborative use that was made of the tape recordings, which increased reliability in the factfinding process, and the absence of a "risk" not fairly assumed by petitioner. [f] The tape recording was made by a participant in the conversation and the opinion emphasized this absence of a third-party intrusion, expressly noting that there was no "electronic eavesdropping on a private conversation which government agents could not otherwise have overheard." * * * As I point out in Part III of this opinion, it is one thing to subject the average citizen to the risk that participants in a conversation with him will subsequently divulge its contents to another, but quite a different matter to foist upon him the risk that unknown third parties may be simultaneously listening in.

While *Lopez* cited *On Lee* without disavowal of its holding, * * * it is entirely accurate to say that we did not there reaffirm it. No decision since *Lopez* gives a breath of life to the reasoning that led to the *On Lee* and *Olmstead* results, and it required little clairvoyance to predict the demise of the basic rationale of *On Lee* and *Olmstead* foreshadowed by our subsequent opinions in *Osborn v. United States*, 385 U.S. 323 (1966), and *Berger v. New York*, 388 U.S. 41 (1967).

[In *Osborn*, agents obtained a court order to wear a body mike and this action was praised by the Supreme Court, which hinted broadly that a warrant procedure could be used to "constitutionalize" electronic eavesdropping.]

* * *

[*Berger v. New York* made it clear that conversations obtained by electronic eavesdropping could no longer be seen as not covered by the Fourth Amendment. Either sufficient safeguards would have to be provided or the practice of electronic eavesdropping would become constitutionally impermissible.]

* * *

Viewed in perspective, then, *Katz* added no new dimension to the law. At most it was a formal dispatch of *Olmstead* and the notion that such problems may usefully be resolved in the light of trespass doctrine, and, of course, it freed from speculation what was already evident, that *On Lee* was completely open to question.

B

But the decisions of this Court since *On Lee* do more than demonstrate that the doctrine of that case is wholly open for reconsideration, and has been since well before *Katz* was decided. They also establish sound general principles for application of the Fourth Amendment that were either dimly perceived or not fully worked out at the time of *On Lee*[:] * * * that verbal communication is protected by

the Fourth Amendment, that the reasonableness of a search does not depend on the presence or absence of a trespass, and that the Fourth Amendment is principally concerned with protecting interests of privacy, rather than property rights. **[g]**

[In Part IIB JUSTICE HARLAN noted that other recent Fourth Amendment decisions, especially *Camara v. Municipal Court*, [this volume], *Terry v. Ohio*, [this volume], and *Chimel v. California*, [this volume], strengthened the understanding that all police intrusions into privacy are covered by the Fourth Amendment, and the central importance of the warrant requirement to validate intrusions into privacy.]

* * *

III
A

That the foundations of *On Lee* have been destroyed does not, of course, mean that its result can no longer stand. Indeed, the plurality opinion today fastens upon our decisions in *Lopez, Lewis* * * * and *Hoffa* * * * to resist the undercurrents of more recent cases emphasizing the warrant procedure as a safeguard to privacy. But this category provides insufficient support. In each of these cases the risk the general populace faced was different from that surfaced by the instant case. No surreptitious third ear was present, and in each opinion that fact was carefully noted.

* * *

The plurality opinion seeks to erase the crucial distinction between the facts before us and these holdings by the following reasoning: if A can relay verbally what is revealed to him by B (as in *Lewis* and *Hoffa*), or record and later divulge it (as in *Lopez*), what difference does it make if A conspires with another to betray B by contemporaneously transmitting to the other all that is said? The contention is, in essence, an argument that the distinction between third-party monitoring and *other* undercover techniques is one of form and not substance. The force of the contention depends on the evaluation of two separable but intertwined assumptions: first, that there is no greater invasion of privacy in the third-party situation, and, second, that uncontrolled consensual surveillance in an electronic age is a tolerable technique of law enforcement, given the values and goals of our political system.

The first of these assumptions takes as a point of departure the so-called "risk analysis" approach of *Lewis*, and *Lopez*, and to a lesser extent *On Lee*, or the expectations approach of *Katz*. * * * While these formulations represent an advance over the unsophisticated trespass analysis of the common law, they too have their limitations and can, ultimately, lead to the substitution of words for analysis. The analysis must, in my view, transcend the search for subjective expectations or legal attribution of assumptions of risk. Our expectations, and the risks we assume, are in large part reflections of laws that translate into rules the customs and values of the past and present.

Since it is the task of the law to form and project, as well as mirror and reflect, we should not, as judges, merely recite the expectations and risks without examining the desirability of saddling them upon society. [h] The critical question, therefore, is whether

under our system of government, as reflected in the Constitution, we should impose on our citizens the risks of the electronic listener or observer without at least the protection of a warrant requirement.

This question must, in my view, be answered by assessing the nature of a particular practice and the likely extent of its impact on the individual's sense of security balanced against the utility of the conduct as a technique of law enforcement. For those more extensive intrusions that significantly jeopardize the sense of security which is the paramount concern of Fourth Amendment liberties, I am of the view that more than self-restraint by law enforcement officials is required and at the least warrants should be necessary. * * *

B

The impact of the practice of third-party bugging, must, I think, be considered such as to undermine that confidence and sense of security in dealing with one another that is characteristic of individual relationships between citizens in a free society. It goes beyond the impact on privacy occasioned by the ordinary type of "informer" investigation upheld in *Lewis* and *Hoffa*. The argument of the plurality opinion, to the effect that it is irrelevant whether secrets are revealed by the mere tattletale or the transistor, ignores the differences occasioned by third-party monitoring and recording which insures full and accurate disclosure of all that is said, free of the possibility of error and oversight that inheres in human reporting.

Authority is hardly required to support the proposition that words would be measured a good deal more carefully and communication inhibited if one suspected his conversations were being transmitted and transcribed. Were third-party bugging a prevalent practice, it might well smother that spontaneity—reflected in frivolous, impetuous, sacrilegious, and defiant discourse—that liberates daily life. Much off-hand exchange is easily forgotten and one may count on the obscurity of his remarks, protected by the very fact of a limited audience, and the likelihood that the listener will either overlook or forget what is said, as well as the listener's inability to reformulate a conversation without having to contend with a documented record. All these values are sacrificed by a rule of law that permits official monitoring of private discourse limited only by the need to locate a willing assistant.

* * *

Finally, it is too easy to forget—and, hence, too often forgotten—that the issue here is whether to interpose a search warrant procedure between law enforcement agencies engaging in electronic eavesdropping and the public generally. By casting its "risk analysis" solely in terms of the expectations and risks that "wrongdoers" or "one contemplating illegal activities" ought to bear, the plurality opinion, I think, misses the mark entirely. *On Lee* does not simply mandate that criminals must daily run the risk of unknown eavesdroppers prying into their private affairs; it subjects each and every law-abiding member of society to that risk. The very purpose of interposing the Fourth Amendment warrant requirement is to redistribute the privacy risks throughout society in a way that produces the results the plurality opinion ascribes to the *On Lee* rule. Abolition of *On Lee* would not end electronic eavesdropping. It would prevent public officials from engaging in that practice unless they first had probable cause to suspect an individual of involvement in illegal activities and had tested their version of the facts before a detached judicial officer. The interest *On Lee* fails to protect is the expectation of the ordinary citizen, who has never engaged in illegal conduct in his life, that he may carry on his private discourse freely, openly, and spontaneously without measuring his every word against the connotations it might carry when instantaneously heard by others unknown to him and unfamiliar with his situation or analyzed in a cold, formal record played days, months, or years after the conversation. Interposition of a warrant requirement is designed not to shield "wrongdoers," but to secure a measure of privacy and a sense of personal security throughout our society.

The Fourth Amendment does, of course, leave room for the employment of modern technology in criminal law enforcement, but in the stream of current developments in Fourth Amendment law I think it must be held that third-party electronic monitoring, subject only to the self-restraint of law enforcement officials, has no place in our society.

[In the remainder of his dissent, JUSTICE HARLAN points out that Title III and the American Bar Association merely followed the court in supporting warrantless body-mikes rather than thinking through the problem from fundamental premises, and that the retroactivity argument of the majority was in error because the Court of Appeals ruled on the basis of emerging principles, not on the basis of *Katz*.]

I would hold that *On Lee* is no longer good law and affirm the judgment below.

[JUSTICE MARSHALL dissented, joining the dissents of JUSTICE DOUGLAS and JUSTICE HARLAN.]

* * * * * * * * * *

COMMENTS

[a] This seemingly straightforward statement of law is the hinge on which the plurality decision turns. Compare it to JUSTICE HARLAN's attempt to show that the basis for the rule was undermined before *Katz*.

[b] That is, the narrow, specific *holding* of *Katz* does not cover the facts of this case.

[c] This is the central question of the case. It is a question that both transcends and affects constitutional questions. In a sense, the issue is whether the incredible efficiencies of modern technology affect the quality of life and whether this in turn changes the contours of constitutional law.

[d] This is an example of the importance of JUSTICE HARLAN's concurrence in *Katz*, stressing that the protected expectation of privacy must be socially "objective."

[e] Compare JUSTICE WHITE's narrow focus on the impact on criminal defendants to JUSTICE HARLAN's broader concern of the impact of warrantless body mikes on the quality of life for law abiding citizens.

[f] JUSTICE HARLAN's fine-tuned case reasoning here is in part an attempt to justify that his majority opinion in *Lopez*, which held admissible the bribe attempt made by the defendant to an IRS agent wearing a body mike, rather than admitting that he reconsidered his earlier position and reversed his opinion.

[g] This is an admission that the path of the law is not absolutely clear as the Court works through and resolves difficult questions.

[h] This eloquent statement of the policy making potential of the Court's cases is remarkable, coming from a Justice who was a paragon of judicial restraint.

Chapter Three

EXIGENCY AND OTHER
SEARCH WARRANT EXCEPTIONS

The subject of search and seizure is explored in further detail in this chapter, which is concerned with a variety of "exceptions" to the Fourth Amendment warrant requirement. As we noted in Chapter Two there are two primary ways of examining the constitutionality of warrantless searches: the "reasonableness" approach and the "warrant and exception" approach.

The warrant-and-exception approach emphasizes the preference for the search warrant and holds that there are a limited number of exceptions to the warrant requirement. The three primary exceptions under this doctrine are hot pursuit, the "automobile" exception, and search incident to arrest. These exceptions share two important attributes. First, each requires that the officer have *probable cause* to believe there is contraband or evidence of a crime in the place searched. Second, each of these searches must be justified by an *exigency*—an urgent situation requiring immediate action.

In the classic hot pursuit case, *Warden v. Hayden*, 387 U.S. 294 (1967), police entered a house five minutes after eyewitnesses reported that the robber entered. They searched the house and found evidence of the crime. To have waited for a warrant in that situation, where probable cause existed and a violent crime suspect had entered moments before, would have been to risk the destruction of evidence and could have led to a more violent confrontation. The Court in *Welsh v. Wisconsin* (1984) placed a limit on the hot pursuit exception: police are barred from entering a home in hot pursuit where the gravity of the crime is not great; in effect there is no exigency in such cases.

The search incident to arrest exception is based both on the need to insure the safety of arresting officers and on the need to preserve evidence. The "scope" of a search incident to arrest is "the area into which an arrestee might reach in order to grab a weapon or evidentiary items." This is defined as the arrestee's "person and the area within his immediate control—construing that phrase to mean the area from within which he might gain possession of a weapon or destructible evidence" (*Chimel v. California* (1969)).   Under the *Chimel* doctrine, officers may reach into areas adjacent to an arrestee, but may not subject an entire premises to a minute search without a search warrant. Likewise, when a person is arrested, the officer may search into pockets and into containers like cigarette packages for any evidence, even if the arrest is for a crime that generates no suspicion of carrying contraband (*United States v. Robinson* (1973)).   An analogous doctrine, the "protective sweep" of *Maryland v. Buie*, 494 U.S. 325 (1990), authorizes police, after arresting a person in a premises, to look into adjoining rooms to see if another person is present. If the police have reasonable suspicion to believe that a confederate is present in the premises, they may "sweep" into all rooms and closets to be sure that a person who could do them harm is not present. *Buie* is an extension of *Chimel*.

The automobile, or vehicle, exception has produced a large body of caselaw and a good deal of confusion. In *Carroll v. United States*, 267 U.S. 132 (1925), the Court upheld a warrantless search of an automobile travelling on the highway and the tearing up of its leather back seat, when the police had probable cause to believe it was transporting "bootleg" liquor. Obtaining a warrant would have been fruitless as the vehicle would quickly be beyond the officers' reach and the contraband gone. *California v. Carney* (1985) added another rationale to the automobile warrantless search exception—the lesser expectation of privacy in vehicles due in part to their nature and in part to their high degree of regulation. In that case the fact that respondent lived in a mobile van capable of being driven away did not confer the protection of a home; a warrantless search was upheld.

If an automobile is immobilized, *e.g.*, on blocks, it cannot be searched under this exception (*Coolidge v. New Hampshire*, 403 U.S. 443 (1971)). Where a footlocker was placed in the trunk of a stationary automobile whose motor was not on, the footlocker could not come under the exception. Its warrantless opening was a violation of the owner's Fourth Amendment right to a judicial warrant when the state searches an "effect" (*United States v. Chadwick* (1977)).

The Court has been bedeviled by the issue of whether a closed container found inside a moving automobile comes under the *Carroll* exception or the *Chadwick* rule. *Chambers v. Maroney*, 399 U.S. 42 (1970) allowed the police, with probable cause, to either search the automobile on the road immediately after it was stopped, or at the police station a short time later where the arrested driver and passengers were taken. In *New York v. Belton* (1981), an officer made a roadside arrest of four men and, having smelled marijuana, went to the passenger compartment to retrieve an incriminating package on the floor. The officer unzipped a jacket pocket and found cocaine. The Supreme Court held that "when a policeman has made a lawful custodial arrest of the occupant of an automobile, he may, as a contemporaneous incident of that arrest, search the passenger compartment of that automobile." Because this case straddled the search incident to arrest and automobile search exceptions, it did not provide a clear precedent for containers in the trunk or other locked areas. The Court appeared to follow the *Chadwick* rule in *Arkansas v. Sanders*, 442 U.S. 753 (1979) and *Robbins v. California*, 453 U.S. 420 (1981) but has decisively followed the *Carroll* approach more recently. *United States v. Ross*, 456 U.S. 798 (1982) held that police may search any part of an automobile if they have a generalized probable cause to believe that contraband is located somewhere in the car. If police have probable cause to believe that contraband is in a closed container in a moving vehicle, the automobile exception allows the opening of the container. While this conflicts with *Chadwick* to some extent, it gives the police a bright line rule. (*California v. Acevedo* (1991)).

Aside from these three exigency-probable cause exceptions, several other warrant exception categories exist. One of the most theoretically productive was the administrative search doctrine. Prior to 1969 the entry into a premises by an administrative officer for a regulatory (non-criminal) inspection could be effected without a warrant (*Frank v. Maryland*, 359 U.S. 360 (1959)). In *Camara v. Municipal Court* (1967) the Court required an "area" warrant for such searches. This form of warrant relaxed the particularity requirement of the Fourth Amendment. Paradoxically, while *Camara* expanded the procedural protection of persons subject to regulatory searches, the flexible reasoning of that case was relied on by the Court as it relaxed both the warrant and the probable cause requirements in the "special needs" cases (see Chapter 2). A warrant for administrative searches is not required if a business is "pervasively regulated" (*Colonnade Catering v. United States*, 397 U.S. 72 (1970) (liquor); *United States v. Biswell*, 406 U.S. 311 (1972) (weapons)), or if a statute provides the standards that would be included in a warrant, *Donovan v. Dewey*, 452 U.S. 594 (1981) (mine inspections).

Consent is an extremely practical exception for law enforcement. Where a person voluntarily consents to a search she "sets aside" the operation of the Fourth Amendment. If police pretend to have a warrant there is no voluntary consent to search because the person has attorned to the authority of the law (*Bumper v. North Carolina*, 391 U.S. 543 (1968)). Any force or intimidation vitiates consent to a search. Police may ask a person if they wish to consent to a search even if the police have no probable cause and need not inform the person that they have Fourth Amendment rights (*Schneckloth v. Bustamonte* (1973)). A person who has joint control (*United States v. Matlock*, 415 U.S. 164 (1974)) or apparent control (*Illinois v. Rodriguez* (1990)) over a place may consent to a search for the other person.

Inventory searches are a *sui generis* category that has been recognized only within the past twenty tears. The inventory is typically a routine search of an impounded vehicle that requires no evidentiary standard. The purpose of the inventory search is to safeguard the property of the owner, protect police against false charges of theft or property, and prevent any danger. A valid inventory search is conducted under a standardized procedure in good faith and does not violate the Fourth Amendment (*Colorado v. Bertine* (1987)). The standardized regulations may nevertheless give officers some latitude in deciding whether to open containers found in an automobile (*Florida v. Wells* (1990)).

A nation has plenary power to protect its borders. At the border police may stop and inspect incoming travellers and containers at random. However, Fourth Amendment protections do extend to a variety of border search situations. Where a nonroutine and intrusive search occurs at the border, such as a body cavity search of a drug smuggler, the Fourth Amendment requires the government to have reasonable suspicion of the violation (*United States v. Montoya de Hernandez* (1985)). No particularized suspicion is required to stop cars at fixed checkpoints at some distance from the border, but probable cause is required to search the vehicles after a brief questioning (*United States v. Martinez-Fuerte*, 428 U.S. 543 (1976)). Customs officers searching for illegal aliens may stop cars in "roving patrols" within 100 miles from the border, but the Court has required reasonable suspicion to stop vehicles (*United States v. Brignoni-Ponce*, 422 U.S. 873 (1976)) and probable cause to search (*Almeida-Sanchez v. United States*, 413 U.S. 266 (1973)). Maritime searches may be made without any level of suspicion or cause (*United States v. Villamonte-Marquez*, 462 U.S. 579 (1983)).

WELSH v. WISCONSIN

466 U.S. 740, 104 S.Ct. 2091, 80 L.Ed.2d 732 (1984)

JUSTICE BRENNAN delivered the opinion of the Court.

Payton v. New York [this volume] (1980), held that, absent probable cause and exigent circumstances, warrantless arrests in the home are prohibited by the Fourth Amendment. But the Court in that case explicitly refused "to consider the sort of emergency or dangerous situation, described in our cases as 'exigent circumstances,' that would justify a warrantless entry into a home for the purpose of either arrest or search." Certiorari was granted in this case to decide at least one aspect of the unresolved question: whether, and if so under what circumstances, the Fourth Amendment prohibits the police from making a warrantless night entry of a person's home in order to arrest him for violation of a nonjailable traffic offense. [a]

I

A

[On a rainy night, Welsh's erratically driven car careened off the road and into a ditch. A passerby stopped, blocked the car with his truck, had someone call the police, and suggested to the apparently intoxicated driver that he wait for assistance. The driver walked off into the night. The police traced Welsh from the abandoned car's registration to his home a short distance away. Welsh's stepdaughter answered the door when the police knocked at 9:00 P.M. They gained entry without consent, found Welsh in bed, and arrested him. [b] At the police station Welsh refused to submit to a breath analysis test.]

B

[Wisconsin law provided that a person who improperly refuses a breath test would have his or her driver's license revoked for sixty days, after a hearing, but that a refusal was proper] if the underlying arrest was not lawful. Indeed, state law has consistently provided that a valid arrest is a necessary prerequisite to the imposition of a breath test. [Such a revocation is a civil/administrative action apart from any conviction for driving while intoxicated (DWI). To determine the legality of arrests the Wisconsin Supreme Court applied federal constitutional standards.]

* * * At the time in question, the Vehicle Code provided that a first offense for driving while intoxicated was a noncriminal violation subject to a civil forfeiture proceeding for a maximum fine of $200; a second or subsequent offense in the previous five years was a potential misdemeanor that could be punished by imprisonment for up to one year and a maximum fine of $500. * * *

C

[At the time of the arrest, the police did not know Welsh had a prior DWI conviction and so the situation legally was such that they arrested him as a first-time offender for a nonjailable traffic offense.] The Supreme

Court of Wisconsin [ruled in favor of the state] * * * relying on the existence of three factors that it believed constituted exigent circumstances: the need for "hot pursuit" of a suspect, the need to prevent physical harm to the offender and the public, and the need to prevent destruction of evidence. * * *

II

It is axiomatic that the "physical entry of the home is the chief evil against which the wording of the Fourth Amendment is directed." * * * And a principal protection against unnecessary intrusions into private dwellings is the warrant requirement imposed by the Fourth Amendment on agents of the government who seek to enter the home for purposes of search or arrest. * * * It is not surprising, therefore, that the Court has recognized, as "a 'basic principle of Fourth Amendment law[,]' that searches and seizures inside a home without a warrant are presumptively unreasonable." * * * See *Coolidge v. New Hampshire*, 403 U.S. 443 (1971) ("a search or seizure carried out on a suspect's premises without a warrant is per se unreasonable, unless the police can show * * * the presence of 'exigent circumstances'"). * * * [c]

Consistently with these long-recognized principles, the Court decided in *Payton v. New York*, that warrantless felony arrests in the home are prohibited by the Fourth Amendment, absent probable cause and exigent circumstances. At the same time, the Court declined to consider the scope of any exception for exigent circumstances that might justify warrantless home arrests, thereby leaving to the lower courts the

initial application of the exigent-circumstances exception. Prior decisions of this Court, however, have emphasized that exceptions to the warrant requirement are "few in number and carefully delineated," * * * and that the police bear a heavy burden when attempting to demonstrate an urgent need that might justify warrantless searches or arrests. Indeed, the Court has recognized only a few such emergency conditions, see, e.g., *United States v. Santana*, 427 U.S. 38 (1976) (hot pursuit of a fleeing felon); *Warden v. Hayden*, 387 U.S. 294 (1967) (same); *Schmerber v. California*, 384 U.S. 757 (1966) (destruction of evidence); *Michigan v. Tyler*, 436 U.S. 499 (1978) (ongoing fire), and has actually applied only the "hot pursuit" doctrine to arrests in the home, see *Santana*.

Our hesitation in finding exigent circumstances, particularly when warrantless arrests in the home are at issue, is especially appropriate when the underlying offense for which there is probable cause to arrest is relatively minor.[d] Before agents of the government may invade the sanctity of the home, the burden is on the government to demonstrate exigent circumstances that overcome the presumption of unreasonableness that attaches to all warrantless home entries. * * * When the government's interest is only to arrest for a minor offense, that presumption of unreasonableness is difficult to rebut, and the government usually should be allowed to make such arrests only with a warrant issued upon probable cause by a neutral and detached magistrate.

* * *

Consistently with this approach, the lower courts have looked to the nature of the underlying offense as an important factor to be considered in the exigent-circumstances calculus. In a leading federal case defining exigent circumstances, for example, the *en banc* United States Court of Appeals for the District of Columbia Circuit recognized that the gravity of the underlying offense was a principal factor to be weighed. *Dorman v. United States*, 435 F. 2d 385, 392 (1970). Without approving all of the factors included in the standard adopted by that court, it is sufficient to note that many other lower courts have also considered the gravity of the offense an important part of their constitutional analysis. **[e]**

[Many references to state and federal cases following this point are given].

We therefore conclude that the common-sense approach utilized by most lower courts is required by the Fourth Amendment prohibition on "unreasonable searches and seizures," and hold that an important factor to be considered when determining whether any exigency exists is the gravity of the underlying offense for which the arrest is being made. Moreover, although no exigency is created simply because there is probable cause to believe that a serious crime has been committed, see *Payton*, application of the exigent-circumstances exception in the context of a home entry should rarely be sanctioned when there is probable cause to believe that only a minor offense, such as the kind at issue in this case, has been committed. **[f]**

Application of this principle to the facts of the present case is relatively straightforward. The petitioner was arrested in the privacy of his own bedroom for a noncriminal, traffic offense. The State attempts to justify the arrest by relying on the hot-pursuit doctrine, on the threat to public safety, and on the need to preserve evidence of the petitioner's blood-alcohol level. On the facts of this case, however, the claim of hot pursuit is unconvincing because there was no immediate or continuous pursuit of the petitioner from the scene of a crime. Moreover, because the petitioner had already arrived home, and had abandoned his car at the scene of the accident, there was little remaining threat to the public safety.   Hence, the only potential emergency claimed by the State was the need to ascertain the petitioner's blood-alcohol level. **[g]**

Even assuming, however, that the underlying facts would support a finding of this exigent circumstance, mere similarity to other cases involving the imminent destruction of evidence is not sufficient. The State of Wisconsin has chosen to classify the first offense for driving while intoxicated as a noncriminal, civil forfeiture offense for which no imprisonment is possible. * * * **[h]** This is the best indication of the State's interest in precipitating an arrest, and is one that can be easily identified both by the courts and by officers faced with a decision to arrest. Given this expression of the State's interest, a warrantless home arrest cannot be upheld simply because evidence of the petitioner's blood-alcohol level might have dissipated while the police obtained a warrant. To allow a warrantless home entry on these facts would be to approve unreasonable police behavior that the principles of the Fourth Amendment will not sanction.

* * *

THE   CHIEF   JUSTICE   would

dismiss the writ as having been improvidently granted and defer resolution of the question presented to a more appropriate case.

[JUSTICE BLACKMUN concurred.]
* * *

JUSTICE WHITE, with whom JUSTICE REHNQUIST joins, dissenting.

[Wisconsin modified the common law rule that a police officer could arrest one for a misdemeanor only on a warrant or if the misdemeanor were committed in the presence of the officer to allow an officer to arrest one who committed a driving offense upon probable cause.]

[JUSTICE WHITE dissented on two grounds. First, because the Wisconsin law defined the proceeding against a first-time drunk driver as civil, the Fourth Amendment exclusionary rule does not apply even if the arrest itself was deemed by the Wisconsin courts as violating the Fourth Amendment rights of the defendant. Secondly, he argued that the gravity of the underlying offense is] a factor to be considered in determining whether the delay that attends the warrant-issuance process will endanger officers or other persons. The seriousness of the offense with which a suspect may be charged also bears on the likelihood that he will flee and escape apprehension if not arrested immediately. But if, under all the circumstances of a particular case, an officer has probable cause to believe that the delay involved in procuring an arrest warrant will gravely endanger the officer or other persons or will result in the suspect's escape, I perceive no reason to disregard those exigencies on the ground that the offense for which the suspect is sought is a "minor" one. [i]
* * *

A warrantless home entry to arrest is no more intrusive when the crime is "minor" than when the suspect is sought in connection with a serious felony. The variable factor, if there is one, is the governmental interest that will be served by the warrantless entry. Wisconsin's Legislature and its Supreme Court have both concluded that warrantless in-home arrests under circumstances like those present here promote valid and substantial state interests. In determining whether the challenged governmental conduct was reasonable, we are not bound by these determinations. But nothing in our previous decisions suggests that the fact that a State has defined an offense as a misdemeanor for a variety of social, cultural, and political reasons necessarily requires the conclusion that warrantless in-home arrests designed to prevent the imminent destruction or removal of evidence of that offense are always impermissible. If anything, the Court's prior decisions support the opposite conclusion. * * *

A test under which the existence of exigent circumstances turns on the perceived gravity of the crime would significantly hamper law enforcement and burden courts with pointless litigation concerning the nature and gradation of various crimes. * * *

This problem could be lessened by creating a bright-line distinction between felonies and other crimes, but the Court—wisely in my view—does not adopt such an approach. There may have been a time when the line between misdemeanors and felonies marked off those offenses involving a sufficiently serious threat to society to justify warrantless in-home arrests under exigent circumstances. But the category of misdemeanors today includes enough serious offenses to call into question the desirability of such line drawing. * * * If I am correct in asserting that a bright-line distinction between felonies and misdemeanors is untenable and that the need to prevent the imminent destruction or removal of evidence of some nonfelony crimes can constitute an exigency justifying warrantless in-home arrests under certain circumstances, the Court's approach will necessitate a case-by-case evaluation of the seriousness of particular crimes, a difficult task for which officers and courts are poorly equipped.

    * * *

    * * * Although first offenders are subjected only to civil forfeiture under the Wisconsin statute, the seriousness

with which the State regards the crime for which Welsh was arrested is evinced by (1) the fact that defendants charged with driving under the influence are guaranteed the right to a jury trial, * * * (2) the legislative authorization of warrantless arrests for traffic offenses occurring outside the officer's presence, * * * and (3) the collateral consequence of mandatory license revocation that attaches to all convictions for driving under the influence. * * * It is possible, moreover, that the legislature consciously chose to limit the penalties imposed on first offenders in order to increase the ease of conviction and the overall deterrent effect of the enforcement effort. * * * [j]

    In short, the fact that Wisconsin has chosen to punish the first offense for driving under the influence with a fine rather than a prison term does not demand the conclusion that the State's interest in punishing first offenders is insufficiently substantial to justify warrantless in-home arrests under exigent circumstances. * * *

* * * * * * * * * *

COMMENTS

[a] In this brief introductory paragraph, JUSTICE BRENNAN lays out the general rule and precedent, the issue that was reserved by that precedent, and the general issue of the case. Such a "packed" introductory paragraph should be read with care as it gives the framework of the case.

[b] In ascertaining the facts of the case, the Supreme Court must scrupulously set out the precise legal facts. The reason for this is that the *holding* of a case is not a general rule of law like a statute, but a rule applicable to the specific fact situation. Where some factual issues are in doubt the Court takes care to insure that the factual predicate of the holding is not in doubt. Thus, JUSTICE BRENNAN avoids the issue of whether the stepdaughter consented to the entry by assuming that no consent was given. This insures that *Welsh* is decided on the issue of the exigency exception to the *Payton* rule, rather than confusing the case with the consent issue. Similarly, the Court decides the case as if Welsh was

arrested for a nonjailable traffic offense, which was taken to be operative fact because it was subjectively believed by the police. This "purifies" the legal issues so that they remain unclouded by factual side issues. This is important in cases decided by the Supreme Court because its decisions must establish rules of general application for the nation.

[c] The repetition of basic rules and the invocation of prior precedent—either by simply giving the citation, by briefly indicating their holdings, or by quoting from them at length in the text of the opinion or in footnotes—serve an important role in the law. In one sense, case opinions present the logic and results of an instance of legal problem solving. In this sense, they are like write-ups of scientific experiments or journal articles presenting the product of scholarship. But opinions are also the presentation of official policies and in this sense are like official proclamations. Unlike the proclamations of presidents or legislatures, which fix on the issues at hand, on present solutions, and on future goals, opinions also establish continuity with the past. By selecting certain past cases to repeat, the present Court gives them new life and impetus. Thus, repetition of earlier rules operates in ways reminiscent of the ritual invocation of prayers to legitimate present decisions by embedding them in a framework of that which has been declared right in the past.

[d] Logically, the existence of an exigency should not turn on the seriousness of the crime but on whether there is probable cause and the suspect will flee or the evidence will be destroyed. However, the exigency concept is *normative* as well as *descriptive*, and so what is perceived as an emergency requiring immediate intervention by state officers without the interposition of a magistrate may indeed turn on its seriousness. Should a similar distinction be made between violent felonies and nonviolent felonies?

[e] The Supreme Court is not a "legal dictator" but is at the apex of a judicial hierarchy set within a legal community. While the Court is responsible for setting rules and has the authority to insist on a final interpretation when there is a conflict among the lower courts, the legitimacy of its opinions depend in part on how sensibly the Court "listens to" and understands lower court opinions. Thus, JUSTICE BRENNAN strengthens his opinion by referring to what many lower courts have done. Also note that on occasion a Court of Appeals opinion can carry great weight because of its thoroughness, the brilliance of its insight, respect for the opinion writer, the fact that many courts follow it, or all of the above.

[f] The generality of this statement and holding leaves open the possibility that in the future it will be applied to nonviolent felonies. However, as this was not the fact in the case, such a holding would be premature.

[g] Does the Court's statement—that there was no exigency after the car was abandoned—partially undermine the holding? That is, if there were an exigency, would the police then be justified in entering a home even for a minor offense?

[h] This implies that if Wisconsin were to make first-time DWI a jailable crime,

perhaps even a lesser felony (with a one- or two-year maximum penalty), and were to declare the crime a serious one because of the threat of drunk driving to life and safety, a future Supreme Court might be constrained to find that an exigency existed under the facts of *Welsh*. This, of course, is speculative, but such speculation often fuels changes in the law.

[i] This view, that the gravity of the offense is only one factor among many that determines whether an exigency exists, adheres more closely to the "logical" and traditional view that sees the need for emergency action depending more on whether evidence will be destroyed or lost than on the gravity of the offense.

[j] Notice that several important and different policy issues are being juggled simultaneously in the dissent. These include: (a) the development of an easy-to-apply rule that is simple to identify (*e.g.*, felony-misdemeanor distinction) versus a rule that is more complex but is less likely to produce unjust results; (b) the extent to which a federal court applying a constitutional rule to a state should determine a factor, such as the seriousness of a crime, by applying the state's views as opposed to its own; and (c) the need to balance the sanctity of the home and its Fourth Amendment protection against the needs of the state to enforce its laws.

CHIMEL v. CALIFORNIA

395 U.S. 752, 89 S.Ct. 2034, 23 L.Ed.2d 685 (1969)

MR. JUSTICE STEWART delivered the opinion of the Court.

This case raises basic questions concerning the permissible scope under the Fourth Amendment of a search incident to a lawful arrest.

* * * Late [one] afternoon * * * three police officers arrived at the * * * home of the petitioner with a warrant authorizing his arrest for [a] burglary. * * * The officers knocked on the door, identified themselves to the petitioner's wife, and asked if they might come inside. She ushered them into the house, where they waited 10 or 15 minutes until the petitioner returned home from work. When the petitioner entered the house, one of the officers handed him the arrest warrant and asked for permission to "look around." The petitioner objected, but was advised that "on the basis of the lawful arrest," the officers would nonetheless conduct a search. No search warrant had been issued.

Accompanied by the petitioner's wife, the officers then looked through the entire three-bedroom house, including the attic, the garage, and a small workshop. In some rooms the search was relatively cursory. In the master bedroom and sewing room, however, the officers directed the petitioner's wife to open drawers and "to physically move contents of the drawers from side to side so that [they] might view any items that would have come from [the] burglary." After completing the search, they seized numerous items— primarily coins, but also several medals, tokens, and a few other objects. The entire search took between 45 minutes and an hour. [a]

[Items seized during the search were admitted in evidence against Chimel at a criminal trial.] * * *

[The Court assumed that the arrest was valid.] This brings us directly to the question whether the warrantless search of the petitioner's entire house can be constitutionally justified as incident to that arrest. The decisions of this Court bearing upon that question have been far from consistent, as even the most cursory review makes evident.

[Dictum in *Weeks v. United States* [this volume] referred in passing to a well known exception to the warrant requirement, "to search the person of the accused when legally arrested."] That statement made no reference to any right to search the *place* where an arrest occurs. * * * Eleven years later the case of Carroll v. United States, 267 U.S. 132 [1925] brought the following embellishment of the *Weeks* statement:

"When a man is legally arrested for an offense, whatever is found upon his person *or in his control* which it is unlawful for him to have and which may be used to prove the offense may be seized and held as evidence in the prosecution." * * * (Emphasis added.)

[Another 1925 case, *Agnello v. United States*, 269 U.S. 20, "still by way of dictum" said:]

"The right without a search warrant contemporaneously to search persons lawfully arrested while committing crime and to search the place where the arrest is made in order to find and seize things connected with the crime as its fruits or as the means by which it was committed, as well as weapons and other things to effect an escape from custody, is not to be doubted." * * *

And in *Marron v. United States*, 275 U.S. 192 [1927], two years later, the dictum of *Agnello* appeared to be the foundation of the Court's decision, [where agents with a search warrant to seize liquor and a still also seized a ledger.   The ledger was seized as incident to the arrest of the illicit producers at the still.]   The Court upheld the seizure of the ledger by holding that since the agents had made a lawful arrest, "[t]hey had a right without a warrant contemporaneously to search the place in order to find and seize the things used to carry on the criminal enterprise." * * *

That the *Marron* opinion did not mean all that it seemed to say became evident, however, a few years later in *Go-Bart Importing Co. v. United States*, 282 U.S. 344 [1931] and *United States v. Lefkowitz* 285 U.S. 452 [1932]. * * * [In these cases the Supreme Court limited the *Marron* ruling to situations where the things seized incident to arrest "were visible and accessible and in the offender's immediate custody."] * * * [I]n *Lefkowitz*, * * * the Court held unlawful a search of desk drawers and a cabinet despite the fact that the search had accompanied a lawful

arrest. * * *

The limiting views expressed in *Go-Bart* and *Lefkowitz* were thrown to the winds, however, in *Harris v. United States*, 331 U.S. 145 decided in 1947. * * *   [Harris] was arrested [on an arrest warrant] in the living room of his four-room apartment, and in an attempt to recover two canceled checks thought to have been used in effecting the forgery, the officers undertook a thorough search of the entire apartment.   Inside a desk drawer they found a sealed envelope marked "George Harris, personal papers."   The envelope, which was then torn open, was found to contain altered Selective Service documents, and those documents were used to secure Harris' conviction for violating the Selective Training and Service Act of 1940.   The Court rejected Harris' Fourth Amendment claim, sustaining the search as "incident to arrest." * * *

Only a year after *Harris*, however, the pendulum swung again.   In *Trupiano v. United States*, 334 u.s. 699 [1948], [the Court invalidated the seizure of evidence at an illegal distillery made without a search warrant but pursuant to arrests.] The opinion stated:
         * * *

"A search or seizure without a warrant as an incident to a lawful arrest has always been considered to be a strictly limited right.   It grows out of the inherent necessities of the situation at the time of the arrest.   But there must be something more in the way of necessity than merely a lawful arrest." * * *

In 1950, two years after *Trupiano*, came *United States v. Rabinowitz*, 339 U.S. 56, the decision upon which California primarily relies in the case now before us. In *Rabinowitz*, federal authorities * * * [armed with an arrest warrant, arrested the defendant] at his one-room business office. At the time of the arrest, the officers "searched the desk, safe, and file cabinets in the office for about an hour and a half," * * * and seized 573 stamps with forged overprints. * * * The Court held that the search in its entirety fell within the principle giving law enforcement authorities "[t]he right 'to search the place where the arrest is made in order to find and seize things connected with the crime * * *'" * * * The test, said the Court, "is not whether it is reasonable to procure a search warrant, but whether the search was reasonable." * * * **[b]**

* * * [The *Rabinowitz*] doctrine, however, at least in the broad sense in which it was applied by the California courts in this case, can withstand neither historical nor rational analysis.
* * *

[The Court then noted that the line of cases supporting the *Rabinowitz* rule was quite wavering. Furthermore, the historic background of the Fourth Amendment was the strongly felt abuses of general warrants, hated by the American colonists, implying that] * * * the general requirement that a search warrant be obtained is not lightly to be dispensed with, and "the burden is on those seeking [an] exemption [from the requirement] to show the need for it * * *'" * * *

Only last Term in *Terry v. Ohio* [this volume], we emphasized that "the police must, whenever practicable, obtain advance judicial approval of searches and seizures through the warrant procedure," * * * and that "[t]he scope of [a] search must be

'strictly tied to and justified by' the circumstances which rendered its initiation permissible." * * * **[c]**

A similar analysis underlies the "search incident to arrest" principle, and marks its proper extent. When an arrest is made, it is reasonable for the arresting officer to search the person arrested in order to remove any weapons that the latter might seek to use in order to resist arrest or effect his escape. Otherwise, the officer's safety might well be endangered, and the arrest itself frustrated. In addition, it is entirely reasonable for the arresting officer to search for and seize any evidence on the arrestee's person in order to prevent its concealment or destruction. And the area into which an arrestee might reach in order to grab a weapon or evidentiary items must, of course, be governed by a like rule. A gun on a table or in a drawer in front of one who is arrested can be as dangerous to the arresting officer as one concealed in the clothing of the person arrested. There is ample justification, therefore, for a search of the arrestee's person and the area "within his immediate control" —construing that phrase to mean the area from within which he might gain possession of a weapon or destructible evidence. **[d]**

There is no comparable justification, however, for routinely searching any room other than that in which an arrest occurs—or, for that matter, for searching through all the desk drawers or other closed or concealed areas in that room itself. Such searches, in the absence of well-recognized exceptions, may be made only under the authority of a search warrant. **[e]** The "adherence to judicial processes" mandated by the Fourth Amendment requires no less.

* * *

It is argued in the present case that it is "reasonable" to search a man's house when he is arrested in it. But that argument is founded on little more than a subjective view regarding the acceptability of certain sorts of police conduct, and not on considerations relevant to Fourth Amendment interests. Under such an unconfined analysis, Fourth Amendment protection in this area would approach the evaporation point. It is not easy to explain why, for instance, it is less subjectively "reasonable" to search a man's house when he is arrested on his front lawn—or just down the street—than it is when he happens to be in the house at the time of arrest. * * * [f] Thus, although "[t]he recurring questions of the reasonableness of searches" depend upon "the facts and circumstances—the total atmosphere of the case," * * * those facts and circumstances must be viewed in the light of established Fourth Amendment principles.

* * *

[The Court noted that the *Rabinowitz* rule creates the possibility for "pretext" arrests, where the police deliberately attempt to arrest a suspect at home so as to avoid the necessity to obtain a search warrant, especially where probable cause does not exist. Thus, in effect, police could operate as if they had general warrants.]

Rabinowitz and *Harris* have been the subject of critical commentary for many years and have been relied upon less and less in our own decisions. It is time, for the reasons we have stated, to hold that on their own facts, and insofar as the principles they stand for are inconsistent with those that we have endorsed today, they are no longer to be followed.

Application of sound Fourth Amendment principles to the facts of this case produces a clear result. The search here went far beyond the petitioner's person and the area from within which he might have obtained either a weapon or something that could have been used as evidence against him. There was no constitutional justification, in the absence of a search warrant, for extending the search beyond that area. The scope of the search was, therefore, "unreasonable" under the Fourth and Fourteenth Amendments, and the petitioner's conviction cannot stand.

Reversed.

[JUSTICE HARLAN concurred.]

[JUSTICE WHITE wrote an elaborate dissenting opinion, joined by JUSTICE BLACK. The gist of the dissent was that the broad search-incident-to-arrest rule of *Rabinowitz* was correct because the searches conducted under it must adhere to a general rule of reasonableness. In this case, the search was reasonable because the arrest alerted Mrs. Chimel, and she would have been in a position to get rid of incriminating evidence after the police had left the house.]

*   *   *   *   *   *   *   *   *   *   *

COMMENTS

[a] It could be argued that the police, by searching an entire house on the authority of having made an arrest, have greater authority than would exist under a warrant, for a magistrate's warrant may establish limits to the search. It was not clear whether the police limited their search of the house to items logically related to the arrest.

[b] This remarkable zigzag history of reversals between broad and narrow interpretations of the scope of the search incident to arrest exception may have reflected changes in the constitution of the Court, the pressure of particular facts, and inattention to the need for consistency. Given the vital function of the Court to establish consistent rules, the need for a definitive ruling is apparent.

[c] The *Chimel* case is here placed within the framework of the Fourth Amendment law "revolution" of the 1960s, which stressed the warrant clause and the need to limit exceptions to the warrant requirement.

[d] JUSTICE STEWART here establishes a "bright-line" rule regarding the scope of a search incident to arrest. Although it has been subject to substantial litigation and has led to occasionally strained results, this rule has offered a workable and reasonable guide to police and courts.

[e] This rule was later expanded by the "protective sweep" doctrine, see *Maryland v. Buie* [this volume].

[f] This may be so, but such conceptions of what was reasonable have obviously motivated numerous members of the Supreme Court in the past to allow broad searches incident to arrest. This area of law can profitably be understood as one where the rules (and the justices' notions of what was reasonable) have been influenced by constitutional norms. The shifts in the Court's rulings reflected a conflict over what was legitimate under the Fourth Amendment on a question where the Amendment did not speak in absolute or precise terms.

UNITED STATES v. ROBINSON

414 U.S. 218, 94 S.Ct. 467, 38 L.Ed.2d 427 (1973)

MR. JUSTICE REHNQUIST delivered the opinion of the Court. [a]

[Officer Jenks, of the District of Columbia Metropolitan Police Department, observed the respondent, Robinson, driving a car in the District of Columbia. Four days earlier, Jenks had checked Robinson's operator permit and as a result had reason to believe that Robinson was operating a motor vehicle after the revocation of his operator's permit, a statutory offense which carried a mandatory minimum jail term and fine. Jenks signaled Robinson to stop the automobile; as Robinson got out of the car, Jenks placed him under arrest for "operating after revocation and obtaining a permit by misrepresentation." The District of Columbia Court of Appeals assumed that Jenks had probable cause to arrest and that he effected a full-custody arrest.]

[In accordance with prescribed departmental procedures, Jenks began to search respondent. He proceeded to pat down Robinson's outer clothing and felt an object in the left breast pocket of the heavy coat Robinson was wearing. Jenks testified that] he "couldn't tell what it was" and also that he "couldn't actually tell the size of it." Jenks then reached into the pocket and pulled out the object, which turned out to be a "crumpled up cigarette package." Jenks testified that at this point he still did not know what was in the package:

"As I felt the package I could feel objects in the package but I couldn't tell what they were. * * * I knew they weren't cigarettes."

The officer then opened the cigarette pack and found 14 gelatin capsules of white powder which he thought to be, and which later analysis proved to be, heroin. Jenks then continued his search of respondent to completion, feeling around his waist and trouser legs, and examining the remaining pockets. The heroin seized from the respondent was admitted into evidence at the trial which resulted in his conviction in the District Court.

[The en banc District of Columbia Circuit Court of Appeals reversed the conviction, holding that the heroin introduced in evidence against respondent had been obtained as a result of a search which violated the Fourth Amendment.]

* * * We conclude that the search conducted by Jenks in this case did not offend the limits imposed by the Fourth Amendment, and we therefore reverse the judgment of the Court of Appeals.

I

It is well settled that a search incident to a lawful arrest is a traditional exception to the warrant requirement of the Fourth Amendment. This general exception has historically been formulated into two distinct propositions. The first is that a search may be made of the *person* of the arrestee by virtue of the lawful arrest. The second is that a search may be made of the area within the control of the arrestee. **[b]**

* * * The validity of the search of a person incident to a lawful arrest has been regarded as settled from its first enunciation, and has remained virtually unchallenged until the present case. * * *

Because the rule requiring exclusion of evidence obtained in violation of the Fourth Amendment was first enunciated in *Weeks v. United States*, [this volume], it is understandable that virtually all of this Court's search-and-seizure law has been developed since that time. In *Weeks*, the Court made clear its recognition of the validity of a search incident to a lawful arrest:

> "What then is the present case? Before answering that inquiry specifically, it may be well by a process of exclusion to state what it is not. It is not an assertion of the right on the part of the Government, always recognized under English and American law, to search the person of the accused when legally arrested to discover and seize the fruits or evidences of crime. This right has been uniformly maintained in many cases." * * *

Agnello v. United States, 269 U.S. 20 (1925), decided 11 years after *Weeks*, repeats the categorical recognition of the validity of a search incident to lawful arrest:

> "The right without a search warrant contemporaneously to search persons lawfully arrested while committing crime and to search the place where the arrest is made in order to find and seize things connected with the crime as its fruits or as the means by which it was committed, as well as weapons and other things to effect an escape from custody, is not to be doubted." * * *

* * *

Thus the broadly stated rule, and the reasons for it, have been repeatedly affirmed in the decisions of this Court since *Weeks v. United States*, * * * nearly 60 years ago. Since the statements in the cases speak not simply in terms of an exception to the warrant requirement, but in terms of an affirmative authority to search, they clearly imply that such searches also meet the Fourth Amendment's requirement of reasonableness.

II

In its decision of this case, the Court of Appeals decided that even after a police officer lawfully places a suspect under arrest for the purpose of taking him into custody, he may not ordinarily proceed to fully search the prisoner. He must, instead, conduct a limited frisk of the outer clothing and remove such weapons that he may, as a result of that limited frisk, reasonably believe and ascertain that the suspect has in his possession. While recognizing that *Terry v. Ohio*, [this volume] dealt with a permissible "frisk" incident to an investigative stop based on less than probable cause to arrest, the Court of Appeals felt that the principles of that case should be carried over to this probable-cause arrest for driving while one's license is revoked. Since there would be no further evidence of such a crime to be obtained in a search of the arrestee, the court held that only a search for weapons could be justified. **[c]**

Terry v. Ohio, * * * did not involve an arrest for probable cause, and it made quite clear that the "protective frisk" for weapons which it approved might be conducted without probable cause. * * *   This Court's opinion explicitly recognized that there is a "distinction in purpose, character, and extent between a search incident to an arrest and a limited search for weapons."

* * *

"* * * An arrest is a wholly different kind of intrusion upon individual freedom from a limited search for weapons, and the interests each is designed to serve are likewise quite different. An arrest is the initial stage of a criminal prosecution.   It is intended to vindicate society's interest in having its laws obeyed, and it is inevitably accompanied by future interference with the individual's freedom of movement, whether or not trial or conviction ultimately follows. The protective search for weapons, on the other hand, constitutes a brief, though far from inconsiderable, intrusion upon the sanctity of the person." * * *

Terry, therefore, affords no basis to carry over to a probable-cause arrest the limitations this Court placed on a stop-and-frisk search permissible without probable cause.

* * *

III

Virtually all of the statements of this Court affirming the existence of an unqualified authority to search incident to a lawful arrest are dicta. **[d]** We would not, therefore, be foreclosed by principles of *stare decisis* from further examination into history and practice in order to see whether the sort of qualifications imposed by the Court of Appeals in this case were in fact intended by the Framers of the Fourth Amendment or recognized in cases decided prior to Weeks. * * *

[JUSTICE REHNQUIST here cited English and American common law cases on point.]

* * *

While these earlier authorities are sketchy, they tend to support the broad statement of the authority to search incident to arrest found in the successive decisions of this Court, rather than the restrictive one which was applied by the Court of Appeals in this case. The scarcity of case law before *Weeks* is doubtless due in part to the fact that the exclusionary rule there enunciated had been first adopted only 11 years earlier in Iowa; but it would seem to be also due in part to the fact that the issue was regarded as well settled.

The Court of Appeals in effect determined that the *only* reason supporting the authority for a *full* search incident to lawful arrest was the possibility of discovery of evidence or fruits.   Concluding that there could be no evidence or fruits in the case of an offense such as that with which respondent was charged, it held that any protective search would have to be limited by the conditions laid down in *Terry* for a search upon less than probable cause to arrest. Quite apart from the fact that *Terry* clearly recognized the distinction between the two types of searches, and that a different rule governed one than governed the other, we find additional reason to disagree with the Court of Appeals.

The justification or reason for the authority to search incident to a lawful arrest rests quite as much on the need to disarm the suspect in order to take him into custody as it does on the need to preserve evidence on his person for later use at trial. * * * The standards traditionally governing a search incident to lawful arrest are not, therefore, commuted to the stricter *Terry* standards by the absence of probable fruits or further evidence of the particular crime for which the arrest is made.

Nor are we inclined, on the basis of what seems to us to be a rather speculative judgment, to qualify the breadth of the general authority to search incident to a lawful custodial arrest on an assumption that persons arrested for the offense of driving while their licenses have been revoked are less likely to possess dangerous weapons than are those arrested for other crimes. It is scarcely open to doubt that the danger to an officer is far greater in the case of the extended exposure which follows the taking of a suspect into custody and transporting him to the police station than in the case of the relatively fleeting contact resulting from the typical *Terry*-type stop. This is an adequate basis for treating all custodial arrests alike for purposes of search justification.

But quite apart from these distinctions, our more fundamental disagreement with the Court of Appeals arises from its suggestion that there must be litigated in each case the issue of whether or not there was present one of the reasons supporting the authority for a search of the person incident to a lawful arrest. We do not think the long line of authorities of this Court dating back to *Weeks*, or what we can glean from the history of practice in this country and in England, requires such a case-by-case adjudication. **[e]** A police officer's determination as to how and where to search the person of a suspect whom he has arrested is necessarily a quick *ad hoc* judgment which the Fourth Amendment does not require to be broken down in each instance into an analysis of each step in the search. The authority to search the person incident to a lawful custodial arrest, while based upon the need to disarm and to discover evidence, does not depend on what a court may later decide was the probability in a particular arrest situation that weapons or evidence would in fact be found upon the person of the suspect. A custodial arrest of a suspect based on probable cause is a reasonable intrusion under the Fourth Amendment; that intrusion being lawful, a search incident to the arrest requires no additional justification. It is the fact of the lawful arrest which establishes the authority to search, and we hold that in the case of a lawful custodial arrest a full search of the person is not only an exception to the warrant requirement of the Fourth Amendment, but is also a "reasonable" search under that Amendment. **[f]**

IV

The search of respondent's person conducted by Officer Jenks in this case and the seizure from him of the heroin, were permissible under established Fourth Amendment law. While thorough, the search partook of none of the extreme or patently abusive characteristics which were held to violate the Due Process Clause of the

Fourteenth Amendment in *Rochin v. California*, [this volume]. **[g]** Since it is the fact of custodial arrest which gives rise to the authority to search, it is of no moment that Jenks did not indicate any subjective fear of the respondent or that he did not himself suspect that respondent was armed. **[h]** Having in the course of a lawful search come upon the crumpled package of cigarettes, he was entitled to inspect it; and when his inspection revealed the heroin capsules, he was entitled to seize them as "fruits, instrumentalities, or contraband" probative of criminal conduct. * * *   The judgment of the Court of Appeals holding otherwise is

    Reversed.

[JUSTICE POWELL concurred, noting that as a custodial arrest is a significant intrusion, the person retains no significant Fourth Amendment interest in the privacy of his person.]

MR. JUSTICE MARSHALL, with whom MR. JUSTICE DOUGLAS and MR. JUSTICE BRENNAN join, dissenting.

    * * *

II

    * * *

The majority also suggests that the Court of Appeals reached a novel and unprecedented result by imposing qualifications on the historically recognized authority to conduct a full search incident to a lawful arrest. Nothing could be further from the truth, as the Court of Appeals itself was so careful to point out.

One need not go back to Black-stone's Commentaries, Holmes' Common Law, or Pollock & Maitland in search of precedent for the approach adopted by the Court of Appeals. Indeed, given the fact that mass production of the automobile did not begin until the early decades of the present century, I find it somewhat puzzling that the majority even looks to these sources for guidance on the only question presented in this case: the permissible scope of a search of the person incident to a lawful arrest for violation of a motor vehicle regulation. **[i]** The fact is that this question has been considered by several state and federal courts, the vast majority of which have held that, absent special circumstances, a police officer has no right to conduct a full search of the person incident to a lawful arrest for violation of a motor vehicle regulation.

[JUSTICE MARSHALL reviewed several recent state and federal cases that held that a search incident to an arrest for motor vehicle violations was limited to a search for weapons.]
    * * *

Accordingly, I think it disingenuous for the Court to now pronounce that what precedents exist on the question "tend to support the broad statement of the authority to search incident to arrest found in the successive decisions of this Court, rather than the restrictive one which was applied by the Court of Appeals in this case." * * *   It is disquieting, to say the least, to see the Court at once admit that "[v]irtually all of the statements of this Court affirming the existence of an unqualified authority to search incident to a lawful arrest are dicta" and concede that we are presented with an open question on which "further examination into history and practice" would be helpful, yet then conduct an examination into prior practice which is not only wholly superficial, but totally inaccurate and misleading.

* * *

* * * * * * * * * *

COMMENTS

[a] A state "companion case," *Gustafson v. Florida*, 414 U.S. 260 (1973), was decided on the same day. It is useful to have a state companion case to a federal case (and vice versa) where a Bill of Rights question arises. Because the "incorporation doctrine" may come into play, it is important to know whether the federal case, decided directly under the particular Amendment, will have the equal impact as a state case in which the constitutional rule is "incorporated into" the due process clause of the Fourteenth Amendment. Some factors were different in *Gustafson* (*e.g.*, there was no department search incident to arrest rule) but the Court treated these differences as not significant. As a result, the *Robinson* rule applies with the same force to state and local law enforcement as to federal officers.

[b] The controlling case on the second issue is *Chimel v. California* [this volume].

[c] There is some logic to this. Can you think of any countervailing policy that limits the ability of the police to exploit a situation, where the police have lawful custody of a person for *one* crime, to find search for contraband or evidence of *another* crime?

[d] In Part I of the opinion the search incident to arrest rule is stated as a firm rule of law. Nevertheless, the Court is justified to characterize all the statements in the cases as dicta because in none of the cases was the issue of search incident to arrest *the* issue on which the decision of the case turned.

[e] The Court is justified in being concerned whether its decision will generate much litigation to test its ruling. The dissent argued that these cases should be determined on a case-by-case basis. The majority's "bright line" rule will avoid litigation over whether an arrest for a non-property crime should include a search for evidence. On the other hand, the ruling places greater unreviewed discretion into police hands.

[f] Compare the majority's holding to the way in which the dissent would frame the issue of the case. It is usually considered more "lawyerly" to focus an issue narrowly, so as not to decide matters not given full consideration by the court. But there is no law that requires this.

[g] This is the "shocks the conscience" case.

[h] This point is put in for a reason. If the extent of the search depended on the officer's subjective assessment of the danger of the situation, it would lead to extensive litigation.

[i] Framing an issue is an art and not a science. While the dissent seeks to narrow the issue of the case to arrests for automobile violations only, the majority views the issue more broadly as the authority in a search incident to any custodial arrest.

MARYLAND v. BUIE

494 U.S. 325, 110 S.Ct. 1093, 108 L.Ed.2d 276 (1990)

JUSTICE WHITE delivered the opinion of the Court.

A "protective sweep" is a quick and limited search of a premises, **[a]** incident to an arrest and conducted to protect the safety of police officers or others. It is narrowly confined to a cursory visual inspection of those places in which a person might be hiding. In this case we must decide what level of justification is required by the Fourth and Fourteenth Amendments before police officers, while effecting the arrest of a suspect in his home pursuant to an arrest warrant, may conduct a warrantless protective sweep of all or part of the premises. The Court of Appeals of Maryland [required] * * * probable cause to believe that a serious and demonstrable potentiality for danger existed. * * * We conclude that the Fourth Amendment would permit the protective sweep undertaken here if the searching officer "possesse[d] a reasonable belief based on 'specific and articulable facts which, taken together with the rational inferences from those facts, reasonably warrant[ed]' the officer in believing," * * * that the area swept harbored an individual posing a danger to the officer or others. We accordingly vacate the judgment below and remand for application of this standard.

I

[Two robbers, one wearing a red running suit, held up a pizza parlor and fled. That day an arrest warrant was obtained against Jerome Buie and his alleged accomplice, Lloyd Allen. Buie's house was placed under surveillance. Two days later, the arrest warrant was executed by seven officers who entered the house, after verifying that Buie was home, and "fanned out through the first and second floors." A corporal shouted down to the basement, and Buie, hiding there, surrendered. A detective then entered the basement, "'in case there was someone else' down there" and spotted the red running suit lying on a stack of clothes in plain view, and seized it. The Maryland Supreme Court ordered the suppression of the suit in evidence on the ground that it was illegally seized because the police had no articulable suspicion or probable cause to believe that an accomplice was in the house where Buie was arrested.]

II

It is not disputed that until the point of Buie's arrest the police had the right, based on the authority of the arrest warrant, to search anywhere in the house that Buie might have been found, including the basement. * * * There is also no dispute that if Detective Frolich's entry into the basement was lawful, the seizure of the red running suit, which was in plain view and which the officer had probable cause to believe was evidence of a crime, was also lawful under the Fourth Amendment. * * * The issue in this case is what level of justification the Fourth Amendment required before Detective Frolich could legally enter the basement to see if someone else was there.

* * *   Maryland, argues that, under a general reasonableness balancing test, police should be permitted to conduct a protective sweep whenever they make an in-home arrest for a violent crime. [b] As an alternative to this suggested bright-line rule, the State contends that protective sweeps fall within the ambit of the doctrine announced in *Terry v. Ohio* [this volume], and that such sweeps may be conducted in conjunction with a valid in-home arrest whenever the police reasonably suspect a risk of danger to the officers or others at the arrest scene. * * *   Respondent argues that a protective sweep may not be undertaken without a warrant unless the exigencies of the situation render such warrantless search objectively reasonable. [c] According to Buie, because the State has shown neither exigent circumstances to immediately enter Buie's house nor an unforeseen danger that arose once the officers were in the house, there is no excuse for the failure to obtain a search warrant to search for dangerous persons believed to be on the premises. Buie further contends that, even if the warrant requirement is inapplicable, there is no justification for relaxing the probable-cause standard. If something less than probable cause is sufficient, respondent argues that it is no less than individualized suspicion—specific, articulable facts supporting a reasonable belief that there are persons on the premises who are a threat to the officers. According to Buie, there were no such specific, articulable facts to justify the search of his basement.

III

It goes without saying that the Fourth Amendment bars only unreasonable searches and seizures. * * * Our cases show that in determining reasonableness, we have balanced the intrusion on the individual's Fourth Amendment interests against its promotion of legitimate governmental interests. * * *   Under this test, a search of the house or office is generally not reasonable without a warrant issued on probable cause. There are other contexts, however, where the public interest is such that neither a warrant nor probable cause is required. * * * [d]

[*Terry v. Ohio* held that an on-the-street "frisk" for weapons was to be tested by the Fourth Amendment's general rule against unreasonable searches because that category of police work required swift action based on the police officer's on-the-spot observation. There was no test other than a balancing of the requirements of privacy against the need for officers to protect themselves and others against violence. Thus, a brief patdown for weapons was authorized when the officer had not a mere hunch but specific and articulable facts to believe that the suspect was carrying a weapon.]

In *Michigan v. Long* [this volume], the principles of *Terry* were applied in the context of a roadside encounter [to the open areas of a car]. * * *   The *Long* Court expressly rejected the contention that *Terry* restricted preventative searches to the person of a detained suspect. In a sense, *Long* authorized a "frisk" of an automobile for weapons.

The ingredients to apply the balance struck in *Terry* and *Long* are present in this case. Possessing an arrest warrant and probable cause to believe Buie was in his home, the officers were entitled to enter and to search anywhere in the house in which Buie might be found. Once he was found, however, the search for him was over, and there was no longer that particular justification for entering any rooms that had not yet been searched. **[e]**

That Buie had an expectation of privacy in those remaining areas of his house, however, does not mean such rooms were immune from entry. In *Terry* and *Long* we were concerned with the immediate interest of the police officers in taking steps to assure themselves that the persons with whom they were dealing were not armed with or able to gain immediate control of a weapon that could unexpectedly and fatally be used against them. In the instant case, there is an analogous interest of the officers in taking steps to assure themselves that the house in which a suspect is being or had just been arrested is not harboring other persons who are dangerous and who could unexpectedly launch an attack. The risk of danger in the context of an arrest in the home is as great as, if not greater than, it is in an on-the-street or roadside investigatory encounter. A *Terry* or *Long* frisk occurs before a police-citizen confrontation has escalated to the point of arrest. A protective sweep, in contrast, occurs as an adjunct to the serious step of taking a person into custody for the purpose of prosecuting him for a crime. Moreover, unlike an encounter on the street or along a highway, an in-home arrest puts the officer at the disadvantage of being on his adversary's "turf." An ambush in a confined setting of unknown configuration is more to be feared than it is in open, more familiar surroundings.

We recognized in *Terry* that "[e]ven a limited search of the outer clothing for weapons constitutes a severe, though brief, intrusion upon cherished personal security, and it must surely be an annoying, frightening, and perhaps humiliating experience." * * * But we permitted the intrusion, which was no more than necessary to protect the officer from harm. Nor do we here suggest, as the State does, that entering rooms not examined prior to the arrest is a *de minimus* intrusion that may be disregarded. We are quite sure, however, that the arresting officers are permitted in such circumstances to take reasonable steps to ensure their safety after, and while making, the arrest. That interest is sufficient to outweigh the intrusion such procedures may entail.

We agree with the State, as did the court below, that a [separate search] warrant was not required. We also hold that as an incident to the arrest the officers could, as a precautionary matter and without probable cause or reasonable suspicion, look in closets and other spaces immediately adjoining the place of arrest from which an attack could be immediately launched. Beyond that, however, we hold that there must be articulable facts which, taken together with the rational inferences from those facts, would warrant a reasonably prudent officer in believing that the area to be swept harbors an individual posing a danger to those on the arrest scene. **[f]** This is no more and no less than was required in *Terry* and *Long*, and as in those cases, we think this balance is the proper one.

We should emphasize that such a

protective sweep, aimed at protecting the arresting officers, if justified by the circumstances, is nevertheless not a full search of the premises, but may extend only to a cursory inspection of those spaces where a person may be found. The sweep lasts no longer than is necessary to dispel the reasonable suspicion of danger and in any event no longer than it takes to complete the arrest and depart the premises.

IV

Affirmance is not required by *Chimel v. California*, [this volume], where it was held that in the absence of a search warrant, the justifiable search incident to an in-home arrest could not extend beyond the arrestee's person and the area from within which the arrestee might have obtained a weapon. First, *Chimel* was concerned with a full-blown search of the entire house for evidence of the crime for which the arrest was made, * * * not the more limited intrusion contemplated by a protective sweep. Second, the justification for the search incident to arrest considered in *Chimel* was the threat posed by the arrestee, not the safety threat posed by the house, or more properly by unseen third parties in the house. To reach our conclusion today, therefore, we need not disagree with the Court's statement in *Chimel*, * * * that "the invasion of privacy that results from a top-to-bottom search of a man's house [cannot be characterized] as 'minor,'" nor hold that "simply because some interference with an individual's privacy and freedom of movement has lawfully taken place, further intrusions should automatically be allowed despite the absence of a warrant that the Fourth Amendment

would otherwise require." * * * The type of search we authorize today is far removed from the "top-to-bottom" search involved in *Chimel*; moreover, it is decidedly not "automati[c]," but may be conducted only when justified by a reasonable, articulable suspicion that the house is harboring a person posing a danger to those on the arrest scene. [g]

V

* * * The Fourth Amendment permits a properly limited protective sweep in conjunction with an in-home arrest when the searching officer possesses a reasonable belief based on specific and articulable facts that the area to be swept harbors an individual posing a danger to those on the arrest scene. * * *

[JUSTICE STEPHENS concurred, stressing that the burden of proving the need for a protective sweep rests on the state. He noted that the facts indicated that at the time of the protective search, Buie had been handcuffed and the police did not have a high sense of danger.]

[JUSTICE KENNEDY also concurred, disagreeing with JUSTICE STEPHENS' characterization of the burden on the police as formidable in this case.]

JUSTICE BRENNAN, with whom JUSTICE MARSHALL joins, dissenting.

Today the Court for the first time extends *Terry v. Ohio* into the home, dispensing with the Fourth Amendment's general requirements of a warrant and probable cause and carving a "reasonable suspicion" exception for protective sweeps in private dwelling. * * *

Terry and its early progeny "permit[ted] only brief investigative stops and extremely limited searches based on reasonable suspicion." * * * But this Court more recently has applied the rationale underlying *Terry* to a wide variety of more intrusive searches and seizures, prompting my continued criticism of the "'emerging tendency on the part of the Court to convert the *Terry* decision'" from a narrow exception into one that "'swallow[s] the general rule that [searches] are reasonable only if based on probable cause.'" * * *

The Court today holds that *Terry*'s "reasonable suspicion" standard "strikes the proper balance between officer safety and citizen privacy" for protective sweeps in private dwellings. * * * I agree with the majority that officers executing an arrest warrant within a private dwelling have an interest in protecting themselves against potential ambush by third parties, * * * but the majority offers no support for its assumption that the danger of ambush during planned home arrests approaches the danger of unavoidable "on-the-beat" confrontations in "the myriad daily situations in which policemen and citizens confront each other on the street." * * * **[h]** In any event, the Court's implicit judgment that a protective sweep constitutes a "minimally intrusive" search akin to that involved in *Terry* markedly undervalues the nature and scope of the privacy interests involved.

While the Fourth Amendment protects a person's privacy interests in a variety of settings, "physical entry of the home is the chief evil against which the wording of the Fourth Amendment is directed." * * * **[i]** The Court discounts the nature of the intrusion because it believes that the scope of the intrusion is limited. The Court explains that a protective sweep's scope is "narrowly confined to a cursory visual inspection of those places in which a person might be hiding," * * * and confined in duration to a period "no longer than is necessary to dispel the reasonable suspicion of danger and in any event no longer than it takes to complete the arrest and depart the premises." * * * But these spatial and temporal restrictions are not particularly limiting. A protective sweep would bring within police purview virtually all personal possessions within the house not hidden from view in a small enclosed space. Police officers searching for potential ambushers might enter every room including basements and attics; open up closets, lockers, chests, wardrobes, and cars; and peer under beds and behind furniture. The officers will view letters, documents and personal effects that are on tables or desks or are visible inside open drawers; books, records, tapes, and pictures on shelves; and clothing, medicines, toiletries and other paraphernalia not carefully stored in dresser drawers or bathroom cupboards. While perhaps not a "full-blown" or "top-to-bottom" search, * * * a protective sweep is much closer to it than to a "limited patdown for weapons" or a "'frisk' of an automobile." * * * Because the nature and scope of the intrusion sanctioned here are far greater than those upheld in *Terry* and

Long, the Court's conclusion that "[t]he ingredients to apply the balance struck in *Terry* and *Long* are present in this case," * * * is unwarranted.   The "ingredient" of a minimally intrusive search is absent, and the Court's holding today therefore unpalatably deviates from *Terry* and its progeny.

In light of the special sanctity of a private residence and the highly intrusive nature of a protective sweep, I firmly believe that police officers must have probable cause to fear that their personal safety is threatened by a hidden confederate of an arrestee before they may sweep through the entire home. Given the state-court determination that the officers searching Buie's home lacked probable cause to perceive such a danger and therefore were not lawfully present in the basement, I would affirm the state court's decision to suppress the incriminating evidence. I respectfully dissent.

* * * * * * * * * *

COMMENTS

[a] JUSTICE WHITE begins the case with a general definition and a statement of the case's general conclusion. This is one technique of opinion writing but not one that is always followed. On the one hand, it is a helpful aid to attorneys desiring to quickly get the gist of a case. On the other hand, it may be designed in this case to "occupy center court" by predisposing the reader and downplaying the facts, which, according to the dissent, may not support the protective sweep rule in this case.   It can also be pointed out that the "protective sweep doctrine," while perhaps reflecting very old police practice, has only in the few years before the *Buie* decision become a distinct area for constitutional adjudication; also the term might have been unfamiliar to segments of the legal community.

[b] Such a rule would weaken the rule of *Chimel v. California* [this volume].

[c] Since there were two robbers and the second had not been seen, should there be a presumption that the accomplice was present, especially since the underlying crime was a crime of violence?

[d] The protective sweep rule is an extension of the *Terry* doctrine which is in turn based on the "reasonableness" approach to Fourth Amendment jurisprudence. What *Terry*, *Long*, and *Buie* have in common is the risk of immediate physical danger to the law enforcement officer in the performance of police duty.

[e] The Court carefully parsed the factual situation: the lawful scope of the police search changed before and after Buie's arrest. After the arrest, danger from Buie was neutralized; however, the potential of danger from a confederate in the house remained.

[f] There are three separate holdings in this paragraph.   First, a warrant is not required to justify a protective sweep.   Third, the reasonable suspicion-articulable facts standard of *Terry* is the proper protective sweep standard. The second holding, sandwiched between the first and third rules, is a dramatic break with an extension of the *Chimel* rule (discussed below by the Court). It says that in every arrest in a premises, the police can automatically look into adjoining rooms and any space large enough to hold a person. This absolute language makes it clear that the police need not have *any* suspicion that another person is hiding in an adjoining room. As a matter of police safety, the rule is reasonable. Just as a search incident to arrest allows for the safety of officers a full search for weapons without any suspicion that the particular person arrested is concealing a weapon, this aspect of *Buie* allows the police in all cases to presume that a dangerous confederate is lurking in adjoining rooms or closets. But this rule is a bold extension of *Chimel* without any justification based on verified dangers to police officers from confederates.

[g] This is true, but it tends to open up much of a searched house to a "plain view" kind of search.

[h] Do you think that the state must specifically prove that in-house ambushes are as dangerous as on-the-street attacks on the police? Would police departments have to authorize or find social science research studies proving the point before such a policy could be held constitutional? Is the application of one's common sense or imagination about the nature of the potential risk of in-house ambush sufficient to support a protective sweep policy?

[i] This point does not seem apt; *Buie* deals with the situation once the police have already entered the premises.

CALIFORNIA v. CARNEY

471 U.S. 386, 105 S.Ct. 2066, 85 L.Ed.2d 406 (1985)

CHIEF JUSTICE BURGER delivered the opinion of the Court.

We granted certiorari to decide whether law enforcement agents violated the Fourth Amendment when they conducted a warrantless search, based on probable cause, of a fully mobile "motor home" located in a public place.

I

[A youth, observed by DEA agents, entered a motor home of Carney and exited an hour and one-quarter later. The agents stopped the youth who told them that he had received marijuana in return for sexual contact. The agents returned to the motor home with the youth. They knocked on the door, Carney stepped out, and with no warrant, an agent] entered the motor home and observed marihuana, plastic bags, and a scale of the kind used in weighing drugs on a table. Carney moved to suppress the evidence. The California Supreme Court reversed Carney's conviction on the ground that although] the agents had probable cause to arrest respondent and to believe that the vehicle contained evidence of a crime * * * the search was unreasonable because no warrant was obtained. * * * [It] held that the expectations of privacy in a motor home are more like those in a dwelling than in an automobile because the primary function of motor homes is not to provide transportation but to "provide the occupant with living quarters." * * *

We granted certiorari. * * * We reverse.

II

* * * This fundamental right [the Fourth Amendment] is preserved by a requirement that searches be conducted pursuant to a warrant issued by an independent judicial officer. There are, of course, exceptions to the general rule that a warrant must be secured before a search is undertaken; one is the so-called "automobile exception" at issue in this case. **[a]** This exception to the warrant requirement was first set forth by the Court 60 years ago in *Carroll v. United States*, 267 U.S. 132 (1925). There, the Court recognized that the privacy interests in an automobile are constitutionally protected; however, it held that the ready mobility of the automobile justifies a lesser degree of protection of those interests. The Court rested this exception on a long-recognized distinction between stationary structures and vehicles:

"[T]he guaranty of freedom from unreasonable searches and seizures by the Fourth Amendment has been construed, practically since the beginning of Government, as recognizing a necessary difference between a search of a store, dwelling house or other structure in respect of which a proper official warrant readily may be obtained, and a search of a ship, motor boat, wagon or automobile, for contraband goods, where it is not practicable to secure a warrant because the vehicle can be *quickly moved* out of the locality or jurisdiction in which the warrant must be sought." [*Carroll*, above] (emphasis added).

The capacity to be "quickly moved" was clearly the basis of the holding in *Carroll*, and our cases have consistently recognized ready mobility as one of the principal bases of the automobile exception. * * * [I]n *United States v. Ross*, [this volume] (1982), we once again emphasized that "an immediate intrusion is necessary" because of "the nature of an automobile in transit. * * *" The mobility of automobiles, we have observed, "creates circumstances of such exigency that, as a practical necessity, rigorous enforcement of the warrant requirement is impossible." * * *

However, although ready mobility alone was perhaps the original justification for the vehicle exception, our later cases have made clear that ready mobility is not the only basis for the exception. The reasons for the vehicle exception, we have said, are twofold. * * * "Besides the element of mobility, less rigorous warrant requirements govern because the expectation of privacy with respect to one's automobile is significantly less than that relating to one's home or office." * * *

Even in cases where an automobile was not immediately mobile, the lesser expectation of privacy resulting from its use as a readily mobile vehicle justified application of the vehicular exception. * * * In some cases, the configuration of the vehicle contributed to the lower expectations of privacy; for example, we held in *Cardwell v. Lewis*, [417 U.S.

583 (1974)] that, because the passenger compartment of a standard automobile is relatively open to plain view, there are lesser expectations of privacy. But even when enclosed "repository" areas have been involved, we have concluded that the lesser expectations of privacy warrant application of the exception. We have applied the exception in the context of a locked car trunk, * * * a sealed package in a car trunk, * * * a closed compartment under the dashboard, * * * the interior of a vehicle's upholstery, * * * or sealed packages inside a covered pickup truck. * * *

These reduced expectations of privacy derive not from the fact that the area to be searched is in plain view, but from the pervasive regulation of vehicles capable of traveling on the public highways. * * * As we explained in *South Dakota v. Opperman*, an inventory search case:

> "Automobiles, unlike homes, are subjected to pervasive and continuing governmental regulation and controls, including periodic inspection and licensing requirements. As an everyday occurrence, police stop and examine vehicles when license plates or inspection stickers have expired, or if other violations, such as exhaust fumes or excessive noise, are noted, or if headlights or other safety equipment are not in proper working order." * * *

The public is fully aware that it is accorded less privacy in its automobiles because of this compelling governmental need for regulation. Historically, "individuals always [have] been on notice that movable vessels may be stopped and searched on facts giving rise to probable cause that the vehicle contains contraband, without the protection afforded by a magistrate's prior evaluation of those facts." * * * In short, the pervasive schemes of regulation, which necessarily lead to reduced expectations of privacy, and the exigencies attendant to ready mobility justify searches without prior recourse to the authority of a magistrate so long as the overriding standard of probable cause is met.

When a vehicle is being used on the highways, or if it is readily capable of such use and is found stationary in a place not regularly used for residential purposes —temporary or otherwise—the two justifications for the vehicle exception come into play. First, the vehicle is obviously readily mobile by the turn of an ignition key, if not actually moving. Second, there is a reduced expectation of privacy stemming from its use as a licensed motor vehicle subject to a range of police regulation inapplicable to a fixed dwelling. At least in these circumstances, the overriding societal interests in effective law enforcement justify an immediate search before the vehicle and its occupants become unavailable.

While it is true that respondent's vehicle possessed some, if not many of the attributes of a home, it is equally clear that the vehicle falls clearly within the scope of the exception laid down in *Carroll* and applied in succeeding cases. Like the automobile in *Carroll*, respondent's motor home was readily mobile. Absent the prompt search and seizure, it could readily have been moved beyond the reach of the police. Furthermore, the vehicle was licensed to "operate on public streets; [was] serviced in public places; * * * and [was] subject to extensive regulation and inspection." * * * And the vehicle

was so situated that an objective observer would conclude that it was being used not as a residence, but as a vehicle.

Respondent urges us to distinguish his vehicle from other vehicles within the exception because it was *capable of functioning as a home*. In our increasingly mobile society, many vehicles used for transportation can be and are being used not only for transportation but for shelter, i. e., as a "home" or "residence." To distinguish between respondent's motor home and an ordinary sedan for purposes of the vehicle exception would require that we apply the exception depending upon the size of the vehicle and the quality of its appointments. Moreover, to fail to apply the exception to vehicles such as a motor home ignores the fact that a motor home lends itself easily to use as an instrument of illicit drug traffic and other illegal activity. In *United States v. Ross*, 456 U.S., at 822, we declined to distinguish between "worthy" and "unworthy" containers, noting that "the central purpose of the Fourth Amendment forecloses such a distinction." We decline today to distinguish between "worthy" and "unworthy" vehicles which are either on the public roads and highways, or situated such that it is reasonable to conclude that the vehicle is not being used as a residence. **[b]**

Our application of the vehicle exception has never turned on the other uses to which a vehicle might be put. The exception has historically turned on the ready mobility of the vehicle, and on the presence of the vehicle in a setting that objectively indicates that the vehicle is being used for transportation. These two requirements for application of the exception ensure that law enforcement officials are not unnecessarily hamstrung in their efforts to detect and prosecute criminal activity, and that the legitimate privacy interests of the public are protected. Applying the vehicle exception in these circumstances allows the essential purposes served by the exception to be fulfilled, while assuring that the exception will acknowledge legitimate privacy interests.

III

[The Court held that because the "DEA agents had fresh, direct, uncontradicted evidence that the respondent was distributing a controlled substance from the vehicle" they had "abundant probable cause" to search and the search was not unreasonable. The judgement of the California Supreme Court was reversed.]

JUSTICE STEVENS, with whom JUSTICE BRENNAN and JUSTICE MARSHALL join, dissenting.

* * *

III

* * * Our prior cases teach us that inherent mobility is not a sufficient justification for the fashioning of an exception to the warrant requirement, especially in the face of heightened expectations of privacy in the location searched. Motor homes, by their common use and construction, afford their owners a substantial and legitimate expectation of privacy when they dwell within. When a motor home is parked in a location that is removed from the public highway, I believe that society is prepared to recognize that the expectations of privacy within it are

not unlike the expectations one has in a fixed dwelling. As a general rule, such places may only be searched with a warrant based upon probable cause. Warrantless searches of motor homes are only reasonable when the motor home is traveling on the public streets or highways, or when exigent circumstances otherwise require an immediate search without the expenditure of time necessary to obtain a warrant.

* * *

In this case, the motor home was parked in an off-the-street lot only a few blocks from the courthouse in downtown San Diego where dozens of magistrates were available to entertain a warrant application. The officers clearly had the element of surprise with them, and with curtains covering the windshield, the motor home offered no indication of any imminent departure. The officers plainly had probable cause to arrest the respondent and search the motor home, and on this record, it is inexplicable why they eschewed the safe harbor of a warrant.
[c]
In the absence of any evidence of exigency in the circumstances of this case, the Court relies on the inherent mobility of the motor home to create a conclusive presumption of exigency.
[d] This Court, however, has squarely held that mobility of the place to be searched is not a sufficient justification for abandoning the warrant requirement. In *United States v. Chadwick*, 433 U.S. 1 (1977), the Court held that a warrantless search of a footlocker violated the Fourth Amendment even though there was ample probable cause to believe it contained contraband. The Government had argued that the rationale of the automobile exception applied to movable containers in

general, and that the warrant requirement should be limited to searches of homes and other "core" areas of privacy. * * * We categorically rejected the Government's argument, observing that there are greater privacy interests associated with containers than with automobiles, and that there are less practical problems associated with the temporary detention of a container than with the detention of an automobile. * * *

* * *

* * * It is perfectly obvious that the citizen has a much greater expectation of privacy concerning the interior of a mobile home than of a piece of luggage such as a footlocker. If "inherent mobility" does not justify warrantless searches of containers, it cannot rationally provide a sufficient justification for the search of a person's dwelling place.

Unlike a brick bungalow or a frame Victorian, a motor home seldom serves as a permanent lifetime abode. The motor home in this case, however, was designed to accommodate a breadth of ordinary everyday living. Photographs in the record indicate that its height, length, and beam provided substantial living space inside: stuffed chairs surround a table; cupboards provide room for storage of personal effects; bunk beds provide sleeping space; and a refrigerator provides ample space for food and beverages. Moreover, curtains and large opaque walls inhibit viewing the activities inside from the exterior of the vehicle. The interior configuration of the motor home establishes that the vehicle's size, shape, and mode of construction should have indicated to the officers that it was a vehicle containing mobile living quarters.

[The dissent suggests that distinguishing between a mobile home and an automobile will not be as difficult to police as the majority makes out. It also points out that the California vehicle code makes some differentiation between ordinary automobiles and motor vehicles designed with living quarters.   For example, drinking alcoholic beverages is allowed in the living quarters of the latter under conditions not allowed in automobiles.]

* * *

*   *   *   *   *   *   *   *   *   *

COMMENTS

[a] The "automobile" exception applies to any mobile vehicle that can move from a place when observed by police who have probable cause to believe that the vehicle contains contraband. Likewise, an automobile on blocks, which is clearly not mobile, cannot be searched under the automobile exception, *Coolidge v. New Hampshire*, 403 U.S. 443 (1971).

[b] The Court would wish to avoid cases where, for example, a person who slept in the back seat of his or her automobile and had no residence, would claim that the car was a house for Fourth Amendment purposes.

[c] The convenience argument is similar to that raised in *United States v. Watson* [this volume], where it was argued that the inspectors had sufficient time to obtain an arrest warrant.

[d] This raises a fundamental point about the nature of the search warrant exceptions: whether they are specific categories or essentially variations on the concept of the "exigency."

UNITED STATES v. CHADWICK

433 U.S. 1, 97 S.Ct. 2476, 53 L.Ed.2d 538 (1977)

MR. CHIEF JUSTICE BURGER delivered the opinion of the Court.

We granted certiorari in this case to decide whether a search warrant is required before federal agents may open a locked footlocker which they have lawfully seized at the time of the arrest of its owners, when there is probable cause to believe the footlocker contains contraband.

(1)

[Amtrak officials in San Diego became suspicious when two men loaded an unusually heavy footlocker leaking talcum powder onto a train. This fit the drug trafficker profile, federal agents were alerted. Federal drug agents, with no arrest or search warrant, were waiting when the train arrived in Boston two days later. A trained dog signaled the presence of a controlled substance inside the footlocker. The agents watched the men take the 200-pound footlocker outside and load it into the trunk of Chadwick's automobile. While the trunk of the car was still open and before the car engine had been started the agents arrested Chadwick and the others. No weapons were found; the key to the footlocker was confiscated. The arrestees and the footlocker were taken to the federal building. The footlocker, which was not suspected of posing any danger, was under the complete control of the federal agents. It could have been stored securely. The footlocker was opened without Chadwick's consent ninety minutes after it was seized and large amounts of marihuana were found.]

[The District Court suppressed the evidence finding that it did not fall into the automobile or the search incident to arrest exceptions to the warrant requirement. The Court of Appeals affirmed the suppression of the seized marihuana. It held that the officers had probable cause and properly seized the trunk but that no exception applied to opening the trunk. The Court of Appeals also rejected the Government's argument that movable personal property which is lawfully seized in a public place should be subject to search without a warrant if probable cause exists to believe it contains evidence of a crime on the grounds that this was not a doctrine established by the Supreme Court.] We granted certiorari. * * * We affirm.

(2)

In this Court the Government again contends that the Fourth Amendment Warrant Clause protects only interests traditionally identified with the home. Recalling the colonial writs of assistance, which were often executed in searches of private dwellings, the Government claims that the Warrant Clause was adopted primarily, if not exclusively, in response to unjustified intrusions into private homes on the authority of general warrants. The Government argues there is no evidence that the Framers of the Fourth Amendment intended to disturb the established practice of permitting warrantless searches outside the home, or to modify the initial clause of the Fourth Amendment by making warrantless searches supported by probable cause *per se* unreasonable.

Drawing on its reading of history, the Government argues that only homes, offices, and private communications implicate interests which lie at the core of the Fourth Amendment. Accordingly, it is only in these contexts that the determination whether a search or seizure is reasonable should turn on whether a warrant has been obtained. In all other situations, the Government contends, less significant privacy values are at stake, and the reasonableness of a government intrusion should depend solely on whether there is probable cause to believe evidence of criminal conduct is present. Where personal effects are lawfully seized outside the home on probable cause, the Government would thus regard searches without a warrant as not "unreasonable." [a]

We do not agree that the Warrant Clause protects only dwellings and other specifically designated locales. As we have noted before, the Fourth Amendment "protects people, not places," *Katz v. United States*, [this volume]; more particularly, it protects people from unreasonable government intrusions into their legitimate expectations of privacy. In this case, the Warrant Clause makes a significant contribution to that protection. The question, then, is whether a warrantless search in these circumstances was unreasonable.

(3)

It cannot be doubted that the Fourth Amendment's commands grew in large measure out of the colonists' experience with the writs of assistance and their memories of the general warrants formerly in use in England. These writs, which were issued on executive rather than judicial authority, granted sweeping power to customs officials and other agents of the King to search at large for smuggled goods. Though the authority to search granted by the writs was not limited to the home, searches conducted pursuant to them often were carried out in private residences. * * *

Although the searches and seizures which deeply concerned the colonists, and which were foremost in the minds of the Framers, were those involving invasions of the home, it would be a mistake to conclude, as the Government contends, that the Warrant Clause was therefore intended to guard only against intrusions into the home. First, the Warrant Clause does not in terms distinguish between searches conducted in private homes and other searches. There is also a strong historical connection between the Warrant Clause and the initial clause of the Fourth Amendment, which draws no distinctions among "persons, houses, papers, and effects" in safeguarding against unreasonable searches and seizures. * * *

Moreover, if there is little evidence that the Framers intended the Warrant Clause to operate outside the home, there is no evidence at all that they intended to exclude from protection of the Clause all searches occurring outside the home. The absence of a contemporary outcry against warrantless searches in public places was because, aside from searches incident to arrest, such warrantless searches were not a large issue in colonial America. Thus, silence in the historical record tells us little about the Framers' attitude toward application of the Warrant Clause to the search of respondents' footlocker. What we do know is that the Framers were men who focused on the wrongs of that day but who intended the Fourth Amendment to safeguard fundamental values which would far outlast the specific abuses which gave it birth.

Moreover, in this area we do not write on a clean slate. [b] Our fundamental inquiry in considering Fourth Amendment issues is whether or not a search or seizure is reasonable under all the circumstances. * * * The judicial warrant has a significant role to play in that it provides the detached scrutiny of a neutral magistrate, which is a more reliable safeguard against improper searches than the hurried judgment of a law enforcement officer "engaged in the often competitive enterprise of ferreting out crime." * * * Once a lawful search has begun, it is also far more likely that it will not exceed proper bounds when it is done pursuant to a judicial authorization "particularly describing the place to be searched and the persons or things to be seized." Further, a warrant assures the individual whose property is searched or seized of the lawful authority of the executing officer, his need to search, and the limits of his power to search. * * *

Just as the Fourth Amendment "protects people, not places," the protections a judicial warrant offers against erroneous governmental intrusions are effective whether applied in or out of the home. Accordingly, we have held warrantless searches unreasonable, and therefore unconstitutional, in a variety of settings. A century ago,

MR. JUSTICE FIELD, speaking for the Court, included within the reach of the Warrant Clause printed matter traveling through the mails within the United States:

"Letters and sealed packages of this kind in the mail are as fully guarded from examination and inspection, except as to their outward form and weight, as if they were retained by the parties forwarding them in their own domiciles. The constitutional guaranty of the right of the people to be secure in their papers against unreasonable searches and seizures extends to their papers, thus closed against inspection, wherever they may be. Whilst in the mail, they can only be opened and examined under like warrant, issued upon similar oath or affirmation, particularly describing the thing to be seized, as is required when papers are subjected to search in one's own household." *Ex parte Jackson*, 96 U. S. 727, 733 (1878).

We reaffirmed *Jackson* in *United States v. Van Leeuwen*, 397 U.S. 249 (1970), where a search warrant was obtained to open two packages which, on mailing, the sender had declared contained only coins. Judicial warrants have been required for other searches conducted outside the home. [Various case examples include electronic interception of a conversation in a public telephone booth, searches of automobiles on private premises and in custody, and searches of hotel rooms and offices.] These cases illustrate the applicability of the Warrant Clause beyond the narrow limits suggested by the Government. They also reflect the settled constitutional principle, discussed earlier, that a fundamental purpose of the Fourth Amendment is to safeguard individuals from unreasonable government invasions of legitimate privacy interests, and not simply those interests found inside the four walls of the home. * * *

In this case, important Fourth Amendment privacy interests were at stake. By placing personal effects inside a doublelocked footlocker, respondents manifested an expectation that the contents would remain free from public examination. No less than one who locks the doors of his home against intruders, one who safeguards his personal possessions in this manner is due the protection of the Fourth Amendment Warrant Clause. There being no exigency, it was unreasonable for the Government to conduct this search without the safeguards a judicial warrant provides.

(4)

The Government does not contend that the footlocker's brief contact with Chadwick's car makes this an automobile search, [c] but it is argued that the rationale of our automobile search cases demonstrates the reasonableness of permitting warrantless searches of luggage; the Government views such luggage as analogous to motor vehicles for Fourth Amendment purposes. It is true that, like the footlocker in issue here, automobiles are "effects" under the Fourth Amendment, and searches and seizures of automobiles are therefore subject to the constitutional standard of reasonableness. But this Court has recognized significant differences between motor vehicles and other property which permit warrantless

searches of automobiles in circumstances in which warrantless searches would not be reasonable in other contexts. * * *

Our treatment of automobiles has been based in part on their inherent mobility, which often makes obtaining a judicial warrant impracticable. Nevertheless, we have also sustained "warrantless searches of vehicles . . . in cases in which the possibilities of the vehicle's being removed or evidence in it destroyed were remote, if not nonexistent." * * *

The answer lies in the diminished expectation of privacy which surrounds the automobile: "One has a lesser expectation of privacy in a motor vehicle because its function is transportation and it seldom serves as one's residence or as the repository of personal effects. . . . It travels public thoroughfares where both its occupants and its contents are in plain view." * * * Other factors reduce automobile privacy. "All States require vehicles to be registered and operators to be licensed. States and localities have enacted extensive and detailed codes regulating the condition and manner in which motor vehicles may be operated on public streets and highways." * * * Automobiles periodically undergo official inspection, and they are often taken into police custody in the interests of public safety. * * *

The factors which diminish the privacy aspects of an automobile do not apply to respondents' footlocker. Luggage contents are not open to public view, except as a condition to a border entry or common carrier travel; nor is luggage subject to regular inspections and official scrutiny on a continuing basis. Unlike an automobile, whose primary function is transportation, luggage is intended as a repository of personal effects. In sum, a person's expectations of privacy in personal luggage are substantially greater than in an automobile.

Nor does the footlocker's mobility justify dispensing with the added protections of the Warrant Clause. Once the federal agents had seized it at the railroad station and had safely transferred it to the Boston Federal Building under their exclusive control, there was not the slightest danger that the footlocker or its contents could have been removed before a valid search warrant could be obtained. The initial seizure and detention of the footlocker, the validity of which respondents do not contest, were sufficient to guard against any risk that evidence might be lost. With the footlocker safely immobilized, it was unreasonable to undertake the additional and greater intrusion of a search without a warrant.

Finally, the Government urges that the Constitution permits the warrantless search of any property in the possession of a person arrested in public, so long as there is probable cause to believe that the property contains contraband or evidence of crime. Although recognizing that the footlocker was not within respondents' immediate control, the Government insists that the search was reasonable because the footlocker was seized contemporaneously with respondents' arrests and was searched as soon thereafter as was practicable. The reasons justifying search in a custodial arrest are quite different. When a custodial arrest is made, there is always some danger that the person arrested may seek to use a weapon, or that evidence may be concealed or destroyed. To safeguard himself and others, and to prevent the loss of evidence, it has been held reasonable for the arresting officer to conduct a prompt, warrantless "search of the arrestee's person and the area 'within his immediate control'—construing that phrase to mean the area from within which he might gain possession of a weapon or destructible evidence." * * *

Such searches may be conducted without a warrant, and they may also be made whether or not there is probable cause to believe that the person arrested may have a weapon or is about to destroy evidence. The potential dangers lurking in all custodial arrests make warrantless searches of items within the "immediate control" area reasonable without requiring the arresting officer to calculate the probability that weapons or destructible evidence may be involved. * * * However, warrantless searches of luggage or other property seized at the time of an arrest cannot be justified as incident to that arrest either if the "search is remote in time or place from the arrest," * * * or no exigency exists. Once law enforcement officers have reduced luggage or other personal property not immediately associated with the person of the arrestee to their exclusive control, and there is no longer any danger that the arrestee might gain access to the property to seize a weapon or destroy evidence, a search of that property is no longer an incident of the arrest.

Here the search was conducted more than an hour after federal agents had gained exclusive control of the footlocker and long after respondents were securely in custody; the search therefore cannot be viewed as incidental to the arrest or as justified by any other exigency. Even though on this record the issuance of a warrant by a judicial officer was reasonably predictable, a line must be drawn. In our view, when no exigency is shown to support the need for an immediate search, the Warrant Clause places the line at the point where the property to be searched comes under the exclusive dominion of police authority. Respondents were therefore entitled to the protection of the Warrant Clause with the evaluation of a neutral magistrate, before their privacy interests in the contents of the footlocker were invaded.

Accordingly, the judgment is

Affirmed.

[JUSTICE BRENNAN, concurring, found it "deeply distressing that the Department of Justice, whose mission is to protect the constitutional liberties of the people of the United States, should even appear to be seeking to subvert them by extreme and dubious legal arguments" in pressing the "probable cause" exception to the warrant requirement.]

[JUSTICE BLACKMUN, joined by JUSTICE REHNQUIST, dissented, arguing that once a person is arrested any attendant packages such a brief cases or footlockers, should be treated under the search incident to arrest rule and be subject to forcible opening by the police.]

* * * * * * * * * * *

COMMENTS

[a] In "special needs" cases such as *New Jersey v. T.L.O.*, [this volume], the reasonableness clause "overrides" the warrant requirement, so to speak. Since this is a case of standard criminal law enforcement, the special circumstances of the "special needs" cases would not apply. The effect of the Government's reasoning then, would be to make reasonableness the primary doctrinal core of the Fourth Amendment and reduce the warrant to a narrow range of cases.

[b] There is a theoretical question of whether constitutional law distorts the Constitution. Some argue that the Court is mistaken in building and relying on doctrines of law and should instead rely on a basic understanding of "the" Constitution. Yet, the CHIEF JUSTICE acknowledges that it is virtually impossible for courts of law to operate without relying on judge-made doctrines. Do you think it would be a good thing for the Court to decide cases on its understanding of the Constitution at the moment of decision without paying attention to past rulings?

[c] Compare the facts of this case to *California v. Acevedo* [this volume], where police, with probable cause to believe a package contained drugs, opened a car trunk and the container only after the car was being driven away. In that case the automobile exception clearly applied as the possibility of flight was real.

NEW YORK v. BELTON

453 U.S. 454, 101 S.Ct. 2860, 69 L.Ed.2d 768 (1981)

JUSTICE STEWART delivered the opinion of the Court.

When the occupant of an automobile is subjected to a lawful custodial arrest, does the constitutionally permissible scope of a search incident to his arrest include the passenger compartment of the automobile in which he was riding? That is the question at issue in the present case.

I

[A New York State Trooper stopped a car carrying four men on the New York Thruway for speeding.] [N]one of the men owned the vehicle or was related to its owner. Meanwhile, the policeman had smelled burnt marihuana and had seen on the floor of the car an envelope marked "Supergold" that he associated with marihuana. He therefore directed the men to get out of the car, and placed them under arrest for the unlawful possession of marihuana. He patted down each of the men and "split them up into four separate areas of the Thruway at this time so they would not be in physical touching area of each other." He then picked up the envelope marked "Supergold" and found that it contained marihuana. After giving the arrestees the warnings required by *Miranda v. Arizona*, [this volume], the state policeman searched each one of them. He then searched the passenger compartment of the car. On the back seat he found a black leather jacket belonging to Belton. He unzipped one of the pockets of the jacket and discovered cocaine. Placing the jacket in his automobile, he drove the four arrestees to a nearby police station.

[Belton was convicted of cocaine possession and appealed.] * * *

The New York Court of Appeals [held] that "[a] warrantless search of the zippered pockets of an unaccessible jacket may not be upheld as a search incident to a lawful arrest where there is no longer any danger that the arrestee or a confederate might gain access to the article." * * * Two judges dissented. They pointed out that the "search was conducted by a lone peace officer who was in the process of arresting four unknown individuals whom he had stopped in a speeding car owned by none of them and apparently containing an uncertain quantity of a controlled substance. The suspects were standing by the side of the car as the officer gave it a quick check to confirm his suspicions before attempting to transport them to police headquarters. * * *" [a] * * *

II

It is a first principle of Fourth Amendment jurisprudence that the police may not conduct a search unless they first convince a neutral magistrate that there is probable cause to do so. This Court has recognized, however, that "the exigencies of the situation" may sometimes make exemption from the warrant requirement "imperative." * * * Specifically, the Court held in *Chimel v. California*, [this volume], that a lawful custodial arrest creates a situation which justifies the contemporaneous search without a warrant of the person arrested and of the immediately surrounding area. Such searches have long been considered valid because of the need "to remove any weapons that [the arrestee] might seek to use in order to resist arrest or effect his escape" and the need to prevent the concealment or destruction of evidence. * * *

The Court's opinion in *Chimel* emphasized the principle that * * * "[t]he scope of [a] search must be 'strictly tied to and justified by' the circumstances which rendered its initiation permissible." * * * Thus while the Court in *Chimel* found "ample justification" for a search of "the area from within which [an arrestee] might gain possession of a weapon or destructible evidence," the Court found "no comparable justification * * * for routinely searching any room other than that in which an arrest occurs—or, for that matter, for searching through all the desk drawers or other closed or concealed areas in that room itself." * * *

Although the principle that limits a search incident to a lawful custodial arrest may be stated clearly enough, courts have discovered the principle difficult to apply in specific cases. Yet, as one commentator has pointed out, the protection of the Fourth and Fourteenth Amendments "can only be realized if the police are acting under a set of rules which, in most instances, makes it possible to reach a correct determination beforehand as to whether an invasion of privacy is justified in the interest of law enforcement." * * * This is because

"Fourth Amendment doctrine, given force and effect by the exclusionary rule, is primarily intended to regulate the police in their day-to-day activities and thus ought to be expressed in terms that are readily applicable by the police in the context of the law enforcement activities in which they are necessarily engaged. A highly sophisticated set of rules, qualified by all sorts of ifs, ands, and buts and requiring the drawing of subtle nuances and hairline distinctions, may be the sort of heady stuff upon which the facile minds of lawyers and judges eagerly feed, but they may be 'literally impossible of application by the officer in the field.'" * * *

In short, "[a] single familiar standard is essential to guide police officers, who have only limited time and expertise to reflect on and balance the social and individual interests involved in the specific circumstances they confront." * * * **[b]**

[*United States v. Robinson*, [this volume], was put forward as an example of a case that laid down "a straightforward rule, easily applied, and predictably enforced" that is within the Fourth Amendment.]

But no straightforward rule has emerged from the litigated cases respecting the question involved here—the question of the proper scope of a search of the interior of an automobile incident to a lawful custodial arrest of its occupants. * * *

When a person cannot know how a court will apply a settled principle to a recurring factual situation, that person cannot know the scope of his constitutional protection, nor can a policeman know the scope of his authority.   While the *Chimel* case established that a search incident to an arrest may not stray beyond the area within the immediate control of the arrestee, courts have found no workable definition of "the area within the immediate control of the arrestee" when that area arguably includes the interior of an automobile and the arrestee is its recent occupant.   Our reading of the cases suggests the generalization that articles inside the relatively narrow compass of the passenger compartment of an automobile are in fact generally, even if not inevitably, within "the area into which an arrestee might reach in order to grab a weapon or evidentiary [i]tem." * * * In order to establish the workable rule this category of cases requires, we read *Chimel*'s definition of the limits of the area that may be searched in light of that generalization.   Accordingly, we hold that when a policeman has made a lawful custodial arrest of the occupant of an automobile, he may, as a contemporaneous incident of that arrest, search the passenger compartment of that automobile.

It follows from this conclusion that the police may also examine the contents of any containers found within the passenger compartment, for if the passenger compartment is within reach of the arrestee, so also will containers in it be within his reach.   [c] * * * Such a container may, of course, be searched whether it is open or closed, since the justification for the search is not that the arrestee has no privacy interest in the container, but that the lawful custodial arrest justifies the infringement of any privacy interest the arrestee may have.   Thus, while the Court in *Chimel* held that the police

could not search all the drawers in an arrestee's house simply because the police had arrested him at home, the Court noted that drawers within an arrestee's reach could be searched because of the danger their contents might pose to the police. * * *

It is true, of course, that these containers will sometimes be such that they could hold neither a weapon nor evidence of the criminal conduct for which the suspect was arrested. However, in *United States v. Robinson*, the Court rejected the argument that such a container—there a "crumpled up cigarette package"—located during a search of Robinson incident to his arrest could not be searched. * * *

The New York Court of Appeals relied upon *United States v. Chadwick*, 433 U.S. 1 [1977], and *Arkansas v. Sanders*, 442 U.S. 753 [1979], in concluding that the search and seizure in the present case were constitutionally invalid.   But neither of those cases involved an arguably valid search incident to a lawful custodial arrest. As the Court pointed out in the *Chadwick* case: "Here the search was conducted more than an hour after federal agents had gained exclusive control of the footlocker and long after respondents were securely in custody; the search therefore cannot be viewed as incidental to the arrest. * * *   [d]

III

It is not questioned that the respondent was the subject of a lawful custodial arrest on a charge of possessing marihuana.   The search of the respondent's jacket followed immediately upon that arrest.   The jacket was located inside the passenger compartment of the car in which the respondent had been a passenger just before he was arrested. The jacket was thus within the area which we have concluded was "within the arrestee's immediate control" within the meaning of the *Chimel* case. The search of the jacket, therefore, was a search incident to a lawful custodial arrest, and it did not violate the Fourth and Fourteenth Amendments. Accordingly, the judgment is reversed.

It is so ordered.

[JUSTICE REHNQUIST and JUSTICE STEVENS concurred separately.]

JUSTICE BRENNAN, with whom JUSTICE MARSHALL joins, dissenting.

* * *

I

* * *

The *Chimel* exception to the warrant requirement was designed with two principal concerns in mind: the safety of the arresting officer and the preservation of easily concealed or destructible evidence. * * *

The *Chimel* standard. * * * places a temporal and a spatial limitation on searches incident to arrest, excusing compliance with the warrant requirement only when the search "'is substantially contemporaneous with the arrest and is confined to the *immediate* vicinity of the arrest.'" * * * When the arrest has been consummated and the arrestee safely taken into custody, the justifications underlying *Chimel's* limited exception to the warrant requirement cease to apply: at that point there is no possibility that the arrestee could reach weapons or

contraband. * * *

In its attempt to formulate a "'single, familiar standard * * * to guide police officers, who have only limited time and expertise to reflect on and balance the social and individual interests involved in the specific circumstances they confront,'" * * * the Court today disregards these principles, and instead adopts a fiction—that the interior of a car is *always* within the immediate control of an arrestee who has recently been in the car. [e]

* * *

II

As the facts of this case make clear, the Court today substantially expands the permissible scope of searches incident to arrest by permitting police officers to search areas and containers the arrestee could not possibly reach at the time of arrest. These facts demonstrate that at the time Belton and his three companions were placed under custodial arrest—which was after they had been removed from the car, patted down, and separated—none of them could have reached the jackets that had been left on the back seat of the car. * * * [f]

* * * Under the approach taken today, the result would presumably be the same even if [the officer] had handcuffed Belton and his companions in the patrol car before placing them under arrest, and even if his search had extended to locked luggage or other inaccessible containers located in the back seat of the car.

* * * [Prior] cases demonstrate that the crucial question under *Chimel* is not whether the arrestee could ever have reached the area that was searched, but whether he could have reached it at the time of arrest and search. If not, the officer's failure to obtain a warrant may not be excused. * * *

III

The Court seeks to justify its departure from the principles underlying *Chimel* by proclaiming the need for a new "bright-line" rule to guide the officer in the field. * * * "[T]he mere fact that law enforcement may be made more efficient can never by itself justify disregard of the Fourth Amendment." Moreover, the Court's attempt to forge a "bright-line" rule fails on its own terms. While the "interior/trunk" distinction may provide a workable guide in certain routine cases—for example, where the officer arrests the driver of a car and then immediately searches the seats and floor—in the long run, I suspect it will create far more problems than it solves. The Court's new approach leaves open too many questions and, more important, it provides the police and the courts with too few tools with which to find the answers.

Thus, although the Court concludes that a warrantless search of a car may take place even though the suspect was arrested outside the car, it does not indicate how long after the suspect's arrest that search may validly be conducted. Would a warrantless search incident to arrest be valid if conducted five minutes after the suspect left his car? Thirty minutes? Three hours? Does it matter whether the suspect is standing in close proximity to the car when the search is conducted? Does it matter whether the police formed probable cause to arrest before or after the suspect left his car? * * *

The Court does not give the police any "bright-line" answers to these questions. More important, because the Court's new rule abandons the justifications underlying *Chimel*, *it offers no guidance to the police officer seeking to work out these answers for himself.* * * *

* * *

[JUSTICE WHITE, joined by JUSTICE MARSHALL dissented on the ground that the search of containers within an automobile was controlled by cases such as *United States v. Chadwick*, [above], and *Arkansas v. Sanders*, [above], which held that containers could not be opened without probable cause. In his dissent, JUSTICE WHITE assumed that the majority opinion applied to locked containers.]

* * * * * * * * * *

COMMENTS

[a] The New York judges' dissent suggests a narrow, fact-based, rationale for upholding the search. Compare this to the majority and dissenting opinions.

[b] A "bright line" rule is of great value to the police. Why is the dissent opposed to the bright line rule that the majority develops here?

[c] In a footnote, JUSTICE STEWART clarified the definition of a container as "any object capable of holding another object" and specified that it included "closed or open glove compartments, consoles, or other receptacles located anywhere within the passenger compartment, as well as luggage, boxes, bags, clothing, and the like." He excluded the trunk. Note that his definition applied to "closed" containers but not "locked" containers. Can the officer pry open a locked glove box? Would this make sense under the *Chimel* rationale?

[d] Does this imply a time limit on the police authority to search?

[e] If it is a fiction that the arrestee has control of the interior of a car, is it a fiction that an arrestee in a house had control of a drawer that is an arms length away?

[f] Do you agree with this factual assertion? Does it make a difference if the trooper stopped a car with only a driver (*i.e.*, no passengers), or if there were several officers at the scene?

CALIFORNIA v. ACEVEDO

500 U.S. 565, 111 S.Ct. 1982, 114 L.Ed.2d 619 (1991)

JUSTICE BLACKMUN delivered the opinion of the Court.

This case requires us once again to consider the so-called "automobile exception" to the warrant requirement of the Fourth Amendment and its application to the search of a closed container in the trunk of a car.

I

[Marijuana seized by the DEA in Hawaii was shipped to Officer Coleman of the Santa Ana, Cal. Police Department. The officer set up a controlled pick up, through Federal Express, to one Jamie Daza, who picked up the package at 10:30 a.m. Daza, package in hand, was followed to his apartment. At 11:45 a.m., Daza left the apartment and dropped the wrapping of the marijuana container into a trash bin. Officer Coleman left the scene to get a search warrant. About 12:05 p.m., other officers saw Richard St. George leave the apartment carrying a half-full blue knapsack. The officers stopped him as he was driving off, searched the knapsack, and found 1 1/2 pounds of marijuana.]

At 12:30 p.m., respondent Charles Steven Acevedo arrived. He entered Daza's apartment, stayed for about 10 minutes, and reappeared carrying a brown paper bag that looked full. The officers noticed that the bag was the size of one of the wrapped marijuana packages sent from Hawaii. Acevedo walked to a silver Honda in the parking lot. He placed the bag in the trunk of the car and started to drive away. Fearing the loss of evidence, officers in a marked police car stopped him. They opened the trunk and the bag, and found marijuana.

* * *

The California Court of Appeal * * * suppressed [the marijuana]. * * * The court concluded that the officers had probable cause to believe that the paper bag contained drugs but lacked probable cause to suspect that Acevedo's car, itself, otherwise contained contraband. Because the officers' probable cause was directed specifically at the bag, the court held that the case was controlled by *United States v. Chadwick*, 433 U.S. 1 (1977), rather than by *United States v. Ross*, 456 U.S. 798 (1982). Although the court agreed that the officers could seize the paper bag, it held that, under *Chadwick*, they could not open the bag without first obtaining a warrant for that purpose. The court then recognized "the anomalous nature" of the dichotomy between the rule in *Chadwick* and the rule in *Ross*. * * * That dichotomy dictates that if there is probable cause to search a car, then the entire car—including any closed container found therein—may be searched without a warrant, but if there is probable cause only as to a container in the car, the container may be held but not searched until a warrant is obtained.

* * *

We granted certiorari, * * * to reexamine the law applicable to a closed container in an automobile, a subject that has troubled courts and law enforcement officers since it was first considered in *Chadwick*.

II

* * * In *Carroll* [*v. United States*, 267 U.S. 132 (1925)], this Court established an exception to the warrant requirement for moving vehicles, for it recognized

> "a necessary difference between a search of a store, dwelling house or other structure in respect of which a proper official warrant readily may be obtained, and a search of a ship, motor boat, wagon or automobile, for contraband goods, where it is not practicable to secure a warrant because the vehicle can be quickly moved out of the locality or jurisdiction in which the warrant must be sought."

* * *

It therefore held that a warrantless search of an automobile based upon probable cause to believe that the vehicle contained evidence of crime in the light of an exigency arising out of the likely disappearance of the vehicle did not contravene the Warrant Clause of the Fourth Amendment. * * * The Court refined the exigency requirement in *Chambers v. Maroney*, 399 U.S. 42 (1970), when it held that the existence of exigent circumstances was to be determined at the time the automobile is seized. The car search at issue in *Chambers* took place at the police station, where the vehicle was immobilized, some time after the driver had been arrested. Given probable cause and exigent circumstances at the time the vehicle was first stopped, the Court held that the later warrantless search at the station passed constitutional muster. The validity of the later search derived from the ruling in *Carroll* that an immediate search without a warrant at the moment of seizure would have been permissible. * * * The Court reasoned in *Chambers* that the police could search later whenever they could have searched earlier, had they so chosen. Following *Chambers*, if the police have probable cause to justify a warrantless seizure of an automobile on a public roadway, they may conduct either an immediate or a delayed search of the vehicle. [a]

In *United States v. Ross*, 456 U.S. 798, decided in 1982, we held that a warrantless search of an automobile under the *Carroll* doctrine could include a search of a container or package found inside the car when such a search was supported by probable cause. The warrantless search of Ross' car occurred after an informant told the police that he had seen Ross complete a drug transaction using drugs stored in the trunk of his car. [b] The police stopped the car, searched it, and discovered in the trunk a brown paper bag containing drugs. We decided that the search of Ross' car was not unreasonable under the Fourth Amendment: "The scope of a warrantless search based on probable cause is no narrower—and no broader—than the scope of a search authorized by a warrant supported by probable cause." * * * Thus, "[i]f probable cause justifies the search of a lawfully stopped vehicle, it justifies the search of every part of the vehicle and its contents that may conceal the object of the search." * * * In *Ross*, therefore, we clarified the scope of the *Carroll* doctrine as properly including a "probing search" of compartments and containers within the automobile so long as the search is supported by probable cause. * * *

In addition to this clarification, *Ross* distinguished the *Carroll* doctrine from the separate rule that governed the search of closed containers. * * * The Court had announced this separate rule, unique to luggage and other closed packages, bags, and containers, in *United States v. Chadwick*, 433 U.S. 1 (1977). In *Chadwick*, federal narcotics agents had probable cause to believe that a 200-pound double-locked footlocker contained marijuana. The agents tracked the locker as the defendants removed it from a train and carried it through the station to a waiting car. As soon as the defendants lifted the locker into the trunk of the car, the agents arrested them, seized the locker, and searched it. In this Court, the United States did not contend that the locker's brief contact with the automobile's trunk sufficed to make the *Carroll* doctrine applicable. Rather, the United States urged that the search of movable luggage could be considered analogous to the search of an automobile. * * *

The Court rejected this argument because, it reasoned, a person expects more privacy in his luggage and personal effects than he does in his automobile. * * * Moreover, it concluded that as "may often not be the case when automobiles are seized," secure storage facilities are usually available when the police seize luggage. * * *

In *Arkansas v. Sanders*, 442 U.S. 753 (1979), the Court extended *Chadwick*'s rule to apply to a suitcase actually being transported in the trunk of a car. In *Sanders*, the police had probable cause to believe a suitcase contained marijuana. They watched as the defendant placed the suitcase in the trunk of a taxi and was driven away. The police pursued the taxi for several blocks, stopped it, found the suitcase in the trunk, and searched it. Although the Court had applied the *Carroll* doctrine to searches of integral parts of the automobile itself, (indeed, in *Carroll*, contraband whiskey was in the upholstery of the seats * * *) [c] it did not extend the doctrine to the warrantless search of personal luggage "merely because it was located in an automobile lawfully stopped by the police." * * * Again, the *Sanders* majority stressed the heightened privacy expectation in personal luggage and concluded that the presence of luggage in an automobile did not diminish the owner's expectation of privacy in his personal items. * * *

In *Ross*, the Court endeavored to distinguish between *Carroll*, which governed the *Ross* automobile search, and *Chadwick*, which governed the *Sanders* automobile search. It held that the *Carroll* doctrine covered searches of automobiles when the police had probable cause to search an entire vehicle but that the *Chadwick* doctrine governed searches of luggage when the officers had probable cause to search only a container within the vehicle. Thus, in a *Ross* situation, the police could conduct a reasonable search under the Fourth Amendment without obtaining a warrant, whereas in a *Sanders* situation, the police had to obtain a warrant before they searched. [d]

The dissent is correct, of course, that *Ross* involved the scope of an automobile search. * * * *Ross* held that closed containers encountered by the police during a warrantless search of a car pursuant to the automobile exception could also be searched.

Thus, this Court in *Ross* took the critical step of saying that closed containers in cars could be searched without a warrant because of their presence within the automobile. Despite the protection that *Sanders* purported to extend to closed containers, the privacy interest in those closed containers yielded to the broad scope of an automobile search.

III

The facts in this case closely resemble the facts in *Ross*. In *Ross*, the police had probable cause to believe that drugs were stored in the trunk of a particular car.* * * Here, the California Court of Appeal concluded that the police had probable cause to believe that respondent was carrying marijuana in a bag in his car's trunk. * * * [b] Furthermore, for what it is worth, in *Ross*, as here, the drugs in the trunk were contained in a brown paper bag.

This Court in *Ross* rejected *Chadwick*'s distinction between containers and cars. It concluded that the expectation of privacy in one's vehicle is equal to one's expectation of privacy in the container, and noted that "the privacy interests in a car's trunk or glove compartment may be no less than those in a movable container."* * * It also recognized that it was arguable that the same exigent circumstances that permit a warrantless search of an automobile would justify the warrantless search of a movable container. * * * In deference to the rule of *Chadwick* and *Sanders*, however, the Court put that question to one side. * * * It concluded that the time and expense of the warrant process would be misdirected if the police could search every cubic inch of an automobile until they discovered a paper sack, at which point the Fourth Amendment required them to take the sack to a magistrate for permission to look inside. We now must decide the question deferred in *Ross*: whether the Fourth Amendment requires the police to obtain a warrant to open the sack in a movable vehicle simply because they lack probable cause to search the entire car. We conclude that it does not.

IV

Dissenters in *Ross* asked why the suitcase in *Sanders* was "more private, less difficult for police to seize and store, or in any other relevant respect more properly subject to the warrant requirement, than a container that police discover in a probable-cause search of an entire automobile?" * * * We now agree that a container found after a general search of the automobile and a container found in a car after a limited search for the container are equally easy for the police to store and for the suspect to hide or destroy. In fact, we see no principled distinction in terms of either the privacy expectation or the exigent circumstances between the paper bag found by the police in *Ross* and the paper bag found by the police here. Furthermore, by attempting to distinguish between a container for which the police are specifically searching and a container which they come across in a car, we have provided only minimal protection for privacy and have impeded effective law enforcement.

The line between probable cause to search a vehicle and probable cause to search a package in that vehicle is not always clear, and separate rules that govern the two objects to be searched may enable the police to broaden their power to make warrantless searches and disserve privacy interests. We noted this in *Ross* in the context of a search of an entire vehicle. Recognizing that under *Carroll*, the "entire vehicle itself * * * could be searched without a warrant," we concluded that "prohibiting police from opening immediately a container in which the object of the search is most likely to be found and instead forcing them first to comb the entire vehicle would actually exacerbate the intrusion on privacy interests." * * * At the moment when officers stop an automobile, it may be less than clear whether they suspect with a high degree of certainty that the vehicle contains drugs in a bag or simply contains drugs. If the police know that they may open a bag only if they are actually searching the entire car, they may search more extensively than they otherwise would in order to establish the general probable cause required by *Ross*.[e]

＊　＊　＊

To the extent that the *Chadwick-Sanders* rule protects privacy, its protection is minimal.[f] Law enforcement officers may seize a container and hold it until they obtain a search warrant. * * * "Since the police, by hypothesis, have probable cause to seize the property, we can assume that a warrant will be routinely forthcoming in the overwhelming majority of cases." * * * And the police often will be able to search containers without a warrant, despite the *Chadwick-Sanders* rule, as a search incident to a lawful arrest. In *New York v. Belton*, [this volume], the Court said:

"[W]e hold that when a policeman has made a lawful custodial arrest of the occupant of an automobile, he may, as a contemporaneous incident of that arrest, search the passenger compartment of that automobile.

"It follows from this conclusion that the police may also examine the contents of any containers found within the passenger compartment." * * *

Under *Belton*, the same probable cause to believe that a container holds drugs will allow the police to arrest the person transporting the container and search it.

Finally, the search of a paper bag intrudes far less on individual privacy than does the incursion sanctioned long ago in *Carroll*. In that case, prohibition agents slashed the upholstery of the automobile. This Court nonetheless found their search to be reasonable under the Fourth Amendment. If destroying the interior of an automobile is not unreasonable, we cannot conclude that looking inside a closed container is. In light of the minimal protection to privacy afforded by the *Chadwick-Sanders* rule, and our serious doubt whether that rule substantially serves privacy interests, we now hold that the Fourth Amendment does not compel separate treatment for an automobile search that extends only to a container within the vehicle.

V

The *Chadwick-Sanders* rule not only has failed to protect privacy but it has also confused courts and police officers and impeded effective law enforcement.
＊　＊　＊

The discrepancy between the two rules has led to confusion for law enforcement officers. For example, when an officer, who has developed probable cause to believe that a vehicle contains drugs, begins to search the vehicle and immediately discovers a closed container, which rule applies? The defendant will argue that the fact that the officer first chose to search the container indicates that his probable cause extended only to the container and that *Chadwick* and *Sanders* therefore require a warrant. On the other hand, the fact that the officer first chose to search in the most obvious location should not restrict the propriety of the search. The *Chadwick* rule, as applied in *Sanders*, has devolved into an anomaly such that the more likely the police are to discover drugs in a container, the less authority they have to search it. We have noted the virtue of providing ""clear and unequivocal" guidelines to the law enforcement profession.'" * * * The *Chadwick-Sanders* rule is the antithesis of a "'clear and unequivocal' guideline." * * *

[The Court reviewed several cases that exemplified the confusion between the two rules.]

Although we have recognized firmly that the doctrine of *stare decisis* serves profoundly important purposes in our legal system, this Court has overruled a prior case on the comparatively rare occasion when it has bred confusion or been a derelict or led to anomalous results. * * * *Sanders* was explicitly undermined in *Ross*, * * * and the existence of the dual regimes for automobile searches that uncover containers has proved as confusing as the *Chadwick* and *Sanders* dissenters predicted. We conclude that it is better to adopt one clear-cut rule to govern automobile searches and eliminate the warrant requirement for closed containers set forth in *Sanders*.

VI

The interpretation of the *Carroll* doctrine set forth in *Ross* now applies to all searches of containers found in an automobile. In other words, the police may search without a warrant if their search is supported by probable cause. The Court in *Ross* put it this way:

"The scope of a warrantless search of an automobile * * * is not defined by the nature of the container in which the contraband is secreted. Rather, it is defined by the object of the search and the places in which there is probable cause to believe that it may be found." * * *

It went on to note: "Probable cause to believe that a container placed in the trunk of a taxi contains contraband or evidence does not justify a search of the entire cab." * * * We reaffirm that principle. In the case before us, the police had probable cause to believe that the paper bag in the automobile's trunk contained marijuana. That probable cause now allows a warrantless search of the paper bag. The facts in the record reveal that the police did not have probable cause to believe that contraband was hidden in any other part of the automobile and a search of the entire vehicle would have been without probable cause and unreasonable under the Fourth Amendment.

Our holding today neither extends

the *Carroll* doctrine nor broadens the scope of the permissible automobile search delineated in *Carroll*, *Chambers*, and *Ross*. It remains a "cardinal principle that 'searches conducted outside the judicial process, without prior approval by judge or magistrate, are *per se* unreasonable under the Fourth Amendment—subject only to a few specifically established and well-delineated exceptions.'" * * * **[g]** We held in *Ross*: "The exception recognized in *Carroll* is unquestionably one that is 'specifically established and well delineated.'" * * *

Until today, this Court has drawn a curious line between the search of an automobile that coincidentally turns up a container and the search of a container that coincidentally turns up in an automobile. The protections of the Fourth Amendment must not turn on such coincidences. We therefore interpret *Carroll* as providing one rule to govern all automobile searches. The police may search an automobile and the containers within it where they have probable cause to believe contraband or evidence is contained.

The judgment of the California Court of Appeal is reversed and the case is remanded to that court for further proceedings not inconsistent with this opinion.

It is so ordered.

[JUSTICE SCALIA concurred on the basis of an "originalist" interpretation of the Fourth Amendment. He would eliminate a general "warrant requirement" except where a warrant was required at common law, and decide all Fourth Amendment search and seizure cases by asking whether or not the search was "reasonable."].

[JUSTICE WHITE dissented, stating that he agreed with most of JUSTICE STEVENS' opinion.]

JUSTICE STEVENS, with whom JUSTICE MARSHALL joins, dissenting.

At the end of its opinion, the Court pays lip service to the proposition that should provide the basis for a correct analysis of the legal question presented by this case: It is "'a cardinal principle that "searches conducted outside the judicial process, without prior approval by judge or magistrate, are *per se* unreasonable under the Fourth Amendment—subject only to a few specifically established and well-delineated exceptions.'" * * *

Relying on arguments that conservative judges **[h]** have repeatedly rejected in past cases, the Court today—despite its disclaimer to the contrary, * * *—enlarges the scope of the automobile exception to this "cardinal principle," which undergirded our Fourth Amendment jurisprudence prior to the retirement of the author of the landmark opinion in *United States v. Chadwick.* * * * **[i]** As a preface to my response to the Court's arguments, it is appropriate to restate the basis for the warrant requirement, the significance of the *Chadwick* case, and the reasons why the limitations on the automobile exception that were articulated in *United States v. Ross,* * * * represent a fair accommodation between the basic rule requiring prior judicial approval of searches and the automobile exception.

I

The Fourth Amendment is a

restraint on Executive power. The Amendment constitutes the Framers' direct constitutional response to the unreasonable law enforcement practices employed by agents of the British Crown. * * * Over the years * * * the Court has recognized the importance of this restraint as a bulwark against police practices that prevail in totalitarian regimes. * * *

This history is, however, only part of the explanation for the warrant requirement. The requirement also reflects the sound policy judgment that, absent exceptional circumstances, the decision to invade the privacy of an individual's personal effects should be made by a neutral magistrate rather than an agent of the Executive. * * *

Our decisions have always acknowledged that the warrant requirement imposes a burden on law enforcement. And our cases have not questioned that trained professionals normally make reliable assessments of the existence of probable cause to conduct a search. We have repeatedly held, however, that these factors are outweighed by the individual interest in privacy that is protected by advance judicial approval. The Fourth Amendment dictates that the privacy interest is paramount, no matter how marginal the risk of error might be if the legality of warrantless searches were judged only after the fact. * * *

In *Chadwick*, the Department of Justice had mounted a frontal attack on the warrant requirement. The Government's principal contention was that "the Fourth Amendment Warrant Clause protects only interests traditionally identified with the home." * * * We categorically rejected that contention, relying on the history and text of the amendment, the policy underlying the warrant requirement, and a line of cases spanning over a century of our jurisprudence. We also rejected the Government's alternative argument that the rationale of our automobile search cases demonstrated the reasonableness of permitting warrantless searches of luggage.

* * *

[JUSTICE STEPHENS reviewed *Arkansas v. Sanders* and *United States v. Ross* in detail.]

In reaching our conclusion in *Ross*, we therefore did not retreat at all from the holding in either *Chadwick* or *Sanders*. * * * We explained repeatedly that *Ross* involved the *scope* of the warrantless search authorized by the automobile exception, * * * and, unlike *Chadwick* and *Sanders*, did not involve the *applicability* of the exception to closed containers. * * *

Thus, we recognized in *Ross* that *Chadwick* and *Sanders* had not created a special rule for container searches, but rather had merely applied the cardinal principle that warrantless searches are per se unreasonable unless justified by an exception to the general rule. * * * *Ross* dealt with the scope of the automobile exception; *Chadwick* and *Sanders* were cases in which the exception simply did not apply.

II

In its opinion today, the Court recognizes that the police did not have probable cause to search respondent's vehicle and that a search of anything but the paper bag that respondent had carried from Daza's apartment and placed in the trunk of his car would have been unconstitutional. * * * Moreover, as I read the opinion, the

Court assumes that the police could not have made a warrantless inspection of the bag before it was placed in the car. * * * Finally, the Court also does not question the fact that, under our prior cases, it would have been lawful for the police to seize the container and detain it (and respondent) until they obtained a search warrant. Thus, all of the relevant facts that governed our decisions in *Chadwick* and *Sanders* are present here whereas the relevant fact that justified the vehicle search in *Ross* is not present.

The Court does not attempt to identify any exigent circumstances that would justify its refusal to apply the general rule against warrantless searches. Instead, it advances these three arguments: First, the rules identified in the foregoing cases are confusing and anomalous. * * * Second, the rules do not protect any significant interest in privacy. * * * And, third, the rules impede effective law enforcement. * * * None of these arguments withstands scrutiny.

The "Confusion"

In the nine years since *Ross* was decided, the Court has considered three cases in which the police had probable cause to search a particular container and one in which they had probable cause to search two vehicles. The decisions in all four of those cases were perfectly straightforward and provide no evidence of confusion in the state or lower federal courts.

* * *

To the extent there was any "anomaly" in our prior jurisprudence, the Court has "cured" it at the expense of creating a more serious paradox. For, surely it is anomalous to prohibit a search of a briefcase while the owner is carrying it exposed on a public street yet to permit a search once the owner has placed the briefcase in the locked trunk of his car. One's privacy interest in one's luggage can certainly not be diminished by one's removing it from a public thoroughfare and placing it—out of sight—in a privately owned vehicle. Nor is the danger that evidence will escape increased if the luggage is in a car rather than on the street. In either location, if the police have probable cause, they are authorized to seize the luggage and to detain it until they obtain judicial approval for a search. [j] Any line demarking an exception to the warrant requirement will appear blurred at the edges, but the Court has certainly erred if it believes that, by erasing one line and drawing another, it has drawn a clearer boundary.

The Privacy Argument

The Court's statement that *Chadwick* and *Sanders* provide only "minimal protection to privacy," * * * is also unpersuasive. Every citizen clearly has an interest in the privacy of the contents of his or her luggage, briefcase, handbag or any other container that conceals private papers and effects from public scrutiny. That privacy interest has been recognized repeatedly in cases spanning more than a century. * * *

Under the Court's holding today, the privacy interest that protects the contents of a suitcase or a briefcase from a warrantless search when it is in public view simply vanishes when its owner climbs into a taxicab. Unquestionably the rejection of the *Sanders* line of cases by today's decision will result in a significant loss of individual privacy.

* * *

The Court also justifies its claim that its holding inflicts only minor damage by suggesting that, under *New York v. Belton*, * * * the police could have arrested respondent and searched his bag if respondent had placed the bag in the passenger compartment of the automobile instead of the trunk. In *Belton*, however, the justification for stopping the car and arresting the driver had nothing to do with the subsequent search, which was based on the potential danger to the arresting officer. The holding in *Belton* was supportable under a straightforward application of the automobile exception. * * * I would not extend *Belton*'s holding to this case, in which the container—which was protected from a warrantless search before it was placed in the car—provided the only justification for the arrest. Even accepting

Belton's application to a case like this one, however, the Court's logic extends its holding to a container placed in the trunk of a vehicle, rather than in the passenger compartment. And the Court makes this extension without any justification whatsoever other than convenience to law enforcement.

The Burden on Law Enforcement

The Court's suggestion that *Chadwick* and *Sanders* have created a significant burden on effective law enforcement is unsupported, inaccurate, and, in any event, an insufficient reason for creating a new exception to the warrant requirement.

* * *

It is too early to know how much freedom America has lost today. The magnitude of the loss is, however, not nearly as significant as the Court's willingness to inflict it without even a colorable basis for its rejection of prior law.

I respectfully dissent.

* * * * * * * * * * *

COMMENTS

[a] A strict reading of the Fourth Amendment would seem to require a warrant in *Chambers v. Maroney*, since the exigency ended. The *Chambers'* rule rested on a concern that if the police have to get a warrant every time they stopped a vehicle with probable cause, innocent passengers would be detained and inconvenienced for very long periods of time. Another way of reading the *Chambers v. Maroney* situation would be to allow a vehicle search on the roadside, but not at the station. If such a rule were in place, it is possible that the decision of *Acevedo*, but not of *Ross*, would have been decided differently.

[b] Note that the *locus* of probable cause differs in *Acevedo* and *Ross*.

[c] The police in *Carroll* actually tore up the leather back seat.

[d] Before *Ross* the Court expressed a feeling of confusion in *Sanders* and in

Robbins v. California, 453 U.S. 420 (1981). *Ross* was a major case that reconciled the *Chadwick* (search of an "effect") and the *Carroll* (automobile exigency exception) lines of cases.

[e] The Court is right to speculate about the ways in which a ruling might reasonably be used on the street to produce a result not intended.

[f] Keep in mind that the *Chadwick* rule is in full force as to "effects" such as trunks and bags. This statement is correct insofar as it applied to searches of containers during the search of an automobile.

[g] It is significant that the Court repeats the classic "warrant-clause-and-exceptions" formula of expounding the Fourth Amendment, favored by liberal justices, rather than the "reasonableness" approach favored by more conservative justices. The "reasonableness" doctrine has been the basis for modifications of the warrant requirement in administrative searches (*Camara v. Municipal Court* [this volume]) and in the "special needs" area (*New Jersey v. T.L.O.* [this volume]).

[h] It is unusual for justices to characterize one another as "conservative" or "liberal" in print. Because a dissent is the statement of the justice who authors it, a dissent may be more freewheeling or idiosyncratic than a majority opinion, which reflects the judgment of each justice who joins the opinion.

[i] He is referring to JUSTICE POWELL.

[j] Throughout these cases the Supreme Court assumes that in the *Chadwick* "effects" situation there can be probable cause to seize the entire container but not to search its contents without a warrant. Reasoning that probable cause to seize includes probable cause to search eliminates one problem, but overlooks the point that with the seizure of the container, any exigency of flight or destruction is over. To treat an "effect" like an automobile could lead to an unravelling of the warrant requirement entirely, so even conservative justices are reluctant to follow this line of reasoning. On the other hand, to subject all containers in automobiles to the *Chadwick* rule weakens the usefulness of the automobile exception. Given this state of affairs, some anomalies will continue to exist.

COLORADO v. BERTINE

479 U.S. 367, 107 S.Ct. 738, 93 L.Ed.2d 739 (1987)

CHIEF JUSTICE REHNQUIST delivered the opinion of the Court.

* * * [A] police officer in Boulder, Colorado arrested * * * Bertine for driving while under the influence of alcohol. After Bertine was taken into custody and before the arrival of a tow truck to take Bertine's van to an impoundment lot, a backup officer inventoried the contents of the van. The officer opened a closed backpack in which he found controlled substances, cocaine paraphernalia, and a large amount of cash. * * * We are asked to decide whether the Fourth Amendment prohibits the State from proving [criminal] charges with the evidence discovered during the inventory of Bertine's van. We hold that it does not.

The backup officer inventoried the van in accordance with local police procedures, which require a detailed inspection and inventory of impounded vehicles. * * * After completing the inventory of the van, the officer had the van towed to an impound lot and brought the backpack, money, and contraband to the police station. * * *

[The Colorado Supreme Court recognized that the United States Supreme Court had held automobile inventory searches constitutional in *South Dakota v. Opperman*, 428 U.S. 364 (1976) and post-arrest inventory searches constitutional in *Illinois v. Lafayette*, 462 U.S. 604 (1983).] The Supreme Court of Colorado felt, however, that our decisions in *Arkansas v. Sanders*, 442 U.S. 753 (1979), and *United States v. Chadwick*, 433 U.S. 1

(1977), holding searches of closed trunks and suitcases to violate the Fourth Amendment, meant that *Opperman* and *Lafayette* did not govern this case. * * * [a]

* * * [I]nventory searches are now a well-defined exception to the warrant requirement of the Fourth Amendment. * * * [b] The policies behind the warrant requirement are not implicated in an inventory search, nor is the related concept of probable cause:

> "The standard of probable cause is peculiarly related to criminal investigations, not routine, noncriminal procedures. * * * The probable-cause approach is unhelpful when analysis centers upon the reasonableness of routine administrative caretaking functions, particularly when no claim is made that the protective procedures are a subterfuge for criminal investigations."* * * [c]

For these reasons, the Colorado Supreme Court's reliance on *Arkansas v. Sanders*, and *United States v. Chadwick*, was incorrect. Both of these cases concerned searches solely for the purpose of investigating criminal conduct, with the validity of the searches therefore dependent on the application of the probable-cause and warrant requirements of the Fourth Amendment.

By contrast, an inventory search may be "reasonable" under the Fourth Amendment even though it is not conducted pursuant to a warrant based upon probable cause. In *Opperman*, this Court * * * found that inventory procedures serve to protect an owner's property while it is in the custody of the police, to insure against claims of lost, stolen, or vandalized property, and to guard the police from danger. In light of these strong governmental interests and the diminished expectation of privacy in an automobile, we upheld the search. * * *

In our more recent decision, *Lafayette*, a police officer conducted an inventory search of the contents of a shoulder bag in the possession of an individual being taken into custody. In deciding whether this search was reasonable, we recognized that the search served legitimate governmental interests similar to those identified in *Opperman*. We determined that those interests outweighed the individual's Fourth Amendment interests and upheld the search.

In the present case, as in *Opperman* and *Lafayette*, there was no showing that the police, who were following standardized procedures, acted in bad faith or for the sole purpose of investigation. In addition, the governmental interests justifying the inventory searches in *Opperman* and *Lafayette* are nearly the same as those which obtain here. [d] In each case, the police were potentially responsible for the property taken into their custody. By securing the property, the police protected the property from unauthorized interference. Knowledge of the precise nature of the property helped guard against claims of theft, vandalism, or negligence. Such knowledge also helped to avert any danger to police or others that may have been posed by the property.

* * *

The Supreme Court of Colorado also expressed the view that the search in this case was unreasonable because Bertine's van was towed to a secure, lighted facility and because Bertine himself could have been offered the opportunity to make other arrangements for the safekeeping of his property. [e] But the security of the storage facility does not completely eliminate the need for inventorying; the police may still wish to protect themselves or the owners of the lot against false claims of theft or dangerous instrumentalities. And while giving Bertine an opportunity to make alternative arrangements would undoubtedly have been possible, we said in *Lafayette*:

> "[t]he real question is not what 'could have been achieved,' but whether the Fourth Amendment *requires* such steps. * * *
>
> The reasonableness of any particular governmental activity does not necessarily or invariably turn on the existence of alternative 'less intrusive' means." [f]

We conclude that here, as in *Lafayette*, reasonable police regulations relating to inventory procedures administered in good faith satisfy the Fourth Amendment, even though courts might as a matter of hindsight be able to devise equally reasonable rules requiring a different procedure.

* * *

Bertine finally argues that the inventory search of his van was unconstitutional because departmental regulations gave the police officers discretion to choose between impounding his van and parking and locking it in a public parking place. * * * [W]e reject [this argument.] Nothing in *Opperman* or *Lafayette* prohibits the exercise of police discretion so long as that discretion is exercised according to standard criteria and on the basis of something other than suspicion of evidence of criminal activity. Here, the discretion afforded the Boulder police was exercised in light of standardized criteria, related to the feasibility and appropriateness of parking and locking a vehicle rather than impounding it. There was no showing that the police chose to impound Bertine's van in order to investigate suspected criminal activity.

While both *Opperman* and *Lafayette* are distinguishable from the present case on their facts, we think that the principles enunciated in those cases govern the present one. The judgment of the Supreme Court of Colorado is therefore reversed.

*   *   *   *   *   *   *   *   *   *   *

COMMENT

[a] This is an example where the decision of the case seems straightforward under one rule (*i.e.*, the inventory search decisions) but is called into question by the logic and implications of another (*i.e.*, the trunk search cases). This conflict exemplifies the extent to which courts seek to establish logical and legal consistency between similar but overlapping areas of law.

[b] In fact, the inventory rules were of very recent vintage at the time of this case. The Court does not categorize the "inventory exception." It could be seen as a spin-off of the *Terry v. Ohio* [this volume] doctrine of reasonable suspicion, but the Court has not taken such a position.

[c] This is not entirely true; Fourth Amendment probable cause analysis has been applied to administrative searches, see *Camara v. Municipal Court* [this volume].

[d] Linking *Opperman* and *Lafayette* may not be apt in all instances, for in *Lafayette* the additional exception of search incident to arrest existed; also, the detention of a defendant without a thorough search presents a much greater opportunity for bad consequences. The majority opinion is weaker if it cannot rely on *Lafayette*.

[e] This point is designed, among other things, to avoid a string of litigation testing when the actual auto impoundment situation does or does not require inventorying; the Court attempts to establish a "bright line" rule.

[f] It can also be argued that less intrusive alternatives enhance Bill of Rights guarantees and individuals' privacy interests, and so is required by the Amendment.

FLORIDA v. WELLS

495 U.S. 1, 110 S. Ct. 1632, 109 L.Ed.2d 1 (1990)

CHIEF JUSTICE REHNQUIST delivered the opinion of the Court.

A Florida Highway Patrol trooper stopped respondent Wells for speeding. After smelling alcohol on Wells' breath, the trooper arrested Wells for driving under the influence. Wells then agreed to accompany the trooper to the station to take a breathalyzer test. The trooper informed Wells that the car would be impounded and obtained Wells' permission to open the trunk. At the impoundment facility, an inventory search of the car turned up two marijuana cigarette butts in an ashtray and a locked suitcase in the trunk. **[a]**   Under the trooper's direction, employees of the facility forced open the suitcase and discovered a garbage bag containing a considerable amount of marijuana.

Wells was charged with possession of a controlled substance. His motion to suppress the marijuana on the ground that it was seized in violation of the Fourth Amendment to the United States Constitution was denied by the trial court. * * * On appeal, the Florida [appellate court held] that the trial court erred in denying suppression of the marijuana found in the suitcase. Over a dissent, the Supreme Court of Florida affirmed. * * * We granted certiorari, * * * and now affirm (although we disagree with part of the reasoning of the Supreme Court of Florida).

The Supreme Court of Florida relied on the opinions in *Colorado v. Bertine* [this volume].   Referring to language in the *Bertine* concurrence

and a footnote in the majority opinion, the [Florida] court held that

> "[i]n the absence of a policy specifically requiring the opening of closed containers found during a legitimate inventory search, *Bertine* prohibits us from countenancing the procedure followed in this instance." * * *

According to the court, the record contained no evidence of any Highway Patrol policy on the opening of closed containers found during inventory searches. * * * **[b]** The court added, however:

> "[T]he police under *Bertine* must mandate either that all containers will be opened during an inventory search, or that no containers will be opened. There can be no room for discretion." * * *

While this latter statement of the Supreme Court of Florida derived support from a sentence in the *Bertine* concurrence taken in isolation, we think it is at odds with the thrust of both the concurrence and the opinion of the Court in that case. We said in *Bertine*:

> "[N]othing in [*South Dakota v.*] *Opperman*[, 428 U.S. 364 (1976),] or [*Illinois* v.] *Lafayette* [this volume] prohibits the exercise of police discretion so long as that discretion is exercised according to standard criteria and on the basis of something other than suspicion

of evidence of criminal activity." *
* * [c]

Our view that standardized criteria, *
* * or established routine, * * * must
regulate the opening of containers
found during inventory searches is
based on the principle that an inventory search must not be a ruse for a
general rummaging in order to discover
incriminating evidence. The policy or
practice governing inventory searches
should be designed to produce an
inventory. The individual police officer
must not be allowed so much latitude
that inventory searches are turned into
"a purposeful and general means of
discovering evidence of crime," *Bertine*,
* * * (BLACKMUN, J., concurring).

But in forbidding uncanalized
discretion to police officers conducting
inventory searches, there is no reason
to insist that they be conducted in a
totally mechanical "all or nothing"
fashion. "[I]nventory procedures serve
to protect an owner's property while it
is in the custody of the police, to
insure against claims of lost, stolen, or
vandalized property, and to guard the
police from danger." * * * A police
officer may be allowed sufficient
latitude to determine whether a
particular container should or should
not be opened in light of the nature of
the search and characteristics of the
container itself. Thus, while policies of
opening all containers or of opening
no containers are unquestionably
permissible, it would be equally permissible, for example, to allow the opening
of closed containers whose contents
officers determine they are unable to
ascertain from examining the containers' exteriors. The allowance of the
exercise of judgment based on concerns
related to the purposes of an inventory

search does not violate the Fourth
Amendment. **[d]**

In the present case, the Supreme
Court of Florida found that the
Florida Highway Patrol had no policy
whatever with respect to the opening
of closed containers encountered
during an inventory search. We hold
that absent such a policy, the instant
search was not sufficiently regulated to
satisfy the Fourth Amendment and that
the marijuana which was found in the
suitcase, therefore, was properly suppressed by the Supreme Court of
Florida. Its judgment is therefore
Affirmed.

JUSTICE BRENNAN, with whom
JUSTICE MARSHALL joins, concurring in the judgment.

I agree with the Court that the
judgment * * * should be affirmed
because the Florida Highway Patrol
had *no* policy at all with respect to
opening closed containers. As the
majority recognizes, * * * the search
was therefore unconstitutional under
any reading of our cases. * * * Our
cases have required that inventory
searches be "sufficiently regulated," * *
* so as to avoid the possibility that
police will abuse their power to conduct such a search. * * *

The facts of this case demonstrate
a prime danger of insufficiently regulated inventory searches: police may
use the excuse of an "inventory search"
as a pretext for broad searches of
vehicles and their contents. In this
case, there was no evidence that the
inventory search was done in accordance with any standardized inventory
procedure. * * * [JUSTICE BREN-
NAN recounted the legal history of the
case in detail, suggesting that the state

police lawyers tried to make it appear, incorrectly, that a policy existed.]

In addition, there was no evidence that an inventory was actually done in this case: the State introduced neither an inventory sheet nor any testimony that the officer actually inventoried the items found in respondent's car. * * * Rather, the testimony at the suppression hearing suggests that the officer used the need to "inventory" as an excuse to search for drugs. * * * [More facts were recited at this point indicating that the officer who searched the car was looking specifically for drugs. It took the police ten minutes to pry open the lock of the suitcase with two knives.]

The majority finds it unnecessary to recount these facts because it affirms the Florida Supreme Court on the narrow ground, clearly established by *Opperman* and *Bertine*, that police may not be given total discretion to decide whether to open closed containers found during an inventory search. With this much I agree. Like JUSTICE BLACKMUN, * * * however, I cannot join the majority opinion because it goes on to suggest that a State may adopt an inventory policy that vests individual police officers with *some* discretion to decide whether to open such containers. * * * This suggestion is pure dictum given the disposition of the case. But as JUSTICE BLACKMUN notes, * * * there is a danger that this dictum will be relied on by lower courts in reviewing the constitutionality of particular inventory searches, or even by local policymakers drafting procedures for police to follow when performing inventories of impounded vehicles. Thus, I write separately to emphasize that the majority's suggestion is incon-

sistent with the reasoning underlying our inventory search cases and relies on a mischaracterization of the holding in *Bertine*. [e]

Our cases clearly hold that an inventory search is reasonable under the Fourth Amendment only if it is done in accordance with standard procedures that *limit* the discretion of the police. * * * In *Bertine*, the Court held that the police may open closed containers found within an impounded vehicle only if the inventory policy mandates the opening of all such containers. * * * Contrary to the majority's assertion today, * * * *Bertine* did not establish that police may exercise discretion with respect to the opening of closed containers during an inventory search. The statement in *Bertine* that "[n]othing in *Opperman* * * * prohibits the exercise of police discretion so long as that discretion is exercised according to standard criteria," * * * was made in response to an argument that the inventory search was unconstitutional because the police had some discretion to determine whether to *impound* the car. The Court's conclusion that the opening of defendant's backpack was constitutional was clearly premised on the city's inventory policy that left no discretion to individual police officers as to the opening of containers found inside a car once it was impounded. * * * JUSTICE BLACKMUN's concurrence in *Bertine* could not be clearer: "[I]t is permissible for police officers to open closed containers in an inventory search *only* if they are following standard police procedures that mandate the opening of such containers in *every* impounded vehicle." * * * (emphasis added).

Opening a closed container constitutes a great intrusion into the privacy of its owner even when the container is found in an automobile. * * * For this reason, I continue to believe that in the absence of consent or exigency, police may not open a closed container found during an inventory search of an automobile. * * * In any event, in *Bertine*, the Court recognized that opening a container constitutes such a great intrusion that the discretion of the police to do so must be circumscribed sharply to guard against abuse. If the Court wishes to revisit that holding, it must wait for another case. Attempting to cast doubt on the vitality of the holding in *Bertine* in this otherwise easy case is not justified.

[JUSTICE BLACKMUN concurred.]

JUSTICE STEVENS, concurring in the judgment.

[JUSTICE STEVENS stated that it was unnecessary for the Court to take this correctly decided case in order to correct a minor flaw, "as countless opinions do."]

It is a proper part of the judicial function to make law as a necessary by-product of the process of deciding actual cases and controversies. But to reach out so blatantly and unnecessarily to make new law in a case of this kind is unabashed judicial activism.

* * * * * * * * * * *

COMMENTS

[a] Compare this statement to that of JUSTICE BRENNAN. Was there an inventory search?

[b] Oddly, the Court does not state the key fact of the case until this point, and then only states it in an oblique manner. Is this just hasty writing or a deliberate framing of the case? Note that JUSTICE BRENNAN's concurrence mentions the lack of a policy at the outset of its opinion.

[c] How clear is this language? Notice that the majority and the concurring justices in this case could not agree on its specific meaning.

[d] Is this paragraph part of the holding of *Wells* or *obiter dictum*?

[e] In other words, the concurrence is designed as "damage control" against what it views as an unwarranted statement injected unnecessarily into the case. Yet, five justices thought the majority's statement about an officer's discretion to open a container was sound.

SCHNECKLOTH v. BUSTAMONTE

412 U.S. 218, 93 S.Ct. 2041, 36 L.Ed.2d 854 (1973)

MR. JUSTICE STEWART delivered the opinion of the Court.

* * *

I

* * * [At 2 a.m. a police officer stopped a car with a headlight and a license plate light burned out. The driver had no driver's license and of the six passengers only Joe Alcala had a license. He said the car belonged to his brother. At the officer's request all the passengers exited the car. Two other officers arrived.] Officer Rand asked Alcala if he could search the car. Alcala replied, "Sure, go ahead." Prior to the search no one was threatened with arrest and, according to Officer Rand's uncontradicted testimony, it "was all very congenial at this time." [Officer] Gonzales testified that Alcala actually helped in the search of the car, by opening the trunk and glove compartment. * * * [The police found stolen checks in the trunk that were used to convict the defendant.]

[The evidence was found to be admissible by the California Court of Appeals and the federal District Court on a writ of habeas corpus. The federal Court of Appeals held that consent was a waiver of Fourth and Fourteenth Amendment rights, which required the state to prove that the respondent knew he had a right to not consent to the search.]

II

* * * [A] search authorized by consent is wholly valid. * * * "[W]hen a prosecutor seeks to rely upon consent to justify the lawfulness of a search, he has the burden of proving that the consent was, in fact, freely and voluntarily given." * * *

The precise question in this case, then, is what must the prosecution prove to demonstrate that a consent was "voluntarily" given. And upon that question there is a square conflict of views. * * * [The federal court of appeals] concluded that it is an essential part of the State's initial burden to prove that a person knows he has a right to refuse consent. The California courts have followed the rule that voluntariness is a question of fact to be determined from the totality of all the circumstances, and that the state of a defendant's knowledge is only one factor to be taken into account in assessing the voluntariness of a consent. * * *

A

The most extensive judicial exposition of the meaning of "voluntariness" has been developed in [cases dealing with the validity of confessions under] the Fourteenth Amendment. * * *
* * *

The significant fact about all of these decisions is that none of them turned on the presence or absence of a single controlling criterion; each reflected a careful scrutiny of all the surrounding circumstances. * * * In none of them did the Court rule that the Due Process Clause required the prosecution to prove as part of its initial burden that the defendant knew he had a right to refuse to answer the questions that were put. While the state of the accused's mind, and the failure of the police to advise the accused of his rights, were certainly factors to be evaluated in assessing the "voluntariness" of an accused's responses, they were not in and of themselves determinative. * * * [a]

B

* * * [We] agree with the courts of California that the question whether a consent to a search was in fact "voluntary" or was the product of duress or coercion, express or implied, is a question of fact to be determined from the totality of all the circumstances. While knowledge of the right to refuse consent is one factor to be taken into account, the government need not establish such knowledge as the *sine qua non* of an effective consent. As with police questioning, two competing concerns must be accommodated in determining the meaning of a "voluntary" consent—the legitimate need for such searches and the equally important requirement of assuring the absence of coercion.

In situations where the police have some evidence of illicit activity, but lack probable cause to arrest or search, a search authorized by a valid consent may be the only means of obtaining important and reliable evidence. * * * And in those cases where there is probable cause to arrest or search, but where the police lack a warrant, a consent search may still be valuable. If the search is conducted and proves fruitless, that in itself may convince the police that an arrest with its possible stigma and embarrassment is unnecessary, or that a far more extensive

search pursuant to a warrant is not justified. In short, a search pursuant to consent may result in considerably less inconvenience for the subject of the search, and, properly conducted, is a constitutionally permissible and wholly legitimate aspect of effective police activity. [b]

But the Fourth and Fourteenth Amendments require that a consent not be coerced, by explicit or implicit means, by implied threat or covert force. For, no matter how subtly the coercion were applied, the resulting "consent" would be no more than a pretext for the unjustified police intrusion against which the Fourth Amendment is directed. * * *

* * * Just as was true with confessions, the requirement of a "voluntary" consent reflects a fair accommodation of the constitutional requirements involved. In examining all the surrounding circumstances to determine if in fact the consent to search was coerced, account must be taken of subtly coercive police questions, as well as the possibly vulnerable subjective state of the person who consents. [c] Those searches that are the product of police coercion can thus be filtered out without undermining the continuing validity of consent searches. In sum, there is no reason for us to depart in the area of consent searches, from the traditional definition of "voluntariness."

The approach of the Court of Appeals * * * would, in practice, create serious doubt whether consent searches could continue to be conducted. [Except for rare cases,] * * * where there was no evidence of any coercion, explicit or implicit, the prosecution would nevertheless be unable to demonstrate that the subject of the search in fact had known of his right to refuse consent.

The very object of the inquiry—the nature of a person's subjective understanding—underlines the difficulty of the prosecution's burden under the rule applied by the Court of Appeals in this case. Any defendant who was the subject of a search authorized solely by his consent could effectively frustrate the introduction into evidence of the fruits of that search by simply failing to testify that he in fact knew he could refuse to consent. * * *

One alternative that would go far toward proving that the subject of a search did know he had a right to refuse consent would be to advise him of that right before eliciting his consent. That, however, is a suggestion that has been almost universally repudiated by both federal and state courts, and, we think, rightly so. For it would be thoroughly impractical to impose on the normal consent search the detailed requirements of an effective warning. [d] Consent searches are part of the standard investigatory techniques of law enforcement agencies. They normally occur on the highway, or in a person's home or office, and under informal and unstructured conditions. The circumstances that prompt the initial request to search may develop quickly or be a logical extension of investigative police questioning. The police may seek to investigate further suspicious circumstances or to follow up leads developed in questioning persons at the scene of a crime. These situations are a far cry from the structured atmosphere of a trial where, assisted by counsel if he chooses, a defendant is informed of his trial rights. * * * And, while surely a closer question, these situations are still

immeasurably far removed from "custodial interrogation" where, in *Miranda v. Arizona*, [this volume] we found that the Constitution required certain now familiar warnings as a prerequisite to police interrogation. * * *

Consequently, we cannot accept the position of the Court of Appeals. * * *

* * *

Conversely, if under all the circumstances it has appeared that the consent was not given voluntarily—that it was coerced by threats or force, or granted only in submission to a claim of lawful authority—then we have found the consent invalid and the search unreasonable. * * *
* * *

In short, neither this Court's prior cases, nor the traditional definition of "voluntariness" requires proof of knowledge of a right to refuse as the *sine qua non* of an effective consent to a search. * * *

C

It is said, however, that a "consent" is a "waiver" of a person's rights under the Fourth and Fourteenth Amendments. The argument is that by allowing the police to conduct a search, a person "waives" whatever right he had to prevent the police from searching. It is argued that under the doctrine of *Johnson v. Zerbst*, [this volume] to establish such a "waiver" the State must demonstrate "an intentional relinquishment or abandonment of a known right or privilege."

But these standards were enunciated in *Johnson* in the context of the safeguards of a fair criminal trial. Our cases do not reflect an uncritical demand for a knowing and intelligent waiver in every situation where a person has failed to invoke a constitutional protection. * * *

* * *

* * * [T]he Court has evaluated the knowing and intelligent nature of the waiver of trial rights in trial-type situations, such as the waiver of the privilege against compulsory self-incrimination before an administrative agency or a congressional committee, or the waiver of counsel in a juvenile proceeding.

The guarantees afforded a criminal defendant at trial also protect him at certain stages before the actual trial [such as a post-indictment lineup], and any alleged waiver must meet the strict standard of an intentional relinquishment of a "known" right. But the "trial" guarantees that have been applied to the "pretrial" stage of the criminal process are similarly designed to protect the fairness of the trial itself. **[e]**

* * *

And in *Miranda v. Arizona*, [this volume], the Court * * * made it clear that the basis for decision was the need to protect the fairness of the trial itself [because of the inherently coercive atmosphere of police custody]. * * *

The standards of *Johnson* were, therefore, found to be a necessary prerequisite to a finding of a valid waiver. * * *

There is a vast difference between those rights that protect a fair criminal trial and the rights guaranteed under the Fourth Amendment. Nothing, either in the purposes behind requiring a "knowing" and "intelligent" waiver of trial rights, or in the practical application of such a requirement suggests

that it ought to be extended to the constitutional guarantee against unreasonable searches and seizures.

A strict standard of waiver has been applied to those rights guaranteed to a criminal defendant to insure that he will be accorded the greatest possible opportunity to utilize every facet of the constitutional model of a fair criminal trial. Any trial conducted in derogation of that model leaves open the possibility that the trial reached an unfair result precisely because all the protections specified in the Constitution were not provided. A prime example is the right to counsel. For without that right, a wholly innocent accused faces the real and substantial danger that simply because of his lack of legal expertise he may be convicted. * * *

The protections of the Fourth Amendment are of a wholly different order, and have nothing whatever to do with promoting the fair ascertainment of truth at a criminal trial. Rather, * * * the Fourth Amendment protects the "security of one's privacy against arbitrary intrusion by the police. . . ." In declining to apply the exclusionary rule of *Mapp v. Ohio* [retroactively], * * * the Court emphasized that "there is no likelihood of unreliability or coercion present in a search-and-seizure case." * * *

Nor can it even be said that a search, as opposed to an eventual trial, is somehow "unfair" if a person consents to a search. **[f]** While the Fourth and Fourteenth Amendments limit the circumstances under which the police can conduct a search, there is nothing constitutionally suspect in a person's voluntarily allowing a search. The actual conduct of the search may be precisely the same as if the police had obtained a warrant. And, unlike those constitutional guarantees that protect a defendant at trial, it cannot be said every reasonable presumption ought to be indulged against voluntary relinquishment. We have only recently stated: "[It] is no part of the policy underlying the Fourth and Fourteenth Amendments to discourage citizens from aiding to the utmost of their ability in the apprehension of criminals." * * *   Rather, the community has a real interest in encouraging consent, for the resulting search may yield necessary evidence for the solution and prosecution of crime, evidence that may insure that a wholly innocent person is not wrongly charged with a criminal offense.

* * * [I]t would be next to impossible to apply to a consent search the standard of "an intentional relinquishment or abandonment of a known right or privilege." To be true to *Johnson* and its progeny, there must be examination into the knowing and understanding nature of the waiver, an examination that was designed for a trial judge in the structured atmosphere of a courtroom. * * * It would be unrealistic to expect that in the informal, unstructured context of a consent search, a policeman, upon pain of tainting the evidence obtained, could make the detailed type of examination demanded by *Johnson*. And, if for this reason a diluted form of "waiver" were found acceptable, that would itself be ample recognition of the fact that there is no universal standard that must be applied in every situation where a person forgoes a constitutional right. * * *

* * *

D

* * * The considerations that informed the Court's holding in *Miranda* are simply inapplicable in the present case. In *Miranda* the Court found that the techniques of police questioning and the nature of custodial surroundings produce an inherently coercive situation [therefore requiring protective warnings to insure that statements were made by the defendant's free choice.] * * *

In this case, there is no evidence of any inherently coercive tactics—either from the nature of the police questioning or the environment in which it took place. Indeed, since consent searches will normally occur on a person's own familiar territory, the specter of incommunicado police interrogation in some remote station house is simply inapposite. [g] There is no reason to believe, under circumstances such as are present here, that the response to a policeman's question is presumptively coerced; and there is, therefore, no reason to reject the traditional test for determining the voluntariness of a person's response. * * *

* * *

E

Our decision today is a narrow one. We hold only that when the subject of a search is not in custody and the State attempts to justify a search on the basis of his consent, the Fourth and Fourteenth Amendments require that it demonstrate that the consent was in fact voluntarily given, and not the result of duress or coercion, express or implied. Voluntariness is a question of fact to be determined from all the circumstances, and while the subject's knowledge of a right to refuse is a factor to be taken into account, the prosecution is not required to demonstrate such knowledge as a prerequisite to establishing a voluntary consent. * * *

[JUSTICE BLACKMUN concurred separately.]

[JUSTICE POWELL, joined by THE CHIEF JUSTICE and JUSTICE REHNQUIST, wrote a concurring opinion arguing for a curtailment of federal habeas corpus in state Fourth Amendment cases.]

[JUSTICES DOUGLAS and BLACKMUN wrote separate dissenting opinions.]

MR. JUSTICE MARSHALL, dissenting. * * *
* * *

I

* * * [T]he Court misstates the true issue in this case. That issue is not, as the Court suggests, whether the police overbore Alcala's will in eliciting his consent, but rather, whether a simple statement of assent to search, without more, should be sufficient to permit the police to search and thus act as a relinquishment of Alcala's constitutional right to exclude the police. This Court has always scrutinized with great care claims that a person has forgone the opportunity to assert constitutional rights. * * * I see no reason to give the claim that a person consented to a search any less rigorous scrutiny. Every case in this Court involving this kind of search has therefore spoken of consent as a waiver. * * *

* * *

A

The Court assumes that the issue in this case is: what are the standards by which courts are to determine that consent is voluntarily given? It then imports into the law of search and seizure standards developed to decide entirely different questions about coerced confessions [which prohibit compelled incriminating statements].
* * * The inquiry in a case where a confession is challenged as having been elicited in an unconstitutional manner is, therefore, whether the behavior of the police amounted to compulsion of the defendant. Because of the nature of the right to be free of compulsion, it would be pointless to ask whether a defendant knew of it before he made a statement; no sane person would knowingly relinquish a right to be free of compulsion. Thus, the questions of compulsion and of violation of the right itself are inextricably intertwined. The cases involving coerced confessions, therefore, pass over the question of knowledge of that right as irrelevant, and turn directly to the question of compulsion.
* * *

B

In contrast, this case deals not with "coercion," but with "consent," a subtly different concept to which different standards have been applied in the past. [h] Freedom from coercion is a substantive right, guaranteed by the Fifth and Fourteenth Amendments. Consent, however, is a mechanism by which substantive requirements, otherwise applicable, are avoided. [Unlike exigency exceptions to the warrant requirement, in consent searches] * * * the needs of law enforcement are significantly more attenuated, for probable cause to search may be lacking but a search permitted if the subject's consent has been obtained. Thus, consent searches are permitted, not because such an exception to the requirements of probable cause and warrant is essential to proper law enforcement, but because we permit our citizens to choose whether or not they wish to exercise their constitutional rights. [i] Our prior decisions simply do not support the view that a meaningful choice has been made solely because no coercion was brought to bear on the subject.

[The majority mistakenly rests its holding on the convenience of the police, a factor that is not relied on in the search incident to arrest or automobile search rationales. Furthermore, it is too easy for the police to demand entry to search without the overt use of force and for courts to uphold these as consent searches.] * * * I cannot believe that the protections of the Constitution mean so little.

II

My approach to the case is straightforward and, to me, obviously required by the notion of consent as a relinquishment of Fourth Amendment rights. I am at a loss to understand why consent "cannot be taken literally to mean a 'knowing' choice." In fact, I have difficulty in comprehending how a decision made without knowledge of available alternatives can be treated as a choice at all.

If consent to search means that a person has chosen to forgo his right to exclude the police from the place they seek to search, it follows that his consent cannot be considered a meaningful choice unless he knew that he could in fact exclude the police. The Court appears, however, to reject even the modest proposition that, if the subject of a search convinces the trier of fact that he did not know of his right to refuse assent to a police request for permission to search, the search must be held unconstitutional. For it says only that "knowledge of the right to refuse consent is one factor to be taken into account." I find this incomprehensible. I can think of no other situation in which we would say that a person agreed to some course of action if he convinced us that he did not know that there was some other course he might have pursued. [j] I would therefore hold, at a minimum, that the prosecution may not rely on a purported consent to search if the subject of the search did not know that he could refuse to give consent. * * *

* * *

* * * [T]here are several ways by which the subject's knowledge of his rights may be shown. [These include the defendant affirmatively showing he knew of his rights by responses to questions, the defendant indicating knowledge of rights by actions, such as a prior refusal to allow a search, or by the police telling the defendant what his rights are.]* * *

The Court's assertions to the contrary notwithstanding, there is nothing impractical about this method of satisfying the prosecution's burden of proof. * * *

* * *

I must conclude, with some reluctance, that when the Court speaks of practicality, what it really is talking of is the continued ability of the police to capitalize on the ignorance of citizens so as to accomplish by subterfuge what they could not achieve by relying only on the knowing relinquishment of constitutional rights. Of course it would be "practical" for the police to ignore the commands of the Fourth Amendment, if by practicality we mean that more criminals will be apprehended, even though the constitutional rights of innocent people also go by the board. But such a practical advantage is achieved only at the cost of permitting the police to disregard the limitations that the Constitution places on their behavior, a cost that a constitutional democracy cannot long absorb.

* * *

* * * * * * * * * *

COMMENTS

[a] A conceptual framework developed in one area of law, here the pre-*Miranda* law of confessions (see Chapter 6, Section A of this volume), can be applied to another, here the law on consent searches. This kind of conceptual borrowing is common in the law and is one reason why knowledge of only one branch of law often does not provide an adequate basis for or appreciation of legal creativity.

[b] To what extent should convenience for the innocent outweigh the more stringent protection of individual rights? How far could such considerations be stretched?

[c] It would appear that the determination of subtle coercion is a fine factual distinction that may in fact deliver substantial discretion to the trier of fact, be it judge or jury.

[d] The dissent disagreed with the majority on this point. Do you think that if Officer Rand said to Alcala, "May I open the trunk; you have a right to refuse under the Fourth Amendment?" that this would be inconvenient? If the officer provided a written waiver form, would it be impractical? Is the real concern that it would reduce the number of consent searches?

[e] While the distinction between the trial, and other stages of the criminal case which are not designed to insure a fair trial, may be valid, does it make sense to say that the consent given to open the trunk in this case was not a waiver of Fourth Amendment rights? If it was a waiver, should the different purposes of trial rights and Fourth Amendment rights lead to different waiver rules?

[f] Is this point entirely honest? Might it not be better to say that in such cases as *Schneckloth* the police take advantage of people, but the failure to inform people of their rights of privacy is worth this deception because of the increases in police efficiency and effectiveness? Does one's sense of the ethics of this situation

depend on whether the search does or does not uncover contraband? Would it make sense for the Court to look to the amount of latitude given, say, to used-automobile salespersons in determining the extent of allowable police deception by silence? Note that Justice Stewart writes positively about the police practice of obtaining consent.

[g] In light of the *Miranda* reasoning, to require a warning whenever the police speak to a citizen and ask if they may enter a home or look into a car trunk might require a formal acknowledgement by the Court that every police-citizen interaction is inherently coercive. Is this accurate? Would such a presumption be wise?

[h] JUSTICE MARSHALL suggests that the lack of voluntary consent may be found even when there is no coercion. Can you think of any examples? Is this separation of consent from coercion psychologically feasible? Does it make sense as a legal rule?

[i] JUSTICE MARSHALL, unlike JUSTICE STEWART, views consent with suspicion.

[j] While JUSTICE MARSHALL's point is generally well-taken, there are situations where a person legitimately makes decisions not knowing every fact or consequence regarding the choice.

ILLINOIS v. RODRIGUEZ

497 U.S. 177, 110 S.Ct. 2793, 111 L.Ed.2d 148 (1990)

JUSTICE SCALIA delivered the opinion of the Court.

In *United States v. Matlock*, 415 U.S. 164 (1974), this Court reaffirmed that a warrantless entry and search by law enforcement officers does not violate the Fourth Amendment's proscription of "unreasonable searches and seizures" if the officers have obtained the consent of a third party who possesses common authority over the premises. The present case presents an issue we expressly reserved in *Matlock*, [above]: Whether a warrantless entry is valid when based upon the consent of a third party whom the police, at the time of the entry, reasonably believe to possess common authority over the premises, but who in fact does not do so.

I

* * *

* * * [P]olice were summoned to the residence of Dorothy Jackson. * * * They were met by Ms. Jackson's daughter, Gail Fischer, who showed signs of a severe beating. She told the officers that she had been assaulted by respondent Edward Rodriguez earlier that day in an apartment on South California. Fischer stated that Rodriguez was then asleep in the apartment, and she consented to travel there with the police in order to unlock the door with her key so that the officers could enter and arrest him. During this conversation, Fischer several times referred to the apartment on South California as "our" apartment, and said that she had clothes and furniture there. It is unclear whether she indicated that she currently lived at the apartment, or only that she used to live there.

The police officers drove to the apartment on South California, accompanied by Fischer. They did not obtain an arrest warrant for Rodriguez, nor did they seek a search warrant for the apartment. At the apartment, Fischer unlocked the door with her key and gave the officers permission to enter. They moved through the door into the living room, where they observed in plain view drug paraphernalia and containers filled with white powder that they believed (correctly, as later analysis showed) to be cocaine. They proceeded to the bedroom, where they found Rodriguez asleep and discovered additional containers of white powder in two open attaché cases. The officers arrested Rodriguez and seized the drugs and related paraphernalia.

[The state courts found that Fischer was not a "usual resident" but rather an "infrequent visitor" at Rodriguez' apartment and that the police therefore did not enter under consent even if they reasonably believed that Fisher possessed the authority to consent at the time of the entry.]

* * *

II

The Fourth Amendment generally prohibits the warrantless entry of a person's home, whether to make an arrest or to search for specific objects.

* * * The prohibition does not apply, however, to situations in which voluntary consent has been obtained, either from the individual whose property is searched, * or from a third party who possesses common authority over the premises. * * * The State of Illinois contends that that exception applies in the present case.

As we stated in *Matlock*, [above], "[c]ommon authority" rests "on mutual use of the property by persons generally having joint access or control for most purposes. . . ." The burden of establishing that common authority rests upon the State. On the basis of this record, it is clear that burden was not sustained. The evidence showed that although Fischer, with her two small children, had lived with Rodriguez beginning in December 1984, she had moved out on July 1, 1985, almost a month before the search at issue here, and had gone to live with her mother. She took her and her children's clothing with her, though leaving behind some furniture and household effects. During the period after July 1 she sometimes spent the night at Rodriguez's apartment, but never invited her friends there, and never went there herself when he was not home. Her name was not on the lease nor did she contribute to the rent. She had a key to the apartment, which she said at trial she had taken without Rodriguez's knowledge (though she testified at the preliminary hearing that Rodriguez had given her the key). On these facts the State has not established that, with respect to the South California apartment, Fischer had "joint access or control for most purposes." To the contrary, the Appellate Court's determination of no

common authority over the apartment was obviously correct.

III

A

[The Court found that the Illinois decision rested on a federal Constitutional basis and not upon an adequate and independent state ground.]

B

On the merits of the issue, respondent asserts that permitting a reasonable belief of common authority to validate an entry would cause a defendant's Fourth Amendment rights to be "vicariously waived." * * *

We have been unyielding in our insistence that a defendant's waiver of his trial rights cannot be given effect unless it is "knowing" and "intelligent." * * * We would assuredly not permit, therefore, evidence seized in violation of the Fourth Amendment to be introduced on the basis of a trial court's mere "reasonable belief"— derived from statements by unauthorized persons—that the defendant has waived his objection. But one must make a distinction between, on the one hand, trial rights that *derive* from the violation of constitutional guarantees and, on the other hand, the nature of those constitutional guarantees themselves. [The Court cited *Schneckloth v. Bustamonte* [this volume] on the distinction between waiver of trial rights and consent to give up Fourth Amendment rights.]

What Rodriguez is assured by the trial right of the exclusionary rule, where it applies, is that no evidence seized in violation of the Fourth Amendment will be introduced at his trial unless he consents. What he is assured by the Fourth Amendment itself, however, is not that no government search of his house will occur unless he consents; but that no such search will occur that is "unreasonable." * * * There are various elements, of course, that can make a search of a person's house "reasonable"—one of which is the consent of the person or his cotenant. [a] The essence of respondent's argument is that we should impose upon this element a requirement that we have not imposed upon other elements that regularly compel government officers to exercise judgment regarding the facts: namely, the requirement that their judgment be not only responsible but correct.

The fundamental objective that alone validates all unconsented government searches is, of course, the seizure of persons who have committed or are about to commit crimes, or of evidence related to crimes. But "reasonableness," with respect to this necessary element, does not demand that the government be factually correct in its assessment that that is what a search will produce. Warrants need only be supported by "probable cause," which demands no more than a proper "assessment of probabilities in particular factual contexts. . . ." * * * If a magistrate, based upon seemingly reliable but factually inaccurate information, issues a warrant for the search of a house in which the sought-after felon is not present, has never been present, and was never likely to have been present, the owner of that house suffers one of the inconveniences we all expose ourselves to as the cost of living in a safe society; he does not suffer a violation of the Fourth Amendment. [b]

Another element often, though not invariably, required in order to render an unconsented search "reasonable" is, of course, that the officer be authorized by a valid warrant. Here also we have not held that "reasonableness" precludes error with respect to those factual judgments that law enforcement officials are expected to make. In *Maryland v. Garrison*, 480 U.S. 79 (1987), a warrant supported by probable cause with respect to one apartment was erroneously issued for an entire floor that was divided (though not clearly) into two apartments. We upheld the search of the apartment not properly covered by the warrant. * * *

The ordinary requirement of a warrant is sometimes supplanted by other elements that render the unconsented search "reasonable." Here also we have not held that the Fourth Amendment requires factual accuracy. A warrant is not needed, for example, where the search is incident to an arrest. In *Hill v. California*, 401 U.S. 797 (1971), we upheld a search incident to an arrest, even though the arrest was made of the wrong person. We said:

> "The upshot was that the officers in good faith believed Miller was Hill and arrested him. They were quite wrong as it turned out, and subjective good-faith belief would not in itself justify either the arrest or the subsequent search. But sufficient probability, not certainty, is the touchstone of reasonableness under the Fourth Amendment and on the record before us the officers' mistake was understandable and the arrest a reasonable response to the situation facing them at the time." * * *

It would be superfluous to multiply these examples. It is apparent that in order to satisfy the "reasonableness" requirement of the Fourth Amendment, what is generally demanded of the many factual determinations that must regularly be made by agents of the government— whether the magistrate issuing a warrant, the police officer executing a warrant, or the police officer conducting a search or seizure under one of the exceptions to the warrant requirement—is not that they always be correct, but that they always be reasonable. * * *

We see no reason to depart from this general rule with respect to facts bearing upon the authority to consent to a search. * * *

Stoner v. California, 376 U.S. 483 (1964), is in our view not to the contrary. There, in holding that police had improperly entered the defendant's hotel room based on the consent of a hotel clerk, we stated that "the rights protected by the Fourth Amendment are not to be eroded . . . by unrealistic doctrines of 'apparent authority.'" * * * [Justice SCALIA determined that there was much ambiguity in *Stoner*, but that *Stoner* did not eradicate consent given by one with apparent authority but did not open the door wide to anyone asserting apparent authority.]

As *Stoner* demonstrates, what we hold today does not suggest that law enforcement officers may always accept a person's invitation to enter premises. Even when the invitation is accompanied by an explicit assertion that the person lives there, the surrounding circumstances could conceivably be such that a reasonable person would doubt its truth and not act upon it without further inquiry. As with other factual determinations bearing upon search and seizure, determination of consent to enter must "be judged against an objective standard: would the facts available to the officer at the moment . . . 'warrant a man of reasonable caution in the belief'" that the consenting party had authority over the premises? * * * If not, then warrantless entry without further inquiry is unlawful unless authority actually exists. But if so, the search is valid.

[The case was reversed and remanded]

JUSTICE MARSHALL, with whom JUSTICE BRENNAN and JUSTICE STEVENS join, dissenting.

* * *

* * * That [consent] searches do not give rise to claims of constitutional violations rests not on the premise that they are "reasonable" under the Fourth Amendment, * * * but on the premise that a person may voluntarily limit his expectation of privacy by allowing others to exercise authority over his possessions. * * * If an individual has not so limited his expectation of privacy, the police may not dispense with the safeguards established by the Fourth Amendment.

* * *

* * * Because the sole law enforcement purpose underlying third-party consent searches is avoiding the inconvenience of securing a warrant, a departure from the warrant requirement is not justified simply because an officer reasonably believes a third party has consented to a search of the defendant's home. In holding otherwise, the majority ignores our long-standing view that "the informed and deliberate determinations of magistrates

* * * as to what searches and seizures are permissible under the Constitution are to be preferred over the hurried action of officers and others who may happen to make arrests." * * * [c]
* * *

A search conducted pursuant to an officer's reasonable but mistaken belief that a third party had authority to consent is thus on an entirely different constitutional footing from one based on the consent of a third party who in fact has such authority. Even if the officers reasonably believed that Fischer had authority to consent, she did not, and Rodriguez's expectation of privacy was therefore undiminished. * * *
* * *

* * * * * * * * * *

COMMENTS

[a] Does the Court make a distinction without a difference? Differences over how far to read the "reasonableness" clause of the Fourth Amendment have been a point of contention between "liberal" and "conservative" justice in many cases. See, e.g., *New Jersey v. T.L.O.* [this volume].

[b] This is a general rule that runs throughout the common law approach to making evidentiary decisions. Even the criminal trial standard of proof beyond a reasonable doubt does not promise that no mistakes will never be made.

[c] This position strongly favoring a warrant is displayed by JUSTICES MARSHALL and BRENNAN in other cases. See *United States v. Watson* [this volume], *United States v. Ross*, 456 U.S. 798 (1982), *California v. Carney* [this volume].

CAMARA v. MUNICIPAL COURT

387 U.S. 523, 87 S.Ct. 1727, 18 L.Ed.2d 930 (1967)

MR. JUSTICE WHITE delivered the opinion of the Court.

In *Frank v. State of Maryland*, 359 U.S. 360 (1959), this Court upheld, by a five-to-four vote, a state court conviction of a homeowner who refused to permit a municipal health inspector to enter and inspect his premises without a search warrant. * * * Since those closely divided decisions, more intensive efforts at all levels of government to contain and eliminate urban blight have led to increasing use of such inspection techniques, while numerous decisions of this Court have more fully defined the Fourth Amendment's effect on state and municipal action. * * * In view of the growing nationwide importance of the problem, we * * * re-examine whether administrative inspection programs, as presently authorized and conducted, violate Fourth Amendment rights as those rights are enforced against the States through the Fourteenth Amendment. * * * [a]

* * *

* * * [A San Francisco housing and health inspector] entered an apartment building to make a routine annual inspection for possible violations of the city's Housing Code. The building's manager informed the inspector that appellant, lessee of the ground floor, was using the rear of his leasehold as a personal residence. Claiming that the building's occupancy permit did not allow residential use of the ground floor, the inspector confronted appellant and demanded that he permit an inspection of the pre-

mises. Appellant refused to allow the inspection because the inspector lacked a search warrant.

The inspector returned * * * without a warrant, and appellant again refused to allow an inspection. A citation was then mailed ordering appellant to appear at the district attorney's office. When appellant failed to appear [he was prosecuted and convicted of violating the San Francisco Housing Code by refusing to permit a warrantless inspection of his residence.] * * *

[Camara argues that the ordinance] is contrary to the Fourth and Fourteenth Amendments in that it authorizes municipal officials to enter a private dwelling without a search warrant and without probable cause to believe that a violation of the Housing Code exists therein. Consequently, appellant contends, he may not be prosecuted * * * for refusing to permit an inspection. * * * [The District Court of Appeal, relying on *Frank*, held that the ordinance does not violate Fourth Amendment rights because it is essentially a civil rather than a criminal search and applies only in a reasonable manner]. Having concluded that *Frank v. State of Maryland*, to the extent that it sanctioned such warrantless inspections, must be overruled, we reverse.

I

* * * The basic purpose of [the Fourth] Amendment, * * * is to safeguard the privacy and security of individuals against arbitrary invasions

by governmental officials. The Fourth Amendment thus gives concrete expression to a right of the people which "is basic to a free society." * * * As such, the Fourth Amendment is enforceable against the States through the Fourteenth Amendment. * * *

* * * [O]ne governing principle, justified by history and by current experience, has consistently been followed: except in certain carefully defined classes of cases, a search of private property without proper consent is "unreasonable" unless it has been authorized by a valid search warrant. * * *

* * * [T]he *Frank* opinion has generally been interpreted as carving out an additional exception to the rule that warrantless searches are unreasonable under the Fourth Amendment. * * *

To the *Frank* majority, municipal fire, health, and housing inspection programs "touch at most upon the periphery of the important interests safeguarded by the Fourteenth Amendment's protection against official intrusion," * * * because the inspections are merely to determine whether physical conditions exist which do not comply with minimum standards prescribed in local regulatory ordinances. Since the inspector does not ask that the property owner open his doors to a search for "evidence of criminal action" which may be used to secure the owner's criminal conviction, historic interests of "self-protection" jointly protected by the Fourth and Fifth Amendments are said not to be involved, but only the less intense "right to be secure from intrusion into personal privacy." * * * **[b]**

We may agree that a routine inspection of the physical condition of private property is a less hostile intrusion than the typical policeman's search for the fruits and instrumentalities of crime. For this reason alone, *Frank* differed from the great bulk of Fourth Amendment cases which have been considered by this Court. But we cannot agree that the Fourth Amendment interests at stake in these inspection cases are merely "peripheral." It is surely anomalous to say that the individual and his private property are fully protected by the Fourth Amendment only when the individual is suspected of criminal behavior. For instance, even the most law-abiding citizen has a very tangible interest in limiting the circumstances under which the sanctity of his home may be broken by official authority, for the possibility of criminal entry under the guise of official sanction is a serious threat to personal and family security. And even accepting *Frank*'s rather remarkable premise, inspections of the kind we are here considering do in fact jeopardize "self-protection" interests of the property owner. Like most regulatory laws, fire, health, and housing codes are enforced by criminal processes. * * * [A]s this case demonstrates, refusal to permit an inspection is itself a crime, punishable by fine or even by jail sentence.

[There are] * * * two other justifications for permitting administrative health and safety inspections without a warrant. First, it is argued that these inspections are "designed to make the least possible demand on the individual occupant." * * * The ordinances authorizing inspections are hedged with safeguards, **[c]** and at any rate the inspector's particular decision to enter must comply with the constitutional standard of reasonableness even if he may enter without a warrant. In addition, the argument proceeds, the warrant process could not function effectively in this field. The decision to inspect an entire municipal area is based upon legislative or administrative assessment of broad factors such as the area's age and condition. Unless the magistrate is to review such policy matters, he must issue a "rubber stamp" warrant which provides no protection at all to the property owner. **[d]**

In our opinion, these arguments unduly discount the purposes behind the warrant machinery contemplated by the Fourth Amendment. Under the present system, when the inspector demands entry, the occupant has no way of knowing whether enforcement of the municipal code involved requires inspection of his premises, no way of knowing the lawful limits of the inspector's power to search, and no way of knowing whether the inspector himself is acting under proper authorization. These are questions which may be reviewed by a neutral magistrate without any reassessment of the basic agency decision to canvass an area. Yet, only by refusing entry and risking a criminal conviction can the occupant at present challenge the inspector's decision to search. * * * The practical effect of this system is to leave the occupant subject to the discretion of the official in the field. This is precisely the discretion to invade private property which we have consistently circumscribed by a requirement that a disinterested party warrant the need to search. * * * We simply cannot say that the protections provided by the warrant procedure are not needed in this context; broad statutory safeguards are no substitute for individ-

ualized review, particularly when those safeguards may only be invoked at the risk of a criminal penalty.

The final justification suggested for warrantless administrative searches is that the public interest demands such a rule: it is vigorously argued that the health and safety of entire urban populations is dependent upon enforcement of minimum fire, housing, and sanitation standards, and that the only effective means of enforcing such codes is by routine systematized inspection of all physical structures. Of course, in applying any reasonableness standard, including one of constitutional dimension, an argument that the public interest demands a particular rule must receive careful consideration. But we think this argument misses the mark. The question is not, at this stage at least, whether these inspections may be made, but whether they may be made without a warrant. * * * In assessing whether the public interest demands creation of a general exception to the Fourth Amendment's warrant requirement, the question is not whether the public interest justifies the type of search in question, but whether the authority to search should be evidenced by a warrant, which in turn depends in part upon whether the burden of obtaining a warrant is likely to frustrate the governmental purpose behind the search. * * * It has nowhere been urged that fire, health, and housing code inspection programs could not achieve their goals within the confines of a reasonable search warrant requirement. Thus, we do not find the public need argument dispositive. **[e]**

In summary, [administrative searches are significant intrusions on Fourth Amendment interest that require the traditional safeguards of a warrant and the reasons in *Frank v. Maryland* are insufficient to justify warrantless searches.] Because of the nature of the municipal programs under consideration, however, these conclusions must be the beginning, not the end, of our inquiry. The *Frank* majority gave recognition to the unique character of these inspection programs by refusing to require search warrants; to reject that disposition does not justify ignoring the question whether some other accommodation between public need and individual rights is essential.

II

* * * [A]ppellant argues * * * that code enforcement * * * warrants should issue only when the inspector possesses probable cause to believe that a particular dwelling contains violations of the minimum standards prescribed by the code being enforced. [f] We disagree.

In [Fourth Amendment warrant cases] "probable cause" is the standard by which a particular decision to search is tested against the constitutional mandate of reasonableness. * * * [Thus, a search for stolen goods] is "reasonable" only when there is "probable cause" to believe that they will be uncovered in a particular dwelling.

Unlike the search pursuant to a criminal investigation, the inspection programs at issue here are aimed at securing city-wide compliance with minimum physical standards for private property. The primary governmental interest at stake is to prevent even the unintentional development of conditions which are hazardous to public health and safety [that effect large areas]. * * * In determining whether a particular inspection is reason-

able—and thus in determining whether there is probable cause to issue a warrant for that inspection—the need for the inspection must be weighed in terms of these reasonable goals of code enforcement. [g]

* * * [T]he only effective way to seek universal compliance with the minimum standards required by municipal codes is through routine periodic inspections of all structures. It is here that the probable cause debate is focused, for the agency's decision to conduct an area inspection is unavoidably based on its appraisal of conditions in the area as a whole, not on its knowledge of conditions in each particular building. [The city argues that a probable cause requirement will eliminate area inspections and destroy reasonable code enforcement.] [h]

[Camara argues that very few] will refuse to consent to such inspections, and second, that individual privacy in any event should be given preference to the public interest in conducting such inspections. The first argument, even if true, is irrelevant to [Fourth Amendment reasonableness.] The second argument is in effect an assertion that the area inspection is an unreasonable search. Unfortunately, there can be no ready test for determining reasonableness other than by balancing the need to search against the invasion which the search entails. [A number of factors] support the reasonableness of area code-enforcement inspections. First, such programs have a long history of judicial and public acceptance. * * * Second, the public interest demands that all dangerous conditions be prevented or abated, yet it is doubtful that any other canvassing technique would achieve acceptable results. Many such conditions * * * are not observable from outside the building and indeed may not be apparent to the inexpert occupant himself. Finally, because the inspections are neither personal in nature nor aimed at the discovery of evidence of crime, they involve a relatively limited invasion of the urban citizen's privacy. * * *

Having concluded that the area inspection is a "reasonable" search of private property within the meaning of the Fourth Amendment, it is obvious that "probable cause" to issue a warrant to inspect must exist if reasonable legislative or administrative standards for conducting an area inspection are satisfied with respect to a particular dwelling. Such standards, which will vary with the municipal program being enforced, may be based upon the passage of time, the nature of the building (*e.g.*, a multi-family apartment house), or the condition of the entire area, but they will not necessarily depend upon specific knowledge of the condition of the particular dwelling. [i] It has been suggested that so to vary the probable cause test from the standard applied in criminal cases would be to authorize a "synthetic search warrant" and thereby to lessen the overall protections of the Fourth Amendment. * * * But we do not agree. The warrant procedure is designed to guarantee that a decision to search private property is justified by a reasonable governmental interest. But reasonableness is still the ultimate

standard. If a valid public interest justifies the intrusion contemplated, then there is probable cause to issue a suitably restricted search warrant. * * * Such an approach neither endangers time-honored doctrines applicable to criminal investigations nor makes a nullity of the probable cause requirement in this area. It merely gives full recognition to the competing public and private interests here at stake and, in so doing, best fulfills the historic purpose behind the constitutional right to be free from unreasonable government invasions of privacy. * * *   [j]

III

[Emergency administrative inspections and searches without a warrant are allowed, for example: seizure of unwholesome food, compulsory smallpox vaccination, health quarantine, and summary destruction of tubercular cattle. Since most citizens comply with administrative inspections, as a practical matter cities will only have to obtain warrants after admission is refused.]

IV

* * * [W]e therefore conclude that appellant had a constitutional right to insist that the inspectors obtain a warrant to search and that appellant may not constitutionally be convicted for refusing to consent to the inspection. * * *

[JUSTICES CLARK, HARLAN, and STEWART dissented.]

* * * * * * * * * * *

COMMENTS

[a] Less than a decade passed between *Frank* and the present case. It is unlikely that the extent or use of administrative searches increased to such a degree that a reconsideration of the constitutional rights of homeowners was needed. It is more likely that the revolution in thinking about rights in the 1960s generated the challenge that resulted in the present case.

[b] Do you agree with the *Frank* Court's reasoning that the Fourth Amendment does not apply to noncriminal government investigations? Why does the Court not explore the history of administrative searches at the time of the framing of the Constitution? Would it be relevant if no such searches occurred? Or if they did, that there were no legal challenges?

[c] Safeguards include the inspector displaying proper credentials and having cause to believe that a problem identified by the ordinance exists.

[d] It could be argued that the review of a magistrate is functional in keeping local government from engaging in excesses out of misplaced enthusiasm for unwise or insensitive inspection programs. The adequacy of review may then depend on the experience and wisdom of the judges. Some judges have had extensive experience in local government. On the other hand, it would not be too hard to conceive of a more adequate review panel consisting of agency experts, local elected officials, and residents.

[e] The warrant requirement will not terminate inspection searches, but may make them more costly. Perhaps the expansion of certain rights occur, or come to be seen as "natural," when society becomes wealthy enough to pay for their enforcement.

[f] What practical effect would this argument have on inspection programs?

[g] The structure of the Court's argument is designed to further the conception of reasonableness and probable cause as flexible categories. This was in line with the innovations in many Fourth Amendment cases decided in the late 1960s.

[h] The opinion is pragmatic—it seeks to fit the Fourth Amendment to the needs of administrative search programs, rather than requiring administrative search programs to adhere to traditional (*i.e.*, criminal) Fourth Amendment requirements.

[i] In other words, a specific finding of probable cause regarding a *particular* premises need not be found. This really stretches traditional notions of particularity and the concept of a general search.

[j] The importance of *Camara* to Fourth Amendment jurisprudence in general lies in this rationale; the reasonableness approach can be expanded to cover novel situations. In light of the extent to which conservative justices later pushed the reasonableness doctrine, *Camara* may have been a strategic error by liberal judges.

UNITED STATES v. MONTOYA DE HERNANDEZ

473 U.S. 531, 105 S.Ct. 3304, 87 L.Ed.2d 381 (1985)

JUSTICE REHNQUIST delivered the opinion of the Court.

Respondent Rosa Elvira Montoya de Hernandez was detained by customs officials upon her arrival at the Los Angeles Airport on a flight from Bogota, Colombia. She was found to be smuggling 88 cocaine-filled balloons in her alimentary canal, and was convicted after a bench trial of various federal narcotics offenses. A divided panel of the United States Court of Appeals for the Ninth Circuit reversed her convictions, holding that her detention violated the Fourth Amendment to the United States Constitution because the customs inspectors did not have a "clear indication" of alimentary canal smuggling at the time she was detained. * * * Because of a conflict in the decisions of the Courts of Appeals on this question and the importance of its resolution to the enforcement of customs laws, we granted certiorari. * * * We now reverse.

* * * At the customs desk she encountered Customs Inspector Talamantes, who reviewed her documents and noticed from her passport that she had made at least eight recent trips to either Miami or Los Angeles. * * * Talamantes and another inspector asked respondent general questions concerning herself and the purpose of her trip. Respondent [spoke no English and had no family or friends in the United States; she said she had come to the United States to purchase goods for her husband's store in Bogota (known as a "source city" for narcotics); she] possessed $5,000 in cash, mostly $50 bills, but had no billfold. She indicated to the inspectors that she had no appointments with merchandise vendors, but planned to ride around Los Angeles in taxicabs visiting retail stores such as J.C. Penney and K-Mart in order to buy goods for her husband's store with the $ 5,000.

Respondent admitted that she had no hotel reservations, but stated that she planned to stay at a Holiday Inn. Respondent could not recall how her airline ticket was purchased. When the inspectors opened respondent's one small valise they found about four changes of "cold weather" clothing. Respondent had no shoes other than the high-heeled pair she was wearing. Although respondent possessed no checks, waybills, credit cards, or letters of credit, she did produce a Colombian business card and a number of old receipts, waybills, and fabric swatches displayed in a photo album. **[a]**

At this point [the inspector]s suspected that respondent was a "balloon swallower," one who attempts to smuggle narcotics into this country hidden in her alimentary canal. Over the years Inspector Talamantes had apprehended dozens of alimentary canal smugglers arriving on Avianca Flight 080. * * * **[b]**

[A female customs inspector took] respondent to a private area and conduct[ed] a patdown and strip search. During the search the female inspector felt respondent's abdomen area and noticed a firm fullness, as if respondent were wearing a girdle. The search revealed no contraband, but the inspector noticed that respondent was wearing two pairs of elastic underpants with a paper towel lining the crotch area.

[As a result, respondent was told she was suspected of smuggling drugs in her alimentary canal. She was placed under observation awaiting a return flight and] was told that if she went to the toilet she would have to use a wastebasket in the women's restroom, in order that female customs inspectors could inspect her stool for balloons or capsules carrying narcotics. The inspectors refused respondent's request to place a telephone call.

[Respondent was detained for the rest of the night, and a Mexican airline refused to transport her because she lacked a proper visa.] She refused all offers of food and drink, and refused to use the toilet facilities. The Court of Appeals noted that she exhibited symptoms of discomfort consistent with "heroic efforts to resist the usual calls of nature."

[After sixteen hours, customs officials obtained a court order from a federal magistrate. Under the order, a physician conducted a rectal examination in a hospital, removing] a balloon containing a foreign substance. Respondent was then placed formally under arrest. By 4:10 a.m. respondent had passed 6 similar balloons; over the next four days she passed 88 balloons containing a total of 528 grams of 80% pure cocaine hydrochloride. [c]
* * *

[The Court of Appeals held that the customs officers needed a "clear indication" of drug possession before engaging in such a lengthy detention and intrusive search at the border. The government argues that the agents had reasonable suspicion which is a sufficient standard.]

The Fourth Amendment commands that searches and seizures be reasonable. What is reasonable depends upon all of the circumstances surrounding the search or seizure and the nature of the search or seizure itself. * * * The permissibility of a particular law enforcement practice is judged by "balancing its intrusion on the individual's Fourth Amendment interests against its promotion of legitimate governmental interests." * * * [d]

Here the seizure of respondent took place at the international border. Since the founding of our Republic, Congress has granted the Executive plenary authority to conduct routine searches and seizures at the border, without probable cause or a warrant, in order to regulate the collection of duties and to prevent the introduction of contraband into this country. * * * This Court has long recognized Congress' power to police entrants at the border. * * *

Consistently, therefore, with Congress' power to protect the Nation by stopping and examining persons entering this country, the Fourth Amendment's balance of reasonableness is qualitatively different at the international border than in the interior. Routine searches of the persons and effects of entrants are not subject to any requirement of reasonable suspicion, probable cause, or warrant, and first-class mail may be opened without a warrant on less than probable cause. * * * Automotive travelers may be stopped at fixed checkpoints near the border without individualized suspicion even if the stop is based largely on ethnicity, * * * and boats on inland waters with ready access to the sea may be hailed and boarded with no suspicion whatever. * * *

These cases reflect longstanding concern for the protection of the integrity of the border. This concern is, if anything, heightened by the veritable national crisis in law enforcement caused by smuggling of illicit narcotics, * * * and in particular by the increasing utilization of alimentary canal smuggling. This desperate practice appears to be a relatively recent addition to the smugglers' repertoire of deceptive practices, and it also appears to be exceedingly difficult to detect. Congress had recognized these difficulties [by providing statutory authority to stop and examine any person or vehicle on which the officer suspects there is contraband].

Balanced against the sovereign's interests at the border are the Fourth Amendment rights of respondent. Having presented herself at the border for admission, and having subjected herself to the criminal enforcement powers of the Federal Government, * * * respondent was entitled to be free from unreasonable search and seizure. But not only is the expectation of privacy less at the border than in the interior, * * * the Fourth Amendment balance between the interests of the Government and the privacy right of the individual is also struck much more favorably to the Government at the border. * * * [e]

We have not previously decided what level of suspicion would justify a seizure of an incoming traveler for purposes other than a routine border search. * * * The Court of Appeals held that the initial detention of respondent was permissible only if the inspectors possessed a "clear indication" of alimentary canal smuggling. * * *

This "clear indication" language comes from our opinion in *Schmerber v. California*, [384 U.S.757 (1966)], but we think that the Court of Appeals misapprehended the significance of that phrase in the context in which it was used in *Schmerber*. The Court of Appeals * * * viewed "clear indication" as an intermediate standard between "reasonable suspicion" and "probable cause." * * * But we think that the words in *Schmerber* were used to indicate the necessity for particularized suspicion that the evidence sought might be found within the body of the individual, rather than as enunciating still a third Fourth Amendment threshold between "reasonable suspicion" and "probable cause." [f]

No other court, including this one, has ever adopted *Schmerber*'s "clear indication" language as a Fourth Amendment standard. * * * We do not think that the Fourth Amendment's emphasis upon reasonableness is consistent with the creation of a third verbal standard in addition to "reasonable suspicion" and "probable cause"; we are dealing with a constitutional requirement of reasonableness, not *mens rea*, * * * and subtle verbal gradations may obscure rather than elucidate the meaning of the provision in question.

We hold that the detention of a traveler at the border, beyond the scope of a routine customs search and inspection, is justified at its inception if customs agents, considering all the facts surrounding the traveler and her trip, reasonably suspect that the traveler is smuggling contraband in her alimentary canal.

The "reasonable suspicion" standard has been applied in a number of contexts and effects a needed balance between private and public interests when law enforcement officials must make a limited intrusion on less than probable cause. It thus fits well into the situations involving alimentary canal smuggling at the border: this type of smuggling gives no external signs and inspectors will rarely possess probable cause to arrest or search, yet governmental interests in stopping smuggling at the border are high indeed. Under this standard officials at the border must have a "particularized and objective basis for suspecting the particular person" of alimentary canal smuggling. * * *

The facts, and their rational inferences, known to customs inspectors in this case clearly supported a reasonable suspicion that respondent was an alimentary canal smuggler. We need not belabor the facts, including respondent's implausible story, that supported this suspicion. * * * The trained customs inspectors had encountered many alimentary canal smugglers and certainly had more than an "inchoate and unparticularized suspicion or 'hunch,'" that respondent was smuggling narcotics in her alimentary canal. The inspectors' suspicion was a "'commonsense conclusio[n] about human behavior' upon which 'practical people,'—including government officials, are entitled to rely." * * *

The final issue in this case is whether the detention of respondent was reasonably related in scope to the circumstances which justified it initially. * * * Here, respondent was detained *incommunicado* for almost 16 hours before inspectors sought a warrant; the warrant then took a number of hours to procure, through no apparent fault of the inspectors. This length of time

undoubtedly exceeds any other detention we have approved under reasonable suspicion. But we have also consistently rejected hard-and-fast time limits, * * * Instead, "common sense and ordinary human experience must govern over rigid criteria." * * *

[Common knowledge about body functions indicates that an ordinary frisk or search cannot detect alimentary canal smuggling. The respondent refused an x-ray examination, falsely claiming to be pregnant.] [T]he customs inspectors were left with only two practical alternatives: detain her for such time as necessary to confirm their suspicions, a detention which would last much longer than the typical "*Terry*" stop, or turn her loose into the interior carrying the reasonably suspected contraband drugs. **[g]**

The inspectors in this case followed this former procedure. They no doubt expected that respondent, having recently disembarked from a 10-hour direct flight with a full and stiff abdomen, would produce a bowel movement without extended delay. But her visible efforts to resist the call of nature, which the court below labeled "heroic," disappointed this expectation and in turn caused her humiliation and discomfort. Our prior cases have refused to charge police with delays in investigatory detention attributable to the suspect's evasive actions, * * * and that principle applies here as well. Respondent alone was responsible for much of the duration and discomfort of the seizure.

Under these circumstances, we conclude that the detention in this case was not unreasonably long. It occurred at the international border, where the Fourth Amendment balance of interests leans heavily to the

Government. At the border, customs officials have more than merely an investigative law enforcement role. They are also charged, along with immigration officials, with protecting this Nation from entrants who may bring anything harmful into this country, whether that be communicable diseases, narcotics, or explosives. * * *

* * * The judgment of the Court of Appeals is therefore

Reversed.

[JUSTICE STEVENS concurred in the judgment.]

JUSTICE BRENNAN, with whom JUSTICE MARSHALL joins, dissenting.

* * *

I.

Travelers at the national border are routinely subjected to questioning, pat-downs, and thorough searches of their belongings. These measures, which involve relatively limited invasions of privacy and which typically are conducted on all incoming travelers, do not violate the Fourth Amendment given the interests of "national self protection reasonably requiring one entering the country to identify himself as entitled to come in, and his belongings as effects which may be lawfully brought in." * * * Individual travelers also may be singled out on "reasonable suspicion" and briefly held for further investigation. * * * **[h]** At some point, however, further investigation involves such severe intrusions on the values the Fourth Amendment protects that more stringent safeguards are required. For example, the length and nature of a detention may, at least

when conducted for criminal-investigative purposes, ripen into something approximating a full-scale custodial arrest—indeed, the arrestee, unlike the detainee in cases such as this, is at least given such basic rights as a telephone call, *Miranda* warnings, a bed, a prompt hearing before the nearest federal magistrate, an appointed attorney, and consideration of bail. In addition, border detentions may involve the use of such highly intrusive investigative techniques as body-cavity searches, x-ray searches, and stomach pumping.

I believe that detentions and searches falling into these more intrusive categories are presumptively "reasonable" within the meaning of the Fourth Amendment only if authorized by a judicial officer. "Though the Fourth Amendment speaks broadly of 'unreasonable searches and seizures,' the definition of 'reasonableness' turns, at least in part, on the more specific commands of the warrant clause." * * *

[This is not an exigency situation where warrants may be dispensed with.] * * *

There is no persuasive reason not to apply these principles to lengthy and intrusive criminal-investigative detentions occurring at the nation's border. To be sure, the Court today invokes precedent stating that neither probable cause nor a warrant ever have been required for border searches. * * * If this is the law as a general matter, I believe it is time that we reexamine its foundations. **[i]** For while the power of Congress to authorize wide-ranging detentions and searches *for purposes of immigration and customs control* is unquestioned, the Court previously has emphasized that far different considerations apply when detentions and searches are carried out *for purposes of investigating suspected criminal activity.* * * * And even if the Court is correct that such detentions for purposes of criminal investigation were viewed as acceptable a century or two ago, * * * we repeatedly have stressed that "this Court has not simply frozen into constitutional law those law enforcement practices that existed at the time of the Fourth Amendment's passage." * * *

[JUSTICE BRENNAN next noted that warrants are required where government agents are involved in administrative searches.] * * *

Something has gone fundamentally awry in our constitutional jurisprudence when a neutral and detached magistrate's authorization is required before the authorities may inspect "the plumbing, heating, ventilation, gas, and electrical systems" in a person's home, investigate the back rooms of his workplace, or poke through the charred remains of his gutted garage, but not before they may hold him in indefinite involuntary isolation at the nation's border to investigate whether he might be engaged in criminal wrongdoing. No less than those who conduct administrative searches, those charged with investigative duties at the border "should not be the sole judges of when to utilize constitutionally sensitive means in pursuing their tasks," because "unreviewed executive discretion may yield too readily to pressures to obtain incriminating evidence and overlook potential invasions of privacy." * * *

Moreover, the available evidence suggests that the number of highly intrusive border searches of suspicious-looking but ultimately innocent travelers may be very high. One physician who at the request of customs officials conducted many "internal searches"—rectal and vaginal examinations and stomach pumping—estimated that he had found contraband in only 15 to 20 percent of the persons he had examined. It has similarly been estimated that only 16 percent of women subjected to body-cavity searches at the border were in fact found to be carrying contraband. It is precisely to minimize the risk of harassing so many innocent people that the Fourth Amendment requires the intervention of a judicial officer. * * *

[JUSTICE BRENNAN then attacked the analogy between border stops and *Terry* stops, arguing that the Court was pushing the "reasonableness" approach beyond a reasonable limit. He also argued that the proper standard for holding someone at the border was probable cause and that without probable cause, the government should not be able to detain a person for observation under the conditions that Mrs. Montoya de Hernandez was subjected to; in such cases where customs agents have suspicion, the person should be denied admission and returned to the country of exit.]

* * * * * * * * * * *

COMMENTS

[a] How plausible was respondent's story? Even if implausible, do you think it generates reasonable suspicion that she was a drug courier? probable cause? a clear indication? In dissent, JUSTICE BRENNAN reminded the Court that it should not use hindsight and decide the case on the fact that the respondent was in fact guilty.

[b] The nature of the agent's suspicion is "statistical." The Court would not allow a "non-border" search of a person based on the like suspicion of an experienced police officer in a "high crime area" or on a college campus where drug use is thought to be high.

[c] Where there is suspicion that a person is a balloon swallower, should a warrant be obtained immediately, so that the period of observation and uncertainty, clearly humiliating and potentially life-threatening, is reduced?

[d] The invocation of the broad "reasonableness" approach usually signals that the Court will require a lower standard of evidence sufficiency of the police than might otherwise be required. However, in light of the following paragraphs, would it have been possible for the Court to have required *no* evidentiary test to restrict the discretion of customs officers?

[e] There may be two reasons the Court now announces the application of the reasonableness principle, two centuries after the founding of the Republic. The most obvious is that prior to the development of the desperate tactic of balloon swallowing, the summary stopping of persons at the border and the complete examination of their luggage were accepted as reasonable by all nations. Only with the need to engage in strip searches, was it necessary for the Court to formally indicate that such searches could not be conducted in a purely random fashion, that is, without any level of suspicion. A related reason, somewhat speculative, is to protect American citizens from unreasonable retaliatory body-cavity searches by customs officials of other nations.

[f] The Court of Appeal's refinement is the way in which common law rules, including rules of constitutional law, grow. The Supreme Court here is nipping this extension of the law in the bud. Given the creative abilities of the attorneys who present cases and of the federal judges, a flowering of the law in this way is a regular feature of our contemporary legal system. The Supreme Court may in some cases feel that such creativity generates too many "legal weeds," rather than "exotic new flowers," requiring judicious judicial pruning.

[g] JUSTICE BRENNAN suggests that where officers have only suspicion, they should exercise another option: return the individual to the country from which she came. Is this acceptable? practical in all cases?

[h] JUSTICE BRENNAN here acknowledges the established rule that nations have plenary powers to inspect and exclude persons and goods at the border. If this doctrine were applied literally, it would be an obstacle to his conclusion that judicial warrants should be required for body cavity strip searches at the border.

[i] JUSTICE BRENNAN is not logically trapped by the precedent that seems to give the government plenary power over persons at the border. He boldly suggests that times have changed; therefore what constitutes proper government action at the border has changed and the law should be modified to take these realities into account. Note, however, that the majority has also changed the statement of what the law is at the border.

Chapter Four

SEARCH AND SEIZURE OF PERSONS:
ARREST AND STOP

The Fourth Amendment prohibits the unreasonable seizure and search of persons, bringing the police processes of arrest and "field interrogation" under constitutional scrutiny.

An arrest occurs when one person deprives another forcibly of his or her freedom of movement. All persons have a legal right to effect a "citizen's arrest" of another person who has committed a crime. However, private citizens and state officers face different consequences for erroneous arrests. A private citizen who arrests another is held strictly accountable for any errors, no matter how reasonable the circumstances of the arrest appear to be.

A State officer is lawfully authorized to make an arrest when she has "probable cause" to believe that a crime has been committed and that it was committed by the suspect. Probable cause is a standard of evidence lower than that needed for the resolution of a civil action (a preponderance of evidence). It exists when a prudent person has reasonable grounds to believe that facts exist that would authorize an arrest (*Beck v. Ohio*, 379 U.S. 89 (1964); *Draper v. United States*, 358 U.S. 307 (1959)). (Probable cause is also the generalized standard that triggers a lawful search and seizure, see Chapter 3 and a "bindover" of a person to stand trial). Police may rely on radio or other secondhand reports of a crime of other law enforcement departments to make an arrest as long as the initial report was based on probable cause (*Whitely v. Warden*, 401 U.S. 560 (1971)).

Where an officer having probable cause mistakenly and in good faith arrests the wrong person (*i.e.*, a mistaken arrest), (a) the officer is not liable for a civil action of wrongful arrest, and (b) any incriminating evidence obtained as a result of the plain view or search incident to arrest doctrines is admissible (*Hill v. California* (1971)). Where an arrest is made without probable cause, any search incident to the arrest violates the Fourth Amendment and the exclusionary rule applies.

On the other hand, a court is not divested of jurisdiction to try a person who has been illegally arrested. Thus, a suspect against whom probable cause exists must stand trial even though officers left their home state, did not use extradition procedures, and may have violated the federal kidnapping statute in arresting the suspect (*Frisbie v. Collins* (1952)). This rule also holds if United States authorities violate international law by having a foreign national arrested in a foreign country (*United States v. Alvarez-Machain* (1992)).

Although the Fourth Amendment on its face requires a judicial warrant to effect an arrest, assuming no exigency situation, the Supreme Court has ruled that no arrest warrant is needed to make an arrest in a public place (*United States v. Watson* (1976)). Because a home is given special protection by the Court, it ruled that an arrest warrant is necessary to effect a lawful arrest of a person in his home where no exigency requires immediate action, even if the police have probable cause to believe that the person has committed a felony (*Payton v. New York* (1980)). Where a person against whom the police have probable cause is arrested in violation of the *Payton* rule, the person is lawfully in police custody but incriminating evidence found in plain view or as a result of a search incident to arrest must be suppressed under the Fourth Amendment exclusionary rule. Likewise, incriminating statements obtained in the house, even after *Miranda* warnings have been given, are inadmissible. But when a suspect arrested in violation of *Payton* is taken to the police station and there given *Miranda* warnings, any statements are admissible as the original illegality of the police has been attenuated (*New York v. Harris* (1990)).

The stereotypical arrest involves police officers physically taking person into custody and handcuffing or otherwise securing the person. An actual touching is not absolutely necessary as long as the person submits to police authority. Arrest can be effected by a variety of physical means, such as shooting a fleeing suspect. In the latter case, the Supreme Court ruled that the common law rule that allows police to use deadly force against fleeing felons who are not believed to have committed a dangerous offense or who are not believed to be dangerous is a violation of the person's Fourth Amendment rights (*Tennessee v. Garner* (1985)). Cases of excessive use of force against police are to be determined under the reasonableness standard of the Fourth Amendment; consequently the motive of the officer is not relevant (*Graham v. Connor*, 490 U.S. 386 (1989)). An arrest may be effected by a roadblock, and the seizure is unreasonable where the police place the roadblock around a blind bend in a road resulting in the suspect fatally crashing into the barrier (*Brower v. County of Inyo*, 489 U.S. 593 (1989)).

An arrested person taken into the custody of a jail or lockup may be subjected to an inventory search of his property for the reasons similar to the automobile inventory cases (Chapter 3): insuring the safety of the prisoner and others, securing the property safely, and avoiding charges of theft against police officers (*Illinois v. Lafayette* (1983)).

The constitutional law of the seizure of persons was fundamentally rearranged by *Terry v. Ohio* (1967), which recognized a less intrusive seizure than arrest, commonly referred to as a "stop and frisk" or "field interrogation." Under *Terry* any forcible stop of a person for questioning is a Fourth Amendment intrusion. It cannot be based on a hunch but must be supported by "reasonable suspicion," a standard of evidence requiring the existence of articulable facts that the person stopped is engaged in or is about to become engaged in criminal activity. Reasonable suspicion may be derived from the totality of the circumstances known to police (*United States v. Cortez*, 449 U.S. 411 (1981)) and may apply to crimes that have already been completed

(*United States v. Hensley*, 469 U.S. 221 (1985)).

The purpose of the brief stop is to question the person so that the officer can confirm or dispel her suspicion. Because police face danger in such encounters, they may pat down the outer clothing of persons stopped under the authority of *Terry* to determine whether the person is armed; such a "frisk" is not for the purpose of securing evidence as is the case in a search incident to arrest. However, other contraband found in "plain view" as a result of such a frisk is admissible (*Minnesota v. Dickerson* (1993), Chapter 2) but where the officer had no reasonable suspicion prior to the "frisk," such evidence is not admissible (*Sibron v. New York* (1967)).

The old practice of "rounding up the usual suspects" against whom articulable suspicion does not exist has been put to an end (*Dunaway v. New York* (1979)). Likewise, the police may not stop drivers at random to check drivers' licenses and vehicle registration unless they have reasonable suspicion or probable cause to believe that the driver committed a driving infraction or a crime (*Delaware v. Prouse* (1979)). The fact that a person was seen in a high crime area does not constitute reasonable suspicion of criminality (*Brown v. Texas*, 443 U.S. 47 (1979)). A statute that required persons walking on a public road, against whom no reasonable suspicion existed, to provide "credible and reliable" evidence of their identification ran afoul the Fourth Amendment (*Kolender v. Lawson* (1983)).

On the other hand, the *Terry* rule has been expanded in later cases. Thus, the basis of reasonable suspicion may be an informer's tip (*Adams v. Williams* (1972)), even an anonymous telephone tip (*Alabama v. White* (1990)). A person may be detained at her home while the police execute a search warrant (*Michigan v. Summers*, (1981)). A stop is a *brief* detention for questioning; if it extends for more than a few moments it "turns into" an arrest that is constitutional only if the police have probable cause to arrest. However, if delay occurs because of evasive action of the suspect the stop may be lawful if the police act diligently and do not delay the process (*United States v. Sharpe*, 470 U.S. 675 (1985) (twenty minutes)). A person questioned briefly by INS agents in a factory has not been seized even though other agents were posted at the exits (*Immigration and Naturalization Service v. Delgado*, 466 U.S. 210 (1984)).

The *Terry* doctrine has supported the constitutionality of airport drug courier profiles (*United States v. Sokolow* (1989)). In airport situations the DEA agents approach suspects and ask them if they will accompany the officers to an office. If the person is not led to believe that she has lost her freedom of movement, the scenario has been treated as a consent search, *e.g.*, where officers politely asked if they could inspect luggage (*United States v. Mendenhall*, 446 U.S. 544 (1980)). However, when agents asked for and retained a person's airline ticket and driver's license, a request to accompany them became a seizure, as the retention of the documents indicated a show of official authority (*Florida v. Royer* (1983)). In *United States v. Place* (1983) the luggage of an air traveller was seized for 90 minutes and transported from LaGuardia to Kennedy airport where a trained dog was present to sniff the baggage for presence of marijuana. The seizure of the luggage exceeded the diligence and time limits of the *Terry* doctrine. A person briefly questioned in the cramped confines of a bus by two law enforcement agents is not seized (*Florida v. Bostick* (1991)).

It is not a seizure for a police cruiser to drive alongside a man who appeared to start running when he saw the police car (*Michigan v. Chesternut*, 486 U.S. 567 (1988)); nor is it a seizure when a police officer runs after a youth with the intention of apprehending the youth (*California v. Hodari D.* (1991)). In both *Chesternut* and *Hodari D.* the suspects "threw down" drugs while the police were following or chasing them; the Court held in both cases that the contraband was abandoned and thus seized in plain view.

UNITED STATES v. WATSON

423 U.S. 411, 96 S.Ct. 820, 46 L.Ed.2d 598 (1976)

MR. JUSTICE WHITE delivered the opinion of the Court.

This case presents questions under the Fourth Amendment as to the legality of a warrantless arrest. * * *

I

[A reliable informant, Khoury, informed postal inspectors that Watson would furnish stolen credit cards. Acting under their instructions, Khoury arranged a meeting with Watson five days later in a restaurant.] Khoury had been instructed that if Watson had additional stolen credit cards, Khoury was to give a designated signal. The signal was given, the officers closed in, and Watson was forthwith arrested. [No stolen credit cards were found on Watson, but some were found in his automobile. The court of appeals ruled that the arrest was a violation of the Fourth Amendment because there was no arrest warrant and no exigency; consequently, evidence obtained from the search of Watson's automobile and seizure of the credit cards had to be excluded as the fruits of an illegal arrest.]

II

* * *

Contrary to the Court of Appeals' view, Watson's arrest was not invalid because executed without a warrant. Title 18 U.S.C. sec. 3061(a)(3) expressly empowers the * * * Postal Service to authorize Postal Service officers and employees "performing duties related to the inspection of postal matters" to

"make arrests without warrant for felonies * * * if they have reasonable grounds to believe that the person to be arrested has committed or is committing such a felony." [a]

* * * Because there was probable cause in this case to believe that Watson had violated [the law], the inspector and his subordinates, in arresting Watson, were acting strictly in accordance with the governing statute and regulations. The effect of the judgment of the Court of Appeals was to invalidate the statute as applied in this case and as applied to all the situations where a court fails to find exigent circumstances justifying a warrantless arrest. We reverse that judgment.

Under the Fourth Amendment, the people are to be "secure in their persons, houses, papers, and effects, against unreasonable searches and seizures,* * * and no Warrants shall issue, but upon probable cause. * * *" Section 3061 represents a judgment by Congress that it is not unreasonable under the Fourth Amendment for postal inspectors to arrest without a warrant provided they have probable cause to do so. This was not an isolated or quixotic judgment of the legislative branch. Other federal law enforcement officers have been expressly authorized by statute for many years to make felony arrests on probable cause but without a warrant. * * *

[b]

* * * [T]here is nothing in the Court's prior cases indicating that under the Fourth Amendment a warrant is required to make a valid arrest for a felony. Indeed, the relevant prior decisions are uniformly to the contrary.

"The usual rule is that a police officer may arrest without warrant one believed by the officer upon reasonable cause to have been guilty of a felony. . . ." * * * Just last Term, while recognizing that maximum protection of individual rights could be assured by requiring a magistrate's review of the factual justification prior to any arrest, we stated that "such a requirement would constitute an intolerable handicap for legitimate law enforcement" and noted that the Court "has never invalidated an arrest supported by probable cause solely because the officers failed to secure a warrant." *Gerstein v. Pugh* [this volume] . * * *

The cases construing the Fourth Amendment thus reflect the ancient common-law rule that a peace officer was permitted to arrest without a warrant for a misdemeanor or felony committed in his presence as well as for a felony not committed in his presence if there was reasonable ground for making the arrest. * * * This has also been the prevailing rule under state constitutions and statutes. * * *

The balance struck by the common law in generally authorizing felony arrests on probable cause, but without a warrant, has survived substantially intact. It appears in almost all of the States in the form of express statutory authorization. * * * [The American Law Institute's *Model Code of Pre-arraignment Procedure* in 1975 adopted] "the traditional and almost universal standard for arrest without a warrant."

* * * Congress has plainly decided against conditioning warrantless arrest power on proof of exigent circumstances. Law enforcement officers may find it wise to seek arrest warrants where practicable to do so, and their judgments about probable cause may be more readily accepted where backed by a warrant issued by a magistrate. * * * But we decline to transform this judicial preference into a constitutional rule when the judgment of the Nation and Congress has for so long been to authorize warrantless public arrests on probable cause rather than to encumber criminal prosecutions with endless litigation with respect to the existence of exigent circumstances, whether it was practicable to get a warrant, whether the suspect was about to flee, and the like. **[c]**

Watson's arrest did not violate the Fourth Amendment, and the Court of Appeals erred in holding to the contrary.

* * *

MR. JUSTICE POWELL, concurring.

* * *

* * * The Government made no effort to show that circumstances precluded the obtaining of a warrant, relying instead for the validity of the arrest solely upon the showing of probable cause to believe that respondent had committed a felony. Respondent contends, and the Court of Appeals held, that the absence of any

exigency justifying the failure to procure a warrant renders this arrest violative of the Fourth Amendment.

* * * [I]t is fair to say, I think, that the prior decisions of the Court have assumed the validity of such arrests without addressing in a reasoned way the analysis advanced by respondent. Today's decision is the first square holding that the Fourth Amendment permits a duly authorized law enforcement officer to make a warrantless arrest in a public place even though he had adequate opportunity to procure a warrant after developing probable cause for arrest. **[d]**

On its face, our decision today creates a certain anomaly. There is no more basic constitutional rule in the Fourth Amendment area than that which makes a warrantless search unreasonable except in a few "jealously and carefully drawn" exceptional circumstances. * * * On more than one occasion this Court has rejected an argument that a law enforcement officer's own probable cause to search a private place for contraband or evidence of crime should excuse his otherwise unexplained failure to procure a warrant beforehand. * * * **[e]**

Since the Fourth Amendment speaks equally to both searches and seizures, and since an arrest, the taking hold of one's person, is quintessentially a seizure, it would seem that the constitutional provision should impose the same limitations upon arrests that it does upon searches. Indeed, as an abstract matter an argument can be made that the restrictions upon arrest perhaps should be greater. A search may cause only annoyance and temporary inconvenience to the law-abiding citizen, assuming more serious dimension only when it turns up evidence of criminality. An arrest, however, is a serious personal intrusion regardless of whether the person seized is guilty or innocent. Although an arrestee cannot be held for a significant period without some neutral determination that there are grounds to do so, * * * no decision that he should go free can come quickly enough to erase the invasion of his privacy that already will have occurred. * * * Logic therefore would seem to dictate that arrests be subject to the warrant requirement at least to the same extent as searches. **[f]**

But logic sometimes must defer to history and **[g]** experience. The Court's opinion emphasizes the historical sanction accorded warrantless felony arrests. In the early days of the common law most felony arrests were made upon personal knowledge and without warrants. * * * By the late 18th century it had been firmly established by Blackstone * * * that magistrates could issue arrest warrants upon information supplied by others. * * * [R]ecognition of the warrant power cast no doubt upon the validity of warrantless felony arrests which continued to be practiced and upheld as before. * * * There is no historical evidence that the Framers or proponents of the Fourth Amendment, outspokenly opposed to the infamous general warrants and writs of assistance, were at all concerned about warrantless arrests by local constables and other peace officers. * * * As the Court today notes, the Second Congress' passage of an Act authorizing such arrests so soon after the adoption of the Fourth Amendment itself underscores the probability that the constitutional provision was intended to restrict entirely different practices.

The historical momentum for acceptance of warrantless arrests, already strong at the adoption of the Fourth Amendment, has gained strength during the ensuing two centuries. Both the judiciary and the legislative bodies of this Nation repeatedly have placed their imprimaturs upon the practice and, as the Government emphasizes, law enforcement agencies have developed their investigative and arrest procedures upon an assumption that warrantless arrests were valid so long as based upon probable cause. * * * Of course, no practice that is inconsistent with constitutional protections can be saved merely by appeal to previous uncritical acceptance. But the warrantless felony arrest, long preferred at common law and unimpeached at the passage of the Fourth Amendment, is not such a practice. Given the revolutionary implications of such a holding, a declaration at this late date that warrantless felony arrests are constitutionally infirm would have to rest upon reasons more substantial than a desire to harmonize the rules for arrest with those governing searches. * * * [h]

Moreover, a constitutional rule permitting felony arrests only with a warrant or in exigent circumstances could severely hamper effective law enforcement. Good police practice often requires postponing an arrest, even after probable cause has been established, in order to place the suspect under surveillance or otherwise develop further evidence necessary to prove guilt to a jury. [Requiring] * * * such additional investigative work could imperil the entire prosecution. Should the officers fail to obtain a warrant initially, and later be required by unforeseen circumstances to arrest immediately with no chance to procure a last minute warrant, they would risk a court decision that the subsequent exigency did not excuse their failure to get a warrant in the interim since they first developed probable cause. If the officers attempted to meet such a contingency by procuring a warrant as soon as they had probable cause and then merely held it during their subsequent investigation, they would risk a court decision that the warrant had grown stale by the time it was used. Law enforcement personnel caught in this squeeze could ensure validity of their arrests only by obtaining a warrant and arresting as soon as probable cause existed, thereby foreclosing the possibility of gathering vital additional evidence from the suspect's continued actions.

In sum, the historical and policy reasons sketched above fully justify the Court's sustaining of a warrantless arrest upon probable cause, despite the resulting divergence between the constitutional rule governing searches and that now held applicable to seizures of the person. * * *

* * *

MR. JUSTICE MARSHALL, with whom MR. JUSTICE BRENNAN joins, dissenting.

By granting police broad powers to make warrantless arrests, the Court today sharply reverses the course of our modern decisions construing the Warrant Clause of the Fourth Amendment. [i] * * * I respectfully dissent.

* * *

* * * The Court reaches its conclusion that a warrant is not necessary for a police officer to make

an arrest in a public place, so long as he has probable cause to believe a felony has been committed, on the basis of its views of precedent and history.   As my Brother POWELL correctly observes, the precedent is spurious.   None of the cases cited by the Court squarely confronted the issue decided today.   Moreover, an examination of the history relied on by the Court shows that it does not support the conclusion laid upon it. * * *
* * *

There is no doubt that by the reference to the seizure of persons, the Fourth Amendment was intended to apply to arrests. * * *

The Court next turns to history. It relies on the English common-law rule of arrest and the many state and federal statutes following it. There are two serious flaws in this approach. First, as a matter of factual analysis, the substance of the ancient common-law rule provides no support for the far-reaching modern rule that the Court fashions on its model. Second, as a matter of doctrine, the longstanding existence of a Government practice does not immunize the practice from scrutiny under the mandate of our Constitution.

The common-law rule was indeed as the Court states it. * * * To apply the rule blindly today, however, makes [little] sense * * * without understanding the meaning of * * * words in the context of their age. For the fact is that a felony at common law and a felony today bear only slight resemblance, with the result that the relevance of the common-law rule of arrest to the modern interpretation of our Constitution is minimal.

* * *   Only the most serious crimes were felonies at common law,

and many crimes now classified as felonies under federal or state law were treated as misdemeanors. * * *

* * * To make an arrest for any of these crimes [misdemeanors] at common law, the police officer was required to obtain a warrant, unless the crime was committed in his presence. Since many of these same crimes are commonly classified as felonies today, however, under the Court's holding a warrant is no longer needed to make such arrests, a result in contravention of the common law.

Thus the lesson of the common law, and those courts in this country that have accepted its rule, is an ambiguous one. Applied in its original context, the common-law rule would allow the warrantless arrest of some, but not all, of those we call felons today.   Accordingly, the Court is simply historically wrong when it tells us that "[t]he balance struck by the common law in generally authorizing felony arrests on probable cause, but without a warrant, has survived substantially intact." As a matter of substance, the balance struck by the common law in accommodating the public need for the most certain and immediate arrest of criminal suspects with the requirement of magisterial oversight to protect against mistaken insults to privacy decreed that only in the most serious of cases could the warrant be dispensed with.   This balance is not recognized when the common-law rule is unthinkingly transposed to our present classifications of criminal offenses. Indeed, the only clear lesson of history is contrary to the one the Court draws: the common law considered the arrest warrant far more important than today's decision leaves it. [j]

* * * [T]he Court's unblinking literalism cannot replace analysis of the constitutional interests involved. While we can learn from the common law, the ancient rule does not provide a simple answer directly transferable to our system. Thus, in considering the applicability of the common-law rule to our present constitutional scheme, we must consider *both* of the rule's two opposing constructs: the presumption favoring warrants, as well as the exception allowing immediate arrests of the most dangerous criminals. The Court's failure to do so, indeed its failure to recognize any tension in the common-law rule at all, drains all validity from its historical analysis.

Lastly, the Court relies on the numerous state and federal statutes codifying the common-law rule. * * * The Court's error on this score is far more dangerous than its misreading of history, for it is well settled that the mere existence of statutes or practice, even of long standing, is no defense to an unconstitutional practice. "[N]o one acquires a vested or protected right in violation of the Constitution by long

use, even when that span of time covers our entire national existence and indeed predates it." * * * Our function in constitutional cases is weightier than the Court today suggests: where reasoned analysis shows a practice to be constitutionally deficient, our obligation is to the Constitution, not the Congress. **[k]**

In sum, the Court's opinion is without foundation. * * * It simply announces, by *ipse dixit*, a rule squarely rejecting the warrant requirement we have favored for so long.

[JUSTICE MARSHALL next undertook an analysis of the Fourth Amendment interests involved in arrests and concluded that (1) the privacy rights of citizens would be better protected by the requirement that an arrest warrant be obtained where feasible in that it would make it more likely that the arrest would be based upon probable cause and (2) the legitimate rights of law enforcement would not be unduly burdened since warrants would not be required where an exigency demanded an immediate arrest.]

* * * * * * * * * * *

COMMENTS

[a] This, of course, cannot be the end of the inquiry. Because the Court of Appeals invalidated the statute on the basis of its reading of the Constitution, the Supreme Court must confront the constitutional issue.

[b] Although the existence of a widespread practice is always of some relevance in deciding constitutional issues, it is not commanding. The very concept of law, in the Western tradition, embodies the understanding that in a conflict between an absolute standard of right and common practice, the common practice must give way.

[c] The majority position, resting on an overwhelmingly common practice, rather than on a strict reading of the Constitution, will not be unpopular but is not as strong an opinion as it could be. Why doesn't the majority rely on the "reasonableness" interpretation of the Fourth Amendment? Reexamine JUSTICE WHITE's opinion after reading JUSTICE POWELL's concurrence. Which explanation do you prefer?

[d] It is interesting to note that a practice could exist for centuries before becoming the subject of a constitutional challenge. This may have as much to do with the acceptance of the legal status quo in the past as with the high level of litigation today.

[e] Admitting and confronting an anomaly in the law tends to make for a more "honest" opinion. Do you think this is the case as to JUSTICE POWELL's concurrence?

[f] JUSTICE POWELL gets to the heart of the dilemma posed by this case. Having posed the issue in this way, isn't the outcome (that when no exigency exists, an officer must get a search warrant) inevitable?

[g] This escape hatch seems to work nicely in this case, but isn't it a dangerous general rule of constitutional interpretation? If used broadly, such a rule would support all kinds of entrenched practices that cannot withstand constitutional scrutiny. While JUSTICE POWELL's point is not entirely illegitimate, knowing when to use such a "rule" is the essence of "constitutional statesmanship."

[h] JUSTICE POWELL goes on to strengthen his "experience" rationale by noting that logical consistency alone may not be the highest desideratum; furthermore, in general terms he gives several good reasons why the no-warrant-with-probable-cause rule makes sense. The essence of a constitutional holding is not that five justices can be mustered for a vote but that the opinion is based on sound reasoning. The reasoning may be subject to dispute, but the justices are bound by their oaths and the traditions of the Court to search for the best reasons that they can produce.

[i] While the majority and concurring opinions have appealed to a long tradition of practice in regard to arrest, JUSTICE MARSHALL appeals to an equally potent practice, the modern movement of broadening the civil liberties of individuals. With a short phrase, JUSTICE MARSHALL appeals to the present and the future, in contrast with the majority's appeal to the past.

[j] JUSTICE MARSHALL's more searching historical analysis is not spurious. While it did not persuade a majority of his colleagues, its thoroughness lays the foundation for a future rehearing of this issue. It is a good example of not accepting a simple explanation of the past as a complete "history." The use of history by the majority and the dissenters is also a vivid example of the fact that the use of history by lawyers and judges in cases is goal oriented, that is, used in order to win a case or explain an opinion. While this does not negate the value of historical examples in legal argument, it does mean that the reader must be aware of this tendentious use of

"legal history."

[k] The majority and the dissent are ultimately separated by a disagreement over constitutional policy. Do you think that the Fourth Amendment should add a layer of inconvenience and judicial review to the arrest decision in order to enhance the rights of citizens? Should the large number of arrests or the possibility that magistrates will rubber-stamp arrest warrants play any part in your judgment? Where justices agree on the plain meaning of a constitutional command, should they obey it at virtually any cost?

PAYTON v. NEW YORK

445 U.S. 573, 100 S.Ct. 1371, 63 L.Ed.2d 639 (1980)

MR. JUSTICE STEVENS delivered the opinion of the Court.

These appeals challenge the constitutionality of New York statutes that authorize police officers to enter a private residence without a warrant and with force, if necessary, to make a routine felony arrest.

* * * In *United States v. Watson*,[this volume] we upheld a warrantless "midday public arrest," expressly noting that the case did not pose "the still unsettled question * * * 'whether and under what circumstances an officer may enter a suspect's home to make a warrantless arrest.'" * * * **[a]** [The highest courts of Florida and New York have upheld warrantless entry into the home to arrest.] The courts of last resort in 10 other States, however, have held that unless special circumstances are present, warrantless arrests in the home are unconstitutional. Of the seven United States Courts of Appeals that have considered the question, five have expressed the opinion that such arrests are unconstitutional.

* * * We now * * * hold that the Fourth Amendment to the United States Constitution, made applicable to the States by the Fourteenth Amendment, * * * prohibits the police from making a warrantless and nonconsensual entry into a suspect's home in order to make a routine felony arrest.

* * *

I

* * * [Police established probable cause that Payton committed a murder during a robbery.] At about 7:30 A.M. [the next day] six officers went to Payton's apartment in the Bronx, intending to arrest him. They had not obtained a warrant. Although light and music emanated from the apartment, there was no response to their knock on the metal door. They summoned emergency assistance and, about 30 minutes later, used crowbars to break open the door and enter the apartment. No one was there. In plain view, however, was a .30-caliber shell casing that was seized and later admitted into evidence at Payton's murder trial.

[The admissibility of the evidence depended upon the constitutionality of the warrantless entry; if unconstitutional, the police had no right to be present and the shell casing would not have been in plain view. The Supreme Court noted that this case did not involve the issues of an entry based upon an exigency or the warrantless entry of a third party's home.]

II

* * * [T]he evil the [Fourth] Amendment was designed to prevent was broader than the abuse of a general warrant. Unreasonable searches or seizures conducted without any warrant at all are condemned by the plain language of the first clause of the Amendment. * * *

The simple language of the Amendment applies equally to seizures of persons and to seizures of property. * * * As the Court reiterated just a few years ago, the "physical entry of the home is the chief evil against which the wording of the Fourth Amendment is directed." * * * And we have long adhered to the view that the warrant procedure minimizes the danger of needless intrusions of that sort.

It is a "basic principle of Fourth Amendment law" that searches and seizures inside a home without a warrant are presumptively unreasonable. Yet it is also well settled that objects such as weapons or contraband found in a public place may be seized by the police without a warrant. The seizure of property in plain view involves no invasion of privacy and is presumptively reasonable, assuming that there is probable cause to associate the property with criminal activity. * * *

* * * [T]his distinction has equal force when the seizure of a person is involved. * * * [A]rrests in public places are valid. * * * [H]owever, * * *

"[a] greater burden is placed * * * on officials who enter a home or dwelling without consent. Freedom from intrusion into the home or dwelling is the archetype of the privacy protection secured by the Fourth Amendment." * * *

* * * [A]bsent exigent circumstances, a warrantless entry to search for weapons or contraband is unconstitutional even when a felony has been committed and there is probable cause to believe that incriminating evidence will be found within. * * * [T]he constitutional protection afforded to the individual's interest in the privacy of his own home is equally applicable to a warrantless entry for the purpose of arresting a resident of the house; for it is inherent in such an entry that a search for the suspect may be required before he can be apprehended. * * * [A]n entry to arrest and an entry to search for and to seize property implicate the same interest in preserving the privacy and the sanctity of the home, and justify the same level of constitutional protection.

* * *

The majority of the New York Court of Appeals, however, suggested that there is a substantial difference in the relative intrusiveness of an entry to search for property and an entry to search for a person. * * * It is true that the area that may legally be searched is broader when executing a search warrant than when executing an arrest warrant in the home. * * * This difference may be more theoretical than real, however, because the police may need to check the entire premises for safety reasons, and sometimes they ignore the restrictions on searches incident to arrest. [b]

But the critical point is that any differences in the intrusiveness of entries to search and entries to arrest are merely ones of degree rather than kind. The two intrusions share this fundamental characteristic: the breach of the entrance to an individual's home. The Fourth Amendment protects the individual's privacy in a variety of settings. In none is the zone of privacy more clearly defined than when bounded by the unambiguous physical dimensions of an individual's home—a zone that finds its roots in clear and specific constitutional terms: "The right of the people to be secure in their * * * houses * * * shall not be violated." That language unequivocally establishes the proposition that "[a]t the very core [of the Fourth Amendment] stands the right of a man to retreat into his own home and there be free from unreasonable governmental intrusion." * * *   In terms that apply equally to seizures of property and to seizures of persons, the Fourth Amendment has drawn a firm line at the entrance to the house.   Absent exigent circumstances, that threshold may not reasonably be crossed without a warrant. [c]

III

* * * New York argues that the reasons that support the *Watson* holding require a similar result here. In *Watson* the Court relied on (a) the well-settled common-law rule that a warrantless arrest in a public place is valid if the arresting officer had probable cause to believe the suspect is a felon; (b) the clear consensus among the States adhering to that well-settled common-law rule; and (c) the expression of the judgment of Congress that such an arrest is "reasonable."   We consider each of these reasons as it applies to a warrantless entry into a home for the purpose of making a routine felony arrest.

* * *

A

* * * [T]he common-law rule on warrantless home arrests was not as clear as the rule on arrests in public places.   Indeed, * * * the weight of authority as it appeared to the Framers was to the effect that a warrant was required, or at the minimum that there were substantial risks in proceeding without one. The common-law sources display a sensitivity to privacy interests that could not have been lost on the Framers. The zealous and frequent repetition of the adage that a "man's

house is his castle," made it abundantly clear that both in England and in the Colonies "the freedom of one's house" was one of the most vital elements of English liberty.

Thus, * * * the relevant common law does not provide the same guidance that was present in *Watson*. * * *

B

A majority of the States that have taken a position on the question permit warrantless entry into the home to arrest even in the absence of exigent circumstances. At this time, 24 States permit such warrantless entries; 15 States clearly prohibit them, though 3 States do so on federal constitutional ground alone; and 11 States have apparently taken no position on the question.

But these current figures reflect a significant decline during the last decade in the number of States permitting warrantless entries for arrest. * * * Virtually all of the state courts that have had to confront the constitutional issue directly have held warrantless entries into the home to arrest to be invalid in the absence of exigent circumstances. * * * Apparently, only the Supreme Court of Florida and the New York Court of Appeals in this case have expressly upheld warrantless entries to arrest in the face of a constitutional challenge. [d]

A long-standing, widespread practice is not immune from constitutional scrutiny.   But neither is it to be lightly brushed aside.   This is particularly so when the constitutional standard is as amorphous as the word "reasonable," and when custom and contemporary norms necessarily play such a large role in the constitutional analysis. In this case, although the weight of state-law authority is clear, there is by no means the kind of virtual unanimity on this question that was present in *United States v. Watson*, with regard to warrantless arrests in public places. * * *

C

No congressional determination that warrantless entries into the home are "reasonable" has been called to our attention. None of the federal statutes cited in the *Watson* opinion reflects any such legislative judgment. Thus, that support for the Watson holding finds no counterpart in this case. * * *

MR. JUSTICE POWELL, concurring in *United States v. Watson*, * * * stated:

> "But logic sometimes must defer to history and experience. The Court's opinion emphasizes the historical sanction accorded warrantless felony arrests [in public places]."

In this case, however, neither history nor this Nation's experience requires us to disregard to the overriding respect for the sanctity of the home that has been embedded in our traditions since the origins of the Republic.

IV

The parties have argued at some length about the practical consequences of a warrant requirement as a precondition to a felony arrest in the home. In the absence of any evidence that effective law enforcement has suffered in those States that already have such a requirement, * * * we are inclined

to view such arguments with skepticism. More fundamentally, however, such arguments of policy must give way to a constitutional command that we consider to be unequivocal.

* * * Thus, for Fourth Amendment purposes, an arrest warrant founded on probable cause implicitly carries with it the limited authority to enter a dwelling in which the suspect lives when there is reason to believe the suspect is within. * * *

MR. JUSTICE WHITE, with whom THE CHIEF JUSTICE and MR. JUSTICE REHNQUIST join, dissenting.

[JUSTICE WHITE concluded that the majority misread history: that in cases of felony the king's authority to enter a home overrode privacy interests and that this royal authority extended to constables.] * * *

[The background, text, and legislative history of the Fourth Amendment demonstrate that the purpose was to restrict the abuses that had developed with respect to warrants; the Amendment preserved common-law rules of arrest. Because it was not considered generally unreasonable at common law for officers to break doors to effect a warrantless felony arrest, the Fourth Amendment was not intended to outlaw the types of police conduct at issue in the present cases.]

[States did not consider the issue of warrantless entry to arrest until late in the 19th century; most have adopted a rule in favor of warrantless entry.]* * *

[Federal statutes authorize] federal agents to make warrantless arrests anywhere, including the home, [that is, federal statutes do not make any exceptions for entries into the home.]

Today's decision rests, in large measure, on the premise that warrantless arrest entries constitute a particularly severe invasion of personal privacy. I do not dispute that the home is generally a very private area or that the common law displayed a special "reverence * * * for the individual's right of privacy in his house." * * * However, the Fourth Amendment is concerned with protecting people, not places, and no talismanic significance is given to the fact that an arrest occurs in the home rather than elsewhere. * * * [e] It is necessary in each case to assess realistically the actual extent of invasion of constitutionally protected privacy. * * * [A]ll arrests involve serious intrusions into an individual's privacy and dignity. Yet we settled in *Watson* that the intrusiveness of a public arrest is not enough to mandate the obtaining of a warrant. The inquiry in the present case, therefore, is whether the incremental intrusiveness that results from an arrest's being *made in the dwelling* is enough to support an inflexible constitutional rule requiring warrants for such arrests whenever exigent circumstances are not present.

Today's decision ignores the carefully crafted restrictions on the common-law power of arrest entry and thereby overestimates the dangers inherent in that practice. At common law, absent exigent circumstances, entries to arrest could be made only for felony. Even in cases of felony, the officers were required to announce their presence, demand admission, and be refused entry before they were entitled to break doors. Further, it seems generally accepted that entries could be made only during daylight

hours. And, in my view, the officer entering to arrest must have reasonable grounds to believe, not only that the arrestee has committed a crime, but also that the person suspected is present in the house at the time of the entry. [f]

These four restrictions on home arrests—felony, knock and announce, daytime, and stringent probable cause—constitute powerful and complementary protections for the privacy interests associated with the home. The felony requirement guards against abusive or arbitrary enforcement and ensures that invasions of the home occur only in case of the most serious crimes. The knock-and-announce and daytime requirements protect individuals against the fear, humiliation, and embarrassment of being aroused from their beds in states of partial or complete undress. And these requirements allow the arrestee to surrender at his front door, thereby maintaining his dignity and preventing the officers from entering other rooms of the dwelling. The stringent probable-cause requirement would help ensure against the possibility that the police would enter when the suspect was not home, and, in searching for him, frighten members of the family or ransack parts of the house, seizing items in plain view. In short, these requirements, taken together, permit an individual suspected of a serious crime to surrender at the front door of his dwelling and thereby avoid most of the humiliation and indignity that the Court seems to believe necessarily accompany a house arrest entry. Such a front-door arrest, in my view, is no more intrusive on personal privacy than the public warrant-less arrests which we found to pass constitutional muster in *Watson*. *

* * [g]

All of these limitations on warrant-less arrest entries are satisfied on the facts of the present cases. * * * Today's decision, therefore, sweeps away any possibility that warrantless home entries might be permitted in some limited situations other than those in which exigent circumstances are present. The Court substitutes, in one sweeping decision, a rigid constitutional rule in place of the common-law approach, evolved over hundreds of years, which achieved a flexible accommodation between the demands of personal privacy and the legitimate needs of law enforcement.

* * *

* * * * * * * * * * *

COMMENTS

[a] The Court often "reserves" an issue to decide a case on the narrowest available issue. This avoids overly general holdings, for a good ruling on a specific issue—carefully studied by the Court—may not provide a good ruling when applied to related issues. Several justices felt that this was the right case to take, to distinguish between an arrest in public and an arrest in one's home.

[b] The Court took up this point in *Maryland v. Buie* [this volume].

[c] This "zone of privacy" standard is in tension with the principle of *Katz v. United States*, [this volume], that the Fourth Amendment protects persons, not places. In view of the *Watson* and *Payton* holdings, it is necessary to say that the *Katz* doctrine has been qualified. In the development of constitutional case law, doctrines often change because of inconsistent decisions of cases over time. Another case that modifies the *Katz* approach is *Rakas v. Illinois* [this volume].

[d] This counting of the rules developed by the states is reminiscent of the tally of States that had adopted the exclusionary rule in the *Wolf* and *Mapp* cases [this volume]. It is an indication that State supreme courts still have a vigorous role to play in the shaping of American constitutional law.

[e] The reliance on the *Katz* doctrine could just as well have been used in *Watson* to require an arrest warrant in nonexigency public arrests.

[f] This ingenuous argument is based on four common law protections. It attempts to connect history to the desired policy result of the dissenting justices, that is, to not burden law enforcement with requirements that appear unnecessary to the dissenters.

[g] JUSTICE WHITE may be presenting an idealized and sanitized version of actual arrest practice, especially when police are making an arrest of a "dope pad" or of someone believed to be armed and dangerous.

NEW YORK v. HARRIS

495 U.S. 14, 110 S.Ct. 1640, 109 L.Ed.2d 13 (1990)

JUSTICE WHITE delivered the opinion of the Court.

[New York police officers, having probable cause to believe Bernard Harris murdered Thelma Staton, went to his apartment and took him into custody, without an arrest warrant and with a display of guns and badges. Proper *Miranda* [this volume] warnings were administered. Harris reportedly admitted that he killed Ms. Staton. He was arrested and taken to the police station where he was again read his *Miranda* warnings and signed a written inculpatory statement. The warnings were administered a third time and Harris was videotaped making incriminating statements to a prosecutor although Harris said he wanted to terminate the interview.]

[The first and third statements were suppressed by the New York Courts; the second written statement made at the police station was admitted into evidence.] The sole issue in this case is whether Harris's second statement * * * should have been suppressed because the police, by entering Harris' home without a warrant and without his consent, violated *Payton v. New York*, [this volume] which held that the Fourth Amendment prohibits the police from effecting a warrantless and nonconsensual entry into a suspect's home in order to make a routine felony arrest. * * * [The intermediate appellate court upheld the conviction].

A divided New York Court of Appeals reversed, * * * [finding that Harris did not consent to the police entry and that the warrantless arrest] violated *Payton* even though there was probable cause. Applying *Brown v. Illinois*, 422 U.S. 590 (1975), and its progeny, the court then determined that the station house statement must be deemed to be the inadmissible fruit of the illegal arrest because the connection between the statement and the arrest was not sufficiently attenuated. * * *

For present purposes, we accept the finding below that Harris did not consent to the police officers' entry into his home and the conclusion that the police had probable cause to arrest him. It is also evident, in light of *Payton*, that arresting Harris in his home without an arrest warrant violated the Fourth Amendment. But, as emphasized in earlier cases, "we have declined to adopt a '*per se* or "but for" rule' that would make inadmissible any evidence, whether tangible or live-witness testimony, which somehow came to light through a chain of causation that began with an illegal arrest." * * * Rather, in this context, we have stated that "[t]he penalties visited upon the Government, and in turn upon the public, because its officers have violated the law must bear some relation to the purposes which the law is to serve." * * * In light of these principles, we decline to apply the exclusionary rule in this context because the rule in *Payton* was designed to protect the physical integrity of the home; it was not intended to grant criminal suspects, like Harris, protection for statements made outside their premises where the police have probable cause to arrest the suspect for committing a crime.

Payton itself emphasized that our holding in that case stemmed from the "overriding respect for the sanctity of the home that has been embedded in our traditions since the origins of the Republic." * * * Although it had long been settled that a warrantless arrest in a public place was permissible as long as the arresting officer had probable cause, * * * *Payton* nevertheless drew a line at the entrance to the home. This special solicitude was necessary because "'physical entry of the home is the chief evil against which the wording of the Fourth Amendment is directed.'" * * * The arrest warrant was required to "interpose the magistrate's determination of probable cause" to arrest before the officers could enter a house to effect an arrest. * * *

Nothing in the reasoning of that case suggests that an arrest in a home without a warrant but with probable cause somehow renders unlawful continued custody of the suspect once he is removed from the house. There could be no valid claim here that Harris was immune from prosecution because his person was the fruit of an illegal arrest. * * * Nor is there any claim that the warrantless arrest required the police to release Harris or that Harris could not be immediately rearrested if momentarily released. Because the officers had probable cause to arrest Harris for a crime, Harris was not unlawfully in custody when he was removed to the station house, given *Miranda* warnings, and allowed to talk. For Fourth Amendment purposes, the legal issue is the same as it would be had the police arrested Harris on his doorstep, illegally entered his home to search for evidence, and later interrogated Harris at the station house. [a] Similarly, if the police had made a warrantless entry into Harris' home, not found him there, but arrested him on the street when he returned, a later statement made by him after proper warnings would no doubt be admissible.

This case is therefore different from *Brown v. Illinois*, * * * *Dunaway v. New York*, [this volume], and *Taylor v. Alabama*, 457 U.S. 687 (1982). In each of those cases, evidence obtained from a criminal defendant following arrest was suppressed because the police lacked probable cause. The three cases stand for the familiar proposition that the indirect fruits of an illegal search or arrest should be suppressed when they bear a sufficiently close relationship to the underlying illegality. * * * We have emphasized, however, that attenuation analysis is only appropriate where, as a threshold matter, courts determine that "the challenged evidence is in some sense the product of illegal governmental activity." * * * [b] [JUSTICE WHITE asserted that in cases such as *Brown v. Illinois* the illegality is the lack of probable cause.]

Harris' statement taken at the police station was not the product of being in unlawful custody. * * *
     * * *

* * * [S]uppressing the statement taken outside the house would not serve the purpose of the rule that made Harris's in-house arrest illegal. The warrant requirement for an arrest in the home is imposed to protect the home, and anything incriminating the police gathered from arresting Harris in his home, rather than elsewhere, has been excluded, as it should have been; the purpose of the rule has thereby

been vindicated. We are not required by the Constitution to go further and suppress statements later made by Harris in order to deter police from violating *Payton*. "As cases considering the use of unlawfully obtained evidence in criminal trials themselves make clear, it does not follow from the emphasis on the exclusionary rule's deterrent value that 'anything which deters illegal searches is thereby commanded by the Fourth Amendment.'" * * * Even though we decline to suppress statements made outside the home following a *Payton* violation, the principal incentive to obey *Payton* still obtains: the police know that a warrantless entry will lead to the suppression of any evidence found, or statements taken, inside the home. If we did suppress statements like Harris', moreover, the incremental deterrent value would be minimal. Given that the police have probable cause to arrest a suspect in Harris' position, they need not violate *Payton* in order to interrogate the suspect. It is doubtful therefore that the desire to secure a statement from a criminal suspect would motivate the police to violate *Payton*. As a result, suppressing a station-house statement obtained after a *Payton* violation will have little effect on the officers' actions, one way or another.

We hold that, where the police have probable cause to arrest a suspect, the exclusionary rule does not bar the State's use of a statement made by the defendant outside of his home, even though the statement is taken after an arrest made in the home in violation of *Payton*. * * *

JUSTICE MARSHALL, with whom JUSTICE BRENNAN, JUS-

TICE BLACKMUN, and JUSTICE STEVENS join, dissenting.
 * * *

I

* * * A police officer who violates the Constitution usually does so to obtain evidence that he could not secure lawfully. The best way to deter him is to provide that any evidence so obtained will not be admitted at trial. Deterrence of constitutional violations thus requires the suppression not only of evidence seized during an unconstitutional search, but also of "derivative evidence, both tangible and testimonial, that is the product of the primary evidence, or that is otherwise acquired as an indirect result of the unlawful search." * * * Not all evidence connected to a constitutional violation is suppressible, however. Rather, the Court has asked "whether, granting establishment of the primary illegality, the evidence to which instant objection is made has been come at by exploitation of that illegality or instead by means sufficiently distinguishable to be purged of the primary taint.'" * * *

Because deterrence is a principal purpose of the exclusionary rule, our attenuation analysis must be driven by an understanding of how extensive exclusion must be to deter violations of the Fourth Amendment. We have long held that where police have obtained a statement after violating the Fourth Amendment, the interest in deterrence does not disappear simply because the statement was voluntary, as required by the Fifth Amendment. * * * [c]

[JUSTICE MARSHALL noted that for the Fourth Amendment attenuation to have any effect, the statement must be voluntary under the Fifth Amendment.] * * * An inquiry into whether a suspect's statement is properly treated as attributable to a Fourth Amendment violation or to the suspect's independent act of will has an irreducibly psychological aspect, and irrebuttable presumptions are peculiarly unhelpful in such a context. Accordingly, we have identified several factors as relevant to the issue of attenuation: the length of time between the arrest and the statement, the presence of intervening circumstances, and the "purpose and flagrancy" of the violation. * * *

We have identified the last factor as "particularly" important. * * * When a police officer intentionally violates what he knows to be a constitutional command, exclusion is essential to conform police behavior to the law. Such a "flagrant" violation is in marked contrast to a violation that is the product of a good-faith misunderstanding of the relevant constitutional requirements. * * * [T]he concern that officers who act in good faith will be overdeterred is nonexistent when, based on a cynical calculus of the likely results of a suppression hearing, an officer intentionally decides to violate what he knows to be a constitutional command.

An application of the *Brown* factors to this case compels the conclusion that Harris' statement at the station house must be suppressed. About an hour elapsed between the illegal arrest and Harris' confession, without any intervening factor other than the warnings required by *Miranda*. * * * This Court has held, however, that "*Miranda* warnings, *alone* and *per se*, * * * cannot assure in every case that the Fourth Amendment violation has

not been unduly exploited." * * * Indeed, in *Brown*, we held that a statement made almost *two* hours after an illegal arrest, and after *Miranda* warnings had been given, was not sufficiently removed from the violation so as to dissipate the taint. * * *

* * *

II

* * * [T]he Court finds suppression unwarranted on the authority of its newly-fashioned per se rule. In the majority's view, when police officers make a warrantless home arrest in violation of *Payton*, their physical exit from the suspect's home *necessarily* breaks the causal chain between the illegality and any subsequent statement by the suspect, such that the statement is admissible regardless of the *Brown* factors.

The Court purports to defend its new rule on the basis of the self-evident proposition that the Fourth Amendment does not necessarily require the police to release or to forgo the prosecution of a suspect arrested in violation of *Payton*. * * * To the Court, it follows as a matter of course from this proposition that a *Payton* violation cannot in any way be the "cause" of a statement obtained from the suspect after he has been forced from his home and is being lawfully detained. Because an attenuation inquiry presupposes some connection between the illegality and the statement, the Court concludes that no such inquiry is necessary here. * * * Neither logic nor precedent supports that conclusion.

A

Certainly, the police were not required to release Harris or forgo his prosecution simply because officers arrested him in violation of *Payton*. But it is a dramatic leap from that unexceptional proposition to the suggestion that the *Payton* violation thus had no effect once the police took Harris from his home. * * *

* * * A person who is forcibly separated from his family and home in the dark of night after uniformed officers have broken down his door, handcuffed him, and forced him at gunpoint to accompany them to a police station does not suddenly breathe a sigh of relief at the moment he is dragged across his doorstep.

Rather, the suspect is likely to be so frightened and rattled that he will say something incriminating. These effects, of course, extend far beyond the moment the physical occupation of the home ends. The entire focus of the *Brown* factors is to fix the point at which those effects are sufficiently dissipated that deterrence is not meaningfully advanced by suppression. The majority's assertion, as though the proposition were axiomatic, that the effects of such an intrusion *must* end when the violation ends is both undefended and indefensible. The Court's saying it may make it law, but it does not make it true.

* * *

* * * * * * * * * *

COMMENTS

[a] The reasoning at this point appears to turn *Payton* into more of a "search and seizure case" than an "arrest case." That is, it seems to follow logically that the police can violate *Payton* with impunity as long as they only wish to arrest the suspect and not to seize anything in the house. Was that the way you read *Payton*? If not, does such a reading now make sense?

[b] What do the words "product of" mean to you? Compare JUSTICE WHITE'S interpretation of these words to that of JUSTICE MARSHALL.

[c] The stress on the deterrence rationale of the exclusionary rule and its attenuation exceptions by JUSTICE MARSHALL clearly marks the policy vision of the majority and the dissent. In contrast the majority coolly maintains that maximum deterrence of police illegality is not required by its rules. What positive value drives the majority position?

TENNESSEE v. GARNER

471 U.S. 1, 105 S.Ct. 1694, 85 L.Ed.2d 1 (1985)

JUSTICE WHITE delivered the opinion of the Court.

This case requires us to determine the constitutionality of the use of deadly force to prevent the escape of an apparently unarmed suspected felon. We conclude that such force may not be used unless it is necessary to prevent the escape and the officer has probable cause to believe that the suspect poses a significant threat of death or serious physical injury to the officer or others.

I

[Officers were dispatched to answer a "prowler" call; Officer Hymon went to the rear of the house and saw] Edward Garner, stopped at a 6-feet-high chain link fence at the edge of the yard. With the aid of a flashlight, Hymon was able to see Garner's face and hands. He saw no sign of a weapon, and, though not certain, was "reasonably sure" and "figured" that Garner was unarmed. * * * He thought Garner was 17 or 18 years old and about 5'5" or 5'7" tall. While Garner was crouched at the base of the fence, Hymon called out "police, halt" and took a few steps toward him. Garner then began to climb over the fence. Convinced that if Garner made it over the fence he would elude capture, Hymon shot him. The bullet hit Garner in the back of the head. Garner was taken by ambulance to a hospital, where he died on the operating table. Ten dollars and a purse

taken from the house were found on his body.

In using deadly force to prevent the escape, Hymon was acting under the authority of a Tennessee statute and pursuant to Police Department policy. The statute provides that "[i]f, after notice of the intention to arrest the defendant, he either flee or forcibly resist, the officer may use all the necessary means to effect the arrest." * * * The Department policy was slightly more restrictive than the statute, but still allowed the use of deadly force in cases of burglary. * * * [a] The incident was reviewed by the Memphis Police Firearm's Review Board and presented to a grand jury. Neither took any action. * * *

Garner's father then brought [a federal tort action] seeking damages under 42 U. S. C. § 1983 for asserted violations of Garner's constitutional rights. The complaint alleged that the shooting violated the Fourth, Fifth, Sixth, Eighth, and Fourteenth Amendments of the United States Constitution. [At the close of trial the court ruled that] Hymon's actions were authorized by the Tennessee statute, which in turn was constitutional. * * *

[After several appellate action, appeal was taken to the Supreme Court by the State of Tennessee, which had intervened to defend the statute.]

II

Whenever an officer restrains the freedom of a person to walk away, he has seized that person. *United States v. Brignoni-Ponce*, 422 U.S. 873, 878

(1975). While it is not always clear just when minimal police interference becomes a seizure, * * * there can be no question that apprehension by the use of deadly force is a seizure subject to the reasonableness requirement of the Fourth Amendment. **[b]**

A

A police officer may arrest a person if he has probable cause to believe that person committed a crime. * * * Petitioners and appellant argue that if this requirement is satisfied the Fourth Amendment has nothing to say about *how* that seizure is made. This submission ignores the many cases in which this Court, by balancing the extent of the intrusion against the need for it, has examined the reasonableness of the manner in which a search or seizure is conducted. To determine the constitutionality of a seizure "[w]e must balance the nature and quality of the intrusion on the individual's Fourth Amendment interests against the importance of the governmental interests alleged to justify the intrusion." * * * We have described "the balancing of competing interests" as "the key principle of the Fourth Amendment." * * * Because one of the factors is the extent of the intrusion, it is plain that reasonableness depends on not only when a seizure is made, but also how it is carried out. * * *

Applying these principles to particular facts, the Court has held that governmental interests did not support a lengthy detention of luggage, *United States v. Place*, [this volume] an airport seizure not "carefully tailored to its underlying justification," *Florida v. Royer*, [this volume], surgery under general anesthesia to obtain evidence,

* * * or detention for fingerprinting without probable cause. * * * On the other hand, under the same approach it has upheld the taking of fingernail scrapings from a suspect, * * * an unannounced entry into a home to prevent the destruction of evidence, * * * administrative housing inspections without probable cause to believe that a code violation will be found, *Camara v. Municipal Court*, [this volume], and a blood test of a drunken-driving suspect. * * * In each of these cases, the question was whether the totality of the circumstances justified a particular sort of search or seizure.

B

The same balancing process applied in the cases cited above demonstrates that, notwithstanding probable cause to seize a suspect, an officer may not always do so by killing him. The intrusiveness of a seizure by means of deadly force is unmatched. The suspect's fundamental interest in his own life need not be elaborated upon. The use of deadly force also frustrates the interest of the individual, and of society, in judicial determination of guilt and punishment. Against these interests are ranged governmental interests in effective law enforcement. It is argued that overall violence will be reduced by encouraging the peaceful submission of suspects who know that they may be shot if they flee. Effectiveness in making arrests requires the resort to deadly force, or at least the meaningful threat thereof. * * *

Without in any way disparaging the importance of these goals, we are not convinced that the use of deadly force is a sufficiently productive means of accomplishing them to justify the killing of nonviolent suspects. * * * The use of deadly force is a self-defeating way of apprehending a suspect and so setting the criminal justice mechanism in motion. If successful, it guarantees that that mechanism will not be set in motion. And while the meaningful threat of deadly force might be thought to lead to the arrest of more live suspects by discouraging escape attempts, the presently available evidence does not support this thesis. The fact is that a majority of police departments in this country have forbidden the use of deadly force against nonviolent suspects. * * * If those charged with the enforcement of the criminal law have abjured the use of deadly force in arresting nondangerous felons, there is a substantial basis for doubting that the use of such force is an essential attribute of the arrest power in all felony cases. * * * Petitioners and appellant have not persuaded us that shooting nondangerous fleeing suspects is so vital as to outweigh the suspect's interest in his own life.

The use of deadly force to prevent the escape of all felony suspects, whatever the circumstances, is constitutionally unreasonable. It is not better that all felony suspects die than that they escape. [c] Where the suspect poses no immediate threat to the officer and no threat to others, the harm resulting from failing to apprehend him does not justify the use of deadly force to do so. It is no doubt unfortunate when a suspect who is in sight escapes, but the fact that the police arrive a little late or are a little slower afoot does not always justify killing the suspect. A police officer may not seize an unarmed, nondangerous suspect by shooting him dead. The Tennessee statute is

unconstitutional insofar as it authorizes the use of deadly force against such fleeing suspects.

It is not, however, unconstitutional on its face. Where the officer has probable cause to believe that the suspect poses a threat of serious physical harm, either to the officer or to others, it is not constitutionally unreasonable to prevent escape by using deadly force. Thus, if the suspect threatens the officer with a weapon or there is probable cause to believe that he has committed a crime involving the infliction or threatened infliction of serious physical harm, deadly force may be used if necessary to prevent escape, and if, where feasible, some warning has been given. As applied in such circumstances, the Tennessee statute would pass constitutional muster. [d]

III

A

It is insisted that the Fourth Amendment must be construed in light of the common-law rule, which allowed the use of whatever force was necessary to effect the arrest of a fleeing felon, though not a misdemeanant. * * * Most American jurisdictions also imposed a flat prohibition against the use of deadly force to stop a fleeing misdemeanant, coupled with a general privilege to use such force to stop a fleeing felon. * * *

The State and city argue that because this was the prevailing rule at the time of the adoption of the Fourth Amendment and for some time thereafter, and is still in force in some States, use of deadly force against a fleeing felon must be "reasonable." [e] It is true that this Court has often looked to the common law in evaluating the reasonableness, for Fourth Amendment purposes, of police activity. * * * On the other hand, it "has not simply frozen into constitutional law those law enforcement practices that existed at the time of the Fourth Amendment's passage." * * * Because of sweeping change in the legal and technological context, reliance on the common-law rule in this case would be a mistaken literalism that ignores the purposes of a historical inquiry.

B

It has been pointed out many times that the common-law rule is best understood in light of the fact that it arose at a time when virtually all felonies were punishable by death. * * * Courts have also justified the common-law rule by emphasizing the relative dangerousness of felons. * * *

Neither of these justifications makes sense today. Almost all crimes formerly punishable by death no longer are or can be. * * * And while in earlier times "the gulf between the felonies and the minor offences was broad and deep," * * * today the distinction is minor and often arbitrary. Many crimes classified as misdemeanors, or nonexistent, at common law are now felonies. * * * These changes have undermined the concept, which was questionable to begin with, that use of deadly force against a fleeing felon is merely a speedier execution of someone who has already forfeited his life. They have also made the assumption that a "felon" is more dangerous than a misdemeanant untenable. Indeed, numerous misdemeanors involve conduct more dangerous than many felonies.

There is an additional reason why the common-law rule cannot be directly translated to the present day. The common-law rule developed at a time when weapons were rudimentary. Deadly force could be inflicted almost solely in a hand-to-hand struggle during which, necessarily, the safety of the arresting officer was at risk. Handguns were not carried by police officers until the latter half of the last century. * * * Only then did it become possible to use deadly force from a distance as a means of apprehension. As a practical matter, the use of deadly force under the standard articulation of the common-law rule has an altogether different meaning—and harsher consequences—now than in past centuries. * * * **[f]**

One other aspect of the common-law rule bears emphasis. It forbids the use of deadly force to apprehend a misdemeanant, condemning such action as disproportionately severe. * * *

In short, though the common-law pedigree of Tennessee's rule is pure on its face, changes in the legal and technological context mean the rule is distorted almost beyond recognition when literally applied.

C

In evaluating the reasonableness of police procedures under the Fourth Amendment, we have also looked to prevailing rules in individual jurisdictions. * * * The rules in the States are varied. * * * Some 19 States have codified the common-law rule, though in two of these the courts have significantly limited the statute. Four States, though without a relevant statute, apparently retain the common-law rule. Two States have adopted the Model

Penal Code's provision verbatim. Eighteen others allow, in slightly varying language, the use of deadly force only if the suspect has committed a felony involving the use or threat of physical or deadly force, or is escaping with a deadly weapon, or is likely to endanger life or inflict serious physical injury if not arrested. Louisiana and Vermont, though without statutes or case law on point, do forbid the use of deadly force to prevent any but violent felonies. The remaining States either have no relevant statute or case law, or have positions that are unclear.

It cannot be said that there is a constant or overwhelming trend away from the common-law rule. In recent years, some States have reviewed their laws and expressly rejected abandonment of the common-law rule. Nonetheless, the long-term movement has been away from the rule that deadly force may be used against any fleeing felon, and that remains the rule in less than half the States. [g]

This trend is more evident and impressive when viewed in light of the policies adopted by the police departments themselves. Overwhelmingly, these are more restrictive than the common-law rule. * * * The Federal Bureau of Investigation and the New York City Police Department, for example, both forbid the use of firearms except when necessary to prevent death or grievous bodily harm. * * * For accreditation by the Commission on Accreditation for Law Enforcement Agencies, a department must restrict the use of deadly force to situations where "the officer reasonably believes that the action is in defense of human life . . . or in defense of any person in immediate danger of serious physical injury." * * * A 1974 study reported that the police department regulations in a majority of the large cities of the United States allowed the firing of a weapon only when a felon presented a threat of death or serious bodily harm. * * * Overall, only 7.5% of departmental and municipal policies explicitly permit the use of deadly force against any felon; 86.8% explicitly do not. * * * In light of the rules adopted by those who must actually administer them, the older and fading common-law view is a dubious indicium of the constitutionality of the Tennessee statute now before us.

D

Actual departmental policies are important for an additional reason. We would hesitate to declare a police practice of long standing "unreasonable" if doing so would severely hamper effective law enforcement. But the indications are to the contrary. There has been no suggestion that crime has worsened in any way in jurisdictions that have adopted, by legislation or departmental policy, rules similar to that announced today. *Amici* note that "[a]fter extensive research and consideration, [they] have concluded that laws permitting police officers to use deadly force to apprehend unarmed, non-violent fleeing felony suspects actually do not protect citizens or law enforcement officers, do not deter crime or alleviate problems caused by crime, and do not improve the crime-fighting ability of law enforcement agencies." * * * The submission is that the obvious state interests in apprehension are not sufficiently served to warrant the use of lethal weapons against all fleeing felons. * * *

Nor do we agree with petitioners and appellant that the rule we have adopted requires the police to make impossible, split-second evaluations of unknowable facts. * * * We do not deny the practical difficulties of attempting to assess the suspect's dangerousness. However, similarly difficult judgments must be made by the police in equally uncertain circumstances. * * * Nor is there any indication that in States that allow the use of deadly force only against dangerous suspects, * * * the standard has been difficult to apply or has led to a rash of litigation involving inappropriate second-guessing of police officers' split-second decisions. Moreover, the highly technical felony/ misdemeanor distinction is equally, if not more, difficult to apply in the field. An officer is in no position to know, for example, the precise value of property stolen, or whether the crime was a first or second offense. Finally, as noted above, this claim must be viewed with suspicion in light of the similar self-imposed limitations of so many police departments.

IV

The District Court concluded that Hymon was justified in shooting Garner because state law allows, and the Federal Constitution does not forbid, the use of deadly force to prevent the escape of a fleeing felony suspect if no alternative means of apprehension is available. * * * This conclusion made a determination of Garner's apparent dangerousness unnecessary. The court did find, however, that Garner appeared to be unarmed, though Hymon could not be certain that was the case. * * * Restated in Fourth Amendment terms,

this means Hymon had no articulable basis to think Garner was armed.

* * * [T]he fact that Garner was a suspected burglar could not, without regard to the other circumstances, automatically justify the use of deadly force. Hymon did not have probable cause to believe that Garner, whom he correctly believed to be unarmed, posed any physical danger to himself or others.

The dissent argues that the shooting was justified by the fact that Officer Hymon had probable cause to believe that Garner had committed a nighttime burglary. * * * While we agree that burglary is a serious crime, we cannot agree that it is so dangerous as automatically to justify the use of deadly force. The FBI classifies burglary as a "property" rather than a "violent" crime. * * * Although the armed burglar would present a different situation, the fact that an unarmed suspect has broken into a dwelling at night does not automatically mean he is physically dangerous. This case demonstrates as much. * * * In fact, the available statistics demonstrate that burglaries only rarely involve physical violence. During the 10-year period from 1973-1982, only 3.8% of all burglaries involved violent crime. * * *

V

* * *

The judgment of the Court of Appeals is affirmed, and the case is remanded for further proceedings consistent with this opinion. * * * JUSTICE O'CONNOR, with whom THE CHIEF JUSTICE and JUSTICE REHNQUIST join, dissenting.

* * *

Because burglary is a serious and dangerous felony, the public interest in the prevention and detection of the crime is of compelling importance. Where a police officer has probable cause to arrest a suspected burglar, the use of deadly force as a last resort might well be the only means of apprehending the suspect. With respect to a particular burglary, subsequent investigation simply cannot represent a substitute for immediate apprehension of the criminal suspect at the scene. * * *

* * *

A proper balancing of the interests involved suggests that use of deadly force as a last resort to apprehend a criminal suspect fleeing from the scene of a nighttime burglary is not unreasonable within the meaning of the Fourth Amendment. * * *

* * * But even if it were appropriate in this case to limit the use of deadly force to that ambiguous class of suspects, I believe the class should include nighttime residential burglars who resist arrest by attempting to flee the scene of the crime. * * * [h]

* * * * * * * * * *

COMMENTS

[a] The operative statute does not talk about "deadly" force but of "all the necessary means," which is a less direct way of encompassing the use of deadly force. As an administrative agency, a police department may issue rules that are less encompassing than a statute as long as the rule does not directly conflict with the law.

[b] Being shot does not fit the stereotypical idea of an arrest that most people hold.

[c] The spirit of a case is often captured in a pithy epigram, such as this one, rather than in its holding.

[d] As the ruling makes clear, the Supreme Court is not limited to only determining whether a law is totally constitutional or unconstitutional, but may generate a rule that preserved the law but narrows its scope by interpretation.

[e] The so-called "jurisprudence of original intent" has been the center of lively debate in criminal procedure in recent decades. Determining the "original intent" of the framers is not mere antiquarianism, but is a way of settling current controversies. This approach is usually propounded by conservatives. See Leonard Levy, *Original Intent and the Framers' Constitution* (New York: Macmillan, 1988). As the discussion here shows, determining original intent is an intricate matter.

[f] This argument also supports the logic of using deadly force against suspects armed with firearms.

[g] When the Court announces a rule with the potential of changing practice in many states it often looks to local practice among the states to gauge how disruptive a new rule would be. See, for example, the Court's statements on the exclusionary rule in *Wolf v. Colorado* [this volume] and *Mapp v. Ohio* [this volume].

[h] In her opinion, JUSTICE O'CONNOR notes that in hindsight the actual case had tragic consequences, but also points out that there was more ambiguity in Officer Hymon's ability to identify Garner as an unarmed teenager than the majority indicated. At bottom, however, the difference between the majority and dissent seems to turn not so much on any technical appraisal of the Fourth Amendment as on a moral calculus, weighing the life of the unarmed fleeing felon against the depredations of burglars.

ILLINOIS v. LAFAYETTE

462 U.S. 640, 103 S.Ct. 2605, 77 L.Ed.2d 65 (1983)

CHIEF JUSTICE BURGER delivered the opinion of the Court.

The question presented is whether, at the time an arrested person arrives at a police station, the police may, without obtaining a warrant, search a shoulder bag carried by that person. [a]

I

[Respondent was arrested by police in Kankakee, Ill., for disturbing the peace as the result of a loud argument with a theater manager. Respondent was handcuffed and taken to the police station.] Respondent carried a purse-type shoulder bag on the trip to the station.

At the police station respondent was taken to the booking room; there, Officer Mietzner removed the hand-cuffs from respondent and ordered him to empty his pockets and place the contents on the counter. After doing so, respondent took a package of cigarettes from his shoulder bag and placed the bag on the counter. Mietzner then removed the contents of the bag, and found 10 amphetamine pills inside the plastic wrap of a cigarette package.

[Respondent was charged with possession of controlled substances. The state justified the search as a valid inventory search.] Officer Mietzner testified that he examined the bag's contents because it was standard procedure to inventory "everything" in the possession of an arrested person. * * * He testified that he was not

seeking and did not expect to find drugs or weapons when he searched the bag, and he conceded that the shoulder bag was small enough that it could have been placed and sealed in a bag, container, or locker for protective purposes. * * * [The State later argued, however,] that the search was valid as a delayed search incident to arrest. Thereafter, the trial court ordered the suppression of the amphetamine pills. * * *

[The Illinois Appellate Court affirmed, ruling that (1) the State delay caused it to waive the search incident to arrest argument, (2) the station-house search of the bag was not a search incident to arrest, and (3) the search was not a valid inventory of respondent's belongings, arguing that there was a greater privacy interest in a purse-type shoulder bag than in an automobile (which provided the precedent for inventory searches).]

* * *

II

The question here is whether, consistent with the Fourth Amendment, it is reasonable for police to search the personal effects of a person under lawful arrest as part of the routine administrative procedure at a police station house incident to booking and jailing the suspect. The justification for such searches does not rest on probable cause, and hence the absence of a warrant is immaterial to the reasonableness of the search. Indeed, we have previously established that the inventory search constitutes a well-defined exception to the warrant requirement. * * * [In] *United States v. Chadwick*, 433 U.S. 1 (1977), * * * we noted that "probable cause to search is irrelevant" in inventory searches and went on to state:

> "This is so because the salutary functions of a warrant simply have no application in that context; the constitutional reasonableness of inventory searches must be determined on other bases." * * *

A so-called inventory search is not an independent legal concept but rather an incidental administrative step following arrest and preceding incarceration. To determine whether the search of respondent's shoulder bag was unreasonable we must "balanc[e] its intrusion on the individual's Fourth Amendment interests against its promotion of legitimate governmental interests." * * *

In order to see an inventory search in proper perspective, it is necessary to study the evolution of interests along the continuum from arrest to incarceration. We have held that immediately upon arrest an officer may lawfully search the person of an arrestee, *United States v. Robinson*, [this volume]; he may also search the area within the arrestee's immediate control, *Chimel v. California*, [this volume]. * * *

An arrested person is not invariably taken to a police station or confined; if an arrestee is taken to the police station, that is no more than a continuation of the custody inherent in the arrest status. Nonetheless, the factors justifying a search of the person and personal effects of an arrestee upon reaching a police station but prior to being placed in confinement are somewhat different from the factors justifying an immediate search at the time and place of arrest.

The governmental interests underlying a station-house search of the arrestee's person and possessions may in some circumstances be even greater than those supporting a search immediately following arrest. Consequently, the scope of a station-house search will often vary from that made at the time of arrest. Police conduct that would be impractical or unreasonable—or embarrassingly intrusive— on the street can more readily—and privately—be performed at the station. For example, the interests supporting a search incident to arrest would hardly justify disrobing an arrestee on the street, but the practical necessities of routine jail administration may even justify taking a prisoner's clothes before confining him, although that step would be rare. * * *

At the station house, it is entirely proper for police to remove and list or inventory property found on the person or in the possession of an arrested person who is to be jailed. A range of governmental interests supports an inventory process. It is not unheard of for persons employed in police activities to steal property taken from arrested persons; similarly, arrested persons have been known to make false claims regarding what was taken from their possession at the station house. A standardized procedure for making a list or inventory as soon as reasonable after reaching the station house not only deters false claims but also inhibits theft or careless handling of articles taken from the arrested person. Arrested persons have also been known to injure themselves—or others—with belts, knives, drugs, or other items on their person while being detained. Dangerous instrumentalities—such as razor blades, bombs, or weapons—can be concealed in innocent-looking articles taken from the arrestee's possession. The bare recital of these mundane realities justifies reasonable measures by police to limit these risks— either while the items are in police possession or at the time they are returned to the arrestee upon his release. Examining all the items removed from the arrestee's person or possession and listing or inventorying them is an entirely reasonable administrative procedure. It is immaterial whether the police actually fear any particular package or container; the need to protect against such risks arises independently of a particular officer's subjective concerns. * * * Finally, inspection of an arrestee's personal property may assist the police in ascertaining or verifying his identity. * * * In short, every consideration of orderly police administration benefiting both police and the public points toward the appropriateness of the examination of respondent's shoulder bag prior to his incarceration. [b]

    * * *

The Illinois court held that the search of respondent's shoulder bag was unreasonable because "preservation of the defendant's property and protection of police from claims of lost or stolen property, 'could have been achieved in a less intrusive manner.' For example, . . . the defendant's shoulder bag could easily have been secured by sealing it within a plastic bag or box and placing it in a secured locker." * * * Perhaps so, but the real question is not what "could have been achieved," but whether the Fourth Amendment *requires* such steps; it is

not our function to write a manual on administering routine, neutral procedures of the station house. Our role is to assure against violations of the Constitution.

The reasonableness of any particular governmental activity does not necessarily or invariably turn on the existence of alternative "less intrusive" means. In *Cady v. Dombrowski*, 413 U.S. 433 (1973), for example, we upheld the search of the trunk of a car to find a revolver suspected of being there. We rejected the contention that the public could equally well have been protected by the posting of a guard over the automobile. In language equally applicable to this case, we held, "[t]he fact that the protection of the public might, in the abstract, have been accomplished by 'less intrusive' means does not, by itself, render the search unreasonable." * * * We are hardly in a position to second-guess police departments as to what practical administrative method will best deter theft by and false claims against its employees and preserve the security of the station house. It is evident that a station-house search of every item carried on or by a person who has lawfully been taken into custody by the police will amply serve the important and legitimate governmental interests involved. [c]

Even if less intrusive means existed of protecting some particular types of property, it would be unreasonable to expect police officers in the everyday course of business to make fine and subtle distinctions in deciding which containers or items may be searched and which must be sealed as a unit. * * *

Applying these principles, we hold that it is not "unreasonable" for police, as part of the routine procedure incident to incarcerating an arrested person, to search any container or article in his possession, in accordance with established inventory procedures.

The judgment of the Illinois Appellate Court is reversed, and the case is remanded for proceedings not inconsistent with this opinion.

It is so ordered.

[JUSTICE MARSHALL, joined by JUSTICE BRENNAN, concurred in the judgment.]

* * * * * * * * * *

COMMENTS

[a] This case should be compared to the automobile inventory cases of *Colorado v. Bertine* and *Florida v. Wells* in Chapter 3. C.

[b] The reasons for a station-house inventory search are similar to those given for automobile inventory searches. If anything, the "danger" rationale is stronger for a station-house search.   The Court cited as support the then leading automobile inventory search case, *South Dakota v. Opperman*, 428 U.S. 364 (1976).

[c] The theoretical basis of the "least intrusive means" argument is that the state should act to protect the privacy of individuals to the greatest extent compatible with its function to protect public security. But in this calculation, as the Court makes clear, practical considerations must be considered, such as the administrative burdens on police departments to secure the property of arrestees so as to maintain their privacy.

TERRY v. OHIO

392 U.S. 1, 88 S.Ct. 1868, 20 L.Ed.2d 889 (1968)

MR. CHIEF JUSTICE WARREN delivered the opinion of the Court.

This case presents serious questions concerning the role of the Fourth Amendment in the confrontation on the street between the citizen and the policeman investigating suspicious circumstances.

Petitioner Terry was convicted of carrying a concealed weapon. * * * Officer McFadden testified that while he was patrolling in plain clothes in downtown Cleveland [one] afternoon * * * his attention was attracted by two men, Chilton and Terry, standing on the corner of Huron Road and Euclid Avenue. * * * [H]e was unable to say precisely what first drew his eye to them. However, he testified that he had been a policeman for 39 years. * * * [H]e had developed routine habits of observation over the years[;] * * * he would "stand and watch people or walk and watch people at many intervals of the day." He added: "Now, in this case when I looked over they didn't look right to me at the time."

* * * He saw [them pace up and down the block five or six times each, pausing frequently to look into the window of a jewelry store and to confer.] After this had gone on for 10 to 12 minutes, the two men walked off together [following a third]. * * *

* * * He testified that * * * he suspected the two men of "casing a job, a stick-up," and that he considered it his duty as a police officer to investigate further. He added that he feared "they may have a gun." * * * Decid-

ing that the situation was ripe for direct action, Officer McFadden approached the three men, identified himself as a police officer and asked for their names. At this point his knowledge was confined to what he had observed. * * * When the men "mumbled something" in response to his inquiries, Officer McFadden grabbed petitioner Terry, spun him around * * * and patted down the outside of his clothing. In the left breast pocket of Terry's overcoat Officer McFadden felt a pistol. * * * At this point, * * * the officer ordered all three men to enter Zucker's store. As they went in, he removed Terry's overcoat completely [and] removed a .38-caliber revolver from the pocket. * * * [Pat downs of Chilton and Katz produced a gun on Chilton but not on Katz.] The officer testified that he only patted the men down to see whether they had weapons, and that he did not put his hands beneath the outer garments of either Terry or Chilton until he felt their guns. * * * [a]

I.

* * * Unquestionably petitioner was entitled to the protection of the Fourth Amendment as he walked down the street in Cleveland. * * * The question is whether in all the circumstances of this on-the-street encounter, his right to personal security was violated by an unreasonable search and seizure.

* * * [T]his question thrusts to the fore difficult and troublesome issues regarding a sensitive area of

police activity[:] * * * the power of the police to "stop and frisk" — as it is sometimes euphemistically termed—suspicious persons. * * *

[The police argue that they need authority to deal with street encounters and that the brief detention of a "stop and frisk" not amounting to arrest should not be governed by the Fourth Amendment. The defendant argues that unless the police have probable cause to arrest, they have no power under the Fourth Amendment to forcibly detain a person temporarily or to frisk them.] [b]

In this context we approach the issues in this case mindful of the limitations of the judicial function in controlling the myriad daily situations in which policemen and citizens confront each other on the street. * * *

The exclusionary rule has its limitations, however, as a tool of judicial control. It cannot properly be invoked to exclude the products of legitimate police investigative techniques on the ground that much conduct which is closely similar involves unwarranted intrusions upon constitutional protections. Moreover, in some contexts the rule is ineffective as a deterrent. Street encounters between citizens and police officers are incredibly rich in diversity. They range from wholly friendly exchanges of pleasantries or mutually useful information to hostile confrontations of armed men involving arrests, or injuries, or loss of life. Moreover, hostile confrontations are not all of a piece. Some of them begin in a friendly enough manner, only to take a different turn upon the injection of some unexpected element into the conversation. Encounters are initiated by the police for a wide variety of purposes, some of which are

wholly unrelated to a desire to prosecute for crime. Doubtless some police "field interrogation" conduct violates the Fourth Amendment. But a stern refusal by this Court to condone such activity does not necessarily render it responsive to the exclusionary rule. Regardless of how effective the rule may be where obtaining convictions is an important objective of the police, it is powerless to deter invasions of constitutionally guaranteed rights where the police either have no interest in prosecuting or are willing to forgo successful prosecution in the interest of serving some other goal.

Proper adjudication of cases in which the exclusionary rule is invoked demands a constant awareness of these limitations. The wholesale harassment by certain elements of the police community, of which minority groups, particularly Negroes, frequently complain, will not be stopped by the exclusion of any evidence from any criminal trial. Yet a rigid and unthinking application of the exclusionary rule, in futile protest against practices which it can never be used effectively to control, may exact a high toll in human injury and frustration of efforts to prevent crime. No judicial opinion can comprehend the protean variety of the street encounter, and we can only judge the facts of the case before us. Nothing we say today is to be taken as indicating approval of police conduct outside the legitimate investigative sphere. Under our decision, courts still retain their traditional responsibility to guard against police conduct which is overbearing or harassing, or which trenches upon personal security without the objective evidentiary justification which the Constitution requires. When such conduct is identified, it must be condemned by the judiciary and its fruits must be excluded from evidence in criminal trials. * * * **[c]**

* * * [W]e turn our attention to the quite narrow question posed by the facts before us: whether it is always unreasonable for a policeman to seize a person and subject him to a limited search for weapons unless there is probable cause for an arrest. * * *

II.

Our first task is to establish at what point in this encounter the Fourth Amendment becomes relevant. That is, we must decide whether and when Officer McFadden "seized" Terry and whether and when he conducted a "search." * * * It must be recognized that whenever a police officer accosts an individual and restrains his freedom to walk away, he has "seized" that person. And it is nothing less than sheer torture of the English language to suggest that a careful exploration of the outer surfaces of a person's clothing all over his or her body in an attempt to find weapons is not a "search." * * * It is a serious intrusion upon the sanctity of the person. * * *

* * * This Court has held in the past that a search which is reasonable at its inception may violate the Fourth Amendment by virtue of its intolerable intensity and scope. * * * The scope of the search must be "strictly tied to and justified by" the circumstances which render its initiation permissible. * * *

* * * We therefore reject the notions that the Fourth Amendment does not come into play at all as a limitation upon police conduct if the officers stop short of something called a "technical arrest" or a "full-blown search." **[d]**

[Thus, by stopping and frisking Terry, Officer McFadden seized and searched him. The next question is whether this seizure and search were unreasonable, that is, whether the officer's action was justified at its inception and whether it was reasonably related in scope to the circumstances which justified the interference in the first place.]

III.

* * * [W]e deal here with an entire rubric of police conduct * * * which historically has not been, and as a practical matter could not be, subjected to the warrant procedure. Instead, the conduct involved in this case must be tested by the Fourth Amendment's general proscription against unreasonable searches and seizures. **[e]**

Nonetheless, the notions which underlie both the warrant procedure and the requirement of probable cause remain fully relevant in this context. * * * [I]n justifying the particular intrusion the police officer must be able to point to specific and articulable facts which, taken together with rational inferences from those facts, reasonably warrant that intrusion. The scheme of the Fourth Amendment becomes meaningful only when it is assured that at some point the conduct of those charged with enforcing the laws can be subjected to the more detached, neutral scrutiny of a judge who must evaluate the reasonableness of a particular search or seizure in light of the particular circumstances. And in making that assessment it is imperative that the facts be judged against an objective standard: would the facts available to the officer at the moment of the seizure or the search "warrant a man of reasonable caution in the belief" that the action taken was appropriate? * * * Anything less would invite intrusions upon constitutionally guaranteed rights based on nothing more substantial than inarticulate hunches, a result this Court has consistently refused to sanction. * * * And simple "'good faith on the part of the arresting officer is not enough.' * * * [f] If subjective good faith alone were the test, the protections of the Fourth Amendment would evaporate, and the people would be 'secure in their persons, houses, papers, and effects,' only in the discretion of the police." * * *

[The Court noted that the police have an interest to prevent and detect crime which necessitates temporary stops of individuals to inquire into suspicious circumstances.]

The crux of this case, however, is not the propriety of Officer McFadden's taking steps to investigate petitioner's suspicious behavior, but rather, whether there was justification for McFadden's invasion of Terry's personal security by searching him for weapons in the course of that investigation. * * * Certainly it would be unreasonable to require that police officers take unnecessary risks in the performance of their duties. American criminals have a long tradition of armed violence, and every year in this country many law enforcement officers are killed in the line of duty. * * *

In view of these facts, we cannot blind ourselves to the need for law enforcement officers to protect themselves and other prospective victims of violence in situations where they may lack probable cause for an arrest. * * *

We must still consider, however, the nature and quality of the intrusion on individual rights which must be accepted if police officers are to be conceded the right to search for weapons in situations where probable cause to arrest for crime is lacking. Even a limited search of the outer clothing for weapons constitutes a severe, though brief, intrusion upon cherished personal security, and it must surely be an annoying, frightening, and perhaps humiliating experience. Petitioner contends that such an intrusion is permissible only incident to a lawful arrest, either for a crime involving the possession of weapons or for a crime the commission of which led the officer to investigate in the first place. However, this argument must be closely examined.

* * * [Terry] says it is unreasonable for the policeman to [disarm a suspect] until such time as the situation evolves to a point where there is probable cause to make an arrest. When that point has been reached, petitioner would concede the officer's right to conduct a search of the suspect for weapons, fruits or instrumentalities of the crime, or "mere" evidence, incident to the arrest.

There are two weaknesses in this line of reasoning, however. First, it fails to take account of traditional limitations upon the scope of searches, and thus recognizes no distinction in purpose, character, and extent between a search incident to an arrest and a limited search for weapons. The former, although justified in part by the acknowledged necessity to protect the arresting officer from assault with a concealed weapon, * * * is also justified on other grounds, and can therefore involve a relatively extensive exploration of the person. A search for weapons in the absence of probable cause to arrest, however, must, like any other search, be strictly circumscribed by the exigencies which justify its initiation. * * * Thus it must be limited to that which is necessary for the discovery of weapons which might be used to harm the officer or others nearby, and may realistically be characterized as something less than a "full" search. * * * [g]

* * * [Second,] [a]n arrest is a wholly different kind of intrusion upon individual freedom from a limited search for weapons, and the interests each is designed to serve are likewise quite different. An arrest is the initial stage of a criminal prosecution. It is intended to vindicate society's interest in having its laws obeyed, and it is inevitably accompanied by future interference with the individual's freedom of movement, whether or not trial or conviction ultimately follows. The protective search for weapons, on the other hand, constitutes a brief, though far from inconsiderable, intrusion upon the sanctity of the person. [h] It does not follow that because an officer may lawfully arrest a person only when he is apprised of facts sufficient to warrant a belief that the person has committed or is committing a crime, the officer is equally unjustified, absent that kind of evidence, in making any intrusions short of an arrest. Moreover, a perfectly reasonable apprehension of danger may arise long before the officer is possessed of adequate information to justify taking a person into custody for the purpose of prosecuting him for a crime. * * *

Our evaluation of the proper balance that has to be struck in this type of case leads us to conclude that there must be a narrowly drawn authority to permit a reasonable search for weapons for the protection of the police officer, where he has reason to believe that he is dealing with an armed and dangerous individual, regardless of whether he has probable cause to arrest the individual for a crime. The officer need not be absolutely certain that the individual is armed; the issue is whether a reasonably prudent man in the circumstances would be warranted in the belief that his safety or that of others was in danger. * * * And in determining whether the officer acted reasonably in such circumstances, due weight must be given, not to his inchoate and unparticularized suspicion or "hunch," but to the specific reasonable inferences which he is entitled to draw from the facts in light of his experience. * * *

IV.

* * * We think * * * a reasonably prudent man would have been warranted in believing petitioner was armed and thus presented a threat to the officer's safety while he was investigating his suspicious behavior. * * * We cannot say [Officer McFadden's] decision at that point to seize Terry and pat his clothing for weapons was the product of a volatile or inventive imagination, or was undertaken simply as an act of harassment; the record evidences the tempered act of a policeman who in the course of an investigation had to make a quick decision as to how to protect himself and others from possible danger, and took limited steps to do so.

* * *

* * * The sole justification of the search in the present situation is the protection of the police officer and others nearby, and it must therefore be confined in scope to an intrusion reasonably designed to discover guns, knives, clubs, or other hidden instruments for the assault of the police officer.

* * *

V.

* * * We merely hold today that where a police officer observes unusual conduct which leads him reasonably to conclude in light of his experience [i] that criminal activity may be afoot and that the persons with whom he is dealing may be armed and presently dangerous, where in the course of investigating this behavior he identifies himself as a policeman and makes reasonable inquiries, and where nothing in the initial stages of the encounter serves to dispel his reasonable fear for his own or others' safety, he is entitled for the protection of himself and others in the area to conduct a carefully limited search of the outer clothing of such persons in an attempt to discover weapons which might be used to assault him. Such a search is a reasonable search under the Fourth Amendment, and any weapons seized may properly be introduced in evidence against the person from whom they were taken.

Affirmed.

[JUSTICES BLACK and WHITE concurred separately.]

MR. JUSTICE HARLAN, concurring.

* * *

* * * [I]f the frisk is justified in order to protect the officer during an encounter with a citizen, the officer must first have constitutional grounds to insist on an encounter, to make a *forcible* stop. * * * I would make it perfectly clear that the right to frisk in this case depends upon the reasonableness of a forcible stop to investigate a suspected crime. [j]

Where such a stop is reasonable, however, the right to frisk must be immediate and automatic if the reason for the stop is, as here, an articulable suspicion of a crime of violence. Just as a full search incident to a lawful arrest requires no additional justification, a limited frisk incident to a lawful stop must often be rapid and routine. There is no reason why an officer, rightfully but forcibly confronting a person suspected of a serious crime, should have to ask one question and take the risk that the answer might be a bullet. * * *

* * *

MR. JUSTICE DOUGLAS, dissenting.

I agree that petitioner was "seized" within the meaning of the Fourth Amendment. I also agree that frisking petitioner and his companions for guns was a "search." But it is a mystery how that "search" and that "seizure" can be constitutional by Fourth Amendment standards, unless there was "probable cause" to believe that (1) a crime had been committed or (2) a crime was in the process of being committed or (3) a crime was about to be committed.

* * * If loitering were in issue and that was the offense charged, there would be "probable cause" shown. But the crime here is carrying concealed weapons; and there is no basis for concluding that the officer had "probable cause" for believing that that crime was being committed. * * *   [A] magistrate would, therefore, have been unauthorized to issue [a warrant], for he can act only if there is a showing of "probable cause." We hold today that the police have greater authority to make a "seizure" and conduct a "search" than a judge has to authorize such action. We have said precisely the opposite over and over again. **[k]**

* * *

To give the police greater power than a magistrate is to take a long step down the totalitarian path. Perhaps such a step is desirable to cope with modern forms of lawlessness. But if it is taken, it should be the deliberate choice of the people through a constitutional amendment. * * *

* * *

* * * * * * * * * *

COMMENTS

[a] The lengthy recitation of facts is designed to "prove" that Officer McFadden's stop of Terry, Chilton, and the third man, Katz, was reasonable; a brief explanation of facts would lead a legal specialist to rapidly conclude that probable cause was not present. No part of an opinion is written with scientific detachment; judicial opinions are intended to be persuasive for a point of view. Why is it important that Officer McFadden had thirty-nine years' experience? Did the officer effect an arrest?

[b] These extreme positions were forcefully presented in amicus curiae, or "friend of the court" briefs by the Americans for Effective Law Enforcement for the police and the National Association for the Advancement of Colored People Legal Defense Fund for the defendant. The first position would, in constitutional terms, unleash the police, while the latter, if strictly applied, would undermine a well-established, if legally vague, practice. These arguments were made at a time of substantial conflict between police and black citizens in the massive urban ghetto riots during the summers of the late 1960s.

[c] This extended discussion about police-citizen encounters and the limits of the exclusionary rule may be seen as an apologia by a liberal justice before making a major concession to the police.

[d] This aspect of the opinion is necessary in order to bring the facts of the case and the stop and frisk practice within the contours of the Fourth Amendment. Counsel for the police argued that the Fourth Amendment simply does not apply. If they won this argument the result would terminate Court oversight of this important area of government-citizen interaction.

[e] Notice how the fundamental distinction between the reasonableness approach

and the warrant clause approach to Fourth Amendment interpretation offers the Court a way of deciding many arrest and search and seizure cases in alternate ways. Is this category merely a convenient mask behind which the justices can carry out their policy preferences?

[f] This is both a key theoretical and a practical point; even if a magistrate cannot rule on certain searches, seizures, arrests or stops before the fact, the articulable standards requirement allows a court to review the stop after the fact.

[g] The problem for JUSTICE WARREN was that the rules regulating arrest were ancient and the probable cause requirement well established. The "limited search for weapons" was a new category, not well known in the law up to that time, although one would not know this simply from reading the opinion.

[h] This distinction may explain why a stop and frisk is not as intrusive as an arrest and full search, but does it adequately explain the constitutional basis of the authority to stop?

[i] The holding explicitly refers to the experience of the officer stopping a person. Does a rookie officer have the experience necessary to stop a suspect? How much experience does it take before an officer is competent to assess a street situation and determine it is suspicious?

[j] Do you think that JUSTICE HARLAN's point was already made in the majority opinion? Or was it necessary to add this point to insure that police would not have their decisions to frisk, given a lawful stop, second-guessed by the courts?

[k] Is JUSTICE DOUGLAS' dissent so one sided that it fails to acknowledge the reasonableness doctrine under the Fourth Amendment? Is there any limit to the reasonableness doctrine? To what extent are the justices entitled to consider the practical realities of what police actually do in deciding their cases?

SIBRON v. NEW YORK

392 U.S. 40, 88 S.Ct. 1889, 20 L.Ed.2d 917 (1968)

MR. CHIEF JUSTICE WARREN delivered the opinion of the Court.

These are companion cases to * * * *Terry v. Ohio*, [this volume] decided today. * * * [a]

* * *

* * * Sibron, * * * was convicted of the unlawful possession of heroin. He moved before trial to suppress the heroin seized from his person by the arresting officer, Brooklyn Patrolman Anthony Martin. * * * Officer Martin testified that while he was patrolling his beat in uniform on March 9, 1965, he observed Sibron "continually from the hours of 4:00 P.M. to 12:00, midnight . . . in the vicinity of 742 Broadway." He stated that during this period of time he saw Sibron in conversation with six or eight persons whom he (Patrolman Martin) knew from past experience to be narcotics addicts. The officer testified that he did not overhear any of these conversations, and that he did not see anything pass between Sibron and any of the others. Late in the evening Sibron entered a restaurant. Patrolman Martin saw Sibron speak with three more known addicts inside the restaurant. Once again, nothing was overheard and nothing was seen to pass between Sibron and the addicts. Sibron sat down and ordered pie and coffee, and, as he was eating, Patrolman Martin approached him and told him to come outside. Once outside, the officer said to Sibron, "You know what I am after." According to the officer, Sibron "mumbled something and reached into his pocket." Simultaneously, Patrolman Martin thrust his hand into the same pocket, discovering several glassine envelopes, which, it turned out, contained heroin.

The State has had some difficulty in settling upon a theory for the admissibility of these envelopes of heroin. [The State dropped an "abandonment" theory.] [b]   Nor did the officer ever seriously suggest that he was in fear of bodily harm and that he searched Sibron in self-protection to find weapons.

* * *

IV.

Turning to the facts of Sibron's case, it is clear that the heroin was inadmissible in evidence against him. The prosecution has quite properly abandoned the notion that there was probable cause to arrest Sibron for any crime at the time Patrolman Martin accosted him in the restaurant, took him outside and searched him. The officer was not acquainted with Sibron and had no information concerning him. He merely saw Sibron talking to a number of known narcotics addicts over a period of eight hours. It must be emphasized that Patrolman Martin was completely ignorant regarding the content of these conversations, and that he saw nothing pass between Sibron and the addicts. So far as he knew, they might indeed "have been talking about the World Series." The inference that persons who talk to narcotics addicts are engaged in the criminal traffic in narcotics is simply not the sort of reasonable inference required to support an intrusion by the police upon an individual's personal security. [c] Nothing resembling probable cause existed until after the search had turned up the envelopes of heroin. It is axiomatic that an incident search may not precede an arrest and serve as part of its justification. * * * Thus the search cannot be justified as incident to a lawful arrest.

If Patrolman Martin lacked probable cause for an arrest, however, his seizure and search of Sibron might still have been justified at the outset if he had reasonable grounds to believe that Sibron was armed and dangerous. *Terry v. Ohio*. * * * We are not called upon to decide in this case whether there was a "seizure" of Sibron inside the restaurant antecedent to the physical seizure which accompanied the search. The record is unclear with respect to what transpired between Sibron and the officer inside the restaurant. It is totally barren of any indication whether Sibron accompanied Patrolman Martin outside in submission to a show of force or authority which left him no choice, or whether he went voluntarily in a spirit of apparent cooperation with the officer's investigation. In any event, this deficiency in the record is immaterial, since Patrolman Martin obtained no new information in the interval between his initiation of the encounter in the restaurant and his physical seizure and search of Sibron outside.

Although the Court of Appeals of New York wrote no opinion in this case, it seems to have viewed the search here as a self-protective search for weapons and to have affirmed on [this] basis. * * * The Court of Appeals has, at any rate, justified searches during field interrogation on the ground that "[t]he answer to the question propounded by the policeman may be a bullet; in any case the exposure to danger could be very great." * * * But the application of this reasoning to the facts of this case proves too much. The police officer is not entitled to seize and search every person whom he sees on the street or of whom he makes inquiries. Before he places a hand on the person of a citizen in search of anything, he must have constitutionally adequate, reasonable grounds for doing so. In the case of the self-protective search for weapons, he must be able to point to particular facts from which he reasonably inferred that the individual was armed and dangerous. * * * Patrolman Martin's testimony reveals no such facts. The suspect's mere act of talking with a number of known narcotics addicts over an eight-hour period no more gives rise to reasonable fear of life or limb on the part of the police officer than it justifies an arrest for committing a crime. Nor did Patrolman Martin urge that when Sibron put his hand in his pocket, he feared that he was going for a weapon and acted in self-defense. His opening statement to Sibron—"You know what I am after"—made it abundantly clear that he sought narcotics, and his testimony at the hearing left no doubt that he thought there were narcotics in Sibron's pocket.

Even assuming *arguendo* that there were adequate grounds to search Sibron for weapons, the nature and scope of the search conducted by Patrolman Martin were so clearly unrelated to that justification as to render the heroin inadmissible. The search for weapons approved in *Terry* consisted solely of a limited patting of the outer clothing of the suspect for concealed objects which might be used as instruments of assault. Only when he discovered such objects did the officer in *Terry* place his hands in the pockets of the men he searched. In this case, with no attempt at an initial limited exploration for arms, Patrolman Martin thrust his hand into Sibron's pocket and took from him envelopes of heroin. His testimony shows that he was looking for narcotics, and he found them. The search was not reasonably limited in scope to the accomplishment of the only goal which might conceivably have justified its inception—the protection of the officer by disarming a potentially dangerous man. Such a search violates the guarantee of the Fourth Amendment, which protects the sanctity of the person against unreasonable intrusions on the part of all government agents.

* * *

* * * The conviction in [*Sibron*] must be reversed, on the ground that the heroin was unconstitutionally admitted in evidence against the appellant.

It is so ordered.

[JUSTICES DOUGLAS, WHITE, FORTAS AND HARLAN, concurred in the result. JUSTICE BLACK, dissenting in *Sibron*, argued that when Sibron put his hand into his pocket, Officer Martin had probable cause to believe that he was reaching for a weapon.]

* * * * * * * * * *

COMMENT

[a] As a "companion case" to *Terry v. Ohio*, *Sibron* established a counterpoint—a stop, frisk and seizure example that does not meet *Terry* standards, and so is constitutionally unreasonable. *Sibron* can be compared to the *Dickerson* "plain feel" case for their similarities as well as contrasts. While *Dickerson* allows a "plain feel" seizure in the abstract, both cases are examples of a close reading of the facts to insure that *Terry* searches do not turn on the absolute subjective sense of reasonableness of the officer.

[b] New York slang—"dropsy case"—applied to cases where police routinely testify that defendants dropped drugs on the ground. If true, this is an abandonment and the officer may seize the evidence in plain view. See *California v. Hodari D.* [this volume]. However, many believe that the overwhelming majority of "dropsy cases," are conducted by illegal searches covered it up by police perjury at suppression hearings and trials.

[c] Does this assertion comport with common sense? Would a "common sense hunch" rule allow police to forcibly stop law abiding people who talk in piblic to friends who are criminally involved?

ADAMS v. WILLIAMS

407 U.S. 143, 92 S.Ct. 1921, 32 L.Ed.2d 612 (1972)

MR. JUSTICE REHNQUIST delivered the opinion of the Court.

Respondent Robert Williams was convicted in a Connecticut state court of illegal possession of a handgun found during a "stop and frisk," as well as of possession of heroin that was found during a full search incident to his weapons arrest. After respondent's conviction was affirmed by the Supreme Court of Connecticut, * * * this Court denied certiorari. * * * Williams' petition for federal habeas corpus relief was denied by the District Court and by a divided panel of the Second Circuit, * * * but on rehearing *en banc* the Court of Appeals granted relief. * * * That court held that evidence introduced at Williams' trial had been obtained by an unlawful search of his person and car, and thus the state court judgments of conviction should be set aside. Since we conclude that the policeman's actions here conformed to the standards this Court laid down in *Terry v. Ohio*, 392 U.S. 1 (1968), we reverse.

Police Sgt. John Connolly was alone early in the morning on car patrol duty in a high-crime area of Bridgeport, Connecticut. At approximately 2:15 a.m. a person known to Sgt. Connolly approached his cruiser and informed him that an individual seated in a nearby vehicle was carrying narcotics and had a gun at his waist.

After calling for assistance on his car radio, Sgt. Connolly approached the vehicle to investigate the informant's report. Connolly tapped on the car window and asked the occupant,

Robert Williams, to open the door. When Williams rolled down the window instead, the sergeant reached into the car and removed a fully loaded revolver from Williams' waistband. The gun had not been visible to Connolly from outside the car, but it was in precisely the place indicated by the informant. Williams was then arrested by Connolly for unlawful possession of the pistol. A search incident to that arrest was conducted after other officers arrived. They found substantial quantities of heroin on Williams' person and in the car, and they found a machete and a second revolver hidden in the automobile.

Respondent contends that the initial seizure of his pistol, upon which rested the later search and seizure of other weapons and narcotics, was not justified by the informant's tip to Sgt. Connolly. He claims that absent a more reliable informant, or some corroboration of the tip, the policeman's actions were unreasonable under the standards set forth in *Terry v. Ohio, supra.*

In *Terry* this Court recognized that "a police officer may in appropriate circumstances and in an appropriate manner approach a person for purposes of investigating possibly criminal behavior even though there is no probable cause to make an arrest." * * * The Fourth Amendment does not require a policeman who lacks the precise level of information necessary for probable cause to arrest to simply shrug his shoulders and allow a crime to occur or a criminal to escape. On the contrary, *Terry* recognizes that it may be the essence of good police work to adopt an intermediate response. * * * A brief stop of a suspicious individual, in order to determine his identity or to maintain the status quo momentarily while obtaining more information, may be most reasonable in light of the facts known to the officer at the time. * * *

The Court recognized in *Terry* that the policeman making a reasonable investigatory stop should not be denied the opportunity to protect himself from attack by a hostile suspect. "When an officer is justified in believing that the individual whose suspicious behavior he is investigating at close range is armed and presently dangerous to the officer or to others," he may conduct a limited protective search for concealed weapons. * * * The purpose of this limited search is not to discover evidence of crime, but to allow the officer to pursue his investigation without fear of violence, and thus the frisk for weapons might be equally necessary and reasonable, whether or not carrying a concealed weapon violated any applicable state law. So long as the officer is entitled to make a forcible stop, and has reason to believe that the suspect is armed and dangerous, he may conduct a weapons search limited in scope to this protective purpose. * * *

Applying these principles to the present case, we believe that Sgt. Connolly acted justifiably in responding to his informant's tip. The informant was known to him personally and had provided him with information in the past. This is a stronger case than obtains in the case of an anonymous telephone tip. [a] The informant here came forward personally to give infor-

mation that was immediately verifiable at the scene. Indeed, under Connecticut law, the informant might have been subject to immediate arrest for making a false complaint had Sgt. Connolly's investigation proved the tip incorrect. Thus, while the Court's decisions indicate that this informant's unverified tip may have been insufficient for a narcotics arrest or search warrant, * * * the information carried enough indicia of reliability to justify the officer's forcible stop of Williams.

In reaching this conclusion, we reject respondent's argument that reasonable cause for a stop and frisk can only be based on the officer's personal observation, rather than on information supplied by another person. [b] Informants' tips, like all other clues and evidence coming to a policeman on the scene, may vary greatly in their value and reliability. One simple rule will not cover every situation. Some tips, completely lacking in indicia of reliability, would either warrant no police response or require further investigation before a forcible stop of a suspect would be authorized. But in some situations—for example, when the victim of a street crime seeks immediate police aid and gives a description of his assailant, or when a credible informant warns of a specific impending crime—the subtleties of the hearsay rule should not thwart an appropriate police response.

While properly investigating the activity of a person who was reported to be carrying narcotics and a concealed weapon and who was sitting alone in a car in a high-crime area at 2:15 in the morning, Sgt. Connolly had ample reason to fear for his safety. [c] When Williams rolled down his window, rather than complying with the policeman's request to step out of the car so that his movements could more easily be seen, the revolver allegedly at Williams' waist became an even greater threat. Under these circumstances the policeman's action in reaching to the spot where the gun was thought to be hidden constituted a limited intrusion designed to insure his safety, and we conclude that it was reasonable. The loaded gun seized as a result of this intrusion was therefore admissible at Williams' trial. * * *

Once Sgt. Connolly had found the gun precisely where the informant had predicted, probable cause existed to arrest Williams for unlawful possession of the weapon. Probable cause to arrest depends "upon whether, at the moment the arrest was made . . . the facts and circumstances within [the arresting officers'] knowledge and of which they had reasonably trustworthy information were sufficient to warrant a prudent man in believing that the [suspect] had committed or was committing an offense." * * * In the present case the policeman found Williams in possession of a gun in precisely the place predicted by the informant. This tended to corroborate the reliability of the informant's further report of narcotics and, together with the surrounding circumstances, certainly suggested no lawful explanation for possession of the gun. Probable cause does not require the same type of specific evidence of each element of the offense as would be needed to support a conviction. * * * Rather, the court will evaluate generally the circumstances at the time of the arrest to decide if the officer had probable cause for his action:

"In dealing with probable cause,

however, as the very name implies, we deal with probabilities. These are not technical; they are the factual and practical considerations of everyday life on which reasonable and prudent men, not legal technicians, act." *Brinegar v. United States*, 338 U.S. 160, 175 (1949).

* * * Under the circumstances surrounding Williams' possession of the gun seized by Sgt. Connolly, the arrest on the weapons charge was supported by probable cause, and the search of his person and of the car incident to that arrest was lawful. * * * The fruits of the search were therefore properly admitted at Williams' trial, and the Court of Appeals erred in reaching a contrary conclusion.

Reversed.

[JUSTICE DOUGLAS, joined by JUSTICE MARSHALL, dissented, on the ground that as Connecticut law allowed persons to carry concealed weapons, there was no way for Officer Connolly to know whether the gun possession was lawful.]

[JUSTICE BRENNAN, dissented in a brief opinion, quoting at length from the dissenting opinion of Chief Judge Henry Friendly of the Second Circuit Court of Appeals. One objection was that *Terry* should not be extended to possessory offenses, but apply only to crimes of violence. There was virtually no corroboration, so the "frisk" which resulted in the seizure of the weapon was the result of a defective tip in that the informant was unnamed, was not shown to be reliable, and gave no information which demonstrated personal knowledge. He raised the specter that the officer could have "manufactured" the informant after the event.] [d]

MR. JUSTICE MARSHALL, with whom MR. JUSTICE DOUGLAS joins, dissenting.

Four years have passed since we decided *Terry* * * * and its companion cases. * * * [e] They were the first cases in which this Court explicitly recognized the concept of "stop and frisk" and squarely held that police officers may, under appropriate circumstances, stop and frisk persons suspected of criminal activity even though there is less than probable cause for an arrest. This case marks our first opportunity to give some flesh to the bones of *Terry et al.* Unfortunately, the flesh provided by today's decision cannot possibly be made to fit on *Terry*'s skeletal framework.

* * *

In today's decision the Court ignores the fact that *Terry* begrudgingly accepted the necessity for creating an exception from the warrant requirement of the Fourth Amendment and treats this case as if warrantless searches were the rule rather than the "narrowly drawn" exception. This decision betrays the careful balance that *Terry* sought to strike between a citizen's right to privacy and his government's responsibility for effective law enforcement and expands the concept of warrantless searches far beyond anything heretofore recognized as legitimate. I dissent.

I

* * *

B. The Court erroneously attempts to describe the search for the gun as a protective search incident to a reasonable investigatory stop. But, as in *Terry*, * * * there is no occasion in this case to determine whether or not police officers have a right to seize and to restrain a citizen in order to interrogate him. The facts are clear that the officer intended to make the search as soon as he approached the respondent. He asked no questions; he made no investigation; he simply searched. There was nothing apart from the information supplied by the informant to cause the officer to search. Our inquiry must focus, therefore, as it did in *Terry* on whether the officer had sufficient facts from which he could reasonably infer that respondent was not only engaging in illegal activity, but also that he was armed and dangerous. The focus falls on the informant.

The only information that the informant had previously given the officer involved homosexual conduct in the local railroad station. [f] * * *

* * *

[JUSTICE MARSHALL also made the points about the weakness of the informant's tip and the lack of personal knowledge of the police officer, that were raised in JUSTICE BRENNAN's dissent.]

Terry did not hold that whenever a policeman has a hunch that a citizen is engaging in criminal activity, he may engage in a stop and frisk. It held that if police officers want to stop and frisk, they must have specific facts from which they can reasonably infer that an individual is engaged in criminal activity and is armed and dangerous. It was central to our decision in *Terry* that the police officer acted on the basis of his own personal observations and that he carefully scrutinized the conduct of his suspects before interfering with them in any way. When we legitimated the conduct of the officer in *Terry* we did so because of the substantial reliability of the information on which the officer based his decision to act.

* * *

[JUSTICE MARSHALL went on to argue that the arrest and search subsequent to the "stop and frisk" was improper.]

* * *

* * * * * * * * * *

COMMENTS

[a] See *Alabama v. White* [this volume] for a case of an anonymous telephone tip.

[b] Was the personal observation by the police officer part of the "holding" of *Terry v. Ohio*?

[c] In a footnote the Court noted that many police officers are killed in the line of duty each year. How relevant is this point?

[d] This is a very hostile attitude towards police. It emerged, however, in an era where hundreds of urban riots (from 1964 to 1972) were blamed on heavy-handed police action against the residents of inner-city slums. In the same period, the consumption of illicit drugs grew to be a problem of enormous proportions; some judges with long memories feared that a new "prohibition era" type of wide-open police enforcement of these possession laws would inevitably result in the widespread intrusion of all people in such neighborhoods, both dealers and the majority of law abiding citizens.

[e] In that period the makeup of the Court changed significantly; four justices appointed by President Nixon, generally more conservative than the justice of the Warren Court. *Adams* is a classic example of how different justices, with different attitudes, can view a case in a different light than the justices who authored and voted for the decision.

[f] This was not disclosed by the majority opinion. Is it relevant that an informant on the streets in a "high crime neighborhood" has previously informed only about one kind of illicit activity?

DUNAWAY v. NEW YORK

442 U.S. 200, 99 S.Ct. 2248, 60 L.Ed.2d 824 (1979)

MR. JUSTICE BRENNAN delivered the opinion of the Court.

* * *

I

[A jail inmate gave a police officer a lead implicating Dunaway to a murder that occurred during a robbery. A detective questioned the inmate] but learned nothing that supplied "enough information to get a warrant" for [Dunaway's] arrest. Nevertheless, [the detective] ordered other detectives to "pick up" petitioner and "bring him in." * * * [a] [Dunaway] was taken into custody; although he was not told he was under arrest, he would have been physically restrained if he had attempted to leave. * * * He was driven to police headquarters in a police car and placed in an interrogation room, where he was questioned by officers after being given the warnings required by *Miranda v. Arizona*, [this volume]. Petitioner waived counsel and eventually made statements and drew sketches that incriminated him in the crime.

* * *

II

We first consider whether the Rochester police violated the Fourth and Fourteenth Amendments when, without probable cause to arrest, they took petitioner into custody, transported him to the police station, and detained him there for interrogation.

* * * There can be little doubt that petitioner was "seized" in the Fourth Amendment sense when he was taken involuntarily to the police station. And respondent State concedes that the police lacked probable cause to arrest petitioner before his incriminating statement during interrogation. Nevertheless respondent contends that the seizure of petitioner did not amount to an arrest and was therefore permissible under the Fourth Amendment because the police had a "reasonable suspicion" that petitioner possessed "intimate knowledge about a serious and unsolved crime." * * * We disagree.

Before *Terry v. Ohio*, [this volume], the Fourth Amendment's guarantee against unreasonable seizures of persons was analyzed in terms of arrest, probable cause for arrest, and warrants based on such probable cause. The basic principles were relatively simple and straightforward: The term "arrest" was synonymous with those seizures governed by the Fourth Amendment. While warrants were not required in all circumstances, the requirement of probable cause, as elaborated in numerous precedents, was treated as absolute. * * * The standard of probable cause thus represented the accumulated wisdom of precedent and experience as to the minimum justification necessary to make the kind of intrusion involved in an arrest "reasonable" under the Fourth Amendment. The standard applied to all arrests, without the need to "balance" the interests and circumstances involved in particular situations.

* * *

Terry for the first time recognized an exception to the requirement that Fourth Amendment seizures of persons must be based on probable cause. That case involved a brief, on-the-spot stop on the street and a frisk for weapons, a situation that did not fit comfortably within the traditional concept of an "arrest." Nevertheless, the Court held that even this type of "necessarily swift action predicated upon the on-the-spot observations of the officer on the beat" constituted a "serious intrusion upon the sanctity of the person, which may inflict great indignity and arouse strong resentment," * * * and therefore "must be tested by the Fourth Amendment's general proscription against unreasonable searches and seizures." * * * However, since the intrusion involved in a "stop and frisk" was so much less severe than that involved in traditional "arrests," the Court declined to stretch the concept of "arrest"—and the general rule requiring probable cause to make arrests "reasonable" under the Fourth Amendment—to cover such intrusions. Instead, the Court treated the stop-and-frisk intrusion as a *sui generis* "rubric of police conduct." * * * And to determine the justification necessary to make this specially limited intrusion "reasonable" under the Fourth Amendment, the Court balanced the limited violation of individual privacy involved against the opposing interests in crime prevention and detection and in the police officer's safety. * * * As a consequence, the Court established "a narrowly drawn authority to permit a reasonable search for weapons for the protection of the police officer, where he has reason to believe that he is dealing with an armed and dangerous individual, regardless of whether he has probable cause to arrest the individual for a crime." * * * Thus, *Terry* departed from traditional Fourth Amendment analysis in two respects. First, it defined a special category of Fourth Amendment "seizures" so substantially less intrusive than arrests that the general rule requiring probable cause to make Fourth Amendment "seizures" reasonable could be replaced by a balancing test. Second, the application of this balancing test led the Court to approve this narrowly defined less intrusive seizure on grounds less rigorous than probable cause, but only for the purpose of a pat-down for weapons.

Because *Terry* involved an exception to the general rule requiring probable cause, this Court has been careful to maintain its narrow scope. * * *

Respondent State now urges the Court to apply a balancing test, rather than the general rule, to custodial interrogations, and to hold that "seizures" such as that in this case may be justified by mere "reasonable suspicion." *Terry* and its progeny clearly do not support such a result. The narrow intrusions involved in those cases were judged by a balancing test rather than by the general principle that Fourth Amendment seizures must be supported by the "long-prevailing standards" of probable cause, * * * only because these intrusions fell far short of the kind of intrusion associated with an arrest. * * * **[b]**

In contrast to the brief and narrowly circumscribed intrusions involved in those cases, the detention of petitioner was in important respects indistinguishable from a traditional arrest. Petitioner was not questioned briefly where he was found. Instead, he was taken from a neighbor's home to a police car, transported to a police station, and placed in an interrogation room. He was never informed that he was "free to go"; indeed, he would have been physically restrained if he had refused to accompany the officers or had tried to escape their custody. The application of the Fourth Amendment's requirement of probable cause does not depend on whether an intrusion of this magnitude is termed an "arrest" under state law. The mere facts that petitioner was not told he was under arrest, was not "booked," and would not have had an arrest record if the interrogation had proved fruitless, while not insignificant for all purposes, * * * obviously do not make petitioner's seizure even roughly analogous to the narrowly defined intrusions involved in *Terry* and its progeny. Indeed, any "exception" that could cover a seizure as intrusive as that in this case would threaten to swallow the general rule that Fourth Amendment seizures are "reasonable" only if based on probable cause. [c]

The central importance of the probable-cause requirement to the protection of a citizen's privacy afforded by the Fourth Amendment's guarantees cannot be compromised in this fashion. * * * Hostility to seizures based on mere suspicion was a prime motivation for the adoption of the Fourth Amendment, and decisions immediately after its adoption affirmed that "common rumor or report, suspicion, or even 'strong reason to suspect' was not adequate to support a warrant for arrest." * * * The familiar threshold standard of probable cause for Fourth Amendment seizures reflects

the benefit of extensive experience accommodating the factors relevant to the "reasonableness" requirement of the Fourth Amendment, and provides the relative simplicity and clarity necessary to the implementation of a workable rule. * * *

In effect, respondent urges us to adopt a multifactor balancing test of "reasonable police conduct under the circumstances" to cover all seizures that do not amount to technical arrests. But the protections intended by the Framers could all too easily disappear in the consideration and balancing of the multifarious circumstances presented by different cases, especially when that balancing may be done in the first instance by police officers engaged in the "often competitive enterprise of ferreting out crime." * * * A single, familiar standard is essential to guide police officers, who have only limited time and expertise to reflect on and balance the social and individual interests involved in the specific circumstances they confront. Indeed, our recognition of these dangers, and our consequent reluctance to depart from the proved protections afforded by the general rule, are reflected in the narrow limitations emphasized in the cases employing the balancing test. For all but those narrowly defined intrusions, the requisite "balancing" has been performed in centuries of precedent and is embodied in the principle that seizures are "reasonable" only if supported by probable cause.

Moreover, two important decisions since *Terry* confirm the conclusion that the treatment of petitioner, whether or not it is technically characterized as an arrest, must be supported by probable cause. [In *Davis v. Mississippi*, 394 U.S. 721 (1969), the Court ruled that the state could not simply pick up suspects without probable cause during an investigation for fingerprinting. The Court noted that fingerprinting is not as intrusive as questioning in that it does not probe into testimonial evidence or the premises, need only be performed once, and is reliable, but reserved the question whether under some circumstances a suspect could be held for fingerprinting on less than probable cause.]

Brown v. Illinois, 422 U.S. 590 (1975), similarly disapproved arrests made for "investigatory" purposes on less than probable cause. Although Brown's arrest had more of the trappings of a technical formal arrest than petitioner's, such differences in form must not be exalted over substance. Once in the police station, Brown was taken to an interrogation room, and his experience was indistinguishable from petitioner's. Our condemnation of the police conduct in *Brown* fits equally the police conduct in this case. * * *

* * * [D]etention for custodial interrogation—regardless of its label —intrudes so severely on interests protected by the Fourth Amendment as necessarily to trigger the traditional safeguards against illegal arrest. We accordingly hold that the Rochester police violated the Fourth and Fourteenth Amendments when, without probable cause, they seized petitioner and transported him to the police station for interrogation.

III

[The Court then found that no attenuation occurred between Dunaway's illegal detention and the incriminating evidence obtained by his questioning simply because *Miranda* warnings were given.]

JUSTICE POWELL took no part in the consideration or decision of this case.

[JUSTICES WHITE and STEVENS concurred.]

[JUSTICE REHNQUIST, joined by THE CHIEF JUSTICE, dissented, arguing that Dunaway accompanied the police voluntarily and that the *Miranda* warnings and Dunaway's voluntary answers to questions purged any primary taint in his initial detention.]

* * * * * * * * * *

COMMENTS

[a] Suspect "round-ups" seem like Grade-"B" detective movies of the 1930s. Jail inmates are often a source of incriminating information against others, but are also known to lie to get favorable treatment.

[b] An historical anomaly is that cavalier detention of suspects, perhaps more socially tolerated (but no more constitutional) before the 1960s "Due Process Revolution," became theoretically feasible under the Constitution only after the

Terry decision.

[c] The Court stretched the "arrest" definition under *Terry;* but this case shows the limits of "redefinition." A "stop" lasts only a few minutes.

DELAWARE v. PROUSE

440 U.S. 648, 99 S.Ct. 1391, 59 L.Ed.2d 660 (1979)

MR. JUSTICE WHITE delivered the opinion of the Court.

The question is whether it is an unreasonable seizure under the Fourth and Fourteenth Amendments to stop an automobile, being driven on a public highway, for the purpose of checking the driving license of the operator and the registration of the car, where there is neither probable cause to believe nor reasonable suspicion that the car is being driven contrary to the laws governing the operation of motor vehicles or that either the car or any of its occupants is subject to seizure or detention in connection with the violation of any other applicable law.

I

[A police officer stopped a car, smelled marijuana smoke coming from the car as he approached it, and seized marijuana in plain view. The officer] testified that prior to stopping the vehicle he had observed neither traffic or equipment violations nor any suspicious activity, and that he made the stop only in order to check the driver's license and registration. The patrolman was not acting pursuant to any standards, guidelines, or procedures pertaining to document spot checks, promulgated by either his department or the State Attorney General. Characterizing the stop as "routine," the patrolman explained, "I saw the car in the area and wasn't answering any complaints, so I decided to pull them off." [The Delaware courts suppressed the evidence on] finding the stop and detention to have been wholly capricious and therefore violative of the Fourth Amendment.

* * * We granted certiorari to resolve the conflict between this decision, which is in accord with decisions in five other jurisdictions, and the contrary determination in six jurisdictions that the Fourth Amendment does not prohibit the kind of automobile stop that occurred here. [a]

* * *

III

The Fourth and Fourteenth Amendments are implicated in this case because stopping an automobile and detaining its occupants constitute a "seizure" within the meaning of those Amendments, even though the purpose of the stop is limited and the resulting detention quite brief. * * * The essential purpose of the proscriptions in the Fourth Amendment is to impose a standard of "reasonableness" upon the exercise of discretion by government officials, including law enforcement agents, in order "'to safeguard the privacy and security of individuals against arbitrary invasions. . . .'" * * * [b] Thus, the permissibility of a particular law enforcement practice is judged by balancing its intrusion on the individual's Fourth Amendment interests against its promotion of legitimate governmental interests. Implemented in this manner, the reasonableness standard usually requires, at a minimum, that the facts upon which an intrusion is based be capable of measurement against "an objective standard," whether this be probable cause or a less stringent test. [c] In those situations in which the balance of interests precludes insistence upon "some quantum of individualized suspicion," other safeguards are generally relied upon to assure that the individual's reasonable expectation of privacy is not "subject to the discretion of the official in the field." * * *

In this case, however, the State of Delaware urges that patrol officers be subject to no constraints in deciding which automobiles shall be stopped for a license and registration check because the State's interest in discretionary spot checks as a means of ensuring the safety of its roadways outweighs the resulting intrusion on the privacy and security of the persons detained. [d]

IV

We have only recently considered the legality of investigative stops of automobiles where the officers making the stop have neither probable cause to believe nor reasonable suspicion that either the automobile or its occupants are subject to seizure under the applicable criminal laws. In *United States v. Brignoni-Ponce,* [422 U.S. 873 (1975)], Border Patrol agents conducting roving patrols in areas near the international border asserted statutory authority to stop at random any vehicle in order to determine whether it contained illegal aliens or was involved in smuggling operations. The practice was held to violate the Fourth Amendment, but the Court did not invalidate all warrantless automobile stops upon less than probable cause. Given "the

importance of the governmental interest at stake, the minimal intrusion of a brief stop, and the absence of practical alternatives for policing the border," * * * the Court analogized the roving-patrol stop to the on-the-street encounter addressed in *Terry v. Ohio,* [this volume], and held:

> "Except at the border and its functional equivalents, officers on roving patrol may stop vehicles only if they are aware of specific articulable facts, together with rational inferences from those facts, that reasonably warrant suspicion that the vehicles contain aliens who may be illegally in the country." * * *

Because "the nature of illegal alien traffic and the characteristics of smuggling operations tend to generate articulable grounds for identifying violators,* * * a requirement of reasonable suspicion for stops allows the Government adequate means of guarding the public interest and also protects residents of the border areas from indiscriminate official interference." * * *

Although not dispositive, these decisions undoubtedly provide guidance in balancing the public interest against the individual's Fourth Amendment interests implicated by the practice of spot checks such as occurred in this case. We cannot agree that stopping or detaining a vehicle on an ordinary city street is less intrusive than a roving-patrol stop on a major highway and that it bears greater resemblance to a permissible stop and secondary detention at a checkpoint near the border. In this regard, we note that *Brignoni-Ponce* was not

limited to roving-patrol stops on lim-
ited-access roads, but applied to any
roving-patrol stop by Border Patrol
agents on any type of roadway on less
than reasonable suspicion. * * * We
cannot assume that the physical and
psychological intrusion visited upon the
occupants of a vehicle by a random
stop to check documents is of any less
moment than that occasioned by a stop
by border agents on roving patrol.
Both of these stops generally entail law
enforcement officers signaling a moving
automobile to pull over to the side of
the roadway, by means of a possibly
unsettling show of authority.   Both
interfere with freedom of movement,
are inconvenient, and consume time.
Both may create substantial anxiety.
For Fourth Amendment purposes, we
also   see   insufficient   resemblance
between sporadic and random stops of
individual vehicles making their way
through city traffic and those stops
occasioned by roadblocks where all
vehicles are brought to a halt or to a
near halt, and all are subjected to a
show of the police power of the
community. "At traffic checkpoints the
motorist can see that other vehicles are
being stopped, he can see visible signs
of the officers' authority, and he is
much less likely to be frightened or
annoyed by the intrusion." * * * [e]

V

[Delaware argued that stop checks
promote public safety. The Court did
not disagree. Nevertheless, the Court
held that without empirical data to
prove that random stops were more
effective in promoting public safety
than stops after an officer observed a
violation,   such   a   program   placed
unlimited discretion in the hands of

patrol officers.] * * *

VI

* * * [The Court examined the
administrative search cases (see *Camara v. Municipal Court* [this volume])
but found that they were not applicable; operating an automobile is not the
same as operating a heavily regulated
business].

An individual operating or traveling in an automobile does not lose all
reasonable   expectation   of   privacy
simply because the automobile and its
use are subject to government regulation.   Automobile travel is a basic,
pervasive, and often necessary mode of
transportation to and from one's home,
workplace, and leisure activities. Many
people spend more hours each day
traveling in cars than walking on the
streets.   Undoubtedly, many find a
greater sense of security and privacy in
traveling in an automobile than they
do in exposing themselves by pedestrian or other modes of travel. Were
the   individual subject to unfettered
governmental intrusion every time he
entered an automobile, the security
guaranteed by the Fourth Amendment
would be seriously circumscribed. * * *
[f]

VII

Accordingly, we hold that except in
those situations in which there is at
least articulable and reasonable suspicion that a motorist is unlicensed or
that an automobile is not registered, or
that either the vehicle or an occupant
is otherwise subject to seizure for
violation of law, stopping an automobile and detaining the driver in order
to check his driver's license and the

registration of the automobile are unreasonable under the Fourth Amendment. This holding does not preclude the State of Delaware or other States from developing methods for spot checks that involve less intrusion or that do not involve the unconstrained exercise of discretion. Questioning of all oncoming traffic at roadblock-type stops is one possible alternative. We hold only that persons in automobiles on public roadways may not for that reason alone have their travel and privacy interfered with at the unbridled discretion of police officers. The judgment below is affirmed.

So ordered.

[JUSTICE BLACKMUN, joined by JUSTICE POWELL, concurred.]

MR. JUSTICE REHNQUIST, dissenting.
* * *

As the Court correctly points out, people are not shorn of their Fourth Amendment protection when they step from their homes onto the public sidewalks or from the sidewalks into their automobiles. But a random license check of a motorist operating a vehicle on highways owned and maintained by the State is quite different from a random stop designed to uncover violations of laws that have nothing to do with motor vehicles. No one questions that the State may require the licensing of those who drive on its highways and the registration of vehicles which are driven on those highways. If it may insist on these requirements, it obviously may take steps necessary to enforce compliance. The reasonableness of the enforcement measure chosen by the State is tested by weighing its intrusion on the motorists' Fourth Amendment interests against its promotion of the State's legitimate interests. * * *

* * * [T]he Court concludes that the contribution to highway safety made by random stops would be marginal at best. The State's primary interest, however, is in traffic safety, not in apprehending unlicensed motorists for the sake of apprehending unlicensed motorists. The whole point of enforcing motor vehicle safety regulations is to remove from the road the unlicensed driver before he demonstrates why he is unlicensed. The Court would apparently prefer that the State check licenses and vehicle registrations as the wreckage is being towed away.

Nor is the Court impressed with the deterrence rationale. * * * The Court arrives at its conclusion [that random spot checks do not deter unlicensed drivers] without the benefit of a shred of empirical data in this record suggesting that a system of random spot checks would fail to deter violators. In the absence of such evidence, the State's determination that random stops would serve a deterrence function should stand. [g]

On the other side of the balance, the Court advances only the most diaphanous of citizen interests. Indeed, the Court does not say that these interests can never be infringed by the State, just that the State must infringe them en masse rather than citizen by citizen. To comply with the Fourth Amendment, the State need only subject *all* citizens to the same "anxiety" and "inconvenien[ce]" to which it now subjects only a few.

For constitutional purposes, the action of an individual law enforcement officer is the action of the State itself, * * * and state acts are accompanied by a presumption of validity until shown otherwise. * * * Although a system of discretionary stops could conceivably be abused, the record before us contains no showing that such abuse is probable or even likely. Nor is there evidence in the record that a system of random license checks would fail adequately to further the State's interest in deterring and apprehending violators. Nevertheless, the Court concludes "[o]n the record before us" that the random spot check is not "a sufficiently productive mechanism to justify the intrusion upon Fourth Amendment interests which such stops entail." * * * I think that the Court's approach reverses the presumption of constitutionality accorded acts of the States. The burden is not upon the State to demonstrate that its procedures are consistent with the Fourth Amendment, but upon respondent to demonstrate that they are not. "On this record" respondent has failed to make such a demonstration.

* * * Absent an equal protection violation, the fact that random stops may entail "a possibly unsettling show of authority," * * * and "may create substantial anxiety," * * * seems an insufficient basis to distinguish for Fourth Amendment purposes between a roadblock stopping all cars and the random stop at issue here. Accordingly, I would reverse the judgment of the Supreme Court of Delaware. **[h]**

* * * * * * * * * * *

COMMENTS

[a] By reconciling conflicting views, a driver passing through different states is not subject to varying "stop rules." Uniformity is valuable in our highly mobile society. Nevertheless, where no federal constitutional principle is involved, local laws often differ.

[b] Does this analysis square with the rule of *California v. Carney* [this volume], *i.e.*, that a person enjoys a lesser expectation of privacy in an automobile than in a home?

[c] Would an arbitrary, but not *capricious,* standard meet the objective test suggested here? Suppose a department required a traffic officer to stop every five-hundredth automobile or stop a vehicle every thirty minutes. That would theoretically eliminate the danger that the police will stop only youths, minorities or "suspicious" looking persons.

[d] Is the Delaware rule reasonable? excessive? outrageous? Does your answer depend on whether you are an officer? have been stopped by the police for no reason?

[e] This reasoning illustrates the weighing process in determining whether an earlier case is good precedent. "Border" cases are different from *Prouse* as they arise in a unique legal setting, where rights are attenuated; they are similar to this case because they deal with the same psychological and confrontational aspects of on-the-road stops. Such factors as the nature of the roads on which border roving patrol occurs becomes relevant to fitting earlier precedent to this case. At bottom, the Court must decide whether the two fact situations are "constitutionally similar"—a judgment that requires the skills of an experienced jurist who has developed a mature understanding of the sociopolitical dynamics of contemporary American society in the light of its historically grounded constitutional policies.

[f] It is often impossible to neatly separate legal conclusions from policy conclusions. This sweeping policy statement is a good example of the Court trying to sense the temper of the American people. Which would *you* prefer: unlimited police authority to stop you to ask for your license on your way to school or work or the *Prouse* rule?

[g] The majority faulted Maryland for basing its stop policies on no empirical evidence. JUSTICE REHNQUIST's position here is tied to his view of the presumption of constitutionality of state law or policy where a Fourth Amendment right is not implicated.

[h] JUSTICE REHNQUIST believes that the personal anxiety generated by a random traffic stop is not a constitutionally valid consideration. Do you agree? Should a general understanding of the psychological reactions of noncriminal citizens who are stopped although there is nothing wrong with their license, registration, or car, play a part in deciding this constitutional question?

KOLENDER v. LAWSON

461 U.S. 352, 103 S.Ct. 1855, 75 L.Ed.2d 903 (1983)

JUSTICE O'CONNOR delivered the opinion of the Court.

This appeal presents a facial challenge to a criminal statute that requires persons who loiter or wander on the streets to provide a "credible and reliable" identification and to account for their presence when requested by a peace officer under circumstances that would justify a stop under the standards of *Terry v. Ohio*, [this volume]. [a] We conclude that the statute as it has been construed is unconstitutionally vague within the meaning of the Due Process Clause of the Fourteenth Amendment by failing to clarify what is contemplated by the requirement that a suspect provide a "credible and reliable" identification. [b] Accordingly, we affirm the judgment of the court below.

I

Appellee Edward Lawson was detained or arrested on approximately 15 occasions between March 1975 and January 1977 pursuant to Cal. Penal Code Ann. §647(e) (West 1970). Lawson was prosecuted only twice, and was convicted once. The second charge was dismissed.

Lawson then brought a civil action in the District Court * * * seeking a declaratory judgment that §647(e) is unconstitutional, a mandatory injunction to restrain enforcement of the statute, and compensatory and punitive damages against the various officers who detained him. The District Court found that §647(e) was overbroad because "a person who is stopped on less than probable cause cannot be punished for failing to identify himself." * * * The District Court enjoined enforcement of the statute. * * *

* * * The Court of Appeals affirmed the District Court determination as to the unconstitutionality of §647(e). * * * The appellate court determined that the statute was unconstitutional in that it violates the Fourth Amendment's proscription against unreasonable searches and seizures, it contains a vague enforcement standard that is susceptible to arbitrary enforcement, and it fails to give fair and adequate notice of the type of conduct prohibited. * * *

The officers appealed to this Court from that portion of the judgment of the Court of Appeals which declared §647(e) unconstitutional and which enjoined its enforcement. * * *

II

In the courts below, Lawson mounted an attack on the facial validity of §647(e). "In evaluating a facial challenge to a state law, a federal court must, of course, consider any limiting construction that a state court or enforcement agency has proffered." * * * As construed by the California Court of Appeal, §647(e) requires that an individual provide "credible and reliable" identification when requested by a police officer who has reasonable suspicion of criminal activity sufficient to justify a *Terry* detention. * * * "Credible and reliable" identification is defined by the State Court of Appeal as identification "carrying reasonable assurance that the identification is authentic and providing means for later getting in touch with the person who has identified himself." * * * In addition, a suspect may be required to "*account for his presence * * ** to the extent that it assists in producing credible and reliable identification . * * *" * * * Under the terms of the statute, failure of the individual to provide "credible and reliable" identification permits the arrest.

III

Our Constitution is designed to maximize individual freedoms within a framework of ordered liberty. **[c]** Statutory limitations on those freedoms are examined for substantive authority and content as well as for definiteness or certainty of expression. * * *

As generally stated, the void-for-vagueness doctrine requires that a penal statute define the criminal offense with sufficient definiteness that ordinary people can understand what conduct is prohibited and in a manner that does not encourage arbitrary and discriminatory enforcement. * * * Although the doctrine focuses both on actual notice to citizens and arbitrary enforcement, we have recognized recently that the more important aspect of the vagueness doctrine "is not actual notice, but the other principal element of the doctrine—the requirement that a legislature establish minimal guidelines to govern law enforcement." * * * Where the legislature fails to provide such minimal guidelines, a criminal statute may permit "a standardless

sweep [that] allows policemen, prosecutors, and juries to pursue their personal predilections." * * *

Section 647(e), as presently drafted and as construed by the state courts, contains no standard for determining what a suspect has to do in order to satisfy the requirement to provide a "credible and reliable" identification. As such, the statute vests virtually complete discretion in the hands of the police to determine whether the suspect has satisfied the statute and must be permitted to go on his way in the absence of probable cause to arrest. An individual, whom police may think is suspicious but do not have probable cause to believe has committed a crime, is entitled to continue to walk the public streets "only at the whim of any police officer" who happens to stop that individual under §647(e). * * * Our concern here is based upon the "potential for arbitrarily suppressing First Amendment liberties. * * *" * * * In addition, §647(e) implicates consideration of the constitutional right to freedom of movement. **[d]**

Section 647(e) is not simply a "stop-and-identify" statute. Rather, the statute requires that the individual provide a "credible and reliable" identification that carries a "reasonable assurance" of its authenticity, and that provides "means for later getting in touch with the person who has identified himself." * * * In addition, the suspect may also have to account for his presence "to the extent it assists in producing credible and reliable identification." * * *

At oral argument, the appellants confirmed that a suspect violates §647(e) unless "the officer [is] satisfied that the identification is reliable." * * * In giving examples of how suspects would satisfy the requirement, appellants explained that a jogger, who was not carrying identification, could, depending on the particular officer, be required to answer a series of questions concerning the route that he followed to arrive at the place where the officers detained him, or could satisfy the identification requirement simply by reciting his name and address. * * *

It is clear that the full discretion accorded to the police to determine whether the suspect has provided a "credible and reliable" identification necessarily "entrust[s] lawmaking 'to the moment-to-moment judgment of the policeman on his beat.'" * * * Section 647(e) "furnishes a convenient tool for 'harsh and discriminatory enforcement by local prosecuting officials, against particular groups deemed to merit their displeasure,'" * * * and "confers on police a virtually unrestrained power to arrest and charge persons with a violation." * * * In providing that a detention under §647(e) may occur only where there is the level of suspicion sufficient to justify a *Terry* stop, the State ensures the existence of "neutral limitations on the conduct of individual officers." * * * Although the initial detention is justified, the State fails to establish standards by which the officers may determine whether the suspect has complied with the subsequent identification requirement.

Appellants stress the need for strengthened law enforcement tools to combat the epidemic of crime that plagues our Nation. The concern of our citizens with curbing criminal activity is certainly a matter requiring the attention of all branches of government. As weighty as this concern is, however, it cannot justify legislation that would otherwise fail to meet constitutional standards for definiteness and clarity. * * * Section 647(e), as presently construed, requires that "suspicious" persons satisfy some undefined identification requirement, or face criminal punishment. Although due process does not require "impossible standards" of clarity, * * * this is not a case where further precision in the statutory language is either impossible or impractical. **[e]**

IV

We conclude §647(e) is unconstitutionally vague on its face because it encourages arbitrary enforcement by failing to describe with sufficient particularity what a suspect must do in order to satisfy the statute. Accordingly, the judgment of the Court of Appeals is affirmed, and the case is remanded for further proceedings consistent with this opinion. **[f]**

It is so ordered.

[JUSTICE BRENNAN both joined in the majority opinion and concurred on the ground that the Court should also hold that the California statute violated the Fourth Amendment.]

[JUSTICE WHITE, joined by JUSTICE REHNQUIST dissented, arguing that the majority incorrectly applied the void for vagueness doctrine.]

*   *   *   *   *   *   *   *   *   *   *

COMMENTS

[a] A "facial" challenge is one to the statute itself, as it is generally applied by the state, and not simply to the particular way in which the statute was applied in this case.

[b] The vagueness doctrine is based on the basic understanding that due process requires that before the state deprives someone of life, liberty or property, the person must be afforded *notice* and a *fair hearing* to challenge the taking. If the statute is vague, the individual is not given adequate notice.

[c] Understanding the theoretical and the historical context of a constitutional provision suggests a direction or attitude that the Court should adopt in deciding a case under the provision. Without some such grounding, constitutional law can become incoherent.

[d] The Court is not simply concerned with the niceties of "notice," but, based on past abuses, with excessive power in the hands of police. In this way, the historic context of policing in America gives substance to the meaning of due process in this case.

[e] The Court hints that a statute may be crafted that allows the police to request identification from a person detained during a *Terry* stop, but does not indicate the contours of such a law. Police can now ask a stopped person to identify herself. The legal consequences of a failure or refusal to provide identification are not clear.

[f] In a footnote the Court indicated that it was not addressing Fourth and Fifth Amendment challenges to the statute because it was not necessary to the decision of the case.

FLORIDA v. ROYER

460 U.S. 491, 103 S.Ct. 1319, 75 L.Ed. 2d 229 (1983)

JUSTICE WHITE announced the judgment of the Court and delivered an opinion, in which JUSTICE MARSHALL, JUSTICE POWELL, and JUSTICE STEVENS joined.

* * *

I

On January 3, 1978, Royer was observed at Miami International Airport by two [Dade County] plainclothes detectives * * * assigned to the county's Organized Crime Bureau, Narcotics Investigation Section. Detectives Johnson and Magdalena believed that Royer's appearance, mannerisms, luggage, and actions fit the so-called "drug courier profile." [a] Royer, * * * purchased a one-way ticket to New York City and checked his two suitcases, placing on each suitcase an identification tag bearing the name "Holt" and the destination "La Guardia." As Royer made his way to the concourse which led to the airline boarding area, the two detectives approached him, identified themselves as policemen working out of the sheriff's office, and asked if Royer had a "moment" to speak with them; Royer said "Yes." [b]

Upon request, but without oral consent, Royer produced for the detectives his airline ticket and his driver's license. The airline ticket, like the baggage identification tags, bore the name "Holt," while the driver's license carried respondent's correct name, "Royer." When the detectives

asked about the discrepancy, Royer explained that a friend had made the reservation in the name of "Holt." Royer became noticeably more nervous during this conversation, whereupon the detectives informed Royer that they were in fact narcotics investigators and that they had reason to suspect him of transporting narcotics.

The detectives did not return his airline ticket and identification but asked Royer to accompany them to a room, approximately 40 feet away, adjacent to the concourse. Royer said nothing in response but went with the officers as he had been asked to do. The room was later described by Detective Johnson as a "large storage closet," located in the stewardesses' lounge and containing a small desk and two chairs. Without Royer's consent or agreement, Detective Johnson, using Royer's baggage check stubs, retrieved the "Holt" luggage from the airline and brought it to the room where respondent and Detective Magdalena were waiting. Royer was asked if he would consent to a search of the suitcases. Without orally responding to this request, Royer produced a key and unlocked one of the suitcases, which one detective then opened without seeking further assent from Royer. Marihuana was found in that suitcase. According to Detective Johnson, Royer stated that he did not know the combination to the lock on the second suitcase. When asked if he objected to the detective opening the second suitcase, Royer said "[n]o, go ahead," and did not object when the detective explained that the suitcase might have to be broken open. The suitcase was pried open by the officers and more marihuana was found. Royer was then told that he was under arrest. Approximately 15 minutes had elapsed from the time the detectives initially approached respondent until his arrest upon the discovery of the contraband.

[Royer was tried for felony possession of marihuana. The trial court found that Royer's voluntarily consented to the search. The District Court of Appeal, reversed, holding that Royer had been involuntarily confined without probable cause; that the involuntary detention had exceeded the limits of *Terry v. Ohio*, [this volume], at the time his consent to the search was obtained; and that the consent to search was therefore invalid because tainted by the unlawful confinement.]

[Under these facts, the Florida Court of Appeals concluded that Royer's confinement was tantamount to arrest.] * * *

At the suppression hearing Royer testified that he was under the impression that he was not free to leave the officers' presence. The Florida District Court of Appeal [agreed, since the State agreed that the officers would not have permitted Royer to leave the room. Detective Johnson testified that he did not have probable cause until the suitcase was opened. The court held that Royer's consent was invalid as a matter of law.]

II

Some preliminary observations are in order. First, it is unquestioned that without a warrant to search Royer's luggage and in the absence of probable cause and exigent circumstances, the validity of the search depended on Royer's purported consent. Neither is it disputed that where the validity of a search rests on consent, the State has the burden of proving that the necessary consent was obtained and that it was freely and voluntarily given, a burden that is not satisfied by showing a mere submission to a claim of lawful authority. * * * [c]

Second, law enforcement officers do not violate the Fourth Amendment by merely approaching an individual on the street or in another public place, by asking him if he is willing to answer some questions. * * * Nor would the fact that the officer identifies himself as a police officer, without more, convert the encounter into a seizure requiring some level of objective justification. * * * The person approached, however, need not answer any question put to him; indeed, he may decline to listen to the questions at all and may go on his way. * * * He may not be detained even momentarily without reasonable, objective grounds for doing so; and his refusal to listen or answer does not, without more, furnish those grounds. * * * If there is no detention—no seizure within the meaning of the Fourth Amendment— then no constitutional rights have been infringed. [d]

Third, it is also clear that not all seizures of the person must be justified by probable cause to arrest for a crime. [The rule of *Terry v. Ohio* was stated.] * * * *Adams v. Williams*, 407 U.S. 143 (1972), applied the same approach in the context of an informant's report that an unnamed individual in a nearby vehicle was carrying narcotics and a gun. * * * *United States v. Brignoni-Ponce*, 422 U.S. 873,

881-882 (1975), was unequivocal in saying that reasonable suspicion of criminal activity warrants a temporary seizure for the purpose of questioning limited to the purpose of the stop. In *Brignoni-Ponce*, that purpose was to verify or dispel the suspicion that the immigration laws were being violated, a governmental interest that was sufficient to warrant temporary detention for limited questioning. Royer does not suggest, nor do we, that a similar rationale would not warrant temporary detention for questioning on less than probable cause where the public interest involved is the suppression of illegal transactions in drugs or of any other serious crime.

Michigan v. Summers, 452 U.S. 692 (1981), involved another circumstance in which a temporary detention on less than probable cause satisfied the ultimate test of reasonableness under the Fourth Amendment. There the occupant of a house was detained while a search warrant for the house was being executed. We held that the warrant made the occupant sufficiently suspect to justify his temporary seizure. The "limited intrusio[n] on the personal security" of the person detained was justified "by such substantial law enforcement interests" that the seizure could be made on articulable suspicion not amounting to probable cause. * * * [e]

Fourth, *Terry* and its progeny nevertheless created only limited exceptions to the general rule that seizures of the person require probable cause to arrest. Detentions may be "investigative" yet violative of the Fourth Amendment absent probable cause. In the name of investigating a person who is no more than suspected of criminal activity, the police may not carry out a full search of the person or of his automobile or other effects. Nor may the police seek to verify their suspicions by means that approach the conditions of arrest. *Dunaway v. New York*, [this volume], * * * made this clear. * * *

[A warrantless Fourth Amendment] * * * search must be limited in scope to that which is justified by the particular purposes served by the exception. For example, a warrantless search is permissible incident to a lawful arrest because of legitimate concerns for the safety of the officer and to prevent the destruction of evidence by the arrestee. * * * Nevertheless, such a search is limited to the person of the arrestee and the area immediately within his control. * * * The reasonableness requirement of the Fourth Amendment requires no less when the police action is a seizure permitted on less than probable cause because of legitimate law enforcement interests. The scope of the detention must be carefully tailored to its underlying justification. [f]

* * * [A]n investigative detention must be temporary and last no longer than is necessary to effectuate the purpose of the stop. Similarly, the investigative methods employed should be the least intrusive means reasonably available to verify or dispel the officer's suspicion in a short period of time. * * * [g] It is the State's burden to demonstrate that the seizure it seeks to justify on the basis of a reasonable suspicion was sufficiently limited in scope and duration to satisfy the conditions of an investigative seizure.

Fifth, * * * statements given during a period of illegal detention are inadmissible even though voluntarily given if they are the product of the illegal detention and not the result of an independent act of free will. * * *

Sixth, if the events in this case amounted to no more than a permissible police encounter in a public place or a justifiable *Terry*-type detention, Royer's consent, if voluntary, would have been effective to legalize the search of his two suitcases. * * * The Florida District Court of Appeal in the case before us, however, concluded not only that Royer had been seized when he gave his consent to search his luggage but also that the bounds of an investigative stop had been exceeded. In its view the "confinement" in this case went beyond the limited restraint of a *Terry* investigative stop, and Royer's consent was thus tainted by the illegality, a conclusion that required reversal in the absence of probable cause to arrest. The question before us is whether the record warrants that conclusion. We think that it does.

III

The State proffers three reasons for holding that when Royer consented to the search of his luggage, he was not being illegally detained. First, it is submitted that the entire encounter was consensual and hence Royer was not being held against his will at all. We find this submission untenable. Asking for and examining Royer's ticket and his driver's license were no doubt permissible in themselves, but when the officers identified themselves as narcotics agents, told Royer that he was suspected of transporting narcotics, and asked him to accompany them to the police room, while retaining his ticket and driver's license and without indicating in any way that he was free to depart, Royer was effectively seized for

the purposes of the Fourth Amendment. These circumstances surely amount to a show of official authority such that "a reasonable person would have believed that he was not free to leave." * * *

Second, the State submits that if Royer was seized, there existed reasonable, articulable suspicion to justify a temporary detention and that the limits of a *Terry*-type stop were never exceeded. We agree with the State that when the officers discovered that Royer was traveling under an assumed name, this fact, and the facts already known to the officers—paying cash for a one-way ticket, the mode of checking the two bags, and Royer's appearance and conduct in general—were adequate grounds for suspecting Royer of carrying drugs and for temporarily detaining him and his luggage while they attempted to verify or dispel their suspicions in a manner that did not exceed the limits of an investigative detention. We also agree that had Royer voluntarily consented to the search of his luggage while he was justifiably being detained on reasonable suspicion, the products of the search would be admissible against him. We have concluded, however, that at the time Royer produced the key to his suitcase, the detention to which he was then subjected was a more serious intrusion on his personal liberty than is allowable on mere suspicion of criminal activity.

By the time Royer was informed that the officers wished to examine his luggage, he had identified himself when approached by the officers and had attempted to explain the discrepancy between the name shown on his identification and the name under which he had purchased his ticket and identified his luggage. The officers were not satisfied, for they informed him they were narcotics agents and had reason to believe that he was carrying illegal drugs. They requested him to accompany them to the police room. Royer went with them. He found himself in a small room— a large closet—equipped with a desk and two chairs. He was alone with two police officers who again told him that they thought he was carrying narcotics. He also found that the officers, without his consent, had retrieved his checked luggage from the airline. What had begun as a consensual inquiry in a public place had escalated into an investigatory procedure in a police interrogation room, where the police, unsatisfied with previous explanations, sought to confirm their suspicions. The officers had Royer's ticket, they had his identification, and they had seized his luggage. Royer was never informed that he was free to board his plane if he so chose, and he reasonably believed that he was being detained. At least as of that moment, any consensual aspects of the encounter had evaporated, and we cannot fault the Florida District Court of Appeal for concluding that *Terry v. Ohio* and the cases following it did not justify the restraint to which Royer was then subjected. As a practical matter, Royer was under arrest. [h] Consistent with this conclusion, the State conceded in the Florida courts that Royer would not have been free to leave the interrogation room had he asked to do so. Furthermore, the State's brief in this Court interprets the testimony of the officers at the suppression hearing as indicating that had Royer refused to consent to a search of his luggage, the officers would have held the luggage

and sought a warrant to authorize the search. * * *

We also think that the officers' conduct was more intrusive than necessary to effectuate an investigative detention otherwise authorized by the *Terry* line of cases. First, by returning his ticket and driver's license, and informing him that he was free to go if he so desired, the officers might have obviated any claim that the encounter was anything but a consensual matter from start to finish. Second, there are undoubtedly reasons of safety and security that would justify moving a suspect from one location to another during an investigatory detention, such as from an airport concourse to a more private area. * * * There is no indication in this case that such reasons prompted the officers to transfer the site of the encounter from the concourse to the interrogation room. It appears, rather, that the primary interest of the officers was not in having an extended conversation with Royer but in the contents of his luggage, a matter which the officers did not pursue orally with Royer until after the encounter was relocated to the police room. The record does not reflect any facts which would support a finding that the legitimate law enforcement purposes which justified the detention in the first instance were furthered by removing Royer to the police room prior to the officers' attempt to gain his consent to a search of his luggage. As we have noted, had Royer consented to a search on the spot, the search could have been conducted with Royer present in the area where the bags were retrieved by Detective Johnson and any evidence recovered would have been admissible against him. If the search proved negative, Royer would have been free to go much earlier and with less likelihood of missing his flight, which in itself can be a very serious matter in a variety of circumstances.

Third, the State has not touched on the question whether it would have been feasible to investigate the contents of Royer's bags in a more expeditious way. The courts are not strangers to the use of trained dogs to detect the presence of controlled substances in luggage. There is no indication here that this means was not feasible and available. If it had been used, Royer and his luggage could have been momentarily detained while this investigative procedure was carried out. Indeed, it may be that no detention at all would have been necessary. A negative result would have freed Royer in short order; a positive result would have resulted in his justifiable arrest on probable cause. **[i]**

We do not suggest that there is a litmus-paper test for distinguishing a consensual encounter from a seizure or for determining when a seizure exceeds the bounds of an investigative stop. Even in the discrete category of airport encounters, there will be endless variations in the facts and circumstances, so much variation that it is unlikely that the courts can reduce to a sentence or a paragraph a rule that will provide unarguable answers to the question whether there has been an unreasonable search or seizure in violation of the Fourth Amendment. Nevertheless, we must render judgment, and we think that the Florida District Court of Appeal cannot be faulted in concluding that the limits of a *Terry*-stop had been exceeded.

IV

The State's third and final argument is that Royer was not being illegally held when he gave his consent because there was probable cause to arrest him at that time. * * * We agree with the Florida District Court of Appeal * * * that probable cause to arrest Royer did not exist at the time he consented to the search of his luggage. The facts are that a nervous young man with two American Tourister bags paid cash for an airline ticket to a "target city." These facts led to inquiry, which in turn revealed that the ticket had been bought under an assumed name. The proffered explanation did not satisfy the officers. We cannot agree with the State, if this is its position, that every nervous young man paying cash for a ticket to New York City under an assumed name and carrying two heavy American Tourister bags may be arrested and held to answer for a serious felony charge. **[j]**

V

Because we affirm the Florida District Court of Appeal's conclusion that Royer was being illegally detained when he consented to the search of his luggage, we agree that the consent was tainted by the illegality and was ineffective to justify the search. The judgment of the Florida District Court of Appeal is accordingly
Affirmed.

[JUSTICE POWELL wrote a brief concurring opinion.]

[JUSTICE BRENNAN concurred in the result. He felt that the discussion of the scope of a *Terry* stop was unnecessary to the decision because the initial seizure of Royer was illegal.]

JUSTICE BLACKMUN, dissenting.

* * *

In my view, the police conduct in this case was minimally intrusive. Given the strength of society's interest in overcoming the extraordinary obstacles to the detection of drug traffickers, such conduct should not be subjected to a requirement of probable cause. * * *

I

* * *

"'[T]he] key principle of the Fourth Amendment is reasonableness—the balancing of competing interests.'" * * * In the case of a seizure less intrusive than a formal arrest, determining whether the less demanding reasonable-suspicion standard will be applied requires balancing the amount of intrusion upon individual privacy against the special law enforcement interests that would be served by permitting such an intrusion on less than probable cause. * * * [k]

* * *

* * * [B]eyond the initial stop and properly limited questioning, further detention and search were based on Royer's consent. Certainly, the intrusion on Royer's privacy was not so extreme as to make the countervailing public interest in greater flexibility irrelevant to the question whether probable cause was required. Consequently, I do not understand why the plurality fails to balance the character of the detention and the degree to which it intruded upon Royer's privacy against its justification as measured by "both the law enforcement interest and the nature of the 'articulable facts' supporting the detention." * * *

II

The officers in this case began their encounter with Royer with reasonable suspicion. They continued their questioning and requested further cooperation only as more facts, heightening their suspicion, came to their attention. Certainly, as any such detention continues or escalates, a greater degree of reasonable suspicion is necessary to sustain it, and at some point probable cause will be required. But here, the intrusion was short-lived and minimal. Only 15 minutes transpired from the initial approach to the opening of the suitcases. The officers were polite, and sought and immediately obtained Royer's consent at each significant step of the process. Royer knew that if the search of the suitcases did not turn up contraband, he would be free to go on his way. Thus, it seems clear to me that "'the police [were] diligently pursuing a means of investigation which [was] likely to resolve the matter one way or another very soon. * * *'" * * *

The special need for flexibility in uncovering illicit drug couriers is hardly debatable. * * *

[JUSTICE REHNQUIST, joined by THE CHIEF JUSTICE and JUSTICE O'CONNOR, dissented, finding that the actions of the police in this case were reasonable under the circumstances:] * * *

Analyzed simply in terms of its "reasonableness" as that term is used in the Fourth Amendment, the conduct of the investigating officers toward Royer would pass muster with virtually all thoughtful, civilized persons not overly steeped in the mysteries of this Court's Fourth Amendment jurisprudence.

Analyzed even in terms of the most meticulous regard for our often con-flicting cases, it seems to me to pass muster equally well.

* * *

* * * * * * * * * *

COMMENTS

[a] As you read the facts, ask yourself if Royer legally consented to anything, and whether or at which stage the officers had either probable cause to arrest or reasonable suspicion to stop.

[b] The profile in this case was based on six elements: Royer carried heavy American Tourister luggage, he was young, apparently between 25-35, he was casually dressed, he appeared pale and nervous, looking around at other people, he paid for his ticket in cash with a large number of bills, and rather than completing the airline identification baggage tag with a name, address, and telephone number, he wrote only a name and the destination. None of these elements is inherently criminal; in combination do you think they are a good basis for a stop-and-frisk? an arrest?

[c] Who has the burden of proof, in a close factual case as this one, may determine which party will win.

[d] This is clear in law. However, as a psychological matter it may be more difficult for most persons to reject a police invitation to speak than to reject a civilian stranger who tries to strike up an unwanted conversation.

[e] These stop and frisk examples bolster the Court's conclusion that there was reasonable suspicion to initially stop and question Royer.

[f] The particularity clause of the Fourth Amendment expresses a common sense understanding that if the police are legitimately given an inch of intrusion, they are likely to "take a mile" if no limits are placed on the scope of the search.

[g] Both JUSTICE BRENNAN, concurring, and the dissenting justices criticized this point, which failed to gain a majority of the Court.

[h] Do you think the police had probable cause to arrest Royer before opening his suitcase?

[i] See *United States v. Place* [this volume].

[j] The dissenters, below, believe that, because of the magnitude of the illegal drug importation problem, the police action in this case was reasonable under the Fourth Amendment. The four justice plurality opinion hints that American beliefs

and habits of liberty are threatened if people can be stopped when police have a good hunch that drugs are being transported. The conclusions of both the plurality and the dissenters are not strictly derived by logic, but contain elements of constitutional policy reasoning.

[k] This reasoning is very close to the "special needs" doctrine that was articulated in *New Jersey v. T.L.O.* [this volume], a doctrine that has not been applied to a straightforward criminal search by law enforcement personnel.

UNITED STATES v. PLACE

462 U.S. 696, 103 S.Ct. 2637, 77 L.Ed.2d 110 (1983)

JUSTICE O'CONNOR delivered the opinion of the Court.

This case presents the issue whether the Fourth Amendment prohibits law enforcement authorities from temporarily detaining personal luggage for exposure to a trained narcotics detection dog on the basis of reasonable suspicion that the luggage contains narcotics. Given the enforcement problems associated with the detection of narcotics trafficking and the minimal intrusion that a properly limited detention would entail, we conclude that the Fourth Amendment does not prohibit such a detention. On the facts of this case, however, we hold that the police conduct exceeded the bounds of a permissible investigative detention of the luggage.

I

[Place appeared suspicious to police officers as he waited in line at the Miami International Airport to purchase a ticket to New York's La Guardia Airport. As Place walked to the gate the officers approached him and requested his airline ticket and some identification.] Place complied with the request and consented to a search of the two suitcases he had checked. Because his flight was about to depart, however, the agents decided not to search the luggage.

[Noting discrepancies on the addresses on the luggage tags, the Miami officers called Drug Enforcement Administration (DEA) authorities in New York to relay their information about Place. Two DEA agents observed Place at La Guardia Airport, believed his behavior was suspicious, and stopped him as he was waiting for a limousine. The police ran a driver's license check on Place that disclosed no offenses. Place refused to consent to a search of his luggage which the agents took. The agents released Place, giving him a telephone number, and took the luggage to Kennedy Airport, where a trained narcotics detection dog positively reacted to the smaller bag by a "sniff test." Approximately 90 minutes elapsed between the seizure of the luggage and the "sniff test"]. Because it was late on a Friday afternoon, the agents retained the luggage until Monday morning, when they secured a search warrant from a Magistrate for the smaller bag. Upon opening that bag, the agents discovered 1,125 grams of cocaine.

[The federal Court of Appeals reversed Place's drug possession conviction, finding that "that the prolonged seizure of Place's baggage exceeded the permissible limits of a *Terry*-type investigative stop and consequently amounted to a seizure without probable cause in violation of the Fourth Amendment."]

We granted certiorari, * * * and now affirm.

II

[The Court first applied a balancing test and held that the State's substantial interest in crime prevention allowed agents to stop individuals for questioning where they had reasonable suspicion, but not probable cause, to believe that the individual was carrying illicit drugs in a container. The next question was whether a limited seizure of a bag was permissible.]

* * *

* * * Specifically, the *Terry* exception to the probable-cause requirement is premised on the notion that a *Terry*-type stop of the person is substantially less intrusive of a person's liberty interests than a formal arrest. In the property context, however, Place urges, there are no degrees of intrusion. Once the owner's property is seized, the dispossession is absolute.

We disagree. The intrusion on possessory interests occasioned by a seizure of one's personal effects can vary both in its nature and extent. The seizure may be made after the owner has relinquished control of the property to a third party or, as here, from the immediate custody and control of the owner. Moreover, the police may confine their investigation to an on-the-spot inquiry—for example, immediate exposure of the luggage to a trained narcotics detection dog—or transport the property to another location. Given the fact that seizures of property can vary in intrusiveness, some brief detentions of personal effects may be so minimally intrusive of Fourth Amendment interests that strong countervailing governmental interests will justify a seizure based only on specific articulable facts that the property contains contraband or evidence of a crime.

In sum, we conclude that when an officer's observations lead him reasonably to believe that a traveler is carrying luggage that contains narcotics, the principles of *Terry* and its progeny

would permit the officer to detain the luggage briefly to investigate the circumstances that aroused his suspicion, provided that the investigative detention is properly limited in scope.

The purpose for which respondent's luggage was seized, of course, was to arrange its exposure to a narcotics detection dog. Obviously, if this investigative procedure is itself a search requiring probable cause, the initial seizure of respondent's luggage for the purpose of subjecting it to the sniff test—no matter how brief—could not be justified on less than probable cause. * * *

The Fourth Amendment "protects people from unreasonable government intrusions into their legitimate expectations of privacy." * * * We have affirmed that a person possesses a privacy interest in the contents of personal luggage that is protected by the Fourth Amendment. * * * A "canine sniff" by a well-trained narcotics detection dog, however, does not require opening the luggage. It does not expose noncontraband items that otherwise would remain hidden from public view, as does, for example, an officer's rummaging through the contents of the luggage. Thus, the manner in which information is obtained through this investigative technique is much less intrusive than a typical search. Moreover, the sniff discloses only the presence or absence of narcotics, a contraband item. Thus, despite the fact that the sniff tells the authorities something about the contents of the luggage, the information obtained is limited. This limited disclosure also ensures that the owner of the property is not subjected to the embarrassment and inconvenience entailed in less discriminate and more intrusive investigative methods. [a]

In these respects, the canine sniff is *sui generis*. We are aware of no other investigative procedure that is so limited both in the manner in which the information is obtained and in the content of the information revealed by the procedure. Therefore, we conclude that the particular course of investigation that the agents intended to pursue here—exposure of respondent's luggage, which was located in a public place, to a trained canine—did not constitute a "search" within the meaning of the Fourth Amendment.

III

There is no doubt that the agents made a "seizure" of Place's luggage for purposes of the Fourth Amendment when, following his refusal to consent to a search, the agent told Place that he was going to take the luggage to a federal judge to secure issuance of a warrant. As we observed in *Terry*, "[t]he manner in which the seizure ... [was] conducted is, of course, as vital a part of the inquiry as whether [it was] warranted at all." * * * We therefore examine whether the agents' conduct in this case was such as to place the seizure within the general rule requiring probable cause for a seizure or within *Terry*'s exception to that rule.

At the outset, we must reject the Government's suggestion that the point at which probable cause for seizure of luggage from the person's presence becomes necessary is more distant than in the case of a *Terry* stop of the person himself. The premise of the Government's argument is that seizures of property are generally less intrusive than seizures of the person. While true in some circumstances, that premise is faulty on the facts we address in this case. The precise type of detention we confront here is seizure of personal luggage from the immediate possession of the suspect for the purpose of arranging exposure to a narcotics detection dog. Particularly in the case of detention of luggage within the traveler's immediate possession, the police conduct intrudes on both the suspect's possessory interest in his luggage as well as his liberty interest in proceeding with his itinerary. The person whose luggage is detained is technically still free to continue his travels or carry out other personal activities pending release of the luggage. Moreover, he is not subjected to the coercive atmosphere of a custodial confinement or to the public indignity of being personally detained. Nevertheless, such a seizure can effectively restrain the person since he is subjected to the possible disruption of his travel plans in order to remain with his luggage or to arrange for its return. Therefore, when the police seize luggage from the suspect's custody, we think the limitations applicable to investigative detentions of the person should define the permissible scope of an investigative detention of the person's luggage on less than probable cause. Under this standard, it is clear that the police conduct here exceeded the permissible limits of a *Terry*-type investigative stop.

The length of the detention of respondent's luggage alone precludes the conclusion that the seizure was reasonable in the absence of probable cause. Although we have recognized the reasonableness of seizures longer than momentary ones, * * * the brevity of the invasion of the individual's Fourth Amendment interests is an

important factor in determining whether the seizure is so minimally intrusive as to be justifiable on reasonable suspicion. Moreover, in assessing the effect of the length of the detention, we take into account whether the police diligently pursue their investigation. We note that here the New York agents knew the time of Place's scheduled arrival at La Guardia, had ample time to arrange for their additional investigation at that location, and thereby could have minimized the intrusion on respondent's Fourth Amendment interests. Thus, although we decline to adopt any outside time limitation for a permissible *Terry* stop, we have never approved a seizure of the person for the prolonged 90-minute period involved here and cannot do so on the facts presented by this case. *
* *

Although the 90-minute detention of respondent's luggage is sufficient to render the seizure unreasonable, the violation was exacerbated by the failure of the agents to accurately inform

respondent of the place to which they were transporting his luggage, of the length of time he might be dispossessed, and of what arrangements would be made for return of the luggage if the investigation dispelled the suspicion. In short, we hold that the detention of respondent's luggage in this case went beyond the narrow authority possessed by police to detain briefly luggage reasonably suspected to contain narcotics.

* * *

[JUSTICE BRENNAN, joined by JUSTICE MARSHALL, concurred in the result, raising concerns about broad interpretations of the *Terry* doctrine, challenging the balancing test reasoning that authorized property seizure on reasonable suspicion, and stating that the dog-sniff issue was decided prematurely.]

[JUSTICE BLACKMUN, joined by JUSTICE MARSHALL, concurred in the judgment, noting that it was not necessary for the court to decide the dog-sniff issue.]

*   *   *   *   *   *   *   *   *   *   *

COMMENTS

[a] Would this reasoning apply to an x-ray scan of bags for weapons where the police have reasonable suspicion?

UNITED STATES v. SOKOLOW

490 U.S. 1, 109 S.Ct. 1581, 104 L.Ed.2d 1 (1989)

CHIEF JUSTICE REHNQUIST delivered the opinion of the Court.

Respondent Andrew Sokolow was stopped by Drug Enforcement Administration (DEA) agents upon his arrival at Honolulu International Airport. The agents found 1,063 grams of cocaine in his carry-on luggage. When respondent was stopped, the agents knew, *inter alia*, that (1) he paid $2,100 for two airplane tickets from a roll of $20 bills; (2) he traveled under a name that did not match the name under which his telephone number was listed; (3) his original destination was Miami, a source city for illicit drugs; (4) he stayed in Miami for only 48 hours, even though a round-trip flight from Honolulu to Miami takes 20 hours; (5) he appeared nervous during his trip; and (6) he checked none of his luggage. A divided panel of the United States Court of Appeals for the Ninth Circuit held that the DEA agents did not have a reasonable suspicion to stop respondent, as required by the Fourth Amendment. * * * We take the contrary view.

This case involves a typical attempt to smuggle drugs through one of the Nation's airports. [Sokolow purchased two round-trip tickets to Miami at the Honolulu Airport] in the names of "Andrew Kray" and "Janet Norian." * * * Respondent paid $2,100 for the tickets from a large roll of $20 bills, which appeared to contain a total of $4,000. He also gave the ticket agent his home telephone number. The ticket agent noticed that respondent seemed nervous; he was about 25 years old; he was dressed in a black jumpsuit and wore gold jewelry; and he was accompanied by a woman, who turned out to be Janet Norian. Neither respondent nor his companion checked any of their four pieces of luggage.

[The suspicious ticket agent notified a police agent who discovered the telephone number was that of a "Karl Herman," who turned out to be Sokolow's roommate; no telephone listing for "Andrew Kray" was found in Hawaii. The officer discovered that return flight was booked for three days after departure and stopovers were identified. DEA agents in a stopover in Los Angeles, noticed that Sokolow appeared nervous. At his return in Honolulu, Sokolow was forcibly detained by DEA agents. He and Norian were "escorted" to a DEA agents where a trained dog sniffed Sokolow's shoulder bag and responded positively. Sokolow was arrested and a warrant was obtained to search his bag. No drugs were found, but "the bag did contain several suspicious documents indicating respondent's involvement in drug trafficking." A further dog-sniff by two dogs "alerted on a medium-sized Louis Vuitton bag." It was evening and Sokolow and Norien were released, but the baggage was detained. A warrant was obtained the next day and a search uncovered 1,063 grams of cocaine.]

[Sokolow's conviction for drug possession was reversed by the federal Court of Appeals. That court held that the DEA agents did not have a reasonable suspicion to justify the stop. It established a two-part test to sustain a stop based on drug courier profiles. First, the State had to show that the suspect was involved in an "ongoing criminal activity," by such facts as the use of an alias or evasive movement through an airport.   The second category, included facts describing "personal characteristics" of drug couriers, such as the cash payment for tickets, a short trip to a major source city for drugs,   nervousness, type of attire, and unchecked luggage.   The two-part test was established because both drug couriers and members of the general public shared the personal characteristics.   That court found no facts of ongoing criminal activity in this case.   A dissenting judge criticized the two-part test as "mechanistic."]

We granted certiorari to review the decision of the Court of Appeals, * * * because of its serious implications for the enforcement of the federal narcotics laws.   We now reverse.

* * * [W]e   assume—without deciding— that a stop occurred here. Our decision, then, turns on whether the agents had a reasonable suspicion that respondent was engaged in wrongdoing when they encountered him on the sidewalk.   In *Terry v. Ohio*, [this volume], we held that the police can stop and briefly detain a person for investigative purposes if the officer has a reasonable suspicion supported by articulable facts that criminal activity "may be afoot," even if the officer lacks probable cause.

The officer, of course, must be able to articulate something more than an "inchoate and unparticularized suspicion or 'hunch.'" * * *   The Fourth Amendment requires "some minimal level of objective justification" for making the stop. * * *   That level of suspicion is considerably less than proof of wrongdoing by a preponderance of the evidence.   We have held that probable cause means "a fair probability that contraband or evidence of a crime will be found," * * * and the level of suspicion required for a *Terry* stop is obviously less demanding than that for probable cause. * * *

The concept of reasonable suspicion, like probable cause, is not "readily, or even usefully, reduced to a neat set of legal rules." * * *   We think the Court of Appeals' effort to refine and elaborate the requirements of "reasonable suspicion" in this case creates unnecessary difficulty in dealing with one of the relatively simple concepts embodied in the Fourth Amendment.   In evaluating the validity of a stop such as this, we must consider "the totality of the circumstances—the whole picture." * * *

The rule enunciated by the Court of Appeals, in which evidence available to an officer is divided into evidence of "ongoing criminal behavior," on the one hand, and "probabilistic" evidence, on the other, is not in keeping with the quoted statements from our decisions.   It also seems to us to draw a sharp line between types of evidence, the probative value of which varies only in degree.   The Court of Appeals classified evidence of traveling under an alias, or evidence that the suspect took an evasive or erratic path through an airport, as meeting the test for showing "ongoing criminal activity." But certainly instances are conceivable in which traveling under an alias would not reflect ongoing criminal activity: for example, a person who wished to travel to a hospital or clinic for an operation and wished to conceal that fact. One taking an evasive path through an airport might be seeking to avoid a confrontation with an angry acquaintance or with a creditor. This is not to say that each of these types of evidence is not highly probative, but they do not have the sort of ironclad significance attributed to them by the Court of Appeals.

On the other hand, the factors in this case that the Court of Appeals treated as merely "probabilistic" also have probative significance. Paying $2,100 in cash for two airplane tickets is out of the ordinary, and it is even more out of the ordinary to pay that sum from a roll of $20 bills containing nearly twice that amount of cash. Most business travelers, we feel confident, purchase airline tickets by credit card or check so as to have a record for tax or business purposes, and few vacationers carry with them thousands of dollars in $20 bills. We also think the agents had a reasonable ground to believe that respondent was traveling under an alias; the evidence was by no means conclusive, but it was sufficient to warrant consideration. While a trip from Honolulu to Miami, standing alone, is not a cause for any sort of suspicion, here there was more: surely few residents of Honolulu travel from that city for 20 hours to spend 48 hours in Miami during the month of July.

Any one of these factors is not by itself proof of any illegal conduct and is quite consistent with innocent travel. But we think taken together they amount to reasonable suspicion. * * * We said in *Reid v. Georgia*, 448 U.S. 438 (1980), * * * "there could, of course, be circumstances in which wholly lawful conduct might justify the suspicion that criminal activity was afoot." * * *

We do not agree with respondent that our analysis is somehow changed by the agents' belief that his behavior was consistent with one of the DEA's "drug courier profiles." * * * A court sitting to determine the existence of reasonable suspicion must require the agent to articulate the factors leading to that conclusion, but the fact that these factors may be set forth in a "profile" does not somehow detract from their evidentiary significance as seen by a trained agent.

[The Court rejected the contention that the DEA agents had to use] the least intrusive means available to verify or dispel their suspicions that he was smuggling narcotics. [The statement of that rule in *Florida v. Royer*, [this volume]], was directed at the length of the investigative stop, not at whether the police had a less intrusive means to verify their suspicions before stopping Royer. The reasonableness of the officer's decision to stop a suspect does not turn on the availability of less intrusive investigatory techniques. Such a rule would unduly hamper the police's ability to make swift, on-the-spot decisions * * * and it would require courts to "indulge in 'unrealistic second-guessing.'" * * *

We hold that the agents had a reasonable basis to suspect that respondent was transporting illegal drugs on these facts. The judgment of the Court of Appeals is therefore reversed, and the case is remanded for further proceedings consistent with our decision.

It is so ordered.

JUSTICE MARSHALL, with whom JUSTICE BRENNAN joins,

dissenting.

* * *

Evaluated against [the reasonable suspicion] standard, the facts about Andrew Sokolow known to the DEA agents at the time they stopped him fall short of reasonably indicating that he was engaged at the time in criminal activity. It is highly significant that the DEA agents stopped Sokolow because he matched one of the DEA's "profiles" of a paradigmatic drug courier. In my view, a law enforcement officer's mechanistic application of a formula of personal and behavioral traits in deciding whom to detain can only dull the officer's ability and determination to make sensitive and fact-specific inferences "in light of his experience," * * * particularly in ambiguous or borderline cases. Reflexive reliance on a profile of drug courier characteristics runs a far greater risk than does ordinary, case-by-case police work of subjecting innocent individuals to unwarranted police harassment and detention. This risk is enhanced by the profile's "chameleon-like way of adapting to any particular set of observations." * * * [JUSTICE MARSHALL here reviewed a large number of federal cases that identify several conflicting categories that constitute the drug courier profile. For example, they have been held to include, in different cases that the profiled suspect was first to deplane, the last to deplane, or deplaned from middle; suspect held one-way tickets, or held round-trip tickets; the flight was nonstop or the flight required a change of planes; the suspect carried no luggage, carried a gym bag, or carried a new suitcase; was traveling alone or was traveling with a companion; acted nervously or acted too calmly.] In asserting that it is not "somehow" relevant that the agents who stopped Sokolow did so in reliance on a prefabricated profile of criminal characteristics, * * * the majority thus ducks serious issues relating to a questionable law enforcement practice, to address the validity of which we granted certiorari in this case. [a]

[JUSTICE MARSHALL went on to compare this case to *Reid v. Georgia*, where a four-part drug courier profile was held insufficient to establish reasonable suspicion, and to evaluate each element of the profile in this case which, "considered either singly or together, are scarcely indicative of criminal activity." He also reviewed cases where the Court found reasonable suspicion to exist, based on articulable facts, and accused the majority of giving "short shrift to constitutional rights" when "drug crimes or antidrug policies are at issue."]

* * * * * * * * * * *

COMMENTS

[a] By deciding the case on the particular facts of the case instead of drug courier profiles in general the Court avoids having to decide cases that involve changes in profiles over time or as used by different law enforcement agencies.

ALABAMA v. WHITE

496 U.S. 325, 110 S.Ct. 2412, 110 L.Ed.2d 301 (1990)

JUSTICE WHITE delivered the opinion of the Court.

Based on an anonymous telephone tip, police stopped respondent's vehicle. A consensual search of the car revealed drugs. The issue is whether the tip, as corroborated by independent police work, exhibited sufficient indicia of reliability to provide reasonable suspicion to make the investigatory stop. We hold that it did.

[One afternoon, a Montgomery Police officer received a telephone call from an anonymous person stating that Vanessa White would be leaving 235-C Lynwood Terrace Apartments at a particular time in a brown Plymouth station wagon with the right taillight lens broken, that she would be going to Dobey's Motel, and that she would be in possession of about an ounce of cocaine inside a brown attaché case. The officer and his partner proceeded to the Lynwood Terrace Apartments, where they saw a brown Plymouth station wagon with a broken right taillight in the parking lot in front of the 235 building. The officers observed respondent leave the 235 building, carrying nothing in her hands, and enter the station wagon. They followed the vehicle as it drove the most direct route to Dobey's Motel. When the vehicle neared Dobey's Motel the police stopped the vehicle. White was asked to step to the rear of her car, she was informed that she was suspected of carrying cocaine in the vehicle. Upon request, White consented to a search of her car. She provided the combination to a locked brown attaché case found in the car which contained some marijuana. During White's arrest processing at the station, three milligrams of cocaine were discovered in her purse.]

[White was convicted of possession of marijuana and cocaine. The Alabama Court of Criminal Appeals of Alabama held that the officers did not have reasonable suspicion to justify the investigatory stop of respondent's car, excluded the drug evidence and reversed White's conviction.] Because of differing views in the state and federal courts over whether an anonymous tip may furnish reasonable suspicion for a stop, we granted the State's petition for certiorari. * * * We now reverse.

Adams v. Williams, 407 U.S. 143 (1972), sustained a *Terry [v. Ohio*, (this volume)] stop and frisk undertaken on the basis of a tip given in person by a known informant who had provided information in the past. We concluded that, while the unverified tip may have been insufficient to support an arrest or search warrant, the information carried sufficient "indicia of reliability" to justify a forcible stop. * * * We did not address the issue of anonymous tips in *Adams*, except to say that "[t]his is a stronger case than obtains in the case of an anonymous telephone tip." * * *

Illinois v. Gates, [this volume], dealt with an anonymous tip in the probable cause context. The Court there abandoned the "two-pronged test" of *Aguilar v. Texas*, 378 U.S. 108 (1964), and *Spinelli v. United States*, [this volume], in favor of a "totality of the circumstances" approach to determining whether an informant's tip establishes probable cause.   *Gates* made clear, however, that those factors that had been considered critical under *Aguilar* and *Spinelli*—an informant's "veracity," "reliability," and "basis of knowledge"—remain "highly relevant in determining the value of his report." * * * These factors are also relevant in the reasonable suspicion context, although allowance must be made in applying them for the lesser showing required to meet that standard.

The opinion in *Gates* recognized that an anonymous tip alone seldom demonstrates the informant's basis of knowledge or veracity inasmuch as ordinary citizens generally do not provide extensive recitations of the basis of their everyday observations and given that the veracity of persons supplying anonymous tips is "by hypothesis largely unknown, and unknowable." * * * This is not to say that an anonymous caller could never provide the reasonable suspicion necessary for a *Terry* stop. But the tip in *Gates* was not an exception to the general rule, and the anonymous tip in this case is like the one in *Gates*: "[it] provides virtually nothing from which one might conclude that [the caller] is either honest or his information reliable; likewise, the [tip] gives absolutely no indication of the basis for the [caller's] predictions regarding [Vanessa White's] criminal activities." * * * By requiring "[s]omething more," as *Gates* did, *ibid.*, we merely apply what we said in *Adams*: "Some tips, completely lacking in indicia of reliability, would either warrant no police response or require further investigation before a forcible stop of a suspect would be

authorized," * * *   Simply put, a tip such as this one, standing alone, would not "'warrant a man of reasonable caution in the belief' that [a stop] was appropriate." *Terry*. * * *

As there was in *Gates*, however, in this case there is more than the tip itself. The tip was not as detailed, and the corroboration was not as complete, as in *Gates*, but the required degree of suspicion was likewise not as high. * * *

Reasonable suspicion is a less demanding standard than probable cause not only in the sense that reasonable suspicion can be established with information that is different in quantity or content than that required to establish probable cause, but also in the sense that reasonable suspicion can arise from information that is less reliable than that required to show probable cause.   *Adams v. Williams*, *supra*, demonstrates as much. We there assumed that the unverified tip from the known informant might not have been reliable enough to establish probable cause, but nevertheless found it sufficiently reliable to justify a *Terry* stop. * * * Reasonable suspicion, like probable cause, is dependent upon both the content of information possessed by police and its degree of reliability.   Both factors—quantity and quality—are considered in the "totality of the circumstances—the whole picture," * * * that must be taken into account when evaluating whether there is reasonable suspicion. Thus, if a tip has a relatively low degree of reliability, more information will be required to establish the requisite quantum of suspicion than would be required if the tip were more reliable. The *Gates* Court applied its totality of the circumstances approach in this manner, taking into account the facts known to the officers from personal observation, and giving the anonymous tip the weight it deserved in light of its indicia of reliability as established through independent police work. The same approach applies in the reasonable suspicion context, the only difference being the level of suspicion that must be established. Contrary to the court below, we conclude that when the officers stopped respondent, the anonymous tip had been sufficiently corroborated to furnish reasonable suspicion that respondent was engaged in criminal activity and that the investigative stop therefore did not violate the Fourth Amendment. [a]

It is true that not every detail mentioned by the tipster was verified, such as the name of the woman leaving the building or the precise apartment from which she left; but the officers did corroborate that a woman left the 235 building and got into the particular vehicle that was described by the caller. With respect to the time of departure predicted by the informant, Corporal Davis testified that the caller gave a particular time when the woman would be leaving, * * * but he did not state what that time was. He did testify that, after the call, he and his partner proceeded to the Lynwood Terrace Apartments to put the 235 building under surveillance. * * * Given the fact that the officers proceeded to the indicated address immediately after the call and that respondent emerged not too long thereafter, it appears from the record before us that respondent's departure from the building was within the time frame predicted by the caller. As for the caller's prediction of respondent's destination, it is true that the officers

stopped her just short of Dobey's Motel and did not know whether she would have pulled in or continued on past it. But given that the four-mile route   driven by respondent was the most direct route possible to Dobey's Motel, * * * but nevertheless involved several turns, * * * we think respondent's destination was significantly corroborated.

The Court's opinion in *Gates* gave credit to the proposition that because an informant is shown to be right about some things, he is probably right about other facts that he has alleged, including the claim that the object of the tip is engaged in criminal activity. * * * Thus, it is not unreasonable to conclude in this case that the independent corroboration by the police of significant aspects of the informer's predictions imparted some degree of reliability to the other allegations made by the caller.

We think it also important that, as in *Gates*, "the anonymous [tip] contained a range of details relating not just to easily obtained facts and conditions existing at the time of the tip, but to future actions of third parties ordinarily not easily predicted." * * * The fact that the officers found a car precisely matching the caller's description in front of the 235 building is an example of the former. Anyone could have "predicted" that fact because it was a condition presumably existing at the time of the call. What was important was the caller's ability to predict respondent's *future behavior*, because it demonstrated inside information—a special familiarity with respondent's affairs. The general public would have had no way of knowing that respondent would shortly leave the building, get in the described car, and drive the most direct route to Dobey's Motel. Because only a small number of people are generally privy to an individual's itinerary, it is reasonable for police to believe that a person with access to such information is likely to also have access to reliable information about that individual's illegal activities. * * * When significant aspects of the caller's predictions were verified, there was reason to believe not only that the caller was honest but also that he was well informed, at least well enough to justify the stop. [b]

Although it is a close case, we conclude that under the totality of the circumstances the anonymous tip, as corroborated, exhibited sufficient indicia of reliability to justify the investigatory stop of respondent's car. We therefore reverse the judgment of the Court of Criminal Appeals of Alabama and remand for further proceedings not inconsistent with this opinion.

So ordered.

JUSTICE STEVENS, with whom JUSTICE BRENNAN and JUSTICE MARSHALL join, dissenting.

Millions of people leave their apartments at about the same time every day carrying an attaché case and heading for a destination known to their neighbors. Usually, however, the neighbors do not know what the briefcase contains. An anonymous neighbor's prediction about somebody's time of departure and probable destination is anything but a reliable basis for assuming that the commuter is in possession of an illegal substance—particularly when the person is not even carrying the attaché case described by the tipster.

The record in this case does not tell us how often respondent drove from the Lynwood Terrace Apartments to Dobey's Motel; for all we know, she may have been a room clerk or telephone operator working the evening shift. It does not tell us whether Officer Davis made any effort to ascertain the informer's identity, his reason for calling, or the basis of his prediction about respondent's destination. Indeed, for all that this record tells us, the tipster may well have been another police officer who had a "hunch" that respondent might have cocaine in her attaché case. [c]

Anybody with enough knowledge about a given person to make her the target of a prank, or to harbor a grudge against her, will certainly be able to formulate a tip about her like the one predicting Vanessa White's excursion. In addition, under the Court's holding, every citizen is subject to being seized and questioned by any officer who is prepared to testify that the warrantless stop was based on an anonymous tip predicting whatever conduct the officer just observed. Fortunately, the vast majority of those in our law enforcement community would not adopt such a practice. But the Fourth Amendment was intended to protect the citizen from the over-zealous and unscrupulous officer as well as from those who are conscientious and truthful. This decision makes a mockery of that protection.

I respectfully dissent.

* * * * * * * * * * *

COMMENTS

[a] Note that in this case, as in *Gates*, nothing that is corroborated is itself an illegal act. Unlike *Gates*, where the travel plans of Lance and Sue Gates were at least out of the ordinary, the facts here are mundane.

[b] At bottom, the existence of *reasonable suspicion* in this case rests on the social assumption that anonymous tips made to police about drug dealing are not likely to be pranks or malicious. The Court implies that this reasoning would not allow these facts to rise to *probable cause* allowing a search because of the greater intrusion on privacy.

[c] This is an unnerving possibility, but as the dissent notes, it is unlikely that such would become a regular police practice. A more likely possibility is that individuals themselves involved in illicit enterprises might use the anonymous tip as a way to undermine competitors. Should the possibility, even the remote possibility, that frustrated officers who are suspicious of drug dealing but have no proof would make anonymous calls be a reason to reject anonymous calls unless accompanied with stronger corroboration than existed in this case?

FLORIDA v. BOSTICK

501 U.S. 429, 111 S. Ct. 2382, 115 L. Ed. 2d 389 (1991)

JUSTICE O'CONNOR delivered the opinion of the Court.

* * *

I

Drug interdiction efforts have led to the use of police surveillance at airports, train stations, and bus depots. Law enforcement officers stationed at such locations routinely approach individuals, either randomly or because they suspect in some vague way that the individuals may be engaged in criminal activity, and ask them potentially incriminating questions. * * * **[a]**

In this case, two officers discovered cocaine when they searched a suitcase belonging to Terrance Bostick. * * * [T]he Florida Supreme Court, whose decision we review here, stated explicitly the factual premise for its decision:

"'Two officers, complete with badges, insignia and one of them holding a recognizable zipper pouch, containing a pistol, boarded a bus bound from Miami to Atlanta during a stopover in Fort Lauderdale. Eyeing the passengers, the officers admittedly without articulable suspicion, picked out the defendant passenger and asked to inspect his ticket and identification. The ticket, from Miami to Atlanta, matched the defendant's identification and both were immediately returned to him as unremarkable. However, the two police officers persisted and explained their presence as narcotics agents on the lookout for illegal drugs. In pursuit of that aim, they then requested the defendant's consent to search his luggage. Needless to say, there is a conflict in the evidence about whether the defendant consented to the search of the second bag in which the contraband was found and as to whether he was informed of his right to refuse consent. However, any conflict must be resolved in favor of the state, it being a question of fact decided by the trial judge.'" * * *

Two facts are particularly worth noting. First, the police specifically advised Bostick that he had the right to refuse consent. * * * **[b]** Second, at no time did the officers threaten Bostick with a gun. * * * [O]ne officer carried a zipper pouch containing a pistol—the equivalent of carrying a gun in a holster—but the court did not suggest that the gun was ever removed from its pouch, pointed at Bostick, or otherwise used in a threatening manner. The dissent's characterization of the officers as "gun-wielding inquisitor[s]," * * * is colorful, but lacks any basis in fact.

[Bostick challenged the seizure of cocaine. The Florida Supreme Court] ruled categorically that "'an impermissible seizure result[s] when police mount a drug search on buses during scheduled stops and question boarded passengers without articulable reasons for doing so, thereby obtaining consent to search the passengers' luggage.'" * *

*

II

The sole issue presented for our review is whether a police encounter on a bus of the type described above necessarily constitutes a "seizure" within the meaning of the Fourth Amendment. The State concedes, and we accept for purposes of this decision, that the officers lacked the reasonable suspicion required to justify a seizure and that, if a seizure took place, the drugs found in Bostick's suitcase must be suppressed as tainted fruit.

Our cases make it clear that a seizure does not occur simply because a police officer approaches an individual and asks a few questions. So long as a reasonable person would feel free "to disregard the police and go about his business," * * * the encounter is consensual and no reasonable suspicion is required. The encounter will not trigger Fourth Amendment scrutiny unless it loses its consensual nature. The Court made precisely this point in *Terry v. Ohio* [this volume]: "Obviously, not all personal intercourse between policemen and citizens involves 'seizures' of persons. Only when the officer, by means of physical force or show of authority, has in some way restrained the liberty of a citizen may we conclude that a 'seizure' has occurred."

Since *Terry*, we have held repeatedly that mere police questioning does not constitute a seizure. [*Florida v. Royer* [this volume] is discussed at this point.]

There is no doubt that if this same encounter had taken place before Bostick boarded the bus or in the lobby of the bus terminal, it would not rise to the level of a seizure. The Court has dealt with similar encounters in airports and has found them to be "the sort of consensual encounter[s] that implicat[e] no Fourth Amendment interest." * * *

Bostick insists that this case is different because it took place in the cramped confines of a bus. A police encounter is much more intimidating in this setting, he argues, because police tower over a seated passenger and there is little room to move around. [c] Bostick claims to find support in language from *Michigan v. Chesternut*, 486 U.S. 567, 573 (1988), and other cases, indicating that a seizure occurs when a reasonable person would believe that he or she is not "free to leave." Bostick maintains that a reasonable bus passenger would not have felt free to leave under the circumstances of this case because there is nowhere to go on a bus. Also, the bus was about to depart. Had Bostick disembarked, he would have risked being stranded and losing whatever baggage he had locked away in the luggage compartment.

The Florida Supreme Court found this argument persuasive, so much so that it adopted a *per se* rule prohibiting the police from randomly boarding buses as a means of drug interdiction. The state court erred, however, in focusing on whether Bostick was "free to leave" rather than on the principle that those words were intended to capture. When police attempt to question a person who is walking down the street or through an airport lobby, it makes sense to inquire whether a reasonable person would feel free to continue walking. But when the person is seated on a bus and has no desire to leave, the degree to which a reasonable person would feel that he or she could leave is not an accurate measure of the coercive effect of the encounter.

Here, for example, the mere fact that Bostick did not feel free to leave the bus does not mean that the police seized him. Bostick was a passenger on a bus that was scheduled to depart. He would not have felt free to leave the bus even if the police had not been present. Bostick's movements were "confined" in a sense, but this was the natural result of his decision to take the bus; it says nothing about whether or not the police conduct at issue was coercive. **[d]**

In this respect, the Court's decision in *INS v. Delgado*, [466 U.S. 210 (1984)], is dispositive. At issue there was the INS' practice of visiting factories at random and questioning employees to determine whether any were illegal aliens. Several INS agents would stand near the building's exits, while other agents walked through the factory questioning workers. The Court acknowledged that the workers may not have been free to leave their worksite, but explained that this was not the result of police activity: "Ordinarily, when people are at work their freedom to move about has been meaningfully restricted, not by the actions of law enforcement officials, but by the workers' voluntary obligations to their employers." * * * We concluded that there was no seizure because, even though the workers were not free to leave the building without being questioned, the agents' conduct should have given employees "no reason to believe that they would be detained if they gave truthful answers to the questions put to them or if they simply refused to answer." *

* *

The present case is analytically indistinguishable from *Delgado*. Like the workers in that case, Bostick's freedom of movement was restricted by a factor independent of police conduct—*i.e.*, by his being a passenger on a bus. Accordingly, the "free to leave" analysis on which Bostick relies is inapplicable. In such a situation, the appropriate inquiry is whether a reasonable person would feel free to decline the officers' requests or otherwise terminate the encounter. This formulation follows logically from prior cases and breaks no new ground. We have said before that the crucial test is whether, taking into account all of the circumstances surrounding the encounter, the police conduct would "have communicated to a reasonable person that he was not at liberty to ignore the police presence and go about his business." * * * Where the encounter takes place is one factor, but it is not the only one. And, as the Solicitor General correctly observes, an individual may decline an officer's request without fearing prosecution. * * * **[e]** We have consistently held that a refusal to cooperate, without more, does not furnish the minimal level of objective justification needed for a detention or seizure. * * *

[The Court remanded the case to Florida to allow the Florida courts to determine with precision whether the facts show that the officers conveyed] a message that compliance with their requests is required. * * *

* * * We do reject, however, Bostick's argument that he must have been seized because no reasonable person would freely consent to a search of luggage that he or she knows contains drugs. This argument cannot

prevail because the "reasonable person" test presupposes an *innocent* person. * * *

[The Court countered several arguments raised by the dissent.]

The dissent reserves its strongest criticism for the proposition that police officers can approach individuals as to whom they have no reasonable suspicion and ask them potentially incriminating questions. But this proposition is by no means novel; it has been endorsed by the Court any number of times. * * *

This Court, as the dissent correctly observes, is not empowered to suspend constitutional guarantees so that the Government may more effectively wage a "war on drugs." * * * If that war is to be fought, those who fight it must respect the rights of individuals, whether or not those individuals are suspected of having committed a crime. By the same token, this Court is not empowered to forbid law enforcement practices simply because it considers them distasteful. The Fourth Amendment proscribes unreasonable searches and seizures; it does not proscribe voluntary cooperation. The cramped confines of a bus are one relevant factor that should be considered in evaluating whether a passenger's consent is voluntary. [f] We cannot agree, however, with the Florida Supreme Court that this single factor will be dispositive in every case.

JUSTICE MARSHALL, with whom JUSTICE BLACKMUN and JUSTICE STEVENS join, dissenting.

* * *

I

[JUSTICE MARSHALL described

the police sweep technique.] Typically under this technique, a group of state or federal officers will board a bus while it is stopped at an intermediate point on its route. Often displaying badges, weapons or other indicia of authority, the officers identify themselves and announce their purpose to intercept drug traffickers. They proceed to approach individual passengers, requesting them to show identification, produce their tickets, and explain the purpose of their travels. Never do the officers advise the passengers that they are free not to speak with the officers. An "interview" of this type ordinarily culminates in a request for consent to search the passenger's luggage. * * *

These sweeps are conducted in "dragnet" style. The police admittedly act without an "articulable suspicion" in deciding which buses to board and which passengers to approach for interviewing. By proceeding systematically in this fashion, the police are able to engage in a tremendously high volume of searches. * * * The percentage of successful drug interdictions is low. * * * [g]

To put it mildly, these sweeps "are inconvenient, intrusive, and intimidating." * * * They occur within cramped confines, with officers typically placing themselves in between the passenger selected for an interview and the exit of the bus. * * * Because the bus is only temporarily stationed at a point short of its destination, the passengers are in no position to leave as a means of evading the officers' questioning. Undoubtedly, such a sweep holds up the progress of the bus. * * * Thus this "new and increasingly common tactic," * * * burdens the experience of traveling by bus with a degree of governmental interference to which, until now, our society has been proudly unaccustomed. * * * [h]

* * *

II

* * *

These facts [of this case] exhibit all of the elements of coercion associated with a typical bus sweep. * * * The officers made a visible display of their badges and wore bright green "raid" jackets bearing the insignia of the Broward County Sheriff's Department; one held a gun in a recognizable weapons pouch. * * * These facts alone constitute an intimidating "show of authority." * * * Once on board, the officers approached respondent, who was sitting in the back of the bus, identified themselves as narcotics officers and began to question him. * * * One officer stood in front of respondent's seat, partially blocking the narrow aisle through which respondent would have been required to pass to reach the exit of the bus. * * *

* * *

* * * Apart from trying to accommodate the officers, respondent had only two options. First, he could have remained seated while obstinately refusing to respond to the officers' questioning. But in light of the intimidating show of authority that the officers made upon boarding the bus, respondent reasonably could have believed that such behavior would only arouse the officers' suspicions and intensify their interrogation. Indeed, officers who carry out bus sweeps like the one at issue here frequently admit that this is the effect of a passenger's refusal to cooperate. * * * The

majority's observation that a mere refusal to answer questions, "without more," does not give rise to a reasonable basis for seizing a passenger, * * * is utterly beside the point, because a passenger unadvised of his rights and otherwise unversed in constitutional law *has no reason to know* that the police cannot hold his refusal to cooperate against him. [i]

Second, respondent could have tried to escape the officers' presence by leaving the bus altogether. But because doing so would have required respondent to squeeze past the *gun-wielding* inquisitor who was blocking the aisle of the bus, this hardly seems like a course that respondent reasonably would have viewed as available to him. The majority lamely protests that nothing in the stipulated facts shows that the questioning officer "*point[ed] [his] gu[n]* at [respondent] or otherwise *threatened* him" with the weapon. * * * (emphasis added).   Our decisions recognize the obvious point, however, that the choice of the police to "display" their weapons during an encounter exerts significant coercive pressure on the confronted citizen. * * * [j] We have never suggested that the police must go so far as to put a citizen in immediate apprehension of *being shot* before a court can take account of the intimidating effect of being questioned by an officer with weapon in hand.

* * * The case on which the majority primarily relies, *INS v. Delgado*, * * * is distinguishable in every relevant respect. In *Delgado*, this Court held that workers approached by law-enforcement officials inside of a factory were not "seized" for purposes of the Fourth Amendment. The Court was careful to point out, however, that

the presence of the agents did not furnish the workers with a reasonable basis for believing that they were not free to leave the factory, as at least some of them did. * * * Unlike passengers confronted by law-enforcement officials on a bus stopped temporarily at an intermediate point in its journey, workers approached by law-enforcement officials at their workplace need not abandon personal belongings and venture into unfamiliar environs in order to avoid unwanted questioning.

Moreover, the workers who did not leave the building in *Delgado* remained free to move about the entire factory, * * * a considerably less confining environment than a bus. Finally, contrary to the officer who confronted respondent, the law-enforcement officials in *Delgado* did not conduct their interviews with guns in hand. * * *

* * *

* * * * * * * * * * *

COMMENTS

[a] There are important implications for law enforcement policy from the basic technique of simply talking to people. Community policing efforts, for example, can include targeting an area and having officers speak to groups of youths or adults on the street for a variety of purposes, ranging from acquaintance and public relations to gathering crime specific information.

[b] This notice is helpful to police to counter the charge that a search is coercive. However, it is possible that this notice can be a polite refrain, spoken quickly in an introductory patter, as if to convey it as *pro forma* information, not to be taken seriously.

[c] The dissent clearly agreed with Bostick's argument. Put yourself in Terry Bostick's seat. How would *you* react to police inquiries while sitting in a bus?

[d] In an airport or on the street, the accosted person can in theory terminate the police inquiry by saying that she does not want to talk *and* by walking away. How does a person in a bus seat terminate the encounter if the police officers do not immediately leave? If you are an officer, how would you react if the passenger said that he had a *right* to not talk?

[e] When the United States joins a case as *amicus curiae* or "friend of the court," its views are given great weight by the Court, as noted by its pointed reference to the "amicus brief" of the United States Solicitor General.

[f] At the end of its opinion, the majority leaves some room to defendants in cases similar to this one to argue that, in *their* particular situation, the close confines of a bus, plus other relevant factors, rendered the situation sufficiently coercive so that a seizure took place.

[g] In a footnote, JUSTICE MARSHALL produced anecdotal evidence that young black males are frequent police targets of such sweeps.

[h] Compare this situation to that of *Kolender v. Lawson* [this volume]. Could police target certain neighborhoods for similar sweeps?

[i] Although the Court does not deal with this point, the widespread ignorance of many American citizens and resident aliens of their constitutional rights gives the police a clear edge in encounters such as these.

[j] The majority and dissent differ to a degree, but the facts of the case seem to be that a gun was not displayed. In other cases, the way in which police weapons are worn or handled could have a bearing on whether the encounter led to a consensual opening of a bag or a seizure.

CALIFORNIA v. HODARI D.

499 U.S. 621, 111 S. Ct. 1547, 113 L.Ed.2d 690 (1991)

JUSTICE SCALIA delivered the opinion of the Court.

Late one evening in April 1988, Officers Brian McColgin and Jerry Pertoso were on patrol in a high-crime area of Oakland, California. They were dressed in street clothes but wearing jackets with "Police" embossed on both front and back. Their un-marked car proceeded west on Foothill Boulevard, and turned south onto 63rd Avenue. As they rounded the corner, they saw four or five youths huddled around a small red car parked at the curb. When the youths, [including Hodari D.], saw the officers' car approaching they apparently panicked, and took flight. * * *

The officers were suspicious and gave chase. McColgin remained in the car * * *; Pertoso left the car, [and chased on foot]. Hodari [emerged from an alley and did not see] Pertoso until the officer was almost upon him, whereupon he tossed away what appeared to be a small rock. A moment later, Pertoso tackled Hodari, handcuffed him, and radioed for assistance. Hodari was found to be carrying $130 in cash and a pager; and the rock he had discarded was found to be crack cocaine.

In the juvenile proceeding brought against him, Hodari moved to suppress the evidence relating to the cocaine. The court denied the motion without opinion. The California Court of Appeal reversed, holding that Hodari had been "seized" when he saw Officer Pertoso running towards him, that this seizure was unreasonable under the Fourth Amendment, and that the evidence of cocaine had to be sup-pressed as the fruit of that illegal seizure. The California Supreme Court denied the State's application for review. We granted certiorari. * * *

As this case comes to us, the only issue presented is whether, at the time he dropped the drugs, Hodari had been "seized" within the meaning of the Fourth Amendment. [a] If so, respondent argues, the drugs were the fruit of that seizure and the evidence concerning them was properly excluded. If not, the drugs were abandoned by Hodari and lawfully recovered by the police, and the evidence should have been admitted. (In addition, of course, Pertoso's seeing the rock of cocaine, at least if he recognized it as such, would provide reasonable suspicion for the unquestioned seizure that occurred when he tackled Hodari. * * *).

We have long understood that the Fourth Amendment's protection against "unreasonable . . . seizures" includes seizure of the person. * * * From the time of the founding to the present, the word "seizure" has meant a "taking possession." * * * For most purposes at common law, the word connoted not merely grasping, or applying physical force to, the animate or inanimate object in question, but actually bringing it within physical control. A ship still fleeing, even though under attack, would not be considered to have been seized as a war prize. * * * To constitute an arrest, however—the quintessential "seizure of the person" under our Fourth Amendment jurisprudence—the mere grasping or application of physical force with lawful authority, whether or not it succeeded in subduing the arrestee, was sufficient. * * * **[b]**

To say that an arrest is effected by the slightest application of physical force, despite the arrestee's escape, is not to say that for Fourth Amendment purposes there is a *continuing* arrest during the period of fugitivity. If, for example, Pertoso had laid his hands upon Hodari to arrest him, but Hodari had broken away and had *then* cast away the cocaine, it would hardly be realistic to say that that disclosure had been made during the course of an arrest. * * *   The present case, however, is even one step further removed.   It does not involve the application of any physical force; Hodari was untouched by Officer Pertoso at the time he discarded the cocaine.   His defense relies instead upon the proposition that a seizure occurs "when the officer, by means of physical force *or show of authority*, has in some way restrained the liberty of a citizen." *Terry v. Ohio*, [this volume] (emphasis added).   Hodari contends (and we accept as true for purposes of this decision) that Pertoso's pursuit qualified as a "show of authority" calling upon Hodari to halt. The narrow question before us is whether, with respect to a show of authority as with respect to application of physical force, a seizure occurs even though the subject does not yield. We hold that it does not.

The language of the Fourth Amendment, of course, cannot sustain respondent's contention. The word "seizure" readily bears the meaning of a laying on of hands or application of physical force to restrain movement, even when it is ultimately unsuccessful. ("She seized the purse-snatcher, but he broke out of her grasp.") It does not remotely apply, however, to the prospect of a policeman yelling "Stop, in the name of the law!" at a fleeing form that continues to flee. That is no seizure. Nor can the result respondent wishes to achieve be produced—indirectly, as it were— by suggesting that Pertoso's uncomplied-with show of authority was a common-law arrest, and then appealing to the principle that all common-law arrests are seizures. An arrest requires *either* physical force (as described above) *or*, where that is absent, *submission* to the assertion of authority. * * *

We do not think it desirable, even as a policy matter, to stretch the Fourth Amendment beyond its words and beyond the meaning of arrest, as respondent urges.   Street pursuits always place the public at some risk, and compliance with police orders to stop should therefore be encouraged. Only a few of those orders, we must presume, will be without adequate basis, and since the addressee has no ready means of identifying the deficient ones it almost invariably is the responsible course to comply.   Unlawful orders will not be deterred, moreover, by sanctioning through the exclusionary rule those of them that are *not* obeyed. Since policemen do not command "Stop!" expecting to be ignored, or give chase hoping to be outrun, it fully suffices to apply the deterrent to their genuine, successful seizures.

Respondent contends that his position is sustained by the so-called *Mendenhall* test, formulated by Justice Stewart's opinion in *United States v. Mendenhall*, 446 U.S. 544, 554 (1980), and adopted by the Court in later cases, see *Michigan v. Chesternut*, 486 U.S. 567, 573 (1988); *INS v. Delgado*, 466 U.S. 210, 215 (1984): "A person has been 'seized' within the meaning of the Fourth Amendment only if, in view of all the circumstances surrounding the incident, a reasonable person would have believed that he was not free to leave." * * * In seeking to rely upon that test here, respondent fails to read it carefully. It says that a person has been seized "only if," not that he has been seized "whenever"; it states a *necessary*, but not a *sufficient* condition for seizure—or, more precisely, for seizure effected through a "show of authority." *Mendenhall* establishes that the test for existence of a "show of authority" is an objective one: not whether the citizen perceived that he was being ordered to restrict his movement, but whether the officer's words and actions would have conveyed that to a reasonable person. Application of this objective test was the basis for our decision in the other case principally relied upon by respondent, *Chesternut*, * * * where we concluded that the police cruiser's slow following of the defendant did not convey the message that he was not free to disregard the police and go about his business. We did not address in *Chesternut*, however, the question whether, if the *Mendenhall* test was met—if the message that the defendant was not free to leave *had* been conveyed—a Fourth Amendment seizure would have occurred. * * *

Quite relevant to the present case, however, was our decision in *Brower v. Inyo County*, 489 U.S. 593, 596 (1989). In that case, police cars with flashing lights had chased the decedent for 20 miles— surely an adequate "show of authority"—but he did not stop until his fatal crash into a police-erected blockade. The issue was whether his death could be held to be the consequence of an unreasonable seizure in violation of the Fourth Amendment. **[c]** We did not even consider the possibility that a seizure could have occurred during the course of the chase because, as we explained, that "show of authority" did not produce his stop. * * * And we discussed * * * an opinion of Justice Holmes, involving a situation not much different from the present case, where revenue agents had picked up containers dropped by moonshiners whom they were pursuing without adequate warrant. The containers were not excluded as the product of an unlawful seizure because "[t]he defendant's own acts, and those of his associates, disclosed the jug, the jar and the bottle— and there was no seizure in the sense of the law when the officers examined the contents of each after they had been abandoned." *Hester v. United States*, 265 U.S. 57, 58 (1924). The same is true here.

In sum, assuming that Pertoso's pursuit in the present case constituted a "show of authority" enjoining Hodari to halt, since Hodari did not comply with that injunction he was not seized until he was tackled. The cocaine abandoned while he was running was in this case not the fruit of a seizure, and his motion to exclude evidence of it was properly denied. We reverse the decision of the California Court of Appeal, and remand for further proceedings not inconsistent with this opinion.

It is so ordered.

JUSTICE STEVENS, with whom JUSTICE MARSHALL joins, dissenting.

The Court's narrow construction of the word "seizure" represents a significant, and in my view, unfortunate, departure from prior case law construing the Fourth Amendment. Almost a quarter of a century ago, in two landmark cases—one broadening the protection of individual privacy, and the other broadening the powers of law enforcement officers— **[d]** we rejected the method of Fourth Amendment analysis that today's majority endorses. In particular, the Court now adopts a definition of "seizure" that is unfaithful to a long line of Fourth Amendment cases. Even if the Court were defining seizure for the first time, which it is not, the definition that it chooses today is profoundly unwise. In its decision, the Court assumes, without acknowledging, that a police officer may now fire his weapon at an innocent citizen and not implicate the Fourth Amendment—as long as he misses his target.

For the purposes of decision, the following propositions are not in dispute. First, when Officer Pertoso began his pursuit of respondent, the officer did not have a lawful basis for either stopping or arresting respondent. * * * Second, the officer's chase amounted to a "show of force" as soon as respondent saw the officer nearly upon him. * * * Third, the act of discarding the rock of cocaine was the direct consequence of the show of force. * * * Fourth, as the Court correctly demonstrates, no common-law arrest occurred until the officer tackled respondent. * * * Thus, the Court is quite right in concluding that the abandonment of the rock was not the fruit of a common-law arrest.

It is equally clear, however, that if the officer had succeeded in touching respondent before he dropped the rock—even if he did not subdue him—an arrest would have occurred. * * * In that event (assuming the touching precipitated the abandonment), the evidence would have been the fruit of an unlawful common-law arrest. The distinction between the actual case and the hypothetical case is the same as the distinction between the common-law torts of assault and battery—a touching converts the former into the latter. Although the distinction between assault and battery was important for pleading purposes, * * * the distinction should not take on constitutional dimensions. The Court mistakenly allows this common-law distinction to define its interpretation of the Fourth Amendment.

At the same time, the Court fails to recognize the existence of another, more telling, common-law distinction—the distinction between an arrest and an attempted arrest. As the Court teaches us, the distinction between battery and assault was critical to a correct understanding of the common law of arrest. * * * ("An arrest requires either physical force . . . *or*, where that is absent, *submission* to the assertion of authority"). However, the facts of this case do not describe an actual arrest, but rather, an unlawful *attempt* to take a presumptively innocent person into custody. Such an attempt was unlawful at common law. Thus, if the Court wants to define the scope of the Fourth Amendment based on the common law, it should look, not to the common law of arrest, but to the common law of attempted arrest, according to the facts of this case. **[e]**

The first question, then, is whether the common law should define the scope of the outer boundaries of the constitutional protection against unreasonable seizures. Even if, contrary to settled precedent, traditional common-law analysis were controlling, it would still be necessary to decide whether the unlawful attempt to make an arrest should be considered a seizure within the meaning of the Fourth Amendment, and whether the exclusionary rule should apply to unlawful attempts.

I

The Court today takes a narrow view of "seizure," which is at odds with the broader view adopted by this Court almost 25 years ago [in *Katz v. United States*, [this volume]]. * * *

* * * Significantly, in the *Katz* opinion, the Court repeatedly used the word "seizure" to describe the process of recording sounds that could not possibly have been the subject of a common-law seizure. * * *

[JUSTICE STEVENS notes here that JUSTICE BLACK's literal reading of the Fourth Amendment in *Katz*, arguing that the *words* of the Fourth Amendment did not apply to eavesdropping, was rejected by the Court.]

The expansive construction of the word "seizure" in the *Katz* case provided an appropriate predicate for the Court's holding in *Terry v. Ohio*, * * * the following year. Prior to *Terry*, the Fourth Amendment proscribed any seizure of the person that was not supported by the same probable cause showing that would justify a custodial arrest. * * * Given the fact that street encounters between citizens and police officers "are incredibly rich in diversity," * * * the Court recognized the need

for flexibility and held that "reasonable" suspicion—a quantum of proof less demanding than probable cause—was adequate to justify a stop for investigatory purposes. * * * As a corollary to the lesser justification for the stop, the Court necessarily concluded that the word "seizure" in the Fourth Amendment encompasses official restraints on individual freedom that fall short of a common-law arrest. Thus, *Terry* broadened the range of encounters between the police and the citizen encompassed within the term "seizure," while at the same time, lowering the standard of proof necessary to justify a "stop" in the newly expanded category of seizures now covered by the Fourth Amendment. * * *

The decisions in *Katz* and *Terry* unequivocally reject the notion that the common law of arrest defines the limits of the term "seizure" in the Fourth Amendment. In *Katz*, the Court abandoned the narrow view that would have limited a seizure to a material object, and instead, held that the Fourth Amendment extended to the recording of oral statements. And in *Terry*, the Court abandoned its traditional view that a seizure under the Fourth Amendment required probable cause, and instead, expanded the definition of a seizure to include an investigative stop made on less than probable cause. Thus, the major premise underpinning the majority's entire analysis today—that the common law of arrest should define the term "seizure" for Fourth Amendment purposes, * * *—is seriously flawed. The Court mistakenly hearkens back to common law, while ignoring the expansive approach that the Court has taken in Fourth Amendment analysis since *Katz* and *Terry*.

II

The Court fares no better when it tries to explain why the proper definition of the term "seizure" has been an open question until today. In *Terry*, in addition to stating that a seizure occurs "whenever a police officer accosts an individual and restrains his freedom to walk away," * * * the Court noted that a seizure occurs "when the officer, by means of physical force or show of authority, has in some way restrained the liberty of a citizen. . . ." * * * The touchstone of a seizure is the restraint of an individual's personal liberty "*in some way*." * * * (emphasis added). Today the Court's reaction to respondent's reliance on *Terry* is to demonstrate that in "show of force" cases no common-law arrest occurs unless the arrestee *submits*. * * * That answer, however, is plainly insufficient given the holding in *Terry* that the Fourth Amendment applies to stops that need not be justified by probable cause in the absence of a full-blown arrest.

In [*Mendenhall*] the Court "adhere[d] to the view that a person is 'seized' only when, by means of physical force or a show of authority, his freedom of movement is restrained." * * * The Court looked to whether the citizen who is questioned "remains free to disregard the questions and walk away," and if she is able to do so, then "there has been no intrusion upon that person's liberty or privacy" that would require some "particularized and objective justification" under the Constitution. * * * The test for a "seizure," as formulated

by the Court in *Mendenhall*, was whether, "in view of all of the circumstances surrounding the incident, a reasonable person would have believed that he was not free to leave." * * * Examples of seizures include "the threatening presence of several officers, the display of a weapon by an officer, some physical touching of the person of the citizen, or the use of language or tone of voice indicating that compliance with the officer's request might be compelled." * * * The Court's unwillingness today to adhere to the "reasonable person" standard, as formulated by JUSTICE STEWART in *Mendenhall*, marks an unnecessary departure from Fourth Amendment case law.

The Court today draws the novel conclusion that even though no seizure can occur *unless* the *Mendenhall* reasonable person standard is met, * * * the fact that the standard has been met does not necessarily mean that a seizure has occurred. * * * (*Mendenhall* "states a *necessary*, but not a *sufficient* condition for seizure . . . effected through a 'show of authority'"). * * *   * * *

Even though momentary, a seizure occurs whenever an objective evaluation of a police officer's show of force conveys the message that the citizen is not entirely free to leave—in other words, that his or her liberty is being restrained in a significant way. * * *

Finally, it is noteworthy that in *Michigan v. Chesternut*, [above], the State asked us to repudiate the reasonable person standard developed in *Terry*, *Mendenhall*, *Delgado*, and *Royer*. We decided, however, to "adhere to our traditional contextual approach," * * * In our opinion, we described Justice Stewart's analysis in *Mendenhall* as "a test to be applied in determining whether 'a person has been "seized" within the meaning of the Fourth Amendment'" and noted that "the Court has since embraced this test." * * * Moreover, in commenting on the virtues of the test, we explained that it focused on the police officer's conduct. * * *

Whatever else one may think of today's decision, it unquestionably represents a departure from earlier Fourth Amendment case law. The notion that our prior cases contemplated a distinction between seizures effected by a touching on the one hand, and those effected by a show of force on the other hand, and that all of our repeated descriptions of the *Mendenhall* test stated only a necessary, but not a sufficient, condition for finding seizures in the latter category, is nothing if not creative lawmaking. Moreover, by narrowing the definition of the term seizure, instead of enlarging the scope of reasonable justifications for seizures, the Court has significantly limited the protection provided to the ordinary citizen by the Fourth Amendment. * * *

III

[In Part III JUSTICE STEVENS applied the *Mendenhall* standard to the facts of this case and concluded that there had been a seizure in violation of the Fourth Amendment since the officers did not have reasonable suspicion or probable cause to chase the boys.]
* * *

* * * In the present case, if Officer Pertoso had succeeded in tackling respondent before he dropped the rock of cocaine, the rock unquestionably would have been excluded as the fruit of the officer's unlawful seizure. Instead, under the Court's logic-chopping analysis, the exclusionary rule has no application because an attempt to make an unconstitutional seizure is beyond the coverage of the Fourth Amendment, no matter how outrageous or unreasonable the officer's conduct may be.

It is too early to know the consequences of the Court's holding. If carried to its logical conclusion, it will encourage unlawful displays of force that will frighten countless innocent citizens into surrendering whatever privacy rights they may still have. * * *

* * *

* * * * * * * * * * *

COMMENTS

[a] In a footnote, JUSTICE SCALIA noted that California conceded that the flight of the youths upon seeing the police was not in itself reasonable suspicion for a *Terry* stop. Although JUSTICE SCALIA thought the point was arguable, he was bound by this concession.

[b] True to his position as an exponent of "original intent jurisprudence,"

JUSTICE SCALIA cites mostly 19th century cases and references for the points in this paragraph.

[c] The Court in that case held that because of the position of the roadblock, the stopping of the chased car amounted to an unreasonable seizure.

[d] The cases are *Katz v. United States* [this volume] and *Terry v. Ohio* [this volume].

[e] JUSTICE STEVENS cleverly takes on the majority's common-law approach on its own grounds and at the very least sows seeds of doubt as to the correctness of the Court's reasoning on that ground. This points to a weakness in deciding current cases on the basis of rules that existed in the past (even if they continue into the present, as do some common law rules). The justices can enter into an historical debate with its own blind alleys and that loses touch with current needs. The issue in constitutional cases is better decided on the basis of constitutional doctrines. While historical materials are important in constitutional cases, they must be used with care.

HILL v. CALIFORNIA

401 U.S. 797, 91 S.Ct. 1106, 28 L.Ed.2d 484 (1971)

MR. JUSTICE WHITE delivered the opinion of the Court.

* * * [F]our armed men robbed a residence in Studio City, California. * * * Alfred Baum and Richard Bader were arrested for possession of narcotics; at the time of their arrest, they were driving petitioner Hill's car, and a search of the car produced property stolen in the Studio City robbery the day before. Bader and Baum both admitted taking part in the June 4 robbery, and both implicated Hill. Bader told the police that he was sharing an apartment with Hill at 9311 Sepulveda Boulevard. He also stated that the guns used in the robbery and other stolen property were in the apartment. [The next day], Baum and Bader again told the police that Hill had been involved in the * * * robbery.

One of the investigating officers then checked official records on Hill, verifying his prior association with Bader, his age and physical description, his address, and the make of his car. The information the officer uncovered corresponded with the general descriptions by the robbery victims and the statements made by Baum and Bader.

Hill concedes that this information gave the police probable cause to arrest him, and the police undertook to do so on June 6. Four officers went to the Sepulveda Boulevard apartment, verified the address, and knocked. One of the officers testified: "The door was opened and a person who fit the description exactly of Archie Hill, as I had received it from both the cards and from Baum and Bader, answered the door. . . . We placed him under arrest for robbery."

The police had neither an arrest nor a search warrant. After arresting the man who answered the door, they asked him whether he was Hill and where the guns and stolen goods were. The arrestee replied that he was not Hill, that his name was Miller, that it was Hill's apartment and that he was waiting for Hill. He also claimed that he knew nothing about any stolen property or guns, although the police testified that an automatic pistol and a clip of ammunition were lying in plain view on a coffee table in the living room where the arrest took place. The arrestee then produced identification indicating that he was in fact Miller, but the police were unimpressed and proceeded to search the apartment—living room, bedroom, kitchen area, and bath—for a period which one officer described as "a couple of hours."

During the course of the search, the police seized several items: rent receipts and personal correspondence bearing Hill's name from a dresser drawer in the bedroom; a starter pistol, two switchblade knives, a camera and case stolen in the Studio City robbery, and two hoodmasks made from white T-shirts, all from the bedroom; a .22-caliber revolver from under the living room sofa; and two pages of petitioner Hill's diary from a bedroom dresser drawer.

* * * Hill was found guilty of robbery on the basis of evidence

produced at the preliminary hearing and the trial.   Eyewitnesses to the robbery were unable to identify Hill; the only substantial evidence of his guilt consisted of the items seized in the search of his apartment.   In sustaining the admissibility of the evidence, the trial judge ruled that the arresting officers had acted in the good-faith belief that Miller was in fact Hill.   The District Court of Appeal agreed that the officers acted in good faith and that the arrest of Miller was valid but nonetheless thought the incident search of Hill's apartment unreasonable under the Fourth Amendment. * * *   The California Supreme Court in turn reversed, sustaining both the arrest and the search. * * * We granted certiorari, * * * and now affirm the judgment of the California Supreme Court.

I

[*Chimel v. California*, [this volume], was not retroactive and so did not apply to this case, which occurred before that decision.]

II

Based on our own examination of the record, we find no reason to disturb either the findings of the California courts that the police had probable cause to arrest Hill and that the arresting officers had a reasonable, good-faith belief that the arrestee Miller was in fact Hill, or the conclusion that "[w]hen the police have probable cause to arrest one party, and when they reasonably mistake a second party for the first party, then the arrest of the second party is a valid arrest." * * *   The police unquestionably had

probable cause to arrest Hill; they also had his address and a verified description.   The mailbox at the indicated address listed Hill as the occupant of the apartment.   Upon gaining entry to the apartment, they were confronted with one who fit the description of Hill received from various sources.   That person claimed he was Miller, not Hill.   But aliases and false identifications are not uncommon.   Moreover, there was a lock on the door and Miller's explanation for his mode of entry was not convincing.   He also denied knowledge of firearms in the apartment although a pistol and loaded ammunition clip were in plain view in the room.   The upshot was that the officers in good faith believed Miller was Hill and arrested him.   They were quite wrong as it turned out, and subjective good-faith belief would not in itself justify either the arrest or the subsequent search. [a] But sufficient probability, not certainty, is the touchstone of reasonableness under the Fourth Amendment and on the record before us the officers' mistake was understandable and the arrest a reasonable response to the situation facing them at the time.

Nor can we agree with petitioner that however valid the arrest of Miller, the subsequent search violated the Fourth Amendment.   It is true that Miller was not Hill; nor did Miller have authority or control over the premises, although at the very least he was Hill's guest.   But the question is not what evidence would have been admissible against Hill (or against Miller for that matter) if the police, with probable cause to arrest Miller, had arrested him in Hill's apartment and then carried out the search at issue.   Here there was probable cause to arrest Hill and the police arrested Miller in Hill's apartment, reasonably believing him to be Hill. In these circumstances the police were entitled to do what the law would have allowed them to do if Miller had in fact been Hill, that is, to search incident to arrest and to seize evidence of the crime the police had probable cause to believe Hill had committed. When judged in accordance with "the factual and practical considerations of everyday life on which reasonable and prudent men, not legal technicians, act," *Brinegar v. United States*, 338 U.S. 160, 175 (1949), the arrest and subsequent search were reasonable and valid under the Fourth Amendment.

[In Part III the Court refused to rule on the issue of whether the introduction of Hill's incriminating diary violated the Fifth Amendment until the state courts decided the question.]

* * *

MR. JUSTICE BLACK concurs in the result.

MR. JUSTICE DOUGLAS took no part in the consideration or the decision of this case.

[JUSTICE HARLAN, joined by JUSTICE MARSHALL, concurred on the Fourth Amendment but dissented on the retroactivity question.]

* * * * * * * * * * *

COMMENT

[a] Good faith *is* a consideration, however, on the issue of whether there is any liability against the police officer for a wrongful entry.

FRISBIE v. COLLINS

342 U.S. 519, 72 S.Ct. 509, 96 L.Ed. 541 (1952)

MR. JUSTICE BLACK delivered the opinion of the Court.

Acting as his own lawyer, the respondent Shirley Collins brought this habeas corpus case in a United States District Court seeking release from a Michigan state prison where he is serving a life sentence for murder. His petition alleges that while he was living in Chicago, Michigan officers forcibly seized, handcuffed, blackjacked and took him to Michigan. He claims that trial and conviction under such circumstances is in violation of the Due Process Clause of the Fourteenth Amendment and the Federal Kidnaping Act, and that therefore his conviction is a nullity.

The District Court denied the writ without a hearing on the ground that the state court had power to try respondent "regardless of how presence was procured." The Court of Appeals, one judge dissenting, reversed and remanded the cause for hearing. * * * It held that the Federal Kidnaping Act had changed the rule declared in prior holdings of this Court, that a state could constitutionally try and convict a defendant after acquiring jurisdiction by force. To review this important question we granted certiorari. 342 U.S. 865.

* * *

This Court has never departed from the rule announced in *Ker v. Illinois*, 119 U.S. 436, 444, that the power of a court to try a person for crime is not impaired by the fact that he had been brought within the court's jurisdiction by reason of a "forcible abduction." No persuasive reasons are now presented to justify overruling this line of cases. They rest on the sound basis that due process of law is satisfied when one present in court is convicted of crime after having been fairly apprized of the charges against him and after a fair trial in accordance with constitutional procedural safeguards. There is nothing in the Constitution that requires a court to permit a guilty person rightfully convicted to escape justice because he was brought to trial against his will.

Despite our prior decisions, the Court of Appeals, relying on the Federal Kidnaping Act, held that respondent was entitled to the writ if he could prove the facts he alleged. The Court thought that to hold otherwise after the passage of the Kidnaping Act "would in practical effect lend encouragement to the commission of criminal acts by those sworn to enforce the law." In considering whether the law of our prior cases has been changed by the Federal Kidnaping Act, we assume, without intimating that it is so, that the Michigan officers would have violated it if the facts are as alleged. This Act prescribes in some detail the severe sanctions Congress wanted it to have. Persons who have violated it can be imprisoned for a term of years or for life; under some circumstances violators can be given the death sentence. We think the Act cannot fairly be construed so as to add to the list of sanctions detailed a sanction barring a state from prosecuting persons wrongfully brought to it by its officers. It may be that Congress could add such a sanction. We cannot.

The judgment of the Court of Appeals is reversed and that of the District Court is affirmed.

It is so ordered.

*   *   *   *   *   *   *   *   *   *

COMMENT

Note that unlike the remedy of the exclusionary rule, where a prosecution may still continue, absent the illegally seized evidence, Collins asks the Supreme Court for a remedy that would terminate the prosecution where an illegal arrest is made by the police.

UNITED STATES v. ALVAREZ-MACHAIN

___ U.S. ___, 112 S.Ct. 2188, 119 L.Ed.2d 441 (1992)

THE CHIEF JUSTICE delivered the opinion of the Court.

The issue in this case is whether a criminal defendant, abducted to the United States from a nation with which it has an extradition treaty, thereby acquires a defense to the jurisdiction of this country's courts. [a] We hold that he does not, and that he may be tried in federal district court for violations of the criminal law of the United States.

[Alvarez-Machain, a citizen and resident of Mexico, was indicted for participating in the kidnap and murder of United States Drug Enforcement Administration (DEA) special agent Enrique Camarena-Salazar and a Mexican pilot working with Camarena, Alfredo Zavala-Avelar. At the direction of DEA officials, Alvarez-Machain was forcibly kidnapped from Mexico and flown to El Paso, Texas, where he was arrested.]

Respondent moved to dismiss the indictment, claiming that his abduction constituted outrageous governmental conduct, and that the District Court lacked jurisdiction to try him because he was abducted in violation of the extradition treaty between the United States and Mexico. * * * The District Court rejected the outrageous governmental conduct claim, but held that it lacked jurisdiction to try respondent because his abduction violated the Extradition Treaty. The district court discharged respondent and ordered that he be repatriated to Mexico. * * *

The Court of Appeals affirmed the dismissal of the indictment and the repatriation of respondent, * * *

[holding] that the forcible abduction of a Mexican national with the authorization or participation of the United States violated the Extradition Treaty between the United States and Mexico. Although the Treaty does not expressly prohibit such abductions, the Court of Appeals held that the "purpose" of the Treaty was violated by a forcible abduction, * * * which, along with a formal protest by the offended nation, would give a defendant the right to invoke the Treaty violation to defeat jurisdiction of the district court to try him. The Court of Appeals further held that the proper remedy for such a violation would be dismissal of the indictment and repatriation of the defendant to Mexico.

* * * We granted certiorari, * * * and now reverse.

Although we have never before addressed the precise issue raised in the present case, we have previously considered proceedings in claimed violation of an extradition treaty, and proceedings against a defendant brought before a court by means of a forcible abduction. We addressed the former issue in *United States v. Rauscher*, 119 U.S. 407 (1886); more precisely, the issue of whether the Webster-Ashburton Treaty of 1842, * * * which governed extraditions between England and the United States, prohibited the prosecution of defendant Rauscher for a crime other than the crime for which he had been extradited. Whether this prohibition, known as the doctrine of specialty, was an intended part of the treaty had been disputed between the two nations for some time. * * * Justice Miller delivered the opinion of the Court, * * * and reached the following conclusion:

"[A] person who has been brought within the jurisdiction of the court *by virtue of proceedings under an extradition treaty*, can only be tried for one of the offences described in that treaty, and for the offence with which he is charged in the proceedings for his extradition, until a reasonable time and opportunity have been given him, after his release or trial upon such charge, to return to the country from whose asylum he had been forcibly taken under those proceedings." * * * (emphasis added).

* * * Unlike the case before us today, the defendant in *Rauscher* had been brought to the United States by way of an extradition treaty; there was no issue of a forcible abduction. [b]

In *Ker v. Illinois*, 119 U.S. 436 (1886), also written by Justice Miller and decided the same day as *Rauscher*, we addressed the issue of a defendant brought before the court by way of a forcible abduction. Frederick Ker had been tried and convicted in an Illinois court for larceny; his presence before the court was procured by means of forcible abduction from Peru. A messenger was sent to Lima with the proper warrant to demand Ker by virtue of the extradition treaty between Peru and the United States. The messenger, however, disdained reliance on the treaty processes, and instead forcibly kidnapped Ker and brought him to the United States. We distinguished Ker's case from *Rauscher*, on the basis that Ker was not brought into the United States by virtue of the extradition treaty between the United States and Peru, and rejected Ker's argument that he had a right under the extradition treaty to be returned to this country only in accordance with its terms. We rejected Ker's due process argument more broadly, holding in line with "the highest authorities" that "such forcible abduction is no sufficient reason why the party should not answer when brought within the jurisdiction of the court which has the right to try him for such an offence, and presents no valid objection to his trial in such court." * * *

In *Frisbie v. Collins*, [this volume], we applied the rule in *Ker* to a case in which the defendant had been kidnapped in Chicago by Michigan officers and brought to trial in Michigan. We upheld the conviction over objections based on the due process clause and the Federal Kidnapping Act. * * *

The only differences between *Ker* and the present case are that *Ker* was decided on the premise that there was no governmental involvement in the abduction, * * * and Peru, from which Ker was abducted, did not object to his prosecution. Respondent finds these differences to be dispositive, * * * contending that they show that respondent's prosecution, like the prosecution of Rauscher, violates the implied terms of a valid extradition treaty. The Government, on the other hand, argues that *Rauscher* stands as an "exception" to the rule in *Ker* only when an extradition treaty is invoked, and the terms of the treaty provide that its breach will limit the jurisdiction of a court. * * * Therefore, our first inquiry must be whether the abduction of respondent from Mexico violated the extradition treaty between the

United States and Mexico. If we conclude that the Treaty does not prohibit respondent's abduction, the rule in *Ker* applies, and the court need not inquire as to how respondent came before it.

In construing a treaty, as in construing a statute, we first look to its terms to determine its meaning. * * * The Treaty says nothing about the obligations of the United States and Mexico to refrain from forcible abductions of people from the territory of the other nation, or the consequences under the Treaty if such an abduction occurs. Respondent submits that Article 22(1) of the Treaty which states that it "shall apply to offenses specified in Article 2 [including murder] committed before and after this Treaty enters into force," * * * evidences an intent to make application of the Treaty mandatory for those offenses. However, the more natural conclusion is that Article 22 was included to ensure that the Treaty was applied to extraditions requested after the Treaty went into force, regardless of when the crime of extradition occurred. [c]

More critical to respondent's argument is Article 9 of the Treaty which provides:

1. Neither Contracting Party shall be bound to deliver up its own nationals, but the executive authority of the requested Party shall, if not prevented by the laws of that Party, have the power to deliver them up if, in its discretion, it be deemed proper to do so.

2. If extradition is not granted pursuant to paragraph 1 of this Article, the requested Party shall submit the case to its competent authorities for the purpose of prosecution, provided that Party has jurisdiction over the offense. * * *

According to respondent, Article 9 embodies the terms of the bargain which the United States struck: if the United States wishes to prosecute a Mexican national, it may request that individual's extradition. Upon a request from the United States, Mexico may either extradite the individual, or submit the case to the proper authorities for prosecution in Mexico. In this way, respondent reasons, each nation preserved its right to choose whether its nationals would be tried in its own courts or by the courts of the other nation. This preservation of rights would be frustrated if either nation were free to abduct nationals of the other nation for the purposes of prosecution. More broadly, respondent reasons, as did the Court of Appeals, that all the processes and restrictions on the obligation to extradite established by the Treaty would make no sense if either nation were free to resort to forcible kidnapping to gain the presence of an individual for prosecution in a manner not contemplated by the Treaty. * * * We do not read the Treaty in such a fashion. Article 9 does not purport to specify the only way in which one country may gain custody of a national of the other country for the purposes of prosecution. In the absence of an extradition treaty, nations are under no obligation to surrender those in their country to foreign authorities for prosecution. * * * Extradition treaties exist so as to impose mutual obligations to surrender individuals in certain defined sets of circumstances, following established procedures. * * * The Treaty thus provides a mechanism which would not otherwise exist, requiring, under certain circumstances, the United States and Mexico to extradite individuals to the other country, and establishing the procedures to be followed when the Treaty is invoked.

The history of negotiation and practice under the Treaty also fails to show that abductions outside of the Treaty constitute a violation of the Treaty. As the Solicitor General notes, the Mexican government was made aware, as early as 1906, of the *Ker* doctrine, and the United States' position that it applied to forcible abductions made outside of the terms of the United States-Mexico extradition treaty. Nonetheless, the current version of the Treaty, signed in 1978, does not attempt to establish a rule that would in any way curtail the effect of *Ker*. Moreover, although language which would grant individuals exactly the right sought by respondent had been considered and drafted as early as 1935 by a prominent group of legal scholars sponsored by the faculty of Harvard Law School, no such clause appears in the current treaty.

Thus, the language of the Treaty, in the context of its history, does not support the proposition that the Treaty prohibits abductions outside of its terms. The remaining question, therefore, is whether the Treaty should be interpreted so as to include an implied term prohibiting prosecution where the defendant's presence is obtained by means other than those established by the Treaty. * * *

Respondent contends that the Treaty must be interpreted against the backdrop of customary international law, and that international abductions are "so clearly prohibited in international law" that there was no reason to include such a clause in the Treaty itself. * * * The international censure of international abductions is further evidenced, according to respondent, by the United Nations Charter and the Charter of the Organization of American States. * * * Respondent does not argue that these sources of international law provide an independent basis for the right respondent asserts not to be tried in the United States, but rather that they should inform the interpretation of the Treaty terms. [d]

* * *

* * * [T]he difficulty with the support respondent garners from international law is that none of it relates to the practice of nations in relation to extradition treaties. In *Rauscher*, we implied a term in the Webster-Ashburton Treaty because of the practice of nations with regard to extradition treaties. In the instant case, respondent would imply terms in the extradition treaty from the practice of nations with regards to international law more generally. Respondent would have us find that the Treaty acts as a prohibition against a violation of the general principle of international law that one government may not "exercise its police power in the territory of another state." * * * There are many actions which could be taken by a nation that would violate this principle, including waging war, but it cannot seriously be contended an invasion of the United States by Mexico would violate the terms of the extradition treaty between the two nations. [e]

In sum, to infer from this Treaty and its terms that it prohibits all means of gaining the presence of an individual outside of its terms goes beyond established precedent and practice. In *Rauscher*, the implication of a doctrine of specialty into the terms of the Webster-Ashburton treaty which, by its terms, required the presentation of evidence establishing probable cause of the crime of extradition before extradition was required, was a small step to take. By contrast, to imply from the terms of this Treaty that it prohibits obtaining the presence of an individual by means outside of the procedures the Treaty establishes requires a much larger inferential leap, with only the most general of international law principles to support it. The general principles cited by respondent simply fail to persuade us that we should imply in the United States-Mexico Extradition Treaty a term prohibiting international abductions.

Respondent and his *amici* may be correct that respondent's abduction was "shocking," * * * and that it may be in violation of general international law principles. Mexico has protested the abduction of respondent through diplomatic notes, * * * and the decision of whether respondent should be returned to Mexico, as a matter outside of the Treaty, is a matter for the Executive Branch. We conclude, however, that respondent's abduction was not in violation of the Extradition Treaty between the United States and Mexico, and therefore the rule of *Ker v. Illinois* is fully applicable to this case. **[f]** The fact of respondent's forcible abduction does not therefore prohibit his trial in a court in the United States for violations of the criminal laws of the United States.

The judgment of the Court of Appeals is therefore reversed, and the case is remanded for further proceedings consistent with this opinion.

So ordered.

JUSTICE STEVENS, with whom JUSTICE BLACKMUN and JUSTICE O'CONNOR join, dissenting.

The Court correctly observes that this case raises a question of first impression. * * * **[g]** The case is unique for several reasons. It does not involve an ordinary abduction by a private kidnaper, or bounty hunter, as in *Ker*, * * * nor does it involve the apprehension of an American fugitive who committed a crime in one State and sought asylum in another, as in *Frisbie v. Collins.* * * * Rather, it involves this country's abduction of another country's citizen; it also involves a violation of the territorial integrity of that other country, with which this country has signed an extradition treaty. **[h]**

A Mexican citizen was kidnaped in Mexico and charged with a crime committed in Mexico; his offense allegedly violated both Mexican and American law. Mexico has formally demanded on at least two separate occasions that he be returned to Mexico and has represented that he will be prosecuted and punished for his alleged offense. It is clear that Mexico's demand must be honored if this official abduction violated the 1978 Extradition Treaty between the United States and Mexico. In my opinion, a fair reading of the treaty in light of [*Rauscher*] and applicable principles of international law, leads inexorably to the conclusion that the District Court, * * * and the Court of Appeals * * * correctly construed that instrument.

I

The Extradition Treaty with Mexico is a comprehensive document containing 23 articles and an appendix listing the extraditable offenses covered by the agreement. The parties announced their purpose in the preamble: The two Governments desire "to cooperate more closely in the fight against crime and, to this end, to mutually render better assistance in matters of extradition." From the preamble, through the description of the parties' obligations with respect to offenses committed within as well as beyond the territory of a requesting party, the delineation of the procedures and evidentiary requirements for extradition, the special provisions for political offenses and capital punishment, and other details, the Treaty appears to have been designed to cover the entire subject of extradition. * * * Moreover, as noted by the Court, * * * Article 9 expressly provides that neither Contracting Party is bound to deliver up its own nationals, although it may do so in its discretion, but if it does not do so, it "shall submit the case to its competent authorities for purposes of prosecution."

Petitioner's claim that the Treaty is not exclusive, but permits forcible governmental kidnaping, would transform these, and other, provisions into little more than verbiage. For example, provisions requiring "sufficient" evidence to grant extradition (Art. 3), withholding extradition for political or military offenses (Art. 5), withholding extradition when the person sought has already been tried (Art. 6), withholding extradition when the statute of limitations for the crime has lapsed (Art. 7), and granting the requested State

discretion to refuse to extradite an individual who would face the death penalty in the requesting country (Art. 8), would serve little purpose if the requesting country could simply kidnap the person. * * * In addition, all of these provisions "only make sense if they are understood as *requiring* each treaty signatory to comply with those procedures whenever it wishes to obtain jurisdiction over an individual who is located in another treaty nation." * * *

It is true, as the Court notes, that there is no express promise by either party to refrain from forcible abductions in the territory of the other Nation. * * * Relying on that omission, the Court, in effect, concludes that the Treaty merely creates an optional method of obtaining jurisdiction over alleged offenders, and that the parties silently reserved the right to resort to self help whenever they deem force more expeditious than legal process. If the United States, for example, thought it more expedient to torture or simply to execute a person rather than to attempt extradition, these options would be equally available because they, too, were not explicitly prohibited by the Treaty. **[i]** That, however, is a highly improbable interpretation of a consensual agreement, which on its face appears to have been intended to set forth comprehensive and exclusive rules concerning the subject of extradition. In my opinion, "the manifest scope and object of the treaty itself," * * * plainly imply a mutual undertaking to respect the territorial integrity of the other contracting party. That opinion is confirmed by a consideration of the "legal context" in which the Treaty was negotiated. * * *

II

[JUSTICE STEVENS argued that the *Rauscher* decision made it clear that a treaty could limit the authority of what the United States could do in the prosecution of a case. There, the treaty limited the crimes for which the courts of the United States could try an extradited person, and therefore Rauscher's conviction of the lesser included crime of cruel treatment, when he was extradited for murder, was void. This was so even though the treaty in that case did not spell out this point with absolute clarity.]

* * *

Although the Court's conclusion in *Rauscher* was supported by a number of judicial precedents, the holdings in these cases were not nearly as uniform as the consensus of international opinion that condemns one Nation's violation of the territorial integrity of a friendly neighbor. It is shocking that a party to an extradition treaty might believe that it has secretly reserved the right to make seizures of citizens in the other party's territory. Justice Story found it shocking enough that the United States would attempt to justify an American seizure of a foreign vessel in a Spanish port. * * *

The law of Nations, as understood by Justice Story in 1824, has not changed. Thus, a leading treatise explains:

"A State must not perform acts of sovereignty in the territory of another State.

. . .

"It is . . . a breach of International Law for a State to send its agents to the territory of another State to apprehend persons accused of having committed a crime. Apart from other satisfaction, the first duty of the offending State is to hand over the person in question to the State in whose territory he was apprehended." * * *

Commenting on the precise issue raised by this case, the chief reporter for the American Law Institute's Restatement of Foreign Relations used language reminiscent of Justice Story's characterization of an official seizure in a foreign jurisdiction as "monstrous:"

"When done without consent of the foreign government, abducting a person from a foreign country is a gross violation of international law and gross disrespect for a norm high in the opinion of mankind. It is a blatant violation of the territorial integrity of another state; it eviscerates the extradition system (established by a comprehensive network of treaties involving virtually all states)." [j]

In the *Rauscher* case, the legal background that supported the decision to imply a covenant not to prosecute for an offense different from that for which extradition had been granted was far less clear than the rule against invading the territorial integrity of a treaty partner that supports Mexico's position in this case. If *Rauscher* was correctly decided—and I am convinced that it was—its rationale clearly dictates a comparable result in this case.

III

A critical flaw pervades the Court's entire opinion. It fails to differentiate between the conduct of private citizens, which does not violate any treaty obligation, and conduct expressly authorized by the Executive Branch of the Government, which unquestionably constitutes a flagrant violation of international law, and in my opinion, also constitutes a breach of our treaty obligations. [The gist of the remainder of Part III of the dissent is that since *Ker* involved a private abduction, it was distinguishable and thus was not precedent in this case.]

IV

As the Court observes at the outset of its opinion, there is reason to believe that respondent participated in an especially brutal murder of an American law enforcement agent. That fact, if true, may explain the Executive's intense interest in punishing respondent in our courts. Such an explanation, however, provides no justification for disregarding the Rule of Law that this Court has a duty to uphold. That the Executive may wish to reinterpret the Treaty to allow for an action that the Treaty in no way authorizes should not influence this Court's interpretation. Indeed, the desire for revenge exerts "a kind of hydraulic pressure . . . before which even well settled principles of law will bend," * * * but it is precisely at such moments that we should remember and be guided by our duty "to render judgment evenly and dispassionately according to law, as each is given

understanding to ascertain and apply it." * * * The way that we perform that duty in a case of this kind sets an example that other tribunals in other countries are sure to emulate.

The significance of this Court's precedents is illustrated by a recent decision of the Court of Appeal of the Republic of South Africa. Based largely on its understanding of the import of this Court's cases—including our decision in *Ker v. Illinois*—that court held that the prosecution of a defendant kidnaped by agents of South Africa in another country must be dismissed. * * * The Court of Appeal of South Africa—indeed, I suspect most courts throughout the civilized world —will be deeply disturbed by the "monstrous" decision the Court announces today. For every Nation that has an interest in preserving the Rule of Law is affected, directly or indirectly, by a decision of this character. [k] As Thomas Paine warned, an "avidity to punish is always dangerous to liberty" because it leads a Nation "to stretch, to misinterpret, and to misapply even the best of laws." To counter that tendency, he reminds us:

> "He that would make his own liberty secure must guard even his enemy from oppression; for if he violates this duty he establishes a precedent that will reach to himself."

I respectfully dissent. [l]

* * * * * * * * * * *

COMMENTS

[a] A treaty is a "compact made between two or more independent nations with a view to the public welfare." *Black's Law Dictionary*, Fifth Edition, p. 1346. Under Article II, §2 of the Constitution, treaties are made by the president with the advice and consent of two-thirds of the Senate. Once a treaty is passed it has the effect of law and is as binding upon the states, under the "supremacy clause," Art. VI, §2, as is the Constitution and United States Statutes.

[b] The majority and the dissent view the applicability of the treaty and the precedents in diametrically opposed ways. Because the DEA chose kidnapping as the preferred way to obtain the person of Alvarez-Machain the Court says that the extradition statute simply does not apply and a precedent like *Rauscher* is not relevant. Aside from the semantic and logical distinctions, what policy differences appear to motivate the majority and dissenting opinions?

[c] Calling its reading of the extradition treaty "more natural" seems, in this case, to be the Court's subjective view; the respondent (and the dissent) does not appear to "strain" to reach its conclusion that an extradition treaty should apply to all removals of criminal suspects from the territory of a nation.

[d] Unlike the primary sources of national or state law (constitution, statutes, supreme court cases), principles of international law are matters of general agreement and thus do not have the same force unless a nation adopts a principle by treaty or by internal statute. Thus, respondent is careful not to argue that the Court is *bound* by the international law principles he cites. Compare this positivistic approach to that of the dissent.

[e] Is this sentence relevant to the argument about extradition?

[f] This is an interesting example of a court reading the law of a case in a narrow, specific, and "legalistic" manner—being guided by the more specific "local" rules even while allowing that other principles of justice or more general rules of international law are to the contrary.

[g] Since there is no clear precedent on point, the Court is free to adopt a rule based on its reasoning about the principles of law involved.

[h] At the outset the dissent seeks to undermine the way in which the majority opinion relies on *Ker* and *Frisbie* by asserting that they are distinguishable from the governing facts of this case. The argument clearly did not carry the majority.

[i] This point is not entirely fair. Note that the District Court rejected respondent's argument that the government's abduction constituted "outrageous conduct." If there had been torture the outrageous conduct argument would be relevant.

[j] Remember that the majority found these rules not to be directly binding on the Court. The allusion to a "comprehensive network of treaties" in the quoted source suggests that in the modern world, some rules of international law have the force of a "world common law," so to speak.

[k] The citation of the South African case is an interesting touch, indicating that American cases that uphold international law standards can be influential in other parts of the world, and that a rejection of these standards can suggest to other nations that actions such as abductions, that weaken international law, are acceptable.

[l] The case ended badly for the United States. Dr. Alvarez-Machain was acquitted of murder and torture in the Los Angeles Federal District Court in December 1992. The judge threw out the case, calling the prosecution's case the "wildest speculation." Another man was convicted. The incident caused much resentment of the United States in Mexico. As a result of the incident the Clinton Administration has promised Mexico that it will not engage in any cross-border kidnapping of Mexican citizens pending a revised extradition treaty. Dr. Alvarez-Machain sued federal law enforcement officials for $20 million in damages for kidnapping, torture, and false imprisonment.

Chapter Five

RIGHT TO COUNSEL

The right to the assistance of counsel is the last of eight rights contained in the Sixth Amendment, which is designed to provide procedures that insure, as far as humanly possible, a fair trial. These rights guarantee to defendants in "all criminal prosecutions" a speedy and public trial, an impartial jury, a jury chosen from the venue of the crime ("the State and district wherein the crime shall have been committed"), notice of the accusations, confrontation of the witnesses against him, subpoena power "for obtaining Witnesses in his favor," and finally, "to have the Assistance of Counsel for his defence." Placing the right to counsel at the end of the list indicates that all the formal rights are meaningless unless a defendant has the services of a committed, trained, professional and competent attorney whose duty it is to represent the defendant to the best of his or her abilities.

The recognition of a right to counsel in the Bill of Rights reflected a colonial heritage of greater trial fairness than existed in England. At the time of the framing of the Constitution the counsel guarantee clearly meant that the State could not prevent a lawyer from appearing in all aspects of the defense of a person haled into court to face criminal charges. This was an advance over the English procedures that placed some restrictions on the role of attorneys at that time.

What the right did not mean in 1791, or for a long time thereafter, was that fundamental fairness required that the State pay for counsel for defendants too poor to hire one. It was not unusual for indigents to appear on their own behalf. Where a poor man defended himself the judge often guided the trial to insure fairness. As an alternative, the judge had the inherent authority to request that members of the bar (designated as "officers of the court") represent an occasional defendant at no fee, as a part of their professional responsibility. This practice was most common in capital cases.

In twentieth-century America, with the rapid growth of urban populations, concerns for justice led to the growth of free legal aid for indigents in civil cases. To a lesser degree municipalities and states provided free counsel in criminal cases, through public defenders' offices and through assigned counsel. Private grants also funded counsel for indigent defendants. This was at first seen as a social service but not a right.

The development of the Constitutional right to counsel involved a critical "incorporation" battle (see Chapter 1) and an expansion of the right to assigned counsel in a wider array of cases. The first great case in this area, *Powell v. Alabama* (1932), was one of the most dramatic cases of the twentieth century. The case arose out of the sensational trial known as the "Scottsboro Boys" case, in an atmosphere of racist, lynch justice in the depression-era South. Although the Court rejected a clear adoption of the incorporation of the Sixth Amendment right to counsel into the due process clause of the Fourteenth Amendment, it did find that the proceedings violated the due process rights of the defendants. They did not receive a fair trial in large measure because no lawyer stood up for them. The case stood for the proposition that in a capital case where special circumstances existed, the State had to provide counsel for the defense. The case specified the valuable and even essential role played by counsel.

The stakes for incorporation increased when, two years after *Powell*, the Court ruled in *Johnson v. Zerbst* (1938), a federal case, that the Sixth Amendment required counsel as a jurisdictional matter. In short, a federal felony trial where the defendant was not represented was unconstitutional and void, unless it could be shown that defendant waived counsel knowingly and intelligently. A few years later, however, the Court refused to extend the same rule to the states. According to *Betts v. Brady* (1942), a trial did not lack due process where an experienced, intelligent, and court-wise adult defended himself for a non-capital crime. *Betts* made it clear that the rule of *Powell* applied only where there were special circumstances in the case requiring counsel.

The Court opened up another line of cases with *Griffin v. Illinois* (1956) by ruling that the equal protection clause was violated where a trial transcript was not made available to an indigent defendant on an appeal. *Griffin* was applied in numerous cases to guarantee free access for indigents, *e.g.*, *Burns v. Ohio*, 360 U.S. 252 (1959) (filing fees to appeal) and *Mayer v. Chicago*, 404 U.S. 189 (1971) (a transcript or record of "sufficient completeness" required in an appeal from an ordinance violation). It is likely that JUSTICE BLACK, the author of the opinion in *Johnson v. Zerbst* and a dissenter in *Betts*, intended his opinion in *Griffin* to be the springboard of a constitutional guarantee to the right of counsel. In *Griffin* he wrote: "There can be no equal justice where the kind of trial a man gets depends on the amount of money he has." This line of reasoning resulted in the holding that an indigent did not receive a fair trial if he was deprived of an expert witness for a necessary part of his defense (*Ake v. Oklahoma* (1985)).

When the Court did incorporate the right to counsel in *Gideon v. Wainwright* (1963) it did so under the theory that the Sixth Amendment right, as pronounced in *Johnson v. Zerbst*, was incorporated into Fourteenth Amendment due process as a fundamental right. *Gideon* was a non-capital felony case. The Sixth Amendment right was extended to misdemeanor cases in *Argersinger v. Hamlin* (1972), where the sentence included imprisonment. The Argersinger right to counsel does not extend to misdemeanor cases where the authorized punishment includes jail but the actual penalty was not incarceration. The Court reasoned that actual imprisonment is a punishment different in kind from fines or the threat of imprisonment.

Faretta v. California (1975) makes it clear that the Sixth Amendment guarantees the *assistance* of counsel, but that the right is personal and may be waived after the person is informed clearly of the right. A defendant has the right to represent herself if she so wishes. Prior to waiving the right the defendant must be informed of the dangers and disadvantages of self-representation; on the other hand, the trial court cannot deny the right of self representation simply because a defendant does not have the knowledge and skill of a trial attorney. Even when a defendant is representing himself, the judge may appoint a standby counsel, but that attorney must not be seen by the jury to interfere with the pro se presentation of the defense (*McKaskle v. Wiggins*, 465 U.S. 168 (1984)).

The Sixth Amendment right extends to sentencing proceedings and to sentencing combined with a revocation (*Mempa v. Rhay*, 389 U.S. 128 (1967)). But with the conclusion of the "criminal prosecution," the Sixth Amendment no longer applies. The constitutional right to counsel at later stages must rely on the more fluid right under the Fourteenth Amendment. Thus, counsel is required at post-sentencing probation revocation hearings (*Gagnon v. Scarpelli*, 411 U.S. 778 (1973)) and parole revocation hearings (*Morrissey v. Brewer*, 408 U.S. 471 (1972)) only if special circumstances exist, which must be determined on a case-by-case basis. Utilizing a balancing analysis, the Court has not extended the right to counsel to any deprivations of liberty that result from prison disciplinary hearings, reasoning that the defendant's interests are less than those of probationers and parolees (*Wolff v. McDonnell*, 418 U.S. 539 (1974)). These are all due process hearings, but the process due depends upon weighing the interests of the individual weighed against the State's interests.

The Court has found that there is "no material difference" between the roles of counsel in juvenile delinquency determinations and adult criminal trials. As a result, *In re Gault*, 387 U.S. 1 (1967) held that "proceedings to determine delinquency which may result in commitment to an institution in which the juvenile's freedom is curtailed, the child and his parents must be notified of the child's right to be represented by counsel retained by them, or if they are unable to afford counsel, that counsel will be appointed to represent the child."

Prison inmates clearly do not have any Sixth Amendment right to counsel. Under the due process right of access to the courts, however, the Court has required that prison systems must not block or censor habeas corpus or other petitions sent by prisoners (*Ex parte Hull*, 312 U.S. 546 (1941)) and may not prohibit the reasonable use of "jailhouse lawyers" (*Johnson v. Avery*, 393 U.S. 483 (1969)) or the use of law students or paralegals (*Procunier v. Martinez*, 416 U.S. 396 (1973)). In *Bounds v. Smith* (1977) the Court stated that the fundamental rule of these cases, the right of access, imposes an affirmative duty on prison authorities to provide the means for prisoners in preparing and filing legal papers. The Court did not require any specific form, but in that case required adequate law libraries.

Douglas v. California (1963), on the basis of the Fourteenth Amendment's due process and equal protection clauses, held that the right to counsel extended to a first appeal of right. *Ross v. Moffitt* (1974) refused to extend this right to later, discretionary appeals, habeas corpus petitions, and other collateral attacks on the conviction. *Ross* held that equal protection reasoning did not apply to these cases and that due process was not offended where court systems provided means to review petitions of inmates. Nor must the state provide free counsel to indigent defendants preparing post-conviction legal challenges while on death-row (*Murray v. Giarratano*, 492 U.S. 1 (1989)).

The right to counsel is the right to the *effective* assistance of counsel. In *Strickland v. Washington* (1984) the Court established a two-prong test: first, the assistance provided must be what is considered reasonably effective in light of the current standards of legal practice in the jurisdiction. If the attorney made an error there is a Sixth Amendment violation only if it caused prejudice to the defendant's case—that *but for* the error the result of the case would have been different. Prejudice is automatically inferred where there is a conflict of interest (*Cuyler v. Sullivan*, 446 U.S. 335 (1980)), although it is not a conflict of interest simply because one attorney represents two defendants in the same case (*Burger v. Kemp*, 483 U.S. 776 (1987)). Ineffective assistance of counsel has been found where the attorney failed to conduct any pretrial discovery and failed to file timely motions to suppress illegally seized evidence (*Kimmelman v. Morrison*, 477 U.S. 365 (1986)), but it is not ineffective assistance for an attorney to refuse to allow a client to commit perjury (*Nix v. Whiteside* (1986)).

In recent years federal prosecutors have been challenging defense counsel. In *Wheat v. United States* (1988) the Court upheld a prosecutor's challenge to an attorney who represented several defendants in a drug conspiracy even though defendants agreed to waive any Sixth Amendment challenges. The Court has upheld the use of the federal drug asset forfeiture law to freeze the assets of a defendant before trial so that his attorney could not be paid out of monies believed to be drug profits (*United States v. Monsanto*, 491 U.S. 600 (1989)) and also held that the post-conviction seizure of such funds (*Caplan & Drysdale v. United States*, 491 U.S. 671 (1989)) did not violate the Sixth Amendment.

POWELL v. ALABAMA

287 U.S. 45, 53 S.Ct. 55, 77 L.Ed. 158 (1932)

MR. JUSTICE SUTHERLAND delivered the opinion of the Court.

[A group of seven black teenagers riding a freight train in Alabama in 1931 got into a fight with a group of seven white youths. The whites were thrown off the train. Two white girls riding the train claimed to have been raped by six of the seven black youths, who were arrested by a sheriff's posse in Scottsboro, Alabama, in an atmosphere of such hostility that the militia was called out to guard the defendants and maintain order. Six days after the arrest, the defendants were indicted. They were not asked whether they had or could obtain lawyers. Their trials were conducted six days after the indictments.] [a]

[No lawyer was directly appointed to defend any of the defendants. Instead, a Tennessee lawyer who came to the trial agreed to help, and several lawyers in the courtroom agreed collectively to conduct the trial. But none of them was directly responsible for the defense, and there was no trial preparation or investigation. JUSTICE SUTHERLAND noted that this imposed "no substantial or definite obligation upon any" of the attorneys.]

[T]he defendants were tried in three several groups. * * * Each of the three trials was completed within a single day. * * * The juries found defendants guilty and imposed the death penalty upon all. * * *

* * *

In this court the judgments are assailed upon the grounds that the defendants, and each of them, were denied due process of law and the equal protection of the laws, in contravention of the Fourteenth Amendment, specifically as follows: * * * they were denied the right of counsel, with the accustomed incidents of consultation and opportunity of preparation for trial. * * *

* * * The record does not disclose [the defendants'] ages, except that one of them was nineteen; but the record clearly indicates that most, if not all, of them were youthful, and they are constantly referred to as "the boys." They were ignorant and illiterate. All of them were residents of other states, where alone members of their families or friends resided.

However guilty defendants, upon due inquiry, might prove to have been, they were, until convicted, presumed to be innocent. It was the duty of the court having their cases in charge to see that they were denied no necessary incident of a fair trial. With any error of the state court involving alleged contravention of the state statutes or constitution we, of course, have nothing to do. The sole inquiry which we are permitted to make is whether the federal Constitution was contravened; * * * and as to that, we confine ourselves, as already suggested, to the inquiry whether the defendants were in substance denied the right of counsel, and if so, whether such denial infringes the due process clause of the Fourteenth Amendment. [b]

* * *

* * * The defendants, young, ignorant, illiterate, surrounded by hostile sentiment, haled back and forth

under guard of soldiers, charged with an atrocious crime regarded with especial horror in the community where they were to be tried, were thus put in peril of their lives within a few moments after counsel for the first time charged with any degree of responsibility began to represent them.

[c]

It is not enough to assume that counsel thus precipitated into the case thought there was no defense, and exercised their best judgment in proceeding to trial without preparation. Neither they nor the court could say what a prompt and thoroughgoing investigation might disclose as to the facts. No attempt was made to investigate. No opportunity to do so was given. Defendants were immediately hurried to trial. * * * Under the circumstances disclosed, we hold that defendants were not accorded the right of counsel in any substantial sense. To decide otherwise, would simply be to ignore actualities. * * * **[d]**

* * * The prompt disposition of criminal cases is to be commended and encouraged. But in reaching that result a defendant, charged with a serious crime, must not be stripped of his right to have sufficient time to advise with counsel and prepare his defense. To do that is not to proceed promptly in the calm spirit of regulated justice but to go forward with the haste of the mob.

* * *

[JUSTICE SUTHERLAND then reviewed the history of right to counsel in England and America. He found that English practice was not an infallible guide to the meaning of due process and fell short of due process in regard to the right to counsel.]

* * * [T]he case of *Hurtado v. California*, [110 U.S. 516 (1884)], where this court determined that due process of law does not require an indictment by a grand jury [stated that] * * * if it had been the purpose of [the 14th] Amendment to perpetuate the * * * grand jury in the states, it would have embodied, as did the Fifth Amendment, an express declaration to that effect.

* * * In the face of the reasoning of the *Hurtado* case, if it stood alone, it would be difficult to justify the conclusion that the right to counsel, being thus specifically granted by the Sixth Amendment, was also within the intendment of the due process of law clause. But the *Hurtado* case does not stand alone. In [a] later case * * * this court held that a judgment of a state court, * * * by which private property was taken for public use without just compensation, was in violation of the due process of law required by the Fourteenth Amendment, notwithstanding that the Fifth Amendment explicitly declares that private property shall not be taken for public use without just compensation. * * *

Likewise, this court has considered that freedom of speech and of the press are rights protected by the due process clause of the Fourteenth Amendment, although in the First Amendment, Congress is prohibited in specific terms from abridging the right. * * *

These later cases establish that notwithstanding the sweeping character of the language in the *Hurtado* case, the rule laid down is not without exceptions. * * * The fact that the right involved is of such a character that it cannot be denied without violating those "fundamental principles of liberty and justice which lie at the base of all our civil and political institutions , * * * is obviously one of those compelling considerations which must prevail in determining whether it is embraced within the due process clause of the Fourteenth Amendment, although it be specifically dealt with in another part of the federal Constitution. * * * **[e]**

It never has been doubted by this court * * * that notice and hearing are preliminary steps essential to the passing of an enforceable judgment, and that they, together with a legally competent tribunal having jurisdiction of the case, constitute basic elements of the constitutional requirement of due process of law. * * * [T]he rule that no one shall be personally bound until he has had his day in court [is] as old as the law, and it meant that he must be cited to appear and afforded an opportunity to be heard. * * *

What, then, does a hearing include? Historically and in practice, in our own country at least, it has always included the right to the aid of counsel when desired and provided by the party asserting the right. The right to be heard would be, in many cases, of little avail if it did not comprehend the right to be heard by counsel. Even the intelligent and educated layman has small and sometimes no skill in the science of law. If charged with crime, he is incapable, generally, of determining for himself whether the indictment is good or bad. He is unfamiliar with the rules of evidence. Left without the aid of counsel he may be put on trial without a proper charge, and convicted upon incompetent evidence, or evidence irrelevant to the issue or otherwise inadmissible. He lacks both the skill and knowledge adequately to prepare his defense, even though he had a perfect one. He requires the guiding hand of counsel at every step in the proceedings against him. Without it, though he be not guilty, he faces the danger of conviction because he does not know how to establish his innocence. If that be true of men of intelligence, how much more true is it of the ignorant and illiterate, or those of feeble intellect. If in any case, civil or criminal, a state or federal court were arbitrarily to refuse to hear a party by counsel, employed by and appearing for him, it reasonably may not be doubted that such a refusal would be a denial of a hearing, and, therefore, of due process in the constitutional sense. **[f]**

* * *

In the light of the facts outlined in the forepart of this opinion—the ignorance and illiteracy of the defendants, their youth, the circumstances of public hostility, the imprisonment and the close surveillance of the defendants by the military forces, the fact that their friends and families were all in other states and communication with them necessarily difficult, and above all that they stood in deadly peril of their lives—we think the failure of the trial court to give them reasonable time and opportunity to secure counsel was a clear denial of due process.

* * *

Judgments reversed.

* * * * * * * * * * *

COMMENTS

[a] This notorious case, known as the "Scottsboro boys' case," was a national cause celebre and the subject of books, films and television plays many years later. It took place in a social atmosphere that included the Great Depression, intense racial hostility, legal segregation, and scores or hundreds of lynchings of African-Americans annually in the South. For a complete rendition of the case, see Dan T. Carter, *Scottsboro: A Tragedy of the American South*, revised edition (Baton Rouge: Louisiana State University Press, 1979); James Goodman, *Stories of Scottsboro* (New York: Pantheon, 1994).

[b] Notice that the Court, in this pre-incorporation period, is careful to give deference to the rights of states to conduct justice in any manner seen fit as long as the rights of citizens under the United States Constitution are not infringed. Notice also that the Court refers to the Fourteenth Amendment but not to the Sixth Amendment.

[c] These facts are not presented simply to heighten the drama of the case. They are the basis of the holding of the case and they will also have significance in the determination of the holdings of subsequent cases, which we will analyze below.

[d] Some ambiguity is possible here, because JUSTICE SUTHERLAND refers to the right to counsel but not directly to the Sixth Amendment. This ambiguity is the basis of JUSTICE BLACK's later claims in *Betts v. Brady* and *Gideon v. Wainwright* [this volume]. It is significant that the mere formal presence of a lawyer does not satisfy the defendant's right to counsel, whether under the Fourteenth or the Sixth Amendment. Although the words of the Court are terse, its dismay at the general conditions of Southern justice in that period is clear.

[e] This discussion compounds the ambiguity of the case. It is not clear whether JUSTICE SUTHERLAND viewed the Sixth Amendment to be "incorporated" into the Fourteenth in the modern sense, or whether he simply understood the Fourteenth Amendment due process clause to include the right to counsel apart from any Sixth Amendment requirement for the federal government.

[f] This statement, although an eloquent analysis regarding the importance of counsel, does not end in a holding that counsel must be afforded an indigent defendant under all circumstances, which was not an issue in this case. Instead, JUSTICE SUTHERLAND held that under all the facts of the case there was a failure to have reasonable time and opportunity to secure counsel. This could be, and later was, seen as a holding that due process (*i.e.*, notice and a fair hearing) was violated.

JOHNSON v. ZERBST

304 U.S. 458, 58 S.Ct. 1019, 82 L.Ed. 1461 (1938)

MR. JUSTICE BLACK delivered the opinion of the Court.

* * *

[Johnson and Bridwell, Marines on leave in Charleston, South Carolina, were convicted in federal court of possessing and uttering counterfeit money. They were represented by counsel at their preliminary hearing.] Upon arraignment, both pleaded not guilty, said that they had no lawyer, and—in response to an inquiry of the court—stated that they were ready for trial. They were then tried, convicted and sentenced, without assistance of counsel.

[After imprisonment, they filed writs of *habeas corpus* claiming a loss of their Sixth Amendment right to counsel.] [a]

"Both petitioners lived in distant cities of other states and neither had relatives, friends, or acquaintances in Charleston. Both had little education and were without funds. They testified that they had never been guilty of nor charged with any offense before, and there was no evidence in rebuttal of these statements." [In a *habeas corpus* hearing, there was disagreement as to whether petitioners requested counsel.] * * * The Assistant District Attorney testified that Bridwell "cross-examined the witnesses"; and, in his opinion, displayed more knowledge of procedure than the normal layman would possess. He did not recall whether Bridwell addressed the jury or not, but the clerk of the trial court testified "that Mr. Johnson [Bridwell?] con-ducted his defence about as well as the average layman usually does in cases of a similar nature." Concerning what he said to the jury and his cross-examination of witnesses, Bridwell testified "I tried to speak to the jury after the evidence was in during my trial over in the Eastern District of South Carolina. I told the jury, 'I don't consider myself a hoodlum as the District Attorney has made me out several times.' I told the jury that I was not a native of New York as the District Attorney stated, but was from Mississippi and only stationed for government service in New York. I only said fifteen or twenty words. I said I didn't think I was a hoodlum and could not have been one of very long standing because they didn't keep them in the Marine Corps. [b]

"I objected to one witness' testimony. I didn't ask him any questions, I only objected to his whole testimony. After the prosecuting attorney was finished with the witness, he said, 'Your witness,' and I got up and objected to the testimony on the grounds that it was all false, and the Trial Judge said any objection I had I would have to bring proof or disproof." [c]

* * *

One. The Sixth Amendment guarantees that "In all criminal prosecutions, the accused shall enjoy the right . . . to have the Assistance of Counsel for his defence." This is one of the safeguards of the Sixth Amendment deemed necessary to insure fundamental human rights of life and liberty. Omitted from the Constitution as originally adopted, provisions of this and other Amendments were submitted by the first Congress convened under that Constitution as essential barriers against arbitrary or unjust deprivation of human rights. The Sixth Amendment stands as a constant admonition that if the constitutional safeguards it provides be lost, justice will not "still be done." It embodies a realistic recognition of the obvious truth that the average defendant does not have the professional legal skill to protect himself when brought before a tribunal with power to take his life or liberty, wherein the prosecution is presented by experienced and learned counsel. That which is simple, orderly and necessary to the lawyer, to the untrained layman may appear intricate, complex and mysterious. Consistently with the wise policy of the Sixth Amendment and other parts of our fundamental charter, this Court has pointed to " . . . the humane policy of the modern criminal law . . ." which now provides that a defendant ". . . if he be poor, . . . may have counsel furnished him by the state . . . not infrequently . . . more able than the attorney for the state."

[The Court here quoted the key passage from *Powell v. Alabama* [this volume] to the effect that a layperson is at a serious loss in a trial without the skilled assistance of a lawyer.] The Sixth Amendment withholds from federal courts, in all criminal proceedings, the power and authority to deprive an accused of his life or liberty unless he has or waives the assistance of counsel. **[d]**

Two. There is insistence here that petitioner waived this constitutional right. The District Court did not so find. It has been pointed out that "courts indulge every reasonable presumption against waiver" of fundamental constitutional rights and that we "do not presume acquiescence in the loss of fundamental rights." A waiver is ordinarily an intentional relinquishment or abandonment of a known right or privilege. The determination of whether there has been an intelligent waiver of the right to counsel must depend, in each case, upon the particular facts and circumstances surrounding that case, including the background, experience, and conduct of the accused.   * * *

The constitutional right of an accused to be represented by counsel invokes, of itself, the protection of a trial court, in which the accused—whose life or liberty is at stake—is without counsel. This protecting duty imposes the serious and weighty responsibility upon the trial judge of determining whether there is an intelligent and competent waiver by the accused. While an accused may waive the right to counsel, whether there is a proper waiver should be clearly determined by the trial court, and it would be fitting and appropriate for that determination to appear upon the record.

Three. The District Court, holding petitioner could not obtain relief by *habeas corpus*, said:

"It is unfortunate, if petitioners lost their right to a new trial through ignorance or negligence, but such misfortune cannot give this Court jurisdiction in a habeas corpus case to review and correct the errors complained of."

The purpose of the constitutional guaranty of a right to counsel is to protect an accused from conviction resulting from his own ignorance of his

legal and constitutional rights, and the guaranty would be nullified by a determination that an accused's ignorant failure to claim his rights removes the protection of the Constitution. True, *habeas corpus* cannot be used as a means of reviewing errors of law and irregularities—not involving the question of jurisdiction—occurring during the course of trial; and the "writ of *habeas corpus* cannot be used as a writ of error." These principles, however, must be construed and applied so as to preserve—not destroy— constitutional safeguards of human life and liberty. The scope of inquiry in *habeas corpus* proceedings has been broadened—not narrowed—since the adoption of the Sixth Amendment. In such a proceeding, "it would be clearly erroneous to confine the inquiry to the proceedings and judgment of the trial court" and the petitioned court has "power to inquire with regard to the jurisdiction of the inferior court, either in respect to the subject matter or to the person, even if such inquiry . . . [involves] an examination of facts outside of, but not inconsistent with, the record." * * *
     * * *

Since the Sixth Amendment constitutionally entitles one charged with crime to the assistance of counsel, compliance with this constitutional mandate is an essential jurisdictional prerequisite to a federal court's authority to deprive an accused of his life or liberty. When this right is properly waived, the assistance of counsel is no longer a necessary element of the court's jurisdiction to proceed to conviction and sentence. If the accused, however, is not represented by

counsel and has not competently and intelligently waived his constitutional right, the Sixth Amendment stands as a jurisdictional bar to a valid conviction and sentence depriving him of his life or his liberty. A court's jurisdiction at the beginning of trial may be lost "in the course of the proceedings" due to failure to complete the court—as the Sixth Amendment requires—by providing counsel for an accused who is unable to obtain counsel, who has not intelligently waived this constitutional guaranty, and whose life or liberty is at stake. If this requirement of the Sixth Amendment is not complied with, the court no longer has jurisdiction to proceed. The judgment of conviction pronounced by a court without jurisdiction is void, and one imprisoned thereunder may obtain release by *habeas corpus*. A judge of the United States—to whom a petition for *habeas corpus* is addressed— should be alert to examine "the facts for himself when if true as alleged they make the trial absolutely void." **[e]**

[Because of the presumption of regularity, the burden of proof in a *habeas corpus* hearing is on the petitioner.]

     * * * [The case was reversed and remanded.]

[JUSTICE REED concurred; JUSTICES McREYNOLDS and BUTLER felt the judgment of the Circuit Court of Appeals should be affirmed.

[JUSTICE CARDOZO took no part in the consideration or decision of the case.]

     *   *   *   *   *   *   *   *   *   *   *

COMMENTS

[a] As a federal case, the Sixth Amendment right is directly invoked, without the overlay of federalism and Fourteenth Amendment due process concerns that were important in *Powell v. Alabama* [this volume].

[b] The quoted paragraphs are from the opinion of the District Court. The testimony gives the impression that the prosecutor appealed to the jury's prejudice against "outsiders." If so, does it seem likely that the prosecutor could have used that tactic if defendants were represented by counsel?

[c] On the whole, the habeas corpus petition indicates that petitioners were not adept in defending themselves. No issue of intent, for example, seems to have been raised.

[d] Quoting from *Powell v. Alabama*, a due process case, shows that the line between the due process right to counsel and the Sixth Amendment right may be narrow.

[e] Jurisdiction is judicial power, conferred by constitution or statute; without jurisdiction a court has no power and right to proceed. By linking constitutional rights to jurisdiction the Supreme Court makes it clear, in no uncertain terms, that a constitutional deprivation is not a "mere procedural error" but a defect that goes to the heart of the process. This activist reasoning was made possible by the approach taken by JUSTICE HOLMES in *Moore v. Dempsey* [this volume].

BETTS v. BRADY

316 U.S. 455, 62 S.Ct. 1252, 86 L.Ed.2d 1595 (1942)

MR. JUSTICE ROBERTS delivered the opinion of the Court.

The petitioner was indicted for robbery in the Circuit Court of Carroll County, Maryland. [a] Due to lack of funds, he was unable to employ counsel, and so informed the judge at his arraignment. He requested that counsel be appointed for him. The judge advised him that this could not be done as it was not the practice in Carroll County to appoint counsel for indigent defendants save in prosecutions for murder and rape.

Without waiving his asserted right to counsel the petitioner pleaded not guilty and elected to be tried without a jury. At his request witnesses were summoned in his behalf. He cross-examined the State's witnesses and examined his own. The latter gave testimony tending to establish an alibi. Although afforded the opportunity, he did not take the witness stand. The judge found him guilty and imposed a sentence of eight years.

* * *

Was the petitioner's conviction and sentence a deprivation of his liberty without due process of law, in violation of the Fourteenth Amendment, because of the court's refusal to appoint counsel at his request? [b]

The Sixth Amendment of the national Constitution applies only to trials in federal courts. The due process clause of the Fourteenth Amendment does not incorporate, as such, the specific guarantees found in the Sixth Amendment although a denial by a state of rights or privileges specifically embodied in that and others of the first eight amendments may, in certain circumstances, or in connection with other elements, operate, in a given case, to deprive a litigant of due process of law in violation of the Fourteenth. Due process of law is secured against invasion by the federal Government by the Fifth Amendment, and is safeguarded against state action in identical words by the Fourteenth. * * * The phrase formulates a concept less rigid and more fluid than those envisaged in other specific and particular provisions of the Bill of Rights. Its application is less a matter of rule. Asserted denial is to be tested by an appraisal of the totality of facts in a given case. That which may, in one setting, constitute a denial of fundamental fairness, shocking to the universal sense of justice, may, in other circumstances, and in the light of other considerations, fall short of such denial. * * *

The petitioner, in this instance, asks us, in effect, to apply a rule in the enforcement of the due process clause. He says the rule to be deduced from our former decisions is that, in every case, whatever the circumstances, one charged with crime, who is unable to obtain counsel, must be furnished counsel by the State. Expressions in the opinions of this court lend color to the argument, but, as the petitioner admits, none of our decisions squarely adjudicates the question now presented.

[JUSTICE ROBERTS reviewed *Powell v. Alabama* and determined that the failure to apply counsel in that case was unfair because of the special circumstances of the case.] * * *

* * * The question we are now to decide is whether due process of law demands that in every criminal case, whatever the circumstances, a state must furnish counsel to an indigent defendant. Is the furnishing of counsel in all cases whatever dictated by natural, inherent, and fundamental principles of fairness? The answer to the question may be found in the common understanding of those who have lived under the Anglo-American system of law. [In federal cases, a lawyer must be appointed for an indigent defendant as a requirement of the Sixth Amendment. [c] Historic evidence from the American colonies and states, as well as recent attempts to provide counsel in England, indicated that in most jurisdictions the provision of an attorney at no charge to the defendant in a noncapital case was in the discretion of the court and not a mandatory right.] [d]

This material demonstrates that, in the great majority of the States, it has been the considered judgment of the people, their representatives and their courts that appointment of counsel is not a fundamental right, essential to a fair trial. On the contrary, the matter has generally been deemed one of legislative policy. In the light of this evidence, we are unable to say that the concept of due process incorporated in the Fourteenth Amendment obligates the States, whatever may be their own views, to furnish counsel in every such case. * * *

In this case there was no question of the commission of a robbery. The State's case consisted of evidence identifying the petitioner as the perpetrator. The defense was an alibi. Petitioner called and examined wit-

nesses to prove that he was at another place at the time of the commission of the offense. The simple issue was the veracity of the testimony for the State and that for the defendant. As Judge Bond says, the accused was not helpless, but was a man forty-three years old, of ordinary intelligence and ability to take care of his own interests on the trial of that narrow issue. He had once before been in a criminal court, pleaded guilty to larceny and served a sentence and was not wholly unfamiliar with criminal procedure. [e] It is quite clear that in Maryland, if the situation had been otherwise and it had appeared that the petitioner was, for any reason, at a serious disadvantage by reason of the lack of counsel, a refusal to appoint would have resulted in the reversal of a judgment of conviction. * * *

To deduce from the due process clause a rule binding upon the States in this matter would be to impose upon them, * * * a requirement without distinction between criminal charges of different magnitude or in respect of courts of varying jurisdiction. * * * "Charges of small crimes tried before justices of the peace and capital charges tried in the higher courts would equally require the appointment of counsel. Presumably it would be argued that trials in the Traffic Court would require it." And indeed it was said by petitioner's counsel both below and in this court, that as the Fourteenth Amendment extends the protection of due process to property as well as to life and liberty, if we hold with the petitioner, logic would require the furnishing of counsel in civil cases involving property.

As we have said, the Fourteenth Amendment prohibits the conviction and incarceration of one whose trial is offensive to the common and fundamental ideas of fairness and right, and while want of counsel in a particular case may result in a conviction lacking in such fundamental fairness, we cannot say that the amendment embodies an inexorable command that no trial for any offense, or in any court, can be fairly conducted and justice accorded a defendant who is not represented by counsel.

The judgment is affirmed.

MR. JUSTICE BLACK, dissenting, with whom MR. JUSTICE DOUGLAS and MR. JUSTICE MURPHY concur.

[The dissent urged the Court to incorporate the Sixth Amendment right to counsel into the due process clause of the Fourteenth. Failing that, JUSTICE BLACK argued that the logic of *Powell v. Alabama*—that it is difficult for any layperson to adequately make a defense in a criminal trial—means that it is always unfair and a due process violation for a felony trial to be conducted without a defense attorney.]

To hold that the petitioner had a constitutional right to counsel in this case does not require us to say that "no trial for any offense, or in any court, can be fairly conducted and justice accorded a defendant who is not represented by counsel." This case can be determined by resolution of a narrower question: whether in view of the nature of the offense and the circumstances of his trial and conviction, this petitioner was denied the procedural protection which is his right under the Federal Constitution. [f] I think he was.

* * *

The right to counsel in a criminal proceeding is "fundamental." *Powell v. Alabama*. * * * It is guarded from invasion by the sixth amendment, adopted to raise an effective barrier against arbitrary or unjust deprivation of liberty by the Federal Government. *Johnson v. Zerbst*. * * *

* * *

A practice cannot be reconciled with "common and fundamental ideas of fairness and right," which subjects innocent men to increased dangers of conviction merely because of their poverty. Whether a man is innocent cannot be determined from a trial in which, as here, denial of counsel has made it impossible to conclude, with any satisfactory degree of certainty, that the defendant's case was adequately presented. No one questions that due process requires a hearing before conviction and sentence for the serious crime of robbery. * * *

Denial to the poor of the request for counsel in proceedings based on charges of serious crime has long been regarded as shocking to the "universal sense of justice" throughout this country. In 1854, for example, the Supreme Court of Indiana said: "It is not to be thought of, in a civilized community, for a moment, that any citizen put in jeopardy of life or liberty, should be debarred of counsel because he was too poor to employ such aid. No Court could be respected, or respect itself, to sit and hear such a trial. The defence of the poor, in such cases, is a duty resting somewhere, which will be at once conceded as essential to the accused, to the Court, and to the public." * * * [g]

* * * * * * * * * *

COMMENTS

[a] Unlike *Powell v. Alabama* [this volume] this was not a capital case; the defendant's liberty was at stake, but not his life.

[b] The question of the appointment of counsel for an indigent as a general right is posed here in a more clear-cut fashion than in the *Powell* case in part because the extreme facts of the earlier case were not present. But it is often the case that when the Court has time to reflect on an issue it clarifies its earlier statements of law.

[c] After *Johnson v. Zerbst* [this volume] the distinction between federal law under the Sixth Amendment and state requirements under the due process clause became sharper, adding an incentive for state defendants to seek the benefits of the federal rule.

[d] In cases where the defendant was unrepresented the judge typically assisted the defendant in presenting his case by offering advice on points of law and how to ask questions from the bench. But in such cases the judge did not interview the defendant in advance to ascertain the defendant's story and, of course, did not in any way investigate a case on the defendant's behalf.

[e] Compare the attributes and circumstances of this defendant to those of the youthful defendants in *Powell v. Alabama*. While the egregious facts of that case were not present in *Betts v. Brady*, the issue of witness veracity often requires the patient cross-examination of many witnesses for long hours in order to make an effective defense.

[f] JUSTICE BLACK indicates a willingness to temper his wishes for a total incorporation with a result, achieved on different grounds, that would afford counsel to the indigent defendant.

[g] Relying on an older state case may be a way of making the point that imposing a Fourteenth Amendment due process right to counsel on the states would not violate reasonable expectations under states' rights.

GRIFFIN v. ILLINOIS

351 U.S. 12, 76 S.Ct. 585, 100 L.Ed. 891 (1956)

MR. JUSTICE BLACK announced the judgment of the Court and an opinion in which THE CHIEF JUSTICE, MR. JUSTICE DOUGLAS, and MR. JUSTICE CLARK join.

Illinois law provides that "Writs of error in all criminal cases are writs of right and shall be issued of course." The question presented here is whether Illinois may, consistent with the Due Process and Equal Protection Clauses of the Fourteenth Amendment, administer this statute so as to deny adequate appellate review to the poor while granting such review to all others. [a]

[After conviction for robbery, petitioners filed for appeal and requested] that a certified copy of the entire record, including a stenographic transcript of the proceedings, be furnished them without cost [on the grounds of their poverty.] * * * As Illinois concedes, it is sometimes impossible to prepare [an appeal] without a stenographic transcript of the trial proceedings. Indigent defendants sentenced to death are provided with a free transcript at the expense of the county where convicted. In all other criminal cases defendants needing a transcript, whether indigent or not, must themselves buy it* * * [b]. The trial court denied the motion. * * *

* * *

Providing equal justice for poor and rich, weak and powerful alike is an age-old problem. People have never ceased to hope and strive to move closer to that goal. This hope, at least in part, brought about in 1215 the royal concessions of Magna Charta: "To no one will we sell, to no one will we refuse, or delay, right or justice. * * * No free man shall be taken or imprisoned, or disseised, or outlawed, or exiled, or anywise destroyed; nor shall we go upon him nor send upon him, but by the lawful judgment of his peers or by the law of the land." These pledges were unquestionably steps toward a fairer and more nearly equal application of criminal justice. In this tradition, our own constitutional guaranties of due process and equal protection both call for procedures in criminal trials which allow no invidious discriminations between persons and different groups of persons. Both equal protection and due process emphasize the central aim of our entire judicial system— all people charged with crime must, so far as the law is concerned, "stand on an equality before the bar of justice in every American court." * * *

Surely no one would contend that either a State or the Federal Government could constitutionally provide that defendants unable to pay court costs in advance should be denied the right to plead not guilty or to defend themselves in court. Such a law would make the constitutional promise of a fair trial a worthless thing. Notice, the right to be heard, and the right to counsel would under such circumstances be meaningless promises to the poor. In criminal trials a State can no more discriminate on account of poverty than on account of religion, race, or color. Plainly the ability to pay costs in advance bears no rational relationship to a defendant's guilt or innocence and could not be used as an excuse to deprive a defendant of a fair trial. * * * [c]

There is no meaningful distinction between a rule which would deny the poor the right to defend themselves in a trial court and one which effectively denies the poor an adequate appellate review accorded to all who have money enough to pay the costs in advance. [d] It is true that a State is not required by the Federal Constitution to provide appellate courts or a right to appellate review at all. * * * But that is not to say that a State that does grant appellate review can do so in a way that discriminates against some convicted defendants on account of their poverty. Appellate review has now become an integral part of the Illinois trial system for finally adjudicating the guilt or innocence of a defendant. Consequently at all stages of the proceedings the Due Process and Equal Protection Clauses protect persons like petitioners from invidious discriminations. * * *

All of the States now provide some method of appeal from criminal convictions, recognizing the importance of appellate review to a correct adjudication of guilt or innocence. Statistics show that a substantial proportion of criminal convictions are reversed by state appellate courts. Thus to deny adequate review to the poor means that many of them may lose their life, liberty or property because of unjust convictions which appellate courts would set aside. Many States have recognized this and provided aid for convicted defendants who have a right to appeal and need a transcript but are unable to pay for it. A few have not.

Such a denial is a misfit in a country dedicated to affording equal justice to all and special privileges to none in the administration of its criminal law. There can be no equal justice where the kind of trial a man gets depends on the amount of money he has. Destitute defendants must be afforded as adequate appellate review as defendants who have money enough to buy transcripts.

* * * We do not hold, however, that Illinois must purchase a stenographer's transcript in every case where a defendant cannot buy it. The Supreme Court may find other means of affording adequate and effective appellate review to indigent defendants. * * * [e]

The judgment of the Supreme Court of Illinois is vacated and the cause is remanded to that court for further action not inconsistent with the foregoing paragraph. MR. JUSTICE FRANKFURTER joins in this disposition of the case.

MR. JUSTICE BURTON and MR. JUSTICE MINTON, whom MR. JUSTICE REED and MR. JUSTICE HARLAN join, dissenting.

While we do not disagree with the desirability of the policy of supplying an indigent defendant with a free transcript of testimony in a case like this, we do not agree that the Constitution of the United States compels each State to do so. * * * It is one thing for Congress and this Court to prescribe such procedure for the federal courts. It is quite another for this Court to hold that the Constitution of the United States has prescribed it for all state courts.

In the administration of local law

the Constitution has been interpreted as permitting the several States generally to follow their own familiar procedure and practice. In so doing this Court has recognized the widely differing but locally approved procedures of the several States. Whether approving of the particular procedures or not, this Court has treated them largely as matters reserved to the States and within the broad range of permissible "due process" in a constitutional sense. **[f]**

Illinois, as the majority admit, could thus deny an appeal altogether in a criminal case without denying due process of law. * * * To allow an appeal at all, but with some difference among convicted persons as to the terms upon which an appeal is exercised, does not deny due process. It may present a question of equal protection. The petitioners urge that point here. **[g]**

Whether the Illinois statute denies equal protection depends upon whether, first, it is an arbitrary and unreasonable distinction for the legislature to make, between those convicted of a capital offense and those convicted of a lesser offense, as to their right to a free transcript. [The dissent argues that because of the finality of the death sentence, it is a rational distinction to give more rights and benefits to those sentenced to death.]

Secondly, certainly Illinois does not deny equal protection to convicted defendants when the terms of appeal are open to all, although some may not be able to avail themselves of the full appeal because of their poverty. Illinois is not bound to make the defendants economically equal before its bar of justice. For a State to do so may be a desirable social policy, but what may be a good legislative policy for a State is not necessarily required by the Constitution of the United States. Persons charged with crimes stand before the law with varying degrees of economic and social advantage. Some can afford better lawyers and better investigations of their cases. Some can afford bail, some cannot. Why fix bail at any reasonable sum if a poor man can't make it?

The Constitution requires the equal protection of the law, but it does not require the States to provide equal financial means for all defendants to avail themselves of such laws.

* * *

* * * * * * * * * *

COMMENT

[a] A writ of error is a writ filed to claim error in a trial as a prelude to taking an appeal. The issue is stated broadly here and is narrowed below.

[b] Stenographic records are not made automatically; they are requested by parties seeking an appeal. They are very expensive; court reporters can charge as much as five dollars per double-spaced page.

[c] Is the equation between the absolute denial of a trial and the denial of a transcript at the discretion of a judge a fair one? Is JUSTICE BLACK exaggerating? or does it make sense to you that an appeal without a full transcript is meaningless?

[d] This statement can be read as an attempt by JUSTICE BLACK to prepare the way for an argument that the right to free counsel for indigents must be granted under the Equal Protection Clause.

[e] This practical limitation after the sweeping language of the opinion seems an odd fit. Notice that this is a 5-to-4 decision, with JUSTICE BLACK specifically indicating JUSTICE FRANKFURTER's concurrence. It may be that JUSTICE FRANK-FURTER agreed to join in JUSTICE BLACK's opinion, making it the majority opinion, if JUSTICE BLACK in return agreed to specify a flexible decision instead of a rigid holding that the state must purchase a transcript in every case.

[f] The disagreement between the majority and the dissenters is over a fundamental constitutional principle: what is the power relationship between the states and the central government, as determined by the Constitution. The Constitution is written in broad terms and does not say anything about procedural matters, such as transcripts for indigents on appeal. It ultimately falls to the justices to say what such concepts as equal protection mean concretely. The wisdom of their judgments ultimately rests on their conceptions of the proper authority relations between citizens, state government, federal government, and the courts.

[g] If a modern state government attempted to eliminate appellate courts, a reasonable argument could be made, in the context of modern legal practice and doctrine, that this would deny due process to all citizens of the state.

GIDEON v. WAINWRIGHT

372 U.S. 335, 83 S.Ct. 792, 9 L.Ed.2d 799 (1963)

MR. JUSTICE BLACK delivered the opinion of the Court. [a]

[Gideon, charged with breaking into a pool hall, a felony, demanded (because of his indigency) and was refused appointed counsel. He conducted his own defense.] He made an opening statement to the jury, cross-examined the State's witnesses, presented witnesses in his own defense, declined to testify himself, and made a short argument "emphasizing his innocence to the charge contained in the Information filed in this case." The jury returned a verdict of guilty, and petitioner was sentenced to serve five years in the state prison. [The Court characterized the facts as essentially the same as *Betts v. Brady* [this volume] and set the case for review to reconsider the *Betts* rule because of the "continuing source of controversy and litigation in both state and federal courts" that the *Betts* rule presented.]
* * * Upon full reconsideration we conclude that *Betts v. Brady* should be overruled.

We have construed [the Sixth Amendment] to mean that in federal courts counsel must be provided for defendants unable to employ counsel unless the right is competently and intelligently waived. [JUSTICE BLACK reviewed *Betts v. Brady*, noting that it held the Sixth Amendment right of counsel not fundamental, and thus not incorporated into the due process clause of the Fourteenth Amendment.]
We accept *Betts v. Brady*'s assumption, based as it was on our prior cases, that a provision of the Bill of Rights which is "fundamental and essential to a fair trial" is made obligatory upon the States by the Fourteenth Amendment. We think the Court in *Betts* was wrong, however, in concluding that the Sixth Amendment's guarantee of counsel is not one of these fundamental rights. Ten years before *Betts v. Brady*, this Court, after full consideration of all the historical data examined in *Betts*, had unequivocally declared that "the right to the aid of counsel is of this fundamental character." *Powell v. Alabama*. * * * While the Court at the close of its *Powell* opinion did by its language, as this Court frequently does, limit its holding to the particular facts and circumstances of that case, its conclusions about the fundamental nature of the right to counsel are unmistakable.
* * *

* * * The fact is that in deciding as it did—that "appointment of counsel is not a fundamental right, essential to a fair trial"—the Court in *Betts v. Brady* made an abrupt break with its own well-considered precedents. In returning to these old precedents, sounder we believe than the new, we but restore constitutional principles established to achieve a fair system of justice. [b] Not only these precedents but also reason and reflection require us to recognize that in our adversary system of criminal justice, any person haled into court, who is too poor to hire a lawyer, cannot be assured a fair trial unless counsel is provided for him. This seems to us to be an obvious truth. Governments, both state and

federal, quite properly spend vast sums of money to establish machinery to try defendants accused of crime. Lawyers to prosecute are everywhere deemed essential to protect the public's interest in an orderly society. Similarly, there are few defendants charged with crime, few indeed, who fail to hire the best lawyers they can get to prepare and present their defenses. That government hires lawyers to prosecute and defendants who have the money hire lawyers to defend are the strongest indications of the widespread belief that lawyers in criminal courts are necessities, not luxuries. The right of one charged with crime to counsel may not be deemed fundamental and essential to fair trials in some countries, but it is in ours. From the very beginning, our state and national constitutions and laws have laid great emphasis on procedural and substantive safeguards designed to assure fair trials before impartial tribunals in which every defendant stands equal before the law. This noble ideal cannot be realized if the poor man charged with crime has to face his accusers without a lawyer to assist him. * * *

The judgment is reversed. * * *

[JUSTICES DOUGLAS and CLARK concurred in separate opinions].

MR. JUSTICE HARLAN, concurring.

I agree that *Betts v. Brady* should be overruled, but consider it entitled to a more respectful burial than has been accorded, at least on the part of those of us who were not on the Court when that case was decided.

I cannot subscribe to the view that *Betts v. Brady* represented "an abrupt break with its own well-considered precedents." * * * In 1932, in *Powell v. Alabama*, * * * a capital case, this Court declared that under the particular facts there presented— "the ignorance and illiteracy of the defendants, their youth, the circumstances of public hostility * * * and above all that they stood in deadly peril of their lives" * * *—the state court had a duty to assign counsel for the trial as a necessary requisite of due process of law. It is evident that these limiting facts were not added to the opinion as an afterthought; they were repeatedly emphasized, * * * and were clearly regarded as important to the result.

Thus when this Court, a decade later, decided *Betts v. Brady*, it did no more than to admit of the possible existence of special circumstances in noncapital as well as capital trials, while at the same time insisting that such circumstances be shown in order to establish a denial of due process. The right to appointed counsel had been recognized as being considerably broader in federal prosecutions [*Johnson v. Zerbst*], but to have imposed these requirements on the States would indeed have been "an abrupt break" with the almost immediate past. The declaration that the right to appointed counsel in state prosecutions, as established in *Powell v. Alabama*, was not limited to capital cases was in truth not a departure from, but an extension of, existing precedent.

The principles declared in *Powell* and in *Betts*, however, have had a troubled journey throughout the years. * * *

[More and more capital and noncapital cases found "special circumstances," even in doubtful instances.] The Court has come to recognize, in other words, that the mere existence of a serious criminal charge constituted in itself special circumstances requiring the services of counsel at trial. In truth the *Betts v. Brady* rule is no longer a reality. **[c]**

This evolution, however, appears not to have been fully recognized by many state courts, in this instance charged with the front-line responsibility for the enforcement of constitutional rights. To continue a rule which is honored by this Court only with lip service is not a healthy thing and in the long run will do disservice to the federal system.

The special circumstances rule has been formally abandoned in capital cases, and the time has now come when it should be similarly abandoned in noncapital cases, at least as to offenses which, as the one involved here, carry the possibility of a substantial prison sentence. (Whether the rule should extend to *all* criminal cases need not now be decided.) This indeed does no more than to make explicit something that has long since been foreshadowed in our decisions.

[JUSTICE HARLAN then stated his disagreement with the majority over the incorporation question, stating that in his opinion, the *Gideon* decision falls under the Fourteenth Amendment only and not the Sixth.]

On these premises I join in the judgment of the Court.

*   *   *   *   *   *   *   *   *   *

COMMENTS

[a] JUSTICE BLACK had the pleasure of writing the opinion in a landmark decision overruling a case that he strenuously dissented in two decades before.

[b] JUSTICE BLACK seems to be stretching a fair reading of the "older precedent" of *Powell v. Alabama* by viewing it as having guaranteed the right of counsel to indigents in *all* felony cases. Compare this reading of precedent to that made in concurrence by JUSTICE HARLAN.

[c] JUSTICE HARLAN correctly points out that in the twenty years between *Betts* and *Gideon*, many narrow decisions began to shift toward granting the right to counsel in more and more cases. He posits a less absolutist view of constitutional rights and constitutional change than does JUSTICE BLACK. In JUSTICE HARLAN's view, the meaning of constitutional provisions can change gradually over time to take into account new social realities. This was anathema to JUSTICE BLACK who strenuously rejected what he saw as judicial lawmaking.

ARGERSINGER v. HAMLIN

407 U.S. 25, 92 S. Ct. 2006, 32 L.Ed.2d 530 (1972)

MR. JUSTICE DOUGLAS delivered the opinion of the Court.

Petitioner, an indigent, was charged in Florida with carrying a concealed weapon, an offense punishable by imprisonment up to six months, a $1,000 fine, or both. The trial was to a judge, and petitioner was unrepresented by counsel. He was sentenced to serve 90 days in jail, and brought this habeas corpus action in the Florida Supreme Court, alleging that, being deprived of his right to counsel, he was unable as an indigent layman properly to raise and present to the trial court good and sufficient defenses to the charge for which he stands convicted. The Florida Supreme Court * * * in ruling on the right to counsel, followed the line we marked out in *Duncan v. Louisiana*, [this volume], as respects the right to trial by jury and held that the right to court-appointed counsel extends only to trials "for non-petty offenses punishable by more than six months imprisonment." * * *

* * * We reverse.

The Sixth Amendment, which in enumerated situations has been made applicable to the States by reason of the Fourteenth Amendment, * * * provides specified standards for "all criminal prosecutions."

One is the requirement of a "public trial." *In re Oliver*, [333 U.S. 257], held that the right to a "public trial" was applicable to a state proceeding even though only a 60-day sentence was involved. * * *

Another guarantee is the right to

be informed of the nature and cause of the accusation. Still another, the right of confrontation. * * * And another, compulsory process for obtaining witnesses in one's favor. * * * We have never limited these rights to felonies or to lesser but serious offenses.

In *Washington v. Texas*, [388 U.S. 14], we said, "We have held that due process requires that the accused have the assistance of counsel for his defense, that he be confronted with the witnesses against him, and that he have the right to a speedy and public trial." * * * Respecting the right to a speedy and public trial, the right to be informed of the nature and cause of the accusation, the right to confront and cross-examine witnesses, the right to compulsory process for obtaining witnesses, it was recently stated, "It is simply not arguable, nor has any court ever held, that the trial of a petty offense may be held in secret, or without notice to the accused of the charges, or that in such cases the defendant has no right to confront his accusers or to compel the attendance of witnesses in his own behalf." * * *
* * *

The right to trial by jury, also guaranteed by the Sixth Amendment by reason of the Fourteenth, was limited by *Duncan v. Louisiana*, [above], to trials where the potential punishment was imprisonment for six months or more. But, as the various opinions in *Baldwin v. New York*, 399 U.S. 66, make plain, the right to trial by jury has a different genealogy and is brigaded with a system of trial to a judge alone. * * *

While there is historical support for limiting the "deep commitment" to trial by jury to "serious criminal cases," there is no such support for a similar limitation on the right to assistance of counsel:

> "Originally, in England, a person charged with treason or felony was denied the aid of counsel, except in respect of legal questions which the accused himself might suggest. At the same time parties in civil cases and persons accused of misdemeanors were entitled to the full assistance of counsel. * * * * * *
>
> "[It] appears that in at least twelve of the thirteen colonies the rule of the English common law, in the respect now under consideration, had been definitely rejected and the right to counsel fully recognized in all criminal prosecutions, save that in one or two instances the right was limited to capital offenses or to the more serious crimes. * * * *" *Powell v. Alabama* [this volume].

The Sixth Amendment thus extended the right to counsel beyond its common-law dimensions. But there is nothing in the language of the Amendment, its history, or in the decisions of this Court, to indicate that it was intended to embody a retraction of the right in petty offenses wherein the common law previously did require that counsel be provided. * * *

We reject, therefore, the premise that since prosecutions for crimes punishable by imprisonment for less than six months may be tried without a jury, they may also be tried without a lawyer.

The assistance of counsel is often a requisite to the very existence of a fair trial. * * *

Both *Powell* [this volume] and *Gideon* [this volume] involved felonies. But their rationale has relevance to any criminal trial, where an accused is deprived of his liberty. *Powell* and *Gideon* suggest that there are certain fundamental rights applicable to all such criminal prosecutions, even those, such as *In re Oliver*, [above], where the penalty is 60 days' imprisonment. * * *

The requirement of counsel may well be necessary for a fair trial even in a petty-offense prosecution. We are by no means convinced that legal and constitutional questions involved in a case that actually leads to imprisonment even for a brief period are any less complex than when a person can be sent off for six months or more. * * * [a]
* * *

[The majority pointed out that because of the huge number of misdemeanor cases there may be a tendency by courts to process them in a perfunctory manner, "regardless of the fairness of the result." Attorneys would be needed to insure the fair treatment of indigent misdemeanor defendants.]

We must conclude, therefore, that the problems associated with misdemeanor and petty offenses often require the presence of counsel to insure the accused a fair trial. MR. JUSTICE POWELL suggests that these problems are raised even in situations where there is no prospect of imprisonment. * * * We need not consider the requirements of the Sixth Amendment as regards the right to counsel where loss of liberty is not involved, however, for here petitioner was in fact sentenced to jail. And, as we said in *Baldwin v. New York*, 399 U.S., at 73, "the prospect of imprisonment for however short a time will seldom be viewed by the accused as a trivial or 'petty' matter and may well result in quite serious repercussions affecting his career and his reputation."

We hold, therefore, that absent a knowing and intelligent waiver, no person may be imprisoned for any offense, whether classified as petty, misdemeanor, or felony, unless he was represented by counsel at his trial.

* * *

We do not sit as an ombudsman to direct state courts how to manage their affairs but only to make clear the federal constitutional requirement. How crimes should be classified is largely a state matter. The fact that traffic charges technically fall within the category of "criminal prosecutions" does not necessarily mean that many of them will be brought into the class where imprisonment actually occurs. [b]

* * *

Under the rule we announce today, every judge will know when the trial of a misdemeanor starts that no imprisonment may be imposed, even though local law permits it, unless the accused is represented by counsel. He will have a measure of the seriousness and gravity of the offense and therefore know when to name a lawyer to represent the accused before the trial starts.

The run of misdemeanors will not be affected by today's ruling. But in those that end up in the actual deprivation of a person's liberty, the accused will receive the benefit of "the guiding hand of counsel" so necessary when one's liberty is in jeopardy. * * *

[JUSTICE BRENNAN concurred, joined by JUSTICES DOUGLAS and STEWART.]

[CHIEF JUSTICE BURGER concurred in the result.]

MR. JUSTICE POWELL, with whom MR. JUSTICE REHNQUIST joins, concurring in the result.

[JUSTICE POWELL urged a more flexible rule, to be applied by the trial judge in all misdemeanor cases, involving jail and non-jail sentences, depending upon the complexity of the legal issues, the likely severity of punishment, and the individual factors peculiar to the case:]

I would hold that the right to counsel in petty-offense cases is not absolute but is one to be determined by the trial courts exercising a judicial discretion on a case-by-case basis. The determination should be made before the accused formally pleads; many petty cases are resolved by guilty pleas in which the assistance of counsel may be required. If the trial court should conclude that the assistance of counsel is not required in any case, it should state its reasons so that the issue could be preserved for review. The trial court would then become obligated to scrutinize carefully the subsequent proceedings for the protection of the defendant. If an unrepresented defendant sought to enter a plea of guilty, the Court should examine the case against him to insure that there is admissible evidence tending to support the elements of the offense. If a case went to trial without defense counsel, the court should intervene, when necessary, to insure that the defendant adequately brings out the facts in his favor and to prevent legal issues from being overlooked. Formal trial rules should not be applied strictly against unrepresented defendants. Finally, appellate courts should carefully scrutinize all decisions not to appoint counsel and the proceedings which follow. **[c]**

* * *

* * * * * * * * * *

COMMENTS

[a] This formulation left open the possibility that counsel was not required in misdemeanors where either no jail sentence was possible or where no jail sentence was imposed. In *Scott v. Illinois*, 440 U.S. 367 (1979) the Court clarified this ambiguity and held that because of the different kind of penalties between jail on the one hand and fine or probation on the other, counsel was a constitutional requirement only if jail was *actually imposed*, as opposed to being authorized.

[b] The Court here trys to quell concerns among local court officials that this ruling will impose excessive costs and administrative problems.

[c] Do you think JUSTICE POWELL's approach is more or less workable than the majority's automatic counsel rule? more or less costly?

FARETTA v. CALIFORNIA

422 U.S. 806, 95 S.Ct. 2525, 45 L.Ed.2d 562 (1975)

MR. JUSTICE STEWART delivered the opinion of the Court.

The Sixth and Fourteenth Amendments of our Constitution guarantee that a person brought to trial in any state or federal court must be afforded the right to the assistance of counsel before he can be validly convicted and punished by imprisonment. * * * The question before us now is whether a defendant in a state criminal trial has a constitutional right to proceed *without* counsel when he voluntarily and intelligently elects to do so. [a] Stated another way, the question is whether a State may constitutionally hale a person into its criminal courts and there force a lawyer upon him, even when he insists that he wants to conduct his own defense. It is not an easy question, but we have concluded that a State may not constitutionally do so.

I

Anthony Faretta was charged with grand theft * * * At the arraignment, the Superior Court Judge assigned to preside at the trial appointed the public defender to represent Faretta. Well before the date of trial, however, Faretta requested that he be permitted to represent himself. Questioning by the judge revealed that Faretta had once represented himself in a criminal prosecution, that he had a high school education, and that he did not want to be represented by the public defender because he believed that office was "very loaded down with . . . a heavy case load." * * *

[The Judge, after questioning Faretta as to his knowledge of legal points and assessing his demeanor] ruled that Faretta had not made an intelligent and knowing waiver of his right to the assistance of counsel, and also ruled that Faretta had no constitutional right to conduct his own defense. * * * Throughout the subsequent trial, the judge required that Faretta's defense be conducted only through the appointed lawyer from the public defender's office. [Faretta was found guilty by the jury and was sentenced to prison.]

II

In the federal courts, the right of self-representation has been protected by statute since the beginnings of our Nation. * * *

With few exceptions, each of the several States also accords a defendant the right to represent himself in any criminal case. The Constitutions of 36 States explicitly confer that right. [b] Moreover, many state courts have expressed the view that the right is also supported by the Constitution of the United States. * * *

In other settings as well, the Court has indicated that a defendant has a constitutionally protected right to represent himself in a criminal trial. For example, * * * the Confrontation Clause of the Sixth Amendment gives the accused a right to be present at all stages of the proceedings where fundamental fairness might be thwarted by his absence. This right to "presence" was based upon the premise that the "defense may be made easier if the accused is permitted to be present at the examination of jurors or the summing up of counsel, *for it will be in his power*, if present, to give advice or suggestion or *even to supersede his lawyers altogether and conduct the trial himself."* * * *

The United States Courts of Appeals have repeatedly held that the right of self-representation is protected by the Bill of Rights. * * *

III

This consensus is soundly premised. The right of self-representation finds support in the structure of the Sixth Amendment, as well as in the English and colonial jurisprudence from which the Amendment emerged.

* * *

The Sixth Amendment does not provide merely that a defense shall be made for the accused; it grants to the accused personally the right to make his defense. It is the accused, not counsel, who must be "informed of the nature and cause of the accusation," who must be "confronted with the witnesses against him," and who must be accorded "compulsory process for obtaining witnesses in his favor." Although not stated in the Amendment in so many words, the right to self-representation—to make one's own defense personally—is thus necessarily implied by the structure of the Amendment. The right to defend is given directly to the accused; for it is he who suffers the consequences if the defense fails. [c]

The counsel provision supplements [the structure and history of the constitutional text]. It speaks of the "assistance" of counsel, and an assistant, however expert, is still an assistant. The language and spirit of the Sixth Amendment contemplate that counsel, like the other defense tools guaranteed by the Amendment, shall be an aid to a willing defendant—not an organ of the State interposed between an unwilling defendant and his right to defend himself personally. [d] To thrust counsel upon the accused, against his considered wish, thus violates the logic of the Amendment. In such a case, counsel is not an assistant, but a master; and the right to make a defense is stripped of the personal character upon which the Amendment insists. It is true that when a defendant chooses to have a lawyer manage and present his case, law and tradition may allocate to the counsel the power to make binding decisions of trial strategy in many areas. * * * This allocation can only be justified, however, by the defendant's consent, at the outset, to accept counsel as his representative. An unwanted counsel "represents" the defendant only through a tenuous and unacceptable legal fiction. Unless the accused has acquiesced in such representation, the defense presented is not the defense guaranteed him by the Constitution, for, in a very real sense, it is not *his* defense. * * *

* * *

IV

There can be no blinking the fact that the right of an accused to conduct his own defense seems to cut against the grain of this Court's decisions holding that the Constitution requires that no accused can be convicted and imprisoned unless he has been accorded the right to the assistance of counsel. [e] * * * For it is surely true that the basic thesis of [the right to counsel] decisions is that the help of a lawyer is essential to assure the defendant a fair trial. And a strong argument can surely be made that the whole thrust of those decisions must inevitably lead to the conclusion that a State may constitutionally impose a lawyer upon even an unwilling defendant.

But it is one thing to hold that every defendant, rich or poor, has the right to the assistance of counsel, and quite another to say that a State may compel a defendant to accept a lawyer he does not want. * * *

* * * To force a lawyer on a defendant can only lead him to believe that the law contrives against him. Moreover, it is not inconceivable that in some rare instances, the defendant might in fact present his case more effectively by conducting his own defense. Personal liberties are not rooted in the law of averages. The right to defend is personal. The defendant, and not his lawyer or the State, will bear the personal consequences of a conviction. It is the defendant, therefore, who must be free personally to decide whether in his particular case counsel is to his advantage. And although he may conduct his own defense ultimately to his own detriment, his choice must be honored out of "that respect for the individual which is the lifeblood of the law." * * *

V

When an accused manages his own defense, he relinquishes, as a purely factual matter, many of the traditional benefits associated with the right to counsel. For this reason, in order to represent himself, the accused must "knowingly and intelligently" forgo those relinquished benefits. * * * Although a defendant need not himself have the skill and experience of a lawyer in order competently and intelligently to choose self-representation, he should be made aware of the dangers and disadvantages of self-representation, so that the record will establish that "he knows what he is doing and his choice is made with eyes open." * * *

* * * [f]

In forcing Faretta, under these circumstances, to accept against his will a state-appointed public defender, the California courts deprived him of his constitutional right to conduct his own defense. Accordingly, the judgment before us is vacated, and the case is remanded for further proceedings not inconsistent with this opinion.

* * *

MR. CHIEF JUSTICE BURGER, with whom MR. JUSTICE BLACKMUN and MR. JUSTICE REHNQUIST join, dissenting.

This case * * * is another example of the judicial tendency to constitutionalize what is thought "good." That effort fails on its own terms here, because there is nothing desirable or useful in permitting every accused person, even the most uneducated and inexperienced, to insist upon conducting his own defense to criminal charges. Moreover, there is no constitutional basis for the Court's holding, and it can only add to the problems of an already malfunctioning criminal justice system. I therefore dissent. **[g]**

* * * [The Court's] ultimate assertion that such a right is tucked between the lines of the Sixth Amendment is contradicted by the Amendment's language and its consistent judicial interpretation.

As the Court seems to recognize, * * * [its] conclusion that the rights guaranteed by the Sixth Amendment are "personal" to an accused reflects nothing more than the obvious fact that it is he who is on trial and therefore has need of a defense. But neither that nearly trivial proposition nor the language of the Amendment, which speaks in uniformly mandatory terms, leads to the further conclusion that the right to counsel is merely supplementary and may be dispensed with at the whim of the accused. Rather, this Court's decisions have consistently included the right to counsel as an integral part of the bundle making up the larger "right to a defense as we know it." * * *

The reason for this hardly requires explanation. The fact of the matter is that in all but an extraordinarily small number of cases an accused will lose whatever defense he may have if he undertakes to conduct the trial himself. * * * **[h]**

* * * Nor is it accurate to suggest * * * that the quality of his representation at trial is a matter with which only the accused is legitimately concerned. * * * Although we have adopted an adversary system of criminal justice, * * * the prosecution is more than an ordinary litigant, and the trial judge is not simply an automaton who insures that technical rules are adhered to. Both are charged with the duty of insuring that justice, in the broadest sense of that term, is achieved in every criminal trial. * * * That goal is ill-served, and the integrity of and public confidence in the system are undermined, when an easy conviction is obtained due to the defendant's ill-advised decision to waive counsel. The damage thus inflicted is not mitigated by the lame explanation that the defendant simply availed himself of the "freedom" "to go to jail under his own banner. . . ." * * * The system of criminal justice should not be available as an instrument of self-destruction. **[i]**

In short, both the "spirit and the logic" of the Sixth Amendment are that every person accused of crime shall receive the fullest possible defense; in the vast majority of cases this command can be honored only by means of the expressly guaranteed right to counsel, and the trial judge is in the best position to determine whether the accused is capable of conducting his defense. True freedom of choice and society's interest in seeing that justice is achieved can be vindicated only if the trial court retains discretion to reject any attempted waiver of counsel and insist that the accused be tried according to the Constitution. * * * **[j]**

[CHIEF JUSTICE BURGER next criticized the majority opinion's analysis of precedent and history and stated that this new right would add to trial and appellate court congestion.]

* * * * * * * * * * *

COMMENTS

[a] The issue is the obverse of the right to counsel, rather than its contrary.

[b] A powerful argument is that a rule is followed by majority of American jurisdictions.

[c] The political basis of this point is clear; the law of criminal procedure is designed directly for the benefit of the individual and only secondarily for the benefit of society. This is consistent with the individualism that is central in our political theory. The creation of rights for "minorities" (here, criminal suspects) that cannot be legislated away by the majority is based on historically grounded fears of governmental excessive use of power. To create a "check and balance" the most interested party—the defendant—is given rights that ultimately benefit a constitutional government.

[d] The basis of the holding ultimately rests on the most basic Constitutional concern that underlies all of criminal procedure—a limitation of the state's power vis-à-vis the individual.

[e] It is important for the coherence of the law for the Supreme Court to reconcile seemingly inconsistent rules.

[f] A defendant cannot simply demand self-representation and the waiver of a lawyer without showing that he knows the rights being relinquished. On the other hand, the defendant cannot be put through a kind of law examination designed to make it very difficult to be granted self-representation.

[g] This is another case where the difference between the majority and the dissenters is less over the substantive issue (the wisdom of self-representation versus appointed counsel) and more over the extent to which certain aspects of trial practice should be enshrined in a constitutional rule.

[h] The dissent suggests that the majority's holding may undermine the right to counsel established in many areas of constitutional law. It also notes that self-representation inevitably means the loss of other trial rights by the defendant. Is this a reasonable price to pay for allowing the autonomy of self-representation?

[i] This is an intriguing and serious counterpoint to the logic of the majority. To what extent does the Court have an obligation to insist that the trial accord with the canons of justice? Can this case be seen as one involving a conflict of rights—the right to a fair trial versus self-representation?

[j] It is more likely in criminal trials that emotionally charged defendants will foolishly relinquish appointed counsel than counsel will be inappropriately thrust on the defendant. Would the discretion of the judge be a "better" solution than a constitutional rule?

DOUGLAS v. CALIFORNIA

372 U.S. 353, 83 S.Ct. 814, 9 L.Ed.2d 811 (1963)

MR. JUSTICE DOUGLAS delivered the opinion of the Court.

[Indigent petitioners were convicted on 13 counts including robbery and assault with intent to commit murder. Their petition for assistance of counsel during the state court appeal was denied.]

* * * [T]he California District Court of Appeal stated that it had "gone through" the record and had come to the conclusion that "no good whatever could be served by appointment of counsel." * * * The District Court of Appeal was acting in accordance with a California rule of criminal procedure which provides that state appellate courts, upon the request of an indigent for counsel, may make "an independent investigation of the record and determine whether it would be of advantage to the defendant or helpful to the appellate court to have counsel appointed. . . . After such investigation, appellate courts should appoint counsel if in their opinion it would be helpful to the defendant or the court, and should deny the appointment of counsel only if in their judgment such appointment would be of no value to either the defendant or the court." * * *

We agree, however, with Justice Traynor of the California Supreme Court, who said that the "[d]enial of counsel on appeal [to an indigent] would seem to be a discrimination at least as invidious as that condemned in *Griffin v. Illinois*," [this volume]. * * * Here the issue is whether or not an indigent shall be denied the assistance of counsel on appeal. In either case the evil is the same: discrimination against the indigent. For there can be no equal justice where the kind of an appeal a man enjoys "depends on the amount of money he has." * * *

In spite of California's forward treatment of indigents, under its present practice the type of an appeal a person is afforded in the District Court of Appeal hinges upon whether or not he can pay for the assistance of counsel. If he can the appellate court passes on the merits of his case only after having the full benefit of written briefs and oral argument by counsel. If he cannot the appellate court is forced to prejudge the merits before it can even determine whether counsel should be provided. At this stage in the proceedings only the barren record speaks for the indigent, and, unless the printed pages show that an injustice has been committed, he is forced to go without a champion on appeal. Any real chance he may have had of showing that his appeal has hidden merit is deprived him when the court decides on an *ex parte* examination of the record that the assistance of counsel is not required.

We are not here concerned with problems that might arise from the denial of counsel for the preparation of a petition for discretionary or mandatory review beyond the stage in the appellate process at which the claims have once been presented by a lawyer and passed upon by an appellate court. [a] We are dealing only with the *first* appeal, granted as a matter of right to rich and poor alike [by California statute] from a criminal conviction. * * * But it is appropriate to observe that a State can, consistently with the Fourteenth Amendment, provide for differences so long as the result does not amount to a denial of due process or an "invidious discrimination." * * * Absolute equality is not required; lines can be and are drawn and we often sustain them. * * * But where the merits of *the one and only appeal* an indigent has as of right are decided without benefit of counsel, we think an unconstitutional line has been drawn between rich and poor.

When an indigent is forced to run this gantlet of a preliminary showing of merit, the right to appeal does not comport with fair procedure. [b] In the federal courts, on the other hand, an indigent must be afforded counsel on appeal whenever he challenges a certification that the appeal is not taken in good faith. * * * The federal courts must honor his request for counsel regardless of what they think the merits of the case may be; and "representation in the role of an advocate is required." * * * In California, however, once the court has "gone through" the record and denied counsel, the indigent has no recourse but to prosecute his appeal on his own, as best he can, no matter how meritorious his case may turn out to be. The present case, where counsel was denied petitioners on appeal, shows that the discrimination is not between "possibly good and obviously bad cases," but between cases where the rich man can require the court to listen to argument of counsel before deciding on the merits, but a poor man cannot. There is lacking that

equality demanded by the Fourteenth Amendment where the rich man, who appeals as of right, enjoys the benefit of counsel's examination into the record, research of the law, and marshalling of arguments on his behalf, while the indigent, already burdened by a preliminary determination that his case is without merit, is forced to shift for himself. The indigent, where the record is unclear or the errors are hidden, has only the right to a meaningless ritual, [c] while the rich man has a meaningful appeal.

We vacate the judgment of the District Court of Appeal and remand the case to that court for further proceedings not inconsistent with this opinion.

It is so ordered.

[JUSTICE CLARK, dissented, arguing that under *Griffin*, California had provided for a fair alternate procedure by authorizing the discretionary appointment of counsel. He pointed out the financial burden the Court was imposing on the states.]

MR. JUSTICE HARLAN, whom MR. JUSTICE STEWART joins, dissenting.

In holding that an indigent has an absolute right to appointed counsel on appeal of a state criminal conviction, the Court appears to rely both on the Equal Protection Clause and on the guarantees of fair procedure inherent in the Due Process Clause of the Fourteenth Amendment, with obvious emphasis on "equal protection." [d] In my view the Equal Protection Clause is not apposite, and its application to cases like the present one can lead only to mischievous results. This case should be judged solely under the Due Process Clause, and I do not believe that the California procedure violates that provision.

EQUAL PROTECTION.

To approach the present problem in terms of the Equal Protection Clause is, I submit, but to substitute resounding phrases for analysis. I dissented from this approach in *Griffin v. Illinois*, [above] and I am constrained to dissent from the implicit extension of the equal protection approach here—to a case in which the State denies no one an appeal, but seeks only to keep within reasonable bounds the instances in which appellate counsel will be assigned to indigents.

The States, of course, are prohibited by the Equal Protection Clause from discriminating between "rich" and "poor" *as such* in the formulation and application of their laws. But it is a far different thing to suggest that this provision prevents the State from adopting a law of general applicability that may affect the poor more harshly than it does the rich, or, on the other hand, from making some effort to redress economic imbalances while not eliminating them entirely.

Every financial exaction which the State imposes on a uniform basis is more easily satisfied by the well-to-do than by the indigent. Yet I take it that no one would dispute the constitutional power of the State to levy a uniform sales tax, to charge tuition at a state university, to fix rates for the purchase of water from a municipal corporation, to impose a standard fine for criminal violations, or to establish minimum bail for various categories of offenses. [e] Nor could it be con-

tended that the State may not classify as crimes acts which the poor are more likely to commit than are the rich. [f] And surely, there would be no basis for attacking a state law which provided benefits for the needy simply because those benefits fell short of the goods or services that others could purchase for themselves.

Laws such as these do not deny equal protection to the less fortunate for one essential reason: the Equal Protection Clause does not impose on the States "an affirmative duty to lift the handicaps flowing from differences in economic circumstances." To so construe it would be to read into the Constitution a philosophy of leveling that would be foreign to many of our basic concepts of the proper relations between government and society. The State may have a moral obligation to eliminate the evils of poverty, but it is not required by the Equal Protection Clause to give to some whatever others can afford.

Thus it should be apparent that the present case * * * is not one properly regarded as arising under this clause. California does not discriminate between rich and poor in having a uniform policy permitting everyone to appeal and to retain counsel, and in having a separate rule dealing *only* with the standards for the appointment of counsel for those unable to retain their own attorneys. The sole classification established by this rule is between those cases that are believed to have merit and those regarded as frivolous. And, of course, no matter how far the state rule might go in providing counsel for indigents, it could never be expected to satisfy an affirmative duty—if one existed— to place the poor on the same level as those who can afford the best legal talent available.

Parenthetically, it should be noted that if the present problem may be viewed as one of equal protection, so may the question of the right to appointed counsel at trial, and the Court's analysis of that right in *Gideon v. Wainwright*, [this volume], decided today, is wholly unnecessary. The short way to dispose of *Gideon v. Wainwright*, in other words, would be simply to say that the State deprives the indigent of equal protection whenever it fails to furnish him with legal services, and perhaps with other services as well, equivalent to those that the affluent defendant can obtain. **[g]**

The real question in this case, I submit, and the only one that permits of satisfactory analysis, is whether or not the state rule, as applied in this case, is consistent with the requirements of fair procedure guaranteed by the Due Process Clause. Of course, in considering this question, it must not be lost sight of that the State's responsibility under the Due Process Clause is to provide justice for all. Refusal to furnish criminal indigents with some things that others can afford may fall short of constitutional standards of fairness. The problem before us is whether this is such a case.

DUE PROCESS.

* * *

[Even if counsel is denied under the California procedure], a full appeal on the merits is accorded to the indigent appellant, together with a statement of the reasons why counsel was not assigned. There is nothing in the present case, or in any other case that has been cited to us, to indicate that the system has resulted in injustice. * * *

* * * [T]he appellate procedures involved here stand on an entirely different constitutional footing [than a criminal trial]. *First*, appellate review is in itself not required by the Fourteenth Amendment, * * * and thus the question presented is the narrow one whether the State's rules with respect to the appointment of counsel are so arbitrary or unreasonable, *in the context of the particular appellate procedure that it has established*, as to require their invalidation. *Second*, the kinds of questions that may arise on appeal are circumscribed by the record of the proceedings that led to the conviction; they do not encompass the large variety of tactical and strategic problems that must be resolved at the trial. *Third*, as California applies its rule, the indigent appellant receives the benefit of expert and conscientious legal appraisal of the merits of his case on the basis of the trial record, and whether or not he is assigned counsel, is guaranteed full consideration of his appeal. It would be painting with too broad a brush to conclude that under these circumstances an appeal is just like a trial. **[h]**

[JUSTICE HARLAN pointed out that the United States Supreme Court does not grant free counsel to indigents who petition the Court for writs of certiorari.]

The Court distinguishes our review from the present case on the grounds that the California rule relates to "the *first appeal*, granted as a matter of right."* * * But I fail to see the significance of this difference. Surely, it cannot be contended that the requirements of fair procedure are exhausted once an indigent has been given one appellate review. * * * [i] Nor can it well be suggested that having appointed counsel is more necessary to the fair administration of justice in an initial appeal taken as a matter of right, which the reviewing court on the full record has already determined to be frivolous, than in a petition asking a higher appellate court to exercise its discretion to consider what may be a substantial constitutional claim.

* * *

I cannot agree that the Constitution prohibits a State, in seeking to redress economic imbalances at its bar of justice and to provide indigents with full review, from taking reasonable steps to guard against needless expense. This is all that California has done. Accordingly, I would affirm the state judgment.

* * * * * * * * * *

COMMENTS

[a] The Court is careful to limit the holding to the specific facts of the case, in part because of the complexity of various levels of discretionary post-conviction proceedings and in part because equality rulings tend to become "absolute" and could produce unintended consequences. The Court pointed out that every indigent petitioner who applied for a writ of certiorari to the United States Supreme Court was not entitled to a lawyer at taxpayer's expense.

[b] Whether the lack of counsel is unfair depends on a view of the role of the lawyer on appeal. Often an appellate attorney must comb through a lengthy trial record with painstaking care seeking errors that can be known only to an expert on many points of law.

[c] This may not be fair to courts which hire staff to review petitions, such as writs of habeas corpus, from indigents. On the other hand, does the Court's ruling put the indigent petitioner in a better position than one with some means who has to weight the financial costs of hiring an attorney to appeal? Should this factor count in a criminal, as opposed to a civil, appeal?

[d] Notice that the majority is not crisply specific as to the grounds for its holding.

[e] Do these analogies answer the point in *Griffin* that equality of treatment should be more exacting in the criminal process than in other areas of life?

[f] This argument can cut both ways; criminal laws against white collar crimes affect the wealthy more heavily than the poor, who have fewer opportunities to commit such crimes.

[g] It is quite likely that in *Griffin*, JUSTICE BLACK intended that the equal protection clause could become the basis of a rule that would guarantee the right to counsel for indigent defendants in state cases.

[h] Compare the points raised here to those raised by the majority in *Ross v. Moffit* [this volume].

[i] This point could be used to favor an indigent arguing for counsel on discretionary post-conviction hearings; see *Ross v. Moffit* [this volume].

ROSS v. MOFFITT

417 U.S. 600, 94 S.Ct. 2437, 41 L.Ed.2d 341 (1974)

MR. JUSTICE REHNQUIST delivered the opinion of the Court.

* * *

I

[In two consolidated cases, indigent, North Carolina, convicted, theft crime defendants appealed to the state court of appeals. They were represented by court-appointed counsel. Both had their convictions affirmed. The Mecklenburg County respondent was denied counsel for discretionary review procedures to the North Carolina Supreme Court. After exhausting state remedies, he applied for habeas relief, which was denied. The Guilford County respondent was represented by a public defender in his discretionary review in the North Carolina Supreme Court, which denied certiorari. This respondent was denied court-appointed counsel to prepare a petition for a writ of certiorari to the United States Supreme Court by the Guilford County Superior Court. Both respondents appealed their denials of counsel to the federal Court of Appeals for the Fourth Circuit.]

The Court of Appeals reversed the two District Court judgments, holding that respondent was entitled to the assistance of counsel at state expense both on his petition for review in the North Carolina Supreme Court and on his petition for certiorari to this Court. Reviewing the procedures of the North Carolina appellate system and the possible benefits that counsel would provide for indigents seeking review in

that system, the court stated:

> "As long as the state provides such procedures and allows other convicted felons to seek access to the higher court with the help of retained counsel, there is a marked absence of fairness in denying an indigent the assistance of counsel as he seeks access to the same court."

* * * [T]he Court of Appeals [said], "[t]he same concepts of fairness and equality, which require counsel in a first appeal of right, require counsel in other and subsequent discretionary appeals."

* * *

II

This Court, in the past 20 years, has given extensive consideration to the rights of indigent persons on appeal. In *Griffin v. Illinois*, [this volume] the first of the pertinent cases, the Court had before it an Illinois rule allowing a convicted criminal defendant to present claims of trial error to the Supreme Court of Illinois only if he procured a transcript of the testimony adduced at his trial. No exception was made for the indigent defendant, and thus one who was unable to pay the cost of obtaining such a transcript was precluded from obtaining appellate review of asserted trial error. * * * The Court in *Griffin* held that this discrimination violated the Fourteenth Amendment.

Succeeding cases invalidated similar

financial barriers to the appellate process, at the same time reaffirming the traditional principle that a State is not obliged to provide any appeal at all for criminal defendants. * * * The cases encompassed a variety of circumstances but all had a common theme. [These included a rule that only a public defender, but not an indigent prisoner, could obtain a free transcript of a hearing on a *coram nobis* application; a rule that a convicted indigent could obtain a free trial transcript only if he satisfied the trial judge that his contentions on appeal would not be frivolous; a filing fee requirement to process a state habeas corpus application by a convicted defendant; and a $20 filing fee to move a state supreme court for leave to appeal from a court of appeals judgment affirming a criminal conviction.] Each of these state-imposed financial barriers to the adjudication of a criminal defendant's appeal was held to violate the Fourteenth Amendment.

The decisions discussed above stand for the proposition that a State cannot arbitrarily cut off appeal rights for indigents while leaving open avenues of appeal for more affluent persons. In *Douglas v. California*, [this volume], however, * * * the Court departed somewhat from the limited doctrine of the transcript and fee cases and undertook an examination of whether an indigent's access to the appellate system was adequate. The Court in *Douglas* concluded that a State does not fulfill its responsibility toward indigent defendants merely by waiving its own requirements that a convicted defendant procure a transcript or pay a fee in order to appeal, and held that the State must go further and provide counsel for the indigent on his first

appeal as of right. It is this decision we are asked to extend today. [a]

* * * [The Court here reviewed the *Douglas* ruling.]

The precise rationale for the *Griffin* and *Douglas* lines of cases has never been explicitly stated, some support being derived from the Equal Protection Clause of the Fourteenth Amendment, and some from the Due Process Clause of that Amendment. Neither Clause by itself provides an entirely satisfactory basis for the result reached, each depending on a different inquiry which emphasizes different factors. "Due process" emphasizes fairness between the State and the individual dealing with the State, regardless of how other individuals in the same situation may be treated. "Equal protection," on the other hand, emphasizes disparity in treatment by a State between classes of individuals whose situations are arguably indistinguishable. We will address these issues separately in the succeeding sections. [b]

III

Recognition of the due process rationale in *Douglas* is found both in the Court's opinion and in the dissenting opinion of MR. JUSTICE HARLAN. The Court in *Douglas* stated that "[w]hen an indigent is forced to run this gantlet of a preliminary showing of merit, the right to appeal does not comport with fair procedure." * * * MR. JUSTICE HARLAN thought that the due process issue in *Douglas* was the only one worthy of extended consideration, remarking: "The real question in this case, I submit, and the only one that permits of satisfactory analysis, is whether or not the state rule, as applied in this case, is consistent with the requirements of fair procedure guaranteed by the Due Process Clause." * * *

We do not believe that the Due Process Clause requires North Carolina to provide respondent with counsel on his discretionary appeal to the State Supreme Court. At the trial stage of a criminal proceeding, the right of an indigent defendant to counsel is fundamental and binding upon the States by virtue of the Sixth and Fourteenth Amendments. * * * But there are significant differences between the trial and appellate stages of a criminal proceeding. The purpose of the trial stage from the State's point of view is to convert a criminal defendant from a person presumed innocent to one found guilty beyond a reasonable doubt. To accomplish this purpose, the State employs a prosecuting attorney who presents evidence to the court, challenges any witnesses offered by the defendant, argues rulings of the court, and makes direct arguments to the court and jury seeking to persuade them of the defendant's guilt. Under these circumstances "reason and reflection require us to recognize that in our adversary system of criminal justice, any person haled into court, who is too poor to hire a lawyer, cannot be assured a fair trial unless counsel is provided for him." * * *

By contrast, it is ordinarily the defendant, rather than the State, who initiates the appellate process, seeking not to fend off the efforts of the State's prosecutor but rather to overturn a finding of guilt made by a judge or jury below. The defendant needs an attorney on appeal not as a shield to protect him against being "haled into court" by the State and stripped of his presumption of innocence, but rather as a sword to upset the prior determination of guilt. This difference is significant for, while no one would agree that the State may simply dispense with the trial stage of proceedings without a criminal defendant's consent, it is clear that the State need not provide any appeal at all. * * * The fact that an appeal *has* been provided does not automatically mean that a State then acts unfairly by refusing to provide counsel to indigent defendants at every stage of the way. * * * Unfairness results only if indigents are singled out by the State and denied meaningful access to the appellate system because of their poverty. That question is more profitably considered under an equal protection analysis. [c]

IV

Language invoking equal protection notions is prominent both in *Douglas* and in other cases treating the rights of indigents on appeal. The Court in *Douglas*, for example, stated:

> "[W]here the merits of *the one and only appeal* an indigent has as of right are decided without benefit of counsel, we think an unconstitutional line has been drawn between rich and poor." * * * (Emphasis in original.)

* * *

Despite the tendency of all rights "to declare themselves absolute to their logical extreme," there are obviously limits beyond which the equal protection analysis may not be pressed without doing violence to principles recognized in other decisions of this

Court. The Fourteenth Amendment "does not require absolute equality or precisely equal advantages," * * * nor does it require the State to "equalize economic conditions." * * * It does require that the state appellate system be "free of unreasoned distinctions," * * * and that indigents have an adequate opportunity to present their claims fairly within the adversary system. * * * The State cannot adopt procedures which leave an indigent defendant "entirely cut off from any appeal at all," by virtue of his indigency, * * * or extend to such indigent defendants merely a "meaningless ritual" while others in better economic circumstances have a "meaningful appeal." * * * The question is not one of absolutes, but one of degrees. In this case we do not believe that the Equal Protection Clause, when interpreted in the context of these cases, requires North Carolina to provide free counsel for indigent defendants seeking to take discretionary appeals to the North Carolina Supreme Court, or to file petitions for certiorari in this Court.

A. [North Carolina has a multi-tiered, appellate system. Convicted defendants have an appeal of right to an intermediate court of appeals, and to the state supreme court in capital cases. A second appeal of right to the Supreme Court is allowed in criminal cases for constitutional issues or in which a judge dissented. In addition, discretionary appeals to the state supreme court are allowed where the issue has significant public interest. North Carolina automatically provides the appointment of counsel on direct appeals taken as of right, but not on discretionary appeals.]

B. The facts show that respondent, in connection with his Mecklenburg County conviction, received the benefit of counsel in examining the record of his trial and in preparing an appellate brief on his behalf for the state Court of Appeals. Thus, prior to his seeking discretionary review in the State Supreme Court, his claims had "once been presented by a lawyer and passed upon by an appellate court." * * * We do not believe that it can be said, therefore, that a defendant in respondent's circumstances is denied meaningful access to the North Carolina Supreme Court simply because the State does not appoint counsel to aid him in seeking review in that court. At that stage he will have, at the very least, a transcript or other record of trial proceedings, a brief on his behalf in the Court of Appeals setting forth his claims of error, and in many cases an opinion by the Court of Appeals disposing of his case. These materials, supplemented by whatever submission respondent may make *pro se*, would appear to provide the Supreme Court of North Carolina with an adequate basis for its decision to grant or deny review. [d]

We are fortified in this conclusion by our understanding of the function served by discretionary review in the North Carolina Supreme Court. The critical issue in that court, as we perceive it, is not whether there has been "a correct adjudication of guilt" in every individual case, * * * but rather whether "the subject matter of the appeal has significant public interest," whether "the cause involves legal principles of major significance to the jurisprudence of the State," or whether the decision below is in probable conflict with a decision of the Supreme

Court. The Supreme Court may deny certiorari even though it believes that the decision of the Court of Appeals was incorrect, * * * since a decision which appears incorrect may nevertheless fail to satisfy any of the criteria discussed above. Once a defendant's claims of error are organized and presented in a lawyerlike fashion to the Court of Appeals, the justices of the Supreme Court of North Carolina who make the decision to grant or deny discretionary review should be able to ascertain whether his case satisfies the standards established by the legislature for such review.

This is not to say, of course, that a skilled lawyer, particularly one trained in the somewhat arcane art of preparing petitions for discretionary review, would not prove helpful to any litigant able to employ him. An indigent defendant seeking review in the Supreme Court of North Carolina is therefore somewhat handicapped in comparison with a wealthy defendant who has counsel assisting him in every conceivable manner at every stage in the proceeding. But both the opportunity to have counsel prepare an initial brief in the Court of Appeals and the nature of discretionary review in the Supreme Court of North Carolina make this relative handicap far less than the handicap borne by the indigent defendant denied counsel on his initial appeal as of right in *Douglas*. And the fact that a particular service might be of benefit to an indigent defendant does not mean that the service is constitutionally required. The duty of the State under our cases is not to duplicate the legal arsenal that may be privately retained by a criminal defendant in a continuing effort to reverse his conviction, but only to assure the indigent defendant an adequate opportunity to present his claims fairly in the context of the State's appellate process. We think respondent was given that opportunity under the existing North Carolina system.

V

Much of the discussion in the preceding section is equally relevant to the question of whether a State must provide counsel for a defendant seeking review of his conviction in this Court. * * * This Court's review, much like that of the Supreme Court of North Carolina, is discretionary and depends on numerous factors other than the perceived correctness of the judgment we are asked to review.

[Also, the source of discretionary appeals to the United States Supreme Court is federal, not state, law.]

The suggestion that a State is responsible for providing counsel to one petitioning this Court simply because it initiated the prosecution which led to the judgment sought to be reviewed is unsupported by either reason or authority. It would be quite as logical under the rationale of *Douglas* and *Griffin*, and indeed perhaps more so, to require that the Federal Government or this Court furnish and compensate counsel for petitioners who seek certiorari here to review state judgments of conviction. Yet this Court has followed a consistent policy of denying applications for appointment of counsel by persons seeking to file jurisdictional statements or petitions for certiorari in this Court. * * * In the light of these authorities, it would be odd, indeed, to read the Fourteenth Amendment to impose such a requirement on the States, and we decline to do so.

VI

We do not mean by this opinion to in any way discourage those States which have, as a matter of legislative choice, made counsel available to convicted defendants at all stages of judicial review. * * * Our reading of the Fourteenth Amendment leaves these choices to the State, and respondent was denied no right secured by the Federal Constitution when North Carolina refused to provide counsel to aid him in obtaining discretionary appellate review.

The judgment of the Court of Appeals' holding to the contrary is
Reversed. [e]

MR. JUSTICE DOUGLAS, with whom MR. JUSTICE BRENNAN and MR. JUSTICE MARSHALL concur, dissenting.

* * *

* * * [T]he indigent defendant proceeding without counsel is at a substantial disadvantage relative to wealthy defendants represented by counsel when he is forced to fend for himself in seeking discretionary review from the State Supreme Court or from this Court. It may well not be enough to allege error in the courts below in layman's terms; a more sophisticated approach may be demanded:

> "An indigent defendant is as much in need of the assistance of

a lawyer in preparing and filing a petition for certiorari as he is in the handling of an appeal as of right. In many appeals, an articulate defendant could file an effective brief by telling his story in simple language without legalisms, but the technical requirements for applications for writs of certiorari are hazards which one untrained in the law could hardly be expected to negotiate.
> "'Certiorari proceedings constitute a highly specialized aspect of appellate work. The factors which [a court] deems important in connection with deciding whether to grant certiorari are certainly not within the normal knowledge of an indigent appellant.* * * *'" * * *

Furthermore, the lawyer who handled the first appeal in a case would be familiar with the facts and legal issues involved in the case. It would be a relatively easy matter for the attorney to apply his expertise in filing a petition for discretionary review to a higher court, or to advise his client that such a petition would have no chance of succeeding.

Douglas v. California was grounded on concepts of fairness and equality. The right to seek discretionary review is a substantial one, and one where a lawyer can be of significant assistance to an indigent defendant. It was correctly perceived below that the "same concepts of fairness and equality, which require counsel in a first appeal of right, require counsel in other and subsequent discretionary appeals." * * *

* * * * * * * * * * *

COMMENTS

[a] This paragraph lays the foundation for the holding in two ways.   First, it characterizes the key element of the *Griffin* line of cases as whether or not an indigent's right to appeal was cut off.   But a close reading of *Griffin* shows that in that case Griffin's actual right to appeal was not cut off.   Second, *Douglas* is not portrayed as a case squarely within the *Griffin* line, but as a departure and extension of those equal protection cases.

[b] By separating the due process and equal protection aspects of *Douglas v. California*, JUSTICE REHNQUIST follows the reasoning established by JUSTICE HARLAN, dissenting in that case.   This also has the effect of toning down the ideological tone of the *Douglas* ruling and allowing for a more precise dissection of the reasoning of these cases.

[c] The due process reasoning offered here is very interesting; it pictures the defendant on discretionary appeal as an attacker rather than an offender.   This is less a matter of a strict legal rule and more a matter of the justice's attitude.   Many are offended by the ability of prisoners to file writs of habeas corpus and believe that once the verdict and appeal of right is concluded, the prisoner should serve time docilely.   What do you think?

[d] The fact that lawyers have already pored over the case and have left a track record does weaken the respondents' cases to some extent.

[e] The opinion can be read in two ways, first as a reasonable limitation on the *Douglas* ruling, second, as the expression of a more conservative Court than the liberal Warren Court which sat from 1961 to 1969.   To the extent that the decision is a reflection of the ideological leanings of justices, it is interesting to compare JUSTICE REHNQUIST's reminder that not every right need be taken to its logical extreme with JUSTICE DOUGLAS' view of fairness and equality.

Does it matter whether the denial of counsel in a post-appeal discretionary rule occurs in a death penalty case? The Supreme Court extended the *Ross v. Moffitt* rule to capital punishment cases in *Murray v. Giarratano*, 492 U.S. 1 (1989). Giarratano, who had to prepare his own writ of certiorari while on death row, was duly executed by the state of Virginia.

STRICKLAND v. WASHINGTON

466 U.S. 668, 104 S.Ct. 2052, 80 L.Ed.2d 674 (1984)

JUSTICE O'CONNOR delivered the opinion of the Court.

* * *

I
A

[Washington, the respondent, was found guilty and sentenced to death for a crime spree that included three murders, torture, kidnapping and theft. He confessed to the police. Against the advice of his experienced, assigned defense lawyer, Washington waived a jury trial and pleaded guilty, telling the judge that he accepted responsibility for his acts. Against counsel's advice, once again, Washington also waived an advisory jury on the death penalty issue.]

* * *

In preparing for the sentencing hearing, counsel spoke with respondent about his background. He also spoke on the telephone with respondent's wife and mother, though he did not follow up on the one unsuccessful effort to meet with them. He did not otherwise seek out character witnesses for respondent. * * * Nor did he request a psychiatric examination, since his conversations with his client gave no indication that respondent had psychological problems. * * * [a]

Counsel decided not to present and hence not to look further for evidence concerning respondent's character and emotional state. That decision reflected trial counsel's sense of hopelessness about overcoming the evidentiary effect of respondent's confessions to the gruesome crimes. * * * It also reflected the judgment that it was advisable to rely on the plea colloquy for evidence about respondent's background and about his claim of emotional stress: the plea colloquy communicated sufficient information about these subjects, and by foregoing the opportunity to present new evidence on these subjects, counsel prevented the State from cross-examining respondent on his claim and from putting on psychiatric evidence of its own.

Counsel also excluded from the sentencing hearing other evidence he thought was potentially damaging. He successfully moved to exclude respondent's "rap sheet." * * * Because he judged that a presentence report might prove more detrimental than helpful, as it would have included respondent's criminal history and thereby undermined the claim of no significant history of criminal activity, he did not request that one be prepared. * * *

At the sentencing hearing, counsel's strategy [stressed Washington's remorse, his acceptance of responsibility, the stress that he claimed he was under at the time of the crime spree, and his apparently clean prior criminal record.] The State put on evidence and witnesses largely for the purpose of describing the details of the crimes. Counsel did not cross-examine the medical experts who testified about the manner of death of respondent's victims. [b]

[The trial judge found that the aggravating circumstances outweighed the mitigating circumstances and sentenced Washington to death.]

* * *

B

* * * Respondent challenged counsel's assistance in six respects. He asserted that counsel was ineffective because he failed to move for a continuance to prepare for sentencing, to request a psychiatric report, to investigate and present character witnesses, to seek a presentence investigation report, to present meaningful arguments to the sentencing judge, and to investigate the medical examiner's reports or cross-examine the medical experts.   In support of the claim, respondent submitted 14 affidavits from friends, neighbors, and relatives stating that they would have testified if asked to do so.   He also submitted one psychiatric report and one psychological report stating that respondent, though not under the influence of extreme mental or emotional disturbance, was "chronically frustrated and depressed because of his economic dilemma" at the time of his crimes. [c]

[The state courts found Washington's six claims of ineffectiveness to be groundless; (1) there was no legal basis for seeking a continuance; (2) state psychiatric examinations of Washington disclosed no mental abnormalities; (3) character witnesses would not have rebutted aggravating circumstances and would have added no mitigating circumstances; (4) a presentence report would have brought out the respondent's prior criminal record, which was otherwise kept out of the proceedings; (5) counsel presented an "admirable" argument for the respondent in light of the overwhelming nature of the aggravating circumstances; and (6) cross-examination of the state's psychiatric witnesses could have led the prosecution, on rebuttal, to undermine Washington's claim that he was under stress when he went on his crime spree.]

* * * [T]he trial court concluded that respondent had not shown that counsel's assistance reflected any substantial and serious deficiency measurably below that of competent counsel that was likely to have affected the outcome of the sentencing proceeding. The court specifically found: "[A]s a matter of law, the record affirmatively demonstrates beyond any doubt that even if [counsel] had done each of the * * * things [that respondent alleged counsel had failed to do] at the time of sentencing, there is not even the remotest chance that the outcome would have been any different.   The plain fact is that the aggravating circumstances proved in this case were completely *overwhelming*. * * *" * * *

The Florida Supreme Court affirmed the denial of relief. * * * **[d]**

C

[The federal court of appeals, on an appeal from a federal habeas corpus action, remanded to determine whether counsel was ineffective in this case on the grounds that counsel did not investigate every plausible line of defense.]

D

[The state of Florida challenged this ruling to the Supreme Court.]

II

In a long line of cases * * * this

Court has recognized that the Sixth Amendment right to counsel exists, and is needed, in order to protect the fundamental right to a fair trial. The Constitution guarantees a fair trial through the Due Process Clauses, but it defines the basic elements of a fair trial largely through the several provisions of the Sixth Amendment, including the Counsel Clause. * * * [e] Thus, a fair trial is one in which evidence subject to adversarial testing is presented to an impartial tribunal for resolution of issues defined in advance of the proceeding. The right to counsel plays a crucial role in the adversarial system embodied in the Sixth Amendment, since access to counsel's skill and knowledge is necessary to accord defendants the "ample opportunity to meet the case of the prosecution" to which they are entitled. * * * [f]

* * * That a person who happens to be a lawyer is present at trial alongside the accused, however, is not enough to satisfy the constitutional command. The Sixth Amendment recognizes the right to the assistance of counsel because it envisions counsel's playing a role that is critical to the ability of the adversarial system to produce just results. An accused is entitled to be assisted by an attorney, whether retained or appointed, who plays the role necessary to ensure that the trial is fair.

For that reason, the Court has recognized that "the right to counsel is the right to the effective assistance of counsel." * * * Government violates the right to effective assistance when it interferes in certain ways with the ability of counsel to make independent decisions about how to conduct the defense. * * *

* * * The benchmark for judging any claim of ineffectiveness must be whether counsel's conduct so undermined the proper functioning of the adversarial process that the trial cannot be relied on as having produced a just result.

[This principle also applies to capital sentencing proceedings, which are trial-like, but not to ordinary sentencing proceedings.]

III

A convicted defendant's claim that counsel's assistance was so defective as to require reversal of a conviction or death sentence has two components. First, the defendant must show that counsel's performance was deficient. This requires showing that counsel made errors so serious that counsel was not functioning as the "counsel" guaranteed the defendant by the Sixth Amendment. [g] Second, the defendant must show that the deficient performance prejudiced the defense. This requires showing that counsel's errors were so serious as to deprive the defendant of a fair trial, a trial whose result is reliable. Unless a defendant makes both showings, it cannot be said that the conviction or death sentence resulted from a breakdown in the adversary process that renders the result unreliable.

A

As all the Federal Courts of Appeals have now held, the proper standard for attorney performance is that of reasonably effective assistance. * * * When a convicted defendant complains of the ineffectiveness of counsel's assistance, the defendant must show that counsel's representation fell below an objective standard of reasonableness.

More specific guidelines are not appropriate.   The Sixth Amendment refers simply to "counsel," not specifying particular requirements of effective assistance.   It relies instead on the legal profession's maintenance of standards sufficient to justify the law's presumption that counsel will fulfill the role in the adversary process that the Amendment envisions.   *   *   *   The proper measure of attorney performance remains simply reasonableness under prevailing professional norms. **[h]**

*   *   *   Counsel's function is to assist the defendant, and hence counsel owes the client a duty of loyalty, a duty to avoid conflicts of interest.   *   *   *   From counsel's function as assistant to the defendant derive the overarching duty to advocate the defendant's cause and the more particular duties to consult with the defendant on important decisions and to keep the defendant informed of important developments in the course of the prosecution. Counsel also has a duty to bring to bear such skill and knowledge as will render the trial a reliable adversarial testing process.   *   *   *

These basic duties neither exhaustively define the obligations of counsel nor form a checklist for judicial evaluation of attorney performance.   In any case presenting an ineffectiveness claim, the performance inquiry must be whether counsel's assistance was reasonable considering all the circumstances.   Prevailing norms of practice as reflected in American Bar Association standards and the like,   *   *   *   are guides to determining what is reasonable, but they are only guides.   No particular set of detailed rules for counsel's conduct can satisfactorily take account of the variety of circumstances faced by defense counsel or the range of legitimate decisions regarding how best to represent a criminal defendant. Any such set of rules would interfere with the constitutionally protected independence of counsel and restrict the wide latitude counsel must have in making tactical decisions.   *   *   *   Indeed, the existence of detailed guidelines for representation could distract counsel from the overriding mission of vigorous advocacy of the defendant's cause. **[i]** Moreover, the purpose of the effective assistance guarantee of the Sixth Amendment is not to improve the quality of legal representation, although that is a goal of considerable importance to the legal system.   The purpose is simply to ensure that criminal defendants receive a fair trial.

Judicial   scrutiny   of   counsel's performance must be highly deferential. It is all too tempting for a defendant to second-guess counsel's assistance after conviction or adverse sentence, and it is all too easy for a court, examining counsel's defense after it has proved unsuccessful, to conclude that a particular act or omission of counsel was unreasonable.   *   *   *   A fair assessment of attorney performance requires that every effort be made to eliminate the distorting effects of hindsight, to reconstruct the circumstances of counsel's challenged conduct, and to evaluate the conduct from counsel's perspective at the time. Because of the difficulties inherent in making the evaluation, a court must indulge a strong presumption that counsel's conduct falls within the wide range of reasonable professional assistance. * * * There are countless ways to provide effective assistance in any given case. Even the best criminal defense attorneys would not defend a particular client in the same way. * * *

The availability of intrusive post-trial inquiry into attorney performance or of detailed guidelines for its evaluation would encourage the proliferation of ineffectiveness challenges. Criminal trials resolved unfavorably to the defendant would increasingly come to be followed by a second trial, this one of counsel's unsuccessful defense. Counsel's performance and even willingness to serve could be adversely affected. Intensive scrutiny of counsel and rigid requirements for acceptable assistance could dampen the ardor and impair the independence of defense counsel, discourage the acceptance of assigned cases, and undermine the trust between attorney and client. [j]

* * * A convicted defendant making a claim of ineffective assistance must identify the acts or omissions of counsel that are alleged not to have been the result of reasonable professional judgment. The court must then determine whether, in light of all the circumstances, the identified acts or omissions were outside the wide range of professionally competent assistance. In making that determination, the court should keep in mind that counsel's function, as elaborated in prevailing professional norms, is to make the adversarial testing process work in the particular case. At the same time, the court should recognize that counsel is strongly presumed to have rendered adequate assistance and made all significant decisions in the exercise of reasonable professional judgment.

* * *

The reasonableness of counsel's actions may be determined or substantially influenced by the defendant's own statements or actions. Counsel's actions are usually based, quite properly, on informed strategic choices made by the defendant and on information supplied by the defendant. In particular, what investigation decisions are reasonable depends critically on such information. * * *

B

An error by counsel, even if professionally unreasonable, does not warrant setting aside the judgment of a criminal proceeding if the error had no effect on the judgment. * * * The purpose of the Sixth Amendment guarantee of counsel is to ensure that a defendant has the assistance necessary to justify reliance on the outcome of the proceeding. Accordingly, any deficiencies in counsel's performance must be prejudicial to the defense in order to constitute ineffective assistance under the Constitution. [k]

In certain Sixth Amendment contexts, prejudice is presumed. Actual or constructive denial of the assistance of counsel altogether is legally presumed to result in prejudice. * * * Prejudice in these circumstances is so likely that case-by-case inquiry into prejudice is not worth the cost. * * * Moreover, such circumstances involve impairments of the Sixth Amendment right that are easy to identify and, for that reason and because the prosecution is directly responsible, easy for the government to prevent.

One type of actual ineffectiveness claim warrants a similar, though more limited, presumption of prejudice. In

Cuyler v. Sullivan, [446 U.S. 335 (1980)], the Court held that prejudice is presumed when counsel is burdened by an actual conflict of interest. In those circumstances, counsel breaches the duty of loyalty, perhaps the most basic of counsel's duties. * * * Prejudice is presumed only if the defendant demonstrates that counsel "actively represented conflicting interests" and that "an actual conflict of interest adversely affected his lawyer's performance." * * * **[l]**

Conflict of interest claims aside, actual ineffectiveness claims alleging a deficiency in attorney performance are subject to a general requirement that the defendant affirmatively prove prejudice. The government is not responsible for, and hence not able to prevent, attorney errors that will result in reversal of a conviction or sentence. Attorney errors come in an infinite variety and are as likely to be utterly harmless in a particular case as they are to be prejudicial. They cannot be classified according to likelihood of causing prejudice. Nor can they be defined with sufficient precision to inform defense attorneys correctly just what conduct to avoid. Representation is an art, and an act or omission that is unprofessional in one case may be sound or even brilliant in another. Even if a defendant shows that particular errors of counsel were unreasonable, therefore, the defendant must show that they actually had an adverse effect on the defense.

* * * [The standard of proving that an attorney's deficient performance resulted in prejudice to the outcome of the defendant's case is that] [t]he defendant must show that there is a reasonable probability that, but for counsel's unprofessional errors, the result of the proceeding would have been different. A reasonable probability is a probability sufficient to undermine confidence in the outcome. **[m]**

In making the determination whether the specified errors resulted in the required prejudice, a court should presume, absent challenge to the judgment on grounds of evidentiary insufficiency, that the judge or jury acted according to law. An assessment of the likelihood of a result more favorable to the defendant must exclude the possibility of arbitrariness, whimsy, caprice, "nullification," and the like. A defendant has no entitlement to the luck of a lawless decisionmaker, even if a lawless decision cannot be reviewed. The assessment of prejudice should proceed on the assumption that the decisionmaker is reasonably, conscientiously, and impartially applying the standards that govern the decision. It should not depend on the idiosyncracies of the particular decisionmaker, such as unusual propensities toward harshness or leniency. Although these factors may actually have entered into counsel's selection of strategies and, to that limited extent, may thus affect the performance inquiry, they are irrelevant to the prejudice inquiry. Thus, evidence about the actual process of decision, if not part of the record of the proceeding under review, and evidence about, for example, a particular judge's sentencing practices, should not be considered in the prejudice determination.

The governing legal standard plays a critical role in defining the question to be asked in assessing the prejudice from counsel's errors. When a defendant challenges a conviction, the question is whether there is a reasonable probability that, absent the errors, the factfinder would have had a reasonable doubt respecting guilt. When a defendant challenges a death sentence such as the one at issue in this case, the question is whether there is a reasonable probability that, absent the errors, the sentencer * * * would have concluded that the balance of aggravating and mitigating circumstances did not warrant death.

In making this determination, a court hearing an ineffectiveness claim must consider the totality of the evidence before the judge or jury. Some of the factual findings will have been unaffected by the errors, and factual findings that were affected will have been affected in different ways. Some errors will have had a pervasive effect on the inferences to be drawn from the evidence, altering the entire evidentiary picture, and some will have had an isolated, trivial effect. Moreover, a verdict or conclusion only weakly supported by the record is more likely to have been affected by errors than one with overwhelming record support. Taking the unaffected findings as a given, and taking due account of the effect of the errors on the remaining findings, a court making the prejudice inquiry must ask if the defendant has met the burden of showing that the decision reached would reasonably likely have been different absent the errors. [n]

IV

* * * [I]n adjudicating a claim of actual ineffectiveness of counsel, a court should keep in mind that the principles we have stated do not establish mechanical rules. Although those principles should guide the process of decision, the ultimate focus of inquiry must be on the fundamental fairness of the proceeding whose result is being challenged. In every case the court should be concerned with whether, despite the strong presumption of reliability, the result of the particular proceeding is unreliable because of a breakdown in the adversarial process that our system counts on to produce just results.

* * *

[In Part V, applying the standards to the facts, the majority concluded that the conduct of Washington's lawyer was reasonable and did not prejudice his case.]

[JUSTICE BRENNAN joined in the Court's opinion, believing that the opinion provided useful guidance, but dissented from the judgment because in capital sentencing, it is essential "that the jury have before it all possible relevant information about the individual defendant whose fate it must determine."]

JUSTICE MARSHALL, dissenting.

* * *

I
A

My objection to the performance standard adopted by the Court is that it is so malleable that, in practice, it will either have no grip at all or will yield excessive variation in the manner in which the Sixth Amendment is interpreted and applied by different courts. To tell lawyers and the lower courts that counsel for a criminal defendant must behave "reasonably" and must act like "a reasonably competent attorney," is to tell them almost nothing. In essence, the majority has instructed judges called upon to assess claims of ineffective assistance of counsel to advert to their own intuitions regarding what constitutes "professional" representation, and has discouraged them from trying to develop more detailed standards governing the performance of defense counsel. In my view, the Court has thereby not only abdicated its own responsibility to interpret the Constitution, but also impaired the ability of the lower courts to exercise theirs. [o]

* * *

B

I object to the prejudice standard adopted by the Court for two independent reasons. First, it is often very difficult to tell whether a defendant convicted after a trial in which he was ineffectively represented would have fared better if his lawyer had been competent. Seemingly impregnable cases can sometimes be dismantled by good defense counsel. On the basis of a cold record, it may be impossible for a reviewing court confidently to ascertain how the government's evidence and arguments would have stood up against rebuttal and cross-examination by a shrewd, well-prepared lawyer. The difficulties of estimating prejudice after the fact are exacerbated by the possibility that evidence of injury to the defendant may be missing from the record precisely because of the incompetence of defense counsel. In view of all these impediments to a fair evaluation of the probability that the outcome of a trial was affected by ineffectiveness of counsel, it seems to me senseless to impose on a defendant whose lawyer has been shown to have been incompetent the burden of demonstrating prejudice. [p]

Second and more fundamentally, the assumption on which the Court's holding rests is that the only purpose of the constitutional guarantee of effective assistance of counsel is to reduce the chance that innocent persons will be convicted. In my view, the guarantee also functions to ensure that convictions are obtained only through fundamentally fair procedures. The majority contends that the Sixth Amendment is not violated when a manifestly guilty defendant is convicted after a trial in which he was represented by a manifestly ineffective attorney. I cannot agree. Every defendant is entitled to a trial in which his interests are vigorously and conscientiously advocated by an able lawyer. A proceeding in which the defendant does not receive meaningful assistance in meeting the forces of the State does not, in my opinion, constitute due process.

* * *

* * * * * * * * * * *

COMMENTS

[a] Character witnesses testify only about the defendant's general reputation in the community. Character witnesses rarely make negative statements about the defendant.

[b] Each element of the defense counsel's presentation is planned out for its tactical and strategic effect.

[c] A defense attorney's duty is not to win an acquittal for a defendant, but to provide the best professional defense allowable under the law. Of course, a defendant's interest is in "winning," and a loss may be attributed to the fault of the lawyer, whether the attorney was or was not incompetent in the performance of his or her duties.

[d] The state judges, the federal district court that upheld the state court on Washington's habeas corpus proceeding, and the Supreme Court's majority all seemed to think that the defense attorney used the right strategy in the face of overwhelming odds; the federal court of appeals, concurring JUSTICE BRENNAN, and dissenting JUSTICE MARSHALL thought that the attorney should have done everything possible in the slim hope that a difficult case could be turned around. If you were in the lawyer's shoes would you have called the character witnesses, asked for a presentence report, and cross-examined the state's psychiatrists?

[e] It is interesting that decades can pass while the Supreme Court works out one issue (the right to appointed counsel for indigents) without reaching another (the standard of effective assistance of counsel). The Court's "agenda" is often set by general social conceptions of what sort of questions are appropriate in a certain era.

[f] Notice how the right to counsel is subordinated to the more fundamental right to a fair trial. This hierarchy is one reason why the majority can feel comfortable in making the standard for effectiveness rather open-ended (see Part III of JUSTICE O'CONNOR's opinion).

[g] Under this prong of the effective-assistance-of-counsel test, a certain level of attorney error may occur without rising to the level of a constitutional wrong.

[h] The majority and dissenting opinions differ over how specific the effectiveness standard should be. There may be no correct answer. JUSTICE MARSHALL, dissenting, correctly notes that the announced standards do not give judges precise guidelines as to what constitutes effective assistance. JUSTICE O'CONNOR is correct in stating that there are practice norms that experienced attorneys and judges can recognize. Which argument would you choose?

[i] This is an interesting point. Many people complain that medicine is practiced "defensively" and expensively by the overuse of standard tests, primarily to avoid liability. JUSTICE O'CONNOR wishes to avoid placing a straitjacket on creative attorneys in developing effective defense strategies.

[j] All appellate courts are sensitive to rulings that would open wide the gates to appeals; this is rarely seen as desirable.

[k] The word "prejudice" is used in a technical sense to describe the second prong of the effective assistance standard, that is, to mean whether counsel's conduct negatively affected the outcome of the case so as to have substantially contributed to the guilty verdict or sentence of death. It does not imply "discrimination" here.

[l] The Court first describes two cases where prejudice is automatically approved: (1) no assistance of counsel and (2) conflict of interest. It then moves on to the general case where prejudice has to be determined by a factual examination of the case.

[m] To better understand the "but for" standard of the prejudice prong, try to state it in a positive way or try to state it in a more complete way.

[n] Because "facts and circumstances" and "totality of the evidence" rules are so open-ended in comparison to so-called "bright-line rules," it is difficult to state in words what they mean; at best, interpretive guidelines can be given, as JUSTICE O'CONNOR does here, with the expectation that the professionals who apply the standards will do so wisely. Is this level of generality an acceptable standard for law?

[o] JUSTICE MARSHALL attacks the "soft underbelly" of the *Strickland* rule—its vagueness or generality. Are the risks of imposing a bright-line rule on the performance of attorneys, as spelled out by JUSTICE O'CONNOR, worth the price of stricter rules, as Justice Marshall desires?

[p] None of JUSTICE MARSHALL's colleagues at the time of this case had his trial experience as an attorney. As chief counsel for the NAACP Legal Defense Fund, he challenged racial segregation laws in courts in the 1930s, 1940s, and 1950s under extremely hostile circumstances. He directed the work of many attorneys in that capacity. As Solicitor General in the 1960s he argued cases before the Supreme Court as the Government's chief litigator. His experience as a trial and appellate lawyer gave his views on matters of trial practice substantial weight.

NIX v. WHITESIDE

475 U.S. 157, 106 S.Ct. 988, 89 L.Ed.2d 123 (1986)

CHIEF JUSTICE BURGER delivered the opinion of the Court.

We granted certiorari to decide whether the Sixth Amendment right of a criminal defendant to assistance of counsel is violated when an attorney refuses to cooperate with the defendant in presenting perjured testimony at his trial.

I

[Whiteside stabbed and killed Calvin Love during a fight in Love's apartment. Whiteside told his lawyers that he thought Love had pulled a gun from under his pillow. He said that Love told his girlfriend to get his "piece." No gun was found during the police investigation, after which Love's family cleaned out the apartment.]

[Whiteside told his lawyer that he was certain Love had a gun, although he had not seen it. About a week before trial Whiteside for the first time told his lawyers that he had seen something "metallic" in Love's hand. He told his lawyers that he feared a jury would not believe his self-defense plea if he said he saw no gun. His lawyers told him that such testimony would be perjury and that it was not necessary to prove that a gun was available but only that Whiteside reasonably believed that he was in danger to make out self-defense. They also told Whiteside that they could not let him commit perjury and that if he did they would impeach his testimony and would seek to withdraw from the case if he insisted on committing perjury.]

[Whiteside testified at trial that he saw no gun but believed that Love had one. He was convicted of second-degree murder and the Iowa Supreme Court affirmed. A federal District Court denied a writ of habeas corpus, but the Circuit Court reversed, ruling that while a defendant has no right to commit perjury, the attorneys' threats to violate their clients' confidences if he testified to a "metallic object" breached the standards of effective representation of *Strickland v. Washington* [this volume]].

II
A

The right of an accused to testify in his defense is of relatively recent origin. Until the latter part of the preceding century, criminal defendants in this country, as at common law, were considered to be disqualified from giving sworn testimony at their own trial by reason of their interest as a party to the case. * * *

By the end of the 19th century, however, the disqualification was finally abolished by statute in most states and in the federal courts. * * * Although this Court has never explicitly held that a criminal defendant has a due process right to testify in his own behalf, cases in several Circuits have so held, and the right has long been assumed. * * * We have also suggested that such a right exists as a corollary to the Fifth Amendment privilege against compelled testimony. * * *

B

In *Strickland v. Washington*, we held that to obtain relief by way of federal habeas corpus on a claim of a deprivation of effective assistance of counsel under the Sixth Amendment, the movant must establish both serious attorney error and prejudice. To show such error, it must be established that the assistance rendered by counsel was constitutionally deficient in that "counsel made errors so serious that counsel was not functioning as 'counsel' guaranteed the defendant by the Sixth Amendment." * * * To show prejudice, it must be established that the claimed lapses in counsel's performance rendered the trial unfair so as to "undermine confidence in the outcome" of the trial. * * *

In *Strickland*, we acknowledged that the Sixth Amendment does not require any particular response by counsel to a problem that may arise. Rather, the Sixth Amendment inquiry is into whether the attorney's conduct was "reasonably effective." To counteract the natural tendency to fault an unsuccessful defense, a court reviewing a claim of ineffective assistance must "indulge a strong presumption that counsel's conduct falls within the wide range of reasonable professional assistance." * * * In giving shape to the perimeters of this range of reasonable professional assistance, *Strickland* mandates that

> "[p]revailing norms of practice as reflected in American Bar Association Standards and the like, . . . are guides to determining what is reasonable, but they are only guides." * * *

Under the *Strickland* standard, breach of an ethical standard does not necessarily make out a denial of the Sixth Amendment guarantee of assistance of counsel. When examining attorney conduct, a court must be careful not to narrow the wide range of conduct acceptable under the Sixth Amendment so restrictively as to constitutionalize particular standards of professional conduct and thereby intrude into the state's proper authority to define and apply the standards of professional conduct applicable to those it admits to practice in its courts. [a] In some future case challenging attorney conduct in the course of a state-court trial, we may need to define with greater precision the weight to be given to recognized canons of ethics, the standards established by the state in statutes or professional codes, and the Sixth Amendment, in defining the proper scope and limits on that conduct. Here we need not face that question, since virtually all of the sources speak with one voice. [b]

C

We turn next to the question presented: the definition of the range of "reasonable professional" responses to a criminal defendant client who informs counsel that he will perjure himself on the stand. We must determine whether, in this setting, [attorney] Robinson's conduct fell within the wide range of professional responses to threatened client perjury acceptable under the Sixth Amendment.

In *Strickland*, we recognized counsel's duty of loyalty and his "overarching duty to advocate the defendant's cause." * * * Plainly, that duty is limited to legitimate, lawful conduct compatible with the very nature of a trial as a search for truth. Although counsel must take all reasonable lawful means to attain the objectives of the client, counsel is precluded from taking steps or in any way assisting the client in presenting false evidence or otherwise violating the law. This principle has consistently been recognized in most unequivocal terms by expositors of the norms of professional conduct since the first Canons of Professional Ethics were adopted by the American Bar Association in 1908. * * * [The CHIEF JUSTICE quoted from the 1908 Canon prohibiting acts in violation of law.] Of course, this Canon did no more than articulate centuries of accepted standards of conduct. * * *

[Contemporary codes of conduct for attorneys state that an attorney shall not knowingly use perjured testimony or false evidence to assist a client, or assist or counsel a client to engage in conduct known to be fraudulent; allow and require an attorney to disclose that his client intends to commit perjury, as an exception from the attorney-client privilege.]

These standards confirm that the legal profession has accepted that an attorney's ethical duty to advance the interests of his client is limited by an equally solemn duty to comply with the law and standards of professional conduct; it specifically ensures that the client may not use false evidence. This special duty of an attorney to prevent and disclose frauds upon the court derives from the recognition that perjury is as much a crime as tampering with witnesses or jurors by way of promises and threats, and undermines the administration of justice. * * *

The offense of perjury was a crime recognized at common law, * * * and has been made a felony in most states by statute, including Iowa. * * * An attorney who aids false testimony by questioning a witness when perjurious responses can be anticipated risks prosecution for subornation of perjury. * * *

It is universally agreed that at a minimum the attorney's first duty when confronted with a proposal for perjurious testimony is to attempt to dissuade the client from the unlawful course of conduct. * * * [A]n attorney's revelation of his client's perjury to the court is a professionally responsible and acceptable response to the conduct of a client who has actually given perjured testimony. Similarly, [various codes of attorney conduct] expressly permit withdrawal from representation as an appropriate response of an attorney when the client threatens to commit perjury. * * * Withdrawal of counsel when this situation arises at trial gives rise to many difficult questions including possible mistrial and claims of double jeopardy.

The essence of the brief *amicus* of the American Bar Association reviewing practices long accepted by ethical lawyers is that under no circumstance may a lawyer either advocate or passively tolerate a client's giving false testimony. This, of course, is consistent with the governance of trial conduct in what we have long called "a search for truth." The suggestion sometimes made that "a lawyer must believe his client, not judge him" in no sense means a lawyer can honorably be a party to or in any way give aid to presenting known perjury. [c]

D

Considering Robinson's representation of respondent in light of these accepted norms of professional conduct, we discern no failure to adhere to reasonable professional standards that would in any sense make out a deprivation of the Sixth Amendment right to counsel. Whether Robinson's conduct is seen as a successful attempt to dissuade his client from committing the crime of perjury, or whether seen as a "threat" to withdraw from representation and disclose the illegal scheme, Robinson's representation of Whiteside falls well within accepted standards of professional conduct and the range of reasonable professional conduct acceptable under *Strickland*.

The Court of Appeals assumed for the purpose of the decision that Whiteside would have given false testimony had counsel not intervened. * * *

* * *

The Court of Appeals' holding that Robinson's "action deprived [Whiteside] of due process and effective assistance of counsel" is not supported by the record since Robinson's action, at most, deprived Whiteside of his contemplated perjury. Nothing counsel did in any way undermined Whiteside's claim that he believed the victim was reaching for a gun. Similarly, the record gives no support for holding that Robinson's action "also impermissibly compromised [Whiteside's] right to testify in his own defense by conditioning continued representation . . . and confidentiality upon [Whiteside's] *restricted* testimony." The record in fact shows the contrary: (a) that Whiteside did testify, and (b) he was "restricted" or restrained only from testifying falsely and was aided by Robinson in developing the basis for

the fear that Love was reaching for a gun. Robinson divulged no client communications until he was compelled to do so in response to Whiteside's post-trial challenge to the quality of his performance. We see this as a case in which the attorney successfully dissuaded the client from committing the crime of perjury.

Paradoxically, even while accepting the conclusion of the Iowa trial court that Whiteside's proposed testimony would have been a criminal act, the Court of Appeals held that Robinson's efforts to persuade Whiteside not to commit that crime were improper, *first*, as forcing an impermissible choice between the right to counsel and the right to testify; and, *second*, as compromising client confidences because of Robinson's threat to disclose the contemplated perjury.

Whatever the scope of a constitutional right to testify, it is elementary that such a right does not extend to testifying *falsely*. * * *

The paucity of authority on the subject of any such "right" may be explained by the fact that such a notion has never been responsibly advanced; the right to counsel includes no right to have a lawyer who will cooperate with planned perjury. A lawyer who would so cooperate would be at risk of prosecution for suborning perjury, and disciplinary proceedings, including suspension or disbarment.
* * *

* * *   An attorney's duty of confidentiality, which totally covers the client's admission of guilt, does not extend to a client's announced plans to engage in future criminal conduct. * * *

* * *

E

We hold that, as a matter of law, counsel's conduct complained of here cannot establish the prejudice required for relief under the second strand of the *Strickland* inquiry.

* * *

[The judgment of the Court of Appeals was reversed.]

[JUSTICE BRENNAN, concurred in the judgment and joined JUSTICE BLACKMUN's concurrence. He noted that all the quotes of professional standards in the majority opinion do not have the force of law.]

JUSTICE BLACKMUN, with whom JUSTICE BRENNAN, JUSTICE MARSHALL, and JUSTICE STEVENS join, concurring in the judgment.

[JUSTICE BLACKMUN's opinion found that there was nothing in attorney Robinson's actions that legally prejudiced Whiteside's case. Thus, there was no reason to engage in a review of the effectiveness branch of the *Strickland* rule. The concurrence also noted that such cases turn on specific facts and that it was inappropriate to attempt to establish blanket rules to cover such situations.]

[JUSTICE STEVENS wrote a brief concurring opinion. He noted that a decision concerning the deterrence of perjury was not necessarily the same as an attorney's actions after a client had given perjured testimony, and that such an issue should be reserved for future consideration.]

* * * * * * * * * * *

COMMENTS

[a] The justices are often cautious about "freezing" what appears to be a good rule into a constitutional form lest it become difficult to modify if negative consequences result from the rule.

[b] The concurring justices react strongly and negatively to the extent to which CHIEF JUSTICE BURGER relies on the codes of conduct promulgated by various bar associations. Here, the CHIEF JUSTICE makes it clear that he is not relying on these codes as the basis of the ruling.

[c] In the practice of law there are times when, to the court, a lawyer's position may seem to be the adoption of a false perspective. In the adversary system the attorney is in charge of determining the nature of the client's case and with marshalling evidence to establish that case, with the client's consent. It is not the role of the judge to second guess the lawyer as long as the attorney stays within the law and the standards of professional conduct.

WHEAT v. UNITED STATES

486 U.S. 153, 108 S.Ct. 1692; 100 L.Ed.2d 140 (1988)

CHIEF JUSTICE REHNQUIST delivered the opinion of the Court.

The issue in this case is whether the District Court erred in declining petitioner's waiver of his right to conflict-free counsel and by refusing to permit petitioner's proposed substitution of attorneys.

I

[Wheat participated in a "far-flung drug distribution conspiracy." He was charged in this conspiracy along with Gomez-Barajas and Bravo, who were represented in their criminal proceedings by attorney Eugene Iredale.] * * * Gomez-Barajas was tried first and was acquitted on drug charges overlapping with those against petitioner. To avoid a second trial on other charges, however, Gomez-Barajas offered to plead guilty to tax evasion and illegal importation of merchandise. At the commencement of petitioner's trial, the District Court had not accepted the plea; Gomez-Barajas was thus free to withdraw his guilty plea and proceed to trial.

Bravo * * * [pled guilty] to one count of transporting * * * marijuana. * * * At the conclusion of Bravo's guilty plea proceedings * * * Iredale notified the District Court that he had been contacted by petitioner and had been asked to try petitioner's case as well. In response, the Government registered substantial concern about the possibility of conflict in the representation. * * * [Hearings were held on this question just before Wheat's scheduled trial date.] [a]

* * * [T]he Government objected to petitioner's proposed substitution on the ground that Iredale's representation of Gomez-Barajas and Bravo created a serious conflict of interest. The Government's position was premised on two possible conflicts. First, [if Gomez-Barajas withdrew his guilty plea and stood trial, Iredale would have to represent Wheat and Gomez-Barajas. Since Wheat was familiar with the sources and size of Gomez-Barajas' income, he was likely to be called as a Government witness at any subsequent trial of Gomez-Barajas.] This scenario would pose a conflict of interest for Iredale, who would be prevented from cross-examining petitioner and thereby from effectively representing Gomez-Barajas.

Second, and of more immediate concern, Iredale's representation of Bravo would directly affect his ability to act as counsel for petitioner. The Government believed that a portion of the marijuana delivered by Bravo * * * eventually was transferred to petitioner. In this regard, the Government contacted Iredale and asked that Bravo be made available as a witness to testify against petitioner, and agreed in exchange to modify its position at the time of Bravo's sentencing. In the likely event that Bravo were called to testify, Iredale's position in representing both men would become untenable, for ethical proscriptions would forbid him to cross-examine Bravo in any meaningful way. By failing to do so, he would also fail to provide petitioner with effective assistance of counsel.

Thus, because of Iredale's prior representation of Gomez-Barajas and Bravo and the potential for serious conflict of interest, the Government urged the District Court to reject the substitution of attorneys.

[Wheat contended that the Government argument concerning a conflict of interest was] highly speculative and bore no connection to the true relationship between the co-conspirators. [Bravo would deny knowing Wheat if called to testify eliminating any need for Iredale to impeach Bravo. Further, it was unlikely that Gomez-Barajas would reject the plea and go to trial on charges of tax evasion and illegal importation; but if he did, Wheat's] lack of involvement in those alleged crimes made his appearance as a witness highly improbable. Finally, and most importantly, all three defendants agreed to allow Iredale to represent petitioner and to waive any future claims of conflict of interest. In petitioner's view, the Government was manufacturing implausible conflicts in an attempt to disqualify Iredale, who had already proved extremely effective in representing Gomez-Barajas and Bravo.

[The district court, after a hearing, found that "an irreconcilable conflict of interest exists." Wheat went to trial with another attorney and was convicted. The Circuit Court affirmed, ruling that the District Court correctly balanced] (1) the qualified right to be represented by counsel of one's choice, and (2) the right to a defense conducted by an attorney who is free of conflicts of interest. * * *

* * *

II

* * * [The Sixth Amendment right to counsel] was designed to assure fairness in the adversary criminal process. * * * [W]e have held that the Sixth Amendment secures the right to the assistance of counsel, by appointment if necessary, in a trial for any serious crime. * * * We have further recognized that the purpose of providing assistance of counsel "is simply to ensure that criminal defendants receive a fair trial," * * * and that in evaluating Sixth Amendment claims, "the appropriate inquiry focuses on the adversarial process, not on the accused's relationship with his lawyer as such." * * * Thus, while the right to select and be represented by one's preferred attorney is comprehended by the Sixth Amendment, the essential aim of the Amendment is to guarantee an effective advocate for each criminal defendant rather than to ensure that a defendant will inexorably be represented by the lawyer whom he prefers. * * *

The Sixth Amendment right to choose one's own counsel is circumscribed in several important respects. Regardless of his persuasive powers, an advocate who is not a member of the bar may not represent clients (other than himself) in court. Similarly, a defendant may not insist on representation by an attorney he cannot afford or who for other reasons declines to represent the defendant. Nor may a defendant insist on the counsel of an attorney who has a previous or ongoing relationship with an opposing party, even when the opposing party is the Government. [b] The question raised in this case is the extent to which a criminal defendant's right under the Sixth Amendment to his chosen attorney is qualified by the fact that the attorney has represented other defendants charged in the same criminal conspiracy.

In previous cases, we have recognized that multiple representation of criminal defendants engenders special dangers of which a court must be aware. While "permitting a single attorney to represent codefendants * * * is not *per se* violative of constitutional guarantees of effective assistance of counsel," * * * a court confronted with and alerted to possible conflicts of interest must take adequate steps to ascertain whether the conflicts warrant separate counsel. * * * As we said: * * *

"Joint representation of conflicting interests is suspect because of what it tends to prevent the attorney from doing. * * * [A] conflict may * * * prevent an attorney from challenging the admission of evidence prejudicial to one client but perhaps favorable to another, or from arguing at the sentencing hearing the relative involvement and culpability of his clients in order to minimize the culpability of one by emphasizing that of another." * * * [c]

Petitioner insists that the provision of waivers by all affected defendants cures any problems created by the multiple representation. But no such flat rule can be deduced from the Sixth Amendment presumption in favor of counsel of choice. Federal courts have an independent interest in ensuring that criminal trials are conducted within the ethical standards of the profession and that legal proceedings appear fair to all who observe them. Both the American Bar Association's

Model Code of Professional Responsibility and its Model Rules of Professional Conduct, as well as the rules of the California Bar Association (which governed the attorneys in this case), impose limitations on multiple representation of clients. * * * Not only the interest of a criminal defendant but the institutional interest in the rendition of just verdicts in criminal cases may be jeopardized by unregulated multiple representation.

For this reason, the Federal Rules of Criminal Procedure direct trial judges to investigate specially cases involving joint representation [and to "take such measures as may be appropriate to protect each defendant's right to counsel."] Although [the rule] does not specify what particular measures may be taken by a district court, one option suggested by the Notes of the Advisory Committee is an order by the court that the defendants be separately represented in subsequent proceedings in the case. * * * This suggestion comports with our instructions * * * that the trial courts, when alerted by objection from one of the parties, have an independent duty to ensure that criminal defendants receive a trial that is fair and does not contravene the Sixth Amendment.

[The Court noted that trial courts could be "whipsawed" by claims of error if they grant or deny prosecutor requests such as the one in this case. If the district court agrees to multiple representation, defendants found guilty will claim conflict of interest. If the court denies the multiple representation, defendants will raise the Sixth Amendment. A waiver by the parties has not prevented Courts of Appeal from taking such cases.] [d]

Thus, where a court justifiably finds

an actual conflict of interest, there can be no doubt that it may decline a proffer of waiver, and insist that defendants be separately represented. * * *

* * * The likelihood and dimensions of nascent conflicts of interest are notoriously hard to predict, even for those thoroughly familiar with criminal trials. It is a rare attorney who will be fortunate enough to learn the entire truth from his own client, much less be fully apprised before trial of what each of the Government's witnesses will say on the stand. A few bits of unforeseen testimony or a single previously unknown or unnoticed document may significantly shift the relationship between multiple defendants. These imponderables are difficult enough for a lawyer to assess, and even more difficult to convey by way of explanation to a criminal defendant untutored in the niceties of legal ethics. Nor is it amiss to observe that the willingness of an attorney to obtain such waivers from his clients may bear an inverse relation to the care with which he conveys all the necessary information to them.

For these reasons we think the district court must be allowed substantial latitude in refusing waivers of conflicts of interest not only in those rare cases where an actual conflict may be demonstrated before trial, but in the more common cases where a potential for conflict exists which may or may not burgeon into an actual conflict as the trial progresses. In the circumstances of this case, with the motion for substitution of counsel made so close to the time of trial, the District Court relied on instinct and judgment based on experience in making its decision. We do not think

it can be said that the court exceeded the broad latitude which must be accorded it in making this decision. Petitioner of course rightly points out that the Government may seek to "manufacture" a conflict in order to prevent a defendant from having a particularly able defense counsel at his side; but trial courts are undoubtedly aware of this possibility, and must take it into consideration along with all of the other factors which inform this sort of a decision.

* * *

[The Court reviewed the factual situation and concluded that the likelihood of a conflict of interest was possible.]

Viewing the situation as it did before trial, we hold that the District Court's refusal to permit the substitution of counsel in this case was within its discretion and did not violate petitioner's Sixth Amendment rights. Other district courts might have reached differing or opposite conclusions with equal justification, but that does not mean that one conclusion was "right" and the other "wrong." The District Court must recognize a presumption in favor of petitioner's counsel of choice, but that presumption may be overcome not only by a demonstration of actual conflict but by a showing of a serious potential for conflict. The evaluation of the facts and circumstances of each case under this standard must be left primarily to the informed judgment of the trial court.

The judgment of the Court of Appeals is accordingly

Affirmed.

JUSTICE MARSHALL, with whom JUSTICE BRENNAN joins,

dissenting.

* * *

[JUSTICE MARSHALL began by noting agreement with the majority's statement of general rules concerning the right to and choice of counsel.]

I do disagree, however, with the Court's suggestion that the trial court's decision as to whether a potential conflict justifies rejection of a defendant's chosen counsel is entitled to some kind of special deference on appeal. The Court grants trial courts "broad latitude" over the decision to accept or reject a defendant's choice of counsel; * * * although never explicitly endorsing a standard of appellate review, the Court appears to limit such review to determining whether an abuse of discretion has occurred. * * * This approach, which the Court supports solely by noting the difficulty of evaluating the likelihood and magnitude of a conflict, accords neither with the nature of the trial court's decision nor with the importance of the interest at stake. **[e]**

The trial court's decision as to whether the circumstances of a given case constitute grounds for rejecting a defendant's chosen counsel—that is, as to whether these circumstances present a substantial potential for a serious conflict of interest—is a mixed determination of law and fact. The decision is properly described in this way because it requires and results from the application of a legal standard to the established facts of a case. * * * Appellate courts traditionally do not defer to such determinations. * * * For this reason, the Court in *Cuyler v. Sullivan*, 446 U.S. 335 (1980), held that a trial court's determination as to whether an attorney had represented

conflicting interests at trial was not entitled to any deference. The determination at issue here, which focuses on the potential for a conflict of interest, is not different in any relevant respect.

The inappropriateness of deferring to this determination becomes even more apparent when its constitutional significance is taken into account. * * * The interest at stake in this kind of decision is nothing less than a criminal defendant's Sixth Amendment right to counsel of his choice. The trial court simply does not have "broad latitude," * * * to vitiate this right. In my view, a trial court that rejects a criminal defendant's chosen counsel on the ground of a potential conflict should make findings on the record to facilitate review, and an appellate court should scrutinize closely the basis for the trial court's decision. Only in this way can a criminal defendant's right to counsel of his choice be appropriately protected.

The Court's resolution of the instant case flows from its deferential approach to the District Court's denial of petitioner's motion to add or substitute counsel; absent deference, a decision upholding the District Court's ruling would be inconceivable. Indeed, I believe that even under the Court's deferential standard, reversal is in order. The mere fact of multiple representation, as the Court concedes, will not support an order preventing a criminal defendant from retaining counsel of his choice. * * * The propriety of the District Court's order thus depends on whether the Government showed that the particular facts and circumstances of the multiple representation proposed in this case were such as to overcome the presumption in favor of petitioner's choice of counsel. I believe it is clear that the Government failed to make this showing. Neither Eugene Iredale's representation of Juvenal Gomez-Barajas nor Iredale's representation of Javier Bravo posed any threat of causing a conflict of interest.

     * * *

[The dissent then provided a detailed analysis of the situation of the three defendants and attorney Iredale to refute the majority's belief that a conflict of interest was a reasonable possibility. The dissent characterized the majority's views as "speculation of the most dubious kind."]

The Court gives short shrift to the actual circumstances of this case in upholding the decision below. These circumstances show that the District Court erred in denying petitioner's motion to substitute or add Iredale as defense counsel. The proposed representation did not pose a substantial risk of a serious conflict of interest. The District Court therefore had no authority to deny petitioner's Sixth Amendment right to retain counsel of his choice. This constitutional error demands that petitioner's conviction be reversed. I accordingly dissent.

[JUSTICE STEVENS wrote a brief dissenting opinion in which JUSTICE BLACKMUN joined.]

*   *   *   *   *   *   *   *   *   *

COMMENTS

[a] The scenario in this case is not likely to arise by a judge *sua sponte* calling attention to a potential conflict, but only by the prosecutor complaining. This practice gives the prosecutor an opportunity to eliminate the most competent opposing defense counsel, while not objecting to less accomplished lawyers.

[b] The existence of various limits on the right to counsel strengthens the Court's decision in this case, as imposing simply another limitation.

[c] The underlying ethic is that an attorney must give full attention and zeal to the representation of the defendant's case; a conflict of interest strikes at the heart of effective representation.

[d] The Court could have eliminated this problem, if it wanted to, by ruling that such waivers would effectively negate any grounds for appeal on the basis of conflict of interest. Such a ruling would be based on a different reading of the right to counsel under the Sixth Amendment.

[e] The decision turns on abuse of discretion. As JUSTICE MARSHALL notes, it is a difficult standard for a defendant to establish. The standard's appropriateness depends largely on how a justice views the nature of the right; the Court wants to give trial judges latitude to avoid unfair trials; the dissenters want to insure that constitutional rights not be undermined by such discretion.

AKE v. OKLAHOMA

470 U.S. 68, 105 S.Ct. 1087, 84 L.Ed.2d 53 (1985)

JUSTICE MARSHALL delivered the opinion of the Court.

The issue in this case is whether the Constitution requires that an indigent defendant have access to the psychiatric examination and assistance necessary to prepare an effective defense based on his mental condition, when his sanity at the time of the offense is seriously in question.

I

[Ake was convicted of murder and sentenced to death. His bizarre behavior led the arraigning court to have him psychiatrically examined at state expense. He was diagnosed as a probable paranoid schizophrenic and was committed to a state hospital for examination with respect to his "present sanity," *i.e.*, his competency to stand trial. He was found incompetent, but after several months of stabilization on Thorazine, an antipsychotic drug, he was found competent to stand trial. Ake's attorney, intending to present an insanity defense, requested the court either to arrange a psychiatric examination, or to provide funds to allow the defense to arrange one for his indigent client. The Court found no constitutional right for the state to provide such assistance. No inquiry had been made into Ake's sanity at the time of the offense during his 3-month stay at the state hospital, so the psychiatrists called to the stand could not comment on Ake's mental state at the time of the crime. Ake's sole defense was insanity. The jurors were instructed that "Ake was to be presumed sane at the time of the crime unless he presented evidence sufficient to raise a reasonable doubt about his sanity at that time." At the sentencing proceeding, the state relied on the testimony of the state psychiatrists who had examined Ake and who had testified at the guilt phase that he was dangerous to society. Ake had no expert witness to rebut this testimony or to introduce on his behalf evidence in mitigation of his punishment. The conviction was affirmed by the state appellate court.]

We hold that when a defendant has made a preliminary showing that his sanity at the time of the offense is likely to be a significant factor at trial, the Constitution requires that a State provide access to a psychiatrist's assistance on this issue if the defendant cannot otherwise afford one. Accordingly, we reverse.

* * *

III

This Court has long recognized that when a State brings its judicial power to bear on an indigent defendant in a criminal proceeding, it must take steps to assure that the defendant has a fair opportunity to present his defense. This elementary principle, grounded in significant part on the Fourteenth Amendment's due process guarantee of fundamental fairness, derives from the belief that justice cannot be equal where, simply as a result of his poverty, a defendant is denied the opportunity to participate meaningfully in a judicial proceeding in which his liberty is at stake. In recognition of this right, this Court held almost 30 years ago that once a State offers to criminal defendants the opportunity to appeal their cases, it must provide a trial transcript to an indigent defendant if the transcript is necessary to a decision on the merits of the appeal. *Griffin v. Illinois*, [this volume]. Since then, this Court has held that an indigent defendant may not be required to pay a fee before filing a notice of appeal of his conviction, * * * that an indigent defendant is entitled to the assistance of counsel at trial, *Gideon v. Wainwright*, [this volume], and on his first direct appeal as of right, *Douglas v. California*, [this volume], and that such assistance must be effective. * * *

Indeed, in *Little v. Streater*, 452 U.S. 1 (1981), we extended this principle of meaningful participation to a "quasi-criminal" proceeding and held that, in a paternity action, the State cannot deny the putative father blood grouping tests, if he cannot otherwise afford them.

Meaningful access to justice has been the consistent theme of these cases. We recognized long ago that mere access to the courthouse doors does not by itself assure a proper functioning of the adversary process, and that a criminal trial is fundamentally unfair if the State proceeds against an indigent defendant without making certain that he has access to the raw materials integral to the building of an effective defense. Thus, while the Court has not held that a State must purchase for the indigent defendant all the assistance that his wealthier counterpart might buy, * * * it has often reaffirmed that fundamen-

tal fairness entitles indigent defendants to "an adequate opportunity to present their claims fairly within the adversary system." * * * To implement this principle, we have focused on identifying the "basic tools of an adequate defense or appeal," * * * and we have required that such tools be provided to those defendants who cannot afford to pay for them.

To say that these basic tools must be provided is, of course, merely to begin our inquiry. In this case we must decide whether, and under what conditions, the participation of a psychiatrist is important enough to preparation of a defense to require the State to provide an indigent defendant with access to competent psychiatric assistance in preparing the defense. Three factors are relevant to this determination. The first is the private interest that will be affected by the action of the State. The second is the governmental interest that will be affected if the safeguard is to be provided. The third is the probable value of the additional or substitute procedural safeguards that are sought, and the risk of an erroneous deprivation of the affected interest if those safeguards are not provided. * * *

A

The private interest in the accuracy of a criminal proceeding that places an individual's life or liberty at risk is almost uniquely compelling. * * * We consider, next, the interest of the State. Oklahoma asserts that to provide Ake with psychiatric assistance on the record before us would result in a staggering burden to the State. * * * We are unpersuaded by this assertion. Many States, as well as the Federal

Government, currently make psychiatric assistance available to indigent defendants, and they have not found the financial burden so great as to preclude this assistance. This is especially so when the obligation of the State is limited to provision of one competent psychiatrist, as it is in many States, and as we limit the right we recognize today. [a]   At the same time, it is difficult to identify any interest of the State, other than that in its economy, that weighs against recognition of this right. The State's interest in prevailing at trial—unlike that of a private litigant—is necessarily tempered by its interest in the fair and accurate adjudication of criminal cases.   Thus, also unlike a private litigant, a State may not legitimately assert an interest in maintenance of a strategic advantage over the defense, if the result of that advantage is to cast a pall on the accuracy of the verdict obtained. [b] We therefore conclude that the governmental interest in denying Ake the assistance of a psychiatrist is not substantial, in light of the compelling interest of both the State and the individual in accurate dispositions.

Last, we inquire into the probable value of the psychiatric assistance sought, and the risk of error in the proceeding if such assistance is not offered. We begin by considering the pivotal role that psychiatry has come to play in criminal proceedings. More than 40 States, as well as the Federal Government, have decided either through legislation or judicial decision that indigent defendants are entitled, under certain circumstances, to the assistance of a psychiatrist's expertise. * * * And in many States that have not assured access to psychiatrists through the legislative process, state courts have interpreted the State or Federal Constitution to require that psychiatric assistance be provided to indigent defendants when necessary for an adequate defense, or when insanity is at issue.

These statutes and court decisions reflect a reality that we recognize today, namely, that when the State has made the defendant's mental condition relevant to his criminal culpability and to the punishment he might suffer, the assistance of a psychiatrist may well be crucial to the defendant's ability to marshal his defense.   [JUSTICE MARSHALL here discusses the role that psychiatrists play in criminal cases.] * * * Through this process of investigation, interpretation, and testimony, psychiatrists ideally assist lay jurors, who generally have no training in psychiatric matters, to make a sensible and educated determination about the mental condition of the defendant at the time of the offense.

Psychiatry is not, however, an exact science, and psychiatrists disagree widely and frequently on what constitutes mental illness, on the appropriate diagnosis to be attached to given behavior and symptoms, on cure and treatment, and on likelihood of future dangerousness. Perhaps because there often is no single, accurate psychiatric conclusion on legal insanity in a given case, juries remain the primary factfinders on this issue, and they must resolve differences in opinion within the psychiatric profession on the basis of the evidence offered by each party. When jurors make this determination about issues that inevitably are complex and foreign, the testimony of psychiatrists can be crucial and "a virtual necessity if an insanity plea is to have any chance of success." By organizing a defendant's mental history, examination results and behavior, and other information, interpreting it in light of their expertise, and then laying out their investigative and analytic process to the jury, the psychiatrists for each party enable the jury to make its most accurate determination of the truth on the issue before them. It is for this reason that States rely on psychiatrists as examiners, consultants, and witnesses, and that private individuals do as well, when they can afford to do so. In so saying, we neither approve nor disapprove the widespread reliance on psychiatrists but instead recognize the unfairness of a contrary holding in light of the evolving practice.

The foregoing leads inexorably to the conclusion that, without the assistance of a psychiatrist to conduct a professional examination on issues relevant to the defense, to help determine whether the insanity defense is viable, to present testimony, and to assist in preparing the cross-examination of a State's psychiatric witnesses, the risk of an inaccurate resolution of sanity issues is extremely high. With such assistance, the defendant is fairly able to present at least enough information to the jury, in a meaningful manner, as to permit it to make a sensible determination.

[To come within the right, a defendant must be] able to make an *ex parte* threshold showing to the trial court that his sanity is likely to be a significant factor in his defense [and] the need for the assistance of a psychiatrist is readily apparent. It is in such cases that a defense may be devastated by the absence of a psychiatric examination and testimony; with such assistance, the defendant might have a reasonable chance of success.

In such a circumstance, where the potential accuracy of the jury's determination is so dramatically enhanced, and where the interests of the individual and the State in an accurate proceeding are substantial, the State's interest in its fisc must yield.

We therefore hold that when a defendant demonstrates to the trial judge that his sanity at the time of the offense is to be a significant factor at trial, the State must, at a minimum, assure the defendant access to a competent psychiatrist who will conduct an appropriate examination and assist in evaluation, preparation, and presentation of the defense. This is not to say, of course, that the indigent defendant has a constitutional right to choose a psychiatrist of his personal liking or to receive funds to hire his own. Our concern is that the indigent defendant have access to a competent psychiatrist for the purpose we have discussed, and as in the case of the provision of counsel we leave to the States the decision on how to implement this right.

B

[A defendant at a capital sentencing proceeding must have the means to counter a prosecution argument of the defendant's dangerousness.]
* * * In such a circumstance, where the consequence of error is so great, the relevance of responsive psychiatric testimony so evident, and the burden on the State so slim, due process requires access to a psychiatric examination on relevant issues, to the testimony of the psychiatrist, and to assistance in preparation at the sentencing phase.

[In Part C the Court found no

precedent in opposition to its ruling and in Part IV the Court found that due process required the appointment of a psychiatrist in this case. A new trial was ordered.]

[CHIEF JUSTICE BURGER concurred in the judgment.]

JUSTICE REHNQUIST, dissenting.

The Court holds that "when a defendant has made a preliminary showing that his sanity at the time of the offense is likely to be a significant factor at trial, the Constitution requires that a State provide access to a psychiatrist's assistance on this issue if the defendant cannot otherwise afford one." * * * I do not think that the facts of this case warrant the establishment of such a principle; and I think that even if the factual predicate of the Court's statement were established, the constitutional rule announced by the Court is far too broad. I would limit the rule to capital cases, and make clear that the entitlement is to an independent psychiatric evaluation, not to a defense consultant.

* * *

* * * * * * * * * * *

COMMENTS

[a] This ruling emphasized the point made frequently in the "equality" cases: that the state need not put the indigent on an equal footing with a wealthy defendant. While there may be a significant difference between one competent psychiatrist provided to an indigent compared to a battery of high paid experts that a very wealthy defendant could afford, the single expert will be sufficient to provide the indigent defendant with a trial that is fundamentally fair.

[b] This basic rule regarding the prosecutor's role limits any pure theory of an adversarial system; the prosecutor is both an advocate and a public officer of justice.

BOUNDS v. SMITH

430 U.S. 817, 97 S.Ct. 1491, 52 L.Ed.2d 72 (1977)

MR. JUSTICE MARSHALL delivered the opinion of the Court.

The issue in this case is whether States must protect the right of prisoners to access to the courts by providing them with law libraries or alternative sources of legal knowledge. In *Younger v. Gilmore*, 404 U.S. 15 (1971), we held *per curiam* that such services are constitutionally mandated. [a] Petitioners, officials of the State of North Carolina, ask us to overrule that recent case, but for reasons explained below, we decline the invitation and reaffirm our previous decision.

I

[North Carolina prison inmates filed civil rights actions under 42 U.S.C. §1983 alleging that they were denied access to the courts in violation of their Fourteenth Amendment rights by the state's failure to provide legal research facilities. [b] A District Court held that a single prison library for a decentralized prison system of seventy-seven facilities in sixty-six counties was "severely inadequate" and violated the prisoners' equal protection rights because some prisoners had no access to legal materials. Given the complexity of providing court access, (whether by providing lawyers, law students, public defenders or law libraries), the court allowed the state to develop a response. The state plan was for establishing seven libraries, staffed with inmates trained as legal researchers, in institutions located across the state; when prisoners in other facilities needed to use a law library, they would be transported to one of the seven facilities and be provided with necessary materials; 350 prisoners a week could be accommodated. Respondents argue that this is inadequate. The state plan was upheld by the District Court.]

In its final decision, the District Court held that petitioners were not constitutionally required to provide legal assistance as well as libraries. It found that the library plan was sufficient to give inmates reasonable access to the courts and that our decision in *Ross v. Moffitt*, [this volume], while not directly in point, supported the State's claim that it need not furnish attorneys to bring habeas corpus and civil rights actions for prisoners.

* * *

Both sides appealed from those portions of the District Court orders adverse to them. The Court of Appeals for the Fourth Circuit affirmed in all respects save one. It found that the library plan denied women prisoners the same access rights as men to research facilities. Since there was no justification for this discrimination, the Court of Appeals ordered it eliminated. The State petitioned for review and we granted certiorari. * * * We affirm.

II

A. It is now established beyond doubt that prisoners have a constitutional right of access to the courts. This Court recognized that right more than 35 years ago when it struck down a regulation prohibiting state prisoners from filing petitions for habeas corpus unless they were found "'properly drawn'" by the "'legal investigator'" for the parole board. *Ex parte Hull*, 312 U.S. 546 (1941). We held this violated the principle that "the state and its officers may not abridge or impair petitioner's right to apply to a federal court for a writ of habeas corpus." * * *

More recent decisions have struck down restrictions and required remedial measures to insure that inmate access to the courts is adequate, effective, and meaningful. Thus, in order to prevent "effectively foreclosed access," indigent prisoners must be allowed to file appeals and habeas corpus petitions without payment of docket fees. * * * Because we recognized that "adequate and effective appellate review" is impossible without a trial transcript or adequate substitute, we held that States must provide trial records to inmates unable to buy them. *Griffin v. Illinois*, [this volume]. Similarly, counsel must be appointed to give indigent inmates "a meaningful appeal" from their convictions. *Douglas v. California*, [this volume].

Essentially the same standards of access were applied in *Johnson v. Avery*, 393 U.S. 483 (1969), which struck down a regulation prohibiting prisoners from assisting each other with habeas corpus applications and other legal matters. Since inmates had no alternative form of legal assistance available to them, we reasoned that this ban on jailhouse lawyers effectively prevented prisoners who were "unable themselves, with reasonable adequacy, to prepare their petitions," from challenging the legality of their confine-

ments. * * * *Johnson* was unanimously extended to cover assistance in civil rights actions in *Wolff v. McDonnell*, 418 U.S. 539, 577-580 (1974). And even as it rejected a claim that indigent defendants have a constitutional right to appointed counsel for discretionary appeals, the Court reaffirmed that States must "assure the indigent defendant an adequate opportunity to present his claims fairly." * * * "[M]eaningful access" to the courts is the touchstone. * * * [c]

Petitioners contend, however, that this constitutional duty merely obliges States to allow inmate "writ writers" to function. They argue that under *Johnson v. Avery*, *supra*, as long as inmate communications on legal problems are not restricted, there is no further obligation to expend state funds to implement affirmatively the right of access. This argument misreads the cases.

In *Johnson* and *Wolff v. McDonnell*, *supra*, the issue was whether the access rights of ignorant and illiterate inmates were violated without adequate justification. Since these inmates were unable to present their own claims in writing to the courts, we held that their "constitutional right to help," * * * required at least allowing assistance from their literate fellows. But in so holding, we did not attempt to set forth the full breadth of the right of access. In *McDonnell*, for example, there was already an adequate law library in the prison. The case was thus decided against a backdrop of availability of legal information to those inmates capable of using it. And in *Johnson*, although the petitioner originally requested lawbooks, * * * the Court did not reach the question, as it invalidated the regulation because of its effect on illiterate inmates. Neither case considered the question we face today and neither is inconsistent with requiring additional measures to assure meaningful access to inmates able to present their own cases.

Moreover, our decisions have consistently required States to shoulder affirmative obligations to assure all prisoners meaningful access to the courts. It is indisputable that indigent inmates must be provided at state expense with paper and pen to draft legal documents, with notarial services to authenticate them, and with stamps to mail them. States must forgo collection of docket fees otherwise payable to the treasury and expend funds for transcripts. State expenditures are necessary to pay lawyers for indigent defendants at trial, * * * and in appeals as of right. * * * This is not to say that economic factors may not be considered, for example, in choosing the methods used to provide meaningful access. But the cost of protecting a constitutional right cannot justify its total denial. Thus, neither the availability of jailhouse lawyers nor the necessity for affirmative state action is dispositive of respondents' claims. The inquiry is rather whether law libraries or other forms of legal assistance are needed to give prisoners a reasonably adequate opportunity to present claimed violations of fundamental constitutional rights to the courts.

B. [A law library is necessary for the legal task confronting prisoners in filing petitions of habeas corpus, as these petitions raise many technical issues of law. Furthermore, prisoners are capable of utilizing law libraries.]

* * *

We hold, therefore, that the funda-mental constitutional right of access to the courts requires prison authorities to assist inmates in the preparation and filing of meaningful legal papers by providing prisoners with adequate law libraries or adequate assistance from persons trained in the law.

C.   * * *

[The Court detailed some of the ways in which prison systems have provided legal access to prisoners, including training inmates as lawyers' paralegal assistants, using law students and volunteer attorneys, hiring lawyers as part time consultants, and hiring full-time staff attorneys.] Nevertheless, a legal access program need not include any particular element we have discussed, and we encourage local experimentation. Any plan, however, must be evaluated as a whole to ascertain its compliance with constitutional standards.

III

Finally, petitioners urge us to reverse the decision below because federal courts should not "sit as co-administrators of state prisons," * * * and because the District Court "exceeded its powers when it puts [sic] itself in the place of the [prison] administrators." * * * While we have recognized that judicial restraint is often appropriate in prisoners' rights cases, we have also repeatedly held that this policy "cannot encompass any failure to take cognizance of valid constitutional claims." * * *

Petitioners' hyperbolic claim is particularly inappropriate in this case, for the courts below scrupulously respected the limits on their role. The District Court initially held only that petitioners had violated the "fundamental constitutional guarantee," * * * of access to the courts. It did not thereupon thrust itself into prison administration. Rather, it ordered petitioners themselves to devise a remedy for the violation, strongly suggesting that it would prefer a plan providing trained legal advisors. Petitioners chose to establish law libraries, however, and their plan was approved with only minimal changes over the strong objections of respondents. Prison administrators thus exercised wide discretion within the bounds of constitutional requirements in this case.

The judgment is

Affirmed.

[JUSTICE POWELL concurred.]

[CHIEF JUSTICE BURGER dissented, emphasizing the practical difficulties raised by the decision. JUSTICE STEWART, joined by THE CHIEF JUSTICE, also wrote a brief dissenting opinion.]

MR. JUSTICE REHNQUIST, with whom THE CHIEF JUSTICE joins, dissenting.

* * *

There is nothing in the United States Constitution which requires that a convict serving a term of imprisonment in a state penal institution pursuant to a final judgment of a court of competent jurisdiction have a "right of access" to the federal courts in order to attack his sentence. [All that *Ex parte Hull* guaranteed is that prison authorities do not ban, censor, or seriously interfere with a prisoner's efforts to write and file a writ of habeas corpus with a court.]

A number of succeeding cases have expanded on this barebones holding that an incarcerated prisoner has a right of physical access to a federal court in order to petition that court for relief which Congress has authorized it to grant. * * * Some [cases], such as *Griffin*, *supra*, and *Douglas v. California*, [this volume] appear to depend upon the principle that indigent convicts must be given a meaningful opportunity to pursue a state-created right to appeal, even though the pursuit of such a remedy requires that the State must provide a transcript or furnish counsel. Others, such as *Johnson v. Avery*, * * * depend on the principle that the State, having already incarcerated the convict and thereby virtually eliminated his contact with people outside the prison walls, may not further limit contacts which would otherwise be permitted simply because such contacts would aid the incarcerated prisoner in preparation of a petition seeking judicial relief from the conditions or terms of his confinement. Clearly neither of these principles supports the Court's present holding: The prisoners here in question have all pursued all avenues of direct appeal available to them from their judgments of conviction, and North Carolina imposes no invidious regulations which allow visits from all persons except those knowledgeable in the law. All North Carolina has done in this case is to decline to expend public funds to make available law libraries to those who are incarcerated within its penitentiaries.

If respondents' constitutional arguments were grounded on the Equal Protection Clause, and were in effect that rich prisoners could employ attorneys who could in turn consult law libraries and prepare petitions for habeas corpus, whereas indigent prisoners could not, they would have superficial appeal. * * * I believe that they would nonetheless fail under *Ross v. Moffitt*. * * * There we held that although our earlier cases had required the State to provide meaningful access to state-created judicial remedies for indigents, the only right on direct appeal was that indigents have an adequate opportunity to present their claims fairly within the adversary system. * * * [d]

In any event, the Court's opinion today does not appear to proceed upon the guarantee of equal protection of the laws, a guarantee which at least has the merit of being found in the Fourteenth Amendment to the Constitution. It proceeds instead to enunciate a fundamental constitutional right of access to the courts, * * * which is found nowhere in the Constitution. But if a prisoner incarcerated pursuant to a final judgment of conviction is not prevented from physical access to the federal courts in order that he may file therein petitions for relief which Congress has authorized those courts to grant, he has been accorded the only constitutional right of access to the courts that our cases have articulated in a reasoned way. * * * Respondents here make no additional

claims that prison regulations invidiously deny them access to those with knowledge of the law so that such regulations would be inconsistent with *Johnson*. * * * Since none of these reasons is present here, the fundamental constitutional right of access to the courts which the Court announces today is created virtually out of whole cloth with little or no reference to the Constitution from which it is supposed to be derived. [e]

Our decisions have recognized on more than one occasion that lawful imprisonment properly results in a retraction [of rights] justified by the considerations underlying our penal system. * * * A convicted prisoner who has exhausted his avenues of direct appeal is no longer to be accorded every presumption of innocence, and his former constitutional liberties may be substantially restricted by the exigencies of the incarceration in which he has been placed. * * * [The logical result of the majority's opinion is that prisoners pursuing appeals must be afforded free lawyers.]

I do not believe anything in the Constitution requires this result, although state and federal penal institutions might as a matter of policy think it wise to implement such a program. * * *

* * * * * * * * * * *

COMMENTS

[a] Some *per curiam* decisions include a written opinion, but for various reasons, do not include a judicial author. Paradoxically, these unsigned opinions of the entire court include routine, run-of-the-mill orders on the one hand and some of the most important decisions on the other. In this case, the *per curiam* decision included no explanatory opinion. This causes some concern that the Court is ruling by fiat, rather than by that explanation that gives legitimacy to caselaw.

[b] The Sixth Amendment right to counsel applies only "[i]n all criminal prosecutions. * * *" As the criminal prosecution, including appeals, has concluded, the Amendment does not apply to prisoners. Therefore, other avenues of relief have been sought.

[c] The cases guaranteeing the right to counsel to persons charged with crime are based in part on the value to the entire society of having justice administered fairly. The meaningful access basis of the rights of prisoners to legal assistance is also based not only on specific benefits and guarantees to prisoners, but on the societal interest in insuring that prisons operate in a constitutional manner.

[d] This statement is cryptic; the "earlier case" that logically preceded *Ross* was *Douglas v. California* [this volume] which held that *counsel* was required on first appeal. It is possible that JUSTICE REHNQUIST was here attempting to shift the understanding of that case so as to eventually overrule it.

[e] It is one thing for cases to expand on the vague words of a Constitutional right. JUSTICE REHNQUIST asserts that the caselaw has no Constitutional foundation. Do you agree?

Chapter Six

CONFESSIONS

Statements obtained from criminal suspects are a very important part of criminal investigation and prosecution. They also raise profoundly serious questions about the fairness and the accuracy of this process. The dilemma is one of the oldest in the criminal process. In many of the most serious crimes, such as murder, there is no conclusive physical or eyewitness evidence against a suspect. Yet, circumstantial evidence points strongly at one person. That person is likely to know more about the offense than others, but he refuses to talk or appears to tell an implausible story. If questioning were prohibited crimes which rip the fabric of society go unpunished. But the history of inquisition, including the regular and lawful use of *judicial* torture in ancient Greece and Rome and in medieval Europe, raises the chilling reality of the unbridled power of State questioning. Indeed, the systematic and ruthless application of psychological pressure makes it probable that innocent persons can be made to confess to crimes they did not commit.

American constitutional law has approached this dilemma by trying to "tame" the confession process by applying judicial limits but not by abolishing the practice. Three separate doctrines have been applied to cases involving suspect's statements: due process (Fifth and Fourteenth Amendments) and the privilege against self-incrimination (Fifth Amendment) for suspects not yet formally charged and the right to counsel (Sixth Amendment) for persons formally charged. Due process cases tended to interfere the least with police practices of interrogation and the Sixth Amendment cases interfere the most.

In medieval and early modern England two major legal traditions—the common law and the civil law systems—operated side by side. In common law courts (*i.e.*, the courts of Common Pleas and King's Bench) testimony was given in open court, verdicts were rendered by a jury and torture was not used. By the Seventeenth Century the rule emerged that a defendant was privileged to not tell what he knew about a crime, *i.e.*, was not required to assist in his own prosecution. The burden of proving guilt fell on the prosecutor, whether a State prosecutor or a private party. At the same time civil law courts such as ecclesiastical (church) courts and prerogative courts of the crown (*e.g.*, the court of star chamber) could question witnesses and parties in secrecy, did not use juries and had the power to use torture to compel the truth from parties.

The victory of Parliament at the end of the Seventeenth Century over the theory and practice of autocratic government also spelled a victory for the common law courts and abolition (*e.g.*, star chamber) or diminution of the jurisdiction of other courts. With the theory of the common law ascendant in the eighteenth century a rule emerged in respect to the pretrial questioning of criminal suspects. By the early nineteenth century it was established law both in England and in the United States that compelled confessions were not admissible in a person's trial. This rule was recognized in federal law (*Bram v. United States*, 168 U.S. 532 (1897)) under the Fifth Amendment rule against self-incrimination.

Thus, when the Supreme Court decided its first *state* confession case, holding in *Brown v. Mississippi* (1936) that a confession obtained by torture violates the Fourteenth Amendment due process clause, it was building on a long legal tradition. This doctrine was extended to non-physical pressure in *Ashcraft v. Tennessee* (1944) where 36 straight hours of questioning was held to offend due process. From the *Brown* decision in 1936 to the *Miranda* case three decades later the Court decided over 30 state confessions cases. In that period it held that a variety of pressure techniques violated due process, such a moving a suspect from one jail to another so that he could not be contacted by family or friends (*Ward v. Texas*, 316 U.S. 547 (1942)); keeping the suspect naked for many hours (*Malinsky v. New York*, 325 U.S. 401 (1945)); holding a suspect for five days without bringing him to a magistrate and subjecting him to relay questioning (*Watts v. Indiana*, 338 U.S. 49 (1949)); having a psychiatrist tell the suspect that he was going to help him (*Leyra v. Denno*, 347 U.S. 556 (1954)); letting a suspect believe that if he confessed he would be saved from a lynch mob (*Payne v. Arkansas*, 356 U.S. 560 (1958)); having a police officer who was an old friend of a suspect tell him that the officer would lose his job if the suspect did not cooperate (*Spano v. New York* (1959)); the use of "truth serum" (*Townsend v. Sain*, 372 U.S. 293 (1963)); and telling a mother that her parental rights would be terminated if she did not talk (*Lynumn v. Illinois*, 372 U.S. 528 (1963)).

As the cases developed the Court put forward more than one theory for the holdings. The more outrageous violations were seen as uncivilized standards not to be tolerated under the flag of fundamental fairness. The cases also raised the fear that undue pressure, not simply torture, could be used to squeeze confessions out of the mouths of innocent suspects by well trained officers who, as zealous participants, lacked objectivity. Finally, the cases also adopted the rationale that even where a coerced confession was consonant with objective evidence, it must be excluded because police must obey the rule of law (*Blackburn v. Alabama*, 361 U.S. 199 (1960); *Rogers v. Richmond*, 365 U.S. 534 (1961)).

The due process clause has not been entirely eclipsed by the application of the Fifth Amendment to confessions after *Miranda*. Statements taken in violation of *Miranda* may be admissible for purposes of impeachment of a witness (*Harris v. New York*, 401 U.S. 222 (1971); *Oregon v. Hass*, 420 U.S. 714 (1975)), but statements that are coerced are not admissible for any purpose (*Mincey v. Arizona* (1978)). Incriminating statements made voluntarily to an undercover agent are not subject to the *Miranda* rule (*Illinois v. Perkins* (1990)) but are not admissible if they are coerced

(*Arizona v. Fulminante* (1991)). *Fulminante* held that the confession in that case was coerced and that its admission influenced the jury and so was not harmless error. However, *Fulminante* also upset what was thought to be a well established rule (*Payne v. Arkansas, supra; Chapman v. California*, 386 U.S. 18 (1967)) by holding, in the abstract, that coerced confessions may be subject to harmless error analysis.

Dissatisfaction with the totality of circumstances adjudication methodology in the due process-confessions cases led the Court to seek other devices to curb overbearing behavior in the interrogation process. In federal cases, for example, the Court excluded statements taken from suspects who had not been brought to a magistrate promptly (*McNabb v. United States*, 318 U.S. 332 (1943); *Mallory v. United States*, 354 U.S. 449 (1957)). Attempts to establish a firm rule that suspects must have the right to counsel at the interrogation stage at first failed to gain a majority of the Court (*Crooker v. California*, 357 U.S. 433 (1958); *Cicenia v. LaGay*, 357 U.S. 504 (1958)). But in *Escobedo v. Illinois*, 378 U.S. 478 (1964), the Court broke new ground by holding, under the right to counsel, that an otherwise voluntary confession was inadmissible when a lawyer's request to see his client (after the client saw and tried to speak to the attorney) was denied.

These approaches were superseded by *Miranda v. Arizona* (1966) which held that a suspect subjected to custodial compulsion who is interrogated is protected by the Fifth Amendment right against self-incrimination; to make the right effective the suspect must be informed of the right and be given an opportunity to waive the right. The *Miranda* rule and its four warnings became the centerpiece of confessions law and generated many cases to interpret it. *Miranda* was the high point and centerpiece of a liberal interpretation of the Bill of Rights. That interpretation was undercut by a more conservative reading of *Miranda* in *Michigan v. Tucker* (1974), which allowed the introduction of evidence derived from statements given after defective *Miranda* warnings on the theory that the *Miranda* warnings were not themselves constitutional rights but merely protective devices of the underlying right against self-incrimination. This interpretation led to several rulings that allowed the use of evidence obtained after defective *Miranda* warnings. In *Oregon v. Elstad* (1985) an incriminating statement was obtained during interrogation where no *Miranda* warnings were given. A second statement obtained after properly administered *Miranda* warnings was held admissible. *New York v. Quarles* (1984) created an exception to *Miranda*, allowing into evidence statements obtained without warnings where the question was prompted by a need to insure "public safety."

Miranda applies when a person is in custody because police custody provides an element of compulsion that is required by the Fifth Amendment. A person surrounded and held captive in his own home is in custody (*Orozco v. Texas*, 394 U.S. 324 (1969)) while a person politely questioned at home by officers is not in custody (*Beckwith v. United States*, 425 U.S. 341 (1976)). Likewise, a person who voluntarily appears at a police station, at police request but at his own convenience, is not in custody (*Oregon v. Mathieson*, 429 U.S. 492 (1977)). *Berkemer v. McCarty*, 468 U.S. 420 (1984) held that *Miranda* does not apply to ordinary traffic stops because the kind of compulsion that derives from the secrecy of police custody does not usually occur in on-the-street stops for traffic violations. When a driver is stopped for investigation of driving while intoxicated, no *Miranda* warnings are necessary before ordering the suspect to perform physical tests of sobriety; warnings are required if a question is asked that has testimonial content, such as asking the suspect the date of his sixth birthday (*Pennsylvania v. Muniz* (1990)). *Muniz* established a "routine booking exception" to *Miranda*. A purely voluntary admission by a person to the police without any custody or interrogation is not covered by *Miranda* and such a statement is admissible (*Colorado v. Connelly*, 479 U.S. 157 (1986)).

Interrogation is defined as direct questioning or its functional equivalent, *i.e.*, any words that the police should know are reasonably likely to elicit an incriminating response from a suspect. A conversation among police in the presence of a suspect that led him to make an incriminating admission is not interrogation (*Rhode Island v. Innis* (1980)). Nor is it interrogation where the police allowed a wife to speak to her husband soon after his arrest on charges of murdering his child, with his full knowledge that the conversation would be monitored by the police; the incriminating statements were not the product of interrogation and they were admissible (*Arizona v. Mauro*, 481 U.S. 520 (1987)).

The state has the burden of proving that a waiver of the right to silence was voluntary. A waiver of rights will not be presumed simply because a defendant made statements after being read *Miranda* warnings (*Tague v. Louisiana*, 444 U.S. 469 (1980)). Waiver is never inferred from silence, but the normal practice of obtaining an express written or oral statement of waiver is not an absolute prerequisite for a valid waiver (*North Carolina v. Butler*, 441 U.S. 369 (1979)).

When a suspect indicates that she does not wish to be interrogated, the questioning must stop. But where the police initiate questioning for a different crime, after again administering *Miranda* warnings and after some time has elapsed, incriminating statements are admissible (*Michigan v. Mosley* (1975)).

A more stringent resumption of questioning rule applies when a suspect requests an attorney; in such case all questioning must cease and the police may not reinterrogate the suspect for the same (*Edwards v. Arizona* (1981)) or different (*Arizona v. Roberson*, 486 U.S. 675 (1988)) crimes unless the suspect "himself initiates further communication, exchanges or conversations with the police." In *Oregon v. Bradshaw*, 462 U.S. 1039 (1983), the Court held that the suspect initiates further conversation by asking, "Well, what is going to happen to me now?" Once a suspect has requested counsel, answering questions about the *Miranda* warnings does not constitute initiating a communication with the police and any incriminating statements are inadmissible (*Smith v. Illinois*, 469 U.S. (1984)). A suspect in custody who does not know that his family had retained a lawyer and who has not invoked the right to counsel does not get the benefit of the *Edwards* rule, even if the attorney contacted the police and was wrongly told that the suspect would not be questioned (*Moran v. Burbine* (1986)).

The last line of cases that respond to police interrogation arise under the Sixth Amendment right to counsel, which applies to a "criminal prosecution" *after* a suspect has been formally charged with a crime. When that occurs the relationship between the State and the individual changes, and the defendant is entitled to a lawyer's help. *Massiah v. United States* (1964) established this rule and declared inadmissible statements obtained from an indicted suspect by an undercover agent who set up a conversation designed to elicit incriminating statements.

The *Massiah* rule was applied in *Brewer v. Williams* (1977). An arraigned murder suspect with a history of mental illness was driven on a 160 mile trip to the place of trial and during the trip subjected to a "Christian burial speech" that was reasonably designed to elicit an incriminating statement. The fact that *Miranda* warnings are administered does not dissipate the violation of the defendant's Sixth Amendment rights. Several cases have since arisen where secret informants have been "planted" with an indicted suspect, either in or out of jail, and were told to listen for incriminating statements. Such jail statements were thrown out in *United States v. Henry*, 447 U.S. 264 (1980) because they were directly elicited by the informant's conversation; but non-elicited incriminating statements to a jail mate who is a passive listener are admissible (*Kuhlman v. Wilson*, (1986)). The *Massiah* rule barred the introduction of incriminating statements when an informant approached an indicted defendant after they were released from jail, and engaged him in conversations about his pending case. In this case the informant was investigating crimes for which the defendant had not yet been charged, but statements made as to the charged crimes were not admissible (*Maine v. Moulton*, 474 U.S. 159 (1985)). Statements obtained in violation of a suspect's right to counsel may be admitted to impeach the testimony of the defendant (*Michigan v. Harvey* (1990)).

BROWN v. MISSISSIPPI

297 U.S. 278, 56 S.Ct. 461, 80 L.Ed. 682 (1936)

MR. CHIEF JUSTICE HUGHES delivered the opinion of the Court.

The question in this case is whether convictions, which rest solely upon confessions shown to have been extorted by officers of the State by brutality and violence, are consistent with the due process of law required by the Fourteenth Amendment of the Constitution of the United States.

Petitioners were indicted for the murder of one Raymond Stewart, whose death occurred on March 30, 1934. They were indicted on April 4, 1934, and were then arraigned and pleaded not guilty. Counsel were appointed by the court to defend them. Trial was begun the next morning and was concluded on the following day, when they were found guilty and sentenced to death. [a]

Aside from the confessions, there was no evidence sufficient to warrant the submission of the case to the jury. [The defendants objected to the confession on voluntariness grounds, but the jury found defendants guilty despite instructions to consider the voluntariness of the confessions. The Mississippi Supreme Court sustained the conviction and determined that the confession did not violate the due process clause of the Fourteenth Amendment.] Two judges dissented. * * * We granted a writ of certiorari.

The grounds of the decision were (1) that immunity from self-incrimination is not essential to due process of law, and (2) that the failure of the trial court to exclude the confessions after the introduction of evidence showing their incompetency, in the absence of a request for such exclusion, did not deprive the defendants of life or liberty without due process of law; and that even if the trial court had erroneously overruled a motion to exclude the confessions, the ruling would have been mere error reversible on appeal, but not a violation of constitutional right. * * *

The opinion of the state court did not set forth the evidence as to the circumstances in which the confessions were procured. That the evidence established that they were procured by coercion was not questioned. The state court said: "After the state closed its case on the merits, the appellants, for the first time, introduced evidence from which it appears that the confessions were not made voluntarily but were coerced." * * * There is no dispute as to the facts upon this point and as they are clearly and adequately stated in the dissenting opinion of Judge Griffith (with whom Judge Anderson concurred)—showing both the extreme brutality of the measures to extort the confessions and the participation of the state authorities—we quote this part of his opinion in full, as follows: * * *

"The crime with which these defendants, all ignorant negroes, are charged, was discovered about one o'clock p.m. on Friday, March 30, 1934. On that night one Dial, a deputy sheriff, accompanied by others, came to the home of Ellington, one of the defendants, and requested him to accompany them to the house of the deceased, and there a number of white men were gathered, who began to accuse the defendant of the crime. Upon his denial they seized him, and with the participation of the deputy they hanged him by a rope to the limb of a tree, and having let him down, they hung him again, and when he was let down the second time, and he still protested his innocence, he was tied to a tree and whipped, and still declining to accede to the demands that he confess, he was finally released and he returned with some difficulty to his home, suffering intense pain and agony. The record of the testimony shows that the signs of the rope on his neck were plainly visible during the so-called trial. A day or two thereafter the said deputy, accompanied by another, returned to the home of the said defendant and arrested him, and departed with the prisoner towards the jail in an adjoining county, but went by a route which led into the State of Alabama; and while on the way, in that State, the deputy stopped and again severely whipped the defendant, declaring that he would continue the whipping until he confessed, and the defendant then agreed to confess to such a statement as the deputy would dictate, and he did so, after which he was delivered to jail.

"The other two defendants, Ed Brown and Henry Shields, were also arrested and taken to the same jail. On Sunday night, April 1, 1934, the same deputy, accompanied by a number of white men, one of whom was also an officer,

and by the jailer, came to the jail, and the two last named defendants were made to strip and they were laid over chairs and their backs were cut to pieces with a leather strap with buckles on it, and they were likewise made by the said deputy definitely to understand that the whipping would be continued unless and until they confessed, and not only confessed, but confessed in every matter of detail as demanded by those present; and in this manner the defendants confessed the crime, and as the whippings progressed and were repeated, they changed or adjusted their confession in all particulars of detail so as to conform to the demands of their torturers. When the confessions had been obtained in the exact form and contents as desired by the mob, they left with the parting admonition and warning that, if the defendants changed their story at any time in any respect from that last stated, the perpetrators of the outrage would administer the same or equally effective treatment.

"Further details of the brutal treatment to which these helpless prisoners were subjected need not be pursued. It is sufficient to say that in pertinent respects the transcript reads more like pages torn from some medieval account, than a record made within the confines of a modern civilization which aspires to an enlightened constitutional government.

"[On the next day] when the defendants had been given time to recuperate somewhat from the tortures to which they had been subjected, [formal confessions were taken by the sheriffs.] Nevertheless the solemn farce of hearing the free and voluntary confessions was gone through with, and these two sheriffs and one other person then present were the three witnesses used in court to establish the so-called confessions, which were received by the court and admitted in evidence over the objections of the defendants duly entered of record as each of the said three witnesses delivered their alleged testimony. There was thus enough before the court when these confessions were first offered to make known to the court that they were not, beyond all reasonable doubt, free and voluntary; and the failure of the court then to exclude the confessions is sufficient to reverse the judgment, under every rule of procedure that has heretofore been prescribed, and hence it was not necessary subsequently to renew the objections by motion or otherwise.

* * *

"[At the trial evidence of the beatings of the defendants was produced.] The defendants were put on the stand, and by their testimony the facts and the details thereof as to the manner by which the confessions were extorted from them were fully developed. * * * [The] deputy was put on the stand by the state in rebuttal, and admitted the whippings. It is interesting to note that in his testimony with reference to the whipping of the defendant Ellington, and in response to the inquiry as to how severely he was whipped, the deputy stated, 'Not too much for a negro; not as much as I would have done if it were left to me.' Two others who had participated in these whippings were introduced and admitted it—not a single witness was introduced who denied it. The facts are not only undisputed, they are admitted, and admitted to have been done by officers of the state, in conjunction with other participants, and all this was definitely well known to everybody connected with the trial, and during the trial, including the state's prosecuting attorney and the trial judge presiding." [b]

1. The State stresses the statement in *Twining v. New Jersey*, 211 U.S. 78, 114, that "exemption from compulsory self-incrimination in the courts of the States is not secured by any part of the Federal Constitution," and the statement in *Snyder v. Massachusetts*, 291 U.S. 97, 105, that "the privilege against self-incrimination may be withdrawn and the accused put upon the stand as a witness for the State." But the question of the right of the State to withdraw the privilege against self-incrimination is not here involved. The compulsion to which the quoted statements refer is that of the processes of justice by which the accused may be called as a witness and required to testify. Compulsion by torture to extort a confession is a different matter.

The State is free to regulate the procedure of its courts in accordance with its own conceptions of policy, unless in so doing it "offends some principle of justice so rooted in the traditions and conscience of our people as to be ranked as fundamental." * * * The State may abolish trial by jury.

[c] It may dispense with indictment by a grand jury and substitute complaint or information. * * * *Hurtado v. California*, 110 U.S. 516. * * * But the freedom of the State in establishing its policy is the freedom of constitutional government and is limited by the requirement of due process of law. Because a State may dispense with a jury trial, it does not follow that it may substitute trial by ordeal. The rack and torture chamber may not be substituted for the witness stand. The State may not permit an accused to be hurried to conviction under mob domination—where the whole proceeding is but a mask—without supplying corrective process. *Moore v. Dempsey* [this volume]. **[d]** The State may not deny to the accused the aid of counsel. *Powell v. Alabama* [this volume]. Nor may a State, through the action of its officers, contrive a conviction through the pretense of a trial which in truth is "but used as a means of depriving a defendant of liberty through a deliberate deception of court and jury by the presentation of testimony known to be perjured." *Mooney v. Holohan*, 294 U.S. 103, 112 [1935]. And the trial equally is a mere pretense where the state authorities have contrived a conviction resting solely upon confessions obtained by violence. The due process clause requires "that state action, whether through one agency or another, shall be consistent with the fundamental principles of liberty and justice which lie at the base of all our civil and political institutions." *Hebert v. Louisiana*, 272 U.S. 312, 316. It would be difficult to conceive of methods more revolting to the sense of justice than those taken to procure the confessions of these petitioners, and the use of the confessions thus obtained as the basis for conviction and sentence was a clear denial of due process.

* * *

* * * The [Mississippi] court thus denied a federal right fully established and specially set up and claimed and the judgment must be

Reversed.

* * * * * * * * * * *

COMMENTS

[a] The swiftness of the criminal justice process is shocking to modern readers, but was common in earlier days, and not viewed in all cases as a failure of justice.

[b] Keep in mind that this brutally frank account of the torture was written by members of the Mississippi Supreme Court who were clearly dismayed and wanted to preserve this shameful account in a public forum.

[c] This was the Court's view in *Palko v. Connecticut* [this volume], an interpretation no longer accepted. See *Duncan v. Louisiana* [this volume].

[d] *Moore v. Dempsey* [this volume] laid the foundation for this case, for *Powell v. Alabama* [this volume], and indeed, for all the due process criminal procedure cases that followed.

ASHCRAFT v. TENNESSEE

322 U.S. 143, 64 S.Ct. 921, 88 L.Ed. 1192 (1944)

MR. JUSTICE BLACK delivered the opinion of the Court.

[Ashcraft was convicted of hiring another to kill his wife and received a 99 year sentence. Police suspicion fell on Ashcraft and he was arrested a week after the murder. Ashcraft was held from Saturday evening until Monday morning. He was questioned "in relays" for thirty-six hours, with virtually no break. He was questioned in relays because the officers became tired. Ashcraft claims that "third degree" methods of brutality were used. The officers denied this. The jury, after receiving a general charge on the standard of voluntariness, determined that his confession was voluntary. Ashcraft complains that the use of the confession violated his right to due process under the Fourteenth Amendment.]

[Under *Lisenba v. California*, 314 U.S. 219 the Supreme Court must make an independent examination of the record in claims arising under the Fourteenth Amendment, and such an assessment is not foreclosed by the findings of the state courts. The Supreme Court refused to resolve factual issues about the use of the "third-degree" and ruled that the confession was involuntary based on the fact that Ashcraft was subjected to thirty-six hours of continuous questioning.]

We think a situation such as that here shown by uncontradicted evidence is so inherently coercive that its very existence is irreconcilable with the possession of mental freedom by a lone suspect against whom its full coercive force is brought to bear. It is inconceivable that any court of justice in the land, conducted as our courts are, open to the public, would permit prosecutors serving in relays to keep a defendant witness under continuous cross examination for thirty-six hours without rest or sleep in an effort to extract a "voluntary" confession. Nor can we, consistently with Constitutional due process of law, hold voluntary a confession where prosecutors do the same thing away from the restraining influences of a public trial in an open courtroom. [a]

The Constitution of the United States stands as a bar against the conviction of any individual in an American court by means of a coerced confession. There have been, and are now, certain foreign nations with governments dedicated to an opposite policy: governments which convict individuals with testimony obtained by police organizations possessed of an unrestrained power to seize persons suspected of crimes against the state, hold them in secret custody, and wring from them confessions by physical or mental torture. So long as the Constitution remains the basic law of our Republic, America will not have that kind of government.

* * *

The judgment affirming Ashcraft's conviction is reversed and the cause is remanded to the Supreme Court of Tennessee for proceedings not inconsistent with this opinion. * * *

* * *

MR. JUSTICE JACKSON, dissenting.

A sovereign State is now before us,
summoned on the charge that it has
obtained convictions by methods so
unfair that a federal court must set
aside what the state courts have done.
Heretofore the State has had the
benefit of a presumption of regularity
and legality. [b] A confession made by
one in custody heretofore has been
admissible in evidence unless it was
proved and found that it was obtained
by pressures so strong that it was *in
fact* involuntarily made, that the individual will of the particular confessor
had been overcome by torture, mob
violence, fraud, trickery, threats, or
promises.   Even where there was
excess and abuse of power on the part
of officers, the State still was entitled
to use the confession if upon examination of the whole evidence it was
found to negative the view that the
accused had "so lost his freedom of
action that the statements made were
not his but were the result of the
deprivation of his free choice to admit,
to deny, or to refuse to answer." * * *

In determining these issues of fact,
respect for the sovereign character of
the several states always has constrained this Court to give great weight
to findings of fact of state courts.
While we have sometimes gone back
of state court determinations to make
sure whether the guaranties of the
Fourteenth Amendment have or have
not been violated, in close cases the
decisions of state courts have often
been sufficient to tip the scales in
favor of affirmance. * * *

As we read the present decision
the Court in effect declines to apply
these well-established principles. * * *

* * *

I.

* * *

This Court never yet has held that
the Constitution denies a State the
right to use a confession just because
the confessor was questioned in custody where it did not also find other
circumstances that deprived him of a
"free choice to admit, to deny, or to
refuse to answer." * * * The Constitution requires that a conviction rest on
a fair trial.   Forced confessions are
ruled out of a fair trial.   They are
ruled out because they have been
wrung from a prisoner by measures
which are offensive to concepts of
fundamental fairness. Different courts
have used different terms to express
the test by which to judge the inadmis-
sibility of a confession, such as
"forced,"   "coerced,"   "involuntary,"
"extorted," "loss of freedom of will."
But always where we have professed to
speak with the voice of the due
process clause, the test, in whatever
words stated, has been applied to the
particular confessor at the time of
confession.

It is for this reason that American
courts hold almost universally and very
properly that a confession obtained
during or shortly after the confessor
has been subjected to brutality, torture,
beating, starvation, or physical pain of
any kind is prima facie "involuntary."
The effect of threats alone may
depend more on individual susceptibility to fear. But men are so constituted
that many will risk the postponed
consequences of yielding to a demand
for a confession in order to be rid of
present or imminent physical suffering.
Actual or threatened violence have no

place in eliciting truth and it is fair to assume that no officer of the law will resort to cruelty if truth is what he is seeking. We need not be too exacting about proof of the effects of such violence on the individual involved, for their effect on the human personality is invariably and seriously demoralizing.

When, however, we consider a confession obtained by questioning, even if persistent and prolonged, we are in a different field. Interrogation per se is not, while violence per se is, an outlaw. Questioning is an indispensable instrumentality of justice. It may be abused, of course, as cross-examination in court may be abused, but the principles by which we may adjudge when it passes constitutional limits are quite different from those that condemn police brutality, and are far more difficult to apply. And they call for a more responsible and cautious exercise of our office. For we may err on the side of hostility to violence without doing injury to legitimate prosecution of crime; we cannot read an undiscriminating hostility to mere interrogation into the Constitution without unduly fettering the States in protecting society from the criminal.
[c]

It probably is the normal instinct to deny and conceal any shameful or guilty act. Even a "voluntary confession" is not likely to be the product of the same motives with which one may volunteer information that does not incriminate or concern him. The term "voluntary" confession does not mean voluntary in the sense of a confession to a priest merely to rid one's soul of a sense of guilt. "Voluntary confessions" in criminal law are the product of calculations of a different order, and usually proceed from a belief that

further denial is useless and perhaps prejudicial. To speak of any confessions of crime made after arrest as being "voluntary" or "uncoerced" is somewhat inaccurate, although traditional.

A confession is wholly and incontestably voluntary only if a guilty person gives himself up to the law and becomes his own accuser. The Court bases its decision on the premise that custody and examination of a prisoner for thirty-six hours is "inherently coercive." Of course it is. And so is custody and examination for one hour. Arrest itself is inherently coercive, and so is detention. When not justified, infliction of such indignities upon the person is actionable as a tort. Of course such acts put pressure upon the prisoner to answer questions, to answer them truthfully, and to confess if guilty.

But does the Constitution prohibit use of all confessions made after arrest because questioning, while one is deprived of freedom, is "inherently coercive"? The Court does not quite say so, but it is moving far and fast in that direction. The step it now takes is to hold this confession inadmissible because of the time taken in getting it.

The duration and intensity of an examination or inquisition always have been regarded as one of the relevant and important considerations in estimating its effect on the will of the individual involved. Thirty-six hours is a long stretch of questioning. That the inquiry was prolonged and persistent is a factor that in any calculation of its effect on Ashcraft would count heavily against the confession. But some men would withstand for days pressures that would destroy the will of another in hours. Always heretofore the ultimate question has been whether the confessor was in possession of his own will and self-control at the time of confession. For its bearing on this question the Court always has considered the confessor's strength or weakness, whether he was educated or illiterate, intelligent or moronic, well or ill, Negro or white.

But the Court refuses in this case to be guided by this test. It rejects the finding of the Tennessee courts and says it must make an "independent examination" of the circumstances. Then it says that it will not "resolve any of the disputed questions of fact" relating to the circumstances of the confession. Instead of finding as a fact that Ashcraft's freedom of will was impaired, it substitutes the doctrine that the situation was "inherently coercive." It thus reaches on a *part* of the evidence in the case a conclusion which I shall demonstrate it could not properly reach on *all* the evidence. And it refuses to resolve the conflicts in the other evidence to determine whether it rebuts the presumption thus reached that the confession is a coerced one.

If the constitutional admissibility of a confession is no longer to be measured by the mental state of the individual confessor but by a general doctrine dependent on the clock, it should be capable of statement in definite terms. If thirty-six hours is more than is permissible, what about 24? or 12? or 6? or 1? All are "inherently coercive." Of course questions of law like this often turn on matters of degree. But are not the states entitled to know, if this Court is able to state, what the considerations are which make any particular degree decisive? How else may state courts apply our tests?

* * *

MR. JUSTICE ROBERTS and MR. JUSTICE FRANKFURTER join in this opinion.

* * * * * * * * * * *

COMMENTS

[a] This case goes beyond *Brown v. Mississippi* [this volume], which was predicated on physical beatings. It is instructive to note that the ruling of this case did not lead to the cessation of coercive police interrogation practices, as can be seen by the summary discussion of due process confessions cases in the chapter introduction that arose after 1944.

[b] At the outset, the dissent, in the eloquent rhetoric typical of JUSTICE JACKSON, indicates the issue to be one of states' rights.

[c] The dissent is not willing to accept the majority's formulation that 36 hours of unbroken questioning is the *equivalent* of physical torture; it would prefer to leave it to the states to correct abuses, seeing correctly that this case would open the door to numerous suits claiming that various police practices amount to the kind of torture that overbears the will of the suspect.

SPANO v. NEW YORK

360 U.S. 315, 79 S.Ct. 1202, 3 L.Ed.2d 1265 (1959)

MR. CHIEF JUSTICE WARREN
delivered the opinion of the Court.

This is another in the long line of cases presenting the question whether a confession was properly admitted into evidence under the Fourteenth Amendment. As in all such cases, we are forced to resolve a conflict between two fundamental interests of society; its interest in prompt and efficient law enforcement, and its interest in preventing the rights of its individual members from being abridged by unconstitutional methods of law enforcement. * * *

[Spano, an immigrant from Italy, was 25 years old, had graduated from junior high school and was regularly employed.

* * * [P]etitioner was drinking in a bar. The decedent, a former professional boxer weighing almost 200 pounds * * * took some of petitioner's money from the bar. Petitioner followed him out of the bar to recover it. A fight ensued, with the decedent knocking petitioner down and then kicking him in the head three or four times. Shock from the force of these blows caused petitioner to vomit. After the bartender applied some ice to his head, petitioner left the bar, walked to his apartment, secured a gun, and walked eight or nine blocks to a candy store where the decedent was frequently to be found. He entered the store in which decedent, three friends of decedent, at least two of whom were ex-convicts, and a boy who was supervising the store were present. He fired five shots, two of

which entered the decedent's body, causing his death. The boy was the only eyewitness; the three friends of decedent did not see the person who fired the shot. Petitioner then disappeared for the next week or so.

[A grand jury indicted Spano for murder and a bench warrant was issued for his arrest.] [a]

[A week later] petitioner called one Gaspar Bruno, a close friend of 8 or 10 years' standing who had attended school with him. Bruno was a fledgling police officer, having at that time not yet finished attending police academy. According to Bruno's testimony, petitioner told him "that he took a terrific beating, that the deceased hurt him real bad and he dropped him a couple of times and he was dazed; he didn't know what he was doing and that he went and shot at him." Petitioner told Bruno that he intended to get a lawyer and give himself up. Bruno relayed this information to his superiors.

The following day, * * * petitioner, accompanied by counsel, surrendered himself to the authorities. * * * His attorney had cautioned him to answer no questions, and left him in the custody of the officers. He was promptly taken to the office of the Assistant District Attorney and at 7:15 p.m. the questioning began, being conducted by Assistant District Attorney Goldsmith, [and five officers.] The record reveals that the questioning was both persistent and continuous. Petitioner, in accordance with his attorney's instructions, steadfastly refused to answer. * * * He asked one officer, Detective Ciccone, if he could speak to his attorney, but that request was denied. * * * He was given two sandwiches, coffee and cake at 11 p.m.

At 12:15 a.m. on the [next morning] after five hours of questioning in which it became evident that petitioner was following his attorney's instructions, on the Assistant District Attorney's orders petitioner was transferred to the 46th Squad, Ryer Avenue Police Station. The Assistant District Attorney also went to the police station and to some extent continued to participate in the interrogation. Petitioner arrived at 12:30 and questioning was resumed at 12:40. * * * But petitioner persisted in his refusal to answer, and again requested permission to see his attorney, this time from Detective Lehrer. His request was again denied.

It was then that those in charge of the investigation decided that petitioner's close friend, Bruno, could be of use. He had been called out on the case around 10 or 11 p.m., although he was not connected with the 46th Squad or Precinct in any way. Although, in fact, his job was in no way threatened, Bruno was told to tell petitioner that petitioner's telephone call had gotten him "in a lot of trouble," and that he should seek to extract sympathy from petitioner for Bruno's pregnant wife and three children. Bruno developed this theme with petitioner without success, and petitioner, also without success, again sought to see his attorney, a request which Bruno relayed unavailingly to his superiors. After this first session with petitioner, Bruno was again directed by Lt. Gannon to play on petitioner's sympathies, but again no confession was forthcoming. But the Lieutenant

a third time ordered Bruno falsely to importune his friend to confess, but again petitioner clung to his attorney's advice. Inevitably, in the fourth such session directed by the Lieutenant, lasting a full hour, petitioner succumbed to his friend's prevarications and agreed to make a statement. Accordingly, at 3:25 a.m. the Assistant District Attorney, a stenographer, and several other law enforcement officials entered the room where petitioner was being questioned, and took his statement in question and answer form with the Assistant District Attorney asking the questions. The statement was completed at 4:05 a.m.

But this was not the end. [The police drove Spano between Manhattan and the Bronx several times to find the bridge from which he had thrown the murder weapon. During the trip Spano made a further incriminating statement to which the officers testified at trial.] **[b]**

Court opened at 10 a.m. that morning, and petitioner was arraigned at 10:15.

At the trial, the confession was introduced in evidence over appropriate objections. The jury was instructed that it could rely on it only if it was found to be voluntary. The jury returned a guilty verdict and petitioner was sentenced to death. The New York Court of Appeals affirmed the conviction over three dissents, * * * and we granted certiorari to resolve the serious problem presented under the Fourteenth Amendment. * * *

* * * [W]e find use of the confession obtained here inconsistent with the Fourteenth Amendment under traditional principles.

The abhorrence of society to the use of involuntary confessions does not turn alone on their inherent untrust-worthiness. It also turns on the deep-rooted feeling that the police must obey the law while enforcing the law; that in the end life and liberty can be as much endangered from illegal methods used to convict those thought to be criminals as from the actual criminals themselves. Accordingly, the actions of police in obtaining confessions have come under scrutiny in a long series of cases. Those cases suggest that in recent years law enforcement officials have become increasingly aware of the burden which they share, along with our courts, in protecting fundamental rights of our citizenry, including that portion of our citizenry suspected of crime. The facts of no case recently in this Court have quite approached the brutal beatings in *Brown v. Mississippi*, [this volume], or the 36 consecutive hours of questioning present in *Ashcraft v. Tennessee*, [this volume]. But as law enforcement officers become more responsible, and the methods used to extract confessions more sophisticated, our duty to enforce federal constitutional protections does not cease. It only becomes more difficult because of the more delicate judgments to be made. Our judgment here is that, on all the facts, this conviction cannot stand.

Petitioner was a foreign-born young man of 25 with no past history of law violation or of subjection to official interrogation, at least insofar as the record shows. He had progressed only one-half year into high school and the record indicates that he had a history of emotional instability. He did not make a narrative statement, but was subject to the leading questions of a skillful prosecutor in a question and answer confession. He was subjected to questioning not by a few men, but by many. They included Assistant District Attorney Goldsmith, [another prosecutor, twelve police detectives and officers and a stenographer.] All played some part, and the effect of such massive official interrogation must have been felt. Petitioner was questioned for virtually eight straight hours before he confessed, with his only respite being a transfer to an arena presumably considered more appropriate by the police for the task at hand. Nor was the questioning conducted during normal business hours, but began in early evening, continued into the night, and did not bear fruition until the not-too-early morning. The drama was not played out, with the final admissions obtained, until almost sunrise. In such circumstances slowly mounting fatigue does, and is calculated to, play its part. The questioners persisted in the face of his repeated refusals to answer on the advice of his attorney, and they ignored his reasonable requests to contact the local attorney whom he had already retained and who had personally delivered him into the custody of these officers in obedience to the bench warrant.

The use of Bruno, characterized in this Court by counsel for the State as a "childhood friend" of petitioner's, is another factor which deserves mention in the totality of the situation. Bruno's was the one face visible to petitioner in which he could put some trust. There was a bond of friendship between them going back a decade into adolescence. It was with this material that the officers felt that they could overcome petitioner's will. They instructed Bruno falsely to state that petitioner's telephone call had gotten him into trouble, that his job was in jeopardy, and that loss of his job would be disastrous to his three children, his wife and his unborn child. And Bruno played this part of a worried father, harried by his superiors, in not one, but four different acts, the final one lasting an hour. * * * Petitioner was apparently unaware of John Gay's famous couplet:

"An open foe may prove a curse,
But a pretended friend is worse,"

and he yielded to his false friend's entreaties.

We conclude that petitioner's will was overborne by official pressure, fatigue and sympathy falsely aroused, after considering all the facts in their post-indictment setting. Here a grand jury had already found sufficient cause to require petitioner to face trial on a charge of first-degree murder, and the police had an eyewitness to the shooting. The police were not therefore merely trying to solve a crime, or even to absolve a suspect. * * * They were rather concerned primarily with securing a statement from defendant on which they could convict him. The undeviating intent of the officers to extract a confession from petitioner is therefore patent. When such an intent is shown, this Court has held that the confession obtained must be examined with the most careful scrutiny, and has reversed a conviction on facts less compelling than these. * * * Accordingly, we hold that petitioner's conviction cannot stand under the Fourteenth Amendment. [c]

The State suggests, however, that we are not free to reverse this conviction, since there is sufficient other evidence in the record from which the jury might have found guilt, relying on

Stein v. New York, 346 U.S. 156. But *Payne v. Arkansas*, 356 U.S. 560, 568, authoritatively establishes that *Stein* did not hold that a conviction may be sustained on the basis of other evidence if a confession found to be involuntary by this Court was used, even though limiting instructions were given. *Stein* held only that when a confession is not found by this Court to be involuntary, this Court will not reverse on the ground that the jury might have found it involuntary and might have relied on it. [d] The judgment must be

Reversed.

MR. JUSTICE DOUGLAS, with whom MR. JUSTICE BLACK and MR. JUSTICE BRENNAN join, concurring.

While I join the opinion of the Court, I add what for me is an even more important ground of decision.

We have often divided on whether state authorities may question a suspect for hours on end when he has no lawyer present and when he has demanded that he have the benefit of legal advice. * * * But here we deal not with a suspect but with a man who has been formally charged with a crime. The question is whether after the indictment and before the trial the Government can interrogate the accused *in secret* when he asked for his lawyer and when his request was denied. [e] This is a capital case; and under the rule of *Powell v. Alabama*, [this volume], the defendant was entitled to be represented by counsel. This representation by counsel is not restricted to the trial. * * *

Depriving a person, formally charged with a crime, of counsel during the period prior to trial may be more damaging than denial of counsel during the trial itself.

We do not have here mere suspects who are being secretly interrogated by the police, * * * nor witnesses who are being questioned in secret administrative or judicial proceedings. * * * This is a case of an accused, who is scheduled to be tried by a judge and jury, being tried in a preliminary way by the police. This is a kangaroo court procedure whereby the police produce the vital evidence in the form of a confession which is useful or necessary to obtain a conviction. They in effect deny him effective representation by counsel. This seems to me to be a flagrant violation of the principle announced in *Powell v. Alabama*, [above] that the right of counsel extends to the preparation for trial, as well as to the trial itself. * * * When he is deprived of that right after indictment and before trial, he may indeed be denied effective representation by counsel at the only stage when legal aid and advice would help him. * * *

[JUSTICE STEWART, concurred on grounds similar to that of JUSTICE DOUGLAS, and was joined by Justices DOUGLAS and BRENNAN.] [f]

* * * * * * * * * * *

COMMENTS

[a] Compare the impact of this fact on the majority opinion and on the concurrence.

[b] Are you at all bothered or troubled by these police tactics? Why? Why not?

[c] Is there a precise holding to this case?

[d] Compare this to *Arizona v. Fulminante* [this volume].

[e] This is a significantly different issue of law than that decided by the majority.

[f] The four concurring justices were presaging the advent of a new approach to confessions law in *Massiah v. United States*, [this volume], *Escobedo v. Illinois*, 378 U.S. 478 (1964) and *Miranda v. Arizona* [this volume].

MINCEY v. ARIZONA

437 U.S. 385, 98 S.Ct. 2408, 57 L.Ed.2d 290 (1978)

MR. JUSTICE STEWART delivered the opinion of the Court.

[A police officer was shot and killed in a volley of shots fired during a drug raid on the home of Rufus Mincey. Mincey was shot and rendered semiconscious. Mincey was convicted for the murder of the officer and for narcotics charges. In this appeal the Supreme Court ruled that a subsequent warrantless search for drugs was in violation of the Fourth Amendment.]

* * *

II

Since there will presumably be a new trial in this case, it is appropriate to consider also the petitioner's contention that statements he made from a hospital bed were involuntary, and therefore could not constitutionally be used against him at his trial.

Mincey was brought to the hospital after the shooting and taken immediately to the emergency room where he was examined and treated. He had sustained a wound in his hip, resulting in damage to the sciatic nerve and partial paralysis of his right leg. Tubes were inserted into his throat to help him breathe, and through his nose into his stomach to keep him from vomiting; a catheter was inserted into his bladder. He received various drugs, and a device was attached to his arm so that he could be fed intravenously. He was then taken to the intensive care unit.

At about eight o'clock that evening, Detective Hust of the Tucson Police Department came to the intensive care unit to interrogate him. Mincey was unable to talk because of the tube in his mouth, and so he responded to Detective Hust's questions by writing answers on pieces of paper provided by the hospital. Hust told Mincey he was under arrest for the murder of a police officer, gave him the warnings required by *Miranda v. Arizona*, [this volume], and began to ask questions about the events that had taken place in Mincey's apartment a few hours earlier. Although Mincey asked repeatedly that the interrogation stop until he could get a lawyer, Hust continued to question him until almost midnight.

After a pretrial hearing, * * * the trial court found that Mincey had responded to this interrogation voluntarily. When Mincey took the witness stand at his trial his statements in response to Detective Hust's questions were used in an effort to impeach his testimony in several respects. On appeal, the Arizona Supreme Court indicated its belief that because Detective Hust had failed to honor Mincey's request for a lawyer, the statements would have been inadmissible as part of the prosecution's case in chief. * * * But, relying on *Harris v. New York*, 401 U.S. 222, and *Oregon v. Hass*, 420 U.S. 714, it held that since the trial court's finding of voluntariness was not "clear[ly] and manifest[ly]" erroneous the statements were properly used for purposes of impeachment. * * *

Statements made by a defendant in circumstances violating the strictures of

Miranda v. Arizona, supra, are admissible for impeachment if their "trustworthiness * * * satisfies legal standards."* * * But any criminal trial use against a defendant of his *involuntary* statement is a denial of due process of law "even though there is ample evidence aside from the confession to support the conviction." * * * If, therefore, Mincey's statements to Detective Hust were not "'*the product of a rational intellect and a free will,*'" * * * his conviction cannot stand. In making this critical determination, we are not bound by the Arizona Supreme Court's holding that the statements were voluntary. Instead, this Court is under a duty to make an independent evaluation of the record. * * * [a]

It is hard to imagine a situation less conducive to the exercise of "a rational intellect and a free will" than Mincey's. He had been seriously wounded just a few hours earlier, and had arrived at the hospital "depressed almost to the point of coma," according to his attending physician. Although he had received some treatment, his condition at the time of Hust's interrogation was still sufficiently serious that he was in the intensive care unit. He complained to Hust that the pain in his leg was "unbearable." He was evidently confused and unable to think clearly about either the events of that afternoon or the circumstances of his interrogation, since some of his written answers were on their face not entirely coherent. Finally, while Mincey was being questioned he was lying on his back on a hospital bed, encumbered by tubes, needles, and breathing apparatus. He was, in short, "at the complete mercy" of Detective Hust, unable to escape or resist the thrust of Hust's interrogation. * * *

In this debilitated and helpless condition, Mincey clearly expressed his wish not to be interrogated. As soon as Hust's questions turned to the details of the afternoon's events, Mincey wrote: "This is all I can say without a lawyer." Hust nonetheless continued to question him, and a nurse who was present suggested it would be best if Mincey answered. Mincey gave unresponsive or uninformative answers to several more questions, and then said again that he did not want to talk without a lawyer. Hust ignored that request and another made immediately thereafter. Indeed, throughout the interrogation Mincey vainly asked Hust to desist. Moreover, he complained several times that he was confused or unable to think clearly, or that he could answer more accurately the next day. But despite Mincey's entreaties to be let alone, Hust ceased the interrogation only during intervals when Mincey lost consciousness or received medical treatment, and after each such interruption returned relentlessly to his task. The statements at issue were thus the result of virtually continuous questioning of a seriously and painfully wounded man on the edge of consciousness.

There were not present in this case some of the gross abuses that have led the Court in other cases to find confessions involuntary, such as beatings, * * * or "truth serums." * * * But "the blood of the accused is not the only hallmark of an unconstitutional inquisition." * * * Determination of whether a statement is involuntary "requires more than a mere color-matching of cases." * * * It requires careful evaluation of all the circumstances of the interrogation.

It is apparent from the record in this case that Mincey's statements were not "the product of his free and rational choice." * * * To the contrary, the undisputed evidence makes clear that Mincey wanted not to answer Detective Hust. But Mincey was weakened by pain and shock, isolated from family, friends, and legal counsel, and barely conscious, and his will was simply overborne. Due process of law requires that statements obtained as these were cannot be used in any way against a defendant at his trial. [b]

* * *

[JUSTICES MARSHALL and BRENNAN concurred in an opinion by JUSTICE MARSHALL.]

[JUSTICE REHNQUIST, dissenting on the confession issue, noted that the trial court found the statements voluntary and pointed to some evidence that indicated that Mincey was alert and able to answer questions. The three hour interrogation was not relentless and grosser forms of abuse were not used.]

* * * * * * * * * *

COMMENTS

[a] These legal standards were all established under the pre-*Miranda* test for the voluntariness of confessions under the Fourteenth Amendment due process clause.

[b] This case indicates that pre-*Miranda* voluntariness standards, under the Due Process Clause of the Fourteenth Amendment, still apply to confessions. It indicates that a confession may be involuntary, not because of extreme police behavior, but because the circumstances may cause otherwise acceptable questioning to undermine a suspect's ability to answer voluntarily.

ARIZONA v. FULMINANTE

499 U.S. 279, 111 S.Ct. 1246, 113 L.Ed.2d 302 (1991)

JUSTICE WHITE delivered an opinion, Parts I, II and IV of which are the opinion of the Court, and Part III of which is a dissenting opinion. [a]

The Arizona Supreme Court ruled in this case that respondent Oreste Fulminante's confession, received in evidence at his trial for murder, had been coerced and that its use against him was barred by the Fifth and Fourteenth Amendments to the United States Constitution. The court also held that the harmless-error rule could not be used to save the conviction. We affirm the judgment of the Arizona court, although for different reasons than those upon which that court relied.

I

[Fulminante was suspected of murdering his 11-year-old stepdaughter, Jeneane Michelle Hunt, whose body was found in the desert, shot twice, and with a ligature around her neck. Her body was decomposed and no physical evidence linked Fulminante to the murder. Fulminante left Arizona for New Jersey, was convicted on a federal firearm possession charge, and was incarcerated in a federal correctional institution in New York. He was befriended by another inmate, Anthony Sarivola, a former police officer involved in loansharking, who became a paid informant for the Federal Bureau of Investigation and masqueraded as an organized crime figure. A prison rumor that Fulminante was suspected of killing his child was used by Sarivola as the basis of obtaining a confession from Fulminante. Fearing assaults from other prisoners for this, Sarivola said he could protect Fulminante but only if he told Sarivola whether he committed the crime. Fulminante admitted to Sarivola that he had driven Jeneane to the desert on his motorcycle, where he choked her, sexually assaulted her, and made her beg for her life, before shooting her twice in the head.]

[At trial this confession and a later confession made by Fulminante to Sarivola's wife were introduced into evidence. Fulminante was convicted. The Arizona Supreme Court held that the confession was coerced; after first ruling that the confession's use was harmless error, it reversed itself and ruled that the United States Supreme Court held that the introduction of a coerced confession required an automatic reversal.]

II

We deal first with the State's contention that the court below erred in holding Fulminante's confession to have been coerced. * * *

In applying the totality of the circumstances test to determine that the confession to Sarivola was coerced, the Arizona Supreme Court focused on a number of relevant facts. First, the court noted that "because [Fulminante] was an alleged child murderer, he was in danger of physical harm at the hands of other inmates." * * * In addition, Sarivola was aware that

Fulminante had been receiving "'rough treatment from the guys.'" * * * Using his knowledge of these threats, Sarivola offered to protect Fulminante in exchange for a confession to Jeneane's murder, * * * and "[i]n response to Sarivola's offer of protection, [Fulminante] confessed." * * * Agreeing with Fulminante that "Sarivola's promise was 'extremely coercive,'" * * * the Arizona Court declared: "[T]he confession was obtained as a direct result of extreme coercion and was tendered in the belief that the defendant's life was in jeopardy if he did not confess. This is a true coerced confession in every sense of the word." * * *

We normally give great deference to the factual findings of the state court. * * * Nevertheless, "the ultimate issue of 'voluntariness' is a legal question requiring independent federal determination." * * *

Although the question is a close one, we agree with the Arizona Supreme Court's conclusion that Fulminante's confession was coerced. The Arizona Supreme Court found a credible threat of physical violence unless Fulminante confessed. Our cases have made clear that a finding of coercion need not depend upon actual violence by a government agent; a credible threat is sufficient. As we have said, "coercion can be mental as well as physical, and . . . the blood of the accused is not the only hallmark of an unconstitutional inquisition." * * * As in *Payne [v. Arkansas*, 356 U.S. 560 (1958)], where the Court found that a confession was coerced because the interrogating police officer had promised that if the accused confessed, the officer would protect the accused from

an angry mob outside the jailhouse door, * * * so too here, the Arizona Supreme Court found that it was fear of physical violence, absent protection from his friend (and Government agent) Sarivola, which motivated Fulminante to confess. Accepting the Arizona court's finding, permissible on this record, that there was a credible threat of physical violence, we agree with its conclusion that Fulminante's will was overborne in such a way as to render his confession the product of coercion. [b]

III

Four of us, JUSTICES MARSHALL, BLACKMUN, STEVENS, and myself, would affirm the judgment of the Arizona Supreme Court on the ground that the harmless-error rule is inapplicable to erroneously admitted coerced confessions. We thus disagree with the Justices who have a contrary view. [c]

The majority today abandons what until now the Court has regarded as the "axiomatic [proposition] that a defendant in a criminal case is deprived of due process of law if his conviction is founded, in whole or in part, upon an involuntary confession, without regard for the truth or falsity of the confession, * * * and even though there is ample evidence aside from the confession to support the conviction. * * *" * * * Today, a majority of the Court, without any justification, * * * overrules this vast body of precedent without a word and in so doing dislodges one of the fundamental tenets of our criminal justice system.

In extending to coerced confessions the harmless error rule of *Chapman v.*

California, [386 U.S. 18 (1967)], the majority declares that because the Court has applied that analysis to numerous other "trial errors," there is no reason that it should not apply to an error of this nature as well. The four of us remain convinced, however, that we should abide by our cases that have refused to apply the harmless-error rule to coerced confessions, for a coerced confession is fundamentally different from other types of erroneously admitted evidence to which the rule has been applied. Indeed, as the majority concedes, *Chapman* itself recognized that prior cases "have indicated that there are some constitutional rights so basic to a fair trial that their infraction can *never* be treated as harmless error," and it placed in that category the constitutional rule against using a defendant's coerced confession against him at his criminal trial. * * * (emphasis added). Moreover, cases since *Chapman* have reiterated the rule that using a defendant's coerced confession against him is a denial of due process of law regardless of the other evidence in the record aside from the confession. * * *

Chapman specifically noted three constitutional errors that could not be categorized as harmless error: using a coerced confession against a defendant in a criminal trial, depriving a defendant of counsel, and trying a defendant before a biased judge. The majority attempts to distinguish the use of a coerced confession from the other two errors listed in *Chapman* first by distorting the decision in *Payne*, and then by drawing a meaningless dichotomy between "trial errors" and "structural defects" in the trial process. Viewing *Payne* as merely rejecting a test whereby the admission of a co-

erced confession could stand if there were "sufficient evidence," other than the confession, to support the conviction, the majority suggests that the Court in *Payne* might have reached a different result had it been considering a harmless-error test. * * * It is clear, though, that in *Payne* the Court recognized that *regardless* of the amount of other evidence, "the admission in evidence, over objection, of the coerced confession vitiates the judgment," because "where, as here, a coerced confession constitutes a part of the evidence before the jury and a general verdict is returned, no one can say what credit and weight the jury gave to the confession." * * * The inability to assess its effect on a conviction causes the admission at trial of a coerced confession to "defy analysis by 'harmless-error' standards," * * * just as certainly as do deprivation of counsel and trial before a biased judge.

The majority also attempts to distinguish "trial errors" which occur "during the presentation of the case to the jury," * * * and which it deems susceptible to harmless-error analysis, from "structural defects in the constitution of the trial mechanism," * * * which the majority concedes cannot be so analyzed. This effort fails, for our jurisprudence on harmless error has not classified so neatly the errors at issue. [d] For example, we have held susceptible to harmless-error analysis the failure to instruct the jury on the presumption of innocence, *Kentucky v. Whorton*, 441 U.S. 786 (1979), while finding it impossible to analyze in terms of harmless error the failure to instruct a jury on the reasonable doubt standard, *Jackson v. Virginia*, 443 U.S. 307, 320, n. 14 (1979). These cases cannot be reconciled by labeling the former "trial error" and the latter not, for both concern the exact same stage in the trial proceedings. Rather, these cases can be reconciled only by considering the nature of the right at issue and the effect of an error upon the trial. A jury instruction on the presumption of innocence is not constitutionally required in every case to satisfy due process, because such an instruction merely offers an additional safeguard beyond that provided by the constitutionally required instruction on reasonable doubt. * * * While it may be possible to analyze as harmless the omission of a presumption of innocence instruction when the required reasonable-doubt instruction has been given, it is impossible to assess the effect on the jury of the omission of the more fundamental instruction on reasonable doubt. In addition, omission of a reasonable-doubt instruction, though a "trial error," distorts the very structure of the trial because it creates the risk that the jury will convict the defendant even if the State has not met its required burden of proof. * * * [e]

[JUSTICE WHITE concedes that confessions taken in violation of the *Massiah* and *Miranda* rules may be subject to harmless error analysis.]

[None of these different kinds of confessions cases] involved a defendant's *coerced* confession, nor were there present in these cases the distinctive reasons underlying the exclusion of coerced incriminating statements of the defendant. First, some coerced confessions may be untrustworthy. * * * Consequently, admission of coerced confessions may distort the truth-seeking function of the trial upon which the majority focuses.

More importantly, however, the use of coerced confessions, "whether true or false," is forbidden "because the methods used to extract them offend an underlying principle in the enforcement of our criminal law: that ours is an accusatorial and not an inquisitorial system—a system in which the State must establish guilt by evidence independently and freely secured and may not by coercion prove its charge against an accused out of his own mouth." * * * This reflects the "strongly felt attitude of our society that important human values are sacrificed where an agency of the government, in the course of securing a conviction, wrings a confession out of an accused against his will," * * * as well as "the deep-rooted feeling that the police must obey the law while enforcing the law; that in the end life and liberty can be as much endangered from illegal methods used to convict those thought to be criminals as from the actual criminals themselves." * * * Thus, permitting a coerced confession to be part of the evidence on which a jury is free to base its verdict of guilty is inconsistent with the thesis that ours is not an inquisitorial system of criminal justice. * * * [f]
* * *

The search for truth is indeed central to our system of justice, but "certain constitutional rights are not, and should not be, subject to harmless error analysis because those rights protect important values that are unrelated to the truth-seeking function of the trial." * * * The right of a defendant not to have his coerced confession used against him is among those rights, for using a coerced confession "abort[s] the basic trial process" and "render[s] a trial fundamentally unfair." * * *

For the foregoing reasons the four of us would adhere to the consistent line of authority that has recognized as a basic tenet of our criminal justice system, before and after both *Miranda* and *Chapman*, the prohibition against using a defendant's coerced confession against him at his criminal trial. *Stare decisis* is "of fundamental importance to the rule of law;" * * * the majority offers no convincing reason for overturning our long line of decisions requiring the exclusion of coerced confessions.

IV

* * * Five of us are of the view that the State has not carried its burden [of proving that the admitted confession was harmless beyond a reasonable doubt] and accordingly affirm the judgment of the court below reversing petitioner's conviction.

A confession is like no other evidence. Indeed, "the defendant's own confession is probably the most probative and damaging evidence that can be admitted against him. . . . [T]he admissions of a defendant come from the actor himself, the most knowledgeable and unimpeachable source of information about his past conduct. Certainly, confessions have profound impact on the jury, so much so that we may justifiably doubt its ability to put them out of mind even if told to do so." * * * While some statements by a defendant may concern isolated aspects of the crime or may be incriminating only when linked to other evidence, a full confession in which the defendant discloses the motive for and means of the crime may tempt the jury

to rely upon that evidence alone in reaching its decision. * * *
* * *

[The remainder of the opinion reviewed the facts of the case a drew the conclusion that the introduction of the confession had an indelible impact on the jury.]

Because a majority of the Court has determined that Fulminante's confession to Anthony Sarivola was coerced and because a majority has determined that admitting this confession was not harmless beyond a reasonable doubt, we agree with the Arizona Supreme Court's conclusion that Fulminante is entitled to a new trial at which the confession is not admitted. Accordingly the judgment of the Arizona Supreme Court is

Affirmed.

CHIEF JUSTICE REHNQUIST, with whom JUSTICE O'CONNOR joins, JUSTICE KENNEDY and JUSTICE SOUTER join as to Parts I and II, and JUSTICE SCALIA joins as to Parts II and III, delivering the opinion of the Court as to Part II, and dissenting as to Parts I and III.

* * *

I

* * *

The admissibility of a confession such as that made by respondent Fulminante depends upon whether it was voluntarily made. * * *

[The CHIEF JUSTICE restated the facts of the case.]
* * *

Exercising our responsibility to make the independent examination of the record necessary to decide this federal question, I am at a loss to see how the Supreme Court of Arizona reached the conclusion that it did. Fulminante offered no evidence that he believed that his life was in danger or that he in fact confessed to Sarivola in order to obtain the proffered protection. Indeed, he had stipulated that "[a]t no time did the defendant indicate he was in fear of other inmates nor did he ever seek Mr. Sarivola's 'protection.'" * * * Sarivola's testimony that he told Fulminante that "if [he] would tell the truth, he could be protected," adds little if anything to the substance of the parties' stipulation. The decision of the Supreme Court of Arizona rests on an assumption that is squarely contrary to this stipulation, and one that is not supported by any testimony of Fulminante. [g]

The facts of record in the present case are quite different from those present in cases where we have found confessions to be coerced and involuntary. Since Fulminante was unaware that Sarivola was an FBI informant, there existed none of "the danger of coercion result[ing] from the interaction of custody and official interrogation." * * * The fact that Sarivola was a government informant does not by itself render Fulminante's confession involuntary, since we have consistently accepted the use of informants in the discovery of evidence of a crime as a legitimate investigatory procedure consistent with the Constitution. * * * The conversations between Sarivola and Fulminante were not lengthy, and the defendant was free at all times to leave Sarivola's company. Sarivola at no time threatened him or demanded that he confess; he simply requested that he speak the truth about the

matter. Fulminante was an experienced habitue of prisons, and presumably able to fend for himself. In concluding on these facts that Fulminante's confession was involuntary, the Court today embraces a more expansive definition of that term than is warranted by any of our decided cases. [h]

II

Since this Court's landmark decision in *Chapman v. California*, * * * in which we adopted the general rule that a constitutional error does not automatically require reversal of a conviction, the Court has applied harmless-error analysis to a wide range of errors and has recognized that most constitutional errors can be harmless. * * * [These include giving unconstitutionally overbroad jury instructions at capital sentencing; admission of evidence at capital sentencing that violated the right to counsel; jury instructions containing an erroneous conclusive and rebuttable presumptions and misstating an element of the offense; erroneously excluding a defendant's testimony about the circumstances of his confession; restricting a defendant's right to cross-examine a witness for bias in violation of the Confrontation Clause; denial of a defendant's right to be present at trial; improper comment on defendant's silence at trial, in violation of the Self-Incrimination Clause; statute improperly forbidding trial court's giving a jury instruction on a lesser-included offense in a capital case in violation of the Due Process Clause; failure to instruct the jury on the presumption of innocence; admission of identification evidence in violation of right to counsel; admission of an out-of-court statement of a nontestifying codefendant in violation of the Sixth Amendment Counsel Clause; admitting a confession obtained in violation of *Massiah v. United States* [this volume]; admission of evidence obtained in violation of the Fourth Amendment; denial of counsel at a preliminary hearing in violation of the Sixth Amendment Counsel Clause.]

The common thread connecting these cases is that each involved "trial error"—error which occurred during the presentation of the case to the jury, and which may therefore be quantitatively assessed in the context of other evidence presented in order to determine whether its admission was harmless beyond a reasonable doubt. In applying harmless-error analysis to these many different constitutional violations, the Court has been faithful to the belief that the harmless-error doctrine is essential to preserve the "principle that the central purpose of a criminal trial is to decide the factual question of the defendant's guilt or innocence, and promotes public respect for the criminal process by focusing on the underlying fairness of the trial rather than on the virtually inevitable presence of immaterial error." * * * **[i]**

In *Chapman v. California, supra,* the Court stated that

"Although our prior cases have indicated that there are some constitutional rights so basic to a fair trial that their infraction can never be treated as harmless error, [citing from a footnote, "* * * *e.g.,* Payne v. Arkansas,* * * * (coerced confession) * * *"] this statement * * * itself belies any belief that all trial errors which violate the Constitution automatically call for reversal."

It is on the basis of this language in *Chapman* that JUSTICE WHITE in dissent concludes that the principle of *stare decisis* requires us to hold that an involuntary confession is not subject to harmless-error analysis. We believe that there are several reasons which lead to a contrary conclusion. In the first place, the quoted language from *Chapman* does not by its terms adopt any such rule in that case. The language that "[a]lthough our prior cases have indicated," coupled with the relegation of the cases themselves to a footnote, is more appropriately regarded as a historical reference to the holdings of these cases. This view is buttressed by an examination of the opinion in

Payne v. Arkansas, * * * which is the case referred to for the proposition that an involuntary confession may not be subject to harmless error analysis. There the Court said:

"Respondent suggests that, apart from the confession, there was adequate evidence before the jury to sustain the verdict. But where, as here, an involuntary confession constitutes a part of the evidence before the jury and a general verdict is returned, no one can say what credit and weight the jury gave to the confession. And in these circumstances this Court has uniformly held that even though there may have been sufficient evidence, apart from the coerced confession, to support a judgment of conviction, the admission in evidence, over objection, of the coerced confession vitiates the judgment because it violates the Due Process Clause of the Fourteenth Amendment." * * *

It is apparent that the State's argument which the Court rejected in *Payne* is not the harmless-error analysis later adopted in *Chapman*, but a much more lenient rule which would allow affirmance of a conviction if the evidence other than the involuntary confession was sufficient to sustain the verdict. This is confirmed by the dissent of Justice Clark in that case, which adopted the more lenient test. Such a test would, of course—unlike the harmless-error test— make the admission of an involuntary confession virtually risk-free for the state. **[j]**

The admission of an involuntary confession—a classic "trial error"—is markedly different from the other two constitutional violations referred to in the *Chapman* footnote as not being subject to harmless-error analysis. One of those cases, *Gideon v. Wainwright*, [this volume] involved the total deprivation of the right to counsel at trial. The other violation, involved in *Tumey v. Ohio*, 273 U.S. 510 (1927), was a judge who was not impartial. These are structural defects in the constitution of the trial mechanism, which defy analysis by "harmless-error" standards. The entire conduct of the trial from beginning to end is obviously affected by the absence of counsel for a criminal defendant, just as it is by the presence on the bench of a judge who is not impartial. Since our decision in *Chapman*, other cases have added to the category of constitutional errors which are not subject to harmless error the following: unlawful exclusion of members of the defendant's race from a grand jury; * * * the right to self-

representation at trial; * * * and the right to public trial. * * * Each of these constitutional deprivations is a similar structural defect affecting the framework within which the trial proceeds, rather than simply an error in the trial process itself. "Without these basic protections, a criminal trial cannot reliably serve its function as a vehicle for determination of guilt or innocence, and no criminal punishment may be regarded as fundamentally fair." * * *

It is evident from a comparison of the constitutional violations which we have held subject to harmless error, and those which we have held not, that involuntary statements or confessions belong in the former category. The admission of an involuntary confession is a "trial error," similar in both degree and kind to the erroneous admission of other types of evidence. The evidentiary impact of an involuntary confession, and its effect upon the composition of the record, is indistinguishable from that of a confession obtained in violation of the Sixth Amendment—of evidence seized in violation of the Fourth Amendment—or of a prosecutor's improper comment on a defendant's silence at trial in violation of the Fifth Amendment. When reviewing the erroneous admission of an involuntary confession, the appellate court, as it does with the admission of other forms of improperly admitted evidence, simply reviews the remainder of the evidence against the defendant to determine whether the admission of the confession was harmless beyond a reasonable doubt.

Nor can it be said that the admission of an involuntary confession is the type of error which "transcends the criminal process." This Court has applied harmless-error analysis to the violation of other constitutional rights similar in magnitude and importance and involving the same level of police misconduct. For instance, we have previously held that the admission of a defendant's statements obtained in violation of the Sixth Amendment is subject to harmless-error analysis. * * * We have also held that the admission of an out-of-court statement by a nontestifying codefendant is subject to harmless-error analysis. * * * The inconsistent treatment of statements elicited in violation of the Sixth and Fourteenth Amendments, respectively, can be supported neither by evidentiary or deterrence concerns nor by a belief that there is something more "fundamental" about involuntary confessions. This is especially true in a case such as this one where there are no allegations of physical violence on behalf of the police. The impact of a confession obtained in violation of the Sixth Amendment has the same evidentiary impact as does a confession obtained in violation of a defendant's due process rights. Government misconduct that results in violations of the Fourth and Sixth Amendments may be at least as reprehensible as conduct that results in an involuntary confession. * * * Indeed, experience shows that law enforcement violations of these constitutional guarantees can involve conduct as egregious as police conduct used to elicit statements in violation of the Fourteenth Amendment. It is thus impossible to create a meaningful distinction between confessions elicited in violation of the Sixth

Amendment and those in violation of the Fourteenth Amendment.

Of course an involuntary confession may have a more dramatic effect on the course of a trial than do other trial errors—in particular cases it may be devastating to a defendant—but this simply means that a reviewing court will conclude in such a case that its admission was not harmless error; it is not a reason for eschewing the harmless-error test entirely. * * *

[Part III was a one paragraph conclusory statement that agreed with the finding of the Arizona Supreme Court in its first decision that the admission of Fulminante's confession was harmless.]

[JUSTICE KENNEDY wrote a pivotal concurring opinion: he agreed with CHIEF JUSTICE REHNQUIST's dissenting opinion that the confession was not coerced; he also agreed with REHNQUIST's majority opinion that as an abstract matter a coerced confession may be subject to harmless error inquiry. But, he jumped the REHNQUIST ship on the application of the harmless error analysis and voted in *this* case with Part III of JUSTICE WHITE's opinion: "I agree with a majority of the Court that admission of the confession could not be harmless error when viewed in light of all the other evidence; and so I concur in the judgment to affirm the ruling of the Arizona Supreme Court."]

*   *   *   *   *   *   *   *   *   *

COMMENTS

[a] JUSTICE WHITE wrote the majority opinion on the issue of whether the confession was coerced (Part II of his opinion); CHIEF JUSTICE REHNQUIST issued the majority opinion on the issue of whether the introduction of a coerced confession can ever be harmless error (Part II of *his* opinion); JUSTICE WHITE then issued the majority opinion on whether the introduction of the confession was harmless in this case (Part IV of his opinion).

[b] How credible is the fear that child abusers in prison face threats of violence from fellow prison inmates?

[c] Since the discussion in this part is a dissent, it may be helpful to first read Part II of CHIEF JUSTICE REHNQUIST's opinion.

[d] This is true; it is an indirect testament to the brilliance, or cleverness, of CHIEF JUSTICE REHNQUIST in creating a new doctrine to achieve a desired result.

[e] This argument logically undercuts the majority's trial error-structural error dichotomy. The majority simply ignored this powerful point. There is no rule of law that requires a justice to meet every argument of a fellow justice with an opposing argument.

[f] This statement of constitutional policy captures the philosophical difference between the REHNQUIST majority and the dissenters on this point.

[g] Nevertheless, the Arizona Supreme Court read the entire record and did not conclude that one stipulation in a suppression hearing negated the conclusion, based on a totality of the circumstances, that the confession was coerced.

[h] If *Massiah* does not apply (see cases in Chapter 6 C.), this paragraph suggests that the police may substitute undercover officers who are good actors to "befriend" suspects (or anyone for that matter) and attempt to get them to make incriminating statements.

[i] Compare the policy of the Court at this point with that stated in JUSTICE WHITE's opinion at comment [f].

[j] Did *Payne* create a precedent?　That was the common belief.　The CHIEF JUSTICE argues that a footnoted statement in *Chapman* and a "proper" reading of *Payne* makes it otherwise.　It is not certain that this paragraph accurately portrays the quotation from *Payne*; that quotation seems to state the harmless error rule even though it was written a few years before *Chapman*.　The CHIEF JUSTICE alludes no further to JUSTICE CLARK's dissent.　That dissent urged the controversial rule of *Stein v. New York*, 346 U.S. 156 (1953), not cited in the *Fulminante* case, that a jury can ignore a coerced confession and rely on other evidence to convict.　*Stein*, which may have been undermined by the time of *Payne*, was repudiated by *Jackson v. Denno*, 378 U.S. 368, 376 (1964), authored by JUSTICE WHITE in 1964.　So, the basis of CHIEF JUSTICE REHNQUIST's opinion may be less than firm.

MIRANDA v. ARIZONA

384 U.S. 436, 86 S.Ct. 1602, 16 L.Ed.2d 694 (1966)

[This is an appeal of four consolidated cases from four jurisdictions. None of the suspects were fully apprised of their constitutional rights, although some were informed of their right to remain silent. In *Miranda v. Arizona*, the defendant, arrested for rape, confessed after being interrogated for two hours at a police station. In *Vignera v. New York* the defendant made an oral admission to police questions about a robbery. In the evening he made another, written confession to a prosecutor. In *Westover v. United States*, the defendant was interrogated by local police and the FBI from at least 9 a.m. to 2 p.m., after having been arrested at 9 p.m. the previous evening for robbery. No warnings were given until noon of that day. In *Stewart v. California* the defendant was held for five days by the police, was interrogated nine times, and was held incommunicado until he confessed. He was then taken before an examining magistrate. There was no evidence of threats or violence in any of these cases. The majority opinion discussed the facts of the cases after fifty pages of constitutional analysis.]

MR. CHIEF JUSTICE WARREN delivered the opinion of the Court.

The cases before us raise questions which go to the roots of our concepts of American criminal jurisprudence: the restraints society must observe consistent with the Federal Constitution in prosecuting individuals for crime. [a] More specifically, we deal with the admissibility of statements obtained from an individual who is subjected to custodial police interrogation and the necessity for procedures which assure that the individual is accorded his privilege under the Fifth Amendment to the Constitution not to be compelled to incriminate himself.

* * *

We start here, as we did in *Escobedo [v. Illinois*, 378 U.S. 478 (1964)], with the premise that our holding is not an innovation in our jurisprudence, but is an application of principles long recognized and applied in other settings. * * * [b]

* * *

Our holding * * * briefly stated is this: the prosecution may not use statements, whether exculpatory or inculpatory, stemming from custodial interrogation of the defendant unless it demonstrates the use of procedural safeguards effective to secure the privilege against self-incrimination. By custodial interrogation, we mean questioning initiated by law enforcement officers after a person has been taken into custody or otherwise deprived of his freedom of action in any significant way. As for the procedural safeguards to be employed, unless other fully effective means are devised to inform accused persons of their right of silence and to assure a continuous opportunity to exercise it, the following measures are required. Prior to any questioning, the person must be warned that he has a right to remain silent, that any statement he does make may be used as evidence against him, and that he has a right to the presence of an attorney, either retained or appointed. The defendant may waive effectuation of these rights, provided the waiver is made voluntarily, knowingly and intelligently. If, however, he indicates in any manner and at any stage of the process that he wishes to consult with an attorney before speaking there can be no questioning. Likewise, if the individual is alone and indicates in any manner that he does not wish to be interrogated, the police may not question him. The mere fact that he may have answered some questions or volunteered some statements on his own does not deprive him of the right to refrain from answering any further inquiries until he has consulted with an attorney and thereafter consents to be questioned. [c]

I.

* * * [All the cases here] share salient features—incommunicado interrogation of individuals in a police-dominated atmosphere, resulting in self-incriminating statements without full warning of constitutional rights. [d]

An understanding of the nature and setting of this in-custody interrogation is essential to our decisions today. The difficulty in depicting what transpires at such interrogations stems from the fact that in this country they have largely taken place incommunicado. From extensive factual studies undertaken in the early 1930s, including the famous Wickersham Report to Congress by a Presidential Commission, it is clear that police violence and the "third degree" flourished at that time. In a series of cases decided by this Court long after these studies, the police resorted to physical brutal-

ity—beatings, hanging, whipping—and to sustained and protracted questioning incommunicado in order to extort confessions. * * *
        * * *

Again we stress that the modern practice of in-custody interrogation is psychologically rather than physically oriented. * * * ["T]his Court has recognized that coercion can be mental as well as physical, and that the blood of the accused is not the only hallmark of an unconstitutional inquisition". * * *

Interrogation still takes place in privacy. Privacy results in secrecy and this in turn results in a gap in our knowledge as to what in fact goes on in the interrogation rooms. A valuable source of information about present police practices, however, may be found in various police manuals and texts which document procedures employed with success in the past, and which recommend various other effective tactics. * * *

The officers are told by the manuals that the "principal psychological factor contributing to a successful interrogation is privacy—being alone with the person under interrogation." * * *

To highlight the isolation and unfamiliar surroundings, the manuals instruct the police to display an air of confidence in the suspect's guilt and from outward appearance to maintain only an interest in confirming certain details. The guilt of the subject is to be posited as a fact. The interrogator should direct his comments toward the reasons why the subject committed the act, rather than court failure by asking the subject whether he did it. Like other men, perhaps the subject has had a bad family life, had an unhappy

childhood, had too much to drink, had an unrequited desire for women. The officers are instructed to minimize the moral seriousness of the offense, to cast blame on the victim or on society. These tactics are designed to put the subject in a psychological state where his story is but an elaboration of what the police purport to know already—that he is guilty. Explanations to the contrary are dismissed and discouraged. * * * [e]
   * * *

When the techniques described above prove unavailing, the texts recommend they be alternated with a show of some hostility. One ploy often used has been termed the "friendly-unfriendly" or the "Mutt and Jeff" act. * * *

The interrogators sometimes are instructed to induce a confession out of trickery. The technique here is quite effective in crimes which require identification or which run in series. In the identification situation, the interrogator may take a break in his questioning to place the subject among a group of men in a line-up [and to coach a witness to identify the suspect] . * * * A variation on this technique is called the "reverse line-up":

"The accused is placed in a line-up, but this time he is identified by several fictitious witnesses or victims who associated him with different offenses. It is expected that the subject will become desperate and confess to the offense under investigation in order to escape from the false accusations."

   * * *

From these representative samples of interrogation techniques, the setting prescribed by the manuals and observed in practice becomes clear. [f] In essence, it is this: To be alone with the subject is essential to prevent distraction and to deprive him of any outside support. The aura of confidence in his guilt undermines his will to resist. He merely confirms the preconceived story the police seek to have him describe. Patience and persistence, at times relentless questioning, are employed. To obtain a confession, the interrogator must "patiently maneuver himself or his quarry into a position from which the desired objective may be attained." When normal procedures fail to produce the needed result, the police may resort to deceptive stratagems such as giving false legal advice. It is important to keep the subject off balance, for example, by trading on his insecurity about himself or his surroundings. The police then persuade, trick, or cajole him out of exercising his constitutional rights.
   * * *

In the cases before us today, given this background, we concern ourselves primarily with this interrogation atmosphere and the evils it can bring. * * *

In these cases, we might not find the defendants' statements to have been involuntary in traditional terms. [g] Our concern for adequate safeguards to protect precious Fifth Amendment rights is, of course, not lessened in the slightest. * * * The fact remains that in none of these cases did the officers undertake to afford appropriate safeguards at the outset of the interrogation to insure that the statements were truly the product of free choice.

It is obvious that such an interrogation environment is created for no purpose other than to subjugate the individual to the will of his examiner. This atmosphere carries its own badge of intimidation. To be sure, this is not physical intimidation, but it is equally destructive of human dignity. * * * Unless adequate protective devices are employed to dispel the compulsion inherent in custodial surroundings, no statement obtained from the defendant can truly be the product of his free choice. [h]

* * *

II.

* * *

* * * In *Malloy [v. Hogan*, 378 U.S. 1 (1964)], we squarely held the privilege [against self-incrimination] applicable to the States, and held that the substantive standards underlying the privilege applied with full force to state court proceedings. * * * [i]

* * *

III.

Today, then, there can be no doubt that the Fifth Amendment privilege is available outside of criminal court proceedings and serves to protect persons in all settings in which their freedom of action is curtailed in any significant way from being compelled to incriminate themselves. We have concluded that without proper safeguards the process of in-custody interrogation of persons suspected or accused of crime contains inherently compelling pressures which work to undermine the individual's will to resist and to compel him to speak where he would not otherwise do so freely. In order to combat these pressures and to permit a full opportunity to exercise the privilege against self-incrimination, the accused must be adequately and effectively apprised of his rights and the exercise of those rights must be fully honored.

It is impossible for us to foresee the potential alternatives for protecting the privilege which might be devised by Congress or the States in the exercise of their creative rule-making capacities. Therefore we cannot say that the Constitution necessarily requires adherence to any particular solution for the inherent compulsions of the interrogation process as it is presently conducted. Our decision in no way creates a constitutional straitjacket which will handicap sound efforts at reform, nor is it intended to have this effect. We encourage Congress and the States to continue their laudable search for increasingly effective ways of protecting the rights of the individual while promoting efficient enforcement of our criminal laws. However, unless we are shown other procedures which are at least as effective in apprising accused persons of their right of silence and in assuring a continuous opportunity to exercise it, the following safeguards must be observed. [j]

At the outset, if a person in custody is to be subjected to interrogation, he must first be informed in clear and unequivocal terms that he has the right to remain silent. For those unaware of the privilege, the warning is needed simply to make them aware of it—the threshold requirement for an intelligent decision as to its exercise. More important, such a warning is an absolute prerequisite in overcoming the inherent pressures of the interrogation atmosphere. * * *

The Fifth Amendment privilege is so fundamental to our system of constitutional rule and the expedient of giving an adequate warning as to the availability of the privilege so simple, we will not pause to inquire in individual cases whether the defendant was aware of his rights without a warning being given. * * *

The warning of the right to remain silent must be accompanied by the explanation that anything said can and will be used against the individual in court. This warning is needed in order to make him aware not only of the privilege, but also of the consequences of foregoing it. It is only through an awareness of these consequences that there can be any assurance of real understanding and intelligent exercise of the privilege. Moreover, this warning may serve to make the individual more acutely aware that he is faced with a phase of the adversary system—that he is not in the presence of persons acting solely in his interest.

The circumstances surrounding in-custody interrogation can operate very quickly to overbear the will of one merely made aware of his privilege by his interrogators. Therefore, the right to have counsel present at the interrogation is indispensable to the protection of the Fifth Amendment privilege. * * * [k]

* * *

In order fully to apprise a person interrogated of the extent of his rights under this system then, it is necessary to warn him not only that he has the right to consult with an attorney, but also that if he is indigent a lawyer will be appointed to represent him. Without this additional warning, the admonition of the right to consult with counsel would often be understood as meaning only that he can consult with a lawyer if he has one or has the

funds to obtain one. * * *

Once warnings have been given, the subsequent procedure is clear. If the individual indicates in any manner, at any time prior to or during questioning, that he wishes to remain silent, the interrogation must cease. [l] At this point he has shown that he intends to exercise his Fifth Amendment privilege; any statement taken after the person invokes his privilege cannot be other than the product of compulsion, subtle or otherwise. Without the right to cut off questioning, the setting of in-custody interrogation operates on the individual to overcome free choice in producing a statement after the privilege has been once invoked. [m] If the individual states that he wants an attorney, the interrogation must cease until an attorney is present. At that time, the individual must have an opportunity to confer with the attorney and to have him present during any subsequent questioning. If the individual cannot obtain an attorney and he indicates that he wants one before speaking to police, they must respect his decision to remain silent.

This does not mean, as some have suggested, that each police station must have a "station house lawyer" present at all times to advise prisoners. It does mean, however, that if police propose to interrogate a person they must make known to him that he is entitled to a lawyer and that if he cannot afford one, a lawyer will be provided for him prior to any interrogation. If authorities conclude that they will not provide counsel during a reasonable period of time in which investigation in the field is carried out, they may refrain from doing so without violating the person's Fifth Amendment privilege so long as they do not question him during that time.

If the interrogation continues without the presence of an attorney and a statement is taken, a heavy burden rests on the government to demonstrate that the defendant knowingly and intelligently waived his privilege against self-incrimination and his right to retained or appointed counsel. * * * Since the State is responsible for establishing the isolated circumstances under which the interrogation takes place and has the only means of making available corroborated evidence of warnings given during incommunicado interrogation, the burden is rightly on its shoulders. **[n]**

An express statement that the individual is willing to make a statement and does not want an attorney followed closely by a statement could constitute a waiver. But a valid waiver will not be presumed simply from the silence of the accused after warnings are given or simply from the fact that a confession was in fact eventually obtained. * * * **[o]**

* * *

The warnings required and the waiver necessary in accordance with our opinion today are, in the absence of a fully effective equivalent, prerequisites to the admissibility of any statement made by a defendant. No distinction can be drawn between statements which are direct confessions and statements which amount to "admissions" of part or all of an offense. The privilege against self-incrimination protects the individual from being compelled to incriminate himself in any manner; it does not distinguish degrees of incrimination. Similarly, for precisely the same reason, no distinction may be drawn between

inculpatory statements and statements alleged to be merely "exculpatory." If a statement made were in fact truly exculpatory it would, of course, never be used by the prosecution. In fact, statements merely intended to be exculpatory by the defendant are often used to impeach his testimony at trial or to demonstrate untruths in the statement given under interrogation and thus to prove guilt by implication. These statements are incriminating in any meaningful sense of the word and may not be used without the full warnings and effective waiver required for any other statement. In *Escobedo* itself, the defendant fully intended his accusation of another as the slayer to be exculpatory as to himself. **[p]**

* * *

Our decision is not intended to hamper the traditional function of police officers in investigating crime. * * *

* * *

In dealing with statements obtained through interrogation, we do not purport to find all confessions inadmissible. Confessions remain a proper element in law enforcement. Any statement given freely and voluntarily without any compelling influences is, of course, admissible in evidence. * * * There is no requirement that police stop a person who enters a police station and states that he wishes to confess to a crime, or a person who calls the police to offer a confession or any other statement he desires to make. Volunteered statements of any kind are not barred by the Fifth Amendment and their admissibility is not affected by our holding today. **[q]**

* * *

[Lengthy, articulate and passionate

dissents were authored by JUSTICES CLARK (concurring in *Stewart v. California*), HARLAN, AND WHITE; only excerpts of JUSTICE WHITE's dissent are printed here.]

MR. JUSTICE WHITE, with whom MR. JUSTICE HARLAN and MR. JUSTICE STEWART join, dissenting. * * *

I.

The proposition that the privilege against self-incrimination forbids in-custody interrogation without the warnings specified in the majority opinion and without a clear waiver of counsel has no significant support in the history of the privilege or in the language of the Fifth Amendment. * * * The rule excluding coerced confessions matured about 100 years [after the privilege against self-incrimination did, and] "there is nothing in the reports to suggest that the theory has its roots in the privilege against self-incrimination. * * *" * * * [r]

Our own constitutional provision provides that no person "shall be compelled in any criminal case to be a witness against himself." These words, when "[c]onsidered in the light to be shed by grammar and the dictionary * * * appear to signify simply that nobody shall be compelled to give oral testimony against himself in a criminal proceeding under way in which he is defendant." * * * Such a construction, however, was considerably narrower than the privilege at common law, and when eventually faced with the issues, the Court extended the constitutional privilege to the compulsory production of books and papers, to the ordinary witness before the grand jury and to witnesses generally. * * * [s]

A few years later the Fifth Amendment privilege was similarly extended to encompass the then well-established rule against coerced confessions: "In criminal trials, in the courts of the United States, wherever a question arises whether a confession is incompetent because not voluntary, the issue is controlled by * * * the fifth amendment. * * *" *Bram v. United States*, 168 U.S. 532, 542. * * *

* * *

Bram, however, itself rejected the proposition which the Court now espouses. The question in *Bram* was whether a confession, obtained during custodial interrogation, had been compelled, and if such interrogation was to be deemed inherently vulnerable the Court's inquiry could have ended there. * * * [T]he Court declared that:

> "* * * the mere fact that the confession is made to a police officer, while the accused was under arrest in or out of prison, or was drawn out by his questions, does not necessarily render the confession involuntary; but, as one of the circumstances, such imprisonment or interrogation may be taken into account in determining whether or not the statements of the prisoner were voluntary" * * *

In this respect the Court was wholly consistent with prior and subsequent pronouncements in this Court. * * * [t]

* * *

Since *Bram*, the admissibility of statements made during custodial interrogation has been frequently reiterated. * * * Without any discussion of the presence or absence of warnings, presumably because such discussion was deemed unnecessary, numerous other cases have declared that "[t]he mere fact that a confession was made while in the custody of the police does not render it inadmissible," * * * despite its having been elicited by police examination. * * *

Only a tiny minority of our judges who have dealt with the question, including today's majority, have considered in-custody interrogation, without more, to be a violation of the Fifth Amendment. And this Court, as every member knows, has left standing literally thousands of criminal convictions that rested at least in part on confessions taken in the course of interrogation by the police after arrest.

II.

* * * [T]he Court has not discovered or found the law in making today's decision, nor has it derived it from some irrefutable sources; what it has done is to make new law and new public policy in much the same way that it has in the course of interpreting other great clauses of the Constitution. This is what the Court historically has done. Indeed, it is what it must do and will continue to do until and unless there is some fundamental change in the constitutional distribution of governmental powers.

But if the Court is here and now to announce new and fundamental policy to govern certain aspects of our affairs, it is wholly legitimate to examine the mode of this or any other constitutional decision in this Court and to inquire into the advisability of its end product in terms of the long-range interest of the country. At the

very least, the Court's text and reasoning should withstand analysis and be a fair exposition of the constitutional provision which its opinion interprets. Decisions like these cannot rest alone on syllogism, metaphysics or some ill-defined notions of natural justice, although each will perhaps play its part. In proceeding to such constructions as it now announces, the Court should also duly consider all the factors and interests bearing upon the cases, at least insofar as the relevant materials are available; and if the necessary considerations are not treated in the record or obtainable from some other reliable source, the Court should not proceed to formulate fundamental policies based on speculation alone. [u]

III.

First, we may inquire what are the textual and factual bases of this new fundamental rule. To reach the result announced on the grounds it does, the Court must stay within the confines of the Fifth Amendment, which forbids self-incrimination only if *compelled*. Hence the core of the Court's opinion is that because of the "compulsion inherent in custodial surroundings, no statement obtained from [a] defendant [in custody] can truly be the product of his free choice," * * * absent the use of adequate protective devices as described by the Court. However, the Court does not point to any sudden inrush of new knowledge requiring the rejection of 70 years' experience. * * * Rather than asserting new knowledge, the Court concedes that it cannot truly know what occurs during custodial questioning, because of the innate secrecy of such proceedings. It extrapolates a picture of what it conceives to be the norm from police investigatorial manuals, published in 1959 and 1962 or earlier, without any attempt to allow for adjustments in police practices that may have occurred in the wake of more recent decisions of state appellate tribunals or this Court. But even if the relentless application of the described procedures could lead to involuntary confessions, it most assuredly does not follow that each and every case will disclose this kind of interrogation or this kind of consequence. Insofar as appears from the Court's opinion, it has not examined a single transcript of any police interrogation, let alone the interrogation that took place in any one of these cases which it decides today. Judged by any of the standards for empirical investigation utilized in the social sciences the factual basis for the Court's premise is patently inadequate. [v]

* * *

Today's result would not follow even if it were agreed that to some extent custodial interrogation is inherently coercive. * * * The test has been whether the totality of circumstances deprived the defendant of a "free choice to admit, to deny, or to refuse to answer," * * * and whether physical or psychological coercion was of such a degree that "the defendant's will was overborne at the time he confessed." * * * The duration and nature of incommunicado custody, the presence or absence of advice concerning the defendant's constitutional rights, and the granting or refusal of requests to communicate with lawyers, relatives or friends have all been rightly regarded as important data bearing on the basic inquiry. * * *

But it has never been suggested, until today, that such questioning was so coercive and accused persons so lacking in hardihood that the very first response to the very first question following the commencement of custody must be conclusively presumed to be the product of an overborne will.

* * *

* * * [E]ven if one assumed that there was an adequate factual basis for the conclusion that all confessions obtained during in-custody interrogation are the product of compulsion, the rule propounded by the Court would still be irrational, for, apparently, it is only if the accused is also warned of his right to counsel and waives both that right and the right against self-incrimination that the inherent compulsiveness of interrogation disappears. But if the defendant may not answer without a warning a question such as "Where were you last night?" without having his answer be a compelled one, how can the Court ever accept his negative answer to the question of whether he wants to consult his retained counsel or counsel whom the court will appoint? And why if counsel is present and the accused nevertheless confesses, or counsel tells the accused to tell the truth, and that is what the accused does, is the situation any less coercive insofar as the accused is concerned? The Court apparently realizes its dilemma of foreclosing questioning without the necessary warnings but at the same time permitting the accused, sitting in the same chair in front of the same policemen, to waive his right to consult an attorney. It expects, however, that the accused will not often waive the right; and if it is claimed that he has, the State faces a severe, if not impossible burden of proof. [w]

All of this makes very little sense

in terms of the compulsion which the Fifth Amendment proscribes. That amendment deals with compelling the accused himself. It is his free will that is involved. Confessions and incriminating admissions, as such, are not forbidden evidence; only those which are compelled are banned. I doubt that the Court observes these distinctions today. By considering any answers to any interrogation to be compelled regardless of the content and course of examination and by escalating the requirements to prove waiver, the Court not only prevents the use of compelled confessions but for all practical purposes forbids interrogation except in the presence of counsel. That is, instead of confining itself to protection of the right against compelled self-incrimination the Court has created a limited Fifth Amendment right to counsel—or, as the Court expresses it, a "need for counsel to protect the Fifth Amendment privilege. * * *" * * * The focus then is not on the will of the accused but on the will of counsel and how much influence he can have on the accused. Obviously there is no warrant in the Fifth Amendment for thus installing counsel as the arbiter of the privilege.

In sum, for all the Court's expounding on the menacing atmosphere of police interrogation procedures, it has failed to supply any foundation for the conclusions it draws or the measures it adopts.

IV.

* * *

In some unknown number of cases the Court's rule will return a killer, a rapist or other criminal to the streets and to the environment which produced him, to repeat his crime whenever it pleases him. As a consequence, there will not be a gain, but a loss, in human dignity. The real concern is not the unfortunate consequences of this new decision on the criminal law as an abstract, disembodied series of authoritative proscriptions, but the impact on those who rely on the public authority for protection and who without it can only engage in violent self-help with guns, knives and the help of their neighbors similarly inclined. * * * [x]

Nor can this decision do other than have a corrosive effect on the criminal law as an effective device to prevent crime. A major component in its effectiveness in this regard is its swift and sure enforcement. The easier it is to get away with rape and murder, the less the deterrent effect on those who are inclined to attempt it. This is still good common sense. If it were not, we should posthaste liquidate the whole law enforcement establishment as a useless, misguided effort to control human conduct.

* * *

* * * * * * * * * *

COMMENTS

[a] The portentous opening sentence is hardly necessary; every case of constitutional criminal procedure involves the extent of state power vis-à-vis the liberty of the individual. Despite this, the statement draws attention to the case as one of

the utmost importance.

[b] This may be one of the most disingenuous statements in the annals of Constitutional law; as the dissents make plain, whether correct as a matter of constitutional interpretation or public policy, this case was clearly an innovation.

[c] This concise and almost statute-like statement of the rules of the case drew the fire of many legal commentators who accused the Court of engaging in "judicial legislation" rather than approaching the case in a customary fashion of resolving a narrow issue utilizing the canons of finding support in precedent and legal reasoning.

[d] The facts are almost irrelevant to the holding of the case. Note what is left out of this summary statement of facts: there is no allusion to physical or psychological coercion, only to statements taken in the secrecy of the police station. This is used as a springboard for a lengthy discussion of the recommended practices in police manuals for obtaining confessions. In the complete reported case, the general points made are supported by lengthy quotes from textbooks and police procedure manuals.

[e] Do these practices strike you as outrageous? If not, are they akin to "high pressure sales tactics" designed to get the suspect to say things that would otherwise remain unsaid?

[f] These examples are not scientifically drawn random samples of police activity; nevertheless, there is no reason to disbelieve that the examples in the manuals were widespread or even typical. Because the specific facts of *Miranda* and its companion cases are not outrageous, the majority's holding depends on the credibility of its generalized factual conclusion: that interrogation in police custody is *inherently* coercive.

[g] Chief Justice Warren here indirectly acknowledges that the case is an innovation.

[h] In this section the CHIEF JUSTICE does not simply describe the setting of police interrogations as background information. The general facts establish a foundation for a legal finding that such practices amount to automatic violations of the right against self-incrimination. This also serves as a launching pad for establishing required "protective devices" in the form of warnings.

[i] Without the incorporation of the self-incrimination clause of the Fifth Amendment into the Fourteenth Amendment in this 1964 case, the decision in *Miranda* would not be possible. Thus, *Malloy* set the foundation for the confessions-warning rule, bringing state action in this area within the purview of the federal constitution.

[j] Under the majority's reasoning, the Court could have made police station house questioning itself a violation of the self-incrimination privilege. This would have disrupted police practices far more than the warnings requirement. The Court suggests that other protective techniques could replace the warnings. This has significance in later cases.

[k] The right to request counsel is not based directly on the Sixth Amendment but is required to protect Fifth Amendment rights.

[l] The suspect's right to invoke the Fifth Amendment is absolute.

[m] This clearly stated residual right of the suspect to cut off interrogation is placed here because the Court feared that in practice police would disregard the substance of the right against self-incrimination once warnings were given and interrogation began. Do you think this level of distrust is justified?

[o] In practice, this means that the police must usually have other evidence, such as a written waiver, to indicate that the defendant waived his rights voluntarily. Some departments routinely make audio- or video-tapes of interrogation sessions.

[p] This paragraph tries to close loopholes in the *Miranda* rules. A suspect might be led to say things he *thinks* will clear him but which instead lead to independent evidence of guilt.

[q] Some commentators have gone so far as to suggest that police interrogation of suspects should be banned. Shortly after the *Miranda* case was issued, many in law enforcement stated that it would end the police practice of interrogation. This has not happened.

The majority opinion devotes a lengthy section, not reprinted here, to a policy defense of its holding, noting that the FBI gives warnings and that English police must give warnings and are ordered not to cross-examine suspects.

[r] JUSTICE WHITE accuses the Court of disregarding the separate historic roots of self-incrimination and confessions and, in effect, rewriting history.

[s] JUSTICE WHITE notes that the Court has not been bound by a strict interpretation of the Fifth Amendment, but has at times expanded the scope of the privilege.

[t] Although *Bram* brought the confession rule within the Fifth Amendment in federal cases, it did not alter the actual test for determining the admissibility of a confession—the voluntariness test.

[u] JUSTICE WHITE is not a reactionary opposed to all constitutional change. He acknowledges the Court's authority to develop new doctrines, but argues that the foundation for such change must be based on shifting precedent or a powerful shift in public sentiment.

[v] JUSTICE WHITE accuses the majority of fabricating the constitutional element of coercion by assuming that the police manuals describe an undeviating reality in every confession situation, without proof of coercion in each specific case.

[w] JUSTICE WHITE reveals a logical flaw in the opinion. If the station house atmosphere is inherently coercive, then it is logically impossible for suspects to voluntarily waive their rights in that atmosphere, even after being informed of their rights. This implies station house lawyers must be appointed to fulfill *Miranda*'s goals. The dissenters were concerned that in subsequent cases, a liberal majority of the Court would move in that direction.

[x] There is always a trade-off between security and liberty in criminal procedure; JUSTICE WHITE sees little gain in civil liberties by limiting the power of the police in this area.

MICHIGAN v. TUCKER

417 U.S. 433, 94 S.Ct. 2357, 41 L.Ed.2d 182 (1974)

MR. JUSTICE REHNQUIST delivered the opinion of the Court.

This case presents the question whether the testimony of a witness in respondent's state court trial for rape must be excluded simply because police had learned the identity of the witness by questioning respondent at a time when he was in custody as a suspect, but had not been advised that counsel would be appointed for him if he was indigent. * * *

I

[A rape victim, tied and gagged, was found by a friend. She could not identify the assailant. The friend noticed a dog in the victim's home; the victim owned no dog. Later, when talking to police, the friend noticed the dog; police followed the dog to respondent Tucker's house and neighbors connected the dog to Tucker, who was arrested.]

* * * Prior to the actual interrogation the police asked respondent whether he knew for what crime he had been arrested, whether he wanted an attorney, and whether he understood his constitutional rights. Respondent replied that he did understand the crime for which he was arrested, that he did not want an attorney, and that he understood his rights. The police further advised him that any statements he might make could be used against him at a later date in court. The police, however, did not advise respondent that he would be furnished counsel free of charge if he could not pay for such services himself.

The police then questioned respondent about his activities on the night of the rape and assault. Respondent replied that during the general time period at issue he had first been with one Robert Henderson and then later at home, alone, asleep. The police sought to confirm this story by contacting Henderson, but Henderson's story served to discredit rather than to bolster respondent's account. [Tucker virtually admitted to Henderson the day after the rape that he had sexual relations with a woman in the neighborhood.]

[Tucker's statements were not admitted into evidence. Henderson's statements, however, were admitted into evidence over counsel's objections, and Tucker was convicted of rape. The police investigation took place before the decision in *Miranda v. Arizona* [this volume] but the trial occurred after the *Miranda* decision was announced. Tucker's conviction was upheld by state courts, but the federal district court, finding that the *Miranda* rules applied, "reluctantly" concluded that Henderson's testimony could not be admitted because Tucker had not been read the warning that he could receive assigned counsel if he could not afford a lawyer. The Court of Appeals affirmed this decision.]

II

* * *

Respondent's argument, and the opinions of the District Court and Court of Appeals, rely upon the Fifth

Amendment right against compulsory self-incrimination and the safeguards designed in *Miranda* to secure that right.   In brief, the position urged upon this Court is that proper regard for the privilege against compulsory self-incrimination requires, with limited exceptions not applicable here, that all evidence derived solely from statements made without full *Miranda* warnings be excluded at a subsequent criminal trial. For purposes of analysis in this case we believe that the question thus presented is best examined in two separate parts. We will therefore first consider whether the police conduct complained of directly infringed upon respondent's right against compulsory self-incrimination or whether it instead violated only the prophylactic rules developed to protect that right.   We will then consider whether the evidence derived from this interrogation must be excluded.

III

The history of the Fifth Amendment right against compulsory self-incrimination, and the evils against which it was directed, have received considerable attention in the opinions of this Court. * * *   At this point in our history virtually every schoolboy is familiar with the concept, if not the language, of the provision that reads: "No person * * * shall be compelled in any criminal case to be a witness against himself. * * *" This Court's decisions have referred to the right as "the mainstay of our adversary system of criminal justice," * * * and as "'one of the great landmarks in man's struggle to make himself civilized.'" * * *

The importance of a right does

not, by itself, determine its scope, and therefore we must continue to hark back to the historical origins of the privilege, particularly the evils at which it was to strike. The privilege against compulsory self-incrimination was developed by painful opposition to a course of ecclesiastical inquisitions and Star Chamber proceedings occurring several centuries ago. * * * Certainly anyone who reads accounts of those investigations, which placed a premium on compelling subjects of the investigation to admit guilt from their own lips, cannot help but be sensitive to the Framers' desire to protect citizens against such compulsion. * * *

Where there has been genuine compulsion of testimony, the right has been given broad scope. [It is applicable at grand jury proceedings, civil proceedings, congressional investigations, juvenile proceedings, and other statutory inquiries; it prevents comment on a defendant's refusal to testify, and was incorporated into the due process clause of the Fourteenth Amendment.]

The natural concern which underlies many of these decisions is that an inability to protect the right at one stage of a proceeding may make its invocation useless at a later stage. * * *

In more recent years this concern—that compelled disclosures might be used against a person at a later criminal trial— has been extended to cases involving police interrogation. Before *Miranda* the principal issue in these cases was not whether a defendant had waived his privilege against compulsory self-incrimination but simply whether his statement was "voluntary." In state cases the Court applied the Due Process Clause of the Fourteenth Amendment, examining the circumstances of interrogation to determine whether the processes were so unfair or unreasonable as to render a subsequent confession involuntary. * * * [a]

Although federal cases concerning voluntary confessions often contained references to the privilege against compulsory self-incrimination, references which were strongly criticized by some commentators, * * * it was not until this Court's decision in *Miranda* that the privilege against compulsory self-incrimination was seen as the principal protection for a person facing police interrogation. This privilege had been made applicable to the States in *Malloy v. Hogan*, [378 U.S. 1 (1964)] and was thought to offer a more comprehensive and less subjective protection than the doctrine of previous cases. In *Miranda* the Court examined the facts of four separate cases and stated:

> "In these cases, we might not find the defendants' statements to have been involuntary in traditional terms. Our concern for adequate safeguards to protect precious Fifth Amendment rights is, of course, not lessened in the slightest. * * * To be sure, the records do not evince overt physical coercion or patent psychological ploys. The fact remains that in none of these cases did the officers undertake to afford appropriate safeguards at the outset of the interrogation to insure that the statements were truly the product of free choice." * * *

Thus the Court in *Miranda*, for the first time, expressly declared that the Self-Incrimination Clause was applica-ble to state interrogations at a police station, and that a defendant's state-ments might be excluded at trial despite their voluntary character under traditional principles.

To supplement this new doctrine, and to help police officers conduct interrogations without facing a contin-ued risk that valuable evidence would be lost, the Court in *Miranda* estab-lished a set of specific protective guidelines, now commonly known as the *Miranda* rules. The Court declared that "the prosecution may not use statements, whether exculpatory or inculpatory, stemming from custodial interrogation of the defendant unless it demonstrates the use of procedural safeguards effective to secure the privilege against self-incrimination." * * * A series of recommended "proce-dural safeguards" then followed. * * *

The Court recognized that these procedural safeguards were not them-selves rights protected by the Constitu-tion but were instead measures to insure that the right against compulsory self-incrimination was protected. As the Court remarked:

> "[W]e cannot say that the Constitu-tion necessarily requires adherence to any particular solution for the inherent compulsions of the inter-rogation process as it is presently conducted." * * * [b]

The suggested safeguards were not intended to "create a constitutional straitjacket," * * * but rather to provide practical reinforcement for the right against compulsory self-incrimina-tion.

A comparison of the facts in this case with the historical circumstances underlying the privilege against compulsory self-incrimination strongly indicates that the police conduct here did not deprive respondent of his privilege against compulsory self-incrimination as such, but rather failed to make available to him the full measure of procedural safeguards associated with that right since *Miranda*. * * * The District Court in this case noted that the police had "warned [respondent] that he had the right to remain silent," * * * and the record in this case clearly shows that respondent was informed that any evidence taken could be used against him. The record is also clear that respondent was asked whether he wanted an attorney and that he replied that he did not. Thus, his statements could hardly be termed involuntary as that term has been defined in the decisions of this Court. Additionally, there were no legal sanctions, such as the threat of contempt, which could have been applied to respondent had he chosen to remain silent. He was simply not exposed to "the cruel trilemma of self-accusation, perjury or contempt." * * *

Our determination that the interrogation in this case involved no compulsion sufficient to breach the right against compulsory self-incrimination does not mean there was not a disregard, albeit an inadvertent disregard, of the procedural rules later established in *Miranda*. The question for decision is how sweeping the judicially imposed consequences of this disregard shall be. This Court said in *Miranda* that statements taken in violation of the *Miranda* principles must not be used to prove the prosecution's case at trial. That requirement was fully complied with by the state court here: respondent's statements, claiming that he was

with Henderson and then asleep during the time period of the crime were not admitted against him at trial. This Court has also said, in *Wong Sun v. United States*, 371 U.S. 471 (1963), that the "fruits" of police conduct which actually infringed a defendant's Fourth Amendment rights must be suppressed. But we have already concluded that the police conduct at issue here did not abridge respondent's constitutional privilege against compulsory self-incrimination, but departed only from the prophylactic standards later laid down by this Court in *Miranda* to safeguard that privilege. Thus, in deciding whether Henderson's testimony must be excluded, there is no controlling precedent of this Court to guide us. We must therefore examine the matter as a question of principle.

IV

Just as the law does not require that a defendant receive a perfect trial, only a fair one, it cannot realistically require that policemen investigating serious crimes make no errors whatsoever. The pressures of law enforcement and the vagaries of human nature would make such an expectation unrealistic. Before we penalize police error, therefore, we must consider whether the sanction serves a valid and useful purpose.

We have recently said, in a search-and-seizure context, that the exclusionary rule's "prime purpose is to deter future unlawful police conduct and thereby effectuate the guarantee of the Fourth Amendment against unreasonable searches and seizures." *United States v. Calandra*, 414 U.S. 338 * * * (1974). We then continued:

"'The rule is calculated to prevent, not to repair. Its purpose is to deter—to compel respect for the constitutional guaranty in the only effectively available way—by removing the incentive to disregard it.'" * * *

In a proper case this rationale would seem applicable to the Fifth Amendment context as well. [c]

The deterrent purpose of the exclusionary rule necessarily assumes that the police have engaged in willful, or at the very least negligent, conduct which has deprived the defendant of some right. By refusing to admit evidence gained as a result of such conduct, the courts hope to instill in those particular investigating officers, or in their future counterparts, a greater degree of care toward the rights of an accused. Where the official action was pursued in complete good faith, however, the deterrence rationale loses much of its force.

We consider it significant to our decision in this case that the officers' failure to advise respondent of his right to appointed counsel occurred prior to the decision in *Miranda*. Although we have been urged to resolve the broad question of whether evidence derived from statements taken in violation of the *Miranda* rules must be excluded regardless of when the interrogation took place, we instead place our holding on a narrower ground. For at the time respondent was questioned these police officers were guided, quite rightly, by the principles established in *Escobedo v. Illinois*, 378 U.S. 478 (1964), particularly focusing on the suspect's opportunity to have retained counsel with him during the interrogation if he chose to do so. Thus, the police asked respondent if he wanted counsel, and he answered that he did not. The statements actually made by respondent to the police, as we have observed, were excluded at trial in accordance with *Johnson v. New Jersey*, 384 U.S. 719 (1966). Whatever deterrent effect on future police conduct the exclusion of those statements may have had, we do not believe it would be significantly augmented by excluding the testimony of the witness Henderson as well.

When involuntary statements or the right against compulsory self-incrimination are involved, a second justification for the exclusionary rule also has been asserted: protection of the courts from reliance on untrustworthy evidence. Cases which involve the Self-Incrimination Clause must, by definition, involve an element of coercion, since the Clause provides only that a person shall not be *compelled* to give evidence against himself. And cases involving statements often depict severe pressures which may override a particular suspect's insistence on innocence. Fact situations ranging from classical third-degree torture, * * * to prolonged isolation from family or friends in a hostile setting, * * * or to a simple desire on the part of a physically or mentally exhausted suspect to have a seemingly endless interrogation end, * * * all might be sufficient to cause a defendant to accuse himself falsely.

But those situations are a far cry from that presented here. The pressures on respondent to accuse himself were hardly comparable even with the least prejudicial of those pressures which have been dealt with in our cases. More important, the respondent did *not* accuse himself. The evidence which the prosecution successfully sought to introduce was not a confession * * * but rather the testimony of a third party who was subjected to no custodial pressures. There is plainly no reason to believe that Henderson's testimony is untrustworthy simply because *respondent* was not advised of *his* right to appointed counsel. Henderson was both available at trial and subject to cross-examination by respondent's counsel, and counsel fully used this opportunity, suggesting in the course of his cross-examination that Henderson's character was less than exemplary and that he had been offered incentives by the police to testify against respondent. Thus the reliability of his testimony was subject to the normal testing process of an adversary trial.

Respondent contends that an additional reason for excluding Henderson's testimony is the notion that the adversary system requires "the government in its contest with the individual to shoulder the entire load." * * * To the extent that this suggested basis for the exclusionary rule in Fifth Amendment cases may exist independently of the deterrence and trustworthiness rationales, we think it of no avail to respondent here. Subject to applicable constitutional limitations, the Government is not forbidden all resort to the defendant to make out its case. It may require the defendant to give physical evidence against himself, * * * and it may use statements which are voluntarily given by the defendant after he receives full disclosure of the rights offered by *Miranda*. Here we deal, not with the offer of respondent's own statements in evidence, but only with the testimony of a witness whom the police discovered as a result of respondent's statements. This recourse to respondent's voluntary statements does no violence to such elements of the adversary system as may be embodied in the Fifth, Sixth, and Fourteenth Amendments.

In summary, we do not think that any single reason supporting exclusion of this witness' testimony, or all of them together, are very persuasive. By contrast, we find the arguments in favor of admitting the testimony quite strong. For, when balancing the interests involved, we must weigh the strong interest under any system of justice of making available to the trier of fact all concededly relevant and trustworthy evidence which either party seeks to adduce. In this particular case we also "must consider society's interest in the effective prosecution of criminals in light of the protection our pre-*Miranda* standards afford criminal defendants." * * * These interests may be outweighed by the need to provide an effective sanction to a constitutional right, * * * but they must in any event be valued. Here respondent's own statement, which might have helped the prosecution show respondent's guilty conscience at trial, had already been excised from the prosecution's case pursuant to this Court's *Johnson* decision. To extend the excision further under the circumstances of this case and exclude relevant testimony of a third-party witness would require far more persuasive arguments than those advanced by respondent.

This Court has already recognized that a failure to give interrogated suspects full *Miranda* warnings does not entitle the suspect to insist that statements made by him be excluded in every conceivable context. In *Harris v. New York*, 401 U.S. 222 (1971), the Court was faced with the question of whether the statements of the defendant himself, taken without informing him of his right of access to appointed counsel, could be used to impeach defendant's direct testimony at trial. The Court concluded that they could, saying:

> "Some comments in the *Miranda* opinion can indeed be read as indicating a bar to use of an uncounseled statement for any purpose, but discussion of that issue was not at all necessary to the Court's holding and cannot be regarded as controlling. *Miranda* barred the prosecution from making its case with statements of an accused made while in custody prior to having or effectively waiving counsel. It does not follow from *Miranda* that evidence inadmissible against an accused in the prosecution's case in chief is barred for all purposes, provided of course that the trustworthiness of the evidence satisfies legal standards." * * *

We believe that this reasoning is equally applicable here. Although *Johnson* enabled respondent to block admission of his own statements, we do not believe that it requires the prosecution to refrain from all use of those statements, and we disagree with the courts below that Henderson's testimony should have been excluded in this case.

Reversed.

[JUSTICE STEWART concurred, suggesting that Justice Brennan's concurrence was essentially similar in reasoning to the majority opinion.]

MR. JUSTICE BRENNAN, with whom MR. JUSTICE MARSHALL joins, concurring in the judgment.

* * *

* * * [T]he element of unreliability—a legitimate concern in *Johnson* because of the inherently coercive nature of in-custody interrogation—is of less importance when the admissibility of "fruits" is at issue. There is no reason to believe that the coercive atmosphere of the station house will have any effect whatsoever on the trustworthiness of "fruits."

Since excluding the fruits of respondent's statements would not further the integrity of the factfinding process and would severely handicap law enforcement officials in obtaining evidentiary substitutes, I would confine the reach of *Johnson v. New Jersey* to those cases in which the direct statements of an accused made during a pre-*Miranda* interrogation were introduced at his post-*Miranda* trial. If *Miranda* is applicable at all to the fruits of statements made without proper warnings, I would limit its effect to those cases in which the fruits were obtained as a result of post-*Miranda* interrogations. * * *
* * *

[JUSTICE WHITE concurred.]

MR. JUSTICE DOUGLAS, dissenting.

* * *

I cannot agree when the Court says that the interrogation here "did not abridge respondent's constitutional privilege against compulsory self-incrimination, but departed only from the prophylactic standards laid down by this Court in *Miranda* to safeguard that privilege." * * * The Court is not free to prescribe preferred modes of interrogation absent a constitutional basis. We held the "requirement of warnings and waiver of rights [to be] fundamental with respect to the Fifth Amendment privilege," * * * and without so holding we would have been powerless to reverse Miranda's conviction. While *Miranda* recognized that police need not mouth the precise words contained in the Court's opinion, such warnings were held necessary "unless other fully effective means are adopted to notify the person" of his rights. * * * There is no contention here that other means were adopted.   The respondent's statements were thus obtained "under circumstances that did not meet constitutional standards for protection of the privilege [against self-incrimination]." * * *

* * * * * * * * * * *

COMMENTS

[a] See the cases in Part A of this chapter.

[b] There may be a difference between "procedural safeguards * * * not themselves rights protected by the Constitution" and procedural safeguards which *must* be applied as a matter of Constitutional imperatives which can be dispensed with only if equivalent or more stringent procedural safeguards are applied. While the actual holding in Part IV was of limited importance, the Court's theory of the *Miranda* doctrine marked a major doctrinal turning point.

[c] The Justices of the Burger Court took a parallel path regarding the *Miranda* doctrine as with the Fourth Amendment exclusionary rule. Neither was overruled, but each was limited. The limitation was accomplished in both cases by interpreting each rule as a utilitarian limitation on specific police abuses, rather than a broadly based ethical rule under a constitutional imperative. See *United States v. Leon* [this volume].

OREGON v. ELSTAD

470 U.S. 298, 105 S.Ct. 1285, 84 L.Ed.2d 222 (1985)

JUSTICE O'CONNOR delivered the opinion of the Court.

This case requires us to decide whether an initial failure of law enforcement officers to administer the warnings required by *Miranda v. Arizona*, [this volume], without more, "taints" subsequent admissions made after a suspect has been fully advised of and has waived his *Miranda* rights. Respondent, Michael James Elstad, was convicted of burglary by an Oregon trial court. The Oregon Court of Appeals reversed, holding that respondent's signed confession, although voluntary, was rendered inadmissible by a prior remark made in response to questioning without benefit of *Miranda* warnings. We granted certiorari, * * * and we now reverse.

I

[A witness to a home burglary of art objects valued at $150,000 implicated Michael Elstad, an 18-year-old neighbor of the victims. Sheriff's officers Burke and McAllister questioned Elstad in his home, midday, in the presence of his mother. An officer stated that he believed Elstad was involved. Elstad replied, "Yes, I was there." No *Miranda* warnings were given at the house. Elstad was taken to Sheriff's headquarters where he was questioned for an hour. He was then read *Miranda* warnings and made a confession. Elstad] concedes that the officers made no threats or promises either at his residence or at the Sheriff's office.

[Elstad was convicted of burglary, and both the statement made at his house and at Sheriff's headquarters were admitted into evidence. The Oregon Court of Appeals ruled that the second confession was tainted by the first, improperly obtained confession.]

* * *

II

The arguments advanced in favor of suppression of respondent's written confession rely heavily on metaphor. One metaphor, familiar from the Fourth Amendment context, would require that respondent's confession, regardless of its integrity, voluntariness, and probative value, be suppressed as the "tainted fruit of the poisonous tree" of the *Miranda* violation. A second metaphor questions whether a confession can be truly voluntary once the "cat is out of the bag." Taken out of context, each of these metaphors can be misleading. They should not be used to obscure fundamental differences between the role of the Fourth Amendment exclusionary rule and the function of *Miranda* in guarding against the prosecutorial use of compelled statements as prohibited by the Fifth Amendment. The Oregon court assumed and respondent here contends that a failure to administer *Miranda* warnings necessarily breeds the same consequences as police infringement of a constitutional right, so that evidence uncovered following an unwarned statement must be suppressed as "fruit of the poisonous tree." We believe this view misconstrues the nature of the protections afforded by *Miranda* warnings and therefore misreads the consequences of police failure to supply them.

A

Prior to *Miranda*, the admissibility of an accused's in-custody statements was judged solely by whether they were "voluntary" within the meaning of the Due Process Clause. * * * [a] The Court in *Miranda* required suppression of many statements that would have been admissible under traditional due process analysis by presuming that statements made while in custody and without adequate warnings were protected by the Fifth Amendment. * * * Voluntary statements "remain a proper element in law enforcement." * * * "Indeed, far from being prohibited by the Constitution, admissions of guilt by wrongdoers, if not coerced, are inherently desirable. * * * Absent some officially coerced self-accusation, the Fifth Amendment privilege is not violated by even the most damning admissions." * * *

Respondent's contention that his confession was tainted by the earlier failure of the police to provide *Miranda* warnings and must be excluded as "fruit of the poisonous tree" assumes the existence of a constitutional violation. This figure of speech is drawn from *Wong Sun v. United States*, 371 U.S. 471 (1963), in which the Court held that evidence and witnesses discovered as a result of a search in violation of the Fourth Amendment must be excluded from evidence. The *Wong Sun* doctrine applies as well when the fruit of the Fourth Amendment violation is a confession. It is settled law that "a confession obtained through custodial interrogation after an illegal arrest should be excluded unless intervening events break the causal connection between the illegal arrest and the confession so that the confession is 'sufficiently an act of free will to purge the primary taint.'" * * *

But as we explained in [*New York v.*] *Quarles* [this volume] and [*Michigan v.*] *Tucker* [this volume], a procedural *Miranda* violation differs in significant respects from violations of the Fourth Amendment, which have traditionally mandated a broad application of the "fruits" doctrine. The purpose of the Fourth Amendment exclusionary rule is to deter unreasonable searches, no matter how probative their fruits. * * * "The exclusionary rule, . . . when utilized to effectuate the Fourth Amendment, serves interests and policies that are distinct from those it serves under the Fifth." * * * Where a Fourth Amendment violation "taints" the confession, a finding of voluntariness for the purposes of the Fifth Amendment is merely a threshold requirement in determining whether the confession may be admitted in evidence. * * * Beyond this, the prosecution must show a sufficient break in events to undermine the inference that the confession was caused by the Fourth Amendment violation.

The *Miranda* exclusionary rule, however, serves the Fifth Amendment and sweeps more broadly than the Fifth Amendment itself. It may be triggered even in the absence of a Fifth Amendment violation. The Fifth Amendment prohibits use by the prosecution in its case in chief only of *compelled* testimony. Failure to administer *Miranda* warnings creates a presumption of compulsion. Consequently, unwarned statements that are otherwise voluntary within the meaning of the Fifth Amendment must nevertheless be excluded from evidence under *Miranda*. Thus, in the individual case, *Miranda*'s preventive medicine provides a remedy even to the defendant who has suffered no identifiable constitutional harm. * * *

But the *Miranda* presumption, though irrebuttable for purposes of the prosecution's case in chief, does not require that the statements and their fruits be discarded as inherently tainted. Despite the fact that patently *voluntary* statements taken in violation of *Miranda* must be excluded from the prosecution's case, the presumption of coercion does not bar their use for impeachment purposes on cross-examination. *Harris v. New York*, 401 U.S. 222 (1971). The Court in *Harris* rejected as an "extravagant extension of the Constitution," the theory that a defendant who had confessed under circumstances that made the confession inadmissible, could thereby enjoy the freedom to "deny every fact disclosed or discovered as a 'fruit' of his confession, free from confrontation with his prior statements" and that the voluntariness of his confession would be totally irrelevant. * * * Where an unwarned statement is preserved for use in situations that fall outside the sweep of the *Miranda* presumption, "the primary criterion of admissibility [remains] the 'old' due process voluntariness test." * * *

[The fruits of an unwarned admission were allowed into evidence in *Michigan v. Tucker* [this volume]]. * * *

We believe that this reasoning applies with equal force when the alleged "fruit" of a noncoercive *Miranda* violation is neither a witness nor an article of evidence but the accused's own voluntary testimony. * * *

Because *Miranda* warnings may inhibit persons from giving information, this Court has determined that they need be administered only after the person is taken into "custody" or his freedom has otherwise been significantly restrained. * * * Unfortunately, the task of defining "custody" is a slippery one, and "policemen investigating serious crimes [cannot realistically be expected to] make no errors whatsoever." * * * If errors are made by law enforcement officers in administering the prophylactic *Miranda* procedures, they should not breed the same irremediable consequences as police infringement of the Fifth Amendment itself. It is an unwarranted extension of *Miranda* to hold that a simple failure to administer the warnings, unaccompanied by any actual coercion or other circumstances calculated to undermine the suspect's ability to exercise his free will, so taints the investigatory process that a subsequent voluntary and informed waiver is ineffective for some indeterminate period. Though *Miranda* requires that the unwarned admission must be suppressed, the admissibility of any subsequent statement should turn in these circumstances solely on whether it is knowingly and voluntarily made.

B

The Oregon court, however,

believed that the unwarned remark compromised the voluntariness of respondent's later confession. It was the court's view that the prior *answer* and not the unwarned questioning impaired respondent's ability to give a valid waiver and that only lapse of time and change of place could dissipate what it termed the "coercive impact" of the inadmissible statement. When a prior statement is actually coerced, the time that passes between confessions, the change in place of interrogations, and the change in identity of the interrogators all bear on whether that coercion has carried over into the second confession. * * * The failure of police to administer *Miranda* warnings does not mean that the statements received have actually been coerced, but only that courts will presume the privilege against compulsory self-incrimination has not been intelligently exercised. * * * **[b]** Of the courts that have considered whether a properly warned confession must be suppressed because it was preceded by an unwarned but clearly voluntary admission, the majority have explicitly or implicitly recognized that [the] requirement of a break in the stream of events is inapposite. In these circumstances, a careful and thorough administration of *Miranda* warnings serves to cure the condition that rendered the unwarned statement inadmissible. The warning conveys the relevant information and thereafter the suspect's choice whether to exercise his privilege to remain silent should ordinarily be viewed as an "act of free will." * * *

The Oregon court nevertheless identified a subtle form of lingering compulsion, the psychological impact of the suspect's conviction that he has let the cat out of the bag and, in so doing, has sealed his own fate. But endowing the psychological effects of *voluntary* unwarned admissions with constitutional implications would, practically speaking, disable the police from obtaining the suspect's informed cooperation even when the official coercion proscribed by the Fifth Amendment played no part in either his warned or unwarned confessions. As the Court remarked * * *:

"[A]fter an accused has once let the cat out of the bag by confessing, no matter what the inducement, he is never thereafter free of the psychological and practical disadvantages of having confessed. He can never get the cat back in the bag. The secret is out for good. In such a sense, a later confession may always be looked upon as fruit of the first. But this Court has never gone so far as to hold that making a confession under circumstances which preclude its use, perpetually disables the confessor from making a usable one after those conditions have been removed." * * * **[c]**

* * *

This Court has never held that the psychological impact of voluntary disclosure of a guilty secret qualifies as state compulsion or compromises the voluntariness of a subsequent informed waiver. The Oregon court, by adopting this expansive view of Fifth Amendment compulsion, effectively immunizes a suspect who responds to pre-*Miranda* warning questions from the consequences of his subsequent informed waiver of the privilege of remaining silent. * * * This immunity comes at a high cost to legitimate law enforcement activity, while adding little desirable protection to the individual's interest in not being *compelled* to testify against himself. * * * When neither the initial nor the subsequent admission is coerced, little justification exists for permitting the highly probative evidence of a voluntary confession to be irretrievably lost to the factfinder.

There is a vast difference between the direct consequences flowing from coercion of a confession by physical violence or other deliberate means calculated to break the suspect's will and the uncertain consequences of disclosure of a "guilty secret" freely given in response to an unwarned but noncoercive question, as in this case. JUSTICE BRENNAN'S contention that it is impossible to perceive any causal distinction between this case and one involving a confession that is coerced by torture is wholly unpersuasive. Certainly, in respondent's case, the causal connection between any psychological disadvantage created by his admission and his ultimate decision to cooperate is speculative and attenuated at best. It is difficult to tell with certainty what motivates a suspect to speak. A suspect's confession may be traced to factors as disparate as "a pre-arrest event such as a visit with a minister," * * * or an intervening event such as the exchange of words respondent had with his father. We must conclude that, absent deliberately coercive or improper tactics in obtaining the initial statement, the mere fact that a suspect has made an unwarned admission does not warrant a presumption of compulsion. A subsequent administration of *Miranda* warnings to a suspect who has given a voluntary but unwarned statement ordinarily

should suffice to remove the conditions that precluded admission of the earlier statement. In such circumstances, the finder of fact may reasonably conclude that the suspect made a rational and intelligent choice whether to waive or invoke his rights.

III

[In this section, the Court rejected the suggestion that in order for a *"Mirandized"* statement to be properly taken after a suspect made an unwarned admission, the police must give an additional warning to the effect that the first statement cannot be used in evidence against the suspect.]
   * * *
   * * * Such a requirement is neither practicable nor constitutionally necessary. * * *

This Court has never embraced the theory that a defendant's ignorance of the full consequences of his decisions vitiates their voluntariness. * * *

IV

When police ask questions of a suspect in custody without administering the required warnings, *Miranda* dictates that the answers received be presumed compelled and that they be excluded from evidence at trial in the State's case in chief. * * * The Court today in no way retreats from the bright-line rule of *Miranda*. We do not imply that good faith excuses a failure to administer *Miranda* warnings; nor do we condone inherently coercive police tactics or methods offensive to due process that render the initial admission involuntary and undermine the suspect's will to invoke his rights once they are read to him. [d] A handful of courts have, however, applied our precedents relating to confessions obtained under coercive circumstances to situations involving wholly voluntary admissions, requiring a passage of time or break in events before a second, fully warned statement can be deemed voluntary. Far from establishing a rigid rule, we direct courts to avoid one; there is no warrant for presuming coercive effect where the suspect's initial inculpatory statement, though technically in violation of *Miranda*, was voluntary. The relevant inquiry is whether, in fact, the second statement was also voluntarily made. As in any such inquiry, the finder of fact must examine the surrounding circumstances and the entire course of police conduct with respect to the suspect in evaluating the voluntariness of his statements. The fact that a suspect chooses to speak after being informed of his rights is, of course, highly probative. We find that the dictates of *Miranda* and the goals of the Fifth Amendment proscription against use of compelled testimony are fully satisfied in the circumstances of this case by barring use of the unwarned statement in the case in chief. No further purpose is served by imputing "taint" to subsequent statements obtained pursuant to a voluntary and knowing waiver. We hold today that a suspect who has once responded to unwarned yet uncoercive questioning is not thereby disabled from waiving his rights and confessing after he has been given the requisite *Miranda* warnings.

The judgment of the Court of Appeals of Oregon is reversed, and the case is remanded for further proceedings not inconsistent with this opinion.

* * *

JUSTICE BRENNAN, with whom JUSTICE MARSHALL joins, dissenting.

* * *

Two major premises undergird the Court's decision. The Court rejects as nothing more than "speculative" the long-recognized presumption that an illegally extracted confession causes the accused to confess again out of the mistaken belief that he already has sealed his fate, and it condemns as "'extravagant'" the requirement that the prosecution affirmatively rebut the presumption before the subsequent confession may be admitted. * * * The Court instead adopts a new rule that, so long as the accused is given the usual *Miranda* warnings before further interrogation, the taint of a previous confession obtained in violation of *Miranda* "ordinarily" must be viewed as *automatically* dissipated. * * *

In the alternative, the Court asserts that neither the Fifth Amendment itself nor the judicial policy of deterring illegal police conduct requires the suppression of the "fruits" of a confession obtained in violation of *Miranda*, reasoning that to do otherwise would interfere with "legitimate law enforcement activity." * * * As the Court surely understands, however, "[t]o forbid the direct use of methods . . . but to put no curb on their full indirect use would only invite the very methods deemed 'inconsistent with ethical standards and destructive of personal liberty.'" * * * If violations of constitutional rights may not be remedied through the well-established rules respecting derivative evidence, as the Court has held today, there is a critical danger that the rights will be rendered nothing more than a mere "form of words." * * *

* * *

I

* * *

If this Court's reversal of the judgment below reflected mere disagreement with the Oregon court's application of the "cat out of the bag" presumption to the particular facts of this case, the outcome, while clearly erroneous, would be of little lasting consequence. But the Court rejects the "cat out of the bag" *presumption entirely* and instead adopts a new rule presuming that "ordinarily" there is *no* causal connection between a confession extracted in violation of *Miranda* and a subsequent confession preceded by the usual *Miranda* warnings. * * * The Court suggests that it is merely following settled lower-court practice in adopting this rule and that the analysis followed by the Oregon Court of Appeals was aberrant. This is simply not so. Most federal courts have rejected the Court's approach and instead held that (1) there is a rebuttable presumption that a confession obtained in violation of *Miranda* taints subsequent confessions, and (2) the taint cannot be dissipated solely by giving *Miranda* warnings. * * * Even more significant is the case among state courts. Although a handful have adopted the Court's approach, the overwhelming majority of state courts that have considered the issue have concluded that subsequent confessions are presumptively tainted by a first confession taken in violation of *Miranda* and that *Miranda* warnings alone cannot dissipate the taint.

The Court today sweeps aside this common-sense approach as "speculative" reasoning, adopting instead a rule that "the psychological impact of voluntary disclosure of a guilty secret" neither "qualifies as state compulsion" nor "compromises the voluntariness" of subsequent confessions. * * * (emphasis added). So long as a suspect receives the usual *Miranda* warnings before further interrogation, the Court reasons, the fact that he "is free to exercise his own volition in deciding whether or not to make" further confessions "ordinarily" is a sufficient "cure" and serves to break any causal connection between the illegal confession and subsequent statements. * * *

The Court's marble-palace psychoanalysis is tidy, but it flies in the face of our own precedents, demonstrates a startling unawareness of the realities of police interrogation, and is completely out of tune with the experience of state and federal courts over the last 20 years. Perhaps the Court has grasped some psychological truth that has eluded persons far more experienced in these matters; if so, the Court owes an explanation of how so many could have been so wrong for so many years.

A

* * *

(2)

Our precedents did not develop in a vacuum. They reflect an understanding of the realities of police interrogation and the everyday experience of lower courts. Expert interrogators, far from dismissing a first admission or confession as creating merely a "speculative and attenuated" disadvantage for

a suspect, * * * understand that such revelations frequently lead directly to a full confession. Standard interrogation manuals advise that "[t]he securing of the first admission is the biggest stumbling block. . . ." * * * If this first admission can be obtained, "there is every reason to expect that the first admission will lead to others, and eventually to the full confession." * * *
* * *

B

The correct approach, administered for almost 20 years by most courts with no untoward results, is to presume that an admission or confession obtained in violation of *Miranda* taints a subsequent confession unless the prosecution can show that the taint is so attenuated as to justify admission of the subsequent confession. * * * Although the Court warns against the "irremediable consequences" of this presumption, * * * it is obvious that a subsequent confession, just like any other evidence that follows upon illegal police action, does not become "sacred and inaccessible." * * * As with any other evidence, the inquiry is whether the subsequent confession "'has been come at by exploitation of [the] illegality or instead by means sufficiently distinguishable to be purged of the primary taint.'" *Wong Sun.* * * *

Until today the Court has recognized that the dissipation inquiry requires the prosecution to demonstrate that the official illegality did not taint the challenged confession, and we have rejected the simplistic view that abstract notions of "free will" are alone sufficient to dissipate the challenged taint. * * * Instead, we have instructed

courts to consider carefully such factors as the strength of the causal connection between the illegal action and the challenged evidence, their proximity in time and place, the presence of intervening factors, and the "purpose and flagrancy of the official misconduct." * * *

The Court today shatters this sensitive inquiry and decides instead that, since individuals possess "'will, perception, memory and volition,'" a suspect's "exercise [of] his own volition in deciding whether or not to make a [subsequent] statement to the authorities" must "ordinarily" be viewed as sufficient to dissipate the coercive influence of a prior confession obtained in violation of *Miranda*. * * * But "[w]ill, perception, memory and volition are only relevant as they provide meaningful alternatives in the causal chain, not as mystical qualities which in themselves invoke the doctrine of attenuation." * * * Thus we have *always* rejected, until today, the notion that "individual will" alone presumptively serves to insulate a person's actions from the taint of earlier official illegality. * * *
* * *

The Court's new approach is therefore completely at odds with established dissipation analysis. A comparison of the Court's analysis with the factors most frequently relied on by lower courts in considering the admissibility of subsequent confessions demonstrates the practical and legal flaws of the new rule.

Advice that earlier confession may be inadmissible. The most effective means to ensure the voluntariness of an accused's subsequent confession is to advise the accused that his earlier admissions may not be admissible and therefore that he need not speak solely out of a belief that "the cat is out of the bag." Many courts have required such warnings in the absence of other dissipating factors, and this Court has not uncovered anything to suggest that this approach has not succeeded in the real world. The Court, however, believes that law enforcement authorities could never possibly understand "the murky and difficult questio[n]" of when *Miranda* warnings must be given, and therefore that they are "ill-equipped" to make the decision whether supplementary warnings might be required. * * *

This reasoning is unpersuasive for two reasons. First, the whole point of *Miranda* and its progeny has been to prescribe "bright line" rules for the authorities to follow. * * * Second, even where the authorities are not certain that an earlier confession has been illegally obtained, courts and commentators have recognized that a supplementary warning merely advising the accused that his earlier confession *may* be inadmissible can dispel his belief that he has nothing to lose by repetition.

* * *

C

* * *

* * * [T]he Court repeatedly suggests that a confession may be suppressed only if the police have used "improper tactics;" * * * this obscure reasoning overlooks the fact that a violation of *Miranda* is obviously *itself* an "improper tactic," one frequently used precisely to undermine the voluntariness of subsequent confessions.

* * *

* * *

In sum, today's opinion marks an evisceration of the established fruit of the poisonous tree doctrine, but its reasoning is sufficiently obscure and qualified as to leave state and federal courts with continued authority to combat obvious flouting by the authorities of the privilege against self-incrimination. I am confident that lower courts will exercise this authority responsibly, as they have for the most part prior to this Court's intervention.

* * *

I dissent.

JUSTICE STEVENS, dissenting.

* * *

For me, the most disturbing aspect of the Court's opinion is its somewhat opaque characterization of the police misconduct in this case. The Court appears ambivalent on the question whether there was any constitutional violation. This ambivalence is either disingenuous or completely law-less. This Court's power to require state courts to exclude probative self-incriminatory statements rests entirely on the premise that the use of such evidence violates the Federal Constitution. The same constitutional analysis applies whether the custodial interrogation is actually coercive or irrebuttably presumed to be coercive. [e] If the Court does not accept that premise, it must regard the holding in the *Miranda* case itself, as well as all of the federal jurisprudence that has evolved from that decision, as nothing more than an illegitimate exercise of raw judicial power. If the Court accepts the proposition that respondent's self-incriminatory statement was inadmissible, it must also acknowledge that the Federal Constitution protected him from custodial police interrogation without first being advised of his right to remain silent. **[f]**

* * *

* * * * * * * * * *

COMMENTS

[a] See the cases in Chapter 6, section A.

[b] A few questions can be posed about this statement. (1) Is this "unintelligent waiver" a *constitutional* violation? (2) Should an "unintelligent waiver" taint later "*Mirandized*" questioning for this reason? (3) Does it undermine the legitimacy of the Court's rule [see the excerpt of JUSTICE STEVENS' dissent, below]? By viewing the *Miranda* warnings as prophylactic rules only, the Court appears to answer the first two questions in the negative. As such, it implicitly answers the third question in the negative.

[c] The Court disapproves of the Oregon court's approach. The Oregon court does not totally eliminate the fruits of subsequent *Mirandized* questioning, but subjects it to the same rules of "dissipating the taint" of the "fruits" of confessions obtained by direct coercion. The Court is distressed that the Oregon approach would hamper police investigation. This attitude stems from its skepticism about the psychological effect of the "cat out of the bag" reasoning. Compare JUSTICE BRENNAN's views on this subject. If you admit an embarrassing fact to a person, how easy is it for you to later deny it?

[d] This caveat signals that the Court is not seeking to overrule the *Miranda* case itself. This goal was mentioned at the time of the *Tucker* case but since that time the Court has been satisfied with the limitations placed on the *Miranda* rule.

[e] "Actually coercive" confessions are those that violate the voluntariness test under the due process clause; "irrebuttably presumed to be coercive" confessions are those excluded under violations of *Miranda*.

[f] JUSTICE STEVENS challenges the foundation of current confessions' jurisprudence in the Supreme Court: that *Miranda* warnings are "mere prophylactic" rules for the true constitutional protection of the Fifth Amendment self-incrimination provision. The doctrine was developed in *Michigan v. Tucker* [this volume] and relied on in *New York v. Quarles* [this volume] and this case. One way of viewing *Miranda* as a constitutional rule is by noting that since a person has Fifth Amendment protection in presumptively coercive custody-interrogation situations, a waiver of the right can only be made knowingly and intelligently. If so, warnings are a constitutional *requirement*, barring an even stronger protection such as a rule prohibiting police interrogation suspect under any circumstances.

NEW YORK v. QUARLES

467 U.S. 649, 104 S.Ct. 2626, 81 L.Ed.2d 550 (1984)

JUSTICE REHNQUIST delivered the opinion of the Court.

* * *

[At 12:30 a.m. two police officers were approached by a woman who] told them that she had just been raped by a black male [whom she described as wearing a jacket with the name "big Ben" printed in yellow letters on the back.] She told the officers that the man had just entered an A & P supermarket located nearby and that the man was carrying a gun.

[The officers spotted the man in the supermarket and arrested him after a brief chase through the aisles. When frisked, the man, Benjamin Quarles, was wearing an empty shoulder holster.] After handcuffing him, Officer Kraft asked him where the gun was. Respondent [Quarles] nodded in the direction of some empty cartons and responded, "the gun is over there." Officer Kraft thereafter retrieved a loaded .38-caliber revolver from one of the cartons, formally placed respondent under arrest, and read him his *Miranda* rights from a printed card. Respondent indicated that he would be willing to answer questions without an attorney present. Officer Kraft then asked respondent if he owned the gun and where he had purchased it. Respondent answered that he did own it and that he had purchased it in Miami, Fla.

[The New York courts found that Quarles was in custody when first interrogated and was read *Miranda* warnings afterwards, thus requiring the suppression of the gun and Quarles's statement.]

* * * The Fifth Amendment itself does not prohibit all incriminating admissions; "[a]bsent some officially *coerced* self-accusation, the Fifth Amendment privilege is not violated by even the most damning admissions." * * * **[a]** The *Miranda* Court, however, presumed that interrogation in certain custodial circumstances is inherently coercive and held that statements made under those circumstances are inadmissible unless the suspect is specifically informed of his *Miranda* rights and freely decides to forgo those rights. The prophylactic *Miranda* warnings therefore are "not themselves rights protected by the Constitution but [are] instead measures to insure that the right against compulsory self-incrimination [is] protected." *Michigan v. Tucker*, [this volume]. * * * **[b]**

In this case we have before us no claim that respondent's statements were actually compelled by police conduct which overcame his will to resist. * * * **[c]** Thus the only issue before us is whether Officer Kraft was justified in failing to make available to respondent the procedural safeguards associated with the privilege against compulsory self-incrimination since *Miranda*.

The New York Court of Appeals was undoubtedly correct in deciding that the facts of this case come within the ambit of the *Miranda* decision as we have subsequently interpreted it. We agree that respondent was in police custody. * * * Here Quarles was surrounded by at least four police officers and was handcuffed when the questioning at issue took place. * * *

[T]here was nothing to suggest that any of the officers were any longer concerned for their own physical safety. * * *

We hold that on these facts there is a "public safety" exception to the requirement that *Miranda* warnings be given before a suspect's answers may be admitted into evidence, and that the availability of that exception does not depend upon the motivation of the individual officers involved. **[d]** In a kaleidoscopic situation such as the one confronting these officers, where spontaneity rather than adherence to a police manual is necessarily the order of the day, the application of the exception which we recognize today should not be made to depend on * * * the subjective motivation of the arresting officer. Undoubtedly most police officers, if placed in Officer Kraft's position, would act out of a host of different, instinctive, and largely unverifiable motives—their own safety, the safety of others, and perhaps as well the desire to obtain incriminating evidence from the suspect.

* * * [W]e do not believe that the doctrinal underpinnings of *Miranda* require that it be applied in all its rigor to a situation in which police officers ask questions reasonably prompted by a concern for the public safety. **[e]** The *Miranda* decision was based in large part on this Court's view that the warnings which it required police to give to suspects in custody would reduce the likelihood that the suspects would fall victim to constitutionally impermissible practices of police interrogation. * * *

The police in this case, in the very act of apprehending a suspect, were confronted with the immediate necessity of ascertaining the whereabouts of a gun which they had every reason to believe the suspect had just removed from his empty holster and discarded in the supermarket. **[f]** So long as the gun was concealed somewhere in the supermarket, with its actual whereabouts unknown, it obviously posed more than one danger to the public safety: an accomplice might make use of it, a customer or employee might later come upon it.

In such a situation, if the police are required to recite the familiar *Miranda* warnings before asking the whereabouts of the gun, suspects in Quarles' position might well be deterred from responding. Procedural safeguards which deter a suspect from responding were deemed acceptable in *Miranda* in order to protect the Fifth Amendment privilege; when the primary social cost of those added protections is the possibility of fewer convictions, the *Miranda* majority was willing to bear that cost. Here, had *Miranda* warnings deterred Quarles from responding to Officer Kraft's question about the whereabouts of the gun, the cost would have been something more than merely the failure to obtain evidence useful in convicting Quarles. Officer Kraft needed an answer to his question not simply to make his case against Quarles but to insure that further danger to the public did not result from the concealment of the gun in a public area. **[g]**

We conclude that the need for answers to questions in a situation posing a threat to the public safety outweighs the need for the prophylactic rule protecting the Fifth Amendment's privilege against self-incrimination. We decline to place officers such as Officer Kraft in the untenable position of having to consider, often in a matter of seconds, whether it best serves society for them to ask the necessary questions without the *Miranda* warnings and render whatever probative evidence they uncover inadmissible, or for them to give the warnings in order to preserve the admissibility of evidence they might uncover but possibly damage or destroy their ability to obtain that evidence and neutralize the volatile situation confronting them. **[h]**

In recognizing a narrow exception to the *Miranda* rules in this case, we acknowledge that to some degree we lessen the desirable clarity of that rule. * * * The exception will not be difficult for police officers to apply because in each case it will be circumscribed by the exigency which justifies it. We think police officers can and will distinguish almost instinctively between questions necessary to secure their own safety or the safety of the public and questions designed solely to elicit testimonial evidence from a suspect.

* * * The exception which we recognize today, far from complicating the thought processes and the on-the-scene judgments of police officers, will simply free them to follow their legitimate instincts when confronting situations presenting a danger to the public safety. * * *

* * *

JUSTICE O'CONNOR, concurring in the judgment in part and dissenting in part.

* * * In [its] holding, the Court acknowledges that it is departing from prior precedent, * * * and that it is "lessen[ing] the desirable clarity of [the *Miranda*] rule." * * * Were the Court writing from a clean slate, I could

agree with its holding. But *Miranda* is now the law and, in my view, the Court has not provided sufficient justification for departing from it or for blurring its now clear strictures. Accordingly, I would require suppression of the initial statement taken from respondent in this case. On the other hand, nothing in *Miranda* or the privilege itself requires exclusion of nontestimonial evidence derived from informal custodial interrogation, and I therefore agree with the Court that admission of the gun in evidence is proper. * * *

* * *

In my view, a "public safety" exception unnecessarily blurs the edges of the clear line heretofore established and makes *Miranda*'s requirements more difficult to understand. In some cases, police will benefit because a reviewing court will find that an exigency excused their failure to administer the required warnings. But in other cases, police will suffer because, though they thought an exigency excused their noncompliance, a reviewing court will view the "objective" circumstances differently and require exclusion of admissions thereby obtained. The end result will be a finespun new doctrine on public safety exigencies incident to custodial interrogation, complete with the hair-splitting distinctions that currently plague our Fourth Amendment jurisprudence. * * * **[i]**

* * *

JUSTICE MARSHALL, with whom JUSTICE BRENNAN and JUSTICE STEVENS join, dissenting.

* * *

I

* * *

[JUSTICE MARSHALL first argued that the New York courts found, as a matter of fact, that there was no threat to public safety at the time Quarles was arrested and accused the majority of ignoring these findings, adding, acidly,] [m]ore cynical observers might well conclude that a state court's findings of fact "deserv[e] a 'high measure of deference,'" * * * only when deference works against the interests of a criminal defendant. [j]

II

[The dissent then agreed with JUSTICE O'CONNOR's concurrence to the effect that a public safety exception would undermine the clarity of the administration of justice for police officers and would lead to mistakes, disagreements, and litigation. JUSTICE MARSHALL then turned to the doctrinal issues.]

III

* * *

A

The majority's error stems from a serious misunderstanding of *Miranda v. Arizona* and of the Fifth Amendment upon which that decision was based. The majority implies that *Miranda* consisted of no more than a judicial balancing act in which the benefits of "enlarged protection for the Fifth Amendment privilege" were weighed against "the cost to society in terms of fewer convictions of guilty suspects." * * * Supposedly because the scales tipped in favor of the privilege against self-incrimination, the *Miranda* Court erected a prophylactic barrier around statements made during custodial

interrogations. The majority now proposes to return to the scales of social utility to calculate whether *Miranda*'s prophylactic rule remains cost-effective when threats to public's safety are added to the balance. * * *

The majority misreads *Miranda*. * * * [k] Whether society would be better off if the police warned suspects of their rights before beginning an interrogation or whether the advantages of giving such warnings would outweigh their costs did not inform the *Miranda* decision. On the contrary, the *Miranda* Court was concerned with the proscriptions of the Fifth Amendment, and, in particular, whether the Self-Incrimination Clause permits the government to prosecute individuals based on statements made in the course of custodial interrogations.

* * *

When *Miranda* reached this Court, it was undisputed that both the States and the Federal Government were constitutionally prohibited from prosecuting defendants with confessions coerced during custodial interrogations. As a theoretical matter, the law was clear. In practice, however, the courts found it exceedingly difficult to determine whether a given confession had been coerced. Difficulties of proof and subtleties of interrogation technique made it impossible in most cases for the judiciary to decide with confidence whether the defendant had voluntarily confessed his guilt or whether his testimony had been unconstitutionally compelled. Courts around the country were spending countless hours reviewing the facts of individual custodial interrogations. * * *

* * * [T]he Court in *Miranda* determined that custodial interrogations are inherently coercive. The Court

therefore created a constitutional presumption that statements made during custodial interrogations are compelled in violation of the Fifth Amendment and are thus inadmissible in criminal prosecutions. As a result of the Court's decision in *Miranda*, a statement made during a custodial interrogation may be introduced as proof of a defendant's guilt only if the prosecution demonstrates that the defendant knowingly and intelligently waived his constitutional rights before making the statement. The now-familiar *Miranda* warnings offer law enforcement authorities a clear, easily administered device for ensuring that criminal suspects understand their constitutional rights well enough to waive them and to engage in consensual custodial interrogation.

In fashioning its "public-safety" exception to *Miranda*, the majority makes no attempt to deal with the constitutional presumption established by that case. [l] The majority does not argue that police questioning about issues of public safety is any less coercive than custodial interrogations into other matters. The majority's only contention is that police officers could more easily protect the public if *Miranda* did not apply to custodial interrogations concerning the public's safety. But *Miranda* was not a decision about public safety; it was a decision about coerced confessions. Without establishing that interrogations concerning the public's safety are less likely to be coercive than other interrogations, the majority cannot endorse the "public-safety" exception and remain faithful to the logic of *Miranda v. Arizona*.

B

[JUSTICE MARSHALL then noted that the facts of Quarles's arrest by four armed officers, handcuffing, and sudden questioning clearly amounted to coercion.] Police and suspect were acting on instinct. Officer Kraft's abrupt and pointed question pressured Quarles in precisely the way that the *Miranda* Court feared the custodial interrogations would coerce self-incriminating testimony.

* * * The "public-safety" exception is efficacious precisely because it permits police officers to coerce criminal defendants into making involuntary statements.

Indeed, in the efficacy of the "public-safety" exception lies a fundamental and constitutional defect. * * * [T]he Court has sanctioned *sub silentio* criminal prosecutions based on compelled self-incriminating statements. I find this result in direct conflict with the Fifth Amendment's dictate that "[n]o person . . . shall be compelled in any criminal case to be a witness against himself."

[The dissent then asserted that there is no constitutional prohibition on police interrogating suspects without warnings to protect the public safety.] * * * All the Fifth Amendment forbids is the introduction of coerced statements at trial. * * * **[m]**

* * * [While the public safety exception may lead to some lost prosecutions, this is not always the case.]

But however frequently or infrequently such cases arise, their regularity is irrelevant. The Fifth Amendment prohibits compelled self-incrimination. * * * [T]his prohibition is the mainstay of our adversarial system of criminal justice. Not only does it protect us against the inherent unreliability of compelled testimony, but it also ensures that criminal investigations will be conducted with integrity and that the judiciary will avoid the taint of official lawlessness. * * * [n] The policies underlying the Fifth Amendment's privilege against self-incrimination are not diminished simply because testimony is compelled to protect the public's safety. The majority should not be permitted to elude the Amendment's absolute prohibition simply by calculating special costs that arise when the public's safety is at issue. [o] Indeed, were constitutional adjudication always conducted in such an ad hoc manner, the Bill of Rights would be a most unreliable protector of individual liberties.

IV

Having determined that the Fifth Amendment renders inadmissible Quarles' response to Officer Kraft's questioning, I have no doubt that our precedents require that the gun discovered as a direct result of Quarles' statement must be presumed inadmissible as well. The gun was the direct product of a coercive custodial interrogation. * * * [p]

* * * * * * * * * *

COMMENTS

[a] It is interesting that although JUSTICE REHNQUIST eventually holds that there was Fifth Amendment coercion in this case he does not lead off with that finding.

[b] The doctrinal conclusion based on *Tucker* is what most sharply divides the majority and the dissent.

[c] What is "actual compulsion"? Does arrest, handcuffing and being asked a short, sharp question amount to psychological pressure? Is "actual compulsion" relevant after *Miranda*? The answer to the last question depends on one's view of whether the *Miranda* warnings are mere protection devices or are of constitutional stature. Compare this to the analysis in *Oregon v. Elstad* [this volume].

[d] There appears to be no established precedent for this exception. Its validity depends upon the persuasiveness of JUSTICE REHNQUIST's reasoning. This is an example of a decision that is both "activist" and "conservative." Recall that JUSTICE WHITE criticized the *Miranda* decision for unwarranted innovation. Of course, *Miranda* parted with a centuries-old common law and constitutional tradition, while the innovation in *Quarles* limits *Miranda*.

[e] The opinion is very explicit in its reference to "doctrinal underpinnings of *Miranda*." What are they? This is a clear example of how the underlying legal theory is used to determine the specific outcome of the case.

[f] The dissent notes that the New York courts closely examined the facts and found no immediate threat to public safety. It is possible that the "necessity" here was fabricated by the Court as a peg on which to hang its new exception?

[g] The deterrence that flows from *Miranda* warnings is inherent in the Bill of Rights; the defendant is informed of rights that she or he *already has*. Can the Court pick and choose which consequences are the acceptable result of the exercise of constitutional rights?

[h] The legitimacy of the Court's balancing approach hinges on the correctness of its *Tucker* reasoning that the warnings are only prophylactic rules. The exception will likely be broadly construed because a narrow rule would supposedly create a risk to the life and safety of officers and innocent bystanders.

[i] One function of the Supreme Court is to maintain the clarity of rules for lower court and agency application. It is not the only function, however, and we can only assume that the majority felt that the need to establish a public safety exception outweighs the need for clarity in this instance.

[j] There are many decision points open to the justices in deciding a case. Here, JUSTICE MARSHALL accuses the majority of straining to twist the case in such a way as to reach a desired goal; this is the accusation of "result-oriented" jurisprudence—a very serious charge in a forum where decisions are supposed to be based on principle. Justices of all ideological or jurisprudential perspectives have been accused of result-oriented jurisprudence.

[k] The Fifth Amendment is supposed to be absolute and not subject to the balancing of the needs of law enforcement against the liberty of the individual, as is the case in Fourth Amendment jurisprudence.

[l] Is JUSTICE MARSHALL correct in saying that the majority has ignored the fundamental constitutional argument? It could be argued that the majority relies on the *Tucker* doctrine, that the *Miranda* warnings do not rise themselves to the level of a constitutional principle.

[m] Thus, if public safety is really in danger, JUSTICE MARSHALL recommends that police flout the *Miranda* requirements but that the evidence thus seized need not be introduced into evidence.

[n] This suggests a practical value derived from a strict adherence to the *Miranda* rule.

[o] In a footnote, JUSTICE MARSHALL compares the *absolute* nature of the privilege against self-incrimination to the Fourth Amendment. The latter only forbids *unreasonable* searches, thus introducing a relative aspect into search and seizure analysis. See Comment [k] above.

[p] This fruits-of-the-poisonous-tree analysis differs from JUSTICE O'CONNOR's concurrence, which is based on the testimonial-nontestimonial distinction in the rule against self-incrimination. The dissent, having fastened instead on the absolute nature of the privilege, logically concludes that fruits of privilege's violation must also be suppressed.

RHODE ISLAND v. INNIS

446 U.S. 291, 100 S.Ct. 1682, 64 L.Ed.2d 297 (1980)

MR. JUSTICE STEWART delivered the opinion of the Court.

In *Miranda v. Arizona*, 384 U.S. 436 [1966] the Court held that, once a defendant in custody asks to speak with a lawyer, all interrogation must cease until a lawyer is present. The issue in this case is whether the respondent was "interrogated" in violation of the standards promulgated in the *Miranda* opinion.

I

[A Providence, R.I., taxicab driver was murdered—killed by a shotgun blast. Four days later another cab driver robbed at shotgun point told police where the robber was dropped off and identified the robber as Innis at the police station. At approximately 4:30 a.m. a motor patrol officer spotted Innis. He was arrested and advised of his *Miranda* rights.]

[Other police officers arrived and again read Innis the *Miranda* warnings. A police Captain arrived and also advised Innis of his *Miranda* rights. He stated that he understood those rights and wanted to speak with a lawyer. Innis was placed in a "caged wagon," a four-door police car with a wire screen mesh between the front and rear seats, to be driven to the central police station by officers Gleckman, Williams, and McKenna. The Captain] instructed the officers not to question the respondent or intimidate or coerce him in any way. . . .

While en route to the central station, Patrolman Gleckman initiated a conversation with Patrolman McKenna concerning the missing shotgun. As Patrolman Gleckman later testified:

"A. At this point, I was talking back and forth with Patrolman McKenna stating that I frequent this area while on patrol and [that because a school for handicapped children is located nearby,] there's a lot of handicapped children running around in this area, and God forbid one of them might find a weapon with shells and they might hurt themselves." * * *

The respondent then interrupted the conversation, stating that the officers should turn the car around so he could show them where the gun was located. [The officers proceeded to the place indicated by Innis and retrieved the shotgun, prior to which the *Miranda* warning was again administered.]
* * *

[The shotgun and Innis' statements were introduced in evidence; he was found guilty of murder. The Rhode Island Supreme Court set aside the conviction on the grounds that the officers interrogated Innis without a valid waiver of his right to counsel. This was viewed as "subtle coercion."]

II

* * *

The Court in the *Miranda* opinion * * * outlined in some detail the consequences that would result if a defendant sought to invoke [its] procedural safeguards. * * *

In the present case, the parties are in agreement that the respondent was fully informed of his *Miranda* rights and that he invoked his *Miranda* right to counsel when he told Captain Leyden that he wished to consult with a lawyer. It is also uncontested that the respondent was "in custody" while being transported to the police station.

The issue, therefore, is whether the respondent was "interrogated" by the police officers in violation of the respondent's undisputed right under *Miranda* to remain silent until he had consulted with a lawyer. In resolving this issue, we first define the term "interrogation" under *Miranda*. * * *

A

The starting point for defining "interrogation" in this context is, of course, the Court's *Miranda* opinion. There the Court observed that "[b]y custodial interrogation, we mean *questioning* initiated by law enforcement officers after a person has been taken into custody or otherwise deprived of his freedom of action in any significant way." * * * (emphasis added). This passage and other references throughout the opinion to "questioning" might suggest that the *Miranda* rules were to apply only to those police interrogation practices that involve express questioning of a defendant while in custody.

We do not, however, construe the *Miranda* opinion so narrowly. The concern of the Court in *Miranda* was that the "interrogation environment" created by the interplay of interrogation and custody would "subjugate the individual to the will of his examiner" and thereby undermine the privilege against compulsory self-incrimination. *

* * The police practices that evoked this concern included several that did not involve express questioning. For example, one of the practices discussed in *Miranda* was the use of lineups in which a coached witness would pick the defendant as the perpetrator. This was designed to establish that the defendant was in fact guilty as a predicate for further interrogation. * * * A variation on this theme discussed in *Miranda* was the so-called "reverse line-up" in which a defendant would be identified by coached witnesses as the perpetrator of a fictitious crime, with the object of inducing him to confess to the actual crime of which he was suspected in order to escape the false prosecution. * * *   The Court in *Miranda* also included in its survey of interrogation practices the use of psychological ploys, such as to "posi[t]" "the guilt of the subject," to "minimize the moral seriousness of the offense," and "to cast blame on the victim or on society." * * *   It is clear that these techniques of persuasion, no less than express questioning, were thought, in a custodial setting, to amount to interrogation.

This is not to say, however, that all statements obtained by the police after a person has been taken into custody are to be considered the product of interrogation.   As the Court in *Miranda* noted:

"Confessions remain a proper element in law enforcement. Any statement given freely and voluntarily without any compelling influences is, of course, admissible in evidence. *The fundamental import of the privilege while an individual is in custody is not whether he is allowed to talk to the police without the benefit of warnings and counsel, but whether he can be interrogated.* * * * Volunteered statements of any kind are not barred by the Fifth Amendment and their admissibility is not affected by our holding today." * * * (emphasis added).

It is clear therefore that the special procedural safeguards outlined in *Miranda* are required not where a suspect is simply taken into custody, but rather where a suspect in custody is subjected to interrogation. [a] "Interrogation," as conceptualized in the *Miranda* opinion, must reflect a measure of compulsion above and beyond that inherent in custody itself.

We conclude that the *Miranda* safeguards come into play whenever a person in custody is subjected to either express questioning or its functional equivalent. That is to say, the term "interrogation" under *Miranda* refers not only to express questioning, but also to any words or actions on the part of the police (other than those normally attendant to arrest and custody) that the police should know are reasonably likely to elicit an incriminating response from the suspect. The latter portion of this definition focuses primarily upon the perceptions of the suspect, rather than the intent of the police. This focus reflects the fact that the *Miranda* safeguards were designed to vest a suspect in custody with an added measure of protection against coercive police practices, without regard to objective proof of the underlying intent of the police. A practice that the police should know is reasonably likely to evoke an incrimi-

nating response from a suspect thus amounts to interrogation. But, since the police surely cannot be held accountable for the unforeseeable results of their words or actions, the definition of interrogation can extend only to words or actions on the part of police officers that they should have known were reasonably likely to elicit an incriminating response.

B

Turning to the facts of the present case, we conclude that the respondent was not "interrogated" within the meaning of *Miranda*. It is undisputed that the first prong of the definition of "interrogation" was not satisfied, for the conversation between Patrolmen Gleckman and McKenna included no express questioning of the respondent. Rather, that conversation was, at least in form, nothing more than a dialogue between the two officers to which no response from the respondent was invited.

Moreover, it cannot be fairly concluded that the respondent was subjected to the "functional equivalent" of questioning. It cannot be said, in short, that Patrolmen Gleckman and McKenna should have known that their conversation was reasonably likely to elicit an incriminating response from the respondent. There is nothing in the record to suggest that the officers were aware that the respondent was peculiarly susceptible to an appeal to his conscience concerning the safety of handicapped children. Nor is there anything in the record to suggest that the police knew that the respondent was unusually disoriented or upset at the time of his arrest.

The case thus boils down to

whether, in the context of a brief conversation, the officers should have known that the respondent would suddenly be moved to make a self-incriminating response. Given the fact that the entire conversation appears to have consisted of no more than a few offhand remarks, we cannot say that the officers should have known that it was reasonably likely that Innis would so respond. This is not a case where the police carried on a lengthy harangue in the presence of the suspect. Nor does the record support the respondent's contention that, under the circumstances, the officers' comments were particularly "evocative." It is our view, therefore, that the respondent was not subjected by the police to words or actions that the police should have known were reasonably likely to elicit an incriminating response from him. **[b]**

The Rhode Island Supreme Court erred, in short, in equating "subtle compulsion" with interrogation. That the officers' comments struck a responsive chord is readily apparent. Thus, it may be said, as the Rhode Island Supreme Court did say, that the respondent was subjected to "subtle compulsion." But that is not the end of the inquiry. It must also be established that a suspect's incriminating response was the product of words or actions on the part of the police that they should have known were reasonably likely to elicit an incriminating response. This was not established in the present case.

For the reasons stated, the judgment of the Supreme Court of Rhode Island is vacated, and the case is remanded to that court for further proceedings not inconsistent with this opinion.

It is so ordered.

[JUSTICE WHITE concurred.]

MR. CHIEF JUSTICE BURGER, concurring in the judgment.

Since the result is not inconsistent with *Miranda* * * * I concur in the judgment.

The meaning of *Miranda* has become reasonably clear and law enforcement practices have adjusted to its strictures; I would neither overrule *Miranda*, disparage it, nor extend it at this late date. * * * **[c]**

MR. JUSTICE MARSHALL, with whom MR. JUSTICE BRENNAN joins, dissenting.

I am substantially in agreement with the Court's definition of "interrogation." * * *

I am utterly at a loss, however, to understand how this objective standard as applied to the facts before us can rationally lead to the conclusion that there was no interrogation. Innis was arrested at 4:30 a.m., handcuffed, searched, advised of his rights, and placed in the back seat of a patrol car. Within a short time he had been twice more advised of his rights and driven away in a four-door sedan with three police officers. Two officers sat in the front seat and one sat beside Innis in the back seat. Since the car traveled no more than a mile before Innis agreed to point out the location of the murder weapon, Officer Gleckman must have begun almost immediately to talk about the search for the shotgun.

The Court attempts to characterize Gleckman's statements as "no more than a few offhand remarks" which could not reasonably have been expected to elicit a response. * * * If the statements had been addressed to respondent, it would be impossible to draw such a conclusion. The simple message of the "talking back and forth" between Gleckman and McKenna was that they had to find the shotgun to avert a child's death.

One can scarcely imagine a stronger appeal to the conscience of a suspect—*any* suspect—than the assertion that if the weapon is not found an innocent person will be hurt or killed. And not just any innocent person, but an innocent child—a little girl—a helpless, handicapped little girl on her way to school. The notion that such an appeal could not be expected to have any effect unless the suspect were known to have some special interest in handicapped children verges on the ludicrous. As a matter of fact, the appeal to a suspect to confess for the sake of others, to "display some evidence of decency and honor," is a classic interrogation technique. * * *

* * *

MR. JUSTICE STEVENS, dissenting.

* * *

I

* * * In my view any statement that would normally be understood by the average listener as calling for a response is the functional equivalent of a direct question, whether or not it is punctuated by a question mark. The Court, however, takes a much narrower view. It holds that police conduct is not the "functional equivalent" of direct questioning unless the police should have known that what they were saying or doing was likely to elicit an incriminating response from the suspect. This holding represents a plain departure from the principles set forth in *Miranda*.

* * *

From the suspect's point of view, the effectiveness of the warnings depends on whether it appears that the police are scrupulously honoring his rights. Apparent attempts to elicit information from a suspect after he has invoked his right to cut off questioning necessarily demean that right and tend to reinstate the imbalance between police and suspect that the *Miranda* warnings are designed to correct. Thus, if the rationale for requiring those warnings in the first place is to be respected, any police conduct or statements that would appear to a reasonable person in the suspect's position to call for a response must be considered "interrogation."

In short, in order to give full protection to a suspect's right to be free from any interrogation at all, the definition of "interrogation" must include any police statement or conduct that has the same purpose or effect as a direct question. Statements that appear to call for a response from the suspect, as well as those that are designed to do so, should be considered interrogation. By prohibiting only those relatively few statements or actions that a police officer should know are likely to elicit an incriminating response, the Court today accords a suspect considerably less protection. Indeed, since I suppose most suspects are unlikely to incriminate themselves even when questioned directly, this new definition will almost certainly exclude every statement that is not punctuated with a question mark from the concept of "interrogation."

The difference between the approach required by a faithful adherence to *Miranda* and the stinted test applied by the Court today can be illustrated by comparing three different ways in which Officer Gleckman could have communicated his fears about the possible dangers posed by the shotgun to handicapped children.   He could have:

> (1) directly asked Innis:
>
> Will you please tell me where the shotgun is so we can protect handicapped schoolchildren from danger?
>
> (2) announced to the other officers in the wagon:
>
> If the man sitting in the back seat with me should decide to tell us where the gun is, we can protect handicapped children from danger.
>
> or (3) stated to the other officers:
>
> It would be too bad if a little handicapped girl would pick up the gun that this man left in the area and maybe kill herself.

In my opinion, all three of these statements should be considered interrogation because all three appear to be designed to elicit a response from anyone who in fact knew where the gun was located.   Under the Court's test, on the other hand, the form of the statements would be critical.   The third statement would not be interrogation because in the Court's view there was no reason for Officer Gleckman to

believe that Innis was susceptible to this type of an implied appeal; * * * therefore, the statement would not be reasonably likely to elicit an incriminating response.   Assuming that this is true, * * * then it seems to me that the first two statements, which would be just as unlikely to elicit such a response, should also not be considered interrogation.   But, because the first statement is clearly an express question, it *would* be considered interrogation under the Court's test.   The second statement, although just as clearly a deliberate appeal to Innis to reveal the location of the gun, would presumably not be interrogation because (a) it was not in form a direct question and (b) it does not fit within the "reasonably likely to elicit an incriminating response" category that applies to indirect interrogation.

As this example illustrates, the Court's test creates an incentive for police to ignore a suspect's invocation of his rights in order to make continued attempts to extract information from him.   If a suspect does not appear to be susceptible to a particular type of psychological pressure, the police are apparently free to exert that pressure on him despite his request for counsel, so long as they are careful not to punctuate their statements with question marks.   And if, contrary to all reasonable expectations, the suspect makes an incriminating statement, that statement can be used against him at trial.   The Court thus turns *Miranda*'s unequivocal rule against any interrogation at all into a trap in which unwary suspects may be caught by police deception.

* * *

* * * * * * * * * * *

COMMENTS

[a] Despite popular opinion, an arrest is perfectly legal without administering *Miranda* warnings.

[b] Compare this factual conclusion to the views of the dissenting Justices. Which view seems to be more realistic?

[c] When first on the Court, CHIEF JUSTICE BURGER vowed to have *Miranda* overturned; this statement is an important signal that this campaign would not be pursued.

MORAN v. BURBINE

475 U.S. 412, 106 S.Ct. 1135, 89 L.Ed.2d 410 (1986)

JUSTICE O'CONNOR delivered the opinion of the Court.

After being informed of his rights pursuant to *Miranda v. Arizona*, [this volume], and after executing a series of written waivers, respondent confessed to the murder of a young woman. At no point during the course of the interrogation, which occurred prior to arraignment, did he request an attorney. While he was in police custody, his sister attempted to retain a lawyer to represent him. The attorney telephoned the police station and received assurances that respondent would not be questioned further until the next day. In fact, the interrogation session that yielded the inculpatory statements began later that evening. The question presented is whether either the conduct of the police or respondent's ignorance of the attorney's efforts to reach him taints the validity of the waivers and therefore requires exclusion of the confessions.

I

[Cranston, R.I. police arrested Burbine and two others for a burglary. Shortly before, they learned from an informant that Burbine was responsible for the murder of Mary Jo Hickey that occurred in Providence, R.I. a few weeks earlier. They informed the Providence Police Department and administered *Miranda* warnings. Burbine refused to sign a written waiver. The two other arrested men implicated Burbine in the murder. At 7:00 p.m. Providence police officers took Burbine into custody and transported him to Providence. At about 7:45 p.m., Burbine's sister called the Public Defender's Office to obtain legal assistance for her brother for the breaking and entering charge, as she was unaware that he was then under suspicion for murder. She reached Assistant Public Defender Allegra Munson, who agreed to represent him. At 8:15 p.m., Ms. Munson telephoned the Cranston police station. Put through to the detective division, she spoke to a male whose identity is not known. She asked if Brian Burbine was being held; the person responded affirmatively. She stated that she "would act as Burbine's legal counsel in the event that the police intended to place him in a lineup or question him. The unidentified person told Ms. Munson that the police would not be questioning Burbine or putting him in a lineup and that they were through with him for the night. Ms. Munson was not informed that the Providence Police were at the Cranston police station or that Burbine was a suspect in Mary's murder.' * * * At all relevant times, respondent was unaware of his sister's efforts to retain counsel and of the fact and contents of Ms. Munson's telephone conversation."]

[In fact, Burbine was questioned by Providence police that evening, each time under properly administered and executed *Miranda* warnings. Burbine confessed orally and in writing. He had access to a telephone which he did not use.]

[Burbine's motion to suppress the statements were denied by the trial court, which found that his statements were voluntary and that there while "Ms. Munson did telephone the detective bureau on the evening in question, * * * 'there was no . . . conspiracy or collusion on the part of the Cranston Police Department to secrete this defendant from his attorney.'" Burbine was found guilty of murder in the first degree by a jury. The Rhode Island Supreme Court affirmed the conviction, ruling by a divided vote, that "[f]ailure to inform respondent of Ms. Munson's efforts to represent him * * * did not undermine the validity of the waivers."]

[The United States District Court denied a writ of habeas corpus, but the Court of Appeals reversed. It found that the police's conduct had fatally tainted respondent's 'otherwise valid' waiver of his Fifth Amendment privilege against self-incrimination and right to counsel. That court did not address any Sixth or Fourteenth Amendments arguments. The "court reasoned that by failing to inform respondent that an attorney had called and that she had been assured that no questioning would take place until the next day, the police had deprived [Burbine] of information crucial to his ability to waive his rights knowingly and intelligently."]

We granted certiorari to decide whether a prearraignment confession preceded by an otherwise valid waiver must be suppressed either because the police misinformed an inquiring attorney about their plans concerning the suspect or because they failed to inform the suspect of the attorney's efforts to reach him. * * * We now reverse.

II

* * *

Respondent does not dispute that the Providence police followed [the *Miranda*] procedures with precision. * * * Nor does respondent contest the Rhode Island courts' determination that he at no point requested the presence of a lawyer. He contends instead that the confessions must be suppressed because the police's failure to inform him of the attorney's telephone call deprived him of information essential to his ability to knowingly waive his Fifth Amendment rights. In the alternative, he suggests that to fully protect the Fifth Amendment values served by *Miranda*, we should extend that decision to condemn the conduct of the Providence police. We address each contention in turn.

A

Echoing the standard first articulated in *Johnson v. Zerbst*, [this volume], *Miranda* holds that "[t]he defendant may waive effectuation" of the rights conveyed in the warnings "provided the waiver is made voluntarily, knowingly and intelligently." * * * The inquiry has two distinct dimensions. * * * First, the relinquishment of the right must have been voluntary in the sense that it was the product of a free and deliberate choice rather than intimidation, coercion, or deception. Second, the waiver must have been made with a full awareness of both the nature of the right being abandoned and the consequences of the decision to abandon it. Only if the "totality of the circumstances surrounding the interrogation" reveals both an uncoerced choice and the requisite level of comprehension may a court properly conclude that the *Miranda* rights have been waived. * * * [a]

Under this standard, we have no doubt that respondent validly waived his right to remain silent and to the presence of counsel. The voluntariness of the waiver is not at issue. As the Court of Appeals correctly acknowledged, the record is devoid of any suggestion that police resorted to physical or psychological pressure to elicit the statements. * * * Indeed it appears that it was respondent, and not the police, who spontaneously initiated the conversation that led to the first and most damaging confession. * * * Nor is there any question about respondent's comprehension of the full panoply of rights set out in the *Miranda* warnings and of the potential consequences of a decision to relinquish them. Nonetheless, the Court of Appeals believed that the "[d]eliberate or reckless" conduct of the police, in particular their failure to inform respondent of the telephone call, fatally undermined the validity of the otherwise proper waiver. * * * We find this conclusion untenable as a matter of both logic and precedent.

Events occurring outside of the presence of the suspect and entirely unknown to him surely can have no bearing on the capacity to comprehend and knowingly relinquish a constitutional right. Under the analysis of the Court of Appeals, the same defendant, armed with the same information and confronted with precisely the same police conduct, would have knowingly waived his *Miranda* rights had a lawyer not telephoned the police station to inquire about his status. [b] Nothing in any of our waiver decisions or in our understanding of the essential components of a valid waiver requires so incongruous a result. No doubt the

additional information would have been useful to respondent; perhaps even it might have affected his decision to confess. But we have never read the Constitution to require that the police supply a suspect with a flow of information to help him calibrate his self-interest in deciding whether to speak or stand by his rights. * * * Once it is determined that a suspect's decision not to rely on his rights was uncoerced, that he at all times knew he could stand mute and request a lawyer, and that he was aware of the State's intention to use his statements to secure a conviction, the analysis is complete and the waiver is valid as a matter of law. The Court of Appeals' conclusion to the contrary was in error.

Nor do we believe that the level of the police's culpability in failing to inform respondent of the telephone call has any bearing on the validity of the waivers. In light of the state-court findings that there was no "conspiracy or collusion" on the part of the police, * * * we have serious doubts about whether the Court of Appeals was free to conclude that their conduct constituted "deliberate or reckless irresponsibility." * * * [c] But whether intentional or inadvertent, the state of mind of the police is irrelevant to the question of the intelligence and voluntariness of respondent's election to abandon his rights. Although highly inappropriate, even deliberate deception of an attorney could not possibly affect a suspect's decision to waive his *Miranda* rights unless he were at least aware of the incident. Compare *Escobedo v. Illinois*, 378 U.S. 478, 481 (1964) (excluding confession where police incorrectly told the *suspect* that his lawyer "'didn't want to see' him"). Nor was the failure to inform respondent of the telephone call the kind of "trick[ery]" that can vitiate the validity of a waiver. *Miranda.* * * * Granting that the "deliberate or reckless" withholding of information is objectionable as a matter of ethics, such conduct is only relevant to the constitutional validity of a waiver if it deprives a defendant of knowledge essential to his ability to understand the nature of his rights and the consequences of abandoning them. Because respondent's voluntary decision to speak was made with full awareness and comprehension of all the information *Miranda* requires the police to convey, the waivers were valid. [d]

B

At oral argument respondent acknowledged that a constitutional rule requiring the police to inform a suspect of an attorney's efforts to reach him would represent a significant extension of our precedents. * * * He contends, however, that the conduct of the Providence police was so inimical to the Fifth Amendment values *Miranda* seeks to protect that we should read that decision to condemn their behavior. Regardless of any issue of waiver, he urges, the Fifth Amendment requires the reversal of a conviction if the police are less than forthright in their dealings with an attorney or if they fail to tell a suspect of a lawyer's unilateral efforts to contact him. Because the proposed modification ignores the underlying purposes of the *Miranda* rules and because we think that the decision as written strikes the proper balance between society's legitimate law enforcement interests and the protection of the defendant's Fifth Amendment rights, we decline

the invitation to further extend *Miranda*'s reach.

At the outset, while we share respondent's distaste for the deliberate misleading of an officer of the court, reading *Miranda* to forbid police deception of an *attorney* "would cut [the decision] completely loose from its own explicitly stated rationale." * * * As is now well established, "[t]he . . . *Miranda* warnings are 'not themselves rights protected by the Constitution but [are] instead measures to insure that the [suspect's] right against compulsory self-incrimination [is] protected.'" [citing *New York v. Quarles*, [this volume] and *Michigan v. Tucker* [this volume]]. Their objective is not to mold police conduct for its own sake. Nothing in the Constitution vests in us the authority to mandate a code of behavior for state officials wholly unconnected to any federal right or privilege. The purpose of the *Miranda* warnings instead is to dissipate the compulsion inherent in custodial interrogation and, in so doing, guard against abridgment of the suspect's Fifth Amendment rights. Clearly, a rule that focuses on how the police treat an attorney —conduct that has no relevance at all to the degree of compulsion experienced by the defendant during interrogation—would ignore both *Miranda*'s mission and its only source of legitimacy. [e]

Nor are we prepared to adopt a rule requiring that the police inform a suspect of an attorney's efforts to reach him. While such a rule might add marginally to *Miranda*'s goal of dispelling the compulsion inherent in custodial interrogation, overriding practical considerations counsel against its adoption. As we have stressed on numerous occasions, "[o]ne of the principal advantages" of *Miranda* is the ease and clarity of its application. * * * We have little doubt that the approach urged by respondent and endorsed by the Court of Appeals would have the inevitable consequence of muddying *Miranda*'s otherwise relatively clear waters. The legal questions it would spawn are legion: To what extent should the police be held accountable for knowing that the accused has counsel? Is it enough that someone in the station house knows, or must the interrogating officer himself know of counsel's efforts to contact the suspect? Do counsel's efforts to talk to the suspect concerning one criminal investigation trigger the obligation to inform the defendant before interrogation may proceed on a wholly separate matter? We are unwilling to modify *Miranda* in a manner that would so clearly undermine the decision's central "virtue of informing police and prosecutors with specificity . . . what they may do in conducting [a] custodial interrogation, and of informing courts under what circumstances statements obtained during such interrogation are not admissible." * * * **[f]**

Moreover, problems of clarity to one side, reading *Miranda* to require the police in each instance to inform a suspect of an attorney's efforts to reach him would work a substantial and, we think, inappropriate shift in the subtle balance struck in that decision. Custodial interrogations implicate two competing concerns. On the one hand, "the need for police questioning as a tool for effective enforcement of criminal laws" cannot be doubted. * * * Admissions of guilt are more than merely "desirable;" * * * they are essential to society's compelling interest in finding, convicting, and punishing those who violate the law. On the other hand, the Court has recognized that the interrogation process is "inherently coercive" and that, as a consequence, there exists a substantial risk that the police will inadvertently traverse the fine line between legitimate efforts to elicit admissions and constitutionally impermissible compulsion. * * * *Miranda* attempted to reconcile these opposing concerns by giving the *defendant* the power to exert some control over the course of the interrogation. Declining to adopt the more extreme position that the actual presence of a lawyer was necessary to dispel the coercion inherent in custodial interrogation, * * * the Court found that the suspect's Fifth Amendment rights could be adequately protected by less intrusive means. Police questioning, often an essential part of the investigatory process, could continue in its traditional form, the Court held, but only if the suspect clearly understood that, at any time, he could bring the proceeding to a halt or, short of that, call in an attorney to give advice and monitor the conduct of his interrogators.

The position urged by respondent would upset this carefully drawn approach in a manner that is both unnecessary for the protection of the Fifth Amendment privilege and injurious to legitimate law enforcement. Because, as *Miranda* holds, full comprehension of the rights to remain silent and request an attorney are sufficient to dispel whatever coercion is inherent in the interrogation process, a rule requiring the police to inform the suspect of an attorney's efforts to contact him would contribute to the protection of the Fifth Amendment privilege only incidentally, if at all. This minimal benefit, however, would come at a substantial cost to society's legitimate and substantial interest in securing admissions of guilt. Indeed, the very premise of the Court of Appeals was not that awareness of Ms. Munson's phone call would have dissipated the coercion of the interrogation room, but that it might have convinced respondent not to speak at all. * * * Because neither the letter nor purposes of *Miranda* require this additional handicap on otherwise permissible investigatory efforts, we are unwilling to expand the *Miranda* rules to require the police to keep the suspect abreast of the status of his legal representation. **[g]**

We acknowledge that a number of state courts have reached a contrary conclusion. * * * We recognize also that our interpretation of the Federal Constitution, if given the dissent's expansive gloss, is at odds with the policy recommendations embodied in the American Bar Association Standards of Criminal Justice. * * * Notwithstanding the dissent's protestations, however, our interpretive duties go well beyond deferring to the numerical preponderance of lower court decisions or to the subconstitutional recommendations of even so esteemed a body as the American Bar Association. * * * **[h]** Nothing we say today disables the States from adopting different requirements for the conduct of its employees and officials as a matter of state law. We hold only that the Court of Appeals erred in construing the Fifth Amendment to the Federal Constitution to require the exclusion of respondent's three confessions.

III

[In Part III the Court dismissed Burbine's argument that the Sixth Amendment right to the assistance of counsel was violated by the facts of this case. It is true that after the first formal charge a defendant has an absolute right to have a lawyer with him in the police station during any interrogation. But no formal charges had yet been preferred against Burbine. The purpose of the Sixth Amendment is "not to wrap a protective cloak around the attorney-client relationship for its own sake," but to assure that a defendant will not be left unguarded against skilled prosecution forces at such time that formal charges are preferred against him and it becomes important to have knowledge of the intricacies of the law. The fact that a suspect is in custody or that this is a "critical stage" does not change this rule. The Court also noted that the true basis of *Escobedo* and *Miranda* rest on the Fifth Amendment rather than on a Sixth Amendment right to counsel.]

IV

Finally, respondent contends that the conduct of the police was so offensive as to deprive him of the fundamental fairness guaranteed by the Due Process Clause of the Fourteenth Amendment. Focusing primarily on the impropriety of conveying false information to an attorney, he invites us to declare that such behavior should be condemned as violative of canons fundamental to the "'traditions and conscience of our people.'" *Rochin v. California*, [this volume] * * *. We do not question that on facts more egregious than those presented here police deception might rise to a level of a due process violation. Accordingly, JUSTICE STEVENS' apocalyptic suggestion that we have approved any and all forms of police misconduct is demonstrably incorrect. We hold only that, on these facts, the challenged conduct falls short of the kind of misbehavior that so shocks the sensibilities of civilized society as to warrant a federal intrusion into the criminal processes of the States.

We hold therefore that the Court of Appeals erred in finding that the Federal Constitution required the exclusion of the three inculpatory statements. Accordingly, we reverse and remand for proceedings consistent with this opinion.

So ordered.

JUSTICE STEVENS, with whom JUSTICE BRENNAN and JUSTICE MARSHALL join, dissenting.

This case poses fundamental questions about our system of justice. As this Court has long recognized, and reaffirmed only weeks ago, "ours is an accusatorial and not an inquisitorial system." * * * The Court's opinion today represents a startling departure from that basic insight.
 * * *

The recognition that ours is an accusatorial, and not an inquisitorial system nevertheless requires that the government's actions, even in responding to this brutal crime, respect those liberties and rights that distinguish this society from most others. * * *

The Court's holding focuses on the period after a suspect has been taken into custody and before he has been charged with an offense. The core of

the Court's holding is that police interference with an attorney's access to her client during that period is not unconstitutional. The Court reasons that a State has a compelling interest, not simply in custodial interrogation, but in lawyer-free, incommunicado custodial interrogation. Such incommunicado interrogation is so important that a lawyer may be given false information that prevents her presence and representation; it is so important that police may refuse to inform a suspect of his attorney's communications and immediate availability. This conclusion flies in the face of this Court's repeated expressions of deep concern about incommunicado questioning. Until today, incommunicado questioning has been viewed with the strictest scrutiny by this Court; today, incommunicado questioning is embraced as a societal goal of the highest order that justifies police deception of the shabbiest kind.
 * * *

Police interference with communications between an attorney and his client is a recurrent problem. [Several cases were cited by JUSTICE STEVENS.] * * * In all these cases, the police not only failed to inform the suspect, but also misled the attorneys.
 * * *

The near-consensus of state courts and the legal profession's Standards about this recurrent problem lends powerful support to the conclusion that police may not interfere with communications between an attorney and the client whom they are questioning. * * *

 * * *

II

[The government has a heavy burden of proving the validity of a waiver of the right to silence when the waiver is made in custody.]

* * * [*Miranda* requires warnings for a valid waiver and *Edwards v. Arizona*, [this volume] holds that waiver is invalid as a matter of law if it is given as a result of police-initiated interrogation after a suspect invokes the right to counsel.] * * * In light of our decision in *Edwards*, the Court is simply wrong in stating that "the analysis is complete and the waiver is valid as a matter of law" when these facts have been established. * * * Like the failure to give warnings and like police initiation of interrogation after a request for counsel, police deception of a suspect through omission of information regarding attorney communications greatly exacerbates the inherent problems of incommunicado interrogation and requires a clear principle to safeguard the presumption against the waiver of constitutional rights. As in those situations, the police deception should render a subsequent waiver invalid.

Indeed, as *Miranda* itself makes clear, proof that the required warnings have been given is a necessary, but by no means sufficient, condition for establishing a valid waiver. As the Court plainly stated in *Miranda*, "any evidence that the accused was threatened, tricked, or cajoled into a waiver will, of course, show that the defendant did not voluntarily waive his privilege. The requirement of warnings and waiver of rights is a fundamental with respect to the Fifth Amendment privilege and not simply a preliminary ritual to existing methods of interrogation." * * *

In this case it would be perfectly clear that Burbine's waiver was invalid if, for example, [the detective] had "threatened, tricked, or cajoled" Burbine in their private pre-confession meeting—perhaps by misdescribing the statements obtained from [the arrested burglars]—even though, under the Court's truncated analysis of the issue, Burbine fully understood his rights. For *Miranda* clearly condemns threats or trickery that cause a suspect to make an unwise waiver of his rights even though he fully understands those rights. In my opinion there can be no constitutional distinction—as the Court appears to draw, * * *—between a deceptive misstatement and the concealment by the police of the critical fact that an attorney retained by the accused or his family has offered assistance, either by telephone or in person.

Thus, the Court's truncated analysis, which relies in part on a distinction between deception accomplished by means of an omission of a critically important fact and deception by means of a misleading statement, is simply untenable. If, as the Court asserts, "the analysis is at an end" as soon as the suspect is provided with enough information to have the *capacity* to understand and exercise his rights, I see no reason why the police should not be permitted to make the same kind of misstatements to the suspect that they are apparently allowed to make to his lawyer. *Miranda*, however, clearly establishes that both kinds of deception vitiate the suspect's waiver of his right to counsel. [i]

As the Court notes, the question is whether the deceptive police conduct "deprives a defendant of knowledge essential to his ability to understand the nature of his rights and the consequences of abandoning them." * * * This question has been resoundingly answered time and time again by the state courts that, with rare exceptions, have correctly understood the meaning of the *Miranda* opinion. The majority's blithe assertion of "no doubt" about the outcome of this case, * * * simply ignores the prevailing view of the state courts that have considered this issue. * * * Unlike the majority, the state courts have realized that attorney communication to the police about the client is an event that has a direct "bearing" on the knowing and intelligent waiver of constitutional rights. As the Oregon Supreme Court has explained: "To pass up an abstract offer to call some unknown lawyer is very different from refusing to talk with an identified attorney actually available to provide at least initial assistance and advice, whatever might be arranged in the long run.   A suspect indifferent to the first offer may well react quite differently to the second." * * *

In short, settled principles about construing waivers of constitutional rights and about the need for strict presumptions in custodial interrogations, as well as a plain reading of the *Miranda* opinion itself, overwhelmingly support the conclusion reached by almost every state court that has considered the matter—a suspect's waiver of his right to counsel is invalid if police refuse to inform the suspect of his counsel's communications.

* * *

* * * * * * * * * *

COMMENTS

[a] At face value this "totality of the circumstances" standard for a valid waiver could plausibly include the circumstances of this case: that a lawyer—unbeknownst to the suspect—had been retained to advise him.

[b] This is an interesting way of reframing the case, moving the reader's attention away from the facts of this case to a hypothetical where no lawyer has been hired. In the remainder of this paragraph the Court fleshes out its suggestion into a general rule of what information is required to be given to effect a valid *Miranda* waiver.

[c] This is because the federal habeas corpus act 28 U.S.C. §2254(d) presumes the correctness of state court findings. See *Kuhlmann v. Wilson*, [this volume].

[d] Do you think this ruling validates police withholding information from suspects? If so, is this the same as the withholding of information that is a normal part of business bargaining?

[e] This paragraph clearly states the attitude of the conservative justices of the Burger-Rehnquist Court. Without seeking to overturn *Miranda*, JUSTICE O'CONNOR gives it a restrictive reading. It would not be out of place for a more liberal justice to argue that since an attorney is the agent of the suspect and an important source of dissipating the compulsion that arises from the custodial atmosphere, that misinformation to the attorney contributes to this compulsion. This argument is made by JUSTICE STEVENS in a portion of his dissent not reprinted.

[f] The practical concern is that literally thousands of legal challenges by attorneys for convicted defendants who confessed would object not only to the relatively rare "unknown lawyer" scenario, but to other factors unknown to the defendant. It would seem relatively easy for courts to limit such challenges to cases involving information about "unknown lawyers," (*i.e.*, the facts in this case) but the Supreme Court clearly does not wish to open up the issue.

[g] The Court honestly confronts the policy implications of its holding and makes it clear that it intends to maintain rules that do not give an "edge" to defendants challenging the validity of confessions under the circumstances of this case.

[h] The Court is quite right in stating that its prime obligation is to its own considered understanding of the dictates of the Constitution. However, in some cases the Court looks to trends in the state courts for guidance. See, *e.g.*, *Wolf v. Colorado* [this volume] and *Mapp v. Ohio* [this volume].

[i] JUSTICE STEVENS seems to be correct in saying that on the waiver issue, it does not matter to the majority whether the police intentionally or ignorantly failed to tell Burbine that an attorney called. It seemed, however, to matter to the Rhode Island judges who found no "conspiracy." Should it make a difference that the police actively seek to hide information or that they do so because of administrative sloppiness?

MICHIGAN v. MOSLEY

423 U.S. 96, 96 S.Ct. 321, 46 L.Ed.2d 313 (1975)

MR. JUSTICE STEWART delivered the opinion of the Court.

[Based on a tip, Detroit police arrested Mosley for robbery, brought him to the Robbery and Breaking and Entering Bureau of the police headquarters building, advised him of his *Miranda* rights, and began questioning him.] When Mosley said he did not want to answer any questions about the robberies, Detective Cowie promptly ceased the interrogation. The completion of the arrest papers and the questioning of Mosley together took approximately 20 minutes. At no time during the questioning did Mosley indicate a desire to consult with a lawyer, and there is no claim that the procedures followed to this point did not fully comply with the strictures of the *Miranda* opinion. Mosley was then taken to a ninth-floor cell block.

Shortly after 6 p.m., Detective Hill of the Detroit Police Department Homicide Bureau brought Mosley from the cell block to the fifth-floor office of the Homicide Bureau for questioning about the fatal shooting of a man named Leroy Williams. * * * Mosley had not been arrested on this charge or interrogated about it by Detective Cowie. Before questioning Mosley about this homicide, Detective Hill carefully advised him of his "*Miranda* rights." Mosley read the notification form both silently and aloud, and Detective Hill then read and explained the warnings to him and had him sign the form. Mosley at first denied any involvement in the Williams murder, but after the officer told him that

Anthony Smith had confessed to participating in the slaying and had named him as the "shooter," Mosley made a statement implicating himself in the homicide. The interrogation by Detective Hill lasted approximately 15 minutes, and at no time during its course did Mosley ask to consult with a lawyer or indicate that he did not want to discuss the homicide. In short, there is no claim that the procedures followed during Detective Hill's interrogation of Mosley, standing alone, did not fully comply with the strictures of the *Miranda* opinion.

[A motion to suppress his incriminating statement was denied and Mosley was convicted by a jury of first-degree murder. The Michigan Court of Appeals, reversed the conviction, holding that the second interrogation of Mosley had been a *per se* violation of the *Miranda* doctrine.]

* * *

* * * The issue in this case * * * is whether the conduct of the Detroit police that led to Mosley's incriminating statement did in fact violate the *Miranda* "guidelines," so as to render the statement inadmissible in evidence against Mosley at his trial. Resolution of the question turns almost entirely on the interpretation of a single passage in the *Miranda* opinion, upon which the Michigan appellate court relied in finding a *per se* violation of *Miranda*:

"Once warnings have been given, the subsequent procedure is clear. If the individual indicates in any manner, at any time prior to or during questioning, that he wishes to remain silent, the interrogation must cease. At this point he has shown that he intends to exercise his Fifth Amendment privilege; any statement taken after the person invokes his privilege cannot be other than the product of compulsion, subtle or otherwise. Without the right to cut off questioning, the setting of in-custody interrogation operates on the individual to overcome free choice in producing a statement after the privilege has been once invoked." * * *

This passage states that "the interrogation must cease" when the person in custody indicates that "he wishes to remain silent." It does not state under what circumstances, if any, a resumption of questioning is permissible. The passage could be literally read to mean that a person who has invoked his "right to silence" can never again be subjected to custodial interrogation by any police officer at any time or place on any subject. Another possible construction of the passage would characterize "any statement taken after the person invokes his privilege" as "the product of compulsion" and would therefore mandate its exclusion from evidence, even if it were volunteered by the person in custody without any further interrogation whatever. Or the passage could be interpreted to require only the immediate cessation of questioning, and to permit a resumption of interrogation after a momentary respite.

It is evident that any of these possible literal interpretations would lead to absurd and unintended results. To permit the continuation of custodial

interrogation after a momentary cessation would clearly frustrate the purposes of *Miranda* by allowing repeated rounds of questioning to undermine the will of the person being questioned. At the other extreme, a blanket prohibition against the taking of voluntary statements or a permanent immunity from further interrogation, regardless of the circumstances, would transform the *Miranda* safeguards into wholly irrational obstacles to legitimate police investigative activity, and deprive suspects of an opportunity to make informed and intelligent assessments of their interests. [a] Clearly, therefore, neither this passage nor any other passage in the *Miranda* opinion can sensibly be read to create a *per se* proscription of indefinite duration upon any further questioning by any police officer on any subject, once the person in custody has indicated a desire to remain silent.

A reasonable and faithful interpretation of the *Miranda* opinion must rest on the intention of the Court in that case to adopt "fully effective means... to notify the person of his right of silence and to assure that the exercise of the right will be scrupulously honored. * * * " * * * The critical safeguard identified in the passage at issue is a person's "right to cut off questioning." * * * Through the exercise of his option to terminate questioning he can control the time at which questioning occurs, the subjects discussed, and the duration of the interrogation. The requirement that law enforcement authorities must respect a person's exercise of that option counteracts the coercive pressures of the custodial setting. We therefore conclude that the admissibility of statements obtained after the person in custody has decided to remain silent depends under *Miranda* on whether his "right to cut of questioning" was "scrupulously honored."

A review of the circumstances leading to Mosley's confession reveals that his "right to cut of questioning" was fully respected in this case. Before his initial interrogation, Mosley was carefully advised that he was under no obligation to answer any questions and could remain silent if he wished. He orally acknowledged that he understood the *Miranda* warnings and then signed a printed notification-of-rights form. When Mosley stated that he did not want to discuss the robberies, Detective Cowie immediately ceased the interrogation and did not try either to resume the questioning or in any way to persuade Mosley to reconsider his position. After an interval of more than two hours, Mosley was questioned by another police officer at another location about an unrelated holdup murder. He was given full and complete *Miranda* warnings at the outset of the second interrogation. He was thus reminded again that he could remain silent and could consult with a lawyer, and was carefully given a full and fair opportunity to exercise these options. The subsequent questioning did not undercut Mosley's previous decision not to answer Detective Cowie's inquiries. Detective Hill did not resume the interrogation about the * * * robbery, but instead focused exclusively on the Leroy Williams homicide, a crime different in nature and in time and place of occurrence from the robberies for which Mosley had been arrested and interrogated by Detective Cowie. Although it is not clear from the record how much Detective Hill knew about the earlier interrogation, his questioning of Mosley about an unrelated homicide was quite consistent with a reasonable interpretation of Mosley's earlier refusal to answer any questions about the robberies. **[b]**

This is not a case, therefore, where the police failed to honor a decision of a person in custody to cut off questioning, either by refusing to discontinue the interrogation upon request or by persisting in repeated efforts to wear down his resistance and make him change his mind. In contrast to such practices, the police here immediately ceased the interrogation, resumed questioning only after the passage of a significant period of time and the provision of a fresh set of warnings, and restricted the second interrogation to a crime that had not been a subject of the earlier interrogation.

[The Court distinguished this case from facts of *Westover v. United States*, 384 U.S. 436, a companion case to *Miranda*. In that case officers from two agencies questioned Westover for an entire night and into the next afternoon about two crimes, without a break, so that the second agency which obtained a confession was the "beneficiary" of the pressure applied during the long questioning by the first agency. No warnings were given to Westover. Thus, the Michigan Court of Appeals was mistaken, in believing that the second questioning of Mosley was "not permitted" by the *Westover* decision.]

For these reasons, we conclude that the admission in evidence of Mosley's incriminating statement did not violate the principles of *Miranda v. Arizona*. Accordingly, the judgment of the Michigan Court of Appeals is vacated, and the case is remanded to that court for further proceedings not inconsistent with this opinion.

It is so ordered.

[JUSTICE WHITE concurred in the result. He wrote that the Court's attempt to establish a "time limit" for when resumption of questioning was allowed under *Miranda* was not a correct approach. Instead, he would judge whether a resumption of questioning was proper solely on the basis of the voluntariness of the suspect's waiver.]

MR. JUSTICE BRENNAN, with whom MR. JUSTICE MARSHALL joins, dissenting.

* * * Today's distortion of *Miranda's* constitutional principles can be viewed only as yet another step in the erosion and, I suppose, ultimate overruling of *Miranda's* enforcement of the privilege against self-incrimination. **[c]**

* * *

* * * [T]he consideration in the task confronting the Court is not whether voluntary statements will be excluded, but whether the procedures approved will be sufficient to assure with reasonable certainty that a confession is not obtained under the influence of the compulsion inherent in interrogation and detention. The procedures approved by the Court today fail to provide that assurance.

* * * [A]s to statements which are the product of renewed questioning, *Miranda* established a virtually irrebuttable presumption of compulsion, * * * and that presumption stands strongest where, as in this case, a suspect, having initially determined to remain silent, is subsequently brought to confess his crime. Only by adequate procedural safeguards could the presumption be rebutted. **[d]**

In formulating its procedural safeguard, the Court skirts the problem of compulsion and thereby fails to join issue with the dictates of *Miranda*. The language which the Court finds controlling in this case teaches that renewed questioning itself is part of the process which invariably operates to overcome the will of a suspect. That teaching is embodied in the form of a proscription on any further questioning once the suspect has exercised his right to remain silent. Today's decision uncritically abandons that teaching. The Court assumes, contrary to the controlling language, that "scrupulously honoring" an initial exercise of the right to remain silent preserves the efficaciousness of initial and future warnings despite the fact that the suspect has once been subjected to interrogation and then has been detained for a lengthy period of time. **[e]**

* * * [S]crupulously honoring exercises of the right to cut off questioning is only meaningful insofar as the suspect's will to exercise that right remains wholly unfettered. The Court's formulation thus assumes the very matter at issue here: whether renewed questioning following a lengthy period of detention acts to overbear the suspect's will, irrespective of giving the *Miranda* warnings a second time (and scrupulously honoring them), thereby rendering inconsequential any failure to exercise the right to remain silent. For the Court it is enough conclusorily to assert that "[t]he subsequent questioning did not undercut Mosley's previous decision not to answer Detective Cowie's inquiries." *

* * Under *Miranda*, however, Mosley's failure to exercise the right upon renewed questioning is presumptively the consequence of an overbearing in which detention and that subsequent questioning played central roles.

I agree that *Miranda* is not to be read, on the one hand, to impose an absolute ban on resumption of questioning "at any time or place on any subject," * * * or on the other hand, "to permit a resumption of interrogation after a momentary respite." * * * But this surely cannot justify adoption of a vague and ineffective procedural standard. * * * *Miranda*'s terms, however, are not so uncompromising as to preclude the fashioning of guidelines to govern this case. Those guidelines must, of course, necessarily be sensitive to the reality that "[a]s a practical matter, the compulsion to speak in the isolated setting of the police station may well be greater than in courts or other official investigations, where there are often impartial observers to guard against intimidation or trickery." * * *

The fashioning of guidelines for this case is an easy task. Adequate procedures are readily available. Michigan law requires that the suspect be arraigned before a judicial officer "without unnecessary delay," certainly not a burdensome requirement. Alternatively, a requirement that resumption of questioning should await appointment and arrival of counsel for the suspect would be an acceptable and readily satisfied precondition to resumption. *Miranda* expressly held that "[t]he presence of counsel . . . would be the adequate protective device necessary to make the process of police interrogation conform to the dictates of the privilege [against self-incrimination]." * * * * The Court expediently bypasses this alternative in its search for circumstances where renewed questioning would be permissible.

* * *

These procedures would be wholly consistent with the Court's rejection of a *"per se* proscription of indefinite duration," * * * a rejection to which I fully subscribe. Today's decision, however, virtually empties *Miranda* of principle, for plainly the decision encourages police asked to cease interrogation to continue the suspect's detention until the police station's coercive atmosphere does its work and the suspect responds to resumed questioning. * * *

[JUSTICE BRENNAN suggested that the facts indicated that both Detectives Cowie and Hill were aware of the robbery-murder and thus suggests that Mosley was set up for the second interrogation, designed to place added pressure on him.]

[In his concluding paragraph, JUSTICE BRENNAN pointed out that states could adopt a "liberal" reading as a matter of *state* constitutional law, and cited several cases that had taken such an approach.]

* * * * * * * * * * *

COMMENTS

[a] This is absurd only from the policy premise found in this sentence, that to permanently terminate questioning would frustrate police work. From the defendant's position, taking the defendant's "No" to mean "No more questioning" is not absurd.

[b] The facts in this case involve reopening questioning for a different crime, and by a different officer, than the subject of the first interrogation. It is not entirely clear whether these facts are to be controlling in future cases.

[c] In the early 1970s CHIEF JUSTICE BURGER announced an intention to overrule the *Miranda* rulings, but he later retreated from this position. However, the Court has since that time significantly reduced the scope of *Miranda*.

[d] JUSTICE BRENNAN does not support a total ban on resumption of questioning, but would allow it only under guidelines not spelled out in *Miranda*.

[e] Given that JUSTICE STEWART dissented in *Miranda*, it is not entirely surprising that in the majority opinion here he does not carry the compulsion argument to the lengths that JUSTICE BRENNAN does.

EDWARDS v. ARIZONA

451 U.S. 477 101 S.Ct. 1880, 68 L.Ed.2d 378 (1981)

JUSTICE WHITE delivered the opinion of the Court.

We granted certiorari in this case, * * * limited to [the question:] "whether the Fifth, Sixth, and Fourteenth Amendments require suppression of a post-arrest confession, which was obtained after Edwards had invoked his right to consult counsel before further interrogation. * * *"

I

On January 19, 1976, a sworn complaint was filed against Edwards in Arizona state court charging him with robbery, burglary, and first-degree murder. An arrest warrant was issued pursuant to the complaint, and Edwards was arrested at his home later that same day. At the police station, he was informed of his rights as required by *Miranda v. Arizona*, [this volume]. Petitioner stated that he understood his rights, and was willing to submit to questioning. After being told that another suspect already in custody had implicated him in the crime, Edwards denied involvement and gave a taped statement presenting an alibi defense. He then sought to "make a deal." The interrogating officer told him that he wanted a statement, but that he did not have the authority to negotiate a deal. The officer provided Edwards with the telephone number of a county attorney. Petitioner made the call, but hung up after a few moments. Edwards then said: "I want an attorney before making a deal." At that point, questioning ceased and Edwards was taken to county jail.

At 9:15 the next morning, two detectives, colleagues of the officer who had interrogated Edwards the previous night, came to the jail and asked to see Edwards. When the detention officer informed Edwards that the detectives wished to speak with him, he replied that he did not want to talk to anyone. The guard told him that "he had" to talk and then took him to meet with the detectives. The officers identified themselves, stated they wanted to talk to him, and informed him of his *Miranda* rights. Edwards was willing to talk, but he first wanted to hear the taped statement of the alleged accomplice who had implicated him. After listening to the tape for several minutes, petitioner said that he would make a statement so long as it was not tape-recorded. The detectives informed him that the recording was irrelevant since they could testify in court concerning whatever he said. Edwards replied: "I'll tell you anything you want to know, but I don't want it on tape." He thereupon implicated himself in the crime.

Prior to trial, Edwards moved to suppress his confession on the ground that his *Miranda* rights had been violated when the officers returned to question him after he had invoked his right to counsel. [The motion was denied and the incriminating statement was introduced in his trial.]

On appeal, the Arizona Supreme Court held that Edwards had invoked both his right to remain silent and his right to counsel during the interrogation conducted on the night of January 19. * * * The court then went on to determine, however, that Edwards had waived both rights during the January 20 meeting when he voluntarily gave his statement to the detectives after again being informed that he need not answer questions and that he need not answer without the advice of counsel: "The trial court's finding that the waiver and confession were voluntarily and knowingly made is upheld." * * *

Because the use of Edward's confession against him at his trial violated his rights under the Fifth and Fourteenth Amendments as construed in *Miranda v. Arizona*, [above] we reverse the judgment of the Arizona Supreme Court.

II

In *Miranda v. Arizona*, the Court determined that the Fifth and Fourteenth Amendments' prohibition against compelled self-incrimination required that custodial interrogation be preceded by advice to the putative defendant that he has the right to remain silent and also the right to the presence of an attorney. * * * The Court also indicated the procedures to be followed subsequent to the warnings. If the accused indicates that he wishes to remain silent, "the interrogation must cease." If he requests counsel, "the interrogation must cease until an attorney is present." * * *

Miranda thus declared that an accused has a Fifth and Fourteenth Amendment right to have counsel present during custodial interrogation. Here, the critical facts as found by the Arizona Supreme Court are that

Edwards asserted his right to counsel and his right to remain silent on January 19, but that the police, without furnishing him counsel, returned the next morning to confront him and, as a result of the meeting, secured incriminating oral admissions. Contrary to the holdings of the state courts, Edwards insists that having exercised his right on the 19th to have counsel present during interrogation, he did not validly waive that right on the 20th. For the following reasons, we agree.

First, the Arizona Supreme Court applied an erroneous standard for determining waiver where the accused has specifically invoked his right to counsel. It is reasonably clear under our cases that waivers of counsel must not only be voluntary, but must also constitute a knowing and intelligent relinquishment or abandonment of a known right or privilege, a matter which depends in each case "upon the particular facts and circumstances surrounding that case, including the background, experience, and conduct of the accused." *Johnson v. Zerbst*, [this volume]. * * *

Considering the proceedings in the state courts in the light of this standard, we note that in denying petitioner's motion to suppress, the trial court found the admission to have been "voluntary," * * * without separately focusing on whether Edwards had knowingly and intelligently relinquished his right to counsel. The Arizona Supreme Court, in a section of its opinion entitled "Voluntariness of Waiver," stated that in Arizona, confessions are prima facie involuntary and that the State had the burden of showing by a preponderance of the evidence that the confession was freely and voluntarily made. The court stated that the issue of voluntariness should be determined based on the totality of the circumstances as it related to whether an accused's action was "knowing and intelligent and whether his will [was] overborne." * * * Once the trial court determines that "the confession is voluntary, the finding will not be upset on appeal absent clear and manifest error." * * * The court then upheld the trial court's finding that the "waiver and confession were voluntarily and knowingly made." * * *

In referring to the necessity to find Edwards' confession knowing and intelligent, the State Supreme Court cited *Schneckloth v. Bustamonte*, [this volume]. Yet, it is clear that *Schneckloth* does not control the issue presented in this case. The issue in *Schneckloth* was under what conditions an individual could be found to have consented to a search and thereby waived his Fourth Amendment rights. The Court declined to impose the "intentional relinquishment or abandonment of a known right or privilege" standard and required only that the consent be voluntary under the totality of the circumstances. The Court specifically noted that the right to counsel was a prime example of those rights requiring the special protection of the knowing and intelligent waiver standard, * * * but held that "[t]he considerations that informed the Court's holding in *Miranda* are simply inapplicable in the present case." * * * *Schneckloth* itself thus emphasized that the voluntariness of a consent or an admission on the one hand, and a knowing and intelligent waiver on the other, are discrete inquiries. [a] Here, however sound the conclusion of the

state courts as to the voluntariness of Edwards' admission may be, neither the trial court nor the Arizona Supreme Court undertook to focus on whether Edwards understood his right to counsel and intelligently and knowingly relinquished it. It is thus apparent that the decision below misunderstood the requirement for finding a valid waiver of the right to counsel, once invoked.

Second, although we have held that after initially being advised of his *Miranda* rights, the accused may himself validly waive his rights and respond to interrogation, * * * the Court has strongly indicated that additional safeguards are necessary when the accused asks for counsel; and we now hold that when an accused has invoked his right to have counsel present during custodial interrogation, a valid waiver of that right cannot be established by showing only that he responded to further police-initiated custodial interrogation even if he has been advised of his rights. We further hold that an accused, such as Edwards, having expressed his desire to deal with the police only through counsel, is not subject to further interrogation by the authorities until counsel has been made available to him, unless the accused himself initiates further communication, exchanges, or conversations with the police. [b]

Miranda itself indicated that the assertion of the right to counsel was a significant event and that once exercised by the accused, "the interrogation must cease until an attorney is present." * * * Our later cases have not abandoned that view. In *Michigan v. Mosley*, [this volume], the Court noted that *Miranda* had distinguished between the procedural safeguards triggered by a request to remain silent and a request for an attorney and had required that interrogation cease until an attorney was present only if the individual stated that he wanted counsel. * * * In *Fare v. Michael C.*, [442 U.S. 707, (1979)] the Court referred to *Miranda*'s "rigid rule that an accused's request for an attorney is *per se* an invocation of his Fifth Amendment rights, requiring that all interrogation cease." And just last Term, in a case where a suspect in custody had invoked his *Miranda* right to counsel, the Court again referred to the "undisputed right" under *Miranda* to remain silent and to be free of interrogation "until he had consulted with a lawyer." *Rhode Island v. Innis*, [this volume]. We reconfirm these views and, to lend them substance, emphasize that it is inconsistent with *Miranda* and its progeny for the authorities, at their instance, to reinterrogate an accused in custody if he has clearly asserted his right to counsel. [c]

In concluding that the fruits of the interrogation initiated by the police on January 20 could not be used against Edwards, we do not hold or imply that Edwards was powerless to countermand his election or that the authorities could in no event use any incriminating statements made by Edwards prior to his having access to counsel. Had Edwards initiated the meeting on January 20, nothing in the Fifth and Fourteenth Amendments would prohibit the police from merely listening to his voluntary, volunteered statements and using them against him at the trial. The Fifth Amendment right identified in *Miranda* is the right to have counsel present at any custodial interrogation. Absent such interrogation, there would have been no infringement of the right that Edwards invoked and there would be no occasion to determine whether there had been a valid waiver. * * *

But this is not what the facts of this case show. Here, the officers conducting the interrogation on the evening of January 19 ceased interrogation when Edwards requested counsel as he had been advised he had the right to do. The Arizona Supreme Court was of the opinion that this was a sufficient invocation of his *Miranda* rights, and we are in accord. It is also clear that without making counsel available to Edwards, the police returned to him the next day. This was not at his suggestion or request. Indeed, Edwards informed the detention officer that he did not want to talk to anyone. At the meeting, the detectives told Edwards that they wanted to talk to him and again advised him of his *Miranda* rights. Edwards stated that he would talk, but what prompted this action does not appear. He listened at his own request to part of the taped statement made by one of his alleged accomplices and then made an incriminating statement, which was used against him at his trial. We think it is clear that Edwards was subjected to custodial interrogation on January 20 within the meaning of *Rhode Island v. Innis*, [above], and that this occurred at the instance of the authorities. His statement, made without having had access to counsel, did not amount to a valid waiver and hence was inadmissible.

* * *

[CHIEF JUSTICE BURGER, concurred in the judgment but disagreed with the ruling as to initiation of discussions by the suspect.

[JUSTICE POWELL, joined by JUSTICE REHNQUIST also concurring in the result but challenged the "initiation" ruling.]

* * * * * * * * * *

COMMENTS

[a] Given the fact that the differentiation between voluntary consent and a waiver was a major issue in *Schneckloth*, the use of the wrong standard by the Arizona court must be seen as careless.

[b] Although the basic rule of terminating questioning was established in *Miranda*, the new *Edwards* rule established here is clearly a further safeguard.

[c] It seems clear from these recitations that the Court does not see itself as innovating here as much as it is simply preserving the *Miranda* ruling from erosion.

PENNSYLVANIA v. MUNIZ

496 U.S. 582, 110 S.Ct. 2638, 110 L.Ed.2d 528 (1990)

BRENNAN, J., delivered the judgment of the Court, except as to Part III-C.

We must decide in this case whether various incriminating utterances of a drunk-driving suspect, made while performing a series of sobriety tests, constitute testimonial responses to custodial interrogation for purposes of the Self-Incrimination Clause of the Fifth Amendment.

I

[Muniz was properly stopped for driving while intoxicated.] * * * [T]he officer asked Muniz to perform three standard field sobriety tests: a "horizontal gaze nystagmus" test, a "walk and turn" test, and a "one leg stand" test. Muniz performed these tests poorly, and he informed the officer that he had failed the tests because he had been drinking. [a]

The patrol officer arrested Muniz and transported him to the [county booking facility]. Following its routine practice for receiving persons suspected of driving while intoxicated, the [booking faciity officer] videotaped the ensuing proceedings. Muniz was informed that his actions and voice were being recorded, but he was not at this time (nor had he been previously) advised of his rights under *Miranda v. Arizona*, [this volume]. Officer Hosterman first asked Muniz his name, address, height, weight, eye color, date of birth, and current age. he responded to each of these questions, stumbling over his address and age. The officer then asked Muniz, "Do you know what the date was of your sixth birthday?" After Muniz offered an inaudible reply, the officer repeated, "When you turned six years old, do you remember what the date was?" Muniz responded, "No, I don't."

Officer Hosterman next requested Muniz to perform each of the three sobriety tests that Muniz had been asked to perform earlier during the initial roadside stop. The videotape reveals that his eyes jerked noticeably during the gaze test, that he did not walk a very straight line, and that he could not balance himself on one leg for more than several seconds. During the latter two tests, he did not complete the requested verbal counts from 1 to 9 and from 1 to 30. Moreover, while performing these tests, Muniz "attempted to explain his difficulties in performing the various tasks, and often requested further clarification of the tasks he was to perform." * * *

Finally, Officer Deyo asked Muniz to submit to a breathalyzer test designed to measure the alcohol content of his expelled breath. Officer Deyo read to Muniz the Commonwealth's Implied Consent Law, * * * and explained that under the law his refusal to take the test would result in automatic suspension of his driver's license for one year. Muniz asked a number of questions about the law, commenting in the process about his state of inebriation. Muniz ultimately refused to take the breath test. At this point, Muniz was for the first time advised of his *Miranda* rights. Muniz then signed a statement waiving his rights and admitted in response to further questioning that he had been driving while intoxicated. **[b]**

Both the video and audio portions of the videotape were admitted into evidence at Muniz's bench trial, along with the arresting officer's testimony that Muniz failed the roadside sobriety tests and made incriminating remarks at that time. Muniz was convicted of driving under the influence of alcohol. * * * Muniz filed a motion for a new trial, contending that the court should have excluded the testimony relating to the field sobriety tests and the videotape taken at the booking center "because they were incriminating and completed prior to [Muniz's] receiving his *Miranda* warnings." * * * The trial court denied the motion, holding that "'requesting a driver, suspected of driving under the influence of alcohol, to perform physical tests or take a breath analysis does not violate [his] privilege against self-incrimination because [the] evidence procured is of a physical nature rather than testimonial, and therefore no Miranda warnings are required.'" * * *

[The appellate court reversed. It ruled that no *Miranda* warnings were required for the field sobriety test and the later tests before the videotape camera; however, it ruled that when the tests began to yield testimonial and communicative statements, *Miranda* warnings were required. Warnings were also required as to the question regarding his sixth birthday and the statements and inquiries he made while performing the physical dexterity and the breathalyzer tests, because they "revealed his thought processes."] After the Pennsylvania Supreme Court denied the Commonwealth's application

for review, * * * we granted certiorari. * * *

II

* * * Although the text [of the Self-Incrimination Clause] does not delineate the ways in which a person might be made a "witness against himself," * * * we have long held that the privilege does not protect a suspect from being compelled by the State to produce "real or physical evidence." * * * Rather, the privilege "protects an accused only from being compelled to testify against himself, or otherwise provide the State with evidence of a testimonial or communicative nature." * * * "[I]n order to be testimonial, an accused's communication must itself, explicitly or implicitly, relate a factual assertion or disclose information. Only then is a person compelled to be a 'witness' against himself." * * *

[*Miranda v. Arizona* was briefly reviewed.] * * *

This case implicates both the "testimonial" and "compulsion" components of the privilege against self-incrimination in the context of pretrial questioning. Because Muniz was not advised of his *Miranda* rights until after the videotaped proceedings at the booking center were completed, any verbal statements that were both testimonial in nature and elicited during custodial interrogation should have been suppressed. * * *

III

In the initial phase of the record proceedings, Officer Hosterman asked Muniz his name, address, height, weight, eye color, date of birth, current age, and the date of his sixth birthday.

Both the delivery and content of Muniz's answers were incriminating. As the state court found, "Muniz's videotaped responses . . . certainly led the finder of fact to infer that his confusion and failure to speak clearly indicated a state of drunkenness that prohibited him from safely operating his vehicle." * * * The Commonwealth argues, however, that admission of Muniz's answers to these questions does not contravene Fifth Amendment principles because Muniz's statement regarding his sixth birthday was not "testimonial" and his answers to the prior questions were not elicited by custodial interrogation. We consider these arguments in turn.

A

We agree with the Commonwealth's contention that Muniz's answers are not rendered inadmissible by *Miranda* merely because the slurred nature of his speech was incriminating. The physical inability to articulate words in a clear manner due to "the lack of muscular coordination of his tongue and mouth" * * * is not itself a testimonial component of Muniz's responses to Officer Hosterman's introductory questions. * * * [The prohibition against self-incrimination] "offers no protection against compulsion to submit to fingerprinting, photographing, or measurements, to write or speak for identification, to appear in court, to stand, to assume a stance, to walk, or to make a particular gesture." * * * "[T]he privilege is a bar against compelling 'communications' or 'testimony,' but that compulsion which makes a suspect or accused the source of 'real or physical evidence' does not violate it." * * * Using this "helpful framework for analysis," * * * we held that a person suspected of driving while intoxicated could be forced to provide a blood sample, because that sample was "real or physical evidence" outside the scope of the privilege and the sample was obtained in manner by which "[p]etitioner's testimonial capacities were in no way implicated." * * * * * *

Under *Schmerber [v. California*, 384 U.S. 757 (1966)] and its progeny, we agree with the Commonwealth that any slurring of speech and other evidence of lack of muscular coordination revealed by Muniz's responses to Officer Hosterman's direct questions constitute nontestimonial components of those responses. Requiring a suspect to reveal the physical manner in which he articulates words, like requiring him to reveal the physical properties of the sound produced by his voice, * * * does not, without more, compel him to provide a "testimonial" response for purposes of the privilege.

B

This does not end our inquiry, for Muniz's answer to the sixth birthday question was incriminating, not just because of his delivery, but also because of his answer's *content*; the trier of fact could infer from Muniz's answer (that he did not *know* the proper date) that his mental state was confused. The Commonwealth and United States as *amicus curiae* argue that this incriminating inference does not trigger the protections of the Fifth Amendment privilege because the inference concerns "the physiological functioning of [Muniz's] brain," * * * which is asserted to be every bit as "real or physical" as the physiological makeup of his blood and the timbre of his voice.

But this characterization addresses the wrong question; that the "fact" to be inferred might be said to concern the physical status of Muniz's brain merely describes the way in which the inference is incriminating. The correct question for present purposes is whether the incriminating inference of mental confusion is drawn from a testimonial act or from physical evidence. In *Schmerber*, for example, we held that the police could compel a suspect to provide a blood sample in order to determine the physical makeup of his blood and thereby draw an inference about whether he was intoxicated. This compulsion was outside of the Fifth Amendment's protection, not simply because the evidence concerned the suspect's physical body, but rather because the evidence was *obtained* in a manner that did not entail any testimonial act on the part of the suspect: "Not even a shadow of testimonial compulsion upon or enforced communication by the accused was involved either in the extraction or in the chemical analysis." * * * In contrast, had the police instead asked the suspect directly whether his blood contained a high concentration of alcohol, his affirmative response would have been testimonial even though it would have been used to draw the same inference concerning his physiology. * * * [c] In this case, the question is not whether a suspect's "impaired mental faculties" can fairly be characterized as an aspect of his physiology, but rather whether Muniz's response to the sixth birthday question

that gave rise to the inference of such an impairment was testimonial in nature.

We recently explained in *Doe v. United States*, 487 U.S. 201 (1988), that "in order to be testimonial, an accused's communication must itself, explicitly or implicitly, relate a factual assertion or disclose information." * * *

"* * * It is the 'extortion of information from the accused,' * * * the attempt to force him 'to disclose the contents of his own mind,' * * * that implicates the Self-Incrimination Clause. . . . 'Unless some attempt is made to secure a communication— written, oral or otherwise—upon which reliance is to be placed as involving [the accused's] consciousness of the facts and the operations of his mind in expressing it, the demand made upon him is not a testimonial one.'" * * *

After canvassing the purposes of the privilege recognized in prior cases, we concluded that "[t]hese policies are served when the privilege is asserted to spare the accused from having to reveal, directly or indirectly, his knowledge of facts relating him to the offense or from having to share his thoughts and beliefs with the Government." * * *

* * * At its core, the privilege reflects our fierce "unwillingness to subject those suspected of crime to the cruel trilemma of self-accusation, perjury or contempt'" * * * that defined the operation of the Star Chamber, wherein suspects were forced to choose between revealing incriminat-

ing private thoughts and forsaking their oath by committing perjury. See *United States v. Nobles*, 422 U.S. 225, 233 (1975) ("The Fifth Amendment privilege against compulsory self-incrimination . . . protects 'a private inner sanctum of individual feeling and thought and proscribes state intrusion to extract self-condemnation'"). * * *

We need not explore the outer boundaries of what is "testimonial" today, for our decision flows from the concept's core meaning. * * * Whatever else it may include, therefore, the definition of "testimonial" evidence articulated in *Doe* must encompass all responses to questions that, if asked of a sworn suspect during a criminal trial, could place the suspect in the "cruel trilemma." This conclusion is consistent with our recognition in *Doe* that "[t]he vast majority of verbal statements thus will be testimonial" because "[t]here are very few instances in which a verbal statement, either oral or written, will not convey information or assert facts." * * * Whenever a suspect is asked for a response requiring him to communicate an express or implied assertion of fact or belief, the suspect confronts the "trilemma" of truth, falsity, or silence and hence the response (whether based on truth or falsity) contains a testimonial component.

* * *

* * * [T]he sixth birthday question in this case required a testimonial response. When Officer Hosterman asked Muniz if he knew the date of his sixth birthday and Muniz, for whatever reason, could not remember or calculate that date, he was confronted with the trilemma. By hypothesis, the inherently coercive environ-

ment created by the custodial interrogation precluded the option of remaining silent. * * * Muniz was left with the choice of incriminating himself by admitting that he did not then know the date of his sixth birthday, or answering untruthfully by reporting a date that he did not then believe to be accurate (an incorrect guess would be incriminating as well as untruthful). The content of his truthful answer supported an inference that his mental faculties were impaired, because his assertion (he did not know the date of his sixth birthday) was different from the assertion (he knew the date was [correct date]) that the trier of fact might reasonably have expected a lucid person to provide. Hence, the incriminating inference of impaired mental faculties stemmed, not just from the fact that Muniz slurred his response, but also from a testimonial aspect of that response.

The state court held that the sixth birthday question constituted an unwarned interrogation for purposes of the privilege against self-incrimination, * * * and that Muniz's answer was incriminating. * * * The Commonwealth does not question either conclusion. Therefore, because we conclude that Muniz's response to the sixth birthday question was testimonial, the response should have been suppressed.

C

The Commonwealth argues that the seven questions asked by Officer Hosterman just *prior* to the sixth birthday question—regarding Muniz's name, address, height, weight, eye color, date of birth, and current age—did not constitute custodial interrogation. * * * [*Miranda* and *Rhode*

Island v. Innis, [this volume] have ruled that "interrogation" means actual "questioning initiated by law enforcement officers" and its "functional equivalent." The latter includes] words or actions that, given the officer's knowledge of any special susceptibilities of the suspect, the officer knows or reasonably should know are likely to "have . . . the force of a question on the accused," * * * and therefore be reasonably likely to elicit an incriminating response.

We disagree with the Commonwealth's contention that Officer Hosterman's first seven questions regarding Muniz's name, address, height, weight, eye color, date of birth, and current age do not qualify as custodial interrogation * * * merely because the questions were not intended to elicit information for investigatory purposes. As explained above, the *Innis* test focuses primarily upon "the perspective of the suspect." * * * We agree with *amicus* United States, however, that Muniz's answers to these first seven questions are nonetheless admissible because the questions fall within a "routine booking question" exception which exempts from *Miranda*'s coverage questions to secure the '"biographical data necessary to complete booking or pretrial services.'" * * * The state court found that the first seven questions were "requested for record-keeping purposes only," * * * and therefore the questions appear reasonably related to the police's administrative concerns. In this context, therefore, the first seven questions asked at the Booking Center fall outside the protections of *Miranda* and the answers thereto need not be suppressed. [d]

IV

During the second phase of the videotaped proceedings, Officer Hosterman asked Muniz to perform the same three sobriety tests that he had earlier performed at roadside prior to his arrest: the "horizontal gaze nystagmus" test, the "walk and turn" test, and the "one leg stand" test. While Muniz was attempting to comprehend Officer Hosterman's instructions and then perform the requested sobriety tests, Muniz made several audible and incriminating statements. Muniz argued to the state court that both the videotaped performance of the physical tests themselves and the audiorecorded verbal statements were introduced in violation of *Miranda*.

The court refused to suppress the videotaped evidence of Muniz's paltry performance on the physical sobriety tests, reasoning that "[r]equiring a driver to perform physical [sobriety] tests . . . does not violate the privilege against self-incrimination because the evidence procured is of a physical nature rather than testimonial." * * * With respect to Muniz's verbal statements, however, the court concluded that "none of Muniz's utterances were spontaneous, voluntary verbalizations," * * * and because they were "elicited before Muniz received his *Miranda* warnings, they should have been excluded as evidence." * * *

We disagree. Officer Hosterman's dialogue with Muniz concerning the physical sobriety tests consisted primarily of carefully scripted instructions as to how the tests were to be performed. These instructions were not likely to be perceived as calling for any verbal response and therefore were not "words or actions" constituting custodial interrogation. * * * The dialogue also contained limited and carefully worded inquiries as to whether Muniz understood those instructions, but these focused inquiries were necessarily "attendant to" the police procedure held by the court to be legitimate. Hence, Muniz's incriminating utterances during this phase of the videotaped proceedings were "voluntary" in the sense that they were not elicited in response to custodial interrogation. * * *

Similarly, we conclude that *Miranda* does not require suppression of the statements Muniz made when asked to submit to a breathalyzer examination. Officer Deyo read Muniz a prepared script explaining how the test worked, the nature of Pennsylvania's Implied Consent Law, and the legal consequences that would ensue should he refuse. Officer Deyo then asked Muniz whether he understood the nature of the test and the law and whether he would like to submit to the test. Muniz asked Officer Deyo several questions concerning the legal consequences of refusal, which Deyo answered directly, and Muniz then commented upon his state of inebriation. * * * After offering to take the test only after waiting a couple of hours or drinking some water, Muniz ultimately refused.

We believe that Muniz's statements were not prompted by an interrogation within the meaning of *Miranda*, and therefore the absence of *Miranda* warnings does not require suppression of these statements at trial. As did Officer Hosterman when administering the three physical sobriety tests, * * * Officer Deyo carefully limited her role to providing Muniz with relevant

information about the breathalyzer test and the Implied Consent Law. She questioned Muniz only as to whether he understood her instructions and wished to submit to the test. These limited and focused inquiries were necessarily "attendant to" the legitimate police procedure, * * * and were not likely to be perceived as calling for any incriminating response.

V

We agree with the state court's conclusion that *Miranda* requires suppression of Muniz's response to the question regarding the date of his sixth birthday, but we do not agree that the entire audio portion of the videotape must be suppressed. Accordingly, the court's judgment reversing Muniz's conviction is vacated, and the case is remanded for further proceedings not inconsistent with this opinion.

It is so ordered.

CHIEF JUSTICE REHNQUIST, with whom JUSTICE WHITE, JUSTICE BLACKMUN and JUSTICE STEVENS join, concurring in part, concurring in the result in part, and dissenting in part.

I join Parts I, II, III-A, and IV of the Court's opinion. In addition, although I agree with the conclusion in Part III-C that the seven "booking" questions should not be suppressed, I do so for a reason different from that of JUSTICE BRENNAN. I dissent from the Court's conclusion that Muniz' response to the "sixth birthday question" should have been suppressed.

The Court holds that the sixth birthday question Muniz was asked required a testimonial response, and that its admission at trial therefore violated Muniz's privilege against compulsory self-incrimination. * * * As an assumption about human behavior, [the conclusion that Muniz felt a need to lie in response to Officer Hosterman's "sixth birthday" question] is wrong. Muniz would no more have felt compelled to fabricate a false date than one who cannot read the letters on an eye chart feels compelled to fabricate false letters; nor does a wrong guess call into question a speaker's veracity. The Court's statement is also a flawed predicate on which to base its conclusion that Muniz' answer to this question was "testimonial" for purposes of the Fifth Amendment.

The need for the use of the human voice does not automatically make an answer testimonial. * * *

The sixth birthday question here was an effort on the part of the police to check how well Muniz was able to do a simple mathematical exercise. Indeed, had the question related only to the date of his birth, it presumably would have come under the "booking exception" to *Miranda v. Arizona.* * * * If the police may require Muniz to use his body in order to demonstrate the level of his physical coordination, there is no reason why they should not be able to require him to speak or write in order to determine his mental coordination. That was all that was sought here. Since it was permissible for the police to extract and examine a sample of Schmerber's blood to determine how much that part of his system had been affected by alcohol, I see no reason why they may not examine the functioning of Muniz' mental processes for the same purpose. Surely if it were relevant, a suspect

might be asked to take an eye examination in the course of which he might have to admit that he could not read the letters on the third line of the chart. At worst, he might utter a mistaken guess. Muniz likewise might have attempted to guess the correct response to the sixth birthday question instead of attempting to calculate the date or answer "I don't know." But the potential for giving a bad guess does not subject the suspect to the truth-falsity-silence predicament that renders a response testimonial and, therefore, within the scope of the Fifth Amendment privilege.

For substantially the same reasons, Muniz' responses to the videotaped "booking" questions were not testimonial and do not warrant application of the privilege. Thus, it is unnecessary to determine whether the questions fall within the "routine booking question" exception to *Miranda* JUSTICE BRENNAN recognizes.
* * *

[JUSTICE MARSHALL concurred with the Court's holding as to the "sixth birthday question" and dissented as to the rest. As he viewed this situation, all the police questions and directions to perform several tests were designed to incriminate the respondent and thus should be preceded by *Miranda* warnings. "The police should have known that the circumstances in which they confronted Muniz, combined with the detailed instructions and questions concerning the tests and the State's Implied Consent Law, were reasonably likely to elicit an incriminating response, and therefore constituted the "functional equivalent" of express questioning. *Rhode Island v. Innis*, 446 U.S. 291, 301 (1980)."]

* * * * * * * * * *

COMMENTS

[a] Given the frequency of automobile drunk driver arrests, this case necessarily has enormous practical impact.

[b] Since Implied Consent laws are valid, would a standard requirement that police officers issue *Miranda* warnings upon stopping suspected intoxicated drivers seriously impede drunk driver law enforcement? Does it make sense to issue a *Miranda* warning for a DUI arrest and still expect the suspect to perform physical tests?

[c] Do you think that a direct question about the suspect's state of inebriation is the same as the "birthday-date" question? If the latter is seen as a physical test, then either *Miranda* warnings must be given for all the physical tests or for none. Compare CHIEF JUSTICE REHNQUIST's dissent on this point.

[d] Notice that this "routine booking exception," is not adopted as the opinion of the Supreme Court. If it were adopted, it could have an enormous practical effect on a practice that occurs in virtually every police department every day. On the one hand, it would insure that booking officers could ask these questions without violating an arrestee's Fifth Amendment rights. On the other hand, it would bring booking practice under judicial scrutiny, creating the possibility that some questions asked at booking would raise constitutional challenges.

ILLINOIS v. PERKINS

496 U.S. 292, 110 S.Ct. 2394, 110 L.Ed.2d 243 (1990)

JUSTICE KENNEDY delivered the opinion of the Court.

An undercover government agent was placed in the cell of respondent Perkins, who was incarcerated on charges unrelated to the subject of the agent's investigation. Respondent made statements that implicated him in the crime that the agent sought to solve. Respondent claims that the statements should be inadmissible because he had not been given *Miranda* warnings by the agent. We hold that the statements are admissible. *Miranda* warnings are not required when the suspect is unaware that he is speaking to a law enforcement officer and gives a voluntary statement.

I

[The November 1984, murder of Richard Stephenson remained unsolved until March 1986,] when one Donald Charlton told police that he had learned about a homicide from a fellow inmate at the Graham Correctional Facility, where Charlton had been serving a sentence for burglary. The fellow inmate was [respondent] Lloyd Perkins. * * * Charlton told police that, while at Graham, he had befriended respondent, who told him in detail about a murder that respondent had committed in East St. Louis. [The details fit the crime,] so [the police] treated Charlton's story as a credible one.

[Perkins was being held in the Montgomery County (Illinois) jail on an aggravated battery charge. Instead of using an electronic listening device, the police decided to place an undercover agent in the cellblock with respondent. Charlton and undercover agent John Parisi, using the alias "Vito Bianco," posed as work release program escapees arrested in the course of a burglary. They were placed in the same cellblock (consisting of 12 cells and a common room) as Perkins, and were instructed to engage Perkins in casual conversation and report anything he said about the Stephenson murder.]

[After Charlton became reacquainted with Perkins, he introduced him to Parisi, who suggested a jail break.] * * * Respondent replied that the Montgomery County jail was "rinky-dink" and that they could "break out." The trio met in respondent's cell later that evening, after the other inmates were asleep, to refine their plan. Respondent said that his girlfriend could smuggle in a pistol. Charlton said "Hey, I'm not a murderer, I'm a burglar. That's your guys' profession." After telling Charlton that he would be responsible for any murder that occurred, Parisi asked respondent if he had ever "done" anybody. Respondent said that he had, and proceeded to describe at length the events of the Stephenson murder. Parisi and respondent then engaged in some casual conversation before respondent went to sleep. Parisi did not give respondent *Miranda* warnings before the conversations.

[Perkins was charged the Stephenson murder. The trial and appellate courts suppressed the statements made to Parisi in the jail on the ground that] *Miranda v. Arizona*, [this volume], prohibits all undercover contacts with incarcerated suspects which are reasonably likely to elicit an incriminating response.

We granted certiorari, * * * to decide whether an undercover law enforcement officer must give *Miranda* warnings to an incarcerated suspect before asking him questions that may elicit an incriminating response. We now reverse.

II

In *Miranda v. Arizona*, * * * the Court held that the Fifth Amendment privilege against self-incrimination prohibits admitting statements given by a suspect during "custodial interrogation" without a prior warning. Custodial interrogation means "questioning initiated by law enforcement officers after a person was been taken into custody. . . ." * * * The warning mandated by *Miranda* was meant to preserve the privilege during "incommunicado interrogation of individuals in a police-dominated atmosphere." * * * That atmosphere is said to generate "inherently compelling pressures which work to undermine the individual's will to resist and to compel him to speak where he would not otherwise do so freely." * * * "Fidelity to the doctrine announced in *Miranda* requires that it be enforced strictly, but only in those types of situations in which the concerns that powered the decision are implicated." * * *

Conversations between suspects and undercover agents do not implicate the concerns underlying *Miranda*. The essential ingredients of a "police-dominated atmosphere" and compulsion are not present when an incarcerated person speaks freely to someone that he believes to be a fellow inmate. Coercion is determined from the perspective of the suspect. * * * When a suspect considers himself in the company of cellmates and not officers, the coercive atmosphere is lacking. * * * There is no empirical basis for the assumption that a suspect speaking to those whom he assumes are not officers will feel compelled to speak by the fear of reprisal for remaining silent or in the hope of more lenient treatment should be confess. [a]

It is the premise of *Miranda* that the danger of coercion results from the interaction of custody and official interrogation. We reject the argument that *Miranda* warnings are required whenever a suspect is in custody in a technical sense and converses with someone who happens to be a government agent. Questioning by captors, who appear to control the suspect's fate, may create mutually reinforcing pressures that the Court has assumed will weaken the suspect's will, but where a suspect does not know that he is conversing with a government agent, these pressures do not exist. The State Court here mistakenly assumed that because the suspect was in custody, no undercover questioning could take place. When the suspect has no reason to think that the listeners have official power over him, it should not be assumed that his words are motivated by the reaction he expects from his listeners. "[W]hen the agent carries neither badge nor gun and wears not 'police blue,' but the same prison gray" as the suspect, there is no "*interplay* between police interrogation and police custody." * * *

Miranda forbids coercion, not mere strategic deception by taking advantage of a suspect's misplaced trust in one he supposes to be a fellow prisoner. As we recognized in *Miranda*, "[c]onfessions remain a proper element in law enforcement. Any statement given freely and voluntarily without any compelling influences is, of course, admissible in evidence." * * * Ploys to mislead a suspect or lull him into a false sense of security that do not rise to the level of compulsion or coercion to speak are not within *Miranda*'s concerns. * * *

Miranda was not meant to protect suspects from boasting about their criminal activities in front of persons whom they believe to be their cellmates. This case is illustrative. Respondent had no reason to feel that undercover agent Parisi had any legal authority to force him to answer questions or that Parisi could affect respondent's future treatment. Respondent viewed the cellmate-agent as an equal and showed no hint of being intimidated by the atmosphere of the jail. In recounting the details of the Stephenson murder, respondent was motivated solely by the desire to impress his fellow inmates. He spoke at his own peril.

The tactic employed here to elicit a voluntary confession from a suspect does not violate the Self-Incrimination Clause. We held in *Hoffa v. United States*, 385 U.S. 293 (1966), that placing an undercover agent near a suspect in order to gather incriminating information was permissible under the Fifth Amendment. In *Hoffa*, while petitioner Hoffa was on trial, he met often with one Partin, who, unbeknownst to Hoffa, was cooperating with law enforcement officials. Partin reported to officials that Hoffa had divulged his attempts to bribe jury members. We approved using Hoffa's statements at his subsequent trial for jury tampering, on the rationale that "no claim ha[d] been or could [have been] made that [Hoffa's] incriminating statements were the product of any sort of coercion, legal or factual." * * * In addition, we found that the fact that Partin had fooled Hoffa into thinking that Partin was a sympathetic colleague did not affect the voluntariness of the statements. * * * The only difference between this case and *Hoffa* is that the suspect here was incarcerated, but detention, whether or not for the crime in question, does not warrant a presumption that the use of an undercover agent to speak with an incarcerated suspect makes any confession thus obtained involuntary.

Our decision in *Mathis v. United States*, 391 U.S. 1 (1968), is distinguishable. In *Mathis*, an inmate in a state prison was interviewed by an Internal Revenue Service agent about possible tax violations. No *Miranda* warning was given before questioning. The Court held that the suspect's incriminating statements were not admissible at his subsequent trial on tax fraud charges. The suspect in *Mathis* was aware that the agent was a government official, investigating the possibility on non-compliance with the tax laws. The case before us now is different. Where the suspect does not know that he is speaking to a government agent there is no reason to assume the possibility that the suspect might feel coerced. (The bare fact of custody may not in every instance require a warning even when the suspect is aware that he is speaking to an official, but we do not have occasion to explore that issue here.)

This Court's Sixth Amendment decisions in *Massiah v. United States*, [this volume], *United States v. Henry*, 447 U.S. 264 (1980), and *Maine v. Moulton*, 474 U.S. 159 (1985), also do not avail respondent. We held in those cases that the government may not use an undercover agent to circumvent the Sixth Amendment right to counsel once a suspect has been charged with the crime. After charges have been filed, the Sixth Amendment prevents the government from interfering with the accused's right to counsel. * * * In the instant case no charges had been filed on the subject of the interrogation, and our Sixth Amendment precedents are not applicable. **[b]**

Respondent can seek no help from his argument that a bright-line rule for the application of *Miranda* is desirable. Law enforcement officers will have little difficulty putting into practice our holding that undercover agents need not give *Miranda* warnings to incarcerated suspects. The use of undercover agents is a recognized law enforcement technique, often employed in the prison context to detect violence against correctional officials or inmates, as well as for the purposes served here. The interests protected by *Miranda* are not implicated in these cases, and the warnings are not required to safeguard the constitutional rights of inmates who make voluntary statements to undercover agents.

We hold that an undercover law enforcement officer posing as a fellow inmate need not give *Miranda* warnings to an incarcerated suspect before asking questions that may elicit an incriminating response. The statements at issue in this case were voluntary,

and there is no federal obstacle to their admissibility at trial. We now reverse and remand for proceedings not inconsistent with our opinion.

It is so ordered.

[JUSTICE BRENNAN concurred in the judgment because he agreed with the specific issue of the case, *i.e.*, "that when a suspect does not know that his questioner is a police agent, such questioning does not amount to 'interrogation' in an 'inherently coercive' environment so as to require application of *Miranda*." However, he did indicate that the deception and manipulation practiced in this case would appear to be a violation of Perkins' due process rights.] **[c]**

JUSTICE MARSHALL, dissenting.

* * *

The Court does not dispute that the police officer here conducted a custodial interrogation of a criminal suspect. Perkins was incarcerated in county jail during the questioning at issue here; under these circumstances, he was in custody as that term is defined in *Miranda*. * * * Perkins' familiarity with confinement * * * does not transform his incarceration into some sort of noncustodial arrangement. *Cf. Orozco v. Texas*, 394 U.S. 324 (1969) (holding that suspect who had been arrested in his home and then questioned in his bedroom was in custody, notwithstanding his familiarity with the surroundings).

While Perkins was confined, an undercover police officer, with the help of a police informant, questioned him about a serious crime. Although the Court does not dispute that Perkins was interrogated, it downplays the nature of the 35-minute questioning by disingenuously referring to it as a "conversatio[n]." * * * The officer's narration of the "conversation" at Perkins' trial, however, reveals that it clearly was an interrogation. * * * The police officer continued the inquiry, asking a series of questions designed to elicit specific information about the victim, the crime scene, the weapon, Perkins' motive, and his actions during and after the shooting. * * * This interaction was not a "conversation"; Perkins, the officer, and the informant were not equal participants in a free-ranging discussion, with each man offering his views on different topics. Rather, it was an interrogation: Perkins was subjected to express questioning likely to evoke an incriminating response. * * *

Because Perkins was interrogated by police while he was in custody, *Miranda* required that the officer inform him of his rights. [d] In rejecting that conclusion, the Court finds that "conversations" between undercover agents and suspects are devoid of the coercion inherent in stationhouse interrogations conducted by law enforcement officials who openly represent the State. * * * *Miranda* was not, however, concerned solely with police *coercion*. It dealt with *any* police tactics that may operate to compel a suspect in custody to make incriminating statements without full awareness of his constitutional rights. * * * Thus, when a law enforcement agent structures a custodial interrogation so that a suspect feels compelled to reveal incriminating information, he must inform the suspect of his constitutional rights and give him an opportunity to decide whether or not to talk.

The compulsion proscribed by *Miranda* includes deception by the police. * * * Although the Court did not find trickery by itself sufficient to constitute compulsion in *Hoffa* * * * the defendant in that case was not in custody. Perkins, however, was interrogated while incarcerated. * * *

Custody works to the State's advantage in obtaining incriminating information. The psychological pressures inherent in confinement increase the suspect's anxiety, making him likely to seek relief by talking with others. * * * In this case, the police deceptively took advantage of Perkins' psychological vulnerability by including him in a sham escape plot, a situation in which he would feel compelled to demonstrate his willingness to shoot a prison guard by revealing his past involvement in a murder. * * *

Thus, the pressures unique to custody allow the police to use deceptive interrogation tactics to compel a suspect to make an incriminating statement. The compulsion is not eliminated by the suspect's ignorance of his interrogator's true identify. The Court therefore need not inquire past the bare facts of custody and interrogation to determine whether *Miranda* warnings are required.

* * *

* * * The exception carved out of the *Miranda* doctrine today may well result in a proliferation of departmental policies to encourage police officers to conduct interrogations of confined suspects through undercover agents, thereby circumventing the need to administer *Miranda* warnings. Indeed, if *Miranda* now requires a police officer to issue warnings only in those situations in which the suspect might feel compelled "to speak by the fear of

reprisal for remaining silent or in the hope of more lenient treatment should he confess," * * * presumably it allows custodial interrogation by an undercover officer posing as a member of the clergy or a suspect's defense attorney. [e] Although such abhorrent tricks would play on a suspect's need to confide in a trusted adviser, neither would cause the suspect to "think that the listeners have official power over him." * * * The Court's adoption of the "undercover agent" exception to the *Miranda* rule thus is necessarily also the adoption of a substantial loophole in our jurisprudence protecting suspects' Fifth Amendment rights.

I dissent.

* * * * * * * * * * *

COMMENTS

[a] This may be so, but one can ask whether every legal rule must be based on social scientific studies of human behavior. Compare JUSTICE MARSHALL's speculation.

[b] Note that the general availability of the techniques used in this case depend largely on the timing of an indictment; once the formal prosecutorial process begins, the *Massiah* doctrine comes into play.

[c] As the due process issue was not raised, it would be premature for the Court to rule on the matter.

[d] That would clearly end the practice indicated by the facts of this case, and would turn inmate-agents or inmate-informants into the "listening posts" as indicated in the *Massiah* line of cases; see *Kuhlman v. Wilson* [this volume].

[e] Do you think these examples are natural extensions of the majority's holding? If you agree with the holding, would you go along with these practices? or do you think that they violate due process?

MASSIAH v. UNITED STATES

377 U.S. 201, 84 S.Ct. 1199, 12 L.Ed.2d 246 (1964)

MR. JUSTICE STEWART delivered the opinion of the Court.

The petitioner was indicted for violating the federal narcotics laws. He retained a lawyer, pleaded not guilty, and was released on bail. While he was free on bail a federal agent succeeded by surreptitious means in listening to incriminating statements made by him. Evidence of these statements was introduced against the petitioner at his trial over his objection. He was convicted, and the Court of Appeals affirmed. We granted certiorari to consider whether, under the circumstances here presented, the prosecution's use at the trial of evidence of the petitioner's own incriminating statements deprived him of any right secured to him under the Federal Constitution. * * *

[Massiah was a merchant seaman suspected of importing drugs. After a search of the ship, he was arrested, arraigned, and subsequently indicted for possession of narcotics, along with a man named Colson. Massiah retained a lawyer,] pleaded not guilty and was released on bail, along with Colson.

A few days later, and quite without the petitioner's knowledge, Colson decided to cooperate with the government agents in their continuing investigation of the narcotics activities in which the petitioner, Colson, and others had allegedly been engaged. Colson permitted an agent named Murphy to install a Schmidt radio transmitter under the front seat of Colson's automobile, by means of which Murphy, equipped with an appropriate receiving device, could overhear from some distance away conversations carried on in Colson's car.

[During a lengthy conversation while sitting in the car with Colson's car, Massiah made incriminating statements heard by Agent Murphy over the radio transmitter. These incriminating statements were used as evidence in Massiah's jury trial. His] convictions were affirmed by the Court of Appeals.

The petitioner argues that it was an error of constitutional dimensions to permit the agent Murphy at the trial to testify to the petitioner's incriminating statements which Murphy had overheard. * * * [Massiah argues that his] Fifth and Sixth Amendment rights were violated by the use in evidence against him of incriminating statements which government agents had deliberately elicited from him after he had been indicted and in the absence of his retained counsel. * * *

In *Spano v. New York*, [this volume], this Court reversed a state criminal conviction because a confession had been wrongly admitted into evidence against the defendant at his trial. In that case the defendant had already been indicted for first-degree murder at the time he confessed. The Court held that the defendant's conviction could not stand under the Fourteenth Amendment. While the Court's opinion relied upon the totality of the circumstances under which the confession had been obtained, four concurring Justices pointed out that the

Constitution required reversal of the conviction upon the sole and specific ground that the confession had been deliberately elicited by the police after the defendant had been indicted, and therefore at a time when he was clearly entitled to a lawyer's help. It was pointed out that under our system of justice the most elemental concepts of due process of law contemplate that an indictment be followed by a trial, "in an orderly courtroom, presided over by a judge, open to the public, and protected by all the procedural safeguards of the law." * * * It was said that a Constitution which guarantees a defendant the aid of counsel at such a trial could surely vouchsafe no less to an indicted defendant under interrogation by the police in a completely extrajudicial proceeding. Anything less, it was said, might deny a defendant "effective representation by counsel at the only stage when legal aid and advice would help him." * * *

Ever since this Court's decision in the *Spano* case, the New York courts have unequivocally followed this constitutional rule. "Any secret interrogation of the defendant, from and after the finding of the indictment, without the protection afforded by the presence of counsel, contravenes the basic dictates of fairness in the conduct of criminal causes and the fundamental rights of persons charged with crime." * * * [a]

This view no more than reflects a constitutional principle established as long ago as *Powell v. Alabama*, [this volume], where the Court noted that "* * * during perhaps the most critical period of the proceedings * * * that is to say, from the time of their arraignment until the beginning of their trial,

when consultation, thoroughgoing investigation and preparation [are] vitally important, the defendants * * * [are] as much entitled to such aid [of counsel] during that period as at the trial itself." * * * And since the *Spano* decision the same basic constitutional principle has been broadly reaffirmed by this Court. * * *

Here we deal not with a state court conviction, but with a federal case, where the specific guarantee of the Sixth Amendment directly applies. * * * We hold that the petitioner was denied the basic protections of that guarantee when there was used against him at his trial evidence of his own incriminating words, which federal agents had deliberately elicited from him after he had been indicted and in the absence of his counsel. It is true that in the *Spano* case the defendant was interrogated in a police station, while here the damaging testimony was elicited from the defendant without his knowledge while he was free on bail. But, as Judge Hays pointed out in his dissent in the Court of Appeals, "if such a rule is to have any efficacy it must apply to indirect and surreptitious interrogations as well as those conducted in the jailhouse. In this case, Massiah was more seriously imposed upon * * * because he did not even know that he was under interrogation by a government agent." * * *

The Solicitor General, [argued that the government had the right and the duty to continue their investigation of the petitioner and his alleged criminal associates even after indictment.]

We may accept and, at least for present purposes, completely approve all that this argument implies, Fourth Amendment problems to one side. We do not question that in this case, as in many cases, it was entirely proper to continue an investigation of the suspected criminal activities of the defendant and his alleged confederates, even though the defendant had already been indicted. All that we hold is that the defendant's own incriminating statements, obtained by federal agents under the circumstances here disclosed, could not constitutionally be used by the prosecution as evidence against *him* at his trial.

Reversed.

MR. JUSTICE WHITE, with whom MR. JUSTICE CLARK and MR. JUSTICE HARLAN join, dissenting.

* * *

[JUSTICE WHITE pointed out that the case resulted in the loss of probative evidence and thus impeded the search for the truth; he was not convinced that this loss was offset by an important countervailing policy such as the rationale for the Fourth Amendment exclusionary rule.]

* * *

Whatever the content or scope of the rule may prove to be, I am unable to see how this case presents an unconstitutional interference with Massiah's right to counsel. Massiah was not prevented from consulting with counsel as often as he wished. No meetings with counsel were disturbed or spied upon. Preparation for trial was in no way obstructed. It is only a sterile syllogism—an unsound one, besides—to say that because Massiah had a right to counsel's aid before and during the trial, his out-of-court conversations and admissions must be excluded if obtained without counsel's consent or presence. The right to

counsel has never meant as much before, * * * and its extension in this case requires some further explanation, so far unarticulated by the Court. [b]

Since the new rule would exclude all admissions made to the police, no matter how voluntary and reliable, the requirement of counsel's presence or approval would seem to rest upon the probability that counsel would foreclose any admissions at all. This is nothing more than a thinly disguised constitutional policy of minimizing or entirely prohibiting the use in evidence of voluntary out-of-court admissions and confessions made by the accused. Carried as far as blind logic may compel some to go, the notion that statements from the mouth of the defendant should not be used in evidence would have a severe and unfortunate impact upon the great bulk of criminal cases.

Viewed in this light, the Court's newly fashioned exclusionary principle goes far beyond the constitutional privilege against self-incrimination, which neither requires nor suggests the barring of voluntary pretrial admissions. * * * The defendant may thus not be compelled to testify at his trial, but he may if he wishes. Likewise he may not be compelled or coerced into saying anything before trial; but until today he could if he wished to, and if he did, it could be used against him. Whether as a matter of self-incrimination or of due process, the proscription is against compulsion—coerced incrimination. Under the prior law, announced in countless cases in this Court, the defendant's pretrial statements were admissible evidence if voluntarily made; inadmissible if not the product of his free will. Hardly any constitutional area has been more carefully patrolled by this Court, and until now the Court has expressly rejected the argument that admissions are to be deemed involuntary if made outside the presence of counsel. * * *

    * * *

Applying the new exclusionary rule is peculiarly inappropriate in this case. At the time of the conversation in question, petitioner was not in custody but free on bail. He was not questioned in what anyone could call an atmosphere of official coercion. What he said was said to his partner in crime who had also been indicted. There was no suggestion or any possibility of coercion. **[c]** What petitioner did not know was that Colson had decided to report the conversation to the police. Had there been no prior arrangements between Colson and the police, had Colson simply gone to the police after the conversation had occurred, his testimony relating Massiah's statements

would be readily admissible at the trial, as would a recording which he might have made of the conversation. In such event, it would simply be said that Massiah risked talking to a friend who decided to disclose what he knew of Massiah's criminal activities. But if, as occurred here, Colson had been cooperating with the police prior to his meeting with Massiah, both his evidence and the recorded conversation are somehow transformed into inadmissible evidence despite the fact that the hazard to Massiah remains precisely the same—the defection of a confederate in crime. * * *

[JUSTICE WHITE suggested that the rule in this case would have negative effects on law enforcement; it would possibly prevent the government from using "cooperative" co-conspirators where a confederate has been indicted and might discourage co-conspirators from coming forward to cooperate with the government.]

    * * * * * * * * * *

COMMENTS

[a] Despite the attention to *Spano* this is not a "confessions" case. While there are some similarities, the element of *coercion* or the coercive atmosphere is missing; thus, the case must be seen as a Sixth Amendment right to counsel case, and not as a Fifth Amendment self-incrimination case.

[b] Taken on its face, JUSTICE WHITE's criticism is sound. Left unsaid by the majority—and what may have motivated the majority's ruling—was that in civil law practice it is unethical for an attorney to contact an opposing party in a case without first contacting opposing counsel. In 1964 it was not entirely clear to the legal profession whether such a rule should be imported into the criminal law.

[c] How voluntary was Massiah's statements in Colson's car? Can it be argued that the deception practiced on Massiah was the equivalent of coercion? Deception by the police does not undermine the validity of confessions nor is the deception involved in undercover work a violation of Fourth or Fifth Amendment rights.

BREWER v. WILLIAMS

430 U.S. 387, 97 S.Ct. 1232, 51 L.Ed.2d 424 (1977)

MR. JUSTICE STEWART delivered the opinion of the Court.

I

* * * [Robert Williams, a mental hospital escapee, turned himself in to Davenport, Iowa, police for the murder of a ten year old girl at a YMCA in Des Moines on December 26, 1968. Williams called McKnight, a lawyer in Des Moines, before surrendering. McKnight spoke to Williams on the phone in the presence of Des Moines police detective Leaming and informed Williams that Des Moines officers would drive to Davenport to pick him up, that they would not interrogate him or mistreat him, and that Williams was not to talk to the officers about the crime. Williams was arraigned (formally charged) for the crime in Davenport. When detective Leaming picked up Williams a Davenport lawyer, Kelly, was denied a request to ride back to Des Moines with them. The Davenport attorney reiterated to Detective Leaming that Williams was not to be questioned on the ride back.]

[On the 160-mile ride back to Des Moines, Williams expressed no desire to be interrogated in the absence of counsel, indicating instead that he would tell the whole story at the end of the trip. However, Leaming knew Williams was a former mental patient who was deeply religious and engaged him in a general discussion. Soon after the trip began, Leaming delivered the so-called] "Christian burial speech." Addressing Williams as "Reverend," the detective said:

"I want to give you something to think about while we're traveling down the road. . . . Number one, I want you to observe the weather conditions, it's raining, it's sleeting, it's freezing, driving is very treacherous, visibility is poor, it's going to be dark early this evening. They are predicting several inches of snow for tonight, and I feel that you yourself are the only person that knows where this little girl's body is, that you yourself have only been there once, and if you get a snow on top of it you yourself may be unable to find it. And, since we will be going right past the area on the way into Des Moines, I feel that we could stop and locate the body, that the parents of this little girl should be entitled to a Christian burial for the little girl who was snatched away from them on Christmas [E]ve and murdered. And I feel we should stop and locate it on the way in rather than waiting until morning and trying to come back out after a snow storm and possibly not being able to find it at all." [a]

Williams asked Detective Leaming why he thought their route to Des Moines would be taking them past the girl's body, and Leaming responded that he knew the body was in the area of Mitchellville—a town they would be passing on the way to Des Moines. Leaming then stated: "I do not want you to answer me. I don't want to discuss it any further. Just think about it as we're riding down the road."

As the car approached Grinnell, a town approximately 100 miles west of Davenport, Williams asked whether the police had found the victim's shoes. When Detective Leaming replied that he was unsure, Williams directed the officers to a service station where he said he had left the shoes; a search for them proved unsuccessful. As they continued towards Des Moines, Williams asked whether the police had found the blanket, and directed the officers to a rest area where he said he had disposed of the blanket. Nothing was found. The car continued towards Des Moines, and as it approached Mitchellville, Williams said that he would show the officers where the body was. He then directed the police to the body of Pamela Powers.

* * *

[This evidence was introduced and used to convict Williams of murder. The Iowa courts ruled that Williams waived his right to counsel, but the lower federal courts, on a writ of habeas corpus, ruled the evidence inadmissible on the alternative grounds of denial of assistance of counsel, a *Miranda* violation, and that his statements were involuntary.]

II

* * *

B

* * *   [JUSTICE STEWART ruled that *Miranda v. Arizona* (this volume) did not apply to this case.] For it is clear that the judgment before us must in any event be affirmed upon the ground that Williams was deprived of a different constitutional right—the right to the assistance of counsel.

This right, guaranteed by the Sixth and Fourteenth Amendments, is indis-

pensable to the fair administration of our adversary system of criminal justice. [It is a] vital need at the pretrial stage. * * *

* * * Whatever else it may mean, the right to counsel granted by the Sixth and Fourteenth Amendments means at least that a person is entitled to the help of a lawyer at or after the time that judicial proceedings have been initiated against him—"whether by way of formal charge, preliminary hearing, indictment, information, or arraignment." * * *

There can be no doubt in the present case that judicial proceedings [by arraignment] had been initiated against Williams before the start of the automobile ride from Davenport to Des Moines. * * * **[b]**

There can be no serious doubt, either, that Detective Leaming deliberately and designedly set out to elicit information from Williams just as surely as—and perhaps more effectively than—if he had formally interrogated him. Detective Leaming was fully aware before departing for Des Moines that Williams was being represented in Davenport by Kelly and in Des Moines by McKnight. Yet he purposely sought during Williams' isolation from his lawyers to obtain as much incriminating information as possible. Indeed, Detective Leaming conceded as much when he testified at Williams' trial. * * * **[c]**

The circumstances of this case are thus constitutionally indistinguishable from those presented in *Massiah v. United States*. * * *

That the incriminating statements were elicited surreptitiously in the *Massiah* case, and otherwise here, is constitutionally irrelevant. * * * Rather, the clear rule of *Massiah* is that once adversary proceedings have commenced against an individual, he has a right to legal representation when the government interrogates him. * * * [d]

III

The Iowa courts recognized that Williams had been denied the constitutional right to the assistance of counsel. They held, however, that he had waived that right during the course of the automobile trip from Davenport to Des Moines. * * *

[The Iowa courts applied a totality-of-circumstances test to ascertain whether Williams waived his right to counsel. The federal courts held that this was the wrong standard under the constitutional guarantee to counsel: there must be an affirmative waiver.] [e]

* * *

The [lower federal courts] were also correct in their understanding of the proper standard to be applied in determining the question of waiver as a matter of federal constitutional law—that it was incumbent upon the State to prove "an intentional relinquishment or abandonment of a known right or privilege." * * * That standard has been reiterated in many cases. We have said that the right to counsel does not depend upon a request by the defendant, * * * and that courts indulge in every reasonable presumption against waiver. * * * This strict standard applies equally to an alleged waiver of the right to counsel whether at trial or at a critical stage of pretrial proceedings. * * * We conclude, finally, that the Court of Appeals was correct in holding that, judged by these standards,

the record in this case falls far short of sustaining petitioner's burden. It is true that Williams had been informed of and appeared to understand his right to counsel. But waiver requires not merely comprehension but relinquishment, and Williams' consistent reliance upon the advice of counsel in dealing with the authorities refutes any suggestion that he waived that right. [He spoke to both the Des Moines and Davenport attorneys numerous times before the trip.] Throughout, Williams was advised not to make any statements before seeing McKnight in Des Moines, and was assured that the police had agreed not to question him. His statements while in the car that he would tell the whole story *after* seeing McKnight in Des Moines were the clearest expressions by Williams himself that he desired the presence of an attorney before any interrogation took place. But even before making these statements, Williams had effectively asserted his right to counsel by having secured attorneys at both ends of the automobile trip, both of whom, acting as his agents, had made clear to the police that no interrogation was to occur during the journey. Williams knew of that agreement and, particularly in view of his consistent reliance on counsel, there is no basis for concluding that he disavowed it. [f]

Detective Leaming proceeded to elicit incriminating statements from Williams. Leaming did not preface this effort by telling Williams that he had a right to the presence of a lawyer, and made no effort at all to ascertain whether Williams wished to relinquish that right. The circumstances of record in this case thus provide no reasonable basis for finding that Williams waived his right to the assistance of counsel.

The Court of Appeals did not hold, nor do we, that under the circumstances of this case Williams *could not*, without notice to counsel, have waived his rights under the Sixth and Fourteenth Amendments. It only held, as do we, that he did not. **[g]**

IV

The crime of which Williams was convicted was senseless and brutal, calling for swift and energetic action by the police to apprehend the perpetrator and gather evidence with which he could be convicted. No mission of law enforcement officials is more important. Yet, "[d]isinterested zeal for the public good does not assure either wisdom or right in the methods it pursues." * * * Although we do not lightly affirm the issuance of a writ of habeas corpus in this case, so clear a violation of the Sixth and Fourteenth Amendments as here occurred cannot be condoned. The pressures on state executive and judicial officers charged with the administration of the criminal law are great, especially when the crime is murder and the victim a small child. But it is precisely the predictability of those pressures that makes imperative a resolute loyalty to the guarantees that the Constitution extends to us all. **[h]**

The judgment of the Court of Appeals is affirmed.

It is so ordered.

[JUSTICES MARSHALL, POWELL and STEVENS concurred in separate opinions.]

MR. CHIEF JUSTICE BURGER, dissenting.

The result in this case ought to be intolerable in any society which purports to call itself an organized society. It continues the Court—by the narrowest margin—on the much-criticized course of punishing the public for the mistakes and misdeeds of law enforcement officers, instead of punishing the officer directly, if in fact he is guilty of wrongdoing. It mechanically and blindly keeps reliable evidence from juries whether the claimed constitutional violation involves gross police misconduct or honest human error. **[i]**

* * *

[Further in his opinion the CHIEF JUSTICE argued that the exclusionary rule should not apply to non-egregious police conduct.]

MR. JUSTICE WHITE, with whom MR. JUSTICE BLACKMUN and MR. JUSTICE REHNQUIST join, dissenting.

* * *

* * * In order to show that a right has been waived * * * the State must prove "an intentional relinquishment or abandonment of a known right or privilege." * * * That respondent knew of his right not to say anything to the officers without advice and presence of counsel is established on this record to a moral certainty. * * *

Respondent relinquished his right not to talk to the police about his crime when the car approached the place where he had hidden the victim's clothes. Men usually intend to do what they do, **[j]** and there is nothing in the record to support the proposition that respondent's decision to talk was anything but an exercise of his own free will. Apparently, without any prodding from the officers, respondent— who had earlier said that he would tell the whole story when he arrived in Des Moines—spontaneously changed his mind about the timing of his disclosures when the car approached the places where he had hidden the evidence. However, even if his statements were influenced by Detective Leaming's above-quoted statement, respondent's decision to talk in the absence of counsel can hardly be viewed as the product of an overborne will. The statement by Leaming was not coercive; it was accompanied by a request that respondent not respond to it; and it was delivered hours before respondent decided to make any statement. Respondent's waiver was thus knowing and intentional. [k]

The majority's contrary conclusion seems to rest on the fact that respondent "asserted" his right to counsel by retaining and consulting with one lawyer and by consulting with another. How this supports the conclusion that respondent's later relinquishment of his right not to talk in the absence of counsel was unintentional is a mystery. The fact that respondent consulted with counsel on the question whether he should talk to the police in counsel's absence makes his later decision to talk in counsel's absence better informed and, if anything, more intelligent.

The majority recognizes that even after this "assertion" of his right to counsel, it would have found that respondent waived his right not to talk in counsel's absence if his waiver had been express—*i.e.*, if the officers had asked him in the car whether he would be willing to answer questions in counsel's absence and if he had answered "yes." * * * But waiver is not a formalistic concept. Waiver is shown whenever the facts establish that an accused knew of a right and intended to relinquish it. Such waiver, even if not express, was plainly shown here. * * *

* * *

MR. JUSTICE BLACKMUN, with whom MR. JUSTICE WHITE and MR. JUSTICE REHNQUIST join, dissenting.

* * *

What the Court chooses to do here, and with which I disagree, is to hold that respondent Williams' situation was in the mold of *Massiah v. United States*, [this volume] that is, that it was dominated by a denial to Williams of his Sixth Amendment right to counsel after criminal proceedings had been instituted against him. The Court rules that the Sixth Amendment was violated because Detective Leaming "purposely sought during Williams' isolation from his lawyers to obtain as much incriminating information as possible." I cannot regard that as unconstitutional *per se*. [l]

First, the police did not deliberately seek to isolate Williams from his lawyers so as to deprive him of the assistance of counsel. * * * The isolation in this case was a necessary incident of transporting Williams to the county where the crime was committed. [m]

Second, Leaming's purpose was not solely to obtain incriminating evidence. The victim had been missing for only two days, and the police could not be certain that she was dead. Leaming, of course, and in accord with his duty, was "hoping to find out where that little girl was," * * * but such motivation does not equate with an intention to evade the Sixth Amendment. * * *

Third, not every attempt to elicit information should be regarded as "tantamount to interrogation." * * * I am not persuaded that Leaming's observations and comments, made as the police car traversed the snowy and slippery miles between Davenport and Des Moines that winter afternoon, were an interrogation, direct or subtle, of Williams. * * * [n]

In summary, it seems to me that the Court is holding that *Massiah* is violated whenever police engage in any conduct, in the absence of counsel, with the subjective desire to obtain information from a suspect after arraignment. Such a rule is far too broad. Persons in custody frequently volunteer statements in response to stimuli other than interrogation. * * * When there is no interrogation, such statements should be admissible as long as they are truly voluntary. * * *
* * *

* * * * * * * * * * *

COMMENTS

[a] Do you think the speech, followed by a long silence, was made deliberately by Detective Leaming to elicit incriminating evidence? Or do you think it was just made to pass the time? If deliberate, does it matter if Detective Leaming planned this earlier or just got the idea for the speech on the trip back to Des Moines?

[b] Once a person has a lawyer does it seem appropriate that the police and prosecutors speak to him *only* through counsel?

[c] JUSTICE BLACKMUN, dissenting below, disagrees. What do you think? Can reasonable persons disagree about this point?

[d] It can be argued that JUSTICE STEWART is expanding the application of *Massiah*; in that case the facts were that the defendant was secretly overheard by informants. The majority, however, sees the absence of counsel as the critical factor.

[e] When federal constitutional rights are being construed, state courts are entitled and even required to apply them, but it is ultimately the responsibility of the federal courts to determine standards and doctrines under the United States Constitution.

[f] Despite all this talking to lawyers, can it be argued that when Williams gave the evidence he then relinquished his right to counsel? JUSTICE WHITE, in dissent, thinks that requiring a specific relinquishment before making an admission in a *Massiah* situation is too formal. Do you agree?

[g] Neither the majority or the dissenting opinions made anything of the fact that

Williams had been a mental patient, other than to note that Detective Leaming was aware of the fact. Do you think that this factor made Williams more susceptible to suggestion? Given that Williams was competent to stand trial, should this factor have played any role in deciding the case?

[h] Compare these remarks to those of CHIEF JUSTICE BURGER on the point. The strict applicability of rules is a troublesome issue of jurisprudence (legal philosophy). How much discretion should police and judges have in applying these rules? Should the strict application of a rule be foregone if injustice will result? Should this be the case when the rule is based on constitutional rights? Is there a point at which the use of discretion means that the law becomes no law at all but the "wise" decision of officials?

[i] Given the horrible facts of the case, it elicited an emotional response from each of the justices who wrote opinions. To what extent should the heinousness of a crime be a determining factor in deciding whether constitutional rights should apply to a defendant? Could you develop a "sliding scale" of the amount of rights a suspect should receive depending upon the seriousness of the crime?

[j] Can this logic be used to justify virtually any legal result where the issue is a party's state of mind?

[k] Is this reasoning ingenuous? It cuts against the rule that a waiver of counsel has to be knowing, voluntary and intelligent as applied in cases like *Johnson v. Zerbst* [this volume].

[l] JUSTICE BLACKMUN pursues a point mentioned in passing by JUSTICE WHITE: may police at all question a formally charged defendant without his lawyer present when he has previously asked for counsel? In civil cases, it is normally considered a breach of ethics for a lawyer to contact the client of her opposing counsel. Should similar consideration apply in criminal law?

[m] Is this consistent with the refusal to allow the lawyer to ride with them?   If JUSTICE BLACKMUN's point is that there are some cases where post-indictment police questioning without defense being counsel present is permissible, should it turn on the fortuitous factors (the need for a trip, the missing body) present here?

[n] Compare the situation here to the facts of *Rhode Island v. Innis* [this volume]. Do you think Detective Leaming's speech was the functional equivalent of interrogation?

KUHLMANN v. WILSON

477 U.S. 436, 106 S.Ct. 2616, 91 L.Ed.2d 364 (1986)

JUSTICE POWELL announced the judgment of the Court and delivered the opinion of the Court with respect to Parts I, IV, and V * * *

* * *

I

[Wilson was arraigned for the murder of a taxi driver, and was placed in a cell with a prisoner named Benny Lee, who had agreed to act as a police informant. The police detective instructed Lee "not to ask * * * any questions, but simply to 'keep his ears open' for the names of the other perpetrators." Lee and Wilson spent several days in the cell together. During that time Wilson spoke about his case, indicating that he had been set up. At one point "Lee advised [Wilson] that this explanation 'didn't sound too good,' but [Wilson] did not alter his story." After a visit from his brother, Wilson began to change his story and told Lee that he and two unidentified men had robbed and killed the cab driver.]

[The trial court, at an evidentiary hearing, held that Lee followed the police instructions and at no time asked Wilson any questions about the crime "and that he 'only listened to [Wilson] and made notes regarding what [Wilson] had to say.' The trial court also found that respondent's statements to Lee were 'spontaneous' and 'unsolicited.'" Lee's testimony was admitted and Wilson was convicted of murder by a jury. New York appellate courts upheld the conviction. Wilson filed a habeas corpus action in the federal District Court, arguing that "that his statements to Lee were obtained pursuant to police investigative methods that violated his constitutional rights" under *Massiah v. United States*, [this volume]. The District Court denied the writ, and a divided Court of Appeals upheld the dismissal. The United States Supreme Court denied a petition for a writ of certiorari. These events took place in the 1970s.]

Following this Court's decision in *United States v. Henry*, 447 U.S. 264 (1980), which applied the *Massiah* test to suppress statements made to a paid jailhouse informant, respondent decided to relitigate his Sixth Amendment claim. * * * [H]e filed in state trial court a motion to vacate his conviction. The judge denied the motion, on the grounds that *Henry* was factually distinguishable from this case [because the jailhouse informant was paid], and that under state precedent *Henry* was not to be given retroactive effect. * * * The [state appellate court] denied respondent leave to appeal.

[Wilson returned to the District Court on a habeas petition, again arguing that Lee's testimony of his incriminating statements violated his Sixth Amendment rights under *Henry*. The District Court found] that *Henry* did not undermine the Court of Appeals' prior disposition of respondent's Sixth Amendment claim. Noting that *Henry* reserved the question whether the Constitution forbade admission in evidence of an accused's statements to an informant who made "no effort to stimulate conversations about the crime charged," * * * the District Court believed that this case presented that open question and that the question must be answered negatively. The District Court noted that the trial court's findings were presumptively correct, * * * and were fully supported by the record. The court concluded that these findings were "fatal" to respondent's claim under *Henry* since they showed that Lee made no "affirmative effort" of any kind "to elicit information" from respondent.

A different, and again divided, panel of the Court of Appeals reversed. * * * The court then reasoned that the circumstances under which respondent made his incriminating statements to Lee were indistinguishable from the facts of *Henry*. * * * Therefore, the court concluded that all of the judges who had considered and rejected respondent's claim had erred, and remanded the case to the District Court with instructions to order respondent's release from prison unless the State elected to retry him.

* * * We now reverse.

[In Parts II and III a plurality of the Court found that the Court of Appeals erred in allowing a subsequent habeas corpus petition by the respondent because the evidence supporting his guilt was nearly overwhelming.]

IV

Even if the Court of Appeals had correctly decided to entertain this successive habeas petition, we conclude that it erred in holding that respondent was entitled to relief under *United States v. Henry*. As the District Court

observed, *Henry* left open the question whether the Sixth Amendment forbids admission in evidence of an accused's statements to a jailhouse informant who was "placed in close proximity but [made] no effort to stimulate conversations about the crime charged." * * * Our review of the line of cases beginning with *Massiah v. United States*, * * * shows that this question must, as the District Court properly decided, be answered negatively.

A

The decision in *Massiah* had its roots in two concurring opinions written in *Spano v. New York*, [this volume] * * *

The Court in *Massiah* adopted the reasoning of the concurring opinions in *Spano* and held that, once a defendant's Sixth Amendment right to counsel has attached, he is denied that right when federal agents "deliberately elicit" incriminating statements from him in the absence of his lawyer. * * * The Court adopted this test, rather than one that turned simply on whether the statements were obtained in an "interrogation," to protect accused persons from "'indirect and surreptitious interrogations as well as those conducted in the jailhouse. In this case, Massiah was more seriously imposed upon . . . because he did not even know that he was under interrogation by a government agent.'" * * * Thus, the Court made clear that it was concerned with interrogation or investigative techniques that were equivalent to interrogation, and that it so viewed the technique in issue in *Massiah*.

In *United States v. Henry*, the Court applied the *Massiah* test to incriminating statements made to a jailhouse informant. The Court of Appeals in that case found a violation of *Massiah* because the informant had engaged the defendant in conversations and "had developed a relationship of trust and confidence with [the defendant] such that [the defendant] revealed incriminating information." * * * This Court affirmed, holding that the Court of Appeals reasonably concluded that the Government informant "deliberately used his position to secure incriminating information from [the defendant] when counsel was not present." * * * Although the informant had not questioned the defendant, the informant had "stimulated" conversations with the defendant in order to "elicit" incriminating information. * * * The Court emphasized that those facts, like the facts of *Massiah*, amounted to "'indirect and surreptitious interrogatio[n]'" of the defendant. * * *

Earlier this term, we applied the *Massiah* standard in a case involving incriminating statements made under circumstances substantially similar to the facts of *Massiah* itself. In *Maine v. Moulton*, 474 U.S. 159 (1985), the defendant made incriminating statements in a meeting with his accomplice, who had agreed to cooperate with the police. During that meeting, the accomplice, who wore a wire transmitter to record the conversation, discussed with the defendant the charges pending against him, repeatedly asked the defendant to remind him of the details of the crime, and encouraged the defendant to describe his plan for killing witnesses. * * * The Court concluded that these investigatory techniques denied the defendant his right to counsel on the pending charges. Significantly, the Court empha-

sized that, because of the relationship between the defendant and the informant, the informant's engaging the defendant "in active conversation about their upcoming trial was certain to elicit" incriminating statements from the defendant. * * * Thus, the informant's participation "in this conversation was 'the functional equivalent of interrogation.'" * * *

As our recent examination of this Sixth Amendment issue in *Moulton* makes clear, the primary concern of the *Massiah* line of decisions is secret interrogation by investigatory techniques that are the equivalent of direct police interrogation. Since "the Sixth Amendment is not violated whenever—by luck or happenstance—the State obtains incriminating statements from the accused after the right to counsel has attached," * * * a defendant does not make out a violation of that right simply by showing that an informant, either through prior arrangement or voluntarily, reported his incriminating statements to the police. Rather, the defendant must demonstrate that the police and their informant took some action, beyond merely listening, that was designed deliberately to elicit incriminating remarks.

B

It is thus apparent that the Court of Appeals erred in concluding that respondent's right to counsel was violated under the circumstances of this case. Its error did not stem from any disagreement with the District Court over appropriate resolution of the question reserved in *Henry*, but rather from its implicit conclusion that this case did not present that open question. That conclusion was based on a fundamental mistake, namely, the Court of Appeals' failure to accord to the state trial court's factual findings the presumption of correctness expressly required by 28 U.S.C. §2254(d). * * *

The state court found that Officer Cullen had instructed Lee only to listen to respondent for the purpose of determining the identities of the other participants in the robbery and murder. The police already had solid evidence of respondent's participation. The court further found that Lee followed those instructions, that he "at no time asked any questions" of respondent concerning the pending charges, and that he "only listened" to respondent's "spontaneous" and "unsolicited" statements. The only remark made by Lee that has any support in this record was his comment that respondent's initial version of his participation in the crimes "didn't sound too good." Without holding that any of the state court's findings were not entitled to the presumption of correctness under §2254(d), the Court of Appeals focused on that one remark and gave a description of Lee's interaction with respondent that is completely at odds with the facts found by the trial court. In the Court of Appeals' view, "Subtly and slowly, but surely, Lee's ongoing verbal intercourse with [respondent] served to exacerbate [respondent's] already troubled state of mind." * * * After thus revising some of the trial court's findings, and ignoring other more relevant findings, the Court of Appeals concluded that the police "deliberately elicited" respondent's incriminating statements. * * * This conclusion conflicts with the decision of every other state and federal judge who reviewed this record, and is clear error in light of the provisions and intent of §2254(d). [a]

V

The judgment of the Court of Appeals is reversed, and the case is remanded for further proceedings consistent with this opinion.

[CHIEF JUSTICE BURGER concurred.]

JUSTICE BRENNAN, with whom JUSTICE MARSHALL joins, dissenting.

[JUSTICE BRENNAN dissented both on the habeas corpus question and on the right to counsel issue.]
* * *

II

The Court holds that the Court of Appeals erred with respect to the merits of respondent's habeas petition. According to the Court, the Court of Appeals failed to accord §2254(d)'s presumption of correctness to the state trial court's findings that respondent's cellmate, Lee, "at no time asked any questions" of respondent concerning the pending charges, and that Lee only listened to respondent's "spontaneous" and "unsolicited" statements. * * * As a result, the Court concludes, the Court of Appeals failed to recognize that this case presents the question, reserved in *Henry*, * * * whether the Sixth Amendment forbids the admission into evidence of an accused's statements to a jailhouse informant who was "placed in close proximity but

[made] no effort to stimulate conversations about the crime charged." * * * I disagree with the Court's characterization of the Court of Appeals' treatment of the state court's findings and, consequently, I disagree with the Court that the instant case presents the "listening post" question.

The state trial court simply found that Lee did not ask respondent any direct questions about the crime for which respondent was incarcerated. * * * The trial court considered the significance of this fact only under State precedents, which the court interpreted to require affirmative "interrogation" by the informant as a prerequisite to a constitutional violation. * * * The court did not indicate whether it referred to a Fifth Amendment or to a Sixth Amendment violation in identifying "interrogation" as a precondition to a violation; it merely stated that "the utterances made by [respondent] to Lee were unsolicited, and voluntarily made and did not violate the defendant's Constitutional rights." * * *

The Court of Appeals did not disregard the state court's finding that Lee asked respondent no direct questions regarding the crime. Rather, the Court of Appeals *expressly accepted* that finding, * * * but concluded that, as a matter of law, the deliberate elicitation standard of *Henry*, * * * and *Massiah*, * * * encompasses other, more subtle forms of stimulating incriminating admissions than overt questioning. The court suggested that the police deliberately placed respondent in a cell that overlooked the scene of the crime, hoping that the view would trigger an inculpatory comment to respondent's cellmate. The court also observed that, while Lee asked respondent no

questions, Lee nonetheless stimulated conversation concerning respondents' role in the Star Taxicab Garage robbery and murder by remarking that respondent's exculpatory story did not "'sound too good'" and that he had better come up with a better one. * * * Thus, the Court of Appeals concluded that respondent's case did not present the situation reserved in *Henry*, where an accused makes an incriminating remark within the hearing of a jailhouse informant, who "makes no effort to stimulate conversations about the crime charged." * * * Instead, the court determined this case to be virtually indistinguishable from *Henry*.

The Sixth Amendment guarantees an accused, at least after the initiation of formal charges, the right to rely on counsel as the "medium" between himself and the State. * * * Accordingly, the Sixth Amendment "imposes on the State an affirmative obligation to respect and preserve the accused's choice to seek [the assistance of counsel]," * * * and therefore "[the] determination whether particular action by state agents violates the accused's right to . . . counsel must be made in light of this obligation." * * * To be sure, the Sixth Amendment is not violated whenever, "by luck or happenstance," the State obtains incriminating statements from the accused after the right to counsel has attached. It is violated, however, when "the State obtains incriminating statements by knowingly circumventing the accused's right to have counsel present in a confrontation between the accused and a state agent." * * * As we explained in *Henry*, where the accused has not waived his right to counsel, the government knowingly circumvents the defendant's right to counsel where it "deliberately elicit[s]" inculpatory admissions, * * * that is, "intentionally creat[es] a situation likely to induce [the accused] to make incriminating statements without the assistance of counsel." * * * **[b]**

In *Henry*, we found that the Federal Government had "deliberately elicited" incriminating statements from *Henry* based on the following circumstances. The jailhouse informant, Nichols, had apparently followed instructions to obtain information without directly questioning *Henry* and without initiating conversations concerning the charges pending against Henry. We rejected the Government's argument that because *Henry* initiated the discussion of his crime, no Sixth Amendment violation had occurred. We pointed out that under *Massiah* * * * it is irrelevant whether the informant asks pointed questions about the crime or "merely engage[s] in general conversation about it." * * * Nichols, we noted, "was not a passive listener; . . . he had 'some conversations with Mr. Henry' while he was in jail and Henry's incriminatory statements were 'the product of this conversation.'" * * *

In deciding that Nichols' role in these conversations amounted to deliberate elicitation, we also found three other factors important. First, Nichols was to be paid for any information he produced and thus had an incentive to extract inculpatory admissions from Henry. * * * **[c]** Second, Henry was not aware that Nichols was acting as an informant. * * * "Conversation stimulated in such circumstances," we observed, "may elicit information that an accused would not

intentionally reveal to persons known to be Government agents." * * * Third, Henry was in custody at the time he spoke with Nichols. This last fact is significant, we stated, because "custody imposes pressures on the accused [and] confinement may bring into play subtle influences that will make him particularly susceptible to the ploys of undercover Government agents." * * * We concluded that by "intentionally creating a situation likely to induce Henry to make incriminating statements without the assistance of counsel, the Government violated Henry's Sixth Amendment right to counsel." * * * **[b]**

In the instant case, as in *Henry*, the accused was incarcerated and therefore was "susceptible to the ploys of undercover Government agents." * * * Like Nichols, Lee was a secret informant, usually received consideration for the services he rendered the police, and therefore had an incentive to produce the information which he knew the police hoped to obtain. Just as Nichols had done, Lee obeyed instructions not to question respondent and to report to the police any statements made by the respondent in Lee's presence about the crime in question. * * * And, like Nichols, Lee encouraged respondent to talk about his crime by conversing with him on the subject over the course of several days and by telling respondent that his exculpatory story would not convince anyone without more work. However, unlike the situation in *Henry*, a disturbing visit from respondent's brother, rather than a conversation with the informant, seems to have been the immediate catalyst for respondent's confession to Lee. * * * While it might appear from this sequence of events that Lee's comment regarding respondent's story and his general willingness to converse with respondent about the crime were not the *immediate* causes of respondent's admission, I think that the deliberate elicitation standard requires consideration of the entire course of government behavior.

[b]

The State intentionally created a situation in which it was forseeable that respondent would make incriminating statements without the assistance of counsel * * *—it assigned respondent to a cell overlooking the scene of the crime and designated a secret informant to be respondent's cellmate. The informant, while avoiding direct questions, nonetheless developed a relationship of cellmate camaraderie with respondent and encouraged him to talk about his crime. While the *coup de grace* was delivered by respondent's brother, the groundwork for respondent's confession was laid by the State. Clearly the State's actions had a sufficient nexus with respondent's admission of guilt to constitute deliberate elicitation within the meaning of *Henry*. I would affirm the judgment of the Court of Appeals.

[JUSTICE STEVENS dissented.]

* * * * * * * * * * *

COMMENTS

[a] While the Court's opinion seems to be a straightforward decision that the facts of this case do not rise to a *Massiah* violation under the rule of *Henry*, it can also be read as an interpretation that applies only on successive habeas corpus petitions under 28 U.S.C. §2254(d).

[b] At these points, the dissenting opinion takes a broader view of the "deliberately-elicited" standard of *Henry* than does the majority. To some extent, one's view of whether Benny Lee was just a "listening post" or an inducement depends on one's view of human psychology. Do you think it is unlikely, possible, or highly likely that a person jailed before trial for a serious crime would divulge incriminating information to a cellmate who was previously a stranger?

[c] The majority ignores the factor of whether the jailhouse informer was paid. On the one hand, the payment of the informer would make no difference to the state of mind of the defendant in ascertaining whether the defendant had been "induced" to make incriminating statements. On the other hand, a paid informant might have a greater incentive to induce a cellmate to divulge incriminating information.

MICHIGAN v. HARVEY

494 U.S. 344, 110 S.Ct. 1176, 108 L.Ed.2d 293 (1990)

CHIEF JUSTICE REHNQUIST delivered the opinion of the Court.

In *Michigan v. Jackson*, 475 U.S. 625 (1986), the Court established a prophylactic rule that once a criminal defendant invokes his Sixth Amendment right to counsel, a subsequent waiver of that right—even if voluntary, knowing, and intelligent under traditional standards—is presumed invalid if secured pursuant to police-initiated conversation. We held that statements obtained in violation of that rule may not be admitted as substantive evidence in the prosecution's case-in-chief. The question presented in this case is whether the prosecution may use a statement taken in violation of the *Jackson* prophylactic rule to impeach a defendant's false or inconsistent testimony. We hold that it may do so.

[Harvey was arrested on July 2 for a sexual assault committed on June 11. He made a statement to an investigating officer, was arraigned, and counsel was appointed for him. More than two months later, Harvey told another police officer that he wanted to make a second statement, but did not know whether he should talk to his lawyer. The officer told Harvey that he did not need to speak with his attorney, because "his lawyer was going to get a copy of the statement anyway." He signed a constitutional rights waiver form, on which he initialed the portions advising him of his right to remain silent, his right to have a lawyer present before and during questioning, and his right to have a lawyer appointed for him prior to any questioning. He answered affirmatively that he understood his constitutional rights. He then gave a statement detailing his version of the events of June 11.]

[At a bench trial, the victim testified to the sexual assault. Harvey testified in his own defense that a fight occurred over a misunderstanding of an exchange of sex for drugs but that no sexual intercourse occurred. On cross-examination, the prosecutor used Harvey's second statement to the police to impeach his testimony. The prosecutor noted that the statement was not given after proper *Miranda* warnings and so could not be used as evidence in the case in chief but only for impeachment. Harvey was convicted.]

[The Michigan Court of Appeals reversed, holding that the second statement was inadmissible even for impeachment purposes, because it was taken in violation of defendant's Sixth Amendment right to counsel under the rule of *Michigan v. Jackson*. "Because the trial 'involved a credibility contest between defendant and the victim,' the court concluded that the impeachment was not harmless beyond a reasonable doubt." The Michigan Supreme Court denied leave to appeal and we granted certiorari.] We now reverse.

To understand this case, it is necessary first to review briefly the Court's jurisprudence surrounding the Sixth Amendment. * * * The essence of this right ["to have the Assistance of Counsel for [one's] defence"], * * * is the opportunity for a defendant to consult with an attorney, and to have him investigate the case and prepare a defense for trial. * * * More recently, in a line of cases beginning with *Massiah v. United States*, [this volume] and extending through *Maine v. Moulton*, 474 U.S. 159 (1985), the Court has held that once formal criminal proceedings begin, the Sixth Amendment renders inadmissible in the prosecution's case-in-chief statements "deliberately elicited" from a defendant without an express waiver of the right to counsel. * * * For the fruits of postindictment interrogations to be admissible in a prosecution's case-in-chief, the State must prove a voluntary, knowing, and intelligent relinquishment of the Sixth Amendment right to counsel. *Patterson v. Illinois*, 487 U.S. 285, * * * (1988). * * * We have recently held that when a suspect waives his right to counsel after receiving warnings equivalent to those prescribed by *Miranda v. Arizona*, * * * that will generally suffice to establish a knowing and intelligent waiver of the Sixth Amendment right to counsel for purposes of postindictment questioning. * * *

In *Michigan v. Jackson*, [above], the Court created a bright-line rule for deciding whether an accused who has "asserted" his Sixth Amendment right to counsel has subsequently waived that right. Transposing the reasoning of *Edwards v. Arizona*, [this volume], which had announced an identical "prophylactic rule" in the Fifth Amendment context, * * * we decided that after a defendant requests assistance of counsel, any waiver of Sixth Amendment rights given in a discussion initiated by police is presumed invalid, and evidence obtained pursuant to such a waiver is inadmissible in the prosecution's case-in-chief. *Jackson*, * * *

Thus, to help guarantee that waivers are truly voluntary, *Jackson* established a presumption which renders invalid some waivers that would be considered voluntary, knowing, and intelligent under the traditional case-by-case inquiry called for by *Brewer v. Williams*.

There is no dispute in this case that respondent had a Sixth Amendment right to counsel at the time he gave the statement at issue. The State further concedes that the police transgressed the *Jackson* rule, because the colloquy between respondent and the investigating officer "cannot be viewed as defendant-initiated interrogation." * * * The question, then, is whether a statement to police taken in violation of *Jackson* can be admitted to impeach a defendant's inconsistent trial testimony. [a]

Michigan v. Jackson is based on the Sixth Amendment, but its roots lie in this Court's decisions in *Miranda v. Arizona*, *supra*, and succeeding cases. *Miranda*, of course, required police interrogators to advise criminal suspects of their rights under the Fifth and Fourteenth Amendments and set forth a now-familiar set of suggested instructions for that purpose. Although recognizing that the *Miranda* rules would result in the exclusion of some voluntary and reliable statements, the Court imposed these "prophylactic standards" on the States, * * * to safeguard the Fifth Amendment privilege against self-incrimination. *Edwards v. Arizona* added a second layer of protection to the *Miranda* rules, holding that "when an accused has invoked his right to have counsel present during custodial interrogation, a valid waiver of that right cannot be established by showing only that he responded to further police-initiated custodial interrogation even if he has been advised of his rights." * * * *Edwards* thus established another prophylactic rule designed to prevent police from badgering a defendant into waiving his previously asserted *Miranda* rights. * * *

Jackson simply superimposed the Fifth Amendment analysis of *Edwards* onto the Sixth Amendment. Reasoning that "the Sixth Amendment right to counsel at a postarraignment interrogation requires at least as much protection as the Fifth Amendment right to counsel at any custodial interrogation," * * * the Court in *Jackson* concluded that the *Edwards* protections should apply when a suspect charged with a crime requests counsel outside the context of interrogation. This rule, like *Edwards*, is based on the supposition that suspects who assert their right to counsel are unlikely to waive that right voluntarily in subsequent interrogations.

We have already decided that although statements taken in violation of only the prophylactic *Miranda* rules may not be used in the prosecution's case-in-chief, they are admissible to impeach conflicting testimony by the defendant. *Harris v. New York*, 401 U.S. 222 (1971); *Oregon v. Hass*, 420 U.S. 714 (1975). The prosecution must not be allowed to build its case against a criminal defendant with evidence acquired in contravention of constitutional guarantees and their corresponding judicially-created protections. But use of statements so obtained for impeachment purposes is a different matter. If a defendant exercises his right to testify on his own behalf, he assumes a reciprocal "obligation to speak truthfully and accurately," * * * and we have consistently rejected arguments that would allow a defendant to "'turn the illegal method by which evidence in the Government's possession was obtained to his own advantage, and provide himself with a shield against contradiction of his untruths.'" * * * **[b]**

There is no reason for a different result in a *Jackson* case, where the prophylactic rule is designed to ensure voluntary, knowing, and intelligent waivers of the Sixth Amendment right to counsel rather than the Fifth Amendment privilege against self-incrimination or "right to counsel." **[c]** We have mandated the exclusion of reliable and probative evidence for *all* purposes only when it is derived from involuntary statements. * * * We have never prevented use by the prosecution of relevant voluntary statements by a defendant, particularly when the violations alleged by a defendant relate only to procedural safeguards that are "not themselves rights protected by the Constitution," * * * but are instead measures designed to ensure that constitutional rights are protected. In such cases, we have decided that the "search for truth in a criminal case" outweighs the "speculative possibility" that exclusion of evidence might deter future violations of rules not compelled directly by the Constitution in the first place. * * *

Respondent argues that there should be a different exclusionary rule for *Jackson* violations than for transgressions of *Edwards* and *Miranda*. The distinction, he suggests, is that the adversarial process has commenced at the time of a *Jackson* violation, and the postarraignment interrogations thus implicate the constitutional guarantee of the Sixth Amendment itself. But nothing in the Sixth Amendment prevents a suspect charged with a crime and represented by counsel from voluntarily choosing, on his own, to speak with police in the absence of an attorney. We have already held that a defendant whose Sixth Amendment right to counsel has attached by virtue of an indictment may execute a knowing and intelligent waiver of that right in the course of a police-initiated interrogation. * * * To be sure, once a defendant obtains or even requests counsel as respondent had here, analysis of the waiver issue changes. But that change is due to the protective rule we created in *Jackson* based on the apparent inconsistency between a request for counsel and a later voluntary decision to proceed without assistance. * * *

In other cases, we have explicitly declined to hold that a defendant who has obtained counsel cannot himself waive his right to counsel. * * * A defendant's right to rely on counsel as a "medium" between the defendant and the State attaches upon the initiation of formal charges, * * * and respondent's contention that a defendant cannot execute a valid waiver of the right to counsel without first speaking to an attorney is foreclosed by our decision in *Patterson.* Moreover, respondent's view would render the prophylactic rule adopted in *Jackson* wholly unnecessary, because even waivers given during *defendant-initiated* conversations would be *per se* involuntary or otherwise invalid, unless counsel were first notified.

Although a defendant may sometimes later regret his decision to speak with police, the Sixth Amendment does not disable a criminal defendant from exercising his free will. To hold that a defendant is inherently incapable of

relinquishing his right to counsel once it is invoked would be "to imprison a man in his privileges and call it the Constitution." * * * This we decline to do. Both *Jackson* and *Edwards* establish prophylactic rules that render some otherwise valid waivers of constitutional rights invalid when they result from police-initiated interrogation, and in neither case should "the shield provided by [the prophylactic rule] be perverted into a license to use perjury by way of a defense, free from the risk of confrontation with prior inconsistent utterances." * * * [d]

Respondent and *amicus* assert, alternatively, that the conduct of the police officer who took Harvey's second statement violated the "core value" of the Sixth Amendment's constitutional guarantee, and under those circumstances, the second statement may not be used even for impeachment purposes. They contend that respondent was affirmatively misled as to his need for counsel, and his purported waiver is therefore invalid. But on the record before us, it is not possible to determine whether Harvey's waiver was knowing and voluntary. The state courts developed no record on that issue, and the Michigan Court of Appeals did not rest its holding on any such determination. There was no testimony on this point before the trial court. The only statement in the trial record concerning the issue of waiver is the prosecutor's concession that the second statement was taken in violation of respondent's *Miranda* rights. But that concession is consistent with the Michigan Court of Appeals' finding that the police violated *Jackson*, which is, after all, only a Sixth Amendment analogue to the *Miranda* and *Edwards* decisions. The

Michigan court made no independent inquiry into whether there had been an otherwise valid waiver of the right to counsel, and respondent's counsel himself conceded that, putting aside the prosecutor's concession, the record is insufficient to determine whether there was a voluntary waiver of Sixth Amendment rights. * * * In short, the issue was never litigated in this case.

Because respondent's counsel did not object at trial to the use of his second statement for impeachment purposes, the State had no occasion to offer evidence to establish that Harvey gave a knowing and voluntary waiver of his right to counsel under traditional standards. [e] On remand, the Michigan courts are free to conduct a hearing on that question. It is the State's burden to show that a waiver is knowing and voluntary, * * * and if all the circumstances in a particular case show that the police have engaged in a course of conduct which would render the waiver involuntary, the burden will not be satisfied. Those facts are not before us, however, and we need not consider the admissibility for impeachment purposes of a voluntary statement obtained in the absence of a knowing and voluntary waiver of the right to counsel.

The judgment of the Michigan Court of Appeals is reversed, and the case is remanded for further proceedings not inconsistent with this opinion.
It is so ordered.

JUSTICE STEVENS, with whom JUSTICE BRENNAN, JUSTICE MARSHALL, and JUSTICE BLACKMUN join, dissenting.

The question presented by this case, as I understand it, is whether the State may initiate a private interview with an indicted and represented defendant to obtain impeachment evidence for use at trial. The answer to that question should be plain: "The Sixth Amendment guarantees the accused, at least after the initiation of formal charges, the right to rely on counsel as a 'medium' between him and the State." * * * This right to rely on counsel applies whether the State is seeking evidence for use in its case in chief, rebuttal evidence, information about trial strategy, or material for use as impeachment.

The Court, couching its conclusion in the language of "prophylactic rules," seemingly answers this question in the affirmative. It reasons as follows: Although *Michigan v. Jackson* * * * is based on the Sixth Amendment, it protects only Fifth Amendment values; [f] the Fifth Amendment does not prohibit the introduction of statements taken after the accused has invoked his right to counsel for use as impeachment; therefore, the Sixth Amendment, as interpreted in *Jackson*, does not prohibit the use of evidence taken in violation of its strictures for impeachment at trial. The Court's syllogism is flawed from the beginning. Only two Terms ago, we made clear that the constitutional rule recognized in *Jackson* is based on the Sixth Amendment interest in preserving "the integrity of an accused's choice to communicate with police only through counsel." *Patterson v. Illinois.* * * * The Court should acknowledge as much and hold that the Sixth Amendment is violated when the fruits of the State's impermissible encounter with the represented defendant are used for impeachment just as it is when the fruits are used in the prosecutor's case in chief.

I

To explain the error of the Court's analysis, it is appropriate to start where the Court does with the difference between the Fifth and Sixth Amendments and the values each serves. The Fifth Amendment protects against compelled self-incrimination. It prevents a criminal defendant from being made "'the deluded instrument of his own conviction.'" * * * Our decisions in *Miranda* and its progeny primarily safeguard that right against "the compulsion inherent in custodial surroundings." * * * The initiation by the police of contact with an unrepresented defendant, after the invocation of the right to counsel during interrogation or at arraignment, creates an irrebuttable presumption that a defendant's waiver of his privilege against compelled self-incrimination is not voluntary. * * * But when that compulsion has been dispelled by the suspect's initiation of interrogation and voluntary waiver of his rights, there is no remaining Fifth Amendment objection to introduction at trial of a statement made outside the presence of counsel. * * *

The Sixth Amendment right to counsel is much more pervasive because it affects the ability of the accused to assert any other rights he might have. It is indisputable that the Amendment assures "'Assistance' at trial, when the accused [is] confronted with both the intricacies of the law and the advocacy of the public prosecutor." * * * That guarantee applies equally whether the defendant is presenting his case or the State is rebutting or impeaching the defendant's evidence. The State's interest in truth-seeking is congruent with the defendant's interest in representation by counsel, for it is an elementary premise of our system of criminal justice "'that partisan advocacy on both sides of a case will best promote the ultimate objective that the guilty be convicted and the innocent go free.'" * * *

The accused's right to the assistance of counsel is not limited to participation in the trial itself. A defendant is entitled to the aid of his lawyer from the time of arraignment "when consultation, thoroughgoing investigation and preparation [are] vitally important," * * * through the time of first appeal. * * * [T]he accused's right to have counsel "for his defence" in a "criminal prosecutio[n]" includes the right to rely on counsel after the government's role has shifted from investigation to accusation and the "defendant finds himself faced with the prosecutorial forces of organized society." * * * Any lesser guarantee would provide insufficient protection against any attempt by the State to supplant "the public trial guaranteed by the Bill of Rights" with a "secret trial in the police precincts." * * *

The Court correctly explains that *Jackson* was based in part on Fifth Amendment concerns extending "the *Edwards* protections" to the situation "when a suspect charged with a crime requests counsel outside the context of interrogation." * * * However, that was not the whole of our opinion. *Jackson* is also firmly and explicitly rooted in our Sixth Amendment decisions holding that an indicted defendant has the "right to rely on counsel as a 'medium' between him and the State" whenever the State attempts to deliberately elicit information from him. * * * *Jackson* made clear that that right applied to the State's initial question whether the defendant would like to waive his constitutional rights as well as to any subsequent questions asking for particular incriminating information. * * * The defendant may waive the right to be free from direct state communication by initiating contact with the State. But if the State initiates communication with a represented defendant outside the presence of counsel any subsequent waiver of the right to rely on counsel is not just "presumed invalid," * * * * it "*is* invalid." *Jackson*, * * * (emphasis added). Preventing the State from directly contacting a represented defendant thus does not, as the Court states, "'imprison a man in his privileges;'" * * * it simply recognizes and gives respect to the defendant's previously invoked choice to communicate with the State only through counsel. As JUSTICE WHITE explained for the Court in *Patterson v. Illinois*, while "an accused [can make] an *initial* election as to whether he will face the State's officers during questioning with the aid of counsel, or go it alone," "the essence" of *Jackson* and our earlier decision in *Edwards v. Arizona* * * * is "[p]reserving the integrity of an accused's choice to communicate with the police only through counsel." * * * Indeed, we expressly noted, in explaining why an unrepresented defendant could waive his Sixth Amendment rights without counsel being present, that "[o]nce an accused has a lawyer, a distinct set of constitutional safeguards aimed at preserving the sanctity of the attorney-client relationship takes effect." * * *

The right to consult with counsel prior to the commencement of an interrogation, moreover, cannot be limited to those interrogations that produce evidence for use in the State's case in chief. The interests of the defendant in the assistance of counsel in his confrontation with the prosecutorial forces of organized society extend to all efforts to elicit information from the defendant whether for use as impeachment or rebuttal at trial or simply to formulate trial strategy. * * * [For example, statements made by a defendant to a state psychiatrist to determine competency to stand trial cannot be used at capital sentencing or on rebuttal in a trial.]

[In Part II, JUSTICE STEVENS argued against treating the rule of *Michigan v. Jackson* only as a prophylactic protection of the Sixth Amendment that need not be given full effect. He argued that the violation in this case was a violation of the defendant's Sixth Amendment right to counsel itself.]

[In Part III, JUSTICE STEVENS noted that he dissented in *Patterson v. Illinois*, arguing that any private interviews of the defendant with prosecution forces should be deemed full violations of the Sixth Amendment. In *Patterson* the Court instead held that a defendant may waive the right to counsel after *Miranda* warnings have been administered, but the validity of the waiver depended on determining what purposes a lawyer can serve at a particular stage of the proceedings. Thus, during a trial a waiver would virtually never be proper. Here, Harvey had been in custody for months and the trial date was approaching. His lawyer would have been able to guide a conference with the police in light of his trial strategy. But the Court says nothing about how strong the presumptions about waiver is at this stage.]

IV

Apparently as a means of identifying rules that it disfavors, the Court repeatedly uses the term "prophylactic rule." * * * It is important to remember, however, that all rules of law are prophylactic. Speed limits are an example; they are designed to prevent accidents. The Sixth Amendment is another; it is designed to prevent unfair trials. An argument that a rule of law may be ignored, avoided, or manipulated simply because it is "prophylactic" is nothing more than an argument against the rule of law itself. The tragedy of today's decision is not merely its denigration of the constitutional right at stake; it also undermines the principle that those who are entrusted with the power of government have the same duty to respect and obey the law as the ordinary citizen.

I respectfully dissent.

* * * * * * * * * *

COMMENTS

[a] From the reported facts, Harvey initiated the *conversation*. But the *interrogation* began only after the police officer, apparently dispensing legal advice without a license, assured Harvey there was no problem with talking with police without counsel present.

[b] An inability to impeach a witness with prior inconsistent statements puts a premium on lying.

[c] The Court establishes a strict parallelism between the Fifth Amendment-*Miranda-Edwards* and the Sixth Amendment-*Massiah-Jackson* rules. This depends on a view of the underlying rights (against self-incrimination; counsel) as equivalent. The Court never explores this point in its opinion but simply assumes it.

[d] In the three prior paragraphs the Court discusses the effect of waiver without mentioning that the waiver in this case was defective.

[e] This is a reminder that counsel's objections at trial are not mere formalities. Valuable rights can be lost or compromised by counsel's failure to object. Attorneys conducting a trial must thus have an extensive expert knowledge of the relevant law.

[f] Is this what the majority meant when it said that the "roots" of *Michigan v. Jackson* "lies in this Court's decisions in *Miranda* * * * and succeeding cases"? The language of carefully crafted Supreme Court opinions still leave room for ambiguity.

Chapter Seven

IDENTIFICATION

The ability to identify the criminal defendant as the person who committed the crime charged is a necessary element in the prosecution of offenders. The process of identification is also the most basic way of clearing those who have been wrongfully identified as perpetrators of crime.

The identification process begins on the street as individuals and police officers seek out the suspect. The process continues in police stations and jails as witnesses view photographs of suspects or view a suspect among others in a lineup. And the process is a critical part of the criminal trial when a witness is asked to identify the alleged perpetrator in open court.

The process of identification is haunted by what is known about the psychology of perception. Human beings do not record what they see and hear with the objective accuracy of cameras or tape recorders. Human perception is filtered through a mental process that can at times distort what occurred. As a result, eyewitnesses have been known to misidentify suspects and defendants. Numerous studies have been written about wrongful convictions that have occurred as a result of misidentification.[*]

The injustice of imprisoning or executing an innocent person tests the system of criminal justice as do few other problems. There are measures that can be taken to reduce misidentification. Ideally, lineups and photo identification should be conducted in a "double blind" manner by officers who have no knowledge of which person is the suspect, but this is not done. Prior to making an identification a suspect can be asked to describe the perpetrator and "create" a portrait using sophisticated computer programs

---

[*]

Edwin M. Borchard, *Convicting the Innocent: Sixty-five Actual Errors of Criminal Justice* (New York: Garden City Publishing Co., 1932); Jerome Frank & Barbara Frank, *Not Guilty* (Garden City, N.Y.: Doubleday, 1957); Hugo Adam Bedeau & Michael Radelet, "Miscarriages of Justice in Potentially Capital Cases," 40 *Stanford Law Review* 21 (1987); C. Ronald Huff, Arye Rattner & Edward Sagarin, *Convicted But Innocent: Wrongful Conviction and Public Policy* (Columbus, Ohio: Ohio State University Press, 1992).

that can replace sketch artists and identification kits. The pre-viewing portrait can then be used as a comparison to the identified suspect. Knowledge of experiments in the psychology of perception can be used to improve the way in which lineups are constructed.

Although the problem of misidentification implicates the fairness of the trial, none of these concerns were seen as constitutional issues prior to the 1960s. The traditional legal approach was for defense counsel on cross-examination to probe for weaknesses in the perception of the eyewitness. In the 1960s, for the first time, constitutional challenges to the identification process were put forward on due process and Sixth Amendment right to counsel grounds. The Supreme Court was receptive to these novel challenges and established constitutional parameters for the identification process.

The right to counsel challenge faced a basic hurdle. The Bill of Rights protects citizens against wrongdoing by government officers. There is no "state action" when a witness misidentifies a defendant. To establish state action, *United States v. Wade* (1967) focused instead on a part of the larger problem of misidentification: police suggestibility. The Right to Counsel extended the "criminal prosecution" requirement of the Sixth Amendment to the pretrial (but post-indictment) lineup under the concept that the lineup was a "critical stage" where events occurred that would have a material effect on the determination of guilt or innocence. *Wade* held that where a post-indictment lineup was conducted without counsel present, the result of the lineup itself must be excluded *and* in the in-court identification is excluded unless the prosecution can show that the witness' initial memory was not tainted by the identification made at the lineup. *Gilbert v. California*, 388 U.S. 263 (1967), decided on the same day as *Wade*, applied the *Wade* rule to a state case and ruled that errors under the rule were subject to harmless error analysis.

These cases upheld the rule that the Fifth Amendment does not apply to the gathering of physical, non-testimonial evidence such as facial or other physical identification via live viewing or photographs, handwriting exemplars, blood samples (*Schmerber v. California*, 384 U.S. 757 (1966)), fingerprints, hair samples, or breathalyzer or urine test results. It is not testimonial to require a suspect to wear a strip of tape or an article of clothing that was worn at the scene of the crime (*Holt v. United States*, 218 U.S. 245 (1910)).

Critics of the *Wade-Gilbert* rule argued that the lineup was unlike any other proceeding where attorneys are required. The role of attorneys at preliminary hearings, trials, sentencing procedures and the like include the presentation and challenging of evidence and the arguing of legal points. All an attorney can do at a lineup or photographic display is to monitor the proceeding for possible suggestibility and complain if she believes that there is something suggestive about the procedure.

A more conservative Supreme Court placed limits on the *Wade* doctrine. *Kirby v. Illinois* (1972) held that the Sixth Amendment required counsel *only* at post-indictment lineups; the criminal process does not begin until the state formally charges a person even though the possibility of suggestibility exists both at pre-indictment and post-indictment lineups. *United States v. Ash* (1973) refused to extend the *Wade-Gilbert* rule to the post-indictment photographic identification process on the grounds that showing photographs, unlike a live lineup, is not subject to the same possibilities of suggestibility;

furthermore, unlike the lineup situation where it is difficult or impossible to reconstruct what happened on cross-examination, the Court found that such reconstruction was easier in respect to photographic identification.

Aside from the right to counsel, the Supreme Court has also held that impermissibly suggestive identification procedures violate the due process rights of suspects. Thus, where the police show only one suspect to a witness, the suggestion is so strong that *this* is the guilty party that the procedure is impermissible suggestive. In such case the identification must be excluded unless the "showup" occurred because of an exigency (*Stovall v. Denno*, 388 U.S. 293 (1967)). Due process was violated where a witness could not identify a suspect at one lineup and at a second lineup the defendant was the only person from the first lineup (*Foster v. California*, 394 U.S. 440 (1969)). The Court has not applied a strict exclusionary rule in such cases but has held that identification resulting from a suggestive process need not be excluded if the totality of the circumstances indicates that the identification was reliable (*Neil v. Biggers*, 409 U.S. 188 (1972)). *Manson v. Brathwaite* (1977) clarified this rule by establishing five factors to test reliability: (1) the opportunity to view the perpetrator, (2) the degree of attention to the perpetrator, (3) the accuracy of the witness' description of the suspect, (4) the witness' level of certainty, and (5) the time between the crime and the confrontation.

UNITED STATES v. WADE

388 U.S. 218, 87 S.Ct. 1926, 18 L.Ed.2d 1149 (1967)

MR. JUSTICE BRENNAN delivered the opinion of the Court.

The question here is whether courtroom identifications of an accused at trial are to be excluded from evidence because the accused was exhibited to the witnesses before trial at a post-indictment lineup conducted for identification purposes without notice to and in the absence of the accused's appointed counsel. [a]

[On September 21, 1964, a federally insured bank was robbed by a man with a small strip of tape on each side of his face who forced a teller and bank officer, at gunpoint, to fill a pillowcase with money. He escaped with an accomplice who had been waiting in a stolen car outside the bank. On March 23, 1965, Wade and two others were indicted for conspiracy and bank robbery.] Wade was arrested on April 2, and counsel was appointed to represent him on April 26. Fifteen days later an FBI agent, without notice to Wade's lawyer, arranged to have the two bank employees observe a lineup made up of Wade and five or six other prisoners and conducted in a courtroom of the local county courthouse. [b] Each person in the line wore strips of tape such as allegedly worn by the robber and upon direction each said something like "put the money in the bag," the words allegedly uttered by the robber. Both bank employees identified Wade in the lineup as the bank robber.

At trial, the two employees, when asked on direct examination if the robber was in the courtroom, pointed to Wade. The prior lineup identification was then elicited from both employees on cross-examination. At the close of testimony, Wade's counsel moved for a judgment of acquittal or, alternatively, to strike the bank officials' courtroom identifications on the ground that conduct of the lineup, without notice to and in the absence of his appointed counsel, violated his Fifth Amendment privilege against self-incrimination and his Sixth Amendment right to the assistance of counsel. The motion was denied, and Wade was convicted. The Court of Appeals for the Fifth Circuit reversed the conviction and ordered a new trial at which the in-court identification evidence was to be excluded, holding that, though the lineup did not violate Wade's Fifth Amendment rights, "the lineup, held as it was, in the absence of counsel, already chosen to represent appellant, was a violation of his Sixth Amendment rights. . . ." * * * We reverse the judgment of the Court of Appeals and remand to that court with direction to enter a new judgment vacating the conviction and remanding the case to the District Court for further proceedings consistent with this opinion. [c]

I.

[In Part I, the Court ruled that no Fifth Amendment violation occurred when Wade was required to participate in the lineup, or by placing strips of tape on his face or by repeating what was said at the robbery. Providing physical evidence of one's identity is not the kind of "testimonial evidence" protected by the privilege against self-incrimination.]

II.

* * * [I]n this case it is urged that the assistance of counsel at the lineup was indispensable to protect Wade's most basic right as a criminal defendant—his right to a fair trial at which the witnesses against him might be meaningfully cross-examined.

The Framers of the Bill of Rights envisaged a broader role for counsel than under the practice then prevailing in England of merely advising his client in "matters of law," and eschewing any responsibility for "matters of fact." The constitutions in at least 11 of the 13 States expressly or impliedly abolished this distinction. * * * This background is reflected in the scope given by our decisions to the Sixth Amendment's guarantee to an accused of the assistance of counsel for his defense. When the Bill of Rights was adopted, there were no organized police forces as we know them today. The accused confronted the prosecutor and the witnesses against him, and the evidence was marshalled, largely at the trial itself. In contrast, today's law enforcement machinery involves critical confrontations of the accused by the prosecution at pretrial proceedings where the results might well settle the accused's fate and reduce the trial itself to a mere formality. In recognition of these realities of modern criminal prosecution, our cases have construed the Sixth Amendment guarantee to apply to "critical" stages of the proceedings. * * * The plain wording of [the counsel] guarantee thus encompasses counsel's assistance whenever necessary to assure a meaningful "defence." [d]

As early as *Powell v. Alabama*, [this

volume], we recognized that the period from arraignment to trial was "perhaps the most critical period of the proceedings. . .," * * * during which the accused "requires the guiding hand of counsel, . . ." * * * if the guarantee is not to prove an empty right. [The Court then noted that earlier cases have identified numerous critical stages where counsel is required: arraignments where rights may be sacrificed (*Hamilton v. Alabama*, 368 U.S. 52 (1961)); post-indictment questioning of or eavesdropping on a defendant (*Massiah v. United States*, [this volume]); pre-indictment questioning by police (*Escobedo v. Illinois*, 378 U.S. 478 (1964) and *Miranda v. Arizona* [this volume]).] [e]

Of course, nothing decided or said in the opinions in the cited cases links the right to counsel only to protection of Fifth Amendment rights. * * * The presence of counsel at such critical confrontations, as at the trial itself, operates to assure that the accused's interests will be protected consistently with our adversary theory of criminal prosecution. * * *

In sum, the principle of *Powell v. Alabama* and succeeding cases requires that we scrutinize *any* pretrial confrontation of the accused to determine whether the presence of his counsel is necessary to preserve the defendant's basic right to a fair trial as affected by his right meaningfully to cross-examine the witnesses against him and to have effective assistance of counsel at the trial itself. It calls upon us to analyze whether potential substantial prejudice to defendant's rights inheres in the particular confrontation and the ability of counsel to help avoid that prejudice.

III.

The Government characterizes the lineup as a mere preparatory step in the gathering of the prosecution's evidence, not different—for Sixth Amendment purposes— from various other preparatory steps, such as systematized or scientific analyzing of the accused's fingerprints, blood sample, clothing, hair, and the like. We think there are differences which preclude such stages being characterized as critical stages at which the accused has the right to the presence of his counsel. Knowledge of the techniques of science and technology is sufficiently available, and the variables in techniques few enough, that the accused has the opportunity for a meaningful confrontation of the Government's case at trial through the ordinary processes of cross-examination of the Government's expert witnesses and the presentation of the evidence of his own experts. The denial of a right to have his counsel present at such analyses does not therefore violate the Sixth Amendment; they are not critical stages since there is minimal risk that his counsel's absence at such stages might derogate from his right to a fair trial. [f]

IV.

But the confrontation compelled by the State between the accused and the victim or witnesses to a crime to elicit identification evidence is peculiarly riddled with innumerable dangers and variable factors which might seriously, even crucially, derogate from a fair trial. The vagaries of eyewitness identification are well-known; the annals of criminal law are rife with instances of mistaken identification. MR. JUSTICE FRANK-FURTER once said: "What is the worth of identification testimony even when uncontradicted? The identification of strangers is proverbially untrustworthy. The hazards of such testimony are established by a formidable number of instances in the records of English and American trials. These instances are recent—not due to the brutalities of ancient criminal procedure." * * * A major factor contributing to the high incidence of miscarriage of justice from mistaken identification has been the degree of suggestion inherent in the manner in which the prosecution presents the suspect to witnesses for pretrial identification. [g] A commentator has observed that "[t]he influence of improper suggestion upon identifying witnesses probably accounts for more miscarriages of justice than any other single factor—perhaps it is responsible for more such errors than all other factors combined." * * * Suggestion can be created intentionally or unintentionally in many subtle ways. And the dangers for the suspect are particularly grave when the witness' opportunity for observation was insubstantial, and thus his susceptibility to suggestion the greatest. [h]

Moreover, "[i]t is a matter of common experience that, once a witness has picked out the accused at the line-up, he is not likely to go back on his word later on, so that in practice the issue of identity may (in the absence of other relevant evidence) for all practical purposes be determined there and then, before the trial." The pretrial confrontation for purpose of identification may take the form of a lineup, also known as an "identification parade" or "showup," as in the present case, or presentation of the suspect alone to the witness. * * * It is obvious that risks of suggestion attend either form of confrontation and increase the dangers inhering in eyewitness identification. But as is the case with secret interrogations, there is serious difficulty in depicting what transpires at lineups and other forms of identification confrontations. * * * For the same reasons, the defense can seldom reconstruct the manner and mode of lineup identification for judge or jury at trial. Those participating in a lineup with the accused may often be police officers; in any event, the participants' names are rarely recorded or divulged at trial. The impediments to an objective observation are increased when the victim is the witness. Lineups are prevalent in rape and robbery prosecutions and present a particular hazard that a victim's understandable outrage may excite vengeful or spiteful motives. In any event, neither witnesses nor lineup participants are apt to be alert for conditions prejudicial to the suspect. And if they were, it would likely be of scant benefit to the suspect since neither witnesses nor lineup participants are likely to be schooled in the detection of suggestive influences. Improper influences may go undetected by a suspect, guilty or not, who experiences the emotional tension which we might expect in one being confronted with potential accusers. Even when he does observe abuse, if he has a criminal record he may be reluctant to take the stand and open up the admission of prior convictions. Moreover, any protestations by the suspect of the fairness of the lineup made at trial are likely to be in vain; the jury's choice is between the accused's unsupported version and that of the police officers present. In short, the accused's inability effectively to reconstruct at trial any unfairness that occurred at the lineup may deprive him of his only opportunity meaningfully to attack the credibility of the witness' courtroom identification. **[i]**

* * *

The potential for improper influence is illustrated by the circumstances, insofar as they appear, surrounding the prior identifications in the three cases we decide today. In the present case, the testimony of the identifying witnesses elicited on cross-examination revealed that those witnesses were taken to the courthouse and seated in the courtroom to await assembly of the lineup. The courtroom faced on a hallway observable to the witnesses through an open door. The cashier testified that she saw Wade "standing in the hall" within sight of an FBI agent. Five or six other prisoners later appeared in the hall. The vice president testified that he saw a person in the hall in the custody of the agent who "resembled the person that we identified as the one that had entered the bank."

The lineup in *Gilbert*, [a companion case], was conducted in an auditorium in which some 100 witnesses to several alleged state and federal robberies charged to Gilbert made wholesale identifications of Gilbert as the robber in each other's presence, a procedure said to be fraught with dangers of suggestion. And the vice of suggestion created by the identification in *Stovall*, *supra*, was the presentation to the witness of the suspect alone handcuffed to police officers. It is hard to imagine a situation more clearly conveying the suggestion to the witness that the one presented is believed guilty by the police. * * *

The few cases that have surfaced therefore reveal the existence of a process attended with hazards of serious unfairness to the criminal accused and strongly suggest the plight of the more numerous defendants who are unable to ferret out suggestive influences in the secrecy of the confrontation. We do not assume that these risks are the result of police procedures intentionally designed to prejudice an accused. Rather we assume they derive from the dangers inherent in eyewitness identification and the suggestibility inherent in the context of the pretrial identification. * * * "[T]he fact that the police themselves have, in a given case, little or no doubt that the man put up for identification has committed the offense, and that their chief pre-occupation is with the problem of getting sufficient proof, because he has not 'come clean,' involves a danger that this persuasion may communicate itself even in a doubtful case to the witness in some way. . . ." * * *

Insofar as the accused's conviction may rest on a courtroom identification in fact the fruit of a suspect pretrial identification which the accused is helpless to subject to effective scrutiny at trial, the accused is deprived of that right of cross-examination which is an essential safeguard to his right to confront the witnesses against him. * * * And even though cross-examination is a precious safeguard to a fair trial, it cannot be viewed as an absolute assurance of accuracy and reliability. Thus in the present context, where so many variables and pitfalls exist, the first line of defense must be the prevention of unfairness and the lessening of the hazards of eyewitness identification at the lineup itself. The trial which might determine the accused's fate may well not be that in the courtroom but that at the pretrial confrontation, with the State aligned against the accused, the witness the sole jury, and the accused unprotected against the overreaching, intentional or unintentional, and with little or

no effective appeal from the judgment there rendered by the witness— "that's the man."

Since it appears that there is grave potential for prejudice, intentional or not, in the pretrial lineup, which may not be capable of reconstruction at trial, and since presence of counsel itself can often avert prejudice and assure a meaningful confrontation at trial, there can be little doubt that for Wade the post-indictment lineup was a critical stage of the prosecution at which he was "as much entitled to such aid [of counsel] . . . as at the trial itself." * * * Thus both Wade and his counsel should have been notified of the impending lineup, and counsel's presence should have been a requisite to conduct of the lineup, absent an "intelligent waiver." * * * No substantial countervailing policy considerations have been advanced against the requirement of the presence of counsel. Concern is expressed that the requirement will forestall prompt identifications and result in obstruction of the confrontations. As for the first, we note that in the two cases in which the right to counsel is today held to apply, counsel had already been appointed and no argument is made in either case that notice to counsel would have prejudicially delayed the confrontations. Moreover, we leave open the question whether the presence of substitute counsel might not suffice where notification and presence of the suspect's own counsel would result in prejudicial delay. And to refuse to recognize the right to counsel for fear that counsel will obstruct the course of justice is contrary to the basic assumptions upon which this Court has operated in Sixth Amendment cases. * * * In our view counsel can hardly impede legitimate law enforcement; on the contrary, for the reasons expressed, law enforcement may be assisted by preventing the infiltration of taint in the prosecution's identification evidence. That result cannot help the guilty avoid conviction but can only help assure that the right man has been brought to justice.

Legislative or other regulations, such as those of local police departments, which eliminate the risks of abuse and unintentional suggestion at lineup proceedings and the impediments to meaningful confrontation at trial may also remove the basis for regarding the stage as "critical." But neither Congress nor the federal authorities have seen fit to provide a solution. What we hold today "in no way creates a constitutional straitjacket which will handicap sound efforts at reform, nor is it intended to have this effect." * * *

V.

We come now to the question whether the denial of Wade's motion to strike the courtroom identification by the bank witnesses at trial because of the absence of his counsel at the lineup required, as the Court of Appeals held, the grant of a new trial at which such evidence is to be excluded. **[j]** We do not think this disposition can be justified without first giving the Government the opportunity to establish by clear and convincing evidence that the in-court identifications were based upon observations of the suspect other than the lineup identification. * * * Where, as here, the admissibility of evidence of the lineup identification itself is not involved, a *per se* rule of exclusion of courtroom identification would be unjustified. * * * A rule limited solely to the exclusion of testimony concerning identification at the lineup itself, without

regard to admissibility of the courtroom identification, would render the right to counsel an empty one. The lineup is most often used, as in the present case, to crystallize the witnesses' identification of the defendant for future reference. We have already noted that the lineup identification will have that effect. The State may then rest upon the witnesses' unequivocal courtroom identification, and not mention the pretrial identification as part of the State's case at trial. **[k]** Counsel is then in the predicament in which Wade's counsel found himself—realizing that possible unfairness at the lineup may be the sole means of attack upon the unequivocal courtroom identification, and having to probe in the dark in an attempt to discover and reveal unfairness, while bolstering the government witness' courtroom identification by bringing out and dwelling upon his prior identification. Since counsel's presence at the lineup would equip him to attack not only the lineup identification but the courtroom identification as well, limiting the impact of violation of the right to counsel to exclusion of evidence only of identification at the lineup itself disregards a critical element of that right.

We think it follows that the proper test to be applied in these situations is that quoted in *Wong Sun v. United States*, 371 U.S. 471 [1963], "'[W]hether, granting establishment of the primary illegality, the evidence to which instant objection is made has been come at by exploitation of that illegality or instead by means sufficiently distinguishable to be purged of the primary taint.' * * *" * * * **[l]** Application of this test in the present context requires consideration of various factors; for example, the prior opportunity to observe the alleged criminal act, the existence of any dis-

crepancy between any pre-lineup description and the defendant's actual
description, any identification prior to
lineup of another person, the identification by picture of the defendant prior to
the lineup, failure to identify the defendant on a prior occasion, and the lapse
of time between the alleged act and the
lineup identification. It is also relevant
to consider those facts which, despite
the absence of counsel, are disclosed
concerning the conduct of the lineup.
[m]

We doubt that the Court of Appeals
applied the proper test for exclusion of
the in-court identification of the two
witnesses. * * * [The judgment of the
Court of Appeals was vacated and the
case remanded for further proceedings].

[CHIEF JUSTICE WARREN and
JUSTICE DOUGLAS concurred,
except for Part I. JUSTICE DOUG-
LAS would have held that compulsory
lineup violates the Fifth Amendment
privilege against self-incrimination, while
the CHIEF JUSTICE agreed with the
opinion of JUSTICE FORTAS, below.]

MR. JUSTICE CLARK, concurring.

With reference to the lineup point
involved in this case I cannot, for the
life of me, see why a lineup is not a
critical stage of the prosecution. Identification of the suspect—a prerequisite to
establishment of guilt—occurs at this
stage, and with *Miranda v. Arizona* * * *
on the books, the requirement of the
presence of counsel arises, unless waived
by the suspect. I dissented in *Miranda*
but I am bound by it now, as we all are.
Schmerber v. California * * * precludes
petitioner's claim of self-incrimination.
I therefore join the opinion of the
Court. [n]

MR. JUSTICE BLACK, dissenting
in part and concurring in part.

[JUSTICE BLACK dissented from
the Court's Fifth Amendment analysis
but concurred with the critical stage
analysis and the application of the Sixth
Amendment right to counsel to the
lineup. However, he found fault with
the Court's remedy both on practical
and constitutional grounds.]
In the first place, even if this Court
has power to establish such a rule of
evidence, I think the rule fashioned by
the Court is unsound. The "tainted
fruit" determination required by the
Court involves more than considerable
difficulty. I think it is practically impossible. How is a witness capable of
probing the recesses of his mind to draw
a sharp line between a courtroom
identification due exclusively to an
earlier lineup and a courtroom identification due to memory not based on the
lineup? What kind of "clear and convincing evidence" can the prosecution
offer to prove upon what particular
events memories resulting in an in-court
identification rest? How long will trials
be delayed while judges turn psychologists to probe the subconscious minds of
witnesses?   All these questions are
posed but not answered by the Court's
opinion. * * *
But more important, there is no
constitutional provision upon which I
can rely that directly or by implication
gives this Court power to establish what
amounts to a constitutional rule of
evidence to govern, not only the Federal
Government, but the States in their trial
of state crimes under state laws in state
courts. * * * [o] The Constitution
deliberately reposed in the States very
broad power to create and to try crimes
according to their own rules and

policies. * * * Before being deprived of this power, the least that they can ask is that we should be able to point to a federal constitutional provision that either by express language or by necessary implication grants us the power to fashion this novel rule of evidence to govern their criminal trials. * * * Neither *Nardone v. United States*, 308 U.S. 338 [1939], nor *Wong Sun v. United States*, * * * both federal cases and both decided "in other contexts," supports what the Court demands of the States today.

* * * I find no such authority in the Due Process Clause. It undoubtedly provides that a person must be tried in accordance with the "Law of the Land." Consequently, it violates due process to try a person in a way prohibited by the Fourth, Fifth, or Sixth Amendments of our written Constitution. But I have never been able to subscribe to the dogma that the Due Process Clause empowers this Court to declare any law, including a rule of evidence, unconstitutional which it believes is contrary to tradition, decency, fundamental justice, or any of the other wide-meaning words used by judges to claim power under the Due Process Clause. * * * **[p]** I have an abiding idea that if the Framers had wanted to let judges write the Constitution on any such day-to-day beliefs of theirs, they would have said so instead of so carefully defining their grants and prohibitions in a written constitution. With no more authority than the Due Process Clause I am wholly unwilling to tell the state or federal courts that the United States Constitution forbids them to allow courtroom identification without the prosecution's first proving that the identification does not rest in whole or in part on an illegal lineup. Should I do so, I would feel that we are

deciding what the Constitution is, not from what it says, but from what we think it would have been wise for the Framers to put in it. That to me would be "judicial activism" at its worst. I would leave the States and Federal Government free to decide their own rules of evidence. That, I believe, is their constitutional prerogative.

I would affirm Wade's conviction.

MR. JUSTICE WHITE, whom MR. JUSTICE HARLAN and MR. JUSTICE STEWART join, dissenting in part and concurring in part.

* * *

The premise for the Court's rule is not the general unreliability of eyewitness identifications nor the difficulties inherent in observation, recall, and recognition. The Court assumes a narrower evil as the basis for its rule—improper police suggestion which contributes to erroneous identifications. The Court apparently believes that improper police procedures are so widespread that a broad prophylactic rule must be laid down, requiring the presence of counsel at all pretrial identifications, in order to detect recurring instances of police misconduct. I do not share this pervasive distrust of all official investigations. None of the materials the Court relies upon supports it. Certainly, I would bow to solid fact, but the Court quite obviously does not have before it any reliable, comprehensive survey of current police practices on which to base its new rule. Until it does, the Court should avoid excluding relevant evidence from state criminal trials.

* * *

I share the Court's view that the

criminal trial, at the very least, should aim at truthful factfinding, including accurate eyewitness identifications. I doubt, however, on the basis of our present information, that the tragic mistakes which have occurred in criminal trials are as much the product of improper police conduct as they are the consequence of the difficulties inherent in eyewitness testimony and in resolving evidentiary conflicts by court or jury. I doubt that the Court's new rule will obviate these difficulties, or that the situation will be measurably improved by inserting defense counsel into the investigative processes of police departments everywhere.

But, it may be asked, what possible state interest militates against requiring the presence of defense counsel at lineups? After all, the argument goes, he *may* do some good, he *may* upgrade the quality of identification evidence in state courts and he can scarcely do any harm. Even if true, this is a feeble foundation for fastening an ironclad constitutional rule upon state criminal procedures. Absent some reliably established constitutional violation, the processes by which the States enforce their criminal laws are their own prerogative. * * *

Beyond this, however, requiring counsel at pretrial identifications as an invariable rule trenches on other valid state interests. One of them is its concern with the prompt and efficient enforcement of its criminal laws. Identifications frequently take place after arrest but before an indictment is returned or an information is filed. The police may have arrested a suspect on probable cause but may still have the wrong man. Both the suspect and the State have every interest in a prompt identification at that stage, the suspect

in order to secure his immediate release and the State because prompt and early identification enhances *accurate* identification and because it must know whether it is on the right investigative track. Unavoidably, however, the absolute rule requiring the presence of counsel will cause significant delay and it may very well result in no pretrial identification at all. Counsel must be appointed and a time arranged convenient for him and the witnesses. Meanwhile, it may be necessary to file charges against the suspect who may then be released on bail, in the federal system very often on his own recognizance, with neither the State nor the defendant having the benefit of a properly conducted identification procedure.

Nor do I think the witnesses themselves can be ignored. They will now be required to be present at the convenience of counsel rather than their own. Many may be much less willing to participate if the identification stage is transformed into an adversary proceeding not under the control of a judge. Others may fear for their own safety if their identity is known at an early date, especially when there is no way of knowing until the lineup occurs whether or not the police really have the right man.

* * *

[JUSTICE FORTAS, joined by CHIEF JUSTICE WARREN and JUSTICE DOUGLAS, concurred with the critical stage analysis of the court but argued that the defendant must be given the opportunity to waive counsel. He agreed that the showing of a defendant at a lineup does not violate the Fifth Amendment right against self-incrimination but that requiring Wade to speak and to wear strips of tape did   constitute a Fifth Amendment violation.]

* * * * * * * * * *

COMMENTS

[a] Unlike confessions and search and seizure cases, this was a novel issue; *Wade* was the first case regarding the constitutionality of lineup procedures decided by the Supreme Court. Note the reference to the post-indictment stage of the criminal proceeding; this becomes critically important in later cases.

[b] Note the lapse of over seven months between the time of offense and the lineup. While far from an ideal condition for the accuracy of witness perception, such time lapses are inevitable in the criminal investigation process

[c] Although the Supreme Court reversed the court of appeals, it did not agree with the trial court that Wade had no right to counsel at the lineup. The court of appeals took an absolute approach, but the Supreme Court's ruling on the remedy is more complex (see Part V).

[d] JUSTICE BRENNAN offers an historically sound reason for not limiting the constitutional role of the defense attorney strictly and narrowly to the trial itself. There is no general disagreement regarding this point among the justices of the Supreme Court. On the other hand, there is disagreement as to precisely when the right to counsel should attach.

[e] This issue is not decided on an ad hoc basis; JUSTICE BRENNAN turns to the constitutional doctrine of the "critical stage" to fit the lineup procedure into it. As with most legal doctrines developed by courts, it began with a phrase in a seminal case (in this case *Powell v. Alabama*).

[f] The science, technology, and techniques of taking, preserving, and analyzing physical evidence are well established and readily available in textbooks; defense attorneys know about these techniques and can ascertain via cross-examination if they were followed. However, the fluid and possibly suggestive aspects of an identification procedure cannot be adequately reproduced by cross-examination, except for the grossest kinds of unfair procedures. This is a central point for the majority. A blanket Sixth Amendment rule requiring attorneys at every aspect of criminal investigation would require the attachment of a defense lawyer to every criminal investigator! A majority of justices would not have imposed such an extreme, costly, and unnecessary requirement. Thus, to win the main point, JUSTICE BRENNAN had to "protect his flanks" here.

[g] Note that JUSTICE BRENNAN here slips the discussion away from the larger problem of eyewitness misidentification to the narrower problem of police officers at a lineup doing something, intentionally or inadvertently, that *suggests* that a suspect is the "right man." He does this to bring the case within the ambit of state action.

[h] Bringing the lineup within the critical-stage analysis of the right to counsel is far from automatic. To make the point as strongly as possible, JUSTICE BRENNAN must convince other justices that the suggestibility problem is so acute that justice is not done if a lawyer is not present at the lineup. He does this by presenting an elaborate analysis of the real, proven dangers of misidentification leading to the conviction of the innocent.

[i] The ability to precisely reconstruct the evidence gathering process is what sets lineups apart from scientific evidence gathering.

[j] The Court here considers the remedy. A blanket exclusionary rule, requested by the defense, would in effect bar the prosecution witnesses from identifying the defendant at the trial. Without such identification, the prosecution would fail. Such a rule is inherently more drastic than one that excludes a confession or illegally obtained evidence, for in such cases, there may be other evidence on which to base a conviction.

[k] On the other hand, if courtroom identification is never barred, the state can disregard the *Wade* right-to-counsel-at lineup rule with impunity.

[l] It is interesting that the test is borrowed from a search and seizure case. What is the "primary illegality" in the lineup situation? What is the "exploitation of that illegality"?

[m] The factors used to determine whether the recollection of identity originated from the crime or the lineup are sufficiently subtle to give the trial court substantial discretion in applying the *Wade* rule to uncounseled lineups.

[n] JUSTICE CLARK's laconic concurrence belies its pivotal importance in supplying the fifth vote for the majority. Although usually conservative on law enforcement issues, his experience as an attorney at times made him sympathetic to the concerns of defendants. His acquiescence in the *Miranda* precedent (by one who dissented in that case) is indicative of a school of thought that once an issue is fully examined and decided by the Court, the losing justices should acquiesce in the case as precedent, rather than fighting a continuous rear guard action against the rule.

[o] This is an example of JUSTICE BLACK's "Bill of Rights fundamentalism." See *Adamson v. California* [this volume].

[p] If *you* were a Supreme Court justice and had the opportunity to establish a rule that you felt, to the core of your beliefs, was wise and just, would you attempt to "stretch" the traditional view of a constitutional rule to do so? Or would you opt for the status quo, even if it would leave a "bad" rule in place? Does it matter that many phrases in the text of the United States Constitution are vague and open-ended?

KIRBY v. ILLINOIS

406 U.S. 682, 92 S.Ct. 1877, 32 L.Ed.2d 411 (1972)

MR. JUSTICE STEWART announced the judgment of the Court and an opinion in which THE CHIEF JUSTICE, MR. JUSTICE BLACKMUN, and MR. JUSTICE REHNQUIST join.

In *United States v. Wade*, [this volume] and *Gilbert v. California*, 388 U.S. 263, this Court held "that a post-indictment pretrial lineup at which the accused is exhibited to identifying witnesses is a critical stage of the criminal prosecution; that police conduct of such a lineup without notice to and in the absence of his counsel denies the accused his Sixth [and Fourteenth] Amendment right to counsel and calls in question the admissibility at trial of the in-court identifications of the accused by witnesses who attended the lineup." * * * Those cases further held that no "in-court identifications" are admissible in evidence if their "source" is a lineup conducted in violation of this constitutional standard. "Only a *per se* exclusionary rule as to such testimony can be an effective sanction," the Court said, "to assure that law enforcement authorities will respect the accused's constitutional right to the presence of his counsel at the critical lineup." * * * In the present case we are asked to extend the *Wade-Gilbert per se* exclusionary rule to identification testimony based upon a police station showup that took place *before* the defendant had been indicted or otherwise formally charged with any criminal offense. [a]

[A man named Willie Shard was robbed by two men who took his wallet.

The next day Kirby was stopped by police and produced checks and identification bearing the name of Willie Shard. Kirby claimed he won the checks in a crap game. Shard was called to the police station and immediately upon entering the room where Kirby and his accomplice sat,] positively identified them as the men who had robbed him two days earlier. No lawyer was present in the room, and neither [Kirby nor his accomplice] asked for legal assistance, or been advised of any right to the presence of counsel.

More than six weeks later, [Kirby and his accomplice] were indicted for the robbery of Willie Shard. * * * A pretrial motion to suppress Shard's identification testimony was denied, and at the trial Shard testified as a witness for the prosecution. In his testimony he described his identification of the two men at the police station * * * and identified them again in the courtroom as the men who had robbed him. * * * [The defendants were found guilty; the appellate courts affirmed, holding the identification admissible because the] the *Wade-Gilbert* per se exclusionary rule is not applicable to pre-indictment confrontations.

* * *

I

We note at the outset that the constitutional privilege against compulsory self-incrimination is in no way implicated here. * * *

* * *

It follows that the doctrine of *Miranda v. Arizona*, [this volume], has no applicability whatever to the issue before us; for the *Miranda* decision was based exclusively upon the Fifth and Fourteenth Amendment privilege against compulsory self-incrimination, upon the theory that custodial *interrogation* is inherently coercive. **[b]**

The *Wade-Gilbert* exclusionary rule, by contrast, stems from a quite different constitutional guarantee—the guarantee of the right to counsel contained in the Sixth and Fourteenth Amendments. Unless all semblance of principled constitutional adjudication is to be abandoned, therefore, it is to the decisions construing that guarantee that we must look in determining the present controversy.

In a line of constitutional cases in this Court stemming back to the Court's landmark opinion in *Powell v. Alabama*, [this volume], it has been firmly established that a person's Sixth and Fourteenth Amendment right to counsel attaches only at or after the time that adversary judicial proceedings have been initiated against him. * * *

This is not to say that a defendant in a criminal case has a constitutional right to counsel only at the trial itself. The *Powell* case makes clear that the right attaches at the time of arraignment, and the Court has recently held that it exists also at the time of a preliminary hearing. *Coleman v. Alabama*, [this volume]. But the point is that, while members of the Court have differed as to existence of the right to counsel in the contexts of some of the above cases, *all* of those cases have involved points of time at or after the initiation of adversary judicial criminal proceedings—whether by way of formal charge, preliminary hearing, indictment, information, or arraignment.

The only seeming deviation from this long line of constitutional decisions was *Escobedo v. Illinois*, 378 U.S. 478. But *Escobedo* is not apposite here for two distinct reasons. First, the Court in retrospect perceived that the "prime purpose" of *Escobedo* was not to vindicate the constitutional right to counsel as such, but, like *Miranda* [*v. Arizona* (this volume)], "to guarantee full effectuation of the privilege against self-incrimination. * * *" * * * Secondly, and perhaps even more important for purely practical purposes, the Court has limited the holding of *Escobedo* to its own facts, * * * and those facts are not remotely akin to the facts of the case before us.

The initiation of judicial criminal proceedings is far from a mere formalism. It is the starting point of our whole system of adversary criminal justice. For it is only then that the government has committed itself to prosecute, and only then that the adverse positions of government and defendant have solidified. It is then that a defendant finds himself faced with the prosecutorial forces of organized society, and immersed in the intricacies of substantive and procedural criminal law. It is this point, therefore, that marks the commencement of the "criminal prosecutions" to which alone the explicit guarantees of the Sixth Amendment are applicable. * * * **[c]**

In this case we are asked to import into a routine police investigation an absolute constitutional guarantee historically and rationally applicable only after the onset of formal prosecutorial proceedings. We decline to do so. Less than a year after *Wade* and *Gilbert* were decided, the Court explained the rule of those decisions as follows: "The rationale of those cases was that an accused is entitled to counsel at any 'critical stage of the *prosecution*,' and that a post-indictment lineup is such a 'critical stage.'" (Emphasis supplied.) * * * We decline to depart from that rationale today by imposing a *per se* exclusionary rule upon testimony concerning an identification that took place long before the commencement of any prosecution whatever.

II

What has been said is not to suggest that there may not be occasions during the course of a criminal investigation when the police do abuse identification procedures. Such abuses are not beyond the reach of the Constitution. As the Court pointed out in *Wade* itself, it is always necessary to "scrutinize *any* pretrial confrontation. * * *" * * * The Due Process Clause of the Fifth and Fourteenth Amendments forbids a lineup that is unnecessarily suggestive and conducive to irreparable mistaken identification. *Stovall v. Denno*, 388 U.S. 293 [1967]; *Foster v. California*, 394 U.S. 440 [1969]. When a person has not been formally charged with a criminal offense, *Stovall* strikes the appropriate constitutional balance between the right of a suspect to be protected from prejudicial procedures and the interest of society in the prompt and purposeful investigation of an unsolved crime.

The judgment is affirmed.

[CHIEF JUSTICE BURGER and JUSTICE POWELL, concurred.]

MR. JUSTICE BRENNAN, with whom MR. JUSTICE DOUGLAS and MR. JUSTICE MARSHALL join, dissenting.

* * * [T]he question in this case is whether, under *Gilbert v. California*, [above], it was constitutional error to admit Shard's testimony that he identified petitioner at the pretrial stationhouse showup when that showup was conducted by the police without advising petitioner that he might have counsel present. *Gilbert* held, in the context of a post-indictment lineup, that "[o]nly a *per se* exclusionary rule as to such testimony can be an effective sanction to assure that law enforcement authorities will respect the accused's constitutional right to the presence of his counsel at the critical lineup." * * * I would apply *Gilbert* and the principles of its companion case, *United States v. Wade*, [above], and reverse.

[JUSTICE BRENNAN analyzed the *Wade* case and concluded that the key to its holding is found in the following passage:] **[d]**

"In sum, the principle of *Powell v. Alabama* and succeeding cases requires that we scrutinize *any* pretrial confrontation of the accused to determine whether the presence of his counsel is necessary to preserve the defendant's basic right to a fair trial as affected by his right meaningfully to cross-examine the witnesses against him and to have effective assistance of counsel at the trial itself. It calls upon us to analyze whether potential substantial prejudice to defendant's rights inheres in the particular confrontation and the ability of counsel to help avoid that prejudice." * * * (emphasis in original).

* * *

The Court then applied that conclusion to the specific facts of the case. "Since it appears that there is grave potential for prejudice, intentional or not, in the pretrial lineup, which may not be capable of reconstruction at trial, and since presence of counsel itself can often avert prejudice and assure a meaningful confrontation at trial, there can be little doubt that for Wade the post-indictment lineup was a critical stage of the prosecution at which he was 'as much entitled to such aid [of counsel] * * * as at the trial itself.'" * * *

While it should go without saying, it appears necessary, in view of the plurality opinion today, to re-emphasize that *Wade* did not require the presence of counsel at pretrial confrontations for identification purposes simply on the basis of an abstract consideration of the words "criminal prosecutions" in the Sixth Amendment. Counsel is required at those confrontations because "the dangers inherent in eyewitness identification and the suggestibility inherent in the context of the pretrial identification," * * * mean that protection must be afforded to the "most basic right [of] a criminal defendant—his right to a fair trial at which the witnesses against him might be meaningfully cross-examined." * * * Indeed, the Court expressly stated that "[l]egislative or other regulations, such as those of local police departments, which eliminate the risks of abuse and unintentional suggestion at lineup proceedings and the impediments to meaningful confrontation at trial may also remove the basis for regarding the stage as 'critical.'" * * * Hence, "the

initiation of adversary judicial criminal proceedings," * * * is completely irrelevant to whether counsel is necessary at a pretrial confrontation for identification in order to safeguard the accused's constitutional rights to confrontation and the effective assistance of counsel at his trial.

> * * *

[In the remainder of his opinion, JUSTICE BRENNAN took the majority to task for erroneously relying on a post-*Wade* case to reinterpret its meaning.]

> * * *

Wade and *Gilbert*, of course, happened to involve post-indictment confrontations. Yet even a cursory perusal of the opinions in those cases reveals that nothing at all turned upon that particular circumstance. In short, it is fair to conclude that rather than "declin[ing] to depart from [the] rationale" of *Wade* and *Gilbert*, * * * the plurality today, albeit purporting to be engaged in "principled constitutional adjudication," * * * refuses even to recognize that "rationale." For my part, I do not agree that we "extend" *Wade* and *Gilbert*, * * * by holding that the principles of those cases apply to confrontations for identification conducted after arrest. Because Shard testified at trial about his identification of petitioner at the police station showup, the exclusionary rule of *Gilbert*, * * * requires reversal. **[e]**

[JUSTICE WHITE dissented.]

* * * * * * * * * * *

COMMENTS

[a] When you read *Wade* [this volume], did the fact that the lineup occurred after the indictment seem to be an important element of the case?

[b] The *Miranda* case had the potential to turn the investigatory process into a more formal, law-directed and quasi-judicial mechanism. The plurality opinion resists this.

[c] Aside from the application of the *Wade* rule, how does a lineup differ before or after an indictment?

[d] In a footnote, JUSTICE BRENNAN challenged the majority's assertion that *Miranda* is not applicable to this case, because, in his view, "*Wade* specifically relied upon *Miranda* in establishing the constitutional principle that controls the applicability of the Sixth Amendment guarantee of the right to counsel at pretrial confrontations."

[e] Both the plurality opinion and the dissenting opinion rest on principles; but the principles differ. Does this make the other opinion unprincipled? Is there a "principled" way to choose between the two positions?

UNITED STATES v. ASH

413 U.S. 300, 93 S. Ct. 2568, 37 L. Ed.2d. 619 (1973)

MR. JUSTICE BLACKMUN delivered the opinion of the Court.

In this case the Court is called upon to decide whether the Sixth Amendment grants an accused the right to have counsel present whenever the Government conducts a post-indictment photographic display, [a] containing a picture of the accused, for the purpose of allowing a witness to attempt an identification of the offender. The United States Court of Appeals for the District of Columbia Circuit, sitting en banc, held, by a [b] 5-to-4 vote, that the accused possesses this right to counsel. * * * The court's holding is inconsistent with decisions of the courts of appeals of nine other circuits. We granted certiorari to resolve the conflict and to decide this important constitutional question. * * * We reverse and remand.

I

[A bank was robbed in August 1965 by two men wearing stocking masks.] * * * The robbery lasted three or four minutes.

A Government informer, Clarence McFarland, told authorities that he had discussed the robbery with Charles J. Ash, Jr., the respondent here. Acting on this information, an FBI agent, in February 1966, showed five black-and-white mug shots of Negro males of generally the same age, height, and weight, one of which was of Ash, to four witnesses. All four made uncertain identifications of Ash's picture. At this time Ash was not in custody and had not been charged. On April 1, 1966 [Ash and co-defendant John L. Bailey were indicted for the bank robbery.] * * *

* * * In preparing for trial, [in May 1968], the prosecutor decided to use a photographic display to determine whether the witnesses he planned to call would be able to make in-court identifications. Shortly before the trial, an FBI agent and the prosecutor showed five color photographs to the four witnesses who previously had tentatively identified the black-and-white photograph of Ash. [c] Three of the witnesses selected the picture of Ash, but one was unable to make any selection. None of the witnesses selected the picture of Bailey which was in the group. This post-indictment identification provides the basis for respondent Ash's claim that he was denied the right to counsel at a "critical stage" of the prosecution.

* * * [At a pretrial hearing, the judge did not rule clearly that the photographic showup was suggestive; he did rule that the Government demonstrated by "clear and convincing evidence" that the in-court identifications were based on observations made during the crime.]

At trial, the three witnesses who had been inside the bank identified Ash as the gunman, but they were unwilling to state that they were certain of their identifications. None of these made an in-court identification of Bailey. [The fourth witness, who saw the robbers outside the bank without their masks, identified Ash and Bailey in court. His identification was impeached by Bailey's counsel showing that the witness had not identified Bailey in the photo identification sessions.] * * * After a conference at the bench, the trial judge ruled that all five color photographs would be admitted into evidence. The Court of Appeals held that this constituted the introduction of a post-indictment identification at the prosecutor's request and over the objection of defense counsel.

[McFarland, the informer (with an extensive criminal record), testified that he had discussed the robbery with Ash before and after the crime and with Bailey afterwards.] **[d]**

The jury convicted Ash [and acquitted Bailey] * * *

The * * * Court of Appeals held that Ash's right to counsel, guaranteed by the Sixth Amendment, was violated when his attorney was not given the opportunity to be present at the photographic displays conducted in May 1968 before the trial. The majority relied on this Court's lineup cases, [*United States v. Wade* [this volume], *Gilbert v. California*, 388 U.S. 263 (1967), and *Stovall v. Denno*, 388 U.S. 293 (1967)].

The majority did not reach the issue of suggestiveness. * * * [It] refrained from deciding whether the in-court identifications could have independent bases, * * * but expressed doubt that the identifications at the trial had independent origins.

* * *

II

[The Supreme Court then reviewed the history of the right to counsel.]

This historical background suggests that the core purpose of the counsel guarantee was to assure "Assistance" at trial, when the accused was confronted with both the intricacies of the law and the advocacy of the public prosecutor.

Later developments have led this Court to recognize that "Assistance" would be less than meaningful if it were limited to the formal trial itself.

This extension of the right to counsel to events before trial has resulted from changing patterns of criminal procedure and investigation that have tended to generate pretrial events that might appropriately be considered to be parts of the trial itself. At these newly emerging and significant events, the accused was confronted, just as at trial, by the procedural system, or by his expert adversary, or by both. * * *

The Court consistently has applied a historical interpretation of the guarantee, and has expanded the constitutional right to counsel only when new contexts appear presenting the same dangers that gave birth initially to the right itself. **[e]**
* * *

The function of counsel in rendering "Assistance" continued at the lineup under consideration in *Wade* and its companion cases. Although the accused was not confronted there with legal questions, the lineup offered opportunities for prosecuting authorities to take advantage of the accused. Counsel was seen by the Court as being more sensitive to, and aware of, suggestive influences than the accused himself, and as better able to reconstruct the events at trial. Counsel present at lineup would be able to remove disabilities of the accused in precisely the same fashion that counsel compensated for the disabilities of the layman at trial. Thus, the Court mentioned that the accused's memory might be dimmed by "emotional tension," that the accused's credibility at trial would be diminished by his status as defendant, and that the accused might be unable to present his version effectively without giving up his privilege against compulsory self-incrimination. * * * It was in order to compensate for these deficiencies that the Court found the need for the assistance of counsel.

* * *

III

[However, *Wade* did not extend the right to counsel to other investigatory and identification procedures, such as fingerprinting, because these were not similar to trial-like confrontations and because any errors made during such procedures could be cured by cross-examination at the trial. The *Wade* case, however, cannot automatically be applied to post-indictment photographic displays.]
* * *

The structure of *Wade*, viewed in light of the careful limitation of the Court's language to "confrontations," makes it clear that lack of scientific precision and inability to reconstruct an event are not the tests for requiring counsel in the first instance. [f] These are, instead, the tests to determine whether confrontation with counsel at trial can serve as a substitute for counsel at the pretrial confrontation. If accurate reconstruction is possible, the risks inherent in any confrontation still remain, but the opportunity to cure defects at trial causes the confrontation to cease to be "critical." * * *
* * *

IV

A substantial departure from the historical test would be necessary if the Sixth Amendment were interpreted to give Ash a right to counsel at the photographic identification in this case.

Since the accused himself is not present at the time of the photographic display, and asserts no right to be present, * * * no possibility arises that the accused might be misled by his lack of familiarity with the law or overpowered by his professional adversary. Similarly, the counsel guarantee would not be used to produce equality in a trial-like adversary confrontation. Rather, the guarantee was used by the Court of Appeals to produce confrontation at an event that previously was not analogous to an adversary trial.

Even if we were willing to view the counsel guarantee in broad terms as a generalized protection of the adversary process, we would be unwilling to go so far as to extend the right to a portion of the prosecutor's trial-preparation interviews with witnesses. Although photography is relatively new, the interviewing of witnesses before trial is a procedure that predates the Sixth Amendment. * * * The traditional counterbalance in the American adversary system for these [prosecutorial] interviews arises from the equal ability of defense counsel to seek and interview witnesses himself. [g]

That adversary mechanism remains as effective for a photographic display as for other parts of pretrial interviews. No greater limitations are placed on defense counsel in constructing displays, seeking witnesses, and conducting photographic identifications than those applicable to the prosecution. Selection of the picture of a person other than the accused, or the inability of a witness to make any selection, will be useful to the defense in precisely the same manner that the selection of a picture of the defendant would be useful to the prosecution. In this very case, for example, the initial tender of the photographic display was by Bailey's counsel, who sought to demonstrate that the witness had failed to make a photographic identification. Although we do not suggest that equality of access to photographs removes all potential for abuse, it does remove any inequality in the adversary process itself and thereby fully satisfies the historical spirit of the Sixth Amendment's counsel guarantee.

[JUSTICE BLACKMUN noted that the potential for abuse arises at every step of the pretrial investigation and prosecution process, not just at the photographic array.] * * *

We are not persuaded that the risks inherent in the use of photographic displays are so pernicious that an extraordinary system of safeguards is required.

We hold, then, that the Sixth Amendment does not grant the right to counsel at photographic displays conducted by the Government for the purpose of allowing a witness to attempt an identification of the offender. [The Court declined to address the due process question without that issue having first been addressed by the lower courts.]

[JUSTICE STEWART concurred in the judgment.]

MR. JUSTICE BRENNAN, with whom MR. JUSTICE DOUGLAS and MR. JUSTICE MARSHALL join, dissenting.

* * *

III

* * *

* * * [A]s in the lineup situation, the possibilities for impermissible suggestion in the context of a photo-graphic display are manifold. * * * Such suggestion, intentional or unintentional, may derive from three possible sources. [h]   First, the photographs themselves might tend to suggest which of the pictures is that of the suspect. For example, differences in age, pose, or other physical characteristics of the persons represented, and variations in the mounting, background, lighting, or markings of the photographs all might have the effect of singling out the accused.

Second, impermissible suggestion may inhere in the manner in which the photographs are displayed to the witness. The danger of misidentification is, of course, "increased if the police display to the witness . . . the pictures of several persons among which the photograph of a single such individual recurs or is in some way emphasized." * * *   And, if the photographs are arranged in an asymmetrical pattern, or if they are displayed in a time sequence that tends to emphasize a particular photograph, "any identification of the photograph which stands out from the rest is no more reliable than an identification of a single photograph, exhibited alone." * * *

Third, gestures or comments of the prosecutor at the time of the display may lead an otherwise uncertain witness to select the "correct" photograph. * * * More subtly, the prosecutor's inflection, facial expressions, physical motions, and myriad other almost imperceptible means of communication might tend, intentionally or unintentionally, to compromise the witness' objectivity. Thus, as is the case with lineups, "[i]mproper photographic identification procedures, . . . by exerting a suggestive influence upon the witnesses, can often lead to an erroneous identification. . . ."

* * * And "[r]egardless of how the initial misidentification comes about, the witness thereafter is apt to retain in his memory the image of the photograph rather than of the person actually seen. . . ." * * * As a result, "'the issue of identity may (in the absence of other relevant evidence) for all practical purposes be determined there and then, before the trial.'" * * *

[JUSTICE BRENNAN then asserted that it is usually not possible for the defense to reconstruct the way in which the photographic identification session was carried out, which is not captured by the mere physical retention of the identification photographs themselves. Also, the fact that the defendant was not present means that a possible witness to irregularities is missing.]

Thus, the difficulties of reconstructing at trial an uncounseled photographic display are at least equal to, and possibly greater than, those involved in reconstructing an uncounseled lineup. * * * As a result, both photographic and corporeal identifications create grave dangers that an innocent defendant might be convicted simply because of his inability to expose a tainted identification. This being so, considerations of logic, consistency, and, indeed, fairness compel the conclusion that a pretrial photographic identification, like a pretrial corporeal identification, is a "critical stage of the prosecution at which [the accused is] 'as much entitled to such aid [of counsel] . . . as at the trial itself.'" * * * [i]

* * *

* * * * * * * * * * *

COMMENTS

[a] The specific reference to the post-indictment stage indicates that the rule of *Kirby v. Illinois* [this volume] does not apply, and the issue is the narrow one of whether the *Wade* [this volume] rule regarding corporeal lineups also applies to photographic identification sessions. The Court generally prefers to rule on narrow and specific issues for fear that an overly broad decision will create unanticipated problems.

[b] Most court of appeals decisions are rendered by three judge panels; the entire bench (*i.e.*, the court sitting en banc) hears cases of unusual significance or to settle conflicts within a Circuit.

[c] Although the showing of photographs to the witnesses on two occasions in this case is not apparently marked by impropriety, the opinion suggests that the second showing tended to "firm up" the recollection process. Even if this was not deliberately intended by the FBI agent, it is a subtle example of the possible suggestiveness of the identification process.

[d] If you were a juror, would you vote for conviction if McFarland's identification were eliminated? That is, would you convict on the basis of these eyewitness identifications alone?

[e] The majority's reasoning is subtle; it must acknowledge that the Sixth Amendment right to counsel is a "dynamic" (*i.e.*, expandable) right that applies to procedures other than the trial itself; yet it must find a basis for limiting the expansion in this case. Carefully note the Court's basis for limiting the right to counsel and compare it to the dissenters' view of this reasoning.

[f] Was this your understanding of *Wade* when you read the case? This point is not so much a matter of historic accuracy of the meaning of *Wade* as it is an example of *stare decisis* at work; more recent cases refine the meaning of prior cases.

[g] The concreteness of this point shores up the rather abstract justification for not including photographic arrays within the *Wade-Gilbert* rule.

[h] The majority and dissenting justices agree that "impermissible suggestion" can occur at a photographic identification session. Yet, they put very different emphases on this possibility. Review their use of language to detect their differences.

[i] JUSTICE BRENNAN turns the majority point about the lack of the defendant at this process around: in his view it undermines the ability of the defense to detect suggestibility, thus increasing the potential for convicting the innocent. If so, this is a potent non-formal reason for extending the right to counsel to the photographic identification procedure.

MANSON v. BRATHWAITE

432 U.S. 98, 97 S.Ct. 2243, 53 L.Ed.2d 140 (1977)

MR. JUSTICE BLACKMUN delivered the opinion of the Court.

This case presents the issue as to whether the Due Process Clause of the Fourteenth Amendment compels the exclusion, in a state criminal trial, apart from any consideration of reliability, of pretrial identification evidence obtained by a police procedure that was both suggestive and unnecessary. This Court's decision in *Stovall v. Denno*, 388 U.S. 293 (1967), and *Neil v. Biggers*, 409 U.S. 188 (1972), are particularly implicated.

I

[Glover, a narcotics undercover police officer, and Brown, an informant, went to an apartment building in Hartford Connecticut, at 7:45 P.M., on May 5, while there was still daylight, to make a controlled narcotics buy. They thought that one Cicero, a known dealer, was selling drugs from a specific apartment. Glover and Brown were observed by backup Officers D'Onofrio and Gaffey. Glover and Brown knocked on the third floor door in an area illuminated by natural light from a window in the hallway. A man opened the door; Brown asked for "two things" of narcotics; Glover handed over a ten-dollar bill and observed the man in the apartment; the door closed; a moment later, the man opened the door and handed Glover two glassine bags of heroin; Glover was within two feet of the seller and observed his face.] [a]

[At headquarters, Glover, who is an African-American, described the seller to D'Onofrio as "a colored man, approximately five feet eleven inches tall, dark complexion, black hair, short Afro style, and having high cheekbones, and of heavy build. He was wearing at the time blue pants and a plaid shirt." D'Onofrio thought that Brathwaite might be the seller, and left a photograph of him at Glover's office. Two days later Glover viewed the photograph for the first time and identified Brathwaite as the seller.]

[At the trial, eight months after the sale, the identification photograph was received in evidence without defense objection. Glover said he had no doubt that the person in the photograph was the seller and he made an in-court identification.] No explanation was offered by the prosecution for the failure to utilize a photographic array or to conduct a lineup. [Brathwaite offered an alibi in defense.]

[The Connecticut Supreme Court upheld the conviction, saying that no "substantial injustice resulted from the admission of this evidence." The federal Court of Appeals ruled, on a habeas corpus petition, that the photograph should have been excluded, regardless of reliability, because the examination of the single photograph was unnecessary, suggestive, and possibly unreliable.]

II

Stovall v. Denno * * * concerned a petitioner who had been convicted * * * of murder. He was arrested the day following the crime and was taken by the police to a hospital where the victim's wife, also wounded in the assault, was a patient. After observing Stovall and hearing him speak, she identified him as the murderer. She later made an in-court identification. * * * On the identification issue, [this] Court reviewed the practice of showing a suspect singly for purposes of identification, and the claim that this was so unnecessarily suggestive and conducive to irreparable mistaken identification that it constituted a denial of due process of law. The Court noted that the practice "has been widely condemned," * * * but it concluded that "a claimed violation of due process of law in the conduct of a confrontation depends on the totality of the circumstances surrounding it." In that case, showing Stovall to the victim's spouse "was imperative." * * * [T]he spouse was the only person who could possibly exonerate the accused; * * * the hospital was not far from the courthouse and jail; * * * no one knew how long she might live; * * * she was not able to visit the jail; and * * * taking Stovall to the hospital room was the only feasible procedure, and, under the circumstances, "'the usual police station line-up * * * was out of the question.'" * * *

Neil v. Biggers, [concerned a rape conviction based] on evidence consisting in part of the victim's visual and voice identification of Biggers at a station house showup seven months after the crime. The victim had been in her assailant's presence for some time and had directly observed him indoors and under a full moon outdoors. She testified that she had "no doubt" that Biggers was her assailant. She previously had given the police a description of the assailant. She had made no identification of others presented at previous showups, lineups, or through

photographs. On federal habeas, the [lower federal courts] held that the confrontation was so suggestive as to violate due process. * * * This Court reversed on that issue, and held that the evidence properly had been allowed to go to the jury. * * * [G]eneral guidelines emerged from these cases "as to the relationship between suggestiveness and misidentification." The "admission of evidence of a showup without more does not violate due process." * * * The Court expressed concern about the lapse of seven months between the crime and the confrontation and observed that this "would be a seriously negative factor in most cases." * * * The "central question," however, was "whether under the 'totality of the circumstances' the identification was reliable even though the confrontation procedure was suggestive." * * * Applying that test, the Court found "no substantial likelihood of misidentification." * * *

III

[The District Court used a two-stage analysis; first, whether the police used an impermissibly suggestive procedure in obtaining the out-of-court identification; second, if they did, whether, under all the circumstances, that suggestive procedure gave rise to a substantial likelihood of irreparable misidentification. The District Court, reviewing the facts, concluded that there was no substantial likelihood of irreparable misidentification. The Court of Appeals confirmed that the exhibition of the single photograph to Glover was "impermissibly suggestive" and felt that, in addition, "it was unnecessarily so." There was no emergency and little urgency. It ruled that in such cases, the identification evidence must be excluded from evidence. "No rules less stringent than these can force police administrators and prosecutors to adopt procedures that will give fair assurance against the awful risks of misidentification." The Circuit Court also cast doubt on the accuracy of Brathwaite's identification by Glover.] [b]

IV

* * *

Since the decision in *Biggers*, the Courts of Appeals appear to have developed at least two approaches to such evidence. * * * The first, or *per se* approach, employed by the Second Circuit in the present case, focuses on the procedures employed and requires exclusion of the out-of-court identification evidence, without regard to reliability, whenever it has been obtained through unnecessarily suggested confrontation procedures. The justifications advanced are the elimination of evidence of uncertain reliability, deterrence of the police and prosecutors, and the stated "fair assurance against the awful risks of misidentification." * * *

The second, or more lenient, approach is one that continues to rely on the totality of the circumstances. It permits the admission of the confrontation evidence if, despite the suggestive aspect, the out-of-court identification possesses certain features of reliability. Its adherents feel that the *per se* approach is not mandated by the Due Process Clause of the Fourteenth Amendment. This second approach, in contrast to the other, is ad hoc and serves to limit the societal costs imposed by a sanction that excludes relevant evidence from consideration and evalua-

tion by the trier of fact. * * * [c]
* * *

There are, of course, several interests to be considered and taken into account. The driving force behind *United States v. Wade*, [this volume], *Gilbert v. California*, 388 U.S. 263, and *Stovall* * * * was the Court's concern with the problems of eyewitness identification. Usually the witness must testify about an encounter with a total stranger under circumstances of emergency or emotional stress. The witness' recollection of the stranger can be distorted easily by the circumstances or by later actions of the police. Thus, *Wade* and its companion cases reflect the concern that the jury not hear eyewitness testimony unless that evidence has aspects of reliability. It must be observed that both approaches before us are responsive to this concern. The *per se* rule, however, goes too far since its application automatically and peremptorily, and without consideration of alleviating factors, keeps evidence from the jury that is reliable and relevant.

The second factor is deterrence. Although the *per se* approach has the more significant deterrent effect, the totality approach also has an influence on police behavior. The police will guard against unnecessarily suggestive procedures under the totality rule, as well as the *per se* one, for fear that their actions will lead to the exclusion of identifications as unreliable.

The third factor is the effect on the administration of justice. Here the *per se* approach suffers serious drawbacks. Since it denies the trier reliable evidence, it may result, on occasion, in the guilty going free. Also, because of its rigidity, the *per se* approach may make error by the trial judge more likely than the totality approach. And in those cases in which the admission of identification evidence is error under the *per se* approach but not under the totality approach—cases in which the identification is reliable despite an unnecessarily suggestive identification procedure—reversal is a Draconian sanction. Certainly, inflexible rules of exclusion that may frustrate rather than promote justice have not been viewed recently by this Court with unlimited enthusiasm. * * *

* * *

The standard, after all, is that of fairness as required by the Due Process Clause of the Fourteenth Amendment. * * * *Stovall*, with its reference to "the totality of the circumstances," * * * and *Biggers*, with its continuing stress on the same totality, * * * did not, singly or together, establish a strict exclusionary rule or new standard of due process. * * *

We therefore conclude that reliability is the linchpin in determining the admissibility of identification testimony for both pre- and post-*Stovall* confrontations. The factors to be considered are set out in *Biggers*. * * * These include the opportunity of the witness to view the criminal at the time of the crime, the witness' degree of attention, the accuracy of his prior description of the criminal, the level of certainty demonstrated at the confrontation, and the time between the crime and the confrontation. Against these factors is to be weighed the corrupting effect of the suggestive identification itself. [d]

V

We turn, then, to the facts of this case and apply the analysis:

1. The opportunity to view. Glover testified that for two to three minutes he stood at the apartment door, within two feet of the respondent. The door opened twice, and each time the man stood at the door. The moments passed, the conversation took place, and payment was made. Glover looked directly at his vendor. It was near sunset, to be sure, but the sun had not yet set, so it was not dark or even dusk or twilight. Natural light from outside entered the hallway through a window. There was natural light, as well, from inside the apartment.

2. The degree of attention. Glover was not a casual or passing observer, as is so often the case with eyewitness identification. Trooper Glover was a trained police officer on duty—and specialized and dangerous duty * * * Glover himself was a Negro and unlikely to perceive only general features of "hundreds of Hartford black males," as the Court of Appeals stated. * * * It is true that Glover's duty was that of ferreting out narcotics offenders and that he would be expected in his work to produce results. But it is also true that, as a specially trained, assigned, and experienced officer, he could be expected to pay scrupulous attention to detail, for he knew that subsequently he would have to find and arrest his vendor. In addition, he knew that his claimed observations would be subject later to close scrutiny and examination at any trial.

3. The accuracy of the description. Glover's description was given to D'Onofrio within minutes after the transaction. It included the vendor's race, his height, his build, the color and style of his hair, and the high cheekbone facial feature. It also included clothing the vendor wore. No claim has been made that respondent did not possess the physical characteristics so described.

D'Onofrio reacted positively at once. Two days later, when Glover was alone, he viewed the photograph D'Onofrio produced and identified its subject as the narcotics seller.

4. The witness' level of certainty. There is no dispute that the photograph in question was that of respondent. Glover, in response to a question whether the photograph was that of the person from whom he made the purchase, testified: "There is no question whatsoever." * * * This positive assurance was repeated. * * * [e]

5. The time between the crime and the confrontation. Glover's description of his vendor was given to D'Onofrio within minutes of the crime. The photographic identification took place only two days later. We do not have here the passage of weeks or months between the crime and the viewing of the photograph.

These indicators of Glover's ability to make an accurate identification are hardly outweighed by the corrupting effect of the challenged identification itself. [Glover was not placed under pressure to make an identification]. * * *

* * *

Surely, we cannot say that under all the circumstances of this case there is "a very substantial likelihood of irreparable misidentification." * * * Short of that point, such evidence is for the jury to weigh. We are content to rely upon the good sense and judgment of American juries, for evidence with some element of untrustworthiness is customary grist for the jury mill. Juries are not so susceptible that they cannot measure intelligently the weight of identification testimony that has some questionable feature.

Of course, it would have been better had D'Onofrio presented Glover with a photographic array including "so far as practicable ... a reasonable number of persons similar to any person then suspected whose likeness is included in the array." * * * But we are not disposed to view D'Onofrio's failure as one of constitutional dimension to be enforced by a rigorous and unbending exclusionary rule. * * *

* * *

The judgment of the Court of Appeals is reversed. * * *

[JUSTICE STEVENS concurred.]

[JUSTICE MARSHALL, joined by JUSTICE BRENNAN dissented, arguing that the majority entirely overlooked the case of *Simmons v. United States*, 390 U.S. 377 (1968), which held "that due process was violated by the later identification if the pretrial procedure had been 'so impermissibly suggestive as to give rise to a very substantial likelihood of irreparable misidentification.' This test focused, not on the necessity for the challenged pretrial procedure, but on the degree of suggestiveness that it entailed."]

* * * * * * * * * * *

COMMENTS

[a] These facts describe a common activity of police in the "war on drugs": the controlled buy. These "wholesale" practices raise concerns that innocent persons

living in poor neighborhoods may be swept into the net along with dealers if police agencies, driven by production values, pay less attention to accuracy in the heated drive to mop up the growing tide of drugs.

[b] The complexity of *Stovall*'s due process approach is shown by the different standards and different factual conclusions drawn by the federal district and circuit courts in this case. This complexity presents the Supreme Court with the responsibility to sort out different ways of approaching identification issues. Thus, it must establish a common methodology for lower courts to use in resolving due process issues in these cases; it does this in the next section.

[c] The Court here summarizes two divergent avenues of interpretation taken by different United States circuit courts: (1) the *per se approach* which requires the trial court to exclude evidence of the suggestive pretrial identification, and (2) the *totality of circumstances approach* which may allow the prosecution to introduce evidence of a suggestive pretrial identification if certain factors are present. The existence of divergent approaches reflects differing policy views among the lower federal judges.

[d] The Court here rejects the *per se* approach and hierarchically ranks reliability as the crticial factor. In policy terms, this places law enforcement above deterring unconstitutional police acts. Although the holding is grounded in precedent and weighs competing factors, an element of policy judgment is inevitable in constitutional adjudication.

[e] The analysis of these factors is for the most part self-explanatory. However, psychologists of perception note that there is no correlation between certainty and accuracy.

Chapter Eight

ENTRAPMENT

The subject of entrapment concerns the constitutional question of the proper relationship between State and individual and the abuse of State power. Nevertheless, the law of entrapment has not evolved from any specific constitutional provision or doctrine, and at the present time does not directly implicate the due process clause.

Entrapment emerged from late 19th century state criminal law cases as a uniquely American limitation on the power to prosecute. In these early cases prosecutions were dismissed when the police appeared to have induced an "otherwise innocent" person into committing crime that the person would not have committed without the inducement. These cases typically arose in the context of the enforcement of "morals" or "victimless" crimes where there was no complainant and the government acted in a somewhat entrepreneurial role.

Lower federal courts began to recognize the defense in the early part of the twentieth century and the defense was recognized as a matter of federal law in *Sorrells v. United States*, 287 U.S. 435 (1932). An undercover Prohibition agent visited Sorrells at his home and cajoled him into selling a personal amount of liquor after playing on his sympathies as a First World War veteran. Three requests had to be made before Sorrells made the sale. The Court unanimously held that the indictment had to be thrown out because of entrapment. But the justices divided into two camps. The majority held that the national prohibition statute could be interpreted as implying a defense of entrapment; otherwise the enforcement of the statute could produce injustice. Dissenting Justices Roberts, Brandeis and Stone argued that no such "defense" could be read into the statute. Instead, they urged the Court to place entrapment on the footing of a rule of public policy.

The Court in *Sherman v. United States* (1958) divided in essentially the same way that it did three decades before in *Sorrells*. It was unanimous in deciding that entrapment occurred when a narcotics informant wore down the sympathy of an apparently recovering addict to obtain a minor amount of drugs, not for a profit motive but apparently to maintain an arrest quota. Five justices upheld the "subjective" test that viewed entrapment as a criminal law defense depending upon the predisposition of the defendant to commit the crime. Four justices urged an objective test to dismiss cases whenever overbearing action by federal officers fell below standards of proper police behavior.

The majority or "subjective" test of entrapment is based on the "legal fiction" that the legislature has created a defense in the substantive criminal law involved. The minority or "objective" test is based on the Court's "supervisory power" to establish rules for the proper ordering of the federal courts. Neither of these bases authorize the federal courts to apply the entrapment defense against cases arising from *state* prosecutions. An important practical difference between the two tests is that entrapment as a criminal law defense must be submitted to the jury for consideration, while under the "objective" test, entrapment is a question to be resolved by a judge in a pretrial motion hearing.

In *United States v. Russell*, 411 U.S. 423 (1973) a federal narcotics agent posed as a supplier of a legal but hard to obtain chemical used in the manufacture of amphetamines. The government therefore supplied an essential ingredient of an illicit drug to a manufacturer. The Court ruled that the gravamen of the entrapment defense was whether the defendant intended to commit the crime and not on the conduct of the government agents. Since the defendant was predisposed to commit the crime and was not induced, the statutory defense was not available to him. The Court came to the same conclusion where a government agent sold heroin to an addict for resale (*Hampton v. United States* (1976)).

In *Russell* and *Hampton* the Court suggested that egregious governmental conduct of entrapment that shocks the conscience may be viewed as a due process violation. Thus far, however, the Court has not applied this constitutional principle to an entrapment case.

Jacobson v. United States (1992) found that entrapment existed. Petitioner lawfully ordered magazines of nude teens not depicting sexual activity. Thereupon, more than one government agency targeted petitioner and for 26 months sent repeated mailings and communications with appeals to join a bogus organization claiming to support free speech and with solicitations to purchase sexually explicit child pornography. The Court held that petitioner's predisposition to break the law was the product of the Government's inducement.

Although the federal entrapment rule adheres firmly to the subjective-criminal law defense standard, some states have adopted the objective-public policy approach or a hybrid approach that combines elements of the two standards. One version of the hybrid approach reduces the scope of the defense: it is not available to any defendant who is predisposed (subjective) and in addition it is not available unless the police conduct fell far below standard undercover techniques (objective). Other states adopt rules that make it more likely that a defendant can successfully claim entrapment: the government conduct makes it likely that a hypothetical person would be lured into wrongdoing (objective element) and, as a result, this particular defendant was induced into the crime (subjective element).

SHERMAN v. UNITED STATES

356 U.S. 369, 78 S.Ct. 819, 2 L.Ed.2d 848 (1958)

MR. CHIEF JUSTICE WARREN delivered the opinion of the Court.

The issue before us is whether petitioner's conviction should be set aside on the ground that as a matter of law the defense of entrapment was established. [a] Petitioner was convicted under an indictment charging three sales of narcotics in violation of 21 U.S.C. sec. 174. * * * [P]etitioner's defense was a claim of entrapment: an agent of the Federal Government induced him to take part in illegal transactions when otherwise he would not have done so.

In late August 1951, Kalchinian, a government informer, first met petitioner at a doctor's office where apparently both were being treated to be cured of narcotics addiction. Several accidental meetings followed, either at the doctor's office or at the pharmacy where both filled their prescriptions from the doctor. From mere greetings, conversation progressed to a discussion of mutual experiences and problems, including their attempts to overcome addiction to narcotics. Finally Kalchinian asked petitioner if he knew of a good source of narcotics. He asked petitioner to supply him with a source because he was not responding to treatment. From the first, petitioner tried to avoid the issue. Not until after a number of repetitions of the request, predicated on Kalchinian's presumed suffering, did petitioner finally acquiesce. Several times thereafter he obtained a quantity of narcotics which he shared with Kalchinian. Each time petitioner told Kalchinian

that the total cost of narcotics he obtained was twenty-five dollars and that Kalchinian owed him fifteen dollars. The informer thus bore the cost of his share of the narcotics plus the taxi and other expenses necessary to obtain the drug. After several such sales Kalchinian informed agents of the Bureau of Narcotics that he had another seller for them. On three occasions during November 1951, government agents observed petitioner give narcotics to Kalchinian in return for money supplied by the Government.

At the trial the factual issue was whether the informer had convinced an otherwise unwilling person to commit a criminal act or whether petitioner was already predisposed to commit the act and exhibited only the natural hesitancy of one acquainted with the narcotics trade. [b] The issue of entrapment went to the jury, and a conviction resulted. Petitioner was sentenced to imprisonment for ten years. * * *

In *Sorrells v. United States*, 287 U.S. 435 (1932), this Court firmly recognized the defense of entrapment in the federal courts. The intervening years have in no way detracted from the principles underlying that decision. The function of law enforcement is the prevention of crime and the apprehension of criminals. Manifestly, that function does not include the manufacturing of crime. Criminal activity is such that stealth and strategy are necessary weapons in the arsenal of the police officer. However, "A different question is presented when the criminal design originates with the officials of the Government, and they implant in the mind of an innocent person the disposition to commit the alleged offense and induce its commission in order that they may prosecute." * * * [c] Then stealth and strategy become as objectionable police methods as the coerced confession and the unlawful search. Congress could not have intended that its statutes were to be enforced by tempting innocent persons into violations. [d]

However, the fact that government agents "merely afford opportunities or facilities for the commission of the offense does not" constitute entrapment. Entrapment occurs only when the criminal conduct was "the product of the *creative* activity" of law-enforcement officials. * * * To determine whether entrapment has been established, a line must be drawn between the trap for the unwary innocent and the trap for the unwary criminal. The principles by which the courts are to make this determination were outlined in *Sorrells*. On the one hand, at trial the accused may examine the conduct of the government agent; and on the other hand, the accused will be subjected to an "appropriate and searching inquiry into his own conduct and predisposition" as bearing on his claim of innocence. * * *

We conclude from the evidence that entrapment was established as a matter of law. In so holding, we are not choosing between conflicting witnesses, nor judging credibility. Aside from recalling Kalchinian, who was the Government's witness, the defense called no witnesses. We reach our conclusion from the undisputed testimony of the prosecution's witnesses.

It is patently clear that petitioner was induced by Kalchinian. The informer himself testified that, believing petitioner to be undergoing a cure for narcotics addiction, he nonetheless sought to persuade petitioner to obtain for him a source of narcotics. In Kalchinian's own words we are told of the accidental, yet recurring, meetings, the ensuing conversations concerning mutual experiences in regard to narcotics addiction, and then of Kalchinian's resort to sympathy. One request was not enough, for Kalchinian tells us that additional ones were necessary to overcome, first, petitioner's refusal, then his evasiveness, and then his hesitancy in order to achieve capitulation. Kalchinian not only procured a source of narcotics but apparently also induced petitioner to return to the habit. [e] Finally, assured of a catch, Kalchinian informed the authorities so that they could close the net. * * * Although he was not being paid, Kalchinian was an active government informer who had but recently been the instigator of at least two other prosecutions. Undoubtedly the impetus for such achievements was the fact that in 1951 Kalchinian was himself under criminal charges for illegally selling narcotics and had not yet been sentenced. It makes no difference that the sales for which petitioner was convicted occurred after a series of sales. They were not independent acts subsequent to the inducement but part of a course of conduct which was the product of the inducement. In his testimony the federal agent in charge of the case admitted that he never bothered to question Kalchinian about the way he had made contact with petitioner. * * *

The Government sought to overcome the defense of entrapment by claiming that petitioner evinced a "ready complaisance" to accede to Kalchinian's request. Aside from a record of past convictions * * * the Government's case is unsupported. There is no evidence that petitioner himself was in the trade. When his apartment was searched after arrest, no narcotics were found. There is no significant evidence that petitioner even made a profit on any sale to Kalchinian. The Government's characterization of petitioner's hesitancy to Kalchinian's request as the natural wariness of the criminal cannot fill the evidentiary void.

[CHIEF JUSTICE WARREN next stated that Sherman's conviction for narcotics sale in 1942 and another for possession in 1946 "are insufficient to prove petitioner had a readiness to sell narcotics at the time Kalchinian approached him. * * * "]

The case at bar illustrates an evil which the defense of entrapment is designed to overcome. **[f]** The government informer entices someone attempting to avoid narcotics not only into carrying out an illegal sale but also into returning to the habit of use. Selecting the proper time, the informer then tells the government agent. The set-up is accepted by the agent without even a question as to the manner in which the informer encountered the seller. Thus the Government plays on the weaknesses of an innocent party and beguiles him into committing crimes which he otherwise would not have attempted. Law enforcement does not require methods such as this.

[CHIEF JUSTICE WARREN went on to reject the position of the dissent, that the case should be decided on the grounds put forward by Justice Roberts in the *Sorrells* case]. * * *

Reversed and remanded.

MR. JUSTICE FRANKFURTER, whom MR. JUSTICE DOUGLAS, MR. JUSTICE HARLAN, and MR. JUSTICE BRENNAN join, concurring in the result. **[g]**

Although agreeing with the Court that the undisputed facts show entrapment as a matter of law, I reach this result by a route different from the Court's.

* * * [T]he basis of this defense, affording guidance for its application in particular circumstances, is as much in doubt today as it was when the defense was first recognized over forty years ago, although entrapment has been the decisive issue in many prosecutions. The lower courts have continued gropingly to express the feeling of outrage at conduct of law enforcers that brought recognition of the defense in the first instance, but without the formulated basis in reason that it is the first duty of courts to construct for justifying and guiding emotion and instinct.

Today's opinion does not promote this judicial desideratum, and fails to give the doctrine of entrapment the solid foundation that the decisions of the lower courts and criticism of learned writers have clearly shown is needed. * * * **[h]**

It is surely sheer fiction to suggest that a conviction cannot be had when a defendant has been entrapped by government officers or informers because "Congress could not have intended that its statutes were to be enforced by tempting innocent persons into violations." **[i]** In these cases raising claims of entrapment, the only legislative intention that can with any show of reason be extracted from the statute is the intention to make criminal precisely the conduct in which the defendant has engaged. That conduct includes all the elements necessary to constitute criminality. Without compulsion and "knowingly," where that is requisite, the defendant has violated the statutory command. If he is to be relieved from the usual punitive consequences, it is on no account because he is innocent of the offense described. In these circumstances, conduct is not less criminal because the result of temptation, whether the tempter is a private person or a government agent or informer.

The courts refuse to convict an entrapped defendant, not because his conduct falls outside the proscription of the statute, but because, even if his guilt be admitted, the methods employed on behalf of the Government to bring about conviction cannot be countenanced. * * * Insofar as they are used as instrumentalities in the administration of criminal justice, the federal courts have an obligation to set their face against enforcement of the law by lawless means or means that violate rationally vindicated standards of justice, and to refuse to sustain such methods by effectuating them. They do this in the exercise of a recognized jurisdiction to formulate and apply "proper standards for the enforcement of the federal criminal law in the federal courts," *McNabb v. United States*, 318 U.S. 332, 341 (1943), an obligation that goes beyond the conviction of the particular defendant before the court. **[j]** Public confidence in the fair and honorable administration of justice, upon which ultimately depends the rule of law, is the transcending value at stake.

The formulation of these standards does not in any way conflict with the statute the defendant has violated, or involve the initiation of a judicial policy disregarding or qualifying that framed by Congress. **[k]** A false choice is put when it is said that either the defendant's conduct does not fall within the statute or he must be convicted. The statute is wholly directed to defining and prohibiting the substantive offense concerned and expresses no purpose, either permissive or prohibitory, regarding the police conduct that will be tolerated in the detection of crime. A statute prohibiting the sale of narcotics is as silent on the question of entrapment as it is on the admissibility of illegally obtained evidence. It is enacted, however, on the basis of certain presuppositions concerning the established legal order and the role of the courts within that system in formulating standards for the administration of criminal justice when Congress itself has not specifically legislated to that end. Specific statutes are to be fitted into an antecedent legal system. **[l]**

* * *

The crucial question, not easy of answer, to which the court must direct itself is whether the police conduct revealed in the particular case falls below standards, to which common feelings respond, for the proper use of governmental power. For answer it is wholly irrelevant to ask if the "intention" to commit the crime originated with the defendant or government officers, or if the criminal conduct was the product of "the creative activity" of law-enforcement officials. Yet in the present case the Court repeats and purports to apply these unrevealing tests. Of course in every case of this kind the intention that the particular crime be committed originates with the police, and without their inducement the crime would not have occurred. But it is perfectly clear from such decisions as the decoy letter cases in this Court, * * * where the police in effect simply furnished the opportunity for the commission of the crime, that this is not enough to enable the defendant to escape conviction. [m]

The intention referred to, therefore, must be a general intention or predisposition to commit, whenever the opportunity should arise, crimes of the kind solicited, and in proof of such a predisposition evidence has often been admitted to show the defendant's reputation, criminal activities, and prior disposition. The danger of prejudice in such a situation, particularly if the issue of entrapment must be submitted to the jury and disposed of by a general verdict of guilty or innocent, is evident. The defendant must either forego the claim of entrapment or run the substantial risk that, in spite of instructions, the jury will allow a criminal record or bad reputation to weigh in its determination of guilt of the specific offense of which he stands charged. [n] Furthermore, a test that looks to the character and predisposition of the defendant rather than the conduct of the police loses sight of the underlying reason for the defense of entrapment. No matter what the defendant's past record and present inclinations to criminality, or the depths to which he has sunk in the estimation of society, certain police conduct to ensnare him into further crime is not to be tolerated by an advanced society. And in the present case it is clear that the Court in fact reverses the conviction

because of the conduct of the informer Kalchinian, and not because the Government has failed to draw a convincing picture of petitioner's past criminal conduct. Permissible police activity does not vary according to the particular defendant concerned; surely if two suspects have been solicited at the same time in the same manner, one should not go to jail simply because he has been convicted before and is said to have a criminal disposition. * * *

This does not mean that the police may not act so as to detect those engaged in criminal conduct and ready and willing to commit further crimes should the occasion arise. Such indeed is their obligation. It does mean that in holding out inducements they should act in such a manner as is likely to induce to the commission of crime only these persons and not others who would normally avoid crime and through self-struggle resist ordinary temptations. This test shifts attention from the record and predisposition of the particular defendant to the conduct of the police and the likelihood, objectively considered, that it would entrap only those ready and willing to commit crime. It is as objective a test as the subject matter permits, and will give guidance in regulating police conduct that is lacking when the reasonableness of police suspicions must be judged or the criminal disposition of the defendant retrospectively appraised. [o] It draws directly on the fundamental intuition that led in the first instance to the outlawing of "entrapment" as a prosecutorial instrument. The power of government is abused and directed to an end for which it was not constituted when employed to promote rather than detect crime and to bring about the downfall of those who, left to themselves, might well have obeyed the law. Human nature is weak enough and sufficiently beset by temptations without government adding to them and generating crime.

* * *

[JUSTICE FRANKFURTER concluded by noting that under an objective test that focuses on police conduct, the issue would be decided before a judge in a hearing before trial, rather than being submitted to the more emotional arena of a jury trial.]

*   *   *   *   *   *   *   *   *   *   *

COMMENTS

[a] Federal criminal statutes contain no provisions for an entrapment defense. As you read the case, ask whether the defense derives from a constitutional interpretation by the Court, from a "common law" interpretation, from statutory interpretation or from the Court's supervisory power?

Criminal law defenses typically involve either a lack of *mens rea* or criminal intent (*e.g.*, insanity, infancy, intoxication) or an impairment of criminal knowledge because of a mistake of fact or duress. Do such considerations apply in the defense of entrapment?

[b] At this point in your reading of the case, do the terms "otherwise unwilling" and "already predisposed" make any sense? Compare your reaction to these terms at this point to your understanding of the terms after you have finished reading the case. Why do you think the facts are recited at such length?

[c] If Sherman was "otherwise innocent" in August, 1951 was he still innocent in November 1951? Was he innocent at the time he sold the heroin? When he sold the heroin, he certainly knew that what he was doing was wrong and a crime. Suppose his motive was to ease the pain and suffering of his new friend Kalchinian. Is a good motive a valid defense to a felony?

[d] If the statute is silent about entrapment, how can the chief justice be so certain about the intent of Congress? Compare CHIEF JUSTICE WARREN's bald statement in this regard to JUSTICE FRANKFURTER's criticism of this "legal fiction" below.

[e] From this paragraph, inducement appears to be the deciding factor in making out the defense of entrapment. The Court does not indicate that a constitutional rationale or its supervisory power is the basis of this defense. Thus, it appears that the Court finds entrapment to be a defense "inherent" in the statute. Is the defense inherent in all criminal statutes? Suppose that during the heyday of the late 1960s a "freelance" government informer infiltrated a radical group made up of immature and volatile persons aged 18 to 21 with no previous history of violence and convinced them to commit violent crimes such as arson, kidnapping or assaults? Would entrapment be inherent in the arson, kidnapping or assault statutes?

[f] Is the "evil" the method used by the government to obtain a conviction? or that it preyed on the weakness of the victim? Would the evil be the same if Sherman regularly sold small quantities of heroin to support a habit? if he sold larger quantities to supplement his income? if he sold as much heroin as he could to become rich?

[g] This is a most interesting lineup of justices; two liberals and two conservatives—two who strenuously opposed the expansion of the incorporation doctrine and two who helped make the due process revolution. Cases are not determined simply by the "alignment" of justices; ideas and doctrines count.

[h] It is the function of the Supreme Court to establish general rules for the guidance of lower courts, not simply to decide individual cases.

[i] This may be true, but legal fictions often serve a useful policy purpose. It is probably the case that it was easier for courts to develop a control on police behavior in this area by resorting to the notion that entrapment was a criminal law defense than to attempt to directly exercise supervisory power over the police.

[j] JUSTICE FRANKFURTER thus believes that the Court should exercise its *supervisory power* to control the practice of entrapment. Even if the police activity is not illegal, is it still appropriate for the Court to prevent "unsavory" practices? If some deceptive practices, such as the use of undercover agents, are necessary to fight consensual crimes, how are the courts to distinguish between legitimate techniques and those to be banned? Might the public be upset with the courts "tying the hands" of the police?

[k] JUSTICE FRANKFURTER is here attempting to head off a criticism that his "objective" approach involved "judicial legislation," an undermining of congressional authority, and a violation of the separation of powers doctrine.

[l] The Rule of Law, the philosophical basis of our legal system, here is suggested as a specific, practical basis for the exercise of the Court's power. Perhaps a majority of the Court did not adopt JUSTICE FRANKFURTER's formulation out of caution that it is difficult to put limits on the Rule of Law as an operational principle.

[m] Here, JUSTICE FRANKFURTER offers a "police conduct" test as a means of determining when there is an entrapment violation. He understands, though, that too stringent a rule will eliminate useful forms of police undercover activity. Thus, the standard of this "objective test" is that entrapment occurs when police conduct falls below standards of governmental conduct according to "common feeling." How objective is a "common feeling" standard? Does it depend on outrage expressed in the public media? On public opinion polls? Or on the less volatile emotion of the judge who is hearing a case? It would appear that there are subjective elements to the "objective rule."

[n] Another weakness with the majority's approach is that it drags a defendant's prior criminal history into the trial; this is usually forbidden by rules of evidence because of its powerful prejudicial effect. Such a rule also detracts from the focus on improper police activity.

[o] This appears to be the source of the labels "objective test" for the position of the concurring justices and "subjective test" for the majority position. Is there really so much difference between acts that will induce "only these persons and not others who would normally avoid crime" and those that induced this particular defendant?

HAMPTON v. UNITED STATES

425 U.S. 484, 96 S.Ct. 1646, 48 L.Ed.2d 113 (1976)

MR. JUSTICE REHNQUIST announced the judgment of the Court in an opinion in which THE CHIEF JUSTICE and MR. JUSTICE WHITE join. [a]

This case presents the question of whether a defendant may be convicted for the sale of contraband which he procured from a Government informant or agent. The Court of Appeals for the Eighth Circuit held he could be, and we agree.

I

Petitioner was convicted of two counts of distributing heroin. * * * The case arose from two sales of heroin by petitioner to agents of the Federal Drug Enforcement Administration (DEA) in St. Louis * * * arranged by one Hutton. * * *

According to the Government's witnesses, * * * Hutton, [an acquaintance of Hampton and a DEA informant,] and petitioner were shooting pool * * * when petitioner, after observing "track" (needle) marks on Hutton's arms told Hutton that he needed money and knew where he could get some heroin. Hutton responded that he could find a buyer and petitioner suggested that he "get in touch with those people." Hutton then called DEA Agent Terry Sawyer and arranged a sale. * * *

[Two sales, for $145 and $500, were then made by Hampton to DEA agents posing as dealers, with Hutton present at each.] * * *

Petitioner's version of events was quite different. According to him, in response to his statement that he was short of cash, Hutton said that he had a friend who was a pharmacist who could produce a non-narcotic counterfeit drug which would give the same reaction as heroin. Hutton proposed selling this drug to gullible acquaintances who would be led to believe they were buying heroin. Petitioner testified that they successfully duped one buyer with this fake drug and that the sales which led to the arrest were solicited by petitioner in an effort to profit further from this ploy. [b]

Petitioner contended that he neither intended to sell, nor knew that he was dealing in heroin and that all of the drugs he sold were supplied by Hutton. His account was at least partially disbelieved by the jury which was instructed that in order to convict petitioner they had to find that the Government proved "that the defendant knowingly did an act which the law forbids, purposely intending to violate the law." [c] Thus the guilty verdict necessarily implies that the jury rejected petitioner's claim that he did not know the substance was heroin, and petitioner himself admitted both soliciting and carrying out sales. [Hampton asked for jury instructions to the effect that entrapment exists when an informer supplies drugs to be sold; that under such circumstances the jury must acquit as a matter of policy, and that the defendant's predisposition is irrelevant when the drugs are supplied by the government.] * * * [d]

The trial court refused the instruction and petitioner was found guilty. *

* * The Court of Appeals * * * affirmed the conviction. * * *

II

In *[United States v.] Russell*, 411 U.S. 423 (1973)] we held that the statutory defense of entrapment was not available where it was conceded that a Government agent supplied a necessary ingredient in the manufacture of an illicit drug. **[e]** We reaffirmed the principle of *Sorrells v. United States*, 287 U.S. 435 (1932 and *Sherman v. United States* [this volume] that the entrapment defense "focus[es] on the intent or predisposition of the defendant to commit the crime," * * * rather than upon the conduct of the Government's agents. We ruled out the possibility that the defense of entrapment could ever be based upon governmental misconduct in a case, such as this one, where the predisposition of the defendant to commit the crime was established.

In holding that "[i]t is only when the Government's deception actually implants the criminal design in the mind of the defendant that the defense of entrapment comes into play," * * * we, of course, rejected the contrary view of the dissents in that case and the concurrences in *Sorrells* and *Sherman*. In view of these holdings, petitioner correctly recognizes that his case does not qualify as one involving "entrapment" at all. He instead relies on the language in *Russell* that "we may some day be presented with a situation in which the conduct of law enforcement agents is so outrageous that due process principles would absolutely bar the government from invoking judicial processes to obtain a

conviction." * * * **[f]**

In urging that this case involves a violation of his due process rights, petitioner misapprehends the meaning of the quoted language in *Russell, supra*. Admittedly petitioner's case is different from Russell's but the difference is one of degree, not of kind. In *Russell* the ingredient supplied by the Government agent was a legal drug that the defendants demonstrably could have obtained from other sources besides the Government. Here the drug which the Government informant allegedly supplied to petitioner both was illegal and constituted the *corpus delicti* for the sale of which the petitioner was convicted. The Government obviously played a more significant role in enabling petitioner to sell contraband in this case than it did in *Russell*. **[g]**

But in each case the Government agents were acting in concert with the defendant, and in each case either the jury found or the defendant conceded that he was predisposed to commit the crime for which he was convicted. The remedy of the criminal defendant with respect to the acts of Government agents, which, far from being resisted, are encouraged by him, lies solely in the defense of entrapment. But, as noted, petitioner's conceded predisposition rendered this defense unavailable to him.

To sustain petitioner's contention here would run directly contrary to our statement in *Russell* that the defense of entrapment is not intended "to give the federal judiciary a 'chancellor's foot' veto over law enforcement practices of which it did not approve. The execution of the federal laws under our Constitution is confided primarily to the Executive Branch of the Government, subject to applicable constitutional and statutory limitations and to judicially fashioned rules to enforce those limitations." * * *

The limitations· of the Due Process Clause of the Fifth Amendment come into play only when the Government activity in question violates some protected right of the *defendant*. **[h]** Here, as we have noted, the police, the Government informant, and the defendant acted in concert with one another. **[i]** If the result of the governmental activity is to "implant in the mind of an innocent person the disposition to commit the alleged offense and induce its commission," * * * the defendant is protected by the defense of entrapment. If the police engage in illegal activity in concert with a defendant beyond the scope of their duties the remedy lies, not in freeing the equally culpable defendant, but in prosecuting the police under the applicable provisions of state or federal law. * * * But the police conduct here no more deprived defendant of any right secured to him by the United States Constitution than did the police conduct in *Russell* deprive Russell of any rights.

Affirmed.

MR. JUSTICE STEVENS took no part in the consideration or decision of this case.

MR. JUSTICE POWELL, with whom MR. JUSTICE BLACKMUN joins, concurring in the judgment.

* * * Hampton contends that the Government's supplying of contraband to one later prosecuted for trafficking in contraband constitutes a *per se* denial of due process. As I do not accept this proposition, I concur in the judgment of the Court and much of the plurality opinion directed specifically to Hampton's contention. I am not able to join the remainder of the plurality opinion, as it would unnecessarily reach and decide difficult questions not before us.

[JUSTICE POWELL saw this case controlled by *Russell* because, in his view, there was no essential legal difference between supplying hard to obtain legal chemicals to manufacture amphetamines and supplying heroin to predisposed defendants.]

But the plurality opinion today does not stop there. In discussing Hampton's due process contention, it enunciates a *per se* rule. * * * The plurality thus says that the concept of fundamental fairness inherent in the guarantee of due process would never prevent the conviction of a predisposed defendant, regardless of the outrageousness of police behavior in light of the surrounding circumstances.

I do not understand *Russell* or earlier cases delineating the predisposition-focused defense of entrapment to have gone so far, and there was no need for them to do so. * * * **[j]**

The plurality's use of the "chancellor's foot" passage from *Russell* * * * may suggest that it also would foreclose reliance on our supervisory power to bar conviction of a predisposed defendant because of outrageous police conduct. Again, I do not understand *Russell* to have gone so far. * * *

MR. JUSTICE BRENNAN, with whom MR. JUSTICE STEWART and MR. JUSTICE MARSHALL concur, dissenting.

[The dissent supports the "objective" test propounded by concurring Justices in *Sorrells* and *Sherman*:] "courts refuse to convict an entrapped defendant, not because his conduct falls outside the proscription of the statute, but because, even if his guilt be admitted, the methods employed on behalf of the Government to bring about conviction cannot be countenanced." * * * The "subjective" approach to the defense of entrapment—followed by the Court today and in *Sorrells*, *Sherman*, and *Russell*—focuses on the conduct and propensities of the particular defendant in each case and, in the absence of a conclusive showing, permits the jury to determine as a question of fact the defendant's "predisposition" to the crime. * * * "Under [the objective] approach, the determination of the lawfulness of the Government's conduct must be made—as it is on all questions involving the legality of law enforcement methods—by the trial judge, not the jury." * * *

In any event, I think that reversal of petitioner's conviction is also compelled for those who follow the "subjective" approach to the defense of entrapment. As MR. JUSTICE REHNQUIST notes, the Government's role in the criminal activity involved in this case was more pervasive than the Government involvement in *Russell*. * * * In addition, I agree with MR. JUSTICE POWELL that *Russell* does not foreclose imposition of a bar to conviction—based upon our supervisory power or due process principles—where the conduct of law enforcement authorities is sufficiently offensive, even though the individuals entitled to invoke such a defense might be "pre-

disposed." * * * In my view, the police activity in this case was beyond permissible limits.

Two facts significantly distinguish this case from *Russell*. First, the chemical supplied in that case was not contraband. * * * In contrast, petitioner claims that the very narcotic he is accused of selling was supplied by an agent of the Government. * * *

Second, the defendant in *Russell* "was an active participant in an illegal drug manufacturing enterprise which began before the Government agent appeared on the scene, and continued after the Government agent had left the scene." * * * In contrast, the two sales for which petitioner was convicted were allegedly instigated by Government agents and completed by the Government's purchase. The beginning and end of this crime thus coincided exactly with the Government's entry into and withdrawal from the criminal activity involved in this case. * * *

* * * Where the Government's agent deliberately sets up the accused by supplying him with contraband and then bringing him to another agent as a potential purchaser, the Government's role has passed the point of toleration. * * * The Government is doing nothing less than buying contraband from itself through an intermediary and jailing the intermediary. * * * There is little, if any, law enforcement interest promoted by such conduct; plainly it is not designed to discover ongoing drug traffic. Rather, such conduct deliberately entices an individual to commit a crime. That the accused is "predisposed" cannot possibly justify the action of government officials in purposefully creating the crime. * * *

* * *

* * * * * * * * * *

COMMENTS

[a] Note that this is a plurality opinion; it does not represent a clear majority of the Court. It will be necessary to examine the concurrence to determine how it differs in its interpretation of the entrapment defense. The difference may not be important to the petitioner in this case, but it is important for the interpretation of entrapment rules in lower federal courts.

[b] It is not clear from the facts of the case whether Hampton could have procured the heroin to sell without Hutton's assistance. It may be relevant for law enforcement policy to know whether the government was dispensing quantities of illegal drugs to many informers and to relatively small-time user-sellers. If this were the case, it would create a vicious circle of government agents selling drugs to low-level users in order to arrest them.

[c] Under the subjective approach, predisposition is an issue to be determined by the jury; under the objective test, the judge determines whether the governmental overreaching amounted to entrapment.

[d] Aside from the legal issues, what is your view of the effectiveness of a law enforcement policy of supplying small or moderate amounts of drugs to a pool-hall habitue in order to make an arrest?

[e] *Russell* was the first entrapment case to reach the Supreme Court after *Sherman*. In *Russell* the government agents became "partners" of a drug manufacturer by supplying a legal, but hard-to-get chemical used in the manufacture of amphetamines.

[f] The due process approach suggested in *Russell* is closely allied to the objective test of entrapment. It would go one step beyond the court's supervisory power as a source of the entrapment rule and seeks the source of the rule in the due process clauses. To the degree that due process encompasses the ethical ideal of "fundamental fairness," such an extension is quite plausible.

[g] Is the difference between supplying a legal chemical and an illegal drug one of degree? Under an objective test, JUSTICE REHNQUIST might be incorrect. However, under the subjective test, he is correct because the real issue is whether the defendant is predisposed to commit the crime. This is an example of how a "factual" conclusion depends in part on the nature of the rule that one is applying. For another distinction, see what JUSTICE POWELL has to say about this point.

[h] It is difficult to see from the phrase "some protected right" how the purported due process entrapment rule could ever come into play with a defendant who is predisposed to commit the crime. If the defendant's other protected right is violated, then the defendant can rely on that violation to challenge the conviction. In such case there is no need for the defendant to challenge the conviction on the basis of outrageous police conduct under a due process theory. This is the point of departure for the concurring justices.

[i] Hampton did act in concert with the informant, Hutton, but did he act in concert with the police if he did not know of their identity as police?

[j] The purpose of JUSTICE POWELL's concurrence is to keep the door open to possible future due process claims in entrapment cases; that is, to thwart the attempt by JUSTICE REHNQUIST to foreclose this avenue.

JACOBSON v. UNITED STATES

___ U.S. ___, 112 S.Ct. 1535, 118 L.Ed.2d 174 (1992)

JUSTICE WHITE delivered the opinion of the Court.

* * * Jacobson was indicted [in 1987] for violating a provision of the Child Protection Act of 1984, * * * (Act), which criminalizes the knowing receipt through the mails of a "visual depiction [that] involves the use of a minor engaging in sexually explicit conduct. * * *" * * * Petitioner defended on the ground that the Government entrapped him into committing the crime through a series of communications from undercover agents that spanned the 26 months preceding his arrest. * * *

Because the Government overstepped the line between setting a trap for the "unwary innocent" and the "unwary criminal," *Sherman v. United States*, [this volume], and as a matter of law failed to establish that petitioner was independently predisposed to commit the crime for which he was arrested, we reverse the Court of Appeals' judgment affirming his conviction.

I

In February 1984, petitioner, a 56-year-old veteran-turned-farmer who supported his elderly father in Nebraska, ordered two magazines and a brochure from a California adult bookstore. The magazines, entitled Bare Boys I and Bare Boys II, contained photographs of nude preteen and teenage boys. [The photographs did not depict sexual activity. The receipt of the magazines was not criminal under federal or Nebraska law at that time.] Within three months, the law with respect to child pornography changed; Congress passed the Act illegalizing the receipt through the mails of sexually explicit depictions of children. In the very month that the new provision became law, postal inspectors found petitioner's name on the mailing list of the California bookstore that had mailed him Bare Boys I and II. There followed over the next 2½ years, repeated efforts by two Government agencies, through five fictitious organizations and a bogus pen pal, to explore petitioner's willingness to break the new law by ordering sexually explicit photographs of children through the mail.

[The Court's opinion contains a lengthy and detailed narrative of the repeated efforts of the government to set up Jacobson into purchasing child pornography through phony front organizations—all operated by government officers—such as the "American Hedonist Society," "Midlands Data Research," "Heartland Institute for a New Tomorrow" (HINT), and by "pen pals" who "mirrored" Jacobson's interests.]

By March 1987, 34 months had passed since the Government obtained petitioner's name from the mailing list of the California bookstore, and 26 months had passed since the Postal Service had commenced its mailings to petitioner. Although petitioner had responded to surveys and letters, the Government had no evidence that petitioner had ever intentionally possessed or been exposed to child pornography. * * *

At this point, a second Government agency, the Customs Service, included petitioner in its own child pornography sting, "Operation Borderline," after receiving his name on lists submitted by the Postal Service. * * *

The Postal Service also continued its efforts in the Jacobson case, writing to petitioner as the "Far Eastern Trading Company Ltd." The letter [indicated that material could be sent that would not be viewed by the U.S. Customs service. Jacobson responded and was charged with and convicted for receiving child pornography (sent by the Government) under the Act. The federal Court of Appeals ruled that Jacobson was not entrapped as a matter of law.] [a]

II

There can be no dispute about the evils of child pornography or the difficulties that laws and law enforcement have encountered in eliminating it. * * * Likewise, there can be no dispute that the Government may use undercover agents to enforce the law. * * *

In their zeal to enforce the law, however, Government agents may not originate a criminal design, implant in an innocent person's mind the disposition to commit a criminal act, and then induce commission of the crime so that the Government may prosecute. * * * Where the Government has induced an individual to break the law and the defense of entrapment is at issue, as it was in this case, the prosecution must prove beyond reasonable doubt that the defendant was disposed to commit the criminal act prior to

first being approached by Government agents. * * *

Thus, an agent deployed to stop the traffic in illegal drugs may offer the opportunity to buy or sell drugs, and, if the offer is accepted, make an arrest on the spot or later. In such a typical case, or in a more elaborate "sting" operation involving government-sponsored fencing where the defendant is simply provided with the opportunity to commit a crime, the entrapment defense is of little use because the ready commission of the criminal act amply demonstrates the defendant's predisposition. * * * Had the agents in this case simply offered petitioner the opportunity to order child pornography through the mails, and petitioner—who must be presumed to know the law—had promptly availed himself of this criminal opportunity, it is unlikely that his entrapment defense would have warranted a jury instruction. * * * [b]

But that is not what happened here. By the time petitioner finally placed his order, he had already been the target of 26 months of repeated mailings and communications from Government agents and fictitious organizations. Therefore, although he had become predisposed to break the law by May 1987, it is our view that the Government did not prove that this predisposition was independent and not the product of the attention that the Government had directed at petitioner since January 1985. * * *

The prosecution's evidence of predisposition falls into two categories: evidence developed prior to the Postal Service's mail campaign, and that developed during the course of the investigation. The sole piece of preinvestigation evidence is petitioner's

1984 order and receipt of the Bare Boys magazines. But this is scant if any proof of petitioner's predisposition to commit an illegal act, the criminal character of which a defendant is presumed to know. It may indicate a predisposition to view sexually-oriented photographs that are responsive to his sexual tastes; but evidence that merely indicates a generic inclination to act within a broad range, not all of which is criminal, is of little probative value in establishing predisposition.

Furthermore, petitioner was acting within the law at the time he received these magazines. * * * Evidence of predisposition to do what once was lawful is not, by itself, sufficient to show predisposition to do what is now illegal, for there is a common understanding that most people obey the law even when they disapprove of it. This obedience may reflect a generalized respect for legality or the fear of prosecution, but for whatever reason, the law's prohibitions are matters of consequence. [c] Hence, the fact that petitioner legally ordered and received the Bare Boys magazines does little to further the Government's burden of proving that petitioner was predisposed to commit a criminal act. This is particularly true given petitioner's unchallenged testimony was that he did not know until they arrived that the magazines would depict minors.

The prosecution's evidence gathered during the investigation also fails to carry the Government's burden. Petitioner's responses to the many communications prior to the ultimate criminal act were at most indicative of certain personal inclinations, including a predisposition to view photographs of preteen sex and a willingness to promote a given agenda by supporting lobbying organizations. Even so, petitioner's responses hardly support an inference that he would commit the crime of receiving child pornography through the mails. Furthermore, a person's inclinations and "fantasies . . . are his own and beyond the reach of government. . . ."

On the other hand, the strong arguable inference is that, by waving the banner of individual rights and disparaging the legitimacy and constitutionality of efforts to restrict the availability of sexually explicit materials, the Government not only excited petitioner's interest in sexually explicit materials banned by law but also exerted substantial pressure on petitioner to obtain and read such material as part of a fight against censorship and the infringement of individual rights. [The government sting operation, HINT, described itself as a lobbying organization to promote sexual freedom and choice.] * * *

Similarly, the two solicitations in the spring of 1987 raised the spectre of censorship while suggesting that petitioner ought to be allowed to do what he had been solicited to do. * * * [B]oth government solicitations suggested that receiving this material was something that petitioner ought to be allowed to do.

Petitioner's ready response to these solicitations cannot be enough to establish beyond reasonable doubt that he was predisposed, prior to the Government acts intended to create predisposition, to commit the crime of receiving child pornography through the mails. * * * The evidence that petitioner was ready and willing to commit the offense came only after the Government had devoted 2½ years to convincing him that he had or should have the right to engage in the very behavior proscribed by law. Rational jurors could not say beyond a reasonable doubt that petitioner possessed the requisite predisposition prior to the Government's investigation and that it existed independent of the Government's many and varied approaches to petitioner. As was explained in *Sherman*, where entrapment was found as a matter of law, "the Government [may not] play on the weaknesses of an innocent party and beguile him into committing crimes which he otherwise would not have attempted." * * *

Law enforcement officials go too far when they "implant in the mind of an innocent person the *disposition* to commit the alleged offense and induce its commission in order that they may prosecute." * * * Like the *Sorrels* [287 U.S. 435 (1932)] court, we are "unable to conclude that it was the intention of the Congress in enacting this statute that its processes of detection and enforcement should be abused by the instigation by government officials of an act on the part of persons otherwise innocent in order to lure them to its commission and to punish them." * * * When the Government's quest for convictions leads to the apprehension of an otherwise law-abiding citizen who, if left to his own devices, likely would have never run afoul of the law, the courts should intervene.

[The judgment of the Court of Appeals, affirming Jacobson's conviction, was reversed.]

JUSTICE O'CONNOR, with whom THE CHIEF JUSTICE and JUSTICE KENNEDY join, and with whom JUSTICE SCALIA joins except as to Part II, dissenting.

Keith Jacobson was offered only two opportunities to buy child pornography through the mail. Both times, he ordered. Both times, he asked for opportunities to buy more. He needed no Government agent to coax, threaten, or persuade him; no one played on his sympathies, friendship, or suggested that his committing the crime would further a greater good. In fact, no Government agent even contacted him face-to-face. The Government contends that from the enthusiasm with which Mr. Jacobson responded to the chance to commit a crime, a reasonable jury could permissibly infer beyond a reasonable doubt that he was predisposed to commit the crime. I agree. * * *

* * *

The second time the Government sent a catalog of illegal materials, Mr. Jacobson ordered a magazine called "Boys Who Love Boys," described as: "11 year old and 14 year old boys get it on in every way possible. Oral, anal sex and heavy masturbation. If you love boys, you will be delighted with this." * * * Along with his order, Mr. Jacobson sent the following note: "Will order other items later. I want to be discreet in order to protect you and me." * * * **[d]**

* * *

[JUSTICE O'CONNOR stated that the established rule of entrapment is that the government must show predisposition to commit the crime at the time the Government first suggests the crime. She argued that the majority changed the rule in that now the Government must show that the defendant's predisposition existed when the Government agent first becomes involved with the defendant.]

* * * * * * * * * *

COMMENTS

[a] What are your views as to the wisdom of the law enforcement policy here? Like the drug area, should some government funding go into treatment?

[b] Does this language justify an indiscriminate mass mailing by the Government of child pornography advertisements, with a follow-up prosecution of everyone who responded and received a copy of the government-supplied depiction of children engaged in sex?

[c] Do you believe this? that criminalizing the mailing of child pornography could deter a former customer from seeking the material?

[d] The majority did not include this level of detail about the material received by Jacobson after 30 months of solicitations. Does it make a difference in your assessment of predisposition when Jacobson was first approached by the Government?

Chapter Nine

THE PRETRIAL PROCESS

In modern times the proceedings between police activity and formal adjudication have become a major arena of criminal procedure. At this stage the defendant is typically represented by an attorney; the activity occurs in the courthouse and in the offices of the prosecutors and attorneys. Pretrial preparation has become far more complex than in the earlier common law period and to a large extent the rights of defendants are determined during the pretrial process. A major reason for this, of course, is that about 10% of all felony charges are resolved by trial (both jury and bench trials) while most are resolved by guilty plea. Therefore, much of the increased pretrial activity occurs with an eye to establishing positions for plea negotiation.

The pretrial process begins with an initial appearance before a magistrate or judge within a day or two of arrest (*Gerstein v. Pugh* (1975); *County of Riverside v. McLaughlin* (1991)). At this stage, and at other points during the pretrial process the court considers the pretrial release of a defendant, either on her own recognizance, under a bail bond, or under a bond offered by the court. The Eighth Amendment does not guarantee pretrial release in absolute terms but does prohibit "excessive" bail (*Stack v. Boyle* (1951)). The Supreme Court has upheld the constitutionality of pretrial preventive detention (*United States v. Salerno* (1987)) thus indicating that the legitimate purposes of refusing bail include insuring the presence of the defendant at trial, preserving the judicial process from tampering, and preventing crimes by putatively dangerous defendants.

The initial appearance is brief. At this hearing an attorney may be secured or the process of obtaining counsel begins. The defendant hears the preliminary charges and pleads. The defendant virtually always pleads not guilty at this stage, although in some jurisdictions guilty pleas are taken to petty offenses and misdemeanors. Charges are rarely dismissed, but the state must show probable cause to hold the defendant. The judge informs the defendant of her rights.

The initial appearance is followed by more formal procedures: the preliminary hearing (also called the preliminary examination) or the grand jury proceeding. The formal purpose of both is to determine whether there is probable cause (or a prima facie case—a slightly higher standard of evidence —in some jurisdictions) to hold the defendant for trial and if so on which charges. The judge in a preliminary hearing hears some evidence by the prosecutor and if the evidence is sufficient the defendant is bound over for trial on formal charges drawn up in a prosecutor's information. Because this is a critical stage of the prosecution the defendant has a right to counsel (*Coleman v. Alabama* (1970)). The grand jury is a citizen's panel traditionally consisting of 23 members. They have subpoena powers and hear the testimony of witnesses conducted by the prosecutor. The defendant and her attorney may not be present in the grand jury room. The grand jury either upholds the prosecutor's charges in a true bill of indictment or dismisses the charges in a no bill.

The prosecutor has great discretion in determining whether or not to charge a defendant and on which charges. On average, prosecutors dismiss about half of all police complaints that are presented to them. The Courts rarely interfere with this discretion. In egregious circumstances courts have dismissed cases where selective prosecution violates the equal protection clause of the Fourteenth Amendment (or an equal protection principle under the Fifth Amendment's due process clause). But in *Wayte v. United States* (1985) the Court found no constitutional violation where sixteen men out of 674,000 who failed to register for the draft were indicted for nonregistration. The government gave nonregistrants' several opportunities to register and did not single out those prosecuted on the basis of their First Amendment activity against draft registration. Where the state brings charges with the vindictive purpose of punishing a defendant for exercising constitutional rights, a court may dismiss the prosecution as a due process violation (*Blackledge v. Perry*, 417 U.S. 21 (1974)).

The prosecutor has a constitutional responsibility under due process to avoid the use of perjured testimony in presenting a case (*Mooney v. Holohan*, 294 U.S. 103 (1935)) and to disclose all evidence favorable to the defense (*Napue v. Illinois*, 360 U.S. 264 (1959)), but only if the evidence is material (*Brady v. Maryland*, 373 U.S. 83 (1963)). The rule of disclosure includes impeachment evidence and the standard to determine materiality is whether there is a reasonable possibility that the outcome of the case would have been different if the evidence had been turned over to the defense (*United States v. Bagley* (1985)).

A pretrial arena of increasing importance are pretrial motions. Motions are requests for court action and may be presented on an almost infinite variety of matters. These include suppression motions under various exclusionary rules, motions for change of venue, motions to compel discovery, to dismiss charges, to challenge prosecutors' charges, etc. Two that rest largely on constitutional grounds are motions to dismiss for violations of the ban on double jeopardy and for violations of the right to a speedy trial.

The Fifth Amendment states, "* * * nor shall any person be subject for the same offence to be twice put in jeopardy of life or limb. * * *" The double jeopardy right applies to the States under the Fourteenth Amendment (*Benton v. Maryland*, 395 U.S. 784 (1969)). The right applies only if jeopardy "attaches." In a jury trial jeopardy attaches when the jury is empaneled and sworn (*Crist v. Bretz*, 437 U.S. 28 (1978)) and in a bench trial when the judge begins to hear evidence, but only where the defendant has waived the right to a jury trial (*Serfass v. United States*, 420 U.S. 377 (1975)). It has long been established that double jeopardy does not apply where a mistrial has been declared (*United States v. Perez*, 22 U.S. (9 Wheat.) 579 (1824)) as long as there is a "manifest necessity" for the retrial, as when a defense attorney in opening statements biased the jurors by asserting that the prosecutor would withhold evidence favorable to the defendant (*Richardson v. United States*, 468 U.S. 317 (1984)).

A single crime scenario which occurs in two states may be tried in both because they are separate sovereigns (*Heath v. Alabama* (1985)). The dual sovereignty rule also allows successive prosecutions in state and federal courts (*Abbate v. United States*, 359 U.S. 187 (1959)), and in the courts of an Indian nation and the federal government (*United States v. Wheeler*, 435 U.S. 313 (1978)), but not between political subdivisions in a single state (*Waller v. Florida*, 397 U.S. 387 (1970)).

The ban on double jeopardy includes the "collateral estoppel" rule, that a decision on an ultimate fact in one case cannot be relitigated in another (*Ashe v. Swenson* (1970)). Where multiple charges are specified against a defendant, a retrial or increased penalty is barred if the crime elements in the second prosecution are the same as those in the first (*Blockburger v. United States*, 284 U.S. 299 (1932)). The *Blockburger* test does apply to a successive prosecution involving a substantive offense and a crime punished under criminal contempt of court; on the other hand a reprosecution is not barred simply because the second prosecution involved the same "conduct" as that charged in the first (*United States v. Dixon* (1993)).

The Sixth Amendment guarantee of a speedy trial was incorporated and made applicable to the states under the due process clause of the Fourteenth Amendment in *Klopfer v. North Carolina*, 386 U.S. 213 (1967). This provision applies only after a prosecution formally commences; delay before formal charges are made may be corrected by criminal statutes of limitation. *Barker v. Wingo* (1972) established a four part test: (1) length of delay, (2) reason for delay, (3) whether defendant made a demand for speedy trial, and (4) the amount of prejudice to defendant's case that resulted from delay. A delay of 8½ years violated the speedy trial right where defendant made no trial demand because he was unaware of the indictment. Where a delay is extremely long, prejudice can be presumed (*Doggett v. United States* (1992)). An 18 month post-indictment delay for investigative purposes did not violate the defendant's right to speedy trial (*United States v. Lovasco* (1977)).

STACK v. BOYLE

342 U.S. 1, 72 S.Ct. 1, 96 L.Ed. 3   (1951)

MR. CHIEF JUSTICE VINSON delivered the opinion of the Court.

[Twelve petitioners were charged with conspiring to violate the Smith Act.] **[a]** Upon their arrest, bail was fixed for each petitioner in the widely varying amounts of $2,500, $7,500, $75,000 and $100,000. On motion of petitioner Schneiderman following arrest in the Southern District of New York, his bail was reduced to $50,000 before his removal to California. On motion of the Government to increase bail in the case of other petitioners, and after several intermediate procedural steps * * * bail was fixed in the District Court for the Southern District of California in the uniform amount of $50,000 for each petitioner.

Petitioners moved to reduce bail on the ground that bail as fixed was excessive under the Eighth Amendment. In support of their motion, petitioners submitted statements as to their financial resources, family relationships, health, prior criminal records, and other information. The only evidence offered by the Government was a certified record showing that four persons previously convicted under the Smith Act in the Southern District of New York had forfeited bail. **[b]** No evidence was produced relating those four persons to the petitioners in this case. At a hearing on the motion, petitioners were examined by the District Judge and cross-examined by an attorney for the Government. Petitioners' factual statements stand uncontroverted.

After their motion to reduce bail was denied, petitioners filed applications for habeas corpus in the same District Court. Upon consideration of the record on the motion to reduce bail, the writs were denied. The Court of Appeals for the Ninth Circuit affirmed. * * *

Relief in this type of case must be speedy if it is to be effective. [Consequently, having the full record, the Court disposed of the grant of certiorari and the merits in one decision.]

First. From the passage of the Judiciary Act of 1789, * * * to the present Federal Rules of Criminal Procedure, Rule 46 (a)(1), federal law has unequivocally provided that a person arrested for a non-capital offense *shall* be admitted to bail. This traditional right to freedom before conviction permits the unhampered preparation of a defense, and serves to prevent the infliction of punishment prior to conviction. * * * Unless this right to bail before trial is preserved, the presumption of innocence, secured only after centuries of struggle, would lose its meaning. **[c]**

The right to release before trial is conditioned upon the accused's giving adequate assurance that he will stand trial and submit to sentence if found guilty. * * * Like the ancient practice of securing the oaths of responsible persons to stand as sureties for the accused, the modern practice of requiring a bail bond or the deposit of a sum of money subject to forfeiture serves as additional assurance of the presence of an accused. Bail set at a figure higher than an amount reasonably calculated to fulfill this purpose is "excessive" under the Eighth Amendment. * * *

Since the function of bail is limited, the fixing of bail for any individual defendant must be based upon standards relevant to the purpose of assuring the presence of that defendant. The traditional standards as expressed in the Federal Rules of Criminal Procedure are to be applied in each case to each defendant. In this case petitioners are charged with offenses under the Smith Act and, if found guilty, their convictions are subject to review with the scrupulous care demanded by our Constitution. * * * Upon final judgment of conviction, petitioners face imprisonment of not more than five years and a fine of not more than $10,000. It is not denied that bail for each petitioner has been fixed in a sum much higher than that usually imposed for offenses with like penalties and yet there has been no factual showing to justify such action in this case. The Government asks the courts to depart from the norm by assuming, without the introduction of evidence, that each petitioner is a pawn in a conspiracy and will, in obedience to a superior, flee the jurisdiction. To infer from the fact of indictment alone a need for bail in an unusually high amount is an arbitrary act. Such conduct would inject into our own system of government the very principles of totalitarianism which Congress was seeking to guard against in passing the statute under which petitioners have been indicted.

If bail in an amount greater than that usually fixed for serious charges of crimes is required in the case of any of the petitioners, that is a matter to which evidence should be directed in a hearing so that the constitutional rights of each petitioner may be preserved. In the absence of such a showing, we are of the opinion that the fixing of bail before trial in these cases cannot be squared with the statutory and constitutional standards for admission to bail.

* * *

[The order below was vacated and the case remanded for a renewed bail hearing. The Court decided that habeas corpus was not the proper method to challenge a bail decision.]

MR. JUSTICE MINTON took no part in the consideration or decision of this case.

By MR. JUSTICE JACKSON, whom MR. JUSTICE FRANKFURTER joins.

* * *

The practice of admission to bail, as it has evolved in Anglo-American law, is not a device for keeping persons in jail upon mere accusation until it is found convenient to give them a trial. On the contrary, the spirit of the procedure is to enable them to stay out of jail until a trial has found them guilty. Without this conditional privilege, even those wrongly accused are punished by a period of imprisonment while awaiting trial and are handicapped in consulting counsel, searching for evidence and witnesses, and preparing a defense. To open a way of escape from this handicap and possible injustice, Congress commands allowance of bail for one under charge of any offense not punishable by death, * * * providing: "A person arrested for an offense not punishable by death shall be admitted to bail * * *" before conviction.

Admission to bail always involves a risk that the accused will take flight. That is a calculated risk which the law takes as the price of our system of justice. We know that Congress anticipated that bail would enable some escapes, because it provided a procedure for dealing with them. * * *

In allowance of bail, the duty of the judge is to reduce the risk by fixing an amount reasonably calculated to hold the accused available for trial and its consequence. * * * But the judge is not free to make the sky the limit, because the Eighth Amendment to the Constitution says: "Excessive bail shall not be required. * * *"

Congress has reduced this generality in providing more precise standards, stating that "* * * the amount thereof shall be such as in the judgment of the commissioner or court or judge or justice will insure the presence of the defendant, having regard to the nature and circumstances of the offense charged, the weight of the evidence against him, the financial ability of the defendant to give bail and the character of the defendant." * * *

These statutory standards are not challenged as unconstitutional, rather the amounts of bail established for these petitioners are alleged to exceed these standards. We submitted no constitutional questions to argument by the parties, and it is our duty to avoid constitutional issues if possible. For me, the record is inadequate to say what amounts would be reasonable in any particular one of these cases and I regard it as not the function of this Court to do so. Furthermore, the whole Court agrees that the remedy pursued in the circumstances of this case is inappropriate to test the question and bring it here. But I do think there is a fair showing that these congressionally enacted standards have not been correctly applied.

It is complained that the District Court fixed a uniform blanket bail chiefly by consideration of the nature of the accusation and did not take into account the difference in circumstances between different defendants. If this occurred, it is a clear violation of Rule 46 (c). Each defendant stands before the bar of justice as an individual. Even on a conspiracy charge defendants do not lose their separateness or identity. While it might be possible that these defendants are identical in financial ability, character and relation to the charge—elements Congress has directed to be regarded in fixing bail—I think it violates the law of probabilities. Each accused is entitled to any benefits due to his good record, and misdeeds or a bad record should prejudice only those who are guilty of them. The question when application for bail is made relates to each one's trustworthiness to appear for trial and what security will supply reasonable assurance of his appearance.

* * *

But the protest charges, and the defect in the proceedings below appears to be, that, provoked by the flight of certain Communists after conviction, the Government demands and public opinion supports a use of the bail power to keep Communist defendants in jail before conviction. Thus, the amount is said to have been fixed not as a reasonable assurance of their presence at the trial, but also as an assurance they would remain in jail. There seems reason to believe that this may have been the spirit to which the courts below have yielded, and it is contrary to the whole policy and philosophy of bail. This is not to say that every defendant is entitled to such bail as he can provide, but he is entitled to an opportunity to make it in a reasonable amount. I think the whole matter should be reconsidered by the appropriate judges in the traditional spirit of bail procedure.

* * *

* * * * * * * * * *

COMMENTS

[a] The Smith Act of 1940 made it a crime to advocate the overthrow of the United States government. At the height of the cold war in the late 1940s and early 1950s there were several major Smith Act trials of leading communists. These were classic political prosecutions and passions ran high in the country. See generally, Stanley I. Kutler, *The American Inquisition: Justice and Injustice in the Cold War* (New York: Hill & Wang, 1982).

[b] Ordinarily, such "evidence" would be quite incredible to support a bail denial request. It is understandable in light of the cold war hysteria then at its peak.

[c] Rights are often interlinked in an "ecology of liberty"; thus the right to bail supports other rights.

UNITED STATES v. SALERNO

481 U.S. 739, 107 S.Ct. 2095, 95 L.Ed.2d 697 (1987)

CHIEF JUSTICE REHNQUIST delivered the opinion of the Court.

The Bail Reform Act of 1984 (Act) allows a federal court to detain an arrestee pending trial if the Government demonstrates by clear and convincing evidence after an adversary hearing that no release conditions "will reasonably assure . . . the safety of any other person and the community." * * * We granted certiorari because of a conflict among the Courts of Appeals regarding the validity of the Act. We hold that, as against the facial attack mounted by these respondents, the Act fully comports with constitutional requirements. * * *

I

[The Act is a response to "the alarming problem of crimes committed by persons on release." Section 3141(a) gives the "judicial officer" discretion to order the pretrial detention of an arrestee; §3142(e) allows pretrial detention if the judge "finds that no condition[s] will reasonably assure the appearance of the person as required and the safety of any other person and the community." Section 3142(f) establishes procedural safeguards, including the presence of counsel and the right to testify, present witnesses, proffer evidence, and cross-examine other witnesses. Under §§ 3142(i) and (f), if the judge finds that no release conditions "can reasonably assure the safety of other persons and the community," the findings of fact must be stated in writing, supported by "clear and convincing evidence."] **[a]**

The judicial officer is not given unbridled discretion in making the detention determination, [but must consider several statutory factors: (1) the nature and seriousness of the charges, (2) the substantiality of the government's evidence against the arrestee, (3) the arrestee's background and characteristics, and (4) the nature and seriousness of the danger posed by the suspect's release. §3142(g). If pretrial detention is ordered,] the detainee is entitled to expedited appellate review of the detention order. §§3145(b), (c). **[b]**

[Salerno, charged with racketeering, was believed to be a high ranking "boss" in an organized crime "family" who had participated in two murder conspiracies. The District Court believed these allegations and granted the Government's detention motion.]

[The Court of Appeals reversed, concluding that due process prevented the detention of persons merely because they were thought to present a danger to the community.] It reasoned that our criminal law system holds persons accountable for past actions, not anticipated future actions. Although a court could detain an arrestee who threatened to flee before trial, such detention would be permissible because it would serve the basic objective of a criminal system—bringing the accused to trial. * * *

II

A facial challenge to a legislative Act is, of course, the most difficult challenge to mount successfully, since the challenger must establish that no set of circumstances exists under which the Act would be valid. The fact that the Bail Reform Act might operate unconstitutionally under some conceivable set of circumstances is insufficient to render it wholly invalid, since we have not recognized an "overbreadth" doctrine outside the limited context of the First Amendment. * * * We think respondents have failed to shoulder their heavy burden to demonstrate that the Act is "facially" unconstitutional. [c]

* * *

A

* * *

Respondents first argue that the Act violates substantive due process because the pretrial detention it authorizes constitutes impermissible punishment before trial. * * * The Court of Appeals assumed that pretrial detention under the Bail Reform Act is regulatory, not penal, and we agree that it is. [d]

As an initial matter, the mere fact that a person is detained does not inexorably lead to the conclusion that the government has imposed punishment. * * * To determine whether a restriction on liberty constitutes impermissible punishment or permissible regulation, we first look to legislative intent. * * * Unless Congress expressly intended to impose punitive restrictions, the punitive/regulatory distinction turns on "'whether an alternative purpose to which [the restriction] may rationally be connected is assignable for it, and whether it

appears excessive in relation to the alternative purpose assigned [to it].'" * * *

We conclude that the detention imposed by the Act falls on the regulatory side of the dichotomy. The legislative history of the Bail Reform Act clearly indicates that Congress did not formulate the pretrial detention provisions as punishment for dangerous individuals. * * * Congress instead perceived pretrial detention as a potential solution to a pressing societal problem. * * * There is no doubt that preventing danger to the community is a legitimate regulatory goal.

Nor are the incidents of pretrial detention excessive in relation to the regulatory goal Congress sought to achieve. The Bail Reform Act [is] carefully limit[ed] * * * to the most serious of crimes[:] * * * crimes of violence, offenses for which the sentence is life imprisonment or death, serious drug offenses, or certain repeat offenders. [e] The arrestee is entitled to a prompt detention hearing, * * * and the maximum length of pretrial detention is limited by the stringent time limitations of the Speedy Trial Act. * * * Moreover, * * * the conditions of confinement envisioned by the Act "appear to reflect the regulatory purposes relied upon by the" Government [requiring] that detainees be housed in a "facility separate, to the extent practicable, from persons awaiting or serving sentences or being held in custody pending appeal." * * * We conclude, therefore, that the pretrial detention contemplated by the Bail Reform Act is regulatory in nature, and does not constitute punishment before trial in violation of the Due Process Clause.

* * * Respondents characterize the

Due Process Clause as erecting an impenetrable "wall" in this area that "no governmental interest—rational, important, compelling or otherwise—may surmount."

We do not think the Clause lays down any such categorical imperative. We have repeatedly held that the Government's regulatory interest in community safety can, in appropriate circumstances, outweigh an individual's liberty interest. For example, in times of war or insurrection, when society's interest is at its peak, the Government may detain individuals whom the Government believes to be dangerous. * * * Even outside the exigencies of war, we have found that sufficiently compelling governmental interests can justify detention of dangerous persons. Thus, we have found no absolute constitutional barrier to detention of potentially dangerous resident aliens pending deportation proceedings. * * * We have also held that the government may detain mentally unstable individuals who present a danger to the public,* * * and dangerous defendants who become incompetent to stand trial. * * * We have approved of postarrest regulatory detention of juveniles when they present a continuing danger to the community. * * * Even competent adults may face substantial liberty restrictions as a result of the operation of our criminal justice system. If the police suspect an individual of a crime, they may arrest and hold him until a neutral magistrate determines whether probable cause exists. * * * Finally, respondents concede and the Court of Appeals noted that an arrestee may be incarcerated until trial if he presents a risk of flight, * * * or a danger to witnesses. [f]

Respondents characterize all of these cases as exceptions to the "general rule" of substantive due process that the government may not detain a person prior to a judgment of guilt in a criminal trial. Such a "general rule" may freely be conceded, but we think that these cases show a sufficient number of exceptions to the rule that the congressional action challenged here can hardly be characterized as totally novel. Given the well-established authority of the government, in special circumstances, to restrain individuals' liberty prior to or even without criminal trial and conviction, we think that the present statute providing for pretrial detention on the basis of dangerousness must be evaluated in precisely the same manner that we evaluated the laws in the cases discussed above.

* * * The Bail Reform Act * * * narrowly focuses on a particularly acute problem in which the Government interests are overwhelming. The Act operates only on individuals who have been arrested for a specific category of extremely serious offenses. * * * Congress specifically found that these individuals are far more likely to be responsible for dangerous acts in the community after arrest. * * * [g]

On the other side of the scale, of course, is the individual's strong interest in liberty. We do not minimize the importance and fundamental nature of this right. But, as our cases hold, this right may, in circumstances where the government's interest is sufficiently weighty, be subordinated to the greater needs of society. We think that Congress' careful delineation of the circumstances under which detention will be permitted satisfies this standard. When the Government proves by clear and convincing evidence that an arrestee presents an identified and articulable threat to an individual or the community, we believe that, consistent with the Due Process Clause, a court may disable the arrestee from executing that threat. * * *

[Justice Rehnquist then went on to establish that the procedures of the Bail Reform Act were] "adequate to authorize the pretrial detention of at least some [persons] charged with crimes," * * * As we stated in *Schall* [*v. Martin*, 467 U.S. 253 (1984)], "there is nothing inherently unattainable about a prediction of future criminal conduct." * * *

B

* * * We think that the Act survives a challenge founded upon the Eighth Amendment.

The Eighth Amendment addresses pretrial release by providing merely that "[e]xcessive bail shall not be required." This clause, of course, says nothing about whether bail shall be available at all. Respondents nevertheless contend that this Clause grants them a right to bail calculated solely upon considerations of flight. They rely on *Stack v. Boyle* [this volume]. * * * In respondents' view, since the Bail Reform Act allows a court essentially to set bail at an infinite amount for reasons not related to the risk of flight, it violates the Excessive Bail Clause. Respondents concede that the right to bail they have discovered in the Eighth Amendment is not absolute. A court may, for example, refuse bail in capital cases. And, as the Court of Appeals noted and respondents admit, a court may refuse bail when the defendant presents a threat to the judicial process by intimidating witnesses. Respondents characterize these exceptions as consistent with what they claim to be the sole purpose of bail—to ensure the integrity of the judicial process.

* * * [W]e reject the proposition that the Eighth Amendment categorically prohibits the government from pursuing other admittedly compelling interests through regulation of pretrial release. * * *

* * * Nothing in the text of the Bail Clause limits permissible government considerations solely to questions of flight. The only arguable substantive limitation of the Bail Clause is that the government's proposed conditions of release or detention not be "excessive" in light of the perceived evil. Of course, to determine whether the government's response is excessive, we must compare that response against the interest the government seeks to protect by means of that response. Thus, when the government has admitted that its only interest is in preventing flight, bail must be set by a court at a sum designed to ensure that goal, and no more. * * * We believe that when Congress has mandated detention on the basis of a compelling interest other than prevention of flight, as it has here, the Eighth Amendment does not require release on bail.
* * *

JUSTICE MARSHALL, with whom JUSTICE BRENNAN joins, dissenting.

This case brings before the Court for the first time a statute in which Congress declares that a person innocent of any crime may be jailed indefinitely, pending the trial of allegations which are legally presumed to be untrue, if the Government shows to the satisfaction of a judge that the accused is likely to commit crimes, unrelated to the pending charges, at anytime in the future. [h] Such statutes, consistent with the usages of tyranny and the excesses of what bitter experience teaches us to call the police state, have long been thought incompatible with the fundamental human rights protected by our Constitution. Today a majority of this Court holds otherwise. Its decision disregards basic principles of justice established centuries ago and enshrined beyond the reach of governmental interference in the Bill of Rights.

* * *

II

* * *

[JUSTICE MARSHALL first attacked the conclusion that detention under the Bail Reform Act is regulatory and not punitive.] The ease with which the conclusion is reached suggests the worthlessness of the achievement. * * *

This argument does not demonstrate the conclusion it purports to justify. Let us apply the majority's reasoning to a similar, hypothetical case. After investigation, Congress determines (not unrealistically) that a large proportion of violent crime is perpetrated by persons who are unemployed. It also determines, equally reasonably, that much violent crime is committed at night. From amongst the panoply of "potential solutions," Congress chooses a statute which permits, after judicial proceedings, the imposition of a dusk-to-dawn curfew on anyone who is unemployed. Since this is not a measure enacted for the purpose of punishing the unemployed,

and since the majority finds that preventing danger to the community is a legitimate regulatory goal, the curfew statute would, according to the majority's analysis, be a mere "regulatory" detention statute, entirely compatible with the substantive components of the Due Process Clause. [i]

The absurdity of this conclusion arises, of course, from the majority's cramped concept of substantive due process. The majority proceeds as though the only substantive right protected by the Due Process Clause is a right to be free from punishment before conviction. The majority's technique for infringing this right is simple: merely redefine any measure which is claimed to be punishment as "regulation," and, magically, the Constitution no longer prohibits its imposition. Because * * * the Due Progress Clause protects other substantive rights which are infringed by this legislation, the majority's argument is merely an exercise in obfuscation.

The logic of the majority's Eighth Amendment analysis is equally unsatisfactory. The Eighth Amendment, as the majority notes, states that "[e]xcessive bail shall not be required." The majority then declares, as if it were undeniable, that: "[t]his Clause, of course, says nothing about whether bail shall be available at all." * * * If excessive bail is imposed the defendant stays in jail. The same result is achieved if bail is denied altogether. Whether the magistrate sets bail at $1 billion or refuses to set bail at all, the consequences are indistinguishable. It would be mere sophistry to suggest that the Eighth Amendment protects against the former decision, and not the latter. [j] Indeed, such a result would lead to the conclusion that there was no need for Congress to pass a preventive detention measure of any kind; every federal magistrate and district judge could simply refuse, despite the absence of any evidence of risk of flight or danger to the community, to set bail. This would be entirely constitutional, since, according to the majority, the Eighth Amendment "says nothing about whether bail shall be available at all."

* * *

* * * [JUSTICE MARSHALL next suggested that the Court failed to consider the issue of whether the Eighth Amendment flatly prohibits the denial of bail for future dangerousness.] The majority does not ask, as a result of its disingenuous division of the analysis, if there are any substantive limits contained in both the Eighth Amendment and the Due Process Clause which render this system of preventive detention unconstitutional. The majority does not ask because the answer is apparent and, to the majority, inconvenient. [k]

III

The essence of this case may be found, ironically enough, in [another] provision of the Act to which the majority does not refer, [p]rovid[ing] that "[n]othing in this section shall be construed as modifying or limiting the presumption of innocence." But the very pith and purpose of this statute is an abhorrent limitation of the presumption of innocence. The majority's untenable conclusion that the present Act is constitutional arises from a specious denial of the role of the Bail Clause and the Due Process Clause in protecting the invaluable guarantee afforded by the presumption of innocence.

* * *

[JUSTICE MARSHALL then posed this puzzle: if an indicted person is detained under the act and is later acquitted, he must be released. Otherwise,] that would allow the Government to imprison someone for uncommitted crimes based upon "proof" not beyond a reasonable doubt. * * * But our fundamental principles of justice declare that the defendant is as innocent on the day before his trial as he is on the morning after his acquittal. Under this statute an untried indictment somehow acts to permit a detention, based on other charges, which after an acquittal would be unconstitutional. The conclusion is inescapable that the indictment has been turned into evidence, if not that the defendant is guilty of the crime charged, then that left to his own devices he will soon be guilty of something else. * * *

* * *

As Chief Justice Vinson wrote for the Court in *Stack v. Boyle*, [this volume] "Unless th[e] right to bail before trial is preserved, the presumption of innocence, secured only after centuries of struggle, would lose its meaning." * * *

* * *

[JUSTICE STEVENS dissented].

* * * * * * * * * * *

COMMENTS

[a] If pretrial detention on the grounds of dangerousness were sought in every case, the time needed to hold these due process hearings might overload the prosecutorial system. This practical impediment could be a real check on the dangers of misusing pretrial detention.

[b] How do these factors limit discretion? Do the first three factors, which are merely formal, add much of a check on the prosecutor?

[c] A "facial" challenge is one that says the law is void "on its face," or in every circumstance, rather than as applied in this case. A law that limits speech or religion is "overly broad" if in some circumstances it might unconstitutionally limit or chill these precious rights. By not extending the concept of "overbreadth" to Eighth Amendment rights, the Court in effect creates a hierarchy of rights, with First Amendment rights receiving greater protection.

[d] In this case, detention—a physical state—can either be "punishment" (not allowed before trial) or "regulation" (allowed before trial). Can Congress and the Court simply label pretrial detention as a "regulation" to get around inconvenient legal obstacles? Why are some payments civil judgments and others criminal fines? What makes a loss a "punishment"?

[e] While limiting preventive detention to the most serious crimes is reasonable, that only indicates that society is willing to accept a greater risk of crime while on bail by those charged with less serious crimes; it does not logically mean that the risk of repeating is any greater.

[f] In this paragraph, the majority finds precedent to support the Act, a critical aspect of the validity and legitimacy of a judicial opinion. Are these examples close enough to the situation of a person held before trial to be suitable precedent or can they be "distinguished"?

[g] Does a congressional finding have to be empirically or scientifically true?

[h] Does adherence to a libertarian spirit of constitutional rights prevent the government from developing new methods to deal with unusually grave threats from criminals? Is JUSTICE MARSHALL being conservative here in that he is not willing to consider any new crime-fighting measures?

[i] Does it make any difference that the Act identifies as potential pretrial detainees individuals who have been *indicted* by the government for crimes? Can this reasoning extend to a draft of all able-bodied males between the ages of seventeen and twenty-one who are not serving in the military into work camps because they are the most crime prone group in society and require supervision for the public safety?

[j] There is apparent illogic here; yet this illogical aspect of the bail provision has been accepted for centuries in the no-bail rule for capital crimes. This would not be the first time that a technically illogical constitutional rule has gained acceptance through a combination of age-old usage and convenience.

[k] Do you agree that Congress and the majority justices have decided to ignore the Bill of Rights? Or is the majority correct in reading the Eighth Amendment as not guaranteeing an absolute right to bail but rather fair bail amounts where granted?

COLEMAN v. ALABAMA

399 U.S. 1, 90 S.Ct. 1999, 26 L.Ed.2d 387 (1970)

MR. JUSTICE BRENNAN announced the judgment of the Court and delivered the following opinion.

Petitioners were convicted in an Alabama Circuit Court of assault with intent to murder in the shooting of one Reynolds after he and his wife parked their car on an Alabama highway to change a flat tire. The Alabama Court of Appeals affirmed, * * * and the Alabama Supreme Court denied review. * * * We granted certiorari. * * * We vacate and remand.

Petitioners * * * argue that the preliminary hearing prior to their indictment was a "critical stage" of the prosecution and that Alabama's failure to provide them with appointed counsel at the hearing therefore unconstitutionally denied them the assistance of counsel.
* * *

II

This Court has held that a person accused of crime "requires the guiding hand of counsel at every step in the proceedings against him," * * * and that that constitutional principle is not limited to the presence of counsel at trial. "It is central to that principle that in addition to counsel's presence at trial, the accused is guaranteed that he need not stand alone against the State at any stage of the prosecution, formal or informal, in court or out, where counsel's absence might derogate from the accused's right to a fair trial."

* * * Accordingly, "the principle of *Powell v. Alabama* [this volume] and succeeding cases requires that we scrutinize *any* pretrial confrontation of the accused to determine whether the presence of his counsel is necessary to preserve the defendant's basic right to a fair trial as affected by his right meaningfully to cross-examine the witnesses against him and to have effective assistance of counsel at the trial itself. It calls upon us to analyze whether potential substantial prejudice to defendant's rights inheres in the particular confrontation and the ability of counsel to help avoid that prejudice." * * * Applying this test, the Court has held that "critical stages" include the pretrial type of arraignment where certain rights may be sacrificed or lost, * * * and the pretrial lineup, * * * *Cf. Miranda v. Arizona*, [this volume], where the Court held that the privilege against compulsory self-incrimination includes a right to counsel at a pretrial custodial interrogation. See also *Massiah v. United States*, [this volume].

The preliminary hearing is not a required step in an Alabama prosecution. The prosecutor may seek an indictment directly from the grand jury without a preliminary hearing. * * * The opinion of the Alabama Court of Appeals in this case instructs us that under Alabama law the sole purposes of a preliminary hearing are to determine whether there is sufficient evidence against the accused to warrant presenting his case to the grand jury, and, if so, to fix bail if the offense is bailable. * * * The court continued:

"At the preliminary hearing * * * the accused is not required to advance any defenses, and failure to do so does not preclude him from availing himself of every defense he may have upon the trial of the case. Also *Pointer v. State of Texas* [380 U.S. 400 (1965)] bars the admission of testimony given at a pre-trial proceeding where the accused did not have the benefit of cross-examination by and through counsel. Thus, nothing occurring at the preliminary hearing in absence of counsel can substantially prejudice the rights of the accused on trial."* * *

This Court is of course bound by this construction of the governing Alabama law. * * *   [a] However, from the fact that in cases where the accused has no lawyer at the hearing the Alabama courts prohibit the State's use at trial of anything that occurred at the hearing, it does not follow that the Alabama preliminary hearing is not a "critical stage" of the State's criminal process. The determination whether the hearing is a "critical stage" requiring the provision of counsel depends, as noted, upon an analysis "whether potential substantial prejudice to defendant's rights inheres in the * * * confrontation and the ability of counsel to help avoid that prejudice." * * * Plainly the guiding hand of counsel at the preliminary hearing is essential to protect the indigent accused against an erroneous or improper prosecution. First, the lawyer's skilled examination and cross-examination of witnesses may expose fatal weaknesses in the State's case that may lead the magistrate to refuse to bind the accused over. Second, in any event, the skilled interrogation of witnesses by an experienced lawyer can fashion a vital impeachment tool for use in cross-examination of the State's witnesses at the trial, or preserve testimony favorable to the accused of a witness who does not appear at the trial.   Third, trained counsel can more effectively discover the case the State has against his client and make possible the preparation of a proper defense to meet that case at the trial. Fourth, counsel can also be influential at the preliminary hearing in making effective arguments for the accused on such matters as the necessity for an early psychiatric examination or bail. [b]

The inability of the indigent accused on his own to realize these advantages of a lawyer's assistance compels the conclusion that the Alabama preliminary hearing is a "critical stage" of the State's criminal process at which the accused is "as much entitled to such aid [of counsel] * * * as at the trial itself." * * *

[The case was remanded to the Alabama courts to determine if actual prejudice was suffered in this case.]

[JUSTICES BLACK, DOUGLAS and WHITE concurred in separate opinions or notes. Justice Blackmun did not participate in the decision.]

[JUSTICE HARLAN concurred with the Court's ruling on the right of counsel, although basing it on due process grounds; he dissented from the scope of the remand order.]

MR. CHIEF JUSTICE BURGER, dissenting.

I agree that as a matter of *sound policy* counsel should be made available to all persons subjected to a preliminary hearing and that this should be provided either by statute or by the rulemaking process.   However, I cannot accept the notion that the Constitution commands it because it is a "criminal prosecution." * * *

MR. JUSTICE STEWART, with whom THE CHIEF JUSTICE joins, dissenting.

* * *

* * * Even the *Miranda* [above] decision does not require counsel to be present at "pretrial custodial interrogation." That case simply held that the constitutional guarantee against compulsory self-incrimination prohibits the introduction at the trial of statements made by the defendant during custodial interrogation if the *Miranda* "guidelines" were not followed. * * *

* * *

The petitioners have simply not alleged that anything that happened at the preliminary hearing turned out in this case to be critical to the fairness of their *trial*. They have not alleged that they were affirmatively prejudiced at the trial by anything that occurred at the preliminary hearing. They have not pointed to any affirmative advantage they would have enjoyed at the trial if they had had a lawyer at their preliminary hearing.

* * *

* * * I would hold, therefore, that the absence of counsel at the preliminary hearing deprived the petitioners of no constitutional rights. Accordingly, I would affirm these convictions.

*   *   *   *   *   *   *   *   *   *   *

COMMENTS

[a]   At this point it would appear that Coleman's argument based on the lack of counsel at the preliminary hearing would fail, since the case at this point is that no incriminating evidence could be used against him.

[b] In order to establish the preliminary hearing as a "critical stage" JUSTICE BRENNAN, for the majority, relied on the general functional importance of this process to defendants.

GERSTEIN v. PUGH

420 U.S. 103, 95 S.Ct. 854, 43 L.Ed.2d 54 (1975)

MR. JUSTICE POWELL delivered the opinion of the Court.

The issue in this case is whether a person arrested and held for trial under a prosecutor's information is constitutionally entitled to a judicial determination of probable cause for pretrial restraint of liberty.

I

[Petitioners were arrested and charged with serious offenses under a prosecutor's information; they remained in jail because the charges against one carried a potential life sentence and another could not make bail.]

In Florida, indictments are required only for prosecution of capital offenses. Prosecutors may charge all other crimes by information, without a prior preliminary hearing and without obtaining leave of court. * * * [Under Florida law then in force, filing an information precluded a preliminary hearing and habeas corpus hearings to test whether probable cause existed to hold suspects. A special procedure allowed for a probable cause hearing after 30 days. Arraignments were often delayed for a month.] As a result, a person charged by information could be detained for a substantial period solely on the decision of a prosecutor.

Respondents * * * filed a class action against Dade County officials in the Federal District Court, claiming a constitutional right to a judicial hearing on the issue of probable cause and requesting declaratory and injunctive relief. * * * Petitioner Gerstein, the State Attorney for Dade County, was one of several defendants.

* * *

II

As framed by the proceedings below, this case presents two issues: whether a person arrested and held for trial on an information is entitled to a judicial determination of probable cause for detention, and if so, whether the adversary hearing ordered by the District Court and approved by the Court of Appeals is required by the Constitution.

A

Both the standards and procedures for arrest and detention have been derived from the Fourth Amendment and its common-law antecedents. * * * The standard for arrest is probable cause, defined in terms of facts and circumstances "sufficient to warrant a prudent man in believing that the [suspect] had committed or was committing an offense." * * * This standard, like those for searches and seizures, represents a necessary accommodation between the individual's right to liberty and the State's duty to control crime. * * *

To implement the Fourth Amendment's protection against unfounded invasions of liberty and privacy, the Court has required that the existence of probable cause be decided by a neutral and detached magistrate whenever possible. The classic statement of this principle appears in *Johnson v. United States*, 333 U.S. 10, 13-14 (1948):

> "The point of the Fourth Amendment, which often is not grasped by zealous officers, is not that it denies law enforcement the support of the usual inferences which reasonable men draw from evidence. Its protection consists in requiring that those inferences be drawn by a neutral and detached magistrate instead of being judged by the officer engaged in the often competitive enterprise of ferreting out crime."

* * *

Maximum protection of individual rights could be assured by requiring a magistrate's review of the factual justification prior to any arrest, but such a requirement would constitute an intolerable handicap for legitimate law enforcement. Thus, while the Court has expressed a preference for the use of arrest warrants when feasible, * * * it has never invalidated an arrest supported by probable cause solely because the officers failed to secure a warrant. * * *

Under this practical compromise, a policeman's on-the-scene assessment of probable cause provides legal justification for arresting a person suspected of crime, and for a brief period of detention to take the administrative steps incident to arrest. Once the suspect is in custody, however, the reasons that justify dispensing with the magistrate's neutral judgment evaporate. There no longer is any danger that the suspect will escape or commit further crimes while the police submit their evidence to a magistrate. And,

while the State's reasons for taking summary action subside, the suspect's need for a neutral determination of probable cause increases significantly. The consequences of prolonged detention may be more serious than the interference occasioned by arrest. Pretrial confinement may imperil the suspect's job, interrupt his source of income, and impair his family relationships. * * * Even pretrial release may be accompanied by burdensome conditions that effect a significant restraint of liberty. * * * When the stakes are this high, the detached judgment of a neutral magistrate is essential if the Fourth Amendment is to furnish meaningful protection from unfounded interference with liberty. Accordingly, we hold that the Fourth Amendment requires a judicial determination of probable cause as a prerequisite to extended restraint of liberty following arrest.

This result has historical support in the common law that has guided interpretation of the Fourth Amendment. * * * At common law it was customary, if not obligatory, for an arrested person to be brought before a justice of the peace shortly after arrest. * * * The justice of the peace would "examine" the prisoner and the witnesses to determine whether there was reason to believe the prisoner had committed a crime. If there was, the suspect would be committed to jail or bailed pending trial. If not, he would be discharged from custody. * * * The initial determination of probable cause also could be reviewed by higher courts on a writ of habeas corpus. * * * This practice furnished the model for criminal procedure in America immediately following the adoption of the Fourth Amendment, * * * and there are indications that the Framers of the Bill of Rights regarded it as a model for a "reasonable" seizure. * * *

B

Under the Florida procedures challenged here, a person arrested without a warrant and charged by information may be jailed or subjected to other restraints pending trial without any opportunity for a probable cause determination. Petitioner defends this practice on the ground that the prosecutor's decision to file an information is itself a determination of probable cause that furnishes sufficient reason to detain a defendant pending trial. Although a conscientious decision that the evidence warrants prosecution affords a measure of protection against unfounded detention, we do not think prosecutorial judgment standing alone meets the requirements of the Fourth Amendment.   Indeed, we think the Court's previous decisions compel disapproval of the Florida procedure. * * *   [I]n *Coolidge v. New Hampshire*, 403 U.S. 443, 449-453 (1971), the Court held that a prosecutor's responsibility to law enforcement is inconsistent with the constitutional role of a neutral and detached magistrate.   We reaffirmed that principle in *Shadwick v. City of Tampa*, 407 U.S. 345 (1972), and held that probable cause for the issuance of an arrest warrant must be determined by someone independent of police and prosecution. * * *   In holding that the prosecutor's assessment of probable cause is not sufficient alone to justify restraint of liberty pending trial, we do not imply that the accused is entitled to judicial oversight or review of the decision to prosecute. Instead, we adhere to the Court's prior holding that a judicial hearing is not prerequisite to prosecution by information. * * *

III

Both the District Court and the Court of Appeals held that the determination of probable cause must be accompanied by the full panoply of adversary safeguards—counsel, confrontation, cross-examination, and compulsory process for witnesses.   A full preliminary hearing of this sort is modeled after the procedure used in many States to determine whether the evidence justifies going to trial under an information or presenting the case to a grand jury. * * *   When the hearing takes this form, adversary procedures are customarily employed. The importance of the issue to both the State and the accused justifies the presentation of witnesses and full exploration of their testimony on cross-examination. This kind of hearing also requires appointment of counsel for indigent defendants.   *Coleman v. Alabama*, [this volume].   And, as the hearing assumes increased importance and the procedures become more complex, the likelihood that it can be held promptly after arrest diminishes. * * *

These adversary safeguards are not essential for the probable cause determination required by the Fourth Amendment.   The sole issue is whether there is probable cause for detaining the arrested person pending further proceedings. This issue can be determined reliably without an adversary hearing.   The standard is the same as that for arrest.   That standard—probable cause to believe the suspect has committed a crime—traditionally has been decided by a magistrate in a nonadversary proceeding on hearsay and written testimony, and the Court has approved these informal modes of proof. * * *

The use of an informal procedure is justified not only by the lesser consequences of a probable cause determination but also by the nature of the determination itself. [a] It does not require the fine resolution of conflicting evidence that a reasonable-doubt or even a preponderance standard demands, and credibility determinations are seldom crucial in deciding whether the evidence supports a reasonable belief in guilt. * * * This is not to say that confrontation and cross-examination might not enhance the reliability of probable cause determinations in some cases. In most cases, however, their value would be too slight to justify holding, as a matter of constitutional principle, that these formalities and safeguards designed for trial must also be employed in making the Fourth Amendment determination of probable cause.

Because of its limited function and its nonadversary character, the probable cause determination is not a "critical stage" in the prosecution that would require appointed counsel. * * *

Although we conclude that the Constitution does not require an adversary determination of probable cause, we recognize that state systems of criminal procedure vary widely. There is no single preferred pretrial procedure, and the nature of the probable cause determination usually will be shaped to accord with a State's pretrial procedure viewed as a whole. While we limit our holding to the precise requirement of the Fourth Amendment, we recognize the desir-

ability of flexibility and experimentation by the States. It may be found desirable, for example, to make the probable cause determination at the suspect's first appearance before a judicial officer, * * * or the determination may be incorporated into the procedure for setting bail or fixing other conditions of pretrial release. In some States, existing procedures may satisfy the requirement of the Fourth Amendment. Others may require only minor adjustment, such as acceleration of existing preliminary hearings. Current proposals for criminal procedure reform suggest other ways of testing probable cause for detention. Whatever procedure a State may adopt, it must provide a fair and reliable determination of probable cause as a condition for any significant pretrial restraint of liberty, and this determination must be made by a judicial officer either before or promptly after arrest.

      * * *

MR. JUSTICE STEWART, with whom MR. JUSTICE DOUGLAS, MR. JUSTICE BRENNAN, AND MR. JUSTICE MARSHALL join, concurring.

I concur in Parts I and II of the Court's opinion, since the Constitution clearly requires at least a timely judicial determination of probable cause as a prerequisite to pretrial detention. * * *

Having determined that Florida's current pretrial detention procedures are constitutionally inadequate, I think it is unnecessary to go further by way of dicta. In particular, I would not, in the abstract, attempt to specify those procedural protections that constitutionally need *not* be accorded incarcerated suspects awaiting trial.

Specifically, I see no need in this case for the Court to say that the Constitution extends less procedural protection to an imprisoned human being than is required to test the propriety of garnishing a commercial bank account; * * * the custody of a refrigerator; * * * the temporary suspension of a public school student; * * * or the suspension of a driver's license. * * *

* * * * * * * * * *

COMMENT

[a] There is another practical concern. Probable cause is said by the courts to be the same "common sense" determination, whether made by police or magistrates. If the Court were to hold that a probable cause hearing before a magistrate required an adversary hearing, it would lead to significant complications in the law concerning police probable cause determinations. The majority apparently decided that such complexity was not worth the potential benefits, discounted against the costs, of adversary probable cause hearings.

COUNTY OF RIVERSIDE v. McLAUGHLIN

500 U.S. 44, 111 S.Ct. 1661, 114 L.Ed.2d 49 (1991)

JUSTICE O'CONNOR delivered the opinion of the Court.

In *Gerstein v. Pugh*, [this volume] this Court held that the Fourth Amendment requires a prompt judicial determination of probable cause as a prerequisite to an extended pretrial detention following a warrantless arrest. This case requires us to define what is "prompt" under *Gerstein*. [a]

I

This is a class action brought under 42 U.S.C. § 1983 challenging the manner in which the County of Riverside, California (County), provides probable cause determinations to persons arrested without a warrant. At issue is the County's policy of combining probable cause determinations with its arraignment procedures. Under County policy, * * * arraignments must be conducted without unnecessary delay and, in any event, within two days of arrest. This two-day requirement excludes from computation weekends and holidays. Thus, an individual arrested without a warrant late in the week may in some cases be held for as long as five days before receiving a probable cause determination. Over the Thanksgiving holiday, a 7-day delay is possible.
* * *

[The federal District Court ruled that to satisfy *Gerstein* a judicial determination of probable cause had to be held within 36 hours of arrest except in emergencies. The Court of Appeals] determined that the County's policy of providing probable cause determinations at arraignment within 48 hours was "not in accord with *Gerstein*'s requirement of a determination 'promptly after arrest'" because no more than 36 hours were needed "to complete the administrative steps incident to arrest." * * *
* * *

III
A

In *Gerstein*, this Court held unconstitutional Florida procedures under which persons arrested without a warrant could remain in police custody for 30 days or more without a judicial determination of probable cause. [*Gerstein* balanced the] important competing interests [of public safety and personal liberty and job and family interests by requiring a "prompt" probable cause hearing.]
* * *

In so doing, we gave proper deference to the demands of federalism. We recognized that "state systems of criminal procedure vary widely" in the nature and number of pretrial procedures they provide, and we noted that there is no single "preferred" approach. * * * Our purpose in *Gerstein* was to make clear that the Fourth Amendment requires every State to provide prompt determinations of probable cause, but that the Constitution does not impose on the States a rigid procedural framework. Rather, individual States may choose to comply in different ways. [b]

Inherent in *Gerstein*'s invitation to the States to experiment and adapt was the recognition that the Fourth Amendment does not compel an immediate determination of probable cause upon completing the administrative steps incident to arrest. Plainly, if a probable cause hearing is constitutionally compelled the moment a suspect is finished being "booked," there is no room whatsoever for "flexibility and experimentation by the States." * * * Incorporating probable cause determinations "into the procedure for setting bail or fixing other conditions of pretrial release"— which *Gerstein* explicitly contemplated, * * *—would be impossible. Waiting even a few hours so that a bail hearing or arraignment could take place at the same time as the probable cause determination would amount to a constitutional violation. Clearly, *Gerstein* is not that inflexible. [c]

Notwithstanding *Gerstein*'s discussion of flexibility, the Ninth Circuit Court of Appeals held that no flexibility was permitted. It construed *Gerstein* as "requir[ing] a probable cause determination to be made *as soon as the administrative steps incident to arrest were completed*, and that such steps should require only a brief period." * * * This same reading is advanced by the dissent. * * * The foregoing discussion readily demonstrates the error of this approach. *Gerstein* held that probable cause determinations must be prompt—not immediate. The Court explained that "flexibility and experimentation" were "desirab[le]"; that "[t]here is no single preferred pretrial procedure"; and that "the nature of the probable cause determination usually will be shaped to

accord with a State's pretrial procedure viewed as a whole." * * * The Court of Appeals and the dissent disregard these statements, relying instead on selective quotations from the Court's opinion. As we have explained, *Gerstein* struck a balance between competing interests; a proper understanding of the decision is possible only if one takes into account both sides of the equation.

The dissent claims to find support for its approach in the common law. It points to several statements from the early 1800's to the effect that an arresting officer must bring a person arrested without a warrant before a judicial officer "'as soon as he *reasonably* can.'"* * * This vague admonition offers no more support for the dissent's inflexible standard than does *Gerstein*'s statement that a hearing follow "promptly after arrest." * * * As mentioned at the outset, the question before us today is what is "prompt" under *Gerstein*. We answer that question by recognizing that *Gerstein* struck a balance between competing interests.

B

Given that *Gerstein* permits jurisdictions to incorporate probable cause determinations into other pretrial procedures, some delays are inevitable. For example, where, as in Riverside County, the probable cause determination is combined with arraignment, there will be delays caused by paperwork and logistical problems. Records will have to be reviewed, charging documents drafted, appearance of counsel arranged, and appropriate bail determined. On weekends, when the number of arrests is often higher and available resources tend to be limited, arraignments may get pushed back even further. In our view, the Fourth Amendment permits a reasonable postponement of a probable cause determination while the police cope with the everyday problems of processing suspects through an overly burdened criminal justice system.

But flexibility has its limits; *Gerstein* is not a blank check. A State has no legitimate interest in detaining for extended periods individuals who have been arrested without probable cause. The Court recognized in *Gerstein* that a person arrested without a warrant is entitled to a fair and reliable determination of probable cause and that this determination must be made promptly.

Unfortunately, as lower court decisions applying *Gerstein* have demonstrated, it is not enough to say that probable cause determinations must be "prompt." This vague standard simply has not provided sufficient guidance. Instead, it has led to a flurry of systemic challenges to city and county practices, putting federal judges in the role of making legislative judgments and overseeing local jailhouse operations. * * *

Our task in this case is to articulate more clearly the boundaries of what is permissible under the Fourth Amendment. Although we hesitate to announce that the Constitution compels a specific time limit, it is important to provide some degree of certainty so that States and counties may establish procedures with confidence that they fall within constitutional bounds. Taking into account the competing interests articulated in *Gerstein*, we believe that a jurisdiction that provides judicial determinations of probable cause within 48 hours of arrest will, as

a general matter, comply with the promptness requirement of *Gerstein*. For this reason, such jurisdictions will be immune from systemic challenges. **[d]**

This is not to say that the probable cause determination in a particular case passes constitutional muster simply because it is provided within 48 hours. Such a hearing may nonetheless violate *Gerstein* if the arrested individual can prove that his or her probable cause determination was delayed unreasonably. Examples of unreasonable delay are delays for the purpose of gathering additional evidence to justify the arrest, a delay motivated by ill will against the arrested individual, or delay for delay's sake. In evaluating whether the delay in a particular case is unreasonable, however, courts must allow a substantial degree of flexibility. Courts cannot ignore the often unavoidable delays in transporting arrested persons from one facility to another, handling late-night bookings where no magistrate is readily available, obtaining the presence of an arresting officer who may be busy processing other suspects or securing the premises of an arrest, and other practical realities. **[e]**

Where an arrested individual does not receive a probable cause determination within 48 hours, the calculus changes. In such a case, the arrested individual does not bear the burden of proving an unreasonable delay. Rather, the burden shifts to the government to demonstrate the existence of a bona fide emergency or other extraordinary circumstance. The fact that in a particular case it may take longer than 48 hours to consolidate pretrial proceedings does not qualify as an extraordinary circumstance. Nor, for that matter, do intervening weekends. A jurisdiction that chooses to offer combined proceedings must do so as soon as is reasonably feasible, but in no event later than 48 hours after arrest.

* * * In advocating a 24-hour rule, the dissent would compel Riverside County—and countless others across the Nation—to speed up its criminal justice mechanisms substantially, presumably by allotting local tax dollars to hire additional police officers and magistrates. There may be times when the Constitution compels such direct interference with local control, but this is not one. As we have explained, *Gerstein* clearly contemplated a reasonable accommodation between legitimate competing concerns. We do no more than recognize that such accommodation can take place without running afoul of the Fourth Amendment.

Everyone agrees that the police should make every attempt to minimize the time a presumptively innocent individual spends in jail. One way to do so is to provide a judicial determination of probable cause immediately upon completing the administrative steps incident to arrest—*i.e.*, as soon as the suspect has been booked, photographed, and fingerprinted. As the dissent explains, several States, laudably, have adopted this approach. The Constitution does not compel so rigid a schedule, however. Under *Gerstein*, jurisdictions may choose to combine probable cause determinations with other pretrial proceedings, so long as they do so promptly. This necessarily means that only certain proceedings are candidates for combination. Only those proceedings that arise very early in the pretrial process—such as bail hearings and arraignments—may be

chosen. Even then, every effort must be made to expedite the combined proceedings. * * *

* * *

JUSTICE MARSHALL, with whom JUSTICE BLACKMUN and JUSTICE STEVENS join, dissenting.

In *Gerstein v. Pugh*, [this volume], this Court held that an individual detained following a warrantless arrest is entitled to a "prompt" judicial determination of probable cause as a prerequisite to any further restraint on his liberty. * * * I agree with JUSTICE SCALIA that a probable-cause hearing is sufficiently "prompt" under *Gerstein* only when provided immediately upon completion of the "administrative steps incident to arrest." * * *

JUSTICE SCALIA, dissenting.

* * *

I

[Justice Scalia argued that the Fourth Amendment drew its meaning from the common law. Citing many eighteenth and nineteenthth century sources, he sought to establish that the framers of the Constitution understood that an arrested person was to be brought before a magistrate as soon as the officer could do so. He further argued that this understanding of the common law was implicit in the reasoning and more general language of *Gerstein v. Pugh* [this volume]. He said that *Gerstein*'s language favoring or allowing states to combine probable cause hearings with other processes was not intended to overrule the Constitutional requirement of a prompt (as-soon-as-possible) hearing.]

II

I have finished discussing what I consider the principal question in this case, which is what factors determine whether the postarrest determination of probable cause has been (as the Fourth Amendment requires) "reasonably prompt." The Court and I both accept two of those factors, completion of the administrative steps incident to arrest and arranging for a magistrate's probable-cause determination. Since we disagree, however, upon a third factor—the Court believing, as I do not, that "combining" the determination with other proceedings justifies a delay—we necessarily disagree as well on the subsequent question, which can be described as the question of the absolute time limit. Any determinant of "reasonable promptness" that is within the control of the State (as the availability of the magistrate, the personnel and facilities for completing administrative procedures incident to arrest, and the timing of "combined procedures" all are) must be restricted by some outer time limit, or else the promptness guarantee would be worthless. * * * At some point, legitimate reasons for delay become illegitimate.

I do not know how the Court calculated its outer limit of 48 hours. I must confess, however, that I do not know how I would do so either, if I thought that one justification for delay could be the State's "desire to combine." There are no standards for "combination," and as we acknowledged in *Gerstein* the various procedures that might be combined "vary widely" from State to State. * * * So as far as I can discern (though I cannot pretend to be able to do better), the Court simply decided that, given the administrative convenience of "combining," it is not so bad for an utterly innocent person to wait 48 hours in jail before being released.

If one eliminates (as one should) that novel justification for delay, determining the outer boundary of reasonableness is a more objective and more manageable task. We were asked to undertake it in *Gerstein*, but declined—wisely, I think, since we had before us little data to support any figure we might choose. As the Court notes, however, *Gerstein* has engendered a number of cases addressing not only the scope of the procedures "incident to arrest," but also their duration. The conclusions reached by the judges in [post-*Gerstein*] cases, * * * are surprisingly similar. I frankly would prefer even more information, and for that purpose would have supported reargument on the single question of an outer time limit. The data available are enough to convince me, however, that certainly no more than 24 hours is needed.

[JUSTICE SCALIA then reviewed numerous cases which uphold a 24 hour rule.]

      * * *

In my view, absent extraordinary circumstances, it is an "unreasonable seizure" within the meaning of the Fourth Amendment for the police, having arrested a suspect without a warrant, to delay a determination of probable cause for the arrest either (1) for reasons unrelated to arrangement of the probable-cause determination or completion of the steps incident to arrest, or (2) beyond 24 hours after the arrest. Like the Court, I would treat the time limit as a presumption; when the 24 hours are exceeded the burden shifts to the police to adduce unforeseeable circumstances justifying the additional delay.

* * *

*   *   *   *   *   *   *   *   *   *   *

COMMENTS

[a] This is a classic example of a case being decided on general principles, leaving important operative details for the future as cases arise.

[b] A later court does not simply *cite* an earlier case as precedent; it *explains* the earlier case in ways that help justify the present ruling.

[c] As against the dissenters who opt for shorter time periods before a *Gerstein* hearing, the majority defends its ruling on the basis of the value of federalism, *i.e.*, a desire to not impose inflexible rules on the states where not mandated by the Constitution.

[d] A precise time limit provides clarity to local jurisdictions and prevents a multiplicity of lawsuits over whether a vague standard is reasonable.

[e] By allowing challenges to unreasonable delays under 48 hours, the Court may by implication be admitting that the Constitution does not provide a clear rule and that they may indeed be engaging in a form of judicial legislation.

WAYTE v. UNITED STATES

470 U.S. 598, 105 S.Ct. 1524, 84 L.Ed.2d 547 (1985)

JUSTICE POWELL delivered the opinion of the Court.

* * *

I

[Under the Selective Service Act, the president issued a proclamation requiring twenty-year old males to register with the Selective Service System (SSS or the Draft). [a] Wayte, the petitioner, fell within that class but did not register. Instead, he wrote letters to government officials, including the president, stating that he would not register on grounds of conscience. Not receiving a reply, Wayte continued to write to government officials notifying them that he was not registering and that he would encourage resistance to draft registration.]

[The Selective Service System adopted a policy of "passive enforcement:" it would enforce the law against only those resisters who advised the SSS they were not registering, instead of actively investigating to find all who failed to register. The SSS wrote to petitioner and other known violators to inform them of their duty to register, request that they comply or explain why not, and warn that a violation could result in criminal prosecution and specified penalties.]

[A year later the SSS] transmitted to the Department of Justice, for investigation and potential prosecution, the names of petitioner and 133 other young men identified under its passive enforcement system. * * * [After further screening out names, the Department of Justice referred the remaining names to the FBI for additional inquiry and to the United States Attorneys for the districts in which the nonregistrants resided. Petitioner's name was one of those referred.] [b]

[Instead of immediate prosecution, FBI agents were sent to interview nonregistrants to persuade them to change their minds; this was known as the "beg" policy. After six months the Justice Department instructed United States Attorneys not to initiate prosecutions under the Act. Instead the] President announced a grace period to afford nonregistrants a further opportunity to register without penalty. * * * Petitioner still did not register. [c]

[The Justice Department then began to prepare to prosecute, even though internal memoranda indicated an awareness that under the "passive enforcement" and "beg" policies, those most likely to be prosecuted were "liable to be vocal proponents of nonregistration" or persons "with religious or moral objections." The department also surmised that it would be accused of retaliating against nonregistrants for exercising First Amendment Rights.] The Department was advised, however, that Selective Service could not develop a more "active" enforcement system for quite some time. * * *

II

[Wayte moved to dismiss the government's prosecution of him on the grounds that he was being targeted for prosecution, out of an estimated 674,000 nonregistrants, for exercising his First Amendment rights and because of discriminatory prosecution policy.]

[Approximately 8.3 million men registered out of 9 million who were required to do so; the SSS referred 286 nonregistrants to the Department of Justice, and of them, 16 were indicted.   Those not indicted were either exempt from the draft, could not be found, or were still under investigation.]

[The district court dismissed the prosecution because it found that others similarly situated to Wayte were not prosecuted and further that he was selected for prosecution on the discriminatory ground of exercising First Amendment rights. **[d]** The court of appeals reversed, agreeing that prosecution of 13 out of 674,000 nonregistrants was a discriminatory choice but finding that the reasons for this discrimination were not impermissible: the government did not prosecute Wayte because of his protest activities, it was simply aware that its passive enforcement policy was more likely to result in the prosecution of protesters. Additionally, the court of appeals found] two legitimate explanations for the Government's passive enforcement system: (i) the identities of nonreported nonregistrants were not known, and (ii) nonregistrants who expressed their refusal to register made clear their willful violation of the law.

Recognizing both the importance of the question presented and a division in the Circuits, we granted certiorari on the question of selective prosecution. * * * We now affirm.

III

In our criminal justice system, the Government retains "broad discretion" as to whom to prosecute. * * * "[S]o long as the prosecutor has probable cause to believe that the accused committed an offense defined by statute, the decision whether or not to prosecute, and what charge to file or bring before a grand jury, generally rests entirely in his discretion." *Bordenkircher v. Hayes*, 434 U.S. 357, 364 (1978). This broad discretion rests largely on the recognition that the decision to prosecute is particularly ill-suited to judicial review. **[e]** Such factors as the strength of the case, the prosecution's general deterrence value, the Government's enforcement priorities, and the case's relationship to the Government's overall enforcement plan are not readily susceptible to the kind of analysis the courts are competent to undertake. Judicial supervision in this area, moreover, entails systemic costs of particular concern. Examining the basis of a prosecution delays the criminal proceeding, threatens to chill law enforcement by subjecting the prosecutor's motives and decision-making to outside inquiry, and may undermine prosecutorial effectiveness by revealing the Government's enforcement policy. All these are substantial concerns that make the courts properly hesitant to examine the decision whether to prosecute.

As we have noted in a slightly different context, however, although prosecutorial discretion is broad, it is not "'unfettered.' Selectivity in the enforcement of criminal laws is * * * subject to constitutional constraints." In particular, the decision to prosecute may not be "'deliberately based upon an unjustifiable standard such as race, religion, or other arbitrary classification,'" * * * including the exercise of protected statutory and constitutional rights. [f] * * *

It is appropriate to judge selective prosecution claims according to ordinary equal protection standards. [g] * * * Under our prior cases, these standards require petitioner to show both that the passive enforcement system had a discriminatory effect and that it was motivated by a discriminatory purpose. * * * All petitioner has shown here is that those eventually prosecuted, along with many not prosecuted, reported themselves as having violated the law. He has not shown that the enforcement policy selected nonregistrants for prosecution on the basis of their speech. Indeed, he could not have done so given the way the "beg" policy was carried out. The Government did not prosecute those who reported themselves but later registered. Nor did it prosecute those who protested registration but did not report themselves or were not reported by others. In fact, the Government did not even investigate those who wrote letters to Selective Service criticizing registration unless their letters stated affirmatively that they had refused to comply with the law. * * * The Government, on the other hand, did prosecute people who reported themselves or were reported by others but who did not publicly protest. These facts demonstrate that the Government treated all reported nonregistrants similarly. It did not subject vocal nonregistrants to any special burden. Indeed, those prosecuted in effect selected themselves for prosecution by refusing to register after being reported and warned by the Government. [h]

Even if the passive policy had a discriminatory effect, petitioner has not shown that the Government intended such a result. The evidence he presented demonstrated only that the Government was aware that the passive enforcement policy would result in prosecution of vocal objectors and that they would probably make selective prosecution claims. As we have noted, however: "'Discriminatory purpose' . . . implies more than . . . intent as awareness of consequences. It implies that the decisionmaker . . . selected or reaffirmed a particular course of action at least in part 'because of,' not merely 'in spite of,' its adverse effects upon an identifiable group." * * * In the present case, petitioner has not shown that the Government prosecuted him *because of* his protest activities. Absent such a showing, his claim of selective prosecution fails. [i]

IV

Petitioner also challenges the passive enforcement policy directly on First Amendment grounds. In particular, he claims that "[e]ven though the [Government's passive] enforcement policy did not overtly punish protected speech as such, it inevitably created a content-based regulatory system with a concomitantly disparate, content-based impact on nonregistrants." * * * This Court has held that when, as here, "'speech' and 'nonspeech' elements are combined in the same course of conduct, a sufficiently important governmental interest in regulating the nonspeech element can justify incidental limitations on First Amendment freedoms." *United States v. O'Brien*, 391 U.S. 367, 376 (1968). * * *

Government regulation is justified

> "if it is within the constitutional power of the Government; if it furthers an important or substantial governmental interest; if the governmental interest is unrelated to the suppression of free expression; and if the incidental restriction on alleged First Amendment freedoms is no greater than is essential to the furtherance of that interest." * * * [j]

In the present case, neither the first nor third condition is disputed.

There can be no doubt that the passive enforcement policy meets the second condition. Few interests can be more compelling than a nation's need to ensure its own security. * * * Unless a society has the capability and will to defend itself from the aggressions of others, constitutional protections of any sort have little meaning. Recognizing this the Framers listed "provid[ing] for the common defence," U.S. Const., Preamble, as a motivating purpose for the Constitution and granted Congress the power to "provide for the common Defence and general Welfare of the United States," Art. I, §8, cl. 1. * * * This Court, moreover, has long held that the power "* * * to classify and conscript manpower for military service is 'beyond question.'" * * * With these principles in mind, the three reasons the Government offers in defense of this particular enforcement policy are sufficiently compelling to satisfy the second *O'Brien* requirement—as to either those who reported themselves or those who were reported by others.

First, by relying on reports of nonregistration, the Government was able to identify and prosecute violators without further delay. Although it still was necessary to investigate those reported to make sure that they were required to register and had not, the Government did not have to search actively for the names of these likely violators. Such a search would have been difficult and costly at that time. Indeed, it would be a costly step in any "active" prosecution system involving thousands of nonregistrants. The passive enforcement program thus promoted prosecutorial efficiency. Second, the letters written to Selective Service provided strong, perhaps conclusive evidence of the nonregistrant's intent not to comply—one of the elements of the offense. Third, prosecuting visible nonregistrants was thought to be an effective way to promote general deterrence, especially since failing to proceed against publicly known offenders would encourage others to violate the law.

The passive enforcement policy also meets the final requirement of the *O'Brien* test, for it placed no more limitation on speech than was necessary to ensure registration for the national defense. Passive enforcement not only did not subject "vocal" nonregistrants to any special burden, * * * but also was intended to be only an interim enforcement system. Although Selective Service was engaged in developing an active enforcement program when it investigated petitioner, it had by then found no practicable way of obtaining the names and current addresses of likely nonregistrants. Eventually, it obtained them by matching state driver's license records with Social Security files. It took some time, however, to obtain the necessary authorizations and to set up this system. Passive enforcement was the only effective interim solution available to carry out the Government's compelling interest.

[JUSTICE POWELL concluded by noting that extended to its logical extreme, Wayte's argument would confer immunity from prosecution on anyone who self-reported, by claiming that the purpose of the prosecution was to punish an individual for protesting.]

V

We conclude that the Government's passive enforcement system together with its "beg" policy violated neither the First nor Fifth Amendment. Accordingly, we affirm the judgment of the Court of Appeals.

It is so ordered.

[JUSTICE MARSHALL dissented, joined by JUSTICE BRENNAN, on the grounds that Wayte had a right to an evidentiary hearing to discover Government documents relevant to his claim of selective prosecution. Wayte claimed that the suppressed evidence supported his claim that the Government had designed a prosecutorial scheme that purposefully discriminated against those who had chosen to exercise their First Amendment right to oppose draft registration. Justice Marshall's lengthy analysis concluded that Wayte met the legal criteria for an evidentiary hearing and that it was, therefore, an abuse of discretion for the appeals court to not allow an evidentiary discovery hearing. Since Wayte was entitled to additional evidence that the government withheld, his claim could not be rejected on the merits until he was granted access to those records.]

* * * * * * * * * *

COMMENTS

[a] Even in the era of the volunteer army, males must register in case the military draft were to be reinstated.

[b] Is it fair, whether legal or not, for the government to prosecute only those who are sufficiently courageous or foolhardy to "ask for it"?

[c] Is prosecutorial policy is partly influenced by politics? To what extent should it be? The draft ended after the enormously unpopular Vietnam War when a large part of the population was disenchanted with the military. It would be hard to imagine a "beg" policy in times of great national unity such as a popular active war.

[d] What is wrong with the government choosing whom to prosecute? If there were a riot, for example, it makes sense to prosecute the leaders. If it is not feasible to prosecute every nonregistrant, does it make sense to prosecute the most visible to increase the deterrent effect of the registration law? Should a collateral consequence be a factor in a prosecutor's policy?

[e] Prosecutorial discretion is the basic rule. How can it be abused? If the courts are not competent to overview prosecution policy, is any other agency? Executive officers, from the president to a mayor? or legislatures, from Congress to a city council or county commission? Can or should public opinion influence prosecutors' policies?

[f] A constitutional standard insures that courts will not substitute their policy judgments for those of prosecutors.   The exception to the general rule exists to prevent flagrant abuses of prosecutorial power.

[g] A federal defendant relies on the Fifth Amendment, which contains a due process clause but no equal protection clause. But the Court applies an "equality standard" as part of due process, as a matter of fundamental fairness.

[h] What does equal treatment mean here?   To Wayte all 674,000 nonregistrants should be treated equally. To the prosecution all who made their status known were treated equally.

[i] The Court enhances the discrimination exception to the general rule of prosecutorial discretion.   The courts will not interfere with a prosecution unless the basis is impermissible *and* the government *intended* to prosecute a crime for that impermissible reason.

[j] Does such a rule devalue the First Amendment? Would the opposite rule make it difficult to maintain order?

UNITED STATES v. BAGLEY

473 U.S. 667, 105 S.Ct. 3375, 87 L.Ed.2d 481 (1985)

JUSTICE BLACKMUN announced the judgment of the Court and delivered an opinion of the Court except as to Part III.

In *Brady v. Maryland*, 373 U.S. 83, 87 (1963), this Court held that "the suppression by the prosecution of evidence favorable to an accused upon request violates due process where the evidence is material either to guilt or punishment." [a] The issue in the present case concerns the standard of materiality to be applied in determining whether a conviction should be reversed because the prosecutor failed to disclose requested evidence that could have been used to impeach Government witnesses.

I

[Bagley, indicted on 15 federal narcotics and firearms charges, filed a discovery motion before trial, requesting the names and addresses of witnesses that the government intended to call at trial, their prior criminal records, and "any deals, promises or inducements made to witnesses in exchange for their testimony." The Government's principal witnesses were O'Connor and Mitchell, state law enforcement officers employed as private security guards who acted as undercover agents for the federal Bureau of Alcohol, Tobacco and Firearms (ATF). The Government's response to the discovery motion did not disclose that any "deals, promises or inducements" had been made to O'Connor or Mitchell. The Government did produce affidavits that detailed the undercover activity of O'Connor and Mitchell.] [b]

[Bagley waived a jury and was tried by the trial judge. O'Connor and Mitchell testified about both the firearms and the narcotics charges. The court found Bagley guilty on the narcotics charges, but not guilty on the firearms charges. After the conviction, Bagley filed a Freedom of Information Act request and discovered that O'Connor and Mitchell were paid under contract for their undercover activity and testimony. Bagley moved for a new trial, arguing that the Government's failure to disclose the contracts, which he could have used to impeach O'Connor and Mitchell, violated his right to due process under *Brady v. Maryland*. The trial judge found that the nondisclosure would have had no effect on the verdict and thus denied the motion for a new trial. The judge reasoned that most of the undercover agents' testimony was on the firearms charges of which Bagley was acquitted; their testimony regarding the narcotics charge tended to be favorable to Bagley's defense that the valium in question was his personal prescription; in that case, impeaching these witnesses would not have helped Bagley.]

[The Court of Appeals reversed, first, because it disagreed with the trial judge's view that the testimony of O'Connor and Mitchell was exculpatory on the narcotics charges. Secondly, the Court of Appeals theorized that "the Government's failure to disclose the requested *Brady* information that respondent could have used to conduct an effective cross-examination impaired respondent's right to confront adverse witnesses" in violation of the rule of *Davis v. Alaska*, 415 U.S. 308 (1974)— that the denial of the right of effective cross-examination is a constitutional error of the first magnitude that requires automatic reversal.]

We granted certiorari, * * * and we now reverse.

II

The holding in *Brady v. Maryland* requires disclosure only of evidence that is both favorable to the accused and "material either to guilt or to punishment." * * * [c]

The *Brady* rule is based on the requirement of due process. Its purpose is not to displace the adversary system as the primary means by which truth is uncovered, but to ensure that a miscarriage of justice does not occur. Thus, the prosecutor is not required to deliver his entire file to defense counsel, but only to disclose evidence favorable to the accused that, if suppressed, would deprive the defendant of a fair trial. * * * [d]

In *Brady* * * * the prosecutor failed to disclose exculpatory evidence. In the present case, the prosecutor failed to disclose evidence that the defense might have used to impeach the Government's witnesses by showing bias or interest. Impeachment evidence, however, as well as exculpatory evidence, falls within the *Brady* rule. * * * Such evidence is "evidence favorable to an accused," * * * so that, if disclosed and used effectively, it may make the difference between conviction and acquittal. * * *

* * *

* * * In *Giglio v. United States*, [405 U.S. 150 (1972)] the Government failed to disclose impeachment evidence similar to the evidence at issue in the present case, that is, a promise made to the key Government witness that he would not be prosecuted if he testified for the Government. This Court said:

> "When the 'reliability of a given witness may well be determinative of guilt or innocence,' nondisclosure of evidence affecting credibility falls within th[e] general rule [of *Brady*]. We do not, however, automatically require a new trial whenever 'a combing of the prosecutors' files after the trial has disclosed evidence possibly useful to the defense but not likely to have changed the verdict. * * * A finding of materiality of the evidence is required under *Brady*. * * * A new trial is required if 'the false testimony could * * * in any reasonable likelihood have affected the judgment of the jury. * * * *'" * * *

Thus, the Court of Appeals' holding is inconsistent with our precedents. [e]

Moreover, the court's reliance on *Davis v. Alaska* for its "automatic reversal" rule is misplaced. In *Davis*, the defense sought to cross-examine a crucial prosecution witness concerning his probationary status as a juvenile delinquent. The defense intended by this cross-examination to show that the witness might have made a faulty identification of the defendant in order to shift suspicion away from himself or because he feared that his probationary status would be jeopardized if he did not satisfactorily assist the police and prosecutor in obtaining a conviction. Pursuant to a state rule of procedure and a state statute making juvenile adjudications inadmissible, the trial judge prohibited the defense from conducting the cross-examination. This Court reversed the defendant's conviction, ruling that the direct restriction on the scope of cross-examination denied the defendant "the right of effective cross-examination" which "would be constitutional error of the first magnitude and no amount of showing of want of prejudice would cure it." * * *

The present case, in contrast, does not involve any direct restriction on the scope of cross-examination. The defense was free to cross-examine the witnesses on any relevant subject, including possible bias or interest resulting from inducements made by the Government. The constitutional error, if any, in this case was the Government's failure to assist the defense by disclosing information that might have been helpful in conducting the cross-examination. As discussed above, such suppression of evidence amounts to a constitutional violation only if it deprives the defendant of a fair trial. Consistent with "our overriding concern with the justice of the finding of guilt," * * * a constitutional error occurs, and the conviction must be reversed, only if the evidence is material in the sense that its suppression undermines confidence in the outcome of the trial.

III

A

It remains to determine the standard of materiality applicable to the nondisclosed evidence at issue in this case. Our starting point is the framework for evaluating the materiality of *Brady* evidence established in *United States v. Agurs* [427 U.S. 97 (1976)]. The Court in *Agurs* distinguished three situations involving the discovery, after trial, of information favorable to the accused that had been known to the prosecution but unknown to the defense. The first situation was the prosecutor's knowing use of perjured testimony or, equivalently, the prosecutor's knowing failure to disclose that testimony used to convict the defendant was false. The Court noted the well-established rule that "a conviction obtained by the knowing use of perjured testimony is fundamentally unfair, and must be set aside if there is any reasonable likelihood that the false testimony could have affected the judgment of the jury." * * * Although this rule is stated in terms that treat the knowing use of perjured testimony as error subject to harmless-error review, it may as easily be stated as a materiality standard under which the fact that testimony is perjured is considered material unless failure to disclose it would be harmless beyond a reasonable doubt. The Court in *Agurs* justified this standard of materiality on the ground that the knowing use of perjured testimony involves prosecutorial misconduct and, more importantly, involves "a corruption of the truth-seeking function of the trial process." * * *

At the other extreme is the situation in *Agurs* itself, where the defendant does not make a *Brady* request and the prosecutor fails to disclose certain evidence favorable to the accused. The Court rejected a harmless-error rule in that situation, because under that rule every nondisclosure is treated as error, thus imposing on the prosecutor a constitutional duty to deliver his entire file to defense counsel. * * *   At the same time, the Court rejected a standard that would require the defendant to demonstrate that the evidence if disclosed probably would have resulted in acquittal. * * * The Court reasoned: "If the standard applied to the usual motion for a new trial based on newly discovered evidence were the same when the evidence was in the State's possession as when it was found in a neutral source, there would be no special significance to the prosecutor's obligation to serve the cause of justice." * * *   The standard of materiality applicable in the absence of a specific *Brady* request is therefore stricter than the harmless-error standard but more lenient to the defense than the newly-discovered-evidence standard.

The third situation identified by the Court in *Agurs* is where the defense makes a specific request and the prosecutor fails to disclose responsive evidence.   The Court did not define the standard of materiality applicable in this situation, but suggested that the standard might be more lenient to the defense than in the situation in which the defense makes no request or only a general request. * * *   The Court also noted: "When the prosecutor receives a specific and relevant request, the failure to make any response is seldom, if ever, excusable." * * *

The Court has relied on and reformulated the *Agurs* standard for the materiality of undisclosed evidence in two subsequent cases arising outside the *Brady* context.   In neither case did the Court's discussion of the *Agurs* standard distinguish among the three

situations described in *Agurs*.   In *United States v. Valenzuela-Bernal*, 458 U.S. 858, 874 (1982), the Court held that due process is violated when testimony is made unavailable to the defense by Government deportation of witnesses "only if there is a reasonable likelihood that the testimony could have affected the judgment of the trier of fact."   And in *Strickland v. Washington*, [this volume], the Court held that a new trial must be granted when evidence is not introduced because of the incompetence of counsel only if "there is a reasonable probability that, but for counsel's unprofessional errors, the result of the proceeding would have been different." * * *   The *Strickland* Court defined a "reasonable probability" as "a probability sufficient to undermine confidence in the outcome." * * *

We find the *Strickland* formulation of the *Agurs* test for materiality sufficiently flexible to cover the "no request," "general request," and "specific request" cases of prosecutorial failure to disclose evidence favorable to the accused: The evidence is material only if there is a reasonable probability that, had the evidence been disclosed to the defense, the result of the proceeding would have been different. A "reasonable probability" is a probability sufficient to undermine confidence in the outcome.

* * *

B

In the present case, we think that there is a significant likelihood that the prosecutor's response to respondent's discovery motion misleadingly induced defense counsel to believe that O'Connor and Mitchell could not be impeached on the basis of bias or interest arising from inducements offered by the Government. * * *

The District Court, nonetheless, found beyond a reasonable doubt that, had the information that the Government held out the possibility of reward to its witnesses been disclosed, the result of the criminal prosecution would not have been different. If this finding were sustained by the Court of Appeals, the information would be immaterial even under the standard of materiality applicable to the prosecutor's knowing use of perjured testimony. [Because the Court of Appeals disagreed with the District Court's factual finding of harmless error, the judgment was reversed; the case was remanded to the Court of Appeals to determine whether the result of the trial would have been different if the inducements offered to O'Connor and Mitchell had been disclosed to the defense.]

JUSTICE POWELL took no part in the decision of this case.

[JUSTICE WHITE, joined by THE CHIEF JUSTICE and JUSTICE REHNQUIST concurred in the judgment. He agreed that Bagley "is not entitled to have his conviction overturned unless he can show that the evidence withheld by the Government was 'material.'" He found no reason to elaborate on the standard, believing that one, flexible, fact-related standard of materiality was sufficient.] [f]

JUSTICE MARSHALL, with whom JUSTICE BRENNAN joins, dissenting.

When the Government withholds from a defendant evidence that might impeach the prosecution's *only witnesses*, that failure to disclose cannot be deemed harmless error. * * *

I

* * *

* * * Whenever the Government fails, in response to a request, to disclose impeachment evidence relating to the credibility of its key witnesses, the truth-finding process of trial is necessarily thrown askew. The failure to disclose evidence affecting the overall credibility of witnesses corrupts the process to some degree in all instances; * * * but when "the 'reliability of a given witness may well be determinative of guilt or innocence,'" * * * and when "the Government's case depend[s] almost entirely on" the testimony of a certain witness, * * * evidence of that witness' possible bias simply may not be said to be irrelevant, or its omission harmless. * * *

II

* * * [In Parts II-A and II-B, JUSTICE MARSHALL reviewed the import of the *Brady* rule. The upshot of his analysis is that the prosecutor's duty is to divulge all evidence that reasonably appears favorable to the defendant, erring on the side of disclosure.]

C

The Court, however, offers a complex alternative. It defines the right not by reference to the possible usefulness of the particular evidence in preparing and presenting the case, but retrospectively, by reference to the likely effect the evidence will have on the outcome of the trial. Thus, the Court holds that due process does not require the prosecutor to turn over evidence unless the evidence is "material," and the Court states that evidence is "material" "only if there is a reasonable probability that, had the evidence been disclosed to the defense, the result of the proceeding would have been different." * * * . Although this looks like a post-trial standard of review * * * it is not. Instead, the Court relies on this review standard to define the contours of the defendant's constitutional right to certain material prior to trial. By adhering to the view articulated in [*Agurs*]—that there is no constitutional duty to disclose evidence unless nondisclosure would have a certain impact on the trial—the Court permits prosecutors to withhold with impunity large amounts of undeniably favorable evidence, and it imposes on prosecutors the burden to identify and disclose evidence pursuant to a pretrial standard that virtually defies definition.

The standard for disclosure that the Court articulates today enables prosecutors to avoid disclosing obviously exculpatory evidence while acting well within the bounds of their constitutional obligation. * * *

* * *

I simply cannot agree with the Court that the due process right to favorable evidence recognized in *Brady* was intended to become entangled in prosecutorial determinations of the likelihood that particular information would affect the outcome of trial. Almost a decade of lower court practice with *Agurs* convinces me that courts and prosecutors have come to pay "too much deference to the federal

common law policy of discouraging discovery in criminal cases, and too little regard to due process of law for defendants." * * * Apparently anxious to assure that reversals are handed out sparingly, the Court has defined a rigorous test of materiality. Eager to apply the "materiality" standard at the pretrial stage, as the Court permits them to do, prosecutors lose sight of the basic principles underlying the doctrine. I would return to the original theory and promise of *Brady* and reassert the duty of the prosecutor to disclose all evidence in his files that might reasonably be considered favorable to the defendant's case. No prosecutor can know prior to trial whether such evidence *will* be of consequence at trial; the mere fact that it might be, however, suffices to mandate disclosure.

D

In so saying, I recognize that a failure to divulge favorable information should not result in reversal in all cases. It may be that a conviction should be affirmed on appeal despite the prosecutor's failure to disclose evidence that reasonably might have been deemed potentially favorable prior to trial. The state's interest in nondisclosure at trial is minimal, and should therefore yield to the readily apparent benefit that full disclosure would convey to the search for truth. After trial, however, the benefits of disclosure may at times be tempered by the state's legitimate desire to avoid retrial when error has been harmless. However, in making the determination of harmlessness, I would apply our normal constitutional error test and reverse unless it is clear beyond a reasonable doubt that the withheld evidence would not have affected the outcome of the trial. See *Chapman v. California*, 386 U.S. 18 (1967). * * *

* * *

In this case, it is readily apparent that the undisclosed information would have had an impact on the defense presented at trial, and perhaps on the judgment. Counsel for Bagley argued to the trial judge that the Government's two key witnesses had fabricated their accounts of the drug distributions, but the trial judge rejected the argument for lack of any evidence of motive. * * * These key witnesses, it turned out, were each to receive monetary rewards whose size was contingent on the usefulness of their assistance. These rewards "served only to strengthen any incentive to testify falsely in order to secure a conviction." * * * To my mind, no more need be said; this nondisclosure could not have been harmless. I would affirm the judgment of the Court of Appeals.

[JUSTICE STEVENS dissented separately.]

* * * * * * * * * * *

COMMENTS

[a] Material evidence is defined as that "quality of evidence which tends to influence the trier of fact because of its logical connection with the issue. Evidence which has an effective influence or bearing on question in issue is 'material.'" *Black's Law Dictionary*, Fifth Edition, p. 881.

[b] The defense request and the government's affidavits were also made under the Jencks Act which requires "the prosecutor to disclose, after direct examination of a Government witness and on the defendant's motion, any statement of the witness in the Government's possession that relates to the subject matter of the witness' testimony."

[c] A rule that required disclosure of evidence favorable to the defendant without a materiality element might require prosecutors to open their entire files to the defense. Some experts recommend this as good practice, but the Supreme Court is reluctant to impose a drastic change in practice on the states.

[d] The Court noted that the *Brady* rule modifies the purely adversary theory of the common law criminal trial. The prosecutor is not simply an adversarial party, but is also a state officer of justice, who must be interested in seeking the truth.

[e] Notice that the Court of Appeals believed the rule to be automatic reversal.

[f] As a result of this concurrence and the dissents, only two justices, BLACK-MUN and O'CONNOR, joined in Part III of the majority opinion.

ASHE v. SWENSON

397 U.S. 436, 90 S.Ct. 1189, 25 L.Ed.2d 469 (1970)

MR. JUSTICE STEWART delivered the opinion of the Court.

In *Benton v. Maryland*, 395 U.S. 784, the Court held that the Fifth Amendment guarantee against double jeopardy is enforceable against the States through the Fourteenth Amendment. The question in this case is whether the State of Missouri violated that guarantee when it prosecuted the petitioner a second time for armed robbery in the circumstances here presented.

[Six men at an early morning poker game were rudely interrupted by three or four masked and armed robbers. The robbers fled in a stolen car. Three men were arrested walking along a road near the abandoned stolen car a short time later and Ashe was arrested by another officer "some distance away."]

The four were subsequently charged with seven separate offenses—the armed robbery of each of the six poker players and the theft of the car. In May 1960 the petitioner went to trial on the charge of robbing Donald Knight, one of the participants in the poker game. At the trial the State called Knight and three of his fellow poker players as prosecution witnesses. Each of them described the circumstances of the holdup and itemized his own individual losses. [Proof of the robbery and losses] was unassailable [and consistent]. * * * But the State's evidence that the petitioner had been one of the robbers was weak. Two of the witnesses thought that there had been only three robbers altogether, and could not identify the petitioner as one of them. Another of the victims, who was the petitioner's uncle by marriage, said that at the "patrol station" he had positively identified each of the other three men accused of the holdup, but could say only that the petitioner's voice "sounded very much like" that of one of the robbers. The fourth participant in the poker game did identify the petitioner, but only by his "size and height, and his actions."

[Ashe's defense consisted entirely of the cross-examination of prosecution witnesses.]

The trial judge instructed the jury that if it found that the petitioner was one of the participants in the armed robbery, the theft of "any money" from Knight would sustain a conviction. He also instructed the jury that if the petitioner was one of the robbers, he was guilty under the law even if he had not personally robbed Knight. The jury—though not instructed to elaborate upon its verdict—found the petitioner "not guilty due to insufficient evidence."

Six weeks later the petitioner was brought to trial again, this time for the robbery of another participant in the poker game, a man named Roberts. The petitioner filed a motion to dismiss, based on his previous acquittal. The motion was overruled, and the second trial began. The witnesses were for the most part the same, though this time their testimony was substantially stronger on the issue of the petitioner's identity. [a] For example, two witnesses who at the first trial had been wholly unable to identify the petitioner as one of the robbers, now testified that his features, size, and mannerisms matched those of one of their assailants. Another witness who before had identified the petitioner only by his size and actions now also remembered him by the unusual sound of his voice. The State further refined its case at the second trial by declining to call one of the participants in the poker game whose identification testimony at the first trial had been conspicuously negative. [b] The case went to the jury on instructions virtually identical to those given at the first trial. This time the jury found the petitioner guilty, and he was sentenced to a 35-year term in the state penitentiary.

[The conviction was upheld by the Missouri Supreme Court; Ashe also lost in a federal habeas corpus proceeding, the federal district court ruling that it was bound by the rule of *Hoag v. New Jersey*, 356 U.S. 464 (1958).]

* * * [T]he operative facts here are virtually identical to those of *Hoag v. New Jersey, supra.* * * *

Viewing the question presented solely in terms of Fourteenth Amendment due process—whether the course that New Jersey had pursued had "led to fundamental unfairness," * * *—this Court declined to reverse the judgment of conviction, because "in the circumstances shown by this record, we cannot say that petitioner's later prosecution and conviction violated due process." * * * The Court found it unnecessary to decide whether "collateral estoppel"—the principle that bars relitigation between the same parties of issues actually determined at a previous trial—is a due process requirement in a state criminal trial, since it accepted New Jersey's determination that the petitioner's previous acquittal did not in any event give rise to such an estoppel. * * * And in the view the Court took of the issues presented, it did not, of course, even approach consideration of whether collateral estoppel is an ingredient of the Fifth Amendment guarantee against double jeopardy.

The doctrine of *Benton v. Maryland, supra,* puts the issues in the present case in a perspective quite different from that in which the issues were perceived in *Hoag v. New Jersey, supra.* The question is no longer whether collateral estoppel is a requirement of due process, but whether it is a part of the Fifth Amendment's guarantee against double jeopardy. [c] And if collateral estoppel is embodied in that guarantee, then its applicability in a particular case is no longer a matter to be left for state court determination within the broad bounds of "fundamental fairness," but a matter of constitutional fact we must decide through an examination of the entire record. * * *

"Collateral estoppel" is an awkward phrase, but it stands for an extremely important principle in our adversary system of justice. It means simply that when an issue of ultimate fact has once been determined by a valid and final judgment, that issue cannot again be litigated between the same parties in any future lawsuit. Although first developed in civil litigation, collateral estoppel has been an established rule of federal criminal law at least since this Court's decision more than 50 years ago in *United States v. Oppenheimer*, 242 U.S. 85 [1916]. As Mr. Justice Holmes put the matter in that case, "It cannot be that the safeguards of the person, so often and so rightly mentioned with solemn reverence, are less than those that protect from a liability in debt." * * * As a rule of federal law, therefore, "[i]t is much too late to suggest that this principle is not fully applicable to a former judgment in a criminal case, either because of lack of 'mutuality' or because the judgment may reflect only a belief that the Government had not met the higher burden of proof exacted in such cases for the Government's evidence as a whole although not necessarily as to every link in the chain." * * *

The federal decisions have made clear that the rule of collateral estoppel in criminal cases is not to be applied with the hypertechnical and archaic approach of a 19th century pleading book, but with realism and rationality. Where a previous judgment of acquittal was based upon a general verdict, as is usually the case, this approach requires a court to "examine the record of a prior proceeding, taking into account the pleadings, evidence, charge, and other relevant matter, and conclude whether a rational jury could have grounded its verdict upon an issue other than that which the defendant seeks to foreclose from consideration." The inquiry "must be set in a practical frame and viewed with an eye to all the circumstances of the proceedings." * * * Any test more technically restrictive would, of course, simply amount to a rejection of the rule of collateral estoppel in criminal proceedings, at least in every case where the first judgment was based upon a general verdict of acquittal.

Straightforward application of the federal rule to the present case can lead to but one conclusion. For the record is utterly devoid of any indication that the first jury could rationally have found that an armed robbery had not occurred, or that Knight had not been a victim of that robbery. The single rationally conceivable issue in dispute before the jury was whether the petitioner had been one of the robbers. And the jury by its verdict found that he had not. The federal rule of law, therefore, would make a second prosecution for the robbery of Roberts wholly impermissible. **[d]**

The ultimate question to be determined, then, in the light of *Benton v. Maryland, supra*, is whether this established rule of federal law is embodied in the Fifth Amendment guarantee against double jeopardy. We do not hesitate to hold that it is. For whatever else that constitutional guarantee may embrace, * * * it surely protects a man who has been acquitted from having to "run the gantlet" a second time. * * *

The question is not whether Missouri could validly charge the petitioner with six separate offenses for the robbery of the six poker players. It is not whether he could have received a total of six punishments if he had been convicted in a single trial of robbing the six victims. It is simply whether, after a jury determined by its verdict that the petitioner was not one of the robbers, the State could constitutionally hale him before a new jury to litigate that issue again.

After the first jury had acquitted the petitioner of robbing Knight, Missouri could certainly not have brought him to trial again upon that charge. Once a jury had determined upon conflicting testimony that there was at least a reasonable doubt that the petitioner was one of the robbers, the State could not present the same or different identification evidence in a second prosecution for the robbery of Knight in the hope that a different jury might find that evidence more convincing. The situation is constitutionally no different here, even though the second trial related to another victim of the same robbery. For the name of the victim, in the circumstances of this case, had no bearing whatever upon the issue of whether the petitioner was one of the robbers.

In this case the State in its brief has frankly conceded that following the petitioner's acquittal, it treated the first trial as no more than a dry run for the second prosecution: "No doubt the prosecutor felt the state had a provable case on the first charge and, when he lost, he did what every good attorney would do—he refined his presentation in light of the turn of events at the first trial." But this is precisely what the constitutional guarantee forbids.

The judgment is reversed. * * *

[JUSTICE BLACK concurred, stating that in his opinion the due process approach in prior cases was never appropriate.]

[JUSTICE HARLAN concurring, noting that the Court's opinion does not include the "same transaction" concept put forward in JUSTICE BRENNAN's opinion.]

MR. JUSTICE BRENNAN, whom MR. JUSTICE DOUGLAS and MR. JUSTICE MARSHALL join, concurring.

I agree that the Double Jeopardy Clause incorporates collateral estoppel as a constitutional requirement and therefore join the Court's opinion. However, even if the rule of collateral estoppel had been inapplicable to the facts of this case, it is my view that the Double Jeopardy Clause nevertheless bars the prosecution of petitioner a second time for armed robbery. The two prosecutions, the first for the robbery of Knight and the second for the robbery of Roberts, grew out of one criminal episode, and therefore I think it clear on the facts of this case that the Double Jeopardy Clause prohibited Missouri from prosecuting petitioner for each robbery at a different trial. *Abbate v. United States*, 359 U.S. 187, 196-201 (1959) (separate opinion).

* * *

In my view, the Double Jeopardy Clause requires the prosecution, except in most limited circumstances, to join at one trial all the charges against a defendant that grow out of a single criminal act, occurrence, episode, or transaction. This "same transaction" test of "same offence" not only enforces the ancient prohibition against vexatious multiple prosecutions embodied in the Double Jeopardy Clause, but responds as well to the increasingly widespread recognition that the consolidation in one lawsuit of all issues arising out of a single transaction or occurrence best promotes justice, economy, and convenience. * * *

* * * Some flexibility in the structuring of criminal litigation is also desirable and consistent with our traditions. But the Double Jeopardy Clause stands as a constitutional barrier against possible tyranny by the overzealous prosecutor. The considerations of justice, economy, and convenience that have propelled the movement for consolidation of civil cases

apply with even greater force in the criminal context because of the constitutional principle that no man shall be vexed more than once by trial for the same offense.   Yet, if the Double Jeopardy Clause were interpreted by this Court to incorporate the "same evidence" test, criminal defendants would have less protection from multiple trials than civil defendants. * * *

The present case highlights the hazards of abuse of the criminal process inherent in the "same evidence" test and demonstrates the necessity for the "same transaction" test.   The robbery of the poker game involved six players. * * * The robbers also stole a car.   Seven separate informations were filed against the petitioner, one covering each of the robbery victims, and the seventh covering the theft of the car.   Petitioner's first trial was under the information charging the robbery of Knight.   Since Missouri has offered no justification for not trying the other informations at that trial, it is reasonable to infer that the other informations were held in reserve to be tried if the State failed to obtain a conviction on the charge of robbing Knight.   Indeed, the State virtually concedes as much since it argues that the "same evidence" test is consistent with such an exercise of prosecutorial discretion.

* * *

The prosecution plainly organized its case for the second trial to provide the links missing in the chain of identification evidence that was offered at the first trial. * * * One must experience a sense of uneasiness with any double-jeopardy standard that would allow the State this second chance to plug up the holes in its case.

The constitutional protection against double jeopardy is empty of meaning if the State may make "repeated attempts" to touch up its case by forcing the accused to "run the gantlet" as many times as there are victims of a single episode.

* * *

MR. CHIEF JUSTICE BURGER, dissenting.

* * * Nothing in the language or gloss previously placed on [the Double Jeopardy Clause] of the Fifth Amendment remotely justifies the treatment that the Court today accords to the collateral-estoppel doctrine. Nothing in the purpose of the authors of the Constitution commands or even justifies what the Court decides today; this is truly a case of expanding a sound basic principle beyond the bounds—or needs—of its rational and legitimate objectives to preclude harassment of an accused.

[The CHIEF JUSTICE stated the facts in a light more favorable to the state.]

II

The concept of double jeopardy and our firm constitutional commitment is against repeated trials "for the same offence." This Court, like most American jurisdictions, has expanded that part of the Constitution into a "same evidence" test. For example, in *Blockburger v. United States*, 284 U.S. 299, 304 (1932), it was stated, so far as here relevant, that

"the test to be applied to determine whether there are two offenses or only one, is whether each provision [*i.e.*, each charge] requires *proof of a fact which the other does not.*" (Emphasis added.)

Clearly and beyond dispute the charge against Ashe in the second trial required proof of a fact—robbery of Roberts—which the charge involving Knight did not. The Court, therefore, has had to reach out far beyond the accepted offense-defining rule to reach its decision in this case. What it has done is to superimpose on the same-evidence test a new and novel collateral-estoppel gloss. **[e]**

* * *

*   *   *   *   *   *   *   *   *   *

COMMENTS

[a] Just as in stage plays, a witness usually turns in a stronger "performance" if given a second opportunity.

[b] Does this tactic strike you as fair? Does it make a difference that this is done by a state's prosecutor?

[c] The intervening years between *Hoag* in 1958 and *Ashe* in 1970, of course, were the years of the "Due Process Revolution" when most important portions of the Bill of Rights were selectively "incorporated" into the Due Process Clause of the Fourteenth Amendment.

[d] The collateral estoppel rule, then, is not that a defendant can never be tried twice, but that another trial may be permissible if the record indicates that a conviction is possible on other evidence.

[e] Assuming that this is correct, (a) does the Supreme Court have authority to do this? (b) from your reading of the case is the majority's rule one that you favor?

HEATH v. ALABAMA

474 U.S. 82, 106 S.Ct. 433, 88 L.Ed.2d 387 (1985)

JUSTICE O'CONNOR delivered the opinion of the Court.

* * *

I

[Larry Heath, an Alabama resident, hired two men to kill his wife. He drove to Georgia where he met the killers and led them back to his Alabama residence. The men] kidnaped Rebecca Heath from her home. The Heath car, with Rebecca Heath's body inside, was later found on the side of a road in Troup County, Georgia. The cause of death was a gunshot wound in the head. The estimated time of death and the distance from the Heath residence to the spot where Rebecca Heath's body was found are consistent with the theory that the murder took place in Georgia. * * *

Georgia and Alabama authorities pursued dual investigations in which they cooperated to some extent. * * * [Heath was indicted first by Georgia authorities. He confessed and pled guilty to murder for a life sentence (with possible parole in seven years) rather than being subjected to a trial that could lead to a death penalty.]

[Several months after the plea, Heath was indicted, convicted and sentenced to life imprisonment in Alabama for capital murder. His objections on double jeopardy grounds were rejected.]

* * *

II

Successive prosecutions are barred by the Fifth Amendment only if the two offenses for which the defendant is prosecuted are the "same" for double jeopardy purposes. Respondent does not contravene petitioner's contention that the offenses of "murder during a kidnaping" and "malice murder," as construed by the courts of Alabama and Georgia respectively, may be considered greater and lesser offenses and, thus, the "same" offense * * * absent operation of the dual sovereignty principle. * * * We therefore assume, *arguendo*, that, had these offenses arisen under the laws of one State and had petitioner been separately prosecuted for both offenses in that State, the second conviction would have been barred by the Double Jeopardy Clause.

The sole remaining question * * * is whether the dual sovereignty doctrine permits successive prosecutions under the laws of different States which otherwise would be held to "subject [the defendant] for the same offence to be twice put in jeopardy." * * * Although we have not previously so held, we believe the answer to this query is inescapable. The dual sovereignty doctrine, as originally articulated and consistently applied by this Court, compels the conclusion that successive prosecutions by two States for the same conduct are not barred by the Double Jeopardy Clause.

The dual sovereignty doctrine is founded on the common-law conception of crime as an offense against the sovereignty of the government. When a defendant in a single act violates the "peace and dignity" of two sovereigns by breaking the laws of each, he has committed two distinct "offences." *United States v. Lanza*, 260 U.S. 377, 382 (1922). As the Court explained in *Moore v. Illinois*, 14 How. 13, 19 (1852), "[a]n offence, in its legal signification, means the transgression of a law." Consequently, when the same act transgresses the laws of two sovereigns, "it cannot be truly averred that the offender has been twice punished for the same offence; but only that by one act he has committed two offences, for each of which he is justly punishable." * * *

In applying the dual sovereignty doctrine, then, the crucial determination is whether the two entities that seek successively to prosecute a defendant for the same course of conduct can be termed separate sovereigns. This determination turns on whether the two entities draw their authority to punish the offender from distinct sources of power. * * * Thus, the Court has uniformly held that the States are separate sovereigns with respect to the Federal Government because each State's power to prosecute is derived from its own "inherent sovereignty," not from the Federal Government. * * * See *Abbate v. United States*, 359 U.S. 187, 193-194 (1959) (collecting cases); *Lanza, supra*. As stated in *Lanza, supra*, at 382:

"Each government in determining what shall be an offense against its peace and dignity is exercising its own sovereignty, not that of the other.

"It follows that an act denounced as a crime by both national and state sovereignties is an offense against the peace and dignity of both and may be punished by each."

* * *

The States are no less sovereign with respect to each other than they are with respect to the Federal Government. Their powers to undertake criminal prosecutions derive from separate and independent sources of power and authority originally belonging to them before admission to the Union and preserved to them by the Tenth Amendment. * * * The States are equal to each other "in power, dignity and authority, each competent to exert that residuum of sovereignty not delegated to the United States by the Constitution itself." * * * Thus, "[e]ach has the power, inherent in any sovereign, independently to determine what shall be an offense against its authority and to punish such offenses, and in doing so each 'is exercising its own sovereignty, not that of the other.'" * * *

The cases in which the Court has applied the dual sovereignty principle outside the realm of successive federal and state prosecutions illustrate the soundness of this analysis. *United States v. Wheeler*, [435 U.S. 313, 320 (1978)] is particularly instructive because there the Court expressly refused to find that only the State and Federal Governments could be considered distinct sovereigns with respect to each other for double jeopardy purposes, stating that "so restrictive a view of [the dual sovereignty] concept * * * would require disregard of the very words of the Double Jeopardy Clause." * * * Instead, the *Wheeler* Court reiterated the principle that the sovereignty of two prosecuting entities for these purposes is determined by "the ultimate source of the power under which the respective prosecutions were undertaken." * * * On the basis of this reasoning, the Court held that the Navajo Tribe, whose power to prosecute its members for tribal offenses is derived from the Tribe's "primeval sovereignty" rather than a delegation of federal authority, is an independent sovereign from the Federal Government for purposes of the dual sovereignty doctrine. * * *

In those instances where the Court has found the dual sovereignty doctrine inapplicable, it has done so because the two prosecuting entities did not derive their powers to prosecute from independent sources of authority. Thus, the Court has held that successive prosecutions by federal and territorial courts are barred because such courts are "creations emanating from the same sovereignty." * * * Similarly, municipalities that derive their power to try a defendant from the same organic law that empowers the State to prosecute are not separate sovereigns with respect to the State. * * * These cases confirm that it is the presence of independent sovereign authority to prosecute, not the relation between States and the Federal Government in our federalist system, that constitutes the basis for the dual sovereignty doctrine.

* * *

III

Petitioner invites us to restrict the applicability of the dual sovereignty principle to cases in which two governmental entities, having concurrent jurisdiction and pursuing quite different interests, can demonstrate that allowing only one entity to exercise jurisdiction over the defendant will interfere with the unvindicated interests of the second entity and that multiple prosecutions therefore are necessary for the satisfaction of the legitimate interests of both entities. This balancing of interests approach, however, cannot be reconciled with the dual sovereignty principle. This Court has plainly and repeatedly stated that two identical offenses are *not* the "same offence" within the meaning of the Double Jeopardy Clause if they are prosecuted by different sovereigns. * * * If the States are separate sovereigns, as they must be under the definition of sovereignty which the Court consistently has employed, the circumstances of the case are irrelevant.

Petitioner, then, is asking the Court to discard its sovereignty analysis and to substitute in its stead his difficult and uncertain balancing of interests approach. * * * The Court's express rationale for the dual sovereignty doctrine is not simply a fiction that can be disregarded in difficult cases. It finds weighty support in the historical understanding and political realities of the States' role in the federal system and in the words of the Double Jeopardy Clause itself, "nor shall any person be subject for the same *offence* to be twice put in jeopardy of life or limb." * * * (emphasis added). * * *

It is axiomatic that "[in] America, the powers of sovereignty are divided between the government of the Union, and those of the States. They are each sovereign, with respect to the objects committed to it, and neither sovereign with respect to the objects committed to the other." * * * It is as well established that the States, "as political communities, [are] distinct and sovereign, and consequently foreign to each other." * * * The Constitution leaves in the possession of each State "certain exclusive and very important portions of sovereign power." The Federalist No. 9, p. 55 (J. Cooke ed. 1961). [a] Foremost among the prerogatives of sovereignty is the power to create and enforce a criminal code. * * * To deny a State its power to enforce its criminal laws because another State has won the race to the courthouse "would be a shocking and untoward deprivation of the historic right and obligation of the States to maintain peace and order within their confines." * * *

Such a deprivation of a State's sovereign powers cannot be justified by the assertion that under "interest analysis" the State's legitimate penal interests will be satisfied through a prosecution conducted by another State. A State's interest in vindicating its sovereign authority through enforcement of its laws by definition can never be satisfied by another State's enforcement of *its* own laws. Just as the Federal Government has the right to decide that a state prosecution has not vindicated a violation of the "peace and dignity" of the Federal Government, a State must be entitled to decide that a prosecution by another State has not satisfied its legitimate sovereign interest. In recognition of this fact, the Court consistently has endorsed the principle that a single act constitutes an "offence" against each sovereign whose laws are violated by that act. The Court has always understood the words of the Double Jeopardy Clause to reflect this fundamental principle, and we see no reason

why we should reconsider that understanding today.

The judgment of the Supreme Court of Alabama is affirmed. * * *

[JUSTICE BRENNAN, joined by JUSTICE MARSHALL, dissented.]

JUSTICE MARSHALL, with whom JUSTICE BRENNAN joins, dissenting.

* * *

II

* * *

A

Under the constitutional scheme, the Federal Government has been given the exclusive power to vindicate certain of our Nation's sovereign interests, leaving the States to exercise complementary authority over matters of more local concern. The respective spheres of the Federal Government and the States may overlap at times, and even where they do not, different interests may be implicated by a single act. See, *e.g.*, *Abbate v. United States*, 359 U.S. 187 (1959) (conspiracy to dynamite telephone company facilities entails both destruction of property and disruption of federal communications network). Yet were a prosecution by a State, however zealously pursued, allowed to preclude further prosecution by the Federal Government for the same crime, an entire range of national interests could be frustrated. The importance of those federal interests has thus quite properly been permitted to trump a defendant's interest in avoiding successive prosecutions or multiple punishments for the same crime. * * * Conversely, because "the States under our federal system have the principal responsibility for defining and prosecuting crimes," * * * it would be inappropriate—in the absence of a specific congressional intent to pre-empt state action pursuant to the Supremacy Clause—to allow a federal prosecution to preclude state authorities from vindicating "the historic right and obligation of the States to maintain peace and order within their confines." * * *

The complementary nature of the sovereignty exercised by the Federal Government and the States places upon a defendant burdens commensurate with concomitant privileges. Past cases have recognized that the special ordeal suffered by a defendant prosecuted by both federal and state authorities is the price of living in a federal system, the cost of dual citizenship. Every citizen, the Court has noted, "owes allegiance to the two departments, so to speak, and within their respective spheres must pay the penalties which each exacts for disobedience to its laws. In return, he can demand protection from each within its own jurisdiction." * * *

B

Because all but one of the cases upholding the dual sovereignty doctrine have involved the unique relationship between the Federal Government and the States, the question whether a similar rule should exempt successive prosecutions by two different States from the command of the Double Jeopardy Clause is one for which this Court's precedents provide all too little illumination. * * *

Where two States seek to prosecute the same defendant for the same crime in two separate proceedings, the justifi-

cations found in the federal-state context for an exemption from double jeopardy constraints simply do not hold. Although the two States may have opted for different policies within their assigned territorial jurisdictions, the sovereign concerns with whose vindication each State has been charged are identical. Thus, in contrast to the federal-state context, barring the second prosecution would still permit one government to act upon the broad range of sovereign concerns that have been reserved to the States by the Constitution. The compelling need in the federal-state context to subordinate double jeopardy concerns is thus considerably diminished in cases involving successive prosecutions by different States. Moreover, from the defendant's perspective, the burden of successive prosecutions cannot be justified as the *quid pro quo* of dual citizenship.

To be sure, a refusal to extend the dual sovereignty rule to state-state prosecutions would preclude the State that has lost the "race to the courthouse" from vindicating legitimate policies distinct from those underlying its sister State's prosecution. But as yet, I am not persuaded that a State's desire to further a particular policy should be permitted to deprive a defendant of his constitutionally protected right not to be brought to bar more than once to answer essentially the same charges. **[b]**
* * *

[In Part III, JUSTICE MARSHALL discussed the danger of collusion between states to do together what they cannot do alone in bringing successive prosecutions.]

*   *   *   *   *   *   *   *   *   *   *

COMMENTS

[a] *The Federalist*, also known as *The Federalist Papers*, were eighty-five newspaper articles explaining and defending the newly drafted Constitution, written by Alexander Hamilton, John Jay, and James Madison, under the pseudonym "Publius," between October, 1787 and May, 1788. The Constitution had to be ratified by special conventions convened in each of the states and its adoption was not guaranteed. These articles were published in New York to convince the voters in the New York convention to ratify the Constitution. Because of the stature of the authors and the brilliance of the articles, *The Federalist* has become a classic of political theory and a vital source for understanding the Constitution.

[b] This case exemplifies the dilemma of federalism in the American scheme of government. The majority stressed the sovereign nature of the states. Yet, that sovereignty is not absolute. The dissenters stressed the fact that the states are bound together into one federal union under one Constitution. The fact that the Bill of Rights, including the Double Jeopardy Clause, applies the same limitations on both the federal and state governments gives some weight to JUSTICE MARSHALL's dissent; from Heath's perspective, it is the case that he was tried twice for the same crime.

UNITED STATES v. DIXON

__ U.S. __, 113 S.Ct. 2849, 125 L.Ed.2d 556 (1993)

JUSTICE SCALIA announced the judgment of the Court and delivered the opinion of the Court with respect to Parts I, II, and IV, and an opinion with respect to Parts III and V, in which JUSTICE KENNEDY joins.

* * *

I

[Dixon was released on bail for second degree murder on the conditions that he would appear and would not commit "any criminal offense." Violation subjected him, under the bail law, to revocation of release and prosecution for contempt of court.] While awaiting trial, Dixon was arrested and indicted [under the criminal code] for possession of cocaine with intent to distribute. [At a contempt hearing police officers testified about the cocaine deal and Dixon's lawyer cross-examined them.] The court concluded that the Government had established "'beyond a reasonable doubt that [Dixon] was in possession of drugs * * * with the intent to distribute.'" * * * The court therefore found Dixon guilty of criminal contempt * * * [and] sentenced [him] to 180 days in jail. * * * (maximum penalty of six months' imprisonment and $1000 fine). [He later moved to dismiss the cocaine indictment on double jeopardy grounds; the trial court granted the motion.]

[In a consolidated case, Foster was found to be in criminal contempt for wife beating in violation of a civil protection order [CPO] that prohibited assault. For repeated violations, Foster was prosecuted by his wife's attorney and found guilty of contempt by committing acts of assault, but acquitted of charges of threat. The Unites States Attorney later filed an indictment against Foster listing one count of simple assault, three counts of threat, and one count of assault with intent to kill. Foster challenged the indictment.] The trial court denied the double-jeopardy claim * * * [a]

[The cases were heard en banc by the District of Columbia Court of Appeals; relying on *Grady v. Corbin*, 495 U.S. 508 (1990), it ruled that both subsequent prosecutions were barred by the Double Jeopardy Clause.] * * * [T]he Government presented the sole question "[w]hether the Double Jeopardy Clause bars prosecution of a defendant on substantive criminal charges based upon the same conduct for which he previously has been held in criminal contempt of court." * * *

II

* * *

The Double Jeopardy Clause, * * * provides that no person shall "be subject for the same offence to be twice put in jeopardy of life or limb." * * * This protection applies both to successive punishments and to successive prosecutions for the same criminal offense. * * * It is well established that criminal contempt, at least the sort enforced through nonsummary proceedings, is "a crime in the ordinary sense." * * *

We have held that constitutional protections for criminal defendants other than the double jeopardy provision apply in nonsummary criminal contempt prosecutions just as they do in other criminal prosecutions. * * * **[b]** We think it obvious, and today hold, that the protection of the Double Jeopardy Clause likewise attaches. * * *

In both the multiple punishment and multiple prosecution contexts, this Court has concluded that where the two offenses for which the defendant is punished or tried cannot survive the "same-elements" test, the double jeopardy bar applies. * * * See, *e.g.*, *Blockburger v. United States*, 284 U.S. 299, 304 (1932) (multiple punishment). * * * The same-elements test, sometimes referred to as the "*Blockburger*" test, inquires whether each offense contains an element not contained in the other; if not, they are the "same offence" and double jeopardy bars additional punishment and successive prosecution. * * * **[c]**

We recently held in *Grady* that in addition to passing the *Blockburger* test, a subsequent·prosecution must satisfy a "same-conduct" test to avoid the double jeopardy bar. The *Grady* test provides that, "if, to establish an essential element of an offense charged in that prosecution, the government will prove conduct that constitutes an offense for which the defendant has already been prosecuted," a second prosecution may not be had. * * * **[d]**

III

A

The first question before us today is whether *Blockburger* analysis permits subsequent prosecution in this new criminal contempt context, where

judicial order has prohibited criminal act. If it does, we must then proceed to consider whether *Grady* also permits it. * * *

We begin with *Dixon*. The statute applicable in Dixon's contempt prosecution provides that "[a] person who has been conditionally released . . . and who has violated a condition of release shall be subject to . . . prosecution for contempt of court." * * * Obviously, Dixon could not commit an "offence" under this provision until an order setting out conditions was issued. The statute by itself imposes no legal obligation on anyone. Dixon's cocaine possession, although an offense under [the criminal code], was not an offense under [the bail law] until a judge incorporated the statutory drug offense into his release order.

In this situation, in which the contempt sanction is imposed for violating the order through commission of the incorporated drug offense, the later attempt to prosecute Dixon for the drug offense resembles the situation that produced our judgment of double jeopardy in *Harris v. Oklahoma*, 433 U.S. 682 (1977) (*per curiam*). There we held that a subsequent prosecution for robbery with a firearm was barred by the Double Jeopardy Clause, because the defendant had already been tried for felony-murder based on the same underlying felony. We have described our terse *per curiam* in *Harris* as standing for the proposition that, for double jeopardy purposes, "the crime generally described as felony murder" is not "a separate offense distinct from its various elements." * * * So too here, the "crime" of violating a condition of release cannot be abstracted from the "element" of the violated condition. The *Dixon* court order incorporated the entire governing criminal code in the same manner as the *Harris* felony-murder statute incorporated the several enumerated felonies. Here, as in *Harris*, the underlying substantive criminal offense is "a species of lesser-included offense." * * *

* * *

Both the Government, * * * and JUSTICE BLACKMUN contend, * * * that the legal obligation in Dixon's case may serve "interests . . . fundamentally different" from the substantive criminal law, because it derives in part from the determination of a court rather than a determination of the legislature. That distinction seems questionable, since the court's power to establish conditions of release, and to punish their violation, was conferred by statute; the legislature was the ultimate source of both the criminal and the contempt prohibition. More importantly, however, the distinction is of no moment for purposes of the Double Jeopardy Clause, the text of which looks to whether the *offenses* are the same, not the interests that the offenses violate. And this Court stated long ago that criminal contempt, at least in its nonsummary form, "is a crime in every fundamental respect." * * * Because Dixon's drug offense did not include any element not contained in his previous contempt offense, his subsequent prosecution violates the Double Jeopardy Clause.

[The analysis also applied to the simple assault charge against Foster.]

B

The remaining four counts in *Foster*, assault with intent to kill * * *

and threats to injure or kidnap, * * * are not barred under *Blockburger*. * * * On the basis of the same episode [where simple assault was charged], Foster was then indicted for * * * assault with intent to kill. Under governing law, that offense requires proof of specific intent to kill; simple assault does not. * * * Similarly, the contempt offense required proof of knowledge of the CPO, which assault with intent to kill does not. Applying the *Blockburger* elements test, the result is clear: These crimes were different offenses and the subsequent prosecution did not violate the Double Jeopardy Clause.

[Similar analysis shows that the three counts of threatening in *Foster* are not the same offense as tried in the contempt hearing.]

IV

Having found that at least some of the counts at issue here are not barred by the *Blockburger* test, we must consider whether they are barred by the new, additional double jeopardy test we announced three Terms ago in *Grady v. Corbin*. They undoubtedly are, since *Grady* prohibits "a subsequent prosecution if, to establish an essential element of an offense charged in that prosecution [here, assault as an element of assault with intent to kill, or threatening as an element of threatening bodily injury], the government will prove conduct that constitutes an offense for which the defendant has already been prosecuted [here, the assault and the threatening, which conduct constituted the offense of violating the CPO]." * * *

We have concluded, however, that *Grady* must be overruled. Unlike *Blockburger* analysis, whose definition of what prevents two crimes from being the "same offence," * * * has deep historical roots and has been accepted in numerous precedents of this Court, *Grady* lacks constitutional roots. **[e]** The "same-conduct" rule it announced is wholly inconsistent with earlier Supreme Court precedent and with the clear common-law understanding of double jeopardy. * * * [This conclusion was followed by a lengthy case analysis aimed primarily at refuting JUSTICE SOUTER's reading of prior cases.]

* * *

CHIEF JUSTICE REHNQUIST, with whom JUSTICE O'CONNOR and JUSTICE THOMAS join, concurring in part and dissenting in part.

[The CHIEF JUSTICE took the position that there was no double jeopardy bar to any of the indictments against Dixon or Foster, and that *Grady* should be overruled.]

* * *

In my view, *Blockburger*'s same-elements test requires us to focus not on the terms of the particular court orders involved, but on the elements of contempt of court in the ordinary sense. Relying on *Harris v. Oklahoma*, * * * a three-paragraph *per curiam* in an unargued case, JUSTICE SCALIA concludes otherwise today, and thus incorrectly finds * * * that the subsequent prosecutions of Dixon for drug distribution and of Foster for assault violated the Double Jeopardy Clause. In so doing, JUSTICE SCALIA rejects the traditional view—shared by every federal court of appeals and state

supreme court that addressed the issue prior to *Grady*— that, as a general matter, double jeopardy does not bar a subsequent prosecution based on conduct for which a defendant has been held in criminal contempt. I cannot subscribe to a reading of *Harris* that upsets this previously well-settled principle of law. Because the generic crime of contempt of court has different elements than the substantive criminal charges in this case, I believe that they are separate offenses under *Blockburger*. I would therefore limit *Harris* to the context in which it arose: where the crimes in question are analogous to greater and lesser included offenses. The crimes at issue here bear no such resemblance.

* * *

* * * The crimes at issue here, however, cannot be viewed as greater and lesser included offenses, either intuitively or logically. A crime such as possession with intent to distribute cocaine is a serious felony that cannot easily be conceived of as a lesser included offense of criminal contempt, a relatively petty offense as applied to the conduct in this case. * * * ([T]he maximum sentence for possession with intent to distribute cocaine is 15 years in prison). Indeed, to say that criminal contempt is an aggravated form of that offense defies common sense. * * *

* * *

JUSTICE WHITE, with whom JUSTICE STEVENS joins, and with whom JUSTICE SOUTER joins as to Part I, concurring in the judgment in part and dissenting in part.

[JUSTICE WHITE took the position that all the indictments against Dixon and Foster were barred by the Double Jeopardy Clause and that

Grady should not be overruled.] * * *

I
A

* * *

The United States' second, more powerful, argument is that contempt and the underlying substantive crime constitute two separate offenses for they involve injuries to two distinct interests, the one the interest of the court in preserving its authority, the other the public's interest in being protected from harmful conduct. * * * It cannot lightly be dismissed. * * * [C]ontempt "proceedings are not intended to punish conduct proscribed as harmful by the general criminal laws. Rather, they are designed to serve the limited purpose of vindicating the authority of the court. In punishing contempt, the Judiciary is sanctioning conduct that violates specific duties imposed by the court itself, arising directly from the parties' participation in judicial proceedings." * * *

The fact that two criminal prohibitions promote different interests may be indicative of legislative intent and, to that extent, important in deciding whether cumulative punishments imposed in a single prosecution violate the Double Jeopardy Clause. * * * But the cases decided today involve instances of successive prosecutions in which the interests of the *defendant* are of paramount concern. To subject an individual to repeated prosecutions exposes him to "embarrassment, expense and ordeal," * * * violates principles of finality, * * * and increases the risk of a mistaken conviction. That one of the punishments is designed to protect the court rather than the public is, in this regard, of scant comfort to the defendant.

It is true that the Court has not always given primacy to the defendant's interest. In particular, the Government directs attention to the dual sovereignty doctrine under which, "[w]hen a defendant in a single act violates the 'peace and dignity' of two sovereigns by breaking the laws of each, he has committed two distinct 'offences.'" *Heath v. Alabama*, [this volume]. * * *

But the dual sovereignty doctrine is limited, by its own terms, to cases where "the two entities that seek successively to prosecute a defendant for the same course of conduct can be termed separate sovereigns." * * * "This determination," we explained, "turns on whether the two entities draw their authority to punish the offender from distinct sources of power," * * * not on whether they are pursuing separate interests. Indeed, the Court has rejected the United States' precise argument in the past. * * * [I]n *Grafton v. United States*, 206 U.S. 333 (1907) [an army private was acquitted in a general court-martial for homicide and then charged with] a criminal complaint in civil court based on the same acts. Seeking to discredit the view that the Double Jeopardy Clause would be violated by this subsequent prosecution, the government asserted that "Grafton committed two distinct offenses—one against military law and discipline, the other against the civil law which may prescribe the punishment for crimes against organized society by whomsoever those crimes are committed." * * * To which the Court responded:

"* * * If * * * a person be tried for an offense in a tribunal deriving its jurisdiction and authority from the United States and is acquitted or convicted, he cannot again be tried for the same offense in another tribunal deriving its jurisdiction and authority from the United States. . . . [T]he same acts constituting a crime against the United States cannot, after the acquittal or conviction of the accused in a court of competent jurisdiction, be made the basis of a second trial of the accused for that crime in the same or in another court, civil or military, of the same government." * * *

Grafton, and the principle it embodies, are controlling. The Superior Court and the District of Columbia Court of Appeals were created by Congress, pursuant to its power under Article I of the Constitution. * * * In addition, the specific power exercised by the courts in this case were bestowed by the Legislature. * * * As we observed * * * "[t]he fact that the allegedly criminal conduct concerns a violation of a court order instead of common law or a statutory prohibition does not render the prosecution any less an exercise of the sovereign power of the United States." * * * It is past dispute, in other words, that "the two tribunals that tried the accused exert all their powers under and by the authority of the same government—that of the United States," * * * and, therefore, that the dual sovereignty doctrine poses no problem. * * *

* * *

II

If, as the Court agrees, the Double Jeopardy Clause cannot be ignored in this context, my view is that the subsequent prosecutions in both *Dixon* and *Foster* were impermissible as to *all* counts. I reach this conclusion because the offenses at issue in the contempt proceedings were either identical to, or lesser included offenses of, those charged in the subsequent prosecutions. JUSTICE SCALIA's contrary conclusion as to some of Foster's counts, which he reaches by exclusive focus on the formal elements of the relevant crimes, is divorced from the purposes of the constitutional provision he purports to apply. Moreover, the results to which this approach would lead are indefensible.

* * *

B

Professing strict adherence to *Blockburger*'s so-called "same elements" test, * * * JUSTICE SCALIA opts for a more circuitous approach. The elements of the crime of contempt, he reasons, in this instance are (1) the existence and knowledge of a court, or CPO; and (2) commission of the underlying substantive offense. * * * Where the criminal conduct that forms the basis of the contempt order is identical to that charged in the subsequent trial, JUSTICE SCALIA concludes, *Blockburger* forbids retrial. All elements of Foster's simple assault offense being included in his previous contempt offense, prosecution on that ground is precluded. * * * The same is true of Dixon's drug offense. * * * I agree with this conclusion, though would reach it rather differently: Because in a successive prosecution case the risk is that a person will have to defend himself more than once against the same charge, I would have put to the side the CPO (which, as it were, triggered the court's authority to punish the defendant for acts already punishable under the criminal laws) and compared the substantive offenses of which respondents stood accused in both prosecutions.

The significance of our disaccord is far more manifest where an element is added to the second prosecution. Under JUSTICE SCALIA's view, the double jeopardy barrier is then removed because each offense demands proof of an element the other does not: Foster's conviction for contempt requires proof of the existence and knowledge of a CPO, which conviction for assault with intent to kill does not; his conviction for assault with intent to kill requires proof of an intent to kill, which the contempt conviction did not. * * * Finally, though he was acquitted in the contempt proceedings with respect to the alleged [earlier simple assault] threats, his conviction under the threat charge in the subsequent trial required the additional proof that the threat be to kidnap, to inflict bodily injury, or to damage property. * * * As to these counts, * * * JUSTICE SCALIA finds that the Constitution does not prohibit retrial.

* * * To focus on the statutory elements of a crime makes sense where *cumulative* punishment is at stake, for there the aim simply is to uncover legislative intent. The *Blockburger* inquiry, accordingly, serves as a means to determine this intent, as our cases have recognized. * * * But, as JUSTICE SOUTER shows, adherence to legislative will has very little to do with the important interests advanced by double jeopardy safeguards against *successive* prosecutions. * * * The central purpose of the Double Jeopardy Clause being to protect against vexatious multiple prosecutions, * * * these interests go well beyond the prevention of unauthorized punishment. The same-elements test is an inadequate safeguard, for it leaves the constitutional guarantee at the mercy of a legislature's decision to modify statutory definitions. * * * Significantly, therefore, this Court [except in one earlier case has] noted that "[t]he *Blockburger* test is not the only standard for determining whether successive prosecutions impermissibly involve the same offense." * * * Rather, "[e]ven if two offenses are sufficiently different to permit the imposition of consecutive sentences, successive prosecutions will be barred in some circumstances where the second prosecution requires the relitigation of factual issues already resolved by the first." * * *

Take the example of Count V in Foster: For all intents and purposes, the offense for which he was convicted in the contempt proceeding was his assault against his wife. The majority, its eyes fixed on the rigid elements-test, would have his fate turn on whether his subsequent prosecution charges "simple assault" or "assault with intent to kill." Yet, because the crime of "simple assault" is included within the crime of "assault with intent to kill," the reasons that bar retrial under the first hypothesis are equally present under the second: These include principles of finality; * * * protecting Foster from "embarrassment" and "expense;" * * * and preventing the government from gradually fine-tuning its strategy, thereby minimizing exposure to a mistaken conviction. * * *

Analysis of the threat charges (Counts II-IV) makes the point more clearly still. In the contempt proceeding, it will be recalled, Foster was *acquitted* of the— arguably lesser-included—offense of threatening "in any manner." As we have stated,

> "the law attaches particular significance to an acquittal. To permit a second trial after an acquittal, however mistaken the acquittal might have been, would present an unacceptably high risk that the Government, with its vastly superior resources, might wear down the defendant so that 'even though innocent he may be found guilty.'"
> * * *

To allow the government to proceed on the threat counts would present precisely the risk of erroneous conviction the Clause seeks to avoid. That the prosecution had to establish the existence of the CPO in the first trial, in short, does not in any way modify the prejudice potentially caused to a defendant by consecutive trials.

To respond, as the majority appears to do, that concerns relating to the defendant's interests against repeat trials are "unjustified" because prosecutors "have little to gain and much to lose" from bringing successive prosecutions and because "the Government must be deterred from abusive, repeated prosecutions of a single offender for similar offenses by the sheer press of other demands upon prosecutorial and judicial resources," * * * is to get things exactly backwards. **[f]** The majority's prophesies might be correct,

and double jeopardy might be a problem that will simply take care of itself. Not so, however, according to the Constitution, whose firm prohibition against double jeopardy cannot be satisfied by wishful thinking.
* * *

[In Part III JUSTICE WHITE wrote that as the case was appropriately settled on his reading of the Double Jeopardy Clause, there was no need to consider the issue of overruling *Grady*. However, he stated agreement with JUSTICES BLACKMUN and SOUTER "that such a course is both unwarranted and unwise."]
* * *

[JUSTICE BLACKMUN concurred with the majority on the ground that contempt is not the same offense as the crimes charged here. He disagreed with overruling *Grady*.]

JUSTICE SOUTER, with whom JUSTICE STEVENS joins, concurring in the judgment in part and dissenting in part.

[JUSTICE SOUTER took the position that all the indictments against Dixon and Foster were barred by the Double Jeopardy Clause and that *Grady* should not be overruled. His reasoning suggests that overruling *Grady* will not have the intended effect because other precedent establish a "same conduct" test.]
* * *

III

The interests at stake in avoiding successive prosecutions are different from those at stake in the prohibition against multiple punishments, and our cases reflect this reality. The protection against successive prosecutions is the central protection provided by the Clause. A 19th-century case of this Court observed that "[t]he prohibition is not against being twice punished, but against being twice put in jeopardy; and the accused, whether convicted or acquitted, is equally put in jeopardy at the first trial." * * * "Where successive prosecutions are at stake, the guarantee serves 'a constitutional policy of finality for the defendant's benefit.'" * * *

The Double Jeopardy Clause prevents the government from "mak[ing] repeated attempts to convict an individual for an alleged offense, thereby subjecting him to embarrassment, expense and ordeal and compelling him to live in a continuing state of anxiety and insecurity." * * * The Clause addresses a further concern as well, that the government not be given the opportunity to rehearse its prosecution, "honing its trial strategies and perfecting its evidence through successive attempts at conviction," * * * because this "enhanc[es] the possibility that even though innocent [the defendant] may be found guilty." * * *

Consequently, while the government may punish a person separately for each conviction of at least as many different offenses as meet the *Blockburger* test, we have long held that it must sometimes bring its prosecutions for these offenses together. If a separate prosecution were permitted for every offense arising out of the same conduct, the government could manipulate the definitions of offenses, creating fine distinctions among them and permitting a zealous prosecutor to try a person again and again for essentially the same criminal conduct. While punishing different combinations of elements is consistent with the Double Jeopardy Clause in its limitation on the imposition of multiple punishments (a limitation rooted in concerns with legislative intent), permitting such repeated prosecutions would not be consistent with the principles underlying the Clause in its limitation on successive prosecution. The limitation on successive prosecution is thus a restriction on the government different in kind from that contained in the limitation on multiple punishments, and the government cannot get around the restriction on repeated prosecution of a single individual merely by precision in the way it defines its statutory offenses. Thus, "[t]he *Blockburger* test is not the only standard for determining whether successive prosecutions impermissibly involve the same offense. Even if two offenses are sufficiently different to permit the imposition of consecutive sentences, successive prosecutions will be barred in some circumstances where the second prosecution requires the relitigation of factual issues already resolved by the first." * * *

An example will show why this should be so. Assume three crimes: robbery with a firearm, robbery in a dwelling and simple robbery. The elements of the three crimes are the same, except that robbery with a firearm has the element that a firearm be used in the commission of the robbery while the other two crimes do not, and robbery in a dwelling has the element that the robbery occur in a dwelling while the other two crimes do not.

If a person committed a robbery in a dwelling with a firearm and was prosecuted for simple robbery, all agree he could not be prosecuted subsequently for either of the greater offenses of robbery with a firearm or robbery in a dwelling. Under the lens of *Blockburger*, however, if that same person were prosecuted first for robbery with a firearm, he could be prosecuted subsequently for robbery in a dwelling, even though he could not subsequently be prosecuted on the basis of that same robbery for simple robbery. This is true simply because neither of the crimes, robbery with a firearm and robbery in a dwelling, is either identical to or a lesser-included offense of the other. But since the purpose of the Double Jeopardy Clause's protection against successive prosecutions is to prevent repeated trials in which a defendant will be forced to defend against the same charge again and again, and in which the government may perfect its presentation with dress rehearsal after dress rehearsal, it should be irrelevant that the second prosecution would require the defendant to defend himself not only from the charge that he committed the robbery, but also from the charge of some additional fact, in this case, that the scene of the crime was a dwelling. If, instead, protection against successive prosecution were as limited as it would be by *Blockburger* alone, the doctrine would be as striking for its anomalies as for the limited protection it would provide. Thus, in the relatively few successive prosecution cases we have had over the years, we have not held that the *Blockburger* test is the only hurdle the government must clear (with one exception * * *).

* * *

*   *   *   *   *   *   *   *   *   *

COMMENTS

[a] Both cases raise questions about the management and exercise of discretion in prosecutors' offices. In Dixon's case, one can ask whether one part of the U.S. Attorney's office knew what another part was doing. In both cases, but especially in Foster's, one can ask why a busy prosecutor's office seeks to indict and try a person who has already been convicted. Does public justice demand reprosecution or are the prosecutors responding to organizational imperatives?

[b] Rights that attach to contempt proceedings include a public trial, the presumption of innocence, proof beyond a reasonable doubt, guarantee against self-incrimination, notice of charges, assistance of counsel, and the right to present a defense.

[c] An "element" here is to be read technically as the essential components of a crime. For example, to make out the crime of theft, each element must be proven: taking; carrying away; personal property; no right of possession; intent to permanently deprive.

[d] "Conduct," for the purpose of the *Grady* rule, is not as technical as the meaning of "element." It encompasses all the activity involved in the criminal incident. Since "conduct" is broader than "elements," the *Grady* rule offers greater protection to defendants.

[e] Does this mean that it is impossible for the Supreme Court to ever establish an expansive view of individual rights? If so, most of the "rights" studied in this volume have no constitutional basis and ought to be overruled.

[f] This argument of the majority, which JUSTICE WHITE counters, does seem on its face to leave the guarantee of individual rights to nothing more substantial than that the State is too busy to bother; the Court typically does not let the guarantee of rights rest only on the good will of the State, as the search warrant cases show.

BARKER v. WINGO

407 U.S. 514, 92 S.Ct. 2182, 33 L.Ed.2d 101 (1972)

MR. JUSTICE POWELL delivered the opinion of the Court.

Although a speedy trial is guaranteed the accused by the Sixth Amendment to the Constitution, this Court has dealt with that right on infrequent occasions. * * * The Court's opinion in *Klopfer v. North Carolina*, 386 U.S. 213 (1967), established that the right to a speedy trial is "fundamental" and is imposed by the Due Process Clause of the Fourteenth Amendment on the States. * * * [a] As MR. JUSTICE BRENNAN pointed out in his concurring opinion in *Dickey [v. Florida*, 398 U.S. 30 (1970)], in none of these cases have we attempted to set out the criteria by which the speedy trial right is to be judged. * * * This case compels us to make such an attempt.

I

[Manning and Barker were arrested, indicted, given appointed counsel, and set for trial in 1958 for murder. Desiring to get a statement from Manning against Barker, the Commonwealth of Kentucky obtained a series of 16 continuances of Barker's trial in order to try Manning first. Barker made no objection to the first 11 continuances. Because of several hung juries and appeals Manning had five trials before being convicted. Barker was free on bond since 1959. After the Commonwealth motion for the twelfth continuance in 1962, Barker's counsel filed a motion to dismiss the indictment, which was denied. Further continuances were granted to the prosecution for reasons including the illness of an ex-sheriff and the unavailability of prosecution witnesses. In 1963 the court announced that the case would be dismissed for lack of prosecution if it were not tried during the next term and a final trial date was set for October 9, 1963. On that date, Barker again moved to dismiss the indictment, and this time specified that his right to a speedy trial had been violated. The motion was denied; the trial commenced with Manning as the chief prosecution witness; Barker was convicted and given a life sentence.]

[The Kentucky Court of Appeals affirmed. The United States District Court rejected a petition for a writ of habeas corpus, but granted Barker leave to appeal *in forma pauperis*. The Court of Appeals affirmed the District Court, ruling that Barker had waived his speedy trial claim for the entire period before February 1963, assuming that was the date of the first motion to dismiss.] In this belief the court was mistaken, for the record reveals that the motion was filed in February 1962. The Commonwealth so conceded at oral argument before this Court. The court held further that the remaining period after the date on which Barker first raised his claim and before his trial—which it thought was only eight months but which was actually 20 months—was not unduly long. In addition, the court held that Barker had shown no resulting prejudice, and that the illness of the ex-sheriff was a valid justification for the delay. We granted Barker's petition for certiorari. * * *

II

The right to a speedy trial is generically different from any of the other rights enshrined in the Constitution for the protection of the accused. In addition to the general concern that all accused persons be treated according to decent and fair procedures, there is a societal interest in providing a speedy trial which exists separate from, and at times in opposition to, the interests of the accused. The inability of courts to provide a prompt trial has contributed to a large backlog of cases in urban courts which, among other things, enables defendants to negotiate more effectively for pleas of guilty to lesser offenses and otherwise manipulate the system. In addition, persons released on bond for lengthy periods awaiting trial have an opportunity to commit other crimes. It must be of little comfort to the residents of Christian County, Kentucky, to know that Barker was at large on bail for over four years while accused of a vicious and brutal murder of which he was ultimately convicted. Moreover, the longer an accused is free awaiting trial, the more tempting becomes his opportunity to jump bail and escape. Finally, delay between arrest and punishment may have a detrimental effect on rehabilitation.

If an accused cannot make bail, he is generally confined, as was Barker for 10 months, in a local jail. This contributes to the overcrowding and generally deplorable state of those institutions. Lengthy exposure to these conditions "has a destructive effect on human character and makes the rehabilitation of the individual offender much more difficult." At times the result may even be violent rioting. Finally, lengthy pretrial detention is costly. * * * In addition, society loses wages which might have been earned, and it must often support families of incarcerated breadwinners.

A second difference between the right to speedy trial and the accused's other constitutional rights is that deprivation of the right may work to the accused's advantage. Delay is not an uncommon defense tactic. As the time between the commission of the crime and trial lengthens, witnesses may become unavailable or their memories may fade. If the witnesses support the prosecution, its case will be weakened, sometimes seriously so. And it is the prosecution which carries the burden of proof. Thus, unlike the right to counsel or the right to be free from compelled self-incrimination, deprivation of the right to speedy trial does not *per se* prejudice the accused's ability to defend himself.

Finally, and perhaps most importantly, the right to speedy trial is a more vague concept than other procedural rights. It is, for example, impossible to determine with precision when the right has been denied. We cannot definitely say how long is too long in a system where justice is supposed to be swift but deliberate. As a consequence, there is no fixed point in the criminal process when the State can put the defendant to the choice of either exercising or waiving the right to a speedy trial. If, for example, the State moves for a 60-day continuance, granting that continuance is not a violation of the right to speedy trial unless the circumstances of the case are such that further delay would endanger the values the right protects. It is impossible to do more than generalize about when those circumstances exist. There is nothing comparable to the point in the process when a defendant exercises or waives his right to counsel or his right to a jury trial. Thus, * * * any inquiry into a speedy trial claim necessitates a functional analysis of the right in the particular context of the case. * * *

The amorphous quality of the right also leads to the unsatisfactorily severe remedy of dismissal of the indictment when the right has been deprived. This is indeed a serious consequence because it means that a defendant who may be guilty of a serious crime will go free, without having been tried. Such a remedy is more serious than an exclusionary rule or a reversal for a new trial, but it is the only possible remedy. [b]

III

Perhaps because the speedy trial right is so slippery, two rigid approaches are urged upon us as ways of eliminating some of the uncertainty which courts experience in protecting the right. The first suggestion is that we hold that the Constitution requires a criminal defendant to be offered a trial within a specified time period. The result of such a ruling would have the virtue of clarifying when the right is infringed and of simplifying courts' application of it. Recognizing this, some legislatures have enacted laws, and some courts have adopted procedural rules which more narrowly define the right. The United States Court of Appeals for the Second Circuit has promulgated rules for the district courts in that Circuit establishing that the government must be ready for trial within six months of the date of arrest, except in unusual circumstances, or the charge will be dismissed. This type of rule is also recommended by the American Bar Association.

But such a result would require this Court to engage in legislative or rulemaking activity, rather than in the adjudicative process to which we should confine our efforts. We do not establish procedural rules for the States, except when mandated by the Constitution. We find no constitutional basis for holding that the speedy trial right can be quantified into a specified number of days or months. The States, of course, are free to prescribe a reasonable period consistent with constitutional standards, but our approach must be less precise. [c]

The second suggested alternative would restrict consideration of the right to those cases in which the accused has demanded a speedy trial. Most States have recognized what is loosely referred to as the "demand rule," although eight States reject it. It is not clear, however, precisely what is meant by that term. Although every federal court of appeals that has considered the question has endorsed some kind of demand rule, some have regarded the rule within the concept of waiver, whereas others have viewed it as a factor to be weighed in assessing whether there has been a deprivation of the speedy trial right. We shall refer to the former approach as the demand-waiver doctrine. The demand-waiver doctrine provides that a defendant waives any consideration of his right to speedy trial for any period prior to which he has not demanded a trial. Under this rigid approach, a prior demand is a necessary condition to the consideration of the speedy trial right.   This essentially was the approach the Sixth Circuit took below.

Such an approach, by presuming waiver of a fundamental right from inaction, is inconsistent with this Court's pronouncements on waiver of constitutional rights.   The Court has defined waiver as "an intentional relinquishment or abandonment of a known right or privilege." * * * Courts should "indulge every reasonable presumption against waiver," * * * and they should "not presume acquiescence in the loss of fundamental rights." * * *

In excepting the right to speedy trial from the rule of waiver we have applied to other fundamental rights, courts that have applied the demand-waiver rule have relied on the assumption that delay usually works for the benefit of the accused and on the absence of any readily ascertainable time in the criminal process for a defendant to be given the choice of exercising or waiving his right.   But it is not necessarily true that delay benefits the defendant.   There are cases in which delay appreciably harms the defendant's ability to defend himself.   Moreover, a defendant confined to jail prior to trial is obviously disadvantaged by delay as is a defendant released on bail but unable to lead a normal life because of community suspicion and his own anxiety.

The nature of the speedy trial right does make it impossible to pinpoint a precise time in the process when the right must be asserted or waived, but that fact does not argue for placing the burden of protecting the right solely on defendants.   A defendant has no duty to bring himself to trial; the State has

that duty as well as the duty of insuring that the trial is consistent with due process.   Moreover, for the reasons earlier expressed, society has a particular interest in bringing swift prosecutions, and society's representatives are the ones who should protect that interest.

It is also noteworthy that such a rigid view of the demand-waiver rule places defense counsel in an awkward position.   Unless he demands a trial early and often, he is in danger of frustrating his client's right.   If counsel is willing to tolerate some delay because he finds it reasonable and helpful in preparing his own case, he may be unable to obtain a speedy trial for his client at the end of that time.   Since under the demand-waiver rule no time runs until the demand is made, the government will have whatever time is otherwise reasonable to bring the defendant to trial after a demand has been made.   Thus, if the first demand is made three months after arrest in a jurisdiction which prescribes a six-month rule, the prosecution will have a total of nine months—which may be wholly unreasonable under the circumstances.   The result in practice is likely to be either an automatic, *pro forma* demand made immediately after appointment of counsel or delays which, but for the demand-waiver rule, would not be tolerated.   Such a result is not consistent with the interests of defendants, society, or the Constitution.

We reject, therefore, the rule that a defendant who fails to demand a speedy trial forever waives his right.   This does not mean, however, that the defendant has no responsibility to assert his right.   We think the better rule is that the defendant's assertion of or failure to assert his right to a speedy trial is one of the factors to be considered in an inquiry into the deprivation of the right. Such a formulation avoids the rigidities of the demand-waiver rule and the resulting possible unfairness in its application. It allows the trial court to exercise a judicial discretion based on the circumstances, including due consideration of any applicable formal procedural rule. It would permit, for example, a court to attach a different weight to a situation in which the defendant knowingly fails to object from a situation in which his attorney acquiesces in long delay without adequately informing his client, or from a situation in which no counsel is appointed. It would also allow a court to weigh the frequency and force of the objections as opposed to attaching significant weight to a purely *pro forma* objection.

In ruling that a defendant has some responsibility to assert a speedy trial claim, we do not depart from our holdings in other cases concerning the waiver of fundamental rights, in which we have placed the entire responsibility on the prosecution to show that the claimed waiver was knowingly and voluntarily made. Such cases have involved rights which must be exercised or waived at a specific time or under clearly identifiable circumstances, such as the rights to plead not guilty, to demand a jury trial, to exercise the privilege against self-incrimination, and to have the assistance of counsel. We have shown above that the right to a speedy trial is unique in its uncertainty as to when and under what circumstances it must be asserted or may be deemed waived. But the rule we announce today, which comports with constitutional principles, places the primary burden on the courts and the prosecutors to assure that cases are brought to trial. We hardly need add that if delay is attributable to the defendant, then his waiver may be given effect under standard waiver doctrine, the demand rule aside.

We, therefore, reject both of the inflexible approaches—the fixed-time period because it goes further than the Constitution requires; the demand-waiver rule because it is insensitive to a right which we have deemed fundamental. The approach we accept is a balancing test, in which the conduct of both the prosecution and the defendant are weighed.

IV

A balancing test necessarily compels courts to approach speedy trial cases on an *ad hoc* basis. We can do little more than identify some of the factors which courts should assess in determining whether a particular defendant has been deprived of his right. Though some might express them in different ways, we identify four such factors: Length of delay, the reason for the delay, the defendant's assertion of his right, and prejudice to the defendant. **[d]**

The length of the delay is to some extent a triggering mechanism. Until there is some delay which is presumptively prejudicial, there is no necessity for inquiry into the other factors that go into the balance. Nevertheless, because of the imprecision of the right to speedy trial, the length of delay that will provoke such an inquiry is necessarily dependent upon the peculiar circumstances of the case. To take but one example, the delay that can be tolerated for an ordinary street crime is considerably less than for a serious, complex conspiracy charge.

Closely related to length of delay is the reason the government assigns to justify the delay. Here, too, different weights should be assigned to different reasons. A deliberate attempt to delay the trial in order to hamper the defense should be weighted heavily against the government. A more neutral reason such as negligence or overcrowded courts should be weighted less heavily but nevertheless should be considered since the ultimate responsibility for such circumstances must rest with the government rather than with the defendant. Finally, a valid reason, such as a missing witness, should serve to justify appropriate delay.

We have already discussed the third factor, the defendant's responsibility to assert his right. Whether and how a defendant asserts his right is closely related to the other factors we have mentioned. The strength of his efforts will be affected by the length of the delay, to some extent by the reason for the delay, and most particularly by the personal prejudice, which is not always readily identifiable, that he experiences. The more serious the deprivation, the more likely a defendant is to complain. The defendant's assertion of his speedy trial right, then, is entitled to strong evidentiary weight in determining whether the defendant is being deprived of the right. We emphasize that failure to assert the right will make it difficult for a defendant to prove that he was denied a speedy trial.

A fourth factor is prejudice to the defendant. Prejudice, of course, should be assessed in the light of the interests of defendants which the speedy trial right was designed to protect. This Court has identified three such inter-ests: (i) to prevent oppressive pretrial incarceration; (ii) to minimize anxiety and concern of the accused; and (iii) to limit the possibility that the defense will be impaired. Of these, the most serious is the last, because the inability of a defendant adequately to prepare his case skews the fairness of the entire system. If witnesses die or disappear during a delay, the prejudice is obvious. There is also prejudice if defense witnesses are unable to recall accurately events of the distant past. Loss of memory, however, is not always reflected in the record because what has been forgotten can rarely be shown.

We have discussed previously the societal disadvantages of lengthy pretrial incarceration, but obviously the disadvantages for the accused who cannot obtain his release are even more serious. The time spent in jail awaiting trial has a detrimental impact on the individual. It often means loss of a job; it disrupts family life; and it enforces idleness. Most jails offer little or no recreational or rehabilitative programs. The time spent in jail is simply dead time. Moreover, if a defendant is locked up, he is hindered in his ability to gather evidence, contact witnesses, or otherwise prepare his defense. Imposing those conse-quences on anyone who has not yet been convicted is serious. It is espe-cially unfortunate to impose them on those persons who are ultimately found to be innocent. Finally, even if an accused is not incarcerated prior to trial, he is still disadvantaged by restraints on his liberty and by living under a cloud of anxiety, suspicion, and often hostility. * * *

We regard none of the four factors identified above as either a necessary or sufficient condition to the finding of a deprivation of the right of speedy trial. Rather, they are related factors and must be considered together with such other circumstances as may be relevant. In sum, these factors have no talismanic qualities; courts must still engage in a difficult and sensitive balancing process. But, because we are dealing with a fundamental right of the accused, this process must be carried out with full recognition that the accused's interest in a speedy trial is specifically affirmed in the Constitution.

V

The difficulty of the task of balancing these factors is illustrated by this case, which we consider to be close. It is clear that the length of delay between arrest and trial—well over five years—was extraordinary. Only seven months of that period can be attributed to a strong excuse, the illness of the ex-sheriff who was in charge of the investigation. Perhaps some delay would have been permissible under ordinary circumstances, so that Manning could be utilized as a witness in Barker's trial, but more than four years was too long a period, particularly since a good part of that period was attributable to the Commonwealth's failure or inability to try Manning under circumstances that comported with due process.

Two counterbalancing factors, however, outweigh these deficiencies. The first is that prejudice was minimal. Of course, Barker was prejudiced to some extent by living for over four years under a cloud of suspicion and anxiety. Moreover, although he was released on bond for most of the

period, he did spend 10 months in jail before trial. But there is no claim that any of Barker's witnesses died or otherwise became unavailable owing to the delay. The trial transcript indicates only two very minor lapses of memory—one on the part of a prosecution witness—which were in no way significant to the outcome.

More important than the absence of serious prejudice, is the fact that Barker did not want a speedy trial. Counsel was appointed for Barker immediately after his indictment and represented him throughout the period. No question is raised as to the competency of such counsel. Despite the fact that counsel had notice of the motions for continuances, the record shows no action whatever taken between October 21, 1958, and February 12, 1962, that could be construed as the assertion of the speedy trial right. On the latter date, in response to another motion for continuance, Barker moved to dismiss the indictment. The record does not show on what ground this motion was based, although it is clear that no alternative motion was made for an immediate trial. Instead the record strongly suggests that while he hoped to take advantage of the delay in which he had acquiesced, and thereby obtain a dismissal of the charges, he definitely did not want to be tried. * * * The probable reason for Barker's attitude was that he was gambling on Manning's acquittal. The evidence was not very strong against Manning, as the reversals and hung juries suggest, and Barker undoubtedly thought that if Manning were acquitted, he would never be tried. * * *

That Barker was gambling on Manning's acquittal is also suggested by his failure, following the *pro forma* motion to dismiss filed in February 1962, to object to the Commonwealth's next two motions for continuances. Indeed, it was not until March 1963, after Manning's convictions were final, that Barker, having lost his gamble, began to object to further continuances. At that time, the Commonwealth's excuse was the illness of the ex-sheriff, which Barker has conceded justified the further delay.

We do not hold that there may never be a situation in which an indictment may be dismissed on speedy trial grounds where the defendant has failed to object to continuances. There may be a situation in which the defendant was represented by incompetent counsel, was severely prejudiced, or even cases in which the continuances were granted *ex parte*. But barring extraordinary circumstances, we would be reluctant indeed to rule that a defendant was denied this constitutional right on a record that strongly indicates, as does this one, that the defendant did not want a speedy trial. We hold, therefore, that Barker was not deprived of his due process right to a speedy trial.

The judgment of the Court of Appeals is

Affirmed.

MR. JUSTICE WHITE, with whom MR. JUSTICE BRENNAN joins, concurring.

* * *

[Delays between charge and trial] may "seriously interfere with the defendant's liberty, whether he is free on bail or not, and that may disrupt his employment, drain his financial resources, curtail his associations, subject him to public obloquy, and create anxiety in him, his family and his friends." *United States v. Marion*, 404 U.S. 307, 320 (1971). * * * [F]or those who desire an early trial, these personal factors should prevail if the only countervailing considerations offered by the State are those connected with crowded dockets and prosecutorial case loads. A defendant desiring a speedy trial, therefore, should have it within some reasonable time; and only special circumstances presenting a more pressing public need with respect to the case itself should suffice to justify delay. Only if such special considerations are in the case and if they outweigh the inevitable personal prejudice resulting from delay would it be necessary to consider whether there has been or would be prejudice to the defense at trial. * * *

Of course, cases will differ among themselves as to the allowable time between charge and trial so as to permit prosecution and defense adequately to prepare their case. But unreasonable delay in run-of-the-mill criminal cases cannot be justified by simply asserting that the public resources provided by the State's criminal-justice system are limited and that each case must await its turn. As the Court points out, this approach also subverts the State's own goals in seeking to enforce its criminal laws.

* * * * * * * * * * *

COMMENTS

[a] This was one of the "incorporation" cases that constituted the "due process revolution" of the 1960s.

[b] The typical understanding of a right as a legal claim includes a notion that it is relatively clear; the discussion in Part II indicates that some rights are far from obvious.

[c] The Supreme Court under CHIEF JUSTICE WARREN was severely criticized for issuing legislative-style rules in *Miranda v. Arizona* [this volume]. It is unlikely that a Court ostensibly less "activist" than the Warren Court would wish to appear to be "legislating."

[d] Notice how JUSTICE POWELL's previous discussion set the stage for the four-factor rule of the case.

DOGGETT v. UNITED STATES

___ U.S. ___, 112 S.Ct. 2686, 120 L.Ed.2d 520 (1992)

JUSTICE SOUTER delivered the opinion of the Court.

In this case we consider whether the delay of 8½ years between petitioner's indictment and arrest violated his Sixth Amendment right to a speedy trial. We hold that it did.

I

[Doggett was indicted for conspiring to import and distribute cocaine in 1980. Before he could be arrested, he left the country for Colombia. The Drug Enforcement Agency alerted all United States Customs stations and a number of law enforcement organizations of Doggett's outstanding arrest warrant. His name was also placed] in the Treasury Enforcement Communication System (TECS), a computer network that helps Customs agents screen people entering the country, and in the National Crime Information Center computer system, which serves similar ends. The TECS entry expired that September, however, and Doggett's name vanished from the system.

In September 1981, [DEA agent] Driver found out that Doggett was under arrest on drug charges in Panama and, thinking that a formal extradition request would be futile, simply asked Panama to "expel" Doggett to the United States. Although the Panamanian authorities promised to comply when their own proceedings had run their course, they freed Doggett the following July and let him go to Colombia, where he stayed with an aunt for several months.

On September 25, 1982, he passed unhindered through Customs in New York City and settled down in Virginia. Since his return to the United States, he has married, earned a college degree, found a steady job as a computer operations manager, lived openly under his own name, and stayed within the law.

Doggett's travels abroad had not wholly escaped the Government's notice, however. In 1982, the American Embassy in Panama told the State Department of his departure to Colombia, but that information, for whatever reason, eluded the DEA, and Agent Driver assumed for several years that his quarry was still serving time in a Panamanian prison. Driver never asked DEA officials in Panama to check into Doggett's status, and only after his own fortuitous assignment to that country in 1985 did he discover Doggett's departure for Colombia. Driver then simply assumed Doggett had settled there, and he made no effort to find out for sure or to track Doggett down, either abroad or in the United States. Thus Doggett remained lost to the American criminal justice system until September 1988, when the Marshal's Service ran a simple credit check on several thousand people subject to outstanding arrest warrants and, within minutes, found out where Doggett lived and worked. On September 5, 1988, nearly 6 years after his return to the United States and 8½ years after his indictment, Doggett was arrested.

He naturally moved to dismiss the indictment, arguing that the Government's failure to prosecute him earlier violated his Sixth Amendment right to a speedy trial. The Federal Magistrate hearing his motion applied the criteria for assessing speedy trial claims set out in *Barker v. Wingo*, [this volume]: "[l]ength of delay, the reason for the delay, the defendant's assertion of his right, and prejudice to the defendant." * * * The Magistrate found that the delay between Doggett's indictment and arrest was long enough to be "presumptively prejudicial," * * * that the delay "clearly [was] attributable to the negligence of the government," * * * and that Doggett could not be faulted for any delay in asserting his right to a speedy trial, there being no evidence that he had known of the charges against him until his arrest. * * * The Magistrate also found, however, that Doggett had made no affirmative showing that the delay had impaired his ability to mount a successful defense or had otherwise prejudiced him. In his recommendation to the District Court, the Magistrate contended that this failure to demonstrate particular prejudice sufficed to defeat Doggett's speedy trial claim.

The District Court took the recommendation and denied Doggett's motion. Doggett then entered a conditional guilty plea * * * expressly reserving the right to appeal his ensuing conviction on the speedy trial claim.

A split panel of the Court of Appeals affirmed. * * * Following Circuit precedent, * * * the court ruled that Doggett could prevail only by proving "actual prejudice" or by establishing that "the first three *Barker* factors weighed heavily in his favor." * * * The majority agreed with the

Magistrate that Doggett had not shown actual prejudice, and, attributing the Government's delay to "negligence" rather than "bad faith," * * * it concluded that *Barker's* first three factors did not weigh so heavily against the Government as to make proof of specific prejudice unnecessary. Judge Clark dissented, arguing, among other things, that the majority had placed undue emphasis on Doggett's inability to prove actual prejudice.

We granted Doggett's petition for certiorari, * * * and now reverse.

II

The Sixth Amendment guarantees that, "[i]n all criminal prosecutions, the accused shall enjoy the right to a speedy . . . trial. . . ." On its face, the Speedy Trial Clause is written with such breadth that, taken literally, it would forbid the government to delay the trial of an "accused" for any reason at all. Our cases, however, have qualified the literal sweep of the provision by specifically recognizing the relevance of four separate enquiries: whether delay before trial was uncommonly long, whether the government or the criminal defendant is more to blame for that delay, whether, in due course, the defendant asserted his right to a speedy trial, and whether he suffered prejudice as the delay's result. * * *

The first of these is actually a double enquiry. Simply to trigger a speedy trial analysis, an accused must allege that the interval between accusation and trial has crossed the threshold dividing ordinary from "presumptively prejudicial" delay, * * * since, by definition, he cannot complain that the government has denied him a "speedy" trial if it has, in fact, prosecuted his case with customary promptness. If the accused makes this showing, the court must then consider, as one factor among several, the extent to which the delay stretches beyond the bare minimum needed to trigger judicial examination of the claim. * * * This latter enquiry is significant to the speedy trial analysis because, as we discuss below, the presumption that pretrial delay has prejudiced the accused intensifies over time. In this case, the extraordinary 8½ year lag between Doggett's indictment and arrest clearly suffices to trigger the speedy trial enquiry; its further significance within that enquiry will be dealt with later.

As for *Barker's* second criterion, the Government claims to have sought Doggett with diligence. The findings of the courts below are to the contrary, however, and we review trial court determinations of negligence with considerable deference. * * * The Government gives us nothing to gainsay the findings that have come up to us, and we see nothing fatal to them in the record. For six years, the Government's investigators made no serious effort to test their progressively more questionable assumption that Doggett was living abroad, and, had they done so, they could have found him within minutes. While the Government's lethargy may have reflected no more than Doggett's relative unimportance in the world of drug trafficking, it was still findable negligence, and the finding stands.

The Government goes against the record again in suggesting that Doggett knew of his indictment years before he was arrested. Were this true, *Barker's*

third factor, concerning invocation of the right to a speedy trial, would be weighed heavily against him. But here again, the Government is trying to revisit the facts. At the hearing on Doggett's speedy trial motion, it introduced no evidence challenging the testimony of Doggett's wife, who said that she did not know of the charges until his arrest, and of his mother, who claimed not to have told him or anyone else that the police had come looking for him. From this the Magistrate implicitly concluded, * * * and the Court of Appeals expressly reaffirmed, * * * that Doggett had won the evidentiary battle on this point. Not only that, but in the factual basis supporting Doggett's guilty plea, the Government explicitly conceded that it had

> "no information that Doggett was aware of the indictment before he left the United States in March 1980, or prior to his arrest. His mother testified at the suppression hearing that she never told him, and Barnes and Riddle [Doggett's confederates] state they did not have contact with him after their arrest [in 1980]." * * *

While one of the Government's lawyers later expressed amazement that "that particular stipulation is in the factual basis," * * * he could not make it go away, and the trial and appellate courts were entitled to accept the defense's unrebutted and largely substantiated claim of Doggett's ignorance. Thus, Doggett is not to be taxed for invoking his speedy trial right only after his arrest.

III

The Government is left, then, with its principal contention: that Doggett fails to make out a successful speedy trial claim because he has not shown precisely how he was prejudiced by the delay between his indictment and trial.

A

We have observed in prior cases that unreasonable delay between formal accusation and trial threatens to produce more than one sort of harm, including "oppressive pretrial incarceration," "anxiety and concern of the accused," and "the possibility that the [accused's] defense will be impaired" by dimming memories and loss of exculpatory evidence. * * * Of these forms of prejudice, "the most serious is the last, because the inability of a defendant adequately to prepare his case skews the fairness of the entire system." * * * Doggett claims this kind of prejudice, and there is probably no other kind that he can claim, since he was subjected neither to pretrial detention nor, he has successfully contended, to awareness of unresolved charges against him.

The Government answers Doggett's claim by citing language in three cases, *United States v. Marion*, 404 U.S. 307, 320-323 (1971), *United States v. MacDonald*, 456 U.S. 1, 8 (1982), and *United States v. Loud Hawk*, 474 U.S. 302, 312 (1986), for the proposition that the Speedy Trial Clause does not significantly protect a criminal defendant's interest in fair adjudication. In so arguing, the Government asks us, in effect, to read part of *Barker* right out of the law, and that we will not do. In context, the cited passages support nothing beyond the principle, which we have independently based on textual and historical grounds, * * * that the Sixth Amendment right of the accused to a speedy trial has no application beyond the confines of a formal criminal prosecution. Once triggered by arrest, indictment, or other official accusation, however, the speedy trial enquiry must weigh the effect of delay on the accused's defense just as it has to weigh any other form of prejudice that *Barker* recognized. * * *

As an alternative to limiting *Barker*, the Government claims Doggett has failed to make any affirmative showing that the delay weakened his ability to raise specific defenses, elicit specific testimony, or produce specific items of evidence. Though Doggett did indeed come up short in this respect, the Government's argument takes it only so far: consideration of prejudice is not limited to the specifically demonstrable, and, as it concedes, * * * affirmative proof of particularized prejudice is not essential to every speedy trial claim. * * * *Barker* explicitly recognized that impairment of one's defense is the most difficult form of speedy trial prejudice to prove because time's erosion of exculpatory evidence and testimony "can rarely be shown." * * * And though time can tilt the case against either side, * * * one cannot generally be sure which of them it has prejudiced more severely. Thus, we generally have to recognize that excessive delay presumptively compromises the reliability of a trial in ways that neither party can prove or, for that matter, identify. While such presumptive prejudice cannot alone carry a Sixth Amendment claim without regard to the other *Barker* criteria, * * * it is part of the mix of relevant facts, and its importance increases with the length of delay.

B

This brings us to an enquiry into the role that presumptive prejudice should play in the disposition of Doggett's speedy trial claim. We begin with hypothetical and somewhat easier cases and work our way to this one.

Our speedy trial standards recognize that pretrial delay is often both inevitable and wholly justifiable. The government may need time to collect witnesses against the accused, oppose his pretrial motions, or, if he goes into hiding, track him down. We attach great weight to such considerations when balancing them against the costs of going forward with a trial whose probative accuracy the passage of time has begun by degrees to throw into question. * * * Thus, in this case, if the Government had pursued Doggett with reasonable diligence from his indictment to his arrest, his speedy trial claim would fail. Indeed, that conclusion would generally follow as a matter of course however great the delay, so long as Doggett could not show specific prejudice to his defense.

The Government concedes, on the other hand, that Doggett would prevail if he could show that the Government had intentionally held back in its prosecution of him to gain some impermissible advantage at trial. * * * That we cannot doubt. *Barker* stressed that official bad faith in causing delay will be weighed heavily against the government, * * * and a bad-faith delay the length of this negligent one would present an overwhelming case for dismissal.

Between diligent prosecution and bad-faith delay, official negligence in bringing an accused to trial occupies the middle ground. While not compel-ling relief in every case where bad-faith delay would make relief virtually automatic, neither is negligence automatically tolerable simply because the accused cannot demonstrate exactly how it has prejudiced him. It was on this point that the Court of Appeals erred, and on the facts before us, it was reversible error.

Barker made it clear that "different weights [are to be] assigned to different reasons" for delay. * * * Although negligence is obviously to be weighed more lightly than a deliberate intent to harm the accused's defense, it still falls on the wrong side of the divide between acceptable and unacceptable reasons for delaying a criminal prosecution once it has begun. And such is the nature of the prejudice presumed that the weight we assign to official negligence compounds over time as the presumption of evidentiary prejudice grows. Thus, our toleration of such negligence varies inversely with its protractedness, * * * and its consequent threat to the fairness of the accused's trial. Condoning prolonged and unjustifiable delays in prosecution would both penalize many defendants for the state's fault and simply encourage the government to gamble with the interests of criminal suspects assigned a low prosecutorial priority. The Government, indeed, can hardly complain too loudly, for persistent neglect in concluding a criminal prosecution indicates an uncommonly feeble interest in bringing an accused to justice; the more weight the Government attaches to securing a conviction, the harder it will try to get it. [a]

To be sure, to warrant granting relief, negligence unaccompanied by particularized trial prejudice must have lasted longer than negligence demonstrably causing such prejudice. But even so, the Government's egregious persistence in failing to prosecute Doggett is clearly sufficient. The lag between Doggett's indictment and arrest was 8½ years, and he would have faced trial 6 years earlier than he did but for the Government's inexcusable oversights. The portion of the delay attributable to the Government's negligence far exceeds the threshold needed to state a speedy trial claim; indeed, we have called shorter delays "extraordinary." * * * When the Government's negligence thus causes delay six times as long as that generally sufficient to trigger judicial review, * * * and when the presumption of prejudice, albeit unspecified, is neither extenuated, as by the defendant's acquiescence,* * * nor persuasively rebutted, the defendant is entitled to relief.

IV

We reverse the judgment of the Court of Appeals and remand the case for proceedings consistent with this opinion.

So ordered.

[JUSTICE O'CONNOR, dissented on the ground that actual prejudice must be shown before a defendant can benefit from the Speedy Trial right.]

JUSTICE THOMAS, with whom THE CHIEF JUSTICE and JUSTICE SCALIA join, dissenting.

* * *

I

We have long identified the "major evils" against which the Speedy Trial Clause is directed as "undue and oppressive incarceration" and the "anxiety and concern accompanying public accusation." *United States v. Marion.* * * * The Court does not, and cannot, seriously dispute that those two concerns lie at the heart of the Clause, and that neither concern is implicated here. Doggett was neither in United States custody nor subject to bail during the entire 8½-year period at issue. Indeed, as this case comes to us, we must assume that he was blissfully unaware of his indictment all the while, and thus was not subject to the anxiety or humiliation that typically accompany a known criminal charge.

Thus, this unusual case presents the question whether, independent of these core concerns, the Speedy Trial Clause protects an accused from two additional harms: (1) prejudice to his ability to defend himself caused by the passage of time; and (2) disruption of his life years after the alleged commission of his crime. [b] The Court today proclaims that the first of these additional harms is indeed an independent concern of the Clause, and on that basis compels reversal of Doggett's conviction and outright dismissal of the indictment against him. As to the second of these harms, the Court remains mum— despite the fact that we requested supplemental briefing on this very point.

I disagree with the Court's analysis. In my view, the Sixth Amendment's speedy trial guarantee does not provide independent protection against either prejudice to an accused's defense or the disruption of his life. I shall consider each in turn.

A

As we have explained, "the Speedy Trial Clause's core concern is impairment of *liberty*." *United States v. Loud Hawk*, * * * (emphasis added). Whenever a criminal trial takes place long after the events at issue, the defendant may be prejudiced in any number of ways. But "[t]he Speedy Trial Clause does not purport to protect a defendant from all effects flowing from a delay before trial." * * * The Clause is directed not generally against delay-related prejudice, but against delay-related prejudice to a defendant's liberty. "The speedy trial guarantee is designed to minimize the possibility of lengthy incarceration prior to trial, to reduce the lesser, but nevertheless substantial, impairment of liberty imposed on an accused while released on bail, and to shorten the disruption of life caused by arrest and the presence of unresolved criminal charges." * * * Thus, "when defendants are not incarcerated or subjected to other substantial restrictions on their liberty, a court should not weigh that time towards a claim under the Speedy Trial Clause." * * *

A lengthy pretrial delay, of course, may prejudice an accused's ability to defend himself. But, we have explained, prejudice to the defense is not the sort of impairment of liberty against which the Clause is directed. "Passage of time, whether before or after arrest, may impair memories, cause evidence to be lost, deprive the defendant of witnesses, and otherwise interfere with his ability to defend himself. *But this possibility of prejudice at trial is not itself sufficient reason to wrench the Sixth Amendment from its proper context.*" * * * (emphasis added). Even though a defendant may be prejudiced by a pretrial delay, and even though the government may be unable to provide a valid justification for that delay, the Clause does not come into play unless the delay impairs the defendant's liberty. "Inordinate delay . . . may impair a defendant's ability to present an effective defense. But the major evils protected against by the speedy trial guarantee exist *quite apart* from actual or possible prejudice to an accused's defense." * * * (emphasis added).

These explanations notwithstanding, we have on occasion identified the prevention of prejudice to the defense as an independent and fundamental objective of the Speedy Trial Clause. In particular, in *Barker v. Wingo*, * * * we asserted that the Clause "was designed to protect" *three* basic interests: "(i) to prevent oppressive pretrial incarceration; (ii) to minimize anxiety and concern of the accused; and (iii) to limit the possibility that the defense will be impaired." * * * Indeed, the *Barker* Court went so far as to declare that of these three interests, "the most serious is the last, because the inability of a defendant adequately to prepare his case skews the fairness of the entire system." * * *

We are thus confronted with two conflicting lines of authority, the one declaring that "limit[ing] the possibility that the defense will be impaired" is an independent and fundamental objective of the Speedy Trial Clause, *e.g.*, *Barker*, * * * and the other declaring that it is not, *e.g.*, *Marion*, *supra*; *MacDonald*, *supra*; *Loud Hawk*, *supra*. The Court refuses to acknowledge this conflict. Instead, it simply reiterates the relevant language from *Barker* and asserts that *Marion*, *MacDonald*, and *Loud Hawk* "support nothing beyond the principle . . . that the Sixth Amendment right of the accused to a speedy trial has no application beyond the confines of a formal criminal prosecution." * * * That attempt at reconciliation is eminently unpersuasive.

It is true, of course, that the Speedy Trial Clause by its terms applies only to an "accused"; the right does not attach before indictment or arrest. * * * But that limitation on the Clause's protection only confirms that preventing prejudice to the defense is not one of its independent and fundamental objectives. For prejudice to the defense stems from the interval between *crime* and trial, which is quite distinct from the interval between *accusation* and trial. If the Clause were indeed aimed at safeguarding against prejudice to the defense, then it would presumably limit *all* prosecutions that occur long after the criminal events at issue. A defendant prosecuted 10 years after a crime is just as hampered in his ability to defend himself whether he was indicted the week after the crime or the week before the trial—but no one would suggest that the Clause protects him in the latter situation, where the delay did not substantially impair his liberty, either through oppressive incarceration or the anxiety of known criminal charges. Thus, while the Court is correct to observe that the defendants in *Marion*, *MacDonald*, and *Loud Hawk* were not subject to formal criminal prosecution during the lengthy period of delay prior to their trials, that observation misses the point of those cases. With respect to the relevant consideration— *the defendants'*

ability to defend themselves despite the passage of time—they were in precisely the same situation as a defendant who had long since been indicted. The initiation of a formal criminal prosecution is simply irrelevant to whether the defense has been prejudiced by delay. [c]

Although being an "accused" is necessary to trigger the Clause's protection, it is not sufficient to do so. The touchstone of the speedy trial right, after all, is the substantial deprivation of liberty that typically accompanies an "accusation," *not* the accusation itself. That explains why a person who has been arrested but not indicted is entitled to the protection of the Clause, * * * even though technically he has not been "accused" at all. And it explains why the lower courts consistently have held that, with respect to sealed (and hence secret) indictments, the protections of the Speedy Trial Clause are triggered *not* when the indictment is *filed*, but when it is *unsealed*. * * *

It is misleading, then, for the Court to accuse the Government of "ask[ing] us, in effect, to read part of Barker right out of the law," * * * a course the Court resolutely rejects. For the issue here is not simply whether the relevant language from *Barker* should be read out of the law, but whether that language trumps the contrary logic of *Marion*, *MacDonald*, and *Loud Hawk*. The Court's protestations notwithstanding, the two lines of authority cannot be reconciled; to reaffirm the one is to undercut the other.

In my view, the choice presented is not a hard one. *Barker*'s suggestion that preventing prejudice to the defense is a fundamental and independent objective of the Clause is plainly dictum. Never, until today, have we confronted a case where a defendant subjected to a lengthy delay after indictment nonetheless failed to suffer any substantial impairment of his liberty. I think it fair to say that *Barker* simply did not contemplate such an unusual situation. Moreover, to the extent that the *Barker* dictum purports to elevate considerations of prejudice to the defense to fundamental and independent status under the Clause, it cannot be deemed to have survived our subsequent decisions in *MacDonald* and *Loud Hawk*.

[The dissent goes on to state that statute of limitation statutes and the due process clause constitute adequate protection to problems of prejudice that are generated by delay. In another part, JUSTICE THOMAS argued that Doggett's life was not disrupted by the years that this prosecution was in limbo and that in any event this is not an interest protected by the Sixth Amendment.]

* * *

* * * * * * * * * *

COMMENTS

[a] JUSTICE SOUTER's previous experience as the Attorney General of New Hampshire gives these comments added weight. In line with the balancing approach to the analysis of the Speedy Trial right, it is appropriate for the Court to consider the deterrent effect of its ruling on law enforcement and prosecutorial practices.

[b] The dissent cites *Marion* to show that the Speedy Trial Right supports two interests but not the prejudice that delay can cause to the proper adjudication. Aside from the verbiage of *Marion*, does this make sense as a matter of the just and proper functioning of the trial system? Does this reading of Sixth Amendment law square with the fact that prejudice was one of the four of the balancing factors of *Barker v. Wingo*?

[c] This line of reasoning is weighty. A formal response is simply that the Sixth Amendment does not attach until a "criminal prosecution" has commenced, as the Court held in *Marion*.

UNITED STATES v. LOVASCO

431 U.S. 783, 97 S.Ct. 2044, 52 L.Ed.2d 752 (1977)

MR. JUSTICE MARSHALL delivered the opinion of the Court.

We granted certiorari in this case to consider the circumstances in which the Constitution requires that an indictment be dismissed because of delay between the commission of an offense and the initiation of prosecution.

I

[In March, 1975, Lovasco was indicted for possessing stolen firearms and for dealing in firearms without a license, crimes alleged to have occurred more than 18 months before the indictment was filed. He moved to dismiss the indictment due to the delay. Lovasco presented a Postal Inspector's report of the investigation that was prepared one month after the crimes were committed, but which also stated that the agents had been unable to confirm or refute Lovasco's factual claim of innocence. Little information was gathered in the next seventeen months.]

To establish prejudice to the defense, respondent testified that he had lost the testimony of two material witnesses due to the delay. [The witnesses died.] Respondent did not state how the witnesses would have aided the defense had they been willing to testify.

The Government made no systematic effort in the District Court to explain its long delay [but asserted that the investigation had continued.]. * * *

[The District Court found that by] the date of the Postal Inspector's report, "the Government had all the information relating to defendant's alleged commission of the offenses charged against him," and that the 17-month delay before the case was presented to the grand jury "had not been explained or justified" and was "unnecessary and unreasonable." The court also found that "[a]s a result of the delay defendant has been prejudiced by reason of the death of [a material witness."] * * * Accordingly, the court dismissed the indictment.

[The Court of Appeals accepted the government's argument that there had been a continuing part-time investigation, but affirmed the District Court's findings.]

We granted certiorari, * * * and now reverse.

II

In *United States v. Marion*, 404 U.S. 307 (1971), this Court considered the significance, for constitutional purposes, of a lengthy preindictment delay. We held that as far as the Speedy Trial Clause of the Sixth Amendment is concerned, such delay is wholly irrelevant, since our analysis of the language, history, and purposes of the Clause persuaded us that only "a formal indictment or information or else the actual restraints imposed by arrest and holding to answer a criminal charge . . . engage the particular protections" of that provision. * * * We went on to note that statutes of limitations, which provide predictable, legislatively enacted limits on prosecutorial delay, provide "'the primary guarantee against bringing overly stale criminal charges.'" * * * But we did acknowledge that the "statute of limitations does not fully define [defendants'] rights with respect to the events occurring prior to indictment," * * * and that the Due Process Clause has a limited role to play in protecting against oppressive delay.

Respondent seems to argue that due process bars prosecution whenever a defendant suffers prejudice as a result of preindictment delay. To support that proposition respondent relies on the concluding sentence of the Court's opinion in *Marion* where, in remanding the case, we stated that "[e]vents of the trial may demonstrate actual prejudice, but at the present time appellees' due process claims are speculative and premature." * * * But the quoted sentence establishes only that proof of actual prejudice makes a due process claim concrete and ripe for adjudication, not that it makes the claim automatically valid. Indeed, two pages earlier in the opinion we expressly rejected the argument respondent advances here:

> "[W]e need not . . . determine when and in what circumstances actual prejudice resulting from preaccusation delays requires the dismissal of the prosecution. Actual prejudice to the defense of a criminal case may result from the shortest and most necessary delay; and no one suggests that every delay-caused detriment to a defendant's case should abort a criminal prosecution." * * *

Thus *Marion* makes clear that proof of prejudice is generally a necessary but not sufficient element of a due process claim, and that the due process inquiry must consider the reasons for the delay as well as the prejudice to the accused.

The Court of Appeals found that the sole reason for the delay here was "a hope on the part of the Government that others might be discovered who may have participated in the theft. . . ." * * * It concluded that this hope did not justify the delay, and therefore affirmed the dismissal of the indictment. But the Due Process Clause does not permit courts to abort criminal prosecutions simply because they disagree with a prosecutor's judgment as to when to seek an indictment. Judges are not free, in defining "due process," to impose on law enforcement officials our "personal and private notions" of fairness and to "disregard the limits that bind judges in their judicial function." * * * Our task is more circumscribed. We are to determine only whether the action complained of—here, compelling respondent to stand trial after the Government delayed indictment to investigate further—violates those "fundamental conceptions of justice which lie at the base of our civil and political institutions," * * * and which define "the community's sense of fair play and decency." * * *

It requires no extended argument to establish that prosecutors do not deviate from "fundamental conceptions of justice" when they defer seeking indictments until they have probable cause to believe an accused is guilty; indeed it is unprofessional conduct for a prosecutor to recommend an indictment on less than probable cause. It should be equally obvious that prosecutors are under no duty to file charges as soon as probable cause exists but before they are satisfied they will be able to establish the suspect's guilt beyond a reasonable doubt. To impose such a duty "would have a deleterious effect both upon the rights of the accused and upon the ability of society to protect itself." * * * From the perspective of potential defendants, requiring prosecutions to commence when probable cause is established is undesirable because it would increase the likelihood of unwarranted charges being filed, and would add to the time during which defendants stand accused but untried. These costs are by no means insubstantial since, as we recognized in *Marion*, a formal accusation may "interfere with the defendant's liberty, . . . disrupt his employment, drain his financial resources, curtail his associations, subject him to public obloquy, and create anxiety in him, his family and his friends." * * * From the perspective of law enforcement officials, a requirement of immediate prosecution upon probable cause is equally unacceptable because it could make obtaining proof of guilt beyond a reasonable doubt impossible by causing potentially fruitful sources of information to evaporate before they are fully exploited. And from the standpoint of the courts, such a requirement is unwise because it would cause scarce resources to be consumed on cases that prove to be insubstantial, or that involve only some of the responsible parties or some of the criminal acts. Thus, no one's interests would be well served by compelling prosecutors to initiate prosecutions as soon as they are legally entitled to do so.

It might be argued that once the Government has assembled sufficient evidence to prove guilt beyond a reasonable doubt, it should be constitutionally required to file charges promptly, even if its investigation of the entire criminal transaction is not complete. Adopting such a rule, however, would have many of the same consequences as adopting a rule requiring immediate prosecution upon probable cause.

First, compelling a prosecutor to file public charges as soon as the requisite proof has been developed against one participant on one charge would cause numerous problems in those cases in which a criminal transaction involves more than one person or more than one illegal act. In some instances, an immediate arrest or indictment would impair the prosecutor's ability to continue his investigation, thereby preventing society from bringing lawbreakers to justice. In other cases, the prosecutor would be able to obtain additional indictments despite an early prosecution, but the necessary result would be multiple trials involving a single set of facts. Such trials place needless burdens on defendants, law enforcement officials, and courts.

Second, insisting on immediate prosecution once sufficient evidence is developed to obtain a conviction would pressure prosecutors into resolving doubtful cases in favor of early—and possibly unwarranted— prosecutions. The determination of when the evidence available to the prosecution is sufficient to obtain a conviction is seldom clear-cut, and reasonable persons often will reach conflicting conclusions. In the instant case, for example, since respondent admitted possessing at least five of the firearms, the primary factual issue in dispute was whether respondent knew the guns were stolen. * * * Not surprisingly, the Postal Inspector's report contained no direct evidence bearing on this issue. The decision whether to prosecute, therefore, required a necessarily subjective evaluation of the strength of the circumstantial evidence available and the credibility of respondent's denial. Even if a prosecutor concluded that the case was weak and further investigation appropriate, he would have no assurance that a reviewing court would agree. To avoid the risk that a subsequent indictment would be dismissed for preindictment delay, the prosecutor might feel constrained to file premature charges, with all the disadvantages that would entail.

Finally requiring the Government to make charging decisions immediately upon assembling evidence sufficient to establish guilt would preclude the Government from giving full consideration to the desirability of not prosecuting in particular cases. The decision to file criminal charges, with the awesome consequences it entails, requires consideration of a wide range of factors in addition to the strength of the Government's case, in order to determine whether prosecution would be in the public interest. Prosecutors often need more information than proof of a suspect's guilt, therefore, before deciding whether to seek an indictment. Again the instant case provides a useful illustration. Although proof of the identity of the mail thieves was not necessary to convict respondent of the possessory crimes with which he was charged, it might have been crucial in assessing respondent's culpability, as distinguished from his legal guilt. If, for example, further investigation were to show that respondent had no role in or advance knowledge of the theft and simply agreed, out of paternal loyalty, to help his son dispose of the guns once respondent discovered his son had stolen them, the United States Attorney might have decided not to prosecute, especially since at the time of the crime respondent was over 60 years old and had no prior criminal record. Requiring prosecution once the evidence of guilt is clear, however, could prevent a prosecutor from awaiting the information necessary for such a decision.

We would be most reluctant to adopt a rule which would have these consequences absent a clear constitutional command to do so. We can find no such command in the Due Process Clause of the Fifth Amendment. In our view, investigative delay is fundamentally unlike delay undertaken by the Government solely "to gain tactical advantage over the accused," * * * precisely because investigative delay is not so one-sided. Rather than deviating from elementary standards of "fair play and decency," a prosecutor abides by them if he refuses to seek indictments until he is completely satisfied that he should prosecute and will be able promptly to establish guilt beyond a reasonable doubt. Penalizing prosecutors who defer action for these reasons would subordinate the goal of "orderly expedition" to that of "mere speed." * * * This the Due Process Clause does not require. We therefore hold that to prosecute a defendant following investigative delay does not deprive him of due process, even if his defense might have been somewhat prejudiced by the lapse of time.

In the present case, the Court of Appeals stated that the only reason the Government postponed action was to await the results of additional investigation. Although there is, unfortunately, no evidence concerning the reasons for the delay in the record, the court's "finding" is supported by the prosecutor's implicit representation to the District Court, and explicit representation to the Court of Appeals, that the investigation continued during the time that the Government deferred taking action against respondent. The finding is, moreover, buttressed by the Government's repeated assertions in its petition for certiorari, its brief, and its oral argument in this Court, "that the delay was caused by the government's efforts to identify persons in addition to respondent who may have participated in the offenses." * * * We must assume that these statements by counsel have been made in good faith. In light of this explanation, it follows that compelling respondent to stand trial would not be fundamentally unfair. The Court of Appeals therefore erred in affirming the District Court's decision dismissing the indictment.

III

In *Marion* we conceded that we could not determine in the abstract the circumstances in which preaccusation delay would require dismissing prosecutions. * * * More than five years later, that statement remains true. Indeed, in the intervening years so few defendants have established that they were prejudiced by delay that neither this Court nor any lower court has had a sustained opportunity to consider the constitutional significance of various reasons for delay. We therefore leave to the lower courts, in the first instance, the task of applying the settled principles of due process that we have discussed to the particular circumstances of individual cases. We simply hold that in this case the lower courts erred in dismissing the indictment. **[a]**

Reversed.

[JUSTICE STEVENS, dissenting, felt the District Court established a firm case of unjustified and unnecessary delay. Therefore, it was improper for the Supreme Court to find that the Government delayed the indictment in order to continue the investigation.]

*   *   *   *   *   *   *   *   *   *

COMMENT

[a] A footnote citing A. Amsterdam, "Speedy Criminal Trial: Rights and Remedies," 27 *Stanford Law Review* 525 (1975), noted reasons for delay, including: law enforcement needs to maintain the "cover" of an undercover informer who develops cases against many suspects; the "sinister" motives of postponing the beginning of defense investigation, or holding a 'club' over the defendant; delay in reporting crimes; delay in identifying the suspect; delay caused by a suspect hiding; delay until a grand jury can be impaneled; and prosecutorial administrative decisions, such as staff assignments and priorities among investigations of known offenses.

Chapter Ten

THE ADJUDICATION PROCESS AND RELATED ISSUES

The determination of guilt or innocence is the immediate goal of the criminal process. The adjudication process encompasses all issues in respect to the criminal trial and plea bargaining. Also included are related topics such as the effect of publicity on the fairness of the trial, the role of the prosecutor and defense counsel, and fairness in jury selection. The law of evidence plays an especially central role in the conduct of jury trials. Of course, the formal rules of criminal procedure and evidence only set the stage for the human dynamics of the trial where the preparation and skill of the attorneys in the practice and the art of litigation bring the drama of the courtroom to life.

The right to trial by jury is enshrined in the Sixth Amendment as it is in the constitutions of every state. But jury trials account for perhaps five percent of all adjudications, with another five percent of criminal cases decided by bench (judge) trials. The vast majority of adjudications are determined by guilty plea. Jury trials have become quite lengthy and cumbersome and are typically reserved for contested cases of heinous crimes. Nevertheless it is constitutionally important for jury trials to be available for most offenses except for the most petty. The Supreme Court has "incorporated" the right to trial as applicable to the states through the due process clause of the Fourteenth Amendment (*Duncan v. Louisiana* [this volume, Chapter 1] (1968)) and implied that a jury is not required for "petty" offenses where the maximum penalty is six months of incarceration or less (*Baldwin v. New York*, 399 U.S. 66 (1970)). Additional statutory penalties, in addition to six months in jail, can take a crime out of the "petty" category, requiring a jury trial (*Blanton v. City of North Las Vegas*, 489 U.S. 538 (1989)).

Federal felony juries follow the traditional common law model, consisting of 12 persons and requiring a unanimous vote to render a guilty or not guilty verdict. Under the Sixth Amendment, as incorporated into the Fourteenth Amendment, the Supreme Court has allowed state juries to vary from this exacting standard. The Court held that a six-person jury was of sufficient size to promote adequate group deliberation, to insulate members from outside intimidation, and to provide a representative cross-section of the community in *Williams v. Florida*, 399 U.S. 78

(1970), but drew the line at five, holding such a jury to violate the Sixth Amendment in *Ballew v. Georgia*, 435 U.S. 223 (1978). The Court has also allowed the states to authorize non-unanimous verdicts for 12 member juries (*Apodaca v. Oregon*, 406 U.S. 404 (1972) (10-2 verdict); *Johnson v. Louisiana*, 406 U.S. 356 (1972) (9-3 verdict)), but has held that a nonunanimous verdict of a six member jury does not sufficiently protect the constitutional values of a trial (*Burch v. Louisiana* (1979)).

One trial value protected by the constitution is the right to be found guilty only on the evidentiary standard of proof of every element of the crime beyond a reasonable doubt (*In re Winship*, 397 U.S. 358 (1970)). This standard is universal in American law in adult felony cases, so its constitutional basis, as an element of due process, was not formally settled until it arose in a juvenile delinquency proceeding. A conviction must be reversed if a trial judge fails to instruct the jury on the reasonable doubt standard as to every element (*Osborne v. Ohio*, 495 U.S. 103 (1990)) or raises the standard of proof to a "moral certainty" (*Cage v. Louisiana*, 111 S.Ct. 328 (1990)). The Court attempted to clarify this standard in *Victor v. Nebraska* (1994). The State has the burden of proof, and it violates due process for a State to turn an element of the crime into a presumption that the defendant must rebut as an affirmative defense (*Mullaney v. Wilbur*, 421 U.S. 684 (1975)). However, certain affirmative defenses such as insanity or diminished capacity or alibi, which require the defendant to establish by a lesser standard than proof beyond a reasonable doubt, pass constitutional muster (*Patterson v. New York*, 432 U.S. 197 (1977)). The right to a jury trial does extend to juvenile delinquency determinations (*McKeiver v. Pennsylvania*, 403 U.S. 528 (1971)).

The selection of a fair jury is critical to justice. Jurors are tested at the voir dire. An unlimited number of jurors may be excused for "cause" (bias) and a limited number my be excused at the request of each attorney under peremptory challenges. The Equal Protection Clause of the Fourteenth Amendment is violated by laws that exclude African-Americans from jury service (*Strauder v. Virginia*, 100 U.S. 303 (1880)), by trial practices that do the same thing (*Neal v. Delaware*, 103 U.S. 370 (1881)), and by the proof that juries virtually exclude African-Americans (*Norris v. Alabama*, 294 U.S. 587 (1935)). Because proof of the Equal Protection violation required proof of intentional discrimination, this standard has not been historically useful in ending the actual exclusion of minorities from juries except in egregious cases (*Whitus v. Georgia*, 385 U.S. 545 (1967)). The exclusion of Mexican-Americans, an identifiable class protected by the Equal Protection Clause, is grounds for reversal (*Castaneda v. Partida*, 430 U.S. 482 (1977)).

The application of the Sixth Amendment impartial jury requirement means that the jury pool must reflect a fair cross-section of the community (*Glasser v. United States*, 315 U.S. 60 (1942)). This has been useful in reducing the exclusion of groups because proof of exclusion did not require proof of intent. Also, violations can be claimed by defendants who are not members of the excluded group. So, under the Sixth Amendment a white defendant asserted that the jury was not impartial when African-Americans were systematically excluded from jury service (*Peters v. Kiff*, 407 U.S. 493 (1972)). The Sixth Amendment is offended by rules that exclude women from jury service unless they specially apply (*Taylor v. Louisiana*, 419 U.S. 522 (1975)). In *Duren v. Missouri*, 439 U.S. 357 (1979), the Court held that the statistical underrepresentation of distinctive groups due to systematic exclusion, in this case women, violated the Sixth Amendment.

Batson v. Kentucky (1986) opened another avenue for eliminating bias on the jury by holding, under the Equal Protection Clause, that a prosecutor may not use peremptory challenges to eliminate African-American jurors from a trial unless the challenge can be shown not to be purposefully discriminatory. The *Batson* rule has been applied to civil cases (*Edmonson v. Leesville Concrete Co.*, 500 U.S. 614 (1991)) and to the use of peremptory challenges by defense attorneys in criminal cases (*Georgia v. McCollum* (1992)). The *Batson* rule has been expanded to include gender (*J.E.B. v. Alabama*, ___ U.S. ___ (1994)).

Earlier Due Process Clause cases held that trial fairness requires that questions about juror bias be allowed where racial bias might be an issue in the case (*Ham v. South Carolina*, 409 U.S. 524 (1973)), but such questions are not required simply because the defendant is black and the victim white (*Ristaino v. Ross*, 424 U.S. 589 (1976)).

The appearance or non-appearance of a defendant at trial can have an effect on the fairness of the case and implicates other rights. Trying a defendant in prison clothes has a negative effect on a jury and raises the due process issue of fairness and whether the proof beyond a reasonable doubt standard is met; a case will be dismissed if a defendant is tried in prison garb after objecting to the practice at trial (*Estelle v. Williams* (1976)). The conspicuous display of security personnel in the courtroom does not violate due process (*Holbrook v. Flynn*, 475 U.S. 560 (1986)). A defendant has a Sixth Amendment right to be confronted with the witnesses against him, but this right can be waived by a defendant who disrupts the trial by wild behavior. In such a case, the defendant can be removed, cited for contempt, or be bound and gagged (*Illinois v. Allen* (1970)).

The right to confrontation is violated when a state rule of evidence operated to prevent cross-examination of a witness (*Chambers v. Mississippi* (1973)). The right has been applied in a series of cases involving the troubling issue of child sexual abuse. In *Coy v. Iowa*, 487 U.S. 1012 (1988) a screen that prevented defendant from viewing the faces of teenage victims violated the face-to-face element of the Confrontation right. But in *Kentucky v. Stincer* (1987) that aspect of the right was not violated where the defendant, but not his counsel, was excluded from an *in camera* hearing to determine the competency of witness-victims who were five and eight years old. *Maryland v. Craig* (1990) ruled that a sex abuse trial met the Confrontation requirement where a six year old victim witness testified via closed circuit television, where cross-examination was available, the defendant could see the face of the witness, and there was a showing of necessity for the use of this procedure.

The hearsay rule has Confrontation Clause implications. In *Idaho v. Wright* (1990) the Court found that the hearsay testimony of a physician who did not preserve an adequate record of his interview with a child victim undermined the statement so that it did not bear a "circumstantial guarantee of trustworthiness." But in *White v. Illinois* (1992) a child's hearsay declarations were admitted under the spontaneous declaration and violent crime victim exceptions to the hearsay rule, without violating the defendant's right to confrontation.

An important trial area is the application of the Fifth Amendment privilege against self-incrimination. The right was incorporated into the Due Process Clause of the Fourteenth Amendment and made applicable in state proceedings (*Malloy v. Hogan*, 378 U.S. 1 (1964); *Murphy v. Waterfront Commission*, 378 U.S. 52 (1964)). The right can be claimed in civil or criminal proceedings. In *Garrity v. New Jersey* (1967) the Court enhanced the protection of the privilege by barring statements that had been compelled at an administrative hearing from being used against the defendant in a criminal prosecution. The Court also held that a person cannot suffer collateral civil consequences, such as the dismissal from one's position as a police officer, for having previously invoked the right to remain silent (*Gardner v. Broderick* (1968)).

The protection given by the right is only against self-incrimination, which can be overcome by the grant of immunity. The Supreme Court has upheld a narrower form of "use immunity" that forbids the use of the defendant's testimony and any evidence derived from it over the broader "transactional immunity" by which the defendant is protected against prosecution for any crimes relating to the compelled testimony (*Kastigar v. United States* (1972)).

The Fifth Amendment privilege does not extend to a corporation (*Hale v. Henkel*, 201 U.S. 43 (1906)), an unincorporated organization like a labor union (*United States v. White*, 322 U.S. 694 (1944)), a partnership (*Bellis v. United States*, 417 U.S. 85 (1974)), or to subpoenas for business documents that have already been voluntarily created (*Fisher v. United States*, 425 U.S. 391 (1976)(documents prepared by defendant's accountant in the possession of defendant's attorney); *United States v. Doe*, 465 U.S. 605 (1984)(defendant's business records in his possession)).

There is no compulsion, for Fifth Amendment purposes, when a statute requires that information be reported that is essential to a public, regulatory purpose, even if the reporting also compels incriminating information (*California v. Byers*, 402 U.S. 424 (1971)(information regarding automobile accident)). The privilege against self-incrimination applies to protect against being compelled to make a testimonial statement, but not to the *production* of testimonial evidence (*Doe v. United States*, 487 U.S. 201 (1988)). In *Baltimore Dept. of Social Services v. Bouknight* (1990) the Court held that the state could compel a mother, who had custody of her child under a department of social services order and supervision, to produce her child in a custody hearing in juvenile court; however, the Court noted that any incriminating evidence that came out of that act of production might not be admissible in a criminal proceeding against the mother.

The Supreme Court legitimated the practice of plea bargaining in several cases in the late 1960s and early 1970s. The government must abide by its plea agreement (*Santobello v. New York* (1972)) as must the defendant (*Ricketts v. Adamson*, 483 U.S. 1 (1987)(must testify not only at initial trial of codefendants but at retrials as well)). Entering a guilty plea is the equivalent of admitting every element of the offense (*McCarthy v. United States*, 394 U.S. 459 (1969)). A waiver of a trial must be made knowingly and voluntarily and a record is required (*Boykin v. United States*, 395 U.S. 238 (1969)). The defendant must be personally addressed by the judge (*McCarthy*) and must be informed of each of the rights given up when the defendant pleads guilty.

Guilty pleas are made under considerable pressure; this is not the kind of pressure that renders pleas involuntary, even if the plea is made to avoid the death penalty (*Brady v. United States*, 397 U.S. 742 (1970)). Due process is not violated when a prosecutor informs a defendant that if the defendant does not plead guilty the prosecutor will also charge the defendant as a habitual offender as allowed under the facts of the case (*Bordenkircher v. Hayes*, 434 U.S. 357 (1978)).

BURCH v. LOUISIANA

441 U.S. 130, 99 S.Ct. 1623, 60 L.Ed.2d 96 (1979)

MR. JUSTICE REHNQUIST delivered the opinion of the Court.

The Louisiana Constitution and Code of Criminal Procedure provide that criminal cases in which the punishment imposed may be confinement for a period in excess of six months "shall be tried before a jury of six persons, five of whom must concur to render a verdict." We granted certiorari to decide whether conviction by a nonunanimous six-person jury in a state criminal trial for a nonpetty offense as contemplated by these provisions of Louisiana law violates the rights of an accused to trial by jury guaranteed by the Sixth and Fourteenth Amendments. * * *

[Burch and a corporation, charged with exhibiting obscene motion pictures, were tried by a six-person jury. Both were found guilty. A poll of the jury after verdict indicated that the jury had voted unanimously to convict the corporation and had voted 5-1 to convict Burch, who was sentenced to seven months in prison.]

Petitioners appealed their convictions to the Supreme Court of Louisiana, where they argued that the provisions of Louisiana law permitting conviction by a nonunanimous six-member jury violated the rights of persons accused of nonpetty criminal offenses to trial by jury guaranteed by the Sixth and Fourteenth Amendments. Though acknowledging that the issue was "close," the court held that conviction by a nonunanimous six-person jury did not offend the Constitution. * * * The court concluded that none of this

Court's decisions precluded use of a nonunanimous six-person jury. "If 75 percent concurrence (9/12) was enough for a verdict as determined in *Johnson v. Louisiana*, 406 U.S. 356 . . . (1972), then requiring 83 percent concurrence (5/6) ought to be within the permissible limits of *Johnson*.'" * * * And our recent decision in *Ballew v. Georgia*, 435 U.S. 223 (1978), striking down a Georgia law allowing conviction by a unanimous five-person jury in nonpetty criminal cases, was distinguishable in the Louisiana Supreme Court's view:

"[In] *Williams [v. Florida*, 399 U.S. 78 (1970)] the court held that a six-person jury was of sufficient size to promote adequate group deliberation, to insulate members from outside intimidation, and to provide a representative cross-section of the community. These values, which *Ballew* held a five-person jury is inadequate to serve, are not necessarily defeated because the six-person jury's verdict may be rendered by five instead of by six persons." * * *

Since the Louisiana Supreme Court believed that conviction by a nonunanimous six-person jury was not necessarily foreclosed by this Court's decisions, it stated that it preferred to "indulg[e] in the presumption of federal constitutionality which must be afforded to provisions of our state constitution." * * *

We agree with the Louisiana Supreme Court that the question

presented is a "close" one. Nonetheless, we believe that conviction by a nonunanimous six-member jury in a state criminal trial for a nonpetty offense deprives an accused of his constitutional right to trial by jury.

Only in relatively recent years has this Court had to consider the practices of the several States relating to jury size and unanimity. *Duncan v. Louisiana*, [this volume], marked the beginning of our involvement with such questions. The Court in *Duncan* held that because trial by jury in "serious" criminal cases is "fundamental to the American scheme of justice" and essential to due process of law, the Fourteenth Amendment guarantees a state criminal defendant the right to a jury trial in any case which, if tried in a federal court, would require a jury under the Sixth Amendment. * * *

[a]

Two Terms later in *Williams v. Florida*, * * * the Court held that this constitutional guarantee of trial by jury did not require a State to provide an accused with a jury of 12 members and that Florida did not violate the jury trial rights of criminal defendants charged with nonpetty offenses by affording them jury panels comprised of only 6 persons. After canvassing the common-law development of the jury and the constitutional history of the jury trial right, the Court concluded that the 12-person requirement was "a historical accident" and that there was no indication that the Framers intended to preserve in the Constitution the features of the jury system as it existed at common law. * * * Thus freed from strictly historical considerations, the Court turned to examine the function that this particular feature performs and its relation to

the purposes of jury trial. * * * The purpose of trial by jury, as noted in *Duncan*, is to prevent government oppression by providing a "safeguard against the corrupt or overzealous prosecutor and against the compliant, biased, or eccentric judge." * * * Given this purpose, the *Williams* Court observed that the jury's essential feature lies in the "interposition between the accused and his accuser of the commonsense judgment of a group of laymen, and in the community participation and shared responsibility that results from that group's determination of guilt or innocence." * * * These purposes could be fulfilled, the Court believed, so long as the jury was of a sufficient size to promote group deliberation, free from outside intimidation, and to provide a fair possibility that a cross section of the community would be represented on it. * * * The Court concluded, however, that there is "little reason to think that these goals are in any meaningful sense less likely to be achieved when the jury numbers six, than when it numbers 12— *particularly if the requirement of unanimity is retained.*" * * * (emphasis added).

A similar analysis led us to conclude in 1972 that a jury's verdict need not be unanimous to satisfy constitutional requirements, even though unanimity had been the rule at common law. Thus, in *Apodaca v. Oregon*, 406 U.S. 404 (1972), we upheld a state statute providing that only 10 members of a 12-person jury need concur to render a verdict in certain noncapital cases. In terms of the role of the jury as a safeguard against oppression, the plurality opinion perceived no difference between those juries required to act unanimously and those permitted to act by votes of 10 to 2. * * * Nor was unanimity viewed by the plurality as contributing materially to the exercise of the jury's common-sense judgment or as a necessary precondition to effective application of the requirement that jury panels represent a fair cross section of the community. * * *

Last Term, in *Ballew v. Georgia*, * * * we considered whether a jury of less than six members passes constitutional scrutiny, a question that was explicitly reserved in *Williams v. Florida*. * * * The Court, in separate opinions, held that conviction by a unanimous five-person jury in a trial for a nonpetty offense deprives an accused of his right to trial by jury. While readily admitting that the line between six members and five was not altogether easy to justify, at least five Members of the Court believed that reducing a jury to five persons in nonpetty cases raised sufficiently substantial doubts as to the fairness of the proceeding and proper functioning of the jury to warrant drawing the line at six. * * *

We thus have held that the Constitution permits juries of less than 12 members, but that it requires at least 6. * * * And we have approved the use of certain nonunanimous verdicts in cases involving 12-person juries. *Apodaca v. Oregon, supra* (10-2); *Johnson v. Louisiana*, 406 U.S. 356 (1972) (9-3). These principles are not questioned here. Rather, this case lies at the intersection of our decisions concerning jury size and unanimity. As in *Ballew*, we do not pretend the ability to discern *a priori* a bright line below which the number of jurors participating in the trial or in the verdict would not permit the jury to function in the manner required by our

prior cases. * * * But having already departed from the strictly historical requirements of jury trial, it is inevitable that lines must be drawn somewhere if the substance of the jury trial right is to be preserved. * * * Even the State concedes as much. * * *

This line-drawing process, "although essential, cannot be wholly satisfactory, for it requires attaching different consequences to events which, when they lie near the line, actually differ very little." *Duncan v. Louisiana.* * * * However, much the same reasons that led us in *Ballew* to decide that use of a five-member jury threatened the fairness of the proceeding and the proper role of the jury, lead us to conclude now that conviction for a nonpetty offense by only five members of a six-person jury presents a similar threat to preservation of the substance of the jury trial guarantee and justifies our requiring verdicts rendered by six-person juries to be unanimous. We are buttressed in this view by the current jury practices of the several States. It appears that of those States that utilize six-member juries in trials of nonpetty offenses, only two, including Louisiana, also allow nonunanimous verdicts. We think that this near-uniform judgment of the Nation provides a useful guide in delimiting the line between those jury practices that are constitutionally permissible and those that are not. * * *

The State seeks to justify its use of nonunanimous six-person juries on the basis of the "considerable time" savings that it claims results from trying cases in this manner. It asserts that under its system, juror deliberation time is shortened and the number of hung juries is reduced. * * * Undoubtedly, the State has a substantial interest in reducing the time and expense associated with the administration of its system of criminal justice. But that interest cannot prevail here. First, on this record, any benefits that might accrue by allowing five members of a six-person jury to render a verdict, as compared with requiring unanimity of a six-member jury, are speculative, at best. More importantly, we think that when a State has reduced the size of its juries to the minimum number of jurors permitted by the Constitution, the additional authorization of non-unanimous verdicts by such juries sufficiently threatens the constitutional principles that led to the establishment of the size threshold that any counter-vailing interest of the State should yield.

The judgment of the Louisiana Supreme Court affirming the conviction of petitioner Burch is, therefore, reversed. * * *

[JUSTICE STEVENS concurred; JUSTICE BRENNAN, joined by JUSTICES STEWART and MARSHALL concurred in the opinion regarding the jury unanimity issue, but dissented to the remand on the grounds that the obscenity statute was overbroad and that the conviction should therefore be overturned.]

* * * * * * * * * *

COMMENTS

[a] In a note the Court stated that the jury rules announced in this and other cases cited applied only to non-petty offenses.
Duncan v. Louisiana "reaffirmed the long-established view that 'petty offenses' may be tried without a jury. * * *" *Baldwin v. New York*, 399 U.S. 66, 69 (1970), defined a non-petty offense (for the purposes of the right to a jury) as "any offense where imprisonment for more than six months is authorized."

BATSON v. KENTUCKY

476 U.S. 79, 106 S.Ct. 1712, 90 L.Ed.2d 69 (1986)

JUSTICE POWELL delivered the opinion of the Court.

This case requires us to reexamine that portion of *Swain v. Alabama*, 380 U.S. 202 (1965), concerning the evidentiary burden placed on a criminal defendant who claims that he has been denied equal protection through the State's use of peremptory challenges to exclude members of his race from the petit jury.

I

Petitioner, a black man, was indicted in Kentucky on charges of second-degree burglary and receipt of stolen goods. [At his trial,] the judge conducted *voir dire* examination of the venire, excused certain jurors for cause, and permitted the parties to exercise peremptory challenges. The prosecutor used his peremptory challenges to strike all four black persons on the venire, and a jury composed only of white persons was selected. [Counsel claimed] that the prosecutor's removal of the black veniremen violated petitioner's rights under the Sixth and Fourteenth Amendments to a jury drawn from a cross section of the community, and under the Fourteenth Amendment to equal protection of the laws. [The judge denied the motion, observing] that the parties were entitled to use their peremptory challenges to "strike anybody they want to." * * *

[Batson's conviction was upheld by the Kentucky Supreme Court, which relied on *Swain*:] a defendant alleging lack of a fair cross section must demonstrate systematic exclusion of a group of jurors from the venire. * * * We granted certiorari, * * * and now reverse.

II

In *Swain v. Alabama*, this Court recognized that a "State's purposeful or deliberate denial to Negroes on account of race of participation as jurors in the administration of justice violates the Equal Protection Clause." **[a]** * * * This principle has been "consistently and repeatedly" reaffirmed, * * * in numerous decisions of this Court both preceding and following *Swain*. We reaffirm the principle today.

A

More than a century ago, the Court decided that the State denies a black defendant equal protection of the laws when it puts him on trial before a jury from which members of his race have been purposefully excluded. *Strauder v. West Virginia*, 100 U.S. 303 (1880). **[b]** That decision laid the foundation for the Court's unceasing efforts to eradicate racial discrimination in the procedures used to select the venire from which individual jurors are drawn. In *Strauder*, the Court explained that the central concern of the recently ratified Fourteenth Amendment was to put an end to governmental discrimination on account of race. * * * Exclusion of black citizens from service as jurors constitutes a primary example of the evil the Fourteenth Amendment was designed to cure.

In holding that racial discrimination in jury selection offends the Equal Protection Clause, the Court in *Strauder* recognized, however, that a defendant has no right to a "petit jury composed in whole or in part of persons of his own race." * * * "The number of our races and nationalities stands in the way of evolution of such a conception" of the demand of equal protection. [c] * * * But the defendant does have the right to be tried by a jury whose members are selected pursuant to non-discriminatory criteria. * * * The Equal Protection Clause guarantees the defendant that the State will not exclude members of his race from the jury venire on account of race, * * * or on the false assumption that members of his race as a group are not qualified to serve as jurors.

Purposeful racial discrimination in selection of the venire violates a defendant's right to equal protection because it denies him the protection that a trial by jury is intended to secure. "The very idea of a jury is a body . . . composed of the peers or equals of the person whose rights it is selected or summoned to determine; that is, of his neighbors, fellows, associates, persons having the same legal status in society as that which he holds." [d] The petit jury has occupied a central position in our system of justice by safeguarding a person accused of crime against the arbitrary exercise of power by prosecutor or judge. * * * Those on the venire must be "indifferently chosen," to secure the defendant's right under the Fourteenth Amendment to "protection of life and liberty against race or color prejudice." * * *

* * *

The harm from discriminatory jury selection extends beyond that inflicted on the defendant and the excluded juror to touch the entire community. [e] Selection procedures that purposefully exclude black persons from juries undermine public confidence in the fairness of our system of justice. Discrimination within the judicial system is most pernicious because it is "a stimulant to that race prejudice which is an impediment to securing to [African-Americans] that equal justice which the law aims to secure to all others."

B

In *Strauder*, the Court invalidated a state statute that provided that only white men could serve as jurors. * * * We can be confident that no State now has such a law. The Constitution requires, however, that we look beyond the face of the statute defining juror qualifications and also consider challenged selection practices to afford "protection against action of the State through its administrative officers in effecting the prohibited discrimination." [f] * * * Thus, the Court has found a denial of equal protection where the procedures implementing a neutral statute operated to exclude persons from the venire on racial grounds, and has made clear that the Constitution prohibits all forms of purposeful racial discrimination in selection of jurors. While decisions of this Court have been concerned largely with discrimination during selection of the venire, the principles announced there also forbid discrimination on account of race in selection of the petit jury. Since the Fourteenth Amendment protects an accused throughout the proceedings bringing him to justice, * * * the State may not draw up its jury lists pursuant to neutral procedures but then resort to discrimination at "other stages in the selection process." * * *

Accordingly, the component of the jury selection process at issue here, the State's privilege to strike individual jurors through peremptory challenges, is subject to the commands of the Equal Protection Clause. Although a prosecutor ordinarily is entitled to exercise permitted peremptory challenges "for any reason at all, as long as that reason is related to his view concerning the outcome" of the case to be tried, * * * the Equal Protection Clause forbids the prosecutor to challenge potential jurors solely on account of their race or on the assumption that black jurors as a group will be unable impartially to consider the State's case against a black defendant. [g]

III

The principles announced in *Strauder* never have been questioned in any subsequent decision of this Court. Rather, the Court has been called upon repeatedly to review the application of those principles to particular facts. A recurring question in these cases, as in any case alleging a violation of the Equal Protection Clause, was whether the defendant had met his burden of proving purposeful discrimination on the part of the State. [h] * * * That question also was at the heart of the portion of *Swain v. Alabama* we reexamine today.

A

[In *Swain* the prosecutor used the State's peremptory challenges to strike the six African-Americans included on the petit jury venire in the trial of an African-American.] While rejecting the defendant's claim for failure to prove purposeful discrimination, the Court nonetheless indicated that the Equal Protection Clause placed some limits on the State's exercise of peremptory challenges. [i]

* * * While the Constitution does not confer a right to peremptory challenges, * * * those challenges traditionally have been viewed as one means of assuring the selection of a qualified and unbiased jury. * * * To preserve the peremptory nature of the prosecutor's challenge, the Court in *Swain* declined to scrutinize his actions in a particular case by relying on a presumption that he properly exercised the State's challenges. [j] * * *

The Court went on to observe, however, that a State may not exercise its challenges in contravention of the Equal Protection Clause. It was impermissible for a prosecutor to use his challenges to exclude blacks from the jury "for reasons wholly unrelated to the outcome of the particular case on trial" or to deny to blacks "the same right and opportunity to participate in the administration of justice enjoyed by the white population." * * * Accordingly, a black defendant could make out a prima facie case of purposeful discrimination on proof that the peremptory challenge system was "being perverted" in that manner. * * * For example, an inference of purposeful discrimination would be raised on evidence that a prosecutor, "in case after case, whatever the circumstances, whatever the crime and whoever the defendant or the victim may be, is responsible for the removal of Negroes who have been selected as

qualified jurors by the jury commission-
ers and who have survived challenges
for cause, with the result that no
Negroes ever serve on petit juries." * *
* Evidence offered by the defendant
in *Swain* did not meet that standard.
While the defendant showed that
prosecutors in the jurisdiction had
exercised their strikes to exclude blacks
from the jury, he offered no proof of
the circumstances under which prosecutors were responsible for striking black
jurors beyond the facts of his own
case. [k]

A number of lower courts following
the teaching of *Swain* reasoned that
proof of repeated striking of blacks
over a number of cases was necessary
to establish a violation of the Equal
Protection Clause. Since this interpretation of *Swain* has placed on defendants a crippling burden of proof,
prosecutors' peremptory challenges are
now largely immune from constitutional scrutiny. [l] For reasons that
follow, we reject this evidentiary formulation as inconsistent with standards
that have been developed since *Swain*
for assessing a prima facie case under
the Equal Protection Clause.

B

[In other equal protection cases
regarding the jury panel (venire)
selection since *Swain*, the Court required a finding of "a racially discriminatory purpose" before finding unconstitutional discrimination. The burden
of proving this is on the defendant.
But once the defendant "has carried
his burden of persuasion," even by
circumstantial evidence, the court "must
undertake 'a sensitive inquiry'" into the
direct and circumstantial evidence.
Thus, even if there is no direct evi-

dence of a discriminatory purpose but
the discriminatory impact is overwhelming, as in the total exclusion of
African-Americans from the venire, a
court may find invidious discrimination
and an equal protection violation.]

* * * Once the defendant makes
the requisite showing, the burden shifts
to the State to explain adequately the
racial exclusion. * * * The State
cannot meet this burden on mere
general assertions that its officials did
not discriminate or that they properly
performed their official duties. * * *
Rather, the State must demonstrate
that "permissible racially neutral selection criteria and procedures have
produced the monochromatic result."
[m] * * *

* * * Proof of systematic exclusion from the venire raises an inference of purposeful discrimination
because the "result bespeaks discrimination."

Since the ultimate issue is
whether the State has discriminated in
selecting the defendant's venire, however, the defendant may establish a
prima facie case [by showing that
African-Americans had long been
excluded from jury panels; that they
were] substantially underrepresented on
the venire from which his jury was
drawn, and that the venire was selected
under a practice providing "the opportunity for discrimination." * * *
[When this combination of factors
occurs, the Court presumes that
purposeful discrimination exists. When
such factors are raised,] the trial court
must undertake a "factual inquiry" that
"takes into account all possible explanatory factors" in the particular case. * *
*

* * * [A] defendant may make a

prima facie showing of purposeful racial discrimination in selection of the venire by relying solely on the facts concerning its selection *in his case.* "* * * A single invidiously discriminatory governmental act" is not "immunized by the absence of such discrimination in the making of other comparable decisions." * * * For evidentiary requirements to dictate that "several must suffer discrimination" before one could object, * * * would be inconsistent with the promise of equal protection to all. [n]

C

The standards for assessing a prima facie case in the context of discriminatory selection of the venire have been fully articulated since *Swain.* * * * These principles support our conclusion that a defendant may establish a prima facie case of purposeful discrimination in selection of the petit jury solely on evidence concerning the prosecutor's exercise of peremptory challenges at the defendant's trial. To establish such a case, the defendant first must show that he is a member of a cognizable racial group, * * * and that the prosecutor has exercised peremptory challenges to remove from the venire members of the defendant's race. Second, the defendant is entitled to rely on the fact, as to which there can be no dispute, that peremptory challenges constitute a jury selection practice that permits "those to discriminate who are of a mind to discriminate." * * * Finally, the defendant must show that these facts and any other relevant circumstances raise an inference that the prosecutor used that practice to exclude the veniremen from the petit jury on account of their race.

This combination of factors in the empaneling of the petit jury, as in the selection of the venire, raises the necessary inference of purposeful discrimination.

In deciding whether the defendant has made the requisite showing, the trial court should consider all relevant circumstances. For example, a "pattern" of strikes against black jurors included in the particular venire might give rise to an inference of discrimination. Similarly, the prosecutor's questions and statements during *voir dire* examination and in exercising his challenges may support or refute an inference of discriminatory purpose. These examples are merely illustrative. We have confidence that trial judges, experienced in supervising *voir dire*, will be able to decide if the circumstances concerning the prosecutor's use of peremptory challenges creates a prima facie case of discrimination against black jurors.

Once the defendant makes a prima facie showing, the burden shifts to the State to come forward with a neutral explanation for challenging black jurors. Though this requirement imposes a limitation in some cases on the full peremptory character of the historic challenge, we emphasize that the prosecutor's explanation need not rise to the level justifying exercise of a challenge for cause. * * * But the prosecutor may not rebut the defendant's prima facie case of discrimination by stating merely that he challenged jurors of the defendant's race on the assumption—or his intuitive judgment—that they would be partial to the defendant because of their shared race. * * * Just as the Equal Protection Clause forbids the States to exclude black persons from the venire on the assumption that blacks as a group are unqualified to serve as jurors, * * * so it forbids the States to strike black veniremen on the assumption that they will be biased in a particular case simply because the defendant is black. The core guarantee of equal protection, ensuring citizens that their State will not discriminate on account of race, would be meaningless were we to approve the exclusion of jurors on the basis of such assumptions, which arise solely from the jurors' race. Nor may the prosecutor rebut the defendant's case merely by denying that he had a discriminatory motive or "affirm[ing] [his] good faith in making individual selections." * * * If these general assertions were accepted as rebutting a defendant's prima facie case, the Equal Protection Clause "would be but a vain and illusory requirement." * * * The prosecutor therefore must articulate a neutral explanation related to the particular case to be tried. The trial court then will have the duty to determine if the defendant has established purposeful discrimination.

IV

The State contends that our holding will eviscerate the fair trial values served by the peremptory challenge. Conceding that the Constitution does not guarantee a right to peremptory challenges and that *Swain* did state that their use ultimately is subject to the strictures of equal protection, the State argues that the privilege of unfettered exercise of the challenge is of vital importance to the criminal justice system.

While we recognize, of course, that the peremptory challenge occupies an important position in our trial procedures, we do not   agree that our decision today will undermine the contribution the challenge generally makes to the administration of justice. The reality of practice, amply reflected in many state- and federal-court opinions, shows that the challenge may be, and unfortunately at times has been, used to discriminate against black jurors. By requiring trial courts to be sensitive to the racially discriminatory use of peremptory challenges, our decision enforces the mandate of equal protection and furthers the ends of justice. In view of the heterogeneous population of our Nation, public respect for our criminal justice system and the rule of law will be strengthened if we ensure that no citizen is disqualified from jury service because of his race. [o]

* * *

V

[The case was remanded to the trial court to find whether there was purposeful discrimination in the use of the peremptories and, if so, whether the prosecutor could supply a neutral explanation. If purposeful, unexplained discrimination is found, the conviction must be reversed.]

JUSTICE MARSHALL, concurring.

I join JUSTICE POWELL's eloquent opinion for the Court, which takes a historic step toward eliminating the shameful practice of racial discrimination in the selection of juries. * * * I nonetheless write separately to express my views. The decision today will not end the racial discrimination that peremptories inject into the jury-selection process. That goal can be accomplished only by eliminating peremptory challenges entirely. [p]

I

* * *

Misuse of the peremptory challenge to exclude black jurors has become both common and flagrant. * * *

II

. . . Cases from [several states] illustrate the limitations of the [Court's] approach. First, defendants cannot attack the discriminatory use of peremptory challenges at all unless the challenges are so flagrant as to establish a prima facie case. This means, in those States, that where only one or two black jurors survive the challenges for cause, the prosecutor need have no compunction about striking them from the jury because of their race. . . . Prosecutors are left free to discriminate against blacks in jury selection provided that they hold that discrimination to an "acceptable" level.

Second, when a defendant can establish a prima facie case, trial courts face the difficult burden of assessing prosecutors' motives. * * * Any prosecutor can easily assert facially neutral reasons for striking a juror, and trial courts are ill equipped to second-guess those reasons. * * *

Nor is outright prevarication by prosecutors the only danger here. "[I]t is even possible that an attorney may lie to himself in an effort to convince himself that his motives are legal." * * * A prosecutor's own conscious or unconscious racism may lead him easily to the conclusion that a prospective

black juror is "sullen," or "distant," a characterization that would not have come to his mind if a white juror had acted identically. . . . [q]

III

The inherent potential of peremptory challenges to distort the jury process by permitting the exclusion of jurors on racial grounds should ideally lead the Court to ban them entirely from the criminal justice system. * * *

[Therefore, neither should defendants be allowed peremptory challenges because they can also "engage in racial discrimination in jury selection."] [r]

Much ink has been spilled regarding the historic importance of defendants' peremptory challenges. * * * But this Court has also repeatedly stated that the right of peremptory challenge is not of constitutional magnitude, and may be withheld altogether without impairing the constitutional guarantee of impartial jury and fair trial. [s] * * * The potential for racial prejudice, further, inheres in the defendant's challenge as well. If the prosecutor's peremptory challenge could be eliminated only at the cost of eliminating the defendant's challenge as well, I do not think that would be too great a price to pay.
* * *

[JUSTICES WHITE, STEVENS, and O'CONNOR concurred separately.]

CHIEF JUSTICE BURGER, joined by JUSTICE REHNQUIST, dissenting.

[Chief Justice Burger's dissent raised the following points. 1. The decision is unusual in that it was based on a constitutional argument that the petitioner did not raise, weakening adherence to precedent and to the Court's normal procedures. 2. The peremptory challenge serves an important function in assuring that the jury will decide a case on the basis of the evidence. 3. Unlike the *Strauder* rule, which properly finds an equal protection violation when classes of persons are excluded from the venire, this case attacks a procedure that is a discrete decision made in a case and tailored to its particular circumstances. 4. The majority's equal protection rule is not the usual rule, because it applies only to race and does not come into play if jurors are excluded on the grounds of sex, religious or political affiliation, mental capacity, or profession, all of which have been protected by equal protection principles. 5. Since the rule is based on equal protection rather than Sixth Amendment principles, it will of necessity be applied to defendants, denying them of the use of peremptory challenges when they believe certain jurors are racially biased. 6. The Court's ruling will inject race into the cases, as attorneys ask prospective jurors overtly to state their race or ethnicity in order to build a record to attack the use of peremptories on the ground of racial bias. In addition the CHIEF JUSTICE raised the following objection to the majority's logic.] **[t]**

Rather than applying straightforward equal protection analysis, the Court substitutes for the holding in *Swain* a curious hybrid. The defendant must first establish a "prima facie case," of invidious discrimination, then the "burden shifts to the State to come forward with a neutral explanation for

challenging black jurors." * * * The Court explains that "the operation of prima facie burden of proof rules" is established in "[o]ur decisions concerning 'disparate treatment.' . . ." * * * The Court then adds, . . . that "the prosecutor must give a 'clear and reasonably specific' explanation of his 'legitimate reasons' for exercising the challenges."

While undoubtedly these rules are well suited to other contexts, particularly where (as with Title VII) they are required by an Act of Congress, they seem curiously out of place when applied to peremptory challenges in criminal cases. Our system permits two types of challenges: challenges for cause and peremptory challenges. Challenges for cause obviously have to be explained; by definition, peremptory challenges do not. . . . Analytically, there is no middle ground: A challenge either has to be explained or it does not. It is readily apparent, then, that to permit inquiry into the basis for a peremptory challenge would force "the peremptory challenge [to] collapse into the challenge for cause." * * * **[u]**

Confronted with the dilemma it created, the Court today attempts to decree a middle ground. To rebut a prima facie case, the Court requires a "neutral explanation" for the challenge, but is at pains to "emphasize" that the "explanation need not rise to the level justifying exercise of a challenge for cause." * * * I am at a loss to discern the governing principles here. A "clear and reasonably specific" explanation of "legitimate reasons" for exercising the challenge will be difficult to distinguish from a challenge for cause. . . . Apparently the Court envisions permissible challenges short of a challenge for cause that are just a little bit arbitrary—but not too much. While our trial judges are "experienced in supervising *voir dire*," * * * they have no experience in administering rules like this.

* * * * * * * * * *

COMMENTS

[a] In a footnote, JUSTICE POWELL noted that Batson invoked his Sixth Amendment right to an impartial jury, surmising that he did this to avoid losing his case on the equal protection precedent of *Swain*, which was against him. Nevertheless, the case would be decided on Fourteenth Amendment equal protection principles, rather than on Sixth Amendment doctrines.

[b] The fact that this struggle has gone on for over a century is powerful testimony to the effect of racism in some aspects of the criminal justice and legal processes. Even a color-blind constitutional principle and positive rulings from the Supreme Court could not override a society holding tenaciously to racist practices. This is another example, not a happy one, of the interaction between law and society.

[c] In a footnote, the Court reaffirmed this, saying, "Indeed, it would be impossible to apply a concept of proportional representation to the petit jury in view of the heterogeneous nature of our society."

[d] Some argue that only a jury made up of people of the same race, or social class, or age group, etc. genuinely constitutes one's "peers." Note that the Court is careful to define persons as having the same *legal* status as peers. As we have no formal aristocracy or royalty in America, all adult citizens are peers. Is this a wise rule for the purposes of jury selection?

[e] This is an unusual acknowledgment from the Court that the policies underlying the decision go far beyond a concern for a properly run jury selection process.

[f] JUSTICE POWELL lays the foundation for the holding: despite the rule that the twelve-person petit jury need not represent a statistical cross-section of the community (a virtual impossibility), the equal protection clause requires the courts to inquire into the *method* of selecting members of the petit jury.

[g] In a footnote, JUSTICE POWELL noted that the Court was not making any ruling on whether the Constitution limited the exercise of peremptory challenges by defense counsel. See *Georgia v. McCollum*, [this volume].

[h] JUSTICE POWELL's strategy in this section is brilliant. He wishes to preserve the peremptory challenge yet allow it to be challenged, where relevant, on the ground that it is being used to perpetuate racial bias. As noted below, neither

JUSTICE MARSHALL, concurring, nor CHIEF JUSTICE BURGER, dissenting, desire such a fine-line ruling. JUSTICE POWELL achieves his goal by shifting the main justification of the ruling from a substantive basis to an evidentiary, burden of proof, footing.

[i] *Swain* is an example where a defendant lost a case but gained a principle that is beneficial to later claimants. The appellate process serves justice, if not the individual defendant.

[j] A legal presumption can be difficult to rebut. In this case, the *Swain* presumption virtually left the peremptory challenge free from interference.

[k] Given the *Swain* rule, the real difference between *Swain* and this case rests not so much on the substantive rule, but on how difficult or easy it is to prove racial discrimination as the basis for exercising a peremptory challenge. *Swain* erected an impossible standard of proof except in the most flagrant cases. So, the difference between the cases makes the right a reality rather than an unobtainable ideal. The law operates not only by ethical substantive rules but in actuality by rules of evidence and procedure.

[l] JUSTICE POWELL takes instruction from the experience of the lower courts that applied the *Swain* rule and found it wanting—an example of the Supreme Court not acting in an autocratic manner toward lower courts.

[m] Note how, once the defendant makes out a case seriously raising the possibility of racial purpose in exercising a peremptory challenge, the burden effectively shifts to the State to prove that its purpose was valid.

[n] These paragraphs indicate more lenient evidentiary rules that may now make it possible for criminal defendants to successfully attack peremptory challenges. The easing up of the evidentiary hurdles virtually changes the substantive rule, at least in its tangible impact on the community.

[o] The choice here is between two values: peremptory challenges or equal protection and the appearance of justice.

[p] JUSTICE MARSHALL's radical solution would deprive prosecutors and defense counsel of peremptory challenges in cases where race is not a factor. Is his remedy worth the price?

[q] JUSTICE MARSHALL arrays powerful evidence suggesting that the Court's new rule in this case will be of greater symbolic than real value to defendants who believe that the prosecutor is unjustly striking jurors.

[r] This is an evenhanded approach; the issue is more racial prejudice in jury selection than prejudice to the defendant.

[s] The fact that the practice of peremptory challenges is not based on a constitutional right makes it easier for the Court to follow JUSTICE MARSHALL's suggestion. Is it possible that trials will be more fair without peremptory challenges by making jurors more appreciative of their role? Or will it allow biased jurors who pass the challenge-for-cause process to serve, undermining the trial's fairness?

[t] In a sense, the CHIEF JUSTICE and JUSTICE MARSHALL agreed that an all-or-nothing rule would be preferable to the majority's "hybrid." The CHIEF JUSTICE, however, wanted "all," while JUSTICE MARSHALL wanted "nothing."

[u] CHIEF JUSTICE BURGER is certainly correct in implying that the nature of peremptory challenges is no longer the same; he exaggerates, though, in suggesting the this case destroys peremptory challenges and turns them into challenges for cause, even in cases where African-American jurors are removed by the prosecutor in a case with an African-American defendant.

GEORGIA v. McCOLLUM

___ U.S. ___, 112 S.Ct. 2348, 120 L.Ed.2d 33 (1992)

JUSTICE BLACKMUN delivered the opinion of the Court.

For more than a century, this Court consistently and repeatedly has reaffirmed that racial discrimination by the State in jury selection offends the Equal Protection Clause. * * * Last Term this Court held that racial discrimination in a civil litigant's exercise of peremptory challenges also violates the Equal Protection Clause. See *Edmonson v. Leesville Concrete Co.*, 500 U.S. 614 (1991). Today, we are asked to decide whether the Constitution prohibits a *criminal defendant* from engaging in purposeful racial discrimination in the exercise of peremptory challenges.

I

[Thomas, William, and Ella McCollum were charged with aggravated assault and simple battery against Jerry and Myra Collins.] Respondents are white; the alleged victims are African-Americans. Shortly after the events, a leaflet was widely distributed in the local African-American community reporting the assault and urging community residents not to patronize respondents' business.

Before jury selection began, the prosecution moved to prohibit respondents from exercising peremptory challenges in a racially discriminatory manner. The State explained that it expected to show that the victims' race was a factor in the alleged assault. According to the State, counsel for respondents had indicated a clear intention to use peremptory strikes in a racially discriminatory manner, arguing that the circumstances of their case gave them the right to exclude African-American citizens from participating as jurors in the trial. Observing that 43 percent of the county's population is African-American, the State contended that, if a statistically representative panel is assembled for jury selection, 18 of the potential 42 jurors would be African-American. With 20 peremptory challenges, respondents therefore would be able to remove all the African-American potential jurors. Relying on *Batson v. Kentucky*, [this volume], the Sixth Amendment, [a] and the Georgia Constitution, the State sought an order providing that, if it succeeded in making out a prima facie case of racial discrimination by respondents, the latter would be required to articulate a racially neutral explanation for peremptory challenges.

The trial judge denied the State's motion, holding that "[n]either Georgia nor federal law prohibits criminal defendants from exercising peremptory strikes in a racially discriminatory manner." * * *

The Supreme Court of Georgia, by a 4-3 vote, affirmed the trial court's ruling. * * *

* * *

II

Over the last century, in an almost unbroken chain of decisions, this Court gradually has abolished race as a consideration for jury service. * * *

* * *

* * * The *Batson* Court held that a defendant may establish a prima facie case of purposeful discrimination in selection of the petit jury based solely on the prosecutor's exercise of peremptory challenges at the defendant's trial. * * *

Last Term this Court applied the *Batson* framework in two other contexts. In *Powers v. Ohio*, 499 U.S. 400 (1991), it held that in the trial of a white criminal defendant, a prosecutor is prohibited from excluding African-American jurors on the basis of race. In *Edmonson v. Leesville Concrete Co.*, [above], the Court decided that in a civil case, private litigants cannot exercise their peremptory strikes in a racially discriminatory manner.

In deciding whether the Constitution prohibits criminal defendants from exercising racially discriminatory peremptory challenges, we must answer four questions. First, whether a criminal defendant's exercise of peremptory challenges in a racially discriminatory manner inflicts the harms addressed by *Batson*. Second, whether the exercise of peremptory challenges by a criminal defendant constitutes state action. Third, whether prosecutors have standing to raise this constitutional challenge. And fourth, whether the constitutional rights of a criminal defendant nonetheless preclude the extension of our precedents to this case.

III
A

The majority in *Powers* recognized that "*Batson* 'was designed "to serve multiple ends,'" only one of which was to protect individual defendants from discrimination in the selection of jurors." * * * As in *Powers* and *Edmonson*, the extension of *Batson* in this context is designed to remedy the harm done to the "dignity of persons" and to the "integrity of the courts." * * *

As long ago as *Strauder* [v. *West Virginia*, 100 U.S. 303 (1880)], this Court recognized that denying a person participation in jury service on account of his race unconstitutionally discriminates against the excluded juror. * * * While "[a]n individual juror does not have a right to sit on any particular petit jury, . . . he or she does possess the right not to be excluded from one on account of race." * * * Regardless of who invokes the discriminatory challenge, there can be no doubt that the harm is the same—in all cases, the juror is subjected to open and public racial discrimination.

But "the harm from discriminatory jury selection extends beyond that inflicted on the defendant and the excluded juror to touch the entire community." * * * One of the goals of our jury system is "to impress upon the criminal defendant and the community as a whole that a verdict of conviction or acquittal is given in accordance with the law by persons who are fair." * * * Selection procedures that purposefully exclude African-Americans from juries undermine that public confidence—as well they should. "The overt wrong, often apparent to the entire jury panel, casts doubt over the obligation of the parties, the jury, and indeed the court to adhere to the law throughout the trial of the cause." * * *

The need for public confidence is especially high in cases involving race-related crimes. In such cases, emotions in the affected community will inevitably be heated and volatile. Public confidence in the integrity of the criminal justice system is essential for preserving community peace in trials involving race-related crimes. * * *

Be it at the hands of the State or the defense, if a court allows jurors to be excluded because of group bias, it is a willing participant in a scheme that could only undermine the very foundation of our system of justice—our citizens' confidence in it. Just as public confidence in criminal justice is undermined by a conviction in a trial where racial discrimination has occurred in jury selection, so is public confidence undermined where a defendant, assisted by racially discriminatory peremptory strikes, obtains an acquittal.

B

The fact that a defendant's use of discriminatory peremptory challenges harms the jurors and the community does not end our equal protection inquiry. Racial discrimination, although repugnant in all contexts, violates the Constitution only when it is attributable to state action. * * * Thus, the second question that must be answered is whether a criminal defendant's exercise of a peremptory challenge constitutes state action for purposes of the Equal Protection Clause.

Until *Edmonson*, the cases decided by this Court that presented the problem of racially discriminatory peremptory challenges involved assertions of discrimination by a prosecutor, a quintessential state actor. In *Edmonson*, by contrast, the contested peremptory challenges were exercised by a

private defendant in a civil action. In order to determine whether state action was present in that setting, the Court in *Edmonson* used the analytical framework summarized in *Lugar v. Edmondson Oil Co.*, 457 U.S. 922 (1982).

The first inquiry is "whether the claimed [constitutional] deprivation has resulted from the exercise of a right or privilege having its source in state authority." * * * "There can be no question" that peremptory challenges satisfy this first requirement, as they "are permitted only when the government, by statute or decisional law, deems it appropriate to allow parties to exclude a given number of persons who otherwise would satisfy the requirements for service on the petit jury." *Edmonson*. * * *

The second inquiry is whether the private party charged with the deprivation can be described as a state actor. * * * In resolving that issue, the Court in *Edmonson* found it useful to apply three principles: 1) "the extent to which the actor relies on governmental assistance and benefits"; 2) "whether the actor is performing a traditional governmental function"; and 3) "whether the injury caused is aggravated in a unique way by the incidents of governmental authority." * * *

As to the first principle, the *Edmonson* Court found that the peremptory challenge system, as well as the jury system as a whole, "simply could not exist" without the "overt and significant participation of the government." * * * [State law encompasses the entire jury selection process.]

In light of these procedures, the defendant in a Georgia criminal case relies on "governmental assistance and benefits" that are equivalent to those

found in the civil context in *Edmonson*.
* * *

In regard to the second principle, the Court in *Edmonson* found that peremptory challenges perform a traditional function of the government: "Their sole purpose is to permit litigants to assist the government in the selection of an impartial trier of fact." * * * **[b]**

Finally, the *Edmonson* Court indicated that the courtroom setting in which the peremptory challenge is exercised intensifies the harmful effects of the private litigant's discriminatory act and contributes to its characterization as state action. These concerns are equally present in the context of a criminal trial. Regardless of who precipitated the jurors' removal, the perception and the reality in a criminal trial will be that the court has excused jurors based on race, an outcome that will be attributed to the State.

Respondents nonetheless contend that the adversarial relationship between the defendant and the prosecution negates the governmental character of the peremptory challenge. Respondents rely on *Polk County v. Dodson*, 454 U.S. 312 (1981), in which a defendant sued, under 42 U.S.C. §1983, the public defender who represented him. The defendant claimed that the public defender had violated his constitutional rights in failing to provide adequate representation. This Court determined that a public defender does not qualify as a state actor when engaged in his general representation of a criminal defendant.

Polk County did not hold that the adversarial relationship of a public defender with the State precludes a finding of state action—it held that this adversarial relationship prevented the attorney's public employment from *alone* being sufficient to support a finding of state action. Instead, the determination whether a public defender is a state actor for a particular purpose depends on the nature and context of the function he is performing. For example, in *Branti v. Finkel*, 445 U.S. 507 (1980), this Court held that a public defender, in making personnel decisions on behalf of the State, is a state actor who must comply with constitutional requirements. And the *Dodson* Court itself noted, without deciding, that a public defender may act under color of state law while performing certain administrative, and possibly investigative, functions. * * * **[c]**

The exercise of a peremptory challenge differs significantly from other actions taken in support of a defendant's defense. In exercising a peremptory challenge, a criminal defendant is wielding the power to choose a quintessential governmental body—indeed, the institution of government on which our judicial system depends. Thus, as we held in *Edmonson*, when "a government confers on a private body the power to choose the government's employees or officials, the private body will be bound by the constitutional mandate of race neutrality." * * * **[d]**

Lastly, the fact that a defendant exercises a peremptory challenge to further his interest in acquittal does not conflict with a finding of state action. Whenever a private actor's conduct is deemed "fairly attributable" to the government, it is likely that private motives will have animated the actor's decision. Indeed, in *Edmonson*, the Court recognized that the private party's exercise of peremptory challenges constituted state action, even though the motive underlying the exercise of the peremptory challenge may be to protect a private interest. * * *

C

[The Court ruled that the State has standing to challenge an equal protection violation by the defendant's discriminatory use of peremptory challenges for the harm done to the integrity of the judicial process, for invidiously undermining bonds of trust between defendant and jurors, and for upholding the rights of excluded jurors who have independent but hard to pursue causes ofaction.]

D

The final question is whether the interests served by *Batson* must give way to the rights of a criminal defendant. As a preliminary matter, it is important to recall that peremptory challenges are not constitutionally protected fundamental rights; rather, they are but one state-created means to the constitutional end of an impartial jury and a fair trial. * * *
* * *

We do not believe that this decision will undermine the contribution of the peremptory challenge to the administration of justice. Nonetheless, "if race stereotypes are the price for acceptance of a jury panel as fair," we reaffirm today that such a "price is too high to meet the standard of the Constitution." *Edmonson*, * * * Defense counsel is limited to "legitimate, lawful conduct." *Nix v. Whiteside* [this volume]. * * * It is an affront to justice to argue that a fair

trial includes the right to discriminate against a group of citizens based upon their race.

Nor does a prohibition of the exercise of discriminatory peremptory challenges violate a defendant's Sixth Amendment right to the effective assistance of counsel. Counsel can ordinarily explain the reasons for peremptory challenges without revealing anything about trial strategy or any confidential client communications. In the rare case in which the explanation for a challenges would entail confidential communications or reveal trial strategy, an *in camera* discussion can be arranged. * * * [e]

Lastly, a prohibition of the discriminatory exercise of peremptory challenges does not violate a defendant's Sixth Amendment right to a trial by an impartial jury. The goal of the Sixth Amendment is "jury impartiality with respect to both contestants." * * *

We recognize, of course, that a defendant has the right to an impartial jury that can view him without racial animus, which so long has distorted our system of criminal justice. We have, accordingly, held that there should be a mechanism for removing those on the venire whom the defendant has specific reason to believe would be incapable of confronting and suppressing their racism. * * *

But there is a distinction between exercising a peremptory challenge to discriminate invidiously against jurors on account of race and exercising a peremptory challenge to remove an individual juror who harbors racial prejudice. * * *

IV

We hold that the Constitution prohibits a criminal defendant from engaging in purposeful discrimination on the ground of race in the exercise of peremptory challenges. Accordingly, if the State demonstrates a prima facie case of racial discrimination by the defendants, the defendants, must articulate a racially neutral explanation for peremptory challenges. The judgment of the Supreme Court of Georgia is reversed and the case is remanded for further proceedings not inconsistent with this opinion.

It is so ordered.

[CHIEF JUSTICE REHNQUIST, concurred, bowing to the precedent of *Edmonson*, although he dissented in that case. JUSTICE THOMAS also concurred in the judgment, but in an opinion expressed "general dissatisfac-tion with our continuing attempts to use the Constitution to regulate peremptory challenges."]

[JUSTICE O'CONNOR, dissented on the grounds that a defendant in a criminal case cannot be said to be engaged in state action. "The Court reaches the remarkable conclusion that criminal defendants being prosecuted by the State act on behalf of their adversary when they exercise peremptory challenges during jury selection."]

[JUSTICE SCALIA, dissenting, argued that *Edmonson* was wrongly decided. Agreeing with JUSTICE O'CONNOR he characterized the extension of state action to a criminal defendant as that case's "reduction to the terminally absurd."]

* * * * * * * * * *

COMMENTS

[a] Under Sixth Amendment cases, a white defendant is entitled to a jury that does not systematically exclude African-Americans (*Peters v. Kiff*, 407 U.S. 493 (1972)), and a male defendant is entitled to a jury that does not operate to suppress the numbers of females who might otherwise serve (*Taylor v. Louisiana*, 419 U.S. 522 (1975)). The Amendment is violated by the gross underrepresentation of women on juries as a result of rules that make non-service easy (*Duren v. Missouri*, 439 U.S. 357 (1979)).

[b] Are there any limits to these words? Since all criminal defense attorneys assist the state in finding the truth, can the private practice of criminal law be banned and all defense lawyers made state workers?

[c] Having established that the state action concept does not apply to every action in the criminal courtroom, do these cases indicate that the Court makes its distinctions on any *principle*?

[d] Can it be said that the defendant "chooses" a governmental body? On a philosophical level it may be the case that the defendant "chooses" to be tried by voluntarily committing a crime, but our law generally adheres to the view that

prosecution, conviction and punishment are compulsory processes. The Court is not entirely clear which "quintessentially governmental body" the defendant chooses. A court is undoubtedly a governmental body, but a jury is not. The jury represents the sovereign people, anterior and superior to the government.

[e] There is a legitimate concern that by inquiring into the use of peremptories the prosecution will try to pry into other aspects of its opponent's case.

VICTOR v. NEBRASKA

__ U.S. ___, 114 S.Ct. 1239, 127 L.Ed.2d 583 (1994)

JUSTICE O'CONNOR delivered the opinion of the Court.

The government must prove beyond a reasonable doubt every element of a charged offense. *In re Winship*, 397 U.S. 358 (1970). **[a]** Although this standard is an ancient and honored aspect of our criminal justice system, it defies easy explication. In these cases, we consider the constitutionality of two attempts to define "reasonable doubt."

I

The beyond a reasonable doubt standard is a requirement of due process, but the Constitution neither prohibits trial courts from defining reasonable doubt nor requires them to do so as a matter of course. * * * **[b]** Indeed, so long as the court instructs the jury on the necessity that the defendant's guilt be proven beyond a reasonable doubt, * * * the Constitution does not require that any particular form of words be used in advising the jury of the government's burden of proof. * * * Rather, "taken as a whole, the instructions [must] correctly conve[y] the concept of reasonable doubt to the jury." * * *

In only one case have we held that a definition of reasonable doubt violated the Due Process Clause. *Cage v. Louisiana*, 498 U.S. 39 (1990) (*per curiam*). There, the jurors were told:

"'[A reasonable doubt] is one that is founded upon a real tangible substantial basis and not upon mere caprice and conjecture. *It must be such doubt as would give rise to a grave uncertainty*, raised in your mind by reasons of the unsatisfactory character of the evidence or lack thereof. A reasonable doubt is not a mere possible doubt. *It is an actual substantial doubt.* It is a doubt that a reasonable man can seriously entertain. What is required is not an absolute or mathematical certainty, but a *moral certainty.*'" Id., at 40 (emphasis added by this Court in *Cage*).

We held that the highlighted portions of the instruction rendered it unconstitutional:

"It is plain to us that the words 'substantial' and 'grave,' as they are commonly understood, suggest a higher degree of doubt than is required for acquittal under the reasonable doubt standard. When those statements are then considered with the reference to 'moral certainty,' rather than evidentiary certainty, it becomes clear that a reasonable juror could have interpreted the instruction to allow a finding of guilt based on a degree of proof below that required by the Due Process Clause." * * * **[c]**

In a subsequent case, we made clear that the proper inquiry is not whether the instruction "could have" been applied in unconstitutional manner, but whether there is a reasonable likelihood that the jury *did* so apply it. * * * The constitutional question in the present cases, therefore, is whether there is a reasonable likelihood that the jury understood the instructions to allow conviction based on proof insufficient to meet the *Winship* standard. * * * [B]oth the Nebraska and the California Supreme Courts held that the instructions were constitutional. We * * * now affirm both judgments.

II

* * *

The jury in Sandoval's [California murder] case was given the following instruction on the government's burden of proof:

> "A defendant in a criminal action is presumed to be innocent until the contrary is proved, and in case of a reasonable doubt whether his guilt is satisfactorily shown, he is entitled to a verdict of not guilty. This presumption places upon the State the burden of proving him guilty beyond a reasonable doubt.
>
> "Reasonable doubt is defined as follows: It is *not a mere possible doubt*; because everything relating to human affairs, and *depending on moral evidence*, is open to some possible or imaginary doubt. It is that state of the case which, after the entire comparison and consideration of all the evidence, leaves the minds of the jurors in that condition that they cannot say they feel an abiding conviction, *to a moral certainty*, of the truth of the charge." * * *

The California Supreme Court rejected Sandoval's claim that the instruction,

particularly the highlighted passages, violated the Due Process Clause. * * *

The instruction given in Sandoval's case has its genesis in a charge given by Chief Justice Shaw of the Massachusetts Supreme Judicial Court more than a century ago:

> "[W]hat is reasonable doubt? It is a term often used, probably pretty well understood, but not easily defined. It is not mere possible doubt; because every thing relating to human affairs, and depending on moral evidence, is open to some possible or imaginary doubt. It is that state of the case, which, after the entire comparison and consideration of all the evidence, leaves the minds of jurors in that condition that they cannot say they feel an abiding conviction, to a moral certainty, of the truth of the charge. The burden of proof is upon the prosecutor. All the presumptions of law independent of evidence are in favor of innocence; and every person is presumed to be innocent until he is proved guilty. If upon such proof there is reasonable doubt remaining, the accused is entitled to the benefit of it by an acquittal. For it is not sufficient to establish a probability, though a strong one arising from the doctrine of chances, that the fact charged is more likely to be true than the contrary; but the evidence must establish the truth of the fact to a reasonable and moral certainty; a certainty that convinces and directs the understanding, and satisfies the reason and judgment, of those who are bound to act conscientiously upon it. This we take to be proof

beyond reasonable doubt." *Commonwealth v. Webster*, 59 Mass. 295, 320 (1850). **[d]**

The *Webster* charge is representative of the time when "American courts began applying [the beyond a reasonable doubt standard] in its modern form in criminal cases." [American courts approved of the *Webster* charge and California incorporated it into its statutory jury instructions.]

* * *

A

Sandoval's primary objection is to the use of the phrases "moral evidence" and "moral certainty" in the instruction. * * * [S]ome understanding of the historical context in which that instruction was written is accordingly helpful in evaluating its continuing validity.

By the beginning of the Republic, lawyers had borrowed the concept of "moral evidence" from the philosophers and historians of the 17th and 18th centuries. * * * James Wilson, who was instrumental in framing the Constitution and who served as one of the original Members of this Court, explained in a 1790 lecture on law that "evidence . . . is divided into two species—demonstrative and moral." * * * Wilson went on to explain the distinction thus:

"Demonstrative evidence has for its subject abstract and necessary truths, or the unchangeable relations of ideas. Moral evidence has for its subject the real but contingent truths and connections, which take place among things

actually existing. . . .

. . . . .

"In moral evidence, there not only may be, but there generally is, contrariety of proofs: in demonstrative evidence, no such contrariety can take place. . . . [T]o suppose that two contrary demonstrations can exist, is to suppose that the same proposition is both true and false: which is manifestly absurd. With regard to moral evidence, there is, for the most part, real evidence on both sides. On both sides, contrary presumptions, contrary testimonies, contrary experiences must be balanced." * * *

* * *

* * * At least one early treatise explicitly equated moral certainty with proof beyond a reasonable doubt. * * *

Thus, when Chief Justice Shaw penned the *Webster* instruction in 1850, moral certainty meant a state of subjective certitude about some event or occurrence. * * * Indeed, we have said that "[p]roof to a 'moral certainty' is an equivalent phrase with 'beyond a reasonable doubt.'" * * *

We recognize that the phrase "moral evidence" is not a mainstay of the modern lexicon, though we do not think it means anything different today than it did in the 19th century. The few contemporary dictionaries that define moral evidence do so consistently with its original meaning. * * *

Moreover, the instruction itself gives a definition of the phrase. The jury was told that "everything relating to human affairs, and depending on moral evidence, is open to some possible or imaginary doubt"—in other words, that absolute certainty is unattainable in matters relating to human affairs.   Moral evidence, in this sentence, can only mean empirical evidence offered to prove such matters—the proof introduced at trial.

This conclusion is reinforced by other instructions given in Sandoval's case. * * *   These instructions correctly pointed the jurors' attention to the facts of the case before them, not (as Sandoval contends) the ethics or morality of Sandoval's criminal acts. Accordingly, we find the reference to moral evidence unproblematic.

[The Court expressed concern that a modern jury might misunderstand the true meaning of "moral certainty" but noted that the linking of that phrase to "an abiding certainty" in this case prevented a due process violation.]
* * *

B

Finally, Sandoval objects to the portion of the charge in which the judge instructed the jury that a reasonable doubt is "not a mere possible doubt." The *Cage* instruction included an almost identical reference to "not a mere possible doubt," but we did not intimate that there was anything wrong with that part of the charge. * * * That is because "[a] 'reasonable doubt,' at a minimum, is one based upon 'reason.'" * * *   A fanciful doubt is not a reasonable doubt. As Sandoval's defense attorney told the jury: "[A]nything can be possible. . . . [A] planet could be made out of blue cheese. But that's really not in the realm of what we're talking about." * * *   That this is the sense in which the instruction uses "possible" is made

clear from the final phrase of the sentence, which notes that everything "is open to some possible or imaginary doubt."   We therefore reject Sandoval's challenge to this portion of the instruction as well.

III

[Victor was convicted of first degree murder and sentenced to death. Included in the charge to the jury was the following]:

"'Reasonable doubt' is such a doubt as would cause a reasonable and prudent person, in one of the graver and more important transactions of life, to pause and hesitate before taking the represented facts as true and relying and acting thereon. It is such a doubt as will not permit you, after full, fair, and impartial consideration of all the evidence, to have an abiding conviction, *to a moral certainty*, of the guilt of the accused. At the same time, absolute or mathematical certainty is not required. You may be convinced of the truth of a fact beyond a reasonable doubt and yet be fully aware that possibly you may be mistaken. You may find an accused guilty upon the *strong probabilities of the case*, provided such probabilities are strong enough to exclude any doubt of his guilt that is reasonable. A reasonable doubt is an *actual and substantial doubt* arising from the evidence, from the facts or circumstances shown by the evidence, or from the lack of evidence on the part of the state, as distinguished from a doubt arising from mere possibility, from bare imagination, or from fanciful conjecture." * * *

On state postconviction review, the Nebraska Supreme Court rejected Victor's contention that the instruction, particularly the emphasized phrases, violated the Due Process Clause. * * *
* * *

A

Victor's primary argument is that equating a reasonable doubt with a "substantial doubt" overstated the degree of doubt necessary for acquittal. We agree that this construction is somewhat problematic. On the one hand, "substantial" means "not seeming or imaginary"; on the other, it means "that specified to a large degree." * * * The former is unexceptionable, as it informs the jury only that a reasonable doubt is something more than a speculative one; but the latter could imply a doubt greater than required for acquittal under *Winship*. Any ambiguity, however, is removed by reading the phrase in the context of the sentence in which it appears: "A reasonable doubt is an actual and substantial doubt . . . *as distinguished from* a doubt arising from mere possibility, from bare imagination, or from fanciful conjecture." * * *

This explicit distinction between a substantial doubt and a fanciful conjecture was not present in the *Cage* instruction. We did say in that case that "the words 'substantial' and 'grave,' as they are commonly understood, suggest a higher degree of doubt than is required for acquittal under the reasonable doubt standard." * * * But we did not hold that the reference to

substantial doubt alone was sufficient to render the instruction unconstitutional. * * * Rather, we were concerned that the jury would interpret the term "substantial doubt" in parallel with the preceding reference to "grave uncertainty," leading to an overstatement of the doubt necessary to acquit. In the instruction given in Victor's case, the context makes clear that "substantial" is used in the sense of existence rather than magnitude of the doubt, so the same concern is not present.

* * *

[Victor also challenged the "moral certainty" language in his charge. As in Sandoval's case, the Court found that the actual charge did not violate Victor's right to due process.]
* * *

IV

The Due Process Clause requires the government to prove a criminal defendant's guilt beyond a reasonable doubt, and trial courts must avoid defining reasonable doubt so as to lead the jury to convict on a lesser showing than due process requires. In these cases, however, we conclude that "taken as a whole, the instructions correctly conveyed the concept of reasonable doubt to the jury." * * * There is no reasonable likelihood that the jurors who determined petitioners' guilt applied the instructions in a way that violated the Constitution. The judgments in both cases are accordingly
Affirmed.

[Although JUSTICE KENNEDY concurred, he made it clear that he had no use for the archaic language of "moral certainty," noting that it could confuse a jury and even stated that its use was "quite indefensible."]

JUSTICE GINSBURG, concurring in part and concurring in the judgment.
* * *

[In her concurrence JUSTICE GINSBURG was quite critical of the instructions given in *Sandoval* and *Victor*. She noted that some federal circuits dispensed with giving definitions of reasonable doubt. She suggested the following instruction as the best available.]
* * *   The Federal Judicial Center has proposed a definition of reasonable doubt that is clear, straightforward, and accurate. That instruction reads:

> "[T]he government has the burden of proving the defendant guilty beyond a reasonable doubt. Some of you may have served as jurors in civil cases, where you were told that it is only necessary to prove that a fact is more likely true than not true. In criminal cases, the government's proof must be more powerful than that. It must be beyond a reasonable doubt.

> "Proof beyond a reasonable doubt is proof that leaves you firmly convinced of the defendant's guilt. There are very few things in this world that we know with absolute certainty, and in criminal cases the law does not require proof that overcomes every possible doubt. If, based on your consideration of the evidence, you are firmly convinced that the defendant is guilty of the crime charged, you must find him guilty. If on the

other hand, you think there is a real possibility that he is not guilty, you must give him the benefit of the doubt and find him not guilty."
* * *

This instruction plainly informs the jurors that the prosecution must prove its case by more than a mere preponderance of the evidence, yet not necessarily to an absolute certainty. The "firmly convinced" standard for conviction, repeated for emphasis, is further enhanced by the juxtaposed prescription that the jury must acquit if there is a "real possibility" that the defendant is innocent. This model instruction surpasses others I have seen in stating the reasonable doubt standard succinctly and comprehensibly.

I recognize, however, that this Court has no supervisory powers over the state courts, * * * and that the test we properly apply in evaluating the constitutionality of a reasonable doubt instruction is not whether we find it exemplary; instead, we inquire only whether there is a "reasonable likelihood that the jury understood the instructio[n] to allow conviction based on proof insufficient to meet" the reasonable doubt standard. * * * **[e]**

JUSTICE BLACKMUN, with whom JUSTICE SOUTER joins in all but Part II, concurring in part and dissenting in part.

* * * The majority today purports to uphold and follow *Cage [v. Louisiana]*, but plainly falters in its application of that case. There is no meaningful difference between the jury instruction delivered at Victor's trial and the jury instruction issued in *Cage* save the fact that the jury instruction

in Victor's case did not contain the two words "grave uncertainty." But the mere absence of these two words can be of no help to the State, since there is other language in the instruction that is equally offensive to due process. I therefore dissent from the Court's opinion and judgment in * * * * *Victor v. Nebraska.*

I

Our democracy rests in no small part on our faith in the ability of the criminal justice system to separate those who are guilty from those who are not. This is a faith which springs fundamentally from the requirement that unless guilt is established beyond all reasonable doubt, the accused shall go free. * * * In *Winship*, the Court recounted the long history of the reasonable doubt standard, noting that it "dates at least from our early years as a Nation." * * * The Court explained that any "society that values the good name and freedom of every individual should not condemn a man for commission of a crime when there is a reasonable doubt about his guilt." * * *

Despite the inherent appeal of the reasonable-doubt standard, it provides protection to the innocent only to the extent that the standard, in reality, is an enforceable rule of law. To be a meaningful safeguard, the reasonable-doubt standard must have a tangible meaning that is capable of being understood by those who are required to apply it. It must be stated accurately and with the precision owed to those whose liberty or life is at risk. Because of the extraordinarily high stakes in criminal trials, "[i]t is critical

that the moral force of the criminal law not be diluted by a standard of proof that leaves people in doubt whether innocent men are being condemned." * *

When reviewing a jury instruction that defines "reasonable doubt," it is necessary to consider the instruction as a whole and to give the words their common and ordinary meaning. * * * It is not sufficient for the jury instruction merely to be susceptible to an interpretation that is technically correct. The important question is whether there is a "reasonable likelihood" that the jury was misled or confused by the instruction, and therefore applied it in a way that violated the Constitution. [f] * * * Any jury instruction defining "reasonable doubt" that suggests an improperly high degree of doubt for acquittal or an improperly low degree of certainty for conviction, offends due process. Either misstatement of the reasonable-doubt standard is prejudicial to the defendant, as it "vitiates all of the jury's findings," * * * and removes the only constitutionally appropriate predicate for the jury's verdict.

A

[JUSTICE BLACKMUN restated the charge in *Cage*, found in Part I of the majority opinion, which includes the phrases "actual substantial doubt" and "moral certainty."]
* * *

* * * The Court [in *Cage*] noted that some of the language in the instruction was adequate, but ruled that the phrases "actual substantial doubt" and "grave uncertainty" suggested a "higher degree of doubt than is required for acquittal under the reason-

able doubt standard," and that those phrases taken together with the reference to "moral certainty," rather than "evidentiary certainty," rendered the instruction as a whole constitutionally defective. * * *

Clarence Victor, * * * also was convicted of first-degree murder and sentenced to death. [The instruction is found in Part II of the majority opinion.] * * *

The majority's attempt to distinguish [the] instruction [in Victor] from the one employed in *Cage* is wholly unpersuasive. Both instructions equate "substantial doubt" with reasonable doubt, and refer to "moral certainty" rather than "evidentiary certainty." And although Victor's instruction does not contain the phrase "grave uncertainty," the instruction contains language that has an equal potential to mislead, including the invitation to the jury to convict based on the "strong probabilities" of the case and the overt effort to dissuade jurors from acquitting when they are "fully aware that possibly they may be mistaken." Nonetheless, the majority argues that "substantial doubt" has a meaning in Victor's instruction different from that in Cage's instruction, and that the "moral certainty" language is sanitized by its context. The majority's approach seems to me to fail under its own logic.

B

First, the majority concedes, as it must, that equating reasonable doubt with substantial doubt is "somewhat problematic" since one of the common definitions of "substantial" is "that specified to a large degree." * * * But

the majority insists that the jury did not likely interpret the word "substantial" in this manner because Victor's instruction, unlike Cage's instruction, used the phrase "substantial doubt" as a means of distinguishing reasonable doubt from mere conjecture. According to the majority, "[t]his explicit distinction between a substantial doubt and a fanciful conjecture was not present in the *Cage* instruction," and thus, read in context, the use of "substantial doubt" in Victor's instruction is less problematic. * * *

A casual reading of the *Cage* instruction reveals the majority's false premise. The *Cage* instruction plainly states that a reasonable doubt is a doubt "founded upon a real tangible substantial basis and not upon mere caprice and conjecture." * * * The *Cage* instruction also used the "substantial doubt" language to distinguish a reasonable doubt from "a mere possible doubt." * * * Thus, the reason the Court condemned the "substantial doubt" language in *Cage* had nothing to do with the absence of appropriate contrasting language; rather, the Court condemned the language for precisely the reason it gave: "[T]he words 'substantial' and 'grave', as they are commonly understood, suggest a higher degree of doubt than is required for acquittal under the reasonable doubt standard." * * * In short, the majority's speculation that the jury in Victor's case interpreted "substantial" to mean something other than "that specified to a large degree" simply because the word "substantial" is used at one point to distinguish mere conjecture, is unfounded and is foreclosed by *Cage* itself.

* * *

In my view, the predominance of potentially misleading language in Victor's instruction made it likely that the jury interpreted the phrase "substantial doubt" to mean that a "large" doubt, as opposed to a merely reasonable doubt, is required to acquit a defendant. It seems that a central purpose of the instruction is to minimize the jury's sense of responsibility for the conviction of those who may be innocent. The instruction goes out of its way to assure jurors that "[y]ou may be convinced of the truth of a fact beyond a reasonable doubt and yet be fully aware that possibly you may be mistaken"; and then, after acquainting jurors with the possibility that their consciences will be unsettled after convicting the defendant, the instruction states that the jurors should feel free to convict based on the "strong probabilities of the case." Viewed as a whole, the instruction is geared toward assuring jurors that although they may be mistaken, they are to make their decision on those "strong probabilities," and only a "substantial doubt" of a defendant's guilt should deter them from convicting. **[g]**

* * *

Considering the instruction in its entirety, it seems fairly obvious to me that the "strong probabilities" language increased the likelihood that the jury understood "substantial doubt" to mean "to a large degree." Indeed, the jury could have a reasonable doubt about a defendant's guilt but still find that the "strong probabilities" are in favor of conviction. Only when a reasonable doubt is understood to be a doubt "to a large degree" does the "strong probabilities" language begin to make

sense. A Nebraska Federal District Court recently observed: "The word 'probability' brings to mind terms such as 'chance,' 'possibility,' 'likelihood' and 'plausibility'—none of which appear to suggest the high level of certainty which is required to be convinced of a defendant's guilt 'beyond a reasonable doubt.'" * * * All of these terms, however, are consistent with the interpretation of "substantial doubt" as a doubt "to a large degree." A jury could have a large and reasonable doubt about a defendant's guilt but still find the defendant guilty on "the strong probabilities of the case," believing it "likely" that the defendant committed the crime for which he was charged.

* * *

Finally, the instruction issued in Victor's case states that a reasonable doubt "is such a doubt as will not permit you, after full, fair, and impartial consideration of all the evidence, to have an abiding conviction, *to a moral certainty*, of the guilt of the accused." In *Cage*, the Court disapproved of the use of the phrase "moral certainty," because of the real possibility that such language would lead jurors reasonably to believe that they could base their decision to convict upon moral standards or emotion in addition to or instead of evidentiary standards. The risk that jurors would understand "moral certainty" to authorize convictions based in part on value judgments regarding the defendant's behavior is particularly high in cases where the defendant is alleged to have committed a repugnant or brutal crime. In *Cage*, we therefore contrasted "moral certainty" with "evidentiary certainty," and held that where "moral certainty" is used in conjunction with "substantial doubt" and "grave uncertainty," the Due Process Clause is violated. * * *

Just as in *Cage*, the "moral certainty" phrase in Victor's instruction is particularly dangerous because it is used in conjunction with language that overstates the degree of doubt necessary to convict. This relationship between the "moral certainty" language, which potentially understates the degree of certainty required to convict, and the "substantial doubt," "strong probabilities," and "possibly you may be mistaken" language which, especially when taken together, overstates the degree of doubt necessary to acquit, also distinguishes Victor's instruction from the one challenged in * * * *Sandoval v. California*. * * * The jury instruction defining reasonable doubt in *Sandoval* used the phrases "moral certainty" and "moral evidence," but the phrases were not used in conjunction with language of the type at issue here—language that easily may be interpreted as overstating the degree of doubt required to acquit. In other words, in Victor's instruction, unlike Sandoval's, all of the misleading language is mutually reinforcing, both overstating the degree of doubt necessary to acquit and understating the degree of certainty required to convict.

This confusing and misleading state of affairs leads me ineluctably to the conclusion that, in Victor's case, there exists a reasonable likelihood that the jury believed that a lesser burden of proof rested with the prosecution. * * * Where, as here, a jury instruction attempts but fails to convey with clarity and accuracy the meaning of reasonable doubt, the reviewing court should reverse the conviction and remand for a new trial. * * *

* * *

* * * * * * * * * * *

COMMENTS

[a] An oddity of American law is that the "proof beyond a reasonable doubt" standard was so well established that the Supreme Court never had an opportunity to declare that it was part and parcel of the due process of law. An opportunity to do so did not arise until 1970, when, in *In re Winship*, a case involving a juvenile delinquency adjudication, the Court firmly established that a defendant's right to not be deprived of life, liberty or property in a criminal matter without due process of law included the reasonable doubt standard.

[b] Not every constitutional rule is explicitly stated in the Constitution. Some implicit rules, like the Fourth Amendment exclusionary rule, are controversial. The "reasonable doubt" rule is not. Why is this so?

[c] To some, it may seem inhumane to allow conviction on less than absolute certainty, especially where the death penalty is involved. Nevertheless, requiring absolute certainty as a matter of law can have drastic consequences. See John H. Langbein, *Torture and the Law of Proof* (Chicago: University of Chicago Press,

1977).

[d] Webster was one of the most celebrated criminal cases of the nineteenth century. Webster was a professor of medicine at Harvard College who killed a creditor with a stick and dismembered and burned the corpse in a laboratory furnace. For an account of the case, see Helen Thompson, *Murder at Harvard* (Boston: Houghton Mifflin, 1977).

[e] As JUSTICE GINSBURG recognizes, it is not entirely appropriate for a majority opinion to suggest an optimal definition of reasonable doubt, but it is appropriate for a concurring opinion to do so.

[f] In this attack on the majority JUSTICE BLACKMUN is saying, in effect, that the majority has put on green eyeshades and used a magnifying glass to interpret the jury instructions so that they would stand, while at the same time clearly dissatisfied with the "moral certainty" language. The larger point is that in a criminal case common law traditions require the courts to interpret the law fairly, but in favor of the defendant in close cases.

[g] JUSTICE BLACKMUN brings an abstract linguistic analysis down to earth. Jury duty in murder cases is an awesome responsibility. The common law sustains a "reasonable doubt" standard because it is shared among the jury members; the standard is high not only for the defendant's sake, but in order to make the decision morally acceptable to jurors. JUSTICE BLACKMUN argues that the standard must not be phrased so as to raise the likelihood of conviction while simultaneously easing the conscience of the jurors. Can you think of historic examples where people have avoided horrible moral consequences with soothing words?

ESTELLE v. WILLIAMS

425 U.S. 501, 96 S.Ct. 1691, 48 L.Ed.2d 126 (1976)

MR. CHIEF JUSTICE BURGER delivered the opinion of the Court.

We granted certiorari in this case to determine whether an accused who is compelled to wear identifiable prison clothing at his trial by a jury is denied due process or equal protection of the laws.

[Williams was convicted by a jury for assault with intent to commit murder with malice based on a fight with a former landlord over property. Unable to post bond, Williams was held in custody while awaiting trial. Williams' request for his civilian clothes was denied and he appeared at the trial in clearly marked prison clothes.] Neither respondent nor his counsel raised an objection to the prison attire at any time.

[The federal District Court on a petition for a writ of habeas corpus held that requiring a defendant to stand trial in prison garb was inherently unfair but denied relief on harmless error grounds. The Court of Appeals, believing that the error did have an effect on the jury, reversed.]

(1)

The right to a fair trial is a fundamental liberty secured by the Fourteenth Amendment. * * * The presumption of innocence, although not articulated in the Constitution, is a basic component of a fair trial under our system of criminal justice. * * *

To implement the presumption, courts must be alert to factors that may undermine the fairness of the factfinding process. In the administration of criminal justice, courts must carefully guard against dilution of the principle that guilt is to be established by probative evidence and beyond a reasonable doubt. *In re Winship*, [this volume.]

The actual impact of a particular practice on the judgment of jurors cannot always be fully determined. But this Court has left no doubt that the probability of deleterious effects on fundamental rights calls for close judicial scrutiny. * * * Courts must do the best they can to evaluate the likely effects of a particular procedure, based on reason, principle, and common human experience.

The potential effects of presenting an accused before the jury in prison attire need not, however, be measured in the abstract. Courts have, with few exceptions, determined that an accused should not be compelled to go to trial in prison or jail clothing because of the possible impairment of the presumption so basic to the adversary system. * * * The American Bar Association's Standards for Criminal Justice also disapprove the practice. * * * This is a recognition that the constant reminder of the accused's condition implicit in such distinctive, identifiable attire may affect a juror's judgment. The defendant's clothing is so likely to be a continuing influence throughout the trial that, not unlike placing a jury in the custody of deputy sheriffs who were also witnesses for the prosecution, an unacceptable risk is presented of impermissible factors coming into play. * * *

That such factors cannot always be avoided is manifest in *Illinois v. Allen*, [this volume], where we expressly recognized that "the sight of shackles and gags might have a significant effect on the jury's feelings about the defendant, . . ." * * *; yet the Court upheld the practice when necessary to control a contumacious defendant. For that reason, the Court authorized removal of a disruptive defendant from the courtroom or, alternatively, binding and gagging of the accused until he agrees to conduct himself properly in the courtroom.

Unlike physical restraints, permitted under *Allen*, *supra*, compelling an accused to wear jail clothing furthers no essential state policy. That it may be more convenient for jail administrators, a factor quite unlike the substantial need to impose physical restraints upon contumacious defendants, provides no justification for the practice. Indeed, the State of Texas asserts no interest whatever in maintaining this procedure.

Similarly troubling is the fact that compelling the accused to stand trial in jail garb operates usually against only those who cannot post bail prior to trial. Persons who can secure release are not subjected to this condition. To impose the condition on one category of defendants, over objection, would be repugnant to the concept of equal justice embodied in the Fourteenth Amendment. * * *

(2)

The Fifth Circuit, in this as well as in prior decisions, has not purported to adopt a *per se* rule invalidating all convictions where a defendant had appeared in identifiable prison clothes.

That court has held, for instance, that the harmless-error doctrine is applicable to this line of cases. * * * Other courts are in accord. * * * In this case, the Court of Appeals quoted the language of MR. JUSTICE DOUGLAS, speaking for the Court in *Harrington v. California*, 395 U.S. 250 (1969):

> "We held in *Chapman v. California* that 'before a federal constitutional error can be held harmless, the court must be able to declare a belief that it was harmless beyond a reasonable doubt.' We said that . . . not all 'trial errors which violate the Constitution automatically call for reversal.'" * * *

In *Chapman v. California*, 386 U.S. 18 (1967), the Court, speaking through MR. JUSTICE BLACK, held:

> "We are urged by petitioners to hold that all federal constitutional errors, regardless of the facts and circumstances, must always be deemed harmful. Such a holding, as petitioners correctly point out, would require an automatic reversal of their convictions and make further discussion unnecessary. We decline to adopt any such rule. All 50 States have harmless-error statutes or rules, and the United States long ago through its Congress established for its courts the rule that judgments shall not be reversed for 'errors or defects which do not affect the substantial rights of the parties.'. . . We conclude that there may be some constitutional errors which in the setting of a particular case are so

unimportant and insignificant that they may, consistent with the Federal Constitution, be deemed harmless, not requiring the automatic reversal of the conviction." * * *

In other situations, when, for example, the accused is being tried for an offense committed in confinement, or in an attempted escape, courts have refused to find error in the practice. * * * "No prejudice can result from seeing that which is already known." * * *

Consequently, the courts have refused to embrace a mechanical rule vitiating any conviction, regardless of the circumstances, where the accused appeared before the jury in prison garb. Instead, they have recognized that the particular evil proscribed is compelling a defendant, against his will, to be tried in jail attire. The reason for this judicial focus upon compulsion is simple; instances frequently arise where a defendant prefers to stand trial before his peers in prison garments. The cases show, for example, that it is not an uncommon defense tactic to produce the defendant in jail clothes in the hope of eliciting sympathy from the jury. * * * This is apparently an accepted practice in Texas courts, * * * including the court where respondent was tried. [a]

Courts have therefore required an accused to object to being tried in jail garments, just as he must invoke or abandon other rights. The Fifth Circuit has held: "A defendant may not remain silent and willingly go to trial in prison garb and thereafter claim error." * * * The essential meaning of the Court of Appeals' decision * * * has been described by that court as

follows:

> "We held * * * that the defendant and his attorney had the burden to make known that the defendant desired to be tried in civilian clothes before the state could be accountable for his being tried in jail clothes. . . ." * * * [b]

Similarly, the Ninth Circuit has indicated that the courts must determine whether an accused "was in fact compelled to wear prison clothing at his state court trial." * * *

(3)

The record is clear that no objection was made to the trial judge concerning the jail attire either before or at any time during the trial. This omission plainly did not result from any lack of appreciation of the issue, for respondent had raised the question with the jail attendant prior to trial. At trial, defense counsel expressly referred to respondent's attire during *voir dire*. The trial judge was thus informed that respondent's counsel was fully conscious of the situation.

Despite respondent's failure to raise the issue at trial, the Court of Appeals held:

> "Waiver of the objection cannot be inferred merely from failure to object if trial in prison garb is customary in the jurisdiction." * * *

The District Court had concluded that at the time of respondent's trial the majority of nonbailed defendants in Harris County were indeed tried in jail clothes. From this, the Court of

Appeals concluded that the practice followed in respondent's case was customary. * * *

However, that analysis ignores essential facts adduced at the evidentiary hearing. Notwithstanding the evidence as to the general practice in Harris County, there was no finding that nonbailed defendants were compelled to stand trial in prison garments if timely objection was made to the trial judge. On the contrary, the District Court concluded that the practice of the particular judge presiding in respondent's case was to permit any accused who so desired to change into civilian clothes. * * *

* * *

Significantly, at the evidentiary hearing respondent's trial counsel did not intimate that he feared any adverse consequences attending an objection to the procedure. There is nothing to suggest that there would have been any prejudicial effect on defense counsel had he made objection, given the decisions on this point in that jurisdiction. Four years before respondent's trial the United States Court of Appeals for the Fifth Circuit had held: "It is inherently unfair to try a defendant for crime while garbed in his jail uniform. . . ." * * * Similarly, the Texas Court of Criminal Appeals had held: "[E]very effort should be made to avoid trying an accused while in jail garb." * * * Prior Texas cases had made it clear that an objection should be interposed. * * *

Nothing in this record, therefore, warrants a conclusion that respondent was compelled to stand trial in jail garb or that there was sufficient reason to excuse the failure to raise the issue before trial. Nor can the trial judge be faulted for not asking the respondent or his counsel whether he was deliberately going to trial in jail clothes. To impose this requirement suggests that the trial judge operates under the same burden here as he would in the situation in *Johnson v. Zerbst*, [this volume], where the issue concerned whether the accused willingly stood trial without the benefit of counsel. Under our adversary system, once a defendant has the assistance of counsel the vast array of trial decisions, strategic and tactical, which must be made before and during trial rests with the accused and his attorney. Any other approach would rewrite the duties of trial judges and counsel in our legal system. [c]

Accordingly, although the State cannot, consistently with the Fourteenth Amendment, compel an accused to stand trial before a jury while dressed in identifiable prison clothes, the failure to make an objection to the court as to being tried in such clothes, for whatever reason, is sufficient to negate the presence of compulsion necessary to establish a constitutional violation.

The judgment of the Court of Appeals is therefore reversed, and the cause is remanded for further proceedings consistent with this opinion.

Reversed and remanded.

MR. JUSTICE STEVENS took no part in the consideration or decision of this case.

[JUSTICE POWELL, joined by JUSTICE STEWART concurred.]

MR. JUSTICE BRENNAN, with whom MR. JUSTICE MARSHALL concurs, dissenting.

[JUSTICE BRENNAN argued that it is the appearance at trial in prison clothes that constituted a due process violation, by undermining the defendant's presumption of innocence, and therefore the element of compulsion, for which there are no precedents, should not be considered as part of the constitutional violation.]

I

* * *

Identifiable prison garb robs an accused of the respect and dignity accorded other participants in a trial and constitutionally due the accused as an element of the presumption of innocence, and surely tends to brand him in the eyes of the jurors with an unmistakable mark of guilt. Jurors may speculate that the accused's pretrial incarceration, although often the result of his inability to raise bail, is explained by the fact he poses a danger to the community or has a prior criminal record; a significant danger is thus created of corruption of the factfinding process through mere suspicion. The prejudice may only be subtle and jurors may not even be conscious of its deadly impact, but in a system in which every person is presumed innocent until proved guilty beyond a reasonable doubt, the Due Process Clause forbids toleration of the risk. Jurors required by the presumption of innocence to accept the accused as a peer, an individual like themselves who is innocent until proved guilty, may well see in an accused garbed in prison attire an obviously guilty person to be recommitted by them to the place where his clothes clearly show he belongs. It is difficult to conceive of any other situation more fraught with risk to the presumption of innocence and the standard of reasonable doubt.

Trial in identifiable prison garb also entails additional dangers to the accuracy and objectiveness of the factfinding process. For example, an accused considering whether to testify in his own defense must weigh in his decision how jurors will react to his being paraded before them in such attire. It is surely reasonable to be concerned whether jurors will be less likely to credit the testimony of an individual whose garb brands him a criminal. And the problem will most likely confront the indigent accused who appears in prison garb only because he was too poor to make bail. In that circumstance, the Court's concession that no prosecutorial interest is served by trying the accused in prison clothes, * * * has an ironical ring.

[The lengthy dissent argued that a knowing, voluntary, and intelligent consent was needed for a defendant to be tried in prison garb. It argued that the failure to object should not be seen as a "procedural default" that blocks a party's ability to challenge a constitutional wrong. It also noted that Williams in fact requested his civilian clothes.]

* * *

* * * * * * * * * *

COMMENTS

[a] The dissent noted that none of the cases cited here involved defendants who had been released on bond.

[b] The failure to adopt a *per se* rule raises some logical problems. Since a jury cannot help but notice and be influenced by a defendant dressed like a "jailbird" it seems incongruous to argue that such a situation is not harmless error.

[c] Despite the apparently logical problem raised in note [b], there is some sense in the Court not placing the responsibility on the trial judge for insuring that every possible error be objected to. Among other things, this case demonstrates the importance of an attorney making timely objections at the trial. This requires that defense counsel have a thorough knowledge of all relevant rules of trial practice, including the constitutional rights of defendants.

ILLINOIS v. ALLEN

397 U.S. 337, 90 S.Ct. 1057, 25 L.Ed.2d 353 (1970)

MR. JUSTICE BLACK delivered the opinion of the Court.

The Confrontation Clause of the Sixth Amendment to the United States Constitution provides that: "In all criminal prosecutions, the accused shall enjoy the right * * * to be confronted with the witnesses against him. * * *" We have held that the Fourteenth Amendment makes the guarantees of this clause obligatory upon the States. *Pointer v. Texas*, 380 U.S. 400 (1965). One of the most basic of the rights guaranteed by the Confrontation Clause is the accused's right to be present in the courtroom at every stage of his trial. * * * The question presented in this case is whether an accused can claim the benefit of this constitutional right to remain in the courtroom while at the same time he engages in speech and conduct which is so noisy, disorderly, and disruptive that it is exceedingly difficult or wholly impossible to carry on the trial.

[Allen was convicted of armed robbery. At his trial he refused court appointed counsel; a stand-by attorney was appointed. Allen questioned a potential juror during voir dire at great length. The judge asked him to confine his questions to the juror's qualifications. In response, Allen threatened the judge's life, tore up a file, and insisted that the court appointed lawyer would not act on his behalf.]

* * *

"* * * The trial judge thereupon stated to the petitioner, 'One more outbreak of that sort and I'll remove you from the courtroom.' This warning had no effect on the petitioner. He continued to talk back to the judge, saying, 'There's not going to be no trial, either. I'm going to sit here and you're going to talk and you can bring your shackles out and straight jacket and put them on me and tape my mouth, but it will do no good because there's not going to be no trial.' After more abusive remarks by the petitioner, the trial judge ordered the trial to proceed in the petitioner's absence. The petitioner was removed from the courtroom. The voir dire examination then continued and the jury was selected in the absence of the petitioner. * * *" * * *

[Allen was given a second chance to be present in the courtroom but again disrupted the proceedings. He was removed from the courtroom during the prosecution's presentation of evidence and was brought in on a few occasions for his identification. On one such occasion he responded "to one of the judge's questions with vile and abusive language." Allen did sit in the courtroom during the defense, conducted by his court appointed lawyer, and behaved himself. The federal court of Appeals ruled that Allen's Sixth Amendment right to be present was absolute and that he should have been kept in the courtroom, even if bound and gagged.]

* * * We cannot agree that the

Sixth Amendment, the cases upon which the Court of Appeals relied, or any other cases of this Court so handicap a trial judge in conducting a criminal trial. The broad dicta in [earlier cases] that a trial can never continue in the defendant's absence have been expressly rejected. *Diaz v. United States*, 223 U.S. 442 (1912). We accept instead the statement of MR. JUSTICE CARDOZO who, speaking for the Court in *Snyder v. Massachusetts*, 291 U.S. 97, 106 (1934), said: "No doubt the privilege [of personally confronting witnesses] may be lost by consent or at times even by misconduct." Although mindful that courts must indulge every reasonable presumption against the loss of constitutional rights, * * * we explicitly hold today that a defendant can lose his right to be present at trial if, after he has been warned by the judge that he will be removed if he continues his disruptive behavior, he nevertheless insists on conducting himself in a manner so disorderly, disruptive, and disrespectful of the court that his trial cannot be carried on with him in the courtroom. Once lost, the right to be present can, of course, be reclaimed as soon as the defendant is willing to conduct himself consistently with the decorum and respect inherent in the concept of courts and judicial proceedings. [a]

It is essential to the proper administration of criminal justice that dignity, order, and decorum be the hallmarks of all court proceedings in our country. The flagrant disregard in the courtroom of elementary standards of proper conduct should not and cannot be tolerated. We believe trial judges confronted with disruptive, contumacious, stubbornly defiant defendants must be given sufficient discretion to meet the circumstances of each case. No one formula for maintaining the appropriate courtroom atmosphere will be best in all situations. We think there are at least three constitutionally permissible ways for a trial judge to handle an obstreperous defendant like Allen: (1) bind and gag him, thereby keeping him present; (2) cite him for contempt; (3) take him out of the courtroom until he promises to conduct himself properly.

I

Trying a defendant for a crime while he sits bound and gagged before the judge and jury would to an extent comply with that part of the Sixth Amendment's purposes that accords the defendant an opportunity to confront the witnesses at the trial. But even to contemplate such a technique, much less see it, arouses a feeling that no person should be tried while shackled and gagged except as a last resort. Not only is it possible that the sight of shackles and gags might have a significant effect on the jury's feelings about the defendant, but the use of this technique is itself something of an affront to the very dignity and decorum of judicial proceedings that the judge is seeking to uphold. Moreover, one of the defendant's primary advantages of being present at the trial, his ability to communicate with his counsel, is greatly reduced when the defendant is in a condition of total physical restraint. It is in part because of these inherent disadvantages and limitations in this method of dealing with disorderly defendants that we decline to hold with the Court of Appeals that a defendant cannot under any possible circumstances be deprived of his right to be present at trial. However, in some situations which we need not attempt to foresee, binding and gagging might possibly be the fairest and most reasonable way to handle a defendant who acts as Allen did here. **[b]**

II

In a footnote the Court of Appeals suggested the possible availability of contempt of court as a remedy to make Allen behave in his robbery trial, and it is true that citing or threatening to cite a contumacious defendant for criminal contempt might in itself be sufficient to make a defendant stop interrupting a trial. If so, the problem would be solved easily, and the defendant could remain in the courtroom. Of course, if the defendant is determined to prevent *any* trial, then a court in attempting to try the defendant for contempt is still confronted with the identical dilemma that the Illinois court faced in this case. And criminal contempt has obvious limitations as a sanction when the defendant is charged with a crime so serious that a very severe sentence such as death or life imprisonment is likely to be imposed. In such a case the defendant might not be affected by a mere contempt sentence when he ultimately faces a far more serious sanction. Nevertheless, the contempt remedy should be borne in mind by a judge in the circumstances of this case.

Another aspect of the contempt remedy is the judge's power, when exercised consistently with state and federal law, to imprison an unruly defendant such as Allen for civil contempt and discontinue the trial until such time as the defendant promises to behave himself. This procedure is consistent with the defendant's right to be present at trial, and yet it avoids the serious shortcomings of the use of shackles and gags. It must be recognized, however, that a defendant might conceivably, as a matter of calculated strategy, elect to spend a prolonged period in confinement for contempt in the hope that adverse witnesses might be unavailable after a lapse of time. A court must guard against allowing a defendant to profit from his own wrong in this way.

III

The trial court in this case decided under the circumstances to remove the defendant from the courtroom and to continue his trial in his absence until and unless he promised to conduct himself in a manner befitting an American courtroom. As we said earlier, we find nothing unconstitutional about this procedure. Allen's behavior was clearly of such an extreme and aggravated nature as to justify either his removal from the courtroom or his total physical restraint. Prior to his removal he was repeatedly warned by the trial judge that he would be removed from the courtroom if he persisted in his unruly conduct, and, as Judge Hastings [of the Federal court of appeals] observed in his dissenting opinion, the record demonstrates that Allen would not have been at all dissuaded by the trial judge's use of his criminal contempt powers. Allen was constantly informed that he could return to the trial when he would agree to conduct himself in an orderly manner. Under these circumstances we hold that Allen lost his right guaranteed by the Sixth and Fourteenth Amendments to be present throughout his trial.

IV

It is not pleasant to hold that the respondent Allen was properly banished from the court for a part of his own trial. But our courts, palladiums of liberty as they are, cannot be treated disrespectfully with impunity. Nor can the accused be permitted by his disruptive conduct indefinitely to avoid being tried on the charges brought against him. It would degrade our country and our judicial system to permit our courts to be bullied, insulted, and humiliated and their orderly progress thwarted and obstructed by defendants brought before them charged with crimes. As guardians of the public welfare, our state and federal judicial systems strive to administer equal justice to the rich and the poor, the good and the bad, the native and foreign born of every race, nationality, and religion. Being manned by humans, the courts are not perfect and are bound to make some errors. But, if our courts are to remain what the Founders intended, the citadels of justice, their proceedings cannot and must not be infected with the sort of scurrilous, abusive language and conduct paraded before the Illinois trial judge in this case. The record shows that the Illinois judge at all times conducted himself with that dignity, decorum, and patience that befit a judge. Even in holding that the trial judge had erred, the Court of Appeals praised his "commendable patience under severe provocation." [c]

We do not hold that removing this defendant from his own trial was the only way the Illinois judge could have constitutionally solved the problem he had. We do hold, however, that there is nothing whatever in this record to show that the judge did not act completely within his discretion. Deplorable as it is to remove a man from his own trial, even for a short time, we hold that the judge did not commit legal error in doing what he did. * * *

MR. JUSTICE BRENNAN, concurring.

* * *

I would add only that when a defendant is excluded from his trial, the court should make reasonable efforts to enable him to communicate with his attorney and, if possible, to keep apprised of the progress of his trial. Once the court has removed the contumacious defendant, it is not weakness to mitigate the disadvantages of his expulsion as far as technologically possible in the circumstances. [d]

[JUSTICE DOUGLAS dissented, urging that the case should have been dismissed for staleness (the trial occurred in 1957), suggested that the insanity defense might have been appropriate in Allen's case, and suggested some dangers of applying the Court's ruling in politically sensitive trials.]

* * * * * * * * * * *

COMMENTS

[a] As occurred in this case, a judge must give a disruptive defendant an opportunity to calm down and accept the continuation of the process. The defense counsel has a role to educate the defendant, who may be "in denial," about the nature of the trial and to impress on her or his client that the "wheels of justice" *will* continue to turn.

[b] One of the most famous examples of a bound and gagged defendant was Bobby Seale, a leader of the Black Panther party, tried with others in the famous "Chicago Seven" political trial in 1969. Seale's case was ultimately severed from the other defendants. Most defendants would not want the jury to see them bound and gagged but in a "political trial" the defendant may desire this to make a point. See Dwight Macdonald, "Introduction," in Mark Levine, George McNamee and Daniel Greenberg, *The Tales of Hoffman: Edited from the Official Transcript* (New York, Bantam, 1969); Tom Hayden, *Trial*, pp. 117-139 (New York: Holt Paperback, 1970).

[c] JUSTICE BLACK's closing statement makes sense only as long as the judicial system is held to be broadly legitimate by the people.

[d] JUSTICE BRENNAN's concurrence alerts us to the fact that advances in video and televising miniaturization, and the widespread adoption of televised trials, now makes it easy for contumacious defendants to view their trials from a jail cell and to communicate with their attorney electronically.

CHAMBERS v. MISSISSIPPI

410 U.S. 284, 93 S.Ct. 1038, 35 L.Ed.2d 297 (1973)

MR. JUSTICE POWELL delivered the opinion of the Court.

Petitioner, Leon Chambers, was tried by a jury in a Mississippi trial court and convicted of murdering a policeman. The jury assessed punishment at life imprisonment, and the Mississippi Supreme Court affirmed, one justice dissenting. . . .

I

[Two Woodville police officers, James Forman and Aaron "Sonny" Liberty, entered a bar to execute an arrest warrant] for a youth named C. C. Jackson. Jackson resisted and a hostile crowd of some 50 or 60 persons gathered. [In the ensuing melee] five or six pistol shots were fired. . . . Liberty [was] shot several times in the back [while Forman was looking in a different direction.] Before Liberty died, he turned around and fired both barrels of his riot gun into an alley in the area from which the shots appeared to have come. The first shot was wild and high and scattered the crowd standing at the face of the alley. Liberty appeared, however, to take more deliberate aim before the second shot and hit one of the men in the crowd in the back of the head and neck as he ran down the alley. That man was Leon Chambers.

[Some evidence by other police officers established circumstantial evidence against Chambers, who was left for dead after being shot. Liberty had been shot with four bullets from a .22-caliber revolver. Chambers was charged with Liberty's killing and maintained his innocence throughout.]

[Gable McDonald, a lifelong resident of Woodville, was in the crowd during the shooting. After the incident he moved away. He returned at the request of "Reverend Stokes" several months later and made a sworn confession to shooting Officer Liberty to Chambers' attorneys. At a preliminary hearing a month later, McDonald repudiated the confession.]

[At trial, Chambers developed two lines of defense, first, that he did not shoot Liberty and, second, that McDonald killed Liberty. In support of the second defense several witnesses implicated McDonald. Chambers tried to prove that McDonald confessed to his attorneys and on other occasions. Chambers claims that he was restricted in making out the second defense because of "the strict application of certain Mississippi rules of evidence."]

II

[The trial court granted Chambers' motion requiring McDonald to appear but ultimately ruled against Chambers' desire to treat McDonald as an adverse witness. The State did not call McDonald to the stand, but Chambers did. The Mississippi courts ruled that McDonald was not an adverse witness because he never accused Chambers of the crime. As a result, Chambers was prevented from putting three witnesses on the stand, Hardin, Turner, and Carter, who would testify that McDonald confessed to them; one would also testify that McDonald said he ditched a .22-caliber revolver and purchased a replacement. Also, Chambers could not cross-examine McDonald on this evidence.]

In sum, then, this was Chambers' predicament. As a consequence of the combination of Mississippi's "party witness" or "voucher" rule and its hearsay rule, he was unable either to cross-examine McDonald or to present witnesses in his own behalf who would have discredited McDonald's repudiation and demonstrated his complicity. Chambers had, however, chipped away at the fringes of McDonald's story . . . But all that remained from McDonald's own testimony was a single written confession countered by an arguably acceptable renunciation. Chambers' defense was far less persuasive than it might have been had he been given an opportunity to subject McDonald's statements to cross-examination or had the other confessions been admitted.

III

The right of an accused in a criminal trial to due process is, in essence, the right to a fair opportunity to defend against the State's accusations. The rights to confront and cross-examine witnesses and to call witnesses in one's own behalf have long been recognized as essential to due process. Mr. Justice Black, writing for the Court in *In re Oliver*, 333 U.S. 257, 273 (1948), identified these rights as among the minimum essentials of a fair trial:

"A person's right to reasonable notice of a charge against him, and an opportunity to be heard in his defense—a right to his day in court—are basic in our system of jurisprudence; and these rights include, as a minimum, a right to examine the witnesses against him, to offer testimony, and to be represented by counsel."

. . . Both of these elements of a fair trial are implicated in the present case.

A

Chambers was denied an opportunity to subject McDonald's damning repudiation and alibi to cross-examination. He was not allowed to test the witness' recollection, to probe into the details of his alibi, or to "sift" his conscience so that the jury might judge for itself whether McDonald's testimony was worthy of belief. * * * The right of cross-examination is more than a desirable rule of trial procedure. It is implicit in the constitutional right of confrontation, and helps assure the "accuracy of the truth-determining process." * * * It is, indeed, "an essential and fundamental requirement for the kind of fair trial which is this country's constitutional goal." * * * Of course, the right to confront and to cross-examine is not absolute and may, in appropriate cases, bow to accommodate other legitimate interests in the criminal trial process. * * * But its denial or significant diminution calls into question the ultimate "'integrity of the fact-finding process'" and requires that the competing interest be closely examined. * * *

In this case, petitioner's request to cross-examine McDonald was denied on the basis of a Mississippi common-law rule that a party may not impeach his own witness. The rule rests on the presumption—without regard to the circumstances of the particular case—that a party who calls a witness "vouches for his credibility." * * * Although the historical origins of the "voucher" rule are uncertain, it appears to be a remnant of primitive English trial practice in which "oath-takers" or "compurgators" were called to stand behind a particular party's position in any controversy. Their assertions were strictly partisan and, quite unlike witnesses in criminal trials today, their role bore little relation to the impartial ascertainment of the facts.

Whatever validity the "voucher" rule may have once enjoyed, and apart from whatever usefulness it retains today in the civil trial process, it bears little present relationship to the realities of the criminal process. It might have been logical for the early common law to require a party to vouch for the credibility of witnesses he brought before the jury to affirm his veracity. Having selected them especially for that purpose, the party might reasonably be expected to stand firmly behind their testimony. But in modern criminal trials, defendants are rarely able to select their witnesses: they must take them where they find them. Moreover, as applied in this case, the "voucher" rule's impact was doubly harmful to Chambers' efforts to develop his defense. Not only was he precluded from cross-examining McDonald, but, as the State conceded at oral argument, he was also restricted in the scope of his direct examination by the rule's corollary requirement that the party calling the witness is bound by anything he might say. He was, therefore, effectively prevented from exploring the circumstances of McDon-

ald's three prior oral confessions and from challenging the renunciation of the written confession.

In this Court, Mississippi has not sought to defend the rule or explain its underlying rationale. Nor has it contended that its rule should override the accused's right of confrontation. Instead, it argues that there is no incompatability between the rule and Chambers' rights because no right of confrontation exists unless the testifying witness is "adverse" to the accused. The State's brief asserts that the "right of confrontation applies to witnesses *against* an accused." Relying on the trial court's determination that McDonald was not "adverse," and on the State Supreme Court's holding that McDonald did not "point the finger at Chambers," the State contends that Chambers' constitutional right was not involved.

The argument that McDonald's testimony was not "adverse" to, or "against," Chambers is not convincing. The State's proof at trial excluded the theory that more than one person participated in the shooting of Liberty. To the extent that McDonald's sworn confession tended to incriminate him, it tended also to exculpate Chambers. And, in the circumstances of this case, McDonald's retraction inculpated Chambers to the same extent that it exculpated McDonald. It can hardly be disputed that McDonald's testimony was in fact seriously adverse to Chambers. The availability of the right to confront and to cross-examine those who give damaging testimony against the accused has never been held to depend on whether the witness was initially put on the stand by the accused or by the State. We reject the notion that a right of such substance in the criminal process may be governed by that technicality or by any narrow and unrealistic definition of the word "against." The "voucher" rule, as applied in this case, plainly interfered with Chambers' right to defend against the State's charges.

B

We need not decide, however, whether this error alone would occasion reversal since Chambers' claimed denial of due process rests on the ultimate impact of that error when viewed in conjunction with the trial court's refusal to permit him to call other witnesses. The trial court refused to allow him to introduce the testimony of Hardin, Turner, and Carter. Each would have testified to the statements purportedly made by McDonald, on three separate occasions shortly after the crime, naming himself as the murderer. The State Supreme Court approved the exclusion of this evidence on the ground that it was hearsay. The hearsay rule, which has long been recognized and respected by virtually every State, is based on experience and grounded in the notion that untrustworthy evidence should not be presented to the triers of fact. Out-of-court statements are traditionally excluded because they lack the conventional indicia of reliability: they are usually not made under oath or other circumstances that impress the speaker with the solemnity of his statements; the declarant's word is not subject to cross-examination; and he is not available in order that his demeanor and credibility may be assessed by the jury. . . . A number of exceptions have developed over the years to allow admission of hearsay statements made under circumstances that tend to assure reliability and thereby compensate for the absence of the oath and opportunity for cross-examination. Among the most prevalent of these exceptions is the one applicable to declarations against interest—an exception founded on the assumption that a person is unlikely to fabricate a statement against his own interest at the time it is made. Mississippi recognizes this exception but applies it only to declarations against pecuniary interest. It recognizes no such exception for declarations, like McDonald's in this case, that are against the penal interest of the declarant. * * *

This materialistic limitation on the declaration-against-interest hearsay exception appears to be accepted by most States in their criminal trial processes, although a number of States have discarded it. Declarations against penal interest have also been excluded in federal courts. * * * Exclusion, where the limitation prevails, is usually premised on the view that admission would lead to the frequent presentation of perjured testimony to the jury. It is believed that confessions of criminal activity are often motivated by extraneous considerations and, therefore, are not as inherently reliable as statements against pecuniary or proprietary interest. While that rationale has been the subject of considerable scholarly criticism, we need not decide in this case whether, under other circumstances, it might serve some valid state purpose by excluding untrustworthy testimony.

The hearsay statements involved in this case were originally made and subsequently offered at trial under circumstances that provided considerable assurance of their reliability.

First, each of McDonald's confessions was made spontaneously to a close acquaintance shortly after the murder had occurred. Second, each one was corroborated by some other evidence in the case—McDonald's sworn confession, the testimony of an eyewitness to the shooting, the testimony that McDonald was seen with a gun immediately after the shooting, and proof of his prior ownership of a .22-caliber revolver and subsequent purchase of a new weapon. The sheer number of independent confessions provided additional corroboration for each. Third, whatever may be the parameters of the penal-interest rationale, each confession here was in a very real sense self-incriminatory and unquestionably against interest. * * * McDonald stood to benefit nothing by disclosing his role in the shooting to any of his three friends and he must have been aware of the possibility that disclosure would lead to criminal prosecution. Indeed, after telling Turner of his involvement, he subsequently urged Turner not to "mess him up." Finally, if there was any question about the truthfulness of the extrajudicial statements, McDonald was present in the courtroom and was under oath. He could have been cross-examined by the State, and his demeanor and responses weighed by the jury. * * *

Few rights are more fundamental than that of an accused to present witnesses in his own defense. * * * In the exercise of this right, the accused, as is required of the State, must comply with established rules of procedure and evidence designed to assure both fairness and reliability in the ascertainment of guilt and innocence. Although perhaps no rule of evidence has been more respected or

more frequently applied in jury trials than that applicable to the exclusion of hearsay, exceptions tailored to allow the introduction of evidence which in fact is likely to be trustworthy have long existed. The testimony rejected by the trial court here bore persuasive assurances of trustworthiness and thus was well within the basic rationale of the exception for declarations against interest. That testimony also was critical to Chambers' defense. In these circumstances, where constitutional rights directly affecting the ascertainment of guilt are implicated, the hearsay rule may not be applied mechanistically to defeat the ends of justice.

We conclude that the exclusion of this critical evidence, coupled with the State's refusal to permit Chambers to cross-examine McDonald, denied him a trial in accord with traditional and fundamental standards of due process. In reaching this judgment, we establish no new principles of constitutional law. Nor does our holding signal any diminution in the respect traditionally accorded to the States in the establishment and implementation of their own criminal trial rules and procedures. Rather, we hold quite simply that under the facts and circumstances of this case the rulings of the trial court deprived Chambers of a fair trial.

The judgment is reversed and the case is remanded to the Supreme Court of Mississippi for further proceedings not inconsistent with this opinion.

It is so ordered.

[JUSTICE WHITE concurred in an opinion that concluded that the Court had jurisdiction in this case because objections based on constitutional issues were raised in the case. He also concurred in the Court's opinion.]

MR. JUSTICE REHNQUIST, dissenting.

Were I to reach the merits in this case, I would have considerable diffi-culty in subscribing to the Court's further constitutionalization of the intricacies of the common law of evidence. I do not reach the merits, since I conclude that petitioner failed to properly raise in the Mississippi courts the constitutional issue that he seeks to have this Court decide.

* * *

* * * * * * * * * *

COMMENT

Critics of the movement to "constitutionalize" rules of criminal procedure often complain that the movement undermines the truth-finding capacity of the trial. *Chambers* is a case where the superimposition of a constitutional rule over a common law rule of evidence has enhanced the truth-finding capacity of the trial.

KENTUCKY v. STINCER

482 U.S. 730, 107 S.Ct. 2658, 96 L.Ed.2d 631 (1987)

JUSTICE BLACKMUN delivered the opinion of the Court.

* * *

I

Respondent Sergio Stincer was indicted * * * and charged with committing first-degree sodomy with T.G., an 8-year-old girl, N.G., a 7-year-old girl, and B.H., a 5-year-old boy. * * * After a jury was sworn, but before the presentation of evidence, the court conducted an in-chambers hearing to determine if the two young girls were competent to testify. [a] Over his objection, respondent, but not his counsel (a public defender), was excluded from this hearing.

The two children were examined separately and the judge, the prosecutor, and respondent's counsel asked questions of each girl to determine if she were capable of remembering basic facts and of distinguishing between telling the truth and telling a lie. * * * T.G., the 8-year-old, was asked her age, her date of birth, the name of her school, the names of her teachers, and the name of her Sunday school. She was also asked whether she knew what it meant to tell the truth, and whether she could keep a promise to God to tell the truth. N.G., the 7-year-old girl, was asked similar questions. * * * The two children were not asked about the substance of the testimony they were to give at trial. [b] The court ruled that the girls were competent to testify. Respondent's counsel did not object to these rulings.

Before each of the girls began her substantive testimony in open court, the prosecutor repeated some of the basic questions regarding the girl's background that had been asked at the competency hearing. * * * T.G. then testified, on direct examination, that respondent had placed a sock over her eyes, had given her chocolate pudding to eat, and then had "put his d-i-c-k" in her mouth. * * * N.G., on direct examination, testified to a similar incident. * * *

On cross-examination, respondent's counsel asked each girl questions * * * similar to those that had been asked at the competency hearing. * * * [C]ounsel did not request that the trial court reconsider its ruling that the girls were competent to testify. The jury convicted respondent of first-degree sodomy for engaging in deviate sexual intercourse and fixed his sentence at 20 years' imprisonment.

[A divided Kentucky Supreme Court found that Stincer's Sixth Amendment rights meant that he had an absolute right to be present at the competency hearing because the hearing "was a crucial phase of the trial."] * * *

II
A

The Sixth Amendment's Confrontation Clause provides: "In all criminal prosecutions, the accused shall enjoy the right * * * to be confronted with the witnesses against him." This right is secured for defendants in state as well as in federal criminal proceedings. * * * The Court has emphasized that "a primary interest secured by [the Confrontation Clause] is the right of cross-examination." * * * The opportunity for cross-examination, protected by the Confrontation Clause, is critical for ensuring the integrity of the fact finding process. Cross-examination is "the principal means by which the believability of a witness and the truth of his testimony are tested." * * * Indeed, the Court has recognized that cross-examination is the "'greatest legal engine ever invented for the discovery of truth.'" * * * [c]

The right to cross-examination, protected by the Confrontation Clause, thus is essentially a "functional" right designed to promote reliability in the truth-finding functions of a criminal trial. [d] The cases that have arisen under the Confrontation Clause * * * fall into two broad, albeit not exclusive, categories: "cases involving the admission of out-of-court statements and cases involving restrictions imposed by law or by the trial court on the scope of cross-examination." * * *

In the first category of cases, the Confrontation Clause is violated when "hearsay evidence [is] admitted as substantive evidence against the defendan[t]," * * * with no opportunity to cross-examine the hearsay declarant at trial, or when an out-of-court statement of an unavailable witness does not bear adequate indications of trustworthiness. * * * For example, * * * an out-of-court statement by an unavailable witness [is] sufficiently reliable to be admitted at trial, consistent with the Confrontation Clause, [if] defense counsel had engaged in full cross-examination of the witness at the preliminary hearing where the statement was made. * * *

The second category involves cases in which the opportunity for cross-examination has been restricted by law or by a trial court ruling. In *Davis v. Alaska*, [415 U.S. 308 (1974)], defense counsel was restricted by state confidentiality provisions from questioning a witness about his juvenile criminal record, although such evidence might have affected the witness' credibility. The Court held that the Confrontation Clause was violated because the defendant was denied the right "to expose to the jury the facts from which jurors . . . could appropriately draw inferences relating to the reliability of the witness." * * * [e] Similarly, in *Delaware v. Van Arsdall*, 475 U.S. 673 (1986), defense counsel was precluded by the trial court from questioning a witness about the State's dismissal of a pending public drunkenness charge against him. The Court concluded: "By thus cutting off all questioning about an event . . . that a jury might reasonably have found furnished the witness a motive for favoring the prosecution in his testimony," the trial court's ruling violated the defendant's rights under the Confrontation Clause.

* * * [T]hese cases reflect the Confrontation Clause's functional purpose in ensuring a defendant an opportunity for cross-examination. * * * Of course, the Confrontation Clause guarantees only "an *opportunity* for effective cross-examination, not cross-examination that is effective in whatever way, and to whatever extent, the defense might wish." * * * This limitation is consistent with the concept that the right to confrontation is a functional one for the purpose of promoting reliability in a criminal trial.

B

* * *

Instead of attempting to characterize a competency hearing as a trial or pretrial proceeding, it is more useful to consider whether excluding the defendant from the hearing interferes with his opportunity for effective cross-examination. No such interference occurred when respondent was excluded from the competency hearing of the two young girls in this case. After the trial court determined that the two children were competent to testify, they appeared and testified in open court. At that point, the two witnesses were subject to full and complete cross-examination, and were so examined. * * * Respondent was present throughout this cross-examination and was available to assist his counsel as necessary. * * * Any questions asked during the competency hearing, which respondent's counsel attended and in which he participated, could have been repeated during direct examination and cross-examination of the witnesses in respondent's presence. * * * [f]

Moreover, the type of questions that were asked at the competency hearing in this case were easy to repeat on cross-examination at trial. Under Kentucky law, when a child's competency to testify is raised, the judge is required to resolve three basic issues: whether the child is capable of observing and recollecting facts, whether the child is capable of narrating those facts to a court or jury, and whether the child has a moral sense of the obligation to tell the truth. * * * Thus, questions at a competency hearing usually are limited to matters that are unrelated to the basic issues of the trial. Children often are asked

their names, where they go to school, how old they are, whether they know who the judge is, whether they know what a lie is, and whether they know what happens when one tells a lie. * * *

In Kentucky, as in certain other States, it is the responsibility of the judge, not the jury, to decide whether a witness is competent to testify based on the witness' answers to such questions. * * * Moreover, appellate courts reviewing a trial judge's determination of competency also often will look at the full testimony at trial.

In this case both T.G. and N.G. were asked several background questions during the competency hearing, as well as several questions directed at what it meant to tell the truth. Some of the questions regarding the witnesses' backgrounds were repeated by the prosecutor on direct examination, while others—particularly those regarding the witnesses' ability to tell the difference between truth and falsehood—were repeated by respondent's counsel on cross-examination. At the close of the children's testimony, respondent's counsel, had he thought it appropriate, was in a position to move that the court reconsider its competency rulings on the ground that the direct and cross-examination had elicited evidence that the young girls lacked the basic requisites for serving as competent witnesses. Thus, the critical tool of cross-examination was available to counsel as a means of establishing that the witnesses were not competent to testify, as well as a means of undermining the credibility of their testimony.

Because respondent had the opportunity for full and effective cross-examination of the two witnesses during trial, and because of the nature of the competency hearing at issue in this case, we conclude that respondent's rights under the Confrontation Clause were not violated by his exclusion from the competency hearing of the two girls.

III

Respondent argues that his rights under the Due Process Clause of the Fourteenth Amendment were violated by his exclusion from the competency hearing. The Court has assumed that, even in situations where the defendant is not actually confronting witnesses or evidence against him, he has a due process right "to be present in his own person whenever his presence has a relation, reasonably substantial, to the fulness of his opportunity to defend against the charge." * * * Although the Court has emphasized that this privilege of presence is not guaranteed "when presence would be useless, or the benefit but a shadow," * * * due process clearly requires that a defendant be allowed to be present "to the extent that a fair and just hearing would be thwarted by his absence." * * * Thus, a defendant is guaranteed the right to be present at any stage of the criminal proceeding that is critical to its outcome if his presence would contribute to the fairness of the procedure. [g]

We conclude that respondent's due process rights were not violated by his exclusion from the competency hearing in this case. We emphasize, again, the particular nature of the competency hearing. No question regarding the substantive testimony that the two girls would have given during trial was asked at that hearing. All the ques-

tions, instead, were directed solely to each child's ability to recollect and narrate facts, to her ability to distinguish between truth and falsehood, and to her sense of moral obligation to tell the truth. Thus, although a competency hearing in which a witness is asked to discuss upcoming substantive testimony might bear a substantial relationship to a defendant's opportunity better to defend himself at trial, that kind of inquiry is not before us in this case. [h]

Respondent has given no indication that his presence at the competency hearing in this case would have been useful in ensuring a more reliable determination as to whether the witnesses were competent to testify. He has presented no evidence that his relationship with the children, or his knowledge of facts regarding their background, could have assisted either his counsel or the judge in asking questions that would have resulted in a more assured determination of competency. On the record of this case, therefore, we cannot say that respondent's rights under the Due Process Clause of the Fourteenth Amendment were violated by his exclusion from the competency hearing. * * *

The judgment of the Supreme Court of Kentucky is reversed.

It is so ordered.

JUSTICE MARSHALL, with whom JUSTICE BRENNAN and JUSTICE STEVENS join, dissenting.

* * *

I

* * * The [Confrontation Clause]

plainly envisions that witnesses against the accused shall, as a rule, testify *in his presence*. I can only marvel at the manner in which the Court avoids this manifest import of the Confrontation Clause. Without explanation, the Court narrows its analysis to address *exclusively* what is accurately identified as simply a primary interest the Clause was intended to secure: the right of cross-examination. * * * This use of analytical blinders is undoubtedly convenient. Since respondent ultimately did receive an opportunity for full cross-examination of the witnesses in his presence, the narrowly drawn standard enables the Court to conclude with relative ease that respondent's confrontation rights were not violated, * * * even though the in-chambers competency hearing admittedly was, in this case, a "crucial" phase of respondent's trial from which he was physically excluded.

Although cross-examination may be a primary means for ensuring the reliability of testimony from adverse witnesses, we have never held that standing alone it will suffice in every case. * * *

Physical presence of the defendant enhances the reliability of the fact-finding process. Under Kentucky law, in a witness competency proceeding the trial judge must assess the witness' ability to observe and recollect facts with accuracy and with committed truthfulness. * * * This determination necessarily requires the judge to make independent factual findings against which can be measured the accuracy of the witness' testimony at the competency proceeding, whether addressing facts such as the witness' name, age, and relation to the defendant, or events concerning the alleged offense

itself. These findings are critical to the trial judge's assessment of the witness' competency to testify, and they often concern matters about which the defendant, and not his counsel, possesses the knowledge needed to expose inaccuracies in the witness' answers. Having the defendant present ensures that these inaccuracies are called to the judge's attention immediately—*before* the witness takes the stand with the trial court's *imprimatur* of competency and testifies in front of the jury as to the defendant's commission of the alleged offense. It is both functionally inefficient and fundamentally unfair to attribute to the defendant's attorney complete knowledge of the facts which the trial judge, in the defendant's involuntary absence, deems relevant to the competency determination. That determination, which turns entirely on the trial court's evaluation of the witness' statements, cannot be made out of the physical presence of the defendant without violating the basic guarantee of the Confrontation Clause. * * *

But more than the reliability of the competency determination is at stake in this case. * * * [T]he constitutional guarantee of the right of confrontation serves certain "symbolic goals" as well:

"[T]he right to confront and cross-examine adverse witnesses contributes to the establishment of a system of criminal justice in which the perception as well as the reality of fairness prevails. To foster such a system, the Constitution provides certain safeguards to promote to the greatest possible degree society's interest in having the accused and accuser engage in open and even contest in a public trial. The Confrontation Clause advances these goals by ensuring that convictions will not be based on the charges of unseen and un-known—and hence unchallenge-able—individuals." [i]

This appearance of fairness is woefully lacking in the present case. The Commonwealth did not request that respondent be excluded from the competency hearing. The trial judge raised this issue *sua sponte*, and only the personal protestations of respondent, a recent Cuban immigrant whose fluency in the English language was limited, preserved the issue for appeal. Neither the prosecuting attorney nor the trial judge articulated any reason for excluding him. From this defendant's perspective, the specter of the judge, prosecutor, and court-appointed attorney conferring privately with the key prosecution witnesses was under-standably upsetting. From a constitu-tional perspective, the unrequested and unjustified exclusion constitutes an intolerable subversion of the symbolic functions of the Confrontation Clause.

* * *

*   *   *   *   *   *   *   *   *   *

COMMENTS

[a] In recent years, prosecutors have become more aggressive in prosecuting sexual assaults against children. Aside from settling an important legal principle, this case affects the trial conduct in a growing number of cases where key witnesses are young children who pose special problems of proof.

[b] Important proceedings can occur in the judge's chambers; the Supreme Court deliberately avoided the question of whether the in-chambers hearing constituted part of the trial.

[c] Confrontation without cross-examination would be meaningless. However, do you think that the mere physical presence of the defendant in the courtroom makes a difference in how witnesses testify and how attorneys and the judge behave?

[d] Is anything added to analysis by calling cross-examination a "functional" right? Could this mean that it is less protected by the Sixth Amendment than the right to be physically present?

[e] Note the strong legislative policy of maintaining the secrecy of juvenile criminal history is overridden by the Constitutional policy of the confrontation clause. What is the basis of that policy? of the policy behind examining the veracity of child witnesses in chambers? Is the policy regarding children's testimony of constitu-tional dimensions?

[f] If much of the in-chambers hearing was repeated in open court in the presence of the defendant, was it necessary for the trial judge to exclude Stincer from the hearing? Do you think that it is essential to examine the competency of a young child in chambers rather than open court? If your answer is yes, why should the child be any more comfortable there than when testifying in open court? Can complete trials be held in-chambers?

[g] Due process tests typically require that all the "facts and circumstances" be examined to determine if the proceeding is "fundamentally unfair."

[h] This sentence would appear to put a real limitation on what can be covered in a hearing in chambers that excludes the defendant.

[i] The common law jury trial is grossly inefficient compared to the European civil law trial. Yet, the jury trial is a model of citizen involvement and fairness largely because of its symbolic aspects. Why is it important that the accused person be able to see everything that goes on that will affect his conviction or acquittal?

MARYLAND v. CRAIG

497 U.S. 836, 110 S.Ct. 3157, 111 L.Ed.2d 666 (1990)

JUSTICE O'CONNOR delivered the opinion of the Court.

This case requires us to decide whether the Confrontation Clause of the Sixth Amendment categorically prohibits a child witness in a child abuse case from testifying against a defendant at trial, outside the defendant's physical presence, by one-way closed circuit television.

I

[In 1986 Sandra Craig was charged with various sexual crimes against a six-year-old girl who had attended a kindergarten and prekindergarten center owned and operated by Craig.]

[Before trial the State sought to invoke a statutory procedure permitting a judge to receive,] by one-way closed circuit television, the testimony of a child witness who is alleged to be a victim of child abuse. To invoke the procedure, the trial judge must first "determin[e] that testimony by the child victim in the courtroom will result in the child suffering serious emotional distress such that the child cannot reasonably communicate." * * * Once the procedure is invoked, the child witness, prosecutor, and defense counsel withdraw to a separate room; the judge, jury, and defendant remain in the courtroom. The child witness is then examined and cross-examined in the separate room, while a video monitor records and displays the witness' testimony to those in the courtroom. During this time the witness cannot see the defendant. The defendant remains in electronic communication with defense counsel, and objections may be made and ruled on as if the witness were testifying in the courtroom.

In support of its motion invoking the one-way closed circuit television procedure, the State presented expert testimony that the named victim, as well as a number of other children who were alleged to have been sexually abused by Craig, would suffer "serious emotional distress such that [they could not] reasonably communicate," * * * if required to testify in the courtroom. * * * The Maryland [courts ruled, on the basis of the expert testimony, that each child would have some or considerable difficulty in testifying in Craig's presence; that one would not be able to communicate effectively; another would probably stop talking and would withdraw and curl up; one would become highly agitated; and another would become extremely timid and unwilling to talk. [a] Over Craig's objection the children testified via one-way closed circuit television after the judge found that the children would experience distress and that Craig retained the essence of the right to confrontation. Mrs. Craig's jury conviction was upheld by one appeals court but reversed by the Court of Appeals of Maryland, which found that under the Maryland statute the inability of the child to testify must be first tested by a face to face confrontation with the accused and that the "high threshold" required by *Coy v. Iowa*, 487 U.S. 1012 (1988) before excluding the accused had not been met.]

We granted certiorari to resolve the important Confrontation Clause issues raised by this case. * * *

II

* * *

We observed in *Coy v. Iowa* that "the Confrontation Clause guarantees the defendant a face-to-face meeting with witnesses appearing before the trier of fact." * * * This interpretation derives not only from the literal text of the Clause, but also from our understanding of its historical roots. * * *

We have never held, however, that the Confrontation Clause guarantees criminal defendants the absolute right to a face-to-face meeting with witnesses against them at trial. Indeed, in *Coy v. Iowa*, we expressly "le[ft] for another day . . . the question whether any exceptions exist" to the "irreducible literal meaning of the Clause: 'a right to *meet face to face* all those who appear and give evidence *at trial*.'" * * * The procedure challenged in *Coy* involved the placement of a screen that prevented two child witnesses in a child abuse case from seeing the defendant as they testified against him at trial. * * * In holding that the use of this procedure violated the defendant's right to confront witnesses against him, we suggested that any exception to the right "would surely be allowed only when necessary to further an important public policy"—*i.e.*, only upon a showing of something more than the generalized, "legislatively imposed presumption of trauma" underlying the statute at issue in that case. * * * We concluded that "[s]ince there ha[d] been no individualized findings that these particular witnesses needed special protection, the judgment [in the case before us] could not be sustained by any conceivable exception." * * * Because the trial court in this case made individualized findings that each of the child witnesses needed special protection, this case requires us to decide the question reserved in *Coy*.

[b]

The central concern of the Confrontation Clause is to ensure the reliability of the evidence against a criminal defendant by subjecting it to rigorous testing in the context of an adversary proceeding before the trier of fact. The word "confront," after all, also means a clashing of forces or ideas, thus carrying with it the notion of adversariness. [c] * * * [T]he right guaranteed by the Confrontation Clause includes not only a "personal examination," * * * but also "(1) insures that the witness will give his statements under oath—thus impressing him with the seriousness of the matter and guarding against the lie by the possibility of a penalty for perjury; (2) forces the witness to submit to cross-examination, the 'greatest legal engine ever invented for the discovery of truth'; [and] (3) permits the jury that is to decide the defendant's fate to observe the demeanor of the witness in making his statement, thus aiding the jury in assessing his credibility." * * *

The combined effect of these elements of confrontation—physical presence, oath, cross-examination, and observation of demeanor by the trier of fact—serves the purposes of the Confrontation Clause by ensuring that evidence admitted against an accused is reliable and subject to the rigorous adversarial testing that is the norm of Anglo-American criminal proceedings.

* * *

We have recognized, for example, that face-to-face confrontation enhances the accuracy of factfinding by reducing the risk that a witness will wrongfully implicate an innocent person. * * * We have also noted the strong symbolic purpose served by requiring adverse witnesses at trial to testify in the accused's presence. * * *

Although face-to-face confrontation forms "the core of the values furthered by the Confrontation Clause," * * * we have nevertheless recognized that it is not the *sine qua non* of the confrontation right. * * * See *Delaware v. Fensterer*, 474 U.S. 15, 22 (1985) (*per curiam*) ("[T]he Confrontation Clause is generally satisfied when the defense is given a full and fair opportunity to probe and expose [testimonial] infirmities [such as forgetfulness, confusion, or evasion] through cross-examination, thereby calling to the attention of the factfinder the reasons for giving scant weight to the witness' testimony"). * * *

For this reason, we have never insisted on an actual face-to-face encounter at trial in *every* instance in which testimony is admitted against a defendant. Instead, we have repeatedly held that the Clause permits, where necessary, the admission of certain hearsay statements against a defendant despite the defendant's inability to confront the declarant at trial. * * * In *Mattox [v. United States*, 156 U.S. 237, 244 (1895)], for example, we held that the testimony of a Government witness at a former trial against the defendant, where the witness was fully cross-examined but had died after the first trial, was admissible in evidence against the defendant at his second trial. * * * We explained:

"There is doubtless reason for saying that . . . if notes of [the witness'] testimony are permitted to be read, [the defendant] is deprived of the advantage of that personal presence of the witness before the jury which the law has designed for his protection. But general rules of law of this kind, however beneficent in their operation and valuable to the accused, must occasionally give way to considerations of public policy and the necessities of the case. To say that a criminal, after having once been convicted by the testimony of a certain witness, should go scot free simply because death has closed the mouth of that witness, would be carrying his constitutional protection to an unwarrantable extent. The law in its wisdom declares that the rights of the public shall not be wholly sacrificed in order that an incidental benefit may be preserved to the accused." * * *

* * * [A] literal reading of the Confrontation Clause would "abrogate virtually every hearsay exception, a result long rejected as unintended and too extreme." * * * Thus, in certain narrow circumstances, "competing interests, if 'closely examined,' may warrant dispensing with confrontation at trial." * * * We have recently held, for example, that hearsay statements of nontestifying coconspirators may be admitted against a defendant despite the lack of any face-to-face encounter with the accused. * * * Given our hearsay cases, the word "confront," as used in the Confrontation Clause, cannot simply mean face-to-face confrontation, for the Clause would then, contrary to our cases,

prohibit the admission of any accusatory hearsay statement made by an absent declarant—a declarant who is undoubtedly as much a "witness against" a defendant as one who actually testifies at trial. [d]

In sum, our precedents establish that "the Confrontation Clause reflects a *preference* for face-to-face confrontation at trial," * * * a preference that "must occasionally give way to considerations of public policy and the necessities of the case." * * * "[W]e have attempted to harmonize the goal of the Clause—placing limits on the kind of evidence that may be received against a defendant—with a societal interest in accurate factfinding, which may require consideration of out-of-court statements." * * * We have accordingly interpreted the Confrontation Clause in a manner sensitive to its purposes and sensitive to the necessities of trial and the adversary process. * * * Thus, though we reaffirm the importance of face-to-face confrontation with witnesses appearing at trial, we cannot say that such confrontation is an indispensable element of the Sixth Amendment's guarantee of the right to confront one's accusers. Indeed, one commentator has noted that "[i]t is all but universally assumed that there are circumstances that excuse compliance with the right of confrontation." * * *

[The Court noted that in other cases, Sixth Amendment rights have not been read absolutely: disruptive defendants may be excluded from their trials; defendants may not be given access to investigative files; surprise defense witnesses have been excluded; counsel and defendant have been prevented from testifying during short breaks in testimony.] We see no reason to treat the face-to-face component of the confrontation right any differently, and indeed we think it would be anomalous to do so.

That the face-to-face confrontation requirement is not absolute does not, of course, mean that it may easily be dispensed with. As we suggested in *Coy*, our precedents confirm that a defendant's right to confront accusatory witnesses may be satisfied absent a physical, face-to-face confrontation at trial only where denial of such confrontation is necessary to further an important public policy and only where the reliability of the testimony is otherwise assured. * * *

III

[Maryland's statutory procedure was deemed superior to that in *Coy* because it preserved all other elements of confrontation that are safeguards of reliability: oath, cross-examination, and observation of the witness' demeanor. Its use is therefore permitted if it is necessary to further an important state interest. The protection of sex crime victims is compelling and could allow, in some cases, the closing of the courtroom to the public and the press. Also, "a State's interest in the physical and psychological well-being of child abuse victims may be sufficiently important to outweigh, at least in some cases, a defendant's right to face his or her accusers in court." Many states have by law allowed for testimony in such cases to be presented without face-to-face confrontations.]

* * *

* * * Accordingly, we hold that, if the State makes an adequate showing of necessity, the state interest in

protecting child witnesses from the trauma of testifying in a child abuse case is sufficiently important to justify the use of a special procedure that permits a child witness in such cases to testify at trial against a defendant in the absence of face-to-face confrontation with the defendant.

The requisite finding of necessity must of course be a case-specific one: The trial court must hear evidence and determine whether use of the one-way closed circuit television procedure is necessary to protect the welfare of the particular child witness who seeks to testify. * * * The trial court must also find that the child witness would be traumatized, not by the courtroom generally, but by the presence of the defendant. * * * Denial of face-to-face confrontation is not needed to further the state interest in protecting the child witness from trauma unless it is the presence of the defendant that causes the trauma. In other words, if the state interest were merely the interest in protecting child witnesses from courtroom trauma generally, denial of face-to-face confrontation would be unnecessary because the child could be permitted to testify in less intimidating surroundings, albeit with the defendant present. Finally, the trial court must find that the emotional distress suffered by the child witness in the presence of the defendant is more than *de minimis, i. e.*, more than "mere nervousness or excitement or some reluctance to testify," * * * We need not decide the minimum showing of emotional trauma required for use of the special procedure, however, because the Maryland statute, which requires a determination that the child witness will suffer "serious emotional distress such that the child cannot reasonably

communicate," * * * clearly suffices to meet constitutional standards.

To be sure, face-to-face confrontation may be said to cause trauma for the very purpose of eliciting truth, * * * but we think that the use of Maryland's special procedure, where necessary to further the important state interest in preventing trauma to child witnesses in child abuse cases, adequately ensures the accuracy of the testimony and preserves the adversary nature of the trial. * * * Indeed, where face-to-face confrontation causes significant emotional distress in a child witness, there is evidence that such confrontation would in fact disserve the Confrontation Clause's truth-seeking goal. * * * [e]

In sum, we conclude that where necessary to protect a child witness from trauma that would be caused by testifying in the physical presence of the defendant, at least where such trauma would impair the child's ability to communicate, the Confrontation Clause does not prohibit use of a procedure that, despite the absence of face-to-face confrontation, ensures the reliability of the evidence by subjecting it to rigorous adversarial testing and thereby preserves the essence of effective confrontation. Because there is no dispute that the child witnesses in this case testified under oath, were subject to full cross-examination, and were able to be observed by the judge, jury, and defendant as they testified, we conclude that, to the extent that a proper finding of necessity has been made, the admission of such testimony would be consonant with the Confrontation Clause.

IV

[The Maryland Court of Appeals held that the closed-circuit television procedure can only be used after a case specific finding is made by the trial judge; that the child witness must first be questioned in the accused's presence; and that the judge find that the child would suffer "severe emotional distress" if he or she were to testify by two-way closed circuit television. That court found that the trial court acted improperly by making its conclusion solely on the basis of expert testimony, without observing the child witnesses in the defendant's presence. The U.S. Supreme Court reversed the Maryland Court of Appeals, stating that "[a]lthough we think such evidentiary requirements could strengthen the grounds for use of protective measures, we decline to establish, as a matter of federal constitutional law, any such categorical evidentiary prerequisites for the use of the one-way television procedure." The case was remanded to determine whether the Maryland Court of Appeals would come to the same conclusion under the Sixth Amendment standards specified by the majority].

JUSTICE SCALIA, with whom JUSTICE BRENNAN, JUSTICE MARSHALL, and JUSTICE STEVENS join, dissenting.

Seldom has this Court failed so conspicuously to sustain a categorical guarantee of the Constitution against the tide of prevailing current opinion. The Sixth Amendment provides, with unmistakable clarity, that "[i]n all criminal prosecutions, the accused shall enjoy the right . . . to be confronted with the witnesses against him." The purpose of enshrining this protection in the Constitution was to assure that none of the many policy interests from time to time pursued by statutory law could overcome a defendant's right to face his or her accusers in court. The Court, however, says:

"We . . . conclude today that a State's interest in the physical and psychological well-being of child abuse victims may be sufficiently important to outweigh, at least in some cases, a defendant's right to face his or her accusers in court. * * *" * * *

Because of this subordination of explicit constitutional text to currently favored public policy, the following scene can be played out in an American courtroom for the first time in two centuries: A father whose young daughter has been given over to the exclusive custody of his estranged wife, or a mother whose young son has been taken into custody by the State's child welfare department, is sentenced to prison for sexual abuse on the basis of testimony by a child the parent has not seen or spoken to for many months; and the guilty verdict is rendered without giving the parent so much as the opportunity to sit in the presence of the child, and to ask, personally or through counsel, "it is really not true, is it, that I—your father (or mother) whom you see before you—did these terrible things?" Perhaps that is a procedure today's society desires; perhaps (though I doubt it) it is even a fair procedure; but it is assuredly not a procedure permitted by the Constitution.

Because the text of the Sixth Amendment is clear, and because the Constitution is meant to protect against, rather than conform to, current "widespread belief," I respectfully dissent.

I

* * * The Court makes the impossible plausible by recharacterizing the Confrontation Clause, so that confrontation (redesignated "face-to-face confrontation") becomes only one of many "elements of confrontation." * * * The reasoning is as follows: The Confrontation Clause guarantees not only what it explicitly provides for—"face-to-face" confrontation—but also implied and collateral rights such as cross-examination, oath, and observation of demeanor (TRUE); the purpose of this entire cluster of rights is to ensure the reliability of evidence (TRUE); the Maryland procedure preserves the implied and collateral rights (TRUE), which adequately ensure the reliability of evidence (perhaps TRUE); therefore the Confrontation Clause is not violated by denying what it explicitly provides for—"face-to-face" confrontation (unquestionably FALSE). This reasoning abstracts from the right to its purposes, and then eliminates the right. It is wrong because the Confrontation Clause does not guarantee reliable evidence; it guarantees specific trial procedures that were thought to *assure* reliable evidence, undeniably among which was "face-to-face" confrontation. Whatever else it may mean in addition, the defendant's constitutional right "to be confronted with the witnesses against him" means, always and everywhere, at least what it explicitly says: the "'right to meet face to face all those who appear and give evidence at trial.'" * * *
* * *

II

* * *

[JUSTICE SCALIA argued that a child witness who is unavailable because of anxiety before a particular witness is not the same as a previously testifying witness who is unavalibale because of death or disappearance.] * * * [The] very object [of the Confrontation Clause] is to place the witness under the sometimes hostile glare of the defendant. "That face-to-face presence may, unfortunately, upset the truthful rape victim or abused child; but by the same token it may confound and undo the false accuser, or reveal the child coached by a malevolent adult." * * * To say that a defendant loses his right to confront a witness when that would cause the witness not to testify is rather like saying that the defendant loses his right to counsel when counsel would save him, or his right to subpoena witnesses when they would exculpate him, or his right not to give testimony against himself when that would prove him guilty.

III

The Court characterizes the State's interest which "out-weigh[s]" the explicit text of the Constitution as an "interest in the physical and psychological well-being of child abuse victims," * * * an "interest in protecting" such victims "from the emotional trauma of testifying." * * * That is not so. A child who meets the Maryland statute's requirement of suffering such "serious emotional distress" from confrontation that he "cannot reasonably communicate" would seem entirely safe. Why would a prosecutor want to call a witness who cannot reasonably communicate? And if he did, it would be the State's own fault. Protection of the child's interest—as far as the Confrontation Clause is concerned—is entirely within Maryland's control. The State's interest here is in fact no more and no less than what the State's interest always is when it seeks to get a class

of evidence admitted in criminal proceedings: more convictions of guilty defendants. That is not an unworthy interest, but it should not be dressed up as a humanitarian one.

* * *

The Court today has applied "interest-balancing" analysis where the text of the Constitution simply does not permit it. We are not free to conduct a cost-benefit analysis of clear and explicit constitutional guarantees, and then to adjust their meaning to comport with our findings. * * *

* * * * * * * * * *

COMMENTS

[a] This is not what happened in this case; this is what an expert predicted would happen. Does it make sense to attempt to allow testimony of a young witness with the accused present and revert to excluding the accused only if a witness in fact ceases to communicate?

[b] The dissent would follow a bright-line rule that requires face-to-face confrontations; the majority makes this element of the Sixth Amendment depend on the facts of the case as determined by the trial judge. This places a major responsibility on trial judges and indicates a large measure of trust in them.

[c] The word "confront" may mean many things. In the context of the Sixth Amendment, the Court reads it to mean several things other than a face-to-face meeting of a witness and accuser in the same courtroom. Do you think this is a basis for withdrawing a face-to-face requirement?

[d] In the light of this well established litany of case law, does an absolute adherence to the face-to-face requirement appear to you weaker than before?

[e] What is your view of the Maryland procedure? Is it affected by your view of the issue of the difficulty of proof in child sexual abuse cases? Some believe that the scourge of child abuse is a national disgrace and that the strongest measures to ferret it out are essential. Others believe that in dealing with the serious issue of child sexual abuse, instances of mass hysteria have led to the conviction of innocent persons.

IDAHO v. WRIGHT

497 U.S. 805, 110 S.Ct. 3139, 111 L.Ed.2d 638 (1990)

JUSTICE O'CONNOR delivered the opinion of the Court.

This case requires us to decide whether the admission at trial of certain hearsay statements made by a child declarant to an examining pediatrician violates a defendant's rights under the Confrontation Clause of the Sixth Amendment.

I

[Laura Lee Wright, jointly charged with Robert L. Giles, her male companion, was convicted of sexual abuse of her two daughters, aged 5½ and 2½ years old at the time the crimes were charged. Laura had a joint custody arrangement with Louis Wright, her ex-husband, who lived with Cynthia Goodman. The older daughter told Goodman that Giles had sexual intercourse with her and that she had seen him have sex with the younger daughter. Goodman reported the story to the police and took the girls to the hospital the next day. A pediatrician, Dr. John Jambura, found evidence of "sexual abuse with vaginal contact" of the girls within two days prior to the examination. At the trial, statements made by the younger daughter (who was found not capable of communicating to the jury) to Dr. Jambura were admitted. On cross-examination Dr. Jambura admitted that he discarded a picture he drew during the examination and that his contemporaneous notes were not detailed.]

[Under Idaho law, hearsay statements are admissible if they do not fit standard hearsay exceptions but have "equivalent circumstantial guarantees of trustworthiness." The statement must be offered as evidence of a material fact, be "more probative on the point for which it is offered than any other evidence which the proponent can procure through reasonable efforts," and must serve the interests of justice.]

[The Idaho Supreme Court reversed Laura Wright's conviction as to her younger daughter because the admission of Dr. Jambura's testimony violated her rights under the Confrontation Clause.]

The Supreme Court of Idaho held that the admission of the inculpatory hearsay testimony violated respondent's federal constitutional right to confrontation because the testimony did not fall within a traditional hearsay exception and was based on an interview that lacked procedural safeguards. * * * The court found Dr. Jambura's interview technique inadequate because "the questions and answers were not recorded on videotape for preservation and perusal by the defense at or before trial; and, blatantly leading questions were used in the interrogation." * * * The statements also lacked trustworthiness, according to the court, because "this interrogation was performed by someone with a preconceived idea of what the child should be disclosing." * * * Noting that expert testimony and child psychology texts indicated that children are susceptible to suggestion and are therefore likely to be misled by leading questions, the court found that "[t]he circumstances surrounding this interview demonstrate dangers of unreliability which, because the interview was not [audio or video] recorded, can never be fully assessed." * * * The court concluded that the younger daughter's statements lacked the particularized guarantees of trustworthiness necessary to satisfy the requirements of the Confrontation Clause and that therefore the trial court erred in admitting them. * * * Because the court was not convinced, beyond a reasonable doubt, that the jury would have reached the same result had the error not occurred, the court reversed respondent's conviction on the count involving the younger daughter and remanded for a new trial. [a] * * *

We granted certiorari, * * * and now affirm.

II

* * *

From the earliest days of our Confrontation Clause jurisprudence, we have consistently held that the Clause does not necessarily prohibit the admission of hearsay statements against a criminal defendant, even though the admission of such statements might be thought to violate the literal terms of the Clause. * * *

Although we have recognized that hearsay rules and the Confrontation Clause are generally designed to protect similar values, we have also been careful not to equate the Confrontation Clause's prohibitions with the general rule prohibiting the admission of hearsay statements. * * * The Confrontation Clause, in other words, bars the admission of some evidence that would otherwise be admissible under an exception to the hearsay rule.

* * * [b]

In *Ohio v. Roberts*, [448 U.S. 56 (1980)] we set forth "a general approach" for determining when incriminating statements admissible under an exception to the hearsay rule also meet the requirements of the Confrontation Clause. * * * We noted that the Confrontation Clause "operates in two separate ways to restrict the range of admissible hearsay." * * * "First, in conformance with the Framers' preference for face-to-face accusation, the Sixth Amendment establishes a rule of necessity. In the usual case . . ., the prosecution must either produce, or demonstrate the unavailability of, the declarant whose statement it wishes to use against the defendant." * * * Second, once a witness is shown to be unavailable, "his statement is admissible only if it bears adequate 'indicia of reliability.' Reliability can be inferred without more in a case where the evidence falls within a firmly rooted hearsay exception. In other cases, the evidence must be excluded, at least absent a showing of particularized guarantees of trustworthiness." * * *

* * *

[For example, hearsay statements of nontestifying but available co-conspirators are constitutionally admissible because the "firmly rooted" exception carries sufficient indicia of reliability.]

[The Court assumed that the younger daughter was an unavailable witness within the meaning of the Confrontation Clause because she was found to be incapable of testifying.]

The crux of the question presented is therefore whether the State, as the proponent of evidence presumptively barred by the hearsay rule and the Confrontation Clause, has carried its burden of proving that the younger daughter's incriminating statements to Dr. Jambura bore sufficient indicia of reliability to withstand scrutiny under the Clause. * * *

* * *

We note at the outset that Idaho's residual hearsay exception, * * * under which the challenged statements were admitted, * * * is not a firmly rooted hearsay exception for Confrontation Clause purposes. * * *

* * *

Although we agree with the court below that the Confrontation Clause bars the admission of the younger daughter's hearsay statements, we reject the apparently dispositive weight placed by that court on the lack of procedural safeguards at the interview.   Out-of-court statements made by children regarding sexual abuse arise in a wide variety of circumstances, and we do not believe the Constitution imposes a fixed set of procedural prerequisites to the admission of such statements at trial.   The procedural requirements identified by the court below, to the extent regarded as conditions precedent to the admission of child hearsay statements in child sexual abuse cases, may in many instances be inappropriate or unnecessary to a determination whether a given statement is sufficiently trustworthy for Confrontation Clause purposes. * * *   Although the procedural guidelines propounded by the court below may well enhance the reliability of out-of-court statements of children regarding sexual abuse, we decline to read into the Confrontation Clause a preconceived and artificial litmus test for the procedural propriety of professional interviews in which children make hearsay statements against a defendant. [c]

The State responds that a finding of "particularized guarantees of trustworthiness" should instead be based on a consideration of the totality of the circumstances, including not only the circumstances surrounding the making of the statement, but also other evidence at trial that corroborates the truth of the statement.   We agree that "particularized guarantees of trustworthiness" must be shown from the totality of the circumstances, but we think the relevant circumstances include only those that surround the making of the statement and that render the declarant particularly worthy of belief. * * * [d]   In other words, if the declarant's truthfulness is so clear from the surrounding circumstances that the test of cross-examination would be of marginal utility, then the hearsay rule does not bar admission of the statement at trial.   The basis for the "excited utterance" exception, for example, is that such statements are given under circumstances that eliminate the possibility of fabrication, coaching, or confabulation, and that therefore the circumstances surrounding the making of the statement provide sufficient assurance that the statement is trustworthy and that cross-examination would be superfluous. * * * [e]

* * *

The state and federal courts have identified a number of factors that we think properly relate to whether hearsay statements made by a child witness in child sexual abuse cases are reliable. [These include spontaneity and consistent repetition; the use of terminology expected of a child of similar age and the lack of motive to fabricate.   Such factors] also apply to whether such statements bear "particularized guarantees of trustworthiness" under the Confrontation Clause. These factors are, of course, not exclusive, and courts have considerable leeway in their consideration of appropriate factors. We therefore decline to endorse a mechanical test for determining "particularized guarantees of trustworthiness" under the Clause. Rather, the unifying principle is that these factors relate to whether the child declarant was particularly likely to be telling the truth when the statement was made.

* * *

* * * "[T]he true danger inherent in [using corroboration to support hearsay] is, in fact, its selective reliability." * * * This concern applies in the child hearsay context as well: Corroboration of a child's allegations of sexual abuse by medical evidence of abuse, for example, sheds no light on the reliability of the child's allegations regarding the identity of the abuser. There is a very real danger that a jury will rely on partial corroboration to mistakenly infer the trustworthiness of the entire statement. Furthermore, we recognized the similarity between harmless-error analysis and the corroboration inquiry when we noted in *Lee [v. Illinois*, 476 U.S. 530 (1986)] that the harm of "admission of the [hearsay] statement [was that it] poses too serious a threat to the accuracy of the verdict to be countenanced by the Sixth Amendment." * * *

* * *

JUSTICE KENNEDY, with whom THE CHIEF JUSTICE, JUSTICE WHITE, and JUSTICE BLACKMUN join, dissenting.

The issue is whether the Sixth Amendment right of confrontation is violated when statements from a child who is unavailable to testify at trial are admitted under a hearsay exception against a defendant who stands accused of abusing her. The Court today holds that it is not, provided that the child's statements bear "particularized guarantees of trustworthiness." * * * I agree. My disagreement is with the rule the Court invents to control this inquiry and with the Court's ultimate determination that the statements in question here must be inadmissible as violative of the Confrontation Clause.

Given the principle, for cases involving hearsay statements that do not come within one of the traditional hearsay exceptions, that admissibility depends upon finding particular guarantees of trustworthiness in each case, it is difficult to state rules of general application. I believe the Court recognizes this. The majority errs, in my view, by adopting a rule that corroboration of the statement by other evidence is an impermissible part of the trustworthiness inquiry. The Court's apparent ruling is that corroborating evidence may not be considered in whole or in part for this purpose. This limitation, at least on a facial interpretation of the Court's analytic categories, is a new creation by the Court; it likely will prove unworkable and does not even square with the examples of reliability indicators the Court itself invokes; and it is contrary to our own precedents. **[f]**

* * *

* * * * * * * * * *

COMMENTS

[a] This is the harmless error rule: if the appellate court believes beyond a reasonable doubt that the jury's conviction verdict was caused by the erroneously introduced evidence, the error was "harmful."

[b] At several points in the law of criminal procedure there is similarity but not identity between a common law rule and a constitutional rule. For example, the common law remedy for illegal entry by state officers was supplemented by the exclusionary rule. Here, the Court is careful to suggest that the constitutional Sixth Amendment interests in a fair trial may not be identical to the interests of the hearsay rule and its exceptions, which balance the search for the truth with the practical needs of conducting trials.

[c] The Court's distinction is of major importance. It affirms the *decision* of the Idaho Supreme Court that the younger daughter's hearsay is too unreliable to satisfy the standards of accuracy required by the Confrontation Clause. But it does not agree with the *opinion* of the Idaho Court. If it did, it would impose the standards of that case on every court in the nation. For example, adopting the Idaho opinion would require the video or audio taping of every physician-child interview in a sex abuse case in order to have such testimony admitted.

[d] Again the Supreme Court agrees but draws an important distinction. Under the state's theory, *any* corroboration in the case could be used to bolster the hearsay and thus allow it into evidence. The Court insists that the totality of circumstances relate only to the making of the statement. Thus, the state cannot bootstrap the hearsay with other elements of the case.

[e] This analogy is especially apt in child sexual abuse cases where the child may be inadvertently "coached."

[f] Does the willingness of the dissenters to allow the use of "bootstrap" corroboration raise the possibility that a larger number of innocent persons would be convicted under the circumstances of this case?

WHITE v. ILLINOIS

__ U.S. __, 112 S.Ct. 736, 116 L.Ed.2d 848 (1992)

THE CHIEF JUSTICE delivered the opinion of the Court.

In this case we consider whether the Confrontation Clause of the Sixth Amendment requires that, before a trial court admits testimony under the "spontaneous declaration" and "medical examination" exceptions to the hearsay rule, the prosecution must either produce the declarant at trial or the trial court must find that the declarant is unavailable. The Illinois Appellate Court concluded that such procedures are not constitutionally required. We agree with that conclusion.

* * *

[White was convicted of sexually assaulting S.G., aged four. Her screams in the early morning hours woke S.G.'s baby sitter, Tony DeVore. S.G. told the baby sitter that White put his hand over her mouth, choked her, threatened to whip her if she screamed and had "touched her in the wrong places," which she identified, by pointing, as the vaginal area. S.G. repeated the same story a half hour later to her mother, Tammy Grigsby, who returned home, and repeated the same story fifteen minutes later to a police officer Terry Lewis. S.G. was taken to a hospital four hours later and she related the same story to Cheryl Reents, an emergency room nurse and to the examining physician, Michael Meinzen.]

S.G. never testified at petitioner's trial. The State attempted on two occasions to call her as a witness but she apparently experienced emotional difficulty on being brought to the courtroom and in each instance left without testifying. * * * The defense made no attempt to call S.G. as a witness and the trial court neither made, nor was it asked to make, a finding that S.G. was unavailable to testify. * * *

Petitioner objected on hearsay grounds to DeVore, Grigsby, Lewis, Reents, and Meinzen being permitted to testify regarding S.G.'s statements describing the assault. The trial court overruled each objection. With respect to DeVore, Grigsby, and Lewis the trial court concluded that the testimony could be permitted pursuant to an Illinois hearsay exception for spontaneous declarations. [a] Petitioner's objections to Reents' and Meinzen's testimony was similarly overruled, based on both the spontaneous declaration exception and an exception for statements made in the course of securing medical treatment. [b] The trial court also denied petitioner's motion for a mistrial based on S.G.'s "presence [and] failure to testify." * * *

[White's conviction was upheld by the Illinois appellate courts; the hearsay declarations were held to have been properly admitted and a challenge based on the Confrontation Clause was rejected. The Illinois courts relied on *Ohio v. Roberts*, 448 U.S. 56 (1980) and *United States v. Inadi*, 475 U.S. 387 (1986) for the proposition that there is no requirement that a declarant must be produced at trial or be proven unavailable before a hearsay declaration may be admitted into evidence.]

[The Court rejected out of hand a

contention raised by the United States. The *amicus curiae* brief of the United States argued that the Confrontation Clause did not apply at all to hearsay declarations because the framers of the Constitution intended the Clause to apply only to the introduction of ex parte affidavits at trial without producing the affiants at trial. Other than that the Confrontation Clause would apply only to out-of-court statements intended to be criminal accusations against a defendant.]

Such a narrow reading of the Confrontation Clause, which would virtually eliminate its role in restricting the admission of hearsay testimony, is foreclosed by our prior cases. * * *

We therefore now turn to petitioner's principal contention that our prior decision in *Roberts* requires that his conviction be vacated. In *Roberts* we considered a Confrontation Clause challenge to the introduction at trial of a transcript containing testimony from a probable-cause hearing, where the transcript included testimony from a witness not produced at trial but who had been subject to examination by defendant's counsel at the probable-cause hearing. In the course of rejecting the Confrontation Clause claim in that case, we used language that might suggest that the Confrontation Clause generally requires that a declarant either be produced at trial or be found unavailable before his out-of-court statement may be admitted into evidence. However, we think such an expansive reading of the Clause is negated by our subsequent decision in *Inadi, supra.*

In *Inadi* we considered the admission of out-of-court statements made by a co-conspirator in the course of the conspiracy. As an initial matter,

we rejected the proposition that *Roberts* established a rule that "no out-of-court statement would be admissible without a showing of unavailability." * * * To the contrary, rather than establishing "a wholesale revision of the law of evidence" under the guise of the Confrontation Clause, * * * we concluded that * * * *Roberts* stands for the proposition that unavailability analysis is a necessary part of the Confrontation Clause inquiry only when the challenged out-of-court statements were made in the course of a prior judicial proceeding. * * * [c]

Having clarified the scope of *Roberts*, the Court in *Inadi* then went on to reject the Confrontation Clause challenge presented there. In particular, we refused to extend the unavailability requirement established in *Roberts* to all out-of-court statements. Our decision rested on two factors. First, unlike former in-court testimony, co-conspirator statements "provide evidence of the conspiracy's context that cannot be replicated, even if the declarant testifies to the same matters in court," * * * Also, given a declarant's likely change in status by the time the trial occurs, simply calling the declarant in the hope of having him repeat his prior out-of-court statements is a poor substitute for the full evidentiary significance that flows from statements made when the conspiracy is operating in full force. * * *

Second, we observed that there is little benefit, if any, to be accomplished by imposing an "unavailability rule." Such a rule will not work to bar absolutely the introduction of the out-of-court statements; if the declarant either is unavailable, or is available and produced for trial, the statements can be introduced. * * *   Nor is an unavailability rule likely to produce much testimony that adds meaningfully to the trial's truth-determining process. * * * Many declarants will be subpoenaed by the prosecution or defense, regardless of any Confrontation Clause requirement, while the Compulsory Process Clause and evidentiary rules permitting a defendant to treat witnesses as hostile will aid defendants in obtaining a declarant's live testimony. * * * And while an unavailability rule would therefore do little to improve the accuracy of factfinding, it is likely to impose substantial additional burdens on the factfinding process. The prosecution would be required to repeatedly locate and keep continuously available each declarant, even when neither the prosecution nor the defense has any interest in calling the witness to the stand. An additional inquiry would be injected into the question of admissibility of evidence, to be litigated both at trial and on appeal. * * *

These observations, although expressed in the context of evaluating co-conspirator statements, apply with full force to the case at hand. We note first that the evidentiary rationale for permitting hearsay testimony regarding spontaneous declarations and statements made in the course of receiving medical care is that such out-of-court declarations are made in contexts that provide substantial guarantees of their trustworthiness. But those same factors that contribute to the statements' reliability cannot be recaptured even by later in-court testimony. A statement that has been offered in a moment of excitement—without the opportunity to reflect on the consequences of one's exclamation—may justifiably carry more weight with a trier of fact than a similar statement offered in the relative calm of the courtroom. Similarly, a statement made in the course of procuring medical services, where the declarant knows that a false statement may cause misdiagnosis or mistreatment, carries special guarantees of credibility that a trier of fact may not think replicated by courtroom testimony. They are thus materially different from the statements at issue in *Roberts*, where the out-of-court statements sought to be introduced were themselves made in the course of a judicial proceeding, and where there was consequently no threat of lost evidentiary value if the out-of-court statements were replaced with live testimony.

The preference for live testimony in the case of statements like those offered in *Roberts* is because of the importance of cross examination, "the greatest legal engine ever invented for the discovery of truth." * * * Thus courts have adopted the general rule prohibiting the receipt of hearsay evidence. But where proffered hearsay has sufficient guarantees of reliability to come within a firmly rooted exception to the hearsay rule, the Confrontation Clause is satisfied.

We therefore think it clear that the out-of-court statements admitted in this case had substantial probative value, value that could not be duplicated simply by the declarant later testifying in court. To exclude such probative statements under the strictures of the Confrontation Clause would be the height of wrong-headedness, given that the Confrontation Clause has as a basic purpose the promotion of the "'integrity of the factfinding process.'" * * * And as we have also noted, a statement that qualifies for admission under a "firmly rooted" hearsay exception is so trustworthy that adversarial testing can be expected to add little to its reliability. * * * Given the evidentiary value of such statements, their reliability, and that establishing a generally applicable unavailability rule would have few practical benefits while imposing pointless litigation costs, we see no reason to treat the out-of-court statements in this case differently from those we found admissible in *Inadi*. A contrary rule would result in exactly the kind of "wholesale revision" of the laws of evidence that we expressly disavowed in *Inadi*. We therefore see no basis in *Roberts* or *Inadi* for excluding from trial, under the aegis of the Confrontation Clause, evidence embraced within such exceptions to the hearsay rule as those for spontaneous declarations and statements made for medical treatment.

As a second line of argument, petitioner presses upon us two recent decisions involving child-testimony in child-sexual assault cases, *Coy v. Iowa*, [487 U.S. 1012 (1988)] and *Maryland v. Craig*, [this volume]. Both *Coy* and *Craig* required us to consider the constitutionality of courtroom procedures designed to prevent a child witness from having to face across an open courtroom a defendant charged with sexually assaulting the child. In *Coy* we vacated a conviction that resulted from a trial in which a child witness testified from behind a screen, and in which there had been no particularized showing that such a procedure was necessary to avert a risk of harm to the child. In *Craig* we

upheld a conviction that resulted from a trial in which a child witness testified via closed circuit television after such a showing of necessity. Petitioner draws from these two cases a general rule that hearsay testimony offered by a child should be permitted only upon a showing of necessity—*i.e.*, in cases where necessary to protect the child's physical and psychological well-being.

Petitioner's reliance is misplaced. *Coy* and *Craig* involved only the question of what *in-court* procedures are constitutionally required to guarantee a defendant's confrontation right once a witness is testifying. Such a question is quite separate from that of what requirements the Confrontation Clause imposes as a predicate for the introduction of out-of-court declarations. *Coy* and *Craig* did not speak to the latter question. As we recognized in *Coy*, the admissibility of hearsay statements raises concerns lying at the periphery of those that the Confrontation Clause is designed to address. * * * There is thus no basis for importing the "necessity requirement" announced in those cases into the much different context of out-of-court declarations admitted under established exceptions to the hearsay rule.

For the foregoing reasons, the judgment of the Illinois Appellate Court is

Affirmed.

[JUSTICE THOMAS, joined by JUSTICE SCALIA, concurred in part and concurred in the judgment. His "originalist" opinion supported the suggestion of the United States' *amicus* brief rejected by the majority.]

*   *   *   *   *   *   *   *   *   *   *

COMMENTS

[a] Illinois law applies the spontaneous declaration exception to a statement relating to a startling event or condition made while the declarant is under the stress of excitement caused by the event or condition.

[b] Illinois law allows the admission of hearsay statements made by victims of serious crimes to medical personnel for purposes of diagnosis or treatment as an exception to the hearsay rule. The statements could include descriptions of the cause of a symptom, pain or sensations, or the inception or general character of the cause or external source of the symptom insofar as reasonably pertinent to diagnosis or treatment.

[c] A witness who testified at a prior hearing might have a change of mind or memory lapse. With a transcript of the prior hearing, an attorney can effectively examine or cross-examine such a witness. If the witness is available but not produced at trial, it deprives the side wishing to cross-examine that witness an opportunity to test the witness' earlier testimony.

GARRITY v. NEW JERSEY

385 U.S. 493, 87 S.Ct. 616, 17 L.Ed.2d 562 (1967)

MR. JUSTICE DOUGLAS delivered the opinion of the Court.

[Appellant police officers were investigated by the state Attorney General for fixing traffic tickets.]

Before being questioned, each appellant was warned (1) that anything he said might be used against him in any state criminal proceeding; (2) that he had the privilege to refuse to answer if the disclosure would tend to incriminate him; but (3) that if he refused to answer he would be subject to removal from office.

Appellants answered the questions. No immunity was granted, as there is no immunity statute applicable in these circumstances. Over their objections, some of the answers given were used in subsequent prosecutions for conspiracy to obstruct the administration of the traffic laws. Appellants were convicted and their convictions were sustained over their protests that their statements were coerced, by reason of the fact that, if they refused to answer, they could lose their positions with the police department. * * *

[The Court granted certiorari on the question of self-incrimination.]

We agree with the New Jersey Supreme Court that the forfeiture-of-office statute is relevant here only for the bearing it has on the voluntary character of the statements used to convict petitioners in their criminal prosecutions.

The choice imposed on petitioners was one between self-incrimination or job forfeiture. Coercion that vitiates a confession under *Chambers v. Florida*, 309 U.S. 227, and related cases can be "mental as well as physical"; "the blood of the accused is not the only hallmark of an unconstitutional inquisition." *Blackburn v. Alabama*, 361 U.S. 199, 206. Subtle pressures * * * may be as telling as coarse and vulgar ones. The question is whether the accused was deprived of his "free choice to admit, to deny, or to refuse to answer." *Lisenba v. California*, 314 U.S. 219, 241. [a]

We adhere to *Boyd v. United States*, [this volume], a civil forfeiture action against property. A statute offered the owner an election between producing a document or forfeiture of the goods at issue in the proceeding. This was held to be a form of compulsion in violation of both the Fifth Amendment and the Fourth Amendment. * * * It is that principle that we adhere to and apply in *Spevack v. Klein* * * *. [b]

The choice given petitioners was either to forfeit their jobs or to incriminate themselves. The option to lose their means of livelihood or to pay the penalty of self-incrimination is the antithesis of free choice to speak out or to remain silent. That practice, like interrogation practices we reviewed in *Miranda v. Arizona*, [this volume], is "likely to exert such pressure upon an individual as to disable him from making a free and rational choice." We think the statements were infected by the coercion inherent in this scheme of questioning and cannot be sustained as voluntary under our prior decisions.

It is said that there was a "waiver." That, however, is a federal question for us to decide. * * *

Where the choice is "between the rock and the whirlpool," duress is inherent in deciding to "waive" one or the other.

"It always is for the interest of a party under duress to choose the lesser of two evils. But the fact that a choice was made according to interest does not exclude duress. It is the characteristic of duress properly so called." * * *

* * * In these cases also, though petitioners succumbed to compulsion, they preserved their objections, raising them at the earliest possible point. * * * The cases are therefore quite different from the situation where one who is anxious to make a clean breast of the whole affair volunteers the information.

Mr. Justice Holmes in *McAuliffe v. New Bedford*, 155 Mass. 216, 29 N.E. 517, stated a dictum on which New Jersey heavily relies:

"The petitioner may have a constitutional right to talk politics, but he has no constitutional right to be a policeman. There are few employments for hire in which the servant does not agree to suspend his constitutional right of free speech, as well as of idleness, by the implied terms of his contract. The servant cannot complain, as he takes the employment on the terms which are offered him. On the same principle, the city may impose any reasonable condition upon holding offices within its control." * * * [c]

The question in this case, however, is not cognizable in those terms. Our question is whether a State, contrary to the requirement of the Fourteenth Amendment, can use the threat of discharge to secure incriminatory evidence against an employee.

We held in *Slochower v. Board of Education*, 350 U.S. 551, that a public school teacher could not be discharged merely because he had invoked the Fifth Amendment privilege against self-incrimination when questioned by a congressional committee:

"The privilege against self-incrimination would be reduced to a hollow mockery if its exercise could be taken as equivalent either to a confession of guilt or a conclusive presumption of perjury. . . . The privilege serves to protect the innocent who otherwise might be ensnared by ambiguous circumstances." * * *

We conclude that policemen, like teachers and lawyers, are not relegated to a watered-down version of constitutional rights. [d]

There are rights of constitutional stature whose exercise a State may not condition by the exaction of a price. Engaging in interstate commerce is one. * * * Resort to the federal courts in diversity of citizenship cases is another. * * * Assertion of a First Amendment right is still another. * * * The imposition of a burden on the exercise of a Twenty-fourth Amendment right is also banned. * * * [e] We now hold the protection of the individual under the Fourteenth Amendment against coerced statements prohibits use in subsequent criminal proceedings of statements obtained under threat of removal from office, and that it extends to all, whether they are policemen or other members of our body politic.

Reversed.

[JUSTICE WHITE dissented.]

MR. JUSTICE HARLAN, whom MR. JUSTICE CLARK and MR. JUSTICE STEWART join, dissenting.

The majority opinion here and the plurality opinion in *Spevack v. Klein*, * * * stem from fundamental misconceptions about the logic and necessities of the constitutional privilege against self-incrimination. I fear that these opinions will seriously and quite needlessly hinder the protection of other important public values. I must dissent here, as I do in *Spevack*.

The majority employs a curious mixture of doctrines to invalidate these convictions, and I confess to difficulty in perceiving the intended relationships among the various segments of its opinion. I gather that the majority believes that the possibility that these policemen might have been discharged had they refused to provide information pertinent to their public responsibilities is an impermissible "condition" imposed by New Jersey upon petitioners' privilege against self-incrimination. From this premise the majority draws the conclusion that the statements obtained from petitioners after a warning that discharge was possible were inadmissible. Evidently recognizing the weakness of its conclusion, the majority attempts to bring to its support illustrations from the lengthy series of cases in which this Court, in light of all the relevant circumstances, has adjudged the voluntariness *in fact* of statements obtained from accused

persons.

The majority is apparently engaged in the delicate task of riding two unruly horses at once: it is presumably arguing simultaneously that the statements were involuntary as a matter of fact, in the same fashion that the statements in [the due process coerced confessions] were thought to be involuntary, and that the statements were inadmissible as a matter of law, on the premise that they were products of an impermissible condition imposed on the constitutional privilege. These are very different contentions and require separate replies, but in my opinion both contentions are plainly mistaken, for reasons that follow. **[f]**

I.

[In this Part JUSTICE HARLAN demonstrates that none of the pressures that are found in the Fourteenth Amendment due process coerced confession cases previously decided by the Supreme Court existed in this case.]

II.

The issue remaining is whether the statements were inadmissible because they were "involuntary as a matter of law," in that they were given after a warning that New Jersey policemen may be discharged for failure to provide information pertinent to their public responsibilities. What is really involved on this score, however, is not in truth a question of "voluntariness" at all, but rather whether the condition imposed by the State on the exercise of the privilege against self-incrimination, namely dismissal from office, in this instance serves in itself to render the statements inadmissible. [g] Absent evidence of involuntariness in fact, the admissibility of these statements thus hinges on the validity of the consequence which the State acknowledged might have resulted if the statements had not been given. If the consequence is constitutionally permissible, there can surely be no objection if the State cautions the witness that it may follow if he remains silent. If both the consequence and the warning are constitutionally permissible, a witness is obliged, in order to prevent the use of his statements against him in a criminal prosecution, to prove under the standards established since *Brown v. Mississippi*, [this volume], that as a matter of fact the statements were involuntarily made. The central issues here are therefore identical to those presented in *Spevack v. Klein*, * * *: whether consequences may properly be permitted to result to a claimant after his invocation of the constitutional privilege, and if so, whether the consequence in question is permissible. For reasons which I have stated in *Spevack v. Klein*, in my view nothing in the logic or purposes of the privilege demands that all consequences which may result from a witness' silence be forbidden merely because that silence is privileged. The validity of a consequence depends both upon the hazards, if any, it presents to the integrity of the privilege and upon the urgency of the public interests it is designed to protect.

It can hardly be denied that New Jersey is permitted by the Constitution to establish reasonable qualifications and standards of conduct for its public employees. Nor can it be said that it is arbitrary or unreasonable for New Jersey to insist that its employees furnish the appropriate authorities with information pertinent to their employment. * * * Finally, it is surely plain that New Jersey may in particular require its employees to assist in the prevention and detection of unlawful activities by officers of the state government. The urgency of these requirements is the more obvious here, where the conduct in question is that of officials directly entrusted with the administration of justice. The importance for our systems of justice of the integrity of local police forces can scarcely be exaggerated. * * * It must be concluded, therefore, that the sanction at issue here is reasonably calculated to serve the most basic interests of the citizens of New Jersey.

The final question is the hazard, if any, which this sanction presents to the constitutional privilege. The purposes for which, and the circumstances in which, an officer's discharge might be ordered under New Jersey law plainly may vary. It is of course possible that discharge might in a given case be predicated on an imputation of guilt drawn from the use of the privilege, as was thought by this Court to have occurred in *Slochower v. Board of Education*. * * * But from our vantage point, it would be quite improper to assume that New Jersey will employ these procedures for purposes other than to assess in good faith an employee's continued fitness for public employment. This Court, when a state procedure for investigating the loyalty and fitness of public employees might result either in the *Slochower* situation or in an assessment in good faith of an employee, has until today consistently paused to examine the actual circumstances of each case. * * * I am unable to see any justification for the majority's abandonment of that process; it is well calculated both to protect the essential purposes of the privilege and to guarantee the most generous opportunities for the pursuit of other public values. The majority's broad prohibition, on the other hand, extends the scope of the privilege beyond its essential purposes, and seriously hampers the protection of other important values. Despite the majority's disclaimer, it is quite plain that the logic of its prohibitory rule would in this situation prevent the discharge of these policemen. It would therefore entirely forbid a sanction which presents, at least on its face, no hazard to the purposes of the constitutional privilege, and which may reasonably be expected to serve important public interests. We are not entitled to assume that discharges will be used either to vindicate impermissible inferences of guilt or to penalize privileged silence, but must instead presume that this procedure is only intended and will

only be used to establish and enforce standards of conduct for public employees. As such, it does not minimize or endanger the petitioners' constitutional privilege against self-incrimination. [h]

I would therefore conclude that the sanction provided by the State is constitutionally permissible. From this, it surely follows that the warning given of the possibility of discharge is constitutionally unobjectionable. Given the constitutionality both of the sanction and of the warning of its application, the petitioners would be constitutionally entitled to exclude the use of their statements as evidence in a criminal prosecution against them only if it is found that the statements were, when given, involuntary in fact. For the reasons stated above, I cannot agree that these statements were involuntary in fact.

I would affirm the judgments of the Supreme Court of New Jersey.

* * * * * * * * * * *

COMMENTS

[a] This is not precisely a police confession case, but the Court draws on the line of due process confession cases to emphasize the coercive nature of the New Jersey law.

[b] *Spevack*, decided the same day as *Garrity*, held that the self-incrimination clause applied to admissions obtained in a state disbarment proceeding.

[c] The term "servant," although somewhat archaic in this context, simply means "employee" in law. *McAuliffe*, decided by JUSTICE HOLMES while on the Supreme Judicial Court of Massachusetts, reflects a nineteenth century sensibility toward public employment.

[d] What is the distinction between the facts of this case and the facts of *Slochower*? Are they constitutionally relevant?

[e] The 24th Amendment banned poll taxes. This recitation of cases that prohibit burdens on the exercise of constitutional rights is a classic example of the process of reasoning by analogy that is the hallmark of the common law system.

[f] The dissent attempts to undermine the majority by attacking its method of reasoning. Ultimately, the dissent rests on the view that there was no direct precedent for the Court's decision. Should the lack of direct precedent prevent the Court from expanding its understanding of a constitutional provision? Do you think that officers who refuse to answer questions about alleged official impropriety should be automatically dismissed from employment? If they do talk, do you agree with the *Garrity* protection?

[g] Is JUSTICE HARLAN's factual assertion entirely correct? It can be argued that the threat of job loss may create a more intense pressure on a suspect than other forms of pressure. Should it matter that the pressure is created by state statute than by the acts and words of a police interrogator?

[h] The dissent portrays a government unable to root out corruption in its ranks; it values order over the Fifth Amendment right of the officer. Yet, the dilemma can be easily resolved by the state passing an appropriate immunity statute. Can you think of any value to be served by maintaining, as JUSTICE HARLAN suggests, a case by case approach to resolving these cases as opposed to the flat rule of the majority?

GARDNER v. BRODERICK

392 U.S. 273, 88 S.Ct. 1913, 20 L.Ed.2d 1082 (1968)

MR. JUSTICE FORTAS delivered the opinion of the Court.

Appellant brought this action in the Supreme Court of the State of New York seeking reinstatement as a New York City patrolman and back pay. He claimed he was unlawfully dismissed because he refused to waive his privilege against self-incrimination. In August 1965, pursuant to subpoena, appellant appeared before a New York County grand jury which was investigating alleged bribery and corruption of police officers in connection with unlawful gambling operations. He was advised that the grand jury proposed to examine him concerning the performance of his official duties. He was advised of his privilege against self-incrimination, but he was asked to sign a "waiver of immunity" after being told that he would be fired if he did not sign. Following his refusal, he was given an administrative hearing and was discharged solely for this refusal, pursuant to * * * the New York City Charter.

The New York Supreme Court dismissed his petition for reinstatement, * * * and the New York Court of Appeals affirmed. * * * We noted probable jurisdiction. * * *

Our decisions establish beyond dispute the breadth of the privilege to refuse to respond to questions when the result may be self-incriminatory, and the need fully to implement its guaranty. See *Spevack v. Klein*, 385 U.S. 511 (1967). * * * The privilege is applicable to state as well as federal proceedings. *Malloy v. Hogan*, 378 U.S. 1 (1964); *Murphy v. Waterfront Commission*, 378 U.S. 52 (1964). The privilege may be waived in appropriate circumstances if the waiver is knowingly and voluntarily made. Answers may be compelled regardless of the privilege if there is immunity from federal and state use of the compelled testimony or its fruits in connection with a criminal prosecution against the person testifying. *Counselman v. Hitchcock*, [142 U.S. 547 (1892)], *Murphy v. Waterfront Commission, supra,* at 79.

The question presented in the present case is whether a policeman who refuses to waive the protections which the privilege gives him may be dismissed from office because of that refusal.

About a year and a half after New York City discharged petitioner for his refusal to waive this immunity, we decided *Garrity v. New Jersey*, 385 U.S. 493 (1967). In that case, we held that when a policeman had been compelled to testify by the threat that otherwise he would be removed from office, the testimony that he gave could not be used against him in a subsequent prosecution. Garrity had not signed a waiver of immunity and no immunity statute was applicable in the circumstances. Our holding was summarized in the following statement (at 500):

"We now hold the protection of the individual under the Fourteenth Amendment against coerced statements prohibits use in subsequent criminal proceedings of statements obtained under threat of removal from office, and that it extends to all, whether they are policemen or other members of our body politic."

The New York Court of Appeals considered that *Garrity* did not control the present case. It is true that *Garrity* related to the attempted use of compelled testimony. It did not involve the precise question which is presented here: namely, whether a State may discharge an officer for refusing to waive a right which the Constitution guarantees to him. The New York Court of Appeals also distinguished our post-*Garrity* decision in *Spevack v. Klein, supra*. In *Spevack*, we ruled that a lawyer could not be disbarred solely because he refused to testify at a disciplinary proceeding on the ground that his testimony would tend to incriminate him. The Court of Appeals concluded that *Spevack* does not control the present case because different considerations apply in the case of a public official such as a policeman. A lawyer, it stated, although licensed by the state is not an employee. This distinction is now urged upon us. It is argued that although a lawyer could not constitutionally be confronted with Hobson's choice between self-incrimination and forfeiting his means of livelihood, the same principle should not protect a policeman. Unlike the lawyer, he is directly, immediately, and entirely responsible to the city or State which is his employer. He owes his entire loyalty to it. He has no other "client" or principal. He is a trustee of the public interest, bearing the burden of great and total responsibility to his public employer. Unlike the lawyer who is directly responsible to his client, the policeman is either responsible to

the State or to no one.

We agree that these factors differentiate the situations. If appellant, a policeman, had refused to answer questions specifically, directly, and narrowly relating to the performance of his official duties, without being required to waive his immunity with respect to the use of his answers or the fruits thereof in a criminal prosecution of himself, * * * the privilege against self-incrimination would not have been a bar to his dismissal. [a]

The facts of this case, however, do not present this issue. Here, petitioner was summoned to testify before a grand jury in an investigation of alleged criminal conduct. He was discharged from office, not for failure to answer relevant questions about his official duties, but for refusal to waive a constitutional right. He was dismissed for failure to relinquish the protections of the privilege against self-incrimination. The Constitution of New York State and the City Charter both expressly provided that his failure to do so, as well as his failure to testify, would result in dismissal from his job. He was dismissed solely for his refusal to waive the immunity to which he is entitled if he is required to testify despite his constitutional privilege. * * *

We need not speculate whether, if appellant had executed the waiver of immunity in the circumstances, the effect of our subsequent decision in *Garrity v. New Jersey, supra*, would have been to nullify the effect of the waiver. New York City discharged him for refusal to execute a document purporting to waive his constitutional rights and to permit prosecution of himself on the basis of his compelled testimony. Petitioner could not have assumed—and certainly he was not required to assume—that he was being asked to do an idlc act of no legal effect. In any event, the mandate of the great privilege against self-incrimination does not tolerate the attempt, regardless of its ultimate effectiveness, to coerce a waiver of the immunity it confers on penalty of the loss of employment. It is clear that petitioner's testimony was demanded before the grand jury in part so that it might be used to prosecute him, and not solely for the purpose of securing an accounting of his performance of his public trust. If the latter had been the only purpose, there would have been no reason to seek to compel petitioner to waive his immunity.

Proper regard for the history and meaning of the privilege against self-incrimination, * * * and for the decisions of this Court, dictate the conclusion that the provision of the New York City Charter pursuant to which petitioner was dismissed cannot stand. Accordingly, the judgment is

Reversed.

[JUSTICE BLACK and JUSTICE HARLAN concurred in the result.]

* * * * * * * * * *

COMMENTS

[a] This does not give a police officer questioned for illegal acts much "wiggle room," as long as the grand jury questions focus on specific behaviors.

KASTIGAR v. UNITED STATES

406 U.S. 441, 92 S.Ct. 1653, 32 L.Ed.2d 212 (1972)

MR. JUSTICE POWELL delivered the opinion of the Court.

This case presents the question whether the United States Government may compel testimony from an unwilling witness, who invokes the Fifth Amendment privilege against compulsory self-incrimination, by conferring on the witness immunity from use of the compelled testimony in subsequent criminal proceedings, as well as immunity from use of evidence derived from the testimony. Petitioners were subpoenaed to appear before a United States grand jury. * * * The Government believed [they] were likely to assert their Fifth Amendment privilege. Prior to the scheduled appearances, the Government applied to the District Court for an order directing petitioners to answer questions and produce evidence before the grand jury under a grant of immunity conferred pursuant to [a federal statute]. Petitioners opposed issuance of the order, contending primarily that the scope of the immunity provided by the statute was not coextensive with the scope of the privilege against self-incrimination, and therefore was not sufficient to supplant the privilege and compel their testimony. The District Court rejected this contention, and ordered petitioners to appear before the grand jury and answer its questions under the grant of immunity.

Petitioners appeared but refused to answer questions, asserting their privilege against compulsory self-incrimination. They were brought before the District Court, and each persisted in his refusal to answer the grand jury's questions, notwithstanding the grant of immunity. The court found both in contempt, and committed them to the custody of the Attorney General until either they answered the grand jury's questions or the term of the grand jury expired. The Court of Appeals * * * affirmed. * * * This Court granted certiorari to resolve the important question whether testimony may be compelled by granting immunity from the use of compelled testimony and evidence derived therefrom ("use and derivative use" immunity), or whether it is necessary to grant immunity from prosecution for offenses to which compelled testimony relates ("transactional" immunity). * * *

I

The power of government to compel persons to testify in court or before grand juries and other governmental agencies is firmly established in Anglo-American jurisprudence. The power with respect to courts was established by statute in England as early as 1562, and Lord Bacon observed in 1612 that all subjects owed the King their "knowledge and discovery." While it is not clear when grand juries first resorted to compulsory process to secure the attendance and testimony of witnesses, the general common-law principle that "the public has a right to every man's evidence" was considered an "indubitable certainty" that "cannot be denied" by 1742. The power to compel testimony, and the corresponding duty to testify, are recognized in the Sixth Amendment requirements that an accused be confronted with the witnesses against him, and have compulsory process for obtaining witnesses in his favor. The first Congress recognized the testimonial duty in the Judiciary Act of 1789, which provided for compulsory attendance of witnesses in the federal courts. MR. JUSTICE WHITE noted the importance of this essential power of government in his concurring opinion in *Murphy v. Waterfront Comm'n*, 378 U.S. 52, 93-94 (1964):

> "Among the necessary and most important of the powers of the States as well as the Federal Government to assure the effective functioning of government in an ordered society is the broad power to compel residents to testify in court or before grand juries or agencies. * * * Such testimony constitutes one of the Government's primary sources of information."

But the power to compel testimony is not absolute. There are a number of exemptions from the testimonial duty, the most important of which is the Fifth Amendment privilege against compulsory self-incrimination. The privilege reflects a complex of our fundamental values and aspirations, and marks an important advance in the development of our liberty. It can be asserted in any proceeding, civil or criminal, administrative or judicial, investigatory or adjudicatory; and it protects against any disclosures that the witness reasonably believes could be used in a criminal prosecution or could lead to other evidence that might be so used. This Court has been zealous to safeguard the values that underlie the privilege.

Immunity statutes, which have historical roots deep in Anglo-American jurisprudence, are not incompatible with these values. Rather, they seek a rational accommodation between the imperatives of the privilege and the legitimate demands of government to compel citizens to testify. The existence of these statutes reflects the importance of testimony, and the fact that many offenses are of such a character that the only persons capable of giving useful testimony are those implicated in the crime. Indeed, their origins were in the context of such offenses, and their primary use has been to investigate such offenses. Congress included immunity statutes in many of the regulatory measures adopted in the first half of this century. Indeed, prior to the enactment of the statute under consideration in this case, there were in force over 50 federal immunity statutes. In addition, every State in the Union, as well as the District of Columbia and Puerto Rico, has one or more such statutes. The commentators, and this Court on several occasions, have characterized immunity statutes as essential to the effective enforcement of various criminal statutes. As Mr. Justice Frankfurter observed, * * * such statutes have "become part of our constitutional fabric." * * *

II

Petitioners contend, first, that the Fifth Amendment's privilege against compulsory self-incrimination, which is that "[n]o person . . . shall be compelled in any criminal case to be a witness against himself," deprives Congress of power to enact laws that compel self-incrimination, even if complete immunity from prosecution is granted prior to the compulsion of the incriminatory testimony. In other words, petitioners assert that no immunity statute, however drawn, can afford a lawful basis for compelling incriminatory testimony. They ask us to reconsider and overrule *Brown v. Walker*, 161 U.S. 591 (1896), * * * [a] decision[] that uphold[s] the constitutionality of immunity statutes. We find no merit to this contention and reaffirm * * * *Brown* * * * [a]

III

Petitioners' second contention is that the scope of immunity provided by the federal witness immunity statute, * * * is not coextensive with the scope of the Fifth Amendment privilege against compulsory self-incrimination, and therefore is not sufficient to supplant the privilege and compel testimony over a claim of the privilege. The statute provides that when a witness is compelled by district court order to testify over a claim of the privilege:

> "the witness may not refuse to comply with the order on the basis of his privilege against self-incrimination; but no testimony or other information compelled under the order (or any information directly or indirectly derived from such testimony or other information) may be used against the witness in any criminal case, except a prosecution for perjury, giving a false statement, or otherwise failing to comply with the order." * * *

The constitutional inquiry, rooted in logic and history, as well as in the decisions of this Court, is whether the immunity granted under this statute is coextensive with the scope of the privilege. If so, petitioners' refusals to answer based on the privilege were unjustified, and the judgments of contempt were proper, for the grant of immunity has removed the dangers against which the privilege protects. * * * If, on the other hand, the immunity granted is not as comprehensive as the protection afforded by the privilege, petitioners were justified in refusing to answer, and the judgments of contempt must be vacated. * * *

Petitioners draw a distinction between statutes that provide transactional immunity and those that provide, as does the statute before us, immunity from use and derivative use. They contend that a statute must at a minimum grant full transactional immunity in order to be coextensive with the scope of the privilege. In support of this contention, they rely on *Counselman v. Hitchcock*, 142 U.S. 547 (1892), the first case in which this Court considered a constitutional challenge to an immunity statute. The statute, a re-enactment of the Immunity Act of 1868, provided that no "evidence obtained from a party or witness by means of a judicial proceeding . . . shall be given in evidence, or in any manner used against him . . . in any court of the United States. . . ." Notwithstanding a grant of immunity and order to testify under the revised 1868 Act, the witness, asserting his privilege against compulsory self-incrimination, refused to testify before a federal grand jury. He was consequently adjudged in contempt of court. On appeal, this Court construed the statute as affording a witness protection only against the use of the specific testimony compelled from him under the grant of immunity. This construction meant that the statute "could not, and would not, prevent the use of his testimony to search out other testimony to be used in evidence against him." Since the revised 1868 Act, as construed by the Court, would permit the use against the immunized witness of evidence derived from his compelled testimony, it did not protect the witness to the same extent that a claim of the privilege would protect him. Accordingly, under the principle that a grant of immunity cannot supplant the privilege, and is not sufficient to compel testimony over a claim of the privilege, unless the scope of the grant of immunity is coextensive with the scope of the privilege, the witness' refusal to testify was held proper. In the course of its opinion, the Court made the following statement, on which petitioners heavily rely:

"We are clearly of opinion that no statute which leaves the party or witness subject to prosecution after he answers the criminating question put to him, can have the effect of supplanting the privilege conferred by the Constitution of the United States. [The immunity statute under consideration] does not supply a complete protection from all the perils against which the constitutional prohibition was designed to guard, and is not a full substitute for that prohibition. In view of the constitutional provision, a statutory enactment, to be valid, must afford absolute immunity against future prosecution for the offence to which the question relates." * * * [b]

Sixteen days after the *Counselman* decision, a new immunity bill was introduced. * * * The bill, which became the Compulsory Testimony Act of 1893, was drafted specifically to meet the broad language in *Counselman* set forth above. The new Act removed the privilege against self-incrimination in hearings before the Interstate Commerce Commission and provided that:

"no person shall be prosecuted or subjected to any penalty or forfeiture for or on account of any transaction, matter or thing, concerning which he may testify, or produce evidence, documentary or otherwise. . . ." * * *

This transactional immunity statute became the basic form for the numerous federal immunity statutes until 1970, when, after re-examining applicable constitutional principles and the adequacy of existing law, Congress enacted the statute here under consideration. The new statute, which does not "afford [the] absolute immunity against future prosecution" referred to in *Counselman*, was drafted to meet what Congress judged to be the conceptual basis of *Counselman*, as elaborated in subsequent decisions of the Court, namely, that immunity from the use of compelled testimony and evidence derived therefrom is coextensive with the scope of the privilege. The statute's explicit proscription of the use in any criminal case of "testimony or other information compelled under the order (or any information directly or indirectly derived from such testimony or other information)" is consonant with Fifth Amendment standards. We hold that such immunity from use and derivative use is coextensive with the scope of the privilege against self-incrimination, and therefore is sufficient to compel testimony over a claim of the privilege. **[c]** While a grant of immunity must afford protection commensurate with that afforded by the privilege, it need not be broader. Transactional immunity, which accords full immunity from prosecution for the offense to which the compelled testimony relates, affords the witness considerably broader protection than does the Fifth Amendment privilege. The privilege has never been construed to mean that one who invokes it cannot subsequently be prosecuted. Its sole concern is to afford protection against being "forced to give testimony leading to the infliction of 'penalties affixed to . . . criminal acts.'" Immunity from the use of compelled testimony, as well as evidence derived directly and indirectly therefrom, affords this protection. It prohibits the prosecutorial authorities from using the compelled testimony in *any* respect, and it therefore insures that the testimony cannot lead to the infliction of criminal penalties on the witness.

* * * The broad language in *Counselman* relied upon by petitioners was unnecessary to the Court's decision, and cannot be considered binding authority. **[d]**

[The opinion next analyzed *Murphy v. Waterfront Comm'n*, 378 U.S. 52 (1964), which held the rule against self-incrimination applicable to the states; held that testimony compelled before a joint state agency by a grant of immunity prevented the use of the testimony in a later federal prosecution; but did not prohibit federal prosecution. While *Murphy* did not deal with the precise issue in this case, its reasoning is useful.]

* * *

* * * As the *Murphy* Court noted, immunity from use and derivative use "leaves the witness and the Federal Government in substantially the same position as if the witness had claimed his privilege" in the absence of a grant of immunity. The *Murphy* Court was concerned solely with the danger of incrimination under federal law, and held that immunity from use and derivative use was sufficient to displace the danger. This protection coextensive with the privilege is the degree of protection that the Constitution requires, and is all that the Constitution requires even against the jurisdiction compelling testimony by granting immunity.

IV

* * *

Petitioners argue that use and derivative-use immunity will not adequately protect a witness from various possible incriminating uses of the compelled testimony: for example, the prosecutor or other law enforcement officials may obtain leads, names of witnesses, or other information not otherwise available that might result in a prosecution. It will be difficult and perhaps impossible, the argument goes, to identify, by testimony or cross-examination, the subtle ways in which the compelled testimony may disadvantage a witness, especially in the jurisdiction granting the immunity.

This argument presupposes that the statute's prohibition will prove impossible to enforce. The statute provides a sweeping proscription of any use, direct or indirect, of the compelled testimony and any information derived therefrom:

"[N]o testimony or other information compelled under the order (or any information directly or indirectly derived from such testimony or other information) may be used against the witness in any criminal case. . . ." * * *

This total prohibition on use provides a comprehensive safeguard, barring the use of compelled testimony as an "investigatory lead," and also barring the use of any evidence obtained by focusing investigation on a witness as a result of his compelled disclosures.

A person accorded this immunity under [the immunity statute] and subsequently prosecuted, is not dependent for the preservation of his rights upon the integrity and good faith of the prosecuting authorities. As stated in *Murphy*:

"Once a defendant demonstrates that he has testified, under a state grant of immunity, to matters related to the federal prosecution, the federal authorities have the burden of showing that their evidence is not tainted by establishing that they had an independent, legitimate source for the disputed evidence." * * *

This burden of proof, which we reaffirm as appropriate, is not limited to a negation of taint; rather, it imposes on the prosecution the affirmative duty to prove that the evidence it proposes to use is derived from a legitimate source wholly independent of the compelled testimony.

This is very substantial protection, commensurate with that resulting from invoking the privilege itself. The privilege assures that a citizen is not compelled to incriminate himself by his own testimony. It usually operates to allow a citizen to remain silent when asked a question requiring an incriminatory answer. This statute, which operates after a witness has given incriminatory testimony, affords the same protection by assuring that the compelled testimony can in no way lead to the infliction of criminal penalties. The statute, like the Fifth Amendment, grants neither pardon nor amnesty. Both the statute and the Fifth Amendment allow the government to prosecute using evidence from legitimate independent sources. [e]

* * *

There can be no justification in reason or policy for holding that the Constitution requires an amnesty grant where, acting pursuant to statute and accompanying safeguards, testimony is compelled in exchange for immunity from use and derivative use when no such amnesty is required where the government, acting without colorable right, coerces a defendant into incriminating himself.

We conclude that the immunity provided by [the statute] leaves the witness and the prosecutorial authorities in substantially the same position as if the witness had claimed the Fifth Amendment privilege. The immunity therefore is coextensive with the privilege and suffices to supplant it. The judgment of the Court of Appeals for the Ninth Circuit accordingly is

Affirmed.

[JUSTICES BRENNAN and REHNQUIST took no part in the consideration or decision of this case; JUSTICE REHNQUIST had worked on the government brief as assistant attorney general].

MR. JUSTICE DOUGLAS, dissenting.

The Self-Incrimination Clause says: "No person . . . shall be compelled in any criminal case to be a witness against himself." I see no answer to the proposition that he is such a witness when only "use" immunity is granted.

* * *

In *Counselman v. Hitchcock*, * * * the Court adopted the transactional immunity test: "In view of the constitutional provision, a statutory enactment, to be valid, must afford absolute immunity against future prosecution for the offense to which the question relates." * * * In *Brown v. Walker*, * * * a case involving another federal prosecution, the immunity statute provided that the witness would be protected "on account of any transaction . . . concerning which he may testify." * * * The Court held that the immunity offered was coterminous with the privilege and that the witness could therefore be compelled to testify, a ruling that made "transactional immunity" part of the fabric of our constitutional law. * * *

This Court, however, apparently believes that *Counselman* and its progeny were overruled *sub silentio* in *Murphy v. Waterfront Comm'n*. * * *

Murphy overruled, not *Counselman*, but *Feldman v. United States*, 322 U.S. 487, which had held "that one jurisdiction within our federal structure may compel a witness to give testimony which could be used to convict him of a crime in another jurisdiction." * * * But *Counselman*, as the *Murphy* Court recognized, "said nothing about the problem of incrimination under the law of another sovereign." * * * That problem is one of federalism, as to require transactional immunity between jurisdictions might

"deprive a state of the right to prosecute a violation of its criminal law on the basis of another state's grant of immunity [a result which] would be gravely in derogation of its sovereignty and obstructive of its administration of justice." * * *

* * *

None of these factors apply when the threat of prosecution is from the jurisdiction seeking to compel the testimony, which is the situation we faced in *Counselman*, and which we face today. The irrelevance of *Murphy* to such a situation was made clear in *Albertson v. Subversive Activities Control Board*, 382 U.S. 70, in which the Court struck down an immunity statute because it failed to measure up to the standards set forth in *Counselman*. Inasmuch as no interjurisdictional problems presented themselves, *Murphy* was not even cited. That is further proof that *Murphy* was not thought significantly to undercut *Counselman*. * * * [f]

* * *

MR. JUSTICE MARSHALL, dissenting.

* * *

* * * But I cannot agree that a ban on use will in practice be total, if it remains open for the government to convict the witness on the basis of evidence derived from a legitimate independent source. The Court asserts that the witness is adequately protected

by a rule imposing on the government a heavy burden of proof if it would establish the independent character of evidence to be used against the witness. But in light of the inevitable uncertainties of the factfinding process, * * * a greater margin of protection is required in order to provide a reliable guarantee that the witness is in exactly the same position as if he had not testified. That margin can be provided only by immunity from prosecution for the offenses to which the testimony relates, *i. e.,* transactional immunity. [g]

* * *

* * * * * * * * * * *

COMMENTS

[a] Attorneys on appeal may advance extreme arguments that would benefit their side; at times such arguments are instrumental in working changes in the law; on the other hand, appellate courts often reject extreme arguments out of hand.

[b] On its face this statement appears to require transactional immunity. Reread the paragraph above and it appears that *Counselman*'s holding was narrower.

[c] The words of the Fifth Amendment speak of a person not being compelled to be "a witness against himself." The prosecution of an immunized witness does not conflict with this wording.

[d] The holding of a case is the rule that is essential to explain the decision in terms of the facts; as the unconstitutional statute in *Counselman* allowed the *use* of compelled testimony, the holding of the case applies to this issue and not to the matter of granting transactional immunity. Compare this view of the case to that presented by JUSTICE DOUGLAS in dissent.

[e] Compare this to the excerpt from JUSTICE MARSHALL's dissent. Is the majority too trusting or is JUSTICE MARSHALL too cynical?

[f] Assume JUSTICE DOUGLAS is technically correct in his reading of prior cases. From this perspective the majority opinion can be seen in a different light. It can be seen as an example of "conservative activism." But it also exemplifies the idea that when the justices appeal to the constitution, they are less bound to prior precedent of the Court than in other kinds of interpretation.

[g] Does the conclusion of the dissenting justices result in a windfall for the defendant?

BALTIMORE DEPT. OF SOCIAL SERV. v. BOUKNIGHT

493 U.S. 549, 110 S.Ct. 900, 107 L.Ed.2d 992 (1990)

JUSTICE O'CONNOR delivered the opinion of the Court.

In this action, we must decide whether a mother, the custodian of a child pursuant to a court order, may invoke the Fifth Amendment privilege against self-incrimination to resist an order of the juvenile court to produce the child. We hold that she may not.

I

Petitioner Maurice M. is an abused child. When he was three months old, he was hospitalized with a fractured left femur, and examination revealed several partially healed bone fractures and other indications of severe physical abuse. In the hospital, respondent Bouknight, Maurice's mother, was observed shaking Maurice, dropping him in his crib despite his spica cast, and otherwise handling him in a manner inconsistent with his recovery and continued health. Hospital personnel notified Baltimore City Department of Social Services (BCDSS), * * * of suspected child abuse. [a] In February 1987, BCDSS secured a court order removing Maurice from Bouknight's control and placing him in shelter care. Several months later, the shelter care order was inexplicably modified to return Maurice to Bouknight's custody temporarily. Following a hearing held shortly thereafter, the juvenile court declared Maurice to be a "child in need of assistance," thus asserting jurisdiction over Maurice and placing him under BCDSS' continuing oversight. BCDSS agreed that Bouknight could continue as custodian of the child, but only pursuant to extensive conditions set forth in a court-approved protective supervision order. The order required Bouknight to "cooperate with BCDSS," "continue in therapy," participate in parental aid and training programs, and "refrain from physically punishing [Maurice]." * * * The order's terms were "all subject to the further Order of the Court." * * * Bouknight's attorney signed the order, and Bouknight in a separate form set forth her agreement to each term. [b]

Eight months later, fearing for Maurice's safety, BCDSS returned to juvenile court. BCDSS caseworkers related that Bouknight would not cooperate with them and had in nearly every respect violated the terms of the protective order. BCDSS stated that Maurice's father had recently died in a shooting incident and that Bouknight, in light of the results of a psychological examination and her history of drug use, could not provide adequate care for the child. * * * On April 20, 1988, the court granted BCDSS' petition to remove Maurice from Bouknight's control for placement in foster care. BCDSS officials also petitioned for judicial relief from Bouknight's failure to produce Maurice or reveal where he could be found. * * * The petition recounted that on two recent visits by BCDSS officials to Bouknight's home, she had refused to reveal the location of the child or had indicated that the child was with an aunt whom she would not identify. The petition further asserted that inquiries of Bouknight's known relatives had revealed that none of them had recently seen Maurice and that BCDSS had prompted the police to issue a missing persons report and referred the case for investigation by the police homicide division. Also on April 20, the juvenile court, upon a hearing on the petition, cited Bouknight for violating the protective custody order and for failing to appear at the hearing. Bouknight had indicated to her attorney that she would appear with the child, but also expressed fear that if she appeared the State would "'snatch the child.'" * * * The court issued an order to show cause why Bouknight should not be held in civil contempt for failure to produce the child.   Expressing concern that Maurice was endangered or perhaps dead, the court issued a bench warrant for Bouknight's appearance. * * *

Maurice was not produced at subsequent hearings. At a hearing one week later, Bouknight claimed that Maurice was with a relative in Dallas. Investigation revealed that the relative had not seen Maurice. The next day, following another hearing at which Bouknight again declined to produce Maurice, the juvenile court found Bouknight in contempt for failure to produce the child as ordered. There was and has been no indication that she was unable to comply with the order. The court directed that Bouknight be imprisoned until she "purge[d] herself of contempt by either producing [Maurice] before the court or revealing to the court his exact whereabouts." * * *

The juvenile court rejected Bouknight's subsequent claim that the contempt order violated the Fifth Amendment's guarantee against self-incrimination. The court stated that the production of Maurice would purge the contempt and that "[t]he contempt is issued not because she refuse[d] to testify in any proceeding . . . [but] because she has failed to abide by the Order of this Court, mainly [for] the production of Maurice M." * * * While that decision was being appealed, Bouknight was convicted of theft and sentenced to 18 months' imprisonment in separate proceedings. The Court of Appeals of Maryland vacated the juvenile court's judgment upholding the contempt order. * * * The Court of Appeals found that the contempt order unconstitutionally compelled Bouknight to admit through the act of production "a measure of continuing control and dominion over Maurice's person" in circumstances in which "Bouknight has a reasonable apprehension that she will be prosecuted." * * * We granted certiorari * * * and we now reverse.

II

The Fifth Amendment provides that "No person . . . shall be compelled in any criminal case to be a witness against himself." The Fifth Amendment's protection "applies only when the accused is compelled to make a *testimonial* communication that is incriminating." * * * The juvenile court concluded that Bouknight could comply with the order through the unadorned act of producing the child, and we thus address that aspect of the order. When the government demands that an item be produced, "the only thing compelled is the act of producing the [item]." * * * The Fifth Amendment's protection may nonetheless be implicated because the act of complying with the government's demand testifies to the existence, possession, or authenticity of the things produced. * * * But a person may not claim the Amendment's protections based upon the incrimination that may result from the contents or nature of the thing demanded. * * * Bouknight therefore cannot claim the privilege based upon anything that examination of Maurice might reveal, nor can she assert the privilege upon the theory that compliance would assert that the child produced is in fact Maurice (a fact the State could readily establish, rendering any testimony regarding existence or authenticity insufficiently incriminating. * * *) Rather, Bouknight claims the benefit of the privilege because the act of production would amount to testimony regarding her control over, and possession of, Maurice. Although the State could readily introduce evidence of Bouknight's continuing control over the child—e. g., the custody order, testimony of relatives, and Bouknight's own statements to Maryland officials before invoking the privilege—her implicit communication of control over Maurice at the moment of production might aid the State in prosecuting Bouknight. [c]

The possibility that a production order will compel testimonial assertions that may prove incriminating does not, in all contexts, justify invoking the privilege to resist production. * * * Even assuming that this limited testimonial assertion is sufficiently incriminating and "sufficiently testimonial for purposes of the privilege," * * * Bouknight may not invoke the privilege to resist the production order because she has assumed custodial duties related to production and because production is required as part of a noncriminal regulatory regime. [d]

The Court has on several occasions recognized that the Fifth Amendment privilege may not be invoked to resist compliance with a regulatory regime constructed to effect the State's public purposes unrelated to the enforcement of its criminal laws. In *Shapiro v. United States*, 335 U.S. 1 (1948), the Court considered an application of the Emergency Price Control Act of 1942 and a regulation issued thereunder which required licensed businesses to maintain records and make them available for inspection by administrators. The Court indicated that no Fifth Amendment protection attached to production of the "required records," which the "'defendant was required to keep, not for his private uses, but for the benefit of the public, and for public inspection.'" * * * The Court's discussion of the constitutional implications of the scheme focused upon the relation between the Government's regulatory objectives and the Government's interest in gaining access to the records in Shapiro's possession:

"It may be assumed at the outset that there are limits which the Government cannot constitutionally exceed in requiring the keeping of records which may be inspected by an administrative agency and may be used in prosecuting statutory violations committed by the record-keeper himself. But no serious misgiving that those bounds have been overstepped would appear to be evoked when there is a sufficient relation between the activity sought to be regulated and the public concern so that the Government can constitutionally regulate or forbid the basic activity concerned, and can constitutionally require the keeping of particular records, subject to inspection by the Administrator." * * *

* * * The Court has since refined those limits to the government's authority to gain access to items or information vested with this public character. The Court has noted that "the requirements at issue in *Shapiro* were imposed in 'an essentially noncriminal and regulatory area of inquiry,'" and that *Shapiro's* reach is limited where requirements "are directed to a 'selective group inherently suspect of criminal activities.'" * * *

California v. Byers, 402 U.S. 424 (1971), confirms that the ability to invoke the privilege may be greatly diminished when invocation would interfere with the effective operation of a generally applicable, civil regulatory requirement. In *Byers*, the Court upheld enforcement of California's statutory requirement that drivers of cars involved in accidents stop and provide their names and addresses. A plurality found the risk of incrimination too insubstantial to implicate the Fifth Amendment, * * * and noted that the statute "was not intended to facilitate criminal convictions but to promote the satisfaction of civil liabilities," * * * was "'directed at the public at large,'" * * * and required disclosure of no inherently illegal activity. * * * **[e]** Justice Harlan, the author of [cases that applied the Fifth Amendment] concurred in the judgment. He distinguished those three cases as considering statutory schemes that "focused almost exclusively on conduct which was criminal." * * * While acknowledging that in particular cases the California statute would compel

incriminating testimony, he concluded that the noncriminal purpose and the general applicability of the reporting requirement demanded compliance even in such cases. * * *

When a person assumes control over items that are the legitimate object of the government's noncriminal regulatory powers, the ability to invoke the privilege is reduced. [This Court has surveyed] a range of cases involving the custody of public documents and records required by law to be kept because they related to "the appropriate subjects of governmental regulation and the enforcement of restrictions validly established." * * * The principle the Court drew from these cases is:

> "[W]here, by virtue of their character and the rules of law applicable to them, the books and papers are held subject to examination by the demanding authority, the custodian has no privilege to refuse production although their contents tend to criminate him. In assuming their custody he has accepted the incident obligation to permit inspection." * * * **[f]**

* * * In *Shapiro*, the Court interpreted this principle as extending well beyond the corporate context, * * * and emphasized that Shapiro had assumed and retained control over documents in which the government had a direct and particular regulatory interest. * * *

These principles readily apply to this case. Once Maurice was adjudicated a child in need of assistance, his care and safety became the particular object of the State's regulatory interests. * * * Maryland first placed Maurice in shelter care, authorized placement in foster care, and then entrusted responsibility for Maurice's care to Bouknight. By accepting care of Maurice subject to the custodial order's conditions (including requirements that she cooperate with BCDSS, follow a prescribed training regime, and be subject to further court orders), Bouknight submitted to the routine operation of the regulatory system and agreed to hold Maurice in a manner consonant with the State's regulatory interests and subject to inspection by BCDSS. * * * [g] In assuming the obligations attending custody, Bouknight "has accepted the incident obligation to permit inspection." * * * The State imposes and enforces that obligation as part of a broadly directed, noncriminal regulatory regime governing children cared for pursuant to custodial orders. * * *

Persons who care for children pursuant to a custody order, and who may be subject to a request for access to the child, are hardly a "'selective group inherently suspect of criminal activities.'" * * * The juvenile court may place a child within its jurisdiction with social service officials or "under supervision in his own home or in the custody or under the guardianship of a relative or other fit person, upon terms the court deems appropriate." * * * Children may be placed, for example, in foster care, in homes of relatives, or in the care of state officials. * * * Even when the court allows a parent to retain control of a child within the court's jurisdiction, that parent is not one singled out for criminal conduct, but rather has been deemed to be, without the State's assistance, simply "unable or unwilling to give proper care and attention to the child and his problems." * * * The provision that authorized the juvenile court's efforts

to gain production of Maurice reflects this broad applicability. * * * ("If a parent, guardian, or custodian fails to bring the child before the court when requested, the court may issue a writ of attachment directing that the child be taken into custody and brought before the court. The court may proceed against the parent, guardian, or custodian for contempt"). This provision "fairly may be said to be directed at . . . parents, guardians, and custodians who accept placement of juveniles in custody." * * *

Similarly, BCDSS' efforts to gain access to children, as well as judicial efforts to the same effect, do not "focu[s] almost exclusively on conduct which was criminal." * * * Many orders will arise in circumstances entirely devoid of criminal conduct. Even when criminal conduct may exist, the court may properly request production and return of the child, and enforce that request through exercise of the contempt power, for reasons related entirely to the child's well-being and through measures unrelated to criminal law enforcement or investigation. * * * This case provides an illustration: concern for the child's safety underlay the efforts to gain access to and then compel production of Maurice. * * * Finally, production in the vast majority of cases will embody no incriminating testimony, even if in particular cases the act of production may incriminate the custodian through an assertion of possession or the existence, or the identity, of the child. * * * These orders to produce children cannot be characterized as efforts to gain some testimonial component of the act of production. The government demands production of the very public charge entrusted to a custodian, and makes the demand for compelling reasons unrelated to criminal law enforcement and as part of a broadly applied regulatory regime. In these circumstances, Bouknight cannot invoke the privilege to resist the order to produce Maurice.

We are not called upon to define the precise limitations that may exist upon the State's ability to use the testimonial aspects of Bouknight's act of production in subsequent criminal proceedings. But we note that imposition of such limitations is not foreclosed. The same custodial role that limited the ability to resist the production order may give rise to corresponding limitations upon the direct and indirect use of that testimony. * * * The State's regulatory requirement in the usual case may neither compel incriminating testimony nor aid a criminal prosecution, but the Fifth Amendment protections are not thereby necessarily unavailable to the person who complies with the regulatory requirement after invoking the privilege and subsequently faces prosecution. * * * In a broad range of contexts, the Fifth Amendment limits prosecutors' ability to use testimony that has been compelled. * * * See * * * *Garrity v. New Jersey*, [this volume]. * * * **[h]**

III

The judgment of the Court of Appeals of Maryland is reversed, and the cases are remanded to that court for further proceedings not inconsistent with this opinion.

So ordered.

JUSTICE MARSHALL, with whom JUSTICE BRENNAN joins, dissenting.

* * *

I

The Court correctly assumes, * * * that Bouknight's production of her son to the Maryland court would be testimonial because it would amount to an admission of Bouknight's physical control over her son. * * * The Court also assumes, * * * that Bouknight's act of production would be self-incriminating. * * * Bouknight's ability to produce the child would conclusively establish her actual and present physical control over him, and thus might "prove a significant 'link in a chain' of evidence tending to establish [her] guilt." * * *

Indeed, the stakes for Bouknight are much greater than the Court suggests. Not only could she face criminal abuse and neglect charges for her alleged mistreatment of Maurice, but she could also be charged with causing his death. The State acknowledges that it suspects that Maurice is dead, and the police are investigating his case as a possible homicide. In these circumstances, the potentially incriminating aspects to Bouknight's act of production are undoubtedly significant.

II

Notwithstanding the real threat of self-incrimination, the Court holds that "Bouknight may not invoke the privilege to resist the production order because she has assumed custodial duties related to production and because production is required as part of a noncriminal regulatory regime." * * * In characterizing Bouknight as Maurice's "custodian," and in describing the relevant Maryland juvenile statutes as part of a noncriminal regulatory regime, the Court relies on two distinct lines of Fifth Amendment precedent, neither of which applies to this litigation.

[In Part II A, JUSTICE MARSHALL argued that "Bouknight is Maurice's mother; she is not, and in fact could not be, his 'custodian' whose rights and duties are determined solely by the Maryland juvenile protection law." Because of this her role was radically different that of corporate agents who have not enjoyed the protection of the Fifth Amendment.]

[In Part II B, JUSTICE MARSHALL argued that the regulatory purpose rationale of the majority did not apply because the clear purpose of the statute and order in this case focused on criminal child abuse.]

[In Part III, JUSTICE MARSHALL took "some comfort in the Court's recognition that the State may be prohibited from using any testimony given by Bouknight in subsequent criminal proceedings."]

* * * * * * * * * *

COMMENTS

[a] This recitation of the terrible facts of child abuse cannot but arouse sympathy in any reader.

[b] These facts emphasize the extent to which the state had control over the raising of Maurice M. at that point; compare this to JUSTICE MARSHALL's emphasis, in dissent, that Bouknight was not a custodian but the child's *mother*.

[c] The facts produce a dilemma. Clearly, the state cannot compel Bouknight to tell about Maurice if she asserts that it could incriminate her. It is also clear that the state can compel a person to submit herself as evidence (for identification purposes) or to allow things like hair samples to be taken. Producing Maurice straddles the line of testimonial and real evidence. Thus, the *act of production* is a testimonial communication; but the state is correct in asserting that the "*contents*" of what is produced is not privileged. In recent years the Court has resolved similar cases involving business records in favor of the state. *United States v. Doe*, 465 U.S. 605 (1984) held that voluntarily created business records of a sole proprietorship are not privileged. However, the Court also held that as the act of production was testimonial, it could be compelled only if the state offered a grant of use immunity.

[d] Here, the Court produces its chief argument to get around the limits of the previous cases, the administrative or regulatory scheme concept. Persons subject to

non-criminal regulatory processes do not have the same high levels of procedural protection as those who are subject to the criminal process.

[e] Since not every person involved in an automobile accident commits a vehicular crime, the *Byers* program is regulatory; but the stop-at-accident-scene requirement applies both to non-criminal drivers and to those whose driving amounted to a crime.

[f] These recent cases have undermined the decision in *Boyd v. United States*, [this volume], although the dicta in that case is still important.

[g] Although voluntary in one sense, after evidence of child abuse, Bouknight could only regain custody of her son under conditions imposed by the state.

[h] While this paragraph does not state a conclusive rule, it strongly implies that any testimonial communication that is compelled from Bouknight's production of Maurice could not be used in a subsequent criminal prosecution.

SANTOBELLO v. NEW YORK

404 U.S. 257, 92 S.Ct. 495, 30 L.Ed.2d 427 (1971)

MR. CHIEF JUSTICE BURGER delivered the opinion of the Court.

We granted certiorari in this case to determine whether the State's failure to keep a commitment concerning the sentence recommendation on a guilty plea required a new trial.

The facts are not in dispute. The State of New York indicted petitioner in 1969 on two felony counts, Promoting Gambling in the First Degree, and Possession of Gambling Records in the First Degree. * * * Petitioner first entered a plea of not guilty to both counts. After negotiations, the Assistant District Attorney in charge of the case agreed to permit petitioner to plead guilty to a lesser-included offense, Possession of Gambling Records in the Second Degree, * * * conviction of which would carry a maximum prison sentence of one year. The prosecutor agreed to make no recommendation as to the sentence.

On June 16, 1969, petitioner accordingly withdrew his plea of not guilty and entered a plea of guilty to the lesser charge. Petitioner represented to the sentencing judge that the plea was voluntary and that the facts of the case, as described by the Assistant District Attorney, were true. The court accepted the plea and set a date for sentencing. * * *

[The sentencing hearing was delayed at least two times until January 9, 1970 because of the absence of a pre-sentence report and a series of motions made by Santobello's new lawyer. The sentencing hearing was conducted by a different judge than the judge who took the plea (who had retired).]

At this appearance, another prosecutor had replaced the prosecutor who had negotiated the plea. The new prosecutor recommended the maximum one-year sentence. In making this recommendation, he cited petitioner's criminal record and alleged links with organized crime. Defense counsel immediately objected on the ground that the State had promised petitioner before the plea was entered that there would be no sentence recommendation by the prosecution. He sought to adjourn the sentence hearing in order to have time to prepare proof of the first prosecutor's promise. The second prosecutor, apparently ignorant of his colleague's commitment, argued that there was nothing in the record to support petitioner's claim of a promise, but the State, in subsequent proceedings, has not contested that such a promise was made.

The sentencing judge ended discussion [by asserting that he was not influenced by the prosecutor's recommendation but by the presentence report and by Santobello's prior criminal history.] The judge then imposed the maximum sentence of one year.

[The intermediate appellate court unanimously affirmed the conviction and the state's highest court denied leave to appeal.] * * *

This record represents another example of an unfortunate lapse in orderly prosecutorial procedures, in part, no doubt, because of the enormous increase in the workload of the

often understaffed prosecutor's offices. The heavy workload may well explain these episodes, but it does not excuse them. The disposition of criminal charges by agreement between the prosecutor and the accused, sometimes loosely called "plea bargaining," is an essential component of the administration of justice. Properly administered, it is to be encouraged. If every criminal charge were subjected to a full-scale trial, the States and the Federal Government would need to multiply by many times the number of judges and court facilities.

Disposition of charges after plea discussions is not only an essential part of the process but a highly desirable part for many reasons. It leads to prompt and largely final disposition of most criminal cases; it avoids much of the corrosive impact of enforced idleness during pretrial confinement for those who are denied release pending trial; it protects the public from those accused persons who are prone to continue criminal conduct even while on pretrial release; and, by shortening the time between charge and disposition, it enhances whatever may be the rehabilitative prospects of the guilty when they are ultimately imprisoned. * * * [a]

However, all of these considerations presuppose fairness in securing agreement between an accused and a prosecutor. It is now clear, for example, that the accused pleading guilty must be counseled, absent a waiver. * * * Fed. Rule Crim. Proc. 11, governing pleas in federal courts, now makes clear that the sentencing judge must develop, *on the record*, the factual basis for the plea, as, for example, by having the accused describe the conduct that gave rise to the charge. [b] The plea must, of course, be voluntary and knowing and if it was induced by promises, the essence of those promises must in some way be made known. There is, of course, no absolute right to have a guilty plea accepted. * * * A court may reject a plea in exercise of sound judicial discretion.

This phase of the process of criminal justice, and the adjudicative element inherent in accepting a plea of guilty, must be attended by safeguards to insure the defendant what is reasonably due in the circumstances. Those circumstances will vary, but a constant factor is that when a plea rests in any significant degree on a promise or agreement of the prosecutor, so that it can be said to be part of the inducement or consideration, such promise must be fulfilled.

On this record, petitioner "bargained" and negotiated for a particular plea in order to secure dismissal of more serious charges, but also on condition that no sentence recommendation would be made by the prosecutor. It is now conceded that the promise to abstain from a recommendation was made, and at this stage the prosecution is not in a good position to argue that its inadvertent breach of agreement is immaterial. The staff lawyers in a prosecutor's office have the burden of "letting the left hand know what the right hand is doing" or has done. That the breach of agreement was inadvertent does not lessen its impact.

We need not reach the question whether the sentencing judge would or would not have been influenced had he known all the details of the negotiations for the plea. He stated that the prosecutor's recommendation did not influence him and we have no reason to doubt that. Nevertheless, we conclude that the interests of justice and appropriate recognition of the duties of the prosecution in relation to promises made in the negotiation of pleas of guilty will be best served by remanding the case to the state courts for further consideration. The ultimate relief to which petitioner is entitled we leave to the discretion of the state court, which is in a better position to decide whether the circumstances of this case require only that there be specific performance of the agreement on the plea, in which case petitioner should be resentenced by a different judge, or whether, in the view of the state court, the circumstances require granting the relief sought by petitioner, i.e., the opportunity to withdraw his plea of guilty. We emphasize that this is in no sense to question the fairness of the sentencing judge; the fault here rests on the prosecutor, not on the sentencing judge. [c]

The judgment is vacated and the case is remanded for reconsideration not inconsistent with this opinion.

MR. JUSTICE DOUGLAS, concurring.

I join the opinion of the Court and add only a word. I agree both with THE CHIEF JUSTICE and with MR. JUSTICE MARSHALL that New York did not keep its "plea bargain" with petitioner and that it is no excuse for the default merely because a member of the prosecutor's staff who was not a party to the "plea bargain" was in charge of the case when it came before the New York court. The staff of the prosecution is a unit and each member must be presumed to know the commitments made by any other member. * * *

These "plea bargains" are important in the administration of justice both at the state and at the federal levels and, as THE CHIEF JUSTICE says, they serve an important role in the disposition of today's heavy calendars. [d]

However important plea bargaining may be in the administration of criminal justice, our opinions have established that a guilty plea is a serious and sobering occasion inasmuch as it constitutes a waiver of the fundamental rights to a jury trial, * * * to confront one's accusers, * * * to present witnesses in one's defense, * * * to remain silent, * * * and to be convicted by proof beyond all reasonable doubt. * * * [T]his Court has recognized that "unfairly obtained" guilty pleas in the federal courts ought to be vacated. In the course of holding that withdrawn guilty pleas were not admissible in subsequent federal prosecutions, the Court opined:

> "[O]n timely application, the court will vacate a plea of guilty shown to have been unfairly obtained or given through ignorance, fear or inadvertence. Such an application does not involve any question of guilt or innocence." * * *

Although [this] dictum concerning grounds for withdrawal of guilty pleas did not expressly rest on constitutional grounds * * * [we] clearly held that a federal prisoner who had pleaded guilty despite his ignorance of and his being uninformed of his right to a lawyer was deprived of that Sixth Amendment right, or if he had been tricked by the prosecutor through misrepresentations into pleading guilty then his due process rights were offended. In *Walker* [v. *Johnston*, 312 U.S. 275], the petitioner was granted an evidentiary hearing to prove his factual claims in anticipation of vacating the plea. * * * In *Machibroda v. United States*, 368 U.S. 487, the defendant alleged that when he threatened to tell his lawyer of private promises made by an Assistant United States Attorney in exchange for a proposed guilty plea, the prosecutor threatened additional prosecutions. Although the Government denied them, the Court held that if the allegations were true, then the defendant would be entitled to have his sentence vacated and the matter was remanded for an evidentiary hearing.

State convictions founded upon coerced or unfairly induced guilty pleas have also received increased scrutiny as more fundamental rights have been applied to the States. After *Powell v. Alabama*, [this volume], the Court held that a state defendant was entitled to a lawyer's assistance in choosing whether to plead guilty. * * * [A] guilty plea obtained without the advice of counsel may not be admitted at a subsequent state prosecution. *White v. Maryland*, 373 U.S. 59. Thus, while plea bargaining is not *per se* unconstitutional, *North Carolina v. Alford*, 400 U.S. 25, 37-38, * * * a guilty plea is rendered voidable by threatening physical harm, * * * threatening to use false testimony, * * * threatening to bring additional prosecutions, * * * or by failing to inform a defendant of his right of counsel. * * * Under these circumstances it is clear that a guilty plea must be vacated.

But it is also clear that a prosecutor's promise may deprive a guilty plea of the "character of a voluntary act." * * * The decisions of this Court have not spelled out what sorts of promises

by prosecutors tend to be coercive, but in order to assist appellate review in weighing promises in light of all the circumstances, all trial courts are now required to interrogate the defendants who enter guilty pleas so that the waiver of these fundamental rights will affirmatively appear in the record. *McCarthy v. United States*, 394 U.S. 459; *Boykin v. Alabama*, 395 U.S. 238. The lower courts, however, have uniformly held that a prisoner is entitled to some form of relief when he shows that the prosecutor reneged on his sentencing agreement made in connection with a plea bargain, most jurisdictions preferring vacation of the plea on the ground of "involuntariness," while a few permit only specific enforcement. * * * As one author has stated, the basis for outright vacation is "an outraged sense of fairness" when a prosecutor breaches his promise in connection with sentencing. D. Newman, Conviction: The Determination of Guilt or Innocence Without Trial 36 (1966).

This is a state case over which we have no "supervisory" jurisdiction; and Rule 11 of the Federal Rules of Criminal Procedure obviously has no relevancy to the problem. [e]

I join the opinion of the Court and favor a constitutional rule for this as well as for other pending or oncoming cases. Where the "plea bargain" is not kept by the prosecutor, the sentence must be vacated and the state court will decide in light of the circumstances of each case whether due process requires (a) that there be specific performance of the plea bargain or (b) that the defendant be given the option to go to trial on the original charges. One alternative may do justice in one case, and the other in a different case.

In choosing a remedy, however, a court ought to accord a defendant's preference considerable, if not controlling, weight inasmuch as the fundamental rights flouted by a prosecutor's breach of a plea bargain are those of the defendant, not of the State.

MR. JUSTICE MARSHALL, with whom MR. JUSTICE BRENNAN and MR. JUSTICE STEWART join, concurring in part and dissenting in part.

I agree with much of the majority's opinion, but conclude that petitioner must be permitted to withdraw his guilty plea. This is the relief petitioner requested, and, on the facts set out by the majority, it is a form of relief to which he is entitled.

* * *

Here, petitioner never claimed any automatic right to withdraw a guilty plea before sentencing. Rather, he tendered a specific reason why, in his case, the plea should be vacated. His reason was that the prosecutor had broken a promise made in return for the agreement to plead guilty. When a prosecutor breaks the bargain, he undercuts the basis for the waiver of constitutional rights implicit in the plea. This, it seems to me, provides the defendant ample justification for rescinding the plea. * * *

* * *

* * * * * * * * * *

COMMENTS

[a] This paragraph marked a revolution in trial practice. Prior to 1966 plea bargaining was seen as unethical and possibly unconstitutional; it occurred *sub rosa*. Academic studies and the discussion of the practice by the President's Commission on Law Enforcement and Administration of Justice (1967) began a process by which plea bargaining became "legitimated." The Supreme Court responded to this change by recognizing the practice.

[b] If this is done conscientiously by the judge it promises that virtually no persons will plead guilty when they are or believe they are innocent. An innocent but pressured defendant might answer yes or no questions improperly; but it is more difficult to convincingly tell about a crime scenario that never occurred.

[c] By mandating that due process requires the prosecutor to keep its promise with the defense, the Court strengthens the system of plea negotiation.

[d] In a note JUSTICE DOUGLAS noted that guilty pleas accounted for 95.5% of all major criminal convictions in New York, and 74.0% in California, citing the President's Commission on Law Enforcement and Administration of Justice, *Task Force Report: The Courts* 9 (1967). The rate of guilty pleas in the federal trial courts was 90.2% of all criminal convictions in the same mid-1960s period.

[e] The due process rationale of the majority opinion is implied rather than stated.

APPENDIX

The Bill of Rights and Fourteenth Amendment

to

The Constitution of the United States

AMENDMENT I

Congress shall make no law respecting an establishment of religion, or prohibiting the free exercise thereof; or abridging the freedom of speech, or of the press; or the right of the people peaceably to assemble, and to petition the Government for a redress of grievances.

AMENDMENT II

A well regulated Militia, being necessary to the security of a free State, the right of the people to keep and bear Arms, shall not be infringed.

AMENDMENT III

No Soldier shall, in time of peace be quartered in any house, without the consent of the Owner, nor in time of war, but in a manner to be prescribed by law.

AMENDMENT IV

The right of the people to be secure in their persons, houses, papers, and effects, against unreasonable searches and seizures, shall not be violated, and no Warrants shall issue, but upon probable cause, supported by Oath or affirmation, and particularly describing the place to be searched, and the persons or things to be seized.

AMENDMENT V

No person shall be held to answer for a capital, or otherwise infamous crime, unless on a presentment or indictment of a Grand Jury, except in cases arising in the land or naval forces, or in the Militia, when in actual service in time of War or public danger; nor shall any person be subject for the same offence to be twice put in jeopardy of life or limb; nor shall be compelled in any criminal case to be a witness against himself, nor be deprived of life, liberty, or property, without due process of law; nor shall private property be taken for public use, without just compensation.

AMENDMENT VI

In all criminal prosecutions, the accused shall enjoy the right to a speedy and public trial, by an impartial jury of the State and district wherein the crime shall have been committed, which district shall have been previously ascertained by law, and to be informed of the nature and cause of the accusation; to be confronted with the witnesses against him; to have compulsory process for obtaining witnesses in his favor, and to have the Assistance of Counsel for his defence.

AMENDMENT VII

In Suits at common law, where the value in controversy shall exceed twenty dollars, the right of trial by jury shall be preserved, and no fact tried by jury, shall be otherwise re-examined in any Court of the United States, than according to the rules of the common law.

AMENDMENT VIII

Excessive bail shall not be required, nor excessive fines imposed, nor cruel and unusual punishments inflicted.

AMENDMENT IX

The enumeration in the Constitution, of certain rights, shall not be construed to deny or disparage others retained by the people.

AMENDMENT X

The powers not delegated to the United States by the Constitution, nor prohibited by it to the States, are reserved to the States respectively, or to the people.

AMENDMENT XIV

Section 1. All persons born or naturalized in the United States, and subject to the jurisdiction thereof, are citizens of the United States and of the State wherein they reside. No State shall make or enforce any law which shall abridge the privileges or immunities of citizens of the United States; nor shall any State deprive any person of life, liberty, or property, without due process of law; nor deny to any person within its jurisdiction the equal protection of the laws.

* * *

Section 5. The Congress shall have power to enforce, by appropriate legislation, the provisions of this article.